THE OXFORD HANDBOOK OF

THE VICTORIAN

NOVEL

D1556420

THE OXFORD HANDBOOK OF

THE VICTORIAN
NOVEL

Edited by
LISA RODENSKY

OXFORD
UNIVERSITY PRESS

OXFORD
UNIVERSITY PRESS

Great Clarendon Street, Oxford, OX2 6DP,
United Kingdom

Oxford University Press is a department of the University of Oxford.
It furthers the University's objective of excellence in research, scholarship,
and education by publishing worldwide. Oxford is a registered trade mark of

Oxford University Press in the UK and in certain other countries

First Edition published in 2013
Impression: 1

British Library Cataloguing in Publication Data
Data available

ISBN 978-0-19-953314-5

Printed and bound in Great Britain by
CPI Group (UK) Ltd, Croydon, CR0 4YY

ACKNOWLEDGEMENTS

My first and greatest debt is owed to this volume's contributors. I am deeply grateful to them for the opportunity to present their work here. I also want to thank Andrew McNeillie, who commissioned me to edit this volume when he was the Senior Commissioning Editor for Literature at Oxford University Press. His encouragement was invaluable. Jacqueline Baker, now Senior Commissioning Editor, has provided equally indispensable support and advice. Oxford's Rachel Platt has helped me in ways too various to list here. Sincere thanks also go to Rosemary Campbell for her careful work on the manuscript and to Jeremy Langworthy for his terrific attention to the page proofs. So too I am grateful to my students Remy Cawley and Elizabeth Sheridan for their assistance with citations and indexing. My thanks must also go to Wellesley College for its support, particularly through the funds provided by the Barbara Morris Caspersen chair. Finally, I want to acknowledge the unflagging encouragement of my colleagues in the English Department at Wellesley College.

Parts of Rachel Sagner Buurma's chapter 'Publishing the Victorian Novel', originally published in 'Anonymity, Corporate Authority, and the Archive: The Production of Authorship in Late-Victorian England', *Victorian Studies* 50 (Fall 2007): 15–42, are reproduced with the kind permission of the Indiana University Press. Parts of Mark Lambert's chapter 'Three Matters of Style', originally published in *Dickens and the Suspended Quotation* (New Haven: Yale University Press, 1981), are reproduced with the kind permission of the Yale University Press.

Contents

PART VII THE NOVEL AND OTHER DISCIPLINES

PART VIII DRAMA, POETRY, AND CRITICISM

PART IX DISTINGUISHING
THE VICTORIAN NOVEL

PART X ENDINGS

LIST OF FIGURES

LIST OF TABLES

LIST OF CONTRIBUTORS

Emily Allen is Associate Professor of English Literature and Associate Dean of the Honors College at Purdue University. She researches and teaches about Victorian literature, theatre, and culture, and is the author of *Theater Figures: The Production of the Nineteenth-Century British Novel* (2003).

Suzy Anger is Associate Professor of English at the University of British Columbia. She is the author of *Victorian Interpretation* (2005), editor of *Knowing the Past: Victorian Literature and Culture* (2001), and co-editor of *Victorian Science as Culture Authority* (2011). She is currently completing a monograph on theories of consciousness and late Victorian fiction.

Rosemarie Bodenheimer is Professor of English at Boston College. She is the author of *The Politics of Story in Victorian Social Fiction* (1988), *The Real Life of Mary Ann Evans: George Eliot, Her Letters and Fiction* (1996), and *Knowing Dickens* (2010). Recently she has been interested in the Dickensian tradition of London writing, as well as in questions about biography.

Julia Prewitt Brown is Professor of English at Boston University and the author of *The Bourgeois Interior: How the Middle Class Imagines Itself in Literature and Film* (2008), *Cosmopolitan Criticism: Oscar Wilde's Philosophy of Art* (1997), *A Reader's Guide to the Nineteenth-Century English Novel* (1985), and *Jane Austen's Novels: Social Change and Literary Form* (1979). She is currently working on a book on the *Bildungsroman* and its afterlife in film.

Julie Buckler is Professor of Slavic Languages and Literatures at Harvard University. She is the author of *The Literary Lorgnette: Attending Opera in Imperial Russia* (2000) and *Mapping St Petersburg: Imperial Text and Cityshape* (2005). Her current book project is titled *Cultural Properties: The Afterlife of Imperial Objects in Soviet and Post-Soviet Russia*.

Rachel Sagner Buurma is Assistant Professor of English Literature at Swarthmore College, where she teaches and researches in the history of the novel, Victorian literature and culture, the history of the book, and 20th-century American literary criticism. Her work has appeared in *Studies in English Literature, English Language Notes, New Literary History*, and *Victorian Studies*. She is currently finishing a book on the literary-critical origins of Victorian novelistic form.

Alison Byerly is the president of Lafayette College. She is the author of two books, *Realism, Representation, and the Arts in Nineteenth-Century Literature* (1998), and *Are We There Yet? Virtual Travel and Victorian Realism* (2012). *Are We There Yet?* connects the Victorian fascination with 'virtual travel' with both the rise of realism in 19th-century fiction, and 21st-century experiments in virtual reality. She has published a number of articles on Victorian media and technology, and also on contemporary technology and its role in higher education and culture.

Marie-Françoise Cachin, Professor emerita, université Paris-Diderot, is a specialist of British publishing history (19th– 20th centuries) and of literary translation. Between 1995 and 2002, she was responsible for a postgraduate degree in literary translation. She is the author of several translations and of a book on translation, *La Traduction* (Paris: Cercle de la librairie, 2007). She has also published many papers on the transnational circulation of texts and British book history, and a book on the history of reading in England entitled *Une nation de lecteurs? La lecture en Angleterre (1815–1945)* (Villeurbanne: Presses de l'enssib, 2010).

Janice Carlisle is Professor of English at Yale University. She has published books and articles on Victorian fiction and autobiography, including a study of the works of John Stuart Mill. Her most recent books are *Common Scents: Comparative Encounters in High-Victorian Fiction* (2004) and *Picturing Reform in Victorian Britain* (2012).

Amanda Claybaugh is Professor of English at Harvard University. She is the author of *The Novel of Purpose* (2007), and she is currently at work on a project about the Civil War and Reconstruction.

Peter Garside is Honorary Professorial Fellow at the University of Edinburgh. He has helped provide a number of bibliographical resources relating to British Fiction in the early 19th century, including *The English Novel, 1770–1829* (2000) and the online database, *British Fiction, 1800–1829* (2004). He has also edited a number of novels belonging to this period, including most recently Walter Scott's *Waverley* (2007). He has also published widely on Romantic literature, Scottish poetry and prose, and the history of the book.

Debra Gettelman is Assistant Professor of English at the College of the Holy Cross, where she teaches and researches Victorian literature and culture, the novel, and the history and psychology of reading. Her work has appeared in *Novel: A Forum on Fiction*, *ELH*, and *Literature Compass*. She is currently completing a book on daydreaming and reading in Victorian literary culture.

Jennifer Green-Lewis is the author of numerous essays on Victorian photography and literature, as well as *Framing the Victorians: Photography and the Culture of Realism* (1996). Her most recent book is *Teaching Beauty in Delillo, Woolf, and Merrill* (with Margaret Soltan, 2008). She teaches courses on Victorian and Modernist literature and visual culture at the George Washington University in Washington, DC, and at the Bread Loaf School of English, Middlebury College, Vermont.

Daniel Hack is Associate Professor of English at the University of Michigan. The author of *The Material Interests of the Victorian Novel* (2005) and articles in such journals as *Critical Inquiry*, *Novel: A Forum on Fiction*, and *Victorian Studies*, he is currently writing a book on the presence of Victorian literature in 19th- and early-20th-century African American literature and print culture.

Kenneth Haynes is Professor of Comparative Literature and Classics at Brown University. He is the author of *English Literature and Ancient Languages* (2003) and has co-edited (with Peter France) *The Oxford History of Literary Translation in English*, vol. 4: 1790–1900 (2006). He is currently editing *The Oxford History of Classical Reception in English Literature*, vol. 5: *After 1880*.

Philip Horne is a Professor in the English Department at University College London. He is the author of *Henry James and Revision: The New York Edition* (1990), and editor of *Henry James: A Life in Letters* (1999). He is co-editor of *Thorold Dickinson: A World of Film* (2008). He has also edited Henry James, *A London Life & The Reverberator*, Henry James, *The Tragic Muse*, Charles Dickens, *Oliver Twist*, and Henry James, *The Portrait of a Lady*. He is Series Editor of the Penguin Classics Henry James, as well as General Editor of the Cambridge University Press edition of *The Complete Fiction of Henry James*. He has written articles on subjects including telephones and literature, the texts of Emily Dickinson, the criticism of F.R. Leavis, and Dickens's style.

Evan Horowitz was once an Assistant Professor of English at the University of North Texas. He was enjoying a fellowship at the Radcliffe Institute for Advanced Study at Harvard when he discovered that he loved Boston too much to leave—so he didn't. A fuller, book-length version of the argument he lays out in these pages is available at <http://www.onceaprofessor.org/>.

Meegan Kennedy teaches 19th-century British science and the novel at Florida State University, where she is an Associate Professor of English and affiliate faculty in the History and Philosophy of Science program. In 2010, she published *Revising the Clinic: Vision and Representation in Victorian Medical Narrative and the Novel* (Ohio State University Press). Her current book project, 'Beautiful Mechanism', examines Victorians' romance with the microscope and its analogue, the eye.

Mark Lambert is the Asher B. Edelman Professor of Languages and Literature Emeritus at Bard College, where he taught courses in British fiction, but also, and most frequently, on medieval literature, Middle English literature, Chaucer, the history of the English language, and Old English. He has also taught at Saint Augustine's College, at Harvard University, and at the University of York. He has published work on Malory (*Malory: Style and Vision in Le Morte Darthur* [1975]); Chaucer ('*Troilus*, I–III: a Criseydan Reading', in *Essays on Troilus and Criseyde* (1979, ed. Mary Salu), 'Telling the Story in *Troilus and Criseyde*' in *The Cambridge Chaucer Companion* (1986, ed. Piero Boitani and Jill Mann)); and on Dickens (*Dickens and the Suspended Quotation*, 1981).

Barbara Leckie is an Associate Professor cross-appointed in the English Department and the Institute for the Comparative Study of Literature, Art, and Culture at Carleton University. She has published *Culture and Adultery: The Novel, the Newspaper, and the Law, 1857–1914* (1999) and is currently completing 'Open Houses: The Architectural Idea, Poverty, and Victorian Print Culture, 1842–92'. She is also the volume editor of *Sanitary Reform in Victorian Britain: End of Century Assessments and New Directions* (Pickering & Chatto, 2013).

George Levine is Emeritus Professor of English, Rutgers University. He has published extensively on Victorian fiction and Victorian culture and science. Among his books are *The Joy of Secularism* (2012), *Darwin the Writer* (2011), *Dying to Know: Scientific Epistemology and Narrative in Victorian England* (2002), and *Darwin and the Novelists* (1992).

William McKelvy, Associate Professor of English at Washington University in St Louis, is the author of *The English Cult of Literature: Devoted Readers 1774–1880* (2007). His articles and reviews, on a wide range of topics and personalities, have appeared in *Essays in Criticism*, the *Journal of British Studies*, *Nineteenth-Century Prose*, *Victorian Literature and Culture*, *Victorian Poetry*, and *Victorian Studies*. He is currently working on his second book, *Copy Rites*, about reproductive aesthetics in the age of steam.

Richard Menke, Associate Professor of English at the University of Georgia, is the author of *Telegraphic Realism: Victorian Literature and Other Information Systems* (2008). He is currently working on a book about the invention of media in late 19th-century literature and culture.

Lynda Mugglestone is Professor of History of English at the University of Oxford, and a Fellow of Pembroke College, Oxford. She has published widely on the history of the English, and on the social, cultural, and ideological issues that dictionary-making can reveal. Recent books include: *Lost for Words: The Hidden History of the Oxford English Dictionary* (2005), *'Talking Proper': The Rise of Accent as Social Symbol* (2007), *Dictionaries: A Very Short Introduction* (2011), *The Oxford History of English* (updated edition, 2012), and, together with Freya Johnston, *Samuel Johnson: The Arc of the Pendulum* (2012). She is currently writing a book on 18th-century language and Samuel Johnson.

James Najarian is an Associate Professor of English at Boston College, where he edits the scholarly journal *Religion and the Arts*. He has published articles in *Victorian Poetry*, *Twentieth-Century Literature*, *Nineteenth-Century Prose*, and other journals. He is the author of *Victorian Keats: Manliness, Sexuality, and Desire* (2002) and is currently working on a study of the idea of the 'Minor Poet' in the 19th century.

Rebecca Edwards Newman has taught 18th- and 19th-century British literature at Bangor University in Wales and Rhodes College in Memphis, Tennessee. Her research interests include Scottish literature and prose fiction of the Romantic and Victorian eras, and she has previously published on Victorian literature and the early 19th-century periodical. She is currently working on a book project on the relationship between the novel and the 19th-century literary magazine.

Patrick R. O'Malley is an Associate Professor of English at Georgetown University. He is the author of *Catholicism, Sexual Deviance, and Victorian Gothic Culture* (2006) as well as essays on religion, gender, and sexuality in the works of writers including John Henry Newman, Oscar Wilde, James Joyce, Thomas Hardy, and Sydney Owenson. He is currently working on an analysis of the representation of history in the works of 19th-century Protestant Irish nationalists.

Christopher Ricks is Warren Professor of the Humanities, and Co-Director of the Editorial Institute at Boston University, having formerly been Professor of English at the University of Bristol and at Cambridge. He was Professor of Poetry at Oxford, 2004–2009. Among the works of Victorian literature that he has edited are *Selected Criticism of Matthew Arnold* (1972), *The Poems of Tennyson* (rev. 1987), *The New Oxford Book of Victorian Verse* (1987), *Palgrave's Golden Treasury* (1991), and Henry James's *What Maisie Knew* (2010), and in other fields, *Inventions of the March Hare: Poems 1990–1917 by T.S. Eliot* (1996), and *The Oxford Book of English Verse* (1999). He is the author of *Milton's Grand Style* (1963), *Tennyson* (rev. 1989), *Keats and Embarrassment* (1974), *The Force of Poetry* (1984), *T.S. Eliot and Prejudice* (1988), *Beckett's Dying Words* (1993), *Essays in Appreciation* (1996), *Allusion to the Poets* (2002), *Reviewery* (2002), *Decisions and Revisions in T.S. Eliot* (2003), *Dylan's Visions of Sin* (2003), and *True Friendship: Geoffrey Hill, Anthony Hecht and Robert Lowell under the sign of Eliot and Pound* (2010).

Solveig C. Robinson is Associate Professor of English and Director of the Publishing and Printing Arts Program at Pacific Lutheran University in Tacoma, Washington. She is the editor of *A Serious Occupation: Literary Criticism by Victorian Women Writers* (2003) and the author of *The Book in Society: An Introduction to Print Culture* (2013). Her articles on Victorian criticism and publishing history have appeared in *Victorian Periodicals Review*, *Victorian Poetry*, and *Book History*. Her current research examines the role of national libraries in defining cultural identity over the course of the 19th and 20th centuries.

Lisa Rodensky is the Barbara Morris Caspersen Associate Professor in the Humanities at Wellesley College. She is the author of *The Crime in Mind: Criminal Responsibility and the Victorian Novel* (2003) and the editor of *Decadent Poetry from Wilde to Naidu* (2006). Her essays have appeared in *Victorian Literature and Culture* and *Essays in Criticism*. She is currently at work on an analysis of the critical vocabulary of the 19th-century novel review.

Jennifer Ruth is Associate Professor of English at Portland State University. She is the author of *Novel Professions: Interested Disinterest and the Making of the Professional in the Victorian Novel* (2006) and a number of articles on the Victorian professional.

Margery Sabin is Lorraine Chiu Wang Professor of English at Wellesley College, where she also serves as Director of the college's interdisciplinary South Asia Studies Program. Her teaching and publications range widely over topics in Victorian and modern British literature, comparative English and French literature, Indian literature in English, modern Irish literature, and the relationship of literature to colonial and post-colonial culture. She is the author of *English Romanticism and the French Tradition* (1976) and *The Dialect of the Tribe: Speech and Community in Modern Fiction* (1987). Her most recent book is *Dissenters and Mavericks: Writings in English about India, 1765–2000* (2002). She is currently writing about varieties of cosmopolitanism in Indian literature.

Talia Schaffer is a professor of English at Queens College CUNY and the Graduate Center CUNY. She is the author of *Novel Craft: Victorian Domestic Handicraft and Nineteenth-Century Fiction* (2011); *The Forgotten Female Aesthetes: Literary Culture in Late-Victorian England* (2001); co-editor with Kathy A. Psomiades of *Women and British Aestheticism* (1999); editor of Lucas Malet's 1901 novel, *The History of Sir Richard Calmady* (2003); and editor of *Literature and Culture at the Fin de Siècle* (2006). She has published widely on non-canonical women writers, material culture, popular fiction, aestheticism, and late-Victorian texts. She is currently working on a book on 'familiar marriage', a rival to romantic unions in Victorian marriage plots.

Jan-Melissa Schramm is a Fellow at Trinity Hall and a Lecturer in the Faculty of English, University of Cambridge, where she teaches Victorian literature. She is the author of *Testimony and Advocacy in Victorian Law, Literature, and Theology* (2000) and *Atonement and Self-Sacrifice in Nineteenth-Century Narrative* (2012). She is co-editor of *Fictions of Knowledge: Fact, Evidence, Doubt* (2011), and she has also written a number of articles on moral and legal thought in the works of Charles Dickens and George Eliot, Victorian satire, and first-person narration. She currently holds a Leverhulme Research Fellowship to complete a monograph provisionally entitled 'Democracy, Censorship, and Victorian Sacred Drama'.

Jonathan Smith is William E. Stirton Professor of English at the University of Michigan-Dearborn. He is the author of *Charles Darwin and Victorian Visual Culture* (2006) and *Fact and Feeling: Baconian Science and the Nineteenth-Century Literary Imagination* (1994), and his articles on science and Victorian fiction have appeared in such venues as *Victorian Studies, Nineteenth-Century Literature, Victorian Literature and Culture*, and *LIT: Literature, Interpretation, Theory*.

Anna Vaninskaya is a Lecturer in Victorian Literature at the University of Edinburgh. She is the author of *William Morris and the Idea of Community: Romance, History, and Propaganda, 1880–1914* (2010), and she has also published many articles and chapters on topics ranging from Chesterton, Orwell, Tolkien, and Stoppard to 19th-century socialism, popular reading, education, and historical cultures. She is currently at work on a second book on Anglo-Russian cultural relations in the early 20th century.

Lynn Voskuil is Associate Professor in the Department of English at the University of Houston, where she teaches Victorian literature, Women's Studies, and Empire Studies. She is the author of *Acting Naturally: Victorian Theatricality and Authenticity* (2004), and her articles have appeared in such journals as *Victorian Studies, ELH, Feminist Studies*, and *Nineteenth-Century Contexts*. Her current book project, entitled 'Horticulture and Imperialism: The Garden Spaces of the British Empire, 1789–1914', explores 19th-century Britain's fascination with tropical plants and horticulture.

INTRODUCTION

LISA RODENSKY

'Handbook' as 'guide' or 'compendium' came into English (from the German *Handbuch*) at the beginning of the 19th century and was then put to use, according to the *OED*, identifying works that offered 'concise information for the tourist'. No doubt the dictionary editors had in mind John Murray's *Hand-Book for Travellers on the Continent* (1836) which inaugurated his series of handbooks (including *A Hand-Book for Travellers in Switzerland and the Alps of Savoy and Piedmont* (1838) and *A Hand-Book for Travellers in Northern Italy* (1842), among many others). At the heart of Murray's venture was the middle-class audience—an audience that could afford to travel (modestly) and buy a (modest) guidebook. This audience also read literature, and Murray took advantage of that fact. The handbooks, reports Barbara Schaff, integrated literary works into the discourse of the travel guide.[1] But tellingly, Murray chose poetry, not novels, as his touchstones (though Scott's *Quentin Durward* (1832) turns up on two occasions and *Waverley* (1814) (indirectly) on one). Schaff argues persuasively that Murray looked to Byron and Shelley as mediators of high culture.

That Murray deployed poetry and not the novel underlines the novel's place in the culture of 1836—also the year that the first instalments of Charles Dickens's *Pickwick Papers* broke onto the scene. Even at the century's end, the novel was still consigned to the margins of literary history, and so too in the manuals and handbooks developed for examination cramming that Anna Vaninskaya describes in her chapter (included here) on the novel in the university. The novel's attempts to assert its cultural authority inform a fair number of the chapters in this *Oxford Handbook of the Victorian Novel*, as do the central facts that underpinned the novel's success—the growth of England as a reading nation and the inventions of technologies that served its readership, the steam-press in particular.

---

[1] Barbara Schaff, 'John Murray's Handbooks to Italy: Making Tourism Literary', in *Literary Tourism and Nineteenth-century Culture*, ed. Nicola J. Watson (Basingstoke: Palgrave Macmillan, 2009). See also James Buzard, 'The Uses of Romanticism: Byron and the Victorian Continental Tour', *Victorian Studies* 35 (Autumn 1991): 29–49.

Every (good) scholarly work guides readers, but a handbook—promising the convenience of manual portability—undertakes to present a broad range of topics without superficiality. For the contributors to such an enterprise, the trick is to balance breadth and depth, where readers rightly expect some condensing of information that covers a topic and also new material or new ways to interpret familiar material, all in the space of a reasonably sized chapter in a single volume (though it is indeed doubtful that any reader will want to travel with *this* handbook, except in its online form). This is a tall order for a Victorian novel handbook in the 21st century. Much (to say the least) has been written on the Victorian novel, and for good reason. Given the significance of the novel to the period and the continuing interest in Victorian studies, it isn't surprising that a number of Victorian novel compendiums are currently in print, not to mention collections on Victorian literature and culture more generally, and many collections on single authors and even on singular works.[2] To contribute meaningfully to this impressive corpus, I present here a combination of familiar but newly imagined topics and topics not often covered in other companions. Some chapters emphasize cultural and historical contexts, others the literary, though this is a matter of degree and not kind, since each of the chapters takes up the novel as both a cultural and literary form and force. With respect to the contextual information that contributors offer, it is no doubt the case that readers will find some repetition. More than one chapter makes note of the rising literacy of the period, for instance. Such repetitions are unavoidable because chapters must stand alone; no reader (except the volume's editor) should be expected to read the book from start to finish. And it must be the case that what might be unnecessary for one reader might be helpful to another. This handbook assumes its audience members are knowledgeable readers of literature, but not that all knowledgeable readers know the same things.

Probably every editor of a Victorian anthology at least considers beginning an introduction by invoking the dates of Victoria's reign to define the period and by extension the period's literature. But who believes that the Victorian novel debuted on 20 June 1837 or took its last curtain call on 22 January 1901? So it is commonsense to think about whether we can distinguish the novel, Victorian-style, by looking at the decades before and after—what we name the 'romantic' period and the 'modern' period (and I don't envy those editors the task of defining those periods, by the way). Some common threads emerge: we contrast romantic idealism with Victorian realism (the heroic

---

[2] For example, Blackwell's *Companion to the Victorian Novel*, ed. Patrick Brantlinger and William B. Thesing (London: Blackwell, 2002) and *Concise Companion to the Victorian Novel*, ed. Francis O'Gorman (London: Blackwell, 2005), Greenwood Press's *Companion to the Victorian Novel*, ed. William Baker and Kenneth Womack (Westport, CT: Greenwood Press, 2002)), and *The Cambridge Companion to the Victorian Novel*, ed. Deirdre David (Cambridge: Cambridge University Press, 2000). The most recent collections of essays covering the period are *The Oxford History of the Novel in English*, vol. 3: *The Nineteenth-Century Novel, 1820–1880*, ed. John Kucich and Jenny Bourne Taylor (Oxford: Oxford University Press, 2012) and *The Oxford History of the Novel in English*, vol. 4: *The Reinvention of the British and Irish Novel, 1880–1940*, ed. Patrick Parrinder and Andrzej Grasiorek (Oxford: Oxford University Press, 2011).

against the domestic) and the moral earnestness of the Victorian against the amoral aes-theticism of the modern. Useful as generalizations, these assertions necessarily break down in particular cases, and we find ourselves needing terms like proto-modernism or romantic realism. Their porousness honours the complexities of works of art that won't abide by categories—and yet the categories help us define preoccupations and dominant impulses of texts in a particular period.[3]

The focus of this handbook is the novel published between 1837 and 1901, very roughly speaking. The overview I give below describes in more detail the handbook's organization in addition to offering brief summaries of and connections among the chapters (though the index is the best source of the many ways the chapters intersect). I have grouped (imperfectly) those chapters together under headings that highlight common threads. Moving through the various sections of this handbook, readers will register how they overlap. The overlapping is sometimes obvious: Jennifer Green-Lewis's chapter on visual culture will coincide with Emily Allen's on the novel and the theatre; Lynn Voskuil's on horticulture crosses Julia Prewitt Brown's on the *Bildungsroman*; Richard Menke and Alison Byerly's chapters on communication and travel technologies intersect with the chapters in the section, 'Commerce, Work, Professions, Status'. How could they not, given how central technological developments were to commerce and work? But like the attempts to define the 'Victorian' itself, the groupings underline a set of concerns even when one could imagine different combinations.

Beyond thematic affinities, the handbook as a whole offers a broad chronological structure—and by 'broad' I also mean 'flawed', since many chapters don't stick to the beginning or end of the period, but travel within it. Nevertheless, I begin with three chapters that attend to the Victorian novel's beginnings and more particularly to the novel's relation to early 19th-century print culture, an area of study that has grown markedly. The seminal work by Richard Altick, John Sutherland, Laurel Brake, Simon Eliot, David McKitterick, and Peter Garside (to name just a few) has opened up this field. Drawing on recent bibliographic work of remarkable scope and detail, Garside's chapter in this handbook considers the much more complex landscape of novel production during the so-called hiatus between 1820 and 1836. While we may be tempted to

---

[3] In their introduction to *The Oxford History of the Novel in English*, vol. 3: *The Nineteenth-Century Novel, 1820–1880*, John Kucich and Jenny Bourne Taylor anticipate objections to the chronological limits of their volume. Redefining the period as 1820–80, the *Oxford History* invokes the major developments in technology and literary production that inaugurated the novel's ascension—and particularly the rise of Walter Scott—to delineate the period's beginning, while the intensified stratification of the novel and its reading public in the 1880s signals the end of what Kucich and Bourne Taylor rightly call 'the great age of the novel' (xviii). In their introduction to *The Oxford History of the Novel in English*, vol. 4: *The Reinvention of the British and Irish Novel, 1880–1940*, Parrinder and Gasiorek pick up where Kucich and Bourne Taylor leave off, with a vision of the last two decades of the 19th century that registers the more rigid distinctions between high-, middle-, and low-brow work. Both of these excellent introductions make persuasive points about this refigured periodization that help readers see the novel's history not in terms of Victoria's reign but in terms of specific cultural forces and the novelist's responses to them. This handbook recognizes the demarcations the *Oxford History* volumes have identified, but this work—more handbook than history—does not address questions of periodization as fully as the *Oxford History* has.

think of this period as one that moves from Walter Scott to Charles Dickens (and Scott is surely the most influential literary force in these years), Garside shows it to be one not of consolidation but of diversification. And though novel production was relatively constant (averaging 78 per year), one registers the spikes and dips with more clarity. The new bibliographic details that Garside brings to bear for the years leading up to the Victorian period will help scholars develop more nuanced and substantiated arguments about the novel's growth into the dominant genre of the 19th century.

The handbook then turns from this pre-history of the Victorian novel to the Victorians' own histories of the novel. The 19th-century novel had achieved some respectability—as Garside and others (Ina Ferris, for instance)[4] have argued, Scott masculinized the novel and its most successful subgenre (historical fiction), demoting female-authored novels in his wake. But the novel's future (as well as its past) was still in question. In 'New Histories of English Literature and the Rise of the Novel, 1835–1859', William McKelvy investigates how, at the beginning of the Victorian period, newly emerging, self-identifying literary historians invoked the 18th-century English novel to distinguish a specifically English literary tradition for a specifically English audience. Indeed, this 'new sense of literary history' (44) depended on literacy—an audience to instruct—and a printing industry that could produce publications cheaply enough for that audience to afford them. As the century unfolded, these Victorian literary historians took the opportunity to include their culture's contemporary novels in an effort to separate the wheat from the chaff, but, as McKelvy argues, the significance of such guidance was not simply that the historians asserted themselves as judgement-makers, but that the Victorian novel—their contemporary novel—was worth making judgements about: that readers should read contemporary novels which became part of a living national literature.

Including the Victorian novel in a national literature (or at least an idea of it) invested the form with legitimacy. But if the novel as a category was worthy of inclusion, not all of its creators (or their creations) were. Who would decide what was good and what not? Such decisions were not to be left to a handful of self-proclaimed literary historians, that's for sure. As Rebecca Edwards Newman describes in 'Genre, Criticism, and the Early Victorian Novel', the last chapter in this first section on 'Beginnings', the years in which the Victorian novel began its rise to power were also the years in which the periodical press expanded its reach and attempted to assert its own power by classifying novels and producing a subgeneric hierarchy. Newman further describes how novelists entered the debates. Finding themselves in competition with periodical critics for the right to determine the generic boundaries and values of their own productions, novelists (and Newman focuses on Edward Bulwer Lytton and Dickens in particular) used both hypertextual apparatus (prefaces, authorial notes) and opportunities within novels to instruct readers about the novel's worth (as a genre), elbowing out (as fully as possible)

[4] Ina Ferris, *The Achievement of Literary Authority: Gender, History, and the Waverley Novels* (Ithaca: Cornell University Press, 1991).

periodical writers who were insinuating themselves as mediators between novels and readers.

The tension—sometimes antagonism—between writers and reviewers was not an especially Victorian impulse. The previous century had its share of it, certainly. What changes in these years (and it's no small change) are the numbers of voices trying to participate in the conversation—not just a few voices in the *Edinburgh Review* or the *Quarterly*, say, but an expanding number of periodical writers—and novelists, and readers (a shift which brings to mind the online 'reviewers' who post their reactions to their blogs moments after completing a book). To this triangle—novelist, reviewer, reader—we add yet more voices, those that Rachel Buurma registers in her 'Publishing the Victorian Novel', the first chapter in the next section of the handbook, which moves forward into topics focusing more extensively on the relations between Victorian publishing, reading, reviewing, quoting, and censoring; Buurma attends to the complex network of relations among publishers, authors, publishers' readers, librarians, and booksellers in the production of novels and refigures the idea of the individual novelist as the sole producer of the novel published under his or her name. Buurma considers instead an alternative model of collective and corporate authorship which takes more fully into account the contributions of (and pressures exerted by) the varied groups trying to be heard.

Recognizing the collectivity of the Victorian novel's authorship necessarily recognizes the expanding and increasingly influential Victorian novel-reading public, and it is that readership which the next chapter in the handbook investigates. There is, as Debra Gettelman explains in 'The Victorian Novel and Its Readers', the well-known narrative of novel-reading history that recounts how Victorian commentators on the period's novel objected to the genre's corruption of an all-too vulnerable readership. But Gettelman, like Buurma, rethinks the ramifications of this interdependence, this porousness. As Buurma reconfigures the idea of individual authorship, so too does Gettelman propose different paradigms for readership. Moving quickly past the usual passages from pundits worrying over the disease of novel reading, Gettelman recovers the evidence showing how and where Victorians identified the novel as a genre which also encouraged readerly individuality and mental liberty. Gettelman explains:

> As readers infused everyday experience with the contents of novels and projected their real experiences into those works of fiction, as they freely appropriated and personalized the latest serial instalments, novel reading in the 19th century ultimately came to be associated in the larger culture with fostering freedom of thought—a 'perfect liberty of reading', as Margaret Oliphant called it, that, whether it was put to better or worse purposes, was imagined to be a distinctively English part of life in the period. [113–14]

The audience that Gettelman zeroes in on was more and more a reading audience, not just of novels but of essays, pamphlets, periodicals, and cheap books on a wide range of topics. Over the last twenty years (or more), work on the dynamics between the Victorian periodical (in particular) and the novel—its sometimes partner, sometimes competitor—has illuminated both institutions. That Dickens was at once a major novelist and periodical editor already provokes us to consider the first in the context of the second (and vice versa). In 'The Victorian Novel and the Reviews', Solveig C. Robinson concentrates on the novel-reviewing practices of the Victorian period, guiding us through the differences between early-, middle-, and late-century reviewing practices and attending to the larger meanings of those differences. Standing back from the period as a whole, Robinson traces the ways in which reviewers were finding their place in relation to the novel, figuring out how to distinguish themselves from the population of readers they sought to instruct, and from advertisers whose puffery tainted reviewing as a practice. In a sense, Robinson's chapter returns us to Newman's, but where Newman examines the novelist's defence against the reviewers, Robinson reconstructs how reviewers inserted themselves into the world of the novel in the first place. The narrative arc Robinson travels on from the beginning of the century to its end reveals an increasing movement towards division, diversity, and hierarchical classification of reviewing itself. Different periodicals established their particular voices and specialities, while, as Robinson notes, the unfolding of the century saw 'the emergence of new, distinct readerships, and . . . the gradual professionalization of literature, which began to differentiate "reviewing" from "literary criticism"' (133). Here one finds both diversification—the various niche readerships emerging for specific periodical publications—and consolidation: periodicals and the novels they reviewed occupied high or low culture, a similar impulse driving the differentiation between reviewing and literary criticism that Robinson articulates. And these increasingly fixed distinctions in the world of the reviews reflected (and also helped produce) the more distinctly established hierarchies among the novels themselves.

The novel's cultural status waxed and waned while the century went forward; different novelists and novels became targets, old targets turned into favourites, favourites became classics. Dickens had become the pre-eminent Victorian novelist securely identified with England and Englishness; George Eliot was a high culture figure and her novels objects of reverence. And yet the legitimacy of Dickens and Eliot, along with William Thackeray, Charlotte and Emily Brontë, Elizabeth Gaskell, and Anthony Trollope surely did not elevate the novel to a status beyond reproach, any more than a much-lauded television show might do now for the rest of the stuff on the other 500 channels. As McKelvy suggests in his earlier chapter, the novel as a genre was breaking into the culture's literary history, but the contemporary novel was still subject to serious scrutiny. In 'The Victorian Novel and the *OED*', Lynda Mugglestone investigates the formative debates about what kind of data should be included in the *OED* and teaches us how those debates reveal the continuing disagreements about the status of the novel. Notwithstanding the unwavering commitment of Frederick Furnivall and James Murray to collecting data for the dictionary from the widest range of readers doing the widest range of reading, reviews of the first fascicles, as well as comments from the *OED* delegates and other insiders, enact continuing fears about the legitimacy of certain novels and novelists—particularly sensation novels. From the detailed archival evidence Mugglestone has unearthed, one registers the intensity of anti-novel prejudices. Mugglestone's work attends closely to the enduring tensions between lexicographers committed to a disinterested collection of citations and those for whom the goal of protecting a particular canon remained paramount. As Mugglestone shows, the range of Victorian novels represented in the *OED* is of a piece with the editors' investment in the living English language. So while reviewers might demote the novels of Mary Elizabeth Braddon or Eliza Lynn Linton as poor reflections of the reading public's tastes, offering no better language than the daily newspaper, those novels could do what a Shakespearean play could not: give evidence of the evolution of English in the 19th century.

Like Gettelman, Buurma, and Robinson, Mugglestone situates the novel within a network of relations involving readers, editors, reviewers, and the novelists themselves. So too Barbara Leckie's chapter on the Victorian novel and censorship, the last chapter in this section, begins by shelving an approach that would focus on censorship trials (indeed only one occurred during the period, as Leckie points out), pitting an author (or publisher) against the state or laws controlling freedom of expression; instead, Leckie thinks about how a range of explicit and implicit regulatory networks—including circulating libraries, reviewers, and publishers—sought to control writers. Leckie considers the ways in which authors themselves understood these pressures in the last twenty years of the 19th century, looking in detail at prefaces to novels. Although Leckie's chapter attends to the last decades of the 19th century, I place it in this first-half of the volume because, like the chapters directly preceding it, this chapter considers the production of the novel and the responses to the novel's content within a complex system of relations. The period from 1880 to the end of the century saw the intensification of purity campaigns, and the tensions within the culture between those moving towards and those moving against free expression came to the fore. Examining three categories of print regulation—'self-censorship (exercised by both authors and readers); family-based censorship (typically exercised by the father and made powerful by the practice of reading out loud); extra-legal institutional censorship (exercised by circulating libraries, public libraries, publishers, and booksellers)' (168–69)—Leckie makes a nuanced case about Victorian print censorship that exposes a network of pressures and not one monolithic force suppressing artistic expression.

Not surprisingly, those late-century authors who felt repressed by the networks Leckie identifies also felt disadvantaged when they compared themselves to their liberated French peers—Émile Zola and Joris-Karl Huysmans, to name just two. The French novel was a force to be reckoned with throughout the period—and attempts to dismiss it as frivolous (or dangerous) didn't stop it from gaining a readership in England. But what of the Victorian novel in France? Marie-Françoise Cachin's chapter begins to answer this question as it produces the essential groundwork for this topic and is the first chapter under 'The Victorian Novel Elsewhere', the section which moves the novel outward, away from England. These chapters recognize that Victorian culture and its most successful literary genre created and capitalized on the expectations and structures (information networks, expansion of empire) that allowed the 20th- and 21st-century novel to claim a global presence.

Focusing on French periodicals that regularly reviewed English novels and the reviewers who attended to such novels, Cachin locates key responses to a wide range of novels of the period. So too Cachin opens up questions about how French publishers selected novels for translation and how translators imagined the work they would do with those novels. By mid-century, Victorian novelists themselves knew the value of a good French translation. In a letter to Emile Montegut, among the important French translators that Cachin discusses, G.H. Lewes requests assistance in finding a good translator for *Adam Bede* (1859), asking: 'if among your literary acquaintances you know of any one who would be competent to translate it'. Not that Eliot and Lewes didn't already have some contenders. Lewes explains:

> We have already had several applications, but it is of consequence to get a good translator, and I think you would be very likely to know of one. A work which has had greater success than Bulwer or Thackeray has ever achieved, and which in less than nine months has sold 10,000 copies, must surely be a good commercial speculation for a French publisher; and if a good translator could be found we are willing to sell the right of translation for 1,000 francs.[5]

In her chapter, Cachin carefully considers how France's own thriving novel culture handled the British novel's challenges to its dominance.

The situation was interestingly different in another 19th-century novel power-house—Russia—but Russia at the beginning of the period, as Julie Buckler reminds us in 'Victorian Literature and Russian Culture: Translation, Reception, Influence, Affinity', had not yet produced its great novel achievements. Timing tells a significant part of this story: that the Victorian novel coalesced before the Russian novel meant that it entered the culture without having to compete with a strong national novel already in place, though it still had the French novel to contend with. And while the Russian public certainly read the canonical authors, Buckler's research shows that 'Russian reception of Victorian literature cast a wide if unsystematic net, such that works and authors from this period translated into Russian extended to the margins of the tradition' (207). Buckler brings to our attention not only a range of authors but also a range of translators and approaches to translation—the good, the bad, and the ugly.

Both Cachin and Buckler analyse the pressures of translation; the absence of such pressure shapes, in its own way, the relations between the Victorian novel and the American novel. Taking up these relations, Amanda Claybaugh tracks the migration of the American novel into England as well as the movement of the English novel into America—a transatlantic crossing facilitated by a shared language and the lack of copyright protections (international copyright laws did not extend to America). Such

---

[5] G.H. Lewes to Emile Montegut, 1 December, 1859, in *The George Eliot Letters*, ed. Gordon. S. Haight, 9 vols. (New Haven: Yale University Press, 1978), 8: 253. Shortly after, on 6 December, Eliot herself wrote to François D'Albert Durade, one of the best English–French translators, reporting that she and Lewes were 'very anxious to get an accomplished translation for "Adam Bede"', adding further that 'I particularly wish my books to be well translated into French, because the French read so little English.' M.E. Lewes to Francois D'Albert-Durade, 6 December 1859, in *George Eliot Letters*, 3: 231.

freer exchange proved more complex as the century unfolded, with the English reviewers coming increasingly to recognize the American novel as less a poorer relation than
a real threat. The closeness also bred the need to define the English novel against the
American, as Claybaugh acutely shows.

There's no denying the impulse to define (and shore up) the Victorian novel as against
novels from other nations, but the novel was also establishing its territory in relation to
other kinds of writing in England itself. The travel memoir occupied an especially significant place in the culture, reflecting the expanding Empire and the appetite for colonial
narratives that displayed the 'exotic'. And yet, as hungry as the Victorians were for these
windows into exotic worlds, the novels of and at home (those we classify loosely under
the rubric of 'domestic novel') kept the empire on the margins, as many post-colonial
critics have observed. This fact provokes Margery Sabin, in her chapter 'Colonial India
and Victorian Storytelling', to frame two key questions:

> why did the mainstream domestic novel pay so little attention to the destabilizing,
> and even subversive, knowledge sometimes coming through writers with deep
> experience of the colonies? And why, in turn, did talented writers among those with
> that experience largely eschew fiction-writing, and (before Kipling) do mostly a
> mediocre job of it when they tried? [250]

By reading the dramatic representations of the interior life in the novel against the
absence of such representations in a range of works by writers who had been in India,
Sabin demonstrates that the novel's investment in internal and external coherence
excluded the fracturing impulses that knowledge of India in particular created. Such
a fracturing in relation to colonial subjects begins to be registered in the post-Mutiny
novels, particularly in Wilkie Collins's *The Moonstone* (1868) and then later, and more
fully, in Kipling's *Kim* (1901), but never so fully as is rendered in Kipling's short stories
and non-fiction of the period.

Sabin's chapter brings to a close this section which investigates, among other things,
what happened to the Victorian novel outside of England and what it brought back from its
travels. The next two chapters in the following section ('Technologies: Communication,
Travel, Visuality') attend more closely to the novel's engagement with movements inside
England. First Richard Menke's 'The Victorian Novel and Communication Networks'
traces the evolution of different information-delivering networks—including Rowland
Hill's reformed postal system and the electric telegraph system. Moving forward into the
years after Hill's system, Menke observes that 'Networked communication became less
an event than a constant, ubiquitous flow' which demonstrated the 'workaday ability of
a communication network to subsume the structure of an entire society' (278) and perhaps—as the wireless telegraph might show—the whole world. Exploring the ways in
which the novel before the 1860s more indirectly registered the power of such networks
and afterwards explicitly registered that power, Menke shows the range of responses to
its possibilities and dangers. The speed and distance that information could dependably
travel influenced the novel, as did the new capacities for people themselves to go other

places. In 'Technologies of Travel and the Victorian Novel' (the volume's next chapter), Alison Byerly explains how the train, boat, bicycle, and, finally, the hot-air balloon shaped the novel's conventions. It is balloon-travel that moves Byerly into her brief discussion of the Victorian obsession with panoramas, a form of virtual travel that allowed Victorians to 'imagine that they were looking at Paris, Bombay, or the Alps. Shifting panoramas, scenes which were slowly unrolled to convey the sense of a journey, were also frequently displayed in London and elsewhere' (310). Here travel intersects profoundly with the developments in visual technologies which brought new ways of seeing and new things to be seen into the culture and its novel.

Victorian visual culture has been a lively topic in Victorian studies for the last two decades (or longer), as have the narrower (though still awesomely large) investigations of the relations between the novel and visual culture. Though Kate Flint's *The Victorians and the Visual Imagination* doesn't limit itself to the novel, the genre occupies a vital place in her analysis of Victorian representations of the visible and the invisible.[6] This interest in visuality and the novel has opened up into research about particular components of the visual culture —illustration and painting, for instance—and their interactions with the novel. The novel was, after all, often an illustrated genre, and when we think of illustration, we immediately call to mind the work of Cruikshank and Phiz. In the best of all possible worlds, one could include chapters on each component part, but in this world I have chosen to focus on what is arguably the most significant visual influence on the novel: photography. In her chapter on the novel and photography, Jennifer Green-Lewis analyses Victorian responses to the growing ubiquity of the photograph. Though the novel as a form preceded the photograph, the latter exerted a marked influence on the world that the Victorian novel inhabited. As Green-Lewis explains, the novel's preoccupation with memory and identity (to name just two topoi) owes much to the cultural practices that the growth of photography stimulated. Green-Lewis asks, 'Is it possible to imagine an artefact that more cogently expresses and defies physical and temporal discontinuity than a photograph?' (315) Readers of novels were also readers of photographs which were 'fast becoming both symbol and substance of reality. If novels were to render the lived reality of their readers they must depict the visible world; and to be visible, as indeed, to be memorable, at mid-century, was to be both photographable and photographed' (318).

The Victorian novel and the photograph grew up together, through the early years of the daguerreotype and the silver-fork novels into the intensely prolific mid-century and on into the end-of-century decadence. So long and varied a period as the Victorian age necessarily divides itself up into different sub-periods—early, middle, late—and as I remarked at the beginning of this introduction, I have tried to honour this broad chronology in my chapter groupings. Figuring out what goes at the beginning and the end of the handbook ('Beginnings' and 'Endings') seemed to me more obvious than what

---

[6] Kate Flint, *The Victorians and the Visual Imagination* (Cambridge: Cambridge University Press, 2000).

I would put in the middle as the 'Middle', but what luck that Janice Carlisle's work has focused on the novels of the 1860s. The decade often comes under investigation in work on the sensation novel—after all, this is the decade of *Lady Audley's Secret* (1862) and *Aurora Floyd* (1863), two novels which were the subject of an 1863 *Fraser's Magazine* review critiquing the 'perverted and vitiated taste' of a public that required ever more excitement.[7] But Carlisle imagines the decade's novels differently. As she argues:

> The conventional view of the sensation novel of the 1860s ... is that the genre works on the reader's nerves, creating morbid feelings of agitation by setting forth plots involving violent crimes and secrets and deceptions. The ways in which these novels depict their characters and the state of their irritated nerves and moving bodies suggest, however, the opposite: this fiction allows its readers to pride themselves on their own relative self-possession, to conclude that they are moving at dignified and seemly rates through lives over which they have relative control. [346]

Carlisle sees this 'complex of relationships' between readers and characters as producing a 'structure of feeling'—a phrase borrowed from Raymond Williams—that more usefully marks novels of the 1860s (338). While thinking of sensation novels as a separate subgenre is illuminating and continues to motivate interesting work, Carlisle's approach thinks beyond that subgeneric category to see new and different connections among mid-century novels.

As does Evan Horowitz's work on the industrial novel, the chapter that kicks off the next section, 'Commerce, Work, Professions, Status'. Instead of searching out 'signs of industry' (factories, masters/workers, riots)—the most obvious elements of what we usually name as the 'industrial novel'—Horowitz locates 'either the revolutionary energy of industrial growth, the new anxiety such growth produced, or both' (366). The critical attention to this particular 'energy' and 'anxiety' in the novels illuminates both the industrial novel as a genre and genre itself. To see genre not only as identifying form and subject matter but also as an impulse or attitude is to recognize that form (novel) and subject matter (industry) insufficiently describe what the Victorian industrial novel is.

Questions about financial profits that remain implicit in Horowitz's chapter take centre stage in George Levine's 'The Protestant Ethic and the "Spirit" of Money: Max Weber, *Silas Marner*, and the Victorian Novel', where Levine attends particularly to Eliot's *Silas Marner* (1861) to show how Victorians squared their Protestantism with their monetary ambitions. For Levine, what most fully illuminates the Victorian reconciliation of lucre and piety is Max Weber's *The Protestant Ethic and the 'Spirit' of Capitalism*. Here Weber exposes the work Protestant ethics must do to disassociate the acquisition of possessions from the pleasure one might take from having them. Levine zeroes in on the complications arising in Victorian novels 'when good characters acquire wealth or morally marginal characters seek it' (381). How is it that the good should do economically well

7 'Popular Novels of the Year', *Fraser's Magazine* 68, no. 404 (August, 1863): 253–69, 262.

and still remain good? Levine argues: 'The irony that Weber pursues in finding religious "spirit" in the history and the continuing practice of capitalist enterprise plays itself out inside the novels. Thus, the secularizing influence of wealth seeps into pious novels almost without exception' (381).

Levine reads the Victorian novelist's simultaneous investments in the conflicting impulses of capitalism and Protestantism through Weber; Jennifer Ruth in her chapter on 'The Victorian Novel and the Professions' attends to a different but related conflict—one between a class-based prejudice against work and the growth of a new professional class of workers. Taking Dickens's *A Tale of Two Cities* (1859) as her central example, Ruth doesn't merely argue that the novel reflects the expansion of the professional class; she maintains that the novel 'contributed to the state's evolution into an entity run by this figure and his cohorts' (397), exploring the complexities Dickens, in particular, exposes as he imagines this rising 'class' and the sometimes-elusive work they performed. Such work the Victorians and their culture judged ambivalently, for to do work was already to raise questions about one's class status—one's respectability.

Respectability is a term so fully attached to 'Victorian' that the one term often implies the other. Kenneth Haynes, in his 'Gentleman's Latin, Lady's Greek', the chapter following Ruth's, considers the ways in which the novel's representation of the classics contributed to 'the formation of different sorts of respectable identities' (415). Quotations from and allusions to the classics in novels might situate a speaker as one thing or another—a gentleman or not, a professional or not, an Anglican or not. And yet Haynes is interested not only in how classical literature policed categories but also in how novelists deployed the classics to challenge boundaries that were themselves becoming less defined.

Chapters in the next grouping implicitly engage professions as well: the scientist, doctor, lawyer, cleric, and horticulturist find their way into work on science, medicine, law, religion, and horticulture. The section begins with what is arguably the field that exerted the most pressure on the Victorian age—science. Jonathan Smith takes on the challenge of describing not just a monolithic Victorian science but varied sciences—biological, geological, thermo-dynamical—in a range of Victorian novels. While Darwinism and literary realism surely inform Smith's work, he attends also to non-realist forms, and as much to the scientific imagination as to novel's science. The movement among genres and scientific subfields in Smith's chapter enacts both the ubiquitous presence of the scientific in the Victorian novel and the novel's influence on scientific discourse.

Smith brings his chapter to a close by gesturing towards the directions in which recent critical work on the novel and sciences has travelled—including work on medicine and psychology. Chapters on these topics follow on from science: first, Meegan Kennedy's chapter on medicine and the novel establishes the common ground upon which Victorian novelists and the fast-developing medical world (including the physicians who published their work in periodicals alongside serialized novels) operated. As with science and law, medicine at once influences and is influenced by the novel. In her contribution, 'Naturalizing the Mind in the Victorian Novel', Suzy Anger narrows her field of inquiry to think through how the debates about the relations between mind and body shaped both the form and content of novels. This work on physiological psychology and narrative exposes the ambivalence novelists felt about representing the mind as controlled by the body.

The discourses that Smith, Kennedy, and Anger put in relation to the novel demonstrate the powerful cultural cross-currents between the novel and these other disciplines. That many of the chapters in this handbook are interdisciplinary speaks to the growth of such work over the last thirty-odd years—not just with respect to the Victorian novel but throughout literary studies. While I doubt that more than a few critics ever isolated the Victorian novel from its culture, recent work now pursues interdisciplinarity more persistently and variedly. Such work makes ready sense. After all, the novel—that loose, baggy monster—brought much of its cultural context directly and indirectly into its pages. These qualities, coupled with the rise of realism, move scholars to consider the ways in which the novel situated itself with and against other institutions. As the handbook shifts from the psychological to the forensic, Jan-Melissa Schramm enters into questions about fiction's competition with the law for authority, and also its attempts to align itself with the law. Drawing our attention to the trial scenes in Elizabeth Gaskell's *Mary Barton* (1848), Schramm approaches their significance from a fresh direction, considering the jury as an organizational structure that would help Gaskell negotiate between the claims of the 'one' (the wrongfully accused defendant, in the case of *Mary Barton*) and the 'many'. Schramm's interpretive lens reveals both the Victorian preoccupation with questions about substitution (when the one stands for the many) and how the literary, theological, and forensic discourses competed with and completed each other in attending to such questions.

So too Patrick O'Malley narrows an enormous field of inquiry—the relations between religion and the novel—by focusing on two novels published thirty years apart: George Eliot's *Romola* (1863) Sarah Grand's *The Heavenly Twins* (1893). While in the earlier chapter on morality and money, George Levine coupled Protestantism and capitalism, O'Malley triangulates Protestantism, Catholicism, and the emerging voices of women. 'Catholicism in Victorian Women's Novels' complicates familiar readings of Catholicism and Protestantism in the novel by considering how Eliot and Grand imagine Catholicism as a rebellious alternative to the domesticity of women that Protestant ideology promotes. This triangulation sharpens our understanding of these compelling representations of Catholicism by showing that they both reinforce a recognizable anti-Catholicism (as foreign, as medieval) and reveal it as a force anticipating modernity.

To think of anti-Catholicism in Victorian novels in terms of a disruptive, protomodern energy is to recall how much some Victorian novelists invested in disciplining those very energies as they arose around them. Drawing together the practices of horticulturists and novelists, Lynn Voskuil underlines not only their shared commitment to improvement and control but also the intensity of the culture's commitment to these values. Though we know well that the Victorians believed in progress, the ubiquitousness and persistence of that belief comes home very powerfully in Voskuil's work. The *Bildungsroman* (a subgenre which Julia Prewitt Brown attends to at more length in her later chapter) integrates horticulture into its plot, as Voskuil shows. Part of what distinguishes the Victorian's horticulture in particular is its dissemination through a popular horticultural press whose audience included both middle- and working-class readers, like the novel itself. And novelists invoked the meanings that the popular horticultural press reinforced—that gardens promoted peaceful, controlled cultivation of self, of others, and of the Other. This last, argues Voskuil, affirms the Victorians's cultivation of empire and the novel's participation in that enterprise.

If novelists understood the narrative possibilities generated by the forces shaping the culture, they also contended with other more direct competitors. The chapters that begin the next section of the handbook place the novel in relation to other genres—first, drama, then poetry, and finally criticism. The novel's apotheosis in the Victorian period is beyond dispute, but Emily Allen in 'The Victorian Novel and Theatre' investigates how the novel's triumph specifically over the theatre marks the novel's history and our interpretation of that history. Of course theatre has its own history, longer than the novel's, and engaging many of the same cultural anxieties we invoke when we discuss the novel. No doubt the theatre appealed to a 19th-century audience eager for spectacle; it might have proved itself the century's dominant form. It didn't. That fact affected, and was affected by, the novel. Moving from the stage back to the page, James Najarian engages the novelist's representations of the poet. His title, 'Verse Versus the Novel', already gestures towards novelists' attempts to demote poets—to turn the unacknowledged legislators of the world into effeminate versifiers (it is no accident that Najarian pits the novel against 'verse' and not poetry, enacting the novelists' strategy of demotion). Starting with Harold Skimpole of Dickens's *Bleak House* (1853), behind whom lurks the poet Leigh Hunt, Najarian uncovers a pattern that suggests the ways in which novelists exploited certain stereotypes of the poet-aesthete to elevate the novel as the culture's moral arbiter.

While Najarian traces the potential competition between the novel and poetry, that relation was also powerfully collaborative. Think, for instance, of George Eliot's essay, 'Notes on Form in Art' (1868) where she appropriates 'poetry' as the term incorporating 'all literary production in which it is the prerogative and not the reproach that the choice and sequence of images and ideas—that is, of relations and groups of relations—are more or less not only determined by emotion but intended to express it'.[8] Here poetry defines the art that creates the closest relation between form and feeling. 'Notes on Form in Art' might provoke readers to think about where and when Victorian novelists incorporate poems into their novels—and Philip Horne turns his mind to that activity in 'Poetic Allusion in the Victorian Novel'. Taking up the novel's poetic allusions, Horne finds in the combined energies of novel and poem a set of possibilities that the novel, absent allusion, could not achieve. Allusion transfuses, and interfuses, and Horne works through how and whether poetic allusion 'can be a means for the prose of novels to gain access to an additional level of suggestiveness about inner processes of the mind—by

---

[8] George Eliot, 'Notes on Form in Art', in *George Eliot: Selected Essays, Poems and Other Writings*, ed. A.S. Byatt and Nicholas Warren (London: Penguin, 1990), 231–6, 232.

offering a depth of reference that is not normally available to the more exclusively functional language' (619)—the language of the everyday that drew so many readers to the novel in the first place.

The fully productive relationship between poetry and the novel that Horne engages demonstrates the power of the novelist to produce out of and with poetry a new creation. And one could think too about instances in which novelists create out of and with other novels. That claim is at the heart of Christopher Ricks's chapter, 'The Novelist as Critic', where the best criticism is also a creative enterprise. Where do we find this in the Victorian novel? Such a question activates the first sections of Ricks's chapter where he singles out the great achievements of Henry James, Dickens, and Charlotte Brontë as creators who revise their own novels and the work of others in ways that reveal their genius. But that visionary-revisionary work overshadows the relatively unexceptional writing of the novelist-critic, the novelist writing about novels non-fictionally, as it were. There are passages of such criticism to be admired, but few, argues Ricks, that rise to the heights that Matthew Arnold or Gerard Hopkins achieve as poet-critics.

After poetry and criticism, the handbook looks more fully inward, to think about quintessentially Victorian forms: first to the *Bildungsroman*, a defining subgenre of the Victorian novel, and then to specific stylistic elements that identify the novel as Victorian. There are, without a doubt, other Victorian subgenres besides the *Bildungsroman* that might rightly claim a place in this volume, and have rightly claimed places in other Victorian novel companions: the historical, silver-fork, Newgate, gothic, sensation, juvenile, and detective novels each contribute meaningfully to our understanding of what the 'Novel' had been in the 18th century, was in the 19th, and would become in the 20th. Various chapters in this volume take up one or more of these (and other) subcategories (particularly Edward's, Horowitz's, Carlisle's, and Schaffer's chapters). I choose to include a separate chapter on the *Bildungsroman* in this section because its preoccupations have grown to be so closely associated with the 19th-century English novel. Indeed, while the first thing we might register about the term *Bildungroman* is its Germanness, the English novelist was quick to appropriate it. As Julia Prewitt Brown observes in 'The Moral Scope of the English *Bildungsroman*', the transformation of the *Bildungsroman* by English novelists enacts its Englishification, as it were. In the hands of the English, the form embodies a range of complex ethical questions—questions that arise not from a general principle but from particular experiences. Ultimately, the *Bildungsroman* became one of the most Victorian of novel subgenres—not so now, when the 'coming of age' narrative gets told most often as memoir or has been monopolized by what booksellers call 'Young Adult fiction'.

The last chapter in this section also takes on the challenge of identifying a specific aspect of a novel that we might defend as Victorian—and what a challenge it is. Are there markers of a Victorian novel-writing style, asks Mark Lambert? There are. In 'Three Matters of Style' Lambert identifies an elaborated style (manifested in Latinate diction, 'elegant variation' of noun phrases, conspicuously formal syntax, complex prepositions) and the 'suspended quotation' (when a narrator interrupts a character) as part of a recognizably Victorian novelistic style. These elements will be found in the 18th- and early

19th-century novel, but the degree to which the Victorian novelist deployed these sty-listic elements distinguishes the Victorian novel. Moreover, Lambert demonstrates how these stylistic elements buttress the novel's investment in the superiority of the narrator. The elaborate style and the suspended quotation elevate the novel's narrator, and define him as a figure unmistakeably Victorian.

The handbook closes with four chapters that zero in on the novel's development in the last decades of the 19th century and the first decade of the 20th. The novelists we most readily identify as Victorian died before the century's turn: Dickens, Thackeray, the Brontës, Eliot, Gaskell, Anthony Trollope, Collins. But the novel surely lived on, though with ever-sharper demarcations between high- and low-brow productions. Eliot's nov-els had achieved critical praise (along with a good measure of financial success), and yet hers were not 'best-sellers', a term that tellingly had entered into the language by 1902 to describe success measured by sales alone, thereby cordoning off sales from other forms of merit. In this respect Dickens was always the hardest case. While some reviewers of the late 1830s had tagged Dickens as a fad whose popularity would fade in time, by 1901 a reviewer of 'Popular Novelists' elevated him to the status of classic.[9] The Victorian novel and its quintessential novelist had not only become legitimate, they had become worthy of study. But as Anna Vaninskaya explores in 'The Novel, Its Critics, and the University: A New Beginning?', the Victorian novel was nowhere on the Oxbridge curriculum and had little place in the debates about literature at university. By tracing the novel's path into England's most elite educational institutions, Vaninskaya picks up, in some respects, where McKelvy (in his chapter at the beginning of this handbook) leaves off, by describing English literary histories at mid-century, moving forward to the late-century work of George Saintsbury. Vaninskaya joins these histories with the manuals designed for those taking civil service and local examinations. The novel was a topic for these examinations, and for Mechanics and Workingmen's Institutions and in women's higher education. Still, Vaninskaya concludes that 'by the 1900s, in relation to the entire sweep (chronological and generic) of English literary history covered by the surveys, and tested in the various exams, the Victorian novel still did not occupy more than a tiny section' (727). In that 'tiny section', the legitimate novelists were being affirmed—Dickens, Thackeray, Charlotte Brontë, Eliot—and those so affirmed would eventually find their way past the guards at the Oxbridge gates.

Of course, the legitimacy of certain Victorian novels presupposes the illegitimacy of others, as the perceived gap between art and schlock widened. George Gissing's *New Grub Street* (1891) enacts the tragedy of the novelist-as-artist who can't support his fam-ily while the popular novelist thrives. In 'The Next Time' (1895), Henry James refigures *The New Grub Street* plot as a short story with a narrator who bemoans the fate of the starving novelist who can't earn a decent pay cheque. Both Gissing and James chart the undoing of the novelist who lacks the capacity (or the willingness) to produce the tried and false so prized by New Grub Street publishers. Although the late 1890s was surely

---

[9] 'The Popular Novel', *Quarterly Review* 194 (1901): 244–73, 246.

the age of the privately printed, exquisitely illustrated books of the literary decadents (think of John Grey's *Silverpoints*), it also gave us the massively successful and schlocky novels of Hall Caine and Marie Corelli.

But classing novels as high- or low-brow was not as easy as Gissing or James might make it seem. Often slotted among the low-brow, money-making productions of the late 19th century that high-brow critics took against were the New Woman novels, but Gissing himself wrote one such novel—*The Odd Women* (1893)—that had some critical and little financial success. Indeed, the 'New Woman novel' category itself presents special definitional challenges. When we think of some other subgenres (gothic, historical, sensation, detective), we don't think of the authors of those subgenres as having a specific political agenda or way of life. Writers of detective novels aren't usually detectives. And yet calling a novel a New Woman novel might also suggest who that author was—except when it didn't. In 'The Victorian Novel and the New Woman', Talia Schaffer not only locates and opens up these categorical complexities, but also reveals how such complexities have provoked particular critical responses in the 19th, 20th, and 21st centuries. So, for instance, the New Critical movement of the 20th century demoted many of these novels as anti-realistic; first-wave feminist critics lauded the works as radical. As Schaffer details, both responses limit the novels in ways that serve particular critical agendas. Moving forward into the 21st century, Schaffer sketches out the fertile work on the New Woman novel in the last decade and the developing critical possibilities for this diverse but identifiable group of texts.

The New Woman novels occupied part of a literary scene that brought the 1800s to a close. The Queen whose name defines the period survived only thirteen months into the 1900s, and though the last days of Victoria were not the last days of the Victorian novel, her end brings us to think about how novelists were registering the movement from one century's writing to another. In the last two contributions (shorter pieces) in this handbook, Rosemarie Bodenheimer and Daniel Hack choose their contender for the 'last Victorian novel', its 'lastness' illuminating most fully what the Victorian novel had come to mean. For while its conventions would ensure its endurance into the next century, they also tagged it as the last century's model. The novels that Bodenheimer and Hack have chosen—Joseph Conrad's *The Secret Agent* (1907) and W.E.B. Du Bois's *The Quest of the Silver Fleece* (1911), respectively—are not of the 19th century but the 20th, and share the point of view of the outsider—at once critical of and indebted to that which came before. Conrad implies his double-vision most tellingly in his Author's Note to *The Secret Agent*, where he defends his pervasively ironic tone as allowing him to say 'all [he] had to say in scorn as well as in pity'. But Conrad's unrelenting irony didn't finally issue in a set of values that the reader might reproduce in her own life. What the novel's first readers objected to was precisely the sense that it offered nothing but irony; readers registered the novel's contempt as a 'gratuitous outrage'.[10] Although Conrad pleaded his innocent intention, Bodenheimer sees Conrad deploying the novel's evocation of

---

[10] Joseph Conrad, *The Secret Agent*, ed. Michael Newton (London: Penguin, 2007), 251, 252.

sympathy as the bomb that finally blows up the Victorian world of the novel and the novel itself.

If asked to conjure a list of candidates for the last Victorian novel, it is possible that other readers might nominate *The Secret Agent*. It is less likely that *The Quest of the Silver Fleece* would come to mind, but it came into at least one reader's mind—fruitfully so. Hack's argument about Du Bois's 1911 American novel shows the Victorian novel's transatlantic grasp and its hold particularly on Du Bois. It is the novel's closing scenes that Hack is most interested in, where Du Bois exposes his predecessors' commitment to the status quo by radicalizing its happy ending.

This ending about endings doesn't aim to close off further thinking about the Victorian novel's end. Neither Hack nor Bodenheimer claim to have the last word on the last Victorian novel. Nor will this be the last Victorian novel handbook. At least it shouldn't be. I hope it won't be. Other editors should have the opportunity to make a list of chapters they want to bring together and then have the great pleasure of working with scholars on those chapters. There are topics missing here about which readers might want to read and scholars might want to write more—on the novel and music, or the novel in Germany, or the subgenres not represented. Or on topics not yet imagined. As the Victorians get further away from us, our versions of their culture and its novel inevitably change. These shifting emphases reflect critical trends, of course, but from such trends emerge more enduring approaches that teach us about the Victorian world and, by extension, our own.

PART I

BEGINNINGS

1

THE EARLY 19TH-CENTURY ENGLISH NOVEL, 1820–1836

PETER GARSIDE

In its first article for January 1820, the *Edinburgh Review* welcomed an entirely new departure in *Ivanhoe*, reviewing it alongside *Novels and Tales of the Author of Waverley* (1819), the first in a series of retrospective collections of Walter Scott's fiction, covering the sequence of Scottish novels from *Waverley* (1814) to *A Legend of Montrose* (1819). Never since Shakespeare, according to the reviewer (Francis Jeffrey) had there been such a case of inventiveness and creative fertility:

> In the period of little more than five years, he has founded a new school of invention; and established and endowed it with nearly thirty volumes of the most animated and original composition that has enriched English literature for a century—volumes that have cast sensibly into the shade all contemporary prose, and even all recent poetry.[1]

Noticeably in the process Jeffrey manages to transmute earlier suggestions by reviewers that the novel was a site of excessive female reproduction into a picture of masculine potency, while at the same time intimating the potential of the novel to match or exceed poetry as a genre. The use of the word 'English', though automatic in the circumstances for Jeffrey, is also telling in the light of Scott's shift with the English medieval *Ivanhoe* to primarily non-Scottish 'chivalric' subjects for his fiction. Correspondence involving Scott and his main associates in the publishing world indicates a calculated effort to expand sales in England, a plan matched by the publisher Archibald Constable's engagement of

Statistical information in this chapter is mainly taken from the two following online sources: P.D. Garside, J.E. Belanger, and S.A. Ragaz, *British Fiction, 1800–1829: A Database of Production, Circulation & Reception*, designer A.A. Mandal, <http://www.british-fiction.cf.ac.uk>; and Peter Garside, Anthony Mandal, Verena Ebbes, Angela Koch, and Rainer Schöwerling, *The English Novel, 1830–1836: A Bibliographical Survey of Prose Fiction Published in the British Isles*, <http://www.cardiff.ac.uk/encap/journals/corvey/1830s/>. Thanks are due to Anthony Mandal for help in producing the figures and tables in the present chapter.
[1] *Edinburgh Review* 33 (1820): 1–54, at 1.

the firm Hurst, Robinson & Co. as his main London associates. Impression numbers, which had reached an unprecedented 10,000 for *Rob Roy* (1818), stretched as high as 12,000 in the early 1820s, with Scott receiving advances in excess of £4,000. At the same time the introduction of the larger and more prestigious octavo format provided an excuse for escalating prices to an optimum 31s 6d (one-and-a half-guineas a volume) with *Kenilworth* (1821). In the new decade Scott also went on to break even his own record of productivity, with the result that on two occasions three titles appeared bearing the same-year imprint (1820 and 1822).

Along with this output, Constable was bringing out collected editions in a range of formats, aimed at different levels of the market, the original *Novels and Tales* being supplemented by other sequences such as *Historical Romances* as fresh titles accumulated. Finally, after Constable's bankruptcy in 1826, the collected Magnum Opus edition, commencing with monthly volumes from June 1829, found a new audience, more earnest and middle class than the original Regency readers, as sales (originally projected at 12,000) soared towards 30,000 per volume.

Certainly it would be hard to overestimate the range of Scott's influence during the 1820s and into the next decade. Among now chartable factors are the establishment of historical romance as the leading fictional mode, as well as a more general masculinization of the novel both in terms of authorship and its readers. At the same time, clearly other more impersonal determinants were at work. New methods of mechanical paper-making and the lifting of war-time restrictions drastically reduced the cost of paper, the main item in publishers' costs, and enhanced the production of larger works of literature such as novels. Less immediately perceptible is a shift in readership, as covert readers of fiction in the 1810s openly embraced a genre now made more respectable, and as a new more extensive wave of younger readers, whose first expectation in imaginative literature was prose fiction, began to make its presence felt. Though Scott's pulling power as an original author had diminished by mid-decade—an early sign was the decision to reduce impression numbers from 12,000 to 10,500 with his *Peveril of the Peak* (1822)—rival novelists, sometimes offering alternative subgenres, clamoured to fill in the space. In Scotland, Constable's list of fiction, mainly comprising Scott titles, was soon exceeded by that of William Blackwood, whose key authors were instrumental in producing a noticeably different kind of 'Scotch novel'. In London, where the publisher Henry Colburn brushed off the crisis in the book trade of 1825–26 with a rapid surge of new titles, emergent forms included the fashionable 'silver fork' novel as initiated by Robert Plumer Ward's *Tremaine, or the Man of Refinement* (1825), and a succession of military-nautical titles, including titles such as George Robert Gleig's *The Chelsea Pensioners* (1829). Two other areas developing rapidly apart from mainstream fiction at this time are the shorter moral-domestic tale, as written by Barbara Hofland [formerly Hoole], and story books for juvenile readers, which could be both religious and informational in tenor. Undoubtedly such transitions reflect deeper changes in the authorship, production, and readership of fiction.

The period 1830–36, leading directly to the accession of Queen Victoria in 1837, links Scott's last published novel, *Tales of My Landlord* (4th series, 1832), with Charles Dickens's *Sketches by 'Boz'* (1836–37), his first work of fiction to be published in book form. Traditionally considered as representing something of a hiatus, this phase is probably best thought of in terms of a number of diverse movements, some apparently contradictory in nature. Seen one way, the course of mainstream fiction served to consolidate some of the main trends evident in the 1820s, with an increasing professionalization of the fiction industry, reinforcement of London's centrality in the market, and tightening of the guinea-and-a-half 'three-decker' (i.e. a novel in three volumes) as the norm for upmarket titles. Elliot Engel and Margaret F. King, however, in *The Victorian Novel before Victoria* (1984), point to a developing urban middle-class outlook, countered by an aristocratic/romantic undertow, reflecting the social tensions in post-Reform Britain, and finding expression in several new modes, notably comic-realistic fiction and the Newgate Novel.[2] Seen on a yet broader scale, the period can be seen as one of variety and richness, marked by diversification rather than any linear upsurge in new titles, and exhibiting a number of transformations in the production and marketing of fiction. The same diversification also points to a fragmentation and extension of the relatively homogenous reading audience which had hitherto underpinned polite fiction, a situation which by the end of the period invited similar acts of imaginative amalgamation to that achieved by Scott in the Romantic era.

RESOURCES

Until recent years, efforts to quantify trends in areas such as output and the gender balance of authorship have been impeded by the imperfect nature of the bibliographical record. The accounts left by the period of itself, including circulating-library and review listings, are diverse but notoriously unreliable. *The English Catalogue of Books 1801–1836*, compiled by Alexander Peddie and Quintin Waddington, a retrospective compilation published in 1914, incorporates information from contemporary catalogues such as William Bent's London trade catalogues, but does not match the comprehensiveness of the regular Publishers' Circulars issued periodically from October 1837, and provides no categorization by genre. Similar kinds of irregularity are carried over into Andrew Block's bibliography *The English Novel 1740–1850*,[3] which compiles its alphabetical listings from a variety of mostly secondary sources, and adopts an elastic policy for inclusion, placing reprints, miscellanies, chapbooks, shilling shockers, quasi-fictional works, and not a few 'ghosts' (i.e. non-existent titles), alongside more standard novels. Other bibliographies have confined themselves to particular kinds of fiction, most notably the Gothic, and more recently women's fiction. Collections of fiction, such as those brought together for the 19th century by Michael Sadleir and Robert Lee Wolff,[4] are necessarily

---

[2] Elliot Engel and Margaret F. King, *The Victorian Novel before Victoria: British Fiction during the Reign of William IV, 1830–37* (London and Basingstoke: Macmillan, 1984).

[3] Andrew Block, *The English Novel 1740–1850* (1939) (London: Dawsons of Pall Mall, 1961).

[4] Michael Sadleir, ed., *XIX Century Fiction: A Bibliographical Record based on his own Collection*, 2 vols. (Cambridge: Cambridge University Press, 1951); Robert Lee Wolff, *Nineteenth-Century Fiction: A Bibliographical Catalogue*, 5 vols. (New York: Garland Publishing, 1981–86).

determined in their structure by the priorities of their collectors and the opportunities available to them, as well as tending to gravitate towards one of two main spheres, the pre-Romantic/Romantic or high Victorian, with the 1830s consequently caught in a kind of no-man's-land between.

A major breakthrough in the quantification of output has been achieved by the publication in 2000 of the two-volume *The English Novel 1770–1829: A Bibliographical Survey of Prose Fiction Published in the British Isles*.[5] Following on from previous such bibliographies charting fiction in the earlier 18th century, its entries (totalling 3,677 for the sixty years covered) are based wherever possible on actual copies of first editions, located through a variety of search methods, with entries only being reconstituted from secondary sources in cases where no copy appears to have survived. In the case of the second volume, covering 1800–29, the number of surviving novels in later years enables a situation where only some forty entries need to be reconstituted, with just two cases for the 1820s. A great boost to this volume was provided by exceptional holdings of Romantic-era novels at Schloss Corvey, in Germany, part of an aristocratic family library rediscovered by scholars in the 1980s. The evident broad-brush accession policy adopted by the library's main collectors (Victor Amadeus, Landgrave of Hesse-Rotenburg, and his second wife Elise) in acquiring the full swathe of contemporary belles-lettres publications in German, English, and French, results in a unique assembly of British fiction comparable to what might have been held by a leading London circulating library such as the Minerva Library. This in turn helped guide the compilers' sense of what in round terms constituted a 'novel' in the eyes of contemporaries, the general policy in *The English Novel* being to exclude items such as miscellanies, very short tales, religious tracts, fiction for young juveniles, and other specialist publications, some of which require their own bibliographical record. While these exclusions, and the absence of primary entries for subsequent editions, arguably have a limiting effect with regard to the full extensiveness of the fiction industry, the greatly enhanced record (both in range and detail) of new novels produced provides a fresh range of opportunity for statistical analysis.

The bibliographical record has been further enhanced by the online *British Fiction 1800–1829: A Database of Production, Circulation, & Reception* [DBF] (<http://www.british-fiction.cf.ac.uk/>), compiled at the Centre for Editorial and Intertextual Research at Cardiff University, and first made publicly available in 2004. On one level, this adds additional primary information to the original entries in the printed Bibliography, as a result of further research, with a number of fresh author attributions, improved information regarding further editions, and the addition of several new entries (making the total count 2,272 titles). The database is searchable over a number of fields. It also offers extensive contextual materials for individual entries, these including advertisements from newspapers, reviews, information from publishing archives and circulating

---

[5] Peter Garside, James Raven, and Rainer Schöwerling, eds., *The English Novel 1770–1829: A Bibliographical Survey of Prose Fiction Published in the British Isles*, 2 vols. (Oxford: Oxford University Press, 2000).

library catalogues, anecdotal records (as found in contemporary memoirs, etc.), and subscription lists where these are found. As a result it becomes possible to view with a new degree of precision elements such as publication costs, author remuneration, impression numbers, and reception.

One further publication now makes it possible to take the bibliographical survey of the novel right up to the advent on the Victorian Age. *The English Novel, 1830–1836* (<http://www.cardiff.ac.uk/encap/journals/corvey/1830s/>), initially released online in 2003, follows the same method as its printed predecessor in providing annual listings of new novels, employing the same criteria for inclusion, with a sum total of 610 entries for the seven years covered. The greater space available, however, allows the extension of individual entries in a number of ways, these including itemization of separate pieces within a work of fiction (a useful provision in view of the increased number of collections of tales at this time) and more extensive records of subsequent editions. At the same time, in responding to the increasingly variegated nature of output, the *English Novel, 1830–1836* provides a series of appendices listing various types of non-standard and quasi-fictional works, such as juvenile literature, multi-genre miscellanies, and heavily didactic/religious tales, comprising as a whole an additional 138 entries. One advantage in keeping the 'mainstream' annual listings separate is that it allows more direct comparison to be made with the bibliographical record for preceding years. Statistical information in the following sections in this chapter apply (unless otherwise stated) to the annual listings in both bibliographies, though data for the years 1800–29 relates to the online *DBF* version, with its slightly larger number of entries and enhanced author attributions.

NUMBERS

Some of the more sanguine commentators on the output of early 19th-century fiction have assumed a generally upward movement, stimulated by moments of exceptional growth, noticeably at the turn of the century, when exasperated reviewers gave up their endeavour to track all titles, and in the early 1830s, supposedly generated by the new technologies and a rising middle-class market. Other commentators, some much closer to events, have pointed to a stuttering of the genre at certain points, and even intimated a terminal decline. Among the latter can be counted James Grant in the second series of *The Great Metropolis* (1837). Grant, a Scottish newspaper editor who had moved to London in the later 1820s, points to a zenith of novel production 'ten or twelve years since', that is about 1825. Compared to this in his eyes there had been a noticeable reduction in the output of new titles more recently, other signs of decline being found in the smaller impressions printed, diminishing sales, and lower author remuneration. In his own experience, four novels published six months ago, two by celebrated authors, had failed to generate sales of more than 350 copies, and three of them somewhat less. Such novels as were produced, moreover, were more likely to be lent rather than purchased individually: 'The truth is, that, with the exception of the works of fifteen or twenty authors, no individual ever now dreams of purchasing a novel for his own reading. The only copies bought are for the circulating libraries.'[6]

The figures for new titles published annually provided by the bibliographies described above offer a picture somewhere between these two poles. In actuality, two of the most significant surges in production had already taken place before 1800; with notable peaks in 1788 (eighty titles with that year's imprint), marked by the rise of a new species of domestic sentimental fiction and the arrival of several new female authors, and in 1799 (99 titles), in a context of ideological ferment and at a highpoint of Gothic fiction. The same period also saw a proliferation of circulating libraries specializing in novels, some of which might possibly have required as many as two new titles a week to satisfy a clientele eager for 'something new'. At the same time, a number of counterweights necessarily limited any exponential growth, negative factors including the ponderous processes involved in producing larger works of literature using movable type and hand presses, and the inability of a relatively small pool of indigenous authors to generate an exceptional number of titles.

By contrast, the pattern for the new century was hardly one of uninterrupted growth. Over the thirty-seven years covered, the average from the total of 2,882 titles is slightly less than seventy-eight novels a year, with only fourteen years passing the eighty mark, and more than half caught in the band between sixty and eighty. Only in three cases is one hundred exceeded; the number in each case standing out from immediately surrounding years, and inviting interpretation in terms of special circumstances. The surge in the year 1808 (111 titles), for example, can be partly explained in terms of widespread controversy surrounding the acrimonious separation of the Prince and Princess of Wales. (Owing to the slowness in production, and a still evident practice of post-dating imprints, it is sometimes useful to look to the preceding year for root causes.) Set against the preceding decade, the 1810s show a marked drop in production, created partly by a backlash against 'low' fiction in more austere times, but governed also by material factors such as the high cost of paper, as well as a marked decline in the production of 'imported' titles in the form of translations of foreign writers. Compared with 1803, in the immediate wake of the Peace of Amiens, when nearly thirty out of seventy-nine titles were translations, mostly from the French, the whole of the 1810s exhibit only thirty-four such works, with indigenous authors as a result supplying a much larger share of output. Noticeably Scott's first venture into the genre with *Waverley* (1814) came at a low point in production (sixty-three titles), followed by an even deeper trough (229 titles only for the four years between 1815–18), though there is a suggestion of recovery (stimulated in part no doubt by the growing reputation of 'the author of *Waverley*') in 1819 with seventy-three titles.

Compared with this the early 1820s represent a period of expansion, reaching a highpoint in 1824 with just under one hundred new titles, reflecting James Grant's sense of a heyday for the novel at this time (see Figure 1.1). While there was some revival in the

---

[6] James Grant, *The Great Metropolis*, 2nd series, 2 vols. (London: Saunders & Otley, 1837), 1: 122–4.

FIGURE 1.1 Publication of new novels, 1820–1836

Sources: British Fiction, 1800–1829 (2004); The English Novel, 1830–1836 (2003)

publication of foreign titles in translation, with an especially interesting crop of German tiles in the mid-1820s, the scale was relatively negligible, and it is at this time that Britain became unmistakably a net exporter of fiction in terms of titles. A drop to seventy-seven titles in 1826 nevertheless registers an element of vulnerability, reflecting larger disturbances during the so-called 'crash' of that year. With the bankruptcy of Archibald Constable (as Scott's publisher, one of the most prominent in the field of upmarket fiction), and a general tendency among the trade in times of crisis to fall back on more traditional kinds of output, the novel at this time might have seemed especially vulnerable. The resilience of the form, however, is evident in a more steady output of eighty titles or more annually between 1827 and 1829.

The previously unanalysed material provided by *The English Novel, 1830–1836* invites a number of questions. The figure of 108 titles for imprint year 1830 might seem to reflect a fairly immediate response to technological change and the new spirit of middle-class reform. However, the following four years fail to sustain this growth, with a noticeable falling back to just sixty-nine titles in 1831. One possible explanation lies in the disruption caused by political agitation leading up to the final passing of the Reform Bills in 1831/32. William Blackwood, writing to his son on 24 October 1831, had little doubt that this was a major cause:

> This cursed Reform Bill has caused a dreadful stagnation in every kind of business for the whole of the year. There never has been so slack a year in our trade ever since I have been in business. Had it not been for the Magazine we should have had nothing to do.[7]

⁷ Cited in Margaret Oliphant, *Annals of a Publishing House: William Blackwood and His Sons*, 2 vols. (Edinburgh: Blackwood, 1897), 2: 104.

Blackwood's reference to *Blackwood's Magazine* suggests another difficulty for the novel at the time, in the shape of the growing popularity of the monthly magazines and a new species of annuals and keepsakes, specializing in smaller items of verse and prose, both of which helped cultivate a new taste for miscellaneous literature. The sudden rise in output of works of fiction to 112 new titles in 1835 might be partly owing to the form having learned to adapt and absorb such changes, in the shape of comic-domestic fiction, illustrated works, collections of tales, and other kinds of compilation. This buoyancy was also aided by an increasingly fluent interchange between British and American fiction markets, with some twenty titles originally published in North America being issued by London publishers in the early 1830s, nine of these in 1835 alone. The upward movement of 1835 is not sustained however in the following year, where output again sinks to below eighty titles (seventy-eight), perhaps partly as a result of a momentary exhaustion, but also in keeping with Grant's negative diagnosis as seen from 1837.

Any full analysis of the situation would be incomplete without reference to the total production of books, though calculation at this level is notoriously difficult, and any comparison between genres is fraught with difficulty, in view of factors such as the different sizes of book concerned. As a whole it would seem that the number of new novels produced reflects book production as a whole, albeit with variations in certain years, and with output of fiction in the earlier 1820s slightly exceeding the general pattern, achieving in the region of 8 per cent of the new book market. As part of his overall analysis of 19th-century book production, Simon Eliot points to a continuing upward trend in the 1830s, with a minor dip in 1831, and a considerable rise in 1832, followed by a slight downturn later in the decade, particularly noticeable in 1836.[8] The latter accords with Grant's pessimism regarding the novel in 1836, a year when according to his own estimate some 1,500 different books were published in London (pointing to a market share for fiction of just over 5 per cent). Noticeably Grant is more upbeat about several other types of publication, including periodical literature and works of 'a light and sketchy kind', though he is more pessimistic still about poetry, 'at a still greater discount in the literary market than novels'.[9]

Another indication of the decline of the genre, in Grant's analysis, lay in the decrease in the impression numbers for first editions (and an absence of subsequent editions except in exceptional cases):

> The authors whose works of fiction a dozen years since commanded a sale from 1,500 to 2,000 copies cannot now command a sale of 500 ... 750 copies ... That indeed is the number usually printed of novels, and other works of fiction, except where the great popularity of the author is supposed likely to carry off a larger impression. One thousand copies of such works ... are considered a large edition.[10]

---

[8] Simon Eliot, *Some Patterns and Trends in British Publishing 1800–1919* (London: Bibliographical Society, 1994), 24.

[9] Grant, *Great Metropolis*, 1: 133–4, 131, 124.

[10] Grant, *Great Metropolis*, 1: 123, 207–8.

Examination of publishers' archives mostly corroborates this account. At the beginning of the century an edition of no more than 500 would have been considered a normality, with only authors of reputation achieving anything higher. In the 1820s, however, there are fairly numerous examples of new or 'middle rank' authors being published in editions of 1500 or more. Longmans printed a first edition amounting to 2,500 of Amelia Opie's *Tales of the Heart* (1820), and regularly authorized impressions of 1750 for works of fiction by Jane and Anna Maria Porter, even when the tide of popularity was starting to turn against them. In Edinburgh William Blackwood at the onset of his novel-producing career risked first editions of 1,500 for James Hogg's *Brownie of Bodsbeck* (1818) and Susan Ferrier's *Marriage* (1818), though at that stage both authors were new to the form. Oliver & Boyd likewise issued 1,500 copies of *Glenfergus* (1820), by Robert Mudie (another first-time novelist), and went on to produce 3,000 copies of John Galt's *Ringan Gilhaize* (1823), having temporarily captured the author from Blackwood. In the 1830s the publishing archives of Richard Bentley provide a dense record of impression numbers, with first editions of new novels generally ranging between 500 and 2,000 copies, in gradations of 250, though in the exceptional case of Maria Edgeworth's last novel, *Helen* (1834), 3,000 were apparently produced. Numbers for imprint year 1836 would seem to show if anything a lessening of confidence, with at least one instance of just 250 copies, and several titles by novelists of reputation being confined to an impression of 750 or 1,000.

AUTHORS

From 1,437 novels belonging to 1820–36, it is possible identify nearly 550 different authors (a figure that includes some ten unidentified pseudonyms). Table 1.1 lists the twelve most productive novelists, followed by the total number of titles per author, amount of volumes involved, and (in the final column) inclusive dates of productivity within the period.

One prominent feature of this list is the absence of any dominant author covering the period as a whole. Both Scott and Galt, the two most productive writers, began their careers as novelists in the mid-1810s, and published their last works in the early 1830s. John Galt's output moved through several phases, from the early London-published *The Majolo* (1815), to the sequence of classic Scottish titles published in Edinburgh during the 1820s, mostly by William Blackwood, and then (from 1830) on to a new period of heightened activity, involving a number of London publishers, culminating in the achievement of no fewer than three titles in both 1832 and 1833. Unlike Scott, all of whose titles were in three or four volumes, Galt's output ranged from short single volumes to conventional three-deckers (a form whose constraints he more than once complained about). Two female authors in the list, Catherine George Ward (afterwards Mason) and Hannah Maria Jones (afterwards Lowndes), on the other hand, specialized for much of the 1820s in a species of serialized fiction, issued first in weekly numbers, and then bound up and re-marketed usually as large single volumes, incorporating engraved

Table 1.1 Most productive authors of novels, 1820–1836

Authors	Novels	Volumes	Imprint Dates
Galt, John[a]	24	48	1820–33
Scott, Sir Walter	17	49	1820–32
Gore, Catherine Grace Frances[b]	16	41	1824–36
Cooper, James Fenimore	14	42	1821–35
James, George Payne Rainsford	13	38	1829–36
Ward, Catherine George[c]	13	19	1820–33
Jones, Hannah Maria[d]	12	12	1821–36
St Clair, Rosalia [pseud.]	11	37	1820–34
Hofland, Barbara	11	21	1820–35
Scargill, William Pitt[e]	11	39	1826–35
Banim, John and Michael[f]	10	27	1824–35
Bulwer Lytton, Edward George	10	27	1827–35

[a] includes 1 newly identified work
[b] includes 1 questionable work (1 vol.)
[c] includes 11 large 1-vol. serialized works
[d] includes 12 large 1-vol. serialized works
[e] includes 4 questionable works (10 vols.)
[f] includes single and jointly authored works
Sources: *British Fiction, 1800–1829* (2004); *The English Novel, 1830–1836* (2003)

illustrations. While at the end of her career in the early 1830s Ward reverted to providing more conventional multi-volume works, Jones continued to produce the same brand of melodramatic domestic fiction for number-specialists such as George Virtue into the Victorian period. Other female stalwarts are the pseudonymous Rosalia St Clair, author of a chain of three- or four-volumed romances for the Minerva Press between 1819 and 1835; and Barbara Hofland, who first emerges as a writer of fiction in 1809, but whose output from the mid-1820s chiefly consisted of shorter moral-domestic tales, published mainly by Longmans, and ranging from *Integrity* (1823) to *Fortitude* (1835). Productive male novelists notable for the regularity of their output across virtually the whole period include James Fenimore Cooper, most of whose three-deckers from *Precaution* (1821) onwards were published in Britain shortly after appearing in North America, though on occasions simultaneously or even ahead of publications there; and the Banim bothers (Michael and John), creators of a sequence of Irish national tales beginning with *Tales, by the O'Hara Family* (1825).

Other prolific novelists can be seen beginning their careers further into the period. After a hesitant start with *Theresa Marchmont* (1824), Catherine Gore produced at least two fashionable novels in four of the years between 1829 and 1836, and went on to publish in all seventy works (including translated and 'edited' titles) over her lifetime. Edward Bulwer Lytton, whose career as a novelist began with the one-volume *Falkland* (1827), enhanced his reputation through a succession of upmarket three-deckers in the early 1830s, leading to *The Last Days of Pompeii* (1834) and *Rienzi* (1835). The historical novelist G.P.R. James first entered the market with *Richelieu, A Tale of France* (1829), this being followed by no fewer than twelve similar works through to 1836, with two titles in 1832 and 1833, and three in 1835: a velocity of output that followed on into the next decade. Other novelists, not included in the list, but whose regularity of output is first seen in the early 1830s, include Frederick Marryat (nine chiefly nautical tales beginning with *The Naval Officer* (1829)), and Frances Trollope (four novels in the wake of her successful non-fictional *Domestic Manners of the Americans* (1832)). Nearer the end of the period under view one catches a glimpse of two writers just at the start of what would prove to be spectacular careers: G.W.M. Reynolds, whose *The Youthful Impostor* (1835) gives little indication of his later sensationalism; and Charles Dickens, whose *Pickwick Papers* was serialized in monthly parts from April 1836, though not made available in book form until the following year.

One of the advantages of having access to full title-page descriptions through the recent bibliographies described above is that it allows a better view of the ways in which authors were projected at their readership when novels were originally published. Over the whole period from 1820 to 1836 less than a third of novels (31.3 per cent in the 1820s; 32.95 per cent for 1830–36) carried an authorial proper name on the title-page of the first edition. Anonymity itself could cover a range of possibilities, from a complete absence of any information, through recognition by means of stated authorship of previous titles (a practice evidently favoured by the circulating libraries), to the consistent use of a pseudonym which effectively acquires the status of a proper name. A strong influence in the case of male anonymity undoubtedly was the example of Scott, who featured on the titles of his novels consistently as 'the author of *Waverley* [etc.]', with the exception of the patently pseudonymous 'Jedediah Cleishbotham' for the *Tales of My Landlord* series, and continued to employ this method even after his enforced outing as the author. Other male novelists whose names are absent on the original title-page during this period include Bulwer Lytton and Benjamin Disraeli, both operating at the upper end of the market.

In the case of female novelists, though anonymity had long offered a shield for those wishing not to jeopardize respectability, a number of authors from the start of the century, such as Maria Edgeworth and Amelia Opie, regularly used their real names, thereby acknowledging a kind of semi-professionalism. The method of description could also change according to circumstances. While Barbara Hofland's first work of fiction was published anonymously, her following novels generally observed the 'by the author of…' pattern; however, by the 1820s 'Mrs Hofland' had become the main signifier, serving in the process as a useful maternal trademark for tales aimed primarily at individual purchasers and juvenile readers. In some instances one senses the publisher's priorities as much as the author's. James Hogg's earlier fictions combined his real name with authorship of the long poem *The Queen's Wake*, his one unequivocal literary success. For *Private Memoirs and Confessions of a Justified Sinner* (1824), however, Longmans were persuaded by Hogg into anonymous publication, a strategy which met with a singular lack of success. In the new decade *Altrive Tales* (1832) was launched as 'by the Ettrick Shepherd', a nomenclature given fresh currency by the author's recent triumphant visit to London; while his last work of fiction, *Tales of the Wars of Montrose* (1835), swollen into three volumes at the behest of its publisher, reverted to the original pattern with 'By James Hogg, Esq., Author of *The Queen's Wake*'. Publishing considerations likewise seem to underlie the unusual appearance of 'Captain Marryat R.N.' on the title of *The Pirate, and the Three Cutters* (1836), a lavishly illustrated volume published by Longmans, while Marryat's other work of fiction that year, the three-decker *Mr. Midshipman Easy*, followed the regular pattern for his novels of identification through previous titles (though the authorship was almost certainly common knowledge at the time).

There were a number of ways by which authorship could be known or guessed at without full disclosure, some of them given new life by the cult of celebrity and practice of 'puffing' works rife in the early 1830s. One fairly common practice was for names to be revealed in paratextual materials such as Dedications and Prefaces. All Mrs Gore's mature novels appeared anonymously, apart from the listing of previous titles, a procedure which placed her on the same footing as male novelists of the 'silver fork' school. However, the Dedication to the Duke of Sussex in her *Polish Tales* (1833) is signed 'C.F. Gore', in a possibly calculated slippage of identity. More brazen still was G.P.R. James, whose name crops up on a number of occasions in this way, and who in 1835 can be found appealing to friends to preserve his anonymity in the 'Advertisement' to *My Aunt Pontypool*, while in *One in a Thousand; or, the Days of Henry Quatre* signing his Dedication to William IV as 'George Payne Rainsford James'. Newspaper advertisements and reviews are likewise found attributing authorship in the case of ostensibly anonymous works. Mary Shelley's *Lodore* (1835) was described on the original title-page as 'By the Author of "Frankenstein"' (in itself a strong mark of identification); an advertisement in *The Star* on 7 April 1835 nonetheless gives it as 'by Mrs. Shelley'. Later editions also could rapidly bring to light full ascriptions, even at a time when the author was still unrevealed in ongoing works: James Fenimore Cooper's *The Pilot* (1824) is thus given as by 'By J.F. Cooper' in the first volume (1832) of Colburn and Bentley's Standard Novels series, while authorship of the Banims' *The Smuggler* (1831) was evidently announced in an advertisement for no. 29 of the same series after a gap of only two years since its original publication.

In broad gender terms the period shows a rising masculinization of the novel in terms of authorship, sustained into the 1830s, and to some extent validating claims about an 'edging out'[11] of women, from a sphere where earlier (notably in the 1790s and 1810s) they had enjoyed a degree of dominance. Figure 1.2 provides a view in percentage terms of the output of titles by named and identified male and female novelists from 1820 to 1836. In the 1820s known male-authored novels outnumber their female counterparts by 426 to 289, with 112 gender-unknown cases, the male category thus claiming more than half (51.5 per cent) of the total number of titles overall. This male surge is immediately apparent in 1820, when male titles outnumber female ones by thirty-four

[11] The term is taken from Gaye Tuchman with Nina E. Fortin, *Edging Women Out: Victorian Novelists, Publishers, and Social Change* (London: Routledge, 1989), which acknowledges the masculine influence of Scott, but whose main analysis begins with 1840–79, as 'the period of invasion' (7).

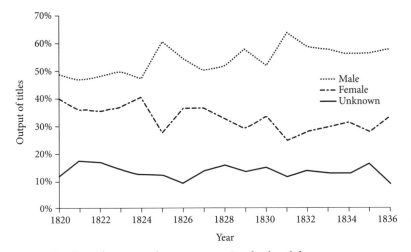

FIGURE 1.2 Authorship of new novels, 1820–1836: Gender breakdown

Sources: British Fiction, 1800–1829 (2004); The English Novel, 1830–1836 (2003)

to twenty-eight, the first year since 1804 to show a clear male dominance. This level is mostly sustained in the following three years, with 117 male-authored works outnumbering eighty-eight by women writers, though in 1824 a measure of equivalence occurs, forty female titles nearly matching forty-seven by males. However in 1825 the balance shifts dramatically again, with for the first time twice as many known male as opposed to female titles (55 to 25), a similar ratio again being evident in 1829 (48 to 24). One outstanding feature of the later 1820s is the high proportion of male novelists writing anonymously, an almost cult-like activity where Scott's influence is again palpable. Another influential factor at this point is the disproportionate amount of male-authored novels coming from Edinburgh, itself then at a high point of production, with only some 15 per cent of output there identifiable as by women writers.

For the period 1830–36 the same trend continues, with novels by male authors outnumbering female ones by 347.5 to 181.5 (the half point reflects a co-authored novel), and male titles again representing more than half the total output, notwithstanding a continuing residue of gender-unknown titles. Moreover, three of the seven imprint years (1831, 1832, and 1835) see twice as many male-authored novels as female ones. Certainly there are signs of women authors finding it difficult to uphold their position, as an older type of domestic fiction faded in popularity at the expense of modes such as military-nautical fiction and the Newgate novel, which by definition proved difficult for them to inhabit. Another notable loss came with the male appropriation of historical romance, first as a result of the unprecedented success of the 'the author of *Waverley*', then through a tighter-seeming, more 'fact'-bound kind of historical fiction, as spearheaded by writers such as Horatio Smith and G.P.R. James. Notwithstanding this growing dominance of male authors, and their occupancy of some of the more prestigious areas of the genre, there are scant signs however as yet of any gender-switching through pseudonym of the kind practised by later novelists.

There are no clear examples of authors at this time reaching financial independence through writing fiction. Walter Scott, by far the biggest earner, ploughed his profits into the seeming security of his estate at Abbotsford, but still maintained his professional legal posts up to and beyond his bankruptcy in 1826. John Galt, who unusually managed to command relatively large payments throughout his career, still maintained his many business interests, and effectively left the literary scene for three years near the end of the 1820s as a result of his activities in Canada. Among those female writers who attained regular and fairly substantial rewards, such as Maria Edgeworth and the Porter sisters, it would be hard to find cases where this represented the core of their social and financial existence. The records of publishing houses and other sources indicate that the optimum period for remuneration came towards the mid-1820s, with a general tailing off afterwards. William Blackwood within one year offered John Gibson Lockhart 1,000 guineas for *Reginald Dalton* (1823), his third work of fiction, and (through her father) Susan Ferrier £1,000 for *Inheritance* (1824). At the start of the new decade the Bentley records indicate payment to Eyre Evans Crowe of £500 for the copyright of *The English at Home* (1830), and a similar sum to Galt for *Lawrie Todd; or, the Settlers in the Woods* (1830). Less prominent novelists were offered more in the region of £100–£200, with the prospect sometimes of half the original sum in the event of a second edition. Other writers entered into 'half profits' agreements, whereby the publisher and author shared any proceeds after costs were deducted, a situation which could lead to a long wait with little or nothing at the end. James Grant in 1837 suggests as not uncommon a situation where the author took the risk of loss, with one recent would-be novelist a loser to the extent of £200, and paints a bleak picture of the lives of those attempting to live by writing alone: 'There are scenes of destitution and misery ever and anon exhibited among literary men—aye, and literary women, too—which would make the heart sick.'[12] Ample proof of the wide-ranging nature of such destitution can be found in the record of appeals to the Royal Literary Fund, where applications relate not just to more obviously vulnerable cases, such as Catherine Ward and Hannah Jones, but to productive male novelists, such as William Pitt Scargill, operating close to the heart of the fashionable carriage trade.[13]

PUBLISHERS AND PRODUCTION

The bulk of fiction in the early 19th century originated from London publishing houses. As a whole in the period under view almost 90 per cent of new novels carry London on their imprint, either as the sole or primary place of publication. The only challenge to

[12] Grant, *Great Metropolis*, 1: 181, 141.
[13] See *The Royal Literary Fund 1790–1918: Archives* (London: World Microfilms, 1994). An overview of the conditions of authorship, based on these records, is provided by Nigel Cross, *The Common Writer: Life in Nineteenth-Century Grub Street* (Cambridge: Cambridge University Press, 1985).

this supremacy came from Scotland, especially in the 1820s, when Edinburgh publishers acted as the managing publishers of some 11.5 per cent of all new fiction. At the same time the 'Scotch novel' became for a while one of the most fashionable of literary items, and went on to have a lasting effect on the history of the novel.

There can be no question that Scott operated as a powerful force in the development of a Scottish fiction industry, which in the earlier century (apart from reprints) had been virtually non-existent. All his novels without fail carried the word Edinburgh at the head of the title-page imprint, followed in earlier instances by the wording 'Printed by James Ballantyne and Co.', this latter reflecting the author's lifelong insistence that his imaginative works should be printed by Ballantyne's firm. The prioritizing of Edinburgh as the place of publication occurs even in those cases where Longmans were technically the managing publishers, though from *The Antiquary* (1816), when Archibald Constable took over the management, its positioning normally reflected the joint reality of an Edinburgh printer and publisher. Even so it would be wrong to regard Constable himself as a major producer of fiction: in the years from 1814 to his bankruptcy in 1826 he managed fewer than thirty titles, the majority by Scott, in the process rejecting approaches from a number of other novelists attracted by the cachet of an Edinburgh imprint. To comprehend fully the optimum period of production, it is necessary to turn to William Blackwood, who was the primary publisher of thirty-five new titles in the 1820s, twice as many as Constable's output, even including the Waverley Novels. Blackwood's productivity as a producer of fiction peaks in the years 1821–25, when his firm was the primary publisher of some twenty-five novels, representing nearly 50 per cent of all new fiction published from Edinburgh (for his full output, and that of other publishers, see Table 1.2). In the 1820s as a whole Blackwood was the fifth-largest publisher of new fiction titles in Britain, most of these with Thomas Cadell, junior, in London as the secondary publisher. An integral part of the operation from the start was *Blackwood's Magazine*, which not only served as a source of material and means of keeping together a body of literary personnel, but also helped shape a core audience, not least in the demographically expanding Central Scottish and Northern English regions. Between 1820 and 1825, more than half Blackwood's fiction titles were generated by just three authors, John Galt, J.G. Lockhart, and John Wilson, all closely connected with the magazine.

Encouraged by the vogue, a number of other Edinburgh booksellers moved into the field, most notably Oliver & Boyd, who published some fifteen titles from Edinburgh in the years 1819–29, mostly with the London firm of Whittaker & Co. as secondary publishers. Other Edinburgh booksellers in the 1820s account for more than forty-five titles, among these being Robert Cadell (Constable's successor, who published titles by Sir Thomas Dick Lauder and Marion and Margaret Corbett, in addition to the later Waverley novels) and William Oliphant (proselytizing evangelical titles, mainly by Grace Kennedy). However in the later 1820s, after the jolt of the failures of 1825–26, production started to decline, as Blackwood fell back on his more regular output, Cadell turned to promoting Scott's Magnum Opus, and Oliver & Boyd found safe ground in textbooks and wholesale distribution. In the period 1830–36 just 3.5 per cent of new novels were managed from Scotland.

Table 1.2 Primary publishers of new novels, 1820–1836

Publishers	Novels	% Total	Imprints Include
Colburn/Bentley	249	17.3	Henry Colburn; Henry Colburn & Co.; Henry Colburn & Richard Bentley; Richard Bentley
Minerva	186	13.0	A.K. Newman & Co.
Longmans	115	8.0	Longman, Hurst, Rees, Orme & Brown; L., H., R., O., B., & Green; L., R., O., B., & G.; L., R., O., B., G., and Longman; Longman & Co.
Whittaker & Co.	89	6.2	G. & W.B. Whittaker; Geo. B. Whittaker; Whittaker, Treacher & Arnot; Whittaker, Treacher & Co.
Saunders & Otley	65	4.5	Saunders & Otley
Smith, Elder, & Co.	51	3.6	Smith, Elder, & Co.
Blackwood	38	2.6	William Blackwood; William Blackwood & Sons
Bull/Churton	36	2.5	Edward Bull; Bull & Churton; Edward Churton
Cochrane/Macrone	32	2.2	Cochrane & Pickersgill; James Cochrane & Co.; Cochrane and Macrone; John Macrone
Virtue	19	1.3	George Virtue; Virtue, Tallis & Co.
Other	557	38.8	
Total	1437		

Sources: *British Fiction 1800–1829* (2004); *The English Novel, 1830–1836* (2003)

An associated factor in this decline was the increasing professionalism of the London trade itself, as a new species of publisher began to take hold of the situation. The two leading producers of new titles in London prior to this, A.K. Newman and Longmans, had operated in distinctly different areas of the book trade. Having taken over the Minerva establishment earlier in the century, A.K. Newman managed to produce a reasonably steady stream of circulating-library fiction, maintaining a rate of up to a third of total output into the early 1820s. In mid-decade, however, the Minerva's market share began to decline rapidly, and in 1829 the concern only brought out nine novels. By this point Newman's titles had acquired a somewhat faded look, many of his (predominantly female) authors being well past any literary celebrity they may once have enjoyed, and the books themselves looking cheap compared with top-range products and being priced accordingly. Newman continued to publish fiction in the 1830s, issuing some forty titles up to 1836, with a slightly varied output, including a number of reprints of American titles, though the odd attempts to mirror immediate literary fashions are far from convincing.

The long-established firm of Longman & Co., whose operations were centrally based in Paternoster Row, issued novels consistently throughout the early 19th century, averaging about ten a year in the earlier 1820s. Apart from an early involvement with Scott, most of their titles came from authors of 'middling' reputation, such as Opie and the Porters, to whom Longmans generally showed creditable loyalty. At the end of the 1820s, however, output dips noticeably (with just two titles for 1829); and while there was a revival of sorts in 1830–36, with just over thirty titles in all, the house could in no way be described as shaping the course of the genre. Some new authors of note were acquired in the new decade, among them James, Harriet Martineau, and Marryat, but more often than not on an occasional basis, rather than as regular authors. A similar pattern can be found in the case of Whittaker & Co., another leading wholesale house, who were primary publishers of approximately ten novels a year in the mid-1820s, notable examples including Mary Shelley's *Valperga* (1823) and Mary Russell Mitford's *Our Village* (1824), followed by some thirty works between 1830–36, when authors included Frances Trollope and Theodore Hook. For the years 1826–29, however, the firm produced only six titles, with none at all in both 1827 and 1828.

It was at this low ebb in the market that Henry Colburn first emerges as a mass producer of fiction. As the proprietor of the English and Foreign Circulating Library in Conduit Street, at the heart of the West End, Colburn at first mostly published translated fiction, before turning to indigenous authors in the 1810s, his lists then containing a number of eye-catching names, notably that of Lady Morgan, though production was limited to no more than a handful of titles annually. At the same time Colburn strengthened his position in the literary world (and capacity for puffing his own wares) through proprietorship of a number of periodicals, notably the *New Monthly Magazine* and the *Literary Gazette*. This in turn led to his disposing of the circulating library in 1824 to concentrate on publishing activities from fresh headquarters in New Burlington Street. Output of fiction by his firm expanded significantly at this point, with thirty new titles in 1826–27, twenty-four in 1828, and no fewer than thirty-four (representing over 40 per cent of total production) in 1829. Six of the 1829 titles also carried on their imprint the name of Richard Bentley, the printer with whom Colburn had entered into full partnership that year. Works issued from New Burlington Street in the late 1820s include three titles that set the mould for a new-style 'silver fork' fiction, as well as Marryat's *The Naval Officer* (1829), and historical novels by James and Smith. Nearly all were in three volumes, in a supposedly octavo format, and retailed at the premium price of 31s 6d.

Before the partnership of Colburn and Bentley foundered in 1832, a further sixty-eight novels had been issued under their joint imprint, the large majority in a similar up-market mould, and involving a variety of celebrity authors, with 'aristocratic' credentials being displayed or intimated at every opportunity. Another achievement, with long-term ongoing effects, was Colburn and Bentley's cloth-backed Standard Novels series, in single volumes, commencing with Cooper's *The Pilot* in February 1831 priced at 6s and continuing until its nineteenth monthly issue before being taken over by Bentley. After the partnership's dissolution, Bentley issued no fewer than seventy-four new novels under his own imprint to 1836, among them W.H. Ainsworth's *Rookwood: A Romance* (1834), adding at the same time a number of authors to those inherited from Colburn. In June 1836, Colburn paid Bentley £3,500 to be released from his exile from the London trade, setting up new premises at Great Marlborough Street, from where he issued three novels with that year's imprint, two of them by Gore (at the onset of a rivalry with Bentley that would carry on to mid-century). At the height of their operations in

1830–36 Bentley and Colburn were responsible for no fewer than 145 new titles, representing almost a quarter of total production of novels for those years.

Two other leading publishers of novels shadowed Colburn in centring their activities on proprietorship of a leading London circulating library. Having purchased Colburn's Conduit Street library in 1824, Saunders & Otley issued a stream of fairly upmarket titles in the later 1820s, including an early female-authored 'silver-fork' fiction, Marianne Spencer Hudson's *Almack's* (1826). In the early 1830s production continued at much the same pace, with a quickening of activity in 1834–35, when the firm issued nearly thirty (twenty-seven) titles, normally in three volumes. High-profile authors assembled by that time included Disraeli, Bulwer Lytton, Gore, and the Countess of Blessington. From 1832 the firm were also publishers of *The Metropolitan Magazine*, under the editorship of Marryat, whose *Jacob Faithful* (1834) and *Peter Simple* (1834) were both serialized there in advance of their publication as full three-deckers. A similar if more fragmented path is found in the case of Edward Bull and his younger partner Edward Churton, whose operations were conducted from the British and Foreign Subscription Library in Holles Street, off Cavendish Square (the terms for which are often appended in their publications). Edward Bull published just four novels in the later 1820s, most notably Henry Neele's *The Romance of History: England* (1828), the first of a line of such post-Scottian productions. An acceleration in output then occurs with nearly ten titles in 1832, immediately prior to Bull entering into partnership with Churton, who first appeared as part of a joint imprint in 1833, before succeeding to the business in 1834 and issuing books under his own name from that point. As a whole the two were responsible for over thirty new novels during 1830–36, aimed at the higher end of the circulating-library market, though with more a more run-of-the mill look about them as time went on. Bell and Churton (then Churton solely) also published *The Court Magazine*, edited for a time by Caroline Norton, whose novel, *The Wife and Woman's Reward* (1835), was nevertheless published by the rival firm of Saunders & Otley.

One other concern leads more directly to the Victorian period proper. Smith, Elder & Co. published their first three works of fiction in 1829, from 65 Cornhill, including the single-volume *Tales and Confessions* by Leitch Ritchie, who, like its founder, originated from Scotland. In the 1830s the firm issued nearly fifty (forty-eight) titles, amongst which are the titles in the 'Library of Romance' series, edited by Ritchie, who attempted to take the lead offered by Bentley's Standard Novels one stage further in offering original (rather than just recently published) works of fiction in single-volume form, priced at 6s. In a prefatory statement in the first of the series, the Banims' *Ghost-Hunter and His Family* (1833), Ritchie promised a monthly sequence of original novels by well-known and unknown authors, translations and adaptations of novels in foreign languages, and reprints and adaptations of American novels. Underlying his remarks one senses a concerted assault on the conventional multi-volume novel with the intention of transforming the fiction industry:

> One effect of the plan will be to diminish the number of novels; for it is manifest, that no work which is not presumed to be calculated for extensive circulation, will be published

at such a price. This will be a benefit even to the book-sellers themselves…for the great majority of existing novels is formed of *unsuccessful* ones. [14]

An element of retreat is nevertheless found in a new prospectus attached to the fourth in the series, John Galt's *The Stolen Child* (1833), which promises a division of titles into parts, allowing the libraries to purchase in sheets and make up smaller volumes of their own. A further faltering is evident in the sixth volume, *The Slave-King* (1833), a translation from Victor Hugo, where a decision to publish bi-monthly henceforth is announced. The series continued as far as its fifteenth volume, William Smith's *Ernesto: A Philosophical Romance* (1835), but clearly without making its intended mark on novel production. Smith, Elder & Co. however continued to publish individual works of fiction, a fair proportion in single volumes, with a bumper crop of thirteen titles (their highest to date) in 1836.

While marked by discord and failed opportunities, the last combination under consideration arguably shows in sharpest relief the possibilities for a new kind of novel. James Cochrane first appears as a publisher of fiction in 1831, issuing that year three titles from his headquarters at 11 Waterloo Place, Pall Mall, the most striking of which is *The Club-Book* (co-published with Pickersgill), a miscellany of shorter pieces mostly by Scottish writers, edited by Andrew Picken. Among the publications of Cochrane's firm in 1832 was James Hogg's *Altrive Tales*, projected as a Magnum-like collection in twelve volumes, but which foundered after the first volume as a result of Cohrane's financial failure that year, leaving Hogg to seek alternative outlets, ultimately leading to the posthumous publication of his *Tales and Sketches* (1836–37) by the Glasgow number-specialists Blackie & Son. After his bankruptcy, Cochrane re-established himself in partnership with John Macrone in 1833, the two names appearing on the imprint of six works of fiction in 1833–34, including John Galt's *Stories of the Study* (1833). The partnership was then dissolved in 1834 (following Cochrane's discovery of his younger partner's adulterous affair with his wife), and the two published separately after that, Cochrane issuing six titles in 1834–35, among them Hogg's *Tales of the Wars of Montrose*, and Macrone thirteen under his own name up to 1836 from new headquarters in St James's Square, his authors including Robert Pierce Gillies, Leitch Ritchie, and Allan Cunningham.

Two of Macrone's last productions—Dickens's *Sketches by 'Boz'* (1836–37), and a fourth edition (1836) of W.H. Ainsworth's *Rookwood* in one volume, likewise illustrated by George Cruikshank—stand out for dynamically bringing into play components which had hitherto mostly stood outside or run parallel with mainstream production. Ultimately Macrone's bankruptcy and premature death in 1837 led to his Dickens property passing to Chapman & Hall (themselves up to that point publishers of just one work of fiction), and the Ainsworth copyright reverting to Bentley, at what would turn out to be one of the most crucial turning-points in the history of the novel.

[14] John and Michael Banim, *The Ghost-Hunter and His Family* (London: Smith, Elder and Co., 1833), ix.

Suggested Reading

Cross, Nigel. *The Common Writer: Life in Nineteenth-Century Grub Street*. Cambridge: Cambridge University Press, 1985.

Eliot, Simon. *Some Patterns and Trends in British Publishing 1800–1919*. London: Bibliographical Society, 1994.

Engel, Elliot and Margaret F. King. *The Victorian Novel before Victoria: British Fiction during the Reign of William IV, 1830–37*. London and Basingstoke: Macmillan, 1984.

Garside, P.D., Anthony Mandal, Verena Ebbes, Angela Koch, and Rainer Schöwerling. *The English Novel, 1830–1836: A Bibliographical Survey of Prose Fiction Published in the British Isles*. <www.cardiff.ac.uk/encap/journals/corvey/1830s>.

Garside, P.D., J.E. Belanger, and S.A. Ragaz. *British Fiction, 1800–1829: A Database of Production, Circulation & Reception*. Designer A.A. Mandal. <http://www.british-fiction.cf.ac.uk>.

Garside, P.D., James Raven, and Rainer Schöwerling, eds. *The English Novel 1770–1829: A Bibliographical Survey of Prose Fiction Published in the British Isles*. 2 vols. Oxford: Oxford University Press, 2000.

Grant, James. *The Great Metropolis*. 2nd series. 2 vols. London: Saunders & Otley, 1837.

Oliphant, Margaret. *Annals of a Publishing House: William Blackwood and His Sons*. 2 vols. Edinburgh: Blackwood, 1897.

Sadleir, Michael, ed. *XIX Century Fiction: A Bibliographical Record Based on His Own Collection*. 2 vols. Cambridge: Cambridge University Press, 1951.

Wolff, Robert Lee. *Nineteenth-Century Fiction: A Bibliographical Catalogue*. 5 vols. New York: Garland Publishing, 1981–86.

2

NEW HISTORIES OF ENGLISH LITERATURE AND THE RISE OF THE NOVEL, 1835–1859

WILLIAM MCKELVY

Where do the novel and the novelist belong in literary history? At the dawn of the Victorian period the answer to that question was not clear. There were signs that some writers of fiction in English were on the way to becoming important figures in general accounts of literary achievement. But there were also indications that the writing of novels was something best done by an author with a primary vocation elsewhere, whether it be law, divinity, the professional domesticity of the genteelly unemployed, or a life of writing in a variety of modes including poetry, drama, and non-fictional prose. To get a sense of the uncertain status of both the novel and the novelist in the 1830s, let us pay a visit to Abbotsford as described in John Gibson Lockhart's *Memoirs of the Life of Sir Walter Scott* (1839) and enquire about the physical location of novels there, the home where the 19th century's most famous novelist before Charles Dickens would earn his comparable fame.

Abbotsford began with the purchase in 1811 of a farmhouse and would evolve, mostly thanks to Scott's literary profits, into a sizeable estate with a Gothic revival mansion completed in 1824. Over the course of hundreds of pages, Lockhart portrays Scott's intimate involvement with the design, construction and decoration of Abbotsford, and the seventh volume of the biography ends with an extended description of the estate in its heyday in 1825. As the tour nears its completion readers are brought into the home's most imposing room, the library containing 'some fifteen to twenty thousand volumes, arranged according to their subjects: British history and antiquities filling the whole of the chief wall; English poetry and drama, classics and miscellanies, one end; foreign literature, chiefly French and German, the other'.[1] The tour then concludes in a smaller attached

---

[1] John Gibson Lockhart, *Memoirs of the Life of Sir Walter Scott*, 2nd edn, 10 vols. (Edinburgh: Cadell, 1839), 7: 405–6. The description of Abbotsford in 1825 had been added to this second edition of the *Memoirs*. The first seven-volume edition had appeared in 1837–38.

room, Scott's private study, an engraving of which served as the volume's frontispiece. This study was, for the English-speaking world in the 1830s and after, the representative site of Scott's extraordinary capacity for literary labour, that which allowed him to construct Abbotsford as well as the writing he was compelled to do following his financial ruin in 1826 when he faced the prospect of being turned out of his beloved home. The solitary writing associated with the study will eventually allow Scott to retain Abbotsford. But with Scott's death, hastened by overwork, this visit to 'the *sanctum* of the Author' is implicitly sombre in tone.[2] For Lockhart's initial readers, all of them aware of the 1826 crash and its aftermath looming in the next volume, the hushed atmosphere of the empty study looks forward to Scott's burial in 1832 in the nearby ruins of Dryburgh Abbey.

The most remembered endeavour in Scott's final years of literary toil was the republication, in forty-eight uniform volumes, of the Waverley Novels (1829–33), an event that has often been cited as a key juncture in the history of the novel in English. 'In collecting and annotating his writings in this way', as Jane Millgate puts it, 'Scott was implicitly assigning to fiction a status previously reserved for poetry and drama.'[3] Said to ennoble the genre at the end and in part at the cost of his life, Scott has long been a crucial figure on the threshold separating the Victorian novel from earlier fiction. Yet in this famous episode in the novel's elevation there is an irony that speaks volumes to scholars with interests in the material history of books including their places of abode. For Scott's final literary labours were dedicated to reclaiming a home that physically memorialized the contemporary novel's subordinate status. In the 1825 account of Abbotsford that would be widely circulated by Lockhart's *Memoirs*, a large selection of novels makes an appearance not in the main library but in the 'charming' and 'cheerful' breakfast-room, and any suspicions that the genre might be generally excluded from the more formal room are confirmed by J.G. Cochrane's exhaustive *Catalogue* (1838) of Scott's books.[4] A guest at Abbotsford in the 1820s could enjoy reading Jane Austen's *Emma: A Novel* (1816). But one would not go to the grand library to find this book. One would go to what Scott would describe as a 'breakfasting parlour, or a *boudoir* if the word be more fashionable, [which] serves the woman-kind of the family for making their tea or sewing their samplers'.[5] The same was true for notable works by other novelists publishing from the 1790s to the 1820s.

---

[2] *Memoirs*, 7: 407.

[3] Jane Millgate, *Scott's Last Edition: A Study in Publishing History* (Edinburgh: Edinburgh University Press, 1987), vii.

[4] J.G. Cochrane's *Catalogue of the Library at Abbotsford* (Edinburgh: T. Constable for the Bannatyne Club, 1838) individually enumerates, 331–36, the 'Novels and Romances, and Light Literature' to be found in the 'Breakfast Parlour'. Authors include Charlotte Smith (1748–1806), Fanny Burney (1752–1840), Ann Radcliffe (1764–1823), Maria Edgeworth (1768–1849), John Galt (1779–1839), Charles Maturin (1782–1824), James Fenimore Cooper (1789–1851), and Mary Shelley (1797–1851). With the main library full of (then) contemporary poetry by authors such as William Wordsworth, Samuel Taylor Coleridge, Lord Byron, Thomas Campbell, and Thomas Moore, it is clear that the contemporary novelists were exiled to the breakfast room on the basis of the literary form itself. For the appearance of the novels and romances in the *Memoirs*, see 7: 404.

[5] Walter Scott, *Reliquiae Trotcosienses, or, The gabions of the late Jonathan Oldbuck Esq. of Monkbarns*, ed. Gerard Carruthers and Alison Lumsden (Edinburgh: Edinburgh University Press, 2004), 42–43.

The *Catalogue* does point to a few exceptions to this rule. Novels by Samuel Richardson and Tobias Smollett could be found in the library in early editions from the 1740s and 1750s. And *Ballantyne's Novelist's Library* (10 vols., 1821–24), a collection of thirty-six novels with biographical memoirs of the authors by Scott, was there as well. Scott's biography of Henry Fielding from that collection, which includes the following statement about the value of prose fiction, would seem to explain why most English novels at Abbotsford were to be found in a room where the day's lightest meal was consumed:

> Excluding from consideration those infamous works, which address themselves directly to awakening the grosser passions of our nature, we are inclined to think, the worst evil to be apprehended from the perusal of novels is, that the habit is apt to generate an indisposition to real history, and useful literature; and that the best which can be hoped is, that they may sometimes instruct the youthful mind by real pictures of life, and sometimes awaken their better feelings and sympathies by strains of generous sentiment, and tales of fictitious woe. Beyond this point they are a mere elegance, a luxury contrived for the amusement of polished life, and the gratification of that half love of literature, which pervades all ranks in an advanced stage of society, and are read much more for amusement, than with the least hope of deriving instruction from them.[6]

The physical segregation of certain kinds of writing at Abbotsford reflected the absence of a model of literary history that unapologetically incorporated contemporary prose fiction into a register of the nation's literary achievements. Another kind of book absent from the main library—indeed absent from Abbotsford altogether during Scott's lifetime—was what we would call a history of English literature, at least one that surveyed writing in English over several centuries and included extensive treatment of poetry, drama, non-fictional prose *and* prose fiction. Three years after Scott's death, in 1835, Robert Chambers made a credible claim to have produced, with his *History of the English Language and Literature*, 'the only History of English Literature which has as yet been given to the world'.[7] And the authors of books surveying a historically organized literary tradition encompassing verse and prose were still pioneers into the 1850s. But things then changed with a startling rapidity, and by the mid-1860s, numerous surveys of this tradition existed in a range of different prices and formats.[8]

---

[6] Walter Scott, 'Prefatory Memoir', in *Ballantyne's Novelist's Library*, 10 vols. (Edinburgh: Ballantyne, 1821–24), 1: xix–xx.

[7] Robert Chambers, *History of the English Language and Literature* (Edinburgh: W. & R. Chambers, 1835), v. Subsequent citations appear in the text.

[8] In addition to Craik's revised histories of 1861 and 1862 discussed below, the first half of the sixth decade of the century alone included the first appearance of the following books: Robert Demaus, *Introduction to the History of English Literature* (Adam & Charles Black: Edinburgh, 1860); William Francis Collier, *A History of English Literature, in a Series of Biographical Sketches* (London: T. Nelson, 1861); Thomas Arnold, *A Manual of English Literature, Historical and Critical* (London: Longman, Longmans, Green, and Co., 1862); David Pryde, *Biographical Outlines of English Literature* (Edinburgh: Bell & Bradfute, 1862); Thomas Budd Shaw, *The Student's Manual of English Literature: A History of English*

The story of the Victorian novel is not simply one of an eventual cultural ascendency that prompted Herbert Paul in 1897 to pen an essay entitled 'The Apotheosis of the Novel under Queen Victoria'.[9] The same literary period that features the rise of the novel to respectability and then literary prominence had access to a new sense of literary history that was embodied by new kinds of books that allowed novel-writing and novel reading to be incorporated into a larger history of English literature. This historiographic transformation was most broadly indebted to the emergence of a reading nation.[10] It was part of a general proliferation of more reading material—made possible by the industrialization of printing—and a rise in the number of readers, particularly a growing class of readers who were content or economically destined to limit that skill to the perusal of works in English. As reading became, ideally, normative—an activity that all Britons could and should engage in—older models of literary history gave way to a new one in which the literary historian became a chronicler of the nation's increasingly monolingual reading habits. At the same time, the new sense of literary history relied on the declining purchase of an older history of fiction that was divorced from national history and concepts of modernization, and frequently tied instead to an ancient construction of authorship and literary authority in which translation and transmission were integral elements of polite literary culture. Even as this older transnational history of fiction continued to exist in various ways in the minds of some readers, the newer short history of the novel would go viral in the handbooks, histories, and manuals of English literature that had so quickly become staples of the Victorian print market.

In 1835 Chambers opened his pioneering *History* by portraying its mission as a humble one: 'to communicate to young persons the rudiments of useful knowledge', but he goes on to suggest that this goal more generally responds to the contemporary expansion of readers and their options as consumers of print. 'Such a work', as Chambers put it, 'cannot fail to be useful to many besides young persons at school,—to all, in short,

Literature. A New Edition, Enlarged and Rewritten. Edited, with notes and illustrations, by William Smith (London: John Murray, 1864); Thomas Budd Shaw, *The Student's Specimens of English Literature. Selected from the Chief English Writers, and Arranged Chronologically, by Thomas B. Shaw. Edited, with additions, by William Smith* (London: John Murray, 1864); Joseph Angus, *The Handbook of English Literature* (London: Religious Tract Society, 1865); and Robert and Thomas Armstrong, *Class-Book of English Literature: with Biographical Sketches, Critical Notices, and Illustrative Extracts* (London: Nelson, 1865).

⁹ *The Nineteenth Century* 41 (May 1897): 769–92.

¹⁰ This term is taken from William St Clair's *The Reading Nation in the Romantic Period* (Cambridge: Cambridge University Press, 2004). While most closely concerned with a surge of reading in the Romantic period, St Clair agrees that Great Britain actually 'became a reading nation' at the end of the Victorian era (13). Richard Altick's classic study, *The English Common Reader: A Social History of the Mass Reading Public, 1800–1900*, 2nd edn (Columbus: Ohio State University Press, 1998), was brought somewhat up to date at the end of the last century with a new foreword by Jonathan Rose. On the rapid industrialization of the print trades at this time, see James Raven, *The Business of Books: Booksellers and the English Book Trade, 1450–1850* (New Haven: Yale University Press, 2007) and David McKitterick, ed., *The Cambridge History of the Book in Britain, 1830–1914* (Cambridge: Cambridge University Press, 2009). On the subjects of literacy and the transition to mass literacy, see David Vincent, *The Rise of Mass Literacy: Reading and Writing in Modern Europe* (Malden, MA: Blackwell, 2000).

whose minds have been awakened to a desire of knowledge; guiding them to the stores of English Literature, and distinguishing for them those works which are most worthy of their attention' (*History*, v). Chambers would bring this history of purposeful consumption full circle by ending his narrative with 'an account of the cheap and popular system of publication, which has formed so remarkable a feature of the passing age'. Describing the making of a number of serial productions—the Library of Useful Knowledge and the Library of Entertaining Knowledge, Constable's Miscellany, Murray's Family Library, Lardner's Cabinet Encyclopedia, and the Edinburgh Cabinet Library—Chambers was insisting that the history of English literature had recently been distinguished by 'the production of books, calculated by their price and modes of production for the less affluent and more numerous portion of the community' (*History*, 269).[11] With most individual volumes in these series priced at five or six shillings, they offered consumers opportunities to own books at about half the retail price of most other new books. And yet, despite the impact of these affordable publishing schemes that had commenced in the 1820s, 'a step still remained to be taken before full advantage of the cheap mode of publication could be said to have been obtained'. The consummation of this trend was reserved for two serial publications, *Chambers's Edinburgh Journal*, priced at 1 1/2d, and *The Penny Magazine*, that had first appeared in 1832 and took advantage of new steam-powered printing machines, mechanized paper production, and stereotyping. These mass-produced and therefore highly affordable weekly miscellanies and others that soon followed, as the *History*'s final sentence put it, now allowed 'a vast mass of literature' to reach 'the middle and lower departments of the community' (*History*, 271).

Chambers here was engaging in self-promotion to be sure. He ended his literary history with the story of the recently started *Journal* that was produced and published by the firm of William & Robert Chambers, a partnership he had formed with his older brother in 1832. But the claim about the dawn of a new literary age *circa* 1832 achieved some credibility as it became embodied in an unprecedented book, a new type of literary history that discloses its findings in response to inquiries about the production and consumption of reading material in English. Just as the Reform Bill of 1832 had expanded voting rights to formerly excluded members of the political community, new mechanized modes of literary production, often celebrated on the pages of works like *Chambers's Edinburgh Journal* and *The Penny Magazine*, admitted new customers into an expanded literary marketplace.[12] This recent event in the history of reading as a social activity was, in Chambers's book, a crucial development in the nation's literary history. An expansion of literary production and consumption, rather than authorial invention, signalled the inception in the 1830s of a new literary epoch.

---

[11] For modern surveys of these series, see Altick, 266–77, Millgate, 91–99, and James Secord, *Victorian Sensation: The Extraordinary Publication, Reception, and Secret Authorship of 'Vestiges of the Natural History of Creation'* (Chicago: University of Chicago Press, 2000), 46–51.

[12] See 'Mechanism of Chambers's Journal', *Chambers's Edinburgh Journal* [hereafter *CEJ*], 6 June, 1835, 149–51 and 'Commercial History of a Penny Magazine', *The Penny Magazine*, nos. 96, 101, 107, 112 (September–December 1833), 377–84, 417–24, 465–72, 505–11.

Chambers described his 1835 history as unique upon its first appearance, a claim that was never challenged by his contemporaries. Most readers today—and just about any likely reader of this book—will find the 1835 *History* all too familiar: it surveys English literary history in seven larger periods, starting with 'From the earliest time till the year 1400' and ending with 'From 1780 till the Present Time'. Along the way during the sixth period, '1727–1780', readers are told that Samuel Richardson, Henry Fielding and Tobias Smollett were the authors in the 1740s of the first English novels still worthy of the general reader's attention. Chambers briefly acknowledges a multilingual and ancient history of prose fiction that could serve as a prologue to this story of innovation. But the more important claim concerned the relative novelty of the English novel: 'the rise of the species of fiction called the *novel*' during a period that was otherwise 'not by any means marked by such striking features of originality or vigour as some of the preceding eras' (*History*, 159, 138).

The appearance of this claim in the first history of English literature (as we know it) needs to be contrasted with an alternative historiography found in works such as John Dunlop's *The History of Fiction* which was first published in 1814 and reissued in a revised second edition in 1816. This three-volume history begins in antiquity, covers chivalric romances of the Middle Ages and divides most of its attention after its discussion of writings in Greek and Latin to works written in Italian, Spanish, and French before coming at the very end of volume three to a brief survey of English novels of the 18th century.[13] Dunlop's *History of Fiction* was a version of literary history that had also recently appeared in condensed form in Anna Letitia Barbauld's 'On the Origin and Progress of Novel-Writing', an essay that served as a general introduction to *The British Novelists*, a fifty-volume collection first published in 1810 and reissued in a second edition in 1820.[14] Often cited by recent critics as an important precursor to the later Waverley edition in its elevation of the novel's status, Barbauld's *British Novelists* stood out as the first extensive collection of novels written exclusively by British authors of recent times: all of the novels were from the 1740s and later, with the exception of Daniel Defoe's *Robinson Crusoe* (1719), which was then offered (and continues to be offered) as a standard anticipation of the modern novel's more celebrated rise at the later period. And yet, *The British Novelists* remains a monument to different claims about prose fiction. It associated the novel in English with a moment of conception in mid-18th-century modernity. At the same time it learnedly demonstrated how the writers and readers of these more recent novels were the heirs of what Mary Ellen McMurran has called 'a long, multicultural history of the novel,

[13] John Colin Dunlop, *The History of Fiction*, 2nd edn, 3 vols. (Edinburgh: Longman, Hurst, Rees, Orme, and Brown, 1816), 3: 457–94.

[14] See Claudia L. Johnson, '"Let Me Make the Novels of a Country": Barbauld's *The British Novelists* (1810/1820)', *Novel* 34(2) (2001 Spring): 163–79 and Michael Gamer, 'A Select Collection: Barbauld, Scott, and the Rise of the (Reprinted) Novel', in *Recognizing the Romantic Novel: New Histories of British Fiction, 1780–1830*, ed. Jillian Heydt-Stevenson and Charlotte Sussman (Liverpool: Liverpool University Press, 2008), 155–91.

encompassing ancient, medieval, Renaissance, and early modern fictions from all over Europe'.[15]

Histories of fiction from the early 19th century generally depicted a genre that was transnational and frequently translated, precisely because it was considered a particularly mobile cultural product that had easily traversed temporal, linguistic, and geographic borders. Underwriting this impression was the persistence of the 'structural agenda of *translatio imperii* and *translatio studii*', the complementary notions, inherited from Greco-Roman culture, that political power, civilization, and learning were transmitted from one location to another.[16] For Dunlop and Barbauld this concept of transmission still had at its core a faith in the finest literary values residing in 'classical' models from the ancient Mediterranean world. While Europe's experience of the Middle Ages was considered in terms of learning's temporary decline, post-medieval European literary culture was correspondingly home to multinational recoveries of classical learning and standards that would subsequently inspire improvements in various vernacular traditions. Regardless of his or her individual mastery of classical languages, the normative reader imagined by Dunlop and Barbauld was situated in a larger literary landscape in which the value and character of vernacular literary cultures were judged in relation to the classical past. Even as they pointed to the 1740s as a moment of literary departures in Britain, Dunlop and Barbauld found in narratives concerning the antiquity and ubiquity of prose fiction a powerful means of vindicating the novel's legitimate literary status.

This literary status was also maintained in part by prices for books that suggested the kind of surplus capital required for the leisure to read regularly for pleasure or the higher education and non-vernacular studies that were experienced by a small percentage of the general population. Dunlop, like Scott a graduate of Edinburgh University and trained to the law, addressed his *History of Fiction*, priced at 10s 6d per volume in its first and second editions, to wealthy antiquarians and bibliophiles. Chambers addressed his 1835 *History*, which cost a total of 2s 6d, to a markedly different audience. This audience had little money to spare and sought improvement and intellectual pleasure beyond the pale of learning cultivated at the nation's universities and other institutions that were built on the prestige of classical learning and biblical studies and the presumption of some familiarity with other modern languages, especially French. For this newer audience it was largely beside the point to chart how innovations in English prose fiction in the 1740s were relatively recent instalments in a multilingual tradition stretching back to antiquity. That genealogy had been of most interest to a different audience in the course of being persuaded that prose fiction was an identifiable literary form with a long history. The new short history of English fiction—as it appeared in Chambers's *History*—was part of a different project that set out to encourage readers of different social standings and with different political and religious affiliations to be united in a common appreciation of

---

[15] Mary Ellen McMurran, 'National or Transnational? The Eighteenth-Century Novel', in *The Literary Channel: The Inter-National Invention of the Novel*, ed. Margaret Cohen and Carolyn Dever (Princeton: Princeton University Press, 2002), 54.

[16] McMurran, 66.

the nation's vernacular literature. And if the older history of fiction was allied to an economic context in which book ownership was a relatively exceptional luxury attending gentility, the new literary history was a product of attempts to lower the cost of reading material of all kinds and to allow 'the people' in general to own and interact with print in private, domestic settings.

The fuller story behind Chambers's *History* reads like one of the many 19th-century novels that depict a character's social and economic dispossession to be followed by acts of self-invention and the recovery of status on modified terms.[17] The second son of a textile manufacturer and merchant, Chambers was a precocious scholar and intended to enter the Church after earning a degree at the University of Edinburgh. His father's bankruptcy ended these plans, and he became instead at the age of sixteen a second-hand bookseller with his initial stock comprised entirely of the books remaining in the possession of his economically distressed family. This 'adventurous project of selling the wreck of the family library, along with his own small parcel of school books' would turn out to be the first step in a literary career that would include being some twenty years later a widely read author and the prosperous proprietor, along with his brother William, of a publishing and printing firm that was, as Robert would put it in 1846, 'one of the great organizations of industry in this country, whereby more paper is blacked in a week than in many other printing-offices in a twelvemonth'.[18]

Before the initial publication of the *Journal* in 1832 and the formation of the corporate entity of W. & R. Chambers, Chambers had been an active participant in Edinburgh's market for print at a particularly eventful time that included in the teens and twenties the remarkable ability of 'The Author of Waverley'—known to literary insiders to be Walter Scott—to dominate the trade in new fiction as published in the expensive multi-volume form. On first publication, Scott's novels were generally priced at slightly more than 10s a volume, making the standard three-volume format normally retail for about 31s, a sum that made individual ownership of new fiction relatively rare and explained the importance of circulating libraries. While one of Scott's final novel's *The Fair Maid of Perth* retailed for 31s 6d at the time of its first publication in June of 1828, a year later one could buy one of Scott's novels in the Waverley edition for a total of 10s, one third of the recent cost. Starting in 1832, the firm of W. & R. Chambers was focused on extending this logic

---

[17] For more on Chambers as a simultaneously innovative producer and historian of print, see my "'This Enormous Contagion of Paper and Print": Making Literary History in the Age of Steam', in *Bookish Histories: Books, Literature and Commercial Modernity 1700–1900*, ed. Ina Ferris and Paul Keen (New York: Palgrave Macmillan, 2009), 61–84. Drawing on extensive archival work, Aileen Fyfe's *Steam-Powered Knowledge: William Chambers and the Business of Publishing, 1820–1860* (Chicago: University of Chicago Press, 2012) situates the commercial initiatives of W. & R. Chambers in the broader context of the age's publishing practices. Other essential studies include Secord's *Victorian Sensation* and Robert J. Scholnick's "'The Fiery Cross of Knowledge": Chambers's Edinburgh Journal, 1832–1844', *Victorian Periodicals Review* 32(4) (1999): 324–58.

[18] William Chambers, *Memoir of Robert Chambers, with Autobiographic Reminiscences of William Chambers* (Edinburgh: W. & R. Chambers, 1873), 141; Robert Chambers, *Select Writings of Robert Chambers*, 7 vols. (Edinburgh: W. & R. Chambers, 1847), 1: iii.

even further as it reminded readers that contemporary publications of all kinds often derived from modes of production that aimed to create relatively few copies to be purchased at high prices. Just as the Waverley Novels were advertised as bargains in contrast to the standard high prices for new fiction, the products of W. & R. Chambers boasted yet another level of affordability in comparison to the world of publishing volumes at five or six shillings a piece.

Published in November of 1835 the *History* appeared as one of two inaugural volumes in a new series, 'Chambers's Educational Course'. Written at a time when Chambers was convinced of the likelihood of the long-term success of W. & R. Chambers, the *History* was a product of the rapid transformation of the firm into an independent entity for the production of unusually affordable reading material. For the first two years of the *Journal*'s publication, the printing of it had been contracted out—as was the norm—to various printers. Starting in January of 1834 the firm had invested in its own steam press which was soon able to produce the requisite number of copies of the *Journal* in something less than a full six-day workweek. Now owners of a printing machine that was at times idle, W. & R. Chambers looked for other works to print and publish and set a precedent in which the *Journal*, in addition to being a successful weekly publication in its own right, became the vehicle for promoting other products such as the *History of the English Language and Literature*.[19] All of the works that rolled off the increasing number of steam presses owned by W. & R. Chambers—there were ten by 1845—were said to be sold at the lowest possible cost and were intended for education and amusement in ways that avoided political partisanship or religious sectarianism.

This underlying purpose was expressed in the prospectus for another series launched at the start of 1838, 'Chambers's People's Editions of Approved Works in All Departments of Literature':

> If the aim of the Publishers be accomplished, the poorest working man in the country will be enabled, from the earnings of a week, to spare as much as will purchase, for his permanent possession and enjoyment, one of the deathless productions of those Intellectual Great who are his brethren in race, and whose names are sparks of Immortality.[20]

Language from the prospectus shortly reappeared in the *Journal* in 'What English Literature Gives Us', a lead article that would point the way to the next great innovation in the making of literary history in the early Victorian period. There Robert Chambers

---

[19] In the case of the *History of the English Language and Literature*, the *Journal* was in one number the vehicle for announcing the work and the new series that it inaugurated only to become the venue in the next number for publishing the first chapter of the *History* as 'Popular Information on Literature: Rise of English Literature'. See *CEJ*, 14 November 1835, 336 and 21 November 1835, 338–39.

[20] *CEJ*, 27 January 1838, 8. The 'People's Editions' soon included four 18th-century novels—Defoe's *Robinson Crusoe* (1838, 1s 8d), Smollett's *Roderick Random* (1838, 1s 8d), Goldsmith's *Vicar of Wakefield* (1839, 8d), and Godwin's *Caleb Williams* (1839, 10d)—as well as the more recent *Cottagers of Glenburnie* (1838, 8d; 1st edn, 1808) by Elizabeth Hamilton. The most expensive novel published in the series was Mary Brunton's *Self-Control: A Novel* (1839; 1st edn, 1811) priced at 2s 2d, a sum that was still

spoke of the 'substantial wealth' represented by English literature and compared that form of wealth to the nation's 'public works' including 'roads', 'bridges', and 'halls of popular assembly':

> England is in both these respects a wealthy country. It has been put by our fathers into our hands, furnished with an amount of physical conveniences and sources of comfort beyond all precedent, and endowed with an intellectual inheritance such as no other country ever had. Evils manifold may affect it, if some will have the case to be so; but, amidst all that troubles her, there still remains, unsullied, intact, ever ready for the solacement of her thinking sons, the deathless productions of her intellectual great.[21]

This great 'intellectual inheritance' was, as Chambers well knew, until recently beyond the grasp of most people. As *Chambers's Edinburgh Journal* had been reminding readers since 1832, limited literacy and the economic structure of the English book trade had often made it impossible for most members of the national community to have access to past and contemporary products of English literary genius.

'What English Literature Gives Us' contains strategic wishful thinking that was satisfied by the *Cyclopaedia of English Literature* (2 vols., 1842–44), a work that Chambers produced with the assistance of Robert Curruthers. An extensive elaboration of the 1835 *History* and incorporating most of that text directly or in some revised form, the *Cyclopaedia* also came with hundreds of pages 'of extracts from our national authors'.[22] Initially published in weekly numbers of double-columned 'sheets' of sixteen pages for 1 1/2d and also sold as a more substantial monthly number (of sixty-four pages) for 7d, the ambitious project was advertised in *Chambers's Edinburgh Journal* as a widely affordable bibliographic surrogate for the libraries and studies that were regular features of the homes of the wealthy: 'For the self-educating everywhere, such a work will be as a whole English Library fused down into one cheap book'. Costing 'five shillings and eight-pence sewed, or seven shillings in boards' the first volume was declared to be in either state 'the cheapest volume of its size ever published in Great Britain'.[23] At 14s, the entire two-volume *Cyclopaedia* in a standard binding was less than half the price of many new novels and 30 per cent cheaper than a single novel published in twenty monthly shilling parts, the format in which Charles Dickens's roughly contemporary *Martin Chuzzlewit* had appeared from January 1843 to July 1844. Heavily illustrated by numerous wood-cuts, the completed *Cyclopaedia* was a national history, a biographical dictionary, a copious anthology and a pictorial tour. With its 1,476 densely printed pages, it was the most

much cheaper than the 6s charged for the same text first published in 1832 as volume XV in Bentley's Standard Novels.

[21] *CEJ*, 26 January 1839, 2. Reprinted in *Select Writings*, 2: 165–72.

[22] 'Preface', *Cyclopaedia of English Literature*, 2 vols. (Edinburgh: W. & R. Chambers, 1842–44), vol. 1 The *Cyclopaedia*'s close relationship to the 1835 *History* is further confirmed by its division of English literary history into the same seven periods outlined below at n. 62.

[23] *CEJ*, 22 October 1842, 320; 7 October 1843, 304.

comprehensive history of English literature and the most comprehensive English literary anthology (encompassing verse and prose) in existence.

The *Cyclopaedia* provided readers with a retrospective pageant of literary achievement. But the book's most urgent historical claim concerned its own production and reception, an event that was framed in terms of a large portion of the community coming into an inheritance that it had traditionally been denied. For the first time, by virtue of the *Cyclopaedia*'s price, a complete literary history and extensive examples 'of the best productions of the English intellect' were being presented for 'the mental advancement of the middle and humbler portions of society'. Addressing an imagined readership that was adding to the recent acquisition of basic literacy a desire to be schooled in the pleasures of the aesthetic imagination and trying to economize on all non-essentials to make room for greater coverage, the *Cyclopaedia* omitted altogether any mention of the ancient history of the novel that had been noted in passing in the 1835 text and began instead with developments in the 17th century.[24] The English novel had become unambiguously new in this literary history invested in 'training the entire people to venerate the thoughtful and eloquent of past and present times'.[25]

Literary historians like Dunlop and Barbauld had spoken of novels in English as a subject matter within the larger topic of prose fiction over the course of hundreds of years and across many cultural boundaries. The *Cyclopaedia* celebrated the English novel as an essential component in the nation's recent history of literary self-expression. Beyond the key innovations of the 1740s, readers only needed to go back to 1719, the year of the publication of Defoe's *Robinson Crusoe*, to understand the history of the English novel in any detail. Here pronounced 'the father or founder of the English novel', Defoe earns this title through the practice of a kind of unprecedented realism: 'In England, the first pictures of real life in prose fiction were given by Defoe, who, in his graphic details, and personal adventures, all impressed with the strongest appearances of truth or probability, has never, in his own walk, been excelled.'[26] The collective accomplishment of the standard triumvirate of the 1740s—Richardson, Fielding, and Smollett—is then described as a narrative synthesis that unites this type of descriptive power with an enhanced capacity to portray different kinds of characters and to manage more complicated plots. And they do so in response to the determinant conditions of commercial modernity and a relative fixation on the bourgeois marriage plot and its complications. 'The gradual improvement in the tone and manners of society, the complicated relations of life, the growing contrasts between town and country manners, and all the artificial distinctions that crowd in with commerce, wealth and luxury', as the *Cyclopaedia* put it, 'banished the heroic romance and gave rise to the novel, in which the passion of love still maintained its place, but was surrounded by events and characters, such as are witnessed in ordinary life, under various aspects and modifications.'[27]

---

[24] *Cyclopaedia* (42–44), 2: 160.
[25] 'Preface', *Cyclopaedia* (42–44), vol. 1.
[26] *Cyclopaedia* (42–44), 1: 617, 2: 160.
[27] *Cyclopaedia* (42–44), 2: 160.

Chambers's status as an innovative literary historian grew out of an ambitious, self-advertised project to succeed commercially in the literary marketplace by harnessing the reproductive capacities of the newest printing technologies. Dependent on mass consumption in order to turn profits, the business model of W. & R. Chambers reflected a faith in the fact that reading and regularly purchasing print were on their way to becoming essential activities for the nation at large, not habits that distinguished the wealthy or learned. A self-made man, Chambers had the vision to understand the mechanical means of his own rise in the world as part of a broader development in a reconceived national literary history that shifted attention to consumption. Chambers articulated the enabling logic here in 'Literary Revolutions', a lead-article that appeared in the *Journal* in 1842. 'The student of English literary history', Chambers begins, 'is familiar with the fact, that every successive age has been distinguished by the development of some species of literature distinct in its character from those which delighted the public in the preceding and subsequent ages.' And he goes on to give an account— starting with Scott's popularization of 'the historical novel'—of the rise and fall of a wide range of literary genres and styles.[28] Assuming that 'the human mind remains fundamentally the same', Chambers wondered why literary modes were constantly changing rather than moving either towards or away from ideals of perfection. The answer was, to him, clear: once a public's taste had been stimulated by a new style, writers would increasingly seek to satisfy that taste and make it 'the predominant literary feature of the time, in short, the fashion'—until the 'next great wit carries away the public mind in a new direction'.[29] Chambers here inaugurates a relativistic understanding of literary history as a potentially ceaseless development of forms and styles driven by habits of literary consumption. Inventive literary production operates in tandem with the changing motivations of readers in search of new kinds of literary encounters.

The open-ended, fundamentally economic sense of history informing the *Cyclopaedia* undergirded Chambers's other great work of the 1840s, the *Vestiges of the Natural History of Creation* which was published in October of 1844, a few months after the completed *Cyclopaedia* was made available. Now recognized as the most important 19th-century explication of evolutionary theory before the appearance of Charles Darwin's *On the Origin of Species* (1859), the *Vestiges*, like the *Cyclopaedia*, was an historical narrative of vast scope, but one focused on natural history instead of national literary history. Its topics 'ranged from the formation of the universe, the record of life and the evolution of new species, to the origin and future destiny of human beings'.[30] The recently published *Cyclopaedia* proclaimed itself to be the instrument for and evidence of a transformation of national life based on the positive exploitation of modern printing technologies. The *Vestiges* enacted a maximized

---

[28] *CEJ*, 28 May 1842, 145. Reprinted in *Select Writings*, 4: 162–68.
[29] *CEJ*, 28 May 1842, 146.
[30] James A. Secord, 'Introduction', in '*Vestiges of the Natural History of Creation' and Other Evolutionary Writings* (Chicago: University of Chicago Press, 1994), ix.

dilation on the same theme of progress. It featured the march 'of mankind from the darkness of barbarism to the day of knowledge and mechanical and social improvement' as the culminating event in a cosmic history of development.[31] What both books have most importantly in common is the programmatic desire to reconcile constant variation with notions of design and higher purpose. In the *Vestiges* that purpose is the will of a beneficent Deity governing biological systems inclined to progressive change. In the *Cyclopaedia*, mechanical improvements offer to the nation at large a form of cultural reconciliation through 'a social and uniting sentiment' derived from 'our common reverence for a Shakespeare, a Milton, a Scott'.[32] The *Cyclopaedia* and the *Vestiges* reached back into the past, but they were also vehicles for a declaration of faith in change itself—in the past, present, and future—as the primary mechanism of history. Chambers's notion of perpetual innovation as described in 'Literary Revolutions' and the *Vestiges* in general embraced an optimistic sense of development that would later be described in the closing lines of *On the Origin of Species* where Darwin would write about 'the endless forms most beautiful and most wonderful' that 'have been, and are being, evolved'.[33]

Wary of compromising the brisk business of W. & R. Chambers with the controversy he rightly suspected would be ignited by the *Vestiges*, Chambers had it published anonymously. Despite having for its inspiration the same essential historical vision, one that could be called anachronistically Darwinian, the *Cyclopaedia* stirred no major controversy. A brief notice in the *Athenaeum* did, however, show how the *Cyclopaedia* practised a form of history that could be considered at least unsettling. Providing 'a connected outline of the history of English literature from its first rude shapings-out, down to the present time—we might almost say to the present hour', Chambers was guilty in the eyes of the reviewer of 'crossing the Rubicon which divides literary history from journalism, and venturing boldly among his contemporaries'.[34] Implying Chambers had a compromised sense of historical tact, the reviewer failed to understand how integral was the contemporaneity of the work. The widening audiences of the 1830s and early 40s—and the authors addressing them—could not be ignored precisely because they were represented as the recent climax of English literary history.

The novel, as a genre, was awarded no undisputed formal superiority at the moment of the *Cyclopaedia*'s publication. But the present times, all too present for the *Athenaeum*, were unique in the (now short) history of novel-writing: 'in no previous period of our literature was there so much respectable talent, knowledge, and imagination embarked in fictitious composition'.[35] Indeed the *Cyclopaedia* dedicates a full hundred pages in the

---

[31] Robert Chambers, '*Vestiges of the Natural History of Creation' and Other Evolutionary Writings*, ed. James A. Secord (Chicago: University of Chicago Press, 1994), 322.
[32] 'Preface', *Cyclopaedia* (42–44), vol. 1.
[33] Charles Darwin, *On the Origin of Species by Means of Natural Selection, or the Preservation of Favoured Races in the Struggle for Life* (London: John Murray, 1859), 490.
[34] *Athenaeum*, 31 August, 1844, 792–93.
[35] *Cyclopaedia* (42–44), 2: 630.

second volume to novelists ranging from Frances Burney to Charles Dickens.[36] These figures active from the 1780s up to the present time were collectively credited with expanding the thematic, formal, and stylistic range of fiction—'extending' the 'dominion' of the novel—while the two greatest novelists in the still unfolding 19th century—Scott and Dickens—were given unquestionable heroic status. In this setting, Dickens was not simply the last writer featured in the section on modern novelists. His career up to the publication of *Martin Chuzzlewit* (1843–44) and *A Christmas Carol in Prose* (1843) was represented as the culmination of a tradition binding the nation's readers to the authors of a native form of recent origins. He was 'next to Scott, the greatest of modern writers of fiction' and 'the most genuine English novelist we have had since Fielding'.[37] What was new here was the appearance of this genealogical claim in the context of a larger literary history that featured the rise of the novel in the 1740s and it subsequent proliferation as a corollary to the nation's march to modernity.

Throughout most of the 1840s the only rival to Chambers's literary histories was George Lille Craik's *Sketches of the History of Literature and Learning in England* (6 vols., 1844–45). Published by Charles Knight as part of his Weekly Volume Series in which readers were offered single 18mo (duodecimo) volumes for 1s 6d bound in cloth, Craik's work was, no less than Chambers's much larger *Cyclopaedia*, yet another venture in the cheap publishing movement.[38] But unlike the *Cyclopaedia*, Craik's history did not significantly incorporate into its narrative its mode of production and consumption. Even though it was completed shortly after the *Cyclopaedia*, Craik's history stopped short in the early 1820s, 'about the close of the reign of George the Third'.[39] His narrative ended, in other words, on the threshold of 'the cheap and popular system of publication' that Chambers had identified as the precursors to the more inventive attempts to reach wider audiences that had begun in the early 1830s. Observing a historiographic convention barring discussion of contemporary writers perhaps had the advantage of lending to his work the appearance of conveying more disinterested historical verdicts. But Craik, as his title implies, also remained partially attached to the concept of *translatio studii* and the older sense of literary history focused on the history of learned writing: his was a history of *Literature and Learning in England*, not of *English Literature*. In Craik's narrative too the novel had a comparatively muted importance. He and Chambers gave similar accounts of the modern English novel's origins in the 1740s, but Craik's literary history did not have a string of stirring sequels to this act of invention. Its coverage of fiction from the 1780s and after required little more than a short paragraph.[40]

[36] *Cyclopaedia* (42–44), 2: 533–633.

[37] *Cyclopaedia* (42–44), 2: 533, 534.

[38] See the *Times*, March 3, 1845, 2, for a full-page advertisement of works published by Charles Knight and Co., including the Weekly Volume series. Like Chambers, Knight was a major agent in the cheap publishing movement as well as an early historian of it. See 'The Modern Epoch of Cheapness' in his *The Old Printer and the Modern Press* (London: J. Murray, 1854), 238–59.

[39] George Lille Craik, *Sketches of the History of Literature and Learning in England*, 6 vols. (London: Charles Knight, 1844–45), 6: 201.

[40] *Sketches*, 5: 151–58 and 6: 103–4, 206.

The first history of English literature to emerge outside of the cheap literature movement was Thomas Budd Shaw's *Outlines of English Literature* (1849) published by John Murray, a traditional publishing house then best known as the proprietor and publisher of the *Quarterly Review* and for its standard editions of Lord Byron's works. Shaw noted the 'singular' fact that no comparable work 'existed in English'. But he also acknowledged that Chambers's earlier works might be considered exceptions, though he insisted that 'Chambers's valuable and complete "Cyclopaedia of English Literature" is as much too voluminous as his shorter sketch is too dry and list-like'.[41] Priced at 12s, the single volume *Outlines* in comfortable octavo format cost nearly five times the price of Chambers's short *History* and close to the price of the vastly larger two-volume *Cyclopaedia*. To a status conscious reader, Shaw's book had the added value of not coming with a helping of humble pie. chambers's literary histories made much of welcoming new arrivals to the book-buying public. Shaw's respectably pricey volume addressed itself to those born into that class.

In Shaw's book, as he explained it, 'only the *greater* names—the greater types of each period—have been examined; whilst the inferior, or merely *imitative*, writers have been unscrupulously neglected'.[42] Correspondingly, most of the twenty-one separate chapters of the *Outlines of English Literature* featured the names of writers ranging from 'Chaucer and His Times' to 'Wordsworth, Coleridge, and the New Poetry'. And in this survey of heroic originality, chapter XIV, entitled 'The Great Novelists', will pronounce the 18th-century rise of the novel to be one of the nation's most distinctive moments of invention:

> We are now arrived at that point in the history of British literature where, in obedience to the ever-acting laws which regulate intellectual as they do physical development, a new species of composition was to originate. As in the material creation we find the several manifestations of productive energy following a *progressive* order,—the lower, humbler, and less organized existences appearing first, and successively making way for kinds more variously and bounteously endowed, the less perfect merging imperceptibly into the more perfect,—so can we trace a similar action of this law in the gradual development of man's intellectual operations. No sooner do certain favourable conditions exist, no sooner has a fit *nidus* or theatre of action been produced, than we behold new manifestations of human intellect appearing in literature, in science, and in art, with as much regularity as, in the primeval eras of the physical world, the animalcule gave way to the fish, the fish to the reptile, the reptile to the bird, the beast, and ultimately to man.[43]

This ardent expression concerning the 18th-century English novel's originality was followed by a later chapter, 'The Modern Novelists', that declared the novel to be 'the

---

[41] Thomas Budd Shaw, *Outlines of English Literature* (London: J. Murray, 1849), iii. Shaw also quotes Chambers at length on Addison, on page 294, from the *Cyclopaedia* (42–44), 1: 606.
[42] *Outlines*, iv, original emphasis.
[43] *Outlines*, 303.

prevailing form, or type, of the present age…just as the epic is the natural form of the heroic or traditionary period'.[44] Using the period's evolutionary thought to mutate what had been a history of literary descent into an epoch-making divergence, Shaw links his close attention to contemporary English fiction to appreciative notions of transformative modernization. He acknowledged the older pan-European tradition of the novel in the major romance languages, but this gesture was a rhetorical prelude to locating an essential if unexplained British originality in the relatively recent works of Defoe, Richardson, Fielding, and Smollett: 'Spain, France, and Italy had all possessed the germ or embryo of prose fiction before it can be said to appear as a substantive, independent, and influential species of literature in Great Britain'.[45]

Like Chambers, Shaw had become an innovative literary historian in part because of his need to improvise a literary career in the wake of financial stress and disappointments in pursuing a more conventional vocational path. The seventh son of a successful architect, Shaw was able to enter Cambridge in 1833 shortly after the death of his father but was declared an insolvent debtor in 1840 after taking his degree and failing to support himself in London as a tutor and miscellaneous writer. Decamping for the Russian capital of St Petersburg, he became there an adjunct Professor of English Literature at the Imperial Alexander Lyceum and co-edited the short-lived *English Review*, a bi-monthly that presented 'in a condensed form, the quintessence of all that is most interesting and instructive in the periodical literature of Great Britain'.[46] Where Chambers's sense of literary history was grounded in his attempts to reach large segments of the public not usually considered reliable literary consumers, Shaw took stock of the nation's literary history for another usefully defamiliarized audience: he needed to describe English literary history's greatest moments for Russian aristocrats and bureaucratic leaders in training, an audience in the 1840s that was generally predisposed to allow that Britain was post-Napoleonic Europe's most advanced, politically stable nation-state.[47] Originally published in 1847 in St Petersburg, Shaw's *Outlines* was a text-book for his students there. It was re-addressed in the 1849 edition to an English audience of substantial means with only minor changes.

The *Outlines* originated in a different context and had a different intended audience in both St Petersburg and in England, but it shared with the *Cyclopaedia* the twin conviction that a superabundance of periodicals, including cheap ones such as *Chambers's Edinburgh Journal*, and the dominance of prose fiction gave to contemporary 19th-century English literary culture its most distinctive features, ones that could be appreciated as legitimate sequels to earlier defining events of English literary history.[48] Shaw's *Outlines* also

---

[44] *Outlines*, 471.

[45] *Outlines*, 303.

[46] *English Review* (1843), 5. For its first two issues, Shaw composed a two-part 'History of Periodical Publication in England' that stretched from the late 17th-century and concluded with an appreciation of 'the vast and brilliant field now occupied by this portion of our literature' (97).

[47] On the reception of the English novel in Russia, see Julia Buckler's chapter in this volume.

[48] The *Outlines* spoke approvingly of 'the publications by Constable and Chambers in Scotland, and the prolific brood of "Family Libraries," "Cabinet Cyclopaedias," and penny journals' (517).

had in common with Chambers's celebrations of the expansion of the reading public a self-congratulatory enthusiasm for a form of bio-mechanical cultural productivity described in the volume's closing lines:

> The English intellect, thanks to the happy freedom of our institutions, and the strong virility of national character, has no dull, dead, periods of feeble imitation and languid servility. The moment it has duly developed itself in one direction, it instantly takes and steadily maintains another: and our literature—essentially the literature of a nation of men—rich in the finest and most unequalled models of every kind and class of excellence—is in every sense worthy of the greatest, freest, and most thoughtful people that the world has ever seen.[49]

Initially standing as the peroration for a series of lectures addressed to all-male students in St Petersburg these claims were likely inspired in part by a teacher's wish to justify the just completed course of instruction. Transferred verbatim to the conclusion of the first English edition of the *Outlines*, they can be read alongside Thomas Babington Macaulay's *History of England*, the first two volumes of which had appeared in November of 1848 as much of Europe was concluding a year of revolutions and counterrevolutions. Like Shaw's volume, Macaulay's *History* was a tribute to England's contemporary greatness as measured by the blessings of commercial modernity and a stable body politic that allowed England to avoid the traumas of 1848. For Macaulay, this solidity and flexibility had been endowed by the events of the late 17th century that culminated in the Glorious Revolution of 1688. Shaw and Chambers were engaged in the related task of portraying the 18th-century rise of the English novel as an essential element in the evolution of modern England's national identity. In the new literary histories, the English novel was the typographic fruit of the late 17th-century political reconfigurations that had allowed England to become a leading, stable European power.

Following Shaw's work, two other single-volume surveys soon appeared. They illustrate how the character of the 18th-century English novel was being contested in the day's new literary histories, even as the genre's essential modernity was now routinely reconfirmed by writers with different agendas. *Sketches of English Literature* appeared in 1852 and is the first comprehensive English literary history to be written by a woman, Clara Balfour. Priced at 7s 6d, Balfour's *Sketches* was addressed to the 'general or the young reader' and especially 'the female reader who snatches from daily duties brief opportunities for reading'.[50] Idealizing a domestic sphere in which the ladies of the house are engaged with woman's work but also able to read for pleasure and instruction,

---

[49] *Outlines*, 539.

[50] Clara Lucas Balfour, *Sketches of English Literature, from the Fourteenth to the Present Century* (London: Longman & Co., 1852), iii. Subsequent citations appear in the text. Balfour's status as trail-blazing literary historian has been largely ignored, though Kristin G. Doern in 'Equal Questions: the "Woman Question" and the "Drink Question" in the Writings of Clara Lucas Balfour, 1808–78', in *Women, Religion, and Feminism in Britain 1750–1900*, ed. Sue Morgan (London: Palgrave, 2002), 159–76, does mention the *Sketches* in the context of her writing and lecturing for the temperance movement.

Balfour speaks with the voice of a well-read, respectable figure addressing younger or less educated women eager to benefit from her guidance. She quickly describes the rise of the modern English novel with the work of Defoe, Richardson, Fielding, Smollett, and Sterne, but seems most intent on making it clear that contact with the last three should be avoided beyond the recollection of their historical roles: with Fielding, his 'aim…was to amuse rather than amend his reader, and the coarseness of his books necessarily restricted them entirely to male readers'; Smollett had 'great wit and a racy humour', but 'the absence of all delicacy made his writings, not withstanding their great intellectual power, revolting to all right-minded persons'; while Sterne's writings 'are equally open to the charge of immorality and coarseness' (278). After efficiently noting the perils to be encountered in these three, Balfour proceeds with a more appreciative and extended discussion of Richardson and Oliver Goldsmith, author of *The Vicar of Wakefield* (1766), followed by a general discourse on 'the utility of works of fiction' that is equally critical of 'those who reject them entirely and those who read them exclusively and indiscriminately' (294–301). Thereafter the various indiscretions associated with some of the founding fathers of the English novel are atoned for by a series of literary refinements and reforms that are often indebted to the work of a long list of female novelists including Fanny Burney, Maria Edgeworth, Jane Austen, and Ann Radcliffe (294–301).

Balfour's brief look back to the 18th-century rise of the novel provides a chance to describe a general improvement of national literary culture that is attributed, in no small part, to the fact that novels were increasingly being addressed to and written by women apparently uninterested in or unable to stomach the coarseness that marred the work of some of the members of the all-male cast presiding over the English novel's modern inception. No less than those by Chambers and Shaw, Balfour's narrative was a chronicle of national progress that featured the making of a more earnest, refined and well-informed reading public moulded by Evangelical religious piety, the increasingly prominent role of women in national life, and technological advances that had 'altered more in the last fifty years than in any three centuries previously' (394).

Balfour concluded by noting how new levels of demand for print had become a leading feature of the period's literary history: 'A reading public makes a demand so vast and continuous, that it has caused a supply unprecedented. The press of our time is as great a marvel as the railroad or the electric telegraph' (401). This superabundance was a topic of her literary history as it reached contemporary times as well as the grounds for the need of histories, such as her own, that assigned value to a seemingly boundless supply of new and republished writings. The age's general 'diffusion of knowledge'—reaching both men and women on increasingly equal terms according to Balfour—was a great gift but one that came with the danger that it might be 'neglected or misused': 'Young people roam in libraries and read at every opportunity; but they too often neglect all system in their reading, and therefore are not much the wiser after all' (403). The fact that Balfour's well-instructed reader could and should legitimately make time for reading contemporary novels was another sign of how English fiction was being incorporated into the period's well-regulated library. Scott's actual library at Abbotsford banished recent fiction and admitted on historical grounds a few works by the native form's founding fathers. Balfour's ideal library reversed this judgement. Coarse mid-18th-century patriarchs were acknowledged by virtue of an historical obligation but ushered away in favour of a large brood of greatly improved descendents of 'the present day', the authors of 'historical, metaphysical, philosophical, conventional, ethical, national, humorous, and domestic fictions, contributed by writers male and female of the very highest reputation' (285).

Not long after the appearance of Balfour's work, William Spalding's *History of English Literature* (1853) was 'offered, as an Elementary Text-Book, to those who are interested in the instruction of young persons' at the low price of 3s 6d.[51] Perhaps with this tender audience in mind, it was more comprehensively critical of the coarseness of the pioneering English novelists of the 1740s and shortly after. 'When we pass from Johnson to the Novelists of his time', Spalding wrote, 'we seem as if leaving the aisles of an august cathedral, to descend into the galleries of a productive but ill-ventilated mine. Around us clings a foul and heavy air, which youthful travellers in the realm of literature cannot safely breathe' (Spalding, *History*, 336). But Spalding was nonetheless convinced that the English novel originated at that time—with the obligatory anticipations by Defoe noted earlier. Where Balfour had documented in detail a reform of fiction largely accomplished by the expanding participation of female writers in the later 18th century, Spalding was not 'inclined to study novels deeply' during this period, and simply named, in addition to praising highly Goldsmith's *Vicar*, eight novelists—four men and four women—active in the period 1760–1800, some of whom 'did much to prepare the way for the greater prevalence of nature and common-sense in this kind of writing' (Spalding, *History*, 349).

Spalding's ultimate destination in the more recent history of the novel was the appearance of Scott's *Waverley* and all that followed from that author: 'By him above all, with two or three precursors and several not unworthy successors' the novel would become a respectable fixture of contemporary literary culture (Spalding, *History*, 363). The unique accomplishments of Scott in Spalding's history included the notion that novel-writing immediately after him was an overshadowed affair. Citing 'the hundreds of novels and romances which have been poured forth in our day' in his overview of the period 1830–52, Spalding said 'it would be rash to seek for any parallel to the multifarious power of Scott' (Spalding, *History*, 399). Spalding nevertheless highlights the work of Dickens and Thackeray among a larger class of authors who aim 'at making the novel illustrate, as far as the form would allow, the questions which agitate society most powerfully'. Despite their admitted differences as writers, they are described as 'the founders of a new school in novel-writing' (Spalding, *History*, 400).

At the heart of Spalding's simplified version of literary history stands his desire or willingness to see a few individuals make transformative innovations in a prolific genre

---

[51] William Spalding, *The History of English Literature; with an Outline of the Origin and Growth of the English Language: illustrated by extracts* (Edinburgh: Oliver & Boyd, 1853), 1. Subsequent citations appear in the text.

with its roots traced to the mid-18th century. This reductive historical narrative would be widely circulated in various guises for well over one hundred years. Some subsequent historians would follow the direction suggested by Balfour and focus on characterizing the manifold and expanding subgenres of English fiction, while others would stay closer to Spalding's approach and use the proliferation (or over-production) of the genre as an occasion to celebrate a few acts of true literary distinction that were achieved despite the commonplace nature of writing a novel. Both approaches paid tribute to Shaw's claim that the novel was the age's representative literary form and both agreed as well that the English novel was indeed new.

Thirteen years after the publication of the first edition of Chambers's *Cyclopaedia*, a second 'New and Improved Edition' began to appear in November of 1857 in the same format: in weekly numbers for 1 1/2d, in monthly parts at 7d, or by the volume, with the slightly longer volumes of this second edition priced at 8s each.[52] With both volumes ready for purchase at the end of October of 1859, the work was advertised in *Chambers's Edinburgh Journal* without the fanfare so much in evidence in the 1840s about unique cheapness. The *Cyclopaedia* remained a remarkable deal given the amount of text and illustrations it offered for its total price of 16s, particularly when compared to the price of much new fiction.[53] But it was no longer aimed primarily at 'the middle and humbler portions of society' seeking 'mental advancement'. Instead it was intended for and embraced by middle-class consumers with expectations that the larger market for books would include more affordable titles, even as many new publications came with a steep duty to be paid by their first owners. The prices and formats that were initially inspired by catering to a new audience in the 1830s and 40s had now become standard options for a larger book buying public.

Comparing the first and second editions of the *Cyclopaedia* allows one to appreciate how rapid was the rise of a number of new novelistic careers that continue to be at the centre of the academic study of Victorian fiction. Completed in July of 1844 and covering events up to the end 1843, the second volume of the first edition had already hailed Dickens as an author 'crowned with unrivalled success'.[54] But the Brontës (Charlotte, Emily, and Anne), Elizabeth Gaskell, Anthony Trollope, and George Eliot are for obvious chronological reasons not to be found in the first edition. William Makepeace Thackeray's barely budding career was rendered in two sentences.[55] Just short of fifteen

---

[52] Most of the expanded scope came from a commitment to including events and publications between 1844 and 1859 into the larger narrative of English literary history. The closing 'Addendum' to the second volume referred to events as late as August 1859. Though this second edition is dated '1858–60', its actual publication dates—1857–59—are used here. The first number of the first volume was published on 7 November 1857; the two volumes complete were available for purchase on 29 October 1859. See *CEJ*, 31 October 1857, 288 and 29 October 1859, 288. It was common to publish books late in the calendar year, in November or December in particular, bearing the date of the approaching year. This habit allowed publications to extend their 'freshness' into a near-term future.

[53] George Eliot's *Adam Bede*, the fictional sensation of the spring of 1859, initially retailed for 31s 6d, just about twice the cost of the *Cyclopaedia*.

[54] *Cyclopaedia* (42–44), 2: 633.

[55] *Cyclopaedia* (42–44), 2: 625.

years later, in the second volume of the second edition, Trollope is recognized as a dis-tinguished chronicler of national characteristics—'There is a degree of reality, vigour, and genuine fresh English feeling about Mr Trollope's novels, which render him remark-able among his contemporaries'—and Thackeray has proven himself 'another master of English fiction', a rival to Dickens in his creative powers if not in his overall popularity.[56] Dickens himself has the many events of his post-1843 career added, and his lucrative public readings, which began in 1858, are said to 'form a new feature in the modern lit-erary life'.[57] The brief, loss-laden careers of the Brontë sisters—with Charlotte taking cen-tre stage—unfold with a level of detail indebted to Gaskell's *The Life of Charlotte Bronte* (1857).[58] Her portrayal of the 'manufacturing population' in her own novels, starting with *Mary Barton* (1848), is praised for throwing 'light on conditions of life, habits, and feelings comparatively new and original in our fictitious literature'.[59] The final contem-porary novelist to earn recognition in the *Cyclopaedia*, George Eliot, does so on the strength of *Adam Bede* alone.[60] Running to a fifth edition as the *Cyclopaedia* was nearing completion, *Adam Bede*'s combination of commercial success and critical acclaim dem-onstrated how an unknown writer could earn fame with what was now considered to be the technical mastery of the 'art' of the novel.[61]

The second edition of the *Cyclopaedia* had also reorganized its coverage of nov-elists to draw attention to what now appeared to be a discrete post-1830 era for the English novel. The first edition of the *Cyclopaedia* surveyed English literary history in seven major periods, with the second volume containing two relatively long periods of 1727–80 and 1780–present, while the second edition included nine periods with the second volume featuring three briefer periods of 1760–1800, 1800–30, and 1830–59.[62] Where the first edition had charted the rise of the novel to be followed by one long generation of novelists active from the 1780s to the early 1840s, the second edition dis-cussed four separate generations of novelists: the inauguration of the form appeared towards the end of volume one and was followed by three additional sections in vol-ume two corresponding to the three periods just noted. The general headnote for the final period of 1830–59 called special attention to the 'rich abundance of our prose fiction' and concluded 'the novel has indeed become a necessity for our social life—an

---

[56] *Cyclopaedia* (57–59), 2: 631, 650.

[57] *Cyclopaedia* (57–59), 2: 650.

[58] *Cyclopaedia* (57–59), 2: 659–62.

[59] *Cyclopaedia* (57–59), 2: 668.

[60] *Cyclopaedia* (57–59), 2: 677.

[61] The *Times*'s review of *Adam Bede*, 12 April 1859, 5, began by declaring it 'a first-rate novel, and its author takes rank at once among the masters of the art'.

[62] In both editions, the first five periods were identical: From the Earliest time–1400, 1400–1558, 1558–1649, 1649–89, 1689–1727. The first volume of the 1842–44 edition stopped at this point, and all of the second volume was taken up by two additional periods: 1727–80, and 1780–the Present. The first volume of the 1857–59 edition added a sixth period (1727–60) to complete the first volume, and devoted all of the second volume to three periods (1760–1800, 1800–30, 1830–59) covering only the past one hundred years of literary history, a disproportional shift towards the present that was justified by the great increase of readers and reading material during that time.

institution'.[63] As the subsection 'Novelists' went on to highlight the talents and prestige of writers such as Dickens, Thackeray, Trollope, the Brontës, Gaskell, Eliot and many others, the *Cyclopaedia* was institutionalizing what would soon be called the 'Victorian novel'. With an Index entry that had not appeared in the first edition, browsing readers in 1859 were also now directed to 'Novels, Rise of'.[64] This addition of 'The Rise of the Novel' to the *Cyclopaedia*'s organizing logic was no minor development if we imagine it as a preliminary step in the phrase's long migration from the back of a book sold to general readers to the title-page of Ian Watt's academic study first published in 1957.

The new literary histories published in the period 1835–59 were responsible for familiarizing readers with a twofold rise of the novel in English: a mid-18th-century moment of formal origins followed by the new genre's recognition, sometime after 1830, as the age's characteristic literary form. Two years after W. & R. Chambers had issued its revision of the *Cyclopaedia*, the publisher Griffin, Bohn and Co. began to do the same for George Craik's *Sketches of the History of Literature and Learning in England* (6 vols., 1844–45) in two different forms: *A Compendious History of English Literature, and of the English Language* (2 vols., 1861) and *A Manual of English Literature, and of the English Language* (1862).[65] Craik mostly recycled his earlier work, but the changes and additions he made reflect and confirm the developments in literary history that have been traced back to key texts by Chambers and Shaw from the 1840s. Most obviously, both new works, by way of their titles, no longer aligned themselves with the older tendency to imagine and document the fate of 'Literature in England'. These were books about *English Literature*. Craik's new material on the history of the English language would also reflect this lexical shift. Historical philology's attention to a long history of English was displacing an earlier inclination, still strong in the 18th century, to regard old varieties of English as rude, irregular, or underdeveloped.[66] In the Victorian era, historical philology would be practised with a formidable level of learning, but this scholarly endeavour had a powerful synergistic relationship with a popular, racialized idealization of the nation—the people themselves—as readers and, in some senses, creatures of English. Even as the common reader of the 19th century was increasingly skilled in one language alone, this reader could proudly be the legatee of a rich and glorious linguistic inheritance that had been entailed in ancient times.

[63] *Cyclopaedia* (57–59), 2: 572.
[64] *Cyclopaedia* (57–59), 2: 812.
[65] The *Compendious History* (24s) was a resetting of the text of the earlier *Sketches* with the addition of more extracts from primary texts, a history of the English language, and a final chapter that extended the history to present times. The *Manual* (7s 6d) was abridged from the *Compendious History* by excising most of its extracts and footnotes. Having Craik's narrative available in these two forms allowed his publisher to sell two versions of what was essentially the same book to two different kinds of consumers.
[66] Craik referred to what we now call Anglo-Saxon or Old English as 'Original English'. See *A Compendious History of English Literature, and of the English Language*, 2 vols. (London: Griffin, Bohn, 1861), 1: 32–41.

Another striking difference was Craik's enthusiastic interest in characterizing English literature of the present times, leading him to close the *Compendious History* with a chapter entitled 'The Victorian Age' that begins with 'the exit of the last of the Georges' in 1830.[67] Where the earlier history (as noted above) had very little to say about late 18th- and early 19th-century fiction, the new version made a strong case for 'the realm of the novel' being 'the widest in the whole world of artistic literature': 'There is nothing, in short, that the novel may not include . . . and there is no end to the number and diversity of the provinces comprehended in it; so that true narrative and imaginative genius, of whatever kind, is always sure to find somewhere in so ample a range its proper region.'[68] Following two other major claims about the Victorian Age—that it was a period in which prose works enjoyed a supremacy and that writing of 'the highest order' was mostly found in 'narrative of one kind or another'—this tribute stands out on the pages of a book that narrated English literary history with an unapologetic inclusion of the English novel as a major development in the nation's modern literary history.[69] Craik might have added that the period's preference for prose narrative combined with the age's high estimation of the novel was borne out by the appearance of new literary histories in the 1840s that had featured the distinctively modern rise of the English novel and had celebrated its 19th-century proliferation.

The deluge of manuals, histories, and handbooks of English literature that would appear in the 1860s and after would increasingly originate in ways that could be related to what has been called 'the rise of English', the history of English studies as a discipline that becomes fully accredited when it achieves a regular departmental profile in colleges and universities in the English-speaking countries of the world. This history has been told many times from various perspectives, and the late-Victorian contemplation of the novel's proper place on English Literature curricula at the university level is described elsewhere in this volume.[70] Attending to an earlier rise of *English Literature* that emerges at the intersection of literary history and book history, the present essay provides a prologue to this better-known history of English studies. In this new perspective, the general academic assent to the 18th-century rise of the English novel did not simply reflect the suitable evidence and plausible argument found in Watt's *Rise of the Novel* and its best critical progeny. It was also rooted in the mass production of books describing that ascent as a crucial stage on the road to becoming a modern reading nation, a flood of paper and ink that would almost completely submerge an earlier transnational history of prose fiction.

---

[67] *Compendious History*, 2: 522.
[68] *Compendious History*, 2: 534.
[69] *Compendious History*, 2: 528, 533.
[70] See Anna Vaninskaya's chapter, 'The Novel, Its Critics and the University: A New Beginning?', in this volume.

Suggested Reading

Balfour, Clara Lucas. *Sketches of English Literature, from the Fourteenth to the Present Century*. London: Longman & Co., 1852.

Chambers, Robert. *Cyclopaedia of English Literature*. 2 vols. Edinburgh: W. & R. Chambers, 1842–44.

———. *History of the English Language and Literature*. Edinburgh: W. & R. Chambers, 1835.

Craik, George Lille. *Sketches of the History of Literature and Learning in England*. 6 vols. London: Charles Knight, 1844–45.

Fyfe, Aileen. *Steam-Powered Knowledge: William Chambers and the Business of Publishing, 1820–1860*. Chicago: University of Chicago Press, 2012.

Gamer, Michael. 'A Select Collection: Barbauld, Scott, and the Rise of the (Reprinted) Novel'. In *Recognizing the Romantic Novel: New Histories of British Fiction, 1780–1830*. Edited by Jillian Heydt-Stevenson and Charlotte Sussman. Liverpool: Liverpool University Press, 2008, 151–91.

Johnson, Claudia L. '"Let Me Make the Novels of a Country": Barbauld's *The British Novelists* (1810/1820)', *Novel* 34(2) Spring (2001): 163–79.

Secord, James A. *Victorian Sensation: The Extraordinary Publication, Reception, and Secret Authorship of 'Vestiges of the Natural History of Creation'*. Chicago: University of Chicago Press, 2000.

Shaw, Thomas Budd. *Outlines of English Literature*. London: J. Murray, 1849.

Spalding, William. *The History of English Literature; with an Outline of the Origin and Growth of the English Language: Illustrated by extracts*. Edinburgh: Oliver & Boyd, 1853.

St Clair, William. *The Reading Nation in the Romantic Period*. Cambridge: Cambridge University Press, 2004.

3

GENRE, CRITICISM, AND THE EARLY VICTORIAN NOVEL

REBECCA EDWARDS NEWMAN

In 1848, the *Metropolitan Magazine* confidently declared the ascendancy of the novel form: 'In all literatures the novel has existed—exists—and will continue to exist…[it] will be read, and its genius and wit, its developments of human character and passion, will fascinate and allure'.[1] Despite its enormous variety, the novel form's pre-eminence in the 19th century is now assured as a touchstone in literary history. Victorian novels offer, in the view of one critic, the 'most typical and widely defining voices' of 19th-century literature; the era's 'defining literary genre' in the words of another.[2] Such assessments are not limited to a 20th-century disciplinary perspective. From the early decades of the 19th century, novelists and critics alike pointed to the possibilities of the novel even while they debated its moral and aesthetic responsibilities. 'Prose Fiction in Britain', wrote David Masson in 1859, 'has received a fresh impulse and has taken on a set of new characteristics, since Dickens and Thackeray became for us its chief representatives'.[3] Following the novelistic achievements of Walter Scott, a perceived shift in the value of the novel and the respectability it conferred upon its authors echoed through the texts and their reception in the wider field of print culture.[4] 'The times are changed now', exclaimed Thackeray's Major Pendennis to his novel-writing nephew, 'there's a run on literature—clever fellows get into the best houses in town'.[5]

But while current scholars and contemporary Victorian criticism now seem to concur in the novel's dominance, this should not efface the furious debates raging since the

---

[1] 'Notices of New Works', *Metropolitan Magazine* 51 (January 1848): 116–18, 116.

[2] Deidre David, ed., *The Cambridge Companion to the Victorian Novel* (Cambridge: Cambridge University Press, 2001), 15; Ian Watt, ed., *The Victorian Novel* (London: Oxford University Press, 1971), v.

[3] David Masson, *British Novelists and Their Styles* [1859] (Boston: D. Lothrop & Co., 1875), 239.

[4] On Scott's significance to the changing status of the novel, see Ina Ferris, *The Achievement of Literary Authority: Gender, History and the Waverley Novels* (Ithaca, NY: Cornell University Press, 1991).

[5] William Thackeray, *Pendennis*, ed. John Sutherland (Oxford: Oxford University Press, 1994), 464.

late 18th century on the value and legitimate contours of the form. Resistance to the novel in that period had been widely marked by a series of factors, from its accepted low status in the hierarchy of literary genres (subordinate to the superior forms of poetry and drama) to its unavoidable identity as a fashionable commodity, a titular 'novelty' without the necessary endurance to achieve canonical posterity. At the same time, as the *Annual Register* warned in 1772, reading novels brought a range of deleterious effects. Such texts might indeed function as 'a kind of literary opium, that lulls every sense into delicious rapture', but they also 'contributed more than any other cause to debauch the morals of the young fair sex'.[6] Female readers in particular stood in danger of moral and intellectual corruption not just from the works of Eliza Haywood and unprincipled French novelists, as the *Annual Register* bemoaned, but from a more widespread novel-istic muse 'tricked out in the trappings of taste'—an unmistakable echo of the contro-versy surrounding Richardson's own 'tricked up' heroine, Pamela, a generation earlier. Such depictions of the novel as a 'prostitution' of literary talent—a means of lowering the standing of writer and form still further—persisted through to the mid-19th century, accompanied by the moral objections of such diversely assorted groups as dissenters, utilitarians, politicians, and writers themselves. And so in 1848, a year which saw the publication of Elizabeth Gaskell's *Mary Barton*, John Henry Newman's *Loss and Gain*, and various parts of Thackeray's *Vanity Fair* and *Pendennis*, Thomas De Quincey could nevertheless denounce writers 'who, *in order* to be popular, must speak through nov-els...That is already to be self-degraded.'[7]

What cannot remain in doubt, in the midst of such polarized views, is that explicit interest in the genre of the novel strengthened dramatically throughout the 19th cen-tury. Readers, novelists, reviewers, and critical commentators were together drawn into a public discussion on the novel form and its 'origin and progress', as Anna Laetitia Barbauld put it in 1810 in the introduction to her fifty-volume edition, *The British Novelists*.[8] These were bold and often controversial declarations on the nature and value of the novel, and they grew in frequency and self-assurance in the course of the early 19th century. In its first twenty years, the *Edinburgh Review* appraised only a handful of novels, but between 1822 and 1850 those figures rose sharply, extending beyond the previously restricted circle of novelists. And in the prefaces, appendices, critical notices, and narratives themselves, novels drew attention to their status in the literary order and issued a self-consciousness that both championed and, at times, undermined the stand-ing of the form. Breaking the flow of the narrative, Catherine's practice of novel reading is insistently defended by Jane Austen's narrator in the fifth chapter of *Northanger Abbey*:

---

    [6] 'An Essay on the Modern Novel', *The Annual Register* (1772): 184–88, 185.

    [7] Thomas De Quincey, 'Review of John Forster's The Life and Adventures of Oliver Goldsmith', *The North British Review* 9 (May 1848): 187–212, 194.

    [8] Anna Letitia Barbauld, *The British Novelists; with an essay; and prefaces, biographical and critical, by Mrs. Barbauld* (London: F.C. & J. Rivington, 1810). Barbauld designated her extensive introductory essay as a critical contribution to the 'origin and progress' of the form.

'Yes, novels; for I will not adopt that ungenerous and impolitic custom so common with novel-writers, of degrading by their contemptuous censure the very performances, to the number of which they are themselves adding.'[9] Yet while the narrator protests that 'no species of composition has been so much decried', *Northanger Abbey* nevertheless proceeds to satirize the effects of Gothic romances upon its own impressionable young heroine—a double-edged endorsement of the form that simultaneously points at the potential dangers of reading the 'wrong' kind of novel.

As this fascination with novelistic 'kind' increased in all forms of print culture, it was also accompanied by a newly awakened interest in 'genre' itself. Conversations on the nature of genre and the novel form often coincided in critical writing, so that one began to articulate the other for the burgeoning audiences of magazines, reviews, and novels. In several respects, 'genre' is a prescient area of consideration in relation to the novel in this period. Just as that form was engaged in a process of development that forced writers to articulate more precisely its parameters and typologies, genre was a word also coming into being in English—an adoption from the French, meaning 'type' or 'sort'—that was only gradually applied in English to the categories of literary composition, and which progressively gained ground in relation to discussions on the novel. As the *Oxford English Dictionary* attests, the earliest usages of 'genre' in 18th-century compositions were italicized to indicate a foreign provenance; the word does not slip comfortably into mainstream usage to refer to literary kind before the middle and latter decades of the 19th century.[10] Instead, terms like 'rank', 'class', 'kind', and 'species' drew attention to a growing need to quantify the value of the novel form, while also highlighting the explicitly taxonomical language that came to structure discourse on its literary categories. Typical of this movement, in 1845 *Hogg's Weekly Instructor* presented an introduction to the novel as a popularly misunderstood and indiscriminate '*species* of literary composition'.[11] In many magazines throughout the 1830s, reviews of contemporary novels were routinely preceded by genealogies of the form, tracing a line of practitioners and texts against which to evaluate the contemporary novel in question. As a result, magazines effectively offered to their readership a practical demonstration of what 'genre' might be: the productive reading of an individual case to determine typology and the necessary understanding of typology to read each singular instance.

Current theories of genre have taken pains to establish the fact that genre does not indicate a prescriptive and rule-governed formalism, in which fixed categories

---

[9] Jane Austen, *Northanger Abbey*, ed. Anne Ehrenpreis (London: Penguin, 1972), 57–58.
[10] The *OED* attributes the first usage of genre to Charles Jenner in 1770. Throughout the 19th century, increasingly frequent mentions of genre painting as an artistic style, and in relation to French literary categories, are made in the middle of the century, but regular references to genre as literary kind do not appear until the later part of the 19th century. By the time of Andrew Lang's article on realism and romance in the *Eclectic Magazine* in 1888, mentions of the 'novel genre' are used without reserve: 'One only begins to object if it is asserted that *this genre* of fiction is the only permissible *genre*, that nothing else is of the nature of art', Andrew Lang, 'Realism and Romance', *The Eclectic Magazine of Foreign Literature, Science and Art* 57 (1888): 259–66, 262.
[11] 'On Novels and Novel-Reading', *Hogg's Weekly Instructor* (25 October 1845): 129–31, 129.

precede literary instances and contain our understanding.[12] Any consideration of the 19th-century novel must therefore shift us away from a sense of the novel as an abstract category and towards a focus on 'genre' as a primarily historical development—a series of classificatory acts that unfold within, respond to, and, in turn, shape the circumstances of that development. To this end, what follows will be framed by two sections that take account of these discussions on the novel-form from different perspectives. The first charts the location of discussions on the novel genre in relation to early 19th-century print culture and the influence of periodical criticism. By outlining the various attempts to legislate an identity for the novel and its 'species' in the decade of Victoria's accession, this section indicates the transformation of those critical discussions into later theories of the novel in the mid-19th century. The second section of this chapter turns its attention to Edward Bulwer Lytton's writings in the 1830s and 1840s; in particular it examines the way in which his early fiction responded to questions of genre, and those acts of critical legislation found in the periodicals. As Bulwer's career attests, 19th-century writers were able to develop in their texts and paratexts an authorial discourse on the novel which attempted to assure the form's high artistic worth and effectively circumvent the power of the reviews by engaging readers in a direct address on the value of the novel.[13]

MAGAZINE CRITICISM AND THE CULTURE OF CLASSIFICATION

When Lady Clarinda declares her intention to publish a fashionable novel in Thomas Love Peacock's satire, *Crotchet Castle* (1831), she is plainly aware of the role the periodical press will play in ensuring its literary success. Open the newspapers, she intimates to Captain Fitzchrome, and 'you will see some morning, that my novel is "the most popular production of the day". This is Mr. Puffall's favourite phrase. He makes the newspapers say it of everything he publishes.'[14] Mr Puffall, the publisher—a thinly disguised caricature of Henry Colburn—promotes his own novels in his own newspapers and magazines through the notorious practice of 'puffing'—the favourable reviewing of one text in another of his publications to ensure commercial success. Despite his association with

---

[12] Carolyn Williams, '"Genre" and "Discourse" in Victorian Cultural Studies', *Victorian Literature and Culture* (1999): 517–20.

[13] Some confusion exists over the name of Edward Bulwer. Although by the end of his career his full name was Edward George Earl Lytton Bulwer Lytton, during the early years he was known as Edward Lytton Bulwer. After receiving a baronetcy in 1838 and inheriting Knebworth in 1843, he hyphenated the patronymic. Within the confines of this chapter, I refer to him as Edward Bulwer or Edward Lytton Bulwer. Andrew Brown, 'Lytton, Edward George Earle Lytton Bulwer, first Baron Lytton (1803–1873)', *Oxford Dictionary of National Biography*, online edn, Oxford University Press, Sept 2004, <http://www.oxforddnb.com/view/article/17314>, accessed 21 July 2010.

[14] Thomas Love Peacock, *Crotchet Castle* (London: T. Hookham, 1831), 98

figures such as Edward Bulwer Lytton and Benjamin Disraeli, by 1831 Henry Colburn had become infamous for manipulating the offices of fair criticism and the novel, implicitly denigrating the value of both and repositioning 'fashionable tales' as the lowest branch of the novel genre. Echoing Thomas Carlyle's 1829 attack on the 'huge subterranean, puffing bellows' of the literature machine, Peacock's novel depicts newspapers and periodicals as principal vehicles for novel production—commercially interested and parasitically positioned to take advantage of an undiscriminating mass readership.[15]

This perceived relationship between the periodical press and the novel form suggests a familiar hierarchical distinction between the book and print journal in the 19th century—one in which reviews and magazines might support the novel but remain insignificant as a literary form or genre in their own right. As *Tait's Magazine* protested in 1833:

> Periodicals are still by many treated as the *et-cetera* and adjectives of literature, because such was their early position; and the name once given, remains unaltered. This is a strange and injurious folly. A few words will suffice to show how important it is that the holders of so much influence should be encouraged.[16]

Over the last twenty years, however, much recent scholarship on middle-class reviews and magazines has begun to reconsider the complex, competitive role that periodicals played in the literary field.[17] And though we often assume that the novel, in sheer numbers at least, dwarfed all other literary forms in terms of popularity, this is not necessarily borne out if we compare it to the success of periodicals. Figures for the number of novels published during the period remain estimates at best, due, in large part, to the proliferation of the novel genre in multiple print formats—from the mighty three-volume triple-decker fiction, to the one-volume edition and of course the serial version, published weekly, monthly or as part of a larger periodical. John Sutherland estimates that 60,000 novels were published between the years 1837 and 1901, though these figures do not include novels published only in serial form as part of other publications (for detailed figures on the years 1820–36, see Peter Garside's chapter in this volume).[18] But figures for the growth of periodicals also match this exponential trajectory: conservative estimates allow that journals, magazines, and reviews increased in number from approximately 265 at the end of the 18th century, to somewhere over 50,000 at the beginning of the twentieth.[19] While the outcomes of these material connections between the novel and the periodical have yet to be fully explored, by 1907, as Simon Eliot has shown,

[15] Thomas Carlyle, *Selected Writings*, ed. Alan Shelston (London: Penguin, 1971), 66.

[16] 'On Periodical Literature', *Tait's Magazine* 3 (1833): 491–96.

[17] See in particular Jon P. Klancher, *The Making of English Reading Audiences 1790–1832* (Madison, WI: University of Wisconsin Press), 1987.

[18] John Sutherland, *The Stanford Companion to Victorian Fiction* (Stanford, CA: Stanford University Press, 1989). On publication data for 1820–36, see Garside's chapter in this volume.

[19] Alvin Sullivan, ed., *British Literary Magazines: [Pt. 1] The Augustan Age and the Age of Johnson, 1698–1788*, *Historical Guides to the World's Periodicals and Newspapers* (Westport, CN: Greenwood Press, 1983), ix.

newspapers and magazines accounted for 28.2 per cent of the total net value of the printing and related industries, as opposed to 5.3 per cent for the total net value of printed books.[20] Indeed, from the mid-19th century, writers were more likely to publish their novels first in magazines or newspapers than as bound three-volume copies—a reflection of the dominance of the periodical and the way it shaped reading habits and perceptions throughout the century.

A significant chapter in this relationship between the novel and periodical criticism takes place in the 1830s and 1840s—those decades so central to the development of the Victorian novel.[21] From the mid-1820s, middle-class magazines exhibited an intensifying interest in the various forms of prose fiction, fuelled equally by their own role as carriers of short and serial fictions, and as commentators on the parameters of the novel. As part of this engagement, magazines began to articulate for their audiences an array of categories and value-judgements that would influence perceptions of the novel's development for the rest of the century. The historical location of this developing discourse is perhaps unsurprising given the recent changes in novel price and availability, including the emergence of Cadell's Author's Edition of the Waverley Novels (1829) in much cheaper 5s copies, and later Colburn and Bentley's highly successful standard novel series, issued at 6s apiece in 1831. Magazines at this time naturally found their attention drawn to a form that was now more physically present than ever before, and in which they undoubtedly held a stake. Serialized autobiographies and fictions had begun to appear in monthly miscellanies such as *Blackwood's* from the 1820s onwards, alongside the spirited mix of contemporary poetry, dramatic extracts, and critical commentary which distinguished the generation of magazines that emerged in the second and third decades of the century. These included the *New Monthly* (1814–), *Blackwood's* (1817–) and the *London* (1820–), later joined by, amongst others, the *Athenaeum* (1828–), the *Metropolitan* (1830–), and *Fraser's* (1830–). These publications demonstrated an interest in the novel that had a series of outcomes for perceptions of the genre. In a representative article in 1834, the *Metropolitan* declared novel-writing to be 'an art that deserves the cultivation of the most exalted genius'.[22] To do this, the magazine concluded, it should be cleansed 'of all that does not legitimately enter into the composition of a novel; the public taste would be thus reformed, every one would, in a short time, be enabled to pronounce with as much certainty, that such a work is a pure novel'.[23] The emphasis here on a necessary 'purity' and 'legitimacy' of genre—a reminder, in Derridean terms, that 'genres are not to be mixed'—can be found across 1830s magazines commenting on the novel's status, and its delineation as a genus with distinct species and forms.[24]

[20] Simon Eliot, *Some Patterns and Trends in British Publishing* (London: The Bibliographical Society, 1994), 105, 157.

[21] Kathleen Tillotson, *Novels of the Eighteen-Forties* (Oxford: Oxford University Press, 1954).

[22] 'On Novels and Novel Writing', *The Metropolitan Magazine* 11 (September 1834): 113–19, 118.

[23] 'On Novels and Novel Writing', 119.

[24] Jacques Derrida, 'The Law of Genre', in *Modern Genre Theory*, ed. David Duff (Harlow: Pearson Educational Ltd, 2000), 219–31, 220.

This commentary on novel-writing in the 1830s and 1840s explicitly situates the discursive context in which novels were produced in the textual exchanges that they engaged in with periodical criticism. Nowhere is this more apparent than in the review articles and editorial commentary of *Fraser's Magazine*, which repeatedly turned its attention to the appropriate structures of the novel: 'The fact is', one review declared, that 'the novel has its rules as well as the epic and the drama, and, indeed, no work of art is without them. Neither can the principle be too often enforced, that libertines are equally objectionable in literature as in life.'[25] William Maginn (an important contributor to *Blackwood's* and later editor of *Fraser's*) here not only offers a specific response to the criminal characters in Bulwer's novels, but also issues a rejoinder to the playful proposition in the author's earlier preface to *The Disowned* (1829)—that the fashionable novel is the 'intellectual libertine of literature', which 'requires no rules' and lies outside the conventions of fiction.[26] Such a position in *The Disowned* explicitly resisted the magazines' classificatory acts and attempted to seal the novel from their regulatory criticism. In this respect, *The Disowned* anticipates a stance novelists would continue to insist upon later in the 19th century: the novel as 'perfectly free', as Henry James claimed in 1884—unbound by any arbitrary laws 'made by critics and readers for their own convenience.'[27] But for the magazine in the 1830s, such stratification offered a means of carving out an order among the 'swarm' of texts before a middle-class reading public, thereby rendering the flood of new literature knowable and classifiable for its audience. In another sense, these magazine avowals of the 'rules' of fiction were also embedded in the legislative and reformist ethos of the early Victorian decades, an atmosphere charged with the rhetoric of a professionalizing legal class and contextualized by a tide of amendments in the political and judicial-penal systems.[28] Such edicts operated in the magazine in various ways, from threats of retribution for those who disobeyed— 'We will soon correct you all/In culprit order at our judgement-seat', chanted one mock-editorial in *Fraser's*—to backhanded praise of a 'successful' break with novelistic conventions—in 1848, a fictional 'Curate' in *Blackwood's* marvelled at *Jane Eyre*, and the way in which, 'in spite of all novel rules, the love heroine of the tale has no physical beauty to recommend her.'[29] Such attempts to position and fix the properties of other literary forms became a generic mark of the magazine itself—the means by which periodicals put in their own bid for critical authority and assisted in the emergence of a discourse of literary criticism.

[25] 'Mr. Edward Lytton Bulwer's Novels; and Remarks on Novel-Writing', *Fraser's Magazine* 1 (June 1830): 509–32, 511.

[26] Bulwer Lytton, Edward Bulwer Lytton, *The Works of Edward Bulwer Lytton, Esq.* 2 vols. (Philadelphia: E. L. Carey & A. Hart, 1836), 1: 185.

[27] Henry James, 'The Art of Fiction', *Longman's Magazine* 4 (1884): 502–52, 517, 512.

[28] See Jan-Melissa Schramm, *Testimony and Advocacy in Victorian Law, Literature, and Theology* (Cambridge: Cambridge University Press, 2000); Rebecca Edwards Newman, '"Prosecuting the Onus Criminus": Early Criticism of the Novel in *Fraser's Magazine*', *Victorian Periodicals Review* 35 (2002): 401–19.

[29] 'A Few Words About Novels—A Dialogue', *Blackwood's Magazine* 64 (October 1848): 459–74, 473.

Novels of the period also participated in this discourse in perceptible ways, regularly exhibiting a narrative consciousness of its external critical demands. As Dickens's narrator in *Oliver Twist* demonstrates, the imaginary critic's voice is woven into the novel's formal structures: 'an author's skill in his craft, being, by ... critics, chiefly estimated with relation to the dilemmas in which he leaves his characters at the end of every chapter'.[30] Readers, as Dickens's narrator insists, must trust the author to break with this critical dictum for 'good and substantial reasons'—an attempt on the part of the novelist to wrest back formal authority from outside the parameters of his text. Thackeray's narrator interjects a similar comment at the end of his satirical novel, *Catherine*, published in *Fraser's* from 1839 to 1840:

> If the critic take the pains to ask why the author, who hath been so diffuse in describing the early and fabulous acts of Mrs. Catherine's existence, should so hurry off the catastrophe ... Solomons [Thackeray's fictional writer] replies that the 'ordinary' narrative is far more emphatic than any composition of his own could be.[31]

In these fictions, the narrator encodes and dismisses critical responses, acknowledging the powerful textual presence of the critic, but relocating authority in the hands of the novelists.

But perhaps the magazines' most salient contribution to the debate on the novel came in the collective outline that critics were to assemble of the novel's various modes and subgenres. Reviews of contemporary novels and more general reflections on the form were accompanied by a language of classification that explicitly anatomized the novel and its place within contemporary print culture. A tacit hierarchy of subgenres was circulated to reading audiences, at the bottom of which continued to be the 'fashionable novel' or so-called 'Almack's' breed of literature, which often adopted as backdrop for its events the exclusive Assembly Rooms in London. These novels detailed the life, manners and adventures of contemporary high society, though often from the detectable vantage-point of an aspirant middle-class writer. In a review of Andrew Picken's Scottish 'tale', *The Dominie's Legacy* (1830), *Fraser's* slammed such productions as the work of 'the Colburnohistorical branch of novel manufacture', connecting fashionable novels with the economic gain for publishers and novelists, and as produced by the effeminacy of an 'emasculated' intellect.[32] As a result, the magazine argued, such productions were 'entirely valueless', eschewing the possibility of moral improvement or philosophical treatment, and linking to that other 'modern' form, the elegant but 'truth-denouncing' 'novel of manners'. Three years earlier, William Hazlitt in the *Examiner* had already coined a name for fictions such as Robert Plumer Ward's *Tremaine* (1825) and Benjamin Disraeli's *Vivian Grey* (1827), which he grouped under the facetious title of 'The Dandy

---

[30] Charles Dickens, *Oliver Twist*, ed. Fred Kaplan (New York: Norton, 1993), 118.
[31] Ikey Solomons [William Thackeray], 'Catherine: A Story', *Fraser's Magazine* 21 (February 1840): 200–212, 210.
[32] 'The Dominie's Legacy', *Fraser's Magazine* 1 (April 1830): 318–35, 321.

School', though following the publication of Bulwer's *Pelham* in 1828, these novels were better known under the pejorative heading of the 'silver-fork' school of fiction. Such acts of naming were typical of magazine and periodical criticism throughout the early 19th century—a parallel to the critical atrocities wreaked on the Cockney school of poetry some years earlier. By 1843, *Blackwood's* could pronounce that '[t]he indescribable absurdities, vices, and follies of the bulk of that class of literature called the fashionable novel, are past the power of catalogue-makers to record', but record them the magazines did, filling their own pages with reams of commentary that confirmed the lowly status of 'fashionable' texts. Thomas Carlyle wryly comments on this phenomenon in Book Three of *Sartor Resartus*, published in *Fraser's* in 1834, in the guise of the bemused Diogenes Teufelsdröckh, who finds that reading such novels threatened 'ruin to the whole of my bodily and intellectual faculties'.[33] Deliverance comes to the German philosopher when he stumbles across the fragment of an old copy of a magazine, torn up to form the packaging for a book he has been sent, and on which is printed 'a Dissertation on this very subject of *Fashionable Novels!*'. The article is evidently an attack, like the one published in *Fraser's*, on the subject of Bulwer's 'fashionable' novel *Pelham*, and Teufelsdröckh notes with approval the full exposure of all elements of the 'dandiacal body'. This incident effectively represents the power of the magazines to intervene in a reader's experience of books—*Fraser's* literally clothes the text in its critique and interrupts its reception— but in this example Carlyle's text nevertheless offers a critique of fashionable novels that implies some continuity with the magazine's represented identity. Figuring as 'waste paper', or a 'defaced stray sheet', the magazine's status is also placed in doubt—a comment on the form's own economic interests and uncertain consecration, and an unavoidable swipe at the larger periodical housing Carlyle's unclassifiable text.

Similar acts and more comprehensive 'systems' of classification could be found across the periodical corpus in relation to emerging subgenres of the novel. Earlier in 1830, Horatio Smith had parodied five different types of novels in his brilliant comic treatise, 'Hints to Young Novel Writers'—the 'sentimental novel', 'the novel of the mysterious and supernatural', 'fashionable novels', 'novels of the intense' (gesturing toward sensational and criminal incidents), and the 'historical novel'.[34] By the following year, the *Literary Gazette* had developed its own classification system of the novel into five different kinds—the 'Romantic' novel ('Horace Walpole, Mrs. Radcliffe, Lewis, and others'), the novel of 'Common Life' ('clever and humorous pictures' by 'Smollett, Goldsmith, Miss Burney, Miss Porters, Mrs. Inchbald, Dr. Moore, and a hundred others'), novels of 'High Life and Fashionable Life' (Richardson and Bulwer), the 'Satirical' novel, and the 'Historical' novel ('here *Scott* is the mighty master').[35] Into these 'foregoing genera', the article concludes, it would be 'tedious to particularise and dwell upon the numerous species', but the piece nevertheless cannot escape outlining seven further species

---

[33] Thomas Carlyle, 'Sartor Resartus, Book III', *Fraser's Magazine* 10 (August 1834): 182–93, 186.

[34] Horace Smith, *The Midsummer Medley for 1830* (London: Colburn & Bentley, 1830).

[35] 'Review of New Books', *The Literary Gazette* (26 November 1831): 753–56.

for its audience, along with elucidating examples. While of course such categorization presented itself throughout the 1830s and 1840s as an objective activity, the symbolic capital that literary magazines attached to each form was inescapable. At the summit of novelistic achievement was most usually the 'historical novel', overshadowed by the genius of Scott and carried forward by novelists such as Bulwer, Ainsworth, and Dickens. *Fraser's* proclaimed it 'the highest, and by far the most *difficult*' form of fiction, closely seconded by the 'didactic' novel, while Archibald Allison, writing in *Blackwood's* in 1845, claimed that 'no art ever was attempted by man more elevated and ennobling than the historical romance'.[36] At the other end of the scale, what Smith had termed 'novels of the intense' were further dissected by magazines throughout the 1830s into the produced categories of 'Newgate' fiction or the 'Jack Sheppard school', a critical grouping that became decisive in apportioning a particular literary value to texts such as *Paul Clifford* (1830), *Eugene Aram* (1832), *Rookwood* (1834), and *Jack Sheppard* (1839–40). In response to these fictions in particular, the legislative tone of magazines condemned novelists for their failure to fall within the proscribed regulations that novel criticism specified—a failure mirrored by the inability of their central characters to live within the laws of society. By 1859, therefore, in his landmark study, *British Novelists and their Styles*, David Masson could identify thirteen different classifications of the forms of the British novel—the majority of them, like the 'Illustrious Criminal Novel', successors of the categories that periodicals and magazines had self-consciously produced and circulated in the 1830s and 1840s.

If, in 1842, *Chambers's Edinburgh Journal* could declare that, 'every successive age has been distinguished by the development of some species of literature distinct in its character', one might nevertheless conclude with some accuracy that no age but the mid-19th century was so distinguished by acts of literary categorization and a public discourse on genre.[37] As the *New Monthly Magazine* wryly remarked in 1841, novel publication and the accompanying mania for classification had reached excessive levels, resulting in

> novels belonging to every kind of society, and almost every distinct profession— historical novels, political novels, religious novels, philosophical novels, fashionable novels, military novels, naval novels—novels of the court and novels of the city— novels of St James's and novels of St Giles's, and novels pertaining to places, person, and things 'that never were on sea or on land'.[38]

This last category, things 'that never were', is distinguished from the categories of experience or occupation that precede it and it offers an embedded reference to a controversy familiar in the late 18th and early 19th centuries between the forms of the romance and

---

[36] Archibald Alison, 'The Historical Romance', *Blackwood's Magazine* 58 (September 1845): 341–56, 347.
[37] 'Literary Revolutions', *Chambers' Edinburgh Journal* (28 May 1842): 145–46, 145.
[38] 'The Old English Gentleman', *The New Monthly Magazine* Part 3 (1841): 276–9, 279.

the novel, which had particular currency in early Victorian literature. In this instance *The New Monthly* discreetly homogenizes the associations of romance and illusive invention into the last of its list of novel-types, yet at the same time it also implicitly endorses the persistence of romance in the novel's ascendancy. And while the foundational myth of the novel—its difference from, and defeat of, romance—was re-transmitted throughout the early 1830s in critical accounts of the form, even in *Fraser's* an authorized genealogy of the novel was ironically presented through its own 'heroic' battles to defeat the forces of superstition:

> Sterne had become the reformer of a simpler creed—Richardson had changed the knightly steed into starch—Fielding and Smollett had sought in real life for objects with which their readers could sympathise, and their ample success awakened a host of imitators. The natural feelings of the human race became the property of this class of authors, the novel became the formidable rival of the romance; and, under the new dispensation, the superstitions of a darker eye were dispelled and vanished slowly away.[39]

Only under the masterful and explicitly masculine hand of Walter Scott, stated *Fraser's*, might romance consent 'to walk within the bounds of reason and nature', triumphantly assuring 'reality' as 'the order of the day'. This preference for realism in novels was championed by *Fraser's* throughout its early years and echoed by the majority of contemporary critics across the magazines and reviews. Yet after Scott's successful transformation of the historical romance, the distinction between romance and novel continued to be troubled by the role such forms played within the nation's literature: in its assessment of Allan Cunningham's *Lord Roldan, A Romance* (1836), the *New Monthly* went on to protest that, despite its present unpopularity, 'To rob our existence of romance would be like shearing the sun of his beams.'[40]

Such accounts manifestly present a complex picture of this debate in 19th-century periodicals, not least because, by the 1830s, these arguments had been circulated in various forms for the best part of a century. A discourse distinguishing the novel from the romance had preceded Clara Reeve's 1785 analysis, *The Progress of Romance*, while Coleridge's lament in 1798 on the 'present taste for romances' would already have been familiar to his readers in the *Critical Review*.[41] Yet magazine criticism of the 1830s and 1840s remains significant not just in its re-transmission of an ideology that shaped the forms of 18th-century fiction. On one hand, this concentrated network of discussions explicitly established the terrain for debates on the novel in the following decades,

---

[39] 'The Dominie's Legacy', 324.

[40] 'Critical Notices', *The New Monthly Magazine* Part 2 (1836): 505–6, 505.

[41] See in particular Ian Duncan, *Modern Romance and Transformations of the Novel: The Gothic, Scott, Dickens* (Cambridge: Cambridge University Press, 2005); Fiona Robertson, 'Romance and the Romantic Novel', in *A Companion to Romance from Classical to Contemporary*, ed. Corinne Saunders (Oxford: Blackwell Publishing, 2004), 287–304.

prefacing the emergence in the 1850s of terms such as 'realism' to mean fidelity of literary representation, and the more careful distinctions drawn in the work of David Masson between the 'Real' and 'Ideal, or romantic' schools of novel-writing. The development of such discussions can also be found in the writings of realist proponents such as George Henry Lewes and George Eliot, who famously pauses her novel, *Adam Bede* (1859), to institute a critical discussion on realism and the merits of the 'common labourer' as opposed to 'picturesque lazzaroni or romantic criminals'.[42] And in the 1860s, echoing the dialogue established in magazine criticism thirty years earlier, Lewes shaped his own more nuanced formulations of realism by re-invoking the discourse of legality that early Victorian periodicals had introduced into public circulation: 'the realistic form of art is a legitimate form. When the subject is high, realism is the highest possible form of art; and when the subject is commonplace, realism gives it a warrant.'[43]

At the same time, the magazines' blended condemnation of and attraction to the elements of romance disclosed an unease about the genre that resonated within the novel itself. *Oliver Twist*, the respectable end of the so-called 'Newgate' fictional canon, also manifests some discomfort about the coexistence of such elements, bearing obvious traces of romance *topoi* that its later authorial voice would attempt to efface. Oliver's origins are unmistakably drawn from the traditions of fairy tale and popular romance in the unfortunate orphan who rises to assume his rightful position of noble birth. Moreover, the miry world of criminal London is cast through overtones of Gothic romance, characterized by 'black mist', 'winding and narrow streets', and descriptions of the monstrous figure of Fagin, who is at home in its squalor: 'As he glided stealthily along, creeping beneath the shelter of the walls and doorways, the hideous old man seemed like some monstrous reptile, engendered in the slime and darkness through which he moved: crawling forth by night, in search of some rich offal for a meal.'[44] Dickens's 1841 preface to the novel, however, explicitly plays down such associations by emphasizing instead the text's connection with realist fiction: 'It appeared to me that to draw a knot of such associates in crime as *really do exist... to shew them as they really are...* would be a service to society.'[45] This response was due in part to various reviews condemning the text as another criminal fiction conditioned by romantic implausibility. In the words of the *Quarterly*, 'The whole tale rivals in improbabilities those stories in which the hero at his birth is cursed by a wicked fairy and protected by a good one; but Oliver himself, to whom all these improbabilities happen, is the most improbable of all. He is represented to be a pattern of modest excellence.'[46] In answer, Dickens subsequently used the third edition to re-frame his text away from romance, averring instead that his novel's purpose was 'the stern and plain truth'—a critique of character and social deprivation in the implicit context of the New Poor Law of 1834. Such authorial redirection is both a

[42] George Eliot, *Adam Bede*, ed. Laura Johnson Wylie (New York: Charles Scribner's Sons, 1917), 178.
[43] George Henry Lewes, 'Causeries', *The Fortnightly Review* (15 April 1866): 636–83.
[44] Dickens, 132.
[45] Dickens, 4, my emphasis.
[46] 'Review of the Oliver Twist; or, The Parish Boy's Progress', *Quarterly Review* 64 (1839): 83–102.

response to a dialogue on genre elicited by periodical criticism and a manifestation of resistance to the critical dictates of reviews. In this manner, the periodicals' interpretative influence upon the early Victorian novel should not be underestimated. While magazines and reviews established themselves as *the* form authorized to comment upon the novel, self-consciously producing readers by hermeneutically framing an audience's consumption of the text, novelists would equally use the novel and the resources of fiction to advance their competing conceptions of the form.

EDWARD BULWER'S NOVEL RESPONSES

In his thirteen various classifications of the British novel, David Masson cannot resist pointing out that 'Edward Bulwer Lytton' scores a mention in over half those categories:

> Sir Bulwer Lytton himself may carry off the palm from all his coëvals in respect of versatility...He has given us novels ranking under at least seven of the thirteen heads enumerated—to wit, the Novel of English Manners, the Fashionable Novel, the Novel of Illustrious Villainy, the Traveller's Novel, the Novel of Supernatural Phantasy, the Art and Culture Novel, and the Historical Novel. I say nothing of any other of Bulwer's merits besides this of his versatility, save that, of all British novelists, he seems to have worked most consciously on a theory of the Novel as a form of literature.[47]

Despite his now-acknowledged centrality in Victorian literature, Edward Bulwer's reputation as a writer continues to encounter the same kinds of controversy that it suffered in his own lifetime. As Masson acknowledged at the time, Bulwer's engagement with the possibilities of the novel and his versatile practices as a novelist set him apart from his contemporaries. Before the ascendancy of Dickens and Thackeray, he was, in the words of Gisella Argyle, 'the principal experimenter in, as well as the theorist on, the craft of fiction', and with a writing career that spanned from the mid-1820s through to the 1870s, the broad popularity of his work ensured that his ideas were in constant circulation throughout the period.[48] Yet in the 1830s, no novelist excited such extremes in contemporary criticism as Bulwer. While *Fraser's* continued to attack 'the vast pretensions, no sense and latent hollowness...of Lytton Bulwerism', *Blackwood's* conversely praised *Pelham* and the 'high-wrought and noble tone' of the novelist's mind'.[49] It is in relation to his novels of this early period, *Paul Clifford* and *Eugene Aram*, that Bulwer began most

---

[47] Masson [1859], 234.

[48] Gisella Argyle, *Germany as Model and Monster: Allusions in English Fiction 1830s–1930s* (Quebec: McGill-Queen's University Press, 2002), 43.

[49] 'The Dominie's Legacy', 318; 'Cloudesley; A Tale', *Blackwood's Magazine* 27 (May 1830): 711–16, 711–12.

clearly to pursue his experimental interests in the fictional form. Much more than the 'Newgate' label so successfully affixed by magazines, these texts explore the generic versatility of the novel in the 1830s and its potential to challenge the interpretative frame that magazines imposed. In this respect, Bulwer's fictions, prefaces, and appendices offered a spirited riposte to the culture of criticism and demonstrate their own marked engagement with the possibilities of the genre.

But what kind of a novel was *Paul Clifford*? A 'Fashionable Novel', claimed *Fraser's* in its earliest review; a novelized 'Newgate Calendar', alleged a later article on *Eugene Aram*; part of the 'gallows school of literature', wrote John Hamilton Reynolds with distaste in 1840.[50] Before the unambiguous articulation of the 'Newgate' category in 1832, in fact no critical consensus had been reached on what typology best described *Paul Clifford*, and this was a problem not merely limited to Bulwer's fifth novel. Previous reviews of *Pelham* had expressly complained of the indeterminacy of its textual classification:

> [Bulwer] has attempted high tragedy…and low comedy…to give true and psychological descriptions of some of the most remarkable men…to portray not only the highest characters, but the lowest grades in the social order…No wonder he has failed, and that miserably.[51]

Charged with producing texts that do not clearly reside within the operational categories available to the novel, Bulwer's fiction consequently subverts a central imperative of genre: that the differences between literary forms, as articulated by criticism, should be based on standards of compulsory separation and purity. In several respects, *Paul Clifford* and *Eugene Aram* do seem contaminated by multiform influences. Romance, melodrama, satire, political burlesque, and historical narrative might variously be identified in the novels, not to mention in *Eugene Aram* an aspiration to tragedy that excited particular outrage in some reviews. And *Paul Clifford*'s nonconformity to a recognized identity also figures in the text at a narrative level where, from the opening pages, the novel's eponymous hero struggles under the weight of his own confused origins.

Paul Clifford tells the story of a young boy whose obscure beginnings position him in the fastness of London's criminal quarters, yet which nevertheless continue to suggest the possibility of his greater nobility. At the outset of the narrative, he is an unnamed object, stranded in the garb of contradictory social signifiers—'somewhat tattered and discoloured', but 'dressed as if belonging to the better classes'—and without a paternal figure or identity to anchor him. The problem for Paul, however, is not so much his obscure identity, or the fear of crossing the law, as the problem of which set of laws should be allowed to define his story. 'If you are like *him*', Paul's dying mother decrees, referring

---

[50] 'Mr. Edward Lytton Bulwer's Novels; and Remarks on Novel-Writing', 532; 'A Good Tale Badly Told', *Fraser's Magazine* 5 (February 1832): 107–13, 107; John Hamilton Reynolds, 'William Ainsworth and Jack Sheppard', *Fraser's Magazine* 21 (February 1840): 227–45, 227.
[51] 'Mr. Edward Lytton Bulwer's Novels; and Remarks on Novel-Writing', 511.

to the genetic laws of inheritance and his undisclosed father, 'I will strangle you.'[52] Ma Lobkins, foster-mother and landlady of The Mug, later commands Paul to learn by the merciless operations of the criminal law, and to avoid being 'scragged' (hanged) by opting for swindling rather than stealing (14). In the course of the narrative, Paul must continue to negotiate a series of social spheres, each governed by its own distinct set of codes, from his childhood den at The Mug, through the worlds of periodical journalism and prison, to a state of eventual lawlessness as highwayman leader of a band of thieves. These worlds are often figured in the text as different written forms, from the genre of criminal biography that Paul encounters in his childhood reading of Dick Turpin, to the body of mass-produced cheap literature that flutters as ephemeral adornments on the walls of the inn. The world of print journalism is incarnated by Mr Peter MacGrawler, 'editor of a magnificent periodical, entitled "The Asinæum"' (10), who outlines the grammatical laws of the 'great science' of criticism—'namely, "to tickle, to slash, and to plaster"'(45): 'To slash is, speaking grammatically, to employ the accusative, or accusing case; you must cut up your book right and left, top and bottom, root and branch. To plaster a book, is to employ the dative, or giving case, and you must bestow on the work all the superlatives in the language' (46). Paul innocently suggests that slashing for the magazine corresponds to committing a capital crime—'I must either pick pockets or write (not gratuitously) for "The Asinæum"'—and narrative events obligingly demonstrate that MacGrawler's roles as editor and common thief are interchangeable. This unmistakable dig at periodical criticism—and at the figure of William Maginn, *Fraser's*' editor, in particular—reverses criticism's own accusations, suggesting that the periodicals' critical judgements are illegitimate or formed without authority. But Paul's encounters with the different worlds of writing, extending from criminal biography and journalism through to ballad forms, prison confessionals, and political addresses, also mark the novel's resistance to any single set of generic conventions. In this manner, Bulwer's fiction anticipates the 20th-century critic, Mikhail Bakhtin, and his account of the play of different social languages, or 'heteroglossia', to be found within the novel form. Just as *Paul Clifford* realizes the diversity of social experience through different forms of writing, it subsequently returns us to the Bakhtinian proposition that 'the novel always includes in itself the activity of coming to know another's word, a coming to knowledge whose process is represented in the novel'.[53] In Bulwer's novel, it is not only encounters with 'another's word', but the formal presentation of those words—the imagination of other genres—that the novel of *Paul Clifford* enacts.

Beyond this engagement with literary form within the bounds of the novel itself, Bulwer's 1830s fictions are also significant for the way in which they explore the resources of the novel as a *print* genre. These texts exploit the material circumstances of book publication by endeavouring to efface or supersede the voice of the magazine with

---

[52] Edward Bulwer Lytton, *Paul Clifford*, ed. Juliet John, 6 vols, vol. 1: *Cult Criminals: The Newgate Novels 1830–47* (London: Routledge, 1998), 4. References hereafter in the text.

[53] Mikhail Bakhin, 'Discourse in the Novel', in *The Dialogic Imagination*, ed. Michael Holquist (Austin: University of Texas Press, 1981), 263.

a powerful directive from the author. This is particularly apparent in Bulwer's expansion of his novelistic prefaces or 'paratexts'—Gerard Genette's term to describe those formal spaces made possible by publication—which assume a critical tone that rivals magazine criticism. As the *London Magazine* had already commented in 1828, Bulwer's introduction to *The Disowned* was 'not an introduction to "The Disowned", so much as a review of *Pelham* and of *Pelham's* reviewers—and a disquisition about "The Disowned" being of a very different nature from his predecessor: in the course of which there are some erudite comments upon novel-writing and reading in general'.[54] *Paul Clifford* did not appear with a formal preface in its first publication, but until 1840, each of its early editions was accompanied by a long 'Dedicatory Epistle', addressed to an anonymous friend, which offered an imagined dialogue between writer and reader.[55] In response to the query that one would 'write nothing else but a novel', the voice of the author considers the merits of alternative kinds of writing, and dismisses in turn forms such as politics, travel-writing, biography, and history. Poetry and philosophy are also rejected for the explicit reason that they are genres in literary decline, overlooked by 'a tide of popular opinion' and unreviewed in the journals. In contrast, the dedication suggests, it is precisely the novel's vast popularity that confers its high value as a genre of writing: as the authorial voice declares, 'in order to write, I must have the hope to be read'(vii). A claim for the status of the novel is therefore made not despite, but because of its popularity, and this is subsequently extended into its ability to facilitate a more direct connection between writer and reader. The novel is the only form which does not require a 'review from the Quarterly' for its successful interpretation and can thereby circumvent the interpretative frames that the periodicals might impose. Accordingly, as the novel's narrator later reiterates in chapter 11—'dear reader, whom we make the umpire between ourself and those who never read—the critics' (115)—*Paul Clifford* unambiguously instructs its audience to eliminate the critical consciousness of the magazines and recognize the high status of the novel genre. 'I beg you to believe', claims the authorial voice, 'that I write novels, not because I cannot write anything else, but because novels are the best possible things to be written' (1.viii).

As a supplement to the dedication, Bulwer did in fact issue a Preface to the second edition in August 1830, which this time launched a more serious attack on the legitimacy of magazine criticism. 'Hath Criticism ever been,—can Criticism ever be—reduced to a science?' the Preface asks, glossing its own presentation of Peter MacGrawler and eroding once again the authority of periodicals. Using the novel's resources in this way could not escape the notice of magazine critics. In contrast to their treatment of Scott, they began to dispute the necessity of such authorial contact and even to instruct

---

[54] 'The Editor's Room', *The London Magazine* 2 (3rd series) (December 1828): 690–710.

[55] *Paul Clifford* went through a number of major editions during the 1830s and 1840s. The first two editions were issued in 1830, the second edition subsequently reprinted a number of times. Significant paratextual changes occur in the second edition (1830), and later editions in 1840 and 1848. During this time the novel was also transformed from a standard three-volume entity into one volume and was printed as part of Colburn & Bentley's cheaper standard novel series.

their readers not to look at prefaces at all. As *Fraser's* argued in a review of Harrison Ainsworth's *Rookwood:*

> What need has a man to extend himself at length through a preface? His work is either good or bad. If the former, it needs no preface; if the latter, it cannot profit by one... for the generality of readers, well aware that such preliminary pages are devoted for the most part to the author's propitiatory or self-laudatory phrases, 'all about' the author's sweet self, very rarely look through them at all. And they are wise in so *not doing.*[56]

Bulwer's later prefaces, however, continued to expand the dimensions of the novel as a print genre, taking full advantage of the form's material success and its repeated editions. Most striking, perhaps, is the revision of *Paul Clifford*'s Preface in 1840, which replaced the attack on criticism with a frame that explicitly pointed to the novel's interest in penal reform. Reorienting the novel away from its widely acknowledged associations with romance and the status of the novel in general, the authorial voice specifies the text's 'double object' with a wholly different emphasis: 'First, to draw attention to...a vicious Prison-discipline and a sanguinary Criminal Code...[Second] to show that there is nothing essentially different between vulgar and fashionable vice.' This foregrounding of a socio-political agenda has certainly been the most durable in cataloguing the interests of the novel since the 19th century, but it also allows us to witness the shift in Bulwer's own arguments about the novel and their reflection of the growing preference for novelistic realism.

This movement towards realism, however, did not lead Bulwer to abandon his ideas on classification and the novel's status. Serious discussions were put forward in 'On the Different Kinds of Prose Fiction', a prefatorial essay to the third edition of *The Disowned* in 1835, which distinguished novels according to a typology of 'narrative' versus 'dramatic' fiction. Three years later these thoughts were developed in a further two-part article, 'On Art in Fiction', in the *Monthly Chronicle*, in which Bulwer again claimed the novel to be high art in its own right, as distinguished from drama and poetry. It is in 1847, however, that Bulwer makes his most substantial contribution in the form of paratext, uniting his interest in the novel's status as a high art genre with a desire to insulate it from the critical interventions of the magazine. 'A Word to The Public' is the extended essay appended to the last of Bulwer's novel's to be given the 'Newgate' title—*Lucretia* (1847). In it, the novelist explicitly takes advantage of the opportunity to forge an intimate and direct contact with his readership. Calling upon his audience to cast aside 'the injury effected by garbled extracts, and wilful misrepresentation' in the reviews, the reader is once again placed to 'adjudicate' between criticism and the text of Bulwer's novels: 'not with a mind steeled against conviction... but rather with a juryman's sincere

---

[56] 'High-Ways and Low-Ways; or Ainsworth's Dictionary, with Notes by Turpin', *Fraser's Magazine* 9 (June 1834): 724–38, 725, original emphasis.

desire to judge for himself'.[57] Specifying instead the importance of an individual critical judgement, the essay effectively produces an ideal reading subject for the novel, whose verdict is formed outside the interpretative and institutional frames of print culture. Within these refigured reader–writer dynamics, the essay subsequently returns to the magazines' contentions on the diminished status of Newgate literature. In response to the critical contention that crime is not 'a legitimate object of fictitious composition', the essay replies that 'Crime, in fact, is the essential material of Tragic drama. Take crime from tragedy, and you annihilate tragedy itself'(306). Drawing together the highly consecrated status of tragedy with the novel, the essay proceeds to outline its own canon of 'tragic classic prose fictions' in the work of Richardson, Goethe, Mackenzie, Godwin, and Scott. As the author's voice makes clear, this uniting of novel with tragedy, that mode used by the 'greatest masters of art', specifies the form as a current inheritor of the Burkean sublime. Thus it is in this paratext that a new theory of tragic fiction is explicitly stated: precisely through its use of crime can the novel renegotiate critical accusations of illegitimacy and reformulate its value, making evident its rank as the most sublime of modern literary forms. From these perspectives, Bulwer's novels and his use of their paratextual spaces consequently mark out an undeniable interest in genre, which brings together a conceptual discourse on the classification of literature with an understanding of the way in which publication and print culture affected those groupings. In the early Victorian decades, these interconnected exchanges between novels and periodical criticism contributed to a definition of genre in which the dynamics of print forms underpinned the theoretical structures of an emerging discipline of literary studies. In this sense, the novel is both the period's 'defining literary genre' and the means by which an understanding of literary genre itself becomes apparent—a complex outcome of the encounters between 19th-century print forms and the textual forum in which those encounters are dramatized and debated.

SUGGESTED READING

Alison, Archibald. 'The Historical Romance'. *Blackwood's Magazine* 58 (September 1845): 341–56.

Anonymous. 'On Novels and Novel-Reading'. *Hogg's Weekly Instructor* 25 (October 1845): 129–31.

Bulwer Lytton, Edward. *Paul Clifford*. Edited by Juliet John. Vol. 1 of *Cult Criminals: The Newgate Novels 1830–47*. London: Routledge, 1998.

Duncan, Ian. *Modern Romance and Transformations of the Novel: The Gothic, Scott, Dickens*. Cambridge: Cambridge University Press, 2005.

Eliot, Simon. *Some Patterns and Trends in British Publishing*. London: The Bibliographical Society, 1994.

---

[57] Edward Bulwer Lytton, *Lucrezia; or, the Children of the Night*, ed. Juliet John., 6 vols., vol. 4: *Cult Criminals: The Newgate Novels 1830–47* (London: Routledge, 1998), 299. References hereafter in the text.

Ferris, Ina. *The Achievement of Literary Authority: Gender, History and the Waverley Novels.* Ithaca: Cornell University Press, 1991.

Klancher, Jon P. *The Making of English Reading Audiences 1790–1832.* Madison: University of Wisconsin Press, 1987.

Masson, David [1859]. *British Novelists and Their Styles.* Boston: D. Lothrop & Co., 1875.

Maginn, William. 'Mr. Edward Lytton Bulwer's Novels; and Remarks on Novel-Writing'. *Fraser's Magazine* 1 (June 1830): 509–32.

Tillotson, Kathleen. *Novels of the Eighteen-Forties.* Oxford: Oxford University Press, 1954.

PART II

PUBLISHING,
READING,
REVIEWING,
QUOTING,
CENSORING

4

PUBLISHING THE VICTORIAN NOVEL[1]

RACHEL SAGNER BUURMA

INTRODUCTION

In a time before Robert Darnton's work on the communications circuit and Pierre Bourdieu's sociology of the field of cultural production offered us the industrial-strength diagrams so useful as aids to understanding the production and consumption of Victorian novels, Royal A. Gettman wrote in his study of the papers of Victorian publisher Bentley that:

> In theory a good book is a self-contained, organic entity, and it should simply be accepted or rejected by a publisher. In actual practice a decision may not be so clear-cut; a book, even an imaginative work like a novel, does not fall from the heavens a complete, crystallized object ... And in theory the greater the genius of the author the larger the likelihood that the manuscript and the book will be identical. In actual practice the printed words may have been touched by other hands.[2]

[1] Thanks to the many readers of material that has made its way into this piece, especially Lara Cohen, Elaine Freedgood, Laura Heffernan, Andrew Miller, Cyrus Mulready, and Megan Ward; special thanks to Lisa Rodensky for her remarkable editorial comments and infinite patience. The staff of the Berg Collection at the New York Public Library and the British Library and the manuscripts room of the British Library deserve thanks for so kindly helping me use manuscript materials from their collections. Many thanks are due to my outstanding research assistant, Anna Tione Levine, who tirelessly worked to help compile the bibliography of sources I read before writing this piece and also helped me think through the genre of the 'handbook' essay. I am indebted to *Victorian Studies* for allowing me to reprint a few pages of material from my essay 'Anonymity, Corporate Authority, and the Archive: The Production of Authorship in Late-Victorian England' (2007).
[2] Royal Gettman. *A Victorian Publisher: A Study of the Bentley Papers* (Cambridge: Cambridge University Press, 1960), 202.

Setting the literary critic's self-contained text penned by the 'lonely writer' against the publishing historian's 'other hands', Gettman demonstrates the great significance of those other hands' work in making Victorian novels. Since (and in fact even before) Gettman's book, literary critics and book historians have multiplied our stories about novelistic meaning and the material forms it takes.[3] A broad, impressionistic survey of the last hundred years of criticism of the Victorian novel turns up some critics for whom novelistic meaning comes into the world out of the intending and controlling head of an autonomous author, and others who assume it passes from a Victorian culture-shaped language through the fingers of the author as mere medium and out onto the printed page; yet another kind of critic sees meaning as a magical property of novelistic form (or formlessness) itself. By contrast, many book historians (even those who study primarily the novel or literature and inhabit literature departments) are very little concerned with the question of literary meaning. John Sutherland probably speaks for many book historians when he writes that despite his interest in the broad historical, biographical, and social contexts of Victorian novels, 'the circumstances that interest me most have to do with the composition, publication, distribution, and consumption of novels. This, it seems to me, constitutes their "life".[4] Sutherland tracks the production of novelistic meaning through attending to the stories within stories embedded within apparently minor allusions within novels or references within author–publisher correspondence; his interests lie more with the stories about the production of works like Charles Reade's *Hard Cash* and George Eliot's *Middlemarch* than in the fictional stories those works contain.[5]

At the intersection of literary publishing history and literary criticism proper we find what we might call, with Leah Price, a 'materialist literary history'[6] which is, in the words of Don McKenzie, 'concerned to show how forms effect meaning', particularly literary meaning. Work in this area, like Price's own study of the relation between the practices of anthologizing and abridgement and novelistic meaning in *The Anthology and the Rise of the Novel* and Priya Joshi's study of the publication and reception of British fiction in India in *In Another Country*, focuses on the way the material forms of books enable the production of literary meaning.[7] The Bourdieuvian approach taken by critics like Peter D. McDonald differs from Sutherland's by working to construct

---

[3] In actual practice, of course, most critics combine some or all of these approaches.

[4] John Sutherland, *Victorian Fiction: Writers, Publishers, Readers* [1995] (Basingstoke: Palgrave Macmillan, 2006], xxv.

[5] Two other examples of this kind of work in the history of the book are Lillian Nayder's *Unequal Partners: Charles Dickens, Wilkie Collins, and Victorian Authorship* (Ithaca: Cornell University Press, 2002) and David Finkelstein's *The House of Blackwood: Author–Publisher Relations in the Victorian Era* (State College: The Pennsylvania State University Press, 2002).

[6] Leah Price, 'The Tangible Page' (review of *The Book History Reader*, ed. David Finkelstein and Alistair McCleery *and Making Meaning: 'Printers of the Mind' and Other Essays* by D.F. McKenzie, ed. by Peter D. McDonald and Michael F. Suarez), *London Review of Books* (31 October 2002): 36–39.

[7] Not about the Victorian novel but important as an example of work at the intersection of literary criticism and book history, Andrew Piper's recent history of the Romantic book *Dreaming in Books: The Making of the Bibliographic Imagination in the Romantic Age* (Chicago: University of Chicago

a structural map of the literary field extrapolated from interactions between individual agents like authors and publishers; this approach promises a robust account of the way cultural status is produced differentially within the social world of literary production.[8]

All of these variously book-history-inflected studies of Victorian novels offer richly detailed accounts of the engagement between publisher and author that goes into the larger scene of novel production. Yet most that I've mentioned centre their case studies around sites of conflict between author and publisher that read the two as autonomous intending individuals each bent on imposing their own particular meaning on the novelistic text and the conditions of its production, while those that pay more attention to the more collaborative aspects of author–publisher work often represent this as a process hidden from the common reader, who sees the author as the novel's single creator. But here I would hope to uncover a wider range of understandings of the way Victorian novelists and publishers co-created novels as material and aesthetic objects by tracking ways publishers and authors worked in concert as often (or more often) as they did in conflict to produce novels which they—as well as their Victorian audiences of both professional and lay readers—often understood to be fully collaborative productions. At both ends of the Victorian era, writers, publishers, editors, publishers' readers, and novel readers themselves expressed their awareness of the collective nature of novel-writing, from Archibald Constable's slightly embarrassed admission that 'I am sometimes half tempted to believe that of these books [the Waverley novels] I am the author'[9] to popular late-Victorian novelist Mary Elizabeth Hawker's serene sense that her publisher T. Fisher Unwin was 'as interested as myself' in preserving the value of her pseudonym.[10] I myself will attempt to keep in mind that novels are collective creations of a range of individuals (the author and her own readers and editors unaffiliated with her publishing house as well as the publisher's house reader, editors, publisher, compositor, printer) whose roles can be—in many cases—traced and untangled but also must be understood as adding up to more than the sum of their parts; I'll assume also that all of

Press, 2009) asks 'How did literature make sense of the book so that it in turn made sense to readers?' and claims that 'Literature makes books as much as books make literature' (11). This last statement is especially relevant for the study of how author–publisher relations work to produce novels, for Piper means not only that literature mediates the reception of print for audiences, but that we must see book-making and literary meaning as interrelated through a constant circuit of production where those readers for whom literature works to make books legible also in turn become producers of knowing books whose forms are mediated by literature.

[8] As McDonald notes in *British Literary Culture and Publishing Practice, 1880–1914* (Cambridge: Cambridge University Press, 1997), a major advantage of the Bourdieuvian perspective is the fact that it offers a model of literary culture that is autonomous from but linked to the economic world. McDonald's work also offers sustained readings of the contents of the novels he discusses.

[9] Thomas Constable, *Archibald Constable and His Literary Correspondents*, 3 vols. (Edinburgh: Edmonston and Douglas, 1873), 2: 140, quoted in Gettman, *A Victorian Publisher*, 154.

[10] Mary Elizabeth Hawker, Letter to T. Fisher Unwin, 22 March 1891 (Mary Elizabeth Hawker, 65 A.L.S. to T. Fisher Unwin, 1891–92, folder 1. Berg Collection of English and American Literature, New York Public Library, New York. Astor, Lenox and Tilden Foundations).

these individuals involved in publishing a novel are unevenly organized around a set of intertwined institutions.[11]

Despite the proliferation of nuanced models for understanding the interplay between material form and literary meaning, Victorian publication practices are still regularly understood to represent simple economic determinism; Fredric Jameson's use of the late-Victorian shift from three-decker to one-volume publication formats as his key example of mechanical causality in *The Political Unconscious* is just the most classic example. Critiquing Althusser's claim that any perception of mechanical causality is the result of false consciousness, Jameson counters with the example of late-Victorian publishing, noting that 'there seems, for instance, to have been an unquestionable causal relationship between the admittedly extrinsic fact of the crisis in late nineteenth-century publishing, during which the dominant three-decker lending-library format was replaced by a cheaper one-volume format, and the modification of the "inner form" of the novel itself'.[12] While offering more complexity and detail, many studies of Victorian novel publication make similar assumptions, tending to assign purely economic agendas to publishers and either moral or aesthetic/artistic agendas to novelists.[13] Yet the interpretive framework that leans upon this truth can have the unintended effect of making us suspect that when persons involved in the publishing process offer aesthetic or ethical motives for their actions that these can be interpreted away, perhaps considered but ultimately demystified as covering up deep economic self-interest. Without naïvely discounting the importance of such economic determinism, I will show here how the questions of morality, economics, and aesthetics surrounding Victorian novel publishing intertwined in ways that resist reduction to a single type of motive and require us to rethink the categories—individual, collective, and corporate—in which Victorians themselves understood the production of literary meaning to occur via the publication process.

The saga of the three-volume novel and the circulating libraries is a case in point. From the middle of the 19th century, the Victorian reader's association of the high-priced three-volume novel with circulating library control of the market for fiction, and her knowledge of the fact that to be successful, novelists had to produce work of a suitable length for circulation in that form, meant that the format itself was read by many as a

---

[11] It is this last assumption—so easy to express in the abstract, so difficult to actively assume in concrete examination of particular instances—that is most often left out of even the most accomplished studies of Victorian novel publishing, and studies of Victorian publishing more generally. Whatever our stated ideas about poststructuralism or 'theory', literary critics and historians of the Victorian period have generally accepted poststructuralism's insight about the composite and socially constructed figure of the author, summed up in Foucault's phrase 'the author-function'. Yet we have been slow to accept the practical, methodological ramifications of this insight.

[12] Fredric Jameson, *The Political Unconscious: Narrative as a Socially Symbolic Act* (Ithaca, NY: Cornell University Press, 1981), 25.

[13] As Lara Langer Cohen points out in the introduction to *The Fabrication of American Literature: Fraudulence in Antebellum Print Culture* (Philadelphia: University of Pennsylvania Press, 2011), this story 'has become a staple of nineteenth-century literary history, in which writers struggle against the tyrannical market, pitting their creative energies against its stultifying power' (10).

concession to the economic over the literary; the 'three-decker' had become a cultural symbol of mechanistic causality and commodified fiction.[14] As the *Saturday Review* noted, such novels, 'the children of circulating libraries', 'are articles of commerce, and are constructed with a view to certain well-established uses and well-ascertained tastes'.[15] Public perception—at least as represented by periodicals like *The Saturday Review*, the *London Times*, and the *Daily News*—was that the three-volume novel was unnecessarily expensive (for readers) and Procrustean (for authors), a diabolical invention of the right-hand side of Darnton's communications circuit. And as quickly as this meaning of the three-decker's form became legible to readers, novelists like Anthony Trollope and William Thackeray began to deploy their consciousness of it as a literary effect designed to both heighten and complicate realism by claiming, for example, that an imposed length and not the fictionality of the representation was the limiting factor on what could be represented.[16]

Further, although the three-volume novel system wasn't really dismantled until the 1890s, by which time the three-decker system had become a losing proposition for the

[14] The Victorian reader did not need to bring this information to her reading of the three-volume format of the novel she happened to be reading because so many of those novels inform her of this through references to their shortness or length, or by referring to their own content as truncated or expanded by the exigencies of the three-volume form (or their resistance to it). These references, especially those that appear before the 1870s, are not necessarily critical of the three-volume form—for Victorian readers the sense that the novel was a commodity written to fit into a certain economically viable form was not necessarily negative (though it could be read so)—but they certainly do insist on bringing it to the reader's attention. On this point see Kelly J. Mays, 'The Publishing World', in *A Companion to the Victorian Novel*, ed. Patrick Brantlinger and William B. Thesing (Malden, MA and Oxford, UK: Blackwell Publishers Ltd, 2002), 11–30, 26–27. Mays's essay delineates another (Bourdieuvian) version of the relationship between the literary and the economic in Victorian publishing, one which sees a mid-Victorian equation of literary and economic success give way to a later-Victorian tension between the two, a tension embodied in increasingly tense relationships between authors and publishers and the proliferation of authors' societies and literary agents. For an account of the impact of Mudie's and the circulating library on the literary marketplace more generally see chapter 2, 'Equipoise and the Three-Decker', in N.N. Feltes's *Modes of Production of Victorian Novels* (Chicago: University of Chicago Press, 1986), 18–35. See also Guinevere L. Griest, *Mudie's Circulating Library and the Victorian Novel* (Bloomington: Indiana University Press, 1970), 55, and Troy Bassett, 'Living on the Margin: George Bentley and the Economics of the Three-Volume Novel, 1865–70', *Book History* 13 (2010): 60–66.

[15] By contrast, the one-volume novel is 'altogether a different type of production', one which 'may not be unfairly described as the accounts which people give of their dreams upon waking from their first sleep'. Instead of being a device for a narrator or chorus to show us all of a world in capitalist descriptive detail, a one-volume novel is 'almost always a literary adaptation' of a device made of mirrors 'so arranged, that when any one entered it he saw his own face in twenty different attitudes', 'One-Volume Novels', *The Saturday Review* (1 January 1859): 11.

[16] See Anthony Trollope's *The Warden* [1855], ed. Geoffrey Harvey (Toronto: Broadview Press, 2001), 94–5, where the authorial narrator notes—fairly neutrally on the one-versus-three-volume issue—that:

> What had passed between Eleanor Harding and Mary Bold need not be told. It is indeed a matter of thankfulness that neither the historian nor the novelist hears all that is said by their heroes or heroines, or how would three volumes or twenty suffice! In the present case so little of this sort have I overheard, that I live in hopes of finishing my work within 300 pages, and of completing that pleasant task—a novel in one volume...

circulating libraries, cultural attitudes towards the respective formats had begun to shift much earlier.[17] The increase in numbers of one- and two-volume novels published in the 1880s seemed to herald, for writers like George Gissing, a style of novel-writing that was 'far more artistic' than that associated with the three-decker. As he wrote to his brother in 1885, just as he himself was 'recasting the first vol. of my novel [*Isabel Clarendon*], & shall make the last two into one',[18] and before the economically motivated circulating library and publisher-led shift away from the three-decker:

> It is fine to see how the old three-vol. tradition is being broken through. Chapman tells me he much prefers two vols., & one vol. is becoming commonest of all. It is the new school, due to continental influence. Thackeray & Dickens wrote at enormous length, & with profusion of detail; their plan is to tell everything, to leave nothing to be divined. Far more artistic, I think, is this later method, of merely suggesting; of dealing with episodes, instead of writing biographies. The old novelist is omniscient; I think it is better to tell a story precisely as one does in real life,—hinting, surmising, telling in detail what *can* so be told, & no more. In fact, it approximates to the dramatic mode of presentment.[19]

The copious prose of Dickens and Thackeray—though in theory quite separable from the three-volume format—seemed to Gissing to have an affinity with it just as the decidedly more modernist-sounding limited perspective and limitation of description seemed to have a close affinity with the increasingly popular single-volume format. A widespread recognition of the ideological content of the three-decker's form—the affiliation of a specific material format with commodification, middle-class-ness, copious description, and omniscience—underlies Gissing's association of changed print format with changed style, and this association offered readers a partial framework for understanding the

and in *The Way We Live Now* the narrator writes of Lady Carbury, an aspiring novelist, as 'false from head to foot', and states:

> It cannot with truth be said of her that she had had any special tale to tell. She had taken to the writing of a novel because Mr. Loiter had told her that upon the whole novels did better than anything else. She would have written a volume of sermons on the same encouragement, and have gone about the work exactly after the same fashion. The length of her novel had been her first question. It must be in three volumes, and each volume must have three hundred pages. But what fewest number of words might be supposed sufficient to fill a page? The money offered was too trifling to allow of very liberal measure on her part. [Anthony Trollope, *The Way We Live Now* [1874–75], ed. John Sutherland (Oxford: Oxford University Press, 1999), 364–65].

[17] Other indications of this cultural response included the issue of new series based on the one-volume format by firms like T. Fisher Unwin, polemics against the three-volume system like George Moore's *Literature at Nurse, or Circulating Morals* (London: Vizetelly, 1885), and the comments of novelists like George Gissing.

[18] George Gissing, *The Collected Letters of George Gissing*, vol. 2: *1881–1885*, ed. Paul F. Mattheisen, Arthur C. Young, and Pierre Coustillas (Athens, OH: Ohio University Press, 1991), 319.

[19] Gissing, 320.

rapid acceleration of the shift from three- to one-volume formats that was precipitated by the circulating libraries and the publishers later in the 1890s.

Understanding how novelists and critics mediated shifts in material print format as much as economically determined changes in the print formats of books affected literary form might be viewed in the light of recent critical work that seeks to recover the complexity of Victorian understandings of novelistic form and meaning. Though the critical tradition has long registered dissent from the view that Victorian novel readers confused realism with reality and responded to fiction in primarily moral and literalist terms (i.e. thought of characters as 'real people' and therefore evaluated novels by ethical rather than aesthetic criteria), recent and ongoing work on both professional reviewing and lay reading of the 19th-century novel has begun the concrete work of expanding such theorizing into an entire field of inquiry, uncovering a world of reception which neither sees Victorian novel readers as benighted creatures whose inability to separate fiction from reality made them endlessly and unresistingly subject to the ideologies encoded in fiction nor attempts to interpret their responses in such a way as to make them form-focused New Critics avant la lettre.[20] The archives that record the histories of author–publisher relations offer us another window into such Victorian understandings of the novel as an aesthetically, morally, and materially meaningful object.

Where do the traces of these Victorian novelist–publisher relationships survive? Certainly in published and unpublished letters, autobiographies, and memoirs—often the first and main sources for studies of author–publisher relations—but also in unbound proofs and morocco-covered dedication copies, readers' reports and book contracts, and stereotype plates and circulating library catalogues, not to mention in the characters, plots, dialogues, and descriptions contained in the novels themselves. Perhaps the best record of prolific Victorian novelist Margaret Oliphant's half-century-long relationship with two generations of Blackwood family publishers can be found not in the thousands of pages of letters exchanged between Oliphant and the Blackwoods (now preserved in the National Library of Scotland), but in the light pencil markings—often little more than underlining and bracketing, accompanied by a few marginal crosses in black ink—which Oliphant's hand sprinkled across the entire Blackwood's publishing archive. These marks are the traces of Oliphant's own use of the archive; at the very end of her long career she wrote volumes one and two of the monumental *Annals of a Publishing House: William Blackwood and his Sons, their Magazine and Friends*, whose very title and subtitle imply a great deal about how late-Victorians saw the publishing house as an institution which

---

[20] See George Levine, *The Realistic Imagination* (Chicago: University of Chicago Press, 1981). On new readings of Victorian reading, see Suzy Anger, *Victorian Interpretation* (Ithaca, NY: Cornell University Press, 2005); Leah Price, *The Anthology and the Rise of the Novel* (Cambridge: Cambridge University Press, 2000) as well as her 'Reading: The State of the Discipline', *Book History* 7 (2004): 303–20; Nicholas Dames, *The Physiology of the Novel* (Oxford: Oxford University Press, 2007); Lisa Rodensky, 'Popular Dickens', *Victorian Literature and Culture* 37, no. 2 (2009): 583–607; Beth Palmer and Adelene Buckland, eds., *A Return to the Common Reader: Print Culture and the Novel, 1850–1900* (Farnham, Surrey, and Burlington, VT: Ashgate, 2011).

both organized and was organized by individuals, families, print forms, and social connections. The difficulty here lies in transforming marginal notes into evidence of author–publisher relations, making a few light lines tell a story. It is more immediately gratifying, more exciting, and very much more dangerous to investigate cases in which such relations go spectacularly wrong, producing epistolary dramas or enduring cultural myths that ask us only to transcribe and pick a side. The story of Caroline Norton's copious (and yet nonetheless archivally incomplete) correspondence with Macmillan's publishing house over the interrupted serialization of her novel *Old Sir Douglas* in *Macmillan's Magazine* between January 1866 and October 1867, which I take up in the first of my three case studies, offers one out of scores of possible examples. Archives like this one seem self-dramatizing because they fit neatly into our own ideas about authorial autonomy and the battle for control between novelist and publisher. While they offer us a very accessible written record, such dramas also tempt us with clearly delineated competing narratives, asking us only to choose between them, and can also distract us from the much broader, less visible field of Victorian novel-publishing-as-usual. But arguably no marginalia or archive of correspondence tells us as much about the publication process of Anthony Trollope's short novel *The Struggles of Brown, Jones, and Robinson* (1861–62), the subject of my second case study, as that novel's own plot does. Finally, I'll examine the everyday and relatively unremarkable correspondence between the T. Fisher Unwin publishing company and author 'Lanoe Falconer' (Mary Elizabeth Hawker) about her novel *Mademoiselle Ixe*, published in Unwin's *Pseudonym Library* series of novels, to show how even late Victorians sometimes saw novel production as a collective activity and assigned novelistic meaning a collective authority.[21]

SERIALIZING: *OLD SIR DOUGLAS* IN *MACMILLAN'S MAGAZINE*

Up to the late 1850s, Victorian novels first appeared before their first readers either as individually bound novels (in one-, three- or the less common two-volume form) or as individually wrapped monthly part-publications.[22] By the early 1860s, part-publications' popularity had diminished, replaced by the less risky initial format of magazine

---

[21] As Andrew Piper writes, 'The more we come to see literature as a social process and not as a singularly generative (or autopoetic) moment, the more we can begin to "recover the collectivity" in Martha Woodmansee and Peter Jaszi's words, [footnote omitted] that informs the making of literature in general and nineteenth-century literature in particular' (9).

[22] The three-volume form, made popular by the publication of Sir Walter Scott's Waverly novels, had been around since the 1820s but came to prominence—and under attack—in the 1850s with the cementing of the reading public's association between the three-decker and Mudie's circulating library. Nevertheless, as Simon Eliot has pointed out, one-volume works of fiction still represented a significant portion of Mudie's stock. See Simon Eliot, 'Fiction and Non-Fiction: One- and Three-Volume Novels in

serialization, in which a few to several chapters of the novel would appear in each weekly, bi-weekly, or monthly issue.[23] Like a successful part-publication, a successful serialization would often be followed by bound-volume publication suitable for circulating libraries and then, over time, a series of increasingly inexpensive formats which ensured not only a kind of 'omnipresence' for the most popular novelists but also a longer period of diffusion and reception than book history's traditional focus on first formats tends to imply.[24] One downside of the 'to be continued' magazine serial model was that disruption or discontinuation caused by either author or publisher always potentially threatened such episodic publication, as when Charles Dickens had to defer *All the Year Round*'s serialization start date for Charles Reade's *Very Hard Cash* from December 1862 to March 1863 due to Reade's difficulties composing,[25] or when the Evangelically flavoured general weekly *Good Words* stopped its announced serialization of Anthony Trollope's *Rachael Ray* due to a dispute about its representation of Evangelicals (negative) and dancing (positive),[26] and Wilkie Collins's *The Moonstone* in *All the Year Round* was nearly interrupted due to the novelist's illness. (Recounting the episode in the preface to the first three-volume edition of that novel, Collins explains that remembering that his audience was waiting for a new instalment each week kept him not only writing, but alive.)[27] And authorial procrastination could always potentially cause disruption, since for every novelist who refused to allow serialization to begin before he had completed a manuscript of the entire work (such as Trollope) there were probably half a dozen who wrote to the episode's publication deadline and rarely beyond (like Dickens or Norton).

Mid-Victorian observers spent considerable time thinking about the effects of these serial formats on the novel's narrative form. Just as Victorian critics noted

---

Some Mudie Catalogues, 1857–94', *Publishing History* 66 (2009): 31–47. Part-publication had long been a popular format for reprints of older works, but Charles Dickens's *Pickwick Papers* (1836–37) famously introduced it as a viable format for new fiction.

[23] The sandwiching of regular novel instalments between the pages of a print vehicle already boasting a certain circulation made selling fiction seem less risky for both author and publisher. The magazine's pre-existing audience offered authors a certain circulation for their novels, and a popular novel promised to increase not only overall magazine sales but also the publisher's prestige, which was linked to publishers' often eponymously named magazines (*Bentley's Magazine*, *Macmillan's Magazine*, *Blackwood's Edinburgh Magazine* are a few examples), and many publishers used their house magazines as a way of launching unknown novelists. Laurel Brake turns this familiar argument about serialization around to also argue that 'the widespread incorporation of the novel into mainstream periodicals in the 1850s and after helped to assure the proliferation and economic viability of the periodical press' (11). The combination meant that with magazine publication of novels 'there was less risk all round for the reader/consumer, the author, and the publisher' (12), Laurel Brake, *Print in Transition, 1850–1910: Studies in Media and Book History* (Basingstoke: Palgrave, 2001).

[24] Mays, 'The Publishing World', 18.

[25] See John Sutherland, 'Dickens, Reade, *Hard Cash*, and Maniac Wives', in *Victorian Fiction*, 55–85.

[26] See Mark Turner, *Trollope and the Magazines: Gendered Issues in Mid-Victorian Britain* (New York: St. Martin's Press, 2000).

[27] Important studies of Victorian serialization are Linda K. Hughes and Michel Lund, *The Victorian Serial* (Charlottesville: University Press of Virginia, 1991) and Graham Law, *Serializing Fiction in the Victorian Press* (Basingstoke: Palgrave Macmillan, 2000).

that the three- and one-volume formats invited different styles, the monthly part-publication and the magazine serial too seemed to demand, or at least encourage, specific formal characteristics. As E.S. Dallas wrote in a *Times* review, Wilkie Collins's

> *The Woman in White* [1859–60] is a novel of the rare old school which must be finished at a sitting. No chance of laying it down until the last page of the last volume has been turned. We have lately gotten into the habit—strange for these fast days—of reading our novels very leisurely. They are constructed on the principle of monthly instalments, and we read a chapter on the 1st of every month, quietly sauntering to the end of the story in about a couple of years. Even the novels which are published complete in three volumes are for the most part built on the same model. It is possible to open the volume at any page and read right on without embarrassment.[28]

Though *The Woman in White* was in fact first serialized in the weekly *All the Year Round*, as Dallas points out at the end of his review, its form reminds him of an earlier order of things. Writing for the large general audience of Great Britain's leading national newspaper, Dallas claims that before serialization novels were coherent intact wholes whose construction encouraged absorbed, through-the-night reading; the new narrative forms of novels built with serialization in mind are, by contrast, so episodic that one can begin them on any page, and the recursive, homogeneous narrative style developed for such episodic material forms has become the general rule for *all* novels. Significantly, for Dallas the novel's narrative form must be understood as linked to, but not determined by, its mode of publication. Unlike Gissing, who imagines the old-fashioned, omniscient, descriptive three-volume novel giving way to the lean, allusive one-volume in a perfect match that aligns material form with literary form and literary form with spirit of the age, for Dallas a new material form has actually caused a disjunction between zeitgeist and literary form. Though serial episodes are short, they— 'strange for these fast days'—encourage a 'leisurely' reading practice; though the older form of the novel offers readers a much longer stretch of text, its tighter construction requires them to cover that textual ground much more quickly. Dallas's description complicates what in this light looks like an oversimplified association between material publication form and narrative/aesthetic form on Gissing's part.[29]

Related questions about novelistic form were central to novelist–publisher–editor discussions about the disrupted publication of Caroline Norton's *Old Sir Douglas* in

---

[28] E.S. Dallas, 'The Woman in White', *The London Times* 30 October 1860: 6.

[29] Dallas would have liked Nicolas Dames's recent analysis of Trollope's chapters, which as Dames explains must be 'understood as a unit of technical interest—something novelists can wrestle with or against—and also a unit of philosophical interest' linked to Trollope's understanding of the way the chapter as a formal unit mediates 'the relationship between segmented experiences (the episode) and a concept of overall education (a life) [as] the central formal problematic of the novel in its classical period', Nicolas Dames, *Literature Compass* 7 (2010): 855–60.

Macmillan's Magazine, which was serialized between January 1866 and October 1867 with a hiatus between June and September of 1866.[30] In April of 1866, with the serialization of Norton's novel well underway, publisher Alexander Macmillan wrote to Norton to explain the non-appearance of one chapter (titled 'Royal Idols') in the most recent May multi-chapter instalment. 'Pardon my saying', he began politely, 'that I think you can hardly have duly considered this chapter, as it has an air of personal pique that would be liable to very severe strictures, and I think most hurtful to yourself. The effect on the minds of all of us who read it was the same surprise and regret and a strong conviction that it would not do to put it in the Magazine under any possible circumstances.'[31] The chapter in question apparently included a negative representation of the Queen's personal conduct, a representation which Macmillan as publisher and David Masson as editor of *Macmillan's* both considered could on no account be included in their magazine. To publish the chapter, as Macmillan argued, would be to put forward such unacceptable views of royalty as his and the magazine's own. Couching his complaint in insistently moral terms—and remaining agnostic on the accuracy of the representation in question—Macmillan explained in this first letter that 'There may be I have no doubt there is very much of pettishness about Court conduct and Kings and Queens may be open to all sorts of reproach. But our Queen who whatever she is in herself... does command our loyalty whatever that may mean.'[32]

The ensuing correspondence between Norton, Macmillan, and Masson dramatizes not primarily the moral conflict one might expect from this opening shot, but more essentially reveals a basic epistemological divide between two entirely different understandings of the interpretability, authority, and function of the novel as understood in relation to its publication format, publisher, and author. Norton conducts the debate by insisting on the primary importance of the unified coherence and aesthetic wholeness of the novel, the self-enclosed fictionality of what it represents, and her own authorial autonomy over that representation, while Macmillan speaks of the novel's moral content, the fact that its characters' views would be read as both Norton's and the magazine's own, and the resulting responsibility for the novel borne by the corporate identity of *Macmillan's* as much as by the individual authority of Norton. Masson's epistolary voice intervenes at the end of the discussion; the single extant letter he contributed shows him

---

[30]   As noted above, at this time magazine serialization was gaining in popularity, and as John Sutherland points out, by the mid-1860s experimental forms of serialization (*Middlemarch*'s eight short books, Trollope's thirty-two weekly 6d parts of the *Last Chronicle of Barset*) were increasingly popular as novelists and publishers came to feel that 'the traditional forms like the three-volume novel and the monthly thirty-two page serial had had their day' (John Sutherland, *Victorian Novelists and Publishers* (Chicago: The University of Chicago Press, 1976), 198). It is worth noting in this regard that at the same time that novelists and critics were increasingly applying ideas about organic form to the novel, the material forms of those novels were increasingly various and disunified.

[31]   Alexander Macmillan to Caroline Norton, [n.d.] April 1866 (Macmillan Archive, Volume CLXXIX, MSS 54964, British Library, London), 5–6.

[32]   Macmillan to Norton, [n.d.] April 1866, 5–6.

marshalling the conflicting terms of the discussion in an attempt to mediate between Macmillan's and Norton's irreconcilable perspectives.[33]

Though she vigorously protested the editorial excision of the relevant chapter of *Old Sir Douglas*, Norton did not do so by defending the morality of the sentiments in question. Rather, as she insisted repeatedly, those sentiments were the words of a single character rather than of the author or the novel or the magazine, unchangeable because like everything in the novel they formed an essential element of the novel as aesthetic whole. As she explained to Macmillan, the integrity of the novel as a work of art requires that if one chapter be removed, the entire serialization be discontinued since 'each of my novels has been written, not as a mere story but with a distinct purpose, and I cannot *unweave* my book because those who differ from me are [startled] at what one of the personages in it is made to say'.[34] In consequence, she continued, 'I am compelled to repeat that it is not a question of omitting a *chapter* but omitting the *book*—if one main purpose of the book is to be objected to.'[35] Macmillan in his reply returns to the moral question ('But I am sure personalities about our Queen would only cause pain and work no amendment', he explains, taking her 'purpose' to be social rather than aesthetic), while Norton's rejoinder again attempted to frame the question in aesthetic terms: 'I cannot have my book published in a mutilated form', she explained, 'Nor would it be *possible* to omit in the way you imagine. The groundwork of the story, the characters in the story, and the opinions advanced in it, are (as I have said) *warp and woof*, and not beans strung on a thread to be pulled off at pleasure.'[36]

Though Norton was far from the first writer to use the well-worn 'warp and woof' metaphor for the integrity of a text, her usage marks what was in 1863 a tension between different ways of thinking about the novel's purpose and structure. Though the 'warp and woof' metaphor had long been used, from the early 19th century it served as a figure for the text's artistry, the revelation of which might destroy the reader's impression of the text's integrity. As a reviewer of Scott's Magnum Opus edition wrote in 1829 of Scott's new prefaces to the novels, 'Why show us the warp and woof of that tapestry which, in its unbetrayed state, was so perfect?'[37] Yet by the 1860s such integrity was something the novel itself rightly displayed, and the figure came to serve as a desirable description of novelistic structure that would be legible to readers. Character, plot, and social

[33] Masson's letter is the last letter on the topic I can find in the BL Macmillan papers or in existing printed Macmillan-related correspondence; clearly more correspondence or perhaps face-to-face discussions continued, however, as the serialization was interrupted only through the summer and resumed in September. In June and July several literary gossip and news columns registered the interruption of the novel's serialization, though none that I have seen hinted at the cause.

[34] Caroline Norton to Alexander Macmillan, 24 April 1866 (Macmillan Archive, Volume CLXXIX, MSS 54964, British Library, London), 79, original emphasis.

[35] Norton to Macmillan, 24 April 1866, 7–9.

[36] Macmillan to Norton, [n.d.] April 1866, 10–11; Norton to Macmillan, [n.d.] April 1866, 12–13, original emphasis.

[37] Review of the *New Edition of the Waverley Novels*, by Sir Walter Scott, *London Magazine* 3 (June 1829): 610–11.

commentary are so tightly woven into the novel's narrative form that, according to Norton, to omit a chapter would be to tear a rent in the fabric of the novel rendering it useless. Despite what the seriality of the publication form might imply about chapters' exchangeability, she insists, her chapters—unlike dried, stored 'beans on a string'—are not interchangeable or extractable.[38] Although she capitulated (to who or what is not clear) in writing *Old Sir Douglas* as a serialized novel (something she does not, as she tells Macmillan, like to do or often do), she resists the serial-linked narrative form that E.S. Dallas a few years earlier implicitly devalued in his praise of *The Woman in White*.

Related to Norton's perception that Macmillan misunderstood her novel's form was her inability to communicate to him the idea that her novel's expressed opinions were distinct from the magazine's editorial perspective, and that her characters' opinions were not—and would not be by readers—identified with her own. As she attempted to explain to Macmillan—not for the first time—'It is perhaps scarcely worth while after saying so much to refer to the argument again that these censures of royalty are in the *mouths of one of the personages* to no more be taken as the Editor's or publisher's views than any other kind of strong language in the mouth of a particular fictional character.'[39] By contrast, for Macmillan the entire content of the magazine was at a certain level editorial content. The flagship magazine of the publishing house and publisher whose name it bore expressed a consistent perspective and embodied a certain decorum from which even the opinions of novelistic characters were not permitted to depart.[40] Although each instalment of the novel emblazoned the words 'By the Hon. Mrs. Norton' just below the title, and despite the fact that, as many scholars have documented, *Macmillan's* was perhaps the first Victorian periodical to consistently feature signed non-fiction (and therefore break from the traditional periodical practice of anonymous publication which subsumed individual writers within a corporate editorial set of opinions and style), nevertheless the sense that the periodical and the publishing house bore ultimate responsibility for the serialized novel's content—were, in fact, as authorial in their relation to the novel as Norton—remained strong.

---

[38] Norton's opposition of the bean-on-string and warp-and-woof metaphors gives new meaning to Henry James's much later use of the two in 'The Figure in the Carpet' (1896) (*Selected Tales*, ed. John Lyon (London: Penguin, 2001)). The young reviewer-narrator offers the textile 'figure in the carpet' metaphor to the established novelist Verecker as a description for the still-unguessed 'intention' that Verecker insists pervades his work. 'It was something, I guessed, in the primal plan; something like a complex figure in a Persian carpet.' As the unnamed reviewer goes on to explain, Verecker 'highly approved of this image when I used it, and he used another himself. "It's the very string," he said, "that my pearls are strung on!"' (295). Norton's dismissive use of the string metaphor allows us to reread what seems at first merely Jamesian stylistic exuberance. Not simply a semi-satirical piling up of figures for an authorial intention expressed as a supposed aesthetic wholeness that (the story implies) can never be truly expressed, carpet vs string is now legible as an opposition between an older and a newer model for the structure of the novel or an oeuvre. Verecker's name thus comes to hint the more strongly at outmoded practices of realism.

[39] Norton to Macmillan, [n.d.] April 1866, 12–13, emphasis in original.

[40] Norton continues in other letters to insist that 'beyond softening the expression,—[or omitting] a name,—or causing these opinions—(which are not given as mine, but as the opinions of one of the

David Masson, editor of *Macmillan's* as well as professor of rhetoric and English literature at the University of Edinburgh and author of *British Novelists and Their Styles* (1859), took up the correspondence where Alexander Macmillan—at least as far as one can tell from the existing record—left off, and in so doing reveals his consciousness of the impasse created by Macmillan's and Norton's radically different orientations towards the novel, literary authority, and publication. Replying to a letter in which Norton had assured Macmillan that 'no one can expect that after more than 30 years successful authorship both with my name and without it, (a severer test of success)—I should submit any work of mine to editorship!',[41] Masson immediately distinguished his approach from Macmillan's by using Norton's own terms in order to mediate between her position and Macmillan's.[42] Assuring her that 'nothing could have been further from my thoughts than the notion that it would be tolerable or becoming in *me* to apply any process of editorship, in any ordinary sense of the word, to anything bearing your name or coming from your pen', he responded to the precise way Norton framed her career-long resistance to editorial intervention in the terms of both her signed and unsigned literary successes.[43] Confirming her claim of autonomy, he wrote that when reading proofs of her work he had always found 'not only the story and the conception of the situations and characters but also the minute touches and details and the exact and artistic texture of the writing perfectly free from any need of correction'.[44] So perfect is Norton's self-editing, he suggests that 'but for my focused habit of reading all proofs before final publication, and also my pleasure in each successive instalment of "Old Sir Douglas"' the 'offending chapter' might easily have made it to press unseen by editorial eyes. 'It was then in no mere exercise or presumption of Editorship', he explained, 'in short, on no *literary* ground

characters in the book), to be disputed and argued against by another of the characters,—I could make no alterations whatever' (Norton to Macmillan, 24 April 1866, 7–9).

[41] Norton to Macmillan, [n.d.] April 1866, 12–13.

[42] Solveig C. Robinson in '"Sir, It is an Outrage": George Bentley, Robert Black, and the Condition of the Mid-list Author in Victorian Britain', *Book History* 10 (2007): 131–68 describes another such drama played out between publisher George Bentley and relatively unknown author Robert Black between 1877 and 1878 during the time that Black's novel *Love or Lucre* was being prepared for the press. Robinson concludes that the violence of Black's reaction to the editorial intervention of publishing house staff was unusual, and generalizes from the evidence of the Bentley archive that such cases were 'exceptions to the rule' of authorial acquiescence in editorial intervention. In this she agrees with Gettman's general sense that most novelists did not much resent even significant alternations to their manuscripts during the publication process (Gettman, *A Victorian Publisher*, 212). In any case, the extensive evidence from the Bentley–Black correspondence Robinson cites does also suggest that Black's main strategy for insisting on authorial control was based not on an appeal to aesthetic criteria but rather on an identification of author with text; Black explicitly disclaims any special literary or artistic merit for his novel, insisting in a legal language of rights that 'an author has an indisputable right to make his own corrects for himself' (Black quoted in Robinson, 140).

[43] David Masson to Caroline Norton, 4 May 1866 (Macmillan Archive, Volume CLXXIX, MSS 54964, British Library, London), 14–15.

[44] Masson to Norton, 4 May 1866, 14–15.

whatsoever—that, when I did read that last chapter, I telegraphed to stop it until we could refer it to you'.[45]

Masson's language seeks to separate the literary from the moral, the unvarying perfection of each instalment's plot, characterization, and style from the incidental referential content of this single disputed chapter.[46] He also takes up the separate question of authorial versus corporate editorial responsibility for the novel's contents, noting that he had carefully considered '[a]ll the reasons which you suggested for *our* [i.e. the *Macmillan's* editorial persona] caring nothing of the matter', as well as her point about 'the dramatic character of the language in the fatal chapter... coming as dialogue in the mouths of the characters in the story'.[47] Having expressed clearly and specifically his understanding of her arguments and the meaning of the way she frames the question, he explained—notably in passive-voiced terms—that after all 'the conviction remained that we, as connected with *Macmillan's Magazine*, should be culpable, and would be held culpable, if, in whatever circumstances and under whatever name, that chapter appeared in its pages'.[48] This entire correspondence occurred between late April and early May; instalments of *Old Sir Douglas* were suspended through June, July (when a small notice appeared in *Macmillan's* notifying readers of the suspension), and August; in September they quietly resumed, and no record seems to exist of the further discussions the three parties must have held. Whatever the final terms of the agreement, the significance for publication history is that we must read Macmillan's short-term personal victory—Norton's excision of 'Royal Idols' and the resumed serialization of *Old Sir Douglas*—alongside the

---

[45] Masson to Norton, 4 May, 1866, 14–15, original emphasis.

[46] George Worth's account of the episode in his *Macmillan's Magazine, 1859–1907: No Flippancy or Abuse Allowed* (Aldershot: Ashgate, 2003) pits a 'strong-willed' (11) Norton against a Macmillan 'Who always replied calmly and politely to Norton's angry letters'. Offering us the Norton–Macmillan correspondence as plot rather than rhetoric, Worth omits Masson's role altogether (except very briefly in a footnote) and reads the episode in terms of ends rather than means, explaining that:

> Norton bristled when Macmillan informed her on 24 April 1866 that he had held back a chapter from the May instalment of her *Old Sir Douglas* because he considered it disrespectful to the Queen... He went on to state his 'sincere hope that you will kindly leave it out of the novel as it appears in the Magazine' because, 'much as I feel it would cause obloquy to us, I should regret much more what I think it would bring to you'. In her reply of the same date Norton was indignant. She maintained that she had written her novel 'with a distinct purpose' and, after a long and often tumultuous career in the public eye, she had come to be indifferent to 'obloquy'... Although Norton did promise to take another look at the revised proofs of the offending chapter, it began to appear that Macmillan had met his match, for the serialized version of 'the book' was actually withdrawn from *Macmillan's* for the next three months. [27]

In framing Norton as merely disrespectful and Macmillan as serenely heroic, Worth exemplifies one of the troubles of accounts of author–publisher relations, comparing them to battles of will for particular outcomes, for if Macmillan did achieve his moral goal of controlling the political content of *Old Sir Douglas*, the terms in which Norton sought to frame the debate were to dominate the literary field by the century's end.

[47] Masson to Norton, 4 May 1866, 14–15, original emphasis.

[48] Masson to Norton, 4 May 1866, 14–15.

longer-term success of Norton's way of looking at novelistic form from the point of view of the autonomous author who controls her enclosed text from a detached position.

As more than one critic has noted, book history and poststructuralism have long shared the insight that the author function is performed by a number of individuals, and that literary texts are both more and less than the sum of the intentions that go into making them. We have almost forgotten—as Macmillan knew in 1865—that the wider Victorian reading audience possessed similar assumptions about the often collective, flexible nature of literary authority.[49] Laurel Brake explains that this scholarly disregard of the 19th-century sense of the difference between the 'collectivism of the serial as a cultural form and the individualism of the book' is due to 'the privileging of books and the marginalization of serials by our author-oriented system of cultural value'.[50] The idea that an author might exercise near-total control over the meaning of her novel while at the same time insisting on a conceptual splitting of textual meaning from authorial intention became one of our critical orthodoxies by the mid-20th century and therefore does not seem unusual when we encounter it in Norton's letters in 1866. Yet at the time her terms were nearly illegible to Macmillan, a signal that the controversy over *Old Sir Douglas*'s serialization was one symptom of a moment of real change in thinking about the relationship between material and literary form.[51]

EDITING AND INVESTING: ANTHONY TROLLOPE'S *THE STRUGGLES OF BROWN, JONES, AND ROBINSON* IN *THE CORNHILL MAGAZINE*

Following the money through the circuits of Victorian author–publisher relations is difficult not only because there were so many ways novelists could be paid for copyright, but also because successful Victorian novelists were often involved in both editorial work and—increasingly as publishing houses continued to incorporate from the 1860s onwards—the financial oversight of publishing houses. Anthony Trollope's

---

[49] In 'Ideas of the Book and Histories of Literature' McDonald notes that despite the similarity of their basic insight about print culture and authorship, the poststructuralists' (Derrida, Foucault) focus on book-related technology has largely been interested in constraints on meaning, while book historians (Donald McKenzie, Roger Chartier) have largely been focused on how print positively effects 'new and different meanings' (Peter D. McDonald, 'The Idea of the Book and Histories of Literature: After Theory?', *PMLA* 121 (January 2006): 217–28).

[50] Laurel Brake, *Print in Transition*, 19.

[51] Norton was far from unique in her problems with Macmillan; Anthony Trollope, for example, had a brief argument with him over the question of expanding his *Macmillan's*-serialized *Sir Harry Hotspur of Humblethwaite* (1870) into a two-volume novel. See Anthony Trollope, *An Autobiography* [1883], ed. Michael Sadleir and Frederick Page (Oxford: Oxford University Press, 1999), 336.

Autobiography provides detailed and regular accounts of how much each of his novels was sold for and to whom as well as a self-approving account of negotiations with publishers over the value of his books, but tends to downplay his other kinds of financial relations with the publishing industry. His first few unpopular novels—*The MacDermots of Ballycloran*, *The Kellys and the O'Kellys*, *La Vendée*—were published on the profit-sharing model, in which the publisher footed the bill for the production of the novel and paid the author a certain contractually determined portion of the profits. In the case of his first three novels, Trollope recounts in his autobiography, no profit meant no payments. But after the publication of *The Warden*, his first novel to achieve respectable sales, Trollope realized that he could negotiate to sell his copyrights outright (before publication for a lump sum and permanently), a method of payment for fiction which, like profit-sharing, was popular. Variations on outright sale also existed, in which an author would sell permission for the publisher to use the copyright for a certain number of years (five, for example) or for certain editions defined by price.[52] Less popular than either of Trollope's models, but still sometimes practised, was the system of publishing on commission, which reversed the profit-sharing model; an author would undertake to pay for all of the costs associated with publication in return for virtually all of the profits, a risky but potentially high-yield venture. The royalty system, in which the novelist was paid a certain contractually determined amount of money per copy sold, did not come into use until later in the 19th century, but then became widely favoured.[53]

Yet novelist–publisher relationships involving money were not limited to the negotiation around payment for novels. The same questions about individual authorship and publisher's institutional responsibility that characterize the Norton–Macmillan relationship arose in even more complex ways in Trollope's life. Though clearly not squeamish when it came to the monetary aspects of his own career as a novelist, his investments in and responsibilities for various publishing ventures seem to have worried him considerably. Late in his life Trollope lamented in a letter to a friend that 'You remember Chapman & Hall. Their business has been turned into a Limited Company, & I am one of the three Directors. Nothing more pernicious and damnable ever occurred, or more likely to break a man's heart.'[54] As early as 1865, Trollope had been involved with the financial organization of the publishing business when he became founding investor in

---

[52] Caroline Norton, for example, told Macmillan while negotiating a deal for reprinting some of her more popular novels in an inexpensive collected works that 'I cannot print under five shillings the vol of "Stuart of Dunleath" being bound by agreement not to do so'; she had sold the rights to the cheap edition to another publisher. Norton to Macmillan, 15 August 1863, 3–4.

[53] For an overview of the different methods publishers had of paying (or not paying) authors, see Simon Eliot, 'The Business of Victorian Publishing', in *The Cambridge Companion to the Victorian Novel*, ed. Deirdre David (Cambridge: Cambridge University Press, 2000), 17–60. Troy J. Bassett's useful chart of three-volume novels published by Bentley between 1865 and 1870 contains a column noting the type of payment agreement for each novel. See 'Living on the Margin: George Bentley and the Economics of the Three-Volume Novel', 60–66.

[54] Anthony Trollope, *The Letters of Anthony Trollope, Volume One, 1835–1870*, ed. N. John Hall (Stanford: Stanford University Press, 1983), 867.

the limited liability company that owned the new *Fortnightly Review.* While Trollope's novels more often than not include a publication subplot (from controversy over newspaper editorializing and anonymous publication in *The Warden* (1855) to novelist Lady Carbury and her trio of editor friends in *The Way We Live Now* (1875)), his short fiction of the 1860s, especially his short novel *The Struggles of Brown, Jones, and Robinson,* are particularly concerned with the overlap between financial and literary forms of responsibility and how (or if) they might be equitably shared between author, editor, and publisher, with a particular emphasis on the problems arising when a clash between a model of the novelist as autonomous individual and the publishing house as corporate authority become involved with questions of money.

The massively unpopular *Struggles,* first published in two instalments in the Thackeray-edited *Cornhill Magazine,* tells the story of the rise and fall of a department store company while thematizing author–editor struggles and the kind of collective responsibility over the fictional text upon which Macmillan and Masson insisted and which Norton resisted in the drama over the publication of *Old Sir Douglas* just a few years later. Parallels between periodical publication and financial firms are built into *Struggles'* narrative; the collective narrative voice of 'we the Firm' employed throughout the novel echoes contemporary debates about periodical anonymity and signature, and raises the broader question about whether periodical-published novels are the responsibility of author, publisher, or a collective amalgamation of the two.[55]

Like Dickens's earlier *Dealings with the Firm of Dombey and Son: Wholesale, Retail, and for Exportation* (1846–48), *Struggles* presents itself as a company history. Unlike *Dombey,* however, *Struggles* is narrated in the first-person plural of the firm's collective voice. In the fictional preface, however, Robinson (the only member of the fictional firm who has not actually invested any money in it) notes that 'It will be observed by the literary and commercial world that, in this transaction, the name of the really responsible party does not show on the title page. I—George Robinson—am that party.'[56] While Robinson insists that he is actually the author of the collectively voiced memoir, he nevertheless reveals that it has been heavily edited, perhaps rewritten. As he recounts in the preface, another firm member complained

> that I can't write English, and that the book must be corrected, and put out by an editor. Now, when I inform the discerning British Public that every advertisement that has been posted by Brown, Jones, and Robinson, during the last three years has come from my own unaided pen, I think few will doubt my capacity to write the 'Memoirs of Brown, Jones, and Robinson' without any editor whatsoever.[57]

---

[55] The title-page of the Smith and Elder 1870 one-volume edition of the novel includes a prefatory image of the entrance to the haberdashery shop with the firm's name on top as the title-page of the novel. graphically representing this doubled way of talking about financial and literary responsibility.

[56] Anthony Trollope, *The Struggles of Brown, Jones, and Robinson. By One of the Firm. Edited by Anthony Trollope* (London: Smith and Elder, 1870), 1.

[57] Trollope, *The Struggles of Brown, Jones, and Robinson,* 5–6.

Robinson gives in at last, however, and 'It was then arranged that one of Smith and Elder's young men should look through the manuscript, and make any few alterations which the taste of the public might require.'[58] Robinson's remarks foreground one common Victorian argument in favour of understanding magazine writing as collectively authored, the argument that almost all published writing is the product of multiple hands and thus should appear as coming from a corporate whole rather than any one individual involved in the writing process. Ending his first-person preface, Robinson again remarks that:

> I have now expressed what few words I wish to say on my own bottom. As to what has been done in the following pages by the young man who has been employed to look over these memoirs and put them into shape, it is not for me to speak. It may be that they might have read more natural-like had no other cook had a finger in the pie. The facts, however, are facts still. They have not been cooked.[59]

Robinson argues that although the prose style may have suffered from this collective writing, the facts are the same. Unlike a company that might 'cook' its books under the protective secrecy of the corporate form, collective writing, he claims, should not cause the reader to be suspicious of the memoir's truthfulness. Editorial intervention is represented as affecting style, not substance; Robinson seeks to preserve himself as the authority behind the text in the face of editorial intervention which is both invisible to the reader and, since it occurs after his act of writing, out of Robinson's control. He claims that corporate or collective authorship is an inaccurate fiction even as he admits that the memoir has been substantially rewritten by one of Smith and Elder's 'young men'.

Trollope's representation of such a transparent reliance upon and disavowal of editorial intervention fits oddly with the terms of publication upon which he insisted for *Struggles*. Just before *Struggles*'s serialization, a letter from George Smith of *Cornhill* publisher Smith and Elder arrived to assure him that after conferring with Thackeray 'I am now however authorized by him to say that "Jones Brown & Robinson" [*sic*] shall be inserted in the "Cornhill Magazine" without any editorial revision.'[60] Trollope replies with satisfaction, writing that 'I should have been unhappy to feel myself severed from the most popular periodical publication of the day.'[61] Invested in an idea of himself as an individual and autonomous author—an idea which required special care to maintain in the context of periodical publication—Trollope's chagrin at editorial intervention and his demands that his text be preserved from such meddling are very much akin to Robinson's feelings about editorial intervention. Yet Robinson, at least, is clearly very much a writer in need of an

---

[58] Trollope, *The Struggles of Brown, Jones, and Robinson*, 6.
[59] Trollope, *The Struggles of Brown, Jones, and Robinson*, 11.
[60] Trollope, *The Letters of Anthony Trollope*, 867.
[61] Trollope, *The Letters of Anthony Trollope*, 868.

editor. This may simply not have seemed like a contradiction to Trollope. Nevertheless, things are complicated further when the 1870 bound-volume edition of the novel adds 'Edited by Anthony Trollope' to the title-page, using the familiar trope of the author as fictional editor in order to bring sense to the republished format. In *Struggles*'s republication, Trollope himself fictionally takes on the editorial power he had in fact so emphatically resisted when it was offered by Thackeray during the novel's initial serialization. As in the novel's own struggles over how to represent financial, authorial, editorial, and publication responsibility, we see in Trollope's negotiations over its conditions of publication his desire at once to maintain a novelist's position of individual authorial autonomy and to fictionally incorporate the editorial role within his own sphere of responsibility. In several other instances—for example in Trollope's involvement with the founding of the *Fortnightly* magazine as a limited liability company and his fictionalization of that founding in the short story 'The Panjandrum'[62]—Trollope continues to replay these conflicting relations in ways that raise but never resolve the practical and theoretical conflicts that arise when one person seeks to play two institutional roles, and when the literary and financial forms of collective responsibility need to be thought about together.

The Publisher's Series and Mary Elizabeth Hawker's and T. Fisher Unwin's *Mademoiselle Ixe* in the Pseudonym Library

While the precipitous fall of the three-volume novel from (perceived) popularity did not occur until the mid-1890s, by at least the 1870s publishers and novelists alike had already begun to notice the aesthetic and economic promise of shorter formats for new novels. In this context the publisher's series—the uniform issuing of a series of one-volume novels by a single publisher, a popular Victorian format for cheap reprints—took on a new life as a form in which new one-volume novels (often by new novelists) could be introduced to the public. John Lane's 'Keynotes' series (named after the novel by 'George Egerton'[63] which initiated the series) and T. Fisher Unwin's 'Pseudonym Library' series were two of the first series of this kind, following in the wake of Samuel Tinsley's apparent partial success in introducing new novels in the one-volume format into his lists in the 1870s.

---

[62] 'The Panjandrum'—both the name of a short story by Trollope and of the magazine founded by the story's characters—dramatizes this conflict between author and editor perfectly by forcing the first-person narrator to untenably inhabit the position of both contributing author of fiction and editor-publisher of the magazine at the same time.

[63] Pseudonym of Mary Chavelita Dunne Bright.

Published, in accordance with the series' unifying principle, under the pseudony-mous name 'Lanoe Falconer', the first novel in the 'Pseudonym Library', *Mademoiselle Ixe* (1890), takes its title from its main character's own pseudonym. This double pseudo-nymity is emphasized by the novel's opening discussion, which centres on the name of the soon-to-arrive governess. As Mrs Merrington explains to a friend, Mademoiselle's last name is spelled 'I-X-E': 'Evelyn says it should be pronounced Ixe, like "eeks" in weeks, but we don't know whether it is a French or a German name.'[64] Although Mrs Merrington pretends to know enough French to judge an earlier, discarded govern-ess's accent as 'quite Parisian', neither she nor her friend Mrs Barnes recognize that Mademoiselle's strange name is the phonetic spelling of the French letter 'x'.[65] The presumably more sophisticated reader of the novel, however, recognizes the name as an obvious pseudonym (and, as it turns out, a nom de guerre in the war of Russian anarchists against the ruling aristocracy), overtly designed to announce itself as such. Effacing her name and replacing it with a marker of its absence, Mademoiselle Ixe simi-larly seems to efface her personality, adapting herself in turns to suit the needs of each member of the family she joins.

Despite all of this emphasis on pseudonymity, *Mademoiselle Ixe* posits and rejects a narrative technique grounded in temporary secrecy and eventual disclosure. Instead, *Ixe* aims to instruct the reader in interpretive strategies that favour collective and corpo-rate understandings of both personal identity and literary authority. The circumstances surrounding the publication of the novel reflect this collective conception of author-ity: author Hawker and publisher Unwin's correspondence concerning *Ixe* treats 'Lanoe Falconer' as a collective entity in which they are jointly invested. Hawker mentions more than once that she knows Unwin to be, as she says in one letter, 'as much interested as myself' in Falconer's literary reputation.[66] And both consciously exceed the bounds of the equally autonomous author (usually understood to be sacrosanct) and literary text by actively shaping the cultural context of their novel's reception; together they worked to ensure that the novel was 'blacked out' by the Russian censor, a circumstance which, in the words of Hawker, 'dramatic fitness demand[ed]'.[67] *Mademoiselle Ixe* both repre-sents and meditates on the complicated Victorian understanding of who authorizes text-ual meaning and of the complex relationship between material and novelistic forms, an understanding which the publication stories surrounding *Old Sir Douglas* and *Struggles*, as well as the (partial) record of the author–publisher relations that produced *Ixe*, also exemplify.

---

[64] Lanoe Falconer [Mary Elizabeth Hawker], *Mademoiselle Ixe*, The Pseudonym Library (London: T. Fisher Unwin, 1891), 3.

[65] Hawker, *Mademoiselle Ixe*, 1.

[66] Mary Elizabeth Hawker, Letter to T. Fisher Unwin, 22 March 1891 (Mary Elizabeth Hawker, 65 A.L.S. to T. Fisher Unwin, 1891–92, folder 1. Berg Collection of English and American Literature, New York Public Library, New York. Astor, Lenox and Tilden Foundations).

[67] Hawker, Letter to Unwin, 22 March 1891, fol. 1.

Substitutions of corporate and collective for individual forms of authority find repeated expression in the novel's plot; *Ixe* regularly raises the possibility of certain kinds of hermeneutically suspicious reading practices, only to show that their reliance upon the category of the individual as their interpretive basis (especially in the marriage plot) must ultimately be replaced with readings that foreground the collective responsibility. One example of this is the character Evelyn's misreading of Mademoiselle's interest in the Russian Count who turns up in the neighbourhood of the English country house in which the novel is primarily set. Evelyn's obliviousness to the fact that Mademoiselle Ixe wishes to kill the Count rather than marry him arises from her inability to distinguish between political and personal motives, between collective interest and self-interest. This failure is registered particularly in Evelyn's misunderstanding of the material form of Mademoiselle's story. When Mademoiselle first encounters the evil Count and turns 'deadly pale', Evelyn immediately (and incorrectly) thinks she understands why: "'There can be no doubt about it," was the verdict of this experienced little novel reader, "she is in love with the Count".'[68] Evelyn, schooled in the old-fashioned, domestic, three-volume novel, mistakes Mademoiselle Ixe's literary form, which turns out to be the distinctively slight, one-volume novella recounting a political rather than a domestic story. Because Evelyn is not aware of current events and knows nothing of 'the throes and pangs which now convulse the national life of countries less happy than her own', she is unable to make the proper interpretation.[69]

While recent criticism seeks to demonstrate that late-Victorian literary culture often understood anonymity or pseudonymity as a ploy designed to heighten the effect of the ultimate disclosure of an author's name and identity—part of a larger pattern (by no means without exception) in studies of print culture—this was of course not the only possible way Victorian readers and writers interpreted such forms of authorship. Contemporary reviews of *Mademoiselle Ixe*, for example, interpret the Pseudonym Library's authorizing structure quite differently, viewing the author as having given up name and even personality for a greater good or an increased collective authority, rather than for the production of a deferred individual celebrity. *The Times* begins its review of the series by remarking that:

> the Pseudonym Library deserves the success it has done much to obtain from the very audacity of the conception. It was a bold and original idea to invite a variety of writers, presumed to be exceptionally gifted, to merge their personalities in that of their publishers, and bring any fame they might gain into a common stock.[70]

While acknowledging the fact that the pseudonymity of the series encourages an unsubstantiated assumption that the writers are 'exceptionally gifted', this article nevertheless

---

[68] Hawker, *Mademoiselle Ixe*, 122.

[69] Hawker, *Mademoiselle Ixe*, 135. The novel proliferates in other examples of such training in collective reading.

[70] Review of 'The Pseudonym Library', *The London Times* (1 September 1891): 6.

emphasizes the collectivizing effects of the series format. The publisher, as *The Times* implies, represents itself as the central authority of the series. The practice of issuing books by different authors in a uniform format and under the unifying publisher's imprint and series title produces a partially corporate authority figure quite different from the individual author who claims unmediated responsibility for his or her text—the person most critics assume underlies Victorian understandings of authorship. The series format necessarily foregrounds the role of the publishing house in selecting the novel, dictating its material form, specifying its genre and range of topics, and editing the text itself. In any given Victorian publisher's series, the publisher's imprint and series title guarantee as much (or more) about a volume as the author's name on the title page does; the Pseudonym Library, as *The Times* review points out, capitalizes on this tendency.

The fields of 19th-century print culture and publishing history continue to grow, generating excellent new work each year, yet we are only slowly beginning to consider the possibility that a culture with such a broad, complex, and changing range of textual production practices may have been provided with an equally impressive range of ideas about material and literary form. Recent work in print culture and publishing history has offered us increasingly detailed accounts of the collaborative nature of 19th-century textual production; most of these studies similarly represent themselves as uncovering modes of collaboration and multiple authorship which were not understood by Victorian readers and writers themselves. Yet as the author–publisher discussions surrounding the serialization of *Old Sir Douglas*, the editing of *The Struggles of Brown, Jones, and Robinson*, and the publication of *Mademoiselle Ixe* make clear, during the 19th century individualism and literary authority were neither as consolidated nor as inextricably linked as 20th-century critics have implied; it was the 20th century that saw the naturalization of the individual author as the dominant or even sole structure for representing literary authority. And a glance at late-Victorian discussions of the shift from one- to three-volume publication or the discussion between a mid-Victorian novelist like Caroline Norton and her publisher shows that Victorian understandings of the interplay between economic, moral, and aesthetic factors that influenced the ways novels were invested with material print forms were both complex and uneven. By paying attention to the literary shaping of understandings of print publication as well as to the ways the material forms of Victorian novels shaped changing understandings of narrative forms in both the 19th century and today, we can continue to trace in more detail the outlines of these still distantly glimpsed formations.

Selected Reading

Altick, Richard. *The English Common Reader*. Chicago: University of Chicago Press, 1957.

Brake, Laurel. *Print in Transition, 1850–1910: Studies in Media and Book History*. Basingstoke: Palgrave, 2001.

Dooley, Allen C. *Author and Printer in Victorian England*. Charlottesville: University of Virginia Press, 1992.

Feltes, Norman N. *Modes of Production of Victorian Novels*. Chicago: University of Chicago Press, 1986.

Griest, Guinevere L. *Mudie's Circulating Library and the Victorian Novel*. Bloomington: Indiana University Press, 1970.

Hughes, Linda K. and Michael Lund. *The Victorian Serial*. Charlottesville: University Press of Virginia, 1991.

Law, Graham. *Serializing Fiction in the Victorian Press*. New York: Palgrave, 2000.

Macdonald, Peter D. *British Literary Culture and Publishing Practice, 1880–1914* Cambridge: Cambridge University Press, 1997.

Oliphant, Margaret, and Mary Porter. *The Annals of a Publishing House: William Blackwood and his Sons, their Magazine and Friends*. Vols. 1–3. Edinburgh and London: William Blackwood and Sons, 1897–98.

Sutherland, J.A. *Victorian Fiction: Writers, Publishers, Readers* [1995]. London: Macmillan, 2006.

———. *Victorian Novelists and Publishers*. Chicago: University of Chicago Press, 1976.

Trollope, Anthony. *An Autobiography* [1882]. Oxford: Oxford University Press, 1999.

Weedon, Alexis. *Victorian Publishing: The Economics of Book Production for a Mass Market, 1836–1916*. Aldershot: Ashgate, 2003.

5

THE VICTORIAN NOVEL
AND ITS READERS

DEBRA GETTELMAN

The best-known and most captivating images of novel reading from the 19th century are by far those that describe, in the most colourful terms possible, the unfortunate effects of reading fiction.[1] Sometimes the damage is imagined to occur to the reader's mind; other times, it is to the novel itself. Rhetoric about how novels corrupt readers' morals and corrode their cognitive capacities—especially when the vulnerable reader referred to is a young woman—intensified as the novel famously rose to power as a literary genre in the 18th century. By the latter 19th century, essays debating (and, more often than not, debasing) the value of reading fiction had become a staple of the periodicals in which much of the period's fiction was first published. Novel readers then, as with scholars now, would have been quite familiar with rhetoric about the 'disease' of novel reading and descriptions of its deteriorative effect on the mental and even physical capacities of addicted, supine readers.[2] In one particularly imaginative account, an 1874 article titled 'The Vice of Reading', Alfred Austin calls such reading 'a softening, demoralizing, relaxing practice', which, 'if persisted in, will end by enfeebling the minds of men and women, making flabby the fibre of their bodies, and undermining the vigour of nations'.[3] Only slightly less well known would have been concerns 19th-century authors voiced about the potential damage readers could inflict on their novels. Thomas Hardy, for instance, repeatedly had uncordial things to say about those 'too genteel' readers—as he refers to them in his first preface to *Tess of the D'Urbervilles* (1891)—who objected to the frank subjects he treated in his

---

[1] For the purposes of this chapter, I use the terms 'fiction' and the 'novel' interchangeably, though I recognize that in the 19th century (as in our own), these categories are unstable.

[2] See Kelly Mays, 'The Disease of Reading and Victorian Periodicals', in *Literature in the Marketplace: Nineteenth-Century British Publishing and Reading Practices*, ed. John Jordan and Robert Patten (Cambridge: Cambridge University Press, 1995), 165–94.

[3] Alfred Austin, 'The Vice of Reading', *Temple Bar Magazine* 42 (September 1874): 251.

fiction.[4] 'What author has not had his experience of such readers?—the mentally and morally warped ones of both sexes, who will, where practicable, so twist plain and obvious meanings as to see in an honest picture of human nature an attack on religion, morals, or institutions', he writes in an 1888 essay, 'The Profitable Reading of Fiction'.[5] Indeed, over the course of the 19th century, as the novel became the predominant genre read by middle-class readers of all ages, publishers frequently restricted its contents in order to appease the tastes and morals of a conventionally minded audience. Hardy famously stopped writing novels in part because of such censorship, and his accusations about the 'warp[ing]' effect that readers' misinterpretations can have on a novel are as scornful and pessimistic as Austin's about the dire consequences that result from the interaction between the novel and its readers.

Rhetoric as vehement as Austin's and Hardy's offers little insight into the actual reading experiences of ordinary novel readers in the Victorian period. But the very frequency of such rhetoric does indicate how much was imagined to be at stake in the ordinary act of picking up a novel to read. What is commonly known about the reception of the novel in the 19th century is that the numbers of both novels and readers—and with them, the novel's cultural presence—grew exponentially. Encounters with works of fiction became a highly visible, omnipresent part of everyday experience for people across a range of social classes. In an often-quoted lecture published in 1870, Anthony Trollope describes novels as having overtaken readers' lives on both material and imaginative levels. 'We have become a novel-reading people', he writes, defined by the fact that, 'We have [novels] in our library, our drawing-rooms, our bedrooms, our kitchens,—and in our nurseries.' For Trollope, novels have permeated not only the houses but the consciousness of Victorian readers until, 'Our memories are laden with the stories which we read, with the plots which are unravelled for us, and with the characters which are drawn for us.'[6] Critical images of novel reading like Austin's—inherited from the 18th century—suggest that fiction acts directly, obviously, and harmfully on its susceptible readers. But what Trollope refers to is something new: a cultural phenomenon that emerges over the course of the 19th century in which the power of novels, whether one thinks of their influence as harmful or salutary, can be measured by the extent to which they become almost imperceptibly ingrained in the subjectivities and material lives of their readers. In contrast to spectacular rhetoric about the 'disease' of novel reading, Trollope's language implies a slow accretion over the preceding decades as novels continually intermingled with their readers' inner lives and daily experiences. In this alternative account that emerges not only from Trollope but—as this chapter will argue—throughout 19th-century commentaries on novel reading, the

---

[4] Thomas Hardy, *Tess of the D'Urbervilles*, ed. David Skilton (Harmondsworth: Penguin, 1985), 35.

[5] Thomas Hardy, 'The Profitable Reading of Fiction', *The Forum* (NY) March 1888; reprinted in *Nineteenth-Century British Novelists on the Novel*, ed. George L. Barnett (New York: Meredith Corp., 1971), 288.

[6] Anthony Trollope, 'On English Prose Fiction as a Rational Amusement', in *Four Lectures*, ed. Morris L. Parrish (London: Constable, 1938), 108.

relation between the novel and its readers starts to look less like mutual antagonism and more like one of George Eliot's webs of mutual dependence: a reciprocal, porous relationship characterized above all by the continuity between readers' experiences of fiction and their own real worlds.

What roles *did* the novel play in the lives of Victorian readers? What roles did Victorian readers play in the production of novels? And to what extent are the answers to these two questions intertwined? Trollope's description of the story-laden memories of Victorian readers is at heart a claim about their subjective experience of books. How readers in the past actually read is a question that book historians and literary critics have frequently posed—and, almost as often, answered by acknowledging the elusiveness of the subjective experience of any individual reader, historical or contemporary. But if it is, indeed, difficult and perhaps impossible to reconstruct the thoughts of a reader in the mid-19th century as she pored over *Jane Eyre*—and how, or whether, her thoughts might differ from those of a reader poring over *Jane Eyre* at any time since—we can trace some of the subjective attitudes Victorian readers expressed about fiction and the roles they imagined it played in their lives. Indeed, as Ian Duncan has suggested in writing about the popularity of the Waverley Novels in the early 19th century, fiction, because of the economic structure of its production, uniquely stirs readers to develop expectations about the meaning it has for their own lives. That is, since the novel as a genre came into existence not because of patronage, but because there was an increasingly large audience who would in some form or another pay to read it, as Duncan puts it, 'a novel *belongs* to the market and the reading public convened there' and thus 'lays itself open to imaginative appropriation by different communities and interests and for divergent intentions'.[7] In what follows, I suggest that in looking across a range of both material and imaginative experiences that the Victorian reading public commonly had with novels—from borrowing circulating library books to resisting unhappy endings—we do find an attitude repeated in the way that readers encountered fiction as well as in how authors and critics thought they ought to approach it. That attitude manifests the culture's propensity to see books and real life as intertwined, the assumption that one could, and should, freely traverse back and forth between the two worlds of fiction and real life. The more that novels permeated Victorian life, the more long-standing concerns about quixotic readers simply imitating what they read gave way to depictions of readers having their own subjectivities which were interdependent with the fiction they read and to theories of reading which privileged such a complex, imaginative intermingling. As readers infused everyday experience with the contents of novels and projected their real experiences into those works of fiction, as they freely appropriated and personalized the latest serial instalments, novel reading in the 19th century ultimately came to be associated in the larger culture with fostering freedom of thought—a 'perfect liberty of reading', as Margaret Oliphant called it, that, whether it

---

[7] Ian Duncan, *Scott's Shadow: The Novel in Romantic Edinburgh* (Princeton: Princeton University Press, 2007), 29 (my emphasis).

was put to better or worse purposes, was imagined to be a distinctively English part of life in the period.[8]

The sense that encounters with fiction were not only an integral, but an integrated part of everyday experience in the 19th century started with a physical world that was rife with print. A number of well-known factors contributed to increase dramatically the production and accessibility of reading material of every sort, particularly periodicals and newspapers, during Victoria's reign. The oft-cited factors that made reading material cheaper for readers to acquire ranged from broad sociological developments to specific legal changes: from increased literacy and urbanization, which meant publishers had a new, lower-end market to appeal to as well as lower distribution costs, to the abolition between 1836 and 1861 of the 'taxes on knowledge', duties which had made newspapers unaffordable for many readers. As Richard Altick notes—in what is still the most influential study of the 19th century's new mass reading public—not just print itself but the very 'appetite for print' permeated both the working class and the bourgeoisie to an unprecedented extent.[9] Indeed, the physical quantity of reading material that was diffused throughout everyday experience, particularly in the urban environments in which an increasing number of people lived, created a culture in which the experience or prospect of reading occupied a larger share of the collective consciousness than ever before. In Bleak House (1853), a novel in which paper documents have become suffocatingly abundant, Charles Dickens suggests how reading-dependent English culture had become by the middle of the century, as he describes Jo's illiteracy: 'It must be a strange state to be like Jo!…To see people read, and to see people write, and to see the postmen deliver letters, and not to have the least idea of all that language—to be, to every scrap of it, stone blind and dumb!'[10] As Dickens along with other observers at the time understood, the prevalence of print shaped the physical world and meant that one increasingly experienced, or expected to experience, that world through reading.

Of the time people spent reading, commentaries from the period repeatedly suggest that fiction occupied more people, for more time, than any other single genre. John Sutherland estimates that approximately 50,000 novel titles were published in the years of Victoria's reign and notes that this estimate may be low, because of the proportion of reading that included fictional elements, or, as Sutherland calls it, 'the fuzzy borders of fiction where it shades into religious-tract, educational and ephemeral periodical reading matter'.[11] Conservative commentators who derided (as F.T. Palgrave does) 'this universal diffusion of literature' and novelists who defended their genre agreed on the fact that Victorian readers of all classes appeared to read fiction above all else.[12]

---

[8] [Margaret Oliphant], 'Novels', Blackwood's 102 (September 1867): 257.

[9] Richard Altick, The English Common Reader, 2d edn (1957; Chicago: University of Chicago Press, 1998), 7.

[10] Charles Dickens, Bleak House, ed. Norman Page (Harmondsworth: Penguin, 1984), 274. On the stylistic elements of the same quotation, see Mark Lambert's 'Three Matters of Style', in this volume.

[11] John Sutherland, Victorian Fiction: Writers, Publishers, Readers (London: Macmillan, 1995), 151.

[12] F.T. Palgrave, 'On Readers in 1760 and 1860', Macmillan's Magazine 1 (April 1860): 488.

As Trollope, though not a disinterested commentator, to be sure, describes the reading taste of middle-class readers in his 1870 lecture, 'Poetry also we read and history, biography and the social and political news of the day. But all our other reading put together hardly amounts to what we read in novels.'[13] Again, just as a new reading sensibility was seen as one of the cognitive effects of the explosion of printed material, the abundance of fiction seemed to be visibly affecting the individual and collective consciousness of Victorian readers. Novels were, according to some commentators, shaping whether and how readers exercised their own imaginations. In describing the scope of Dickens' cultural impact shortly after the novelist's death, for instance, his friend and biographer John Forster points to how many people Dickens helped to exert their imaginations at all. He describes how the serial publication of Dickens's fiction improved the faculties of working-class readers in a step by step, 'month by month' way: 'There were crowds of people at this time who could not tell you what imagination meant, who were adding month by month to their limited stores the boundless gains of imagination.'[14] As David Vincent has traced, among the kind of newly literate, working-class readers Forster refers to, the activity of reading imaginative stories was gradually replacing the activity of listening to them. The vast popularity of fiction among such readers helped to bring about a real sociological shift—a cognitive effect felt beyond the minds of individual readers—in which the exercise of imagination increasingly depended on print culture, rather than being stimulated by an oral culture.[15]

Several innovations in publishing and book distribution that found great success during the middle of the 19th century also helped to integrate novels fluidly into everyday life. Although they were separate innovations, the growth of the circulating library, railway bookstall, and serial publication all fostered a dynamic in which novels were frequently moving physically and psychically in and out of the flow of readers' daily lives. The high cost of books meant that, from the 18th century onward, an increasing number of readers paid an annual fee to borrow their books from subscription libraries, rather than buying them. The majority of what readers borrowed, of course, was fiction, whether from Mechanics' Institutes libraries, which were available to working-class readers beginning in the 1820s, or from the enormously successful Mudie's Select Library, which provided more middle-class readers with the books they read than any other venue did between its founding in 1842 and the end of the century.[16] Mudie's explicitly encouraged what was, for them, a profitable dynamic of fiction cycling in and out of the Victorian household: the company is known for having used its influence over publishers to ensure that novels continued to be published in three separate, expensive volumes that needed to be borrowed until nearly the end of the

[13] Trollope, 'English Prose Fiction', 108.

[14] John Forster, *The Life of Charles Dickens*, 2 vols. (1872–74; London: Dent, 1969), 1: 97.

[15] David Vincent, *Literacy and Popular Culture: England 1750–1914* (Cambridge: Cambridge University Press, 1989), 217.

[16] As Guinevere Griest puts it, '"Mudie" meant fiction, or more specifically, novels.' See *Mudie's Circulating Library and the Victorian Novel* (Bloomington: Indiana University Press, 1970), 37.

century. Typical references to Mudie's in print took forms which emphasized the sense of books in constant motion—the 'box from Mudie's', the vans coming and going to and from New Oxford Street—while Mudie's itself advertised that it offered 'a constant succession of the principal books of the season'.[17] Such references to the coming-and-going aspect of Mudie's were certainly not always positive. Trollope equates the library with the undiscriminating, rapid consumption of novels in a lecture published in 1868, in which he writes of the young woman who gradually becomes addicted to fiction:

> Everybody has a subscription at Mudie's. It was very natural that some light reading should be required... But when I saw the first cargo that came down I did feel a little alarm. There were four three-volume novels, and I had not written one of them myself;—fine spirit-stirring stories in which everybody lost everybody, and the rest were all murdered. I soon found that the box had come back again and that the set had been changed.[18]

The period's other commercially successful innovation in book distribution, W.H. Smith's bookstalls in railway terminals, also began in the 1840s and helped to bring about the publication of cheap paperback editions. By marketing novels as something one read in the temporal and physical space between destinations, W.H. Smith's similarly if more subtly conveyed a sense of fiction as something portable, that travelled physically as well as psychologically throughout Victorian life.

Publication in parts, one of the most commonly recognized publishing trends that made fiction more accessible in the 19th century, meant that a good deal of contemporary fiction was designed with a cyclical reading experience in mind. The economic appeal of reading a story in serially published instalments was, of course, that it required less outlay up front. 'Many will pay 5s. at a time who will not pay 30s. at once', Edward Bulwer Lytton wrote to his publisher, John Blackwood. The appeal was also aesthetic: Bulwer was negotiating the publication of his new novel in volume as well as serialized form—which could be in a magazine or, less commonly, separately published parts—because, as he put it, 'It seems to me that there are two classes of readers—the one who like the serial form the other who prefer waiting till the whole is completed.'[19] In their important work on the serial, Linda Hughes and Michael Lund have argued that Victorian readers indeed developed a preference for this form because of the resonance of its dominant ethos of gradual, continual, uniform progress and development.[20] In

[17] *The Reader*, 30 July 1864.

[18] Anthony Trollope, 'Higher Education of Women', in *Four Lectures*, ed. Morris L. Parrish (London: Constable, 1938), 83.

[19] Edward Bulwer Lytton to John Blackwood, undated letter written in 1849; quoted in Sutherland, *Victorian Fiction*, 110.

[20] The serial as they describe it was 'a literary form attuned to fundamental tendencies in the age at large', tendencies also evident in the economics, evolutionary theory, and theories of moral character of the time. See Linda K. Hughes and Michael Lund, *The Victorian Serial* (Charlottesville: University of Virginia Press, 1991), 8.

practice, serialization meant that novels punctuated, and were punctuated by, real life on several levels. Within a periodical, the pages on which a novel appeared would often have been interspersed with advertisements, other articles, and even other novels (*The Cornhill*'s widely read first issues in 1860 featured serialized novels by both Trollope and Thackeray). Periodicals and serials literally circulated in and out of a reader's daily, weekly, or monthly experience; during the temporal gaps between instalments, readers could think, talk, and read about a number of fictional worlds even as they were going about their own lives. Realist fiction, in fact, encouraged this. Serially published novels famously were structured to build suspense about the ongoing story, and, as Caroline Levine has argued, suspense for realist authors meant training readers to suspend judgement, to fill these pauses with speculations, rather than conclusions, and to develop sceptical habits of mind that they carried back into their lives.[21]

Novel reading was also consistently viewed as an activity which extended into other spheres of life because there were simply more people reading than ever before, to the point that 'novel readers' comprised an important social and economic category apart from the discrete act or psychological after-effects of reading. The dramatic increases during the 19th century both in the number of novels published and in rates of literacy have been seen as interdependent phenomena, a key example of the reciprocally influential relationship between readers and novels in the period. Among less well-educated consumers, an interest in fiction spurred would-be readers to want to learn: imaginative literature provided (in Vincent's words) 'the greatest and most persistent incentive for gaining a command of the tools of literacy, and their first and most satisfying application'.[22] Meanwhile, newly equipped printers entering the market and producing less costly reading material found fiction to be the most reliable return on their investment, so that novels became, in turn, the reading material most accessible to working-class readers.[23] Middle-class commentators emphasized this connection and tended to discuss new readers as novel readers: as a social body that universally acquired literacy only to put it to the use of reading fiction (despite the fact that, as Jonathan Rose has shown, the self-stated goal of many working-class autodidacts was to develop their sense of intellectual independence).[24] Wilkie Collins, for instance, in his 1858 essay 'The Unknown Public', describes an audience which buys what he calls penny-novel journals and reads for 'its amusement more than for its information'.[25] Collins concludes that this 'monster audience of at least three millions!' is important economically as well as aesthetically, for (he reasons) if this body of fiction readers could eventually respond

[21] See Caroline Levine, *The Serious Pleasures of Suspense: Victorian Realism and Narrative Doubt* (Charlottesville: University of Virginia Press, 2003).

[22] Vincent, *Literacy and Popular Culture*, 226.

[23] Vincent, *Literacy and Popular Culture*, 197.

[24] See Jonathan Rose, *The Intellectual Life of the British Working Classes* (New Haven: Yale University Press, 2001), 12–57.

[25] Wilkie Collins, 'The Unknown Public', *Household Words* (21 Aug 1858): 218.

to a reputable work, the result would be a tremendous windfall as well as real aesthetic influence.[26] Other novelists, and particularly Dickens, saw themselves as writing for a public not defined by their class, but rather brought together—however temporarily—by their status as novel readers. Dickens is known for referring to his readers as a social body en masse: he comments in the preface to *Bleak House* on never having had so many readers—and then, three years later in the preface to *Little Dorrit* (1857), on having even more. Across various groups concerned with novel readers, then—from authors and publishers who benefited financially from them to critics who disparaged newly literate readers—novel reading was frequently viewed as an activity whose importance lay in its economic and social consequences beyond the act of reading.

Debate, discussion, and controversy about the accessibility of fiction throughout all classes of Victorian life, particularly surrounding the development of free libraries, was another way in which novels had an ongoing presence in the Victorian public consciousness. Overall, as we have seen, because of new publishing formats, new markets of readers, and new distribution forms, over the course of the 19th century books became less prohibitively expensive, and thus more freely accessible; this accessibility was also partly the result of the Public Libraries Act in 1850, which made possible literally free access in an attempt 'to make good books available to all'.[27] In practice, of course, public libraries could still be somewhat prohibitive to their targeted audience, potential readers from the lower-middle and working classes. In a 1905 report, Lady Bell writes of how a woman 'whose outer garment might be a ragged shawl' might be intimidated by the required process of 'going up an imposing flight of stairs, getting a ticket, giving a name, looking through a catalogue, having the book entered, etc.'[28] It is well known that, also in practice, public libraries primarily provided a means of obtaining fiction, despite their supporters' original intention to foster self-improvement. As Altick notes, by the 1890s the majority of free libraries reported that between 65 per cent and 90 per cent of the books that circulated were fiction.[29] Free libraries, then, in the latter part of the century in particular offered an occasion to reiterate long-standing concerns about the extent to which supposedly more impressionable readers, such as working-class and women readers, chose fiction over other genres. The effect of such discussions about where readers got their books, whether the focus was on Mudie's or the public libraries, was to articulate and reinforce the sense that novels were simply everywhere, both materially and imaginatively—often by voicing a desire to restrict this unprecedented accessibility.

The sense that novels were circulating freely across social boundaries and the question of whether any reader should be able to approach novels in such an uncontrolled, free way

[26] Collins, 'Unknown Public', 221.

[27] Mary Hammond, *Reading, Publishing and the Formation of Literary Taste in England, 1880–1914* (Aldershot: Ashgate, 2006), 28.

[28] Lady F. Bell, 'What People Read', *Independent Review*, 7, pt 27 (1905): 433; quoted in Vincent, *Literacy and Popular Culture*, 212.

[29] Altick, *English Common Reader*, 231.

also surface in portrayals of reading within some contemporary novels. In his influential work on representations of reading in 19th-century British fiction, Patrick Brantlinger has shown how anxieties about 'the near universal literacy Britain had achieved by the 1890s' and the emergence of a mass audience for the novel haunted several genres of fiction written for a middle-class readership.[30] What made Victorian novelists anxious was not knowing how their books would be read, an underlying condition of authorship that was exacerbated by having an audience that was larger, less knowable, and contained more newly literate readers than at any time in the past.[31] Concern about controlling how readers read was not only motivated by class anxiety, however. The material availability of fiction, which only increased as the 19th century went on, contributed to the sense that a reader's actual encounter with a novel was not so easily limited. Moreover, Altick describes the English tendency to disavow the unscripted, uncontrolled quality of pleasure reading—to see 'the ordinary reader's right to browse at will' as a frivolous purpose; this attitude had several sources, including a long-standing puritanical influence, a 'deep-seated prejudice against random reading', which was heightened by the utilitarian ethos of the time.[32] This background helps to explain why Victorian fiction so often tries to control how it is read. What Garrett Stewart has called the 'relentless micromanagement of reaction in nineteenth-century narrative' includes the Victorian novel's characteristic direct addresses to the reader and the inscribing of specific readerly responses into its pages—addresses that on occasion demand that readers accept the author's more radical ideas.[33] Arguably the best known such address in all of Victorian fiction is Jane Eyre's bald declaration in the conclusion of that novel, 'Reader, I married him.' Brontë's revealing the socially unconventional, cross-class marriage between Rochester and his former governess in such a bold, almost defiant tone has been shown to be part of a series of direct addresses in the novel in which she anticipates, and attempts to cut off pre-emptively, a conventionally minded reader's response.[34] Within their novels, then, Victorian authors reveal a consciousness that readers could respond in less than desirable ways to the fiction they read—a practice of thinking independently which is partly known to us now because of the anxious commentary it generated.

I have been suggesting that the particular ways in which novels became more physically accessible in the Victorian period resulted in a shared attitude towards fiction as—for better, or worse—something that wove freely in and out of daily, or weekly, or monthly experience for a wide population of readers and even became integrated into the way Victorian readers exercised their imaginative faculties. I want to turn now to

[30] Patrick Brantlinger, *The Reading Lesson: The Threat of Mass Literacy in Nineteenth-Century British Fiction* (Bloomington: Indiana University Press, 1998), 193.

[31] Brantlinger, *Reading Lesson*, 16.

[32] Altick, *English Common Reader*, 132–33.

[33] Garrett Stewart, *Dear Reader: The Conscripted Audience in Nineteenth-Century British Fiction* (Baltimore: Johns Hopkins University Press, 1996), 21.

[34] See Sylvère Monod, 'Charlotte Brontë and the Thirty "Readers" of *Jane Eyre*', in *Jane Eyre*, ed. Richard J. Dunn (New York: W.W. Norton, 1971), 496–507.

how a related attitude, specifically a sense that novel reading was an expression of read-erly freedom, appears across Victorian descriptions of the act of novel reading itself. In the second half of the 19th century, when readers from many different social groups were often reading the same novels, critics writing reviews of new fiction and essays about Victorian literary culture emphasized subjective differences in ways of reading as a legitimate basis for distinguishing between classes of readers.[35] This section focuses on the great deal that those critics as well as novelists in the latter 19th century had to say about the expectations, assumptions, and mental faculties that novel readers should (and should not) bring to bear on the act of reading. Again, since it is so difficult to reconstruct the actual mental experiences of historical readers, I am simply interested in recovering some of the period's commonly expressed attitudes towards novel reading—and towards the psychological experience of novel reading. As this section will show, one prevalent attitude among Victorian literary commentators was to regard novel reading as a participatory, cooperative act which equally encourages and depends on the reader's freedom of thought—sometimes seeing this as an unfortunate reality, but largely as a desired purpose of reading fiction. Novels, then, were perceived not only as mixed up with the real lives and thoughts of their readers, but as part of a distinctively English culture that valued reading as an expression of individuality and mental liberty.

As we saw in the beginning of this chapter, many of the descriptions of what was thought to be going on in the novel reader's mind that circulated in the Victorian press were actually supporting a broader, long-standing critique of the corrupting effect fiction had on readers' minds and morals. In such descriptions, as in 18th-century accounts, *how* fiction corrupts is by encouraging its readers to read novels in an imita-tive, quixotic manner, to take the fictional world as a model for their own real lives—particularly when those readers are young women. But with one key difference: the Victorian way of conceiving of imitative reading tended to view this uncritical reading practice less as a result of the mesmerizing and uncontrollable power of novels than as a consequence of the reader's lack of mental exertion. Indeed, the real concern that we find in 19th-century literary culture was not so much with the contents of what readers were imagining, as whether, and how much, novel readers were exercising their own faculties. The difference can be seen in how a similar sentiment is framed in two 18th- and 19th-century commentaries. In a *Rambler* essay from 1750 on modern and ancient romances, Samuel Johnson attributes the 'mischie[f]' of reading romances to the combi-nation of their utterly compelling contents and an assumption that copying from exam-ple is the natural reaction of the fiction reader's imagination:

> If the power of example is so great, as to take possession of the memory by a kind of violence, and produce effects almost without the intervention of the will, care ought

---

[35] See Debra Gettelman, "'Those Who Idle Over Novels": Victorian Critics and Post-Romantic Readers', in *A Return to the Common Reader: Print Culture and the Novel, 1850–1900*, ed. Beth Palmer and Adelene Buckland (Farnham, England: Ashgate, 2011).

to be taken that, when the choice is unrestrained, the best examples only should be exhibited; and that which is likely to operate so strongly, should not be mischievous or uncertain in its effects.[36]

Johnson's most vehement language is not about the reader's imagination, though it operates 'strongly', but about the 'mischievous' and 'violent' way in which a work of fiction hijacks that imagination, almost against the reader's will. Critics writing in the latter 19th century, on the other hand, often assign responsibility for quixotic reading to women readers who, in allegedly identifying directly with the heroines they read about, are not reading critically but—in this case, problematically—adopting another's words, thoughts, and actions. As one anonymous reviewer writes about the female novel reader in *The Saturday Review* in 1866, 'She has a dangerous habit of identifying situations of a novel with the circumstances of her own life, and of speaking and acting as she thinks a young lady in a novel would speak or act'.[37] On one level such charges merely show how much anxiety there was about what desires and thoughts love stories might stir in women readers. But this writer's focus also suggests how Victorian literary observers were also preoccupied, more broadly, with evaluating the depth and complexity of the reader's mental exertion. He goes on to emphasize imitative novel reading as a problem that depends on the reader, rather than on the book, in explaining the reasons why women readers are more imitative than men: they read more novels, have less of a range of real-life experience, and are more imaginative—only their imaginations are stocked with characters from novels, 'peopled with the airy creations of romance'.[38] So widespread were images of the unsophisticated, unthinking woman reader that, as Kate Flint has shown persuasively, women novelists at times used their own fiction to counter them. In *The Doctor's Wife* (1864), Mary Elizabeth Braddon satirizes the image of the quixotic reader who reads largely clichéd romances in her heroine Isabel Gilbert, who 'wanted to be a heroine,—unhappy perhaps, and dying early'.[39] With her frequent literary allusions, Braddon, Flint argues, calls on her readers to use their own literary knowledge, to read in a knowing, interpretive way, and thus to recognize their difference from such an imitative stereotype.[40]

Concerns that readers were not being reflective enough and the question of what role novels played in either fostering or countering such tendencies also went beyond these expressions of anxiety about certain populations of readers. At times when critics objected that novel readers were not putting their own minds to work,

   [36] Samuel Johnson, *Rambler* 4 in *The Yale Edition of the Works of Samuel Johnson: The Rambler*, ed. W.J. Bate and Albrecht B. Strauss, 14 vols. (New Haven: Yale University Press, 1969), 3:22; quoted in Mary Poovey, *The Proper Lady and the Woman Writer: Ideology as Style in the Works of Mary Wollstonecraft, Mary Shelley, and Jane Austen* (Chicago: University of Chicago Press, 1984), 182.
   [37] 'Novels, Past and Present', *The Saturday Review* (14 April 1866): 440.
   [38] 'Novels, Past and Present', 440.
   [39] Mary Elizabeth Braddon, *The Doctor's Wife* (Oxford: Oxford University Press, 1998), 28.
   [40] See Kate Flint, *The Woman Reader 1837–1914* (Oxford: Oxford University Press, 1993), 274–93.

they were pointing to a broader sociological condition, the well-known sense that many Victorians felt themselves to be living in an unreflective, materialistic age. The author of an article on 'Books and Their Uses' that appeared in *Macmillan's* in 1859 complains not just about novel reading, but the volume of reading in general in 'this much written-for age'. Reading is not by nature problematic, but becomes so when it is practised in a way that substitutes for thinking for oneself: 'There still remains a question whether the craving for books may not be a disease, and whether we may not live too little in ourselves, and too much in others... It is also unprofitable always to see things reflected in another man's mind.'[41] Particularly during the 1860s and 1870s, when critics were responding to popular 'sensation novels' that were thought to thrill readers on a visceral level, the long-standing complaint that novel reading was mentally numbing, that it led to a state of what Wordsworth had called 'savage torpor', became a staple in Victorian periodicals. Critics, of course, routinely likened novel reading to mindless, bodily consumption: Austin refers to novels as 'the worst form of mental food'; Oliphant, to them as a narcotic substance, a 'stimulant'; and Henry Mansel, future dean of St Paul's, calls the novel 'the dram or the dose, rather than... solid food'.[42]

Such harsh depictions of the damaging effects of popular novels have been the focus of many studies and are the most familiar images we have of Victorian reading. But if Victorians largely agreed that imagination, spirituality, and the very sense of humanity seemed to be threatened by living within an increasingly industrialized world, not everyone saw novels as the cause of or as exacerbating such cognitive erosion. Rather, as I have been suggesting, an alternative, more positive account emerges from a variety of 19th-century commentaries, including from defenders who emphasized the restorative power of novels and construed reading as an opportunity to exercise valued faculties that seemed to have little exercise elsewhere. Dickens, famously, claimed his magazine *Household Words* provided an antidote to the age's 'utilitarian spirit' and its 'iron binding of the mind to grim realities'; in describing the magazine's purpose in its initial number, he focuses on his wish to keep his readers' imaginative faculties active, to 'tenderly cherish that light of fancy which is inherent in the human breast'.[43] For the writer Thomas Arnold, it is those who do not read novels, businessmen, who need to be brought to read them in order to learn 'that there are things which mere practical energy cannot accomplish, and which no amount of money can buy—spiritual powers—faculties of observation, imagination, memory, description...'.[44]

---

[41] 'Books and Their Uses', *Macmillan's* 1 (December 1859): 110.

[42] [Alfred Austin], 'Our Novels: The Sensational School,' *Temple Bar* 29 (June 1870): 424; Margaret Oliphant, 'Sensation Novels,' *Blackwood's Edinburgh Magazine* 91 (May 1862): 565; [Henry Mansel], 'Sensation Novels,' *Quarterly Review* 113 (April 1863): 485. See also Janice Radway, 'Reading is Not Eating: Mass-Produced Literature and the Theoretical, Methodological, and Political Consequences of a Metaphor,' *Book Research Quarterly* 2, 3 (Fall 1986): 7–29.

[43] Charles Dickens, 'A Preliminary Word', *Household Words*, 30 March 1850.

[44] Thomas Arnold, 'Recent Novel Writing', *Macmillan's* 13 (January 1866): 208.

Both within novels and outside of them, then, we see various suggestions for how readers can and should exercise their faculties, use their minds in ways that are not simply active, but critical and sophisticated. The first of these reading activities, as I will call them, involves creating deep and multifaceted bridges between fiction and real life. For one, the predominant aesthetic of the novel at the time, realism, implicitly invited readers to see continuities between the work of fiction and the surrounding world. Realist novelists such as Charlotte Brontë, Eliot, Trollope, and Dickens also explicitly directed readers, in prefaces as well as in moments of direct address within their novels, in how they should not simply be connecting the real and fictional worlds, but using what they learn from fiction to read their own world more imaginatively, critically, or compassionately.[45] Eliot is probably best known for articulating this realist ideal of imaginative continuity, as she famously addresses her readers for an entire chapter of *Adam Bede* (1859), titled 'In Which the Story Pauses A Little', to explain that her aim in creating an imperfect fictional world is to develop the reader's sympathetic feelings towards those similarly imperfect, 'real breathing men and women' outside of the novel's pages. When critics and reviewers, too, frequently praised novels for hewing closely to real life, they were modelling a process of reading which involved continual, active comparison in the reader's mind. In a review of *Jane Eyre*, Eliot's partner George Henry Lewes goes one step further than this and suggests that a good book is one that asks the reader to continue thinking comparatively beyond its pages: 'The story is not only of singular interest, naturally evolved, unflagging to the last, but it fastens upon your attention, and will not leave you. The book closed, the enchantment continues. With the disentanglement of the plot, and the final release of the heroine from her difficulties, your interest does not cease... Reality—deep, significant reality—is the great characteristic of the book.'[46] In this case, Lewes largely judges the merit of the story based on how long it occupies the reader's mind and how extensively the reader is able to compare the story with real life—processes stirred up in the reader's mind, even if they come from qualities located in the novel itself.

A second reading activity which Victorian novelists and critics encouraged was to participate in imaginatively constructing the fictional world, even when this meant the reader imported images from beyond its pages. Like the process of reading comparatively, this practice of appealing and sometimes deferring to 'the reader's own imagination' (in Hardy's words) involves a continual traversing of the boundary between the reader's real world and the fictional world; again, too, Victorian writers had praise for both novels that spark such a sophisticated, creative process in the reader's mind and readers who engage in it. Hardy's writing about his readers suggests that he was especially aware of their capacity to shape a work of fiction to their own specifications.

[45] On the significance of the novel's evocation of compassion in relation to the law, see Jan-Melissa Schramm's chapter in this volume.

[46] [G.H. Lewes], unsigned review, *Fraser's Magazine* 36 (December 1847), 691–92; in Miriam Allott, ed., *The Brontës: The Critical Heritage* (London: Routledge, 1974), 84.

In the same essay in which he rails against 'mentally and morally warped' readers for misinterpreting his frank critiques of conventional morality, he describes a quite different and desirable outcome that can result from the reader's turning over, interpreting, and mentally adding to the novel's pages. The aim of reading for pleasure, he says,

> should be the exercise of a generous imaginativeness, which shall find in a tale not only all that was put there by the author, put he it never so awkwardly, but which shall find there what was never inserted by him, never foreseen, never contemplated. Sometimes these additions which are woven around a work of fiction by the intensitive [sic] power of the reader's own imagination are the finest parts of the scenery.[47]

Hardy describes the process of reading as, ideally, an 'exercise' which actually completes the novel: the fictional world is created partly (and sometimes 'awkwardly') by the author and partly by *whatever* mental images the work sparks in the reader's mind. From our perspective, three-volume, Victorian realist novels appear to leave the reader little room for imagination, so it is perhaps surprising to find not only Hardy but literary commentators and novelists in the middle of the 19th century, the golden age of realism, suggesting that the ideal way to read fiction is to add to a novel's already dense pages. Indeed, a number of Victorian writers themselves were concerned for a variety of reasons about whether contemporary novels gave readers ample opportunity to exercise what Hardy appealingly calls a 'generous imaginativeness'. This capacity to reflect, recall, or indulge in reverie was, as we have seen, thought to be increasingly lost in an ever more industrialized, mechanized culture, particularly in contrast to the immense value that Romantic-era literature had placed on any imagination, the author's or the reader's.[48] The author of an 1860 article on Richardson, Austen and Scott, who urges novel readers to take up these earlier writers of fiction once again, bases his argument in part on the fact that they knew how to leave enough to the reader's imagination. He praises Scott for, like Austen, too, 'leaving his persons and their sayings and doings to work out their own impression on the reader, as they might do in actual life'.[49] Contemporary novels, as this writer describes them, entrust little to the contemporary reader, while the sophisticated reader, whom authors trust, reads novels in a way that is anachronistic and endangered. Note the paradox here: the novel was a medium whose growth had come in so many ways from Britain's industrialization in the 19th century, and novel reading was at times treated as offering a space in which readers could cultivate their own imaginativeness and resist the mental effects of living within such a culture. Such a paradox enacts a central contradiction between collectivity and individuality that I have been sketching here. Writers saw novel readers as at once a mass that shared attitudes and as individuals whose very individuality might be nurtured by novels.

---

[47] Hardy, 'Profitable Reading', 279.
[48] See David Perkins, 'Romantic Reading as Revery', *European Romantic Review* 4 (1994): 183–99.
[49] 'British Novelists—Richardson, Miss Austen, Scott', *Fraser's Magazine* 61 (January 1860): 37.

Victorian novel readers appeared to share this attitude about the importance of their own creative responses to the novels they read. We know this because enough readers were evidently re-imagining the fiction they read to suit their own expectations that several Victorian novelists—who did not always like their readers' responses—explore this reading activity, with all its attendant problems, within their fiction. As we have seen, publication practices like serialization meant that novel readers had some experience of fictional stories as something fluid, which they could themselves imaginatively manipulate and carry on during the temporal gaps between instalments. Readerly creativity posed a particular problem, however, for Eliot because her realistic endings often frustrated readers who had developed ideal, wished-for endings of their own. As her publisher, John Blackwood described Eliot's feelings about the public's response to *Daniel Deronda*, 'It was hard upon her that people should be angry with her for not doing what *they* expected with her characters.'[50] I want briefly to focus on Eliot's characterization of reading in one of her novels, *The Mill on the Floss* (1860), which tellingly mirrors how—in Eliot's experience, at least—some Victorian readers were treating fiction as a springboard to their own further imagining. Throughout the novel, Eliot portrays both physical books and literary stories as things that get indelibly marked and personalized, with results that can be either deeply enriching or terribly destructive. After Mr Tulliver loses his lawsuit and the family's belongings are auctioned, Maggie's first real experience of loss is concentrated in seeing an empty wall where there had been a bookshelf. What she mourns, however, is the loss of Tom's additions to their personal copy of a fictional work: 'Our dear old *Pilgrim's Progress* that you coloured with your little paints... —I thought we should never part with that while we lived—everything is going away from us—the end of our lives will have nothing in it like the beginning!'[51] Eliot was ambivalent about her readers' creativity throughout her career: on the one hand, as we saw above, her readers persistently conjured their own, wished-for happier endings; on the other hand, she acknowledges the genuine affective value that comes from the personal images a novel evokes in the reader, as in Maggie's deep affection for Bunyan.[52] What Eliot underscores in *The Mill on the Floss*, which was written relatively early in her career, is simply that readers persist in using books in ways that are separate from their authors' intentions. Books of all sorts are misinterpreted, unread, or used for purposes that other characters consider illegitimate, from Mr Tulliver's inscribing a desire for vengeance in the family Bible (despite Maggie's objections) to Maggie's thinking she has found the key to happiness in Thomas à Kempis. A 19th-century novel, in fact, becomes the subject of the novel's most detailed description of how and why a reader might replace the author's design with his or her own. As Maggie comments on the Walter Scott novel Philip Wakem carries while walking in the Red Deeps:

---

[50] Quoted in Carol Martin, *George Eliot's Serial Fiction* (Columbus: Ohio State University Press, 1994), 235.

[51] George Eliot, *The Mill on the Floss* (Harmondsworth: Penguin, 2003), 252.

[52] For a discussion of Eliot's ambivalence, see Debra Gettelman, 'Reading Ahead in George Eliot', *Novel: A Forum on Fiction* 39 (Fall 2005): 25–47.

'The Pirate'…O, I began that once; I read to where Minna is walking with Cleveland, and could never get to read the rest. I went on with it in my own head, and I made several endings; but they were all unhappy. I could never make a happy ending out of that beginning. Poor Minna! I wonder what is the real end.[53]

Maggie's '[going] on with it in [her] own head', the appropriation that accompanies and ultimately seems to overtake her reading of Scott, is not exactly positive here: she desires a happy ending, and can't be bothered even to finish the novel. But Eliot also does, on another level, sympathize with Maggie's reading—with her belief that reading should be practised as an expression of one's personal thoughts and desires—because Maggie, after all, tragically struggles to find an outlet for such expression elsewhere.

From a variety of motives and causes, then, Victorian novel readers tended to treat novels as something that one *could* take such liberties with. On the one hand, by the latter 19th century, much of the critique of novel reading was focusing on how readerly affect was too predominant, to the point of crowding out any other, more aesthetically discriminating response. But I want to end by noting that the portrayal of novel reading as an inevitably appropriative activity, which we find both within and surrounding Victorian fiction, was also spoken of with nationalistic pride by some influential contemporary observers. Novel reading, as 19th-century readers practised it, finally became an emblem of a larger English outlook that valued mental liberty. In an 1867 article in *Blackwood's* that discusses the recent glut of sensation fiction, Oliphant praises the usual moral wholesomeness of English novels, as compared with French fiction, because such wholesome fiction has had a positive, broader effect on how 'the national mind' approaches its reading. She writes:

It has increased that perfect liberty of reading which is the rule in most cultivated English houses…It has made us secure and unsuspicious in our reception of everything, or almost everything, that comes to us in the form of print. This noble confidence has been good for everybody concerned. It has put writers on their honour, and saved readers from that wounding consciousness of restraint or danger which destroys all delicate appreciation.[54]

Oliphant may be arguing for the value of English prudery, but to do so she invokes something she evidently regards as a real sociological phenomenon: the unique freedom with which middle-class English readers choose their books and discuss them with all members of the family. This lack of constraint takes the outward forms of browsing in a literal sense and ranging in conversation, as well as, even more importantly for Oliphant, enabling a more subtle and seemingly contradictory capacity to pay close attention, to respond with aesthetic discrimination ('delicate appreciation'). Taken for granted as 'the

---

[53] Eliot, *Mill on the Floss*, 317–18.
[54] [Margaret Oliphant], 'Novels', *Blackwood's* 102 (September 1867): 257.

rule in most cultivated English houses,' such freedom is a necessary condition for books to provoke higher thinking. If novels were to become less wholesome, she writes, 'We should no longer be able to discuss, as we do now continually, the books that we are reading and the thoughts that we are thinking.'[55] In this ideal (and decidedly not French) world that she describes, reading, thinking, and the expression of one's own thoughts overlap 'continually'.

If Oliphant sees novel reading as an activity in which one can exercise the very English right of the individual to think independently, Trollope suggests that reading novels has a role in initially instilling such a habit. In one of the several lectures and articles Trollope wrote defending the novel as a genre, he refers to how in other countries:

> It has been in accordance with the manners of the upper classes that the girl should be brought to marry the man almost out of the nursery,—or rather, perhaps, out of the convent,—without having enjoyed any of that freedom of thought which the reading of novels and poetry will certainly produce.[56]

There is in fact some truth to Trollope's chauvinism, for what distinguished England from other countries in the 19th century was the reach of its industrialization, which in several ways contributed to the Victorian reader's sense of the freedom of novel reading. Novels became vastly more accessible to readers, in formats that invited readerly speculation and produced a sense that one was continually traversing the barrier between everyday life and fiction, while authors urged those living in such an industrialized culture to keep imagination alive through appropriating what they read. The paradox of English nationalism is of course that individuality and freedom of thought are the very qualities that define the collective national character, and within the lively Victorian debate about novel reading, the novel's most promising effect may have been its potential to cultivate free readers who were at once more themselves and more English.[57]

SUGGESTED READING

Altick, Richard. *The English Common Reader*. Chicago: University Of Chicago Press, 1957.
Brantlinger, Patrick. *The Reading Lesson: The Threat of Mass Literacy in Nineteenth-Century British Fiction*. Bloomington: Indiana University Press, 1998.
Flint, Kate. *The Woman Reader 1837–1914*. Oxford: Oxford University Press, 1993.
Griest, Guinevere. *Mudie's Circulating Library and the Victorian Novel*. Bloomington: Indiana University Press, 1970.
Hammond, Mary. *Reading, Publishing and the Formation of Literary Taste in England, 1880–1914*. Aldershot: Ashgate, 2006.

---

[55] [Oliphant], 'Novels', 258.
[56] Anthony Trollope, 'Novel-Reading', *Nineteenth Century*, January, 1879; reprinted in George L. Barnett, *Nineteenth-Century British Novelists on the Novel* (New York: Meredith Corp., 1971), 216–17.
[57] Thanks to Lisa Rodensky for this suggestion.

Hughes, Linda K. and Michael Lund. *The Victorian Serial*. Charlottesville: University of Virginia Press, 1991.

Levine, Caroline. *The Serious Pleasures of Suspense: Victorian Realism and Narrative Doubt.* Charlottesville: University of Virginia Press, 2003.

Rose, Jonathan. *The Intellectual Life of the British Working Classes*. New Haven: Yale University Press, 2001.

Stewart, Garrett. *Dear Reader: The Conscripted Audience in Nineteenth-Century British Fiction.* Baltimore: Johns Hopkins University Press, 1996.

Vincent, David. *Literacy and Popular Culture: England 1750–1914.* Cambridge: Cambridge University Press, 1989.

6

THE VICTORIAN NOVEL AND THE REVIEWS[1]

SOLVEIG C. ROBINSON

OVERVIEW

Characterizing the relationship between the Victorian novel and the reviews is a daunting task. While the *Critical Heritage* volumes have long provided inform-ation about the reception of canonical authors, and the Wellesley Project and subse-quent scholarship has unmasked many of the anonymous reviewers who wrote for the high-culture 19th-century periodicals, many questions still remain about the inter-relationships between the better-known novelists and reviewers of the age—and the roles played by the lesser writers and periodicals have only begun to be examined.[2] However, the combination of renewed interest in the history of the book and digitiza-tion projects that are helping to restore historical texts to a broader circulation is yield-ing valuable new information about Victorian publishing practices. Along with new studies of 19th-century periodicals, scholars have also produced a number of new stud-ies of 19th-century reviewing practices and of readership more generally. This recent work makes it possible to define some of the trends and tendencies in Victorian novel

---

[1] Many thanks to the participants in the 'Marketing the Book' Workshop at the VSAWC-VISAWUS Joint Conference on 'Victorian Markets and Marketing', Vancouver, BC, October 15–17, 2009, for their helpful comments and suggestions.

[2] Both *The Wellesley Index to Victorian Periodicals, 1824–1900*, 5 vols., ed. Walter E. Houghton (Toronto: University of Toronto Press, 1966–89) and the *Critical Heritage* volumes published by Routledge & Kegan Paul in London are invaluable research tools. The following *Critical Heritage* volumes were consulted for this article: *The Brontës*, ed. Miriam Allott (1974); *George Eliot*, ed. David Carroll (1971); *Dickens*, ed. Philip Collins (1971); *Gissing*, ed. Pierre Coustillas and Colin Partridge (1972); *Thomas Hardy*, ed. R.G. Cox (1970); *Arnold Bennett*, ed. James Hepburn (1981); *Robert Louis Stevenson*, ed. Paul Maxner (1981); *Wilkie Collins*, ed. Norman Page (1974); *Anthony Trollope*, ed. Donald Smalley (1969); and *Thackeray*, ed. Geoffrey Tillotson and Donald Hawes (1968).

reviewing and to suggest how the complex influences and intertextualities helped shape both the novels themselves and their contemporary reception.

Victorian novel-reviewing practices are difficult to encapsulate, as indeed is the definition of what constituted a 'review'. Published commentary on Victorian novels ranged widely in length and quality. At the bottom were very short notices of books published, the so-called 'book paragraphs' that were essentially forms of advertising placed by the publishers and used to fill columns. Just above these were brief plot synopses of current fiction (often under generic headings like 'New Books' or 'Our Library Table') and articles that amounted to condensed versions of novels, consisting primarily of long extracts stitched together with minimal commentary. More thoughtful, and approaching the kind of reviews more common today, were in-depth discussions of single novels or series, particularly by major writers such as Walter Scott, Charles Dickens, W.M. Thackeray, or George Eliot, or by especially popular writers, such as Mary Elizabeth Braddon or Wilkie Collins. At the top were extended critical essays about individual works, authors, or subgenres (such as sensation or New Woman fiction), as well as comparative reviews (often national or historical in nature). While today's readers might expect most Victorian reviews to be of the complete three-volume versions of novels, in fact Victorian critics also reviewed the most recent instalments of serialized fiction, the vehicles (usually monthly magazines) in which those instalments were appearing, and reviews written by other reviewers.

Besides varying widely in length, format, and content, Victorian novel reviews also appeared in a broad range of venues, from high-culture quarterlies to daily newspapers. In the 1830s and 1840s, the quarterly reviews—particularly the *Edinburgh* and the *Quarterly*—were generally accepted to be the most influential sources of commentary on literature. By the 1850s and through the 1860s, weekly and monthly magazines were in the ascendant, with the *Athenaeum, Examiner, Saturday Review, Spectator, Pall Mall Gazette*, and *Fortnightly Review* considered essential reading for literary news, and the monthly magazines—most notably the *Cornhill, Blackwood's, Macmillan's*, and *Temple Bar*—serving as primary sources for both new fiction and the latest judgements about it. From the mid-century on, daily newspapers were also important vehicles for reviews, which appeared in everything from the establishment *Times* to the mass-audience *Illustrated London News*. Provincial papers typically printed round-ups of reviews published elsewhere (summaries that quoted liberally from their sources), along with occasional original essays. Periodicals targeted at particular audiences—whether defined by class, gender, age, politics, religion, or pastimes—offered reviews to their particular readers, noting which novels were likely to appeal to, say, evangelical girls, bicycle-riding clerks, free-thinking bohemians, or weary men of the world.

Reviews were intended to spark readers' interest in the literature of the day, to provide guidance about which works were likely to interest and amuse (or shock and offend), and—often—to render a judgement on a work's artistic and moral value (whether good or bad). Reviews were considered to be a very significant form of advertising (a business that came of age at the same time), a notion that was reinforced by the fact that reviews frequently appeared alongside the actual advertisements (the 'book lists') placed by the publishers or by Mudie's Circulating Library—which lists, of course, also might include excerpts from published reviews. As Andrew King explains: 'The interaction between advertising and extracting [from works being reviewed]...operates in the interest of both the network as a whole and the individual producer who organizes it: for the producer, it fills empty pages without costs beyond printing; for members of the network it is an advertisement.'[3] The relationship between reviews and advertising was underpinned by the fact that from mid-century on, all of the major fiction houses owned their own magazines in which they could feature and promote their works. Indeed, the close relationship between publishing and advertising was one of the perennial concerns of reviewers, with early Victorian writers fomenting against the long-established practice of 'puffing' and later writers trying to create more distance between commercial, 'popular' fiction and aesthetic, 'literary' or 'high-culture' fiction. Not incidentally, both early and later critics were simultaneously trying to distinguish their own individual critical practices from those of their predecessors and contemporaries.

What such critical debates meant to the general readers of Victorian novels is unclear. Evidence of reviews influencing readers to obtain or avoid particular titles is hard to come by, although studies such as Richard Altick's classic *The English Common Reader*, Kate Flint's *The Woman Reader, 1837–1914*, and Jonathan Rose's *The Intellectual Life of the British Working Classes*, along with ongoing projects like the Reading Experience Database (RED), provide some useful information, as do correspondence columns in various periodicals and the occasional letters from readers to authors.[4] In his biography of Mary (Mrs Humphry) Ward, John Sutherland describes a rare instance of an author witnessing a reader's response to her own work, in this case the novel *Robert Elsmere* (1888), which at that point in time had hardly been reviewed and was finding its readers due to word of mouth rather than critical acclaim. Ward was waiting in a train when a fellow passenger rushed along the platform waving a book. The passenger joined Ward in the carriage and then leaned out the window to exclaim to her friend: 'They told me no chance for weeks—not the slightest! Then—just as I was standing at the counter [of Mudie's], who should come up but somebody bringing back the first volume...as I was *there* I laid hands on it, and here it is.' She proceeded 'to devour the pages of the familiar green volume.'[5]

As this anecdote suggests, it is important to remember that until the end of the century, most readers procured their book-form novels from Mudie's and other circulating

[3] Andrew King, '*Reynolds's Miscellany*, 1846–1849: Advertising Networks and Politics', in *G.W.M. Reynolds: Nineteenth-Century Fiction, Politics, and the Press*, ed. Anne Humpherys and Louis James (Aldershot: Ashgate, 2008), 67.

[4] See Richard D. Altick, *The English Common Reader: A Social History of the Mass Reading Public, 1800–1900*, 2nd edn (Columbus: Ohio State University Press, 1998); Kate Flint, *The Woman Reader, 1837–1914* (Oxford: Oxford University Press, 1993); Jonathan Rose, *The Intellectual Life of the British Working Classes* (New Haven: Yale University Press, 2001); and The Reading Experience Database (RED), 1450–1945 (<http://www.open.ac.uk/Arts/RED/>).

[5] Quoted in John Sutherland, *Mrs Humphry Ward: Eminent Victorian, Pre-Eminent Edwardian* (Oxford: Oxford University Press, 1991), 126.

libraries, so that their choices were circumscribed by the selection guidelines of the main distributors. Guinevere Griest suggests that Charles Mudie's tastes may have been a greater influence on readers than any reviewers' opinions: 'If he did not actually ban a book from his shelves (as he did Reade's *Cream*, Mrs. Edwards's *Morals of Mayfair*, and Moore's early novels), he might make only token purchases, remove it from his advertised lists, or see that his assistants advised against it.'[6] (The Public Library Act was passed in 1850, but many districts were reluctant to fund libraries at all, let alone to purchase novels for them, so public libraries began to fill some of the demand for fiction only in the later decades.) On the other hand, most readers (including Mudie) would gain their initial acquaintance with many novels through the serialized versions, so they would in some sense already know what they were getting when they secured a given volume.

In his study of the Victorian press, Aled Jones raises the crucial question of what kind of influence the press had on readers, and vice versa, noting that the Victorians themselves wondered 'whether the press reflected or created public opinion, whether...it represented shifts in public mood or whether it determined the direction and extent of those discernable changes in popular attitudes'.[7] Wilkie Collins, in a letter to publisher William Tinsley about Mudie's disappointing initial order for *The Moonstone*, reveals how complex and interwoven the influences of reviewers, distributors, and readers could be:

> we have only to wait a few weeks—until the book has time to get *talked about*. I don't attach much importance to the reviews—except as advertisements which are inserted for nothing. But the impression I produce on the general public of readers is the lever that will move anything—provided the impression is favourable. If this book does what my other books have done, in the way of *stimulating the first circle of readers among whom it falls*—that circle will widen to a certainty. It all depends on this.[8]

Despite this complicated web of influences, however, the general consensus among historians is that at the beginning of the Victorian era, the educated, generalist 'men of letters' who reviewed novels and other works for the influential quarterlies constituted 'a popular source of authority, with this authority often assuming a moral as well as an intellectual dimension'.[9] The writers and readers of the quarterlies were generally from the same social milieu, and the reviewers assumed a sage-like role. Readers seem to have

[6] Guinevere Griest, *Mudie's Circulating Library and the Victorian Novel* (London: David & Charles, 1970), 214–15.

[7] Aled Jones, *Powers of the Press: Newspaper, Power and the Public in Nineteenth-Century England* (Aldershot: Scolar Press, 1996), 87.

[8] Wilkie Collins to William Tinsley, 11 July 1868; quoted in J.A. Sutherland, *Victorian Novelists and Publishers* (London: Athlone Press, 1976), 46.

[9] Carol Atherton, *Defining Literary Criticism: Scholarship, Authority, and the Possession of Literary Knowledge, 1880–2002* (Houndmills: Palgrave Macmillan, 2005), 4.

read reviews as much for the quality and style of the prose as for the actual judgements on literature. However, this kind of authority was gradually eroded, both by the fragmentation of the publishing market that coincided with the emergence of new, distinct readerships, and by the gradual professionalization of literature, which began to differentiate 'reviewing' from 'literary criticism'. According to Carol Atherton, 'Late-Victorian intellectuals could not rely on the existence of a socially homogenous public sphere of readers who shared both their cultural values and the type of knowledge on which their work was based. Instead, they turned to the universities to provide them with a new kind of intellectual community.'[10] (On the novel in the university, see Anna Vaninskaya's chapter below.) While more educated readers may have turned to the new university literature departments for guidance, Paul Delany suggests that general readers came to rely more on the reviewers in mass-circulation papers to make the kinds of judgements for them that Mudie had made earlier in the century.[11]

Novel Reviewing in the 1830s and 1840s

The quarterly reviews dominated the literary world until the 1840s. Created in the mid-18th century, the quarterlies became what Joanne Shattock calls the 'mandarin periodical form': 'Authoritative, ultra-respectable and at times highly influential, they were from the outset prestigious enterprises.'[12] Led by the *Edinburgh Review* and the *Quarterly Review*, the quarterlies featured longer, more serious articles with lengthy quotations. Articles in quarterlies were almost always anonymous (although the identity of contributors was frequently an open secret—William Hazlitt and Thomas Babington Macaulay were known as closely associated with the *Edinburgh*, for instance), with the goal being to present a generally consistent editorial perspective and tone while helping readers make sense of the literature and ideas of the day.

One of the major challenges for the quarterlies at the beginning of the Victorian age was to shed the discredited reviewing practices of earlier eras, the most notorious of which was 'puffery', or the exaggerated commendation of literary works. Nicholas Mason notes that while puffing was well established by the late 17th century, it acquired new strength as the publishing industry began to expand in the Romantic era. Under the cover of anonymity, it became common practice for reviewers to praise their friends' works, often at the behest of the author. Authors might even review their own works—as Walter Scott did in the case of *Tales of My Landlord*. Mason warns that such

[10] Atherton, *Defining Literary Criticism*, 4.
[11] Paul Delany, *Literature, Money and the Market: From Trollope to Amis* (Houndmills: Palgrave, 2002), 106.
[12] Joanne Shattock, *Politics and Reviewers: The 'Edinburgh' and the 'Quarterly' in the Early Victorian Age* (London: Leicester University Press, 1989), 5.

practices mean scholars should take care when generalizing about the reception of texts based on reviews: the reviews may not give an accurate picture of an author's or work's popularity.[13] Andrew King adds that it is easy to underestimate the complex economics of puffing. In his analysis of *Reynolds's Miscellany* in the late 1840s, King discusses Reynolds's practice of intentionally blurring the lines between advertisements, extracts, reviews, and 'notices' of books, and observes that

> Authors were willing to provide material from already published works free of charge (rather than take Reynolds to court for breach of copyright) in return for recommendation of the full-length work. What was essential...was that the origins of the extracts be acknowledged and, preferably, praised. Such puffing...can and should be seen as the result of cooperation in the face of economic adversity.[14]

The quarterlies' reputation for partisanship was at least partly responsible for the rise of some of the more influential weeklies, most notably the *Athenaeum*. Its founding editor, Charles Dilke, was determined to steer clear of puffery, and he established a firm policy of refusing any gifts (including books) from either publishers or authors in order to preserve the paper's independence. Dilke also published articles exposing the effects of puffery, noting that it deceived both readers and booksellers, who would order books on the mistaken belief that they were in demand. In his 1941 analysis of the *Athenaeum*, Leslie Marchand argues that the review's claims of unbiased judgement were largely borne out:

> With few exceptions it did condemn bad books and praise good ones. And what is more important, when it failed, the fault could be laid to shortness of vision and not to party or commercial bias. It was not long before the public began to realize this, and intelligent readers everywhere came to trust its judgment of books, more than that of any other literary journal.[15]

While not all readers would agree with Marchand's judgements about which books were 'good' and 'bad', the fact remains that although the *Athenaeum*'s reputation fell in subsequent decades, it remained an important source of information about the literary world.

As for the content of early Victorian novel reviews, there was a certain degree of continuity from the Romantic era. Where the Romantics had emphasized the importance of individual intensity of feelings and insights, the early Victorian critics tempered that

---

[13] Nicholas Mason, '"The Quack Has Become God": Puffery, Print, and the "Death" of Literature in Romantic-Era Britain', *Nineteenth-Century Literature* 60 (1) (June 2005): 29–30.

[14] King, '*Reynolds's Miscellany*, 1846–1849', 67.

[15] Leslie Marchand, *The Athenaeum: A Mirror of Victorian Culture* (Chapel Hill: University of North Carolina Press, 1941), 138; see also 232–35.

notion, wanting to see such insights applied to the good of society.[16] Dickens's novels, which exploded on to the literary scene in the late 1830s, provide a useful case study for both the continuities and slight shifts in emphasis in reviewing practices during this time. Dickens definitely benefited from puffing: the *Critical Heritage* volume reveals that his friend (and unofficial agent) John Forster reviewed him both favourably and often in the pages of the *Examiner*: Forster noticed *Nicholas Nickleby* nine separate times while the novel was in serialization in 1837–39, and he also put himself forward in late 1844 to review *The Chimes* for the *Edinburgh Review*. But many of Dickens's early reviewers did not have such close ties to the author. Taken en masse, their reviews are concerned with how Dickens fits into the unfolding tradition of English fiction (comparisons with Fielding and Smollett are common), the effects of serialization and how it might impact the value and reception of literature more generally, and the reasons for Dickens's popularity. All of these issues are touched on in a November 1838 review of *Oliver Twist* in the *Spectator*. Addressing the question of why popular and critical assessments of *Oliver Twist* had diverged, the reviewer explains: 'The answer will be, that they [the general readers] have been moved by *parts*: we [the critics] are speaking of the work considered as *a whole*, and testing it by reference to time, and those models of enduring art.' Dickens's sympathy for the downtrodden and his reformist tendencies met with approval by early Victorian reviewers, as being consonant with a social conscience.

The early reception of the Brontës' novels also illuminates some of the continuities and shifts between Romantic and Victorian reviewing. Reviewers of *Jane Eyre* and *Wuthering Heights* noted the intensity and individuality of the characters (especially Jane, Heathcliff, and sometimes Rochester) and of the style of the two novels. (*Agnes Grey* drew less comment but was recognized as having affinities with the others.) But while the early reviewers were usually impressed by the novels' Romanticism, they were also often puzzled and concerned about where that tended. For example, in April 1848 a critic in the High Church *Christian Remembrancer* refused to brand *Jane Eyre* as 'immoral or antichristian' but urged the author to channel her power in the direction of moral good, rather than ambiguity: 'Let her be a little more trustful of the reality of human goodness, and a little less anxious to detect its alloy of evil. She will lose nothing in piquancy, and gain something in healthiness and truth.' Similarly, an unnamed reviewer in the popular *Douglas Jerrold's Weekly Newspaper* in January 1848 claimed that *Wuthering Heights* was 'a strange sort of book,—baffling all regular criticism' but 'impossible to begin and not finish'; furthermore, it was 'impossible to lay it aside afterwards and say nothing about it'. Clearly daunted by a novel that didn't conform to established patterns, the reviewer expressed concern that there seemed to be no real *purpose* towards which the novel was driving ('we have discovered none but mere glimpses of hidden morals or secondary meanings'). The reviewer urged the author to turn 'his' power 'to better account. We are quite confident that the writer...wants but the practised skill to make a great artist.'

---

[16] Marchand, *The Athenaeum*, 232–35.

NOVEL REVIEWING IN THE 1850S AND 1860S

In the 1850s, the elimination of the last 'taxes on knowledge' (the taxes on advertising and newspapers) spurred an enormous growth in periodicals. George Worth notes that the result was a 'widening breach' between those who read the old high-culture quarterlies and those who read the new mass periodicals like *Cassell's Illustrated Family Paper* or the *London Journal*.[17] Into that breach tumbled a host of weekly reviews, most notably the new and sprightly *Saturday Review of Politics, Literature, Science and Art* (established in 1855), but also a number of older reviews that were now under new editors, including the *Athenaeum*, *Spectator*, and *Examiner*. Also relatively new on the scene were monthly magazines owned and managed by publishing houses. According to Deborah Wynne, these magazines were designed 'to appeal to all family members' and therefore featured 'an integrated approach to magazine design, making no divisions into sections specifically directed at particular readers'.[18] The magazines not only satisfied middle-class readers' appetite for a combination of thoughtful information and quality diversion suitable for reading aloud in the home, but they were a powerful vehicle for advertising. John Sutherland explains that

> The peculiar organisation of English fiction publishing meant a necessarily heavy expenditure on advertising . . . When firms became rich enough it was practicable to have their own house journal . . . so as to give the house's products adequate exposure. These journals were ideal for selling fiction as well, and at costs even lower than monthly numbers could achieve.[19]

The best and most influential of the publishers' magazines were *Blackwood's Edinburgh Magazine* (established in 1817, and popularly known simply as 'Maga', its success predated that of the other house magazines), *Macmillan's* (established 1859), *Cornhill* (founded 1860 by Smith, Elder), and *Temple Bar* (founded 1860 by Bentley's, which also published *Bentley's Miscellany* until 1868). But even relatively downmarket publishers like John Maxwell and William Tinsley offered their own magazines (*Belgravia*, founded 1866 and edited by Maxwell's wife M.E. Braddon, and *Tinsley's*, founded 1868). The magazines' primary appeal for readers was their generous portions of new fiction—up to three serialized novels might run in each magazine at any given time, plus shorter works—as well as their regular and fairly in-depth reviews of current and classic literature.

---

[17] George Worth, *Macmillan's Magazine, 1859–1907: 'No Flippancy or Abuse Allowed'* (Aldershot: Ashgate, 2003), 2.

[18] Deborah Wynne, *The Sensation Novel and the Victorian Family Magazine* (Houndmills: Palgrave, 2001), 16.

[19] Sutherland, *Victorian Novelists and Publishers*, 37.

The weekly and monthly magazines became central to the ongoing debates about the evolution and direction of fiction. They were often edited, at least nominally, by novelists. Besides Dickens (whose *Household Words* and later *All the Year Round* were worlds unto themselves), other editor-novelists included Harrison Ainsworth, M.E. Braddon, G.A. Sala, and Thackeray. Many novelists also served as reviewers, including Edward Bulwer Lytton, George Eliot, Henry James, Geraldine Jewsbury, George Meredith, and Margaret Oliphant. These novelists were understandably keen to participate in the social and critical debates about the evolving practice and popularity of fiction—and not unsurprisingly, they usually weighed in to defend practices and subgenres most closely aligned with their own work. So, for example, George Eliot's 1857 review 'Silly Novels by Lady Novelists' in the *Westminster Review* excoriates both formulaic subgenres and the vanity of bad writers, thereby helping to place in relief the kind of realist fiction that she herself was just beginning to produce; Oliphant's 1862 'Sensation Novels' in *Blackwood's* blames Charlotte Brontë for inventing the type of wilful heroine that was now wreaking havoc in works like *Aurora Floyd*, *Lady Audley's Secret*, and *East Lynne*—a type of heroine that Oliphant's tamer, 'domestic' fiction did not encompass; and Sala's 'The "Sensational" in Literature and Art', published in *Belgravia* in 1868, argues that sensation fiction is actually within the solid mainstream of the English literary tradition—a sentiment surely very pleasant to the ears of *Belgravia*'s editor, M.E. Braddon.

While some of the reviews at mid-century were signed (either with names, initials, or pseudonyms), anonymous reviewing remained the norm. As I noted in the introduction to *A Serious Occupation*, anonymous publication 'helped to preserve a sense of corporate identity for the different periodicals: the *Saturday Review* or *Blackwood's Edinburgh Review*, for example, presented an outward consistency reinforced by the magazine's suppression of its individual contributors' identities'.[20] A by-product of this practice, however, was that individuals from all ranks of life, and of both sexes, might aspire to the role of reviewer. While writers with specialization or particular language skills might be sought out to review particular works (especially non-fiction), novel reviewing could be done—at least in theory—by anyone who read fiction. Geraldine Jewsbury was just one reviewer who explicitly capitalized on the fact that she could represent the average (woman) novel reader.

As the examples given above might suggest, one of the main critical concerns in the 1850s and 1860s was with genre. On the one hand, the rise of the realist novel encouraged a more sober, analytical examination of Victorian society through fiction, a tendency that expressed itself in the more didactic social problem novels, like Disraeli's *Sybil* or Gaskell's *North and South*. On the other hand, the taste for novels of contemporary life also gave rise to sensation fiction, whose tendencies were generally conceded to be anything but sober. Reviewers debated fiercely about which kind of fiction was to be encouraged, and novels that seemed

[20] Solveig C. Robinson, Introduction to *A Serious Occupation: Literary Criticism by Victorian Women Writers* (Peterborough: Broadview Press, 2003), xii–xiii.

to straddle the two modes—for example, Gaskell's and Eliot's accounts of fallen women in *Ruth* and *Adam Bede*—drew some of the strongest and widest-ranging criticism.

The increasing importance of realism mid-century created problems for Dickens, whose exaggerated characters evoked complaint. A review of *Bleak House* in *Bentley's Miscellany* in October 1853 is fairly representative, marking the 'tendency to disagreeable exaggeration' as the novel's worst quality and expressing a clear taste for a more linear plot with fewer, more naturalistic characters:

> [supernumerary] characters are only serviceable in fiction, when they represent a class, and something is gained to morality, if nothing to art. When, on the other hand, they are exaggerated exceptions, and represent nothing which we have ever seen, or heard, or dreamt of, we cannot but regard them as mere excrescences which we would like to see pruned away.

Henry Chorley, whose review appeared in the *Athenaeum* the previous month, was more generous, but even he drew the line at the elderly Smallweeds, whose infirmities he found cruelly depicted in ways 'which are losing their hold on the popular taste even at the minor theatres'; he also criticized the death of Krook, which 'would be false and repugnant in point of Art, even if it were scientifically true'. Dickens also received some fierce critiques of *Hard Times*, whose overt didacticism troubled as many critics as were cheered by its politics.

By contrast, rising star George Eliot benefited from the growing taste for realism. The *Spectator* praised *The Mill on the Floss*, noting in April 1860 that 'Few persons in the novel-dramas which make so much of our literature now-a-days are so distinctly embodied and vividly coloured as the Maggie Tulliver who has just been introduced as a new guest in so many thousand English homes.' While Dickens had created some 'true portraits' of individual children, Eliot 'reminds us of what nearly all children are'. The often barbed *Saturday Review* was similarly complimentary in its April 1861 assessment of *Silas Marner*, particularly commending Eliot for her depictions of the poor and lower middle classes, in which she far surpassed Scott: 'this writer is without rival, and no phase of life could be harder to draw'. In a lengthy October 1863 article on Eliot's novels published in the *Home and Foreign Review*, Richard Simpson more fully expressed mid-century views on realism:

> When novels contain true pictures of character,—when they hold up a true mirror to man's nature,—they become glasses for readers to see themselves by. It is easy to read any novel frivolously—for its adventures, its intrigue, its hurried action, or its emotional power; or to read it for its literary merits only—for its brilliancy, its wit, or its artistic unity. But novels which paint character truly lead, through self-examination, to self-knowledge.

Eliot, Simpson states, is a 'searching but indulgent moralist' who thereby illuminates our common human nature and explores 'the critical question of the relations between passion and duty, reason and feeling, man and mankind, the soul and God'.

Although his ambitions as a moralist were not so far-reaching as Eliot's, Anthony Trollope was also praised for the ways in which in his novels reflected contemporary life. For example, in March 1864 the *Athenaeum* stated approvingly that the characters of *The Small House at Allingham* were 'all living, human beings', and a review the following month in the *Spectator* described the novel as an 'admirable representation of our modern social world'. Trollope was also praised for the naturalness of his fiction. In an April 1861 review of *Framley Parsonage*, the *Examiner* explained that the 'value' of Trollope's novels rested in characters who were 'the result of shrewd observation cleverly expressed in every-day phrase'. As this last comment suggests, however, reviews of realist novels could be double-edged. While readers clearly enjoyed these 'mirrors' of human nature and society, reviewers increasingly wondered if there was sufficient creativity or artistry in them. For example, while the *Examiner* generally commended *Framley Parsonage*, the reviewer also expressed reservations about what kind of writer Trollope was, describing Trollope as 'not in the highest sense a man of genius' and claiming 'there is not a touch of original fancy' or 'invention' in any of his novels. In May 1864, the *Saturday Review* expressed a similar concern, saying that while Trollope's line in fiction was 'a very pleasant one', it nevertheless 'may not be the highest of all possible lines'. Already in the 1860s, such comments about creativity and art in relation to realist fiction were pointing the way towards aestheticism, and it not surprising that in March 1873 it would be Henry James who suggested that *Middlemarch* surely marked the 'limit' of what he was already calling the 'old-fashioned English novel': 'If we write novels so', he asked rhetorically in the *Galaxy*, 'how shall we write History?'

The relative mildness of these critiques of realist fiction is thrown into relief when compared with critiques of the sensation novel, which emerged in the 1860s. The genre was ushered in by Wilkie Collins's *The Woman in White* (1859–60) and was followed in quick succession by Ellen Wood's *East Lynne* (1861) and M.E. Braddon's *Lady Audley's Secret* (1862) and *Aurora Floyd* (1863). Many reviewers, especially early on, praised the ingenuity of the plots. For example, in an August 1860 review of *The Woman in White*, the *Saturday Review* noted that 'Nobody ever leaves one of [Collins's] tales unfinished. That is a great compliment to his skill. But then very few feel at all inclined to read them a second time. Our curiosity once satisfied, the charm is gone.' In what appears to have been a rejoinder, the *Spectator* in early September observed that 'To keep the reader's attention fairly and equably on the alert through a continuous story that fills three volumes of the ordinary novel form, is no common feat', and concluded that 'from his first page to his last the interest is progressive, cumulative, and absorbing'. The *North British Review* paid a similar compliment about compelling plotting to Braddon in September 1865, stating that 'What is conspicuous above all is the skill with which she groups her materials.' However, the review contained a sting: Braddon's skill in plotting enabled her to deal with 'revolting topics' in such a manner 'as to hinder the startled reader from tossing her volume away in disgust'.

Many reviews of sensation fiction were as hyperbolic as some of the works they criticized. Critics frequently had recourse to disease metaphors, as H.L. Mansel did in his influential *Quarterly Review* article in April 1863. Mansel's 'Sensation Novels' ran over thirty pages and indicted the genre for 'preaching to the nerves instead of the judgment' and for stimulating 'the cravings of a diseased appetite'. Kate Flint observes that sensation fiction was thought to be particularly dangerous for women readers, because 'it suggested exactly what hypocrisy, manipulation, and concealed desires lay present behind the socially respectable façade of decorum' and showed up 'the very boredom of this existence'.[21] This explains in part Margaret Oliphant's denunciation in *Blackwood's* in September 1867 of heroines who 'marry their grooms in fits of sensual passion...pray their lovers to carry them off from husbands and homes they hate...[and] give and receive burning kisses and frantic embraces, and live in a voluptuous dream'. Despite the fulminations against the novels in the mainstream press, Deborah Wynne points out that, ironically, it was the newly popular family magazines that were the primary disseminators of the genre. Wynne claims that the respectable nature of these magazines was key to the legitimization of sensation fiction in the 1860s, because the magazines' readers were considered to be 'educated and domestic family members, rather than sensation-seekers after cheap thrills'.[22]

Bradley Deane suggests that sensation fiction was the catalyst for a late-century break between popular and aesthetic or literary culture. Worry about the effects of sensation fiction on the reading public generated calls for a 'critical constabulary' that would take responsibility for 'sorting the proper novelists from the cultural gatecrashers': 'Taking it upon themselves to define and protect the precincts of legitimate culture, these critics asserted the public's inability to do so, with the consequence that public enthusiasm and literary merit began to part ways'.[23] Deane suggests that during this period critics moved away from 'their previous role as consumer advocates...to become outspoken opponents of the literary market itself', and that as a result a new function of criticism emerged: one that was to 'chart the boundaries of legitimate culture and preserve them from the impulses of the reading masses', a movement encapsulated in Matthew Arnold's dictum to 'know the best that is known and thought'.[24] To the extent that this actually happened, it might be considered a kind of retrograde motion: a reversion to some of the literary and critical ideals espoused by the old quarterlies.

NOVEL REVIEWING IN THE 1870S TO 1890S

The relationship between the novel and the reviews was recalibrated again towards the end of the Victorian era. One factor driving this recalibration was the huge increase in potential readers, an increase driven both by overall population growth and by the

---

[21] Flint, *The Woman Reader*, 276–77.

[22] Wynne, *The Sensation Novel*, 1.

[23] Bradley Deane, *The Making of the Victorian Novelist: Anxieties of Authorship in the Mass Market* (London: Routledge, 2003), 60.

[24] Deane, *The Making of the Victorian Novelist*, 67, 71.

literacy gains accruing from the 1870 Education Act. Where in 1800 Britain's population had been approximately 10 million, with a literacy rate of only approximately 50 per
cent, by 1891 the population had more than trebled, to about 33 million, and the literacy
rate had soared to approximately 93 per cent. This meant a potential reading audience
of nearly 31 million, a sixfold increase from the beginning of the century. Supplying
books to these new readers—and guiding their choices—became a major undertaking.
An 1872 article entitled 'The Art of Novel Writing' in the *Gentleman's Magazine* divided
the contemporary flood of novels into three categories—those with a purpose, those
whose emphasis was on character, and 'ordinary' novels—and observed that the latter
group could be 'found everywhere, and lies within the reach of all who are able to read.
None so ignorant as not to find a book of this sort to suit his capacity; none so poor as
not to be able to afford himself this amusement.' Just as publishers were offering books to
meet the needs of every possible kind of novel reader, so too were hundreds of new periodicals being launched to attract increasingly particularized groups of readers, whether
women, children, members of different social and economic classes, specialists, or hob-
byists. Most of these new periodicals offered reviews that sought to best meet their particular readers' perceived needs and tastes.

Not only were there more readers with more particular tastes to satisfy, but there
were also more opportunities for those readers to purchase novels for themselves. The
decline of the three-volume novel—so dominant in earlier decades—and its replacement with a shorter, one-volume form meant that the novel became affordable, and that
the relationship between the novel and the reviews had to be recalibrated. The format
change accompanied a change in the business relationships between publishers and the
circulating libraries that effectively broke Mudie's monopoly on the purchase of new fiction and simultaneously brought prices down so that middle-class readers could afford
to purchase new novels when they were issued. This is turn generated new opportunities for publishers to market their books directly to readers. As Jonathan Rose puts it,
late-century publishers 'found it profitable to aim more narrowly at niche audiences—
imperialist fiction for smoking-room gentlemen, feminist fiction for suffragettes, cheap
romances for working girls, and modernist fiction for a growing cadre of avant-garde
readers'.[25]

As publishers endeavoured to market their books directly to readers, advertising of
individual titles began first to supplement and then to supplant the long-established
listings of new books. Whereas the lists merely offered titles, the advertising of individual books created opportunities for promotion that could reach the public even
before a review could be published. The first novel to receive a modern-style advertising blitz is widely regarded to have been H. Rider Haggard's *King Solomon's Mines*
(1885). Cassell's plastered London with posters declaring it to be 'The most amazing
book ever written', and according to Haggard's biographer D.S. Higgins, 'People began

---

[25] Jonathan Rose, 'Was Capitalism Good for Victorian Literature?', *Victorian Studies* 46 (Spring
2004): 495.

to believe it. What was this book? They must know.'[26] Ever-increasing numbers of readers now could be swayed to read—or avoid—certain novels based on advertising alone, without resort to critical opinion. A clever or salacious title might be employed to drive sales, even if reviewers pointed out that the book was not particularly interesting or well-written, as in the case of Grant Allen's *The Woman Who Did* (1895). Indeed, bad reviews themselves could be used to sell books: in her Introduction to the Oxford Popular Fiction edition of Allen's novel, Sarah Wintle points to a *Punch* cartoon from March 1895 that pivots on this irony. In response to an author who wonders why her publisher has reprinted a review calling her book 'the foulest novel that ever yet defiled the English tongue', the publisher declares, 'You must remember we've paid you a large price for your book, and brought it out at great expense—and we naturally wish to sell it.'[27]

This effort to market books directly to readers produced the phenomenon of the 'best seller' by at least the mid-1880s, and one important consequence was that the perceived value of an individual title or author was recalculated. As Paul Delany observes, books were increasingly ranked by sales or consumer choice, rather than by status. Late-century novelists like Arnold Bennett or H.G. Wells achieved a success 'defined by volume of sales, advertising, and sensitivity to the popular mood'; this was a definition of 'success' that might have nothing to do with 'accolades bestowed by the traditional intelligentsia'[28]—although certainly some novelists, like George Gissing, garnered both. Also at this time, the decline of Mudie's created a new need for novel reviewers, especially for the new mass-circulation papers, where a cadre of new reviewers tried to fill the vacuum left by the disappearance of Mudie's 'Select' list of fiction.[29]

Yet another important development was the general shift from anonymous to signed articles and reviews. Previous generations of reviewers had been (mostly) willing to subsume themselves into the editorial 'we' of the given publications for which they wrote, and readers had been (mostly) willing to accept the corporate voices of the various reviews and magazines to which they subscribed. But with the rise of the New Journalism and its greater emphasis on personality, periodicals of all kinds increasingly featured signed articles. At least in theory, it became easier to identify critical points of view with individual reviewers, although pseudonyms still covered a variety of ills. (In at least one instance, the use of pseudonyms gave new life to the age-old practice of self-puffery: Arnold Bennett reviewed his own *A Man from the North* in *Hearth and Home* in March 1898 under the by-line 'Sarah Volatile'.) By-lines also helped mark the rise of the professional, 'expert' critic—individuals like Leslie Stephen, Andrew Lang, George Saintsbury, Edmund Gosse, and Walter Besant, whose authority to write about fiction was derived more from education and other credentials than from practical

---

[26] D.S. Higgins, *Rider Haggard: The Great Storyteller* (London: Cassell, 1981), 83.

[27] Sarah Wintle, Introduction to Grant Allen, *The Woman Who Did* (Oxford: Oxford University Press, 1995), 2.

[28] Delany, *Literature, Money and the Market*, 100.

[29] Delany, *Literature, Money and the Market*, 110.

experience as novelists or from their status as 'ordinary' readers of fiction. As Ian Small explains, the 1870s signalled a crisis of critical authority: prior to that there had been 'no specialized body of knowledge' that constituted literary criticism and 'no specialist practitioners';[30] thereafter, readers and writers increasingly distinguished between 'criticism' and 'reviewing', as Grant Allen did in an article in the *Fortnightly Review* in 1882 entitled 'Decay of Criticism'. Already, 'criticism' had become a high-culture form, requiring both judgement and specialist knowledge; mere 'reviewing', in Allen's assessment, had become 'wholly unauthoritative'.[31]

The last decades of the Victorian age saw changes not only in who was reading and reviewing, but also in what was available to read. A broad range of new fictional subgenres emerged, from high-culture forms, including works influenced by naturalism or aestheticism, to a variety of new popular subgenres, including science fiction and children's literature (especially boys' adventure tales). Somewhere in between fell the much-discussed New Woman novels, the faith-and-doubt novels like Ward's *Robert Elsmere* and Edna Lyall's *Donovan*, progressive political and scientific fiction like William Morris's *News from Nowhere*, and the somewhat more esoteric works by authors like Marie Corelli. As might be expected, reviews of these various works were often strongly stamped by the vehicles in which the reviews appeared, and novelists' innovations or observance of tradition were applauded or excoriated according to the perceived needs and tastes of the reading audience to which the periodicals were directed. At every level, however, reviews performed a similar kind of cultural work. In his analysis of the 'Books and Bookmen' columns of the *Star*, a mainly political paper founded in 1888, Jock Macleod suggests that even in reviews aimed at more popular audiences, the aim was to draw readers 'into the immediacy and relevance of cultural markers that signified advanced literary culture, rather than the world of popular romance or adventure'. Macleod claims that the *Star* asked its readers 'to consider themselves part of the "cultural" nation (and by implication, the "national" culture), rather than as members of a culturally excluded Demos'.[32]

Not surprisingly, some trends in fiction were more likely to be applauded in high-culture and avant-garde periodicals than in the traditional family magazines or the mass-market press. Naturalism was one such trend, and the reception of Gissing's *New Grub Street* illuminates the differences in critical response across the cultural spectrum. At the more high-culture end, in May 1891 the *Spectator* called *New Grub Street* 'a novel which many may fail to enjoy, but which few competent critics can fail to admire, even if they admire under protest', while the *Saturday Review* described it as 'almost terrible in its realism' and admired its send-up of the contemporary literary marketplace: 'it estimates to a nicety the literary pabulum which the general public enjoys'. In contrast, the

---

[30] Ian Small, *Conditions for Criticism: Authority, Knowledge, and Literature in the Late Nineteenth Century* (Oxford: Clarendon Press, 1991), 136.

[31] Quoted in Small, *Conditions for Criticism*, 95–96.

[32] Jock Macleod, 'Between Politics and Culture: Liberal Journalism and Literary Cultural Discourse at the *Fin de Siècle*', *English Literature in Transition, 1880–1920* 51(1) (2008): 9.

following month the more middlebrow *Murray's Magazine* grudgingly admired Gissing's ability to draw characters, but concluded that the novel was 'not Art, and we trust that it is not Life'. Still lower on the cultural hierarchy, in the mass-market *Illustrated London News* in May 1891, L.F. Austin observed that *New Grub Street* would be 'repugnant to all who hold that the true aim of the artist is to represent the beautiful and to idealise the facts of common life'. Despite suggesting that Gissing's work might offer 'refreshment to the jaded reader of the average novel', Austin was reluctant to recommend it more generally. 'Will Mr Mudie's subscribers relish the process' by which Amy Reardon grew from 'romantic belief in struggling genius to the mature worldliness of a comfortable drawing room' he asked. 'If so, English novelists may venture to draw from life'. The implied threat—'If not . . .'—is simply left hanging.

The critical reception of Hardy's novels also reflects the high-culture versus popular-culture divide. While 'The Anti-Marriage League'—Margaret Oliphant's January 1896 denunciation of *Jude the Obscure* (and Allen's *Woman Who Did*) in *Blackwood's*—may be one of the best-known reviews of the Victorian age, her reservations about both Hardy's naturalism and the New Woman qualities of Sue Bridehead were not unique among reviewers for middle-brow periodicals. Reviewers in more high-culture journals, however, found much more to praise. For example, in a round-up review of Hardy's works in the *Westminster Review* in January 1896, D.F. Hannigan compared Hardy to Fielding, Balzac, Flaubert, Turgenev, George Eliot, and Dostoyevsky, and declared him to be 'the greatest living English writer of fiction'. Other high-culture reviewers were careful to distinguish themselves from more 'ordinary'—and thus less discerning—readers. Writing in the *Academy* in April 1887, William Wallace distanced himself from 'the ordinary clients of Mr. Mudie, who feel dissatisfied unless Virtue passes a Coercion Bill directed against Vice at the end of the third volume', and strongly defended Hardy's *The Woodlanders* for its exploration of the 'Unfulfilled Intention of the actual world' and its strong plot and characters, concluding that the novel offered readers 'a Coleridgian sabbath of the soul'. Havelock Ellis, writing in the avant-garde *Savoy* in October 1896, apologized for his belated reassessment of Hardy's latest novels and explained that the reason for the delay was that 'Mr. Hardy was becoming a popular novelist.' In an elaborate extended metaphor, Ellis rather preciously explained that 'it may be a foolish fancy, but I do not like drinking at those pools which are turbid from the hoofs of my fellow creatures; when I cannot get there before the others I like to wait until a considerable time after they have left'. The 'great stampede' of ordinary readers fleeing from *Jude the Obscure* had suggested it was now safe to reacquaint himself with Hardy's work.

Like naturalism, aestheticism in fiction divided reviewers on class grounds. High-culture journals found much to praise in the notion of 'art for art's sake', and with greater frequency they moved towards critical essays that addressed literary craft, more than reviews of fiction per se, as in the case of Vernon Lee's 'On Literary Construction' in the *Contemporary Review* in September 1895. On the other hand, more middle-brow journals scoffed at what they perceived as an elevation of style over substance. Henry James's writing was one focus for such critical debates. For example, the *Spectator* in

September 1890 noted that James's works were valued by a 'little company of superior persons' who were sure to enjoy *The Tragic Muse* because of its 'Jamesian peculiarities by which they are charmed and the profane crowd repelled'; in particular, the reviewer notes that

> Though the book is a very long one, there is even less of that vulgar element known as 'the story' than usual; indeed, were the narrative summarised, it would be seen that Mr. James has all but realised that noble but perhaps unattainable ideal,—a novel without any story at all.

But what was seen as a virtue in the pages of the *Spectator* was described as a fault in the middle-class family magazines. In 'A Gossip on Romance', published in *Longman's* in November 1882, Robert Louis Stevenson observed ironically that 'It is thought clever to write a novel with no story at all, or at least a very dull one.' And Margaret Oliphant registered a degree of exasperation in a review of James's *A London Life* in her June 1889 'Old Saloon' column for *Blackwood's*:

> The art of the American cosmopolitan is at all times conspicuous as art. It is impossible to lose sight of the skill with which he whips up the very light materials at this command, and makes a graceful something out of nothing ... His pleasure in these processes manifestly surpasses his pleasure in either the characters or the story.

The arguably more popular subgenre of New Woman novels posed another kind of problem for reviewers. Did they touch on important questions of contemporary life in such a way as to point the direction for a rising generation of more politically and socially engaged women, as some of the more progressive magazines, like W.T. Stead's *Review of Reviews* (July 1894), suggested? Or did they mark the decline of civilization and manners, as a critic in the more mainstream *All the Year Round* (December 1894) claimed?

The debate over the merits of high-culture versus popular forms of fiction was occasionally complicated by works that looked like one thing but might be the other. A particularly interesting case was Stevenson's *Dr Jekyll and Mr Hyde*, which was published very unobtrusively in 1886 as a paper-covered shilling booklet. The *Academy* recognized immediately that it was a significant work: in his January 1886 review of the slender book, James Ashcroft Noble remarked that

> in spite of the paper cover and the popular price, Mr. Stevenson's story distances so unmistakably its three-volume and one-volume competitors, that its only fitting place is the place of honour. It is, indeed, many years since English fiction has been enriched by any work at once so weirdly imaginative in conception and so faultlessly ingenious in construction as this little tale.

While this upmarket praise was sweet, it was a review in the *Times* a few days later that publisher Charles Longman credited with sparking off the book's popularity. Although writing for a much broader (but still mostly educated) audience, the *Times*'s reviewer also noted the novel's strengths of style even while seeming to place it firmly in the once-suspect genre of sensation fiction.

Perhaps one of the most telling developments of the fin de siècle was the re-emergence of an old periodical genre, the miscellany review of reviews. From the popular penny weekly *Tit-Bits*, launched in 1881, to the sixpenny monthly *Review of Reviews*, launched in 1889, these digests of news items and reviews from elsewhere (the *Review of Reviews* also featured condensed versions of novels) were testaments to the inability of readers to keep their heads above the tide of new books. While Arnold Bennett may have boasted that he could look at a pile of books and write a 1,500-word column about them in under an hour,[33] most readers could not. Without reviewers to contain the floods, even the most educated members of the public and the novelists themselves would find it difficult to navigate the waters of Victorian fiction.

Suggested Reading

Altick, Richard D. *The English Common Reader: A Social History of the Mass Reading Public, 1800–1900*. 2nd edn. Columbus: Ohio State University Press, 1998.

Deane, Bradley. *The Making of the Victorian Novelist: Anxieties of Authorship in the Mass Market*. London: Routledge, 2003.

Delany, Paul. *Literature, Money and the Market: From Trollope to Amis*. Houndmills: Palgrave, 2002.

Flint, Kate. *The Woman Reader, 1837–1914*. Oxford: Oxford University Press, 1993.

Rose, Jonathan. *The Intellectual Life of the British Working Classes*. New Haven: Yale University Press, 2001.

Small, Ian. *Conditions for Criticism: Authority, Knowledge, and Literature in the Late Nineteenth Century*. Oxford: Clarendon Press, 1991.

Sutherland, J.A. *Victorian Novelists and Publishers*. London: Athlone Press, 1976.

Wynne, Deborah. *The Sensation Novel and the Victorian Family Magazine*. Houndmills: Palgrave, 2001.

---

[33] Delany, *Literature, Money and the Market*, 120.

7

THE VICTORIAN NOVEL
AND THE *OED*

LYNDA MUGGLESTONE

The *OED* was, as Arnold Bennett famously remarked, the longest serial publication ever written.[1] Wilkie Collins's *No Name* had, for instance, been serialized in forty-four parts in 1862–63; Gaskell's *Wives and Daughters* appeared in eighteen lengthy instalments between August 1864 and January 1866; and Trollope's *The Last Chronicle of Barset* (1866–67) was completed in thirty-two parts, each of which cost 6d. In contrast, the first fascicle of the *OED*, edited by James Murray, appeared in 1884, narrating the varied histories of words from *A-Ant*. Its second, covering the words from *Ant* to *Batten* appeared one year later. By 1890, the dictionary, now under the shared editorship of James Murray and Henry Bradley (who had been appointed as editor in 1888), had merely reached C. Seven years later, now having reached D and E, the third volume was formally dedicated to Queen Victoria by Oxford University Press. By 1901, the year of Victoria's death, the dictionary had four editors, variously at work on parts of J, K, L, and O. Only in 1928, and after forty-four years, was the final fascicle published though—in a neatly modernist twist—this would not be the section containing *Z-Zygt* (which had appeared in 1921), but instead that covering *Wise* to *Wyzen* (a Scottish or northern form of *weasand*, meaning 'gullet' or 'oesophagus'). By this point, the dictionary—still under its original title of *A New English Dictionary on Historical Principles*—encompassed some 15,490 pages, 178 miles of type, 50,000,000 words, almost 500,000 definitions, and nearly 2 million quotations.[2]

---

[1] 'Books and Persons,' *Evening Standard* 5 January 1928 ('The OED was the longest sensational serial ever written'). Bennett was a long-term purchaser of the first edition as published in parts. See Hans Aarsleff, 'The Original Plan for the *OED* and its Background.' *Transactions of the Philological Society* 88 (1990): 151–61, 151.

[2] James Murray, Henry Bradley, William Craigie, and C.T. Onions, eds., *A New English Dictionary on Historical Principles*, 10 vols. (Oxford: Clarendon Press, 1884–1928).

Victorian writers repeatedly grappled with metaphors which might convey the complex nature of the *OED* and the immensity of the labours which it required. Quintessentially Johnsonian images of the 'poet doomed…to wake a lexicographer'[3] were now dispelled. Murray was instead depicted as toiling in a 'word-factory', a 'literary workshop', or a 'lexicographical laboratory' in images resonant of Victorian industrial process and scientific precision. As the children's writer Jennett Humphreys observed in 1882, Murray's scriptorium was, in essence, the 'trade premises' of the dictionary 'where the philological raw material, spread abundantly and heterogeneously, could be ground out by division and sub-division'. Other metaphors explored the dictionary as a building or physical structure; it was a 'linguistic colossus', Richard Grant wrote in a commendatory letter to Murray in 1884 after reading the closely printed pages of *A-Ant*.[4] For the *Athenaeum* the dictionary was a 'noble monument of the great Victorian era', emblematic of intellectual advance and national achievement. For the *Scotsman* in October 1891, it was a 'pyramid'—a wonder of the lexicographical world—against which other dictionaries were depicted as 'tents', ephemeral constructions which will 'cease to be before the builders of the "New" come near the six-and-twentieth tier of that colossal structure'.

While the *OED* as building thereby dwarfed all predecessors and competitors, its foundations, in a further metaphorical extension, were represented by a vast body of quotations collected by an extraordinary volunteer endeavour among the ordinary reading public. As the phonetician and philologist Henry Sweet stressed in a letter to Oxford University Press, written in April 1877, it was these laboriously gathered citations, each occupying a single rectangular 'slip' of paper, which formed the 'essential groundwork' of the dictionary.[5] Murray acquired two tons of them when he took over the editorship of the dictionary in 1879; by 1903, a further four tons had accumulated in the various dictionary offices in Oxford. Quotational evidence of this kind, deriving from literary and non-literary texts across a textual span of some eight centuries, was to be salient to the new philological science which the *OED* embodied. 'The great advance of Philology of late years has completely changed the conditions of a good dictionary', as Sweet declared in his letter to Oxford University Press: 'What is now required is fullness of citations and historical method, or, in other words, *a full number of citations from every period of the language.*'

Rather than emanating from the literary preferences—or antipathies—of the lexicographer (Samuel Johnson had, for instance, firmly excluded Hobbes as a source of evidence for his dictionary of 1755 on the grounds that he 'did not like his principles'), quotations in the *OED* would instead derive from innumerable voluntary acts of reading

---

[3] Samuel Johnson, *A Dictionary of the English Language* (London: W. Strahan, 1755), Preface.

[4] All citations from Murray's private letters and papers are—unless otherwise stated—taken from the uncatalogued Murray Papers, Bodleian Library, Oxford.

[5] Henry Sweet to Bartholomew Price, 20 April 1877. Sweet's letter, written in his role as President of the London Philological Society, sought to persuade the Delegates of Oxford University Press to undertake publication of the dictionary. It is reproduced in full in K.M. Elisabeth Murray, *Caught in the Web of Words* (New Haven: Yale University Press, 1977), 342–46.

among novels and plays, pamphlets, poems, and newspapers, tracts on science, travel, or theology (among a range of other texts). 'Persons of all estates and conditions, of both sexes and all ages, not merely of the leisured classes, but...busy men and women' had 'collected and copied out' quotations in search of the vital evidence of usage, as Murray noted in a lecture he gave to the London Institute in 1910. As Murray also pointedly remarked, even if Johnson had 'not risen to the idea of inviting the 18th century public to help him with the collection of quotations', readers all over the world had, in contrast, abundantly 'contribute[d] their stones to the mighty cairn which we are raising to the honour of our country's language'. The Victorian *OED* emblemized the collective endeavour of a new era, in which empiricism, evidence, and objectivity were prime characteristics of a modern, and scientific, lexicography.

VICTORIAN READERS AND
THE ART OF READING

While the dictionary's editors crafted the final form of each sense and sense-division,[6] it was Victorian readers who hence established much of its 'raw materials', sending, for example, over a thousand quotations a day to Murray's Oxford scriptorium in the early 1880s. As the *Times* remarked in October 1897, 'it is doubtful whether history records any instance of literary co-operation at all comparable with that...for the work over which Dr. Murray and Mr. Bradley preside'. This programme of volunteer endeavour began long before the first fascicle of the dictionary appeared. Public appeals for readers and reading first appeared in journals and newspapers in the late 1850s when the London Philological Society asked for assistance with what was at this point envisaged merely as a supplement to existing English dictionaries (recording new words and senses, as well as forms which might simply have been omitted in earlier works).[7] The gaps in knowledge which these early endeavours revealed, however, swiftly made plain that a far larger enterprise would be required. A formal proposal for a dictionary now defined by its newness, of both methodology and evidence, was established by 1859.[8] Within a few months, as Herbert Coleridge recorded in his role as the dictionary's

---

[6] Volunteers—who included within their ranks Victorian writers such as Charlotte Yonge and William Rossetti—also assisted with sub-editing the assembled quotations, placing them into a provisional order of sense and sense-development. Rossetti was also an important reader, sending in 5,000 quotations to the dictionary by the time the first volume was completed.

[7] For the early history of the *OED* project, see Lynda Mugglestone, *Lost for Words: The Hidden History of the Oxford English Dictionary* (New Haven: Yale University Press, 2005) and 'The Oxford English Dictionary: 1857–1928', in *The Oxford History of English Lexicography*, ed. A.P. Cowie, 2 vols. (Oxford: Oxford University Press, 2009), 1: 230–60.

[8] See *Proposal for the Publication of a New English Dictionary by the Philological Society* (London: Trübner, 1859).

first editor, 147 readers were at work in Britain while more than 400 works were being searched for relevant quotations.[9]

Though the reading programme temporarily fell into abeyance in the mid-1870s, the sheer abundance of evidence it provided over the wider history of the dictionary critically underpinned the nature of the *OED*'s achievements. 'The perfection of the dictionary is in its data', Murray stressed, and his own *Appeal to the English-Speaking and English-Reading Public* (widely circulated after his appointment as editor)[10] provided a vital renaissance for the project in this respect. Early in 1880 Murray could report to the Philological Society that 503 readers were now at work in Britain (and 148 more in America), with 881 books in the process of being read. A total of 295,000 citations had already been received. By May 1880, this had risen to 754 readers, with 1,568 books either having been read or in the process of being read, from which 361,670 citations had been despatched to the dictionary. By 1901, reading had extended to over 100,000 books, and a tally of *circa* 5,000,000 quotations. Murray had over 200 quotations for the word *hand* alone (including evidence from Sir Arthur Conan Doyle's *Micah Clarke* (1889), as well as from popular historical novelists such as Edward Peacock).[11] Material for the word *passage* covered some nine inches of closely packed slips in which Victorian novels were again prominent. Stevenson's *The Strange Case of Dr Jekyll and Mr Hyde* was, for example, used to provide evidence for the increasingly rare use of *passage* in the sense 'The passing of people': 'Even on Sunday, when it [the street] was comparatively empty of passage'. Mary Elizabeth Braddon's *The Cloven Foot* (1879) likewise substantiates the construction *of passage* ('I am only in town as a bird of passage'), while Frederick Marryat's *Mr Midshipman Easy* was, appropriately, the source of an 1836 citation illustrating *passage* in its sense of 'journey; a voyage across the sea from one point to another'. Citational evidence for words beginning with I, as Murray noted in a letter in 1897, occupied a daunting seventeen yards.

THE FACTS OF THE LIVING LANGUAGE

Murray's *Appeals* of 1879–80 drew particular attention to the reading which was required for the dictionary within contemporary writing—the texts of the Victorian

---

[9] As Coleridge also admitted, the standard of reading—and extraction—at this point was somewhat variable; only thirty could be classed as 'first-rate contributors, who … work with a thorough and intelligent appreciation of the nature of the scheme' (see his *A Letter to the Very Rev. the Dean of Westminster, 30 May 1860*, which was appended to Richard Chenevix Trench's *On Some Deficiencies in our English Dictionaries* (London: John W. Parker & Sons, 1860), 73.

[10] James Murray, *An Appeal to the English-Speaking and English-Reading Public to Read Books and Make Extracts for the Philological Society's New Dictionary* (Oxford: Clarendon Press, 1879). Murray issued three editions of the *Appeal* between April 1879 and January 1880.

[11] Peacock's historical novel *Ralf Skirlaugh, the Lincolnshire Squire* which was published in 1870 in three volumes hence substantiates the colloquial sense 'used of a person in reference to his ability or skill in doing something' (*OED*1 s.v. 9): 'he was a good hand at singlestick'.

period itself. Here 'much remains to be done', Murray noted: a 'large number' of books 'remained unrepresented, not only of those published during the last ten years, while the Dictionary has been in abeyance, but also of earlier date'.[12] Unlike texts from Middle English which required painstaking attention to original spelling as well as familiarity with earlier stages of the language, contemporary texts were, in this sense, importantly seen as open to all. 'Anyone can help', Murray urged. 'This is work in which anyone can join', the *Academy* echoed in May 1879: 'even the most indolent novel-reader will find it little trouble to put a pencil mark against any word or phrase that strikes him, and he can afterwards copy out the content at this leisure'. Murray's own pupils and colleagues at Mill Hill School (where he continued to teach until 1885) amply proved the point, sending in over 5,000 citations from a wide range of Victorian novels; Dickens's *Dombey and Son* was, for instance, read by C.F. Neville (who submitted 200 quotations from this novel alone), A.E. Gatward meanwhile tackled *Our Mutual Friend*, E.A. Blaxell read Kingsley's *The Water Babies*, while H. Jackson read *Yeast* (a work which would provide over 100 citations in the published dictionary).

A list of books accompanying the 1879 *Appeal* proffered a diverse range of writers and source texts for the Victorian period, literary and non-literary. Among the former were works by Matthew Arnold, Charlotte Brontë, De Quincey, and Disraeli (only *Sybil*, Murray noted, had been read by April 1879 though *Vivian Grey* would have been covered by June).[13] Explicit mention was also made of the novels of George Eliot, Charlotte Yonge, Charles Kingsley, Margaret Oliphant, and Frederick Marryat. As Murray stressed, the aim was inclusivity not exclusivity. 'Offers to read any other book not yet read will be welcome', he added at the end of the list. As Murray here made plain, any text could act as a source for the dictionary, though, as we will see, the linguistic practices of Victorian novelists—canonical or otherwise—were often to be of particular interest, as well as utility. Frederick Furnivall, who succeeded Coleridge as editor in 1861, had, for example, repeatedly stressed the dictionary's commitment to ongoing history—together with the duty of the lexicographer to 'get at the facts of the living language'.[14] While Furnivall sent thousands of newspaper citations to this dictionary with this in mind, recent Victorian novels could be equally useful. Relevant citations would frequently conclude an entry or sense in the *OED*'s first edition, supplying vital evidence of ongoing change in lexical and semantic practice.

To look at the entry for a word such as *grandiose* in the *OED* is, for instance, to see a historical narrative which is profoundly embedded in Victorian writing. Citations from Thackeray, De Quincey, Dickens, and George Eliot track the emergence and consolidation of its second sense ('Of speech, style, deportment, etc. Characterized by formal stateliness; often in disparaging sense: Aiming at an effect of grandeur, pompous'), as in

---

[12] Murray, *Appeal* (1879), 3.

[13] *Vivian Grey* was read by H.P. Bull of Hereford, who assembled 1,200 citations from this one text (over 460 of these would be used in the published edition).

[14] Fredrick Furnivall to Bartholomew Price, 1 June 1882 (Murray Papers).

Dickens's satirical probing in *Our Mutual Friend* in 1865 ('What is it that we call it in our grandiose speeches?') or Eliot's description of Julius Klesmer's visit to the Meyricks in *Daniel Deronda* ('His grandiose air was making Mab feel herself a ridiculous toy to match the cottage piano'). Similar is the entry for *brutalize* where quotations from Robert Louis Stevenson (*Travels with a Donkey in the Cevennes*: 'God forbid... that I should brutalise this innocent creature') and Eliza Lynn Linton ('He would have died outright had he been brutalized in any way', from *The Autobiography of Christopher Kirkland* in 1885) verify shifts in meaning within the final decades of Victorian England, here in the third sense which Murray identified for this word: 'To treat as a brute, or brutally.'

The act of reading Victorian novels per se, and the art of reading them for the dictionary, were nevertheless to be clearly distinguished. The latter was a deliberate process of textual scrutiny, its focus intently fixed on language and on lexicographic purpose. 'To peruse books, newspapers, etc., for quotations suitable for inclusion as illustrative examples in a dictionary', as a sub-sense included in a later *OED Supplement* formally confirms.[15] To *read* in these terms was, as this suggests, essentially an active process, one enacted upon texts which were, as another element in the metalanguage of the *OED* makes plain,[16] to be 'extracted'. Specific—and extensive—instructions were provided. Murray's 1879 'Directions to Readers for the Dictionary', for example, comprised twelve separate directives, together with an additional page of explanatory notes and two illustrative specimens of how quotations were to be noted down, giving precise details of text, date, page number, and form of the word being illustrated. Being a *reader* in Victorian England was, as a result, to be equally polysemous, encompassing both the person who might read for pleasure or study as well as, in terms of the gathering of evidence for the dictionary, the person who was engaged in a process of linguistic documentation. The latter was also intentionally removed from subjective engagements with style, argument, or literary merit.

While a novel such as Eliot's *Silas Marner* might therefore be enjoyed, as contemporary reviewers noted, for its 'strong intellectual impress' as well as its 'feminine insight and finish',[17] reading for the dictionary enacted a transformative process by which the fictional narrative became part of the 'fabric of facts' from which, as Murray stressed in 1884,[18] the *OED* was to be constructed. Eliot's use of *aberration* in describing Miss Nancy's well-regulated existence ('The very pins on her pincushion were stuck in after a

---

[15] This was added by Robert Burchfield in the *Supplements* to the *OED* (4 vols.) which appeared between 1972 and 1986. Murray's own words, quoted by K.M. Elisabeth Murray in her biography of her grandfather (*Caught in the Web*, 146) appropriately provided the first citation: 'I don't for words of that kind believe in the quotation test at all... because you know that not one millionth of current literature is read, & that it is the veriest chance or succession of chances which has caught *carriageless*... & missed a thousand others as good.'

[16] See e.g. Murray's request in the 1879 *Appeal* for 'help from readers' in 'reading and extracting the books which still remain unexamined'.

[17] See R.H. Hutton, unsigned review of *Silas Marner*, *The Economist* (27 April 1861): 455, reprinted in David Carroll, *George Eliot: The Critical Heritage* (New York: Barnes and Noble, 1971), 175.

[18] James Murray, 'Thirteenth Annual Address of the President to the Philological Society', *Transactions of the Philological Society* 19 (1884): 509.

pattern from which she was careful to allow no aberration') was, for example, rendered into empirical evidence for the ongoing figurative usage of this form in the very first fascicle of the dictionary. In a similar way, the use of *acquaintance* in depicting Dunstan Cass's concern for external circumstance ('He might meet some acquaintance in whose eyes he would cut a pitiable figure') provided the most recent evidence, again in the first fascicle, within the respective entry's final sense ('A person or persons with whom one is acquainted'). 'Every fact faithfully recorded, and every inference correctly drawn from the facts, becomes a permanent accession to human knowledge', as Murray affirmed in a lecture in 1910, talking of the evidence which textual relocations of this kind gave. The works of Dickens, Thackeray, Hardy, Oliphant, Marryat, and Wilkie Collins, and of emi-nently popular novelists such as Rhoda Broughton, Eliza Lynn Linton, or Dinah Craik were all subject to this process of generic transformation. Abstracted from their original context, the assembled quotations came to participate in a descriptive—and essentially realist—history of language and language use in English, covering both 'ordinary' as well as 'extraordinary' words. Whereas Johnson had initially envisaged quotations in his *Dictionary* of 1755 as operating within wider moral and didactic schema,[19] for the *OED* they were to be far more functional. As linguistic witnesses, they merely testified to the usage of a particular form or shade of meaning within the historical sweep of language. If some usages are labelled as 'literary' (i.e. as particularly distinctive of usage confined to a literary register, as in Dickens's use of *couched* in *The Old Curiosity Shop*: 'The driver was couched on the ground beneath'), the vast majority were not. Instead, as Murray explained in a letter in August 1883, the quotations were intended to be '*illustrations* (not *examples*) of how and where the usage arose ... They show the history of the form.'[20]

It is as part of this process of rendering fiction into linguistic fact that Thackeray's *Vanity Fair* (1848) acts as evidence for the unremarkable *greengroceries* ('Mr. Raggles himself had to supply the greengroceries') as well as the more inventive *giftling* ('a small gift'), or by which Dickens's writing can substantiate the creative use of *candlestick-wards* as an adverb (used in chapter XXVIII of *Bleak House* where it was duly spotted by an attentive reader), as well as serving as historical witness to the otherwise unremarkable diction of *door* or *dolly*. Collins's *Woman in White* (1860) is, here with a certain liter-ary appropriateness, used to provide a citation for *affrightedly* ('Looking up and down the road affrightedly'), as well as the most recent evidence for *clandestine* in the first edition of the *OED* ('I obtained access by clandestine means', as Count Fosco explains of the way in which he came to read Marian's journal). Anthony Trollope's novels were particularly popular, with well over 1,000 citations spread over the published diction-ary from the rarity of *bekiss* (for which Trollope was the sole Victorian witness) to the everyday realities of *arm-hole*, diligently noted by one contributor in reading Trollope's

---

[19] As Johnson stated in his *Plan of a Dictionary of the English Language* (London: J. and P. Knapton, 1747), they were to be selected not merely for 'immediate use' but also that they 'may give pleasure or instruction by conveying some elegance of language, or, some precept of prudence, or piety' (31).

[20] James Murray to Benjamin Jowett, 24 August 1883 (Murray Papers).

Belton Estate of 1865 ('With his thumbs fixed into the armholes of his waistcoat'). At the other extreme is lexical evidence which illustrated the diffusion or appropriation of Victorian scientific discourse into narrative fiction, as in Eliza Lynn Linton's striking use of *congelation* ('The freezing of an animal body or member, so as to make it numb or dead') in *The Autobiography of Christopher Kirkland* (1885): 'I felt only the congelation, the paralysis, the death of life.' Victorian novels across the spectrum, and their assiduous reading by a variety of dictionary volunteers, could, as such instances suggest, provide a highly fertile resource for lexicographic exploration, documenting both change and continuity in Victorian English.

Whereas Herbert Coleridge had commented in 1860 on the apparent 'indifference to the modern literature' by readers for the dictionary,[21] Murray's experience was, as this suggests, rather different. Extant evidence on the making of the dictionary enables us to track the ways in which the works of Victorian novelists were assimilated within the patterns of active reading undertaken by volunteers. While the first edition of Murray's *Appeal*, for example, noted that Eliot's *Middlemarch* remained unread, a later annotated copy of the *Appeal* (preserved in the Murray Papers in the Bodleian Library) confirms a swift response. The title of the novel is now firmly crossed through in black ink (it was read by Miss B.E. McAllum in Newcastle who would submit some 250 citations by 1884). Instead, the June 1879 *Appeal* now urged a reading of Eliot's *Theophrastus Such*, while the January 1880 edition removed Eliot entirely from the dictionary reading which was still required. Similar is the note which, in the original *Appeal* of 1879, had stated that Margaret Oliphant's novels remained unread; this too was emended by hand in the annotated copy of the *Appeal* in the Murray Papers as readers responded to the circulated request for help. The Reverend J. Crake of Huddersfield would, for instance, undertake Oliphant's *Chronicles of Carlingford*, sending hundreds of citations to the dictionary by 1884. W. Douglas, another assiduous reader who had despatched 33,000 quotations to Murray by this point, read other popular Victorian novels such as Mary Elizabeth Braddon's *Lady Audley's Secret* and the works of Mrs Henry Wood (alongside those of Darwin and Spenser, and a range of scientific texts from which evidence was also derived). Meanwhile, C.F. Grieg in Kent sent off 1,100 citations extracted from the novels of Charlotte Yonge and C. Gray in Wimbledon tackled Trollope, Kingsley, and Captain Marryat, amassing some 17,000 citations from these and other works. Thackeray's *Henry Esmond* was scrutinized in detail by Mrs Colenso in Norwich, eventually yielding 250 citations (another reading by P.L. Bailey in Edinburgh added hundreds more). The statement in the January 1879 *Appeal* that, of Brontë's works, only *Jane Eyre* had been read for the dictionary was also subject to swift revision; *Villette* was read by Miss H. Lucas in Harrowgate, from which she provided—together with her reading of Arnold's *Mixed Essays*—some 800 citations. Miss Hardcastle in Sydenham also

---

[21] See Coleridge's letter appended to Trench, 75.

devoted herself to Brontë's novels in a further exercise of female industry and its often forgotten significance for the making of the *OED*.

CANONS AND CANONICITY

For Murray, the emphasis on texts—whether literary or non-literary—as sources of purely empirical evidence on language in use would, in the ideal world, render qualitative or canonical concerns irrelevant. 'Slips from any current book, review, or other work are acceptable', as he noted in the 1879 *Appeal*, emphasizing the remit of inclusivity—the dictionary as 'inventory' of language—which had been seen as pre-eminent since the very beginning (see Mugglestone 2005, 2009). As Richard Chenevix Trench had argued in the two formative lectures for the dictionary project which he delivered to the London Philological Society in November 1857, the dictionary-maker was no longer to be regarded as a critic, proffering opinions on the legitimacy or otherwise of various words or senses. Instead, the prime role of the lexicographer was as a historian whose approach to language was marked by impartiality and objectivity, as well as by scientific rigour. 'It is, let me once more repeat, for those who use a language to sift the bran from the flour, to reject that and retain this', Trench exhorted.[22] Usage—and evidence on usage—was pre-eminent. In this light, the subjective discriminations of 'good' and 'bad' usage which could characterize earlier lexicography—as in Johnson's entry for *shabby* (a word which, he declared 'ought not to be admitted into the language') or *roundabout* (which, his dictionary states, should be excluded from books)—were firmly rejected. The true responsibility of the lexicographer, Trench countered, was simply to construct an 'inventory of the language' or—in yet another generic transformation—a 'biography' of each word or sense in which 'impartial hospitality' alone would influence the information to be included.

For Victorian readers, both those who read for the dictionary and those who merely sought information within its pages, this remit could challenge habitual expectations about authority, evidence, and the very nature of lexicography. As the contemporary reception of the *OED* confirms, the use of evidence from Victorian novels—and especially from modern, popular, and eminently non-canonical texts—repeatedly emerged as a topos of particular concern. Rhoda Broughton's use of *acrobatically*, for example, appeared prominently in the first fascicle of the *OED*, having been cited from her novel *Second Thoughts*: 'Most of them are standing acrobatically on their heads.' Dated 1880, this attested a new adverbial extension from *acrobatic*, itself a relatively recent word within Victorian English (Murray had traced the latter to 1861 in Bishop George Smith's *Ten Weeks in Japan*: 'One of the actors came forth before the crowd of holiday-makers and performed a variety of acrobatic evolutions'). For the philologist

---

[22] Trench, 8.

(and historical lexicographer), citations such as that by Broughton fulfilled important criteria. Just as Trench had specified in his lectures, 'it is in every case desirable that the *first* authority for a word's use in the language... should be adduced'.[23] In terms of the dictionary entry as biography, Broughton's novel hence provided a 'register of... birth' for a hitherto unrecorded form, as did her use of the superlative *accentedest* in her earlier novel *Nancy* (1873): '"Algy!" repeat I, in a tone of the profoundest, accentedest surprise.'

Early reviewers could, however, raise rather different concerns, especially in rela-tion to the ability of writers such as Broughton, associated with popular sensation fiction for much of her career, to be considered as an 'authority' for language at all. A lengthy review in *John Bull* in February 1884, for example, cited *acrobatically* as a word 'so completely the coinage of the present day that we are surprised to meet with [it] in such good company'. While modernity—the use of all too recent history— could, as here, be used to provide one source of critical opposition, principles of per-ceived canonicity and the vexed issue of legitimate authority clearly provided others. *Acrobatically* was a form verified only by 'the somewhat questionable authority of Miss Rhoda Broughton', the reviewer continued, raising the evidently problematic issue of 'how far the right of coining words... can properly be conceded to the female novelist'. While the reviewer acknowledged that such entries undoubtedly demonstrated the assiduity of 'the various readers who have lent their services in the compilation of lists of words', the question of whether such efforts had been misdirected clearly served to evoke palpable unease.

Such anxieties—on canonicity and the nature of appropriate evidence for the dictionary—were replicated on many occasions within both the public and private reception of the *OED*. As *The Times* also noted in reviewing this first fascicle in 1884, 'though a scientific dictionary should be by no means Della Cruscan in its selection of words, it should surely maintain as far as possible a classical standard in its selection of authors quoted'. The use of *The Pirates of Penzance* in the entry for *all* ('A pirati-cal maid of all work') had, for instance, evidently disturbed popular precepts about what dictionaries could or should do in substantiating the facts of usage. The preced-ing quotation—from Dickens's *Oliver Twist* ('Brittles was a lad of allwork')—tellingly attracted no such comment. A similar dichotomy was in evidence in responses to *sourish*, used by Eliot in *Adam Bede* ('I believe he meant right at bottom; but... he was sourish-tempered') which was deemed unexceptionable in reactions to the dic-tionary, and *maturish*, verified by a single citation from George Meredith's *Diana of the Crossways* ('She played... the maturish young woman smitten by an adorable youth'). 'What justification is there for "maturish—somewhat mature"?' demanded the *Yorkshire Post*, clearly resistant to the notion that Meredith's usage might provide justification enough. A literary double standard can be all too perceptible, illustrat-ing too how a canon for the 19th-century novel was clearly in the process of being

---

[23] Trench, 29.

established, including where its parameters might be seen to lie. Neologisms by popular novelists such as Joseph Shorthouse attract marked scepticism, as in his use of *enspiritualize* in *Sir Percival*. Included by Henry Bradley in the *OED* in 1891, a review in the *Athenaeum* firmly castigated 'the insertion of … useless modern coinages' from which 'nothing is gained'—either by the dictionary or those who consulted its pages in search of properly authoritative information. As in the *OED*'s earlier definition of *authority* ('The quotation or book acknowledged, or alleged, to settle a question of opinion or give conclusive testimony'), the interpretative latitude between 'acknowledged' and 'alleged' seemed to offer considerable scope for popular debate. 'Perhaps the compilers have not been as fastidious as some would wish in the selection of the illustrative quotations, especially for words of modern origin and usage', as another review in *The Times* ventured in 1889.

Comments of this kind repeatedly foregrounded issues of divergent acceptability and divergent value within Victorian writing and reception, as well as raising equally evaluative concerns about the ability of certain Victorian novelists to act as sources of evidence or authority within the dictionary at all.[24] Could Jerome K. Jerome really act as a witness to the use of *rag*, a letter to the *TLS* in 1904 likewise demanded, highly critical of the fact that 'literature' for Murray and his co-editors seemed to signify anything that was written, rather than acting as a signal of qualitative worth. Such concerns remained, of course, at odds with the fundamental credo of the dictionary. 'All, all shall enter', Frederick Furnivall had declared in a circular to the Philological Society in 1863.[25] The democracy of words which he envisaged for the dictionary was, he stressed, in no way to be a 'National Portrait Gallery' of English worthies—but a sphere in which descriptive equality instead governed an overarching ideal of linguistic inclusivity, embracing 'all the members of the race of English words'. Murray's determined inclusion of Broughton (as well as his use of newspapers and other popular or ephemeral texts) can on many occasions be seen to emblematize his reluctance to engage with the kind of hierarchical principles of 'best writers' and 'polite authors' which featured in Johnson's earlier dictionary.[26] Here too, as its own original title confirms, the *OED* would indeed be deliberately 'new'. As Murray argued in his lectures, Johnson's decision to provide 'support and illustration of every word and sense, as far as possible, by quotations drawn from accredited writers' was, here in a critical evaluation of a rather different kind, merely evidence of what Murray deemed to be Johnson's 'characteristic failure' in terms of lexicography.

---

[24] Interestingly, reservations about the admissibility or otherwise of poetic citations are rarely expressed, suggesting a perceptual generic positioning of the 'poetic' within the categories of 'high' and non-ephemeral writing.

[25] Fredrick Furnivall, *Circular to the Members of the Philological Society* (London: The Philological Society, 1863), 3.

[26] See e.g. the full title of Johnson's 1755 dictionary: *A Dictionary of the English Language: in which the Words are Deduced from their Originals, and Illustrated in their Different Signification by Examples from the Best Writers.*

DESCRIPTIVISM AND DISSENT

Such self-evident tensions in terms of the relative validity of different source materials were perhaps still more pertinent in their presence behind the scenes and in the making of the dictionary in itself. Here too descriptivism—especially as manifested in the decision to record the shifting language of late Victorian England—could seem both controversial as well as unduly liberal. Broughton's use of *accentedest*, for example, inserted by Murray in the proofs of the first fascicle, attracted the censure of one of Murray's most valued critical readers for the dictionary, Henry Hucks Gibbs. It was a 'horrid word', Gibbs objected to Murray in a letter written in July 1882—surely a species of 'solecism' which 'should not find entrance without a note of reprobation'. Editorial responsibility in this content, he advised, should indubitably mean editing out—or, as Gibbs added, 'When Miss Broughton writes English I should quote her, but else …'. Innovative usage here was perceived to slide into error, lexical creativity into aberration in a process of reception which was clearly very different to that accorded to creative nonce-formations by Dickens or Thackeray. Broughton's *accentedest* was 'only slovenly writing', Gibbs instead opined.

Such faults, Gibbs contended, could be traced to the very nature of Victorian print culture which he characterized by its 'easy printing and multitude of books'. While 'there are many indefensible words used in all periods', he noted, Victorian novelists were in this respect perhaps especially culpable 'because of the rapidity with which men can now write and print and of the omnivorous greed which makes readers swallow everything'.[27] Even given descriptive principles, he argued, surely it was still the business of the lexicographer 'to reject some rubbish which passes for words'. Contesting fundamental precepts of the dictionary, Gibbs hence questioned whether each and every word really needed to be accorded a linguistic 'life-history' or a record of its date of birth: 'it is well—very well—to fix the first entry of a word into the language; but', he cautioned, 'you must be quite sure that it *has* entered … and is not a mere vagrant knocking at the door'.

Exchanges such as these can offer illuminating insights into conceptions of canonicity, literary value, and attitudes to 'proper' lexicography in Victorian England. In particular, Gibbs's long-standing commitment to a dictionary which, as Trench had contended in his 1857 lectures, was to be a 'lexicon totius Anglicitatus' (and in which it is the expressed 'duty' of the lexicographer 'to make the inventory complete'), sits uneasily with his accusations of 'vagrancy' or 'rubbish' in the lexis of popular Victorian writing, and with his resistance to the carefully factual exposition which characterized Murray's replies. Gibbs would, for example, take similar issue with *accidented* ('Characterized by accidents'), which was attested in Stevenson's *New Arabian Nights* and duly quoted by

---

[27] Henry Hucks Gibbs to James Murray, 20 July 1882 (Murray Papers).

Murray in the dictionary ('The highest and most accidented of the sandhills immedi-ately adjoined: and from these I could overlook Northmour'). The fact that the word was additionally supported by a quotation from the *Daily News* (sent in by Furnivall from his morning newspaper) did not, in Gibbs's view, lend the proposed entry further cred-ibility. Murray's use of citations from Mary Elizabeth Braddon, judged another 'hasty writer' by Gibbs (and, as such, yet another casualty of the 'easy printing' of Victorian England) was to be equally problematic. Braddon 'grinds out novels by the yard, and does not give her self time to think about whether she is using good English or not', Gibbs argued in another forceful letter, giving this as his prime 'objection to her as an *authority*, where better can be had'.[28]

As here, the popularity and productivity of the Victorian novelists could be con-structed as active demerits. If 'great writers' were prototypically assumed to craft their prose, slowly honing their words into perfected order, writers such as Braddon or Linton, as Gibbs made plain in the same letter, '*have not time* to be sure of their work'. As a result, as another qualitatively loaded metaphor in his letters indicates, even if novelists of this kind 'have good horses in their stable, they bring out some sorry hacks sometimes'. *Hack* in this sense, as the *OED* would later eloquently explain, is used '*depreciatively*', to sig-nify 'a sorry or worn out horse; a jade'. For Murray, Gibbs continued, the lesson was clear: 'take in preference to them instances if you can from people who give themselves time to think'—though, as Gibbs added in a further comment laden with gendered atti-tudes to usage and validity, even this precept was to be used with caution: 'Many who do think have not the faculty of writing clear intelligible English. Witness my cousin Miss Yonge—popular as she is.'

Such images of qualitative discrimination are, of course, equally embedded in other Victorian discourses in which sensation fiction was, in particular, often to be castigated for its status as purely commercial commodity, as well as for its transgressive engage-ment with issues of morality, propriety, or feminine decorum. As Henry Longueville Mansel had stated in the *Quarterly Review* in 1863, 'no divine influence can be imagined as presiding over the birth' of works of this kind 'beyond the market-law of demand and supply; no more immortality is dreamed of than for the fashions of the current season'.[29] The ephemerality of such works was further reified by a presumed absence of enduring value. As Mansel continued in terms which closely presage Gibbs's own strictures on quotation sources and the *OED*:

> A commercial atmosphere floats around works of this class, redolent of the manufactory and the shop...These circumstances of production naturally have their effect on the quality of the articles produced. Written to meet an ephemeral demand, aspiring only to an ephemeral existence, it is natural that they should have recourse to rapid and ephemeral methods of awakening the interest of their readers.

[28] Henry Hucks Gibbs to James Murray, 3 May 1883 (Murray Papers).
[29] H.L. Mansel, 'Sensation Novels', *Quarterly Review* 113 (April 1863): 481–514.

Writing of this kind could, of course, attract other opinions (Henry James, for instance, rigorously defended Braddon against all charges of 'slovenly English').[30] Nevertheless, the literary (and indeed moral) quality of the Victorian sensation novel was repeatedly questioned; the novels of Mary Elizabeth Braddon and Ellen Wood are not 'works of art', an article on 'Novel Writing: How it is Done' similarly expounded in *The Ladies' Treasury* in 1886, again drawing attention to the speed of production (and implied hastiness) which characterized popular fiction of this kind.[31] An article in 1892 disparagingly depicted such texts as the chosen reading of 'young misses' who 'do not get beyond the 'lovely tales' of Mrs Braddon or Mrs Henry Wood's *East Lynne* which', the writer adds, 'seems to be a standard work among a certain class'.[32] The productivity (and commercial success) of Dickens—as well the speed of writing which serial publication imposed—meanwhile remained exempt from scrutiny and comments of this kind, as did his pre-eminent status as literary authority within the *OED* as well as outside it.[33]

The fact that such antipathies towards certain types of writing (and, by extension, certain types of evidence) could be shared by the Delegates of Oxford University Press added further tensions in this respect within the making of the *OED*. The Delegates' edict of 1883, for example, called for 'Quotations illustrative of modern literary words to be taken as far as possible from great writers'. While in harmony with the kind of literary scruples discussed above, this clearly sits at odds with the original 1859 *Proposal's* insistence that 'we accept as authorities all English books', as well as challenging the early principle, articulated by Herbert Coleridge, that 'the literary merit or demerit of any particular writer…is a subject upon which the Lexicographer is bound to be almost indifferent'.[34] Modern quotations (those which appear in texts after 1880) were viewed with similar distrust by the Delegates; untried by time, the forms they illustrated were, yet again, seen as potentially ephemeral and hence unworthy of lexicographical record (unless, of course, they happened to be legitimized within a 'famous quotation'). The request that words or senses of this kind should be avoided in the making of the dictionary prompted an irate response form Murray, here in an undated sheet of notes which remains in the Murray Papers. 'I refuse', Murray stated categorically. As he continued, 'To an enormous number of men the "modern instances" are the favourite feature, as I know from the visitors who

---

[30]   Henry James, 'Miss Braddon', *The Nation* 9 (November 1865): 593–95, 595: 'Let not the curious public take for granted that, from a literary point of view, her works are contemptible. Miss Braddon writes neither fine English nor slovenly English; not she. She writes what we may call very knowing English. If her readers have not read George Eliot and Thackeray and all the great authorities, she assuredly has.'

[31]   C.J. Hamilton, 'Novel Writing: How It Is Done', *The Ladies' Treasury: A Household Magazine* (1886): 83.

[32]   L.M.H.C. 'Words and Workers', *The Monthly Packet* (1892): 42.

[33]   Dickens stands as one of the ten most cited writers in the *OED*, based on the statistics available from the second edition of the *OED* (1989). While Shakespeare and the Bible take clear precedence in terms of number of citations, Dickens—along with Sir Walter Scott—are the only novelists included in this ranking, though citations from Scott (at over 16,000) are almost double those for Dickens (at just over 8,500).

[34]   Cited in K.M. Elisabeth Murray, *Caught in the Web*, 195, from a draft report of the Dictionary Committee *circa* 1860 at Oxford University Press.

have inspected the proofs'; the *OED* was, he stressed, intended to be a 'scientific dictionary', not a subjective exercise in literary appreciation. Or as Murray trenchantly informed
the Philological Society in his Presidential Address of 1884, in reality 'the only rule' for
the dictionary was 'to take the best quotation you had for the word you had to illustrate,
and not be so silly as to choose a poor quotation because it had a big name tacked on
to it'.[35] As this suggests, the canonical imperatives urged upon Murray in relation to the
Victorian novel could, at least at times, be steadfastly rejected.

Debates of this kind, enacted behind the scenes in the making of the dictionary as well
as in the columns of journals and newspapers, hence offer a number of significant insights
not only into Murray's commitment to the 'impartial hospitality' which acted as one of the
hallmarks of the *OED*, but also into the ways in which the recurrent preconceptions about
the overwhelming presence of 'great writers' within the *OED* might also be approached.[36].
As a number of critics have noted, it is clear that quotations from such sources can dominate in the patterns of evidence deployed in the published text. In this context, it should of
course be remembered that the citations included in any entry represent those selected as
illustrative examples for publication; the underlying analysis of meaning and use in each
entry depended on a far wider range of evidence (much of which still exists in the archival resources of the *OED*). Nevertheless, citations from 'great writers', given the reading
preferences of volunteers, are abundantly represented in the dictionary's files, as well as in
the dictionary itself. Under *citizen*, for example, one can find a narrative history of development characterized by writers such as Macaulay and Ruskin, Walpole, Emerson, and
Gladstone. Charlotte Brontë, Leslie Stephen, and Nathaniel Hawthorne likewise document
the various uses of *divert*. As such patterns of evidence suggest, however critical Murray
might have been in his lectures of the canonical precedents set by Johnson, it seems clear
that hierarchical associations of the 'best writers' ('writers of the first reputation' were to be
preferred to 'those of an inferiour rank', as Johnson had argued)[37] often continued to influence how readers selected both reading and data for the dictionary, as well as influencing
other widely shared judgements about editing and expendability within it.

Conversely, it remains equally clear that non-canonical and popular writers such as
Braddon, Collins, or R.S. Surtees were also both read for the dictionary and liberally
cited within it, as well as being resolutely defended in their role—and significance—as
witnesses to Victorian linguistic history. Just as Murray argued for the salience of citations from newspapers ('they show how the language grows—they make visible the
actual steps which for earlier stages we must reconstruct by inference'),[38] the same

[35] Murray, 'Thirteenth Annual Address', 372.

[36] See e.g. Jürgen Schäfer, *Documentation in the O.E.D.: Shakespeare and Nashe as Test Cases* (Oxford:
Oxford University Press, 1980); Charlotte Brewer, 'The Use of Literary Quotations in the Oxford English
Dictionary', *Review of English Studies* n.s. 61 (2010): 91–125; though see also John Considine, 'Literary
Classics in *OED* Quotation Evidence', *Review of English Studies* n.s. 60 (2009): 515–37 for other views.

[37] See Johnson, *Plan*, 30–31.

[38] James Murray to Bartholomew Price, Secretary to the Delegates of Oxford University Press, 9
June 1882 (Murray Papers). The letter is discussed in Lynda Mugglestone, ed. *Lexicography and the OED:
Pioneers in the Untrodden Forest* (Oxford: Oxford University Press, 2002), 13–14.

arguments could—for the lexicographer and linguist—equally extend to the popular and potentially ephemeral literary text.[39] It is not Eliot or Dickens but Eliza Lynn Linton's *My Love* which provides the only evidence in the Victorian *OED* for the colloquial *bumbler* ('He is a bit of a bumbler when all is said and done'). Similarly, it is Linton who, in 1885, provides late-Victorian confirmation of 'colossally' in the sense 'hugely, extremely' in *The Autobiography of Christopher Kirkland* (a novel which also serves to attest the idiomatic use of *cocoanut*: 'You need not bother that silly cocoanut of yours', as the eponymous hero is informed). Late Victorian uses of *kid* (to mean a child), of the topical *bloomerized*, or *kick* (to mean a new style) are likewise all attested in her work. In the same way, over 1,000 quotations from Braddon's work appear throughout the dictionary's first edition, as under *apoplectically* where her novel *Asphodel* (1881) supplies the only cited evidence ('The Rector was sighing, somewhat apoplectically'), or *gaudy* where a citation from *Joshua Haggard's Daughter* (1876) accompanies an earlier one from Dickens's *Nicholas Nickleby*. Surtees would be cited over 500 times, while Broughton too would make regular appearances, not only in *accentedest* and *acrobatically*, the entries for which remained unchanged—against Gibbs's advice—in the final text of the first fascicle, but also under *bemaster* and *circumstance, figuratively*, and *impolite* (amid hundreds of other examples). Ellen Wood would similarly appear with striking frequency (almost 400 citations appear in the published text), while Yonge—in spite of Gibbs's reservations—emerges as one of the most cited female writers within the dictionary. Writing the dictionary could be a careful balancing act, between canonical and non-canonical, and linguistic principles and popular language attitudes. As Murray insisted in a carefully revised response to the Delegates in October 1883:

> if the Dictionary is to be made at all, it must be by taking the best of the materials we have, even though that best consist of newspaper quotations, and quotations after 1875…I am sure the Delegates will give me credit for inserting 'famous quotations' under every word, *when we have them*. [original emphasis][40]

HISTORIANS AND CRITICS

As Murray repeatedly sought to impress upon both Gibbs and the Delegates, the editor of a modern dictionary was 'not to sit in judgement on words & decide on their merits'. If Stevenson, in writing *Treasure Island*, had, in the opinion of one critical reader, used 'bad English' (surely an adverb had been used instead of an adjective in 'The air … smelt more

[39] Speed of production could, as here, be a virtue, bringing one closer to contemporary and idiomatic English untrammelled by extensive revision.

[40] Objections of this kind would recur in communications from the Delegates, especially in the various battles over size and cost of the dictionary in 1893 and 1896.

freshly than down beside the marsh'), Murray's view remained intransigently empirical. Stevenson's quotation was to be included, the evaluative—and prescriptive scruples—dismissed. The sense was both clear and descriptively supported. Similar were objections raised to the use of *like* in the sense 'as' by Darwin, Morris, and Jerome K. Jerome; 'untaught or careless', 'merely vulgar'; 'none of these are of authority for correct modern prose', state a set of annotations in the margin of the relevant proof sheet. Subjectivities of this kind were again swiftly dispelled; evidence from all three appears, unmodified, in the published entry.

Critical judgement was not, on the other hand, to be abdicated entirely. If quotations provided the facts, the lexicographer's interpretative skill was also salient. Victorian novelists here offered many puzzles for the philologist. Did Eliot in using *euphuism* in *Felix Holt* ('Those are your roundabout euphuisms that dress up swindling') really intend to signify the kind of affected style of writing which had its origin in Lyly? Or was her intended—and rather different—meaning instead that of *euphemism*? Bradley, editing the word in the late 1880s, decided that the latter was the most likely explanation, labelling Eliot's citation as 'erroneous', together with a similar use by Gaskell in *Wives and Daughters* in 1866: '"If anything did—go wrong, you know", said Cynthia, using a euphuism for death.' Both, in other words, were seen as usages which had been inadvertently deployed. Even here, however, the descriptive status of evidence was maintained. The facts are cited, and interpretation is objectively founded, based on careful textual examination.[41]

Problematic interpretations of a different kind surrounded the word *brean* in Stevenson's *The Merry Men*. 'A child might have read their dismal story, and yet it was not until I touched that actual piece of mankind that the full horror of the charnel brean burst upon my spirit' stated the printed text, in a citation sent in by an assiduous reader. For Murray, however, the meaning remained opaque, resisting definition even after lengthy consideration. Contemporary Victorian writers in this respect offered particular advantages since they could—as indeed happened on this occasion—be contacted directly by the lexicographer in search of help. Murray wrote to Stevenson in February 1887 to 'ask…for light on this dark word' which had been sent to the dictionary by 'some industrious reader'. 'Can you tell us anything about the meaning and source…and where else we can find it?', he requested. Stevenson's reply indeed elucidated *brean* with ease, bringing Murray's quest to an end (together with the potential inclusion of *brean* in the relevant fascicle). As Stevenson explained, *brean* had in fact come into existence merely through his failure to read the proofs with sufficient attention ('that proof was never read; hence these tears', as he began his letter to Murray). The real word, and that which he had originally written, was 'ocean'.

---

[41] That interpretations of a more prescriptive nature can intervene elsewhere is of course a casualty of the very nature of a dictionary as human formation, especially where issues of on-going linguistic change are concerned. See further Mugglestone, '"An Historian not a Critic": The Standard of Usage in the *OED*', in *Lexicography and the OED: Pioneers in the Untrodden Forest*, ed. Lynda Mugglestone (Oxford: Oxford University Press, 2002) and *Lost for Words*, chapter 5.

Similar processes of discovery and elucidation attended thousands of other words, again spanning both canonical and non-canonical writers. Mary Elizabeth Braddon was contacted about *arolla* as used in her novel *Asphodel* (1881), George Eliot about *adust* in *Romola* ('He was tired and adust with long riding'), and Charlotte Yonge about *free-lance* which seemed to signify a type of medieval mercenary in her novel *The Lances of Lynwood*. Murray wrote to Edmund Gosse about the identity of a 'Claude Lorraine glass', and to Meredith about his perplexing use of the word *pilkins* in *The Ordeal of Richard Feverel*. In each case precise information was returned. Eliot replied with reference to her stylistic preference for the rhythm of *adust* ('In a dusty condition, affected by dust') against that of *dusty*. 'So explained by the author quoted', as the entry in the first edition of the *OED* attested.[42] Gosse wrote an extremely full reply in July 1889, recommending further sources of information where Murray might procure the evidence needed for the dictionary. Meredith provided a particularly illuminating history for *pilkins* (even if one which couldn't be included in the dictionary entry). It 'came to me from a person…on a wayside bench outside a village alehouse among the South Downs', he explained. Meredith had sat down next to him and, as he noted, they had begun 'talking of a case something like to that mentioned in the novel, these "pilkins" being a coarse grain. As the word was new to me I told him to repeat it—with him it was quite familiar.' Whether *pilkins* should also be included as an entry in the *OED* was, at least to Meredith, in doubt: 'Probably it was merely local, & it might be rejected', he surmised.[43] Mary Elizabeth Braddon likewise provided a full account of *arolla* and how she had come to use it. Rather than being imaginary, as Murray had originally surmised, she had encountered it in some books borrowed from the Royal Geographical Society while doing some preparatory reading for her novel. As Murray's entry in the first fascicle was hence able to confirm, it designated the 'name given in French Switzerland to the *Pinus* cembra', a sense which was precisely illustrated by the accompanying citation from Braddon: 'Where huge arollas of a thousand years' growth spread their black branches against the snow-line'. Charlotte Yonge meanwhile provided the vital information that *freelance* was not a Victorian innovation, but had an earlier history in Scott's *Ivanhoe* from where she had borrowed it.

Such processes of discovery repeatedly confirmed the validity of what the *OED* sought to achieve, as well as further establishing its superiority over earlier works. Textual accuracy—the true accountability of a dictionary to both history and evidence—was salient. As historian and as critic Murray looked back at Johnson and was astonished at the fallibilities of literary evidence which had attended his work. All too often, as Murray stated

[42] The entry for *adust* (adj.) was revised in December 2011 on *OED Online*, and the reference to Eliot's communication was removed at the same time.

[43] An undated letter in the *OED* archives at Oxford University Press from George Meredith to James Murray. Murray in fact decided to retain *pilkins* in the *OED*, labelling it 'local', and giving Meredith's *The Ordeal of Richard Feverel* as the sole evidence for its use: 'He swears soam o' our chaps steals pilkins'; 'The Bantam said he had seen Tom secreting pilkins in a sack.' Its inclusion does, however, also lend support to arguments about the privileging of words used in literary texts within the *OED*.

in a lecture in 1910, Johnson's citations are 'merely an echo of the original'. Indeed, 'it was only very slowly, and with reluctance, that we realised that the caution "Verify your references" was just as needful in the case of Johnson as of any man who ever lived'. The fictive identity of Stevenson's *brean* proved Murray's point (against scores of similar lexical 'ghosts' which appeared unchallenged in Johnson's text), as well as further countering the Delegates' scruples about modern evidence, and the documentation of ongoing lexical and semantic change. Instead, the range, abundance, and diversity of Victorian writing would prove of incontestable value for the dictionary. Novelists across the literary spectrum—read and extracted by the Victorian reading public—would in this respect aid in establishing countless narratives of lexical and semantic history in a text which was itself widely—and rightly—regarded as an emblematic triumph of Victorian industry and achievement.

SUGGESTED READING

Brewer, Charlotte. 'The Use of Literary Quotations in the Oxford English Dictionary'. *Review of English Studies* n.s. 61 (2010): 91–125.

Considine, John. 'Literary Classics in *OED* Quotation Evidence'. *Review of English Studies* n.s. 60 (2009): 515–37.

Mugglestone, Lynda. '"An Historian not a Critic": The Standard of Usage in the *OED*'. In *Lexicography and the OED: Pioneers in the Untrodden Forest*. Edited by Lynda Mugglestone. Oxford: Oxford University Press, 2002, 189–206.

——, ed. *Lexicography and the OED: Pioneers in the Untrodden Forest*. Oxford: Oxford University Press, 2002.

——. *Lost for Words: The Hidden History of the Oxford English Dictionary*. Yale: Yale University Press, 2005.

——. 'The Oxford English Dictionary; 1857–1928'. In *The Oxford History of English Lexicography*. Edited by A.P. Cowie. 2 vols. Oxford: Oxford University Press, 2009, 1: 230–60.

Murray, James. *The Evolution of English Lexicography*. Oxford: Clarendon Press, 1900. <http://ezproxy.ouls.ox.ac.uk:2118/archive/paper-romanes/>.

Murray, K. M. Elisabeth. *Caught in the Web of Words. James A. H. Murray and the Oxford English Dictionary*. London and New Haven: Yale University Press, 1977.

Schäfer, Jürgen. *Documentation in the O.E.D.: Shakespeare and Nashe as Test Cases*. Oxford: Oxford University Press, 1980.

Taylor, Dennis. *Hardy's Literary Language and Victorian Philology*. Oxford: Clarendon Press, 1993.

8

THE NOVEL AND CENSORSHIP IN LATE-VICTORIAN ENGLAND

BARBARA LECKIE

In the Victorian period, the only print censorship trial targeting a novel occurred in the fall of 1888. The journalist-turned-publisher, Henry Vizetelly, was brought to trial for the publication of provocative English translations of Emile Zola's novels.[1] Shortly after the trial, the National Vigilance Association published a pamphlet, 'Pernicious Literature', documenting the parliamentary debate, the trial, and the press response. The House of Commons debate includes 'a very painful incident' related by Samuel Smith to illustrate the potential dangers of reading Zola. A boy comes across two open pages of a Zola novel in a store window and stops to read: '[t]he matter', Smith claims, 'was of such a leprous character that it would be impossible for any young man who had not learned the divine secret of self control to have read it without committing some form of outward sin within twenty-four hours after'.[2] While an extreme example, this short anecdote captures many of the fears and assumptions animating appeals for print censorship or regulation in the Victorian period: it assumes a direct link between reading and social action; it highlights a category of vulnerable reader (here it is a boy but the most prominent vulnerable reader in the period was typically a young female reader);

---

[1] These editions were provocative because they were inexpensive and translated (thus making them accessible to a broader audience than usual), their titles were known for their sensational appeal (*Madame Bovary*, for example, was one of the novels published by Vizetelly in translation), and they included front matter and Prefaces deliberately highlighting the editions' unexpurgated character, boldness, and 'realism'.

[2] National Vigilance Association, 'Pernicious Literature', in *Documents of Modern Literary Realism*, ed. George J. Becker (Princeton: Princeton University Press, 1963), 335.

and it highlights the availability of the reading material (here it is a store window but cheap publications were equally problematic as were translations that made material available to broader publics.)

The history of the English novel and print censorship remains to be written. This history would be a very short account, however, if it were dedicated only to legal versions of censorship and an impossibly long account if it adopted the broadest possible definition of censorship (variations on 'culture is censorship'). The challenge, then, is to comprehend print censorship in a manner flexible enough to embrace the range of ways in which it worked in Victorian England but still specific enough to retain its ties to the law. In this chapter I want to focus on the English novel and print censorship in the last two decades of the 19th century; it is in this period that many writers and commentators confront and contest restrictions on novelistic representations, and they articulate, concisely and astutely, many factors that contribute to calls for censorship that are, nevertheless, not always aligned with legal censorship.

It is also in this period, as noted above, that censorship and the law come together explicitly in the one legal trial that targets novels—English translations of Zola's novels—in the 19th century. In both contexts—print commentaries and the legal trial—it was censorship for obscene libel (that is, representations of sex and sexuality) that commanded the attention of the censors in these latter decades as opposed to religion (blasphemy) and politics (sedition). I focus here on an overlooked forum for the scrutiny of censorship: Prefaces to novels.[3] Prefaces to novels afford a wonderful opportunity to study the relationship between print censorship and the novel, in general, and print censorship and *this* novel (the novel for which the Preface is written), in particular. They have the institutional authority of the novel itself as well as the marginal *frisson* following from their paratextual status. Many novel Prefaces, in short, engaged explicitly with the question of censorship and the novel and offer some of the most comprehensive, explosive, and incisive dimensions of print censorship in the period.

PRINT CENSORSHIP IN VICTORIAN ENGLAND

Print censorship has long been overlooked as a resonant category in Victorian England in part because of the absence of prominent censorship trials. But it exercised a powerful force on writers, publishers, booksellers, and readers themselves and, I want to argue, was vitally important to the definition and development of the novel. The print censorship debates, as the Prefaces I turn to below illustrate, understood censorship less in

---

[3] For an extended analysis of Prefaces in Vizetelly novel editions and a treatment of the Vizetelly trials see Barbara Leckie, '"A Preface is Written to the Public": Print Censorship, Novel Prefaces, and the Construction of a New Reading Public in Late-Victorian England', *Victorian Literature and Culture* 37 (2009): 447–62.

terms of the law (and a single repressive or restrictive force) and more in terms of censorship as a complicated network of relations, or what Ian Hunter and colleagues call a 'diversity of regulatory mechanisms'.[4] That is, targets of censorship in the late-Victorian censorship debates knew well the toll that censorship exerted on their production and publication, even in the absence of legal force and sensational trials.

In 19th-century England, then, print censorship was inseparable from the production and reception of printed matter and the markets in which such works circulated. The censorship and regulation of print culture, in other words, was not only, or even primarily, related to the legal restriction of printed matter (although such legal cases were important). Further, the controls on print did not typically manifest themselves as the repression of an author or, what Edward de Grazia calls, the 'assault on genius'. Rather, print censorship in 19th-century England is best understood, I want to suggest, in the interrelated contexts of the production of the book (its expense, its size, its prefatory material, its reprint status, its language, its expurgation where relevant, and so on), the reception of the work (the class, gender, age, nationality, and place of readers), and its markets (the periodical journals, the annuals, the newspapers, the circulating libraries, the railway stations, and so on). In this context we can identify the following forms of print regulation: self-censorship (exercised by both authors and readers); family-based censorship (typically exercised by the father and made powerful

---

[4] Ian Hunter, David Saunders, and Dugald Williamson, *On Pornography* (London: Macmillan, 1992), 71. Theoretical approaches to censorship fall into two broads camps. Pre-1985 criticism tends to follow a freedom versus the law model; post-1985 criticism, often influenced by Foucault, tends to focus on networks and a constellation of different factors. In this context, Walter Kendrick, *The Secret Museum: Pornography in Modern Culture* (New York: Viking, 1987) and Ian Hunter et al., *On Pornography* offer the most nuanced accounts of censorship in Victorian print culture, but important gaps and omissions remain as new questions are also raised. The pre-1985 criticism tends to privilege the author's right to free speech; it assumes that the government or state restricts expression and that the goal should be, instead, freedom of expression. The post-1985 group can be further divided into critics who consider the relationship between censorship and language. Most of these theorists take issue with 'free speech' not because they are opposed to freedom of speech but rather because they question the capacity of speech ever to be free. Pierre Bourdieu, for example, refers to a political field which 'produces an effect of censorship by limiting the universe of political discourse, and thereby the universe of what is politically thinkable' (Pierre Bourdieu, *Language and Symbolic Power*, trans. Gino Raymond and Matthew Adamson (Cambridge, MA: Harvard University Press, 1991), 172). And Judith Butler defines implicit censorship as the 'implicit operations of power that rule out in unspoken ways what will remain unspeakable' (Judith Butler, *Excitable Speech: A Politics of the Performative* (New York: Routledge, 1997), 130). Interestingly, their comments closely echo late-Victorian commentary on censorship. For a range of approaches to print censorship in the Victorian period see: Lucy Bland, *Banishing the Beast: English Feminism and Sexual Morality, 1885–1914* (London: Penguin Books, 1991); Edward DeGrazia, *Girls Lean Back Everywhere: The Law of Obscenity and the Assault on Genius* (New York: Random House, 1992); Alan Hunt, *Governing Morals: A Social History of Moral Regulation* (Cambridge: Cambridge University Press, 1999); Paul Hyland and Neil Sammells, eds., *Writing and Censorship in Britain* (London: Routledge, 1992); Peter Keating, *The Haunted Study: A Social History of the English Novel, 1875–1914* (London: Secker, 1989); Robin Myers and Michael Harris, eds., *Censorship and the Control of Print in England and France, 1600–1910* (Winchester: St Paul's, 1992); Lisa A. Sigel, *Governing Pleasures: Pornography and Social Change, 1815–1914* (New York: Rutgers University Press, 2002); and Alan Travis, *Bound and Gagged: A Secret History of Obscenity in England* (London: Profile, 2000).

by the practice of reading out loud); extra-legal institutional censorship (exercised by circulating libraries, public libraries, publishers, and booksellers); as well as legal censorship.

In the context of legal censorship, the three most prominent trials of the period were the *Hicklin v. Regina* trial (for the publication of *The Confessional Unmasked*, a critique of Catholicism) (1868); the Bradlaugh-Besant trial (for the republication of Knowlton's *Fruits of Philosophy*, a birth control manual) (1877–78); and the Vizetelly trial (1888). These trials addressed religious, scientific, and literary writings respectively and articulated fundamental aspects of censorship that reflected all levels of print regulation in Victorian England (that is, they cannot be understood only in their legal context but rather, I would argue, have to be addressed in terms of the production, reception, and markets of the works in question).

The latter decades of the 19th century on which I am focusing here revive a view of the novel that had dominated in the latter decades of the eighteenth and early decades of the nineteenth centuries. In that period, an Evangelical zeal drove several censorship campaigns and also animated an aversion to the novel often articulated in periodical essays, for instance, that promoted the perception of the novel as, by definition and almost without exception, immoral and potentially dangerous, even as—or, more likely, because—the readership for novels was on the rise. While the wholesale critique of the novel had softened in the 1880s and 1890s, fears related to the novel from this earlier period were inflamed again by what was perceived to be at once a broadening of the topics novels chose to address, in part imported from French novels as the references to Zola translations above illustrate, and a broadening of the audiences for whom the novel was available.[5]

This sensitivity to audience reflects a persistent feature of the censorship debates in the Victorian period. In the legal sphere, the Obscene Publications Act (1857) and the Hicklin Standard (1868) defined the approach to print censorship that obtained through the 20th century. In both of these approaches, audience was key to the evaluation of censorship. The Obscene Publications Act alerted the evaluator's attention to material that was distributed, as *The Times* put it in an editorial on 29 June 1857, in 'low thoroughfares' to 'the young, the ignorant, and the vicious', and the Hicklin Standard defined 'the test of obscenity' in terms of works that may 'deprave and

---

[5] The impact of the French novel on defining appropriate boundaries for the English novel was enormous. Long associated with everything corrupt, the licence in range of representation practised by French novelists provoked considerable anxiety in English novelists, readers, and publishers. As I illustrate in this chapter, in the latter decades of the century many novelists began to contest what they perceived to be the narrowness of English literary licence, but it is important to acknowledge that many more novelists participated in the implicit print restrictions than contested them. The rising influence of French authors (Baudelaire, Huysmans, Zola, the Goncourt brothers, etc.) intrigued English novelists who wished to be valued not only for the story they told but also for the art they created. The growth of new and alternative publishing houses in the latter decades of the century (Vizetelly, Bodley Head, John Lane) is also part of this story. On the Victorian novel in France, see Marie-Françoise Cachin's chapter in this volume.

corrupt those whose minds are open to such immoral influences, and into whose hands a publication of this sort might fall'.[6] In the passage preceding this citation, literary quality is explicitly excluded from consideration and in a later section authorial intention is similarly discounted. The only factors worthy of attention when evaluating obscenity, then, are the content of the work in combination with its anticipated readership.

It was in this context that novelists had learned to calibrate carefully their representations so as to ensure the widest possible circulation for their works. But several things changed in the 1880s. The contrast between, as Henry James put it, 'that which they [people] see and that which they speak of, that which they feel to be a part of life and that which they allow to enter literature,'[7] was becoming more starkly visible. This visibility, in part, was due to the liberty granted newspapers in their publications of, if not sexually explicit, then sexually suggestive material. It was in the 1880s that W.T. Stead, for example, launched his 'Maiden Tribute' inquiry into what he called 'the white slave trade' with detailed exposés of the purchase of young girls for sexual trafficking.[8] It was also in the 1880s that one saw a renewed fascination in the titillation afforded by the transcription in the press of detailed divorce cases which again dealt with sexual material. And it was in the 1880s that circulating libraries began to lose their grip on a public that had until this period been satisfied to let these libraries determine the appropriate range of novelistic representation.

In response to this expansion of print freedom in the press, vice societies (ironically led by W.T. Stead himself) sought to suppress an extension of print freedom in other venues (especially the novel);[9] and novelists, the most persistent of whom was George Moore, sought to gain for themselves a similar freedom of expression in their own genre. Novelists began to take greater risks and also to thematize the restrictions they confronted, at the same time as vice societies exerted greater zeal and energy in their suppression. It was this combination, in part, that led to the Vizetelly trials of 1888 and 1889. Without the energy and dedication of George Moore to print freedom, cheap Zola translations might not have been published at this time; but also without the attention and scrutiny of vice societies, in this case the National Vigilance Association, they might not have been prosecuted.

[6] *Law Reports*, '*Regina* v. *Hicklin*', Queen's Bench Cases, vol. 3. (London: William Clowes, 1867–68): 360–79, 371.

[7] Henry James, 'The Art of Fiction', in *Essays on Literature: American Writers, English Writers*, ed. Leon Edel and Mark Wilson (New York: The Library of America, 1984), 670.

[8] See Judith Walkowitz's *City of Dreadful Delight* (Chicago: University of Chicago Press, 1992) for a good analysis of the Maiden Tribute case, in particular, and 1880s London, in general.

[9] There are also several studies of social purity movements of the period that address questions of censorship: Lucy Bland's *Banishing the Beast*, Alan Hunt's *Governing Morals*, and Stefan Petrow's *Policing Morals: The Metropolitan Police and the Home Office, 1870–1914* (Oxford: Clarendon Press, 1994). Finally, Jeffrey Weeks's important *Sex, Politics, and Society: The Regulation of Sexuality since 1800* (London: Longman, 1981) treats pornography, social purity movements, and many other issues related to sexuality.

In this chapter I want to highlight the efforts of three novelists in the early 1890s to redefine the censorship debates in a manner more congenial to their literary production in the wake of the revival of censorship agitation in the 1880s. Their efforts are bracketed by the Vizetelly trials and both the 1895 trial of Oscar Wilde for gross indecency and the 1898 trial of George Bedborough for selling Havelock Ellis's *Sexual Inversion*. These latter two trials do not address novel censorship directly and yet they contributed to ongoing revisions of the intersections between the English novel, print censorship, and the reading public. It is noteworthy that the two trials related to print culture—the Vizetelly and Bedborough trials—target the publisher and bookseller respectively and not the authors. The period I address here is also shaped by recent interventions in the censorship debates by Henry James and George Moore. James's 'The Art of Fiction' and 'The Future of the Novel', among other works, take issue with print restrictions imposed on the novelist.[10] Moore's series of novel prefaces, polemical works, and essays deal much more directly with print censorship and the perceived damage exacted by circulating libraries on the vitality and growth of the English novel.[11]

NOVEL PREFACES: OSCAR WILDE, THOMAS HARDY, AND GRANT ALLEN, 1890–95

Wilde's Preface to *The Picture of Dorian Gray*, Hardy's Prefaces to *Tess* and *Jude the Obscure*, and Allen's Preface to *The British Barbarians* respond to the print censorship debates in very different ways. These were not just debates between a censorship and anti-censorship position but also a debate *within* the anti-censorship position. Wilde advances an art-for-art's sake position that attempts to remove the novel from the debate by severing the connection between art and society and, despite other statements to the contrary, denying the moral force of literature. Hardy, by contrast, focuses on current modes of publication and the construction of the novel-reading audience. And Grant Allen explicitly launches a 'protest' against prevailing systems of print production, interpretations of 'purity', and readership restrictions. Taken together, these Prefaces foreground the next century's struggle with perennial questions about art and its responsibilities to and freedom from its reading audience.

---

[10] See Barbara Leckie, *Culture and Adultery: The Novel, the Newspaper, and the Law, 1857–1914* (Philadelphia: University of Pennsylvania Press, 1999) for a discussion of Henry James and George Moore in the context of print censorship.

[11] Moore is best known for his 1885 *Literature at Nurse, or Circulating Morals: A Polemic on Victorian Censorship*, ed. Pierre Coustillas (Hassocks: Harvester, 1976), but he also discusses censorship at length in novel prefaces, letters to the editor, and other print forums.

Useless Art

Wilde's entanglement with Victorian law, of course, is best known in the context of the 1895 libel and gross indecency trials.[12] But as Richard Ellman, Peter Keating, and Regenia Gagnier suggest in passing, Wilde's Preface to *Dorian Gray* can be read as a statement not only of his aesthetic position but also as a response to the political climate of print censorship; or rather, aestheticism is never entirely separable from the social and political context in which it arises. This Preface is a response to early reviews of Wilde's novel; in this respect, it speaks to that novel's reception history.[13] Unlike most Prefaces, however, it was first published independently, in *The Fortnightly Review* in March 1891, and it was republished a month later in the first edition of *Dorian Gray*.[14]

This Preface does not invoke censorship explicitly but it can be read as a strategic response to protect the novelist by insisting on severing the connection, prominent in social purity discourse and in the Zola example with which I open, between reading and action. Instead of arguing that novels had a positive social and moral function, Wilde refused the terms of the debate.[15] By writing his Preface as a series of aphorisms Wilde already challenged the standard format of an English Preface. Not surprisingly, his Preface is closer in style to antecedents of the art-for-art's sake movement. Théophile Gautier's Preface to *Mademoiselle de Maupin*, for example, like Wilde's, was written in response to negative reviews of an article he wrote outlining his aesthetic position.

The Preface to Gautier's novel severs the connection not only between reading and action, but also between representation and the author. 'It is ridiculous to say that a man

---

[12]   In *Modernism and the Theater of Censorship* (New York: Oxford University Press, 1996), Adam Parkes notes that these trials can also be read as 'obscenity trials' (11).

[13]   Wilde's novel was first published in *Lippincott's Monthly Magazine* in the year following the second Vizetelly trial. When Wilde published the novel in book form he significantly revised a great deal of the text, arguably censoring his own work in response to the many negative reviews the first version of the novel received. During the Wilde trials, the prosecuting attorney notably always cited from the *Lippincott's* version, claiming that the later novel had been 'purged'. See H. Montgomery Hyde, *The Trials of Oscar Wilde* (New York: Dover, 1962), 111. The controversy in response to the first version of the novel took place primarily in the pages of the *Scots Observer* (to which Wilde also contributed) and is discussed in some detail by Regenia Gagnier in her *Idylls of the Marketplace: Oscar Wilde and the Victorian Public* (Stanford: Stanford University Press, 1986) and others. The relationship between Wilde's novel and Vizetelly's trials is discussed briefly by Lawrence Danson, 'Wilde as Critic and Theorist', in *The Cambridge Companion to Oscar Wilde*, ed. Peter Raby (Cambridge: Cambridge University Press, 1997): 80–95, 86–8, and Anne Margaret Daniel, 'Wilde the Writer', in *Palgrave Advances in Oscar Wilde Studies*, ed. Frederick S. Roden (New York: Palgrave, 2004), 36–71, 46–7.

[14]   See Laurel Brake, 'The Discourses of Journalism: "Arnold and Pater" Again—and Wilde', in *Pater in the 1990s*, ed. Laurel Brake and Ian Small (Greensboro: ELT Press, 1991), 43–61 for a good discussion of the climate of censorship in the 1880s and 1890s and for a treatment of Wilde's Preface in this context.

[15]   As Peter Keating notes in *The Haunted Study*, when Wilde wrote in his Preface, '"There is no such thing as a moral or an immoral book. Books are well written or badly written. That is all", he was not only proclaiming aesthetic doctrine, he was also openly mocking the law' (243). Wilde's art-for-art's sake defence, Keating notes, would not be acceptable in a British court for another sixty years.

is a drunkard because he describes an orgy, a rake because he describes debauchery'.[16] He is especially scathing when he turns to what he terms the 'utilitarian critics'. Like other Prefaces, and the censorship debates as a whole, Gautier also compares the evaluation of his alleged immorality to classic writers who have preceded him. He mocks the question the utilitarian critic asks: 'What is the use of this book?', and he writes: 'No, you imbeciles, no, idiotic and goitrous creatures that you are, a book does not make jellied soup; a novel is not a pair of seamless boots.'[17] His comments on usefulness and beauty resonate with Wilde's own thinking on these issues:

> Nothing beautiful is indispensable to life…Nothing is really beautiful unless it is useless; everything useful is ugly, for it expresses a need, and the needs of man are ignoble and disgusting, like his poor weak nature. The most useful place in the house is the lavatory …pleasure seems to me the goal of life, and the only useful thing in the world.[18]

Consider the Preface to Wilde's novel in the context of these comments and the general climate of print censorship:

> The artist is the creator of beautiful things.
> To reveal art and conceal the artist is art's aim.
> The critic is he who can translate into another manner or a new material his impression of beautiful things.
> The highest as the lowest form of criticism is a mode of autobiography.
> Those who find ugly meanings in beautiful things are corrupt without being charming. This is a fault.
> Those who find beautiful meanings in beautiful things are cultivated. For these there is hope.
> They are the elect to whom beautiful things mean only beauty.
> There is no such thing as a moral or an immoral book. Books are well written, or badly written. That is all.[19]

If most critiques of censorship in the period put their focus on print production, circulation, markets, and reception, Wilde inflects the debate differently. He seeks to keep the focus on art and to mock the focus on the reader. In Wilde's terms, it is neither the artist nor the book itself that produces an immoral work, it is the reader figured as the critic.

---

[16] Théophile Gautier, *Mademoiselle de Maupin*, trans. Joanna Richardson (Harmondsworth: Penguin, 1981), 34. This point is also made in 'The Soul of Man Under Socialism'. The Wilde trials, in many ways, point to the failure of novelists to dictate the terms of the debate when it came to the law. To write about a drunkard was to name one's self a drunkard, so to speak.

[17] Gautier, *Mademoiselle de Maupin*, 36.

[18] Gautier, *Mademoiselle de Maupin*, 39.

[19] Oscar Wilde, *The Picture of Dorian Gray*, ed. Norman Page (Peterborough, ON: Broadview, 1998), 41. Subsequent citations appear in the text.

Criticism, then, is a form of autobiography in so far as it may betray the critic's immoral thoughts. Art in and of itself has no use-value—the famous last line of the Preface is 'All art is quite useless' (42)—and the question of a work's morality is accordingly, and often contradictorily, sidelined. The aesthetic argument—the value of art as art—anticipates the most successful response to print censorship that would develop in the modernist period. Instead of highlighting the need to protect the reader, the emphasis slowly shifted to the need to protect art (a category that had been eclipsed by the category of the reader in the earlier debates).

'Household Reading'

Where Wilde refuses the moral terms of the censorship debates that position art in relation to its social function, Hardy, like George Moore, refuses the construction of a default reader who dictates the limits of acceptable representation. Unlike Wilde, then, he takes up the debate on its own terms and within the proscribed boundaries. Hardy is keenly attuned to the ways in which conditions of production impinge on what a writer can say. Hardy writes his first Preface to *Tess* in 1891. His views on print regulation, however, are fully elaborated in an 1890 symposium on 'Candour in English Fiction' that was published in the *New Review*.[20] When 'observers and critics remark, as they often remark, that the great bulk of English fiction of the present day is characterized by its lack of sincerity, they usually omit to trace this serious defect to external, or even eccentric causes'. Instead of focusing on the imagination or insight of the author, Hardy suggests, one should consider 'the conditions under which our popular fiction is produced'.[21] In 'representations of the world, the passions ought to be proportioned as in the world itself' (16). Encapsulating the main points in the censorship debates to date, he stresses the impact of 'the magazine and the circulating library' on shaping literary production tailored to 'what is called household reading, which means, or is made to mean, the reading either of the majority in a household or of the household collectively' (17).[22] The result is a form of implicit censorship:

> What this practically amounts to is that the patrons of literature—no longer Peers with a taste—acting under the censorship of prudery, rigorously exclude from the pages they regulate subjects that have been made, by general approval of the best

[20] The other participants were Walter Besant and Eliza Lynn Linton. Both writers, like Hardy, discussed audience and public opinion and both deplored 'the barriers set up by Mrs. Grundy', E. Lynn Linton, 'Candour in English Fiction', *New Review* 2 (January 1890): 11–14, 11.

[21] Thomas Hardy, 'Candour in English Fiction', *New Review* 2 (January 1890): 15–21, 15. Subsequent citations appear in the text.

[22] This comment echoes the persistent lament through George Moore's writings on censorship: the novel is severely diminished, he argues, by the dominion of the young female reader as the default reader in the context of whom print restrictions are dictated.

judges, the cases of the finest imaginative compositions since literature rose to the dignity of an art. [18]

The author, Hardy argues, inevitably ends up submitting to 'the Grundyist and sub-scriber' (19). 'It behooves us', he continues, 'to inquire how best to circumvent the present lording of nonage over maturity, and permit the explicit novel to be more gener-ally written' (21). Hardy proposes three possibilities: (1) books bought and not borrowed (classes of books rather than a 'general audience'); (2) serials in newspapers 'read mainly by adults'; and (3) develop magazines for adults. He does not, then, take issue with print regulation for young readers. Havelock Ellis cynically reflects on this point in his review of *Jude*. What might happen, he wonders, if the young were to read Hardy? 'Consider how sad it would be if the young should come to suspect, before they are themselves married, that marriage after all may not always be a box of bonbons. Remember the Young Person.'[23]

The Prefaces to Hardy's *Tess* are written between 1891, when the novel was first pub-lished, and 1912. They take up the issues of literary production and reception already discussed in his essay on 'Candour'. Here is the Preface to the first edition in its entirety:

> The main portion of the following story appeared—with slight modifications—in the *Graphic* newspaper; other chapters, more especially addressed to adult readers, in the *Fortnightly Review* and the *National Observer*, as episodic sketches. My thanks are tendered to the editors and proprietors of those periodicals for enabling me now to piece the trunk and limbs of the novel together, and print it complete, as originally written two years ago.
>
> I will just add that the story is sent out in all sincerity of purpose, as an attempt to give artistic form to a true sequence of things; and in respect of the book's opinions and sentiments, I would ask any too genteel reader, who cannot endure to have said what everybody nowadays thinks and feels, to remember a well-worn sentence of St Jerome's: If an offence come out of the truth, better is it that the offence come than that the truth be concealed.[24]

Hardy first focuses here on the mode of publication: novels published in serial publica-tions are inevitably shaped by the periodical's anticipated readership. The *Graphic* news-paper does not permit the range of representation that is possible in periodicals like the *Fortnightly Review* and *National Observer* addressed to 'adult readers'. Even though he does not refer directly to the young female reader, his reference to the 'too genteel reader' anticipates his focus on readers in later Prefaces.

The second paragraph focuses on the representation of truth: Hardy refers to his 'sin-cerity of purpose' and puts into play 'true' or 'truth' three times in this short passage. He

---

[23] Havelock Ellis, 'Concerning *Jude the Obscure*', *Savoy Magazine* 6 (October 1896): 35–49, 45.
[24] Thomas Hardy, *Tess of the d'Urbervilles*, ed. John Paul Riquelme (Boston: Bedford, 1998), 24–25. Subsequent citations appear in the text.

clearly invokes possible objections to the book (in the form of the 'genteel reader'), and the implicit call to censorship that underwrites such objections ('who cannot endure to have said'). He closes with an appeal that interests of truth override petitions for concealment.[25] The differences between Hardy and Wilde in this context are also interesting: where Hardy privileges truth in terms of the value of exposé, Wilde privileges truth in terms of the value of art.

For the fifth edition, in 1892, Hardy rewrites the Preface entirely. In this Preface he traces the novel's reception history, noting that the majority of reviewers praised his novel. The Preface, however, focuses on the minority of readers who were unhappy with it; they are divided into three groups: reviewers who address 'subjects fit for art' (25); reviewers who feel that the novel reflects only life at the end of the 19th century and does not do more than that; and the 'genteel' reader to whom Hardy referred in his original Preface.

The first sentence of this Preface is noteworthy for the contortions it makes not to say what it is saying:

> This novel being one wherein the great campaign of the heroine begins after an event in her experience which has usually been treated as fatal to her part of protagonist, or at least the virtual ending of her enterprises and hopes, it was quite contrary to avowed conventions that the public should welcome the book, and agree with me in holding that there was something more to be said in fiction than had been said about the shaded side of a well-known catastrophe. [25]

The reference to sex with Alec as 'an event' or the description of the chapters following the 'event' as 'the shaded side of a well-known catastrophe' suggests that even in the Preface, Hardy understood that he could not say all. If Tess was an attempt to say something more in fiction about sex, then the Preface remained a site in which that something would not be said directly to the 'public' whose 'avowed conventions' made candour impossible. Where Wilde parodies the unsayable, Hardy circumlocutes. It is in the Preface to *Jude the Obscure*, however, written in 1895, that Hardy confronts the construction of the reader most directly.

Again Hardy draws his reader's attention to the restrictions imposed by serial publication:

> The history of this novel (whose birth in its present shape has been much retarded by the necessities of periodical publication) is as follows. [He recounts the year he began writing the text, when he finished it, and its publication in *Harper's*.] But, as in the case of *Tess of the D'Ubervilles*, the magazine version was for various reasons abridged and modified in some degree, the present edition being the first in which the whole appears as originally written. [38]

---

[25] Several critics, of course, did not agree with Hardy. See, for example, Caine's 'New Watchwords', *Contemporary Review* (1890): 471–72.

Where Hardy justified his account in *Tess* by reference to sincerity and truth, here he writes:

> For a novel addressed by a man to men and women of full age; which attempts to deal unaffectedly with the fret and fever, derision and disaster, that may press in the wake of the strongest passion known to humanity, and to point, without a mincing of words, the tragedy of unfulfilled aims, I am not aware that there is anything in the handling to which exception can be taken. [38]

If the 1912 Preface to *Tess*, with its account of the book-burning by the bishop, has garnered the most critical attention, one can see from these earlier Prefaces Hardy's efforts to wrestle with print restrictions. For the most part he accepts the terms of the print regulation debate—the vulnerability of the young female reader and the focus on morality—but attempts to refigure them in a manner more conducive to his own novelistic production. His novels are not written for young women, he claims, and they are moral. Where social purity movements were attempting to define 'moral' in one way, novel Preface writers during this period were giving the term a broader inflection, although, unlike Wilde, most did not reject the terms of the debate altogether.

A Hill-top Novel

In the same year as the Wilde trial and Hardy's *Jude*, Grant Allen published *The British Barbarians*[26] and wrote the most explicit protest against print regulation that I have found in a Preface written in English. Before turning to this Preface I want to consider an exchange on print regulation in which Allen was involved that predates it by four years. In June 1891, a year after Hardy's 'Candour in Fiction', Allen published an essay, 'Letters in Philistia', in the *Fortnightly Review*. He argues against restrictions placed on writers and notes that English fiction is not known abroad as French and Russian fiction is. 'The British public is, in one word, stodgy.'[27] He further notes that W.E. Henley once referred to him mockingly as 'the man who isn't allowed'. According to Allen, Henley missed his point. He explains: 'It isn't that *I* am not allowed: it is that *we* are not allowed...men can't write as they would...because the public and its distributing agents dictate to them so absolutely how and what they are to produce that they can't escape from it.' He continues:

> The definiteness of the demand, indeed, has become almost ludicrous. Rigid contracts are nowadays signed beforehand for the protection of such and such a piece of work, consisting, let us say, of three volumes, divided into twenty-six weekly parts; each part comprising two chapters, to average two thousand five hundred words

---

[26] Grant Allen, *The British Barbarians: A Hill-Top Novel* (London: Lane, 1895).
[27] Grant Allen, 'Letters in Philistia', *Fortnightly Review* (June 1891): 947–62, 950.

apiece. Often enough, a clause is even inserted in the agreement that the work shall contain nothing that may not be read aloud in any family circle. Consider what, in the existing condition of English bourgeois opinion, that restriction means![28]

This family-based censorship—captured also in Hardy's phrase 'household reading'— was hotly debated in the period. The number of writers who raise this issue and either suggest that such regulation is over or that it persists more powerfully than ever testifies to its hold on the public imagination. Trollope, for example, argued in his *Autobiography* that unlike the restrictions placed on fiction fifty years ago, 'There is…no such embargo now [in 1876].'[29] Stead replied directly to Allen's article in a piece for the *Review of Reviews* in which he rejected the claim that English novelists were forced to negotiate serious print restrictions:

> It is sheer nonsense to pretend that in England a man cannot say what he will…I have never hesitated to discuss in the frankest and freest manner possible all questions which Mrs Grundy taboos, discussing them in the hearing of the whole people, regardless of the shrieks of the prude…It is not plain speech and free speech that the English public dislikes, it is unclean speech, speech that is used to corrupt the mind and deprave the imagination that the British Philistia, if it be Philistia, protests against—and rightly protests—and will go on protesting.[30]

As the driving force behind the Maiden Tribute exposé Stead felt that he knew what he was talking about. He suggests that there is ample 'liberty' for the British novelist; what is missing is 'genius'. And he distinguishes here between 'free speech' (which is applauded) and 'unclean speech' (which corrupts). He continues on to note that free speech related to 'social problems' is merited but draws the line when it leads to what he calls 'depravity' (in his example, 'depravity' is equated with not fully acknowledging the seriousness of adultery).[31]

Undeterred by these responses, Allen took up the issue of print regulation again in his 1895 preface to *The British Barbarians*. Both *The British Barbarians* (written in 1889) and *The Women Who Did* (written in early 1893 and published a few months before *The British Barbarians* publication in 1895) represent adulterous relationships, as did 'Ivan Greet's Masterpiece', the title story of the collection published in 1893. In the Preface to this collection, Allen writes: 'I sent [the title story to the *Graphic*], I confess, in fear and trembling, and was agreeably surprised when the editor had the boldness to print it unaltered.'[32] He then notes that two other stories that dealt with

---

[28] Allen, 'Philistia', 953. These debates, moreover, are exacerbated by the differing views on press censorship and theatre censorship; different rules and attitudes obtain in the categories of press, theatre, and the novel.

[29] Anthony Trollope, *An Autobiography* (Edinburgh: Blackwood, 1883), 125.

[30] W.T. Stead, 'Philistia and Mr. Grant Allen', *Review of Reviews* 3 (June 1891): 585.

[31] Stead, 'Philistia', 585.

[32] Grant Allen, *Ivan Greet's Masterpiece etc.* (London: Chatto, 1893), n.p.

adultery were rejected by every journal he sent them to, 'declined by the whole press of London'.[33] This previous experience likely animates his attitude to censorship in the Preface to *The British Barbarians*. His novel, which he calls a 'hill-top novel' (written freely from his hill top), 'raises a protest in favour of purity'. Allen reverses the terms of the purity movement so important to many of his contemporaries; he claims that his novel is 'pure' in a period when the field is otherwise 'flooded with stories of evil tendencies'. Purity, for Allen, refers to the author who writes what he or she thinks and does not try to moderate his or her subject matter and views in light of an anticipated readership.

The reason other novelists have not raised similar protests, he argues, is due to their reliance on a mode of publication—serialization in magazines and newspapers— that limits what the novelist can say. He groups together 'Catholic readers', 'Wesleyan Methodist subscribers', 'the young person', and the 'British matron' as the readers responsible for the novel's 'ridiculous timidity' and argues that the representation of 'truth' (which Allen upholds) should not in any way curtail a novel's 'circulation'. The excessive caution exercised by editors as they take into consideration the anticipated response of their potential readers results in a situation in which 'it is almost impossible to get a novel printed in an English journal unless it is warranted to contain nothing at all to which anybody, however narrow, could possibly object, on any grounds what- ever, religious, political, social, moral, or aesthetic'. Literature, Allen claims, following Thomas Hardy, is 'the expression of souls in revolt'.[34] The mode of publication, he argues, accordingly prevents the production of literature.

Further, Allen reverses the terms of the relationship between censorship and the reader. He states explicitly that he wants to write for girls and women but does not want to limit the range of his representation in this context. Wise men are wise already; it is the boys and girls and women who most need 'suggestion and instruction'. Instead of using the reader's innocence as a gauge that disqualifies her from reading the novel, it is her very innocence and need for instruction that makes the reading of the novel so important.[35]

Allen admittedly expresses his radical positions with respect to print freedom in the context of a conservative framework: he celebrates the genius of the individual author; and while he reverses the terms of the purity movement he maintains the pure/impure opposition. He is nevertheless clearly suggesting that writers should not be limited by unnecessarily restrictive publication conditions and readers should not be unnecessarily

---

[33] Allen, *Ivan*, n.p.

[34] Ever vulnerable to critique, *The British Barbarians* was parodied by H.D. Traill in a work entitled *The Barbarous Britishers, A Tip-Top Novel* (London: Lane, 1896), which includes a Preface that mocks the terms of Allen's Preface to his novel: 'Do not imagine for a moment that I have said anything which I don't think. Absurd as some of my opinions may seem, I really hold them. What I have complained of is, that I have all along entertained more absurd opinion still, which, owing to the cowardly clinging of Editors to common-sense, I have had to suppress' (2).

[35] This was an argument that had also been made in response to print censorship in the 1860s.

protected.[36] In this Preface, then, Allen at once demonstrates the force of social purity discourse in the literary culture but attempts to redefine the terms of this discourse to counter its print regulation arguments.[37]

In conclusion, these Prefaces, and others written in the 1880s and 1890s, exhibit an acute awareness of print restrictions. Each of these novelists tried to recast the terms of the censorship debate in different ways. Wilde situated his response in the context of aestheticism and a rejection of the utilitarian approach to literature; Hardy wrote against modes of publication and claimed that his novels were not written for young readers; and Allen similarly protested against modes of publication but claimed that the novel should be for the young. These foci on the reader and modes of publication remind us that print regulation was never simply about legal repression of an author. At the same time, one can see in Hardy, Allen, and Wilde a shift to a focus on art. For Hardy this shift is translated in terms of 'sincere' art and for Allen it is translated in terms of 'pure' art; it is only in Wilde, however, that this focus on art disrupts the terms of the debate as it renders qualities of sincerity and purity irrelevant to the 'uselessness' of art.

If Wilde retorts by privileging the aesthetic, Hardy by privileging the adult reader, and Allen by privileging the purity of art and all readers, I want to close with two reversals of censorship attitudes that speak to the complexity of the censorship field in the period. The first involves a moment in the Vizetelly trial and its aftermath. The prosecution collects twenty-one offending passages from Zola's *La Terre* and reads them aloud to the jury members for their evaluation. After hearing only a few of these passages, the jury, presumably repulsed, requests not to have to listen to them all, Vizetelly abruptly pleads guilty, and the trial comes to a rapid close. Only five years later, in 1893, the British government and press, representatives of the same population that could not bear in 1888 this tiny sampling of Zola's work, welcome Zola to England with an 'enthusiastic reception' and 'sounds of ringing cheers'.[38]

My second example occurs in a novel, Mary Cholmondeley's *Red Pottage*, published in 1899. In this novel, Cholmondeley's central character, Hester, is a novelist. She writes a novel that her brother, a reverend, reads. Deeply disturbed by the novel's content, even as he is impressed by the force of its style, the reverend feels it is his duty to burn the

---

[36] In 1926 *The Woman Who Did* (Boston: Little Brown, 1926) was explicitly advertised in terms of its positioning with respect to the censorship debates. The novel was not itself censored but its engagement with censorship issues is announced on the cover of the text. It reads: 'The present seemingly endless discussion as to what is or what is not fit to print makes timely this new edition of a famous novel which set the literary world by the ears when it was first published in 1895.'

[37] Allen's novel was not well received (although interestingly, most reviewers devoted half their reviews to commentary on the preface). The *New York Times* reviewer wrote: 'Mr. Grant Allen repeats over and over again how utterly fearless he is, and declares that he is disseminating the highest truth … From the mock stiltedness of the preface, you know what Mr. Grant Allen was after' (18 December 1895, 10).

[38] Henry Vizetelly, *Glances Back over Seventy Years: Reminiscences* (London: Vizetelly,1893), 432.

novel. This is one of the more flagrant descriptions of censorship in the 19th-century English novel and an ironic commentary on the outward crime that may be committed within twenty-four hours of reading. But it is also a brilliant dénouement both to Cholmondeley's novel and to the story of English print censorship. Cholmondeley enacts a representation of censorship and the dictates of the vulnerable reader, by way of the vulnerable male reader, and a powerful critique and undoing of such censorship: for if Hester's brother burns her book, we read this account in *Red Pottage*, a novel that itself closely resembles that burned novel of the narrative. Hester's novel, then, is simultaneously burned and revived. Both of these reversals no doubt owe a debt to the ongoing explorations of censorship enacted in a range of cultural forums. In short, a consideration of late-Victorian novel Prefaces illustrates the ways in which authors and publishers negotiated the new climate of print censorship in the context of the rise and influence of social purity movements, changing understandings of the social role of the novel, new novel forms, and new and contested conditions of literary production and publication.

Suggested Reading

Brake, Laurel. 'The Discourses of Journalism: "Arnold and Pater" Again—and Wilde'. In *Pater in the 1990s*. Edited by Laurel Brake and Ian Small. Greensboro: ELT Press, 1991, 43–61.

Bristow, E.J. *Vice and Vigilance: Purity Movements in Britain since 1700*. Dublin: Gill, 1977.

Butler, Judith. *Excitable Speech: A Politics of the Performative*. New York: Routledge, 1997.

Cox, Don Richard, ed. *Sexuality and Victorian Literature*. Knoxville: University of Tennessee Press, 1984.

De Grazia, Edward. *Girls Lean Back Everywhere: The Law of Obscenity and the Assault on Genius*. New York: Random, 1992.

Ellis, Havelock. 'Concerning *Jude the Obscure*'. *Savoy Magazine* 6 (October 1896): 35–49.

Gagnier, Regenia. *Idylls of the Marketplace: Oscar Wilde and the Victorian Public*. Stanford: Stanford University Press, 1986.

Hardy, Thomas. 'Candour in English Fiction'. *New Review* 2 (January 1890): 15–21.

Hunt, Alan. *Governing Morals: A Social History of Moral Regulation*. Cambridge: Cambridge University Press, 1999.

Hunter, Ian, David Saunders, and Dugald Williamson. *On Pornography*. London: Macmillan, 1992.

Hyland, Paul and Neil Sammells, eds. *Writing and Censorship in Britain*. London: Routledge, 1992.

Keating, Peter. *The Haunted Study: A Social History of the English Novel, 1875–1914*. London: Secker, 1989.

Kendrick, Walter. *The Secret Museum: Pornography in Modern Culture*. New York: Viking, 1987.

Leckie, Barbara. '"A Preface is Written to the Public": Print Censorship, Novel Prefaces, and the Construction of a New Reading Public in Late-Victorian England'. *Victorian Literature and Culture* 37 (2009): 447–62.

Leckie, Barbara. *Culture and Adultery: The Novel, the Newspaper, and the Law, 1857–1914*. Philadelphia: University of Pennsylvania Press, 1999.

Marcus, Steven. *The Other Victorians: A Study of Sexuality and Pornography in Mid Nineteenth-Century England*. New York: Basic, 1966.

Mason, Michael. *The Making of Victorian Sexuality*. Oxford: Oxford University Press, 1994.

Myers, Robin and Michael Harris, eds. *Censorship and the Control of Print in England and France, 1600–1910*. Winchester: St Paul's, 1992.

Thomas, Donald. *A Long Time Burning: The History of Literary Censorship in England*. London: Routledge, 1969.

Travis, Allan. *Bound and Gagged: A Secret History of Obscenity in Britain*. London: Profile, 2000.

Walkowitz, Judith. *City of Dreadful Delight: Narratives of Sexual Danger in Late-Victorian London*. Chicago: University of Chicago Press, 1992.

Weeks, Jeffrey. *Sex, Politics, and Society: The Regulation of Sexuality since 1800*. London: Longman, 1981.

Wilde, Oscar. *The Picture of Dorian Gray*. Edited by Norman Page. Peterborough, ON: Broadview, 1998.

PART III

THE VICTORIAN NOVEL ELSEWHERE

9

VICTORIAN NOVELS
IN FRANCE

MARIE-FRANÇOISE CACHIN

The relationship between France and Britain has not always been cordial to say the least, but at the beginning of the Victorian era, a few years after the end of the Napoleonic wars, the situation between the two nations was showing signs of improvement. A long tradition of cultural exchanges has always existed across the Channel in spite of political disagreements and warfare, and each country remains interested in the literary production of the other. In France, if the great classics of English literature like Shakespeare, Milton, and Byron are no longer studied at school, Victorian writers like Dickens, Wilde, and Stevenson are relatively well-known names. But the introduction of British novels to France has never been and can never be systematic. The number of and investment in British novels depend on both the state of France's own novel production and whether the French reading public finds anything worth reading in British novels.

Several questions immediately arise as one investigates the presence of Victorian fiction in France: how was the fiction introduced? Through what channels? How many Victorian novels were published in France? And how were they produced? In thinking about how the fiction was introduced, we need, of course, to look at the parts played by translators and publishers. By examining translation and advertising (for instance), we come to understand not only the ways in which writers and works were selected as worthy of publication, but also the ways the works were altered and how consequently they were reviewed and received by the reading public.

FRENCH MEDIATORS OF THE VICTORIAN NOVEL

Periodicals

The transmission and circulation of foreign works need mediators, and several French periodicals importantly negotiated between the Victorian novel and French readers. At the beginning of the 19th century, major British reviews like the *Edinburgh Review* and the *Quarterly Review* attracted the attention of French publishers and critics because they published both long reviews and extracts of British books. Some of the articles published in these prestigious British reviews came to be known and read in France. As a consequence, French periodicals were launched along the same lines and contributed to the discovery of English novelists by the French reading public. Two of these French reviews played a prominent part in that respect.

The first was the *Revue britannique*, a monthly founded in 1825, and its very name clearly indicates that it was mostly concerned with Britain. It reproduced (in French) articles from various British magazines, such as *The New Monthly Magazine* or *The Westminster Review*, and also extracts from successful novels of the time. From 1829, one man, Amédée Pichot, played a prominent part in the *Revue britannique*. Pichot had himself started in 1825 a periodical entitled *L'Echo britannique*, which merged into the *Revue britannique* in 1835. Remaining at the head of the *Revue britannique* from 1839 till his death in 1877 when his son Pierre-Amédée took over, Pichot made a significant contribution to the popularization of British culture through his articles on and his translations of British novelists. Between 1825 and 1901 when the *Revue britannique* folded, French readers enjoyed a good sample of what was being published across the Channel, particularly as regards fiction, which according to some was in its golden age. Throughout the period, there were articles dealing with general subjects, such as 'Les femmes auteurs en Angleterre' ('Women Writers in England')[1] or 'Les romanciers anglais contemporains: Miss Thackeray, Charles Dickens'.[2] Others were devoted to a particular writer, like Thackeray,[3] or more frequently to reviews of British novels, generally in translation, like Dickens's *A Christmas Carol*[4] or Charles Kingsley's *Alton Locke*[5] in 1851.

---

[1] 'Le femmes auteurs en Angleterre', *Revue britannique* (November 1836): 89–107.

[2] 'Les romanciers anglais contemporains: Miss Thackeray, Charles Dickens', *Revue britannique* (July, 1869): 37–60.

[3] Amédée Pichot, 'William Thackeray et ses ouvrages', *Revue Britannique* (March 1855) : 173–84.

[4] E.D. Forgues, 'Correspondance Politique et Littéraire de La Revue Britannique', *Revue britannique* (January 1844): 220–21. On this notice, see *The Annotated Christmas Carol*, ed. Michael Patrick Hearn (New York: W.W. Norton, 2005), 37.

[5] E.D Forgues, 'Poète et tailleur (Autobiographie d'Alton Locke)', *Revue britannique* (February 1851): 323–72.

After 1860, famous magazines like the *Cornhill Magazine* or *Macmillan's Magazine*, which had just started, could provide the *Revue britannique* with all kinds of articles, short stories, or extracts from recent novels, thus allowing the French reading public to become acquainted with the literary production of the time.

The *Revue des deux mondes*, a fortnightly review which still exists today, stood second to the *Revue britannique* as a promoter and mediator of British fiction. It was founded in 1829 by François Buloz in order to incite French people to look outside their own country, the two worlds of the title being France versus the rest of the world! The proportion devoted to culture and literature was significant from the start and British literature was in the hands of a few major critics. One of them, Philarète Chasles, was a librarian and a professor specializing in foreign literature, who contributed to the *Revue des deux mondes* with papers such as 'Du roman en Angleterre depuis Walter Scott' ('The English Novel since Walter Scott'),[6] or reviews of Thackeray's and Disraeli's works. He was also a major contributor to the *Journal des débats politiques et littéraires*, another periodical well known for its interest in mainstream literature leading to the regular publication of serials. It had several correspondents in Britain and a few novelists like Anthony Trollope, Rudyard Kipling, and H. Rider Haggard as occasional contributors, which was the best way of finding out about recent English books. No doubt Hippolyte Taine remains the best-known contributor to the *Revue*, along with his 1856 essay on Dickens, which he reprinted eight years later in *Histoire de la littérature anglaise*.[7]

The *Revue* published the work of other significant French writers on the Victorian novel as well, including Paul-Emile Daurand Forgues and Émile Montégut. Forgues, who signed his articles 'Old Nick', spoke fluent English, met Dickens in 1844 and was a friend of Wilkie Collins. He wrote several pieces for the *Revue des deux mondes*, for instance an article on women novelists—and Dinah Mulock in particular—in England ('La Roman de femme en Angleterre'), one on the religious novel that took as its key example George Eliot's *Scenes of Clerical Life* ('La Vie cléricale en Angleterre') and one on the contemporary English novel in 1867.[8] Montegut, writing later in the century, authored two books on English literature, *Essais sur la littérature anglaise* and *Ecrivains modernes de l'Angleterre*.[9] Towards the end of the century, Thérèse Bentzon became a regular contributor for the review, writing an article on the new

---

[6] Philarète Chasles, 'Du Roman en Angleterre depuis Walter Scott,' *Revue des deux mondes* (March 1845): 5–23. Scott garnered considerable popularity in France.

[7] Hippolyte Taine, 'Charles Dickens: son talent et ses oeuvres', *Revue des deux mondes* (January 1856): 618–47 and *Histoire de la littérature anglaise*, 4 vols. (Hachette: Paris, 1864). On Taine's approach to reviewing, see John Philip Couch, *George Eliot in France: A French Appraisal of George Eliot's Writings, 1858–1960* (Chapel Hill: University of North Caroline Press, 1967), 2–3 and 8–9.

[8] E.D. Forgues, 'Le Roman de femme en Angleterre: Miss Mulock', *Revue des deux mondes* (February 1860): 797–831; 'La Vie cléricale en Angleterre: Scenes of Clerical Life' (May 1858): 306–31, and 'Le Roman anglais contemporain' (June 1867): 1007–26. On Forgues' review of *Scenes of Clerical Life*, see Couch, 14–15.

[9] *Essais sur la littérature anglaise* (Paris: Hachette, 1883); *Ecrivains modernes de l'Angleterre* (Paris: Hachette, 1885).

English novels in 1888 and reviewing the works of Stevenson and Kipling. Another contributor, Téodor de Wyzewa, of Polish origin, was a specialist in European literature.[10] Among his articles are 'Une nouvelle histoire du roman anglais' ('A New History of the English Novel') and later a review of G.K. Chesterton's *Charles Dickens* (1906), 'Un nouveau livre anglais sur Charles Dickens' ('A New English Book on Charles Dickens').[11] Each of these critics contributed to the diffusion of British novels not only through the various periodicals in which they wrote but also through the books they published on the subject.

Beyond offering up criticism and reviews, periodicals acted as mediators through the publication of short stories and Victorian novels, either in long serials or in shortened versions or in extracts. Thus the *Revue britannique* published *David Copperfield* as a serial between May 1849 and December 1851 (with an interruption between February and October 1851), Thackeray's *Pendennis* between June and September 1851, and Charlotte Yonge's *La Colombe dans le nid de l'aigle* (*The Dove in the Eagle's Nest*) between February and October 1866.[12] It seems that the *Revue des deux mondes* favoured extracts rather than complete novels, if we judge from George Meredith's *Sandra Belloni* or Ouida's *Lady Tattersall*, which appeared in only one issue each. On the other hand, many periodicals published some of Dickens's short stories: 'Notre voisin' (January 1852, 'Our Next-Door Neighbour') in *L'Artiste*, 'L'Election du bedeau' (April 1855, The Election of the Beadle), 'L'Auberge de Houx' (October 1860, 'The Holly-Tree Inn'), and 'Poursuite à mort' (October 1863, 'Hunted Down') in *L'Illustration*. *Le Moniteur universel* is the only one to give a complete novel, *Martin Chuzzlewit* (under that very title), published between January and October 1854. As in British magazines, publishing a serialized novel was a test before its publication in volume form. However, the two printed texts could quite often be rather different. This is what happened with Mary Elizabeth Braddon's *Run to Earth* published in 1868, translated into French under the title *La Chanteuse des rues*, first appearing as a serial in *Le Rappel* (a newspaper) in 1873, and then published in two volumes by Louis Hachette (about whom more anon) the following year. A close examination of the two texts reveals that the end of the serialized version differs significantly from that of the volume text, as will be shown below.[13]

---

[10] On Wyzewa, see Elga Liverman, *A Critic Without a Country* (Geneva: Droz, 1961).

[11] 'Une nouvelle histoire du roman anglais', *Revue des deux mondes* (April 1900): 935–46; 'Un nouveau livre anglais sur Charles Dickens', *Revue des deux mondes* (February 907): 937–46.

[12] Besides these famous novelists, M.G. Devonshire gives a long list of serials by anonymous authors published in the *Revue britannique* in her book *The English Novel in France 1830–1870* (London: University of London Press, 1929), 452–53. Information gathered from this book has proved very useful for this chapter. Devonshire's book remains a key reference in spite of its early date.

[13] Limitations of space prevent me from offering a more detailed examination of advertising in periodicals, but, needless to say, the advertisements they printed contributed to the diffusion of the British novel in French culture. Later in the chapter I take up the advertisement of British novels in publishers' catalogues.

Translators[14]

As we have seen, many if not all of the periodicals' critics were translators. This helped the introduction of British fiction into France in two ways: as critics, they were able to suggest which texts should be translated and why, and they could explain the potential interest and the qualities justifying the translation; as translators, they acted as mediators between two languages as well as two cultures. In that respect their responsibility concerning the task of translation was important, as will be shown later in this chapter. Given their dual position, one should not forget how influential and decisive these critic-translators were as intermediaries between English novelists and French publishers.

Publishers

Publishers naturally had significant control over the success of the English novel in France, and while some chose to make English novels translated into French available to the reading public, a few also published English novels in English. For instance, the publisher Louis-Claude Baudry launched a series called 'Ancient and Modern British Authors', which was advertised in the *Journal des débats* in 1831. Between 1831 and 1851 Baudry published some 450 volumes which were sold much more cheaply than in London as he published them in pirated editions.[15] Booksellers like Augustin Renouard with a series advertised in the *Journal des débats* in 1831 and entitled 'Ancient and Modern British Authors', or Lequien with his 'Best British Authors', also contributed to the diffusion of the Victorian novel in France, not only for the British living there, but also for English-speaking French readers interested in British culture. In that respect the most famous and the most interesting figure is Giovanni Antonio Galignani, the owner of a 'cabinet de lecture' (circulating library) in Paris who was a shameless publisher of pirated editions of Dickens and other writers of the time until 1851, when the Anglo-French Copyright Treaty, followed by the International Copyright Act in 1852, established the legal framework for the reprinting of books in both countries. Galignani's library had a catalogue of some 30,000 titles in 1836. The last publisher of British fiction in English who must be mentioned was not French but German. Unlike Galignani, Bernard Tauchnitz paid his authors for their works. Tauchnitz's series of British and American authors was available in France and allowed French readers to discover Victorian novels in their original language.[16]

---

[14] More will be said later about the translators as authors of translations.

[15] Information found in Diana Cooper-Richet, 'La Librairie étrangère à Paris au XXe siècle', *Actes de la recherche en sciences sociales*, no. 126/127 (March 1999), 67.

[16] On Tauchnitz's influence, see Christa Jansohn, 'The Impact of Bernhard Tauchnitz's Book Series "Collection of British and American Authors" on the Continent', *Angermion: Yearbook for Anglo-German*

But most publishers willing to publish British novels necessarily offered them in translation. In France, in the mid-19th century, translations became an important part of some publishers' catalogues. The most significant publisher of translations was unquestionably Gervais Charpentier who launched a 'Bibliothèque anglaise' in 1839, which included translations of works by Oliver Goldsmith, Henry Fielding and Anthony Trollope (printed as 'Troloppe' in the series). Various series of foreign literature developed progressively, the best-known being the 'Bibliothèque des meilleurs romans étrangers' ('Library of the Best Foreign Novels') launched by Hachette, already a major French publisher.

Louis Hachette was convinced that foreign literature had to be part of his publishing business. He set out to imitate W.H. Smith's Railway Libraries, launching several series, grouped under the name of 'Bibliothèque des chemins de fer' in 1856. One of these, easily recognizable by its yellow cover (a reminder of the English yellowbacks), was devoted to classic French works and foreign works. Hachette published a few English novels in the 'Littérature étrangère' section of his 'Bibliothèque des chemins de fer'. The catalogue for 1856 included novels like Charlotte Brontë's *Jane Eyre* (published as by Currer Bell), Elizabeth Gaskell's *Ruth* and *Cranford* (published as by Mme Gaskell), and Thackeray's *Œuvres* (Works) in five volumes: *Henry Esmond*, *Histoire de Pendennis*, *La Foire aux vanités*, *Le Livre des snobs*, and *Mémoires de Barry Lyndon*, which means that these writers were already known in France. During the same period, there existed a series owned by the French printer Charles Lahure for which works by Thackeray and Bulwer Lytton were translated. This series, called 'Bibliothèque des meilleurs romans étrangers' ('Library of the Best Foreign Novels'), was soon merged with Hachette's 'Littérature étrangère' series, keeping the name of Lahure's collection. It was difficult for Lahure to refuse this merger, given that in 1856 Hachette had signed an exclusive contract with Dickens who was already quite famous in France. The great English novelist's first book was serialized in England between March 1836 and October 1837, published as one volume in November and then quickly and freely translated into French under the title of *Le Club des Pickwickistes*; several reviews of the book, including one attributed to Philarète Chasles, also appeared in 1838. According to this contract, Hachette paid Dickens for the exclusive translation rights to eleven of Dickens's novels already in print, as well as all the short stories appearing in *Household Words*. The novelist was also entitled to ban all other previously published translations. Hachette realized that he needed to have a special editor for these translations and he therefore signed an agreement with Paul Lorain, who was to choose the translators and supervise their work when not translating himself, as was the case for *Nicholas Nickleby*.

The 'Bibliothèque des meilleurs romans étrangers' is undoubtedly one of the most important series of foreign literature in France in the 19th century. But other publishers were interested in British novels, as appears from some of the publishers' catalogues in

Literary Criticism, Intellectual History and Cultural Transfers/Jahrbuch für Britisch-Deutsche Kulturbeziehungen 3 (2010): 161–83.

the Bibliothèque nationale de France. However scarce and incomplete they may be, these archives reveal the growing significance of Victorian novels in France and clearly prove that in the second half of the 19th century, more publishers developed their foreign catalogues. This was the case of the publishers Michel Lévy Frères who, according to their 1865 catalogue, published novels by Dickens, Thackeray, Ainsworth, Bulwer Lytton, and Thomas Mayne-Reid, while books by Dinah Craik, Ouida, and George W.M. Reynolds featured in the 1876 catalogue. In the last decades of the century, the same evolution is apparent for the publisher Plon, who published Sabine Baring-Gould, Braddon, Ouida, Stevenson, and Margaret L. Woods. Interestingly, the publisher Mercure de France launched a series exclusively devoted to foreign writers ('Collection d'auteurs étrangers') which included Kipling, Wells, and Meredith.

VICTORIAN NOVELS IN FRANCE

Evolution of production

Besides publishers' catalogues, other documents can be used in order to draw up a more general picture of the Victorian writers available to the French reading public and the kind of novels which were translated and promoted in France in the 19th century. What follows is based on the volumes of the *Bibliographie de la France* for 1851, 1861, 1871, 1881, 1891, and 1901, which in theory list every new work published in the year. However, while legal deposit did exist in France at the time, this does not mean that the actual yearly production of books can be ascertained because, as clearly stated in volume III of the *Histoire de l'édition française*, some books could be listed twice, particularly if they were published in two volumes, and some might be simply or deliberately omitted.[17] Books published in English (as opposed to English books in translation) are mentioned in a specific category in the 1851 volume of the *Bibliographie de la France*, a category which disappears afterwards. Moreover, works serialized in magazines were not listed unless they were then republished in volume form later on.

It is therefore difficult to give precise numbers of the Victorian novels published in France in the 19th century. For the years 1836–48, one can use the information given by M.G. Devonshire in her study *The English Novel in France 1830–1870*, amounting to a total of 549 titles for this period of thirteen years, with two peak years: seventy-three titles in 1837 and eighty-one in 1838. The lowest figure appears in 1848 and can be easily explained by the political turmoil taking place in France that year. It is obvious that

---

[17] Martyn Lyons, 'Les Best-sellers', in *Histoire de l'édition française*, ed. Roger Chartier and Henri-Jean Martin, vol. 3: *Le temps des éditeurs. Du Romantisme à la Belle-Epoque* (Fayard—Cercle de la Librairie, 1990), 410–11.

such fluctuations reflect the political situation or the social agitation of the times. The *Bibliographie de la France* shows that novels by well-known authors such as Goldsmith, Sterne, Defoe, and Scott were reprinted throughout the century. For example, in 1851, Scott's complete works were published in several volumes by different publishers and his name remained present till the end of the century. The only Victorian writer mentioned in 1851 is Dickens, with *David Copperfield*, published for the first time in French translation by Amédée Pichot as *Le Neveu de ma tante* ('My Aunt's Nephew') in three volumes. Ten years later, only five new Victorian writers (apart from Dickens) out of a total number of twenty-four translations are mentioned: Ainsworth, Bulwer-Lytton, Lady Georgiana Fullerton (given in the *Bibliographie* as Mme Fullerton), the Irish author Charles Lever, and Mayne-Reid (with eight titles). The increase in writers in 1871 is noteworthy, passing from six to ten, although the total number of titles—twenty-six—is only slightly higher. The newcomers are Braddon and Mrs Henry Wood, all the other novelists (Ainsworth, Charlotte Brontë (listed as Currer Bell), Dickens, Disraeli, Fullerton, Mayne-Reid, Trollope, and Thackeray) having already been published in France. In 1881, the increase is spectacular with a list of twenty-one British novelists and forty-five titles. Among the new names found in the *Bibliographie de la France*, such as R.D. Blackmore, Rhoda Broughton, Dinah Mulock ('Mrs Craik'), Douglas Jerrold, Amelia B. Edwards, Mrs W.C. Elphinstone Hope, J.H. Ewing, S.J. Whyte-Melville, and Charlotte Yonge, some had been previously published in France. But what must be underlined here is the widening range of authors, reflecting the introduction of different kinds of fiction, such as sensation novels or children's fiction. Conversely, the 1891 volume of the *Bibliographie de la France* shows a decrease of both authors and titles, with only thirteen novelists and thirty-seven titles. Moreover, two of the novels mentioned are abridged school texts, George Eliot's *The Mill on the Floss* and *Silas Marner*.[18] The former, a French translation that kept the English title, was published by Garnier, while the latter was published in a series called 'Classiques anglais' by Belin Frères, a publisher of school texts. The new authors reflect the evolution of the production towards more Irish novelists like Miriam Alexander ('Miss Alexander'), Margaret Hungerford ('Mrs Hungerford') and William O'Brien ('W. O'Brien'), and the presence of the popular lady novelist Ouida. The last volume of the *Bibliographie de la France* studied for this paper, dated 1901, is most interesting not for the numbers of authors and titles, which remain rather stable (fifteen novelists and thirty-four titles), but for the introduction of the major late-Victorian novelists: Hardy, Kipling, Stevenson, Wells, and Conan Doyle, and also for the disappearance of Walter Scott, who had hitherto always featured in the different volumes of the *Bibliographie de la France*.

Examining these figures, one is struck by the relatively limited number of Victorian novels translated into French. It is true that throughout the 19th century, France itself was blessed with many great novelists: Victor Hugo, Stendhal, Balzac, George Sand, and

---

[18]   These two novels had been published in translation before, *The Mill on the Floss* as *La Famille Tulliver, ou le moulin sur la Floss* in 1881 and *Silas Marner* with this title also in 1881.

Flaubert, to name only some of the most famous ones. This is one of the possible explanations for the decrease of Victorian novelists and it may explain Elisabeth Parinet's remark that the French did not show any great and sustained curiosity towards foreign literatures until the end of the century.[19] However, almost all the major Victorian novelists seem to have been translated at least once by 1900. But how were they chosen? This is what will now be discussed.

Selection

Undoubtedly, intermediaries did play an important part in the selection of novels to be translated into French. British literary magazines were a useful and reliable source of information and they were certainly carefully read by translators and publishers. But some publishing companies also had correspondents in London who could report on the publication and the success of good novels. For just as publishers will decide to print only those manuscripts which they consider to be potentially successful books, in the case of translations a second selection necessarily takes place in the foreign country concerned. Publishers will always look for the best foreign texts available. As M.G. Devonshire proclaims: 'The French did not trouble to import into France second-rate English novels', though she soon rightly adds that 'the French did not reject all the dross',[20] particularly if they had sold well in England, one might add! It is always difficult to know whether a foreign text will suit a reading public with a different cultural background. Publishers are well aware that there are many factors facilitating the introduction of foreign literature, in particular readers' horizons of expectation which will favour the response to the translated text or not, as the case may be. They will prefer critically acclaimed novels as well as bestsellers which in their opinion will sell well and therefore be profitable, whatever their literary qualities may be.

This is probably the reason why Louis Hachette, following the aforementioned contract which he had just signed with Dickens, decided to inform the novelist about his project of a series devoted to the best foreign novels. In 1856, Hachette sent Dickens a letter announcing his son's visit with a list of English writers whom he thought the most esteemed and most likely to be appreciated in France. He asked Dickens to read, modify, and complete the list if necessary in order to plan his future publications in the best possible way. The list included the following writers: Ainsworth, Bulwer, Carlyle, Disraeli (given as D'Israeli), Fullerton, Catherine Gore (given as Mrs Gore), Jerrold, Julia Kavanagh (given as Miss Kavanagh), Lewes, Macaulay, Thackeray, Samuel Warren, Anne Marsh-Caldwell (given as Mrs Marsh), Jewsbury, and Wilkie Collins. In his reply,

[19] Elisabeth Parinet, *Une histoire de l'édition à l'époque contemporaine, XIXe—XXe siècle*, Collection Points Histoire (Paris: Éditions du Seuil, 2004), 93.
[20] Devonshire, 6–7.

Dickens wrote: 'All these ladies and gentlemen, with the exception of one name[21] against which I have put a cross I know. Do you wish a letter of introduction to each?' adding: 'I return your list with the addresses of several of the writers mentioned in it, written against their names.'[22] Most of these novelists can be found in Hachette's catalogues for the 'Bibliothèque des meilleurs romans étrangers', confirming that Dickens's advice proved most useful, though Hachette's list shows that the French publisher was well aware of the situation of the novel in Britain at the time.

According to Devonshire, the French tended to separate Victorian novels into different genres: historical romances, fashionable novels, social novels, sea novels, religious novels, sensational novels, children's literature, etc. This categorization is clearly reflected in some of the articles published in the *Revue des deux mondes*: 'Le roman politique en Angleterre', 'Études sur le roman anglais: IV: Le Roman de mœurs judiciaires', 'Le Socialisme et la littérature démocratique en Angleterre', 'Le Roman de mœurs industrielles en Angleterre', 'Le Roman de la nouvelle réforme en Angleterre', and 'La Renaissance du roman historique anglais en Angleterre'.[23] It therefore seems likely that publishers chose according to the genre that they thought most appropriate and suited to their catalogues. The publisher Firmin-Didot obviously selected morally unobjectionable novels like Maxwell Gray's (a pseudonym for Mary Gleed Tuttiett) *L'Héritage des Gledesworth* or George Eliot's *Silas Marner* for his series 'Bibliothèque des mères de famille'. Children's novels in translation were generally published in series devoted to the genre, like Hachette's famous 'Bibliothèque rose illustrée'.

However, on the whole and throughout the century, publishers tended to focus on individual authors rather than on genres. This is clear in the case of Dickens and his exclusive contract with Hachette, but the publisher also selected other Victorian novelists like Elizabeth Gaskell, Mary Elizabeth Braddon, G.A. Lawrence, Whyte Melville, Anthony Trollope, and Mrs Henry Wood, who all had their collected works (Œuvres) published in several volumes in the 'Bibliothèque des meilleurs romans étrangers'. The list of the Victorian novelists published by Hachette clearly shows a mixture of writers of high literary quality like Dickens, Thackeray, Gaskell, or Trollope, and of popular sensational novelists like Braddon, Collins, and Wood. One feels Hachette's choice was more in favour of the favourite authors of Victorian circulating libraries. According to the

[21] The name Dickens identified was Warren's, probably Samuel Warren. The other less familiar names in the list are those of women novelists: Georgiana Fullerton, Julia Kavanagh, Anne Marsh Caldwell.

[22] Dickens to Louis Hachette, 9 June 1856, in *The Letters of Charles Dickens*, ed. Graham Storey and Kathleen Tillotson, 12 vols. (Oxford: Clarendon Press, 1997), 8: 133.

[23] Philarète Chasles 'Le Roman politique en Angleterre', *Revue des deux mondes* (April 1845): 1011–21; [Anonymous], 'Études sur le roman anglaise: IV: Le roman de mœurs judiciaires', *Revue des deux mondes* (June 1847): 1106–1130; Émile Montégut, 'Le Socialisme et la littérature Démocratique en Angleterre', *Revue des deux mondes* (April 1851): 430–58; Émile Montégut, 'Le Roman de mœurs industrielles en Angleterre', *Revue des deux mondes* (September 1855): 115–46; Thérèse Bentzon, 'Le Roman de la nouvelle réforme en Angleterre', *Revue des deux mondes* (December 1889): 649–81; and Téodor de Wyzewa, 'La Renaissance du roman historique anglais en Angleterre', *Revue des deux mondes* (January 1890): 184–201.

French book historian Jean-Yves Mollier, the weakness of Hachette's catalogue in this respect can be explained by the absence of a systematic search for future great novelists, contrary to the practice of publishers like Mercure de France or Stock at the beginning of the 20th century who chose to promote groundbreaking new authors like Kipling and Wells.[24]

Translation

Not surprisingly, French translators moved quickly to translate novels for publishers when the author in question was famous or the novel to be translated had sold well in England. The time between the novel's original publication and its publication in translation could be very short and might be even shorter for subsequent novels by the same author. A brief analysis of these time spans for some thirty Victorian novelists, based on the *Bibliographie de la France* and on the general catalogue of the Bibliothèque nationale de France, reveals, not unsurprisingly, that they could vary considerably. It all depended on the first title introduced into France. For example, the first French translation of Bulwer-Lytton's *The Last Days of Pompeii*, published in England in 1834, was published the very same year by Mame. Wilkie Collins's *The Woman in White*, published in England in 1860, was translated by E.D. Forgues as *La Femme en blanc* the following year and published by Dentu. A one-year time span can be noted for other Victorian novels like George Eliot's *Adam Bede*; Charles Reade's *It Is Never Too Late To Mend*; Mrs Henry Wood's *East Lynne*, first published in France in 1862 under the title *Lady Isabel* (described in the Bibliothèque nationale de France general catalogue as given 'en prime', i.e. a free copy, by the periodical *La Patrie*); and Charlotte Yonge's *The Daisy Chain*, published in 1856 in England and in 1857 in France. Perhaps the time span was so short because all these novels, except *Adam Bede*, were rather of the sensational or otherwise popular genre.

A time span of two to five years between the original novel and its French translation can be noted for Benjamin Disraeli's *Sybil*, Elizabeth Gaskell's *Cranford*, Thomas Hardy's *The Trumpet Major*, R.L. Stevenson's *Treasure Island*, and H.G Wells's *Ann Veronica*. But there are a few cases when the time span is unusually long, generally for books whose positive reception in France would have been harder to predict, such as R.D. Blackmore's *Lorna Doone*, published in England in 1869, but translated only in 1904, probably because it was considered too prolix and complicated. That such a highly complex and original novel as *Wuthering Heights*, published in 1847, was first translated into French only in 1892 under the undecipherable title *Un Amant*, is understandable. It is more difficult to understand why Charlotte Brontë's *Jane Eyre* was only translated seven years after its original publication, though *Shirley* (1849) was translated as early as 1850,[25] and William Thackeray's *Barry Lyndon* after fourteen years.

---

[24] See Jean-Yves Mollier, *Louis Hachette* (Paris: Fayard, 1999).
[25] Even more surprising, the first translation of *Villette* published in England in 1853 did not appear in France until 1932.

As may have been noticed, the first book to come to France was not necessarily the first one written by the author. Similarly the publication of the first French translation did not necessarily mean that the rest of the novelist's works would follow. Here again it would be a question of popularity and success. It also depended on the publishers, who generally did not manage to secure all the rights to the novelist's extant and future works, as Hachette did with Dickens. The same was true of translations and original publications, that is to say that any French publisher could decide to publish an English novelist's work if not yet translated or even to propose a new translation of it, especially before the 1851 treaty on copyright between France and Britain. Some Victorian novelists, especially in the first years of their introduction into France, could find themselves translated by many different translators and published by almost as many French publishers. A few examples will illustrate this point.

Jane Eyre (1847) was first translated in 1854 by Mme Lesbazeilles Souvestre under the title *Jeanne Eyre, ou les Mémoires d'une institutrice* and published by D. Giraud. The same translation was used with the heroine's name re-established as 'Jane Eyre' by Hachette in 1862. In the meantime, another version of the novel appeared in 1855 in Hachette's 'Bibliothèque des chemins de fer'. In the catalogue of the Bibliothèque nationale de France, the book is presented as '*Jane Eyre, ou Mémoires d'une gouvernante*, de Currer Bell (C. Brontë) imité par Old Nick (P.-E. Daurand-Forgues)'. During this period, a translation did not necessarily mean the faithful rendering of the original text. A novel could therefore be either translated or adapted or imitated. Whatever the strategy, there was never any guarantee about the result in French! In that respect, according to the leading French scholar Sylvère Monod, the first translations of Dickens's novels were often faulty and unsatisfactory in many ways.[26] Monod illustrates his point with references to *Oliver Twist*, *Dombey & Son*, and *David Copperfield*, among other novels, exposing the great number of suppressions and modifications, such as in *Dombey* the merging together of Chapters 7 and 8, or the changes in the characters' names, Cuttle becoming Cottle or Richards, Richardine. As regards *David Copperfield*, he gives more precise examples, like the line 'engaging to call upon me the next day' translated by Amédée Pichot as 'il m'engagea à aller le rejoindre trois jours après'.

The beginning of the career of *Oliver Twist* in France was somewhat chaotic. It began with a first edition in four volumes published by G. Barba in 1841 under the title *Olivier Twist, ou l'Orphelin du dépôt de mendicité* in a translation by Ludovic Bénard. In 1850, Barba published *Les Voleurs de Londres*, a translation of *Oliver Twist* by Emile Gigault de La Bédollière, who also translated Walter Scott, James Fenimore Cooper, Frederick Marryat, and Thomas Mayne Reid. In 1864, a third and better translation by Alfred Gérardin was published by Hachette, following his contract with Dickens. The case of *Dombey & Son* is even more convoluted. First translated into French by Paul Hennequin

---

[26] Sylvère Monod, 'Les Premiers Traducteurs français de Dickens', in *Romantisme* no. 106 (1999): 119–28. In *George Eliot in France*, 182–3, Couch offers a side-by-side comparison of extracts from François D'Albert Durade's translation of *The Mill on the Floss* with the English original.

and published in Belgium between 1847 and 1851, the novel was in the meantime translated in France and published in 1848 by Baudry who had previously published an
English edition of the novel. The translation was begun by Benjamin Laroche who had
no respect whatsoever for the original text, suppressing a chapter or combining two in
one! The work was next taken up by Alfred Nettement, who was slightly more scrupu-
lous, and the final translated novel was published by Cadot. Hachette's authorized translation of *Dombey & Son* was done by a woman, Alix Bressant; although at times faulty,
it nonetheless became the standard translation and had been reprinted twelve times by
1910. No other translation of this novel was done before 1937. Finally, one should say
a word about Amédée Pichot's translation of *David Copperfield*. According to Monod,
Pichot was always ready to suppress or add passages whenever he felt he could improve
Dickens's text. He doubtless thought that the title which he chose for this novel, *Le Neveu
de ma tante*, was much better than the original one.

Translations of Mary Elizabeth Braddon's sensation novels offer yet more evidence
of how and when Victorian novels reached the French reading public. Once she was
discovered, on account of her enormous success in Britain, her books were very rapidly
translated, most of them by Charles Bernard-Derosne, and published by Hachette in the
'Bibliothèque des meilleurs romans étrangers'. She probably was as popular in France as
in England, as appears from the fact that in 1864 Hachette published three of her novels: *Le Testament de John Marchmont*, *La Trace du serpent* and *Le Triomphe d'Eleanor*.
The case of her novel *Run to Earth* deserves special attention, because, as mentioned
previously, it was first serialized in French under the title *La Chanteuse des rues* in the
newspaper *Le Rappel*, before being published by Hachette in Charles Bernard-Derosne's
translation. But if one compares the text of the serial with the text of the volume edition,
one soon realizes that the former offers a freer interpretation of the original while the
latter remains more faithful. In the serial, chapters were much shorter and their titles
different; for instance the first chapter as published by Hachette was entitled 'Le Songe',
whereas in the serial it was divided into two chapters, the first entitled 'Une belle fille
dans un mauvais lieu' and the second one 'Le Rêve sinistre'. Descriptions were usually
shorter in the serial, probably to avoid slowing down the pace of the story proper. It soon
became impossible for me to follow the two translated texts side by side and the two
endings appeared completely different. It seems as if it did not really matter if the readers of the serial got the exact text of the novel or not. It also means that in such cases, the
Victorian novel would lose a lot of its authenticity, its originality, and its literary qualities. Indeed, with respect to *Run to Earth*, one wonders whether anything at all of the
original text reached its foreign readers.

Fortunately, the situation changed, and even in the course of the century the quality
of translations improved and the French reading public had access to Victorian novels which reflected their British originals more accurately. Rudyard Kipling and H.G.
Wells, for instance, were translated more regularly by the same translators and published
mostly by the same publishers. Most of Kipling's novels were translated into French by
Louis Fabulet and Robert d'Humières together and published by Mercure de France.
Wells was often translated by Henry D. Davray, who was also a critic at the periodical of

the same name. Publishers tried to find good translators and to enlist their services as often as possible.

Finally, a few words must be said about children's fiction. Victorian novels for children constitute a relatively significant proportion of the books introduced into France in the 19th century. But when and how were they translated? Thomas Mayne-Reid's adventure novels for boys provide a fascinating case study. In 'La Plus Etrange Aventure de Mayne-Reid: sa traduction', Thierry Chevrier finds first that forty-four of Mayne-Reid's novels were translated into French by forty-eight different translators.[27] He adds that thirty-five out of these forty-four were translated several times, with the most famous one, *The Scalp Hunters*, being translated a grand total of seven times! Chevrier explains that Mayne-Reid was introduced to France by one Allyre Bureau who was granted permission to translate *The Scalp Hunters* by the author himself. Bureau's translation was published in five relatively expensive volumes with the title *Les Chasseurs de chevelures* by Locard-Davi and de Vresse, then in a cheaper edition by the 'Librairie nouvelle' in 1854. Another translation was done later by Emile de la Bédollière and published the same year by Gustave Barba in his series 'Le Panthéon littéraire illustré'. Chevrier also draws an interesting list of the translations of the novel *Rifle Rangers* between 1854 and 1961, all with different titles: *Le Corps franc des rifles* (Cadot, 1854), *Les Tirailleurs au Mexique* (Barba, 1854), *Volontaires et guerilleros au pays d'Anahuac* (Lecène et Houdin, 1891), *La Compagnie des francs-rôdeurs* (A.L. Guyot, 1901), *Anahuac, terre des aventures* (Tallandier, 1928), *Les Aventures du Capitaine Haller* (Tallandier, 1952), *Les Rangers* (Robert Laffont, 1961) and *Les Francs-Tireurs* (GP, 1980). Chevrier then points out the various flaws in the translations, particularly the early ones, though he underlines the difficulty of the task at times. For example, in Madame Burée's 1872 translation of *The Castaways* (1869) 'rotten onions' (des oignons pourris) is translated by 'le goût de l'ognon [*sic*] roussi'. Translations of children's fiction are often in fact adaptations, because the cultural references which cannot always be understood by young foreign readers have to be modified or explained.

The introduction of Victorian novels into France therefore strongly depended (and still depends) on the skill and conscientiousness of the translators, who were then and are now expected to give a faithful rendering of the original text. But in some cases, and in particular as regards children's novels, the only possibility was to adapt it for the target readers. One striking example of this is Lewis Carroll's *Alice's Adventures in Wonderland* (1865). Translated into French in 1869, it was actually published by Macmillan, the publisher of Carroll's original novel. The translator Henri Bué was a teacher of French and German at Bradfield and his father was a friend and colleague of Carroll's. In a case like this, the text presents such difficulties that its translations are inevitably adaptations. The problem occurs for example when Carroll refers to nursery rhymes or when he invents names for the courses studied by the Mock Turtle at school: 'Uglification' in

[27] T. Chevrier, 'La Plus Etrange Aventure de Mayne-Reid: sa traduction', in *Le Rocambole*, Bulletin des Amis du roman populaire, no. 11, 'Stratégies de traduction' (Summer 2000), 26.

Henri Parisot's translation (considered as one of the best so far) becomes 'Mortification', 'Seaography' 'la Sous-l'eau-graphie' and 'Laughing and Grief' 'le Patin et le Break', etc. Many translations of Carroll's masterpiece continue to be realized and published today, simply because no translation is satisfactory enough to render not only the words themselves, but also all the cultural references embedded in the story. New translators want to take up the challenge.

Publication

There is little doubt that publishers, like editors, act as mediators of the translated text. The way the book is published—its paratext, to use Gérard Genette's word—has to be taken into account as we examine the transmission and reception of Victorian novels in France.

So, for example, in 19th-century French editions of Victorian novels, the title-page usually offers a set phrase which varies according to the strategy chosen: 'traduit' or 'imité' or 'adapté' de l'anglais. This shows that publishers did not try to hide the foreign origin of the book, conversely to what may happen nowadays. Linked with this point is the question of the title, which can be either a literal translation, or a more or less accurate one. In the first half of the 19th century, Christian names would often be Frenchified, with *Jane* Eyre becoming *Jeanne* Eyre, and *Mary* Barton becoming *Marie* Barton for example. The title of the translation could be changed whenever the literal meaning would not be clear for a French reader, or because the French publishers might wish to make it more attractive and understandable, as was often the case for popular novels. Charles Reade's *Hard Cash* became *L'Argent fatal* and Mary Elizabeth Braddon's *Only a Clod* was changed into *Le Brosseur du lieutenant*, a far cry from the original title indeed! The use of subtitles was not uncommon in order to suggest the theme of the novel more clearly, as seen previously for *Jane Eyre*. An 1881 French edition of *The Mill on the Floss* became *La Famille Tulliver, ou le moulin sur la Floss*. But in some cases, the solution chosen was not always the simplest one. Thus, the first translation of *Great Expectations* by Ch. Bernard-Derosne, published in the newspaper *Le Temps* was entitled *Les Grandes Espérances du nommé Philip Pirrip, vulgairement appelé Pip*. *A Tale of Two Cities*, Dickens's novel on the French Revolution, was often translated and printed with various titles modelled on Balzac and Hugo, like *Paris et Londres en 1793*, or *Un drame sous la Révolution*. However, in spite of the publishers' efforts to make it attractive for French readers, the novel met with little success. Braddon's *Henry Dunbar* was subtitled 'Histoire d'un réprouvé' ('The Story of an Outcast'). One final interesting example is that of the children's bestseller *Tom Brown's Schooldays*, which Hachette printed without the author's name but with a subtitle meant to suggest the contents of the book: *Tom Brown. Scènes de la vie de collège en Angleterre*.

Another device used by French publishers to help the introduction of Victorian novels into France is a well-known one: Prefaces. These are always very useful to mediate the foreign work, and in the 19th century they were often written by translators as a means of justifying their translation strategy. Thus Amédée Pichot explained in his Preface to *David Copperfield* that he chose to shorten certain scenes and rid the text of all of Dickens's anglicisms in order to avoid shocking French readers! In other cases, Prefaces were used to introduce the writer and stress the quality of his/her novels. Some were written by French commentators, others were by the writer himself and then translated. Prefaces could also come from series editors. In a special series called 'Romans et aventures célèbres', each volume consisted of two or three texts by different writers, each with its own introduction. One of these volumes included 'Dans l'alcôve' by Douglas Jerrold, 'Le Vaisseau fantôme' by Frederick Marryat (given there as 'Capitaine Marryat') and 'La Case de l'Oncle Tom' by Harriet Beecher Stowe (given there as 'Beecher-Stow'). This sort of Preface helped in introducing foreign writers to French readers, consequently providing some biographical information as well as a short comment on their works. If H. Duclos, the author of the three Prefaces, was rather kind to Jerrold, he clearly voiced his hostility towards Marryat's aggressive preference for his own country, speaking of his 'partialité agressive', and adding that it might be the reason for his success in England. One wonders why it was decided to publish him in France! Mary Elizabeth Braddon's very short Preface to *Henry Dunbar*, translated for the French edition, was of a different kind, because she wrote it to complain about critics who revealed the plots of her novels: 'The story of "Henry Dunbar" pretends to be nothing more than a story, the revealment [*sic*] of which is calculated to weaken the interest of the general reader, for whose amusement the tale is written.'

Before turning to the reception of Victorian novels by the French reading public in the 19th century, it is worth looking at the way these books were advertised in some publishers' catalogues, whose function is to present a publisher's production to the retailers. In order to promote new titles and to shed light on the publisher's choices, extracts from reviews might be included. The Librairie Amyot catalogue for 1854 contained several quotations concerning Dickens taken from periodicals of the time. For example, a quotation praising the translation of *The Cricket on the Hearth* under the title *Le Cricri du foyer* is taken from *Le Journal des débats*. It was followed by a short paragraph from *Le Moniteur*, describing the story as a masterpiece. Further down, an extract from *Le Semeur* was quoted in praise of Disraeli's *Les Deux Nations (Sybil)*, referring to the success of the book in England. Again the announcement of the publication of Lady Georgiana Fullerton's *Ellen Middleton* was accompanied with a quotation from *Le Semeur*, indicating that the author was the daughter of Lord Granville, former British ambassador in Paris. It also pointed out the qualities of the novel—the purity of her style, the novel's endearing scenes, the well-drawn pictures of English upper society, etc.—all of which justified its publication in France. The same sort of comments, but written by the publisher himself, can be found in the 1838 catalogue for Charles Gosselin, who published Walter Scott and Fenimore Cooper in France. One of the comments concerned Frederick Marryat's novels, highlighting their popularity in Britain as evidenced by the publication in Belgium of pirated editions of M. Defauconpret's marvellous translations. This is a surprising remark considering Defauconpret's reputation as a very faulty translator, occasionally passing off English novels he had translated as his own work with the words 'by the translator of Walter Scott's historical novels' on the covers!

Publishers' comments thus paved the way for other critics' reviews and contributed to the reception of Victorian novels in France.

Reception

Evaluating the reception of Victorian novels in France in the 19th century is not an easy task, for sales figures are in short supply. The only option is to rely on published reviews, which were somewhat limited and irregular. However, periodicals like the *Revue des deux mondes*, the *Revue britannique*, the *Journal des débats* and the *Revue critique des livres nouveaux* provide enough information to get an idea of the critics', if not the readers' response, to Victorian fiction. Besides, not infrequently, some of the reviews dealt with the original books, such as those published by Tauchnitz, when the French editions were not yet available. This was particularly the case with the *Revue des deux mondes*,

The most striking characteristic of these reviews is the use of comparisons with other English or French novelists. For example, E.D. Forgues' 1851 review of Charles Kingsley's novel *Alton Locke* in the *Revue britannique* referred to Dickens, Disraeli, and Gaskell, because, like him, they wrote about social problems.[28] The conclusion of the review of *Middlemarch* published in the same periodical in 1872 ends with the unexpected remark that George Sand is not superior to George Eliot.[29] Forgues even compared her to Stendhal.[30] In 1895, in a long article on Mrs Humphry Ward, the reviewer of the *Revue des deux mondes* compared her with Jane Austen and George Sand.[31] These comparisons were obviously useful to attract readers. Whether a novel would suit the French reader's taste or not was a recurrent theme. The reviewer of Kipling's novel *Kim* in the *Revue des deux mondes* wrote that the English liked the book because they liked picaresque novels, implicitly suggesting that it could not be appreciated in France, and he went so far as to criticize Kipling's contempt for everything that is not English.[32] Ward's *Marcella* was described as her best novel translated into French because it was more suitable for the French reading public.[33] Otherwise, the different demands, different characteristics, and different kinds of reading in England and in France were underlined. Such comments were often stereotypical and therefore not always convincing. Interesting reasons for a novelist's success in France were often given. As regards Gaskell, her fame was thought to be due to an interest in English social history on the part of the French

[28] E.D. Forgues, 'Poète et tailleur (Autobiographie d'Alton Locke)', 323. For a more detailed account of Gaskell's French reception, see Annette B. Hopkins, 'Mrs. Gaskell in France: 1849–1900', *PMLA* 53 (June 1938): 545–74.

[29] Amédée Pichot, 'Correspondance de Londres', *Revue britannique* (November 1872): 468–79, 477.

[30] Discussed in Devonshire, 374–75.

[31] G. Bonet-Maury, 'Madame Humphry Ward', *Revue des deux mondes* (March 1895): 651–67, 651.

[32] Théodor de Wyzewa, 'Le Nouveau Roman de M. Rudyard Kipling', *Revue des deux mondes* (October 1901): 936–46.

[33] G. Bonet-Maury, 'Madame Humphry Ward', 663.

reading public and if only two of Reade's books, *It Is Never Too Late To Mend* and *Hard Cash* were successful, it was because they were reform novels.[34]

A general lack of enthusiasm for Victorian novels on the part of critics was not unusual, even when they commented on the best British novelists of the times. The main reproach concerned the length of novels, due as we know to the modes of publication in England, particularly the three-deckers. 'Too long' is a recurrent criticism, bearing either on English fiction in general or on particular books, and this failing is associated with boredom, another recurrent term, applied not only to second-rate works, but also to works that already had critical success in England. For instance the term was used for Trollope's novels as well as for Kipling's *Kim*, described as a 'long roman d'un ennui mortel' (a long mortally boring novel) in the review quoted previously.[35] Ward's *The History of David Grieve* was said to be too long because of too many digressions, something for which Reade was also criticized.[36] The multiplicity of characters was considered another mark against Ward's and Kipling's novels. It is worth noting that in *La Revue critique des livres nouveaux*, comments on translations were sometimes given. The translation of *Adam Bede* by M. D'Albert-Durade was said to have been done with remarkable talent, while in the review of *Silas Marner* two years later it was considered less satisfactory.[37]

Fortunately there were also positive, if not extravagantly laudatory, reviews of the greatest Victorian novels. In the *Revue critique des livres nouveaux*, for April 1858, the reviewer praised *Jane Eyre* for being interesting to the point of being unputdownable, and described it as 'hors ligne', meaning outstanding: 'la forme n'est pas moins belle que le fond; le style est admirable de clarté, de précision, de force et de couleur' (the manner is not less beautiful than the matter; her style has wonderful clarity, precision, strength and colour).[38] Philarète Chasles wrote that both Charlotte's Brontë's personality and works appealed greatly to the French. In his review of *Vanity Fair* in the *Revue des deux mondes* in February 1849, he considered Thackeray's book as the best novel of the times, though he could not refrain from criticizing its occasional prolixity and other weaknesses, such as the lack of 'concentration and concision'.[39] But for the French, the greatest and the most praised of all Victorian novelists was unquestionably Dickens, though it took him some time to be appreciated, possibly on account of poor translations.[40] His popularity began to grow from 1850 to 1855,

[34]   E.D. Forgues, 'Une réforme par le roman', *Revue des deux mondes* (February 1864): 669, cited in Devonshire, 357.

[35]   'Le Nouveau Roman de M. Rudyard Kipling', 940.

[36]   G. Bonet-Maury, 'Madame Humphry Ward', 660.

[37]   'George Elliot'[sic], *Revue critique des livres nouveaux* (January 1861): 21–22.

[38]   '*Jane Eyre* par Currer Bell', *Revue critique des livres nouveaux* 18 (April 1858): 165–68, 166.

[39]   Philarète Chasles, 'Le Roman de moeurs en Angleterre—W.M. Thackeray, La Foire aux vanités', *Revue des deux mondes* 45 (February 1849): 953.

[40]   See also Joseph T. Flibbert, 'Dickens and the French Debate Over Realism: 1838–1856', *Comparative Literature* 23 (1971): 18–31, where Flibbert argues that the negative critical reaction to Dickens in France before the 1850s arose out of French critical resistance to 'the 'realistic' portrayal of common subjects, the tendency to describe the vulgarity and the misery of humble people rather than idealize their condition' (19). Flibbert sees this resistance as part and parcel of a strong French critical preference for

which explains the number of his publications in France.[41] Devonshire draws up a list of his novels in print in France between 1849 and 1870 which amounts to nearly a hundred titles.[42] This list shows that the titles most favoured by French readers were *David Copperfield, Oliver Twist, Little Dorrit, Hard Times, Dombey & Son*, and *The Old Curiosity Shop*, with more than five editions each over a little more than twenty years.

As regards popular fiction, and particularly sensation novels, reviews expressed a certain reserve in their judgements but could not help noting their success in France. Thus, in the *Revue des deux mondes* in June 1863, E.D. Forgues was highly critical of them, while admitting that Braddon knew how to use the devices of the melodrama. But he nonetheless praised Collins for being the more literary of the two.[43] That such writers were appreciated by French readers is unquestionable, since the novels of Braddon, Collins, Wood, Ouida, and so on, were regularly reviewed by both the *Revue des deux mondes* and by the *Revue britannique*. Thérèse Bentzon's review of Ouida's novel *La Branche de lilas* in the *Revue des deux mondes* in September 1873 is quite surprising, coming from a woman, in suggesting that the novelist's boldness in dealing with adultery could well have come from her French origins, but so could her numerous literary qualities, 'la verve de son style, la témérité naturelle de sa si brillante imagination, sa légèreté de plume' (the vigour of her style, the natural boldness of her brilliant imagination, the lightness of her writing) which were considered rare in her country.[44] It is clear that the reason why Hachette continued publishing these writers in his 'Bibliothèque des meilleurs romans étrangers' was their success with the French reading public.

CONCLUSION

What is the situation of Victorian novels in France today? The main Victorian novelists continued to be in print in French translations, in various types of editions throughout the 20th century and after. Novels which are considered classics can be found in abridged and/or bilingual series to be used as school texts. A case in point is *Jane Eyre* which was published by the children's publisher Ecole des loisirs in a series called 'Classiques abrégés' in 2008, but unfortunately the translation used is that by

English romantic literature, as well as a tendency to 'identify realism in literature with democratic and revolutionary forces which, they feared, would lead to political and social chaos' (19).

  [41] Flibbert attributes this shift to Hippolyte Taine's essays on Dickens. See 'Dickens and the Debate Over Realism', 19.

  [42] Devonshire, 313–15.

  [43] E.D. Forgues, 'Miss M.E. Braddon et le roman à sensation', *Revue des deux mondes* (June 1863): 953–77.

  [44] Thérèse Bentzon, '*La Branche de lilas* par Ouida', *Revue des deux mondes* (September 1873): 64–66. An excerpt from the novel follows the review.

Mme Desbazeille-Souvestre for Hachette in 1862, whose quality is questionable. Two series have specialized in the publication of complete works—or at least of the major novels—of a given author. The first is the famously elegant scholarly hardback series 'La Pléïade', published by Gallimard, which includes the Brontë sisters, Dickens, Kipling, Conrad, Stevenson, and Wilde in its catalogue. The other is a more popular paperback series called 'Bouquins', in which novels by the Brontës, Lewis Carroll, Dickens, Kipling, Haggard, Stevenson, and Conan Doyle can be found. Apart from these two series, it is possible to find a few French publishers who will occasionally put one or two more or less forgotten Victorian novels in their catalogues. For there are many Victorian novels which were never translated and remain unknown. It is difficult to assess the success of such books because most of the time they are minor works and often unfortunately published in an old faulty translation for financial reasons. This is the case with the publisher Phebus who has recently published Blackmore's *Lorna Doone*. However Phebus has also launched a paperback series called 'Libretto' in which successful Victorian novelists like Anne Brontë, Collins (seven titles), Hardy, and Stevenson can be found.

In other words, the Victorian novel is still present in France in the 21st century, above all through its most popular authors. However, the canonical works are not completely forgotten today and continue to be read, either in English or in French, by the more educated category of readers, undoubtedly with great delight. And translators and publishers will certainly continue to provide French readers with new and possibly better editions of both well-known and forgotten Victorian novels.

Suggested Reading

Chevrier, Thierry. 'La Plus Etrange Aventure de Mayne-Reid: sa traduction'. In *Le Rocambole*, Bulletin des Amis du roman populaire, no. 11. 'Stratégies de traduction' (Summer 2000), 26.

Couch, John Philip. *George Eliot in France: A French Appraisal of George Eliot's Writings, 1858–1960*. Chapel Hill: University of North Caroline Press, 1967.

Devonshire, M.G. *The English Novel in France, 1830–1870*. London: University of London Press, 1929.

Flibbert, Joseph T. 'Dickens and the French Debate Over Realism: 1838–1856'. *Comparative Literature* 23 (1971): 18–31.

Hopkins, Annette B. 'Mrs. Gaskell in France: 1849–1900'. *PMLA* 53 (June 1938): 545–74.

Jansohn, Christa. 'The Impact of Bernhard Tauchnitz's Book Series "Collection of British and American Authors" on the Continent', *Angermion: Yearbook for Anglo-German Literary Criticism, Intellectual History and Cultural Transfers/Jahrbuch für Britisch-Deutsche Kulturbeziehungen* 3 (2010): 161–83.

Lyons, Martyn. 'Les Best-sellers'. In *Histoire de l'édition française*. Edited by Roger Chartier and Henri-Jean Martin. Vol. 3: *Le Temps des éditeurs. Du Romantisme à la Belle-Epoque* (Fayard—Cercle de la Librairie, 1990), 410–11.

Mollier, Jean-Yves. *Louis Hachette*. Paris: Fayard, 1999.

Monod, Sylvère. 'Les Premiers Traducteurs français de Dickens'. *Romantisme* no. 106 (1999): 119–28.

Parinet, Elisabeth. *Une histoire de l'édition à l'époque contemporaine, XIXe–XXe siècle*. Collection Points Histoire. Paris: Éditions du Seuil, 2004.

Sassoon, Donald. *The Culture of the Europeans from 1800 to the Present*. London: HarperCollins, 2006.

Taine, Hippolyte. *Histoire littérature anglaise*. 4 vols. Paris: Hachette, 1864.

10

VICTORIAN LITERATURE AND RUSSIAN CULTURE: TRANSLATION, RECEPTION, INFLUENCE, AFFINITY

JULIE BUCKLER

Victorian England did not know Russian literature until the 1880s, but educated Russians developed an avid interest in English literature during the second half of the 18th century. Thus, before Russians took 19th-century classics such as Dickens, Thackeray, the Brontës, Trollope, and George Eliot to their hearts, they had read Sterne, Fielding, Richardson, Smollett, Defoe, and Ann Radcliffe in translation, and were passionate about Lord Byron and Sir Walter Scott.[1] France was the primary Western model for modern Russian culture, but Britain too exerted a considerable influence, with formal diplomatic and trade relations established in the mid-16th century.[2] Gallomania reigned in Russia from the second half of the 18th century into the early 19th century when French was central to the education and social culture of the Russian aristocracy, but Napoleon's invasion of Russia in 1812 caused a marked cultural shift. The rule of Tsar Alexander I (1801–25) was associated with a 'cult of all things English', although

---

[1] Ernest J. Simmons, *English Literature and Culture in Russia (1553–1840)* (Cambridge: Harvard University Press, 1935) is an extremely useful source for the three centuries preceding the Victorian period. See also Iu. D. Levin, *The Perception of English Literature in Russia: Investigations and Materials*, trans. Catherine Phillips (Nottingham: Astra Press, 1994) for information about Enlightenment-era English periodicals in Russian translation, the reception of English poetry in the culture of Russian sentimentalism, and on Shakespeare in Russia. Levin produced a great deal of scholarship on this topic published by the Institute of Russian Literature (Pushkin House) of the USSR Academy of Sciences, but only the essays in the aforementioned volume have been translated into English.

[2] See the introduction to Priscilla Meyer, *How the Russians Read the French: Lermontov, Dostoevsky, Tolstoy* (Madison: University of Wisconsin Press, 2008). See also Thomas Barran, *Russia Reads Rousseau, 1762–1825* (Evanston: Northwestern University Press, 2002).

this trend had its roots in the latter part of the 18th century, when aristocratic Russians began to travel abroad, including to England.[3] So, for example, during the first part of the 1830s, Alexander Pushkin planned to write a Russian dandy novel to be titled *A Russian Pelham*, and the opening chapter of his novel-in-verse *Eugene Onegin* dwells upon the hero's English-style dress and calculated rudeness.[4]

Anyone familiar with the late Victorian and Edwardian periods will know something about the enthusiastic reception of Turgenev, Tolstoy, Dostoevsky, and Chekhov in England—accompanied by critical assessments from the likes of Matthew Arnold, Henry James, D.H. Lawrence, and Virginia Woolf.[5] The English reception of Russian literature at this stage was nevertheless culturally 'shallow', since translators' efforts were concentrated on a few major Russian writers. Many significant writers from 19th-century Russia remained little known to English readers, among them Goncharov, Leskov, Pisemsky, Ostrovsky, and Saltykov-Shchedrin.

The story of how Russians read English literature, and more particularly, how 19th-century Russians encountered and understood Victorian literature, will likely be less familiar to users of this Handbook. Russians were reading Victorian literature more or less from its beginnings in the late 1830s. And in contrast to the English reception of Russian literature that began some half-century later, the Russian reception of Victorian literature cast a wide if unsystematic net, such that the works and authors translated into Russian extended to the margins of the tradition. Virtually all of the works of better-known Victorian writers (the Brontës, Collins, Dickens, Eliot, Thackeray, Trollope, as well as Bulwer Lytton, Gaskell, Gissing, Kipling, Meredith, and Stevenson) were translated into Russian, and multiple editions of a given work might appear over the course of the 19th century, sometimes in more than one translation. American

---

[3] A.G. Cross, 'Russian Perceptions of England, and Russian National Awareness at the End of the Eighteenth and the Beginning of the Nineteenth Centuries', in *Anglo-Russica: Aspects of Cultural Relations Between Great Britain and Russia in the Eighteenth and Early Nineteenth Centuries: Selected Essays* (Oxford: Berg, 1993), 90–91. Cross notes the 1803 appearance of the term *angloman* (Anglomaniac) in the dictionary *Novyi slovotolkovatel'*, defined as 'a person who is astonished by, and imitates to ludicrous excess, everything that is done in England'. The writer Nikolai Karamzin (1766–1826) recalled, 'There was a time when having met almost no Englishmen, I was enraptured by them and imagined England to be the country most attractive to my heart...It seemed to me that to be brave was to be English, magnanimous also, a real man also. Novels, if I'm not mistaken, were the main source for such an opinion' (*Sochineniia*, vol. 2 (SPb, 1848), 773). See also the anthology *'Ia bereg pokidal tumannyi Al'biona...': Russkie pisateli ob Anglii. 1646–1945*, ed. O.A. Kaznina and A.N. Nikoliukin (Moscow: Rosspen, 2001).

[4] Sam Driver provides good background on this topic in his 'The Dandy in Pushkin', *Slavic and East-European Journal* 29(3) (1985): 243–57.

[5] Perhaps Donald Davie put it best in his 1972 essay 'Mr. Tolstoy, I presume? The Russian Novel through Victorian Spectacles', in *Slavic Excursions: Essays on Russian and Polish* (Manchester: Carcanet, 1990) when he wrote: '[The] awakening of the Anglo-Saxon people to Russian literature—something which happened to all intents and purposes between 1885 and 1920—should rank as a turning point no less momentous than the discovery of Italian literature by the generations of the English Renaissance. The teacher of Russian literature to English-speaking youth today is a beachcomber along sands still wet from the incursion of that tidal wave' (276).

writers such as Fenimore Cooper, Twain, and Bret Harte were also extremely popular. Non-canonical Victorian writers such as Frederick Marryat, Mary Elizabeth Braddon, 'Ouida', Mrs Henry Wood, Walter Besant, William Harrison Ainsworth, Charles Kingsley, Eliza Lynn Linton, Charles Reade, Augustus Mayhew, and James Payn were amply translated into Russian. John Edward Jenkins and the infamous Thomas Mayne Reid were better known in Russia than at home in England, the latter much beloved in both imperial and Soviet Russia.[6] There are, however, some inexplicable lacunae in the corpus of Russian translations, one being Thomas Hardy, represented only by an 1893 translation of *Tess of the D'Urbervilles*.

'... TOOK A PAPER-KNIFE AND AN ENGLISH NOVEL FROM HER HANDBAG'

An iconic moment from Tolstoy's *Anna Karenina* may serve as an image for the relationship between the Russian reader and English literature of the Victorian period. On the train from Moscow to St Petersburg, all aflutter from her first encounters with Vronsky, Anna attaches a lamp to the armrest of her seat and loses herself in an unnamed English novel:

> Anna Arkadyevna read and understood, but it was unpleasant for her to read, that is, to follow the reflection of other people's lives. She wanted too much to live herself. When she read about the heroine of the novel taking care of a sick man, she wanted to walk with inaudible steps round the sick man's room; when she read about a Member of Parliament making a speech, she wanted to make that speech; when she read about how Lady Mary rode to hounds, teasing her sister-in-law and surprising everyone with her courage, she wanted to do it herself. But there was nothing to do, and so, fingering the smooth knife with her small hands, she forced herself to read.[7]

The fictional novel that Anna reads in this scene is a composite of Trollope, Eliot, and others, with its hero striving 'to attain the English notion of happiness—a baronetcy and an estate'. Anna will live out this fantasy later in the novel, when she and Vronsky set themselves up in English style at their thoroughly modern estate Vozdvizhenskoe, but she will not attain the fulfilment of her readerly desires.

Amy Mandelker has artfully characterized the preceding passage from Anna Karenina as exemplifying the way in which 'otherness' was intrinsic to Russian reading, which so

    [6] Kenneth E. Harper and Bradford A. Booth, 'Russian Translations of Nineteenth-Century English Fiction', *Nineteenth-Century Fiction* 8(3) (1953): 188–97.
    [7] *Anna Karenina*, trans. Pevear and Volokhonsky (London: Penguin Books, 2002), 99–100.

often involved a foreign text. The text could be in a foreign language (the text's original language, or sometimes translated into an intermediary language such as French from, say, English or German) or the text might be translated directly into Russian.[8] All of these possibilities created an overriding sense of 'otherness.' Even reading a work of *Russian* literature in Anna's time meant being sensitive to the ways in which a given work responded to its Western antecedents or influences, individual and generic. The rapidity with which Russia mounted its own literary tradition during the 18th and 19th centuries, a tradition that asserted a distinct identity in both formal and thematic terms, was nevertheless accompanied by 'an agonizing self-consciousness of its own derivative nature and a struggle for originality.'[9]

Anxieties about Russian cultural inferiority were accompanied by defensive rhetorical table-turnings, Dostoevsky being perhaps the prime offender. In 1873, Dostoevsky wrote that foreigners could never truly understand Gogol, Pushkin, or Turgenev, and that the greater and more original a Russian author was, the longer he would remain unrecognized abroad:

> I am convinced, we understand Dickens in Russia almost as well as the English do...And yet, how original is Dickens, and how very English! What, then, must one conclude from that? Is this understanding of other nations a special gift that the Russians possess to a higher degree than [other] Europeans?[10]

In 1876, Dostoevsky even more outrageously asserted the particular receptivity of Russians to foreign literature:

> [E]very European poet, thinker and philanthropist is always most fully and intimately understood and accepted in Russia in all the countries of the world apart from his own...This Russian attitude to world literature is a phenomenon almost unparalleled...among other nations throughout world history. [It] really is our national Russian peculiarity...every poet innovator of Europe, everyone who appears there with a new idea and a new source of strength, cannot fail immediately to become a Russian poet as well, cannot bypass Russian thought, cannot fail to become almost a Russian force.[11]

A recent study on the influence of English literature on the Russian modernist aesthetic renaissance uses the work of cultural semiotician Yuri Lotman as a framework

---

[8]   This practice of mediated translations went both ways in Russian–English literary relations. The earliest translations of Russian literary works into English during the 19th century were frequently made through French or German intermediary versions.

[9]   Amy Mandelker, *Framing Anna Karenina: Tolstoy, the Woman Question, and the Victorian Novel* (Columbus: Ohio State University Press, 1993), 129.

[10]   F.M. Dostoevskii, *Polnoe sobranie sochinenii*, 12 vols. (SPb, 1894–95), t. 21, 68–69.

[11]   F.M. Dostoevskii, *PSS*, t. 10, ch. 10, 204–205.

for thinking about the dynamics of the 'ingrafting' Dostoevsky describes.[12] According to Lotman's model of cultural assimilation, foreign texts provide a vital stimulus for the creative development of a new national literary tradition, which constitutes itself in relation to the outside influence.[13] When considering the cultural assimilation of Victorian literature in Russia, however, it is important to keep in mind the significant differences between Victorian middle-class nationalism and the left-leaning Russian intelligentsia's scepticism toward liberal-capitalist and bourgeois values.[14] The Russian intelligentsia confronted the challenge of modernizing Russia with their particular brand of Romantic idealism and Utopian socialism, perhaps most fully embodied in Nikolai Chernyshevsky's 1862 novel *What Is to Be Done?*, which imagines humanity's joyous future in a sexually open social commune. The Great Reforms of the 1860s produced limited results, however, and the increasingly conservative retrenchment of the Russian government during the remainder of the imperial period widened the gulf between official conservative cultural nationalism and alienated radical alternatives. But neither radicals nor conservatives favoured the development of capitalism in Russia, a place that did not foster the development of middle ground.

Despite defensive rhetoric and wishful thinking, Russians felt alienated from the Western cultures they so strove to emulate, and were often seen by their European counterparts as crudely unassimilable. A familiar figure from English literature vividly illustrates this cultural predicament. The frame story of Mary Shelley's *Frankenstein* (1818) takes place in Russia, when the young explorer Robert Walton sails northward from Arkhangelsk and encounters the monster and his creator in the icy wastes. (Dr Frankenstein declares, 'Amidst the wilds of Tartary and Russia, although he still evaded me, I have ever followed in his track'.) Richard Freeborn offers a reading of Shelley's novel that ties the monster to Russian cultural identity in its isolation from 'the sources of…European heritage and the world of civilized men to which he sought to belong'. Ivan Kireevsky's 1830 essay 'The Nineteenth Century' and Petr Chadaaev's 1829 Philosophical Letters both emphasize Russia's exclusion from the heritage of classical antiquity as well as the absence of a Russian Renaissance culture, historical factors that rendered Russia neither truly Western nor fully Eastern. In this spirit, Freeborn writes:

> How frightening he [the monster] might seem to those Russians intelligent and sensitive enough to recognize his presence in their lives! How hideous might seem this European idea, this animated corpse, whose 'dull yellow eye' might slowly open and scrutinize them! Only then perhaps would those who did not flee from the sight of the monster…recognize in that 'dull yellow eye' covert signs of their own dilemma

---

[12]   Rachel Polonsky, *English Literature and the Russian Aesthetic Renaissance* (Cambridge: Cambridge University Press, 1998), 2–5.

[13]   Yuri Lotman, *Izbrannye stat'i*, vol. 1 (Tallin, 1992), 112–17.

[14]   See chapter 1 of Olga Stuchebrukhov, *The Nation as Invisible Protagonist in Dickens and Dostoevsky: Uncovering Hidden Social Forces within the Text* (Lewiston: Edwin Mellon Press, 2006) for a comparison of British and Russian nationalisms, both political and cultural.

and begin slowly to acknowledge that his loneliness and homelessness and craving for a past were monstrous reflections of a specifically Russian condition.

Russia was a country 'uninfluenced by the universal education of the human race, rootless, existing in an immature, childlike state of soulless quiescence and characterized chiefly by being alone in the world, inaccessible to the sum total of human ideas and incapable of contributing to it', seemingly repudiated by its Creator and seeking to revenge itself.[15] Freeborn links Victor Frankenstein's creation of a 'new man' to the Utopian fantasies that inspirited Russian radicals, revolutionaries, and socialist realists.[16]

Bram Stoker's *Dracula* offers a complementary iconic figure for Russia in the British literary imagination, this time from the later period of Imperial Gothic. According to Jimmie E. Cain, Jr, a deep-seated fear of Russia shapes both *Dracula* (1897) and *The Lady of the Shroud* (1909). Russophobia in Victorian England was a product of imperial rivalry in the Near East and Central Asia, exacerbated by the Crimean War of 1854–56. Stoker's *Dracula* offers a happy fictional solution by

> ameliorating the stain on England's reputation eventuating from her problematic incursion against Russia in the Crimean War and…dissipating the anxieties engendered by Russia's designs on British India and Central Asia…by portraying a force of imperial warriors pledged to England who defeat a primitive Eastern invader, pursue him to his homeland, and destroy him on his native soil.[17]

This victory counters the reverse colonization that is Dracula's primary aim in Britain.

Stoker's *Dracula* can also be seen as a response to the thousands of Bulgarian, Polish, Romanian, and Russian Jews who immigrated to England to escape pogroms and state-sponsored anti-Semitism during the 1880s and 1890s. These Jewish immigrants were perceived as alien invaders from the East who sought to contaminate the blood of the British nation. Even greater levels of cultural anxiety were provoked by exiled Russian revolutionary terrorists, and the potential havoc they might wreak on British

[15] Richard Freeborn, 'Frankenstein's Last Journey', *Oxford Slavonic Papers* (1985): 113–17.

[16] In another essay, 'Frankenstein and Bazarov', *New Zealand Slavonic Journal* (1994) Freeborn makes this link explicit by casting the hero of Turgenev's novel *Fathers and Children* as a 19th-century Prometheus, with his emphasis on science.

[17] Jimmie E. Cain, Jr, *Bram Stoker and Russophobia: Evidence of the British Fear of Russia in Dracula and The Lady of the Shroud* (Jefferson, NC: McFarland & Co., 2006), Cain writes, 'Dracula's strategy is nothing less than genocide via rape, practiced by the Russians of Stoker's time among the Turks and by their Serbian brethren among the Bosnian Muslims in the early 1990s. Dracula symbolizes the possibility of deracination and racial contamination…' (138). See also John Howes Gleason, *The Genesis of Russophobia in Great Britain: A Study of the Interaction of Policy and Opinion* [1950] (New York: Octagon Books, 1972) which focuses on the period 1815–41. For an interesting account of the exploitation of Nikolai Gogol's novel *Dead Souls*, published in English in 1854 under the title *Home Life in Russia by a Russian Noble* as a 'forgery and purposeful distortion' with many omissions and additions for anti-Russian propaganda purposes, see Carl Lefevre, 'Gogol and Anglo-Russian Literary Relations during the Crimean War', *American Slavic and East European Review* 8(2) (April 1949): 106–25.

soil. And indeed, the number of Russian political emigrants grew from a trickle to a steady stream after the 1881 assassination of Tsar Alexander II. Major Marxists and anarchists such as Georgy Plekhanov, Peter Kropotkin, Vera Zasulich, Sergius Stepniak, and Lenin all spent time living in Britain. English fictional works featuring Russian revolutionaries on British soil became popular during this period, among them William Le Queux's *A Secret Service: Strange Tales of a Nihilist* (1896), Fred Whishaw's *A Russian Vagabond* (1898), Isabel Meredith's *A Girl Among the Anarchists* (1903), E.L. Voynich's *Olive Latham* (1904), and C. De Lone's *Petrovich's Revenge* (1909).[18] Reception of major Russian realists aside, canonical and popular literary works reveal the diverse images produced by reflections of Russia in the British literary imagination.

TRANSLATION AND RECEPTION

The inception of modern Russian letters in the 18th century grew from the energetic practice of translation, although literary norms of the time often blurred the boundaries between translation, adaptation, imitation, and downright plagiarism. English literature first came to Russia in French and German translations, rendered into Russian from these intermediary languages, and sometimes resulting in a decades-long delay between the original publication of a work like Richardson's *Clarissa Harlowe* (1748) and its reception in Russian translation during the early 1790s. This characteristic delay in translation and reception grew shorter during the Pre-Romantic period, and the gap then closed almost completely with Russia participating more or less in the 'real-time' reception of Sir Walter Scott and Lord Byron.

Most 19th-century Russian writers honed their literary skills with early experiments in translation—Dostoevsky famously started off with a translation of Balzac's *Eugénie Grandet* and Tolstoy tried his hand at Sterne's *Sentimental Journey*, most likely working from a French version. But it was not until 1840 or so that literary translation in Russia truly became part of the commercial and professional practices of the newly forming literary market.[19] Writer and critic Nikolai Chernyshevsky remarked in 1857, 'Translated

---

[18] See John Slatter, 'Bears in the Lion's Den: The Figure of the Russian Revolutionary Emigrant in English Fiction, 1880–1914,' *Slavonic and East European Review* 77(1) (January 1999): 30–53. See also Barbara Arnett Melchiori, *Terrorism in the Late Victorian Novel* (London: Croom Helm, 1985) and A.G. Cross, *The Russian Theme in English Literature from the Sixteenth Century to 1980* (Oxford: Willem A. Meeuws, 1985). The best-known exemplars of this subgenre are, of course, Polish-born Joseph Conrad's *The Secret Agent* (1907) and *Under Western Eyes* (1911), the latter set in St. Petersburg and Geneva, and perhaps the earliest example is Oscar Wilde's play *Vera, or The Nihilist* (1880). See my essay 'Melodramatizing Russia: Nineteenth-Century Views from the West', in *Imitations of Life: Two Centuries of Melodrama in Russia*, ed. Louise McReynolds and Joan Neuberger (Durham: Duke University Press, 2002).

[19] For a historical survey on the subject, see chapter 1 of Maurice Friedberg, *Literary Translation in Russia: A Cultural History* (University Park, PA: Pennsylvania State University Press, 1997). See also Iu. D. Levin, *Russkie perevodchiki XIX veka i razvitie khudozhestvennogo perevoda* (Leningrad: Nauka, 1985).

literature is of enormous importance to us. Until Pushkin it was incomparably more important than original [Russian] writing. And even now it is by no means certain whether original [Russian] writing has become more important than translations.'[20]

While translations of foreign literature did appear in stand-alone editions, Russian readers most frequently encountered translations of Western literature, along with instalments of new works by Turgenev, Dostoevsky, Tolstoy, and others, in the monthly 'thick journals' that were an essential part of 19th-century Russian cultural life. These monthly journals were published right up to the 1917 Bolshevik Revolution, although the heyday of major Russian prose fiction ended around 1880.[21] Circulation figures were small by Western European standards; in the 1860s, the decade when daily public newspapers became a fixture in Russia, the most popular journals had 3,500–7,000 subscribers each.[22] Despite these seemingly small numbers, however, it is impossible to overestimate the importance of Russian journals in the intellectual and cultural life of the period, especially in the encyclopaedic nature of their content and the ideal of enlightenment to which they were dedicated. Each journal had its own ideological cast, placing a major emphasis on belles-lettres—Russian literature, foreign literature in translation, and literary criticism—and also including articles on a broad range of topics from domestic and international politics, economics, agriculture, industry, science, history, arts, and religion. From the later 1840s onward, it was usual for each issue of a thick journal to include translations of significant or popular contemporary foreign literary works from French, German, English, Italian, and Polish.

A great deal of English literature from the Victorian period appeared in Russian translation during the 19th century, encompassing nearly all of the major authors and works, along with many works from the margins of the canon.[23] Russian translators also paid significant attention to English poetry.[24] This relatively comprehensive

---

[20] N.G. Chernyshevskii, *Polnoe sobranie sochinenii*, t. 4 (Moscow, 1948), 503–4.

[21] Deborah A. Martinsen, ed., *Literary Journals in Imperial Russia* (Cambridge: Cambridge University Press, 1997). See also chapter 2 'The Tradition', in Robert Maguire, *Red Virgin Soil: Soviet Literature in the 1920s* (Evanston: Northwestern University Press, 2000). The primary journals in question were *Library for Reading* (*Biblioteka dlia chteniia*, 1834–65), *The Contemporary* (*Sovremennik*, 1836–66), *Notes of the Fatherland* (*Otechestvennye zapiski*, 1839–84), *Russian Herald* (*Russkii vestnik*, 1856–1906), *Herald of Europe* (*Vestnik Evropy*, 1866–1918), *Russian Wealth* (*Russkoe bogatstvo*, 1876–1918), and *Russian Thought* (*Russkaia mysl'*, 1880–1918).

[22] M. Mazaev, 'Zhurnal', *Entsiklopedicheskii slovar'*, ed. A.F. Brokgauz and I.A. Efron, xii (St Petersburg, 1894), 64–65. For information about the daily press, see Louise McReynolds, *The News under Russia's Old Regime: The Development of a Mass-Circulation Press* (Princeton: Princeton University Press, 1991). For information about literacy in imperial Russia, see Jeffrey Brooks, *When Russia Learned to Read: Literacy and Popular Culture, 1861–1917* (Princeton: Princeton University Press, 1985).

[23] An extremely useful source for tracking these translations in a general way is the 1971 Variorum Reprint of the Dikson-Meizer *Bibliograficheskii ukazatel' perevodnoi belletristiki* (SPb, 1897) and the Braginskii *Bibliograficheskii ukazatel' perevodnoi belletristiki v russkikh zhurnalakh za piat' let 1897–1901 gg.* (SPb, 1902).

[24] For a sampling, see the bilingual anthology *Angliiskaia poeziia v russkikh perevodakh (XIV–XIX veka)*, ed. M.P. Alekseev, V.V. Zakharov, and B.B. Tomashevskii (Moscow: Progress, 1981), which starts with ballads and Chaucer and goes as far as Gerard Manley Hopkins and Oscar Wilde.

coverage of English literature was, however, mitigated by haphazard and freewheeling translation practices. Russian thick journals did not pay fees to foreign authors, since they were not legally obliged to do so, and Russian translators received paltry compensation, which meant that foreign works in translation were profitable for Russian publishers. Thus due to primarily practical considerations, many 19th-century translations into Russian were abridged in seemingly unsystematic or even perverse fashion. Some works were published in 'digest' form, with commentary by the translator linking translated excerpts and plot summaries. Moreover, the state censorship could insist that problematic passages be eliminated, while the editorial board of the particular journal might choose to excise passages that did not correspond to its ideological orientation. Many translations produced in 19th-century Russia were products of literary hackwork, rendered in haste in return for poor pay. Only with the onset of the modernist period did a more responsible and even artistic conception of translation came to the fore in Russia.

The single most prolific Russian translator of Victorian prose fiction was Irinarkh Vvedensky (1813–55), who provided Russian readers with a steady stream of English novels in the 1840s to 1850s, more than 5,000 printed pages in total.[25] Vvedensky began with *The Vicar of Wakefield* in 1845, and during the period 1847–52 translated *Dombey and Son*, *The Pickwick Papers*, *David Copperfield*, *The Haunted Man*, *Vanity Fair*, *Jane Eyre*, and Caroline Norton's *Stuart of Dunleath*. Posthumous assessments of Vvedensky's work fault him for making an extraordinary number of mistakes in translation and for the liberties he took with the original texts. Vvedensky himself considered this free approach to foreign texts a legitimate method for attuning himself to the author's spirit, and firmly believed that a truly worthy 'translation' should not be strictly faithful. In an 1849 letter to Charles Dickens that appeared in his translation of *Dombey and Son*, Vvedensky wrote, 'I understood you as an Englishman and at the same time, in my thoughts, I had you move to Russian soil, and made you express your ideas as you would if you lived under Russian skies.'[26] Vvedensky liked to insert his own commentary and additions throughout, in phrases and even entire sentences he rendered in a literary idiom similar to the foreign author's own style. He was also fond of adding pithy Russian-style proverbs as folksy authorial interjections at the end of specific passages ('It's easy enough to solve someone else's problems!').[27] Vvedensky represents a complex figure in the Russian literary landscape of the mid-19th century. He took liberties with the texts he translated that would not be tolerated today, but he also raised Russian consciousness about the degree to which prose translation could be a literary art rather than a mechanistic operation.

---

[25] For a detailed account of Vvedensky's literary career, see Iu. D. Levin, 'Irinarkh Vvedenskii i ego perevodcheskaia deiatel'nost', in *Epokha realizma: iz istorii mezhdunarodnykh sviazei russkoi literatury*, ed. M.P. Alekseev (Leningrad: Nauka, 1982).

[26] This letter was reprinted in the journal *Kolos'ia*, 1884, no. 11. Also quoted in part in Levin, *Russkie perevodchiki*, 127 and in Maurice Friedberg, *Literary Translation in Russia: A Cultural History* (University Park, PA: Pennsylvania State University Press, 1997), 150.

[27] Levin, 'Irinarkh Vvedenskii i ego perevodcheskaia deiatel'nost', 131.

British periodicals frequently culled for literary works for translation into Russian included *The Athenaeum, Atlantic Monthly, Canadian Monthly, The Cornhill Magazine, Fortnightly Review, Quarterly Magazine, St. James's Magazine, Scribner's Monthly, Temple Bar,* and *Westminster Review.* It is fascinating to map specific British authors of the Victorian period onto the ideological orientation of the Russian journals that published them—the conservative *Russian Herald,* liberal *Herald of Europe,* and radical *Word,* for example. Prominent authors such as Dickens and Eliot appeared in all the journals, whereas writers who made social discontent their primary focus were showcased in *Notes of the Fatherland* (Owens Blackburn, E.A. Dillwyn, Mrs Fawcett, James Greenwood), and John Edward Jenkins and Grenville Murray were shared with other journals of a radical stripe. The *Russian Herald* and *Herald of Europe* favoured writers of conservative or moderate tendencies such as Trollope, Bulwer Lytton, and Wilkie Collins.[28]

English realist prose was extremely congenial to Russian readers beginning in the 1840s, when Russian literature turned increasingly towards its own realist themes and methods, initially favouring physiological sketches associated with writers of the so-called 'Natural School' such as Nikolai Nekrasov. Sympathy for the downtrodden, broad humanitarian ideals, social awareness, and protagonists of non-noble origin were the order of the day, and early Victorian literature met this agenda. Russian critics tended to see the triumvirate of Dickens, Thackeray, and Charlotte Brontë as representative of separate trends in English literature, and they declared the new 19th-century English literary tradition greatly superior to that of the 18th century.[29] A reviewer in *Notes of the Fatherland* in 1859 heralded 'a multitude of serious talents who have left earlier writers far behind them', noting, 'Thackeray is wittier and more elegant than Swift...Dickens is more artistic than Fielding...Charlotte Bronte...is more profound and interesting than Richardson.'[30] But it should also be noted that interest in the Victorian novelists—with the exception of Dickens—was matched or exceeded by the avidity with which Russians read Victor Hugo, Balzac, Stendahl, Flaubert, and George Sand during the second third of the 19th century.

Dickens was far and away the most popular and influential Victorian writer in Russia.[31] Moreover, since Dickens had a documented impact on the creative development of both Dostoevsky and Tolstoy, the quantity of critical literature about Dickens

---

[28] I.P. Foote, 'Otechestvennye zapiski and English Literature, 1868–84', *Oxford Slavonic Papers* 6 (1973): x–xx, 32.

[29] Olga Demidova, 'The Reception of Charlotte Bronte's Work in Nineteenth-Century Russia', *Modern Language Review* 89 (1994): 689–96. Russian thick journals also covered other aspects of cultural life in Victorian England, surveying the writings and activities of John Stuart Mill, Herbert Spencer, Henry George, Benjamin Disraeli, and William Gladstone, taking a vital interest in Darwin, and following broad socio-political issues such as education, industrialization, free trade, and women's rights.

[30] *Otechestvennye zapiski*, vol. 126, no. 9, section 3 (1859), 69.

[31] Note the importance of Dickens as a much-read author during the Soviet period as well, evidenced by the new and monumental thirty-volume edition of his works in Russian translation that was completed in 1963, with 600,000 sets printed.

in Russia is incommensurably larger than for any other Victorian writer.[32] Dickens's first Russian translator was the aforementioned Irinarkh Vvedensky who wrote to the author in June 1849: 'For ten years your name has enjoyed enormous fame in Russia and you are read with great zeal from the banks of the Neva to the remotest limits of Siberia.'[33] *The Pickwick Papers* (1836) was first translated into Russia in 1838 and *Nicholas Nickleby* (1838–39) in 1840, both in abridged form. Excerpts from *Sketches by Boz* (1836) appeared in various periodicals in 1839. The first complete translation of a Dickens novel—*Oliver Twist* (1837–39) in 1841—definitively established Dickens's reputation in Russia. From this point on, Russian translations appeared very quickly after the publication of each instalment in England.

Women's issues in Victorian literature were particularly timely for Russian readers, with this topic figuring in Russian literature from the 1840s and 1850s onwards, and Russian women writers began publishing works of prose fiction from the 1830s (Karolina Pavlova, Maria Zhukova, E.A. Gan, Avdotia Panaeva). *Jane Eyre* (1847) appeared in Russian translation in 1849 in the journal *Notes of the Fatherland* (Vvedensky rendered the title as *Dzhenni Eir*).[34] Dostoevsky read it while imprisoned in the Peter-Paul Fortress, and declared the novel 'exceptionally fine'.[35] In 1852, a reviewer in *Library for Reading* characterized Jane Eyre in romantic terms as

> written in an extraordinarily compressed, picturesque, and energetic style... the fresh and fiery creation of a young talent of powerful imagination and diverse experience, torn from its creator's soul without inducements or advance calculations, without

[32] The primary Russian-language monograph on this subject is I. Katarskii, *Dikkens v Rossii*, which emphasizes the middle of the 19th century, and along with Dickens's reception by Russian critics and the Russian reading public, pays particular attention to Dickens's influence on Tolstoy's early works (1850s) and on Dostoevsky's works from the 1840s to the 1850s, his pre-exilic period. See also the major bibliographic resource *Charl'z Dikkens. Bibliografiia russkikh perevodov i kriticheskoi literatury na russkom iazyke, 1838–1960*, which includes both translations of Dickens's works and critical literature in Russian for the 122-year period surveyed.

[33] *Kolos'ia*, 1884, no. 11, 275–76. The Soviet-era translator Kornei Chukovsky provided a generous assessment of Vvedensky's accomplishments as a translator of Dickens, as follows: 'What does it matter if he is a liar and an ignoramus who distorts nearly every sentence? The fact is that without him we would have no Dickens at all. He alone brought us closer to [Dickens's] work, immersed us in his flavor, infected us with his temper. He did not understand Dickens's words, but he understood Dickens himself... We heard Dickens's real voice, and we came to love it. In his translations Vvedensky seems to have dressed himself up in Dickens's costume and mask; he appropriated his gestures and manner of walking... Of course, one cannot tolerate a translator's adding his own words to the text [*otsebiatina*], but some of Vvedensky's [additions] are so much in the spirit of Dickens, are so much in harmony with his general tone, that one hates to cross them out. Indeed, one wonders whether Dickens would have crossed them out himself, had he chanced upon them!' See Kornei Chukovskii, *Iskusstvo perevoda* (Leningrad: Academia, 1930), 61–62.

[34] *Jane Eyre* had, in fact, been available to Russian readers since the year of its publication in Tauchnitz's English-language edition. And in 1857, a second Russian translation titled 'Dzhenni Eir, or the Notes of a Governess' done by Sof'ia Koshlakova was published as a stand-alone edition.

[35] See Dostoevsky's letter to his brother from 14 September, in his 30-volume collected works, vol. 28 (Book 1), 161.

pretensions to effect—torn, as are all the first creations of talented people, stormily and almost involuntarily, perhaps even against the will of its author.[36]

Shirley was translated in 1851 and *Villette* in 1853, both published in *Library for Reading*, and *The Professor* in 1857 in *Notes of the Fatherland*. Interest in Charlotte Brontë and her work increased after her death in 1855, marked by several dedicated review-essays in Russian periodicals. Interest in Brontë was renewed at the end of the 19th century, with the 1895 publication of O. Peterson's Russian monograph about the Brontë sisters.[37]

During the same mid-century period, other Victorian women writers were quickly rendered in Russian translation whenever their new works appeared in print.[38] Elizabeth Gaskell's *Cranford* was translated in 1855 (*Notes of the Fatherland*), *North and South* in 1856 (*Russian Herald*), *My Lady Ludlow* in 1859 (*Notes of the Fatherland*), *Mary Barton* in 1861 (*Time*), *The Dark Night's Work* in 1863 (*Library for Reading*), *Ruth* in 1864 (*Time*), and *Wives and Daughters* in 1867 (*Notes of the Fatherland*).

George Eliot's *Adam Bede* first appeared in Russian in 1859 (in both *Russian Herald* and *Notes from the Fatherland*) and Eliot's work was frequently treated in Russian literary criticism during the decade that followed.[39] Russian critic Petr Veinberg provided a judicious assessment of Eliot in an 1869 review essay, declaring her a humanitarian rather than tendentious writer, who, despite her 'social-democratic' leanings, placed a greater emphasis on moral rather than political issues in her novels.[40] *Scenes of Clerical Life* was translated in 1860 (*Russian Herald*), *Mill on the Floss* in 1860 (*Notes of the Fatherland*), *Silas Marner* in 1861 (*Russian World*), *Felix Holt* in 1867 (*Library of the Best Foreign Novels and Stories in Russian Translation*), *Middlemarch* in 1872–73 (*Notes of the Fatherland*), *Daniel Deronda* in 1876 (*Deed*), and *The Lifted Veil* in 1879 (*Notes of the Fatherland*).[41] Five separate editions of *Middlemarch* in Russian translation appeared

[36] Korrer Bell i ego dva romana: 'Shirley' i 'Jean [sic] Eyre,' *Biblioteka dlia chteniia*, t. 116, no. 11, otd. 2 (1852), 36.

[37] O. Peterson, *Semeistvo Bronte (Kerrer, Ellis, i Akton Bell)* (SPb, 1895).

[38] See Alexander Druzhinin, 'Pis'ma ob angliiskoi literature. Zhenshchiny-pisatel'nitsy', *Sovremennik*, 1853, t. 41, no. 10, otd. 4, for a critical survey of contemporary English women writers. Druzhinin (1824–64) was a respected literary critic, perhaps the Russian critic most knowledgeable about Victorian literature during the first two decades of its Russian reception. See also a very long article (137 pages) by M.K. Tsebrikova, 'Anglichanki-romanistki', *Otechestvennye zapiski*, t. 201 (1871), nos. 8–9, 11, for an assessment of Victorian women novelists.

[39] Olga Demidova, 'Charlotte Bronte, Elizabeth Gaskell, and George Eliot in Russian: A Bibliography (1849–1989)', *Oxford Slavonic Papers* 29 (1996): 44–60.

[40] P. Veinberg, 'Dzhordzh Elliot', *Otechestvennye zapiski*, t. 186, no. 10, otd, 1869. 2.

[41] A curious episode in the Russian reception of George Eliot was the 1886 publication of an article by Sofia Kovalevskaya, a mathematician (and future professor at the University of Stockholm), who visited George Eliot in 1869 and 1880 and described her impressions for Russian readers. See *Russkaia mysl'*, no. 6 (1886), 93–108. For an English translation, see Raymond Chapman and Eleanora Gottlieb, 'A Russian View of George Eliot', *Nineteenth-Century Fiction* 33(3) (1978): 348–65. Kovalevskaya, by her own account, offered George Eliot the following criticism of the latter's novels: 'I was always struck by one feature . . . all her heroes and heroines die too opportunely, precisely at the moment when the psychological plot becomes complicated to the degree of extreme tension, when the reader wants to

before 1875. Russian critics lauded Eliot for precisely those literary qualities most valued in Russia's own emerging national literature—seriousness of purpose, psychological realism, positivism, deep understanding of a specific socio-cultural setting, and a commitment to the moral and spiritual development of her readers. During the years that followed Eliot's death in 1880, several substantial essays surveying her entire oeuvre appeared in Russian thick journals, including an 1884 two-part 'Life and Works' piece of some eighty pages by Russian publisher and journalist Alexei Suvorin.[42]

While English fiction in translation continued to appear in Russian journals throughout the 19th century, the interest of Russian writers and critics in these works declined somewhat, beginning in the 1860s. It is easy to speculate on the reason for this. Turgenev began publishing his novels in the later 1850s, starting with *Rudin* (1857), and continuing with *The Nest of Gentlefolk* (1859), *On the Eve* (1860), *Fathers and Children* (1862), *Smoke* (1867), and *Virgin Soil* (1877). Dostoevsky produced a number of short works during the 1840s, and was in Siberian exile from 1849 to 1859. Once Dostoevsky returned to St. Petersburg, he began publishing his 'mature' works and garnering critical notice over the course of the 1860s—*Notes from Underground* (1864), *Crime and Punishment* (1866), *The Idiot* (1868), *The Possessed* (1872), *The Raw Youth* (1875), and *Brothers Karamazov* (1881). Tolstoy's literary debut occurred in 1852, but his real literary celebrity begins in 1865, when *War and Peace* began to appear in instalments, and *Anna Karenina* followed in 1873–77. During the 1830s to the 1850s, Russian fictional prose emphasized short works, with a few notable exceptions (Lermontov's 1841 *Hero of Our Time* and Gogol's 1842 *Dead Souls*). But by the 1860s, Russian readers were paying primary attention to the astonishing new novels coming from Russian writers. And while the assessments of Russian critics often included impressionistic comparative references to past and present British, French, and German writers, Russians preferred to emphasize what they saw as the radically original and distinctively national qualities in these new works.

INFLUENCES AND AFFINITIES

Existing scholarship on the relationship between Russian and English literature during the Victorian period tends to emphasize influence and affinity. Some of the most notable pairings in this regard are Dostoevsky and Dickens, Tolstoy and Dickens, Tolstoy and George Eliot, Tolstoy and Elizabeth Gaskell, Tolstoy and Thomas Hardy, Tolstoy

know in what way life will disentangle the consequences of this or that action; suddenly death appears and the knot is untied.' In response, George Eliot reportedly asked, 'Have you really not noticed that it actually happens that way in life?...It has already happened so many times that faith in death has given me the courage to live!'

[42] A.S. Suvorin, 'Dzhordzh Eliot. Ocherk zhizni i sochinenii', *Vestnik Evropy*, 1884, t. 3, no. 5, 138–79; no. 6, 469–511.

and Mrs Henry Wood, Turgenev and Thackeray. Extending the purview to include American literature yields pairings such as Turgenev and Henry James, Turgenev and Harriet Beecher Stowe.

Not surprisingly, critics have focused primarily on the affinities between Dostoevsky and Dickens in scholarly work on the Russian–Victorian connection, with Dickens exerting a significant influence on Dostoevsky during both his pre- and post-exilic periods, *Crime and Punishment* representing a critical reading of *Hard Times*, and so forth.[43] Olga Stuchebrukhov finds a shared ambivalence towards modernity in both Dickens and Dostoevsky, a yearning for community distinct from that embodied by the modern nation-state. As exemplified by *Bleak House* and *The Possessed*, as well as works published in periodicals such as *Household Words*, *All the Year Round*, and *Diary of a Writer*, both authors sought to shift the novel and journalism away from linear time and secular content to provide moral lessons in creating an image of the ideal nation. While Dickens uses allegory to locate the centre of change in the outside world, striving towards a higher reality through a politically and civically conscious nationalism, Dostoevsky employs symbolism to situate the potential for change in the individual consciousness, advocating a cultural nationalism dependent on inner moral and spiritual enlightenment.[44]

In a self-proclaimed 'reverse influence study', Loralee MacPike claims that Dostoevsky radically 'recreated' Dickens by reading him, such that 'Dickens' creations are transmogrified; his [Dickens'] fascinated abhorrence of evil becomes a strange dance of celebration of the powers of the human soul'.[45] MacPike asserts that through Dostoevsky's reading of Dickens, 'we find a Dickens invisible to the eye of the critic who focuses on the English author alone', and thus she investigates what can be learned about Dickens through his influence on Dostoevsky rather than adding her voice to the scholarly throng that sees Dostoevsky as an advancement or improvement on Dickens.[46]

---

[43] Dickens was the author Dostoevsky most often chose to read during his decade of Siberian exile (1849–59) and *The Insulted and Injured* (1861) is often cited as his most Dickensian work. For more information about Dickens and Dostoevsky's later works, see Irina Gredina and Philip Allingham, 'Dickens's Influence upon Dostoevsky, 1860–1870; or, One Nineteenth-Century Master's Assimilation of Another's Manner and Vision', on The Victorian Web, <http://www.victorianweb.org/>.

[44] Stuchebrukhov, 1–9.

[45] Of course, Dickens could not actually have read Dostoevsky, since the only translation of Dostoevsky before 1870 was in German, a language Dickens did not know. Dickens was fluent in French, but the French translations of Dostoevsky all came out after 1870 and translations of Dostoevsky into English began only in 1886.

[46] MacPike, *Dostoevsky's Dickens: A Study of Literary Influence* (London: George Prior Publishers, 1981), 1–3. MacPike summarizes the scholarship in this vein as follows: 'N.M. Lary, in *Dostoevsky and Dickens*, finds Dickens a Dostoevky manqué; Donald Fanger's *Dostoevsky and Romantic Realism* traces in Dostoevsky the culmination of Dickens' attempts to romanticize and thus transform reality; Stefan Zweig, in *Three Masters: Balzac, Dickens, Dostoevsky*, transl. Eden and Cedar Paul (New York: Viking Press, 1930) sees Dostoevsky as the acme of psychological realism and Dickens as but an intermediate step. Even the late Igor Katarsky, whose primary interest is Dickens, finds it necessary in *Dickens in Russia* to treat Dostoevsky as an advancement over the earlier writer.' Fanger notes a reverse trend, whereby Dostoevsky is seen as lacking the 'generous and humane perspective of his less narrowly obsessed English confrere', Donald Fanger, *Dostoevsky and Romantic Realism* (Chicago: University of Chicago Press, 1985), 252.

Dickens also exerted a primary influence on Tolstoy, who read a Russian translation of *David Copperfield* at age twenty-three, in 1851. The direct influence of *David Copperfield* is evident in Tolstoy's 1852 fictional autobiography *Childhood*, in which, as Tolstoy's biographer A.N. Wilson expresses it, some of Tolstoy's own recent adult memories and impressions are 'Copperfielded' into an imagined distant past.[47] Tolstoy's fondness for Dickens was unabated more than fifty years later, when he declared Dickens 'the greatest novelist of the nineteenth century'.[48] And *David Copperfield* remained a particular favourite, cited in *What Is Art?* as truly 'universal', with Dickens's body of work characterized as the highest form of Christian art.[49] A portrait of Dickens hung over Tolstoy's desk at his family estate Yasnaya Polyana, and Tolstoy seems to have taken inspiration from Dickens at many different moments in his life as a writer.[50] Tolstoy's wife Sofia Andreevna noted in her diary on 23 October 1878, 'Lyova said today that he had read so much historical material that he would like a rest and read Dickens's *Martin Chuzzlewit* for a change. I know that when Lyova begins to read English novels he is sure to start writing again himself.'[51]

Commonly invoked Russian-Victorian influences and affinities prove misleading or merely superficial when subjected to closer analysis. Shoshana Knapp points out that although Tolstoy greatly admired George Eliot, he 'invented' his own version of her, 'just as he invented his own Shakespeare, his own Beethoven and Wagner'.[52] This is a much more productive way to think about the two authors than the unreflective inventorying of Eliot references culled from Tolstoy's letters and diaries. (For example, an 1891 letter Tolstoy wrote to M.M. Lederle lists the works that made the most substantial impression on him between the ages of thirty-five and fifty and includes the notation 'George Eliot. Novels. Great impression.')[53] Some affinities are drawn so broadly or are so integrally

[47] A.N. Wilson, *Tolstoy: A Biography* (New York: W.W. Norton, 1988), 95. For more on the influence of Dickens on Tolstoy's *Childhood*, see Andrew Baruch Wachtel, *The Battle for Childhood: Creation of a Russian Myth* (Stanford: Stanford University Press, 1990).

[48] PSS, 75: 24.

[49] PSS, 30: 160–61.

[50] The bibliography for Philip Rogers, 'Scrooge on the Neva: Dickens and Tolstoj's Death of Ivan Ilich', *Comparative Literature* 40 (1988): 193–218, includes all of the major studies of the Tolstoy–Dickens connection up to the late 1980s.

[51] S.A. Tolstaia, *Dnevniki*, 2 vols. (Moscow: GIXL, 1978), 1: 99–100.

[52] Shoshana Knapp, 'Tolstoj's Reading of George Eliot: Visions and Revisions', *Slavic and East-European Journal* 27 (1983): 318–26. Knapp goes on to note that Tolstoy 'owned a copy of *Middlemarch*, but he never mentioned the novel in his writings. *Daniel Deronda* he did not even own. His special favorites, on the other hand, include *Scenes of Clerical Life*, which can be characterized by the melodramatic techniques and programmatic aesthetics she later outgrew, and *Felix Holt, the Radical*, which has been condemned by even her admirers as an ill-informed excursion into politics. Tolstoj's respect for her works, furthermore, was sustained for 50 years, and increased with time, particularly after his "conversion"; the late Tolstoj still loved the early George Eliot, the odd George Eliot, the unpopular George Eliot... [H]is reading of George Eliot remained selective and interpretative; he found what he sought, and disregarded the rest.'

[53] PSS, vol. 66, pp. 67–68. For a survey of Tolstoy's reading materials, see Galina Alekseeva, 'Describing Tolstoy's Private Library: English Books at Iasnaia Poliana', *Tolstoy Studies Journal* 13 (2001): 98–107.

connected to the nature of the literary genre in question (the realist novel) as to be unpersuasive. Still, it is hard to argue against the Tolstoyan resonance of *Middlemarch*'s closing line: 'for the growing good of the world is partly dependant on unhistoric acts; and that things are not so ill with you and me as they might have been, is half owing to the number who lived faithfully a hidden life, and rest in unvisited tombs'. This way of seeing the world is everywhere expressed in *War and Peace*, in which Tolstoy asserts that history is not made by kings and generals, but rather by ordinary people going about the business of their lives, making no conscious attempt to influence the course of history.

One affinity strategy positions a particular Russian writer within a constellation of writers from the Victorian tradition. Josie Billington juxtaposes Gaskell and Tolstoy, but ends up defining Tolstoy by adding George Eliot and Thomas Hardy to the mix. Billington sees in the acknowledged greatness of Tolstoy's realism the 'neglected hallmarks of Gaskell's own genius', namely 'a capacity for being as slow as the life she pictures; for sheerly inhabiting the multitudinous forms within life; and for faithfully rendering the dense complexity of life's matter and its amorphous resistance to category or formal solution'. Gaskell's *Wives and Daughters* is 'the nearest equivalent we have in England to Tolstoy's *Anna Karenina*'. For Billington, Tolstoy is

> the great missing figure of the English Victorian period, and as such is a crucial addition…to any course on Victorian literary studies. For not only does Tolstoy comprise within himself everything that the English nineteenth century was suffering from—the absence of God, the loss of absolute meaning and the consequent 'homelessness,' as Lukács puts it, of the human soul. In earnestly seeking a religious resolution to these problems and a return to a spiritual absolute, Tolstoy also helps us to see how secular a project Victorian realism essentially was.[54]

Another form of constellating emphasizes works and genres rather than individual writers. Thus Amy Mandelker situates *Anna Karenina* between French and English novels of adultery, arguing that Tolstoy's novel ultimately offers a revisionist critique of both: '*Anna Karenina* is not a realist novel, although it has come to be read that way. Rather, it reflects on every level, both thematic and formal, Tolstoy's polemic with realism and with Victorian literature, and his quest for mythopoesis as an alternative.'[55] Tolstoy probed the Victorian literary convention of treating women as artworks whose beauty results in

---

[54] Josie Billington, *Faithful Realism: Elizabeth Gaskell and Leo Tolstoy. A Comparative Study* (Lewisburg: Bucknell University Press, 2002), 9–10. As restated, '[R]eading Tolstoy is precisely the same as turning around inside a combination of different minds and modes of thinking and being essential to a consideration of later nineteenth- and early twentieth-century novel writing in England. For Tolstoy is not either George Eliot or Gaskell just because he is both modes. On the one hand, he is the restless seeker after truth, struggling to free from the mass and detail of life some rescuing thought or meaning with all the seriousness of George Eliot, to save his sanity and his life. And yet, on the other hand, Tolstoy is as wryly subdued and accepting as is Gaskell when the absolute becomes absorbed amidst the mundane contingencies of an ordinary life' (142).

[55] Mandelker, *Framing Anna Karenina*, 67.

their fall: 'Even more than Proust and Joyce, Tolstoy indicts the pornographic modalities of the Western aesthetic tradition and recasts the portrait of the beautiful in iconic terms.'[56] Ultimately, 'Tolstoy rewrites the Victorian realist, domestic novel according to his own aesthetic principles, subverting mimesis and realist aesthetics by...the creation of an elaborate system of imagery that...serves to elevate symbolism over verisimilitude, iconicity over conventionality.'[57]

Victorians and the Russian Novel

The reception of Russian literature by Victorian critics and readers is the more familiar side of the story. Rather than recapitulating the particulars here, I would merely mention some of its most notable aspects.[58]

Eugène-Melchior de Vogüé's 1886 *Le Roman russe* was translated into English almost immediately upon publication and proved highly influential, launching the tradition (bemoaned by all Russian literary specialists) of invoking the 'mysterious soul of Russia'. Of Russian literature, de Vogüé declared

> Realism is the proper and perfect instrument which it has employed, applied with equal success to material and spiritual life. Although this realism may occasionally lack method and taste, and is at the same time both diffuse and subtle, it is invariably natural and sincere, ennobled by moral sentiments, aspirations toward the Divine, and sympathy for humanity...[T]he Russian character...has...such intense sympathy for human nature, for the humblest creatures, for the forsaken and unfortunate. This spirit decries reason and elevates the brute, and inspires the deepest compassion in the heart.[59]

Russian literature thus came to be seen by Victorian readers as a wholesome and morally improving alternative to the too-graphic writings of French naturalists and fin-de-siècle decadents.

---

[56] Mandelker, *Framing Anna Karenina*, 9.

[57] Mandelker, Framing *Anna Karenina*, 11. For a fascinating bit of literary speculation, see Denis Goubert, 'Did Tolstoy Read East Lynne?' *Slavonic and East European Review* 58(1) (January 1980): 22–39.

[58] A very good place to start is Harold Orel's 1954 'Victorians and the Russian Novel: A Bibliography', *Bulletin of Bibliography* 21 (1954): 61–63, which provides separate sections for historical background, translations of Russian novels, critical articles and monographs, reading tastes in Victorian England, and the Victorian reception of French Naturalism, to which Russian literature was often favourably compared. Chapter 1 ('Translation Culture') of Rachel May, *The Translator in the Text: On Reading Russian Literature in English* (Evanston: Northwestern University Press, 1994) gives an excellent narrative survey of the history of the reception of Russian literature from the first part of the 19th century up to the end of the Soviet period and references a great deal of the secondary literature on the topic.

[59] Eugène-Melchior de Vogüé, *The Russian Novelists* (Haskell House, 1974), 267–69.

When the reception of Russian literature by Victorian England began in earnest during the 1880s, Victorian literature itself was perceived as already in decline.[60] (Ironically, this would also be true of Russian literature, with 1881, the publication date of *Brothers Karamazov*, regarded as the traditional endpoint for the end of Russian realism's greatest period.)[61] Because of the decades lost to translation and cultural transmission, however, Russian literature produced during the 1860s–1870s seemed very fresh to Victorian readers of the 1880s–1890s.

A new surge of interest in Russian literature among English readers followed the 1905 revolution in Russia, lasting until the mid-1920s. Maurice Baring published his 1910 *Landmarks in Russian Literature*, lavishing praise on Dostoevsky and Gogol, and declaring Turgenev rather conventional. Baring also posited the now familiar pairing of Tolstoy and Dostoevsky as perfect counterparts:

> Tolstoy and Dostoevsky shine and burn in the firmament of Russian literature like two great planets, one of them as radiant as the planet Jupiter, the other as red and ominous as the planet Mars. Beside either of these the light of Turgenev twinkles, pure indeed, and full of pearly luster, like the moon faintly seen in the East at the end of an autumnal day.[62]

No account of the relationship between Victorian culture and Russian literature is complete without recognizing Constance Garnett, who translated more than seventy volumes of Russian literature during the period 1893–1934, making most works of the major Russian prose writers available to English-language readers.[63] Garnett began with Turgenev, producing a fifteen-volume collected edition of his works in 1894–99. Her translations of Tolstoy's major works appeared during the first years of the twentieth century. And Garnett was instrumental in making Dostoevsky more palatable to English intellectuals (who had previously found him too 'rough' and 'Russian'), and the critical tide began to turn in his favour with her translation of *Brothers Karamazov* in 1912, which she followed with another eleven volumes over the next eight years. Garnett then moved on to Chekhov and produced sixteen volumes of his stories, plays, and letters.

[60] In contrast, Russian literature was published in English translation significantly earlier in America, beginning in the late 1860s, with significant critical notice paid in American journals by American critics. See May, 18–19.

[61] Dostoevsky died in 1881 and Turgenev in 1883. Tolstoy had renounced fictional literature as a result of his religious conversion at the end of the 1870s, and although he continued to produce some works of short fiction and one very bad novel (*Resurrection*, 1899), his primary energies for writing from the post-conversion period were directed at essays on religious and socio-political themes, and reading materials for newly literate Russian peasants.

[62] Maurice Baring, 'Tolstoy and Turgenev', *Quarterly Review*, CCXI, July 1909, 181.

[63] May, *The Translator in the Text*, discusses Garnett on pp. 25–26 and 31–42 and gives some fascinating examples of her translation practices. Note that Isabel Hapgood, an American journalist and traveller, also published numerous translations of Russian literature into English during the same period.

By present standards, Garnett's technique as a translator is much criticized, perhaps most famously by Joseph Brodsky, who quipped, 'The reason English-speaking readers can barely tell the difference between Tolstoy and Dostoevsky is that they aren't reading the prose of either one. They're reading Constance Garnett.'[64] Garnett's translations domesticated and smoothed out Russian prose, as Rachel May describes,

> erasing those idiosyncrasies of narrative voice and dialogue that different authors possessed. Gogol's pounding repetitions, Dostoevsky's constant interruptions of the text or his tendency to put one character's words in another's mouth, Tolstoy's interminable sentences, Turgenev's tendency to allow his narrator's voice to echo the dialect of the character being described—all were smoothed over, brought closer to an ideal of good English.[65]

Nevertheless, Garnett's translations, somewhat edited and updated, and are still widely read today.

A set of attitudes toward Russian culture came into focus during the late Victorian period, setting the tone for the more systematic production of Anglo-American literary criticism and scholarship during the twentieth century. Russian writers were lauded for sincerely acknowledging human suffering, for considering the most serious metaphysical and spiritual questions, and for representing human life on a vast and panoramic canvas, as large as Russia itself.[66] But along with 'sincerity', the unpolished literary style of 19th-century Russian writers was also seen as reflecting the half-barbarous state of their homeland, as in this representative statement by Arthur Symons on the Russian temperament:

> Civilisation has no roots in him. Laws have been made for chaining him down, as if he were a dangerous wild beast, and the laws were made by those who knew his nature and had determined to thwart it. If he cannot have his way, he is always ready to be a martyr.[67]

In spite of such retrograde statements (which resemble assessments made by various 18th- and 19th-century foreign observers of Russia), the alleged superiority of Russian literature over Victorian literature became fixed as a staple notion of 20th-century Anglo-American comparative literary criticism, as in Harry Levin's assessment that 'the limitations of range and depth that the Victorian novel shows by comparison with

---

[64] As cited in David Remnick, 'The Translation Wars', *New Yorker*, 7 November 2005.

[65] May, 40.

[66] Note Matthew Arnold's famous declaration, '[T]he truth is we are not to take Anna Karenina as a work of art; we are to take it as a piece of life. A piece of life it is. The author has not invented and combined it he has seen it; it has all happened before his inward eye, and it was in this wise it happened' ('Count Leo Tolstoy', *Fortnightly Review* 42 (1887): 785).

[67] Arthur Symons, *Studies in Prose and Verse* (London: Martin Secker, 1904), 171.

the French or the Russian may ultimately reflect the greater stability of English institutions, untroubled by revolution in the recent past and not seriously liable to it in the near future'.[68] In all its aspects, Russian literature was important to Victorian readers as, in Harold Orel's words, 'a deeply felt experience', and represented one of the most important literary traditions for English readers during the late 19th and early 20th centuries.[69]

Although Russians read Victorian literature several decades before Victorians read Russian literature, it is fair to say that the currents of influence ran powerfully in both directions. In fact, it might be said that each culture discovered the other's literature at the moment when it was most needed. Russians read English 18th-century fiction at a moment when their own national literature, prose in particular, was in very rudimentary form, and they took to heart the excellent instruction these works provided on narration, setting, and character. Similarly, 19th-century English authors, Dickens foremost among them, inspired the major Russian literary talents of the time to set off boldly on their own creative paths. In turn, the 19th-century Russian greats exerted significant influence on the English modernists, and perhaps more importantly, reminded English readers at the turn of the 20th century of literature's potential power to act as a progressive force in the world. By the middle of the 20th century, the literature of each culture was ensconced in the literary canon of the other, seen to illustrate both vivid national particularity *and* universality.

Suggested Reading

Billington, Josie. *Faithful Realism: Elizabeth Gaskell and Leo Tolstoy. A Comparative Study.* Lewisburg: Bucknell University Press, 2002.

Blumberg, Edwina J. 'Tolstoy and the English Novel: A Note on Middlemarch and Anna Karenina'. *Slavic Review 30* (1971): 561–69.

Buckler, Julie. 'Melodramatizing Russia: Nineteenth-Century Views from the West'. In *Imitations of Life: Two Centuries of Melodrama in Russia*. Edited by Louise McReynolds and Joan Neuberger. Durham: Duke University Press, 2002.

Cruise, Edwina. 'Tracking the English Novel in Anna Karenina: Who Wrote the English Novel That Anna Reads?' *Anniversary Essays on Tolstoy*. Edited by Donna Tussing Orwin. Cambridge: Cambridge University Press, 2010.

Demidova, Olga. 'The Reception of Charlotte Brontë's Work in Nineteenth-Century Russia', *Modern Language Review 89* (1994), 689–96.

Friedberg, Maurice. *Literary Translation in Russia: A Cultural History*. University Park: Pennsylvania State University Press, 1997.

Goubert, Denis. 'Did Tolstoy Read East Lynne?' *Slavonic and East European Review* 58(1) (January 1980): 22–39.

[68] Harry Levin, *The Gates of Horn: A Study of Five French Realists* (New York: Oxford University Press, 1963), 79.

[69] Harold Orel, 'English Critics and the Russian Novel: 1850–1917', *The Slavonic and East European Review* 33(81) (June 1955): 469. See also Orel's 'The Forgotten Ambassadors: Russian Fiction in Victorian England', *American Slavic and East European Review* 12(3) (October 1953): 371–77.

Gredina, Irina and Philip Allingham, 'Dickens's Influence upon Dostoevsky, 1860–1870; or, One Nineteenth-Century Master's Assimilation of Another's Manner and Vision'. The Victorian Web. <http://www.victorianweb.org/>.

Harper, Kenneth E. and Bradford A. Booth. 'Russian Translations of Nineteenth-Century English Fiction'. *Nineteenth-Century Fiction* 8(3) (December 1953): 188–97.

Jones, W. Gareth, ed. *Tolstoi and Britain*. Washington, DC: Berg, 1995.

Knapp, Shoshana. 'Tolstoj's Reading of George Eliot: Visions and Revisions'. *Slavic and East-European Journal* 27 (1983): 318–26.

LeBlanc, Ronald D. *The Russianization of Gil Bas: A Study in Literary Appropriation*. Columbus: Slavica Publishers, 1986.

Levin, Iu. D. *The Perception of English Literature in Russia: Investigations and Materials*. Translated by Catherine Phillips. Nottingham: Astra Press, 1994.

MacPike, Loralee. *Dostoevsky's Dickens: A Study of Literary Influence*. London: George Prior Publishers, 1981.

Mandelker, Amy. *Framing Anna Karenina: Tolstoy, the Woman Question, and the Victorian Novel*. Columbus: Ohio State University Press, 1993.

May, Rachel. *The Translator in the Text: On Reading Russian Literature in English*. Evanston: Northwestern University Press, 1994.

Polosky, Rachel. *English Literature and the Russian Aesthetic Renaissance*. Cambridge: Cambridge University Press, 1998.

Rogers, Philip. 'Lessons for Fine Ladies: Tolstoj and George Eliot's *Felix Holt, the Radical*'. *Slavic and East-European Journal* 29 (1985): 379–92.

Wellek, Rene. 'The Nineteenth-Century Russian Novel in English and American Criticism'. In *The Russian Novel from Pushkin to Pasternak*. Edited by John Garrard. New Haven: Yale University Press, 1983.

11

THE VICTORIAN NOVEL AND AMERICA

AMANDA CLAYBAUGH

While the preceding two chapters followed Victorian novels as they travelled to France and to Russia, this chapter focuses instead on American novels as they arrived in Great Britain. Their arrival was recorded in thousands of reviews. All the major Victorian periodicals and many of the minor ones reviewed American novels, sometimes in brief capsule reviews and sometimes in long review essays, sometimes alongside British novels and sometimes on their own. Through these reviews, the literary establishment of Britain struggled to determine whether American novels are different from British—and, if so, how. At times, these reviewers come to conclusions too eccentric to be taken seriously, as when a writer for the *Edinburgh Review* argued that American authors, because of their climate and the nervous energy it produces, are less suited to the novel than to the literary sketch.[1] And at other times, the generalizations made by one reviewer contradict those made by another, and it becomes clear that reviewers would often reach for whatever term of praise or abuse came most readily to hand: American novels were pious, but also sensational; American style was crude, but also ornate; American novelists wrote with a moral purpose, but also out of a pure commitment to art.

These contradictions and eccentricities notwithstanding, some general trends emerge. In the first half of the 19th century, British reviewers tended to treat American novels as oddities, subjecting them to patronizing praise and condescending advice. In the second half of the century, however, they began to see the American novel as a fully fledged rival to the British, and their conception of what was distinctively British about British literature changed as a result. This change in the reception of the American novel was partly caused, I will show, by developments in the transatlantic literary marketplace. But it was also catalysed, I will argue, by two unlikely pairs of novelists—Nathaniel Hawthorne

---

[1] Rowland E. Prothero, 'American Fiction', *Edinburgh Review* 173 (January 1891): 33.

and Harriet Beecher Stowe, Henry James and William Dean Howells—and by a notorious pair of essays in the *Century* magazine.

The American Novel Before the Civil War

Through most of the 19th century, until 1891, the United States Congress refused to ratify any international copyright treaty. As a consequence, there was a largely unimpeded traffic in English-language books across the Atlantic: a publisher in one nation was free to reprint works from the other without securing permission from their authors, much less offering those authors compensation. In theory, this traffic in books could go in both directions; in practice, particularly before the 1870s, British reprints were much more popular in America than the reverse.

Many efforts were made to put an end to reprinting. British publishers and British authors were outraged by reprinting because they did not profit from the widespread American circulation of British books, and they would periodically lobby Congress to ratify a copyright treaty. In 1837, for instance, Thomas Carlyle, Maria Edgeworth, and Robert Southey did so, and when Charles Dickens visited America a few years later, he would take up the task. His *Pickwick Papers* (1836–37) had been a phenomenal success in both Britain and America, but that success was made newly visible for him in the crowds of admirers that thronged around him throughout his American tour, gathering in the thousands to greet his steamer or bid farewell to his railway car, lining up in the hundreds to shake his hand. The sight of so many readers from whom he had made not one penny seems to have prompted Dickens into advocacy. At the first of the public dinners held in his honour, Dickens offered a toast to the day when US authors would profit from the sale of their works in Britain—and British authors, from the sale of their works in the United States. At the second dinner, he rose and asked 'leave to whisper in your ear two words: *International Copyright*'.[2]

American authors, too, were outraged by reprinting, recognizing that it deprived them of readers. Not only were British authors better known than American authors, but their books were cheaper when reprinted than were American books under copyright. Under these conditions, it was very difficult for American authors to attract an audience, much less to support themselves through their writing: before the 1850s, only two American authors, Washington Irving and James Fenimore Cooper, made significant profits from their books.[3]

---

[2] Quoted in Edgar Johnson, *Charles Dickens: His Tragedy and Triumph*. 2 vols. (New York: Simon and Schuster, 1952), 1: 381.

[3] Elizabeth Barnes, 'Novels', in *An Extensive Republic: Print, Culture, and Society in the New Nation, 1790–1840*, ed. Robert A. Gross and Mary Kelley, *A History of the Book in America* (Chapel Hill: University of North Carolina Press, 2010), 443.

Protesting these conditions, American authors gave voice to an emerging literary nationalism. Ralph Waldo Emerson, for instance, warned that America would not develop a national literature until Americans stopped reprinting British books. 'Every book we read, every biography, play, romance, in whatever form, is still English history and manners', Emerson observed in his *English Traits* (1856). 'So that a sensible Englishman once said to me, "as long as you do not grant us copyright, we shall have the teaching of you".'[4] In the course of freeing themselves from British influence, a number of American authors were willing to make common cause with their British rivals. Irving joined Dickens in petitioning Congress in the 1840s, and in the 1880s, the British Author's Society (founded by Walter Besant and chaired by Alfred Tennyson, George Meredith, and Thomas Hardy) worked in tandem with the American Copyright League (led by James Russell Lowell and Mark Twain).

There were good reasons for fearing, as Emerson and other literary nationalists had warned, that the transatlantic traffic in books was hindering the development of American literature. Certainly, reprinting brought American readers and writers into contact with a literary culture that was largely indifferent to them, at least in the first decades of the 19th century. American readers were deeply immersed in British literature, having almost immediate access to all the most important British books, with bestsellers like *The Pickwick Papers* famously circulating within eighteen hours of reaching American shores. But British readers came across American books much less frequently and took them much less seriously. To be sure, Cooper's novels and Irving's short stories and travel writings were often read and admired, but for the most part, American literature was viewed in a patronizing light.

American novelists were seen, by British critics, as specializing in two genres, neither of which was held in high regard on either side of the Atlantic. The first was the religious or didactic novel, what was called at the time, 'the novel of purpose'. American novels were typified, one reviewer observed, by a 'gentle dullness and mild zeal of a semi-religious character'.[5] Another observed that no novelists are as moral as American lady novelists.[6] The second genre was the supernatural. The American people were seen as generally shrewd, but their novels, as one reviewer described them, were often filled with 'strange religious transcendentalism, and psychomancy, and all sorts of mystic extravagances'.[7] Other reviewers suggested that such extravagances were typical of a young and immature literature, implicitly contrasting the American novel with a British novel then in full-flower.

Alongside these descriptions of what American novels usually were, we can find many claims about what they should be: British reviewers preferred that American novels focus on distinctively American subjects. At times, reviewers enjoyed marvelling at the exotic social practices of the Americans, as when one novel was praised for describing 'Vegetarians, Temperance people, believers in Women's Rights, or Abolitionists', all

---

[4] Ralph Waldo Emerson, *English Traits* (1856) (Cambridge: Harvard University Press, 1929), 36.

[5] 'American Novels', *Athenaeum* (January 12, 1856): 40.

[6] 'Notices to Correspondents', *Reynolds's Miscellany* 338 (December 30, 1854): 368.

[7] 'Rev. of Faith Gartney's Girlhood', *Saturday Review* (December 2, 1865): 710.

in the heat of their respective campaigns.[8] More often, however, they enjoyed learning about America's regions and regional customs. Indeed, there was a strong expectation that American novels serve as a kind of travel guide to those parts of the country that British readers could not visit for themselves. As soon as America's cities, railroads, and rivers had all been described to British satisfaction, reviewers called on American novelists to describe those rural districts still 'unvisited by the tourist from the Old World'.[9] Such descriptions would come to be called 'local colour writing', and there was a fashion in local colour as there was in all things. Early in the century, there had been a vogue for two figures in particular, the Yankee and the Indian. But as early as the 1840s, one reviewer was confessing himself exhausted with 'tales of the prairie and the Red Indian', while another was observing that not all Americans were Yankees and suggested that some other national groups might be described.[10] As the century went on, new sources of local colour would be found. In the 1880s, for instance, British reviewers would celebrate the discovery of New Orleans and Tennessee as subjects for novels.[11] And in the 1890s, they would take a similar interest in novels about California, particularly in those that depicted what one reviewer referred to as 'the delightful Chinaman'.[12]

Coupled with this British preference for American novels about American subjects was the presumption that American novelists were unqualified to write about anything else. British critics were particularly annoyed when American novelists presumed to write about British society. Reviewing a now-forgotten novel about life among the elite, one critic dryly noted that it is a 'curious illustration of republicanism' that American novelists should be so quick to write about lords and baronets.[13] Other reviewers pitied American authors, who were said to have trouble understanding British society because of the general primitiveness of their own. Such authors fail, one reviewer concludes, because of 'a vulgarity that is innate'.[14]

In addition to strong preferences about American subject matter, British critics made strong complaints about American language and style. Coventry Patmore, the poet, was one of the first to note that American English was diverging from British English and to caution the nation's authors against it. They are 'abusing their noble inheritance of a pure, sweet, and powerful language', he warned, 'which will become a chronic and even an incurable disease'.[15] This was an unusual complaint at the time Patmore was making it, but it would become more and more common as the century went on. In the 1880s and 1890s, a number of reviewers would note the divergence of American from British

[8] 'Rev. of Hannah Thurston', *Saturday Review* (November 28, 1863): 769.

[9] 'Rev. of The Americans at Home', *British Quarterly Review* 21 (January 1855): 61.

[10] 'Journal of American Literature', *Critic* (June 27, 1846): 743. [Frederick Hardman], 'The Writings of Charles Sealsfield', *Foreign Quarterly Review* 74 (July 1846): 419.

[11] 'Two Southern Stories', *Saturday Review* (January 10, 1885): 61.

[12] 'Novels', *Saturday Review* (March 8, 1890): 293.

[13] 'Rev. of Helen Leeson: A Peep at New York Society', *Critic* (December 15, 1855): 426.

[14] 'Rev. of Trumps: A Novel', *Athenaeum* (June 8, 1861): 761.

[15] Coventry Patmore, 'American Novels', *North British Review* 20 (November 1853): 98–99.

English. One reviewer was typical in noting, only half-jokingly, that American novels will soon need to be translated for those who speak 'only English and a few other dead or old-world tongues'.[16] And another reviewer warns, after praising Stephen Crane highly, that readers will have to learn a new language to read him, since he uses words such as 'bug' and 'snickered'.[17] Nor was this reviewer alone in his peevishness about minor variations in language: many would complain about American words like 'executed', 'interviewed', 'non-committal', 'worriment', 'materialize', 'realize', and 'orotund'.

Where American language was seen as overly crude, American style was seen as overly crafted, particularly in the antebellum period. Some British reviewers observed a rhetorical style learned in the pulpit or in the lecture hall, with novelists aiming to do no more than 'to weave smooth sentences and rounded periods'.[18] Other reviewers noted a style that was ornate, even extravagant. 'The language is generally at a high pitch of rhetoric', one reviewer observed, and 'though sometimes eloquent, is more frequently an unpruned overgrowth of high-sounding words'.[19] Later in the century, the terms of the complaint would reverse. Reviewers would say that American novels are 'a little wanting in polish' and could learn 'refinement' from the 'Old Country', but could offer the old country in turn 'an example of courage and spirit'.[20] Thirty years later, another reviewer would make a similar observation, saying that American novels had 'little style, and little sense of proportion', as with all novels from a young country.[21]

Thus, the British view of American novels during the first half of the 19th century—the expectation that they would be either supernatural or purposeful, the hope that they would focus on American life rather than attempting to depict life elsewhere, and the sense that their style and even their language were somehow distinct—was informed by a conviction that the American novel was not yet the equal of the British. But changes were at work that would soon ensure that the American novel, and American literature more generally, would be taken more seriously.

Some of these changes had to do with the growth of the American publishing industry, a development that was deeply indebted to reprinting. Reviled as it was by American authors, the reprinting of British books nonetheless laid the foundations for a fully developed American literature to emerge. It did so, first, by creating a large reading public. The literacy rate among Americans was much higher than in Europe, and the cheap supply of British books meant that Americans were accustomed not simply to reading, but to reading fiction. Moreover, they were accustomed to buying novels, rather than borrowing them from libraries as British readers would do. Even one of the most vehement advocates for international copyright law, Edmund Gosse, admitted that the

[16] George Saintsbury, 'New Novels', *Aca demy* (January 26, 1889): 54.
[17] 'American Fiction', *Athenaeum* (May 22, 1897): 678.
[18] 'Journal of American Literature', *Critic* (April 4, 1846): 357.
[19] 'Rev. of Rutledge and The Household of Bouverie; Or, the Elixir of Gold', *Athenaeum* (September 15, 1860): 353.
[20] 'Novels and Novelettes', *Athenaeum* (December 11, 1869): 176.
[21] 'American Fiction', *Athenaeum* (November 5, 1898): 641.

reprinters, whom he disparaged as 'book-pirates', had made the purchasing of books a national habit of the Americans.[22]

Secondly, reprinting created an American publishing industry. Publishing requires significant investments of capital upfront: the reprinting of popular British books, which almost guaranteed profits, made such investments less risky and thereby enabled small publishing houses to grow larger and new ones to emerge. The American publishing industry expanded dramatically over the first half of the 19th century. By 1850, more books were being published in America than in Britain, and Harper Brothers in New York was larger than any London publishing house. As a result, by mid-century, the two nations had achieved a rough equilibrium, which the literary historian John Sutherland has succinctly described: 'copy for copy, American publishers vastly outproduced English; title for title, English novelists vastly outproduced American'.[23] British observers were keenly aware of this development, and contemporary reviews are filled with figures that tried to capture the sheer size of the American publishing industry: millions of volumes of Dickens, 250,000 copies of *Bleak House* (1852–53) alone; four times as much William Makepeace Thackeray than in Britain; and more than a 100,000 copies of *Jane Eyre* (1848). These reviewers recognized that the American publishing industry was not only larger than the British, but had become the largest in the world.[24] What was good for American publishers would ultimately be good, as the scholar Meredith McGill has recently argued, for American novelists as well. By mid-century, with the readers eager and the presses humming, the conditions were in place for the emergence of a national literature.

This emergence was heralded by two figures, one of whom was Harriet Beecher Stowe. Stowe had written her first novel, *Uncle Tom's Cabin* (1851), in the hopes of persuading readers of the evils of slavery, and as readers wept over its depictions of slave families torn apart, many did become committed abolitionists. But the novel also succeeded in persuading American publishers that there was a large market for American novels. Within its first week of publication, *Uncle Tom's Cabin* had sold 10,000 copies; within its first year, 300,000; and it would be the first novel to sell more than 1 million copies—all, in a nation whose total population was only 24 million.

Much the same thing happened in Britain. When *Uncle Tom's Cabin* was first reprinted in Britain, in the summer of 1852, reviewers were well aware of its phenomenal American popularity. At first, they found that popularity inexplicable. They expected, as one reviewer put it, to see 'the advent of a great genius of fiction', but found instead only 'a composition of average merit'.[25] But the novel soon became as popular with its British audience as it had been with American readers, and the reviews duly reported, for

[22] Edmund Gosse, 'The Protection of American Literature', *Fortnightly Review* 48 (July 1890): 60.
[23] John Sutherland, *Victorian Novelists and Publishers* (Chicago: University of Chicago Press, 1976), 17.
[24] [Romeo Elton], 'Quarterly Review of American Literature', *Eclectic Review* 3 (February 1858): 185.
[25] 'Rev. of Uncle Tom's Cabin', *Critic* (June 1, 1852): 293.

instance, that one publisher employed '400 men, women, and children' merely to bind the many copies of *Uncle Tom's Cabin* being reprinted, and that the many reprintings of the novel had exhausted London's stocks of paper.[26] Nor was *Uncle Tom's* success limited to books. It had pervaded, as another reviewer observed, all corners of British culture, from conversation to commerce, from drama to dance: 'Uncle Tom's Cabin hangs on every lip. Uncle Tom's Cabin flares on every wall; Uncle Tom's Cabin gives name to all sorts of articles, vendible, edible, potable and portable; to dramas at theaters; to polkas, mazurkas, quadrilles, waltzes, and ballads'.[27]

Such extraordinary popularity created its own standards of greatness. British reviewers continued to believe that the novel was poorly constructed (they were particularly troubled that its two plots did not intersect), but this did not keep several from judging *Uncle Tom* to be the greatest work of American literature. Moreover, as the months went by and the novel's popularity continued unabated, British reviewers began to consider *Uncle Tom* alongside British novels—and to acknowledge that *Uncle Tom* was outpacing them as well. It was not merely an American success, but rather 'the book of two hemispheres', the 'greatest literary feat of any age or country', and finally, 'the most marvellous literary phenomenon that the world has witnessed'.[28]

There was a sense, then, that *Uncle Tom's Cabin* had thrown 'English authorship into a temporary eclipse', and the author most shadowed by this eclipse was the one Stowe resembled most closely: Charles Dickens.[29] Stowe's sentimental heroines were judged to be more affecting, even, than Dickens's, while her characters in general were judged to be just as comic.[30] Indeed, one of the earliest British reviews of *Uncle Tom's Cabin* read it as a comic novel à la *Pickwick Papers*, one that invited readers to 'laugh along with their black friends, perhaps as heartily as they may have done with the immortal Wellers'.[31] Stowe was the better psychologist, one reviewer suggested, while several argued that she was also the more committed reformer.[32] This last comparison was thrown more starkly into relief when *Bleak House* began appearing in serial parts. Critics were disappointed that *Bleak House* lazily attacked an abuse, the inefficiency of the Chancery courts, that had long ago been remedied, while at the same time satirizing those women, like Stowe, who were energetically campaigning to end the ongoing abuse of Africans.[33] For a brief time, then, Stowe put Dickens 'quite thoroughly into the shade'.[34]

[26] 'Topics of the Week', *Literary Gazette* (October 9, 1852): 764.

[27] 'Rev. of Uncle Tom's Cabin', *Musical World* (October 9, 1852): 649.

[28] 'American Slavery and "Uncle Tom's Cabin"', *North British Review* 18 (November 1852): 235; 'Rev. of Uncle Tom's Cabin', *Tait's Edinburgh Magazine* (November 1852): 703; 'Rev. of Uncle Tom's Cabin', *Edinburgh Review* 101 (April 1855): 3.

[29] 'The Man of Business', *Leisure Hour* (May 19, 1853): 333.

[30] 'Rev. of Uncle Tom's Cabin', *Rambler* 3 (November 1852): 422.

[31] 'Rev. of Uncle Tom's Cabin', *Examiner* (May 29, 1852): 341.

[32] 'Rev. of Uncle Tom's Cabin', *Blackwood's Edinburgh Magazine* 74 (October 1853): 401.

[33] 'Rev. of Uncle Tom's Cabin, Bleak House, Slavery and the Slave Trade', *Athenaeum* (February 12, 1853): 188.

[34] 'Rev. of Uncle Tom's Cabin', *Musical World* (October 9, 1852): 649.

Stowe would continue to follow in Dickens's path. In 1853, she came to Britain on a tour that mirrored Dickens's tour of America a decade earlier. When she landed in Liverpool, she found the docks filled with people who wanted to be the first to catch a glimpse of her, and she was feted in a series of dinners, as Dickens had been. She did not, as he had done, make speeches in favour of international copyright law, but she did take the money entrusted to her for the benefit of the slaves and keep it as compensation for lost profits. And British reviewers enjoyed pointing out that now Americans could better understand the evils of reprinting, since *Uncle Tom*'s success was largely due, one reviewer wryly noted, to 'the law, or no law, of international copyright'.[35]

While Stowe demonstrated that American novels could be popular, a second novelist, Nathaniel Hawthorne, demonstrated that they could be artful as well. Hawthorne came to British attention quite early. His first collections of short stories, published in the 1840s, were quickly reprinted in Britain, and they were warmly, if not widely, reviewed. He was taken to be one of the few original authors America had yet produced, equal to the much-admired Washington Irving, and he was particularly praised, as Irving had been, for his imagination and his style. This pattern continued into the 1850s with the reprinting of Hawthorne's first two novels, *The Scarlet Letter* (1850) and *The House of the Seven Gables* (1851).[36] It was only with his third novel, *The Blithedale Romance* (1852), that he came to widespread British attention. *Blithedale* was reviewed much more widely than the first two novels had been, and Hawthorne, who had previously been seen as Irving's equal, was now seen as standing in a class of his own. He was, in the words of a typical review from the time, 'the highest, deepest, and finest imaginative writer whom America has yet produced'.[37] This is a striking change in reception, and it cannot be attributed to the novel itself: *Blithedale* is interesting, but clearly less accomplished than *Scarlet Letter* and *House of the Seven Gables*.

The change should be attributed, I would argue, to Harriet Beecher Stowe. *The Blithedale Romance* was published just as the *Uncle Tom* mania was reaching its height, and it stood as an example of American artistry to counter American popularity. Indeed, one reviewer made this comparison explicitly:

> From fact we pass to fiction, and to the examination of Hawthorne's last production, in order to which we must brush aside the whole brood of negro tales now swarming amongst us. *Uncle Tom* has become a notoriety, and the success of the book is the great literary fact of the day ... *The Blithedale Romance* will never attain the popularity which is vouchsafed ... to some of its contemporaries, but it is unmistakably the finest production of genius in either hemisphere.[38]

[35] 'Rev. of Uncle Tom's Cabin', *Prospective Review* (October 1852): 490.
[36] 'Rev. of Mosses from an Old Manse', *Athenaeum* (August 8, 1846): 807.
[37] 'Rev. of The Blithedale Romance', *Athenaeum* (July 10, 1852): 741.
[38] 'Contemporary Literature of America', *Westminster Review* 58 (October 1852): 592.

But even as reviewers emphasized Hawthorne's artistry, they also suggested that his was an artistry of an unfamiliar kind. Unlike his morally serious mid-Victorian rivals, but oddly like the decadent writers who would emerge at the century's end, Hawthorne was seen as uniting an 'intense admiration of beauty' with an attraction toward the perverse and diseased.[39] One reviewer described him as 'linger[ing] amid what is morbid'; another, as 'walk[ing] abroad always at night', and a third made the same point more pungently: 'He is in his element when dissecting a corpse, and smelling putrefaction.'[40]

More generally, Hawthorne was seen as pursuing the beautiful to the exclusion of any morality. His 'rich perception of the beautiful' is 'sadly deficient in moral depth and earnestness', one reviewer observed, while another noted that he has a keen 'eye for the beautiful', but only 'dim perceptions of the right, the good, and the true'.[41] Nonetheless, reviewers found Hawthorne's beauties so enchanting that they forgave him the morbidity. He continued to be judged 'unquestionably a man of genius', and reviewers were willing to accept that his 'peculiar genius' lay in 'the power he possesses to be haunted, and in his turn to haunt the reader'.[42]

As the decade went on, Hawthorn's standing only rose. His next book, a campaign biography for his old friend Franklin Pierce, was reviewed fairly widely in Britain simply because he had written it. And in 1854, the news that President Pierce had appointed Hawthorne US consul to Liverpool was widely and approvingly reported in the British press. While in Britain, Hawthorne was lionized, honoured in public dinners, and introduced to all the leading literary and cultural figures. By the time *The Marble Faun* (1860) was published, under the title *Transformation* in Britain, reviewers heralded it as a work that transcended nation and as 'one of the most remarkable novels that 1860 is likely to give us, whether from English, French, or American sources'.[43]

But Hawthorne would shock his British admirers with his final book, a collection of essays about his experiences in Britain entitled *Our Old Home* (1863). As the title suggests, Hawthorne describes British culture with warm appreciation, seeing it as the origin of his own. But the essays are interspersed with critical remarks about the English, most egregiously, for British reviewers, the observation that English men and women are less attractive than Americans. 'He seems to have really thought us ill-looking', spluttered one reviewer.[44] In response, British reviewers accused Hawthorne of ingratitude, claiming that they had admired him even before the Americans had done, and they attributed

[39] Victor, 'Nathaniel Hawthorne', *Theatrical Journal* 15 (February 1854): 44.

[40] Sir Nathaniel, 'American Authorship', *New Monthly Magazine* 98 (June 1853): 203; 'Contemporary Literature of America', *Westminster Review* 58 (October 1852): 594; 'Rev. of The Blithedale Romance', *New Quarterly Review* 1 (October 1852): 414.

[41] 'Contemporary Literature of America', *Westminster Review* 58 (October 1852): 594; 'Rev. of The Blithedale Romance', *New Quarterly Review* 1 (October 1852): 415.

[42] [R. H. Hutton], 'Nathaniel Hawthorne', *National Review* 11 (October 1860): 460; 'Nathaniel Hawthorne', *Eclectic Review* 3 (May 1860): 549.

[43] 'Rev. of Transformation', *Athenaeum* (March 3, 1860): 296.

[44] 'Rev. of Our Old Home', *Christian Remembrancer* 47 (January 1864): 167.

this ingratitude to cultural insecurity. 'He is jealous of us', suggested one reviewer, while another noted that Hawthorne must be afflicted by the 'sense of injury' that all Americans share.[45] *Our Old Home* briefly lowered Hawthorne's standing in Britain, but his sudden death a year later, and the eulogies it prompted, reminded reviewers of their previous esteem. A spate of essays surveying Hawthorne's entire career restored *Our Old Home* to its properly minor position, and critics forgave Hawthorne his criticisms of the British, attributing them now to his disappointment that Britain had not taken the Union side during the Civil War. One reviewer spoke for them all when he concluded, 'we shall miss him as much as his fellow country-men will'.[46]

Together, then, Stowe and Hawthorne pointed towards a new era of equality in transatlantic literary relations, one in which American novels might be as popular as the British or, possibly, even more artful. But this era was postponed by the outbreak of the Civil War. Little fiction of note was published during the war, and when the American literary world reconstituted itself in the war's aftermath, a new set of authors and a new set of concerns would come to the fore.

The American Novel After the Civil War

The Civil War ended in 1865, and by the late 1860s, American publishers had returned to publishing fiction—and, increasingly, to watching it be reprinted in Britain. Reprinting became more predictable in the second half of the century. In part, this was because publishers were now willing to enter into what were called 'courtesy of the trade' agreements: through these, they paid authors for the exclusive right to print the authors' work, confident that such agreements would be honoured by rival publishers. In this way, a *de facto* system of international copyright came into being. At the same time, authors who were popular enough to be certain of an audience in both nations learned to make better use of the existing copyright laws, arranging to have their works released both in America and in Britain (most often, in British Canada) on the same day and thereby securing copyright in both places.

These changes in publishing made American novels a familiar part of the British literary world. This change is registered in the reviews. During the antebellum period, there had been scattered reviews on particularly noteworthy works and authors, but in the postbellum period American literature became a routine object of attention: the *Saturday Review* devoted a column every month to American literature and the *Athenaeum* to American fiction, while the *Westminster Review* printed a long essay every year on works by Americans. To some extent, critics continued to dismiss American novels, as when

---

[45] 'Rev. of Our Old Home', *Examiner* (October 17, 1863): 663; 'Hawthorne on England', *Blackwood's Edinburgh Magazine* 94 (November 1863): 615.

[46] 'Nathaniel Hawthorne, Mr. Senior, and Mr. W. J. Fox', *Reader* (June 11, 1864): 735.

one claimed that the rare pleasure of discovering that a novel is actually good comes most rarely when the novel is by an American, while another called America 'a paradise for writers...without special gifts'.[47] But by the late 1860s, most reviewers were coming to think of American novels as consistently acceptable, if rarely excellent. One reviewer observed that there was now a steady supply of American fiction of 'the second or third class', while a generation later, another critic would be observing along the same lines that Americans produce more novels of 'average merit' than do the British.[48] And by the 1880s, most reviewers had begun treating the American novel with a grudging respect. One praised American novels as being 'nearly always intelligent work and very often pleasant reading', while another noted that there is no more need for bad English novels, since better ones are arriving from America by the barrelful.[49] The rise of American novels was often seen in relation to a perceived decline in British fiction, following the deaths of its major practitioners. One reviewer noted that there is a new interest in American literature because English literature 'has so little to boast of', while another expressed the hope that the emergence of an American rival would prompt English writers to do their best.[50] Still, the tone of decline persisted. America 'has no Walter Scott, no Thackeray, no George Eliot', one reviewer observed. 'Neither, it may be added, has England.'[51]

Thus, the general Victorian view of postbellum American novels as nearly the equal of British novels, or perhaps even better than a British novel in decline. This was not enough, however, to satisfy an ambitious new school of American novelists, under the leadership of William Dean Howells. Now largely forgotten, Howells was the single most important figure in the postbellum literary world. Not only was he a prolific novelist and playwright in his own right, but he also presided over the two most influential literary magazines, first editing the *Atlantic Monthly* and then writing the review essays for *Harper's Monthly*. From these positions, he shaped literary opinion, determining which American writers would be published and read. Among the authors he championed most strongly were his good friends Mark Twain and Henry James. Twain does not often appear in British discussions of the American novel, since he was considered by the British to be a humorist rather than a novelist. But James, along with Howells, defined what British reviewers took the American novel to be.

The two caused a small stir through their commitment to what was called 'the international theme', stories about leisured Americans encountering European culture for the first time. At the centre of these stories could often be found a so-called 'American girl', a young woman whose mix of independence and innocence distinguishes her from

[47] George Saintsbury, 'New Novels', *Academy* (January 17, 1885): 42; 'Novels of the Week', *Athenaeum* (May 24, 1890): 670.

[48] 'Novels and Novelettes', 776; L.R.F. O., 'Fiction', *Speaker* (July 21, 1900): 446.

[49] W. E. Henley, 'New Novels', *Academy* (June 23, 1883): 434; 'Reviews and Views', *Merry England* 3 (September 1884): 354.

[50] 'American Fiction', *London Quarterly Review* 1 (Oct. 1883): 186; 'Letters in America', *Scottish Review* 1 (Nov. 1882): 31.

[51] Prothero, 'American Fiction', 65.

her European sisters. In part, the American girl simply reflected the fact that social mores were less restrictive in America, where young women were permitted to conduct their courtships at least somewhat on their own. But the figure was also used to illustrate broader national differences, as a perceptive British critic recognized:

> [The American girl] speaks for more than herself; she throws a light on American social institutions and ideas, such as not even the travelling notes of observant and philosophical members of parliament give us; and through her we are constantly getting deeper insight into the working of the wonderful social and political fabric that those energetic and fearless descendants of ours are building out of old-English manners.[52]

The most famous example of the international theme and the most famous American girl can be found in James's *Daisy Miller* (1878). This novella recounts the adventures of a young American woman as seen through the eyes of a somewhat older American man. He is at first entranced by Daisy's daring, by her readiness to stay up talking with him late at night or to travel with him without a chaperone, but he is soon shocked to find her taking up with obscure Italian men and touring the Coliseum with them alone in the moonlight: in this way, he discovers that his years in Europe have made him a European. The novel proved to be quite controversial in America, where it was often read as an attack on his native country by an author who had made his life abroad. The controversy made *Daisy Miller* the bestselling of all James's works, although he did not profit from it at all, having mishandled the copyright.

British reviewers were taken aback by the international theme, which reversed the conventions of local colour writing and presented Britain and Europe as exotic locales for the entertainment of American readers. The genre heralded a new cultural confidence among Americans, and British reviewers responded defensively, arguing that Howells, James, and their circle were forced to write about Europe for lack of any better subject at home. One reviewer observed that America is a place that defies novelists in its 'very simplicity' and that it therefore makes sense that American authors would turn to an older civilization for subject matter.[53] Another reviewer sympathized with the paucity of subjects for American novels, noting that now that the Indians are extinct and the Wild West written out, there is nothing for novelists to do but import Europeans to write about.[54] And a third distinguishes true American literature, by authors such as George Washington Cable and Bret Harte, which describes the nation's regions and offers British readers the pleasures of the exotic, from 'spurious' American literature, by Howells and James, who 'neglect their own country altogether' and populate their novels with 'plaster images brought back from Venice, Paris or London'.[55]

[52] Agnes Macdonnell, 'The American Heroine', *Macmillan's Magazine* 32 (October 1875): 548.
[53] 'Rev. of The American', *Examiner* (August 11, 1877): 1013.
[54] 'American Society in American Fiction', *Edinburgh Review* 156 (July 1882): 175.
[55] [Louis John Jennings], 'American Novels', *Quarterly Review* 155 (January 1883): 203.

British reviewers took an even dimmer view of the American girl. As early as the 1870s, they were observing that the female characters in American novels were every year becoming 'more disagreeable'.[56] The American girl was disagreeable because she was self-confident, certain that she was 'capable of resolving every problem, and deciding on every action' without any assistance.[57] Indeed, so self-assured was this figure that more than one reviewer described her in martial terms: 'From San Francisco to Finland, they run about the world, without a touch of *mauvaise honte*, in every circle at their ease, flaunting the flag of the American girl, conquering and to conquer', writes one reviewer, while another observes, more pithily, 'The Young Girl is a being who can go everywhere and do everything, like the British Army.'[58] Even more disagreeable than the girls themselves, to the mind of many British reviewers, was the American fascination with them. Reviewers commonly complained that American novelists were 'altogether too much occupied with "young girls"'.[59] And one went so far as to claim that the question of the American girl had become, for her countryman, the equivalent to the riddle of the sphinx. As a result, 'a great and pacific people sits, conjectural and contemplative, at the feet of a being known to American literature as "The Young Girl"'.[60] But where American readers were endlessly fascinated, British readers had grown, another reviewer insisted, simply bored.[61]

It is worth noting that the American girl would have a surprising afterlife. Once the American vogue for fiction about the American girl had abated, British writers began to make the figure their own. In the late 1880s and 1890s, American girls appeared in a number of British essays on social and cultural themes, almost always as an admirable figure of female autonomy. One writer praised young American women for their cultivation and the seriousness with which they pursue their art, while another argued that the freedom of their upbringing has made them capable of judging and acting for themselves.[62] The American girl is praised for being more knowledgeable and more capable than even full-grown Victorian women. She 'understands how to look after herself', because she, unlike her English sisters, has 'travelled, and mixed with men and women, and had her experiences'.[63] All of this sounds rather familiar: it echoes contemporary depictions of the New Woman. The American girl, I would argue, became a less threatening alternative to the New Woman for those who wanted to argue for greater female autonomy: the two figures were combined in those late-century Victorian writings that describe the American girl as jealous of her 'rights' and always wanting more.[64]

[56] 'American Literature', *Saturday Review* (June 26, 1875): 837.
[57] F.P. Verney, 'The Americans Painted by Themselves', *Contemporary Review* 46 (October 1884): 547.
[58] 'Rev. of American Literature: an Historical Sketch', *Athenaeum* (January 20, 1883): 80; 'The American Sphinx', *Saturday Review* (December 2, 1882): 728.
[59] 'Rev. of In the Distance', *Saturday Review* (April 1, 1882): 399.
[60] 'The American Sphinx', *Saturday Review* (December 2, 1882): 728.
[61] 'Novels of the Week', *Athenaeum* (January 5, 1884): 16.
[62] 'Americans Abroad', *Chamber's Journal* (October 8, 1887): 650; J. Acton Lomax, 'American and English Girls', *National Review* 12 (February 1889): 774.
[63] 'The American Girl', *London Journal* (September 26, 1896): 279.
[64] 'The American Woman, As Seen Through German Spectacles', *Review of Reviews* 5 (June 1892): 585.

If Howells and his circle introduced new content to the 19th-century novel, they more importantly altered its form. British reviewers were made aware of their formal ambitions through a pair of essays published in the November 1882 issue of the *Century Magazine*. The first was written by Howells, and it was a celebration of James. Howells began by admitting that James is appreciated more by critics than by ordinary readers, and he devoted the rest of the essay to explaining why this was so: James could be difficult because he was more interested in analysis than in storytelling, a preference that Howells defended by noting that all stories have already been told and so there was nothing left to learn but what an author thought of them. With the preference for analysis over story-telling came a favouring of character over plot, as the recently published *Portrait of a Lady* (1881) demonstrated: the novel ended when the character of its protagonist had been fully explored, even though the plot was not yet done.

Howells celebrated James as a way of defending what he calls the 'new school' of the novel. This new school was characterized by its form, its preference for analysis over storytelling and character over plot, but equally by the realism of its representations, its attention to ordinary persons and experiences. Indeed, it would be called 'realist' as often as it would be called 'modern' and 'new'. In Howells's view, this new school of nov-elists marked a significant development over what the novel had been before, as he made clear in the essay's most notorious passage:

> The art of fiction has, in fact, become a finer art in our day than it was with Dickens and Thackeray. We could not suffer the confidential attitude of the latter now, nor the mannerism of the former, any more than we could endure the prolixity of Richardson or the coarseness of Fielding. These great men are of the past—they and their methods and interests; even Trollope and Reade are not of the present. The new school derives from Hawthorne and George Eliot rather than any others; but it studies human nature much more in its wonted aspects, and finds its ethical and dramatic examples in the operation of lighter but not really less vital motives.[65]

Clearly, Howells was making a case for the postbellum American novel, singling out Hawthorne and James and, implicitly, himself. But he made the case, crucially, on generational grounds: on one side, Richardson and Fielding, Dickens and Thackeray; on the other, Hawthorne, but also Eliot, as well as French realists such as Alphonse Daudet.

Howells's essay made a bold enough claim in its own right, but its effect was magnified by appearing in the same issue as an essay explicitly about transatlantic relations, written by Charles Dudley Warner, a New England man of letters. The subject of this essay was putatively Britain, but Warner devoted most of it to decrying the outsized influence that Britain has had over America. Making the same point that Emerson had made decades

---

[65] William D. Howells, 'Henry James, Jr.,' *Century* XXV (November 1882): 28.

earlier, Warner observes that Americans have been reading British books, and thereby imbibing British ideas, since the nation's founding:

> For more than fifty years after our independence, we imported our intellectual food,—with the exception of politics, and theology in certain forms—and largely our ethical guidance from England. We read English books, or imitations of the English way of looking at things; we even accepted the English caricatures of our own life as genuine—notably in the case of the so-called typical Yankee. It is only recently that our writers have begun to describe our own life as it is, and that readers begin to feel that our society may be as interesting in print as that English society which they have been all their lives accustomed to read about … for half a century English writers, by poems and novels, controlled the imagination of this country.[66]

The rest of the essay continued this declaration of literary independence. Warner praised American authors for realizing that a nation must develop a culture along 'its own lines' (141), and he observed that, as a result, American and English literature, indeed even American and English language, were diverging from one another. For this reason, American literature could only be judged by American readers—and if the English failed to see that Washington Irving's *Knickerbocker's History* (1809) and James Russell Lowell's *Bigelow Papers* (1848, 1867) were equal to anything the English had written, then their own cultural narrowness was to blame.

This pair of essays prompted an outraged response, voiced through long review essays and brief remarks made in passing for much of the following year. The outrage attached most obviously to Warner's literary nationalism, as we can see in an essay by Margaret Oliphant. She began by revealing that British critics have long been willing to view American literature with an indulgent eye, not realizing how little American authors believed indulgence was needed. But the recent reprinting of magazines like the *Century* had revealed to British readers how the American literary world viewed itself, and Oliphant could barely comprehend what she had learned. She refused to believe that anyone, not even those living across thousands of miles of salt water, could find Irving and Lowell superior to Shakespeare and Milton, Addison and Pope. And she asked with heavy irony whether Warner would be capable of reading her reply, written as it was in English English. (Here, she stands apart from the many British reviewers since Coventry Patmore who had agreed that the languages were diverging.) As to Warner's claim that British reviewers were incapable of understanding American works, Oliphant dismissed it as the adolescent whining of a 'tyro of eighteen' who complains that he is not understood by his father.[67] Oliphant was not alone. Even an essay written by a British critic to warn his countrymen that they were being too 'touchy' in their response to Warner nonetheless repeated Oliphant's claims, noting that it was laughable to say that American

---

[66] Charles Dudley Warner, 'England', *Century* XXV (November 1882): 141.

[67] [Margaret Oliphant], 'American Literature in England', *Edinburgh Review* 157 (January 1883): 140.

literature had superseded the English canon—and that there would be no profit in the reprinting of British books if the two Englishes had truly diverged.[68]

Howells's essay invited equally strong objections, albeit on aesthetic grounds. There were some complaints about the subject matter of the novels he championed. While Howells thought of himself as writing about the everyday, critics tended to find in the modern novel an unseemly attention to the low. Amy Levy, for instance, complained that no subject is too sordid or trivial to become the subject of a modern novel, although she would soon go on to write two such novels herself. And there were many complaints about form. *The Portrait of a Lady* that Howells had praised so highly was, for British reviewers, the proof of why analysis should not be put above storytelling or character above plot:

> Mr. James, in his latest completed work—'The Portrait of a Lady'—carries out unflinchingly the theories of his school. There is no story. The book is one of the longest of recent times—767 closely-printed pages; and there is not a single interesting incident in it from beginning to end. No one can possibly care, for a single moment, what becomes of any of the characters... Three volumes of 'analysis' in small type is somewhat trying, even to the most sternly cultivated aestheticism. The characters are described at enormous length by Mr. James; then they describe themselves; then they are described by the other characters. Between them all, it would be strange if their 'points' were not sufficiently brought out.[69]

This reviewer then went on to note that Howells was even worse in this respect than James: for while James could sometimes be seduced away from his faith in plotlessness, Howells never was. Levy, too, criticized Howells and James on formal grounds as well, complaining that their ideal narrator 'never leaves us alone for an instant; he is forever labelling, explaining, writing'.[70]

The controversy over the essays in the *Century* had immediate consequences for James and Howells's careers. It broke out in the very year that each had published his first major novel, Howells's *A Modern Instance* (1882) as well as James's *Portrait of a Lady*, and over-shadowed the reception of both. But the controversy had surprising long-term effects, as well. Although the initial responses were careful to distinguish Howell's generational argument from Warner's national one, subsequent responses conflated the two. As a result, the new novel or realist novel quickly came to be seen as distinctively American. A review of a Howells novel, *A Foregone Conclusion*, saw it as typical not of Howells, but of his nation, calling it 'one of those American novels' that is 'subtle and full of analysis'.[71] Often, Howells was not even mentioned and the formal principles he had defended were

[68] 'International Touchiness', *Saturday Review* (February 3, 1883): 138.
[69] [Louis John Jennings], 'American Novels', *Quarterly Review* 155 (January 1883): 213.
[70] Amy Levy, 'The New School of American Fiction', *Temple Bar* 70 (March 1884): 384.
[71] 'New Novels', *Academy* (May 20, 1882): 355.

simply assigned to the American novel more generally. Noting that a certain novel 'runs down with a vague conclusion', one reviewer reminded himself that in American novels this is 'thought to be rather a beauty than a defect'.[72] Another reviewer made the same point by witty inversion, expressing disbelief that a particular novel was American since it does, in fact, have a plot.[73] Through the rest of the century, British critics repeatedly identified the preference for analysis over narration, character over plot, as well as the commitment to realism, as specifically American traits.

This had two interesting effects. The first was a recoding of the American novel in British critical discourse: where the antebellum American novel had been associated with local colour and moral purpose, the postbellum American novel was increasingly seen as artful and introspective. As a result, a novel like Miriam Coles Harris's *Phoebe* (1884), a novel of piety and moral purpose, is described as un-American because it lacks the slow movement and introspection of the James school.[74] And a novel like Albert Aiken's *The Man from Texas* (1879), filled with local colour, is dismissed as atypical of American novels because it has more 'incident' than 'polish'.[75] With this recoding of the American novel as artistic came a sense that it had somehow become more sophisticated than its British counterpart, more aligned with the artistic movements on the Continent. This posed a serious challenge to the supremacy of the British novel, and reviewers responded to it in two ways. Some dismissed the novels of the Howells school as still immature, betraying the insecurity of a young culture that nervously insists on following the 'literary etiquette books'.[76] Others attacked these novels instead as old beyond their years. One reviewer noted that the works of Howells and James show that the American novel, which had not yet approached its middle age, now means to skip it entirely.[77] And another reviewer agreed that American fiction has 'taken on the infirmities of old age' without having abandoned 'the crudities of youth'.[78] Having arrived at this new conception of the American novel, a number of reviewers claimed to find traces of it in the earlier period: one attributed the self-consciousness of the postbellum novel to transcendentalism, another to the influence of Hawthorne, the first American novelist to be seen as artful.[79]

But if the *Century* controversy changed how Victorian critics viewed the American novel, it changed how they viewed the British novel as well. Many literary historians have long placed late Victorian writings in the context of the contemporary translation of French realism, but the late Victorians were clearly responding to American novelists as well, in particular to Howells. Because Howells advocated realism and analysis,

---

72 'Novels of the Week', *Athenaeum* (October 26, 1889): 555.
73 'Novels of the Week', *Athenaeum* (August 2, 1884): 143.
74 'Four American Novels', *Saturday Review* (August 30, 1884):283.
75 'Belles Lettres', *Westminster Review* 123 (January 1885): 291.
76 George Saintsbury, 'The Present State of the Novel', *Fortnightly Review* 42 (September 1887): 412.
77 A. Orr, 'International Novelists and Mr. Howells', *Contemporary Review* 37 (May 1880): 742.
78 'A Set of Five Story Books', *Saturday Review* (May 25, 1889): 641.
79 'Letters in America', *Scottish Review* 1 (November 1882) 51; Prothero, 'American Fiction', 49.

the critics attacking him ended up defending storytelling and romance, so that a novel in which young boys run away to become pirate captains and Indian chiefs is described by one reviewer as a 'beautiful unconscious protest against Mr. Howells and realism'.[80] Moreover, Victorian reviewers came to see the storytelling and romance they were defending as distinctively British. By the 1890s, they had recognized an equilibrium between the two literary worlds, with the Americans exporting realism and the British, romance.[81]

In 1891, the United States Congress finally ratified an international copyright law, but it ended up making less of a difference than its supporters hoped, in part for technical reasons. American printers and compositors, who belonged to a powerful trade union, had ensured that US copyright protections would be extended only to those British texts that had been printed in the United States from type set by Americans. This required British publishers to commit to two separate typesettings and printings, which they were only willing to do for authors certain to sell well in America. As a consequence, only about five per cent of British books were copyrighted in the United States, at least according to contemporary observers. But this was not the only reason that international copyright failed to make a difference. By the time the treaty was ratified, the literary exchange between America and Britain had gone on for so long that the two nations remained bound to one another even after copyright intervened.

Cross-currents and National Literatures

Today, literary scholars tend to divide British from American literature without thinking, but this was something that no Victorian reviewer would have done. Those reviewers took it for granted that American literature, unlike the literatures of France, or Russia, or Germany, could never be truly foreign to Britain. The connections between the two nations ran deeper than language and were less contingent than reprinting: they could only be expressed through metaphors of family. And so the Americans are continuously described as 'our brothers', as 'Transatlantic cousins', as 'kin beyond the sea', with full recognition that familial feelings comprise hatred and rivalry as well as loyalty and love.[82]

Victorian reviewers not only remind us of the important connections between British and American literature, they also provide us with two models for conceptualizing the relation between them. Some reviewers argued that it made no sense to treat the two as

---

[80] 'Mr. Chambers and Popular Literature', *Saturday Review* (May 26, 1883): 657.
[81] W. Robertson Nicoll, 'The Present State of American Literature', *Bookman* 11 (December 1896): 62–63.
[82] Patmore, 'American Novels', 109; Richard F. Littledale, 'New Novels', *Academy* (June 2, 1877): 482; 'Americans Abroad', 649.

distinct. 'The very notion of literatures in one language is', Coventry Patmore insisted, 'an absurdity.'[83] For him, the phrase 'English literature' comprised all the writings of the Anglophone world, even as he acknowledged that this literature still flourished best at what he puckishly called 'headquarters'.[84] Nor was Patmore alone in this view. Other reviewers, too, spoke of the two branches, British and American, of English literature, or considered together 'every department of British prose fiction at home or across the sea', or parenthetically modified the phrase 'English fiction' to include American fiction as well.[85] This view also shapes books such as S. Austin Allibone's *Critical Dictionary of English Literature and British and American Authors* (1858–72), Percy Russell's *Guide to British and American Novels* (1894), or the *History of English Prose Fiction* (1882), which included, as a matter of course, a chapter on American authors. For this school of critics, it makes perfect sense that an American woman would answer the question 'who are your poets?' with a list that includes Chaucer, Shakespeare, and Milton.[86] For in this view, Americans are equal heirs to that tradition: any poem 'written in the English language, whether produced in England or in some other part of the vast English-speaking world, is an English poem'.[87] From these reviewers, we can learn not to presume too quickly that there are differences between British and American literature, and they are the predecessors to the many critics who focus on Anglo-American literature without drawing distinctions.

   Other reviewers recognize that the two literatures, while emerging out of a shared literary and cultural tradition, are nonetheless struggling to be distinct. This position has been taken up more recently by present-day scholars. Lawrence Buell, for instance, has argued that American literature emerged in a context of cultural dependence, shaped by a British inheritance that it both emulated and rejected, uncertain of a British approval that it both desired and disdained. This, he notes, is typical of the literatures of former colonies, and for this reason, he has called the literature of 19th-century America the first post-colonial literature.[88] There is much support for Buell's argument in literary history, from Emerson's 'American Scholar' (1837), which called for an end to 'our day of dependence, our long apprenticeship to the learning of other lands', through Young America's many calls for a national literature that the whole world will admire, to the Preface to Walt Whitman's *Leaves of Grass*, which opens with an image of European literature being carried, like a corpse, out the door.[89] But there is evidence as well in the contemporary

   [83] Patmore, 'American Novels', 82.

   [84] Patmore, 'American Novels', 21.

   [85] 'Letters in America', *Scottish Review* 1 (Nov. 1882), 31; 'Every Man His Own Mrs. Nickleby', *National Observer* (August 25, 1894): 387; The Bookworm, 'Bibliographical', *Academy* (April 21, 1900): 326.

   [86] 'Rev. of American Literature: an Historical Sketch', *Athenaeum* (January 20, 1883): 79.

   [87] Theodore Watts, 'The Future of American Literature', *Fortnightly Review* 49 (June 1891): 917.

   [88] Lawrence Buell, 'American Literary Emergence as Postcolonial Phenomenon', *American Literary History* 4, no. 3 (Autumn 1992): 411–42.

   [89] Ralph Waldo Emerson, 'The American Scholar', in *The Complete Works of Ralph Waldo Emerson*, 2 vols. (London: Bell and Daldy, 1866), 2: 174; John O'Sullivan, 'Democracy and Literature', *United States Democratic Review* 11 (August 1842): 196.

Victorian reviews, which reveal the post-colonial dynamic from the other side. Most reviewers patronized American literature when not dismissing it or attacking it, and they tended to presume that all American novels fell into one of two categories: a few that were 'crudely original', while the rest were 'feebly imitative'. [90] One reviewer noted that American literature merely imitates European, so much so that its only true characteristic was 'the absence of a character'.[91] Another critic made much the same point, noting that the greatest works of American literature could have been written by Europeans.[92]

More recently, a critic of this century, Paul Giles, has argued that British literature struggled with the idea of America as much as American literature did with the idea of Britain. In Giles's account, the legacy of an Anglo-American world split by the American Revolution has been divided between Britain and America. America is associated with the rebellious impulses, in particular religious dissent and political republicanism, while Britain is associated with the more consensual values of a state church and a constitutional monarchy. And so British authors take up the subject of America as a way of resolving political issues of their own.[93] Certainly, the Victorian reviews shared this view of the relation between the two cultures, and the reviewers who think of America and Britain as part of a shared culture tend to emphasize the Puritans as its point of origin. One reviewer, for instance, noted that the men and women who travelled from Old England to New England were happy to carry their English customs with them; and this is why, he observed, it is possible to see that the customs of the Americans are the customs of the England of Elizabethan times, from folk dancing and housekeeping to lynching.[94] And another, acknowledging differences between Americans and the British, nonetheless located the origin of American culture in John Milton, America's first and chief author.[95] Taken together, Buell and Giles throw into relief what the Victorian reviews themselves reveal: that the English-language novel was one of the domains in which both Britain and America struggled to define themselves, a struggle that took place with, through, and against one another. In the process, the British novel came to a new self-conception, and the American novel came into its own.

SUGGESTED READING

Buell, Lawrence. 'American Literary Emergence as a Postcolonial Phenomenon'. *American Literary History* 4, no. 3 (Autumn 1992): 411–42.

Casper, Scott E. *The Industrial Book: 1840–1880*. Vol. 3 of *A History of the Book in America*. Chapel Hill: University of North Carolina Press, 2007.

---

[90] Prothero, 'American Fiction', 38.

[91] 'Journal of American Literature', *Critic* (April 4, 1846): 357

[92] 'Journal of American Literature', *Critic* (September 19, 1846): 347.

[93] Paul Giles, *Atlantic Republic: The American Tradition in English Literature* (Oxford: Oxford University Press, 2006), 1.

[94] 'Rev. of The Americans at Home', 73.

[95] 'Retrospective Survey of American Literature', *Westminster Review* (January 1852): 289.

Giles, Paul. *The Atlantic Republic: The American Tradition in English Literature*. New York: Oxford University Press, 2006.

Gross, Robert A. and Mary Kelly, eds. *An Extensive Republic: Print, Culture, and Society in the New Nation, 1790–1840*. Chapel Hill: University of North Carolina Press, 2010.

McGill, Meredith. *American Literature and the Culture of Reprinting, 1834–1853*. Philadelphia: University of Pennsylvania Press, 2003.

Sutherland, John. *Victorian Novelists and Publishers*. Chicago: University of Chicago Press, 1976.

12

COLONIAL INDIA AND VICTORIAN STORYTELLING

MARGERY SABIN

To take up anew the topic of colonialism in the Victorian novel requires awareness of the once radical but now virtually orthodox position on this subject in literary criticism. The marks of an allegedly monolithic imperial discourse have become easy to summarize since Edward Said forcefully laid them out in *Orientalism* (1978) and, later, *Culture and Imperialism* (1993).[1] Said includes all genres of writing in his indictment of European imperial consciousness:

> In your narratives, histories, travel tales, and explorations, your consciousness was represented as the principal authority, an active point of energy that made sense not just of colonizing activities but of exotic geographies and peoples. Above all, your sense of power scarcely imagined that those 'natives' who appeared either subservient or sullenly uncooperative were ever going to be capable of finally making you give up India or Algeria. Or of saying anything that might perhaps contradict, challenge, or otherwise disrupt the prevailing discourse.[2]

Said rightly challenges ways in which earlier literary history granted autonomy from colonial politics and history to the 19th-century 'domestic' novel by writers such as Austen, Dickens, the Brontës, Gaskell, George Eliot, Wilkie Collins, and others. Read with an interrogative eye, the marginality of colonial experience for these novelists could be exposed as not innocent but tacitly and often overtly complicit with England's

---

[1] Edward W. Said, *Orientalism* (New York: Pantheon, 1978); *Culture and Imperialism* (New York: Alfred Knopf, 1993).

[2] *Culture and Imperialism*, xxi.

drive for global dominance.[3] Said is also right to observe the pervasive chauvinism that sustained what Francis Hutchins has called 'the illusion of permanence' about British imperial power.[4]

Yet now that the categories of imperial discourse in the Victorian period have become rather fixed in place, both historians and literary critics are turning attention to more complex cultural interactions between colonizers and colonized cultures than the initial indictments in postcolonial criticism featured.[5] For this inquiry, distinctions among genres are valuable. The rich repertory of non-fiction writing that flourished with the reading public in both the early and late Victorian periods—memoirs, travel journals, histories, war reportage—includes texts which fit less easily into generalizations about imperial discourse than do the novels. Although the authors of these writings, like all authors everywhere, proceed from their own active points of energy (in Said's phrase), and no doubt we may discern in their writings established categories of thought and language, long immersion in foreign cultures also frequently disrupt and subvert the assumptions of novelists for whom England was taken for granted as home.

Jonah Raskin, in *The Mythology of Imperialism*, finds vivid figurative language to sum up the inveterate attachment to England as 'home' in the Victorian novel:

> In Victorian novels the colonies are usually places to transfer burned out characters, or from which to retrieve characters... For the Victorians existence meant existence in England... Going to India was like falling off a cliff. The Englishman coming back to London felt like a fish thrown back into the sea after flopping about on land.[6]

Yet in *Kim*, Kipling's narrator offers a contrary metaphor when he calls the Indian scene 'the smiling river of life'.[7] Kipling's stories of India received such extravagant applause in England in the 1890s because for the first time a writer seemed to combine immersion

---

[3] See, for examples, *Culture and Imperialism*, xii and *passim*; Suvendrini Perera, *The English Novel from Edgeworth to Dickens* (New York: Columbia University Press, 1991), 7–8 and *passim*; Patrick Brantlinger, *Rule of Darkness: British Literature and Imperialism, 1830–1914* (Ithaca and London: Cornell University Press, 1988), 3–16 and *passim*.

[4] Francis G. Hutchins, *The Illusion of Permanence: British Imperialism in India* (Princeton, NJ: Princeton University Press, 1967).

[5] See, for examples, Sara Suleri, *The Rhetoric of English India* (Chicago: University of Chicago Press, 1992); Bart Moore-Gilbert, ed., *Writing India, 1757–1990: The Literature of British India* (Manchester, UK: Manchester University Press, 1996); Homi K. Bhabha, *The Location of Culture* (London and New York: Routledge, 1994); C.L. Bayly, *Indian Society and the Making of the British Empire* (Cambridge, UK: Cambridge University press, 1988); William Dalrymple, *White Mughals: Love and Betrayal in Eighteenth-Century India* (New York: Viking Penguin, 2003), *The Last Mughal: the Fall of a Dynasty: Delhi 1857* (New York: Vintage, 2008); Ambreen Hai, *Making Words Matter: The Agency of Colonial and Postcolonial Literature* (Athens, OH: Ohio University Press, 2009).

[6] Jonah Raskin, *The Mythology of Imperialism* (New York: Random House, 1971), 17–18; quoted by Perera, 2.

[7] Rudyard Kipling, *Kim* [1901], ed. Edward Said (New York: Penguin, 1987), 109. Subsequent citations appear in the text.

in a colonial culture from years as a journalist with a fiction-making imagination. How this combination informed his fiction has only recently begun to be fully explored.[8]

Two fresh questions for studies of the Victorian novel are these: why did the mainstream domestic novel pay so little attention to the destabilizing, and even subversive, knowledge sometimes coming through writers with deep experience of the colonies? And why, in turn, did talented writers among those with that experience largely eschew fiction-writing, and (before Kipling) do mostly a mediocre job of it when they tried? To probe these questions with some specificity and depth, I choose not to attempt another compendious survey of the vast field of Victorian colonial literature of the sort now available in several excellent versions,[9] preferring to examine more closely the distinctiveness of selected texts and their relations to each other. The colonial geography of this chapter will also be limited to the Indian sub-continent: the largest and most dynamic location of British colonial expansion in the Victorian period, and the biggest source of writing activity, at least until Africa came to the fore at the end of the century.

Elizabeth Gaskell's 1853 novel, *Cranford*, suggests how colonial experience was not only consigned to the margins of the Victorian novel but also figured within it as a competing form of storytelling. The novel's colonial character, Peter Jenkyns, is a forgotten and absent figure through most of the novel. As a young man, this prankster son of the town's severe and scholarly Rector, had fled his family, town, and nation after a brutal paternal flogging for a prank too shocking to be excused. Disguised in the dress of his pre-eminently respectable, unmarried sister, he had displayed himself to the observation of his mostly female neighbours coddling something in the shape of a baby for which there was no decent explanation. Only years later, when the Rector and the older sister have died, does his unexpected return (with money from his indigo plantation) rescue his remaining aged sister from penury and dependence on kindly neighbours. Even more interesting to this mainly female community, however, is the entertainment Peter (now called Aga Peter) provides: He 'told more wonderful stories than Sindbad the sailor; and ... was quite as good as an Arabian night any evening'.[10]

Gaskell follows Raskin's outline of the Victorian novel's use of India to provide escape (or punishment) for scapegrace progeny, while at the same time enabling them later to assist more worthy relatives at home through the money they can bring back. What this model does not include is realistic political, social, or cultural detail. Aga Peter's

---

[8] See Suleri, 11–132; Hai, 21–96; Zohreh Sullivan, *Narratives of Empire: The Fictions of Rudyard Kipling* (Cambridge, UK: Cambridge University Press, 1993).

[9] Leading examples of such surveys include: Patrick Brantlinger, 'Race and the Victorian Novel', in *The Cambridge Companion to the Victorian Novel*, ed. Deirdre David (Cambridge UK: Cambridge University Press, 2001), 149–68; Deirdre David, 'Empire, Race, and the Victorian Novel', in *A Companion to the Victorian Novel*, ed. Patrick Brantlinger and William B. Thesing (Malden MA, Oxford: Blackwell, 2002), 84–100; Cannon Schmitt, '"The Sun and Moon Were Made to Give Them Light": Empire in the Victorian Novel', in *A Concise Companion to the Victorian Novel*, ed. Francis O'Gorman (Malden, MA, Oxford: Blackwell, 2005), 4–24.

[10] Elizabeth Gaskell, *Cranford* [1853], ed. Elizabeth Porges Watson, Oxford World's Classics (London: Oxford University Press, 1972), 154. Subsequent citations appear in the text.

imprisonment by the Burmese in Rangoon after an unnamed siege figures as an ordeal, but without any political content. Nor does his account of his later success as an indigo planter feature any social details beyond what might be gleaned from his preference for sitting on the floor cross-legged and handling his food in strange ways.

Patrick Brantlinger included Aga Peter's stories in *Cranford* with the sea adventures of Captain Marryat, as paradigmatic 'imperial adventure tales' that only seem antithetical, but belong to 'a single system of discourse, the literary equivalent of imperial domination abroad and liberal reformation at home'.[11] Other details of *Cranford*, however, suggest that Aga Peter's Indian stories represent a competitive rather than reinforcing discursive presence in relation to the novel's interest in the art of plain and realistic storytelling.[12] Gaskell's narrator regards Aga Peter's Indian stories and the community's enthusiasm for them with affectionate but sceptical incredulity. When he includes 'cherubim' among the successful targets of a shooting expedition, she concludes that he remains the prankster he was as a youth, in the same class as the phony magician Signor Brunoni, with a set of tricks he too brought back from India. Gaskell, by contrast, is defining a form of domestic realism that can raise interest in a mode of life even abnormally devoid of 'tricks'.

Among the non-fiction colonial writers from India at this time, one who might have shocked more than entertained the ladies of *Cranford* is Fanny Parkes. Her travel journal of more than twenty years of 'Wanderings' in India (written as postings to her mother in England) received its single printing in 1850.[13] The fragmentary and chronological form of the travel genre precisely suits Fanny's resilience, curiosity, and capacity for growth. Freedom from the demands of a long narrative form allows her to avoid the strain of fitting strange foreign persons and places into a superimposed design. The calendar alone orders her own sequences of distress and exuberance.

Married to a lower-level administrator, Fanny regularly left her confined life as a *memsahib* for her favoured activity of 'vagabondising over India' (303), and it is the record of these 'wanderings' that registers the diverse details of Indian life, from the daily routines in a Mughal *zenana* to the variety of preferences in sleeping furniture among different social classes. Her myriad realistic details diminish the exoticism of Indian life without erasing vast cultural differences. Equally important, comparisons lead her increasingly to criticize British practices, especially in relation to women.

---

[11] Brantlinger, *Rule of Darkness*, 12–13.

[12] More in a spirit of nostalgia than of domestic reform, Gaskell in the essay 'The Last Generation' describes the method in which she is recalling the small-town English community of her youth that she later fictionalizes in *Cranford*: 'every circumstance and occurrence…is strictly and truthfully told without exaggeration', *Sartain's Union Magazine* 5 (July 1849), reprinted in Appendix I, *Cranford*, 161.

[13] Fanny Parkes, *Wanderings of a Pilgrim in Search of the Picturesque, During Four-and-Twenty Years in the East; With Revelations of Life in the Zenana* (Pelham Richardson: London, 1850); substantial selections from this long out-of-print volume has been newly edited (with an excellent introduction) by William Dalrymple under the title *Begums, Thugs and Englishmen* (New Delhi: Penguin India, 2002). Subsequent citations appear in the text.

Fanny's female voice gives a distinctive timbre even to adventures that are more familiar from the male colonial archive. 'Vagabondising over India' liberates Parkes from the
female domestic norm, whether Indian or English. A long sequence of journal entries,
for example, records the adventures of her fifty-one-day river trip from Allahabad to
Agra in a small boat on the perilous Jumna river, with only a native crew for company.
She presents herself on this voyage as a strange kind of hybrid: in part, a gallant captain, supervising and sustaining the flagging morale of her crew by eloquent pep talks
in Hindustani through one ordeal after another: sandbars, torrents of cold rain, violent
winds, leakage, and other dire threats to the boat. She also likes to show herself working
beside the crew:

> We had to take down a part of the aft-cabin, and to take up some boards before we
> could get at it: and when found, we had nothing on board fit to stop it. At last it was
> effectually stopped with towels, torn up and forced in tight, and stiff clay beaten down
> over that. I thought it might last until our arrival at Kalpee, where proper repairs
> might take place. [164]

At other moments, she is the *memsahib*, admiring picturesque ruins and landscapes on
the shores. Not least of the 'picturesque' sights she describes is her own figure on deck,
dressed against the winter cold in a variety of motley costumes, such as 'a pair of Indian
shawls, snow boats, and a velvet cap'(169). Like her complex role, her costume is neither entirely English nor Indian, not entirely male or female—a combination of her own
invention that duplicates her mixed identity of *memsahib*, captain, and crew.

Parkes's narrative departs more pointedly from the imperial discourse of the male
seafaring adventure when she shows how her river journey alienated her from the
conventional colonial society she rejoins once arrived at the destination of Agra. After
almost two months virtually isolated from English compatriots, she becomes a critical
observer of the colonialized scene at the famous monument of the Taj Mahal: 'European
ladies and gentleman have the band to play on the marble terrace, and dance quadrilles
in front of the tomb!' she laments: 'Can you imagine anything more detestable?'(184).
Further on in Agra, she is even more offended by the desecration of Mughal structures
and callous disregard for Indian religious sensitivity:

> some wretches of European officers—to their disgrace be it said—made the beautiful
> room a cook-room! and the ceiling, the fine marbles and the inlaid work, are all one
> mass of blackness and defilement! Perhaps they cooked the *su'ar*, the hog, the unclean
> beast, within the sleeping apartments of Noorjahan—the proud, the beautiful
> Sultana! [186]

Parkes's tenderness towards Mughal royalty was no doubt greatly influenced by her
sojourns at the establishments of one Colonel James Gardner and his son, a more substantial, real-life version of Gaskell's Aga Peter in *Cranford*. (Gardner's son was, like
Peter, an indigo planter.) Fanny's dearest male friend in India, Gardner was one of the

last of the 'white Moghuls', in William Dalrymple's memorable phrase for Englishmen who ventured deep 'Indianization' at the end of the 18th and early 19th century.[14] His hectic military career (at one time fighting on *both* sides of colonial battles during the Maratha wars) had yielded by the time of Parkes's visits in the mid-1830s to old age and a retirement devoted to storytelling about the complexities of his earlier life. His romantic elopement with a young Delhi princess and the bi-cultural upbringing of his children and grandchildren animate stories which Fanny herself ardently reports and even directly enters through the Colonel's hospitality. She spends time with his wife and other women in his *zenana* and attends the extravaganza of his granddaughter's wedding, also to a scion of Delhi royalty. Fanny repeatedly urged Gardner to write his remarkable 'biography', but he declined because 'If I were to write it, you would scarcely believe it; it would appear fiction'(104). The never-written biography of Colonel Gardner links him to an earlier generation when romantic and cultural immersion in Indian life was still respectable, if never common, for high-ranking English military and administrative figures.[15]

Parkes joins herself to this waning subgroup, though as a woman she emerges as even more unconventional and considerably less respectable than her forebears.[16] Her most exotic feat is to establish herself as an independent woman, boldly going her own way. Her husband gets only perfunctory mention in her journals, most often when he is encouraging her once again to set off on her 'vagabondising'.

Although Fanny was not immune to the glamour of a week-long Mughal wedding, she found her most congenial female society when she visited the Marathas, and established what became her closest female friendship in India, with the dowager ex-queen of Gwalior, Baiza Bai, who had ruled Sindh as widow until deposed by an insurrection set in motion by her adopted son. This was still high-class Indian life, but in manifest decline as power was increasingly being seized by the British in one after another territory at this time in the 1830s. Rescued, so to speak, from the worse fate of death by the treacherous insurgents, Baiza Bai had now paradoxically become a prisoner of the British, who did nothing to restore her power but instead protected her life by holding her in forced exile from her home, tightly controlling her movements, even while indulging her in some of her customary royal luxuries.

Parkes is not naïve about this intricate political situation, but subordinates it to her main subject: her experience with the Maratha women. She reports with delight that not only the ex-queen, but also her teenage granddaughter and her whole female retinue

[14] Dalrymple, *White Mughals*.

[15] Parkes quotes from and comments on the tribute to Gardner, in the *Asiatic Journal* of 1844: '"His autobiography would be a work of the highest value," stated this respectable public organ of colonial India, "affording a picture of Indian manners and Indian policy with which few besides himself have ever had the opportunity of becoming so intimately acquainted"' (211).

[16] Two more conventional women's journals from colonial India were written by Emily and by Fanny Eden, sisters of the Governor General, Lord Auckland. Dalrymple compares their writing unfavourably to Parkes's and comments on the Eden sisters' social disdain for Fanny Parkes. See Dalrymple, 'Introduction' to *Begums, Thugs, and Englishmen*, ix–xii.

retain the spirit of female warriors and rulers, despite the loss of their real power. 'Were I an Asiatic', she comments with enthusiasm, 'I would be a Mahratta!'(265).

Scenes of camaraderie and spirited fun differentiate these sections of the journal from anything either in the male colonial archive or the Victorian domestic novel. Unlike the display of 'native' women for male delectation, a staple in imperial discourse, these women appear sporting themselves for their own entertainment. Amused to see an English lady 'who would ride crooked!' (246), they assemble to watch the spectacle of Fanny riding into camp side-saddle. Baiza Bai then laughingly challenges her to don Maratha riding costume to try her own horse and saddle. Fanny is more than game; properly dressed, mounted, with her feet firmly in 'the great iron stirrups', she gallops off: '*En cavalier*, it appeared so safe, as if I could have jumped over the moon'(246). In writing, she adds a more historical complaint, about 'Queen Elizabeth, and her stupidity in changing the style of riding for women'. The fun continues when Fanny reverses the challenge for one of the Maratha ladies to try her side-saddle in English riding habit: 'how ugly she looked! "She is like a black doctor!" exclaimed one of the girls' (247).

This irreverent mockery of English style by both Fanny and the Maratha women goes well outside the Orientalist image of life in the *zenana*. So does Fanny's more melancholy sympathy for the loss of freedom represented by their confinement for sport in an 'enclosure', a kind of playground controlled by British power. The sympathy and counsel she is called upon to provide the ex-queen show Parkes crossing cultures in a different way, when she dresses her sympathy in the form of a Hindustani proverb: '"Jiska lathe ooska bhains"—i.e. "He who has the stick, his is the buffalo!"' (265).

Sympathy, in the form of tough proverbial wisdom, recurs in other conversations she recounts, especially concerning the sad lot of women the world over—with or without colonialism: 'Whether the melon falls on the knife or the knife on the melon, the melon is the sufferer' (248) is her contribution to a conversation comparing the lot of widows in England and India. Real differences are there, of course, but Fanny regularly presents them with the same tough and humorous impartiality. When one of the Maratha ladies wants to know whether she has arranged a substitute female companion for her husband when she has to go away to England after her father's death, Fanny (who has without a qualm left her husband for months at a time in India) teasingly invites this very lady to take her place, before explaining to her the rather different views of the English on such subjects: 'our ideas appeared as strange to her as hers were to me; and she expressed herself grieved that I should omit what they considered a duty' (340).

Fanny Parkes's free and open spirit in her journals would have seemed more than passing strange, not only to the ladies of Cranford, but to any Victorian reader or heroine, even Jane Eyre, for all her asserted boldness. Perhaps that is why Parkes's book failed to pass into a second edition in 1850. Brontë's novel, published in 1848, already disconcerted some Victorian readers by its heroine's boldness; *Jane Eyre* remains famous for Jane's declaration of women's right to action and liberty, spoken to herself out of an attic window at Thornfield: 'It is vain to say human beings ought to be satisfied with tranquility: they must have action; and they will make it if they cannot find it' (125).[17] Yet Jane's yearning for new fields of action takes her no farther than from Thornfield to the relatively nearby village of Morton, and only that far when she is fleeing Rochester's bigamous (or worse) proposal. Jane assertively opposes whatever she thinks she knows about foreign relationships between men and women. Earlier, still ignorant of Rochester's married condition, she teasingly casts him in the role of a Turk, and banters about how, as a 'missionary', she would stir up mutiny against him in his seraglio (300). Later, she refuses the actual opportunity to accompany St John Rivers as a missionary's wife. St John presents that proposal as an action based on resolve to serve God by saving the souls of pagans. Although Jane later accords St John a pre-posthumous tribute directly out of the textbook of Evangelical imperialism, she herself chooses survival at home with a loving, reformed (though maimed) Rochester.

A common puzzlement about *Jane Eyre* concerns the curious decline of her earlier longing for action. The exuberant representation of female action in Fanny Parkes's Indian journals makes Jane's difference more conspicuous, while also suggesting another instance of competition between imperial and domestic discourses. Initially, Rochester is the type of tainted colonial traveller all but destroyed by his colonial misadventures, even though he reshapes his experiences into stories that enthral Jane. St. John exemplifies the opposite type: the colonial 'Greatheart' on a mission to serve God, even at the cost of his own life. For Jane, by contrast, the longing for a wider field of action and experience is very soon fulfilled by the interior adventure of her passionate love. Brontë's metaphoric language transfers to Jane's interior life all the danger, thrill and drama that Fanny Parkes attaches to her riverboat adventures or gallops *en cavalier*. The 'varied field of hopes and fears, of sensations and excitement' that Jane already longed to explore at the end of her stay at Lowood school becomes internalized into the landscape of her inner life, both waking and in dreams and drawings based on dreams. Gaskell, in quite a different style, had also granted the outwardly impassive ladies of Cranford intensities of longing and disappointment, if perceptible only through stifled sobs. Her later novels, such as *North and South*, endow her characters with greater intensities of interior life; George Eliot does the same for male as well as female characters, deepening the moral dimension attached to the capacity for interiority in the development of the English domestic novel.

Brontë's boldness is to give both Rochester and Jane an adventurous metaphoric vocabulary for emotion: he warns Jane early on that some day she is likely to come 'to a craggy pass of the channel, where the whole of life's stream will be broken up into whirl and tumult, foam and noise'(161). After Jane faces the truth of Rochester's own story, his prophecy is realized: 'eddying darkness seemed to swim round me, and reflection came in as black and confused a flow…I seemed to have laid me down in the dried-up bed of a great river; I heard a flood loosened in remote mountains, and felt the torrent come' (331). Bronte differentiates Jane's inner drama from Rochester's prediction by joining

---

[17] Charlotte Brontë, *Jane Eyre* [1847], ed. Michael Mason (New York and London: Penguin, 1996). Subsequent citations appear in the text.

her metaphoric flood to the language of Psalm 49: 'the waters came into my soul … the floods overflowed me'. A protective religious faith different from St. John's wilful resolve strengthens Jane's inner journey.

The internal drama that becomes the highest form of 'action' in the Victorian novel is almost entirely absent from non-fiction colonial narratives. Proverbial metaphors displace the drama of the individual inner life by a less personal dynamic of power—the knives and the stick. The proverbs have a toughness that resists melodrama and pathos. In their fatalism, proverbs also may seem conservative, resigned to the futility of protest or reform. From the perspective of colonial politics, Brontë's celebration of her English heroine's internal adventure is perhaps the most chauvinistic English feature of her novel, in that the primacy of the individual life of feeling comes to signify England's civilized superiority over colonial cultures.

The absence of any persuasive interiority is one of the characteristics that makes Phillip Meadows Taylor's Indian story, *Confessions of a Thug* (1839), such an exotic murder narrative. One of the most popular Victorian novels to come directly out of the colonial experience, it lies somewhere in-between a work of imaginative fiction and a historical document, while its peculiar mixture of styles shows the difficulty of making an English novel out of material that seems to resist its conventions and values.

The true mystery of the crimes presented in such minute detail in *Confessions of a Thug* arises from there being no internal source for the homicidal violence of its Thug narrator, Ameer Ali. It is true that *Confessions of a Thug* became a bestseller in an era when interior dramas were not the main draw for crime novels; conventional motives such as greed or revenge sufficed for 'penny dreadful' popular fiction. Taylor, however, does aspire to create a more complex human character for his narrator. At the same time, he is drawing on contemporary public documents about Thuggee with their own restrictive narrative structures. As a result, the novel ends up a compendium of styles that leaves the reader more uncertain than before about what form of inner life could generate and sustain serial murder on an almost unimaginable scale—Ameer Ali counts more than 150 murders to his own account.[18]

Taylor had first-hand experience in the prosecution of Thuggee as an associate of William H. Sleeman in the early 1830s. After a disappointing transfer of his post to Hyderabad where he had earlier served the Nizam, Taylor turned to constructing a novel out of the investigatory material he and Sleeman had collected.[19] Taylor had at hand the

---

[18] Javed Majeed also notices what he calls 'competing' narrative styles in the novel, but tends to see them as 'subverting' the imperial discourse through a narrator who 'achieves a status independent of the author's interference, amounting to a challenging rival to the narrative of mastery and control', 'Meadows Taylor's *Confessions of a Thug*', in *Writing India*, 103. My reading differentiates Taylor more thoroughly from the English interlocutor within the novel, and sees the narrator, Ameer Ali, as less of a rival than a projection of Taylor's own diverse tastes, experiences, and interests.

[19] Details of this collaboration, as well as of the whole Thuggee campaign are presented by Martine Van Woerkens, *The Strangled Traveler: Colonial Imaginings and the Thugs of India* [1995], trans. from French by Catherine Tihanyi (Chicago and London: University of Chicago Press, 2002). See also Mary Poovey, 'Ambiguity and Historicism: Interpreting *Confessions of a Thug*', *Narrative* 12(1) (January 2004): 3–21.

already structured courtroom narratives of Thuggee practice, replete with detail: from the initial enticement of travelling couriers, traders, and other groups who moved along the perilous roads of central India, through the ritual of strangling and robbery, to the final disposal of dismembered corpses in remote burial places. The eerie absence of interiority in these depositions in part increased public horror at the idea of India's religious barbarism. The inhuman coldness of the depositions, however, was in part an artefact of the judicial structure. In such cases, the prosecution relied on participant informers, called 'Approvers', selected for their ability to deliver detailed information about places, times, and other participants.[20] Confessions of feelings—whether of motives or remorse—were not part of the court protocol, as Sleeman explained in a letter: 'I listened with all the coldness of a magistrate who wanted merely to learn facts and have nothing whatever to do with feelings.'[21]

In Taylor's novel, the Sahib police official occasionally responds to Ameer Ali's confession with some form of official righteousness, but Taylor devises for his already imprisoned narrator a self-presentation that quite radically departs from the popular stereotypes of Thuggee as a fanatical Hindu cult for whom worship of a Hindu goddess of destruction has supplanted normal feelings. For a start, Ameer Ali is a Muslim who invokes Allah as often as any Hindu goddesses, but who is lax in his devotions to either religion. Taylor's other departures from stereotype humanize Ameer Ali along lines especially congenial to Taylor himself.[22] Whereas Sleeman had worked to penetrate the system of Thuggee by decoding (and publishing) the lexicography of Thug argot,[23] Taylor's Sahib pays tribute to Ali Ameer's elegant Urdu: 'pure and fluent, perhaps a little affected from his knowledge of Persian'.[24] This colonial police official is a discriminating linguist and observer of native style, as when he admires Ameer Ali's courtly manner, hardly equalled 'even by the Mahomedan [sic] noblemen, with many of whom I have associated'. He does not explain his own credentials, but Taylor himself, in conversation and other writings, was known to enjoy describing his own noble associations in India.[25]

---

[20] Shahid Amin analyses the judicial protocol of the British colonial court in India in 'Approver's Testimony, Judicial Discourse: the Case of Chauri Chaura,' in *Subaltern Studies* 5, Writings on South Asian History and Society, ed. Ranajit Guha (Delhi: Oxford University Press, 1987), 166–202. Margery Sabin responds to this analysis in 'In Search of Subaltern Consciousness,' *Prose Studies* 30(2) (August 2008): 184–87.

[21] Quoted by Van Woerkens, 231.

[22] For analogy of Thug narrator to Philip Meadows Taylor himself, see Poovey, 8–9.

[23] Van Woerkens, 219–33, describes and criticizes Sleeman's publication of *Ramaseeana*, a lexicography and ethnographic study of Thuggee secret language. Van Woerkens, *passim*, prefers what she calls Taylor's 'imaginative discourse' to Sleeman's presumption to grasp the reality of Thuggee, and India generally, through rational investigation. I present a more favourable judgement of Sleeman in 'William Henry Sleeman and the Suttee Romance,' in *Dissenters and Mavericks: Writings about India in English: 1765–2000* (New York: Oxford University Press, 2002), 69–88.

[24] Philip Meadows Taylor, *Confessions of a Thug* [1839] (New York: Oxford University Press, 1986), 266. Subsequent citations appear in the text.

[25] See Van Woerkens, 193–97.

In *Confessions of a Thug*, Taylor supplements the spare deposition style by borrowing freely from both Oriental and English storytelling to create a hybrid 'character' for his murderer. From English fiction he devises a family plot for Ameer Ali that adds a familiar novelistic pathos: it begins when, orphaned by a Thuggee attack on his own parents, he is spared and then adopted by the leader of the band who tenderly cared for him in place of a son he had himself lost. Like Oliver Twist, Ameer was ignorant of his true parentage, but in this case, the orphan's new family and community are loving, even though his surrogate father is leader of the gang. After the adolescent Ameer accidentally learns of their 'profession', loyalty and ideals of manly courage make him eager to pass the initiation tests for grown-up participation. He succeeds and embarks on his illustrious career of Thuggee. The scattered emotional moments in the rest of the narrative all play variations on the theme of familial sentiment. Even the Sahib is moved by Ameer's tears when he recounts the death of one of his children. Taylor draws on a rather different source of human interest from Oriental romance in the long interludes of erotic intrigue, including one that shifts into the family plot, when it results in Ameer's marriage to a beauty he rescues from a cruel older husband.

Other, even more implausible, additions to Taylor's Thuggee narrative make Ameer Ali a connoisseur of the Oriental picturesque. He is not so intent on his homicidal business that he cannot pause to admire sights which evoke bygone Mughal glory, such as the view of Hyderabad from the crest of a slope: 'Before me … lay the city, its white terraced houses gleaming brightly in the sunlight … The Char Minar and Mecca Musjid rose proudly from the masses of buildings by which they were surrounded' (163). Hyderabad was the city where Taylor did most of his own business, and he was a connoisseur of such scenes. It seems equally the colonial traveller, Taylor, rather than a Thug named Ameer Ali, who takes detailed pleasure in the theatrical spectacle of a 'Mohorum'[26] procession from an upstairs window of a house:

> Host after host poured through the narrow street; men of all countries, most of them bearing naked weapons which flashed in the torch-light … others again in fantastic dresses formed themselves into groups, and, as they ran rather than walked along, performed strange and uncouth antics; … here and there would be seen a man painted like a tiger, a rope passed round his waist, which was held by three or four others, while the tiger made desperate leaps and charges into the crowd, which were received with shouts of merriment. [179]

Perhaps the most persuasive version of theatricality in *Confessions of a Thug* pertains to Ameer Ali himself. The profession of Thug required an unending sequence of costumed

---

[26] Also transliterated as Mohurrum, this important Shi'a festival is a holiday of mourning for the deaths of the martyrs Hasan and Hussein, killed in the Battle of Karbala in 680 CE in a struggle over the Prophet's succession. During the colonial period, the procession became identified with outbreaks of violence between Muslims and Hindus in India, as in Kipling's story, 'On the City Wall', discussed later in this chapter.

performances to entice unwitting travellers to the site of their destruction. The skill of these impostures comes across as the most absorbing feature of Thuggee ritual for Ameer (and for Taylor also). Disguise and deceptive performance are everywhere to be encountered in Taylor's India: the source of its vitality as well as danger. A master of the art, Ameer Ali dons and sheds costumes with delighted ease. In this way, Taylor's professional Thug, with his taste and talent for imposture, presages Kipling's secret agent Kim, in an art that diverts rather than invites attention to the true identity and inner life of character. Performance becomes a satisfying and strategic alternative to interiority, aligned with a particularly Indian kind of storytelling art.[27]

Theatrical disguise and storytelling merge explicitly late in *Confessions of a Thug* in a scene where a group of Rokurreas are targeted for their treasure.[28] Ameer characterizes Rokurreas as themselves cunning in 'deceit and stratagem', so that handling them is really a contest of wit. Ameer appeals to the Sahib to appreciate here the real 'excitement which possesses the soul of a Thug':

> Here had we kept company with Rokurreas for twenty days; we had become intimate; they told their adventures, we told ours; the evenings passed in singing or telling tales, until one by one we sunk down wearied upon our carpets. Cannot you appreciate the intense interest with which we watched their every movement, nay every word which fell from them, and our alarms, as sometimes our minds misgave us that we were suspected? [424–25]

In passages like these Taylor transforms the coldly gruesome discourse of Thuggee court depositions into 'intense interest' for the popular novelist. The line is not that long in colonial storytelling between Aga Peter to Ameer Ali and thence to Kipling's Kim.[29]

In between comes the Rebellion of 1857 and its brutal suppression, which both British and Indian historians mark as a watershed year in Anglo-Indian colonial relations. What began as revolt by sepoys in the lower ranks of the Indian army quickly expanded into a violent rebellion through large areas of north and central India. It took the British two years of at least equal violence to regain control. One result was the official transfer of governance from the East India Company to Parliament, within a newly constituted British Empire under the rule of newly titled Queen-Empress Victoria. The political implications of 1857 and its aftermath continue to be explored and debated. Most pertinent

[27] Robert Garis associates the 'genius' of Dickens with a performative energy at odds with the style that literary criticism has come to identify with the 'serious' English novel in the Victorian era. See *The Dickens Theatre* (Oxford: Clarendon Press, 1965), 3–5 and *passim*.

[28] I am grateful to Neelima Shukla-Bhatt for identifying 'Rokurrea' as a Victorian transliteration of 'Rokadia': a name for the trade of treasure courier.

[29] Majeed (93) remarks the anticipation of *Kim* in Ameer Ali's skill and pleasure in verbal and other forms of disguise. He sees the effect in Taylor's novel to be a 'discrediting of indigenous forms of elaboration' and a hierarchy on the basis of language usage that places 'Oriental hyperbole' below 'English plain speaking'. This forcing of the text into conformity with an official colonial policy leads to Majeed's eventual separation of Taylor, as author, from the narrator he has created with so much zest.

to the concerns of this chapter is a fall from the kind of freewheeling engagement in India of adventurous individuals, such as Fanny Parkes and Phillip Meadows Taylor, who became forced to choose sides in a vastly more embattled separation between rulers and ruled. To be sure, such individuals were exceptional even before 1857, but the savagery of those years infused a new intensity of racial contempt and desire for vengeance into English and Anglo-Indian public opinion.[30] In a strongly argued re-examination of post-1857 British culture, Christopher Herbert looks beyond the xenophobic discourse of triumphal vengeance to locate, in a variety of now-neglected but once best-selling texts, challenges to the dominant hysteria.[31] Signs of new self-doubt about the superiority of English civilization show in Herbert's examples of 'sometimes dizzying rhetorical instability'(136), written against the current of policies and popular rhetoric that had become more aggressive and self-justifying.

A crucial text for Herbert is William Henry Russell's widely read dispatches in the *Times* from the towns and villages suspected as treasonous strongholds during the suppression of rebellion in 1858–59. Russell's reportage became a two-volume bestseller, *My Diary in India*,[32] which went through three large editions in its first year of publication (1860). In contrast to the inspiriting adventures of earlier travellers' tales and journals, Russell shapes an anguished encounter with the 'horror' of British racism and vengeful atrocity, prefiguring and, Herbert suggests, possibly influencing, the imagery and shape of Conrad's end-of-century novel, *Heart of Darkness*.[33]

In the decades following the trauma of 1857, British imperial expansion and the popular opinion that supported it famously hardened, with an open drive for global power replacing earlier rationales of reform and progress. The novels of these decades, however, show a darkening of tone, often if not always directly related to colonial subjects. Looked at from Herbert's perspective of lost confidence in the 'civilization' that Britain was forcibly imposing elsewhere, the dark and decaying state of the ancient cathedral town of Cloisterham, in Dickens's *Mystery of Edwin Drood*, for example, stands out for its sinister underground passages that correspond to the secret depths in the heart of its choirmaster, John Jasper. His opium addiction brings one of the major products of colonial commerce deep into the English countryside and Church. A consciousness of British racism, new to Dickens's fiction, appears in the frightening version of a lynch mob that pursues the dark-skinned outsider, Neville, chased down as a suspect in the disappearance of the eponymous Edwin Drood. Although Neville finds some sympathetic friends

---

[30] Patrick Brantlinger gives a full account of the 'polarization of good and evil' in the Mutiny literature in his chapter, 'The Well at Cawnpore: Literary Representations of the Indian Mutiny of 1857', in *Rule of Darkness*, 199–224.

[31] Christopher Herbert, *War of No Pity: The Indian Mutiny and Victorian Trauma* (Princeton: Princeton University Press, 2008).

[32] William Howard Russell, *My Diary in India, 1858–9*, 2 vols. (London: Routledge, 1860). Edward Thompson draws heavily on Russell's reportage for evidence of British atrocity in *The Other Side of the Medal* (1925), ed. Mulk Raj Anand (New Delhi: Sterling, 1989).

[33] Herbert, 65–67, 292 n. 4.

when he escapes to London, the unfinished novel breaks off with his decline into what seems fatal hopelessness.

Wilkie Collins's crime novel of the preceding year, *The Moonstone*, has a more cheerful surface, but its narrative structure—divided among several unreliable narrators—and its historical back story of a theft that dates from the early years of colonial conquest, offers another example of a fiction that hints at crimes that the society has no way to integrate into coherent consciousness. In this novel, the ostracized racial outcast, the medical assistant Ezra Jennings, has the honour of intuitively solving the present crime mystery, but like Dickens's Neville, there is no place in the plot for him but an early death. The decent and respectable English characters thrive at the end, but without any evident internal growth or virtually any internal drama at all.

Collins avoids direct reference to the brutal events of 1857 in *The Moonstone* by backdating his plot to the years 1848–50 and confining the criminal investigation in question to the domestic crime of a jewel theft from a respectable English household. More brutal criminality is relegated to the distant past of colonial history through the Prologue, 'Extracted from a family paper',[34] that traces the Victorian family's possession of a fabulous Indian jewel to British looting at the time of the savage victory over the fierce ruler, Tipu Sultan, in the battle of Seringapatam in 1798. Further in the past, Mughal powers had already stolen this jewel from its sacred place in a Hindu temple, so that the British have only perpetuated rather than inaugurating the violence of history.

Seringapatam consolidated English power over Muslim rule in south India at the end of what might be regarded as the remote and lawless past, but in the novel Seringapatam also seems to stand in for more recent campaigns of British conquest, such as the annexation of the Punjab after the brutal conflicts of the Sikh wars in the late 1840s. Set in the context of ongoing imperial conquests after the events of 1857, the domestic tranquillity of the family's upper-middle-class Victorian family appears as a kind of wilful ignorance, a chosen oblivion, which the unexpected inheritance of the jewel disrupts. The family has disowned the reckless uncle who looted the jewel a half-century earlier; his bequest of the jewel may represent more revenge than forgiveness. Part of the novel's 'joke' is the respectable family's unwillingness to refuse the legacy of colonial spoils, even though they regard it as an intrusion into their 'innocent' domestic privacy. The novel's attractive young hero, Franklin, light-heartedly refers to his bad uncle as 'the wicked Colonel', but when the family servant, Betteredge, foreseeing only trouble from this gift, wants to throw it into the neighbouring quicksands, Franklin jocularly exposes the materialism that overrides any qualms about an inheritance from colonial crimes: "'If you have got the value of the stone in your pocket," answered Mr Franklin, "say so, Betteredge, and in it goes!'" (53).

Collins is an indulgent as well as shrewd observer of a kind of superficial decency and frivolity that allow the Victorian upper class to enjoy its privileges unburdened by

---

[34] Wilkie Collins, *The Moonstone* [1868], ed. J.I.M. Stewart (London: Penguin, 1998). Subsequent citations appear in the text.

distressing awareness of darker underpinnings or complications. This convenient habit of inattention becomes a more incriminating ethical and psychological limitation in the wake of the servant girl Rosanna's suicide note, which indicts Franklin's obliviousness of her unrequited passion as a chief reason for her despair. Collins's plot links neglect of social class suffering to dissociation from colonial wrongs. In both areas of Victorian life, his charming characters have a not so innocent propensity to avert attention from disturbing realities. Franklin eventually recognizes, through the subtle guidance of Ezra Jennings, that an opiate administered by the novel's true villain, the Evangelical hypocrite, Godfrey Ablewhite, had made him the unwitting thief. Franklin's public re-enactment of his opiate sleepwalking, theatrically establishes his innocence and finally clears the way to a happy domestic union with Rachel. Ablewhite is chased down and gets the death he deserves, and the jewel is taken back to its Hindu place by the Brahmin stalkers who have been following the plot with almost comically stereotyped stealth. In terms of the novel's distribution of judgement, Ablewhite's greed and hypocrisy lowers him beneath the 'wicked Colonel' of the 18th century, who at least granted the jewel the power of a curse; Ablewhite takes possession of it with the merely materialistic goal of having it cut up into profitable pieces in Amsterdam.

The decline of colonial exploitation into an exclusively materialistic crime identifies *The Moonstone* with late Victorian colonialism. The only character who thinks in any other way is the eccentric Indophile and explorer, Murthwaite, who seems the true inheritor of the 18th-century Colonel's 'love of the marvellous'. He is welcome in the household in the marginally respectable role of traveller and storyteller. His knowledge of Indian languages and ritual, his boredom in England, and his incongruous admiration for the likely ruthlessness of the Brahmin stalkers make him the fitting witness and narrator of the diamond's final return to its original place, an event that moves outside the range of the family's concern. By the end of the novel, other forms of inheritance guarantee the prosperity of the young couple, who in their renewed self-absorption forget entirely about the jewel or any aspect of colonial relations.

The Moonstone is a superbly entertaining novel, with its multiple satirized narrators and characters. Its lightness of tone keeps it quite far from a denunciation of empire, since its hypocritical Evangelical villain is a type that doesn't require an empire for its machinations. From Herbert's perspective on later Victorian culture, what stands out in Collins's colonial detective novel is the exposé of oblivion as the desired state of respectable Victorian society. Opium, the familiar marker of Oriental contamination, has been domesticated here into laudanum, a seemingly benign sleeping sedative. In this novel, laudanum works as an alibi for innocent unconsciousness. Collins himself, as an author eager to please his contemporary audience, divests himself of responsibility for anything offensive in his book through the same alibi. His Preface comments that he was unaware during much of the novel's composition because he wrote it while he himself was under opium sedation for painful illness![35]

---

[35] 'Preface to the Revised Edition', May 1871, reprinted in *The Moonstone*, 29–30. A longer version of this interpretation of *The Moonstone* appears in my *Dissenters and Mavericks*, 89–110.

The presence or absence of conscious awareness has a great bearing on judgements of responsibility, not only for legal attributions of guilt, but also for the representation of choices.[36] At age twenty-four, Rudyard Kipling chose to return to England after seven years in India—from 1882 to 1889. Twelve years later he published *Kim*, a coming-of-age novel in which the issue of choice is notably opaque. Kipling was driven back to his unloved 'homeland' partly by the toll of debilitating illness and partly by the ambition to leave behind the journalistic work of his adolescence in India and shine in an adult metropolitan literary career. Letters from this period suggest that for Kipling, English adulthood, no matter how spectacularly successful, involved considerable restriction and loss. *Kim* only hints at this disappointment by the connotations in the language of Kim's epiphany near the end, where acceptance of adulthood seems to happen virtually apart from choice: 'with an almost audible click he felt the wheels of his being lock up anew on the world without'(331). Kim was never a promising acolyte for his beloved lama's belief in freedom from the 'wheel of life', but the mechanical 'click' at the end seems to separate him also from the 'river of life' that so thrilled him in his earlier travels through India. From this perspective, the famous celebratory descriptions of those Indian scenes—the best writing in the novel—take on an elegiac character: for the writer looking back, if not for the character Kim, who is still at the edge of loss.

Kim omits any Wordsworthian ruminations about loss and abundant recompense. Like other colonial chroniclers featured in this chapter, Kipling avoids interiority throughout the novel, and even calls attention to its absence. In the scene at the army camp, where the boy's identity papers in an amulet-bag around his neck first identify him as Kimball O'Hara, son of a former 'colour-sergeant' with this very Irish regiment, the question of Kim's internal state is raised by the kindly priest Father Victor, who faces a choice about the orphan's schooling: 'The priest leaned forward. "I'd give a month's pay to find out what's goin' on inside that little round head of yours." "There is nothing," said Kim, and scratched it' (153). Kim's head is not as empty as it seems; the narrative goes on with his internal 'wondering' about what his horse-trader friend, Mahbub Ali, knows or not, what he will do, and how much Kim should tell him of what is happening. But these instrumental and strategic speculations ironically prove pointless within a page when Mahbub seems fortuitously to turn up, followed on the next page by Colonel Creighton, the British 'handler' of this group. It becomes obvious that they are already keeping an eye on Kim, so that his questions and speculations are, in a sense, insignificant; from this point on whatever is in his mind is subordinated to the government's surveillance and control of his every movement.

The question of 'what's goin' on inside' has often been addressed to Kipling's Indian writings more generally, though not in the first flash of his celebrity. Kipling's sensational arrival on the London literary scene in 1889, with seven volumes of stories already

---

[36] Lisa Rodensky, in *The Crime in Mind: Criminal Responsibility and the Victorian Novel* (New York: Oxford University Press, 2003) explores the representation of consciousness as a crux in the relationship of criminal liability in Victorian law and fiction.

published in India,[37] fixed public attention on the novelty of his intriguing plots and characters and the brilliant evocation of unfamiliar colonial situations. The English reader could enjoy *frissons* of wonder, laughter, sorrow, or even horror without stopping to scrutinize possible ambiguities or uncertainties. The blaze of Kipling's celebrity blocked out inquiry into what, if anything, he actually had in mind. It was only later, after Kipling came forward as one of the most strident of imperial apologists in the inter-war period of the 1920s and 1930s, that the hidden implications of Kipling's earlier writing became suspect.[38] It was then only too easy for postcolonial critics in the 1970s and 1980s to fit Kipling's Indian fiction neatly into the categories of Orientalism and imperial discourse. In the past two decades, the opening up of these categories themselves have generated fresh critical speculation about this elusive writer, author of the most substantial literary fiction about colonialism in the Victorian period.

In *Kim*, uncertainty about what is in this boy's head matters to Father Herbert because still unbeknownst to the boy, the seemingly impecunious old lama has offered to pay for the schooling of his little *chela*; the lama trustingly sees no problem in the prospect of his Anglo-Indian schooling. Nor does Kim want to think that the roles of *chela* and *sahib* are incompatible. At first, his ability to juggle multiple identities supports this optimism. At St Xavier's school, he learns to read and write (at the lama's expense), and undergoes even more arduous out-of-school training arranged by native experts under the supervision of Colonel Creighton, who has already selected Kim as a promising secret agent precisely because of his agility as a racial chameleon. Initially, Kim is even allowed holidays with the lama 'vagabonding over India' (215) in the Colonel's derogatory phrase (oddly echoing Fanny Parkes's travel enthusiasm). Even when Kim has been fully enrolled as a servant of empire, the lama continues to believe that the mission of his remaining life is to teach his beloved *chela* the art of transcending worldly desire. The novel ends without Kim disabusing him of this notion, and without Kipling revealing his own view of this possibility.

The reader, however, is in a position to notice the contradiction between the lama's pursuit of Buddhist detachment and Colonel Creighton's engagement of Kim in the Great Game of empire. All along there has been the related and unresolved incongruity between Kim's relish for the abundant human vitality alongside 'the smiling river

[37] Kipling's seven volumes, published in the Indian Railway Series in India were: *Plain Tales from the Hills; Soldiers Three; The Story of the Gadsby's; In Black and White; Wee Willie Winkie; The Phantom Rickshaw; Under the Deodars.* Angus Wilson, in *The Strange Ride of Rudyard Kipling: His Life and Works* (New York: Viking, 1977) gives a good account of Kipling's Indian years, including the popular notice accorded the early stories published in the *Civil and Military Gazette* between November 1886 and June 1887, thirty-nine of which were reprinted in *Plain Tales from the Hills* (Wilson, 113). The Indian Railway Series was reissued in England in 1890.

[38] See e.g. a strong critique of Kipling's politics by George Orwell, 'Rudyard Kipling' [1942], in *Collected Essays, Journalism, and Letters of George Orwell*, ed. Sonia Orwell and Ian Angus, 4 vols. (New York: Harcourt Brace, 1968), 2: 184–97. For Randall Jarrell's notable effort to revive interest in Kipling's art, see 'On Preparing to Read Kipling', in *Kipling, Auden and Co: Essays and Reviews, 1935–1964* (New York: Farrar Straus and Giroux, 1961) reprinted in *Rudyard Kipling: Modern Critical Reviews*, ed. Harold Bloom (New York: Chelsea House, 1987), 9–22.

of life' and the lama's search for the 'River of the Arrow', which will grant him freedom from the 'Wheel of Things' (59). Kipling presents Kim's mind as increasingly disabled from conscious reflection about these choices and dilemmas in the second half of the novel, even as in other ways his training has all been directed to sharpening his mental powers. In the final crisis of the book, when his 'handlers', Mahbub Ali and Hurree Babu, rather cynically indulge what they regard as the lama's harmless fantasies, Kim has been rendered literally unconscious by the woman of Kulu through mysterious medicinal brews and hypnotic massage, so that he 'slid ten thousand miles into slumber—thirty-six hours of it—sleep that soaked like rain after drought'(324). Kim needs this cure because his uneasiness about deceiving the lama by hiding his government mission during their long trek in the northern mountains has reduced him to a kind of hysterical aphasia:

> 'I have—I have ... *Hai mai!* But I love thee ... and it is all too late ... I was a child ... Oh, why was I not a man?' Overborne by strain, fatigue, and the weight beyond his years, Kim broke down and sobbed at the lama's feet. [320]

Kim's broken speech here corresponds to a deeper confusion, in that it is precisely his coming manhood and the loss of childhood that has impelled him to deceive the lama on their Himalayan expedition. Kim's repeated question in the novel, 'Who is Kim?', becomes ironic by the end of the novel when the identity indicated by his name will be replaced by a coded number 'in one of the locked books of the Indian Survey Department' (69): Mahbub Ali is C25:1B; Hurree is R17, and the unnamed Mahratta, recognizable on a train through the exchange of secret passwords, is E23. Rather than opening the way to more communicative language for speech or thought, manhood in the Great Game substitutes for personal identity a coded number that is no more communicative than aphasia.

Kim's 'holidays' in the last two-thirds of the novel are thus marked as double events: they appear to prolong the childhood play of Kim's free movement through India and enjoyment of its many coloured spectacle of peoples and places, yet within the construction of the plot this freedom becomes illusory. The shrewd horse-trader, Mahbub Ali answers the question of how far Kim should be indulged in his holidays by comparing him to a high spirited 'colt' being trained for higher performance:

> 'There is no holding the young pony from the game,' said the horse-dealer ... 'If permission be refused to go and come as he chooses, he will make light of the refusal. ... only once in a thousand years is a horse so well fitted for the game as this our colt. And we need men.' [215]

To use the same word 'game' for both the Great Game of competition between Russia and England for power in the Northwest border territory and for Kim's holiday play drains moral seriousness from imperial politics, while also minimizing the difference between Kim's earlier joy (articulated with Dickensian echo as a 'stupendous lark') (131) and the circumscribed interludes of refreshment permitted in a training regimen.[39]

It is unclear how much Kipling means to distinguish Kim's later from his earlier pleasures. In the initial chapters, the narrator renders Kim's joy as his rapturous freedom on the Grand Trunk road: 'this was life as he would have it—bustling and shouting, the buckling of belts, and beating of bullocks, and creaking of wheels, lighting of fires and cooking of food, and new sights at every turn of the approving eye' (121). Much later in the book the narrator gives equally lyric tribute to Kim's 'pure delight' when travelling with Mahbub on their Great Game mission in the mountains: 'climbing, dipping, and sweeping about the growing spurs; the flush of the morning laid along the distant snows' (193–94). That in the first travel Kim was still a 'free' agent, while later he is on assignment and under surveillance makes little difference in the narrator's lyrical affirmation. The external spectacle of India is equally pleasing to 'the approving eye' in both descriptive passages.

Kim is furthermore eager rather than reluctant to excel in his Great Game assignment and proud of his prowess at progressing into manhood: he is conscious of his age (sixteen) and of his sprouting moustache. He never resists his transition to adulthood—a resistance that is made to seem pointless, in any case, since the wheel of human and natural life to which the novel as a whole is so firmly attached, cannot be stopped. During his recuperative sleep near the end of the narrative, Mother Earth takes over from the woman of Kulu to infuse the boy-man with 'the seed of life': 'His head lay powerless upon her breast, and his opened hands surrendered to her strength' (332).

Kipling independently chose his own passage from adolescence to adulthood when he left India for England in 1889. Thereafter, India became permanently associated for him with childhood and adolescence. Sara Suleri offers the phrase 'atrophic adolescence' to name what she sees as a condition of arrested development in the British imperial imagination more generally; she calls attention to the immaturity associated with the English colonial enterprise in writings from Burke to Kipling.[40]

Kipling himself was an immature seventeen in 1882, when he went from school in England to take up the job his father had arranged for him as 'sub-editor' on *The Civil and Military Gazette*, an Anglo-Indian newspaper in Lahore. Contrary to Raskin's comment, that for the Victorians, 'Going to India was like falling off a cliff', Kipling in 1882 was returning to the family of his earliest years after a childhood of misery boarded in a grim English family in what he called 'The House of Desolation'.[41] Catapulted into

---

[39] In calling attention to 'lark' as an English word, Kipling's narrator seems deliberately to invoke the famous Dickens phrase, 'What larks!' (or as young Pip writes 'wot larx'), repeated several times in *Great Expectations* to characterize the innocent and loving fun between Pip and Joe Gargery, which Pip loses when he leaves the forge to become a gentleman in London.

[40] Suleri, 111.

[41] Kipling uses the phrase 'House of Desolation' in *Something of Myself* to name the houseold in Swansea where he was boarded from October 1871 to April 1877. See *Kipling: Something of Myself and Other Autobiographical Writings*, ed. Thomas Pinney (Cambridge, UK: Cambridge University Press, 1990), 7; The same unhappy childhood house provides the setting of the autobiographical story, 'Baa

responsibilities that made him not so much an apprentice as '50% of the editorial staff' (in his own phrase), he used his fluency in Hindustani and indefatigable enthusiasm to venture—on and off duty—into situations inaccessible to most other Anglo-Indians.

Out of the special circumstances of this immersion, Kipling precociously invented a literary persona and a prose style brilliantly adaptable to a more complicated relationship to Anglo-India than the elegiac novel of 1901 included. The self-contained brevity of the short story, like a newspaper article, letter, or journal entry, legitimates a fragmentary form of narrative, without requiring a novel's sustained development of character and plot. Kipling embraced this freedom to perfect a style of terse, worldly-wise insinuation that he knows more than he ever cares to tell. Abrupt turns of events and sudden, often ironic or ambiguous endings control and mask rather than explore feelings.

Kipling's letters from the 1880s are more expansive and display more openly his moods and his precocious talent for mimicry, self-mockery, and enthusiastic but gruelling labour. In one letter, he reproduces at length an afternoon with a wily old Afghan who tries to bribe him with money, then horses, then a beautiful girl to use his influence to help him get released from confinement in Lahore as an enemy combatant. The letter turns comic as Kipling stages the encounter, devising high-flown English equivalents for both the Afghan's Hindustani mixture of flattery, plea, and insult and his own performance of British righteousness. Deflating off-stage asides set off the artifice on both sides, ending with the question to his aunt in England: 'Wasn't it a rummy adventure for a Sunday morning?'[42]

The entertainment in many of Kipling's Indian letters rests on his implicit confidence in the absence of any serious threat to British power at this point in the 1880s. 'The illusion of permanence' liberated Kipling to immerse himself in 'rummy' adventures with all kinds of Indian characters rarely featured in earlier Victorian writing. In the letters he converts his pleasure into a duty to understand these 'queer people' as

> men with a language of their own which it is your business to understand, and proverbs, which it is your business to quote (this is a land of proverbs) and bywords and allusions which it is your business to master; and feelings which it is your business to enter into and sympathize with. Then they'll believe in you and do things for you and let you do things for them.[43]

An impure mixture of opportunism and genuine enthusiasm plays down the brute fact that a foreign occupation sustained by political and military power was providing him with rare privileges as well as pleasures. Despite his bouts of illness and exhaustion,

---

Baa Black Sheep', first published in the *Week's News*, 21 December 1888) and later collected in the volume *Wee Willie Winkie* in *The Writings in Prose and Verse of Rudyard Kipling*, 36 vols. *(New York: Scribners, 1897–1937)* 6: 323–68.

[42] Letter to Edith Macdonald, 4 February 1884, in *The Letters of Rudyard Kipling*, ed. Thomas Pinney, 6 vols. (Iowa City: Iowa University Press, 1990), 1: 57.

[43] Letter to Margaret Burne-Jones, 28 November 1885–11 January 1886, in *Letters*, 1: 101.

faith in what he calls 'the holy inkpot' sustained him to draw seemingly endless creative inspiration from the mobility he managed to achieve.

Underlying anxiety about this boundary-crossing comes out only through the ironies and ambiguities in the Indian stories. Children—both Indian and English—often die and Anglo-Indian adults who get excessively entangled in native life tend to be horribly punished: by insanity, mutilation, bad dreams, or death. Those who stay sheltered within colonial enclaves, whether in hill station retreats, desolate army or civil outposts, or the clubs of a city like Lahore, succumb to boredom, dissipation, and disease. Most of the stories invite only limited sympathy for the characters, while the narrator, often reduced to a mere conduit for a story told to him, imperturbably withholds judgement. The reader, like Father Victor in *Kim* is left to speculate what is actually in the author's mind.

In the very brief 'Story of Muhammad Din', for example, a first-person narrator less appealing than the Kipling of the letters recalls the pathos of a child's death in a way that makes him seem only superficially benign and sympathetic. The child, Mohammed Din, is rather special in that, although he is the son of a servant, he displays an as-yet unbroken independent spirit. At the opening, he has transgressed by entering the narrator's dining room, inspecting the pictures and other objects there, and inducing his father to request that he be given an old chipped polo ball. After silently assenting to the father's scolding for this brashness, the narrator bestows the old polo ball as a gift in a rather lordly gesture. The rest of the plot is spare. The narrator and child meet and exchange formal, conventional greetings on the neutral ground of the garden, where the child lisps 'Talaam *Tahib*' and the narrator responds '*Salaam*, Muhammad Din'.[44] But in his own garden strolls the narrator stumbles upon a little architectural construction (no doubt imitated from the colonial prints in the house). The boy has designed a construction, with the polo-ball half-buried in dust, at the centre of a courtyard and with a protective wall constructed out of bits of broken brick and china. 'Heaven knows that I had no intention of touching the child's work then or later' (310) the narrator insists, but he does in fact heedlessly step on it in one of his garden strolls. Despite that crisis, and another scolding from his father, the child begins again to construct an even more elaborate edifice. Now the narrator is more engaged, and still without directly communicating with the child, begins to look forward to watching this growing creation as one of the main pleasures of his garden walk.

The end, characteristically for Kipling, is abrupt. One day, the boy simply isn't there. He turns out to have succumbed to fever and despite quinine 'and an English doctor', dies within a few days. The doctor says: 'They have no stamina, these brats'(311). The final sentence turns back to the narrator: 'A week later, though I would have given much to have avoided it, I met on the road to the Mussulman burying-ground Imam Din, accompanied by one other friend, carrying in his arms, wrapped in a white cloth, all that

---

[44] 'Story of Muhammad Din', *Plain Tales from the Hills*, in *Writings in Prose and Verse*, 1: 309–12, 309. Subsequent citations appear in the text.

was left of little Muhammad Din' (312). That's all. The story is hardly more than a sketch, and the final sentence emphasizes the narrator's retreat as much as the pathos of the child's death. This *sahib* has almost involuntarily become very interested in an Indian child, but has never dropped his colonial decorum. First he is haughty, then heedless, and finally, despite a sense of loss, avoids any show of feeling but retreats to the confines of his private domain. The symbolism of the child's work can be taken as a little rehearsal for some future Indian generation's construction of itself, albeit on models of India imitated from English prints. The plot dooms the potential architect to early death.

The final impulse to 'avoid' any direct involvement with Mohammad Din—dead or alive—raises the larger questions of how much of the real trouble (or promise) of Indian life the young Kipling himself was willing to engage with and how much the reader is free to blame the narrator's impulse to avoid. What sympathy is elicited seems split between the doomed Indian child and the self-protective adult *sahib*.

'On the City Wall', a story from late in Kipling's time in India (December 1888) comes closer to acknowledging the political ambiguity of the narrator's position. Although the view from this wall shows a picturesque vista of river, fort, and city, the wall itself is remarkable for the heterogeneous group of Indians who meet there to converse and enjoy the hospitality of beautiful Lalun, identified as a kind of courtesan who can stand for India itself.[45] It is in this light that her admirers—an Anglified Mohammedan, plus unnamed Shiahs, Sufis, wandering Hindu priests, Pundits, Sikhs, and others—also seem to represent India's multiplicity. What the English narrator is doing in Lalun's salon remains unexplained. Enough of an insider to know that the songs in praise of her are coded versions of subversive political messages, his own politics remain incoherent: he both admires Lalun and the songs in her praise, yet cynically dismisses the notion of Indian nationalists and English liberals alike that India might ever govern itself: 'It will never stand alone, but the idea is a pretty one' (305).

The main dreamer in the story is the young Mohammedan, Wali Dad, seemingly incapacitated by too much English-style education for any activity other than lolling about Lalun's salon and borrowing books from the narrator. When a celebration of the Mohurrum holiday within the city deteriorates into a Hindu–Muslim riot, Wali Dad's compulsion to join the frenzy exposes the thin veneer of his sophistication. 'Wali Dad left my side with an oath, and shouting: "*Ya Hasan! Ya Hussain!*" plunged into the thick of the fight, where I lost sight of him' (330). In contrast to the picturesque Mohurram procession described in *Confessions of a Thug*, Kipling presents a communal riot that makes everyone look bad. The British troops called out to suppress the violence openly welcome the opportunity to have 'a little fun' with their weapons. Their undisguised appetite for violence seems as much a reversion to primitive racial identity as Wali Dad's frenzy: 'The Garrison Artillery, who to the last cherished a wild hope that they might be

---

[45] 'On the City Wall', *In Black and White* in *Writings in Prose and Verse*, 4: 302–39. Subsequent citations appear in the text.

allowed to bombard the City at a hundred yards' range, lined the parapet above the East gateway and cheered themselves hoarse' (331).

Kipling separates the narrator from this atavism, but he has his own quieter drama. Earlier, the story had identified a fort visible from the city wall where an old imprisoned Sikh warrior of many lost battles against the British could sometimes be seen on the ramparts. Once famous as a 'tiger' in the Sikh wars, he is now treated indulgently by his captors as a throwback to hostilities that have now yielded to an era of more settled British power.[46] The narrator prefers the idea of Khem Singh to the idle and affected Wali Dad, but their actual meeting implicates him in unexpected complicity. After withdrawing back to the city wall from the hysteria of the riot, the narrator recalls being hustled in the imperfect light by Lalun to help her lift over the wall a heavy figure, cursing 'in an unknown tongue'. With a combination of flattery and urgent alarm, Lalun convinces the narrator to escort the unknown figure out through the gates of the city. And he does. Only in a kind of epilogue does he ruefully admit that without his awareness he has been co-opted into aiding Khem Singh's escape from prison.

Kipling characteristically adds a few extra tricks to the end of the story. The narrator's discovery of his complicity with an enemy of empire loses significance because Khem Singh himself willingly returns to prison once he himself seems to recognize that the days of Indian heroism are gone: 'It is not good out yonder' (338), he later tells the narrator. Still, in a last ambiguous turn, Singh draws a map on the sand where his new friend, the now identified *sahib*, might help the escape of another prisoner. The narrator stops without judgement of further possibilities of rebellion, only glancing ruefully at where infatuation with Lalun had led. A light-hearted tone gives the impression that he could resume his equivocal position on the wall without falling into a single racial role, as did Wali Dad, the British soldiers, and even Khem Singh.

The repudiation of conscious struggles of feeling or judgement on the surface of Kipling's fiction contributed to his popularity as a writer of manly actions and adventures. Meditative vigils and struggles of allegiance were the properties of feminine, domestic, and elite literature in the Victorian period. Yet Kipling's techniques of displacement, irony, symbolism, and ambiguity point his fiction past Victorian realism to effects associated more often with modernism.

In the first half of the 19th century, so-called domestic novelists developed a hierarchy of values that placed dramas of consciousness above the external adventures of colonial travellers, administrators, and white Mughals such as Gaskell's Aga Peter, Fanny Parkes, her friend, James Gardner, and Meadows Taylor. Their adventures in India alienated them from England, even though their opportunities depended on colonial privileges as much as on their own bold spirits. The hostilities of the Mutiny punctured the *naïveté* in that often attractive version of early Victorian colonial narrative. As Herbert

---

[46] Khem Singh alludes to the Rebellion of 1857, but also to the 'Kuka rising', a defeated Sikh rebellion in 1871–72 against the annexation of the Punjab that the British had accomplished after fierce fighting in 1849.

persuasively demonstrates, later non-fiction reporters and historians such as Russell and Kaye fall into contradictions, or rely on irony and fractured narratives to handle the challenge to coherent reflection about the nation's increasing and hardened expansionist drive. In this chapter, I select Wilkie Collins and Rudyard Kipling as examples of writers who thematize as well as enact the breakdown of consciousness in late Victorian fiction. In *The Moonstone*, the amiable hero, Franklin, steals the sacred Indian jewel under the influence of opium, so he is officially not responsible for colonial plunder handed down from an earlier era. Kipling's narratives evade consciousness. Drugged sleep saves Kim from having to face the cost of entering manhood as an agent of empire. In 'On the City Wall', confused distraction leads Kipling's narrator into unwitting collusion with an enemy of empire. The author about to take on his adult English identity back in England disowns the subversive impulse. Only while still an adolescent in India, could he sit on the wall, as it were, through his double-voiced skills. Even two decades and a World War later, English writers such as E.M. Forster and Edward Thompson, still struggled with the challenge of colonialism to the consciousness that was so cherished a feature of English Victorian identity.

Suggested Reading

Bhabha, Homi K. *The Location of Culture*. London and New York: Routledge, 1994.

Brantlinger, Patrick. *Rule of Darkness: British Literature and Imperialism, 1830–1914*. Ithaca and London: Cornell University Press, 1988.

Dalrymple, William. *The Last Mughal: The Fall of a Dynasty, Delhi 1857*. New York: Vintage, 2008.

Herbert, Christopher. *War of No Pity: The Indian Mutiny and Victorian Trauma*. Princeton and Oxford: Princeton University Press, 2008.

Hutchins, Francis G. *The Illusion of Permanence: British Imperialism in India*. Princeton: Princeton University Press, 1967.

Moore, Gilbert, Bart, ed. *Writing India 1757–1990: The Literature of British India*. Manchester UK: Manchester University Press, 1996.

Parry, Benita. *Delusions and Discoveries: Studies on India in the British Imagination, 1880–1930*. Berkeley: University of California Press, *circa* 1972.

Said, Edward. *Culture and Imperialism*. New York: Alfred E. Knopf, 1993.

Suleri, Sara. *The Rhetoric of English India*. Chicago and London: University of Chicago Press, 1992.

Sullivan, Zohreh T. *Narratives of Empire: The Fictions of Rudyard Kipling*. New York: Cambridge University Press, 1993.

PART IV

TECHNOLOGIES: COMMUNICATION, TRAVEL, VISUALITY

13

THE VICTORIAN NOVEL AND COMMUNICATION NETWORKS

RICHARD MENKE

The 19th century saw the development of an astonishing range of media innovations, many of which have only recently been superseded by digital technologies. The pace and the specifically Victorian span of these advances are particularly striking when it comes to the century's revolution in communication networks, from Rowland Hill's new Penny Post, to the electric telegraphs of William Cooke and Charles Wheatstone, to telephony and the early years of wireless transmission. Postal reform and electric telegraphy were developed in the late 1830s and implemented during the next decade; the Scotsman Alexander Graham Bell demonstrated his telephone to Queen Victoria in 1878; the half-Irish Guglielmo Marconi came to England to develop and finance his research on wireless telegraphy in the 1890s. The universalizing Penny Post, the lightning-fast electric telegraph, the haunting voice on the telephone, and the mystical and all-pervading 'wireless'—over the course of the era, these innovations increased the speed, universality, and ineffableness of telecommunication and helped generate the rich media environment of the 20th century.

It is hardly surprising to find that Victorian novels set in the 19th century should take the age's communication networks for granted. But the presence of these networks becomes particularly meaningful in light of the ideological value that novels about Victorian social divisions often place on intercommunication as well as the more general popularity of plots that hinge upon communications and miscommunications. The ending of Elizabeth Gaskell's *Cranford* (1851–53) imagines a letter that fetches a long-lost brother back from India and takes the village of Cranford out of the exclusive 'possession of the Amazons', the ladies who constitute its genteel society; the resolution of Anthony Trollope's *John Caldigate* (1878–79) rests in part on the detection of a forged Australian postmark.[1] (Trollope's decision here to draw upon his own long career as a postal official is unusual, but the weight this novel places on a letter and its history is not.)[2] By the final third of the century, the intercontinental telegraph cables that began to operate in 1866 would even become a sort of technological substrate for Henry James's transatlantic novels. In fact, as this chapter will suggest, the 1860s present something of a dividing line for the relationships between novels and Victorian communication networks. Although in many ways works from the first half of the Victorian period share a common logic with Victorian communication networks, novels from the 1870s and afterwards tend to invoke and explore such networks more directly.

The Victorian age's revolution in networked communication aptly demonstrates not simply how technological innovations can reshape culture but also how thoroughly technologies are a part of the cultures that generate and use them. For these crucial Victorian communication networks reflect and enact the developing values that we also find elsewhere in Victorian culture, especially in novels. For one thing, the era's communication systems offered both analogues and material evidence for the connections of interest and interchange that linked the members of a society, and for the networks of relation postulated by contemporary novels, with their frequent inclination to organize multiple plot strands and large casts of characters. Indeed, by the mid-19th century, communication networks offered an especially compelling parallel for a complex structure of social relationships, thanks to continuing redefinitions of the meanings not only of *network* but also of *communication* itself.

The English word *network* has always denoted both woven objects and structures that resembled them, such as blood vessels. But in the 19th century, the term took on new metaphorical and practical significance. The *Oxford English Dictionary* documents a new tendency to use the term to describe not simply nets and net-like objects but also connections among non-material things, a practice the *OED* illustrates first of all with quotations from two of the century's most productive literary metaphorists, Coleridge (1817) and Emerson (1856). At the same time, large-scale, interconnected physical structures from river systems to transportation lines also came to be described as 'networks'.[3] These senses of the transcendent and the physically extensive merged in the new network of the electric telegraph, a device that used an ever-growing system of wires to channel the mysterious force of electricity. This network, and questions about its resemblance to or difference from the organic networks of the body, galvanized Victorian sci-

---

[1] Elizabeth Gaskell, *Cranford* [1853], ed. Elizabeth Porges Watson (Oxford: World's Classics, Oxford University Press, 1980), 1.

[2] R.H. Super's *Trollope at the Post Office* (Ann Arbor: University of Michigan Press, 1981) provides a thorough account of Trollope's postal career. On *John Caldigate*, postal communication, and colonialism, see Eileen Cleere, *Avuncularism: Capitalism, Patriarchy, and Nineteenth-Century British Culture* (Stanford, CA: Stanford University Press, 2004), 199–201.

[3] On the era's transportation revolutions, see Alison Byerly's chapter in this volume.

ence and engineering.[4] More expansively, the network ideal in the 19th century could represent the growth of globalization, standardization, and interdependence.[5]

What did it take to turn a means of connection into a Victorian communication network? Rowland Hill's plan to reform the British postal system offers a notable example of the emerging logic of 19th-century networks because it transformed an institution that was much older than the 19th century, and because postal reform required no great technological leap. By the early 19th century, the British Post Office was already a large and striking organization, but it took the work of the postal reformer Hill and others to turn it into a coherent communication network.[6] This change entailed a dramatic rethinking of the entire postal system, from its everyday mechanics to its basic rationale. Before Hill's reforms, postal rates were essentially considered a form of taxation. High postal charges led large cities to create cheaper local letter delivery services modelled on London's old Penny Post (which had by then become the Twopenny Post, thanks to rate increases), but these urban services were separate from both the Inland Post Office in charge of the national letters and the Foreign Post Office, which handled international ones. In London, each office had its own staff and bureaucracy, so that three parallel postal systems fanned out over the city.

Moreover, the complexities of this institutional structure were surpassed by the elaborate schedule of postal charges based on distance and other factors; even London's Twopenny Post cost threepence for outer districts. Once a letter was delivered, its postage was collected from its recipient, a practice that made distribution grindingly slow. In essence, from start to finish, the Post Office handled each letter individually, as a discrete object: ascertaining the rate between its origin and destination, calculating its particular charge, and trying to collect its fee, so that even payment for postage became a unique, contingent event. Rowland Hill's great insight was to realize that, despite all of this complexity, the actual cost to transport a letter was minimal.[7] Instead of assessing postage based on distance, the Post Office should charge a small, uniform tariff, a standard fee

[4] Laura Otis has richly demonstrated the importance of the network, as metaphor and reality, for scientists and novelists alike, *Networking: Communicating with Bodies and Machines in the Nineteenth Century*, (Ann Arbor: University of Michigan Press, 2001).

[5] Armand Mattelart, *Networking the World, 1794–2000*, trans. Liz Carey-Libbrecht and James A. Cohen (Minneapolis: University of Minnesota Press, 2000). Mattelart even describes a Utopian 'cult of the network' in the era, *The Invention of Communication*, trans. Susan Emmanuel (Minneapolis: University of Minnesota Press, 1996), 85.

[6] For useful histories of the British Post Office in the 19th century, see Howard Robinson, *The British Post Office: A History* (Princeton: Princeton University Press, 1948; Westport, CT: Greenwood, 1970) as well as Charles R. Perry, *The Victorian Post Office: The Growth of a Bureaucracy* (Woodbridge: Royal Historical Society Office, 1992). In the following paragraphs, I have drawn on their accounts, as well as on the work of Gavin Fryer and Clive Akerman, eds., *The Reform of the Post Office in the Victorian Era and Its Impact on Social and Economic Activity*, 2 vols. (London: Royal Philatelic Society, 2000), and on my discussion of the postal network in *Telegraphic Realism: Victorian Fiction and Other Communication Systems* (Stanford, CA: Stanford University Press, 2008), 31–43.

[7] Rowland Hill, *Post Office Reform: Its Importance and Practicability* [1837], in Fryer and Akerman, *Reform of the Post Office*, 1: 11.

for the letter to enter the system, and should concentrate on reducing the costs and complexity of the system itself. Hill predicted the Post Office would thrive by charging a low rate, a penny, to encourage universal use of the postal network.

Standardization, universality, and freedom from distance: Hill justified these new principles on the basis of efficiency and cost reduction, yet they precisely echo the emerging norms of communication networks. Here is further testimony to the interplay between culture and innovation. At its core, postal reform meant that rather than treating letters as unique objects with individual histories and trajectories, the Post Office should treat them as uniform articles to be processed in a comprehensive system. A host of changes follow from this principle. To begin with, the fare to enter the system should be provided by a letter's sender, ensuring that all letters are paid for before they begin their journeys. Since the charges are uniform, they can be prepaid in an impersonal way, by a special envelope or a small piece of sticky paper; as an afterthought, Hill suggests the invention of the postage stamp. Houses would need more uniform street addresses, for efficient sorting and delivery, as well as mailboxes or mail-slots on doors. Trollope's famous suggestion of public pillar-boxes to receive letters would later help complete the system.

In the standard rhetoric of the electric telegraph's enthusiasts, the telegraphic network would soon be credited with abolishing distance. But by 1840 the British postal network had already done the same thing; Hill's reforms brought all of the country into the same, single postal zone. For the postal system, the consequences of the new penny postage were spectacular. From 1840 to 1901, while the population of the United Kingdom rose from 26.5 million to 41.5 million, the annual number of letters handled by the Post Office rose from 169 million to 2,323 million, now in addition to more than 400 million postcards and 500 million telegrams.[8] Networked communication became less an event than a constant, ubiquitous flow. In concrete terms, the success of early Victorian postal reform would even lead—via Parliament's 1868 decision to nationalize the electric telegraph industry for the sake of establishing low, simple charges—to the government's future responsibilities for telephony and broadcast networks. More obliquely, postal reform emphasized the workaday ability of a communication network to subsume the structure of an entire society, an ability that resonates with the ambition and the social interests of realist novels. Writing in his *Autobiography* about his work as a postal surveyor, Trollope revives the literal implication of the network as a net, noting that his great 'object was to create a postal network which should *catch* all recipients of letters'—potentially, that is, to include everyone.[9]

For the Victorians, the network becomes a general figure for organizing the real interchanges, the unseen or imperfectly visible systems of connections and disconnections,

[8] B.R. Mitchell, *British Historical Statistics* (Cambridge: Cambridge University Press, 1988), 12–13, 563–64, 566.

[9] Anthony Trollope, *An Autobiography* [1883], ed. Michael Sadleir and Frederick Page (Oxford: World's Classics, Oxford University Press, 1989), 88.

that underlie the everyday social world. Walter Bagehot draws on this figure in his 1856 reflections on the 'difficulty' of governing or comprehending a complex, liberal society:

> Any body can understand a rough despotic community;—a small buying class of nobles, a small selling class of traders, a large producing class of serfs, are much the same in all quarters of the globe; but a free intellectual community is a *complicated network* of ramified relations, interlacing and passing hither and thither, old and new, some of fine city weaving, others of gross agricultural production. You are never sure what effect any force or any change may produce on a frame work so exquisite and so involved.[10] [emphasis added]

For Bagehot, the 'network' or 'frame work' expresses the problem of modern social complexity, yet also—by naming this complexity and offering an image for its structure—provides one solution. Furthermore, not only his contrast between varied contemporary communities and uniform pre-industrial ones but also his distinction between 'fine' and 'gross' threads of relation aptly suggests that—even with its universalizing promise—a mid-Victorian 'network' did not necessarily specify a homogeneous, identity-crushing grid of relations.

The word *communication* begins with the idea of sharing something or making it common, and this core meaning suited the idea of a connecting network.[11] Yet over the course of the Victorian era, the sense of *communication* shifted in light of the new networks that so dramatically increased its speed and reach. At the same time as Hill was reforming the Post Office, the brand-new electric telegraph system was beginning to take shape, at first along the backbone of the recently established railway network. In contrast to the sudden impact of penny postage, it would take years for electric telegraphy to become a tool for everyday communication, although it was soon adopted by the railways and then by journalism and business. As it came into public awareness and use, it would redefine what it meant to communicate.

In one influential formulation, the electric telegraph represents a turning point in the history of communication because it decisively divided transmission from physical transportation, and 'freed communication from the constraints of geography' even more effectively than making the entire country into a single postal zone.[12] By setting aside geography, the telegraph allowed *communication* to begin assuming its full

---

[10] Walter Bagehot, 'The Character of Sir Robert Peel' [1856], in *The Collected Works of Walter Bagehot*, ed. Norman St John-Stevas, 15 vols. (London: Economist, 1965–86), 3: 254–55.

[11] Raymond Williams, 'Communication', in *Keywords: A Vocabulary of Culture and Society*, rev. edn (New York: Oxford University Press, 1983), 72–73.

[12] James W. Carey, 'Technology and Ideology: The Case of the Telegraph', in *Communication as Culture: Essays on Media and Society* (Boston: Unwin Hyman, 1989), 204. Carey takes the separation of transport from communication as a hallmark of electric telegraphy, but for a fascinating account of their continued relationship, and a thoughtful critique of Carey's work, see John Durham Peters, 'Technology and Ideology: The Case of the Telegraph Revisited', in *Thinking with James Carey: Essays on Communications, Transport, History*, ed. Jeremy Packer and Craig Robertson (New York: Peter Lang, 2006), 137–55.

contemporary meaning, with little sense that communicating should require contact or proximity (the implication that survives when we speak of rooms that communicate). Looking back on the era, the naturalist Alfred Russel Wallace identified the independence of 'communication' from 'locomotion' as one of the defining features of the 19th century.[13] Even more than celebrations of the railway network or of the postal system, Victorian writing about the telegraph network expresses the idea that a communication network could rewire the material and discursive connections that seemed to bind the nation, the Empire, and the globe.

Victorian communication networks encouraged a wider impression of new contiguities and expanding relations, a sense that the stream of communication itself both produced and embodied human interconnection. This is part of the reason that the electric telegraph sponsored notably inaccurate fantasies of the coming peace between the nations. It also meant that communication networks could represent the ties of global commerce and empire which they helped to sustain, an association that spans the entire period. While Gaskell's *Cranford* imagines the postal network as the prosaic yet mysterious connection between a quiet English village and far-off India, H.G. Wells's late-Victorian scientific romances would extend the workings of real imperial networks to imagine wireless communications by colonizing Martians or human explorers of the moon.[14]

From a repository for Utopian longings to a tool of knowledge and control: novels' approaches to the imaginative possibilities opened up by long-distance communication networks cover a similar range. Apart from characters' exchanges of letters, early Victorian novels tend to approach communication networks indirectly but at times with an implicit notion of their potential power. In this context, for instance, the cosmic communication between Jane and her far-off lover Rochester in Charlotte Brontë's *Jane Eyre* (1847) emerges as part of a wider discourse of telecommunication in the 1840s, even down to its representation of a textual message (a novel's writing, a telegram's alphabetic content) as a mystical, unmediated voice accessed by something like a new sense. When Brontë introduces Jane's moment of mystical contact with her love as 'not like an electric shock; but ... quite as sharp, as strange, as startling', she disclaims electricity as the literal vehicle of communication but explicitly tells us to imagine Jane's experience along similar lines.[15]

With *Jane Eyre*'s most extravagant disruption of its outward realism, the novel adopts the human voice as a vehicle of long-distance transmission and seems to prefigure telephony by several decades. Yet, if we understand the mandate of realistic fiction as

---

[13] Alfred Russel Wallace, *The Wonderful Century: Its Successes and Its Failures* (London: Swan Sonnenschein, 1898), 19.

[14] On Wells and communication technologies, see Aaron Worth, 'Imperial Transmissions: H. G. Wells, 1897–1901', *Victorian Studies* 53 (2010): 65–89.

[15] Charlotte Brontë, *Jane Eyre* [1857], ed. Margaret Smith (Oxford: World's Classics, Oxford University Press, 2000), 419. For further elaboration of the connections between *Jane Eyre* and telegraphy in the late 1840s, see Menke, *Telegraphic Realism*, 77–88.

representing the actual world by following out its logic, the moment appears neither wholly opposed to realism nor entirely uncanny in its anticipation of a future communication device. 'It has always been one of the primary tasks of art to create a demand whose hour of full satisfaction has not yet come', asserts Walter Benjamin in a celebrated essay on art and technology; this creation comes about when—as Brontë's novel does at its climax—a form of art 'strains after effects which can be easily achieved only with a changed technical standard'.[16]

The suggestion of a networked world could also encourage reflections on what reality might look like as a stream of flowing everyday discourse. Thinking about the telegraph wires running under London between the central telegraph office and the railway stations, one early writer on the telegraph claims that

> it is almost impossible for any ruminating being to walk the streets without occasionally pausing to reflect not only on the busy bustling scenes which glide before his eyes, but on those which, at very different rates, are at the same moment flowing beneath his feet.
>
> In our metropolis, there is scarcely a street which does not appear to take pride in exposing as often as possible to public view a series of pipes of all sizes, in which fire of various companies, pure water of various companies, and unmentionable mixtures, abominable to all, pass cheek by jowl with infinitely less trouble than the motley human currents flow above them. But…there is certainly no [pipe] which has more curious contents than the three-inch iron pipe of the Electric Telegraph Company; and yet, of all the multitudes who walk the streets, how few of them ever care to reflect what a singular contrast exists between the slow pace at which they themselves are proceeding, and the rate at which beneath their feet forty-five electric wires are transmitting in all directions, and to a variety of distances, intelligence of every possible description![17]

This conception imagines not terse, disconnected telegrams pulsing along the line, but a textual flow, forming 'scenes' that resemble the mundane cityscape outside and above, only in a condensed and accelerated form. The 'scenes' on the wire must go in serial form, in the kind of sequence that a ruminating author might elaborate into a narrative. If Victorian novels could look like networks, the contents of Victorian networks could look like electrified novels.

The flow of stories on the telegraph wires regularizes human interaction in a way that parallels other forms of shared, channelled flow (gas, water, waste), but which is also a dramatically altered and concentrated version of what is happening above. Some of the

---

[16] Walter Benjamin, 'The Work of Art in the Age of its Technical Reproducibility: Second Version', in *The Work of Art in the Age of its Technical Reproducibility, and Other Writings on Media*, ed. Michael W. Jennings, Brigid Doherty, and Thomas Y. Levin, and trans. Edmund Jephcott et al. (Cambridge, MA: Belknap and Harvard University Press, 2008), 38.

[17] Frances Bond Head, *Stokers and Pokers, or, the London and North-Western Railway, the Electric Telegraph, and the Railway Clearing-House* (London: Murray, 1849), 125.

early metaphorical uses of the word *network* applied it to the circulatory system or to river systems, but the term is also primed to carry implications of a built structure—*net work*—that handles 'flow': canals, railways, pipes, electric wires. The model of communication as a controlled, channelled 'flow' comes to be generalized in large part from the electric telegraph and from Victorian understanding of its network. Yet this model also shapes the conceptual transformation of the mail from a handling of unique objects to a management of the postal flow. Creating fictional analogues for his experiences with the postal bureaucracy, Trollope assigns the young protagonists of *The Three Clerks* (1858) to the government departments of Internal Navigation and of Weights and Measures, offices responsible for standardizing trade and regulating the flow of vessels and goods across canals and rivers. The tasks are not so different from postal work. Like business and transport networks, communication networks became part of what has been called the 'control revolution' in the 19th century, the modernization of processing and control that turned the industrial era into a nascent information age.[18]

The telegraph first brought this revolution of managed flow to the railway network, maximizing the use of the same tracks for different routes, including for trains travelling in opposite directions. By the final decades of the century, the development of duplex and multiplex telegraphy would bring the same kind of innovation to the telegraphic network itself. But in fact, the idea of interweaving streams of discourse within a single physical medium was anticipated by mid-Victorian novelists such as Dickens, Trollope, and Eliot. For the idea of society as a network of relations could help justify literary forms such as the multi-plot novel, a work whose storylines link an entire range of characters, and one of the distinctive forms of 19th-century fiction.

Undoubtedly, the best-known appearance of a network in a Victorian novel is George Eliot's invocation of the 'web' in *Middlemarch* (1871–72). This image represents the organized connection of person to person, story to story—and also, as a recurrent connecting metaphor within the text, helps to enact that linkage. In the novel's crucial announcement of this controlling image, the narrator explicitly links it to the contemporary world of multiplicity and haste, and to the Victorian novel:

> A great historian, as he insisted on calling himself, who had the happiness to be dead a hundred and twenty years ago…glories in his copious remarks and digressions as the least imitable part of his work, and especially in those initial chapters to the successive books of his history, where he seems to bring his arm-chair to the proscenium and chat with us in all the lusty ease of his fine English. But Fielding lived when the days were longer (for time, like money, is measured by our needs), when summer afternoons were spacious, and the clock ticked slowly in the winter evenings. We belated historians must not linger after his example…I at least have so much to do in unravelling certain human lots, and seeing how they were woven and

---

[18] James R. Beniger, *The Control Revolution: Technological and Economic Origins of the Information Society* (Cambridge, MA: Harvard University Press, 1986).

interwoven, that all the light I can command must be concentrated on this particular web, and not dispersed over that tempting range of relevancies called the universe.[19]

Eliot's 'woven and interwoven' web of 'human lots' closely recalls Bagehot's 'network of ramified relations, interlacing and passing hither and thither'. But, true to her novel's commitment to lived complexity, and to Eliot's multiple ways of developing the web metaphor and the human connections it crystallizes, *Middlemarch* remains conscious of the status of its links as both sustaining interconnections and constricting bonds. And while the narrator awards the weave of human connection an objective existence in the world of *Middlemarch*, the novel will offer only a view of a 'particular web', and perhaps only an imperfect view at that. Like the Victorian postal reformers, *Middlemarch*'s 'historian' recasts an existing cultural form, the novel, as a 19th-century network.

For early- and mid-Victorian novelists, such unspoken implications and anticipations often characterize the relationships between fiction and the era's existent or emergent communication networks. In the second half of the Victorian period, however, the connections between novels and networks become more self-conscious and overt. By the 1870s, the rapturous response to the first permanent transatlantic telegraph link as well as the nationalization of the telegraph system and reduction of its charges had given telegraphy new prominence as a public topic and a daily reality. Moreover, these decades brought an accelerating emergence of newer technological media, including the typewriter, the phonograph, the telephone, and—at the end of the period—wireless telegraphy. For this was the era of the great 'invention of invention' by Thomas Edison and others, the establishment of new organizations and routines for systematically creating, improving, mass producing, and selling new technologies.

A later work by Walter Bagehot suggests that such rapid technological innovation might not only characterize the era but also hold wider implications for intellectual and social life:

> One peculiarity of this age is the sudden acquisition of much physical knowledge. There is scarcely a department of science or art which is the same, or at all the same, as it was fifty years ago. A new world of inventions—of railways and of telegraphs— has grown up around us which we cannot help seeing; a new world of ideas is in the air and affects us, though we do not see it.[20]

These first lines of *Physics and Politics* (1867–72) point to the growth of transportation and communication networks as a parallel for the new connections between scientific knowledge and everyday life. Literature too was beginning to get the message; from the 1870s onward, many works of fiction include actual communication networks as explicit

[19] George Eliot, *Middlemarch* [1872], ed. David Carroll (Oxford: World's Classics, Oxford University Press, 2008), 132.

[20] Walter Bagehot, *Physics and Politics* (1867–72), in *The Collected Works of Walter Bagehot*, ed. Norman St John-Stevas, 15 vols. (London: Economist, 1974), 7: 17.

subjects and explore them in detail. At first most of these works are either stories written for telegraph workers or breathless explorations of technology intended for the young.[21] Furthermore, some of the most detailed exploration of particular communication technologies occurs not in novels but in short stories such as Trollope's 'The Telegraph Girl' (1877). But as novels take up the 'new world' of inventions and ideas, they express and respond to this growing awareness in several fashions. In their pages, communication technologies may provide models for supernatural experiences, opportunities for close examination of actual forms of communication, or—perhaps most surprisingly— occasions for a critique of the late-Victorian trade in writing. These three possibilities emerge in a variety of works from the last third of the century.

Jane Eyre appropriates the framework of long-distance communication to represent the not-quite-electric shock of mystical communion, but later in the century tele-technologies emerge as more systematic and sustained paradigms for psychic and occult experience. It is only superficially paradoxical that one result of the increased awareness of real media and communication networks should be the entrée they seemed to offer into mystical dimensions. After all, to justify the reality of these realms, psychic theory and novels alike could imaginatively push the expanding possibilities of actual communication just a step or two further. The coining of the word *telepathy* (1882) by the writer and psychic researcher Frederic Myers reflects this logic, combining a prefix associated with long-distance electrical signalling (via telegraph and now the telephone, patented in 1876) with a root signifying 'feeling'.[22]

In fiction, novels by Marie Corelli offer perhaps the most intense application of this paradigm (with the writing of George du Maurier, another author of late-Victorian bestsellers, as a close rival). Her first novel, *A Romance of Two Worlds* (1886), tells the story of a female pianist whose nervous collapse is resolved when a mysterious figure named Heliobas helps her discover the 'Electric Creed' or 'Electric Principles of Christianity'.[23] Early in the novel, the network illustrates the internal psychic disruption of the heroine's mind, the disturbance of

> that wondrous piece of human machinery, the nervous system; that intricate and
> delicate network of fine threads—electric wires on which run the messages of

---

[21] On telegraphers' fiction, see Otis, *Networking*, 136–46, as well as Katherine Stubbs, 'Telegraphy's Corporeal Fictions', in *New Media, 1740–1915*, ed. Lisa Gitelman and Geoffrey P. Pingree (Cambridge, MA: MIT Press, 2003), 91–111. R.M. Ballantyne's juvenile novels *Post Haste: A Tale of Her Majesty's Mails* (1880) and *The Battery and the Boiler, or, Adventures in the Laying of Submarine Electric Cables* (1883) offer lengthy examinations of the postal system and telegraph network in the midst of their young heroes' adventures with the domestic and imperial Victorian communication infrastructures; see Menke, *Telegraphic Realism*, 175–80.

[22] For a compelling history of the origins and fortunes of telepathy in late-Victorian culture, see Roger Luckhurst, *The Invention of Telepathy, 1870–1901* (Oxford: Oxford University Press, 2002).

[23] Marie Corelli, *A Romance of Two Worlds* [1886] (Prime Classics, 2004), 157; subsequently cited in the text. On Corelli and psychic communication, see Jill Galvan, *The Sympathetic Medium: Feminine Channeling, the Occult, and Communication Technologies, 1859–1919* (Ithaca, NY: Cornell University Press, 2010), 1–2, 85–98.

thought, impulse, affection, emotion. If these threads or wires become, from any subtle cause, entangled, the skill of the mere medical practitioner is of no avail to undo the injurious knot, or to unravel the confused skein. (38)

But, in parallel with the new realities of telegraphy, the same image allows the novel to postulate electrical links from an individual nervous system to realms more distant than any physical connection could reach, as if by a new wire on the telepath network: 'Granting human electricity to exist, why should not a communication be established, like a sort of spiritual Atlantic cable, between man and the beings of other spheres and other solar systems?' (114). Corelli would continue to pursue the telepathic possibilities of electrical communication in related novels such as *Ardath* (1889) and *The Soul of Lilith* (1892), but—albeit in a non-theological mode—the alignment between telegraphy and telepathy would continue to shape fiction as varied as Bram Stoker's *Dracula* (1897) and Henry James's *In the Cage* (1898).

If these two works have recently become the most frequently considered in critical accounts of the relationships between Victorian literature and communication networks, the reason may lie in their multifaceted approaches to this relationship. James and Stoker create complexity in part by combining the telepathic tinge of rapid long-distance communication with a heightened interest in the actual mechanics of media and the psychology of ordinary information exchange. Seizing on the supernatural overtones of communication networks, *Dracula* places its eponymous villain at the heart of what has been called an 'undead network' that channels the flows of blood and information.[24] Yet even as it assembles this occult network, the novel also draws attention to the specific properties of media and to the text's own putative status as a mosaic of different media— journals kept in shorthand, business and personal letters, telegrams, phonographic recordings, newspaper clippings—unified as a typescript by Mina Harker.[25] James's *In the Cage*, with its keen psychological portrait of a young telegraphist who becomes obsessed with a love affair between her customers, might seem to have little in common with Stoker's horror story. But it too shows a subtle awareness of the real mechanics of media (in its fixation on the acoustic telegraph's clicking 'sounder', for instance) and the everyday psychodynamics of information work, at the same time as it draws on the mediumistic possibilities that surround a sensitive telegraph worker who considers herself particularly receptive to her customers' secret stories.[26]

---

[24] Geoffrey Winthrop-Young, 'Undead Networks: Information Processing and Media Boundary Conflicts in *Dracula*', in *Literature and Science*, ed. Donald Bruce and Anthony Purdy (Amsterdam: Rodopi, 1994), 107–29.

[25] Jennifer Wicke provides the earliest and most influential analysis of media in *Dracula* in 'Vampiric Typewriting: *Dracula* and its Media', *ELH* 59 (1992): 467–93. On *Dracula*'s networks, see also Otis, *Networking*, 194–219.

[26] For critical explorations of the occult or psychic subtexts of telegraphy in *In the Cage*, see Pamela Thurschwell, *Literature, Technology, and Magical Thinking, 1880–1920* (Cambridge: Cambridge University Press, 2001), 86–114; and Galvan, *Sympathetic Medium*, 26–60.

As novels begin to probe new communication forms, they also start drawing special attention to the limitations of media, to miscommunications, and technological failure. A critical telegram goes astray in *Dracula*; later on, the intimate voice of a phonographic diary, however 'cruelly true' it may be in its fidelity to real speech, must be transcribed via typewriter in order to become a useful source of information.[27] *In the Cage* features another lost telegram, one that is recovered only thanks to the exquisite memory of its heroine. In Thomas Hardy's self-consciously up-to-date *A Laodicean* (1881), a distorted photograph and a forged telegram incriminate the blameless hero even in the eyes of the novel's intelligent, telegraph-wielding heroine.

Such insistence on the flaws, limits, or dubiousness of technological media may help support a final form of engagement between novels and communication networks in the last decades of the century: the invocation of tele-technologies and other new media as part of a critical account of what would later come to be called the mass media. This critique animates the most famous Victorian quotation about the connections between novels and networked communication, a line from the opening pages of George Gissing's *New Grub Street* (1891). In a speech to his sister, the shrewd, cheerful, and opportunistic Jasper Milvain criticizes a fellow writer's lack of business sense:

> '...Now, look you: if I had been in Reardon's place, I'd have made four hundred at least out of "The Optimist"; I should have gone shrewdly to work with magazines and newspapers and foreign publishers, and—all sorts of people. Reardon can't do that kind of thing, he's behind his age; he sells a manuscript as if he lived in Sam Johnson's Grub Street. But our Grub Street of to-day is quite a different place: *it is supplied with telegraphic communication*, it knows what literary fare is in demand in every part of the world, its inhabitants are men of business, however seedy.'
> 'It sounds ignoble,' said Maud.[28] [emphasis added]

The passage gives Gissing's novel its very name and announces its great themes far in advance of its plot. But although the novel will for the most part treat Jasper as a regrettably accurate guide to the contemporary world of letters, his specific claims here seem puzzling, even misleading.

In fact, the telegraph isn't much in evidence in Gissing's Grub Street, and little seems to hinge on foreign publishers, since the novel doesn't represent publishing as an especially international industry. Rather, for Milvain in this speech, globalization stands in for mass culture (today's Grub Street 'knows what literary fare is in demand in every part of the world'), and 'telegraphic communication' stands in for the reduction of published writing to its saleable medium. What defines the Grub Street of today? Not merely the hackwork of selling words, which was already summed up in the Grub Street of Johnson,

[27] Bram Stoker, *Dracula* [1897], ed. Maud Ellman (Oxford: World's Classics, Oxford University Press, 1998), 222.

[28] George Gissing, *New Grub Street* [1891], ed. John Goode (Oxford: World's Classics, Oxford University Press, 1993), 9; subsequently cited in the text.

but the collapse of the supposed autonomy of the literary sphere as even a polite fiction. As *New Grub Street* proceeds, this collapse will be associated with a new, mass audience, with the readership that makes the journal *Chit Chat* (an analogue of George Newnes's real *Tit-Bits*) a success even beyond its target market of the 'quarter-educated' (460). And for Gissing, this new regime of letters is also expressed by the reduction of writing to the outward form in which it appears, to its bare medium. This reduction is the process that has the young novelist Edwin Reardon cranking out the requisite number of volumes instead of imagining stories, and the prospective editor of *Chit Chat* planning its content in terms of 'chit-chatty information—bits of stories, bits of description, bits of scandal, bits of jokes, bits of statistics, bits of foolery', all broken into items of 'two inches at the utmost' (460).

Milvain's comments about the novel in a world of telegraphs are obviously flippant. Nevertheless, they point to a more general logic in late Victorian writing, a logic by which Victorian novelists can treat the telegraph and other media technologies as part of a recognizable complex that combines general anxieties about a mass audience with a specific attention to the external properties of media *as* media. To this end, we can note the way that *In the Cage* conflates mastery of the electric telegraph with stories from vulgar, borrowed 'ha'penny novels'—'greasy, in fine print and all about fine folks'—in the fantasies of its young telegraphist.[29] But late Victorian novels are especially likely to treat other forms of writing as mere communication media when they are imagining the fortunes of characters who are writers or novelists themselves.

A scene from *A Writer of Books* (1898), a 'new woman' novel by George Paston (Emily Morse Symonds), wittily exemplifies this turn to media technologies as terms for criticizing print publications. Defying middle-class propriety, the novel's eponymous heroine has allowed a young, male stranger to take her to dinner, just in case as a novelist she ever needs 'to send her hero to such a place' as this 'little foreign restaurant'.[30] As she prepares to leave her dinner companion, he disappointedly suggests a newspaper column as a place of textual assignation: "'Oh, but I say,'" he expostulated. "'You're not going off like that? You'll let me see you again. Any time you want an outing, just put a line in the *Telephone*, the agony column, you know'" (46). Casually but pointedly, the novel names 'the *Telephone*' as the printed site where a hapless young man might hope to re-establish a missed romantic connection. Calling the print organ for such an incident the *Telephone* makes clear the modernity of the incident, and its mediation by vehicles that promise more broadly to extend the logic of freewheeling sociability into a sense of anonymous public intimacy—indeed, of public sexuality. A 'line in the *Telephone*': Paston punningly suggests how the dynamics of advertising to a potential intimate

---

[29] Henry James, *In the Cage* [1898], in *Complete Stories, 1892–98* (New York: Library of America, 1996), 866, 837.

[30] George Paston [Emily Morse Symonds], *A Writer of Books* [1898] (Chicago: Academy Chicago, 1999), 41; subsequently cited in the text.

might even echo the structure of Victorian telephony, with its switchboard of connections to be forged between private parties on a public network.

In one rich and comic moment, *A Writer of Books* has deftly aligned the more dubious
possibilities of the late-Victorian press with a new communication network in order to
satirize the sensibility of that press. Only a few pages earlier, the story's novelist-heroine
has met the 'literary critic of the *Phonograph*'—a 'sentimental' journal intended for
'lower middle-class readers' and named after another late-Victorian media invention
(22, 34). When the middle-aged, married critic makes a grotesque pass at her amidst
talk of protecting her delicate womanhood, the heroine recognizes the kind of mindless
repetition that might invest writing with the aurality of a broken record: 'I seem to have
heard something like that before…Or rather I have read it in the *Daily Phonograph*'
(56). Once again, a critique of the outlook of the mass press proceeds by identifying the
press with a newer medium and using the properties of this medium to indict the press.

As I have indicated, novels from the final decades of the century often treat communication networks explicitly: as models for paranormal experience, as subjects for close
imaginative investigation, as critical tropes for the late-Victorian culture industry. If
earlier works are more diffuse in their engagement with these networks, they nonetheless share a broad tendency to approach networks as at once a confirmation of the social
ties between persons and a means for investigating those ties. Throughout the period,
when novels examine the abilities and constraints of real and imagined communication networks, they also find ways to think about the social properties and mechanics
of Victorian novels, their own promises to assemble textual exchanges into a form of
public connection.

Suggested Reading

Clayton, Jay. *Charles Dickens in Cyberspace: The Afterlife of the Nineteenth Century in Postmodern
    Culture*. Oxford: Oxford University Press, 2003.
Galvan, Jill. *The Sympathetic Medium: Feminine Channeling, the Occult, and Communication
    Technologies, 1859–1919*. Ithaca: Cornell University Press, 2010.
Golden, Catherine J. *Posting It: The Victorian Revolution in Letter Writing*. Gainesville: University
    Press of Florida, 2009.
Menke, Richard. *Telegraphic Realism: Victorian Fiction and Other Information Systems*. Stanford:
    Stanford University Press, 2008.
Otis, Laura. Networking: *Communicating with Bodies and Machines in the Nineteenth Century*.
    Ann Arbor: University of Michigan Press, 2001.
Robinson, Howard. *The British Post Office: A History*. Princeton: Princeton University Press,
    1948. Westport: Greenwood, 1970.
Thomas, Kate. *Postal Pleasures: Sex, Scandal, and Victorian Letters*. New York: Oxford University
    Press, 2012.
Worth, Aaron. *Imperial Media: Colonial Networks and Information Technologies in the British
    Literary Imagination, 1857–1918*. Columbus: Ohio State University Press, forthcoming.

14

TECHNOLOGIES OF TRAVEL AND THE VICTORIAN NOVEL

ALISON BYERLY

The Victorians liked to think of themselves as people who were going places, literally and figuratively. The 19th century saw an unprecedented expansion of opportunities for travel, both within the country and around the globe. The invention of the steam engine led quickly to the development of new modes of transportation that would change the face of England, and change its relationship to the rest of the world. The development of the railway network from the late 1830s through to the 1860s allowed people of all classes to travel across the country more rapidly and less expensively than ever before. At the same time, the growth of the steamship industry, beginning with the maiden voyage of the *SS Great Western* in 1838, began an era of regularly scheduled transatlantic crossings that added America to the list of formerly remote places—such as India, Africa, and China—that were becoming far more accessible to British travellers.

The expansion of cultural geography enabled by these new technologies of travel had a profound effect on literary forms of the period, particularly the novel. The Romantic poets of the late 1700s and early 1800s had already incorporated a strong sense of place into their poetry, and over the course of the 19th century novels too became increasingly focused on evocations of specific places. The 19th century also saw tremendous growth in the evolving genre of travel literature. As real travel became more widespread, interest in reading about travel expanded as well. Popular travel literature included Sir Richard F. Burton's *Personal Narrative of a Pilgrimage to Mecca and El-Medinah* (1855) and numerous accounts of his African explorations; Isabella Bird Bishop's accounts of her travels over many years in the American Rocky Mountains, Japan, Tibet, China, Korea, and Morocco; and David Livingstone's bestselling 1857 *Missionary Travels and Research in South Africa*.

Critical analyses of Victorian travel literature often see exotic travel accounts as a kind of imaginative appropriation that reflects or nostalgically recreates the acts of political appropriation that constitute British imperialism in the 19th century. Within the field of Victorian studies, Mary Louise Pratt's *Imperial Eyes: Travel Writing and Transculturation* established an understanding of the way in which the signifying practices of travel writing both 'encode and legitimate the aspirations of economic expansion and empire', and at times, 'betray them'.[1] Other critics have focused so forcefully on the legitimizing role of travel writing within an imperialist agenda that they may seem, argues Steve Clark, to 'render the whole genre intrinsically invidious'.[2]

But the Victorian interest in travel literature was not limited to accounts of foreign travel. The development of new domestic travel networks meant the Victorians came to enjoy accounts and guidebooks describing familiar places in and around England. New technologies spawned new subgenres of travel literature that focused on the experience of specific modes of travel. The popularity of boating on the Thames, for example, is reflected in dozens of guidebooks, periodical articles, maps, and even poems about the pleasures of this leisurely form of travel. By contrast, the more rapid and utilitarian travel of the railway led to an enormous number of practical guidebooks designed to help readers negotiate the complexities of railway stations and timetables, as well as to many articles, essays, and short stories depicting this new form of experience. As I have argued elsewhere, the development and refinement of the guidebook genre, with its emphasis on the integration of personal narrative and topographical depiction, influenced the elaborate landscape depictions that characterize many Victorian novels.[3] Moreover, the inclusive rhetoric with which these guidebooks attempted to make the reader feel a sense of participation in the journeys described found an echo in the direct address with which Victorian novelists invited readers to enter their fictional worlds.

In fact, the development of these new technologies of travel had a crucial effect on the development of the Victorian novel. The sense of expanding space that characterized the period created a larger canvas for the novelist, and the increased mobility of people of all classes allowed for a broader cast of characters. The circumscribed world of the typical Jane Austen novel, in which all of the action takes place in a handful of upper-class drawing rooms within ten miles of each other, would be replaced by the panoramic urban landscapes of Dickens, teeming with people of all classes, gathered from British colonies all over the globe.

This chapter will both examine the ways in which a range of Victorian novels represent specific forms of travel, and map some of the routes that expanded the fictional landscapes of the period. These new technologies of travel enabled industrialization, economic development, and some of the most significant cultural shifts of the Victorian

---

[1] Mary Louis Pratt, *Imperial Eyes: Travel Writing and Transculturation* (Boston: Routledge, 1992), 5.

[2] Steve Clark, 'Introduction', in *Travel Writing and Empire: Postcolonial Theory in Transit*, ed. Steve Clark (London: Zed Books, 1999), 1–28, 3.

[3] Alison Byerly, *Are We There Yet? Virtual Travel and Victorian Realism* (Ann Arbor: University of Michigan Press, 2013). This chapter draws throughout on my examination there of different modes of travel, which in *Are We There Yet?* are presented there within the larger context of changing perceptions of the relationship between the self and the fictional worlds conjured through literature and other forms of art and media.

age. The novel itself was shaped by the types of travel it depicted: realist fiction evolved alongside the train and the steamboat. As we will see, the effects of travel technology are both broad and particular. In the most general sense, these new technologies enabled the wider perspective on the world that informs so many great novels of the period. On a more localized level, they were integral to the complex plots of Victorian fiction, which often hinged on lovers being separated and reunited across vast distances, wastrel sons being exiled to India and returning again, or London detectives being able to catch a train to the country in order to examine fresh footprints at the scene of a crime.

Paradoxically, increased mobility led to renewed interest in the local and the particular. Juliet McDonagh has suggested that 'mobility, as the condition of modernity…is both the concealed provocation and secret subject of realism', as it fuelled the 'obsessive fascination with local places that dominated the British novel from the nineteenth century onward'.[4] Whether in Thomas Hardy's depictions of the countryside he called 'Wessex', Elizabeth Gaskell's evocations of the slums of Manchester, or George Gissing's critiques of the suburbs springing up around London, British novelists focused close attention on the specific and increasingly divergent cultures of town, country, and the places in between. The ability to describe, and the appetite for, these almost anthropological studies of different localities were crucial to the development of the realist novel. James Buzard sees the Victorian novel as embodying an 'autoethnographic imagination' in which the narrative voice cultivates an 'outsider's insideness' that resembles the anthropologist's role as 'participant-observer'.[5] One has only to think of George Eliot's narrators to understand how central this development is to the rise of the realist novel. Eliot's commitment to a narrator who situates herself squarely inside the place she is describing, and inside the minds of its inhabitants, while also maintaining the capacity to describe it with scientific accuracy, speaks to the way in which place becomes a proxy for identity.

The dominant technology of the period was of course the railway, a technology that profoundly altered England's sense of itself. As we will see, Victorian novelists depicted the railway as both an extraordinary achievement and a looming threat, and this ambivalence manifests itself in novels by George Eliot, Charles Dickens, Anthony Trollope, Bram Stoker, Conan Doyle, and Mary Elizabeth Braddon. Beyond the rails, steamships, both large ocean liners and the smaller steam launches that cruised the Thames, play a role in several Victorian novels, including the works of Thackeray, Dickens, and Trollope. At the close of the century, a simple yet also revolutionary mechanism for travel, the bicycle, offered new mobility and freedom for women in particular. The *fin-de-siècle* works of Jerome K. Jerome, George Gissing, and Conan Doyle all make use of this convenient new form of urban transport. And, finally, a daring new form of travel, the hot-air balloon, offered select passengers a unique, birds-eye perspective

---

[4] Josephine McDonagh, 'Space, Mobility, and the Novel', in *A Concise Companion to Realism*, ed. Matthew Beaumont (Chichester: John Wiley and Sons, 2010), 50–67, 66, 63.

[5] James Buzard, *Disorienting Fiction: The Autoethnographic Work of Nineteenth-Century British Novels* (Princeton: Princeton University Press, 2005), 11, 10.

on the world, widely promulgated in articles, illustrations, and early photographs, that influenced landscape descriptions in a number of Victorian novels.

At the start of the 19th century, most travel in and around England took place on foot, on horse, or by coach. The limitations of pedestrian travel are movingly visible in the long, weary journeys of Hetty Sorrel, the seduced dairymaid of Eliot's *Adam Bede*; of Brontë's Jane Eyre, after she has left the home of Mr Rochester; and of Michael Henchard and his homeless family, in the opening pages of Thomas Hardy's *The Mayor of Casterbridge*. Travel on horseback, a mode of transportation generally available only to young, active gentlemen, also appears occasionally in novels by Eliot, Hardy, and others, but representations of riding generally lack the specific emotional or thematic resonance associated with walking.

Coaches and carriages drive a number of novels in the first half of the century, particularly those of Austen and Thackeray. Because coaches were expensive, slow, and dependent on the highly variable quality of roads, coach journeys are usually a powerful marker of upper-class status. In *Emma*, for example, Emma chides Mr Knightley for deigning to walk a short distance rather than taking his carriage, and impecunious members of Austen's society are often reduced to the humiliation of relying on offered rides in other people's carriages. Coach journeys generally signal moments of decisive separation, perhaps most dramatically in Thackeray's *Vanity Fair*, when Becky Sharpe, departing school, flings her presentation copy of Dr Johnson's Dictionary out of the window as she drives away.

These earlier modes of transportation enact a reality in which the majority of people spent their entire lives within a limited geographic range. When a person did leave home for London, for the colonies, or for America, that departure was understood to be more or less permanent. There were few opportunities for travel back and forth across long distances. The railway would change all of that. The speed of railway travel made it the ultimate symbol of the pace of modern life. In a nostalgic description in *Felix Holt: The Radical* of the stage-coach culture of 'five and thirty years ago', Eliot contrasts the leisurely pace of a coach journey—and by extension, her own narrative—with the modern, experimental technology represented by pneumatic trains:

> Posterity may be shot, like a bullet through a tube, by atmospheric pressure from Winchester to Newcastle: that is a fine result to have among our hopes; but the slow old-fashioned way of getting from one end of our country to the other is the better thing to have in the memory. The tube-journey can never lend much to picture or narrative...[6]

Pneumatic trains had at one time seemed a logical next development for the railways, and an 1864 illustration from the *Illustrated London News* shows a 'working model' of a 'pneumatic railway for passengers' exhibited in the grounds of the Crystal Palace at

---

[6] George Eliot, *Felix Holt* [1866], ed. Peter Coveney (London: Penguin, 1987), 75.

Sydenham. It did indeed shoot passengers through a tube over a distance of 600 yards in 50 seconds.[7] Eliot would comment again on the pace of modern life in *Daniel Deronda*, where the novel's many train journeys are contrasted with Deronda's rowing trips on the Thames, which provide an opportunity for reflection that is implicitly contrasted with the hurried transportation afforded by the railway. At the very end of the century, Eliot's vision of tube travel would be partially realized, as the railway lines that first went partially underground in 1863 were followed in 1890 by deep-tunnel lines, including the 1900 Central Line known as the 'Twopenny Tube'—a nickname that was then extended to the entire London Underground system.

'THE ANNIHILATION OF SPACE AND TIME': THE COMING OF THE RAILWAY

In the 21st century, trains have an aura of quaintness that makes it difficult to remember that for 19th-century travellers, they represented cutting-edge technology. For us, the word 'railway' tends to conjure up images of gleaming Victorian locomotives exhibited in museums, charming rural branch lines sprawled across the English landscape, or eccentric railway enthusiasts poring over timetables. Our continued association of railways with an earlier age reflects the fact that railways were perceived, even then, as unmistakably *of* that age. For the Victorians, they were the quintessential symbol of emerging modernity. As we will see, allusions to rail travel in Dickens and Eliot serve as symbols of progress that allowed those novelists to comment on the changes taking place in the world around them. More frequent and detailed representations of train travel in later works by Doyle, Braddon, and Stoker seek to align their fictional worlds with the urban and suburban landscapes of modern British life. These varied depictions share, however, an emphasis on the almost magical power of technology to separate the physical experience of getting from one place to another from the imaginative experience of travel.

As Wolfgang Schivelbusch demonstrated in his pioneering work *The Railway Journey: Trains and Travel in the Nineteenth Century* (1977), the rapid growth of the railways throughout Europe and America altered 'the traditional space-time consciousness' of every society it touched.[8] The Victorians frequently referred to the railway's 'annihilation of space and time'—an evocation of Alexander Pope's lines, 'Ye Gods! annihilate but space and time/And make two lovers happy'—to convey the sense in which this form of travel profoundly altered people's sense of their relationship to, and control over, the

---

[7] *Illustrated London News* (September 10, 1864): 275–76

[8] Wolfgang Schivelbusch, *The Railway Journey: Trains and Travel in the Nineteenth Century*, trans. Anselm Hollo. Originally published as *Geschichte der Eisenbahnreise*, 1977 (Oxford: Basil Blackwell, 1980), 37.

world around them. Karl Marx would use this phrase in 1857 to encapsulate the contradictions of capitalism, writing in the *Grundrisse*: 'While capital... must strive to tear down every barrier... to exchange and conquer the whole earth for its markets, it strives on the other side to annihilate this space with time'.[9] The ability of the railway to eliminate what geographers call 'the friction of distance' was an enormous benefit to trade and industrial development, and in Victorian literature the railway is often viewed as inextricably linked with the rise of commodity culture.

Schivelbusch coined the phrase 'the machine ensemble' to describe the way in which 'the speed and mathematical directness with which the railroad proceeds through the terrain destroys the close relationship between the traveler and the traveled space',[10] and the critic John Ruskin, who objected strenuously to the effect of railway construction on the landscape, as well as to the experience itself, famously described the sensation as 'being sent on the railway like a parcel'.[11] Ruskin complained that the railway degraded the scenic experience of travel, insisting that it was impossible to visually apprehend and appreciate landscape when it passed by so rapidly. The vastly increased speed of train travel certainly had an effect on travellers' perceptions of distance, or, more abstractly, of space in general. Places did not seem as far apart when they could be reached so easily. Stephen Kern has explored this phenomenon in the period from 1880 to 1918, pointing out that the first trains and then 'technical innovations including the telephone, wireless telegraph, x-ray, cinema, bicycle, [and] automobiles' led to a 'reorientation' of thinking about space and time, while such 'independent cultural developments... as the stream-of-consciousness novel, psychoanalysis, Cubism, and the theory of relativity shaped consciousness directly'.[12]

For better or worse, railways represented Progress. Among the reforms that are a source of conflict in the small provincial town featured in Eliot's *Middlemarch*, the coming of the railway stands as an image of the inevitability of change. As Caleb Garth pragmatically tells a group of angry countrymen, the railway 'will be made whether you like it or not'.[13] On an individual level, the inflexibility of a train that is limited to a fixed track makes it an apt image in the novel for the inevitable collision between the divergent perspectives of Rosamond and Lydgate. Their growing estrangement is described starkly as a 'total missing of each other's mental track'. Eliot notes that Rosamond was very quick to see 'causes and effects which lay within the track of her own tastes and interests', but she is stubbornly blind to things that she does not wish to see.[14] Eliot's application of this broad technological metaphor to subjective human experience is one indication of how completely the railway had permeated contemporary culture.

---

[9] Karl Marx, *Grundrisse: Foundations of the Critique of Political Economy*, trans. Martin Nicolaus (Harmondsworth: Penguin, 1993), 539.

[10] Schivelbusch, 58.

[11] John Ruskin, *Modern Painters* [1843–60], 5 vols. (London: Cook and Wedderburn, 1904), 3: 370–71.

[12] Stephen Kern, *The Culture of Time and Space: 1880–1910* (London: Weidenfeld and Nicolson, 1983), 1.

[13] George Eliot, *Middlemarch* [1872] (London: Penguin Books, 1994), 859.

[14] Eliot, *Middlemarch*, 587, 588.

The railway was seen as having a profound, tangible effect on human experience that was symptomatic of many 'shocks of the new'. Nicholas Daly has traced a connection between the advent of the railways and the development of both sensation drama and sensation fiction, suggesting that the nervousness brought about by the 'heightened time-consciousness' of train travellers has its analogue in the frenzied pace of plot developments in sensation fiction, which often depend on a 'rapid succession of diverse locations'.[15]

At the most basic logistical level, the need for coordination among railway timetables on lines maintained by many different operators created a national push for standard time that had a profound effect on cultural attitudes towards time. This pressure resulted in the adoption of Greenwich mean time by most of the nation when the Royal Observatory, in conjunction with the South Eastern railway, began telegraphing time-signals in 1852.[16] Many contemporary commentators noted the way in which life seemed to speed up, as expectations for punctuality were heightened and businesses began to operate more rigidly and efficiently within prescribed time frames. One interesting effect of this sense of increased speed was a corresponding pressure to make productive use of the time 'saved'.

Conan Doyle's Sherlock Holmes revels in the speed of railway travel, and calculates the journey time carefully: "'We are going well,' said he, looking out of the window, and glancing at his watch. "Our rate at present is fifty-three and a half miles an hour"'. When Watson protests that he has seen no quarter-mile posts, Holmes replies, 'Nor have I. But the telegraph poles on this line are sixty yards apart, and the calculation is a simple one.'[17] Holmes makes good use of travel time to converse with Watson or with clients; one such conversation begins when he notes with satisfaction, 'We have a clear run here of seventy minutes... I want you, Mr. Hall Pycroft, to tell my friend your very interesting experience.'[18]

The many film adaptations of Doyle's stories have created an inextricable visual association of 1890s London with hansom cabs, but in fact Sherlock Holmes is promiscuous in his use of different modes of transportation: hansom cabs, trains, bicycles, and even occasional boats on the Thames all have a role in his constant journeys around London and the surrounding countryside. Many of Doyle's stories begin with a bored and restless Holmes receiving a telegram, or a visitor, at home in Baker Street. The new problem acts as a catalyst that sends Holmes energetically into action, often jumping on the next train out to the suburb where a crime has taken place. The stories depict a rapid alternation

---

[15] Nicholas Daly, 'Railway Novels: Sensation Fiction and the Modernization of the Senses', *English Literary History* 66 (1999): 461–87, 473. See also Nicholas Daly, *Sensation and Modernity in the 1860s* (Cambridge: Cambridge University Press, 2009).

[16] See Kern, 11–15, and Michael Freeman, *Railways and the Victorian Imagination* (New Haven: Yale University Press, 1999).

[17] Sir Arthur Conan Doyle, *The Adventures of Sherlock Holmes* [1887–93] (Ware: Wordsworth Classics, 1996), 291

[18] Doyle, 332.

between stasis and movement, boredom and intense activity, that dramatizes a central condition of modernity: the way in which freer circulation of information paradoxically increases, rather than decreases, the perceived need for travel.

Although coach travel was incompatible with reading, railway travel was not, and the railways contributed to a general expansion in recreational reading during this period, as people of all classes bought books at the railway station to help them pass the time.[19] Railway bookstalls initially limited themselves to guidebooks and popular novels, but a number of publishers soon established special cheap editions of more reputable works. The establishment of 'Routledge's Railway Library', 'Bentley's Railroad Library', 'Murray's Railway Reading', and 'Longman's Travellers' Library' made a mark on the publishing patterns of the day, creating a competitive market for inexpensive literature appealing to middle-class taste. These series might include popular novels as well as collections of short stories, humorous sketches, essays, and poems.

The development of literature intended specifically for railway reading led to claims that the railway, like many other aspects of modern life, was having a negative effect on people's capacity for sustained attention and thoughtful reflection. In one anonymous 1849 article, the author complains that 'the headlong bustle and the toil of life...leave men small leisure save to skim the surface of books'. The pandering of writers to this limited attention span has, according to this author, led to 'a quantity of literature, if literature it can be called, fit for little else, save to be read in a railway carriage or steamboat'.[20]

Elizabeth Gaskell satirizes the perceived threat that railway reading posed to the Victorian reader's attention span in *Cranford* (1853). Although she doesn't invoke a railway novel, she uses Dickens' *Pickwick Papers* to provoke the old spinster Miss Jenkyns' conservative response to the new literary tastes that made the *Pickwick* part-publications—often associated by reviewers with newspaper ephemera—so popular. Set in 1842, the book's opening chapter dwells at length on a dispute between Miss Jenkyns and Captain Brown that arises when he praises the writing of a contemporary author, 'Boz', whom she considers a vulgar upstart not to be compared with her favourite, Dr Johnson. Soon after, Captain Brown is killed in a railway accident. He is sitting by the tracks, absorbed in a book, when his attention is caught too late by a child who has wandered into a train's path. He dies in the act of saving her. When Miss Jenkyns reads in the newspaper account (though committed to Dr Johnson, she is not above reading the newspaper) that "'the gallant gentleman was deeply engaged in a number of 'Pickwick,' which he had just received," she sighs sadly, "poor, dear, infatuated man!"'[21] Although the well-worn criticism of 'railway literature' was that it demanded too little attention, Brown meets his Maker because he is immersed in *Pickwick*, not because he is skimming its surface. But while Gaskell may gently mock Miss Jenkyns's old-fashioned resistance

[19] Richard D. Altick, *The English Common Reader* (Chicago: University of Chicago Press, 1957), 89, 305; Jack Simmons, *The Victorian Railway* (New York: Thames & Hudson, 1991), 245–49; Schivelbusch, 66–71.

[20] 'Railway Literature', *Dublin University Magazine* 34 (1849), 281.

[21] Elizabeth Gaskell, *Cranford; and other Tales* [1853] (London: Smith, Elder, and Co., 1906), 21.

to the 'new' that Dickens represents, it remains the case that Brown is indeed killed in a railway accident. The accident attests to an underlying ambivalence. *Pickwick* deserves the attention it gets from the gallant Captain Brown, but the railroad has its dangers, as does the industrial life it represents.

At stake here is not simply whether one should read Johnson or Dickens (though that's an important matter); attitudes towards the railway stood as markers for attitudes towards the larger political questions that both upset England's stability and nurtured its belief in progress. In *Sybil, or The Two Nations* (1845), Disraeli describes the railway as a key cultural artefact, and a touchstone for the varying political opinions of different characters. When a railway station is compared unfavourably with a picturesque monastery, the radical Stephen Morley responds, 'The railways will do as much for mankind as the monasteries did.'[22] By contrast, conservative Lord de Mowbray complains that the railway 'has a very dangerous tendency to equality' (105), which is perhaps one reason, in addition to the intrusiveness of a branch line, that Lord Marney also opposes it. His lady reports, 'There is nobody so violent against railroads as George', but admits that his opposition ceased when the railroad agreed to his terms.[23] This admission obviously exposes Lord Marney's hypocrisy but also demonstrates his pragmatism—like suffrage and other reforms, the railroad was coming, whether one liked it or not, so one might as well get on board and make a profit.

Perhaps no well-known Victorian novelist figured the railroad more frequently in his novels than Trollope, who was a regular rail traveller himself and famously wrote many of his novels, beginning with *Barchester Towers* (1857), while riding on the train. His novels reflect his detailed understanding of the cultural changes introduced by the railway and the discomfort those changes could produce. For instance, the contemporary debates about whether railways should offer Sunday excursion trains, which competed with church attendance, animates a scene in *Barchester Towers*: when Mr Slope and Dr Grantly debate this point, Dr Grantly acknowledges that it is a question the market would decide, noting, 'if you can withdraw the passengers, the company, I dare say, will withdraw the trains'.[24] Trollope's sympathies would be echoed in even more up-to-date terms by Wilkie Collins, who has a character in *The Moonstone* (1868) remark bitterly: 'The established Sunday tyranny, which is one of the institutions of this free country, so times the trains so as to make it impossible to ask anybody to travel to us from London.'[25] Jennings's passing reference to this controversy both demonstrates Collins's commitment to literary realism and reveals his own liberal resistance to what he saw as a retrograde religious tyranny set against the democracy that the train provided to its increasingly mobile passengers.

Trollope's *The Prime Minister* (1873) depicts the railway as part of a whole network of urban transportation options. When the ruined financier Ferdinand Lopez leaves his

[22] Benjamin Disraeli, *Sybil, or The Two Nations* [1845] (London: Longmans, 1913), 96.
[23] Disraeli, 118.
[24] Anthony Trollope, *Barchester Towers* [1857], 2 vols. (New York: Dodd, Mead, 1906), 1: 45.
[25] Wilkie Collins, *The Moonstone* [1868], ed. J.I.M. Stewart (Harmondsworth: Penguin, 1986), 410.

house for the last time, Trollope describes the path he takes to his final destination in detail: 'It was raining hard, and when he got into the street he looked about for a cab, but there was none to be found. In Baker Street he got an omnibus which took him down to the underground railway, and by that he went to Gower Street.'[26] He remarks airily to a waitress, 'It's a bore, you know, coming out in the rain when there are no cabs.' When Lopez makes his way to the mythical Tenway Junction (based on Willdesden Junction, opened in 1866), Trollope emphasizes the confusion of the scene, but implies that there is an inner logic to the mechanism that is not visible to the individual traveller. The junction has 'direct communication with every other line in and out of London', like a kind of central switchboard, and while it seems impossible to the traveller to imagine that 'the best trained engine should know its own line', trains 'flash' in and out like lightning, each landing in its appointed place.

The whole scene is 'quite unintelligible to the uninitiated', but experienced travellers finally come to recognize that 'over all this apparent chaos there is presiding a great genius of order' (231). That 'great genius of order' is the railway system and Trollope himself, whose expert plotting is just as masterful. The reader too participates in the pleasures of this knowledge, following the network of the plot with increasing expertise. We wait for the train with Lopez, who wanders on the platform long enough to attract attention, but though he is warned by an onlooker to stay away from the track, nevertheless, 'With quick, but still with gentle and apparently unhurried steps, he walked down before the flying engine—and in a moment had been knocked into bloody atoms' (235). In short, he commits suicide, but though his death seems a just punishment for his actions, the combined brutality and scientific modernity of this final phrase perfectly sums up the conflicted attitude of the Victorians in the face of what was often called 'the railway monster'.

The Victorian novel thus manifests both the gains and losses associated with the railway, and with the increasing complexity of the industrialized world. In Mary Elizabeth Braddon's *Lady Audley's Secret* (1862), trains play an important role in allowing Robert Audley to pursue his investigation, and a 'Bradshaw' is an indispensible guide. Braddon notes:

> Robert had consulted a volume of *Bradshaw*, and had discovered that Villebrumeuse lay out of the track of all railway traffic, and was only approachable by diligence from Brussels. The mail for Dover left London Bridge at nine o'clock, and could be easily caught by Robert and his charge, as the seven o'clock up-train from Audley reached Shoreditch at a quarter past eight.[27]

Braddon's painstaking, one might even say unnecessary, level of detail about this element of the plot conveys a simple pleasure in mastering this modern discourse. At this

[26] Anthony Trollope, *The Prime Minister* [1871], 2 vols. (London: Oxford University Press, 1952); 2: 230.
[27] Mary Elizabeth Braddon, *Lady Audley's Secret* [1862], ed. David Skilton (Oxford: Oxford University Press, 1987), 382–83.

point in the novel, our respect for Audley has increased tenfold: a man who was once a useless and often inert dilettante, a reader of French novels, has become a dedicated and successful truth-seeker: his understanding of timetables helps him to nail the would-be murderer. Instead of relying on an obscure knowledge of, say, other languages, or other areas of expertise that might be provided by his education, Audley uses knowledge available to ordinary, middle-class readers. By integrating the railway into her plot, Braddon not only grounds her novel in realistic detail, but also aligns her hero with the train-going reader, and, by contrast, suggests the helplessness of the decaying aristocracy represented by the duped Sir Michael Audley.

And yet, Robert Audley hardly enjoys his train travels. Indeed, he often barely notices what's around him when he is on the train. We see in *Lady Audley's Secret*, and in the Victorian period more generally, the beginning of a recognizably modern attitude towards travel, in which the traveller does not focus on the journey, which seems too pass too quickly to absorb. Instead, the traveller attempts to pass the time in other ways. When the journey itself is described, it is usually in relation to a character's conversations or thoughts. Robert Audley's experience of a train journey that forms part of his investigation is conditioned by his mental efforts to make sense of a puzzling situation:

> The shrieking engine bore him on the dreary northward journey, whirling him over desert wastes of flat meadow-land and bare corn-fields, faintly tinted with fresh sprouting green. This northern road was strange and unfamiliar…and the wide expanse of the wintry landscape chilled him by its aspect of bare loneliness. The knowledge of the purpose of his journey blighted every object upon which his absent glances fixed themselves for a moment; only to wander wearily away; only to turn inwards upon that far darker picture always presenting itself to his anxious mind.[28]

While landscapes that mirror a character's innermost thoughts are as old as fiction itself, this passage is noteworthy in its interplay between Audley's harried mental state and the rapid, fragmentary nature of the scene that surrounds him. He is passively borne over an 'unfamiliar' landscape, but has no time to become familiar with it; his 'absent' glance lights on objects for a moment before wandering away. The description seems to locate this failure of attention in Audley, whose anxiety has 'blighted' everything he sees, but it also seems as if the unfixable vastness of the landscape that whirls past him augments his sense of powerlessness. The railway journey both represents and contributes to a sense of instability that results from Audley's sensory overload.

Many depictions of railway travel emphasize the dizzying, disorienting nature of the experience. Dickens's novels and essays include numerous references to railway travel that both celebrate the innovation it represents, and recognize the dangers inherent in its power. Although *Dombey and Son* centres on a shipping firm, and its plot depends

---

[28] Braddon, 242.

upon a number of maritime incidents, such as ships being lost and sailors presumed drowned, the novel is arguably more focused on the railway than on sea travel.

Among many references to the railway throughout *Dombey and Son*, three set-pieces offer contrasting visions of rail travel: the long passage in chapter 20 in which Dombey thinks about his lost son and sees the railway engine as an image of the 'remorseless monster, Death'; the elaborate description of 'Staggs's Gardens', a neighbourhood that 'had hesitated to acknowledge the railway in its straggling days ... and now boasted of its prosperous relation'; and the dramatic description, near the end of the novel, of Carker's ghastly death on a railway track.[29]

Each of these passages reinforces an already established set of associations, but cumulatively, they demonstrate the contradictions implicit in these associations. The railway was often described as a kind of monster, and depicted as such in contemporary cartoons, a characterization that conveyed its power, its danger, and the degree to which the rapid growth of the railway made it seem like a living entity. As Dombey muses about his son Paul, he sees a symbolic aspect to the journey he is taking: 'The very speed at which the train was whirled along mocked the swift course of the young life that had been borne away so steadily and so inexorably to its foredoomed end.' The predetermined itinerary of the rail journey becomes, here and elsewhere, an image for one's life's journey—a journey with only one possible destination. 'The power that forced itself upon its iron way—its own—defiant of all paths and roads, piercing through the heart of every obstacle, and dragging living creatures of all classes, ages, and degrees behind it, was a type of the triumphant monster, Death' (280). Here the democracy of travel ('all classes, ages, and degrees') turns into the inevitability of doom in all lives. This association is fully realized in chapter 55, when the fleeing Carker falls under a train, his last sight 'the red eyes, bleared and dim, in the daylight, close upon him', until he is 'beaten down, caught up, and whirled away upon a jagged mill, that spun him round and round, and struck him limb from limb ...' (779). The passage strikingly juxtaposes the familiar image of the train as a monster, whose red eyes seem to signal the deliberate attack of a sentient being, with an image of the train as a brutal machine that flings Carker's body mindlessly about. Though we may see this fate as a just punishment for the evil-doing Carker, we also recoil at the violence of his last moments, just as we feel repulsed by the description of Bill Sikes' death in *Oliver Twist*, which includes the image of his dog's brains being dashed out against the ground. [30]

The ambivalence we feel manifests itself also in the long passage Dickens devotes to describing the positive effect of a new railway in the area known as Staggs's Gardens. Its rotting houses, waste-heaps, and rutted roads were replaced by signs of prosperity

---

[29]   Charles Dickens, *Dombey and Son* [1848] (New York: Oxford University Press, 1974), 354, 218; subsequent citation appear in the text. On Staggs's Gardens and industrialism more generally, see Evan Horowitz's chapter below.

[30]   Some critics have seen the novel's explicit connection of the railway with death as an indictment of the industrial world. Others argue, such as Murray Baumgarten, argue that this 'linkage is subjective and takes place in Dombey's stunted imagination', 'Railway/Reading/Time: *Dombey & Son* and the Industrialized World', *Dickens Studies Annual* 19 (1990): 65–89, 71.

that encapsulate a burgeoning commodity culture: 'There were railway patterns in its drapers' shops, and railway journals in the windows of its newsmen. There were railway hotels, office-houses, lodging-houses, boarding-houses; railway plans, views, wrappers, bottles, sandwich-boxes, and timetables...there was even a railway time observed in clocks, as if the sun itself had given in' (218).

But Harland S. Nelson suggests that Dickens's description of Staggs's Gardens emphasizes a 'dehumanization of the neighborhood', showing the power of 'a great force that turns everything upside down in its passing', while F.S. Schwarzbach sees *Dombey and Son* as demonstrating 'Dickens's recognition of the revolutionary social importance of the railway and the developing industrial technology it symbolized', but suggests that the description of Staggs's Gardens displays a very equivocal optimism: 'The railway universe that replaces Staggs's Gardens may be for the best after all—perhaps.'[31]

The association of this modern technology with real physical danger was not unique to Dickens, but was perhaps felt more strongly given his own personal experience. In a famous postscript to *Our Mutual Friend*, Dickens refers to his involvement in the deadly Staplehurst accident on the South Eastern Railway in 1865, in which ten passengers were killed. Dickens escaped without injury, but re-entered his precariously dangling railway carriage to retrieve his manuscript of *Our Mutual Friend*. In a personal account of the accident in a letter to a friend Dickens also described his efforts to free fellow-passengers from the carriage. By identifying himself as Charles Dickens, he was able to claim the attention of a railway guard and persuade him to give up the key that was needed to unlock the doors of the carriage. He also assisted several dying passengers. Jill Matus sees this episode as symptomatic of a phenomenon she calls 'railway trauma', noting that railway accidents were seen as productive of a specific and identifiable psychological trauma in survivors, a form of trauma linked to the kind of 'overwhelming and unassimilable' events made possible by the material technologies of modernity.[32]

Train disasters came to seem routine enough to become a clichéd plot device in many late-century Victorian novels. George Gissing's *New Grub Street* (1891) for example, includes a down-on-his-luck doctor who explains that the source of his decline was the mental breakdown he suffered as a result of losing his wife and child in a rail accident: 'One minute I was talking with them...my wife was laughing at something I had said; the next, there were two crushed, bleeding bodies at my feet.'[33] There, the suddenness of the disaster reinforces the novel's relentless emphasis on the difficulty of controlling one's own career and destiny in the face of the larger social forces at work in the increasingly commercialized London of the novel.

---

[31] Harland S. Nelson, 'Staggs's Gardens: The Railway Through Dickens's World', *Dickens Studies Annual* 3 (1974): 41–53, 50, 52; F.S. Schwarzbach, *Dickens and the City* (London: Athlone Press, 1979), 113.

[32] Jill Matus, 'Trauma, Memory, and Railway Disaster: The Dickensian Connection', *Victorian Studies* 43 (2001): 413–36, 414–15; see also Matus, *Shock, Memory, and the Unconscious in Victorian Fiction* (Cambridge: Cambridge University Press, 2009).

[33] George Gissing, *New Grub Street* [1891], ed. Bernard Bergonzi (Harmondsworth: Penguin Books, 1968), 443.

In the train disaster, then, Gissing describes a common occurrence in daily life and gestures towards the railway's symbolic meanings. Where Dickens in Dombey and Son invites readers to see the train as an emblem of the inevitability of death, Gissing's train accident reveals the power of chance. The structure of 'One minute...the next', enacts the moment-by-moment unpredictability of late 19th-century life, and, by extension, modernity. But while Gissing's train accident signals unpredictability, it is precisely the ability to master travel, and exploit its predictability, that allows the vampire hunters to defeat Bram Stoker's Dracula. In some ways, Dracula brings us back to Lady Audley's Secret, where Robert Audley's understanding of train timetables helps him vanquish Lady Audley. So too Stoker depicts rail travel as a modern convenience that is critical to the heroes' ability to foil Dracula's plans. Not unlike Braddon in Lady Audley's Secret, Stoker grounds his supernatural tale in the details of train travel. The novel is obsessive in its insistence on recording characters' movements, both through descriptions of voyages by sea or rail, and through casual references to the timing of trains, as when Dr Seward says, 'I took my way to Paddington, where I arrived about fifteen minutes before the train came in.'[34] While it would be difficult to label a novel about the supernatural a work of realism, the book blends its fantastic story with a quasi-documentary emphasis on timetables, facts, and statements that gives it a surprisingly realistic feel.

As critics have noted, travel forms the central axis and motivation for the novel. Stephen Arata has suggested that Dracula, which appeared at a time of perceived 'cultural decay' in Britain, 'enacts the period's most important and pervasive narrative of decline, a narrative of reverse colonization'.[35] Arata sees the novel as a blending of two genres, the Gothic and the travel narrative, and points out that Jonathan Harker's journal description of his trip to Transylvania displays many of the standard tropes of Victorian travel. In fact, he argues that Harker and Dracula present mirror images of each other in their movement through the geography of the novel: Harker is an 'Orientalist travelling East', while Dracula is presented as an 'Occidentalist travelling West'.[36]

Stoker employs every form of travel imaginable to complete the book's journeys: Harker's journey to Transylvania, the Count's journey back, and the many trips taken by the friends of Lucy Westenra in the course of investigating the Count's movements and, finally, destroying him. The many choices available to the modern traveller are acknowledged in Mina's detailed memorandum on the subject of how Count Dracula might be expected to return: 'Ground of inquiry.—Count Dracula's problem is to get back to his own place...(b) How is he to be taken?—Here a process of exclusion may help us. By road, by rail, or by water?' (417).

While many of the book's most dramatic journeys are sea voyages, rail travel occupies a central thematic position. As Arata has noted, one of Harker's first meetings with

[34] Bram Stoker, Dracula [1897], ed. Maurice Hindle (Harmondsworth: Penguin Books, 2003), 262 ; subsequent citations appear in the text.
[35] Stephen D. Arata, 'The Occidental Tourist: Dracula and the Anxiety of Reverse Colonization,' Victorian Studies 33 (1990): 621–45, 623.
[36] Arata, 638.

the Count finds him reading, 'of all things in the world, an English Bradshaw's Guide' (34), which Arata sees as part of his successful impersonation of an English gentleman, a role which, as Harker himself demonstrates, includes a 'fetish for punctual trains'.[37] The Count himself makes good use of the rail networks, sending coffins of earth by the Great Northern Railway after they have arrived from overseas, their receipt at King's Cross Station dutifully noted by an exchange of letters between his solicitors and his shipping agents (119–20). Later, Harker is able to track Dracula through the King's Cross station master (272).

Mina Harker, in addition to being skilled in such areas of modern technology as type-writing and stenography, is also a self-described 'train fiend', able to inform Seward, having made a study of local timetables, that any train to Castle Dracula would 'go by Galatz, or any rate through Bucharest', and that the next train to Galatz leaves at 6:30 the following morning (402). Mina had noted earlier, after a conversation with Van Helsing: 'he was surprised at my knowledge of the trains offhand, but he does not know that I have made up all the trains to and from Exeter, that I may help Jonathan in case he is in a hurry' (224). Her facility in this regard aligns her with other modern, scientific approaches that are used against the ancient vampire.

The success with which the vampire-hunters exploit modern technologies of travel highlights Dracula's exclusion from the mobility that is a primary characteristic of the modern world. Because he is tied to the native earth he must sleep on during the day-light hours, he is, in Van Helsing's words, 'more prisoner than the slave of the galley, than the madman in his cell' (287). In the end, they manage to destroy the Count by denying him the resting place that he would need if he were to be transplanted to foreign soil, what Van Helsing calls 'his earth-home, his coffin-home, his hell-home' (287), and pur-suing him to his real home in Transylvania.

Full Speed Ahead: Steamships and Steam Launches

Though the railway stands as the ultimate symbol of speed in this period, the develop-ment of steam-powered ships offers a straightforward test case of the effect of taking an existing mode of travel and simply speeding it up. The new steamships travelled many of the same ocean routes that sailing ships had travelled, and steam launches the same river or canal waterways that smaller craft had travelled for centuries. Nevertheless, the speed with which these journeys could now be accomplished stood in stark contrast to the leisurely pace previously associated with water travel.

---

[37] Arata, 638.

Ships had always offered a practical way of transporting goods and people, and were the dominant mode of long-distance transportation before the coming of the railway. As ships became less necessary for utilitarian purposes, they became more highly valued for recreational purposes, and boat travel on small crafts became a very popular pastime over the course of the century. This form of travel changed rapidly, however, with the addition of steam.

The *SS Great Western* was the first purpose-built steamship to initiate regularly scheduled transatlantic crossings, starting in 1838, when it managed to cross the Atlantic in the unprecedented time of just under three weeks. Competing shipping lines soon sprang up, and in the 1840s, the Cunard Line ran *Britannia*-class steamships across the Atlantic on a highly dependable schedule dictated by government mail contracts. The *Britannia* and ships like it were smaller and less comfortable than the *Great Western*, and when Dickens and his wife crossed from Liverpool to Boston in 1842, he wrote that 'nothing smaller for sleeping in was ever made except coffins'.[38]

River journeys became a real tourist industry once steamers made these journeys faster, and railways made it easier to follow a river in one direction and return home. Dickens, Thackeray, and Trollope all took such journeys, and their travel notes and essays include detailed comparisons between the Thames, the Mississippi, and the Rhine. In their fiction, such trips represent early examples of a kind of banal tourism that was an entirely new cultural development. As James Buzard has shown, many forms of 19th-century travel had a self-consciously programmed quality to them, hence the recurrent image of 'the beaten track', which succinctly designates the space of the "touristic" as a region in which all experience is predictable and repetitive'.[39] Patrick Brantlinger has described a 'waning of adventure' in late 19th-century imperialism in terms that acknowledge the paradox: 'Despite or perhaps because of the greatness of the major Victorian explorers, exploration after the 1870s rapidly declined into mere travel, Cook's Tours came into vogue, and the "penetration" of Africa and Asia turned into a sordid spectacle of tourism and commercial exploitation'.[40] Short trips up the Thames might be a pale imitation of heroic explorations of the Nile, but they were certainly a cheaper and easier form of travel.

I begin here by looking at representations of one of the more exclusive forms of river travel, affordable only to the relatively wealthy. William Thackeray, who had travelled the Rhine as a young man in 1830, used it as a setting for fashionable travel in several of his novels. *Vanity Fair* includes the 'Am Rhein' chapter that describes the progress of Amelia, Jos, Georgy, and Dobbin through the Rhineland. Nobody says much about the scenery; Amelia sketches, Jos drinks, Georgy orders the servants about, and Dobbin follows faithfully behind. *The Newcomes*, too, features a Rhineland trip during which

---

[38] Charles Dickens, *American Notes for General Circulation* [1842] in *American Notes and Pictures from Italy* (New York: Oxford University Press, 1974), 3.

[39] James Buzard, *The Beaten Track: European Tourism, Literature, and the Ways to 'Culture' 1800–1918* (Oxford: Clarendon Press, 1993), 4.

[40] Patrick Brantlinger, *Rule of Darkness: British Literature and Imperialism, 1830–1914* (Ithaca: Cornell University Press, 1988), 37–38.

Clive sketches the scenery but finds Ethel even more picturesque. Thackeray wrote an entire novella, *The Kickleburys on the Rhine* (1850), satirizing the pretensions of British travellers taking a trip that had already become a touristic cliché. The ship's ambitious socialites, flirtatious daughters, and bored husbands conspicuously fail to enjoy, or even notice, any of the river's fabled sights. At Bonn, the narrator looks at the hotel register and notes, 'Why, everybody is on the Rhine! Here are the names of half one's acquaintance', confirming that the main purpose of the trip was to perform a standard social ritual.[41] Throughout *The Kickleburys on the Rhine*, Thackeray contrasts the idealized scenery through which the travellers pass with their mundane observations about the other passengers' clothing, or the quality of the beef served at dinner.

In contrast to the fashionable world of European tours represented by the Rhine, the Thames was a more workaday river, and depictions of the Thames in Victorian fiction have more middle- and working-class associations. Its status as a working river would be challenged, however, by the development of a craze for recreational boating on the Thames in the latter half of the century. As a major shipping artery, the London Thames had always been crowded with a variety of vessels, more so in the 18th and early 19th centuries than by the mid- to late-1800s. Britain's extensive canal network not only provided critical transport for goods, it contributed to a strong tradition of recreational boating that made the Thames a very popular destination for those seeking a brief outing. The railway made it possible to take a one-way boating excursion and return home by train, greatly increasing the popularity of day-long and multi-day boating trips. The upper waterways became more difficult to negotiate later in the century, as amateurs in small boats began to clog the river and steam launches entered the scene, much to the dismay of the small boaters.

Many accounts of river travel include hostile commentary on the growing nuisance presented by steam launches, which not only disrupted smaller craft with their large wakes, but also annoyed seekers of pastoral peace by transporting large and rowdy parties. Godfrey Turner describes them as 'the most unpopular and best-hated craft on the Thames', a 'one-sided convenience, esteemed by the selfish, the lazy, and the fast'.[42] Charles Dickens Jr's *Dictionary of the Thames*, written by the son of the novelist in 1887, refers slightingly to the 'people who pay their L5 5s. a day for the hire of a launch, and whose idea of a holiday is the truly British notion of getting over as much ground as possible in a given time'.[43]

As many contemporary cartoons demonstrate, steam launches were seen as catering to a more mixed population than other forms of tourist travel. Given the limited holiday time available to the working classes, and the effort made to tempt them into

[41] William M. Thackeray, *The Kickleburys on the Rhine. By M.A. Titmarsh* (London: Smith, Elder, 1850), 33.

[42] Godfrey Turner, quoted in *The Royal River: The Thames from Source to Sea* (London and New York: Cassell and Co., 1885), 169.

[43] Charles Dickens Jr (the Younger), *Dickens's Dictionary of the Thames* (London: Macmillan, 1887). Facsimile rpt. Old House Books, Moretonhampstead, 1994), 237.

steam and rail excursions with cheaper fares, one- or two-day boat excursions certainly had great appeal for workers and their families, as well as for aspirants to middle-class gentility who could afford a few days on the Thames more easily than a month on the Rhine. The rhetoric of the steam-launch debate not only echoed the class fears raised by cheap excursion trains, it may seem familiar to 21st-century readers accustomed to the debates played out today between cross-country skiers and snowmobilers, or canoers and jet-skiers. Genteel travellers rowing traditional Thames boats maintained their right to a quiet, peaceful river environment, while proponents of the steam launches argued for easier, more rapid access to the river for larger groups of people.

Among river purists, the preference for speed was perceived as a threat to the entire ethos of recreational travel. The speed of the steam launch is not the utilitarian speed of efficient commuter transportation to a specific and necessary destination, but speed primarily for its own sake, for the pleasure of dramatic movement and the sensation of mastering the terrain that passes so quickly. From the point of view of those with time to spare, the primary virtues of paddling or canoeing upriver are the enforced slowness of the pace, the peaceful ambience, the relative isolation, and the opportunity, even necessity, of looking thoughtfully at the slowly changing scene. The exciting pace, rapidly shifting landscape, and highly social atmosphere of the steam launch seemed a rejection of the very values that drew boaters to the Thames to begin with.

Though printed commentary and satiric cartoons in this period universally condemn steam launches and the inconsiderate louts riding them, this mode of river travel increased dramatically in popularity during the 1870s and 1880s. Perhaps the most realistic perspective is provided by Jerome K. Jerome, author of the humorous bestseller *Three Men in a Boat* (1889). While rowing his own boat, his narrator complains endlessly about the launches, and humorously describes his own deliberate efforts to get in the way of steamers; but he later appreciates the convenience of getting a tow from a friend's steam launch, and then complains, with self-conscious irony, about the 'wretched small boats' that keep blocking their way.[44]

Some river enthusiasts objected to steam launches on principle, not just because of their effect on other boats, but because it was felt that they provided an inferior experience to the passengers themselves. As James Buzard notes of 19th-century travel in general, 'critics tended to hold the tangible evidence of modernization in travel (improved roads, carriages, steamboats, railways) responsible for destroying the true character of travel…they allegedly laid waste the self-improving potential of valid travel'.[45] As different as Thackeray's travel on the Rhine is from Jerome's day on the Thames, both Thackeray and Jerome suggest that river travel had become a parody of itself, and that the actual experience seldom matched the idealized image of cultured recreation associated with it.

---

[44] Jerome K. Jerome, *Three Men in a Boat; Three Men on the Bummel* [1889, 1890], ed. Geoffrey Harvey (Oxford: Oxford University Press, 1998), 137.

[45] Buzard, *Beaten Track*, 32.

DECLARATION OF INDEPENDENCE: THE BICYCLE CRAZE

Few inventions of the period had a more revolutionary effect than the simple piece of technology known as the 'safety bicycle'. The 19th century saw refinements of bicycle design that turned it from a dangerous novelty item into a popular form of individual transport. Its contribution to increased mobility for women in particular made it a cultural icon in the 1880s and 1890s. Earlier in the century there had been brief vogues for 'pedestrian curricles' or 'velocipedes', then for the high-wheeler known as the 'penny-farthing'. But the development of a steel-framed, chain-driven, well-balanced, rubber-tyred machine that could be mass produced at reasonable cost made bicycles enormously popular among young adults, particularly in urban areas. The fact that it offered women an opportunity to travel long distances without male escort, and without negotiating public transit, led to its identification with the emergence of what was called the 'New Woman', the modern woman of the *fin de siècle*. The 'New Woman' might be a suffragette, a typist, or simply a young woman with more independent aspirations than in the past. But this new image or stereotype of female assertiveness was strongly identified with the development of the bicycle. American feminist Susan B. Anthony famously said, in an interview published in the *New York World* of 2 February 1896:

> Let me tell you what I think of bicycling. I think it has done more to emancipate woman than any one thing in the world. I rejoice every time I see a woman ride by on a wheel. It gives her a feeling of self-reliance and independence the moment she takes her seat; and away she goes, the picture of untrammelled womanhood.[46]

The independence afforded by bicycle travel is evident in a number of Conan Doyle stories. Most obviously, 'The Adventure of the Solitary Cyclist' hinges on the independence, but also vulnerability of a young woman who is followed by a man on a bicycle when she cycles to the train station for a weekly visit home. 'The Adventure of the Priory School' includes a controversial deduction by Holmes asserting that the direction of a bicycle can be determined by its tracks; numerous fans have debated the plausibility of his deduction. Doyle himself was well known as a cycling enthusiast. He cycled regularly, and wrote: 'I can only speak words of praise for the bicycle, for I believe that its use is commonly beneficial and not at all detrimental to health, except in the matter of beginners who overdo it.'[47]

---

[46] 'Champion of Her Sex', *New York Sunday World* (2 February 1896): 10.

[47] Arthur Conan Doyle, 'Cycling Notes', *Scientific American* (18 January 1896): 38. According to David Herlihy, in *Bicycle: The History* (New Haven: Yale University Press, 2006), 227, Doyle and his wife enjoyed riding a tandem bicycle together.

Given George Gissing's interest in the position of women in *fin-de-siècle* British culture, it is not surprising that bicycles are commonplace in his works. One short story
features an assertive young woman who fits the New Woman image: 'The baronet's
daughter had come into town on her bicycle, as was declared by the short skirt, easy
jacket, and brown shoes, which well displayed her athletic person. She was a tall, strongly
built girl of six-and-twenty, with a face of hard comeliness and magnificent tawny hair'.[48]
The young woman's bicycle may be a source of independence, but it is also a class marker
that creates a conflict with the story's heroine, the well-educated and equally independent, but less well-off daughter of the lodge-keeper. The baronet's daughter's sneer about
those who can't afford bicycles leads May to shut the lodge gate in her face when she
cycles through, and she is forced to apologize to the haughty young woman in order to
keep her father from losing his job as lodge-keeper. While the other forms of transportation we have seen have tended to enlarge the travel options of middle- and working-class
people, the bicycle is here presented as something of a luxury.

This sense of the bicycle as a trendy luxury item is reinforced by Jerome K. Jerome,
who followed up on the enormous success of *Three Men in A Boat* with his 1900 book,
Three Men on the Bummel, which features a cycling tour in Germany. As in his earlier
work, Jerome shows a knack for catching the wave of a current trend. The contemporary
bicycle craze is well represented in discussions of different brands of bicycles and the
various features that are advertised. When Harris walks in with a cycling-paper in his
hand, the narrator immediately says, 'Leave it alone.' When Harris asks what he means, J.
replies: 'That brand-new, patent, revolution in cycling, recordbreaking, Tomfoolishness,
whatever it may be, the advertisement of which you have there in your hand.' Harris
responds defensively, 'If every man talked like that there would be no advancement
made in any department of life. If nobody ever tried a new thing the world would come
to a standstill.' But J. reminds him how he was nearly blown up by a 'patent-lamp'.[49] Here,
the bicycle seems to be the Victorian equivalent of an iPad or flat-screen TV; a new piece
of technology that inspires men to want upgrades.

ABOVE THE FRAY: HOT-AIR BALLOONS

The bicycle gave Victorians another way to get around, and yet the view they took in
from the bicycle could not have been markedly different from that which they might see
from a coach or slow train. But another new form of travel offered both a slow, peaceful
journey and unique perspective that had never before been seen. With the expansion of
hot-air balloon flights from the early 1800s onward, people were able for the first time

---

[48] George Gissing, 'A Daughter of the Lodge', in *A House of Cobwebs, and Other Stories* (London:
Archibald Constable and Co., 1906), 182.

[49] Jerome K. Jerome, *Three Men in a Bummel* (Rockville, MD: Serenity, 2009), 31.

to see what the world looked like from the air. Though the number of actual balloon travellers was relatively small, descriptions and illustrations of the experience proliferated rapidly, and it soon became commonplace to talk about the panoramic views of major cities that were now available. James Glaisher, whose 1871 book *Travels in the Air* is the most comprehensive account of ballooning experiences from this period, describes the view from the balloon as 'like a grand natural panorama'.[50] This broad, topographic perspective allows him to see the relationship between the centre of the city and the suburbs, the city and the country, this country and its neighbour across the channel. Balloon travellers often described London as being like a vast map or model, its constituent parts visible for the first time. These descriptions of broad, panoramic vistas soon appeared in fictional worlds as well.

Elaine Freedgood, in *Victorian Writing about Risk*, suggests that the popularity of balloon travel reflects its status as a leisurely alternative to the rapid pace of modern life: 'Ballooning not only became a means of escape from new and restrictive configurations of time and space, it also provided access, albeit brief, to a region of the air that was unsullied by the pace of activity on the ground'.[51] While balloonists were hailed as heroes, balloon travel was not itself difficult; it was a pleasant, passive activity that offered the opportunity to distance oneself from the hubbub of modern life. For the Victorian novelist, it provided a model for the kind of perspective that allowed them to look into the hearts and lives of many different characters from the omniscient perspective of a narrator like, for instance, 'Boz'.

The frontispiece to Dickens' *Sketches by Boz* (1836), which depicts a balloon ascending into the air while the crowd below looks up in admiration, suggests that the author intends to present a kind of panoramic overview of the London scene. Cruikshank's drawing portrays Boz as a lofty presence surveying a world that cannot be viewed in its entirety by those who live in it, but must be seen from above to be fully comprehended. This image provides a concrete personification of the omniscient narrative voice of the 19th-century novel. The panoramic visual perspective embodied in accounts of balloon journeys finds its parallel in the characteristic narrative perspective of Victorian fiction.

The sense of Olympian detachment from the world that pervades many balloon accounts offers a possible model for the famous passage in Thomas Hardy's *Tess of the D'Urbervilles* that compares Tess to a fly. At the end of a description of Tess's descent into the Valley of Froom, Hardy writes: 'Not quite sure of her direction Tess stood still upon the hemmed expanse of verdant flatness, like a fly on a billiard-table of indefinite length, and of no more consequence to the surroundings than that fly'.[52] The idea of humans seeming like flies to greater powers is not new, of course. In the Preface to later editions of *Tess*, Hardy uses the Shakespearean quotation 'as flies to wanton boys are we to the

---

[50] James Glaisher, *Travels in the Air* (London: Richard Bentley, 1871), 20.
[51] Elaine Freedgood, *Victorian Writing about Risk: Imagining a Safe England in a Dangerous World* (Cambridge: Cambridge University Press, 2000), 81.
[52] Thomas Hardy, *Tess of the D'Urbervilles* [1891] (London: Macmillan, 1912), 136.

gods;/They kill us for their sport' to illuminate his controversial closing statement to the novel, that 'The President of the Immortals' had 'ended his sport with Tess'.[53] Hardy's image has a specifically visual quality, however, that seems indebted to the aerial perspectives that had become familiar to himself and his readers. The reader is forced to move from the 'bird's-eye perspective before [Tess]'[54] to a bird's-eye perspective that includes Tess, thus positioning himself or herself somewhere above the action of the novel—though, of course, this seemingly superior position offers us no fuller understanding of Tess than any other position in the novel.

Balloon travel is explicitly invoked in a well-known passage from Charlotte Brontë's *Villette* (1853) where Brontë's famously retiring heroine, Lucy Snowe, talks about the effect of her assuming a masculine role in the school vaudeville. Lucy has not only performed the male part with enthusiasm, she has followed her performance by extraordinarily bold remarks in a discussion with her friend Dr John:

> ...for the second time that night I was going beyond myself—venturing out of what I looked on as my natural habits...On rising that morning, had I anticipated that before night I should have acted the part of a gay lover in a vaudeville; and an hour after, frankly discussed with Dr. John the question of his hapless suit, and rallied him on his illusions? I had no more presaged such feats than I had looked forward to an ascent in a balloon, or a voyage to Cape Horn.[55]

Lucy has generally preferred the role of spectator to that of spectacle, yet she takes pleasure in having this role temporarily inverted. Brontë links the image of a balloon ascent with an allusion to 'rounding the Horn', a famously difficult feat of maritime navigation, to convey Lucy's astonishment at the action she has performed. The absurdly exaggerated images magnify the distance between Lucy's normal, restricted sphere of action and the expanded world of masculine exploration that provides a stage for such heroic exploits. Like a balloon journey, Lucy's theatrical experience allows her to see beyond her usual horizon.

Balloon travel was frequently compared to another typically Victorian activity associated with travel: the viewing of enormous panoramas depicting popular landscape scenes. Panoramas were so popular in the 19th century that many cartoons and essays satirized the 'panoramania' that seemed to have gripped the country. Dedicated venues were built to exhibit 360-degree, circular panoramas that allowed dozens of spectators at a time to stand in the middle of a huge room and imagine that they were looking at Paris, Bombay, or the Alps. Moving panoramas, scenes which were slowly unrolled to convey the sense of a journey, were also frequently displayed in London and elsewhere.

---

[53] Hardy, *Tess*, 449.
[54] Hardy, *Tess*, 133.
[55] Charlotte Bronte, *Villette*, ed. Herbert Rosengarten and Margaret Smith (Oxford: Clarendon Press, 1984), 211.

The sprawling vistas typically depicted in these huge paintings owed much to the aerial views publicized by balloon travellers, and such representations were part of a trend that was manifested also in the popularity of magic lantern slides, stereoscopic views, and other forms of optical technology that catered to a growing demand for 'virtual travel': for representations, in literature and in other media, that imaginatively transport the reader to another place.[56]

As we have seen, the Victorian age saw enormous changes in transportation technology. The increased mobility of people of all classes is reflected in the wider canvas of the fiction of the period, and contributed to the evolution of literary realism, a genre dedicated to showing, not idealized characters and situations, but ordinary people, and realistic places. As the Victorians expanded their own orbits, they expanded the borders of their fictional universes as well. At the same time, they were keenly aware that the changes represented by industrialization and modernity also had the potential to diminish the value of the individual and weaken the bonds of community. Thus, their representations of the new technologies that enabled these changes embody the same contradictions as travel itself: in the Victorian novel we see that travelling by railway, steamship, bicycle, or balloon is always a journey to the unfamiliar, but one that in the end evokes a new understanding of one's own place in the world.

Suggested Reading

Buzard, James. *Disorienting Fiction: The Autoethnographic Work of Nineteenth-Century British Novels*. Princeton: Princeton University Press, 2005.

——. *The Beaten Track: European Tourism, Literature, and the Ways to 'Culture' 1800–1918*. Oxford: Clarendon Press, 1993.

Byerly, Alison. *Are We There Yet? Virtual Travel and Victorian Realism*. University of Michigan Press, 2013.

Daly, Nicholas. *Literature, Technology, and Modernity, 1860–2000*. Cambridge: Cambridge University Press, 2004.

Freedgood, Elaine. *Victorian Writing About Risk: Imagining a Safe England in a Dangerous World*. Cambridge: Cambridge University Press, 2000.

Freeman, Michael. *Railways and the Victorian Imagination*. New Haven and London: Yale University Press, 1999.

Jennings, Humphrey and Mary-Lou Jennings. *Pandaemonium, 1660–1886: The Coming of the Machine Age as Seen by Contemporary Observers*. London: Papermac, 1995.

Kern, Stephen. *The Culture of Time and Space, 1880–1918*. Cambridge: Harvard University Press, 2003.

Matus, Jill. *Shock, Memory, and the Unconscious in Victorian Fiction*. Cambridge: Cambridge University Press, 2009.

---

[56] I explore this idea in detail in *Are We There Yet? Virtual Travel and Victorian Realism*, as well as in "'A Prodigious Map Beneath His Feet': Virtual Travel and the Panoramic Perspective', *Nineteenth-Century Contexts* 29 (June/September 2007): 151–69.

Menke, Richard. *Telegraphic Realism: Victorian Fiction and Other Information Systems*. Palo Alto: Stanford University Press, 2008.

Schivelbusch, Wolfgang. *The Railway Journey: Trains and Travel in the Nineteenth Century*. Translated by Anselm Hollo. Originally published as *Geschichte der Eisenbahnreise*, 1977. Oxford: Basil Blackwell, 1980.

15

VICTORIAN PHOTOGRAPHY
AND THE NOVEL

JENNIFER GREEN-LEWIS

'As I never saw my father or my mother, and never saw any likeness of either of them (for their days were long before the days of photographs), my first fancies regarding what they were like, were unreasonably derived from their tombstones.' Pip's interesting parenthetical on the first page of *Great Expectations* (1861) reminds the reader of a small but significant fact about the time 'long before the days of photographs': for the vast majority of people, the pre-photographic age was also the age of posthumous visual oblivion. Retaining a visible presence after death, or simply when absent, was, before the 1840s, largely the prerogative of the well-to-do, as well as some middle-class people who could afford to be painted, sketched, or silhouetted. Pip's long dead working-class parents have left no visual marker of themselves, other than their one remaining child; hence, his imaginative association of them, and his dead siblings, with their gravestones.

Pip's aside reminds us that for a great number of people in the mid-19th century, the most significant function of the photograph was to counter death; its magical promise was not merely to arrest time, but to visually restore time's lost subjects to their loved ones. The camera's early use as a means of recording the likeness of a dead child makes sense in this context (Figure 15.1), as does the later popularity of spirit photography. Such images were powerful embodiments of loss and desire visibly fused by a significantly *invisible* technology. Indeed, the invisibility of the images' means of production— the absence of authorial intrusion in the form of, say, stylistic interference—was initially an important contributor to their emotional force as well as their indexical authority. Daguerreotypes and calotypes did more than merely image the dead; for their possessors, they affirmed the once unmediated physical presence of their subjects as surely as a fingerprint, and kept them visually in the present tense.

It is, of course, a desire for visual presence that occasions Pip's mention of photographs in *Great Expectations*, but the reference may also have been a nod to Dickens's close friend Chauncey Hare Townshend, the person to whom *Great Expectations* is dedicated, and, according to Mark Haworth-Booth, the foremost collector of photographs

FIGURE 15.1 Anonymous, tintype of child, post-mortem. Stanley Burns Tintype Collection, Gernsheim Collection, Harry Ransom Humanities Research Center, The University of Texas at Austin.

in Britain at the time after the Prince consort. Townshend's fascination with visual objects of all kinds is suggested by the contents of his study, which apparently included 'a hand glass, a brass kaleidoscope, five stereoscopes…a large stereoscope, and cases of stereoscopic slides (both glass and mounted on card)'.[1] Dickens's own interest in photography as a curiosity is suggested by the publication of several articles on the subject during his tenure as editor of *Household Words*. His gifts to Townshend included not only the original manuscript of *Great Expectations*, but also a crystal ball, reflecting their shared interest in alternative ways of seeing the world: a world that might be broken by Townshend's kaleidoscope into splinters of colour, or magnified by the glass, or given depth and dimension by the stereoscope, so that the past or the future—perhaps most

---

[1] Mark Haworth-Booth, ed., *The Golden Age of Victorian Photography 1839–1900* (New York: Aperture, 1984), 118.

especially the past—might be glimpsed and recalled by the technologically enhanced workings of the human eye.

Much as photography was a symbol of modernity, its earliest subjects suggested another source of its fascination. Daguerre's famous images of fossils (1839), like Fox Talbot's calotypes of the bust of Patroclus (1843), or mid-century images of ancient ruins by photographers such as Francis Frith, Constantine Athanassiou, Maxime Du Camp, and Armand Pierre Seguier, embodied an extraordinary confrontation of the ages (Figures 15.2–15.5). Through photography, modernity was at the service of antiquity, able to preserve it for generations to come; as Baudelaire wrote, it might 'rescue from oblivion those tumbling ruins, those books, prints and manuscripts which time is devouring, precious things whose form is dissolving and which demand a place in the archives of our memory'.[2] Indeed, many pioneer Victorian photographers had their cameras focused on the past as an antidote to forgetting, a remedy for that dissolution of form to which Pip's parents and siblings have succumbed in *Great Expectations*.[3]

Richard Terdiman writes that the Victorians worried 'intricately about *forgetting*' and argues, moreover, that their fears took literary form in the plots of their novels, which 'present themselves as the diegesis of history's stress: much more under the sign of a tense exploration of the past's disjunction from the present than under the more traditional guise of rehearsing some consecrated mythology symbolic of the community's consciousness of itself'.[4] Novelistic representation of the present moment's relationship to past history, in other words, increasingly reflected a view of the Victorian present as newly and disturbingly discontinuous from the past.

Is it possible to imagine an artefact that more cogently expresses and defies physical and temporal discontinuity than a photograph? The *fact* of the photograph affirms the moment's having ceased to be, its pastness; its separation from present flux. At the same time, the *experience of reading* the photograph affirms the opposite: the subject exists in the ever present. Elizabeth Barrett's sense of the daguerreotype in 1843 as a human 'facsimile' ('It is not merely the likeness which is precious ... but the association and the sense of nearness involved in the thing ... the fact of the very shadow of the person lying there fixed for ever!')[5] was shared by many, as sales figures for daguerreotypes throughout the 1840s attest. It is hardly surprising that early photography shows a heightened sensitivity to the ambiguities of its mnemonic relationship to the passage of time, both in its choice of subject matter as well as its early critical discourse. Indeed, as this chapter will suggest, photography's most significant contribution to the 19th-century novel may

---

[2] Charles Baudelaire, 'The Salon of 1859', reprinted in *Photography in Print: Writings from 1816 to the Present*, ed. Vicki Goldberg (New York: Simon and Schuster, 1981): 123–26, 125

[3] For a discussion of Victorian photography's interest in old things, see Green-Lewis, '"Already the Past": The Backward Glance of Victorian Photography', *English Language Notes* 44, no. 2 (Fall/Winter 2006): 25–43.

[4] Richard Terdiman, *Present Past: Modernity and the Memory Crisis* (Ithaca, NY: Cornell University Press, 1993), 14, 25.

[5] Haworth-Booth, 25.

FIGURE 15.2 Louis Jacques Mandé Daguerre, *Collection de coquillages et divers*, 1839. ©Musée des arts et métiers-CNAM, Paris/photo Studio CNAM.

lie in the structure that the cultural response to it provided for organizing our thoughts about the past.

While all creative work of the period must be considered within the wider culture of realism, the rapid rise and extraordinary reach of Victorian photography gave a particular substance and shape to that culture's relationship with notions of the real. What the novel represented even by mid-century was a world in which photography had already begun to shape the experience of being human. Further, photography was not merely another, new, way of representing reality; it actually provided many of its viewers with a *standard* of what was real. Whether Victorian authors made self-conscious use of photography or not, the works they produced were subject to that standard; the degree to which their novels seemed 'real' was at least in part a result of their relationship to photography's peculiar, yet familiar, register. Nancy Armstrong proposes that by the mid-1850s, 'fiction equated seeing with knowing and made visual information the basis for the intelligibility of a verbal narrative'; as a result of this, 'In order to be realistic, literary realism referenced a world of objects that either had been or could be photographed.'[6] Most Victorian viewers seem at least initially to have regarded photographs as reliable

---

[6] Nancy Armstrong, *Fiction in the Age of Photography: The Legacy of British Realism* (Cambridge and London: Harvard University Press, 1999), 7.

FIGURE 15.3 William Henry Fox Talbot, *Bust of Patroclus* (*The Pencil of Nature*, 1844–46, Plate V). Gernsheim Collection, Harry Ransom Humanities Research Center, The University of Texas at Austin. File # 964:0340:0005.

testimony to the real world, and thus as affirming a view of that world as visually accessible, and thereby both knowable and, to some degree, stable. Fiction's occasional engagement with the subject of photography or its makers suggests an interest in the material culture of the modern world as well as an ongoing preoccupation with the interplay among images, words, and things.

But Victorian fiction's very attention to that interplay—its consideration of the complexities of truth-telling, as well as the creativity and unpredictability of this visual medium whose limits were as yet unknown—suggests that photography's appeal was also due to its imaginative association with the *un*known, the *un*real, the *un*stable. Certainly, photography's relationship to the workings of memory, as metaphor, vehicle, and symbol, seems to have been fed by its metaphysical as well as its empirical associations. In thinking through the ways in which photography shaped the Victorian novel it is important to acknowledge its play with dreams and desires—its conceptual power—as well as its material presence and documentary capabilities, and to recognize that its shaping force in nineteenth-century literature was, as a result, far from uniform.

Photography was not the only cause of, or symbol for, Victorian literature's heightened visual sensitivity. As critics have effectively demonstrated, a whole range of optical

FIGURE 15.4 Francis Frith, *The Statues of the Plain, Thebes*, 1858. Gernsheim Collection, Harry Ransom Humanities Research Center, The University of Texas at Austin. File # 964:0495:0016.

technologies helped develop and ready a nation of observers; the Victorians were fully prepared to read Daguerre's images by the time of their public introduction in 1839.[7] Further, by the mid-1850s, the experience of reading photographs was part of ordinary life. Novels were being produced for, and consumed by, an increasingly middle-class population for whom a photograph was fast becoming both symbol and substance of reality. If novels were to render the lived reality of their readers they must depict the visible world; and to be visible, as indeed, to be memorable, at mid-century, was to be both photographable and photographed.

This is no mere metaphor, though photography's metaphorical reach is striking. When the critic Elizabeth Rigby praised *Vanity Fair* (1848) for being 'pre-eminently a novel of the day...a literal photograph of the manners and habits of the nineteenth century,

---

[7] See Jonathan Crary, *Techniques of the Observer: On Vision and Modernity in the Nineteenth Century* (Cambridge, MIT Press, 1990). For a useful accounting of the 19th-century expansion of visual technologies see Joss Marsh, 'Spectacle', in *A Companion to Victorian Literature and Culture*, ed. Herbert Tucker (Malden, MA and Oxford: Blackwell, 1999): 276–88.

FIGURE 15.5 Francis Frith, *The Hypaethral Temple, Philae*, 1857. Gernsheim Collection, Harry Ransom Humanities Research Center, The University of Texas at Austin. File # 964:0495:0010.

thrown on to paper by the light of a powerful mind',[8] she seems to be commenting on that novel's similarity to real life, its documentary faithfulness, as though the novel were a kind of window on the real world. Stylistically speaking, *Vanity Fair* is probably not what a modern reader would call photographic: it makes little pretence at the objectivity or authorial distance that supposedly characterizes a photograph. Thackeray's narrator intrudes at various moments, both visually (in illustrations) and textually (in digressions, asides, and commentary). The novel is farcical, over-the-top, and its puppet characters are hardly lifelike. For the postmodern reader, *Vanity Fair's* brand of realism is more theatrical than photographic; its recital of a world of stuff is full of the pleasures of association and unruly imagination, and offers none of the tidy visual-linguistic correspondences that might today be identified as 'documentary'—if, in fact, that's what Elizabeth Rigby meant by 'literal photograph'.

[8] Elizabeth Rigby, '*Vanity Fair*—and *Jane Eyre*', *Quarterly Review* 84, no. 167 (December 1848): 153–85, <http://faculty.plattsburgh.edu/peter.friesen/default.asp?go=252> (accessed February 2010).

But perhaps it is worth asking what exactly Rigby *did* mean? If we borrow Charlotte Brontë's famous distinction that, because it lacked 'sentiment' and 'poetry,' she found Jane Austen's writing to be 'more real than true,'[9] perhaps it was not that Rigby found *Vanity Fair real* but that she found it *true*; that Thackeray engaged with more than merely surface realities and instead rendered substantive truths about human beings. Rigby's metaphor, in fact, may express a view of photography as something that disrupts or intensifies our understanding of the world, as much as it may be said to reflect it.

Brontë herself turned to the camera for a metaphor, when she tried to describe the kind of detail she found in Austen; but unlike Rigby, her choice conveys disappointment rather than enthusiasm: 'I had not seen *Pride and Prejudice*', she wrote, 'and then I got the book. And what did I find? An accurate daguerrotyped [*sic*] portrait of a common-place face; a carefully fenced, highly cultivated garden, with neat borders and delicate flowers; but no glance of a bright vivid physiognomy, no open country, no fresh air...', Brontë concludes, 'Miss Austen is only shrewd and observant.'[10] For Brontë, Austen's faithfulness to detail aligns her with the science, and not the art, of representation; her accomplishment is merely technical, and thus limited. The accuracy of the daguerreo-type is small virtue, given what Brontë perceives as a significant lack in Austen of emotional realism.

The point here is obviously not whether a camera-made image is either or more true or real, but that by 1848, the year in which both Rigby and Brontë wrote, photography evidently provided a model of representation against which literature might be mean-ingfully measured. The idea that literature might be like a photograph, for better or worse—that, in fact, thinking about a photograph might help the reader think about writing—suggests a newly energized effort to describe the progress of realism in gen-eral and the novel in particular.[11] In her own exploration of the relationship between images and 'abstract or collective terms' (as she terms it, 'the picture writing of the mind'), George Eliot famously wrote of Dickens that 'while he can copy Mrs. Plornish's collo-quial style with the delicate accuracy of a sun picture...he scarcely ever passes from the humorous and external to the emotional and tragic, without becoming as transcendent in his unreality as he was a moment before in his artistic truthfulness.'[12] (As with Brontë and her Austen-as-daguerreotype metaphor, what Eliot deems 'photographic' in Dickens

---

[9] Brontë to George Lewes, 18 January 1848, in *The Letters of Charlotte Brontë*, vol. 2: 1848–1851, ed. Margaret Smith (Oxford: Clarendon Press, 2000), 14.

[10] Brontë to George Lewes, 12 January 1848, in *The Letters of Charlotte Brontë*, 10.

[11] The effort to describe the work of realism in terms of the visual arts may have been energized by photography, but it was of course far from new, painting having previously provided critics with analogies for describing a work's achievement. See, for example, Walter Scott's review of Austen's *Emma* (1816), a novel which recalled for him 'the merits of the Flemish school of painting'; or Anna Barbauld's 1804 characterization of Richardson as having 'the accuracy and finish of a Dutch painter' (both quoted in Ruth Bernard Yeazell, *Art of the Everyday: Dutch Painting and the Realist Novel* (Princeton, NJ: Princeton University Press, 2008), 1–2).

[12] George Eliot, 'The Natural History of German Life', [1859] in *Selected Essays, Poems and Other Writings*, ed. A.S. Byatt (London: Penguin Classics, 2005), 107, 111.

suggests limited, rather than comprehensive, truths. Dickens has, as it were, an eye (or an ear) for the outer; he can 'copy' as well as a camera can; but he is blind (or deaf)— 'transcendent in his unreality'—in his efforts to convey the inner life. A similar note was struck by a less exalted critic in the *North British Review* (1845) who complained of

> ludicrous minuteness in the trivial descriptive details [which] induces us to compare Mr. Dickens' style of delineation to a photographic landscape. There, everything within the field of view is copied with unfailing but mechanical fidelity. Not a leaf, or stone, or nail is wanting, or out of place; the very bird is arrested as it flits across the sky...He lavishes as much attention on what is trivial or useless as on the more important part of the picture, as if he could not help painting everything with equal exactness.[13]

The analogy was a popular if occasionally pejorative one: in *Bleak House*, a reviewer for the *Illustrated London News* (1853) found 'many intellectual daguerreotypes to carry away'.[14] 'So crowded is the canvas which Mr. Dickens has stretched and so casual the connexion that gives to his composition whatever unity it has', ran another unsigned review of the novel in the *Spectator*, 'that a daguerreotype of Fleet Street at noon-day would be the aptest symbol to be found for it; though the daguerreotype would have the advantage in accuracy of representation.'[15] Dickens's prose is figured as the consequence of a kind of literary accident, as though the author has set his camera down and merely taken everything before it with minimal editorial interference—and not before, curiously, having stretched a painter's canvas for his 'composition'. Here, as elsewhere at mid-century, the reviewer of fiction slides without comment between the figurative languages of painting and photography. Just as the *North British Review* finds Dickens cannot help 'painting' something that looks like 'a photographic landscape', so 'canvas' serves the *Spectator*'s *reviewer* as the initial metaphor, ultimately trumped by 'daguerreotype'. Rather than making obsolete or superseding the writing-as-painting metaphor, photography seems, initially at least, to have merely offered another version of it.

Meanwhile canvas, daguerreotype, and novel alike all appear to overwhelm with their excessive detail, notwithstanding the fact that a 'profound fascination with precision' was 'a dominant characteristic of Victorian intellectual life'.[16] Certainly, photography's contribution to seeing and documenting was reified for many in its astonishing detail. Writing in 1859, Oliver Wendell Holmes recorded his wonder that his

> stereoscopic views of the arches of Constantine and of Titus give not only every letter of the old inscriptions, but render the grain of the stone itself. On the pediment

---

[13] Thomas Cleghorn, 'Writings of Charles Dickens', *North British Review* (May, 1845): 186–91; Philip Collins, ed., *Dickens: The Critical Heritage* (London: Routledge, 1971), 190.

[14] Unsigned review, *Illustrated London News* (September 24, 1853), 247; Collins, 282.

[15] George Brimley, from an unsigned review, *Spectator* (September 24, 1854): 923–25; Collins, 284.

[16] Haworth-Booth, 10.

of the Pantheon may be read, not only the words traced by Agrippa, but a rough inscription above it, scratched or hacked into the stone by some wanton hand during an insurrectionary tumult.[17]

As one practitioner enthused in 1853:

> Not only does [the daguerreotype] delineate every object presented to its operation, with perfection in proportions, perspective, and tint...but it delineates objects which the visual organs of man would overlook, or might not be able to perceive, with the same particularity, with the same nicety, that it depicts the most prominent feature in the landscape.

In this way the camera is superhuman: 'it acts with a certainty and extent, to which the powers of human faculties are perfectly incompetent. And thus may scenes of the deepest interest, be transcribed and conveyed to posterity, not as they appear to the imagination of the poet or painter, but as they actually are.'[18]

The writer's evaluation of daguerreotypes as things 'as they actually are' implies a belief that reality resides in the details, a belief shared by many viewers similarly delighted by the newly enhanced power of the eye. 'I once looked at a small daguerreotype of a landscape through a magnifying glass', wrote a reviewer in 1854 for the American children's magazine *The Schoolmate*; 'every little object appeared distinct and life-like. The leaves could be plainly seen upon the trees, and little birds appeared upon the branches, which no one supposed were in the picture. In a distant house, every brick could be counted.'[19]

Delight in the counting of tiny bricks and birds and, by extension, in the potential visual accumulation of all the small things that ultimately make up the larger world, was matched by excitement at new mobility and depth of vision. The visual prosthetic of the camera (and, in turn, of the magnifying glass held over the daguerreotype) allowed the human gaze to explore the world more thoroughly than it ever had, both up close and at a distance; photography enabled the gaze to go, indeed, as far as the moon itself. As the *Schoolmate* article goes on to explain:

> Mr. Whipple, the daguerreotypist of Boston, has been very successful in daguerreotyping the moon...[his] crystalotype of the moon ranks among the wonders of the age, and, by its easy reproduction, enables every person, whose cultivated taste leads them to care for such things, to possess a picture of the moon, actually drawn by herself. The picture, let us observe, is a faithful copy of the lunar

---

[17]   Oliver Wendell Holmes, 'The Stereoscope and the Stereograph' [1859], reprinted in Goldberg, 100–114, 108.

[18]   A. Bisbee, *The History and Practice of Daguerreotyping* [1853] (New York: Arno, 1973): 19–20.

[19]   'Daguerreotypes of the Moon', *The Schoolmate* (January 1854) 75, <http://www.merrycoz.org/smate/MOON.HTM> (accessed February 2010).

features—as faithful as an ordinary daguerreotype of a friend's face. Nothing more curious has ever fallen under our notice.[20]

The celebration of the moon's 'self-portrait', and its rhetorical erasure of the famous photographer, John Adams Whipple, in the process, has a fairly obvious counterpart in theories of literary realism that overlook the 19th-century novel's self-consciousness about authorial agency. Indeed, it is easy to see how the history of the novel has collided with the history of photography most frequently in discussions that centre on the representation of the object world, which is commonly assumed to be the subject or primary domain of realism. In their identification of certain works as more real than others ('more real than true'), many Victorian readers assented to views of the world that appeared to correspond with photography's own. When photographs show up as objects in novels, are given as gifts, passed around among characters, or propped on mantelpieces, they signal adherence to a standard of verisimilitude in representation. But they also suggest their author's self-consciousness about the status of the novel itself as a representing object in competition with other such objects. The novelistic use of photographs as symbolic furniture, tokens of reality, functioned much as brand-names do in novels today: photographs 'fixed' their owners in terms of taste and aspiration by situating them temporally and economically.

Sherlock Holmes's pursuit of a compromising photograph in 'A Scandal in Bohemia' (1891) embeds the short story in its age, Conan Doyle's plot hanging on the detail that a cabinet photograph is too big to fit in a lady's purse. Like the photograph of Mrs Manston in Hardy's *Desperate Remedies* (1871), Irene Adler's image is as much a product and marker of modern material culture as it is the object of pursuit and desire. Likewise with Amy Levy's *The Romance of a Shop* (1888), a novel which is remarkable largely for its treatment of photography as a valid and workable career choice. Levy's story concerns four sisters who set up a studio and become photographers after they are left penniless on the death of their father. While the women shock their aunt and provide some small scandal for the neighbourhood with their decision to support themselves by working, photography itself does not seem to be itself the cause of eccentricity—indeed, even after her marriage, one sister, Lucy, maintains a successful photographic practice of her own. Photography rather provides independence, and serves primarily to identify the women as modern, as does Levy's practice of frequently quoting recent fiction. One could argue, in fact, that Levy's style is where photography really leaves its mark on *The Romance of a Shop*, its many cultural references creating a collage of contemporary tastes and

---

[20] John Adams Whipple's 'yankee ingenuity' was arguably best demonstrated by his installation of a 'steam engine in his gallery to run the buffers, heat the mercury, fan the clients waiting their turn, and revolve a gilded sunburst over the street entrance', Beaumont Newhall, *The History of Photography* (New York: Museum of Modern Art, Little, Brown, 1986), 33. He was not the first to train his camera on the moon, however: Douwe Draaisma notes that the first daguerreotype of the moon was made as early as 1840 by John William Draper: Douwe Draaisma, *Metaphors of Memory: A History of Ideas About the Mind*, trans. Paul Vincent (Cambridge: Cambridge University Press, 1995), 116.

technologies. Each chapter is marked with epigraphs, and characters continually recall snippets of poems and novels, including works by Brontë and Eliot. Gertrude (if this were *Little Women*, she would be Jo), reads *The British Journal of Photography*; there is mention of lithographs, slides, and sketches; Lucy's future husband, Frank Jermyn, is an engraver for a newspaper called *The Woodcut*, and a war correspondent.

Largely because of these references, presumably reflecting Levy's interest in the material details of the lives of her characters, the novel has the same flat quality as Wells's later *Tono-Bungay* (1909), which is similarly shaped by its author's attention to surface verisimilitude. Perhaps it is unsurprising that, in the decades after the daguerreotype had yielded in popularity to the reproducible photograph, ekphrastic appearances of the photograph rarely convey Elizabeth Barrett's feelings of 'association' and 'nearness'. Although Hardy's short story 'An Imaginative Woman' (1898) offers a notable exception in its play with the magically fertile image of the poet Robert Trewe, in his novels photographs are as likely to emphasize a public as a private relationship and embody distance rather than intimacy, while the careless marketing or dissemination of photographs by their owners (as in *Jude the Obscure*, 1895) seems to symbolize the characters' modernist rootlessness. In Hardy, to own a photograph is not necessarily to know its subject, but rather the reverse, affirming Daniel Novak's claim that for some Victorians, 'rather than capturing identity, photography effaces it'.[21]

Curiously, it is Levy, however, and not Hardy, whose work directly engages with photography's primary work of memorialization. When, in *The Romance of a Shop*, Gertrude is assigned to photograph the recently deceased Lady Watergate, Levy's description of the corpse essentially reproduces the image Gertrude is about to make: 'A woman lay, to all appearance, sleeping there, the bright October sunlight falling full on the upturned face, on the spread and shining masses of matchless golden hair.'[22] Gertrude's assignment is not to document the fact of death. Although on occasion post-mortem photographs might show their subjects in their coffins, the dead were more frequently represented, like Lady Watergate, 'to all appearance, sleeping'—in the case of children, often in their mother's arms. Gertrude's job is rather to bear photographic witness to the fact that the subject had once *lived*. As an essayist in 1889 put it, 'faces vanish like the dreams of night /But live in portraits drawn by beams of light'.[23] The post-mortem photograph was not a truth-teller so much as an aide-mémoire: a means of recalling a subject and resisting a loss.

Hard as it is to document specific changes in readers' memory-making processes throughout the 19th century, it is arguable that how they reconstructed and recollected

[21] Daniel Novak, *Realism, Photography, and Nineteenth-Century Fiction* (Cambridge: Cambridge University Press, 2008), 118.

[22] Amy Levy, *The Romance of a Shop* [1888], ed. Susan David Bernstein (Ontario, Canada: Broadview, 2006), 86.

[23] Friese Green, 'Fox Talbot: His Early Experiments', *The Convention Papers,* supplement to *Photography* 1.36 (1889): 6. Quoted in Jennifer Green-Lewis, *Framing the Victorians: Photography and the Culture of Realism* (Ithaca, NY: Cornell University Press, 1996), 44.

their pasts is just as significant for a history of literary realism as the degree to which realism references objects in a recognizable world. Certainly the Victorian novel's preoccupation with themes of identity, inheritance, memory, and loss, marked a shift in habits of viewing and remembering that were permanently fused by the advent of photography. While literary realism, as Armstrong argues, 'showed readers how to play the game of modern identity from the position of observers',[24] modern identity also necessitated engagement with the images not merely of things, but of things recalled. Part of the connective tissue among Victorian readers was the shared experience of observing *and* remembering.

Gertrude's photograph of the deceased clearly enacts that experience, and indeed the passage concludes with another version of it: Gertrude-as-camera takes a mental photograph of the grieving husband. His face 'formed a picture which imprinted itself as by a flash on Gertrude's overwrought consciousness, and was destined not to fade for many days to come'.[25] Levy's conflation of photograph with both memory and the flash of sudden insight is suggestive, though, by 1888, unoriginal: Henry James had already crafted a scene for Isabel Archer in *Portrait of a Lady* (1881) in which a moment of great insight impresses itself upon the passive but receptive heroine: 'the thing made an image', wrote James, 'lasting only a moment, like a sudden flicker of light'.[26] In fact, flash lighting was for a long time part of the concept, if not the practice, of photography. Fox Talbot published an announcement of his own experiments with artificial light—'illuminating [subjects] with a sudden electric flash'—as early as 1851.[27] And in his reading of *Bleak House* (1852–53), Ronald Thomas finds evidence that Dickens's famous detective, Inspector Bucket, with his sudden mental flashes of insight, 'stands in for the dreamed-of but as yet unrealized photographic technology in the novel'.[28] While the technology of flash itself continued to evolve (flash powder, for example, was not developed until the late 1880s), so the 'language of flash', as Kate Flint terms it, became 'both the language of revelation and recollection'.[29] With or without flash, James's and Levy's metaphor of mind as

[24] Armstrong, 26.

[25] Levy, 87.

[26] Henry James, *A Portrait of a Lady* [1881], eds. Geoffrey Moore and Patricia Crick (New York: Penguin, 1983), 408.

[27] 'On the Production of Instantaneous Photographic Images', *Athenaeum* (December 6, 1851), cited in Ivan Kreilkamp, 'One More Picture: Robert Browning's Optical Unconscious', *ELH* 73 (2006): 409–34, 427.

[28] Ronald Thomas, 'Making Darkness Visible: Capturing the Criminal and Observing theLaw in Victorian Photography and Detective Fiction', in *Victorian Literature and the Victorian Visual Imagination*, ed. Carol Christ and John O Jordan (Berkeley: University of California Press, 1995): 134–68, 144. Haworth-Booth makes a similar argument about Inspector Bucket's 'enumerative, all-encompassing sort of vision', 19–20.

[29] Kate Flint, 'Photographic Memory', *Romanticism and Victorianism on the Net* 53 (February 2009), <http://id.erudit.org/iderudit/029898ar> (accessed February 2010). In her reading of Levy's novel, Flint notes that early experiments with *blitzlichtpulver*, 'the first widely used flashpowder', was 'enthusiastically written up in the photographic press…in language that…drew parallels between the science of photography and the sudden, awe-inspiring shock of illumination produced by natural lightning' (9).

a receptive photographic plate is a historically appropriate if essentially unaltered component of Aristotle's metaphor of memory as a drawing or imprint, which was popular during the 18th century and still much in use throughout the 19th.

The degree to which Victorians believed those images to be 'fixed' on memory's plate varied. Writing in 1846 of some spectacular scenery in Scotland, Dickens's friend Townshend was 'quite sure that the impression upon my mind, made by what I beheld yesterday, can never be effaced'.[30] In his 1856 work on the physiology of memory, J.W. Draper found photography to be a useful metaphor for the permanence of memory: 'I believe that a shadow never falls upon a wall without leaving thereupon its permanent trace—a trace which might be made visible by resorting to proper processes. All kinds of photographic drawing are in their degree examples of the kind'.[31] The critic E.S. Dallas's conception of mind in *The Gay Science* (1866) as gateway to a repository of memory similarly affirmed the permanence of mental impressions: 'Absolute as a photograph, the mind refuses nought. An impression once made upon the sense, even unwittingly, abides for ever more'.[32] Even if those impressions were not readily available to the mind, they continued to exist. Hermann Ebbinghaus argued in 1885 that 'Mental states of every kind ... which were at one time present in consciousness and then have disappeared from it, have not with their disappearance absolutely ceased to exist'; instead, 'they continue to exist, stored up, so to speak, in the memory'.[33]

As prevalent throughout the Victorian period, however, was the concern with memory's impermanence, a fear effectively expressed well before photography's invention in the memorable terms of John Locke that 'The pictures drawn in our minds, are laid in fading colors'.[34] This was, of course, the primary challenge for photography's pioneers; much of the early narrative of photographic history concerns their initial failures to preserve its magical images and implicitly affirms the superior lasting power of both paintings and novels. In *The Pencil of Nature* (1844–46), Fox Talbot wrote of his desire to fix the 'fairy pictures' of a camera obscura, 'creations of a moment, and destined as rapidly to fade away'.[35] And indeed, his ultimate success in 'the art of fixing a shadow' was a triumph of will over mutability: at last, he wrote, 'we may receive on paper the fleeting shadow, arrest it there and in the space of a single minute fix it there so firmly as to be no more capable of change'.[36]

Levy does not say what became of Lady Watergate's portrait, whether it was displayed on the piano, or hidden away in a drawer. As photographic prints superseded

    [30] Haworth-Booth, 14.

    [31] Draaisma, 120.

    [32] Kate Flint, *The Victorians and the Visual Imagination* (Cambridge: Cambridge University Press: 2000), 143.

    [33] Herman Ebbinghaus, *Memory: A Contribution to Experimental Psychology* [1885], trans. Henry Ruger and Clara Bussenius (New York: Dover, 1964), 1.

    [34] John Locke, *An Essay Concerning Human Understanding* (1689), ed. Kenneth P. Winkler (Indianapolis: Hackett, 1996), 61.

    [35] Newhall, *History*, 19.

    [36] W.H. Fox Talbot, 'Some Account of the Art of Photogenic Drawing', *London and Edinburgh Philosophical Magazine and Journal of Science* 14 (March 1839), reprinted in Goldberg, 36–48, 41.

daguerreotypes in private collections, however, a popular new option for storage and retrieval emerged. A Victorian descendant of the scrapbook, the photograph album rendered the passage of time both as object and narrative, giving shape and solidity to the mysterious and life-conferring act of recollection. Albums were, as Patrizia Di Bello writes, 'an important aspect of the visual culture of the time, crucial sites in the elaboration and codification of the meaning of photography, as a new, modern visual medium'. Women's private albums in particular, which frequently included materials and techniques from scrapbooking, 'operated as tactile as much as visual objects. They juxtapose photographic images and other mnemonic traces, always pointing to some-thing that no longer is—as it was when photographed—with the here-and-now of tactile experience.'[37]

Looking ahead to the end of the 19th century and the commercialization of the hand-held camera, Nancy West writes that 'Kodak taught amateur photographers to apprehend their experiences and memories as objects of nostalgia, for the easy availabil-ity of snapshots allowed people for the first time in history to arrange their lives in such a way that painful or unpleasant aspects were systematically erased.'[38] It seems equally plausible that Kodak's success in this regard lay in a thriving album culture ready to accommodate its images.

Dickens makes no reference in *David Copperfield* (1850) to the camera or its artefacts, but stylistically there is no mistaking the shift into photography's present tense. The past, accessible throughout the novel in pictorial form, is both stable and determinate. Take, for example, the visual album of school memories that David shows us in chapter 7. In this early retrospective, a mature David is recalling his school days to the reader as a series of individual images that gain resonance because of the repetitive ritual of their display: 'Here I sit at the desk again', he begins; and then, 'Here I sit at the desk again'; 'Here I am in the playground'—and so on.[39]

The novel's shift to the present tense is markedly pictorial in its effect; the stasis of the moment out of narrated time emphasizes the image; but here it is primarily the *repetition* of images that produces, and reproduces, the sensation of remembering. Twenty-two chapters later, David makes similar use of visual repetition in his depiction of Steerforth asleep. The moment, chronologically, precedes David's knowledge of his friend's future betrayal, but in formal terms it already contains the weight of its future significance: 'I was up with the dull dawn', David recalls, 'and, having dressed as quietly as I could, looked into his room. He was fast asleep; lying, easily, with his head upon his arm, as I had often seen him lie at school.' Just in case we haven't picked up on the visual alert,

[37] Patrizia Di Bello, *Women's Albums and Photography in Victorian England: Ladies, Mothers and Flirts* (Hampshire, England: Ashgate, 2007), 2, 3.

[38] Nancy Martha West, *Kodak and the Lens of Nostalgia* (Charlottesville, VA: University Press of Virginia, 2000), 1.

[39] Charles Dickens, *David Copperfield* [1850], ed. Jerome H. Buckley (New York and London: Norton, 1989), 83. Subsequent citations appear in the text.

he adds: 'The time came in its season, and that was very soon, when I almost wondered that nothing troubled his repose, as I looked at him. But he slept—let me think of him so again—as I had often seen him sleep at school' (370). This is, of course, déjà-vu, with its immediate recall of the phrase 'as I had often seen him lie at school', and its echo of the end of chapter 6 when David watches Steerforth asleep, 'his head reclining easily on his arm'; but it also contributes to the final accretion of the fully realized image in chapter 55 of the drowned Steerforth on the beach, who lies 'with his head upon his arm, as I had often seen him lie at school' (81, 669).

David's self-consciousness about such moments is marked, as noted above, by a shift in tenses that occurs whenever moments are taken out of narrative progression. Similar 'album scenes' in fact occur regularly throughout the novel, stylistically set off from the text but also flagged for the reader by their chapter titles: 'A Retrospect'; 'Another Retrospect'; 'A Last Retrospect'. The first titled retrospect is another one of school days, individual moments lifted from 'the silent gliding on of my existence—the unseen, unfelt progress of my life...'. Looking 'back upon that flowing water', David seeks for representative images of his life, 'marks along its course, by which I can remember how it ran'. We see him first as a boy in the Cathedral; we move from that moment to a later one when 'I am higher in the school'. Time steals on, he writes, 'unobserved'; there is 'A blank... and what comes next! *I* am the head boy, now...' (230, 231). And so on. In discrete moments—moments presented visually to the reader as optical rather than lived experience—David recounts his 'progress to seventeen'. Time is, in this way, observed.

The death of Dora also gets its own album of visual moments: chapter 53 shifts to the present with the framing device of a pause: 'there is a figure in the moving crowd before my memory, quiet and still, saying... Stop to think of me—turn to look upon the little blossom, as it flutters to the ground!'(643). The cessation of narrative ('I do. All else grows dim, and fades away. I am again with Dora...') is once again pictorially defined against the more generalized past. In Dora's album, David separates out the times of day ('It is morning' gives way to 'It is evening' and the inevitable 'It is night'), naturalizing Dora's death, but rendering her progress towards it in static terms, like a narrative painting, or a series of photographs that may be made to tell a story. At the end, memory fails: 'for a time', concludes the chapter, 'all things are blotted out of my remembrance' (648).

The novel thus reproduces David's past not as process, but rather in the form of images that do not change. The moments are unaltered, as static and as monumental as David's last glimpse of his mother at the gate as he heads off to school. 'I was in the carrier's cart when I heard her calling to me', he recalls. 'I looked out, and she stood at the garden gate alone, holding her baby up in her arms for me to see. It was cold still weather; and not a hair of her head, or a fold of her dress, was stirred, as she looked intently at me, holding up her child.' Here the stillness of the day provides the visual conditions for producing the fixed moment to which David will return—as, indeed, he immediately does: 'So I lost her. So I saw her afterwards, in my sleep at school—a silent presence near my bed—looking at me with the same intent face—holding up her baby in her arms' (110). The reproduction of the image through, as it were, instant replay—a visual echo—produces both the déjà-vu of memory and the burden of hindsight on which much of the emotional force of the novel rests.

It is not a coincidence that this overtly pictorial novel should be so equally overtly engaged with the work of revisiting and reconstructing the past. Pictorialism in novels—the descriptive making of scenes, in which readers and sometimes narrators are positioned as observers, such as the opening of *Adam Bede* (1859), for example—is frequently an occasion for reflection on the relationship of present to past, as though such reflection can only take place out of the normal pace of narrative. Scene making of the kind that Dickens does, when (say) in *David Copperfield* he alerts the reader to a painting by Ostade as a way of imagining the emigrants below deck, about to set sail, frames moments that already have a cultural freight attached to them. For Dickens in this instance, as for George Eliot generally, it is painting and not photography that invites reflection. Certainly, the formative presence of painting in Victorian novels can hardly be over-emphasized. Its language and its metaphors; an interest in scale, perspective, and the use of colour; the inclusion of painting as a subject and artists as characters— these are everywhere in the pages of Victorian fiction, poetry, and literary criticism.[40]

In such an intensely visually oriented culture, it is hardly possible to fully separate out photography's influence on the novel as distinct from the many other popular visual technologies of the period. Nonetheless, the ubiquity of photographs, coupled with their specifically mnemonic emphasis, meant that during the last half of the 19th century, almost all Victorians experienced visual access to their individual and collective pasts. It is arguably as a result of that access—which so effectively naturalized the relationship between reading images and remembering—that photography became an inextricable part of the novel's own history.

For the novel, of course, depends very heavily on memory, and not just textual memory, but also memory of our own perceptions. Reading novels is a process of recall as well as of recognition, in which readers are asked to remember their own experiences and emotions, in order to imagine something like them.[41] It is logical that any implicit direction that readers might receive from a novel on how to imagine a perception (David's last sight of his mother, for example) would be shaped by contemporary visual technology, because any such direction must depend upon historically and culturally determined mental processes of creating images. Put simply: our image-making mental processes when we read are deferential to those processes by which we make images when we're *not* reading.

Looking at photographs, which was a popular pastime by the mid-century, and in a matter of decades part of ordinary daily existence in a commercial culture, dramatically shaped those image-making mental processes. Maurice Halbwachs has argued that 'No

---

[40] For an overview see Jeffrey Spear, 'The Other Arts: Victorian Visual Culture', in *A Companion to the Victorian Novel*, ed. Patrick Brantlinger and William B. Thesing (Malden, MA: Blackwell, 2002), 189–206. For recent more in-depth discussions of the formative role of painting and illustration in Victorian novels, see Kate Flint, *The Victorians and the Visual Imagination*; Julia Thomas, *Pictorial Victorians: The Inscription of Values in Word and Image* (Athens, OH: Ohio University Press, 2004); and Ruth Bernard Yeazell.

[41] See Elaine Scarry's discussion of novels as structures of production that aim to give rise to the perception of what is imitated—*Reading by the Book* (New Jersey: Princeton University Press, 2001).

memory is possible outside frameworks used by people living in society to determine and retrieve their recollections.'[42] If he is right, then it is surely no exaggeration to say that for much of the Victorian period, photography was part of the framework of determination and retrieval that made memory possible. *David Copperfield*'s invitation to read and reread images from David's memory and its fascination with stilled moments textually framed, were informed by a culture which had already recast the activity of reading pictures of the past in photography's terms. *David Copperfield* self-identifies as a realist text, not because Dickens renders a world of things that corresponds precisely to his readers' world of objects—in fact, he doesn't—but because David's mode of envisioning his world corresponds to the Victorians' own practices of looking at images. Nineteenth-century readers had a way of understanding, or making sense of, David's memories, forged by the culture of looking—looking at albums, at magic lantern shows, at stereographs, panoramas, and visual wonders of all kinds—of which photography was, by the mid-century, the most popular and widely disseminated form. The practice of keeping scrapbooks and photographic albums is thus one obvious model for David's form of memorializing.[43] Through the borrowed practice of cutting out moments from the flow of time, and inserting them into spaces to be both read and reread, *David Copperfield* implicitly identifies the stasis of pictures with the past, and invites a nostalgic response to them.

Indeed, nostalgia, with its 'retrospects, expectations, ellipses, elisions, reminders', its 'languages of time', as Nicholas Dames puts it, seems to be both the emotional context and purpose of this particular novel.[44] For as much as novels generally depend, as noted earlier, on memory, so Victorian novels also depend, as Dames shows so well, on memory's failure. The 'nostalgic evasion' of truth that he argues characterizes the Victorian period,[45] and the frequent substitution for it with something more pleasing, both central to the workings of nostalgia generally, are on display in *David Copperfield*, whose pictorial moments serve as substitutes for the original. By the time David writes of the memory of Steerforth asleep with his head on his arm, Steerforth is dead and gone; he is shrunk to the dimensions of a single image, forever young and innocent, forever a schoolboy. David's memory-picture of Steerforth is an example of forgetting posing as remembering, just as the stasis of his memory of Clara Copperfield, 'holding up her baby in her arms', allows David to forget her real failure as a mother to protect him from the abuses of Mr Murdstone.[46]

---

[42] Maurice Halbwachs, *On Collective Memory*, trans. Lewis Coser (Chicago: University of Chicago Press, 1992), 43.

[43] For discussion of the culture of the album see Alan Thomas, *The Expanding Eye: Photography and the Nineteenth-Century Mind* (London: Croom Helm, 1978), 43–64; and Patrizia Di Bello.

[44] Nicholas Dames, *Amnesiac Selves: Nostalgia, Forgetting, and British Fiction, 1810–1870* (Oxford: Oxford University Press, 2001), 11.

[45] Dames, 11.

[46] Nicholas Dames has observed that a 'peculiarity unique to Victorian narratives' is 'the equation of remembrance to a pleasurable sort of forgetting' (5). Certainly the poignancy of Steerforth's death depends upon that 'pleasurable sort of forgetting'.

It is as though Dickens has taken a leaf out of a book by Henry Peach Robinson, one of the best-known and most successful Victorian pictorial photographers. 'The pleasures of memory are enormously increased', wrote Robinson in one of his many practical works for the aspiring photographer, 'if to your mental picture-gallery you can add a gallery of truthful aids to memory'. But then he goes on to argue for the benefits of selective recall. The art of photography, he argues, has no obligation to be anything but beautiful; and 'Memory, like the sundial, need mark no hours but the bright ones.'[47] Not for Robinson the post-mortem photograph; notwithstanding his famous and much discussed play on the genre with the exhibition of his photograph 'Fading Away' (1858), his energies were consciously directed away from the perceived unpleasantness of both the modern and the real.[48] As he lamented, 'A passion for realism is the affectation of the hour in art and literature, and is making some of our novels so dirty—in the name of art—that one scarcely likes to mention even the titles of them' (65). At the same time, however, Robinson's work was frequently textually inspired; the art of photography, he felt, lay in its 'poetry, sentiment, story'—what he called the 'literary part of a picture'.[49]

Robinson's work, remarkable for its extensive use of combination printing, provides an interesting visual analogue for *David Copperfield*'s series of images in chapter 64, 'A Last Retrospect'. Combination printing involves making multiple prints from a variety of negatives out of which the final image is crafted, and involves extensive manipulation (in the form of scissors, glue, masking tape, and additional exposures) on the part of the photographer.[50] Rather than offering the reader a linear, or chronologically driven, conclusion, David follows instead Robinson's practice of reducing 'temporal links to spatial contiguity', as Novak describes it,[51] lifting his characters out of their chronological narrative to relocate them in the present as collage. David looks back 'once more—for the last time—before I close these leaves', to give the reader what is functionally a combination print: 'I see myself, with Agnes at my side...I see our children and our friends around us...' (734). Each image is held before the reader, in apparently random order: 'Here is my aunt...here comes Peggotty...I see an old man making giant kites...Who is this bent lady...what English lady is this...', and so on, in a triumphant present tense of just desserts that ends with the face of Agnes. Robinson's early defence of his photographic manipulations ('I maintain that I can get nearer to the truth...with several negatives than with one')[52] speaks to his belief in the centrality of agency in successful photography, the essential fictionalizing that is necessary to effective truth-telling. In the cutting

[47] H.P. Robinson, *The Elements of a Pictorial Photograph* [1896] (New York: Arno, 1973), 138.

[48] For an extended reading of Robinson's most infamous work, see Jennifer Green-Lewis, 'Not Fading Away: Photography in the Age of Oblivion', *Nineteenth-Century Contexts* 22 (2001): 559–85.

[49] Robinson, *Elements*, 13–14.

[50] See Beaumont Newhall's description of the extraordinarily painstaking details involved in making some of the more ambitious images, such as Oscar Rejlander's 'The Two Ways of Life' (1857); Newhall, *History*, 74.

[51] Novak, 14.

[52] Robinson, 'Composition NOT Patchwork', *The British Journal of Photography* 7: 121 (July 2, 1860), 190. Quoted in Novak, 4.

and the pasting, the re-photographing, Robinson's aim was, he later wrote, 'not truth exactly, much less fact; it is effect'.[53] Fiction and reality in his photographs are neither distinct nor fully independent of each other; to the pictorial photographer, as Novak asserts, 'photographic fictions are both *more* realistic and more *photographic*'.[54]

David Copperfield's final juxtaposition of images results in a peculiar disruption of temporality, a kind of levelling of pictures to the absolute present, which participates in the aesthetics of Robinson's combination printing, as well as those of the photo-collage in the private album. Somewhere between the prescribed spaces of the later snapshot albums and the earlier free play of the scrapbook, the popular practice of photo-collage offers another model for thinking about photography's potential in the creation of *unreality*, or indeed representational anarchy. The social context of Victorian photo-collage (like much of Dickens's work) is both comedic and performative. As Marta Weiss notes:

> Often displayed in fashionable drawing rooms, these volumes belonged to the same atmosphere of performance and sociability as tableaux vivants and the photographs they inspired…not only was the construction of a photo-collage comparable to other photographic practices that combined the apparently factual medium of photography with fictional subject matter, but motifs of performance—from the enactment of social roles to more overt forms of theatricality—also recurred in many of these albums.[55]

But where does this leave the Victorian reader of *David Copperfield*, who is also the reader of albums and collages, of publicly displayed combination prints and privately possessed post-mortem photographs, of glass-covered daguerreotypes and paper photographic prints? If we consider Dickens's grand finale of portraits in that novel as a kind of literary collage or combination print, why is the reading experience not disrupted or undermined by the synaptic chaos of the closing chapter?

Perhaps it is that long-time readers of serialized works enjoyed this kind of repetitive contact with the familiar images of persons. Perhaps, more subtly, it has something to do with the kind of forgetting that reading any novel necessitates. After all, 'novelistic totality', as Novak persuasively argues, depends on 'the ability to forget both the text's composite history and the reader's role in constructing the text through the act of reading'.[56] Reading Victorian novels, as much as it requires some feat of memory—all those characters! all those plots!—also engages us in some feat of forgetting; a naturalization, as it were, of the highly acculturated act of reading at a given moment in history. The naturalization of the photograph in the process of reading images from one's past

[53] Robinson, *Elements*, 81.
[54] Novak, 4.
[55] Marta Weiss, 'The Page as Stage', in *Playing with Pictures: The Art of Victorian Photocollage*, Elizabeth Siegel, with essays by Patrizia Di Bello and Marta Weiss (Art Institute of Chicago and Yale University Press, 2010), 37–48, 37.
[56] Novak, 32.

involves a similar suspension of memory, if not an absolute forgetting of our own status as reading subjects. In addition to its function as a cipher of modernity, its metaphysical playfulness, and its work as a normative standard of visual representation, photography may have shaped the Victorian novel most by providing it with structures for reading, retrieving, and organizing the past, thus giving us, as well as the Victorians, a formal way of thinking about identity through time.

Suggested Reading

Armstrong, Nancy. *Fiction in the Age of Photography: The Legacy of British Realism*. Cambridge and London: Harvard University Press, 1999.

Bisbee, A. *The History and Practice of Daguerreotyping* [1853]. New York: Arno, 1973.

Conan Doyle, Arthur. *Sherlock Holmes: The Major Stories with Contemporary Critical Essays*. Edited by John Hodgson. Boston and New York: Bedford Books, 1994.

Dames, Nicholas. *Amnesiac Selves: Nostalgia, Forgetting, and British Fiction, 1810–1870*. Oxford: Oxford University Press, 2001.

Di Bello, Patrizia. *Women's Albums and Photography in Victorian England: Ladies, Mothers and Flirts*. Hampshire: Ashgate, 2007.

Dickens, Charles. *David Copperfield* [1850]. New York and London: Norton, 1990.

———.*Great Expectations* [1861]. New York and London: Penguin Classics, 1996.

Draaisma, Douwe. *Metaphors of Memory: A History of Ideas About the Mind*. Translated by Paul Vincent. Cambridge: Cambridge University Press, 1995.

Ebbinghaus, Herman. *Memory: A Contribution to Experimental Psychology* (1885). Translated by Henry Ruger and Clara Bussenius. New York: Dover, 1964.

Flint, Kate. 'Photographic Memory'. *Romanticism and Victorianism on the Net* 53 (February 2009). <http://id.erudit.org/iderudit/029898ar> (accessed February 2010).

———. *The Victorians and the Visual Imagination*. Cambridge: Cambridge University Press, 2000.

Goldberg, Vicki, ed. *Photography in Print: Writings from 1816 to the Present*. New York: Simon and Schuster, 1981.

Green-Lewis, Jennifer. *Framing the Victorians: Photography and the Culture of Realism*. Ithaca, NY: Cornell University Press, 1996.

Haworth-Booth, Mark, ed. *The Golden Age of Victorian Photography 1839–1900*. New York: Aperture, 1984.

Kreilkamp, Ivan. 'One More Picture: Robert Browning's Optical Unconscious'. *ELH* 73 (2006): 409–34.

Levy, Amy. *The Romance of a Shop* [1888]. Edited by Susan David Bernstein. Ontario: Broadview, 2006.

Newhall, Beaumont, ed. *Photography: Essays and Images*. New York: Museum of Modern Art, 1980.

———. *The History of Photography*. New York: Museum of Modern Art. New York: Little, Brown, 1986.

Novak, Daniel. *Realism, Photography, and Nineteenth-Century Fiction*. Cambridge: Cambridge University Press, 2008.

Terdiman, Richard. *Present Past: Modernity and the Memory Crisis*. Ithaca, NY: Cornell University Press, 1993.

Weiss, Marta, 'The Page as Stage'. *Playing with Pictures: The Art of Victorian Photocollage.* Elizabeth Siegel, with essays by Patrizia Di Bello and Marta Weiss. Art Institute of Chicago and Yale University Press, 2010, 37–48.

West, Nancy Martha, *Kodak and the Lens of Nostalgia.* Charlottesville, VA: University Press of Virginia, 2000.

PART V

THE MIDDLE

16

NOVELS OF THE 1860S

JANICE CARLISLE

Britain in the 1860s produced a strikingly high number of inventions and innovations, and it witnessed an impressive variety of inaugurations. Among the many that might be cited are these representative instances. In the area of technology and transport: the laying of the North Atlantic cable and the building of the first all-iron warship, the opening of the first station on the London underground, and the commencement of the Thames embankment. In labour relations: the initial efforts at collective bargaining, the founding of the London Trades Council, and the first meetings of the Trades Union Congress and of the First International. In commercial and industrial endeavours: the opening of the first department store in London, the founding of Morris, Marshall, Faulkner, & Co., as well as the invention and production of the British breech-loading rifle. In politics and legislation: the confederation of Canada as part of the Empire, the nationalization of the telegraph as a branch of the Post Office, the near doubling of the electorate with the passage of the Second Reform Act, and the enactment of measures that not only stipulated the conditions of labour in small factories but also attempted to regulate the quality of various kinds of schools and food stuffs. In social and professional associations: the founding of the Football Association, the Charitable Organization Society, along with the institution of the Queensbury rules in boxing. Finally, in intellectual and religious life: the first use of the word *evolution* in the fifth edition of *Origin of Species*, the development of the electromagnetic theory of light, the disestablishment of the Irish Church, and the founding of a range of lastingly significant periodicals, including the *Cornhill*, *Fortnightly Review*, *Pall Mall Gazette*, *Beehive*, and *Graphic*.

Such evidence attests that, despite a good deal of unrest and violence—Fenian uprisings and bombings, Sheffield 'outrages', and the bloody suppression of a rebellion in Jamaica—the 1860s were nothing if not years of firsts and foundings, a sustained and varied array of technological, industrial, and commercial developments. If one were to define what would have been called in an earlier decade 'the spirit of the age', it would be that of a mobile, vibrant, energetic culture—from hindsight a watershed of important changes, remarkable in the ways that they foretold a future of continuing transformations that would result in the more highly commodified, centralized, professionalized, and codified society of the 20th century. Although the mid-Victorian period was not quite an age of equipoise—a golden age of optimism or even complacency, a characterization still favoured by some historians—the decade of the 1860s, its high-Victorian epitome, was marked by a sense of purposeful invention and satisfying accomplishment.[1] In those years the emergence of the new was distinctive, hard to miss, and impossible to dismiss.

When one looks at the fiction of the 1860s, however, that spirit seems almost nowhere in evidence. Rarely does any novel of the decade remind its readers, even when it is set in the present, that such energies are worth remark, such developments worth inclusion, though trains and 'telegraphic messages' do function as necessary adjuncts to plots that require the rapid movement of people and information. What then is the relation between novels written in the 1860s and the context in which they were written? I have provided one answer to that question in *Common Scents*, a study of the osmology of high-Victorian fiction, the system of odours that testify to the central values of the 1860s, which in turn reflect the economic developments that were moving towards the corporate capitalism fully established by the end of the century and away from the family-owned businesses of earlier decades.[2] Instead of pursuing a sensory approach here, I want to focus instead on questions raised by Raymond Williams in 'The Analysis of Culture', a chapter of *The Long Revolution* (1961), where he tests the explanatory potential of what he famously called a 'structure of feeling' by taking as his example the case of the 1840s.

---

[1] For such developments see the comprehensive historical account of the period by K. Theodore Hoppen, *The Mid-Victorian Generation, 1846–1886* (Oxford: Oxford University Press, 1998). On the debate over the age of equipoise, so called after a book by W.L. Burn, *The Age of Equipoise: A Study of the Mid-Victorian Generation* New York: Norton, 1965), see Ian Inkster et al., eds., *The Golden Age: Essays in British Social and Economic History 1850–1870* (Burlington: Ashgate, 2000); Martin Hewitt, ed., *An Age of Equipoise? Reassessing Mid-Victorian Britain* (Aldershot: Ashgate, 2000). Nicholas Daly treats the 1860s as a watershed in terms of both technological and literary development—see *Literature, Technology, and Modernity, 1860–2000* (Cambridge: Cambridge University Press, 2004), 3, 43—as do, for different reasons: Catherine Gallagher, *The Industrial Reformation of English Fiction, 1832–1867: Social Discourse and Narrative Form* (Chicago: University of Chicago Press, 1985), chapter 9; Lynda Nead, *Victorian Babylon: People, Streets, and Images in Nineteenth-Century London* (New Haven: Yale University Press, 2000); Karen Chase and Michael Levenson, *The Spectacle of Intimacy: A Public Life for the Victorian Family* (Princeton: Princeton University Press, 2000), 'Conclusion'. Daly lists a number of innovations in the 1860s (4).

[2] Janice Carlisle, *Common Scents: Comparative Encounters in High-Victorian Fiction* (New York: Oxford University Press, 2004), chapters 1 and 2. A profound longing for but rejection of materiality marks the over eighty novels whose representations of scents I examine. Among middle-class, male characters, this feeling presents itself as an apparently idiopathic suffering, a form of melancholia involving symptoms of irritability and restlessness, because such men have been cut off from the substances produced and sold by tradesmen, artisans, and small shopkeepers. From this perspective the connection between the fiction of the 1860s and the institutional politics of the time is indirect but telling: the values embodied in the osmology of high-Victorian fiction play out in the major political event of the decade, the passage of the Second Reform Act of 1867 (see *Common Scents*, 'Afterword'). For the ways in which this process was represented in visual terms, see my study of the relationships between art and parliamentary politics, *Picturing Reform in Victorian Britain* (Cambridge: Cambridge University Press, 2012).

The analyst of culture, according to Williams, should look for 'patterns of a character-istic kind', patterns whose similarities in a wide range of dissimilar fields and endeavours reveal the 'relationships between elements in a whole way of life'.[3] When he outlines the goal of the cultural historian, Williams defines what he later in the essay labels a 'struc-ture of feeling': 'The most difficult thing to get hold of, in studying any past period, is this felt sense of the quality of life at a particular place and time: a sense of the ways in which the particular activities combined into a way of thinking and living' (48, 47). That 'felt sense', that 'way of thinking and living', cannot be directly apprehended after its moment as a vital, living context has passed, but Williams argues that literary texts, like other forms of 'documentary culture', can provide telling, if necessarily limited and selective, understandings of such a structure of feeling. Poems and novels and essays embody 'the particular living result of all the elements in the general organization' of a given time (49, 48)—in other words, the 'felt sense' of the relationships that make up 'a whole way of life', the feeling that is structured by them. Texts are able to serve this purpose because they convey not only 'public ideals but [also] ... their omissions and consequences', thereby evidencing the two principal components of a given structure of feeling, both the 'domi-nant social character' of a period, the values and attitudes and ideals that characterize the major and most powerful sectors of a culture, and the impress on those living in that culture of 'the real factors' at work in it (63, 66). Williams identifies a harsh conflict between values and realities as the chief characteristic of the 1840s: 'the morality of the industrial and commercial middle class', in which the importance of money and status and success and family is preeminent, as opposed to the lived experience of 'man alone, afraid, a victim' (61, 68); and it is this complex of values, material realities, and emotions that constitutes the structure of feeling of that decade.[4] The implications of Williams's model of culture are further specified when, in the final essay of *The Long Revolution*, he discusses the role of class in the 1960s and asks 'what it is there to do' (317). Applied to the 1860s, Williams's questions become: What do the novels of that decade identify as its characteristic structure of feeling? What do they accomplish for the readers of this fic-tion? What are they there to do?

To suggest answers to such questions here, I consider a representative group of novels from the 1860s, novels that range from the very well known, such as Charles Dickens's *Great Expectations* (1860–61) and *Our Mutual Friend* (1864–65), and the securely canonical—*Felix Holt, The Radical* (1866) by George Eliot, *The Moonstone* (1868) by Wilkie Collins, and Anthony Trollope's *Phineas Finn: The Irish Member* (1867–69)—to

---

[3] Raymond Williams, *The Long Revolution* (New York: Columbia University Press, 1961), 47, 46. Hereafter cited in the text by page number. For other uses of Williams's term in relation to a novel published in the 1860s, see John P. Farrell, 'The Partners' Tale: Dickens and *Our Mutual Friend*', *ELH* 66 (1999): 759–99; Pam Morris, 'A Taste for Change in *Our Mutual Friend*: Cultivation or Education?' in *Rethinking Victorian Culture*, ed. Juliet John and Alice Jenkins (London: Macmillan, 2000), 179–94.

[4] Williams's explanation of this concept is admittedly contradictory. At times it seems to be simply an affective response to the dominant social character of a period, but his discussion begins and ends in 'The Analysis of Culture' with the more elaborate formulation that I outline here.

the relatively minor, such as Mary Elizabeth Braddon's *Lady Audley's Secret* (1861–62) and Margaret Oliphant's *Salem Chapel* (1862–63), to the distinctly obscure *Lizzie Lorton of Greyrigg* (1866) by Eliza Lynn Linton.[5] In these novels, many conditions presented in the 1840s and 1850s as requiring urgent amelioration are treated as if they have already been adequately addressed. The legal black hole that is the Court of Chancery in *Bleak House* (1852–53) becomes the source of salvation for a character in *Salem Chapel*: to be made a ward of Chancery in the later novel is to escape being a pawn in the violent games played by one's warring parents. More important, these texts confirm and extend the implications of Amanda Claybaugh's argument about the gradual replacement, principally during the 1850s, of the predominantly 'reformist' goals of earlier Victorian fiction with a more general sense of 'purpose'. In discussing one of Dickens's first sketches, Claybaugh outlines a strategy evident in later novels when they render the systemic as if it were only personal : 'the cautionary temperance tale … transforms the present fact of economic inequality into a prior history of individual choices unwisely made'.[6] By the 1860s such changes in register and relevance are features of all kinds of fiction beyond the more narrowly didactic.

More specifically, in novels of this decade, wider cultural, social, political, economic, and technological trends are displaced onto plights generated by plots of private interests—the abduction of a sister, the loss of a wallet, or the suspected theft of a precious gem—plots that are so extreme and often so unlikely that they can scarcely seem representative. Thus, Gabriel Betteredge, the chief servant and arguably the most important narrator in *The Moonstone*, remarks of the entry of 'a devilish Indian Diamond' into 'our quiet English house', 'Who ever heard the like of it—in the nineteenth century, mind; in an age of progress, and in a country which rejoices in the blessings of the British constitution? Nobody ever heard the like of it, and, consequently, nobody can be expected to believe it.' In those rare instances in which the developments characteristic of the decade are evidenced, they are often reflected in characters defined by their idiosyncratic personal traits, by their unusual dispositions and wayward temperaments. As Robert Audley of *Lady Audley's Secret* puts the point, his is 'an age of eccentricity'.[7] Paradoxically, however, because so many characters in these novels are identified as eccentric, their similar affective responses constitute the kind of pattern to which Williams asks the cultural critic to attend, thereby pointing towards the structure of feeling of the 'age of progress' and the 'age of eccentricity' during which they were created.

Two of the affective conditions typical of such atypical characters involve their feeling frenzied or being unpleasant. Opposed to the dominant social character of the decade,

---

[5] The arguments formulated here were developed in response to a graduate seminar in which these novels were the central texts. I am grateful to the following students for their lively and stimulating conversations: Natalie Prizel, Christopher Hurshman, Ruth Gilligan, Lawrence Benn, Angela M. Parker, and Lauren Gerber.

[6] Amanda Claybaugh, *The Novel of Purpose: Literature and Social Reform in the Anglo-American World* (Ithaca: Cornell University Press, 2007), 34, 61.

[7] Wilkie Collins, *The Moonstone*, ed. Sandra Kemp (London: Penguin, 1998), 46. Mary Elizabeth Braddon, *Lady Audley's Secret*, ed. David Skilton (Oxford: Oxford University Press, 1987), 196.

then, which portrays a culture moving with relative confidence into the future that it was creating for Britain, the primary affective conditions that emerge from its fiction are decidedly negative, verging on the pathological in one case and tending towards incivility in the other. Moreover, such emotions, experienced equally by male and female characters, indirectly register the dominant social character of the decade so that they can both acknowledge and manage the forces prominent in high-Victorian culture. Depictions of frenetic and unpleasing thoughts and behaviours invite the readers of novels of the 1860s to feel superior to the fictional character displaying them, while at the same time identifying technological speed and the inescapable distinctions of a class system as the chief features of the 1860s. The transformative, purposeful, forward-moving culture of that decade depended, as these novels testify, on maintaining basic social categories that define one person as better than another. By making it possible for readers to experience a sense of superiority, these novels define that sense as a significant component of the structure of feeling typical of the 1860s, the 'felt sense' of 'the whole organization'. Yet they also suggest that literary texts are 'there to do', as Williams argues, not only the work of representing the two components of that structure, the dominant social character and the affective consequences of the material realities unrecognized by it; these novels also provide oddly liberating, though not necessarily progressive, perspectives on such forces.

FRENZY AND FEVER

The frantic, frenzied, and feverish quality of the experience depicted in novels of the 1860s emerges from depictions of both physical and mental action—movements of restless bodies back and forth and back again through space, movements of unquiet minds from one thought to another. Physical agitation, in an age-old convention of romance, often acts out mental agitation, restlessness made often excruciatingly painful because the characters exist in plots that require them to wait helplessly for the unfolding of events over which they have no control. Perhaps because Miss Havisham has insisted that the young Pip attend her every other day for eight or ten months so that he can walk her back and forth from one of her two rooms in Satis House to the other, the adult Pip moves about propelled by 'restlessness and disquiet of mind', so much so that he finds himself 'wandering, wandering, wandering' around the house in Richmond where Estella is staying: 'O the many, many nights and days through which the unquiet spirit within me haunted' that dwelling. Later on he idles, in an apparently endless period of delay, as he waits to spirit Magwitch away from England; 'condemned to inaction and a state of constant restlessness and suspense, I rowed about in my boat, and waited, waited, waited, as I best could'.[8] The heroes of *Our Mutual Friend* are only slightly less prone to perpetual motion. Harmon tries repeatedly to retrace the steps that have led to

---

[8] Charles Dickens, *Great Expectations*, ed. Janice Carlisle (Boston: Bedford, 1996), 256, 280, 350.

his having been thrown into the Thames, and he finds himself turning circles, unable to distinguish the wall and doorway for which he is looking from all the walls and doorways that he sees. Wrayburn transforms such circular movement into a vicious trick that he plays on the schoolmaster Headstone, 'goad[ing him] to madness', making him 'chafe and fret at every pore', by leading him, night after night, up one street and down another, into dead ends and around corners.[9] In other novels the geographic extent of such wanderings widens significantly. In *Lady Audley's Secret*, Robert Audley, intent on solving the mystery of the disappearance of his friend George Talboys, travels back and forth throughout England, east and west, north and south[10]—only to discover that none of his destinations has given him a clue to George's actual whereabouts.

The plot of *Salem Chapel* makes frenetically purposeless action seem more frantic and more pointless than even that of *Lady Audley's Secret*. Arthur Vincent has come to Carlingford to minister to the members of a nonconformist congregation and, no less important, to use his gifts of oratory and his forward-looking theological training to improve his social position. As if to divert his attention from the lady to whose hand he, Pip-like, should not presume, his sister Susan is abducted by a villainous gentleman, and Vincent is forced temporarily to give up his duties at the chapel so that he can search for his sister. For all his frantic travel, mostly by rail at night, from one part of the country to another—first to London, then to back to Carlingford, back to London, to his hometown of Lonsdale, back to Carlingford, up north to a town between Morpeth and Durham, then to Dover, and finally to Folkestone—he is constantly on the move, but consistently too late. In the end, he accomplishes exactly nothing. Susan simply shows up at his lodgings in Carlingford, and his mother, not Vincent, is the one who sees and recognizes the largely unconscious 'it' into which Susan's similarly enforced and frantic journeying has turned her.[11] The villain's opportunity to encounter Susan results from the remarkable fact that there are in England three towns called Lonsdale, 'in Derbyshire,...in Devonshire, [and] in Cumberland' (107). The least feverish of the characters in the fiction that I am treating here is Phineas Finn, and even he often journeys between London and Ireland, between London and one country house or another, and between London and one electoral district or another. Like the Lonsdales of *Salem Chapel*, those destinations become frustratingly muddled because they have, in what must be a kind of joke on the vaunted differences between the constituent parts of the United Kingdom, such similar names: Loughshane (Ireland), Loughlinter (Scotland), and Loughton (England). In many ways the fictional world of *Phineas Finn* is as unlike that of *Salem Chapel* as possible, but they have similarly confusing geographical coordinates.

---

[9] Charles Dickens, *Our Mutual Friend*, ed. Adrian Poole (London: Penguin, 1997), 359, 533.

[10] Daly cites this example in his discussion of railway culture and speed in sensation novels (*Literature, Technology, and Modernity*, 48). As will become apparent, the conclusion that he reaches is the opposite of the one that I propose here.

[11] Margaret Oliphant, *Salem Chapel*, Intro. Penelope Fitzgerald (New York: Penguin, Virago Press, 1986), 262. See Carlisle, *Common Scents*, 108–11.

Characterized as the opposite of Phineas, Vincent demonstrates the link between the body in motion and the mind in a fever. Like the figure glimpsed through the window of the *maison de santé* at the end of *Lady Audley's Secret*, a 'restless creature, who paced perpetually backwards and forwards' (386), Vincent, in the mould of Pip and Harmon, moves his body as a way of acting out the 'indescribable commotion in all his thoughts' (133). Vincent cannot control or contain his distress. Except for those moments when the novel depicts the more stationary physical form but equally restless thoughts of his mother as she endures the 'sickening, intolerable suspense' of waiting for news of her daughter (246), his hysteria becomes, for large sections of the narrative, the main emotion that the reader is asked to experience because the story so consistently records his point of view. Vincent, who is described as having fallen into a 'sweet delirium' of love for a beautiful and kindly lady, is driven 'frantic' by the thought of his defiled sister (350, 209); and he comes to resemble no other character more than the sister who has been driven to physical 'fever' and 'frenzy' by the violations with which she has been threatened and damaged but not destroyed, the sister who has been transformed, according to her brother's thinking, by a 'frightful, tropical blaze of passion, anguish, and woe' (270, 289). The treatment of Susan's fever in *Salem Chapel*—a physical illness like those suffered by Pip in *Great Expectations* and Mr Candy in *The Moonstone*—is telling. The doctor called in to attend Susan unaccountably sees in her a woman capable of the worst crimes, but he tries to qualify that hasty condemnation by remarking that she is 'the most curious psychological puzzle', 'the most singular case he had ever met with' (411–12).

Widespread enough to be considered a form of contagious psychological disease, then, mental fevers in these novels of the 1860s are nonetheless typically identified as unusual, the result of the eccentricities of a character's 'nature' or the extremities of a character's situation. Lady Audley, in trying to pre-empt Robert's claims that she has attempted murder, tells Sir Michael, himself a victim of a conventional 'fever' of love (332), that his nephew suffers from a 'psychological peculiarity', only to be herself labelled four times the 'unnatural' one whose 'wretchedness' is of 'an abnormal nature' (288, 313–14, 295). Lady Audley is ultimately so exceptional a case that no simple diagnosis of insanity or criminality seems adequate to explain her actions—thus all the critical debate over the identity of her 'secret'. The eponymous character of *Lizzie Lorton* is equally unusual. A young lady reared without the restraining influence of a mother in a region of the Lake District that is remote enough to be untouched by all the changes that have turned neighbouring districts into popular tourist resorts, Lizzie is nothing if not unconventional. So intensely passionate that she resembles a 'savage', she is a 'wild' and 'reckless' creature mastered by 'the terrible fever of her despair'. In the final crisis of the story—the exact nature of which I will not reveal lest I spoil the considerable pleasures of the novel for those who have not read it—Lizzie finds herself moving so restlessly about that 'all the most unhappy features of her character were in greatest prominence at this moment', the implication being that she would not be endangered if she did not have so many unusual and 'unhappy features' in her 'character'.[12]

---

[12] Eliza Lynn Linton, *Lizzie Lorton of Greyrigg* (New York: Harper and Brothers, 1866), 80, 165, 167, 163.

Fever and fret are also functions of individual nature in *The Moonstone*. For days after the apparent theft of his cousin Rachel Verinder's gem, Franklin Blake wanders elusively around the house because, according to Betteredge's humorous account, a combination of English heritage and Continental training has given the young man a unique disposition: he is English, French, and German by turns, capable of having 'twenty different minds' in twenty minutes (71). The plot of the novel depends on another of Blake's 'constitutional peculiarit[ies]', his 'nervous sensitiveness', a 'condition' of highly strung nerves that allows them to be acted upon in unusual and, to a layperson's eye, unpredictable ways by a relatively moderate dose of opium (424, 411, 389). The fate of the diamond remains unknown, not only because Blake takes off on a long journey 'wandering' to unspecified destinations in the 'East' (296), but also because his cousin Rachel, not for nothing his relative, is herself constitutionally peculiar. In her case a 'hot and tempestuous' temperament is driven to distraction because she has information that she cannot share but the effects of which on her she cannot conceal. 'Frantic' and 'feverish' to the point of 'hysterics', she is frequently in a 'pitiable' state of 'nervous agitation'. During one particularly intense 'hysterical passion', she completely loses control over her behaviour and emits a 'cry of fury' and gives into a 'frenzy of rage' (217–18, 187, 355, 352). The mystery of the moonstone and thus Rachel's plight, tellingly enough, result from the fact that the doctor who has attended her birthday celebration has succumbed to a bodily 'fever', during which 'delirium' his thoughts wander in a way that only his assistant can follow and only then with great effort. Even Betteredge, that eminently sensible and stolid serving man, feels himself taken over, set on the move, by 'detective-fever' (161).

Why all these enflamed, fretful, fevered characters? Why all this frantic, even frenzied movement? One answer to these questions might emerge from the relatively few times when comments on the technology of transport enter into these texts. The narrator of *Salem Chapel* remarks, when Vincent returns from one of his fruitless journeys, that the 'haze of din and smoke and speed' experienced by 'railway travellers' 'abstracts [them] from all the world', a description that, oddly enough, is used later to explain Susan's perilous fever when she is depicted as 'a solemn speechless creature, abstracted already out of this world and all its influences', 'abstracted' from 'this world' on her way to death (142, 403). The postscript to *Our Mutual Friend* contains another equation between railway travel and the ultimate 'abstraction' of mortality when Dickens refers to the 'terribly destructive accident' at Staplehurst that occurred when the train in which he was travelling leapt from its tracks (799). Speed and the absence of life are also conjoined in another text in which one might least expect to find such a connection. The 'Author's Introduction' to *Felix Holt* offers this remarkable prelude to the action of the novel, which is set in 1832–33:

> Posterity may be shot, like a bullet through a tube, by atmospheric pressure from Winchester to Newcastle...[But such a] tube-journey can never lend much to picture and narrative; it is as barren as an exclamatory O! Whereas the happy outside

[coach] passenger seated on the box from the dawn to the gloaming gathered enough stories of English life…to make episodes for a modern Odyssey.[13]

The subject here is pointedly not railway travel, but in an odd prophecy of the tube system that opened in London at the end of the 19th century, the 'author' envisions a future form of transportation as a tube, a circular form of nullity, a barren 'O!' that cannot contain stories, that cannot sustain the kind of human life worth being recorded in a novel. Lamenting the passing of the old coaching days is a trope in the literature of the 1860s—W.M. Thackeray makes semi-comic, semi-pathetic use of it in one of his *Roundabout Papers*—but the introduction to *Felix Holt* dabbles in science fiction to project any anxieties that might attach to the present onto a deeply disturbing, empty future in which neither novelists nor readers will find much to interest them.

These passages in novels as different as *Salem Chapel*, *Our Mutual Friend*, and *Felix Holt* are more or less divorced from the narratives that give rise to them, displacing into the realm of commentary or afterword one of the distinctive features of the 1860s, its identity as the time of the second great Victorian boom in railway speculation and building that followed that of the 1840s, a trend that in 1865 reached a peak with annual investments of £28 million.[14] Nicholas Daly and Wolfgang Schivelbusch before him have convincingly linked specific ways of reading to such developments, Daly stressing the increased speeds of modern industrial culture and Schivelbusch, the alienating and enervating conditions created by train travel.[15] Viewed as a structure of feeling evidenced by the characters of the fiction of the 1860s, however, that relation between technology and reading might be construed differently. By paying attention to the speed of the thoughts and movements of the characters in these novels, readers might be given the opportunity to feel relatively unmoved by the ever-increasing celerity of the times in which they were living. Instead of being, as Daly puts it, 'acclimatiz[ed]' to the 'the accelerated railway age' and 'synchronize[d]…with industrial modernity'[16] by moving frenetically in the manner of Robert Audley and Arthur Vincent, readers are offered an imaginative education that teaches them to feel superior to the effects of such technology. Presumably participating, at least indirectly, in a world of energetic, purposeful striving and generally satisfying accomplishment, the reader of the 1860s would have been invited to recognize frenzy and fever as affective responses that are extreme, unrestrained, and untoward, responses that it might be acceptable to indulge vicariously and imaginatively while reading a novel, but not emotions appropriate to one's own daily life. Speeds that are represented as too fast in novels of this decade therefore define by

---

[13] George Eliot, *Felix Holt, The Radical*, ed. Peter Coveney (London: Penguin, 1987), 75–76.

[14] Hoppen, *The Mid-Victorian Generation*, 291.

[15] Daly, *Literature, Technology, and Modernity*, 6–7; Wolfgang Schivelbusch, *The Railway Journey: Trains and Travel in the 19th Century*, trans. Anselm Hollo (New York: Urizen, 1980), chapter 7. Both discuss Dickens's involvement in the Staplehurst accident (Daly, 34–5; Schivelbusch, 137–8).

[16] Daly, *Literature, Technology, and Modernity*, 7, 37.

contrast the pace of events in the reader's life as almost necessarily slower and consequently less unnerving. Both male and female audience members might have enjoyed the opportunity to think of themselves as people made of sterner, more imperturbable stuff than characters like Philip Pip and Rachel Verinder. The conventional view of the sensation novel of the 1860s—a category that includes, among the novels treated here, *Lady Audley's Secret, Salem Chapel, Lizzie Lorton,* and *The Moonstone,* if not, by virtue of several of their subplots, *Great Expectations, Our Mutual Friend,* and *Felix Holt*—is that the genre works on the reader's nerves, creating morbid feelings of agitation by setting forth plots involving violent crimes and secrets and deceptions.[17] The ways in which these novels depict their characters and the state of their irritated nerves and moving bodies suggest, however, the opposite: this fiction allows its readers to pride themselves on their own relative self-possession, to conclude that they are moving at dignified and seemly rates through lives over which they have relative control. As a structure of feeling, then, this complex of relationships encompasses not only speed and agitation but also its affective superior, calm.

UNPLEASANTNESS

Readers are invited to disavow the experience of a character like Arthur Vincent and to distance themselves from his emotions because he, like so many characters in the novels of the 1860s, is simply so surpassingly unpleasant. Not even the torments of uncertainty and fear that he suffers in *Salem Chapel* can explain why Vincent's distraction repeatedly issues in discourtesy. The scenes in which he confronts those who might help him find his sister Susan are so melodramatic that the stage practices of the period could hardly have done justice to them. Vincent plays the part less of the determined rescuer of endangered femininity than of the mad avenger. He thrusts people aside, rushes into houses and inns, shouts and carries on. Even before he reaches such extremes, he picks up a ragged street urchin by his collar and, 'with a certain unconscious fury, [swings] him impatiently off the pavement' (34)—an action that makes Bucket's badgering of Jo in *Bleak House* seem positively humane. Similarly, Vincent grasps a housekeeper by the arm and roughly pushes her about until she screams. Yet such violence against others, acted out by a man of the cloth, dissenting though that cloth may be, is confirmed by his behaviour on more pacific occasions. His parishioners expect that he will join them in the humble rituals of daily life, visiting and drinking tea; but Vincent, as the butterman Tozer recognizes, refuses to be a pastor who 'sits down pleasant to his tea, and makes hisself friendly' (240). Vincent cannot even muster 'pleasant looks' for the members of

---

[17] The classic statements of such a view come from Margaret Oliphant, 'Sensation Novels', *Blackwood's*, 91 (1862): 564–84; and D.A. Miller, *The Novel and the Police* (Berkeley: University of California Press, 1988). See also Winifred Hughes, *The Maniac in the Cellar* (Princeton: Princeton University Press, 1980).

his congregation (436). Treating his mother contemptuously as a person who could not possibly understand his ideas or even his feelings, he is, sad to say, repeatedly unkind to her, the only person who comprehends and shares his anxiety and pain.

The list of characters with whom, like Vincent, it is hard for the reader to sympathize or wholeheartedly to identify is almost as long as an accounting of the innovations of the decade during which such figures were created. Not for nothing is a minor character in *Our Mutual Friend* ironically called Pleasant Riderhood, although, as the narrator points out, she is 'not so very, very bad' (346), despite her running of a pawnshop that allows her to victimize sailors in need of a little cash. In being 'not so very, very bad', she is certainly much better than her betters or her equals: Podsnap, the Veneerings, the Lammles, Fascination Fledgby, Rogue Riderhood, old Hexam and his son Charley, Headstone, Wrayburn, the dissembling Boffin, and Wegg—all these figures do little to make themselves pleasant to anyone around them. *Great Expectations* offers a similarly lengthy catalogue of unfeeling, self-absorbed, self-satisfied, and decidedly unpleasant characters: aggrieved women like Mrs Joe and Miss Havisham, toadies like Sarah Pocket and her confreres, along with Pumblechook, Jaggers and the Wemmick of the Old Bailey and Newgate, Dolge Orlick, and Bentley Drummle, all seem intent on behaving towards other characters with as little consideration and sometimes as much cruelty as possible. Their behaviour may be as off-putting to the reader as it is distressing and annoying to other characters. Part of the daring of the novels that Dickens completed in the 1860s is his willingness to present major characters who are self-conscious about and who therefore themselves experience the unpleasantness to which they subject others. Estella's 'beauty', with its unfading and 'indescribable charm', may seem less striking to readers of *Great Expectations* than it is to Pip since she is a woman who, by her own account, has 'no heart' and who treats others accordingly (428, 226). As a nasty, rude child, Estella teaches Pip what the words *coarse* and *common* mean when she uses them to describe him, a lesson that he is later happy to prove that he has learned by marshalling them against Joe (73, 147). The roles of both Pip and Estella in *Great Expectations* are to some extent combined and taken over by the unreformed Bella in *Our Mutual Friend*. John Harmon's father chooses her to be his son's marital punishment because she is such a petulant, selfish, and demanding young girl: her tantrums when she does not get what she wants are the only behaviour that the old Harmon has seen of her.

Other novels display similar characterizations. Any concern that readers of *Felix Holt* might have for the maternal sufferings of the unloved and unappreciated Mrs Transome is likely to dissipate when the narrator explains at the beginning of the novel that this unnatural mother wishes that her first son had died long before he does, and at the end that she wishes that her second son had never been born (98, 490). Like Mrs Transome, Mrs Holt in her whining and lamenting goes well beyond the usual clichés about querulous, interfering mothers, and the son for whom the novel is named is only marginally more pleasant than she is. Felix Holt is less the ideal working man than a simple prig, self-satisfied and pompous, unable to imagine what others might actually need since he is so ready, like Mrs Transome with her home-made medicines, to prescribe for them what he thinks they need. Harold Transome is no better, and Esther Lyon presumably would remain wed to her 'fine ladyism' and her finicky disdain for others if Felix Holt were not so ready to denounce her attitudes in the most abrupt and discourteous of fashions (153). The so-called real young lady of *The Moonstone* is equally unappealing. Even before the loss of her prized jewel and her resulting hysterical rages, Rachel Verinder, according to Betteredge's conventional judgements, is a 'girl' who indulges in 'secrecy, and self-will', a 'girl' who is 'stiff-necked' and all-too-prone to 'judge…for herself' (64–65). Moreover, Rachel continually opens herself to 'odious misconstruction' (280), quite often because she is being so odious. Even apparently pleasant characters join the ranks of the unpleasant. Lady Audley's blond sweetness, the reader quickly learns, simply disguises her murderous ambitions. Although Phineas Finn is the exception to the rule when it comes to disagreeable characters—'It was simply his nature to be pleasant', explains the narrator[18]—the handsome Irishman is the cause of unpleasantness in others: Lady Laura reveals her worst qualities to both Finn and her husband, the nouveau-riche Robert Kennedy, because she is so openly fond of Finn; and Kennedy's only partially unjustified jealousy of Finn turns him into a monster of Evangelical propriety, ultimately forcing his wife to live as a disgraced woman on the Continent so that she can escape his cold and demeaning attempts to manage her behaviour. Taken as a group, such disobliging and disagreeable characters seem to be the most prominent denizens of the fiction of the 1860s.

The implications of this phenomenon are illuminated by the characterization of Phineas Finn precisely because, as the narrator stresses, his pleasantness is so exceptional. The party functionaries of the novel, Rattler and Bonteen, are filled with envy by Finn's easy and sustained successes, successes achieved in part by his taste for hard bureaucratic work, in part by his physical charms, but more conclusively by the willingness of others to invite him into their company. And no wonder: when the social world is composed at one extreme of men like the egregious Quintus Slide, editor of a working-class newspaper, and, at the other, of the prideful, old earl of Brentford and his unruly son, Lord Chiltern, who would not prefer spending time with Phineas? What is true of Finn can be applied more generally in reverse to responses provoked by other figures in novels of the 1860s. Because reading is an imaginative form of entering into another's company, spending time with one unpleasant character after another is exactly what the fiction of the decade asks one to do. The novel that features Lizzie Lorton, perhaps the most disagreeable of the lot, embodies in the relations of its characters the kind of discomfort that readers may well feel in her presence. Negations of the term *pleasant* are used again and again by other characters and by Lizzie herself to explain what it means to spend time with her. When Margaret Elcombe, a more-than-conventionally good and therefore appropriately self-disciplined young lady, points out that two of their acquaintances, the rector and his mother, 'make one's days very, very pleasant', she counsels Lizzie to behave so that she will be able to continue to enjoy their company; but

---

[18] Anthony Trollope, *Phineas Finn: The Irish Member*, ed. Jacques Berthoud (Oxford: Oxford University Press, 1991), 1: 118.

Lizzie picks up on Margaret's adjective and turns it into an infinitive that expresses what she cannot and will not do: 'People have to take me as I am: I could not change myself to please any one.' Characters who find themselves taking a walk with Lizzie do not have a 'pleasant' time of it, nor does she: 'I am not a particularly pleasant companion', she notes, in another instance of accurate self-evaluation (87, 82, 86). Unlike the inhabitants of her village who can scarcely avoid meeting her in a drawing room or on the streets, readers of the novel named for her are not forced to be in her company. Why would they not choose immediately to leave it?

One answer to such a question inheres in the structural similarity between representations of fever and fret in the novels of this decade and the great number of unpleasant characters in them. When George Bernard Shaw categorized a group of his works as 'plays unpleasant', he was referring to the nature of the social problems that animate their conflicts—prostitution, slum dwellings—but when characters of the 1860s are represented as being unpleasant, they, like those feeling febrile or frantic, are portrayed as atypical cases, as outliers rather than instances of a norm. Labelling herself 'reckless' and 'wicked', Lizzie explains her exceptionality by claiming that she could have been a military or revolutionary heroine or a traveller to distant lands. She could never be, she claims, conventionally 'good': 'I am not that kind of girl' (87). Just as Lizzie Lorton sees her ungovernable spirit as a virtue that sets her apart from and above other women, Rachel Verinder reveals her sense of her own moral superiority because she considers her pointless and irrational silence about Franklin's apparent theft of her diamond as an act of noble self-sacrifice that she alone is capable of sustaining. Even though the misery that Pip's ambitions cause him to suffer somewhat mitigates the effects of his making himself thoroughly unpleasant, particularly when he mistreats Joe, Pip thinks of himself as singled out, raised up from his original status by a unknown 'Fortune' that has turned him into a person so anomalous that he cannot find a category for his identity: 'I was a blacksmith's boy but yesterday; I am—what shall I say I am—today?' (236). Yet, if such characters are taken together, not one by one as each of them would want to be considered, they act out the implications of a structure of feeling that is ironically replicated in the responses that readers are invited to have to them. One case in particular demonstrates how that might be so.

Of all the characters in these novels from the 1860s, the one who bears away the prize as the most determinedly disagreeable and disobliging is Mrs Wilfer of *Our Mutual Friend*, and her depiction identifies what motivates the unpleasantness of many of those who are similarly characterized. As the wife of a clerk living in 'very small and very mean' lodgings, Mrs Wilfer nonetheless exhibits an unalterable 'gloomy majesty' that is manifested by her 'lofty glare' (308). On the occasion of the anniversary of her wedding to the mate whose life she makes decidedly uncomfortable, she uses the register of physical height to express her sense that she has wed a man beneath her: because she is a tall woman afraid of not being able to reach the intellectual heights of a tall man, she has married 'a little man'. This explanation of why Mrs Wilfer cannot enjoy her anniversary or make it a pleasant occasion for anyone in her family is wonderfully ludicrous, mistaking, as it does, a physical trait for a mental quality, but her point is clear: she is majestic and lofty because she thinks herself the superior of those around her, and while she casts this recognition in terms of intellect, it is a matter of class. The discrepancy between her lot and her sense of self importance is premised not only on her parents' and her own physical height but on the bizarre idea that the three copper-plate engravers who frequented her parents' home were 'the wits of the day' (451), a claim that turns that home into an elite salon. She openly treats the Boffins with contempt because she wants to make evident her own superiority to any status that their new money might have accorded them. Mrs Wilfer acts in distinctively unappealing ways because she feels superior both to her own circumstances and to those whom she is mistreating. In a similar fashion, being better than others is to a character of the 1860s, more often than not, a matter of social superiority. Being unpleasant therefore typically acts out the unattractive contempt that he or she feels for supposed social inferiors.

Through her exaggerations and her unchanging responses, Mrs Wilfer therefore epitomizes the attitudes of many of the other characters created during the 1860s. Arthur Vincent treats those below him, parishioners and housekeepers and ragged boys and even mothers, with the disdain that those who feel aggrieved by their class positions usually console themselves, and he cannot make himself 'pleasant' to his congregants, as one parishioner realizes, because the young man thinks himself 'a deal too high' for them (240). Similarly, the old, retired minister of *Salem Chapel* rightly sees that Vincent is suffering from a 'fever' of ambition (30). He has come to Carlingford convinced that his exceptional education at the dissenting seminary of Homerton will ensure his social success among the town's gentry. When he rails against the privileges of an established Church, the narrator comments, 'It was the natural cry of a man who had entered life at disadvantage, and chafed, without knowing it, at all the phalanx of orders and classes above him, standing close in order to prevent his entrance' (76). Estella evidences similar feelings in *Great Expectations*, although she frames her awareness of class differences in terms of clothing and manners. Her 'air of completeness and superiority' (226) reflects her contempt for those who she mistakenly thinks are not as well born as she is. Similarly, Mrs Joe twice bemoans being a blacksmith's wife because that status is beneath her. There are, I grant, in these novels a number of pleasant characters— Mortimer Lightwood, Joe and Biddy, Mrs Vincent, Betteredge, the Rev. Lyon, Herbert Pocket, Violet Effingham, Philip Gascoigne—but they are so either because they have a place high enough in the social hierarchy to be content with it, as is the case with the last three in my list, or because, as is the case with the rest, they have no designs on or desires for stations higher than their own. Such figures escape the major characteriological flaw of the decade, as do those, such as Lizzie Hexam of *Our Mutual Friend*, who are allowed to rise by the plots that they inhabit. Yet even characters whose class status should not make them susceptible to meanness also indulge in unpleasantness to make clear their superiority to others. Rachel Verinder treats the detective Cuff with open discourtesy, and Robert Audley displays his contempt for the retired soldier on half pay who for years has tended his best friend's son after he was abandoned by both mother and father. The one time that Franklin Blake is genuinely discourteous occurs when a fisherman's daughter asks him, 'When you see a poor girl in service, do you feel no remorse?' and he answers, 'Certainly not. Why should I?' (309).

As Raymond Williams trenchantly points out, class as a 'system' based on 'the reality of differential treatment' is registered more specifically and explicitly when one looks down than when one looks up: the ability to imagine that one really deserves to be numbered among those hazily figured as one's superiors depends on making quite precise discriminations between oneself and one's inferiors (319–21). The problems attendant upon a class system may have been almost as obvious in the 1860s as they had been in earlier decades, but contemporaries liked to believe that such problems were confined to the past, that they had been largely assuaged by increased opportunities for all kinds of self-improvement. Thus, what Williams might have recognized as a dominant value of the 1860s, its belief that the individual who tries hard enough will be rewarded with social advancement, conflicted with the 'real factors' of class distinctions that continued to put people at painful and insuperable disadvantages. The action of *The Moonstone* is set in 1848 to highlight a temporal irony: one of its characters can say, 'the day is not far off when the poor will rise against the rich' (192), but its readers know, from the vantage point of the 1860s, that that is not going to be the case: the poor and the disenfranchised will continue to know their places. Walter Bagehot's famous theory of class as 'a system of *removable inequalities*'—inequalities that would remain as characteristics of the system but which could be overcome by particularly hardworking and deserving individuals—was a creation of the late 1850s,[19] but it was equally, if not more, pertinent in the following decade. Margaret Elcombe in *Lizzie Lorton* actually quotes Bagehot when her more conservative aunt pontificates that 'God made different classes, and meant us to keep them': according to Margaret, 'as all the causes which make classes are removable, I do not think they are absolutely appointed by divine law' (102). The causes of social distinction remain, even though they are not the effect of divine dispensation.

Everyday life in Britain during the 1860s, more variously than Gaul in Caesar's times, was divided into three parts: three kinds of schools and therefore three educational commissions, three kinds of railway carriages, three kinds of seats in a theatre, three kinds of rooms in a single pub. All the innovations and inventions to which I refer at the beginning of this chapter came about in the context of relative social, economic, and political stability, but that happy fact was the result, I think, not of the blurring or softening of class divisions, as the argument about the age of equipoise typically runs, but of their hardening, their becoming more entrenched than ever in a now fully established system of industrial capitalism and in an array of new social and political alliances that often codified old standards of value. Cultural prophets like Thomas Carlyle and John Ruskin were becoming more and more intemperate in the 1860s, not only because the former was growing old and the latter less sane, but also because those around them were now so quick to claim erroneously that social and economic problems, such as unequal educational opportunities and the abuse of the children doing factory labour, had simply disappeared. To the extent that a class system continued to determine the quality of

---

[19] Walter Bagehot, *The Collected Works of Walter Bagehot*, ed. Norman St John-Stevas, 15 vols. (London: Economist, 1965–1986), 2: 308.

everyday life, contemptuous characters who identify themselves as above those around them are 'there to do' the cultural work of neutralizing and limiting the effects of that apparently intractable system through a kind of homeopathic narrative medicine: novelists of the 1860s invite their readers to feel superior to characters who respond in such a fashion to other characters. Thus, in one sense both the experience depicted in a novel written in that decade and the imaginative apprehension of that experience affirm the inescapability and perhaps the justice of hierarchical distinctions.

Because the extreme case of Mrs Wilfer is extremely comic, it elucidates how such a process works. She epitomizes Henri Bergson's well-known idea that comedy involves 'something mechanical encrusted on the living'. In every scene in which she appears, Mrs Wilfer acts as if she were a machine capable of doing only one thing: glaring at others from the 'lofty' height of her 'gloomy majesty'. Of all Dickens's characters, she is perhaps the one who most justifies George Henry Lewes's complaint that they react like pithed, 'brainless frogs', creatures 'always...moved with the same springs, and uttering the same sounds'.[20] Mrs Wilfer is rigid both in posture and in thought: her youngest daughter Lavinia is driven to admit, 'isn't she enough to make one want to poke her with something wooden, sitting there bolt upright in a corner?' Later on, Lavinia hopelessly laments, 'I wish to goodness, Ma...that you'd loll a little', a wish that is never granted (448, 783). In her responses to her husband, Mrs Wilfer simply cannot come down from her 'pedestal' (664). Like characters overwhelmed by their own feverish thoughts and actions, Mrs Wilfer prides herself on being idiosyncratic, temperamentally unique, as her ideas about height and wit reveal, but in this instance her behaviour elicits the superiority implicit in laughter or amusement rather than the sense of superiority inherent in calm and self-possession. More specifically, she evokes in the reader the kind of self-satisfaction that, according to Thomas Hobbes, accompanies laughter, an unlovely self-applause created by 'the apprehension of some deformed thing in another'.[21] She is a source of amusement, not of concern or identification. In that sense Mrs Wilfer, like other unpleasant characters who populate the novels of the 1860s, offers readers the pleasures of meanness, the satisfactions of feeling mean about a character who herself behaves in a mean-spirited way to those around her. The comic qualities that excite a sense of contempt in the reader, however, also make possible an equality between that reader and the victims of her conviction that she is elevated above them. Again in a homeopathic fashion, the reader's response may, in effect, cancel out Mrs Wilfer's, putting the reader imaginatively on the level of the figures for whom she feels scorn. Mrs Wilfer raises the status of her victims, Rumpty Wilfer and the Boffins, by making them the figures with whom the reader is asked to identify. By excluding from concern an unsympathetic character obsessed with her own superiority, the reader is

---

[20]   Henri Bergson, *Laughter: An Essay on the Meaning of the Comic*, trans. Cloudesley Brereton and Fred Rothwell (New York: Macmillan, 1911), 37; George Henry Lewes, 'Dickens in Relation to Criticism', *Fortnightly Review* 17 o.s., 11 n.s. (1872): 149, 148.

[21]   Thomas Hobbes, *Leviathan, or the Matter, Form, and Power of a Commonwealth, Ecclesiastical and Civil*, Intro. Henry Morley (London: George Routledge, 1885), 34.

given an opportunity to ignore both the causes and the effects of a system of class discriminations. As a result, class as the determinative social reality of the decade, through
a form of what Williams in another context calls 'magical solutions' (68), seems simply
to disappear.

Just as Mrs Wilfer and Lavinia verbally abuse the latter's suiter, George Sampson, so
that he can function as a 'diversion' from more troubling topics, novels in the 1860s displace the fever of technological advancement and the intractability of class distinctions
onto characters identified as eccentric and, in some cases, singled out for laughter. This
strategy was both widely employed and evidently popular. The novels that I treat here
were successes in their own times. Even *Lizzie Lorton* and *Salem Chapel* were for both
Eliza Lynn Linton and Margaret Oliphant, respectively, the books that marked high
points in their careers in terms of the sales that they garnered and the respect that they
enjoyed; and all but those two are now canonical texts. The pleasures of feeling better
than others—the calm that the reader feels in the face of the frenzy that torments Arthur
Vincent, the meanness of feeling superior to the meanness in himself that makes Pip so
unhappy—apparently had some purchase on the reading public and must still appeal to
professional readers who now teach and write about this fiction. Not that the pleasure of
indulging a seemingly well-justified conviction of one's superiority is the only response
that this fiction invites. The novels of the 1860s contain enough aesthetic appeal, compelling plots, inventive language, and engaging characters to give joy to any number of
diversely disposed members of differently constituted audiences. Yet the characteristic
that makes this fiction distinctively appealing is its ability to create in its readers the
sense that they are relatively untouched by the conditions and forces to which its characters are so signally subject.

Victorian readers who found themselves feeling better than characters whose
thoughts and behaviour are frenzied or who are unpleasant could therefore disavow
any personal connection between their own lots and the larger social or cultural conditions that occasion such qualities. Paradoxically, then, the structure of feeling, the sense
of lived experience, embodied in these novels not only takes account of the dominant
social character and its 'omissions and consequences'; that structure is also constituted
by attitudes and affects that attempt to ignore them. Indulging in the pleasures offered
by such a narrative strategy must be even more appealing now than it was 150 years
ago. To the extent that 21st-century readers recognize—how could they not?—that people and information now move at speeds exponentially more rapid than they did in the
mid-19th century, to the extent that members of a such an audience, particularly in the
United States at least, are tempted to assume incorrectly that contemporary culture has
risen above the irrationalities of class distinctions, to such extents imaginative participation in the experiences offered by the fiction of the 1860s would make deeply satisfying,
even more than it was originally, a response of superiority to characters oppressed or
deformed by such conditions. Thus, in that sense as well, the forward-looking tendencies of the decade of the 1860s fully, if indirectly, characterize novels that, in their own
distinctively innovative and inventive ways, foretell the economic and social developments of the future.

Suggested Reading

Christensen, Allan Conrad. *Nineteenth-Century Narratives of Contagion: 'Our Feverish Contact'*. London: Routledge, 2005.

Dames, Nicholas. *The Physiology of the Novel: Reading Neural Science and the Form of Victorian Fiction*. Oxford: Oxford University Press, 2007.

Freedgood, Elaine. *Victorian Writing about Risk: Imagining a Safe England in a Dangerous World*. Cambridge: Cambridge University Press, 2000.

Gallagher, Catherine. *The Body Economic: Life, Death, and Sensation in Political Economy and the Victorian Novel*. Princeton: Princeton University Press, 2006.

Kaplan, Cora. "'What We Have Again to Say': Williams, Feminism, and the 1840s'. In *Cultural Materialism: On Raymond Williams*. Edited by Christopher Prendergast. Minneapolis: University of Minnesota Press, 1995, 211–36.

Menke, Richard. *Telegraphic Realism: Victorian Fiction and Other Information Systems*. Stanford: Stanford University Press, 2008.

Simpson, David. 'Raymond Williams: Feeling for Structure, Voicing "History"'. In *Cultural Materialism: On Raymond Williams*. Edited by Christopher Prendergast. Minneapolis: University of Minnesota Press, 1995, 29–50.

Winter, Alison. *Mesmerized: Powers of Mind in Victorian Britain*. Chicago: University of Chicago Press, 1998.

Wood, Jane. *Passion and Pathology in Victorian Fiction*. Oxford: Oxford University Press, 2001.

PART VI

COMMERCE, WORK, PROFESSIONS, STATUS

17

INDUSTRIALISM AND THE VICTORIAN NOVEL

EVAN HOROWITZ

Ninety-nine times out of a hundred, when someone writes 'X is the most important event in millennia of human history' or 'Y fundamentally altered the structure of society', the proper response is to roll your eyes. These are the sort of grand, rhetorical flourishes that writers employ to add vigour to their claims and colour to their prose. The problem, though, is that once in a while these kinds of claims must actually be true. Something must really be the most important event in millennia of human history, and some things probably do transform the very structure of society. How, then, to say as much without sounding strident and hyperbolic? This is one—and only the first—problem with talking about industrialism. It really was the most economically and socially revolutionary occurrence in modern human history, but every attempt to express this fact ends up sounding hollow, obstreperous, or clichéd.

The second, perhaps even more daunting difficulty is that everyone seems to feel they already know about industrialism. Even if you can demonstrate that your rhetoric isn't hollow, and even if you can show that industrialism really does represent an epochal change, you still have to make it seem like a topic worthy of new investigation and analysis—something more than the old story of classes and factories, divisions of labour and alienation, steam-engines, spinning jennies, and novels by Disraeli and Gaskell. That old story, told and retold in various ways by Thomas Carlyle, Friedrich Engels, Louis Cazamian, E.P. Thompson, Raymond Williams, Catherine Gallagher, and others, is so entrenched in literary studies that it seems virtually immune to challenge. But it is, as I say, an old story, with many and growing cracks in its foundation.

The time has come, in fact, to do away with this old story, and for two reasons. First, because it is no longer consistent with the best information we have about industrial life. Second, it never did justice to the complex relationship between industrialism and literature, tending instead to focus attention on a very narrow literary subgenre, the one that has come to be called the industrial novel (or, as I will call it, the social problem novel), including such explicitly class-conscious books as *Hard Times*, *Felix Holt*, *Sybil*, *Shirley*,

Alton Locke, and *North and South*. Surely, there is something inadequate about a theory of industrialism which makes a handful of specialized texts the truest literary expression of a great, epochal historical event. These things are simply not commensurate. If industrialism is that rare thing which can honestly be called 'the most important event in millennia of human history', we should expect its effect on literature to be similarly important and dramatic. There should be traces of it across every genre—in lyric and epic, and essay and play, and quite certainly the novel, both minor and major.

The aim of this chapter is to tell a new story about industrialism, one that accounts for recent historical research and that makes room for a richer understanding of industrial literature. To this end, what follows will be divided into two sections:

- 'The Old Story'—which describes the continuing value of the social problem novel.
- 'The New Story'—which builds a new account of the industrial novel.

Counterintuitive though it may seem, what I am going to show in 'The New Story' is that industrialism means something more than the rise of industry. It refers to a change in the horizon of economic life, the end of the Malthusian trap and the emergence of a new, mutually reinforcing relationship between population growth and economic progress. This broader perspective—emphasizing social and economic dynamics rather than the artefacts of industry—affords a more comprehensive understanding of the relationship between industrialism and the novel.

THE OLD STORY

The so-called social problem novel has been the locus of inquiry for over a century now—ever since Louis Cazamian published his path-breaking book *The Social Novel in England: Dickens, Disraeli, Mrs Gaskell, Kingsley*. Not only have those same authors continued to anchor this genre of criticism, but so too has Cazamian's basic focus on the 'social' implications of industrial change been the guiding star. When Raymond Williams took up the subject in his own influential book, *Culture and Society* (1958), he emphasized the shift from an old ethic of social responsibility to the merely transactional relationships that governed society under industrial capitalism—and he suggested, further, that part of the value of 19th-century literature derived from its ability to sustain certain aspects of the old structure of feeling. Catherine Gallagher, too, in *The Industrial Reformation of English Fiction: Social Discourse and Narrative Form* (1985), foregrounded a series of vibrant 19th-century debates about shifting social relationships: from the role of the worker to the value of the family to the expanding population of voters. For each of these critics, in other words, it is the new terrain of social debate and class conflict that grounds the inquiry into industrial change itself. And, in each case, the novels they treat as exemplary are those which explicitly thematize such debates and conflicts. As Gallagher herself puts it, 'The works most immediately affected were those we now call the "industrial novels," Gaskell's *Mary Barton* and *North and South*, Charles Kingsley's *Alton Locke*, Charles Dickens's *Hard Times*, and George Eliot's *Felix Holt*.[1]

As I have said, it is the goal of this chapter to show that this short list of relatively minor texts is simply incommensurate with the real impact of industrialism, but I don't mean to suggest that such texts are without value—and certainly not that the readings offered by Williams, Gallagher, and others are anything but profound. These kinds of novels capture at least one crucial aspect of industrial change: the remapping of the fault lines of social conflict and the emergence of that new structure of solidarity which we call class. Industrialism's cities and factories didn't just produce new products, they also produced new forms of social cohesion; they enabled new affective bonds among people in disparate places with similar working conditions. Piecemeal labourers and daily-wage-earners began to think of themselves as belonging to the working classes; shopkeepers, managers, and capitalists to the middle classes; land-owners and title-holders to the upper classes; and, lest we forget, writers and intellectuals to the professional classes. As industrialism wrought its varied changes, these kinds of horizontal allegiances played an increasingly prominent role both in everyday life and in the social imaginary.

One of the things that social problem novels do extremely well is to make these new class categories visible as stereotypes. That may sound like a dubious achievement but the transformation of class into type helps to illustrate the stakes and strategies of class struggle. Benjamin Disraeli's *Sybil* provides a particularly grotesque example of how this works in its fantastical account of the town of Wodgate, where 'capital is insistently resisted' and 'Labour reigns supreme'.[2] What might, in the hands of a Ruskin or a Morris, be the setting for a Utopian experiment, is in Disraeli a communal abyss. Without capitalists to organize production—or churches to enforce values—the most skilled labourers rule despotically over a shapeless mass of barely-human cogs. These worker-aristocrats are, Disraeli tells us, 'ruthless tyrants' who 'habitually inflict upon their subjects punishments more grievous than the slave population of our colonies were ever visited with'—not the least of which involves 'cutting their heads open with a file or lock' (163). As one would expect, the results are hardly salutary, and the people who suffer under this tyranny far removed from the proverbial 'respectable working man':

> It is not that the people are immoral, for immorality implies some forethought; or ignorant, for ignorance is relative; but they are animals; unconscious; their minds a blank; and their worst actions only the impulse of a gross or savage instinct. There

[1] Louis Cazamian, *The Social Novel in England, 1830–1850: Dickens, Disraeli, Mrs Gaskell, Kingsley* (London: Routledge and Kegan Paul, 1973); Catherine Gallagher, *The Industrial Reformation of English Fiction* (Chicago: University of Chicago Press, 1985), xi; Raymond Williams, *Culture and Society, 1780–1950*, 2nd edn (London: Chatto and Windus, 1959).

[2] Benjamin Disraeli, *Sybil: Or the two nations* [1845], ed. Sheila Smith (Oxford: Oxford Paperbacks, 1998), 163. Subsequent citations appear in the text.

are many in this town who are ignorant of their very names; very few who can spell them. It is rare that you meet with a young person who knows his own age; rarer to find the boy who has seen a book, or the girl who has seen a flower. Ask them the name of their sovereign, and they will give you an unmeaning stare; ask them the name of their religion, and they will laugh: who rules them on earth, or who can save them in heaven, are alike mysteries to them. [164]

In this dictatorship of the proletariat, the working people are reduced to unconscious beasts, their humanity stripped bare by the brutality of 'Labour's' laws. It is at once a horrifying vision of the world without capitalism, a dire warning against granting power to the working classes, and an earnest appeal to take up the rich man's burden and help those who suffer under such conditions. Notice, to that last end, how the early image of an immoral 'people' morphs into the much more sympathetic picture of an illiterate young boy and a girl who—weep!—has never seen a flower. Who, Disraeli asks us, will save these souls if we capitulate to the demands of workers?

The force of this question—who will save the workers?—is actually central to Disraeli's novel as a whole, as is the effort to find an answer. If, as I said before, one of the great strengths of the social problem novel is its ability to map social conflict through class-types, one of its great ambitions is to resolve social conflict by placing these class-types on a narrative path towards resolution. In *Sybil*, this means finding some worthy upper-class characters who can restore order through responsibility. A new generation of aristocrats must arise to accept the full burden of paternalism and *noblesse oblige*. The degree of artifice required to make this solution narratively possible is high indeed, involving a multitude of timely deaths and a collection of hidden documents. And the decidedly idiosyncratic result speaks to the more generally idiosyncratic way that the social problem novels tend to imagine harmony. None of the existing, real-world proposals will do: not Chartism, Owenism, Saint-Simonianism, Fourierism, Marxism, Laissez-faire Capitalism, or otherwise. Always a more original and more nuanced solution must be developed. *Sybil*'s answer—that we have to build a new aristocracy from scratch, and that we can do so narratively by killing off some existing aristocrats and promoting others in their place—is already quite quixotic, but it is more than matched by its peers.

Dickens's *Hard Times*, for instance, is another social problem novel with its own, quite different but still eccentric ideal. It, too, has its share of class stereotypes and children in desperate need of saving, but it also has something that Disraeli's text lacks: a menacing middle-class ideology. There are very few middle-class figures in *Sybil*—strikingly few, given the otherwise wide ambit. But Dickens's focus on the men and masters of the imagined, industrial city of Coketown attracts him towards a different set of problems—and then to a different kind of solution. He is troubled by the rank hypocrisy of self-aggrandizing capitalists, like Josiah Bounderby, and riled by the degradation of upright working men, like Stephen Blackpool, but above all what he finds intolerable is the bourgeois instrumentalization of everyday life, the unimaginative and inhuman evaluation of all things in terms of their measurable, factual utility. Here, for instance, is

Dickens's picture of the good-hearted but dangerously-misguided Mr Gradgrind, calculating the answers to all of life's problems while sitting alone in his study:

> In that charmed apartment, the most complicated social questions were cast up,
> got into exact totals, and finally settled—if those concerned could only have been
> brought to know it. As if an astronomical observatory should be made without any
> windows, and the astronomer within should arrange the starry universe solely by
> pen, ink, and paper, so Mr. Gradgrind, in *his* Observatory (and there are many like
> it), had no need to cast an eye upon the teeming myriads of human beings around
> him, but could settle all their destinies on a slate, and wipe out all their tears with one
> dirty little bit of sponge.[3]

This, too, is a stereotype, as crude in its way as Disraeli's Wodgate. Only this time it is not
'Labour' which rules over 'teeming myriads' and narrows the scope of human being. It is
a deficient utilitarian philosophy, unable in its mathematical precision to reckon with the
real complexity of lived experience. Here, as throughout the novel, Dickens insists that
the only way to address the 'most complicated social questions' of industrial change is by
social-izing, by talking to others and experiencing something of what they experience—
rather than turning them into numbers and crunching them about. That, at least, is part
of the solution on offer in *Hard Times*, as when Gradgrind's own daughter, Louisa, goes to
visit the 'dwellings of the Coketown hands' and finds herself changed by the experience of
coming 'face to face' (155) with the workers inside (just as we, his readers, are meant to be
changed by our face-to-face encounters with Dickens's motley cast of characters).

But the more profound demand of *Hard Times* is that we confront the dehumanizing
force of utilitarianism by embracing the unreal, the irrational, and the imaginary. In place
of sterile facts, we need fertile fancies, and children's books in place of blue ones. Against
the threat of an all-consuming ideology of utility and statistics—born of accountants'
tables and concretized in the industrial city—Dickens celebrates the immeasurable and
the irreducible. And he anoints as the champion of this alternate view, the young Sissy
Jupe, offspring of a fanciful circus-performer, who makes Mr Gradgrind feel 'that there
was something in this girl which could hardly be set forth in a tabular form' (92). It is
Sissy who brings balance to bourgeois ideology and whose offspring carry with them the
novel's greatest hope for a more human future:

> But, happy Sissy's happy children loving her; all children loving her; she, grown learned
> in childish lore; thinking no innocent and pretty fancy ever to be despised; trying hard
> to know her humbler fellow-creatures, and to beautify their lives of machinery and
> reality with those imaginative graces and delights, without which the heart of infancy
> will wither up, the sturdiest physical manhood will be morally stark death, and the
> plainest national prosperity figures can show, will be the Writing on the Wall. [287]

---

[3] Charles Dickens, *Hard Times for These Times* [1854], ed. Kate Flint (London: Penguin, 2003), 95.

In Sissy's future world, one can be 'learned in childish lore', can value 'pretty fancy', and even substitute 'imaginative graces and delights' for Gradgrind's once-beloved 'national prosperity figures'. It is the resolution of a fairy tale, and that is very much the point, fairy tales being the sugar to industrialism's acid. Yet, like Disraeli's ideal of a new nobility, Dickens's Utopia is not without its eccentricity. Notice, for instance, that in the world of Sissy's children there will still be lots of 'machinery and reality', and plenty of 'humbler fellow-creatures' to get to know. The harsh landscape of industrial work and urban poverty are left virtually untouched; only their impact is tempered by the availability of new distractions. It is a very one-sided kind of response—where grinding poverty is made less onerous by circuses alone, and little bread—and that is but one of its weaknesses. It also takes a remarkably long time, a full generation in fact. No character who has been committed to the ascendancy of fact can ever be fully redeemed. Mr Gradgrind may find a new, more charitable world-view and his daughter, Louisa, may escape the worst errors of her early life, but happy children and grandchildren are denied them. Their line has to effectively die out, so that Sissy's more promising offspring can shape the future in their stead.

One thing that Dickens and Disraeli share, then, is an insistence that the social conflicts of industrial life be solved by means both public and private, through politics and ideology but also romance and reproduction. In Disraeli, not only must the bad aristocrats be killed off, but the good aristocrats who replace them must then intermarry to ensure that their good values pass down to posterity. In Dickens, the most tainted characters must either remain unmarried (and thus, unable to procreate) or else turn widowers (for the same reason). Either way, the public, political resolution of social problems is mirrored by a private, romantic resolution—and this mirroring is actually a standard feature of the social problem novel more generally.

In fact, it is the breakdown of this generic expectation which makes George Eliot's *Felix Holt: The Radical* such an interesting, and problematic, member of the genre. There is very little industrial activity in Eliot's novel. What takes its place is an acute attention to the rise of political radicalism—another of the social movements set off by industrial change. More precisely, the novel describes the faltering efforts of one character, the eponymous Felix, to reform the very meaning of the term radical. Felix aims to be 'a demagogue of a new sort; an honest one, if possible, who will tell the people they are blind and foolish, and neither flatter them nor fatten on them'.[4] If this seems unlikely to attract votes, that's a secondary concern for Felix. Unlike the other self-proclaimed Radicals in the novel, Felix isn't interested in votes; he thinks the Chartist-style attention to suffrage a kind of sham, and voting rights for workers dangerously premature. His principal interests are moral, rather than political: he wants to teach workers to drink less, spend their wages better, and generally 'go to some roots a good deal lower down than the franchise' (264). Perhaps not surprisingly, his moral bullying doesn't get him very far. In fact, it gets him into quite a bit

---

[4] George Eliot, *Felix Holt, the Radical* [1866], ed. Lynda Mugglestone (London: Penguin Books, 1995), 262. Subsequent citations appear in the text.

of trouble. When, at one point, he sees the local working people drawn into a violent mob, he tries to intervene—only to end up killing one person and ensuring the death of a second. And though he, himself, is eventually pardoned for those crimes, his broader efforts to build a new kind of radicalism cannot be so easily redeemed. No working men flock to his cause, no acolytes emerge to help preach the good word, and no great transformation is enabled by his activities. Whatever social problems exist at the beginning of this novel still exist at the end—and will continue to exist into the foreseeable future.

The only real resolution is a private one. Throughout the novel, Felix's public-house proselytizing has been matched, and sometimes dwarfed, by his parlour-room pros-elytizing. Rather than actually helping local workers, he seems to prefer talking about helping local workers—and never more so than when sitting beside the beautiful, if rather less earnest, Esther Lyon. As I have already said, this talk doesn't much aid the cause of radical social improvement, but it does have its effect: it reforms Esther. She, and she alone, embraces Felix's ideas of sobriety and austerity, turning away from the seductions of luxury and wealth to marry Felix and support his destiny as a wandering Radical. That, as I say, is a kind of success, but it is a purely private kind, far below Felix's stated ambition. A happy marriage—as opposed to a happy society—is the most that this *soi-disant* Radical can accomplish. Unlike Dickens and Disraeli, who use private resolutions to reflect and ramify their broader public and political ideas, Eliot keeps the private quite distant from the big social questions which had seemed to be the novel's focus. At the end, Felix and Esther walk off the stage together, arm in arm, but it is not because their work is done; quite the contrary, it is because they have learned that their work cannot be done. The industrializing world, and its workers, simply aren't ready. Private happiness has no public correlate, which gives this industrial novel its own, bleak eccentricity.

There is another way to read the broken ending of *Felix Holt*, however. It may not be a sign of failure, some inability to wed plot and politics, private and public, per-sonal and social. It may be more a matter of indifference. Felix and Esther walk off together, in this reading, because they have learned to care more about personal hap-piness then public happiness. Private resolution proves more important to them than the details of industrial exploitation, and that makes a kind of sense within the uni-verse of the Victorian novel more generally. Sure, there are a handful of books which engage, directly, with issues of politics, factory-life, utilitarianism, and the structure of social conflict under industrialism, and understandably those novels have a cer-tain appeal for literary scholars; yet, it must be acknowledged that the overwhelming majority of Victorian literature simply did not take this route. It, too, was immersed in industrial life, and it too was shaped by the conditions of industrial change, but only rarely did it take the form of a social problem novel. Victorian novelists found, instead, other ways to tie the fictional to the industrial, other techniques for building narratives out of the industrial world. And if we want to understand the full scope of this effort we have to follow Felix and Esther away from the social problem novel and begin, instead, a new story.

THE NEW STORY

The best way to begin this new story is by returning to the most basic questions. What was industrialism? When and where did it begin? What effects did it have on the economy, and on society at large? Fortunately for us, we don't have to build our own answers. Even as literary scholars have largely shifted their attention, historians have continued to develop new insights into what they consider not just the most important event of the 19th century but a 'materialist crossing of the Jordan', 'a phenomenon unprecedented in human history', and 'the greatest transformation in human history since the remote times when men invented agriculture and metallurgy, writing, the city and the state'.[5] Using a variety of approaches and datasets, what they have found is that industrialism is best understood as a kind of tipping point, a threshold moment in economic history before which there was one mode of economic life and after which another, wholly different one. Industry itself—by which is meant the organization of production into larger units, the greater use of machine labour, the reliance on steam-power, and the increasing functionalization of work—was a contributing factor in this leap from the pre-industrial, but it was hardly the only factor. Trade played an important role, as did colonialism, and the relative peace of the post-Napoleonic period. Weighing these various factors—and a host of others—has been a major concern of historical scholarship, but by far the most important thing for literary studies is just to recognize the broader, system-wide transformation.

Industrialism introduced a wholly new economic system, and by that I don't mean a new mode of production (to use the old Marxist terminology). I mean, instead, the end of the Malthusian trap. More and more scholarship is revealing that Thomas Malthus was essentially correct about the zero-sum nature of early economic life. From the beginnings of civilization right through to the 18th century, wealth and population were mutually antagonistic: increases in wealth bred increases in population which cannibalized all benefits; decreases in wealth forced declines in population by whatever means necessary, be it starvation, plague, or emigration. In the Malthusian world, there was no stable way for economic gains to be enjoyed by individual subjects or citizens. With the arrival of industrialism, however, this all changed. A new, positive-sum dynamic took hold of economic life, finally enabling an overall rate of growth sufficient to improve the lives of individuals. After millennia of stagnation, what economists call 'modern economic growth' finally began, and it brought real, distributed improvements in the social welfare of the populace at large.[6]

---

[5] Gregory Clark, *A Farewell to Alms: A Brief Economic History of the World* (Princeton: Princeton University Press, 2007), 193; Joel Mokyr, *The Enlightened Economy: An Economic History of Britain, 1700–1850* (New Haven: Yale University Press, 2009), 3–4; Eric Hobsbawm, *The Age of Revolution 1789–1848*, 1st edn (New York: Vintage Books, 1996), 1.

[6] The best, most recent account of this comes from Clark.

To be safe, one shouldn't get too roisterous about these kinds of claims. Obviously, industrialism didn't bring an end to penury or human suffering. The misery described by Engels and Mayhew, Booth and Rowntree, Dickens and Hardy was real enough, and there is still a vibrant argument among economists about when the great gains of industrialism began transforming the lives of the poor and the working classes (1800? 1850? 1860?—few would push the date beyond that). Abominable poverty, horrific health conditions, and greatly suffering masses —these things persisted into the industrial era. Indeed, in some ways they become more visible (because more concentrated in larger, urban agglomerations). Yet, they were also on their way out. Today's best evidence on prices and wages show that by mid-century, at the latest, Victorian industrialism was bringing real, material gains to virtually every segment of the population, from the disreputable poor all the way to the disreputable rich. Whereas for thousands of years, Jesus's pronouncement (repeated by Dickens in *Hard Times*) that 'the poor you will have always with you' had been basically true; by Dickens's own time, it was not. If poverty was still a part of Victorian life, it was no longer an inevitable or eternal part.

Perhaps the most important thing to recognize, from the standpoint of the Victorian novel, is that this great, economic transformation began in England (and parts of Scotland). Traces of industry one could find throughout the world—railways in France and factories in the US and machine-labour in China and India—but industrialism as a whole came first to England; and it didn't arrive elsewhere until the very end of the 19th-century. England faced the revolutionary energies of industrial change decades before any other nation on earth, and it therefore faced them very much alone. 'Sixty, eighty years ago', Engels wrote in the early 1840s, 'England was a country like every other, with small towns, few and simple industries, and a thin but proportionally large agricultural population. Today it is a country like no other...'.[7] If there was one thing about which the Victorians were certain, it was that theirs was an era of unprecedented change. As John Stuart Mill put it: 'The conviction is already not far from being universal, that the times are pregnant with change; and that the nineteenth century will be known to posterity as the era of one of the greatest revolutions of which history has preserved the remembrance, in the human mind, and in the whole constitution of human society.'[8] Thomas Carlyle, himself a great contributor to this genre of Victorian auto-diagnosis, summarized the situation beautifully: 'works of that sort are a characteristic of our era'.[9] The Victorian, in other words, can be characterized as an age obsessed with characterizing itself; and the most basic reason for this was that the social and economic landscape of Victorian England was fundamentally different from every other human society (past and present).

---

[7] Friedrich Engels, *The Condition of the Working Class in England* [1845], ed. David McLellan (Oxford: Oxford University Press, 2009), 28.

[8] John Stuart Mill, 'The Spirit of the Age', in *The Spirit of the Age*, ed. Gertrude Himmelfarb (New Haven: Yale University Press, 2007), 52.

[9] Fred Kaplan, *Thomas Carlyle: A Biography* (Ithaca NY: Cornell University Press, 1983), 297.

The new story of industrialism has, at its centre, a Victorian protagonist. This is a point whose importance for Victorian studies cannot be overstated. It makes the Victorian era something more than an interesting moment in British history; it makes it a unique moment in world history, during which the new economic system which would eventually span the globe was being tried out in one small and restless place. Put differently, industrialism is something more than a Victorian context; it is a sign of Victorian distinction, a way to understand not only the integrity of the Victorian world, but its singularity.

If the Victorian world was unique, however, that hardly means it was better. In purely material terms, an argument of that sort might be maintained: by ending the Malthusian trap, industrialism did set Victorian society on a path towards greater material well-being. But industrialism also disrupted a balance that had governed societies for thousands of years. If it made possible, for the first time, real, distributed, economic growth, it also thrust people into new kinds of social relationships, the effect of which could be jarring, if not occasionally terrifying. The basic dynamics which had governed economic and social life since history began were no longer operative, and the exact nature of the new dynamics still unclear. As I have said, this was not all bad: wealth was increasing, communities were growing, jobs were multiplying, etc. And yet, the fact that these changes had never been experienced—and that Victorian England was experiencing them very much alone—left the beneficiaries of industrialism feeling rather like its guinea pigs. What, exactly, lay at the end of all this change? What novel social arrangements were being generated? Would the newly minted railways and steam-engines be replaced by newer innovations—and those, in turn, replaced by ever-newer ones? Would posterity—as George Eliot wondered—be one day 'shot, like a bullet through a tube, by atmospheric pressure from Winchester to Newcastle' (*Felix Holt*, 3)? These sorts of questions, the Victorians could neither escape nor answer—and for that reason their experience of industrialism was tinged with ambivalence, a vague, if pressing anxiety about the unspoken costs of industrial development.

It is at this point that we can begin to turn this new story of industrialism into a new account of industrial literature. And that's because the ambivalence I am describing—the strange mix of boundless confidence and free-floating unease which industrialism inspired—helped the Victorian novel negotiate its relation to industrialism at large. In the old story, remember, if we wanted to track a novel's engagement with industrial life, we looked for signs of industry: factories and railways; class-types and class conflicts; sub-human labourers and noble aristocrats (Disraeli); heartless utilitarians and imaginative orphans (in Dickens); self-proclaimed radicals and beer-swilling miners (Eliot); not to mention the thoughtless managers, saccharine workers, officious union-leaders, or the noble women whose sympathy could heal all social discord. In the new story, however, this approach won't work because the meaning of industrialism is no longer bounded by industry. Instead, we need to seek out topoi which reflect either the revolutionary energy of industrial growth, the new anxiety such growth produced, or both.

There are two topoi that stand out, and they match the two most prominent aspects of post-Malthusian life: economic growth, on the one hand, and population growth, on the other. Or to put it in the terms that became most potent for Victorian literature: progress and social formlessness.

It is easy to understand why industrial change should have inspired a new belief in progress. By a kind of seductive slippage, real improvements in social welfare seemed to portend further improvements, and ever more just beyond those. Early, modest advances carried with them a promise of later, larger ones—and great indeed was the appeal of that promise. The Victorian social theorist, Herbert Spencer, argued that 'Progress…is not an accident but a necessity.'[10] Thomas Babington Macaulay wrote that 'the history of England is emphatically the history of progress.'[11] And Mill, too, insisted that the trajectory of history 'is, and will continue to be, saving occasional and temporary exceptions, one of improvement'. Of all these, however, perhaps the best, clearest expression comes from the more radical Frederic Harrison:

> We all feel a-tiptoe with hope and confidence. We *are* on the threshold of a great time, even if our time is not great itself. In science, in religion, in social organization, we all know what great things are in the air. 'We shall see it, but not *now*'—or rather our children and our children's children will see it…It is *not* the age of money bags and cant, soot, hubbub, and ugliness. It is the age of great expectation and unwearied striving after better things.[12]

Harrison's emphatic italics, along with his confident 'We all', tell the tale. There may be 'soot, hubbub, and ugliness' in Victorian society, but these are not its defining features. What matters—far more than present conditions—is the lure of the future, and the future looked to Harrison like a 'great time' full of 'better things'. If asked what these 'better things' would be, Mill, Macaulay, or Spencer might have loudly disagreed, but they all would have embraced Harrison's core conviction that society has moved, is moving, and will continue to move in a desirable direction. As yet another Victorian intellectual put it, 'amidst the varied reflections which the nineteenth century is in the habit of making on its condition and its prospects, there is one common opinion in which all parties coincide—that we live in an era of progress'.[13]

What the Victorians meant by progress was rather different from their predecessors. Godwin, Condorcet, Priestley, and the other enlightenment champions of progress had their own, quite sanguine, visions of the future, but mostly they meant the distant future, whereas the Victorians had a narrowed time frame, something more like decades than centuries. And whereas 18th-century philosophers tended to imagine progress as governed by the warm presence of God, Providence, Reason, or Science, the Victorians saw

[10] Herbert Spencer, *Social Statics* (New York: D. Appleton and Company, 1899), 32.
[11] Walter Edwards Houghton, *The Victorian Frame of Mind, 1830–1870* (New Haven and London: Yale University Press, 1957), 39.
[12] Frederic Harrison, 'A Few Words about the Nineteenth Century', *Fortnightly Review* 31, no. 184 (1 April 1882): 411–26, 415.
[13] James Anthony Froude, 'On Progress', *Fraser's Magazine* 12, no. 2 (December 1870): 671–90, 671.

only the dominion of industrialism. It was the new energy of industrial growth, in other words, that gave the Victorian conception of progress its great force. By the same token, however, the ambivalence which industrialism activated became, also, an ambivalence about progress. For the Victorians, the most pressing concern was simply: where is all this progress leading? The enlightenment philosophers had known how to answer. 'To Perfection', they would have said, or 'to Harmony' or 'to Truth'. The Victorians, in contrast, worried that even if they reached such noble ends, they would somehow be kept restlessly moving towards promises of ever-greater perfection. 'Ever climbing up the climbing wave' is how Tennyson described it—and he was a believer in progress. Paired, as it were, with industrialism itself, the idea of progress which shaped Victorian life comprised something of the excitement that came with unprecedented material growth and also something of the unease that came with entering—alone—this uncharted historical territory.

Precisely because it was paired with industrialism, because it carried the same weight of ambivalence, progress became a proxy for novelists, an indispensable tool for grappling with the promise and strain of the industrial world. We have looked at the response of one of those novelists already, but if we want to understand Dickens's place in the new story of industrial literature, we have to shift from the earnest admonitions of *Hard Times* to the slightly earlier *Dombey and Son*, and focus, more specifically, on a sequence of descriptive passages which show the full, tortured path from industrialism to progress and then disquiet. We begin with a picture of Staggs's Gardens, a London neighbourhood in the throes of industrial turmoil:

> The first shock of a great earthquake had, just at that period, rent the whole neighbourhood to its centre. Traces of its course were visible on every side. Houses were knocked down; streets broken through and stopped; deep pits and trenches dug in the ground; enormous heaps of earth and clay thrown up; buildings that were undermined and shaking, propped by great beams of wood. Here, a chaos of carts, overthrown and jumbled together, lay topsy-turvy at the bottom of a steep unnatural hill; there, confused treasures of iron soaked and rusted in something that had accidentally become a pond. Everywhere were bridges that led nowhere; thoroughfares that were wholly impassable; Babel towers of chimneys, wanting half their height; temporary wooden houses and enclosures, in the most unlikely situations; carcases of ragged tenements, and fragments of unfinished walls and arches, and piles of scaffolding, and wildernesses of bricks, and giant forms of cranes, and tripods straddling above nothing...In short, the yet unfinished and unopened Railroad was in progress; and, from the very core of all this dire disorder, trailed smoothly away, upon its mighty course of civilization and improvement.[14]

The arrival of the railway is like nothing so much as a natural disaster. What had been (one is invited to presume) a poor but still orderly community becomes a chaos of

[14] Charles Dickens, *Dombey and Son* [1848], ed. Andrew Sanders (London: Penguin Books, 2002), 78–79. Subsequent citations appear in the text.

mangled and indifferent parts: carts, chimneys, bricks, wood, iron bars, and tempo-rary houses. All this 'dire disorder' is presumably part of a process of reconstruction, but at this point there is no trace of that, only the 'topsy-turvy', 'unnatural', 'confused', 'rusted', 'temporary', 'unfinished', 'impassable' landscape—somewhere between 'wil-dernesses' and 'Babel'. For that reason, it is hard to treat Dickens's talk about the 'mighty course of civilization and improvement' as anything but heavy irony. If that were the last word, we might just add this passage to the old pantheon of industrial literature, what with its familiar emphasis on the destructive force of machinery, its keen attention to division and disruption, and its more general transformation of fic-tion into hortatory.

As it happens, though, this is not the last word. Some six years and 150 pages later, *Dombey and Son* returns to Staggs's Gardens, or at least the area which had once borne that name:

> There was no such place as Staggs's Gardens. It had vanished from the earth. Where the old rotten summer-houses once had stood, palaces now reared their heads, and granite columns of gigantic girth opened a vista to the railway world beyond. The miserable waste ground, where the refuse-matter had been heaped of yore, was swallowed up and gone; and in its frowsy stead were tiers of warehouses, crammed with rich goods and costly merchandise. The old by-streets now swarmed with passengers and vehicles of every kind: the new streets that had stopped disheartened in the mud and waggon-ruts, formed towns within themselves, originating wholesome comforts and conveniences belonging to themselves, and never tried nor thought of until they sprung into existence. Bridges that had led to nothing, led to villas, gardens, churches, healthy public walks. The carcasses of houses, and beginnings of new thoroughfares, had started off upon the line at steam's own speed, and shot away into the country in a monster train. [244–45]

Great as the surprise may be, there really does seem to have been a 'mighty course of civ-ilization and improvement'. To be sure, there are some lingering problems: the fact that Staggs's Gardens had 'vanished from the earth' is certainly one concern, as are terms like 'carcasses' and 'swarmed' streets, especially alongside the ressentiment of 'palaces', 'rich goods', and 'costly merchandise'. But 'wholesome comforts and conveniences', sound nice, especially when you are told that such conveniences were 'never tried nor thought of' before the railway. And not only are all the formerly half-built bridges and roadways now complete, but they lead to 'villas, gardens, churches, healthy public walks'. Utopia it is not, but the new Staggs's Gardens (or the ex-Staggs's Gardens) is still a tremendous, material improvement. Gentrification we might call it, only with the caveat that gentrifi-cation can involve both the displacement of the poor and sometimes also their economic gain. Such gains had never been possible before, but industrialism made them possible, enabling just the kind of shared benefits we see here.

As ever with industrial progress, however, these real improvements invite a new set of concerns—not, I should say, that the comforts of Staggs's Gardens are somehow apoc-ryphal, or even that they depend on the exploitation of toiling millions. No, the deepest concern is that all this change and progress has generated a restless drive for further change and endless progress:

> To and from the heart of this great change, all day and night, throbbing currents rushed and returned incessantly like its life's blood. Crowds of people and mountains of goods, departing and arriving scores upon scores of times in every four-and-twenty hours, produced a fermentation in the place that was always in action…Night and day the conquering engines rumbled at their distant work, or, advancing smoothly to their journey's end, and gliding like tame dragons into the allotted corners grooved out to the inch for their reception, stood bubbling and trembling there, making the walls quake, as if they were dilating with the secret knowledge of great powers yet unsuspected in them, and strong purposes not yet achieved. [245–46]

Once the railway takes hold, it cannot be stopped; it remakes everything in its own image. Not only do the trains rush to and fro, but so too do the 'crowds of people' and the 'mountains of goods'. The most telling bit is in that last line, where the dragons dilate with the 'secret knowledge of great powers yet unsuspected in them'. If there is one surety in all this change, it is that more change will come. Staggs's Gardens has gone from a ramshackle construction site to a place of 'wholesome comforts' but its course is not finished; it may continue forever towards an end that cannot be seen. These railway dragons seem to know, too well, that they are not done mutating, that someday they will cease to be railways and metamorphose into automobiles or airplanes or rockets: something faster, more powerful, and ever more promising. And Dickens's concern, it would seem, is that we will continue to follow those faster vehicles on more rapid trips along shifting routes until we no longer know how to stop, rest, or find even a moment of calm.

This was one of the great anxieties activated by industrialism: a concern that economic progress was not just something taking place around people, but inside of them. It was turning the Victorians into industrial people: restless types who could thrive only in a world of open-ended, if not endless development; agitated men and women who could see in calm and tranquillity only boredom and stasis. When looking for traces of industrialism in the Victorian novel, these are symptoms worth noting: characters discontented with anything but future happiness, places defined not by what they are but what they are becoming, plotlines that would rather open out into the great unsaid than close themselves in a final, satisfying resolution.

The other thing to note, when looking for traces of industrialism in the Victorian novel, is social formlessness. If the anxieties of progress reflect one axis of industrial change, namely economic growth, anxieties of social formlessness reflect the other: population growth. Industrialism, remember, refers to the breaking of a trap, and that trap had two pinching halves: limits to economic welfare on the one side, and limits to population on the other. Escaping from the Malthusian world meant not only that the economy could grow in a sustainable way but that populations could grow alongside. Nineteenth-century England saw nearly a tripling in population, from some 10 million to over 30 million. Even more importantly—for lived experience as for Victorian writing—was the bias towards large communities. Whereas, in 1800, London was the only city with over 100,000 people, by 1900 there were over thirty cities of that size.[15] And one consequence of this shift from village life to towns and cities was a change in the conception of society itself. This is the reason that the category of the 'social' gained a new kind of empirical coherence and attracted new scientific interest (as Mary Poovey has described so eloquently).[16] It is also the reason the word 'social' became so politically contentious: Robert Owen talked about social-ism as versus individual-ism; William Lovett thought 'social reformation' was the key to 'social happiness'; Engels thought the key to change was 'social war'.[17] More than anything else, radical change meant radical social change.

If we wanted, we could follow these debates about the need for social change back to the same social problem novels that we left in the previous section. That would certainly be one way to integrate them into this new story of industrialism. Ultimately, though, such a path would still be too narrow, and if we want to clear a broader one we need to think less specifically about social conflict and more basically about everyday social experience. The sheer number of people that an average 19th-century Englishman encountered on a daily basis was orders of magnitude higher than the number his grandfather did. More to the point, the amount of information required to keep track of those new people was similarly enormous. Social life had given way to something more like a social system, something so abstract that it was difficult to fathom, directly. Indeed, a whole new language developed to make sense of this apparent senselessness: the language of statistics. Yet, for all its power, statistics was not particularly well suited to literary expression. Instead, the most forceful, the most memorable, the most characteristic literary response to the expanding scope of social interaction was simply to give voice to the experience of unfathomability.

There are, I should say, good examples of this in the social problem novel itself. In fact, if we start there and then move into the wider seas of the Victorian novel, we can get a good sense for how, precisely, the new approach to industrialism expands our understanding of industrial literature. Here, to begin with, is another passage from Disraeli's *Sybil*:

> There is no community in England; there is aggregation, but aggregation under circumstances which make it rather a dissociating than a uniting principle…A density of population implies a severer struggle for existence, and a consequent repulsion of elements brought into too close contact. In great cities men are brought together by the desire of gain. They are not in a state of co-operation, but of isolation, as to the making of fortunes; and for all the rest they are careless of neighbours. [71–72]

[15] Harold James Perkin, *Origins of Modern English Society* (London: Routledge, 1991), 117.

[16] Mary Poovey, *Making a Social Body: British Cultural Formation, 1830–1864* (Chicago: University of Chicago Press, 1995).

[17] William Lovett, *Chartism: A New Organization of the People* [1840] (Leicester: Leicester University Press, 1969).

Once upon a time, Disraeli tells us, there was a sense of community in England. Today, unfortunately, there is none. In what amounts to a bitter paradox, the increasing 'density of population' has made society more diffuse, rather than more tightly integrated. So where cooperation once reigned, now isolation prevails; and where fellow-feeling once governed, now there is only an anarchy of aggregation. The sentiment here is bleak but hardly idiosyncratic. It is something that you find in Carlyle, F.D. Maurice, Cooke Taylor, and Marx—to name just a few. Indeed, if there's one thing to note about this quotation from Disraeli it is that it seems familiarly essayistic—perhaps even prosaic. Where, we might ask, are its more literary features? Where are the techniques and strategies that give literature its unique intellectual and aesthetic powers (figural language, mixed perspective, polysemy, emplotment, etc.)? Disraeli's lines may tell us something about industrialism, but what do they tell us about industrialism *and the novel*?

Contrast, for instance, this famous extract from *Hard Times*:

> Seen from a distance in such weather, Coketown lay shrouded in a haze of its own, which appeared impervious to the sun's rays. You only knew the town was there, because you knew there could have been no such sulky blotch upon the prospect without a town. A blur of soot and smoke, now confusedly tending this way, now that way, now aspiring to the vault of Heaven, now murkily creeping along the earth, as the wind rose and fell, or changed its quarter: a dense formless jumble, with sheets of cross light in it, that showed nothing but masses of darkness. [111]

What was description in Disraeli, becomes figuration in Dickens. It is not people that we see here, but haze, soot, and smoke; disaggregated particles standing in for disaggregated individuals. Society, community—these things are present only by loose implication: in the word 'masses' for instance, or the presupposed fact that every town must have its townspeople. You might even be tempted to dismiss the connection between this 'dense formless jumble' of 'soot and smoke' and the dense formless structure of industrial society if it weren't reinforced by passages throughout the novel (not least of all those far-distant 'teeming myriads of human beings' that Gradgrind surveys from his observatory.) The great genius of this moment in Dickens lies in its ability to use the figural resources of literature to square the circle of industry, industrialism, and society. Factories produce soot; factories attract alienated hands; soot becomes a figure for the new mass of alienated hands—a doubled figure, in fact, connected both through the metonymic chain of factory-soot-hand and the metaphor system of formless, indistinct things.

It is an elegant, literary solution, and it found a broad resonance in Victorian literature—well beyond the confines of the social problem novel (sometimes, beyond the genre of the novel itself, as for instance in the smoky world of Tennyson's *Idylls of the King*). Dickens himself returned to it for the opening tableau of his later *Bleak House*, where in fact he gave his anaphora of 'fog' a new figural potential. Unlike the soot in *Hard Times*, which is so thickly negative and so baleful to all coherence, this fog seems to compose a kind of integument, a thin tissue binding the city together. *Bleak House's* fog, in other words, is both a metaphor for incoherence and a testament to incipient solidarity.

Something of this same duality also shapes George Eliot's *Middlemarch*, the novel she wrote immediately after *Felix Holt*. In fact, thinking about fog in these terms—as a widespread and evolving figure for the restructuring of society under the pressure of industrialism—provides a new way of understanding Eliot's social vision. To simplify a bit, the word most often associated with this vision is probably organic. Society, she is wont to say, is held together like a web, or moves together like a river, or, in one of *Middlemarch*'s richest poetic epigraphs, sings together on waves of sound:

> How will you know the pitch of that great bell
> Too large for you to stir? Let but a flute
> Play 'neath the fine-mixed metal: listen close
> Till the right note flows forth, a silvery rill:
> Then shall the huge bell tremble—then the mass
> With myriad waves concurrent shall respond
> In low soft unison.[18]

If it is not immediately clear that these lines are about social form, rather than, say, the acoustics of bells, the evidence is nonetheless there—most directly in that pointed word 'mass', and most profoundly in the final cadence, where the 'mass' is made a chorus of individuals, singing in 'low soft unison'. Though the whole of society may seem over-grown or unwieldy, the right cause, the right ideal, the right note will show its resounding harmony.

Fog is different, even if it, too, stands in for unwieldy society. As Lydgate, for instance, struggles to advance his fledgling medical practice, he is routinely frustrated by the ignorant chatter of the townspeople. Yet, he decides not to intercede, believing instead that it would be 'as useless to fight against the interpretations of ignorance as to whip the fog' (449). Fog is his figure for the great, impenetrable, resistless, and stupid world of the many. And for him at least, this fog is never lifted; if anything, it gains in force as the novel progresses. In the end, it is just this foggy and diffuse world of gossip—specifically, the wafting presumption of Lydgate's association with Bulstrode—which seals Lydgate's fate and conclusively ends his ability to work his calling. And there is fog, as well, in Lydgate's personal life. It races him home, one could say, for it is already there when he returns to escape from the 'infamous suspicions' (756) that have ruined his public reputation. Confessing his failure to his wife, and hoping to be forgiven, he finds instead a 'chill fog which had gathered between them' (757). Right or wrong, public opinion has seeped across the threshold, consenting as it were not just to the failure of his profession but to the equal failure of his marriage.

The chattering voices that make up *Middlemarch*'s fog are not exactly those of a chorus resounding with the sound of a single bell. Here, the resonance is more baleful than

---

[18] George Eliot, *Middlemarch* [1871–72], ed. Rosemary Ashton (New York: Penguin Books, 1994), 293. Subsequent citations appear in the text.

beautiful, and its effect on the people we care about most is particularly lamentable. Yet, there also seems to be a grudging respect for its breadth and authority. The idle many who compose this fog are not put down, as they might easily be with a stroke of the authorial pen or the rising of a fictional sun. Instead, they are allowed their victory. And part of the question, in Eliot, is whether that is a just victory, or simply an inevitable one. How much should we value this potent social fog, with all its energy of inchoate organization? No doubt, we would prefer a world in which both the crowd and our Lydgate can emerge triumphant, but what if that is not among the choices. What if the desire for social cohesion—and the fear of that diffuse, disaggregated society that Disraeli and Dickens both espy—means that we must take coherence as we find it. Put differently, what happens if, when the bell starts trembling, we discover that we don't much like the sound it makes—or that it drowns out the voice of a favourite singer. This is the kind of vexed, social question that only becomes visible through the *Middlemarch* fog.

More generally, these were the terms—fog, smoke, formless, mob—which Eliot and her peers used to capture the social transformations of industrialism. In order to see this, however—in order to connect the figures of social formlessness with the unfolding of industrial change—we have to rethink the meaning of industrialism itself. In particular, we have to recognize that it involves something more than the rise of industry, with its factories, machines, and class conflicts. Its most revolutionary effects were tied, instead, to the emergence of a new economic and demographic dynamic beyond the reach of Malthus and his long-effective trap. Focusing on this broader dynamic allows us to finally escape the hold of the social problem novel and expose a wider field of influence. Only if we replace the old, outdated story of industrialism with a new, updated version, in other words, can we produce a more complete account of industrialism and the Victorian novel.

SUGGESTED READING

Benjamin, Walter. 'On the Theory of Knowledge, Theory of Progress'. In *The Arcades Project.* Edited by Tiedemann. Translated by H. Eiland and Kevin McLaughlin. Cambridge: Belknap Press, 2002, 456–88.

Bizup, Joseph. *Manufacturing Culture: Vindications of Early Victorian Industry.* Victorian Literature and Culture Series. Charlottesville: University of Virginia Press, 2003.

Brantlinger, Patrick. *The Spirit of Reform: British Literature and Politics, 1832–1867.* Cambridge: Harvard University Press, 1977.

Buckley, Jerome Hamilton. *The Triumph of Time: A Study of the Victorian Concepts of Time, History, Progress, and Decadence.* Cambridge: Belknap Press, 1966.

Clark, Gregory. *A Farewell to Alms: A Brief Economic History of the World.* Princeton: Princeton University Press, 2007.

Gagnier, Regenia. *The Insatiability of Human Wants: Economics and Aesthetics in Market Society.* Chicago: University of Chicago Press, 2000.

Gallagher, Catherine. *The Industrial Reformation of English Fiction: Social Discourse and Narrative Form, 1832–1867.* Chicago: University of Chicago Press, 1985.

Jameson, Fredric. 'Progress Versus Utopia; Or, Can We Imagine the Future'. *Science Fiction Studies* 9, no. 2 [27] (1982): 147–58.

Lukács, Georg. 'Realism in the Balance'. In *Aesthetics and Politics*. Edited by Fredric Jameson.London: Verso, 1980, 28–59.

Mokyr, Joel. *The Enlightened Economy: An Economic History of Britain, 1700–1850*. New Haven: Yale University Press, 2009.

Perkin, Harold James. *The Origins of Modern English Society 1780–1880*. London: Routledge & Kegan Paul, 1969.

Poovey, Mary. *Making a Social Body: British Cultural Formation, 1830–1864*. Chicago: University of Chicago Press, 1995.

Williams, Raymond. *Culture and Society, 1780–1950*. 2nd edn. London: Chatto and Windus, 1959.

18

THE PROTESTANT ETHIC AND THE 'SPIRIT' OF MONEY: MAX WEBER, *SILAS MARNER*, AND THE VICTORIAN NOVEL

GEORGE LEVINE

When I was young and simple I thought the nineteenth-century novel was driven by love; but now, in my more complicated riper years, I see that it's also driven by money, which indeed holds a more central place in it than love does, no matter how much the virtue of love may be waved idealistically aloft.

(Margaret Atwood, *Payback*)

I

Who upon first reading those famously love-driven novels *Wuthering Heights* and *Jane Eyre* is swept up by Heathcliff's finances or Rochester's balance sheet? We don't immediately register that Heathcliff gains power by (somehow) gaining wealth, so that even the Victorian novel most profoundly preoccupied with irrational and perhaps even supernatural forces and most contemptuous of mere wealth depends on wealth to develop its plot.[1] So too the romance between Rochester and Jane may obscure but cannot erase the fact that it is deeply inflected by class; Jane manages real independence only when she inherits unexpected money. She marks her virtue by giving away three-quarters but

---

[1] 'The crux of *Wuthering Heights*', says Terry Eagleton, 'must be conceded by even the most remorselessly mythological and mystical of critics to be a social one,' *Myths of Power: A Marxist Study of the Brontes* (New York: Barnes and Noble, 1975), 100.

definitely not *all* of that money, and only then acquires the power to both love and master Rochester and enter the class she had despised. Atwood is right to note that money 'holds a more central place than love' in the Victorian novel.

The Victorian novel was built primarily out of its profitability. Here at least Dr Johnson was completely right: 'No man but a blockhead ever wrote except for money'. No woman either. Although also an extraordinary virtuoso exploration of a child's consciousness, *David Copperfield* is obsessed with money; happiness depends, as Micawber repeatedly puts it, on sixpence, whether asset or debit. David's story traces a rise from near poverty and oppression to wealth acquired through writing—what else?—novels, and the book can be taken as an exemplum of the novel as money-maker, at the same time as it is a story *about* money, and about novel-writing as a way to middle-class comfort and respectability.[2]

Thackeray confronts more directly than Dickens the crucial role money plays in novel-writing. David's contemporary, Pendennis, must learn the lesson of money in a more cynically counter-romantic way. Although he begins in a very different social place than David, and although he gets an Oxbridge education, he too has to gain his fortune (and his bride) through novel-writing. He escapes debt and disaster, but also false romantic expectations that would have had him marry down instead of up, a catastrophe—seen as a catastrophe—that badly damages Penn's friend Warrington. Here, quite explicitly, Atwood's perception is confirmed: whatever the Victorian novel might want us to believe about romance, money is far more important.

A marriage that is not conditional on or related to economic questions is rare in Victorian novels. Romance and money are so thoroughly intermingled that in many cases the very substance and form of the book depends on the entanglement (or disentanglement). Even so 'modernist' and psychological a novel—to take a surprisingly obvious example—as Henry James's *Portrait of a Lady* hangs absolutely on the relation between money and marriage. One thinks, among dozens of more centrally Victorian examples, of Margaret Oliphant's *The Perpetual Curate*, whose primary drama arises from the curate's relative poverty, which leaves him unwilling or unable to propose to his beloved Lucy. As counterpoint to this drama, however, there is the story of the new Rector's wife, Mrs Morgan, who finds herself disappointed in her husband's behaviour and wondering if his long wait for marriage had soured his nature, and, as a consequence, whether it wouldn't have been better for their relationship if they had married young, broke, and in love. The book is characteristically evasive about the answer—and it is this kind of evasiveness with which I will be concerned in much of this chapter. Here

---

[2] D.A. Miller sees the Victorian novel as a kind of handbook for the new bourgeoisie, a confirmation of 'the novel reader in his identity as a "liberal subject"', *The Novel and the Police* (Berkeley: University of California Press, 1988), x. While I do not follow Miller into his Foucauldian understanding of an inescapably containing system, some of the novel's strategies for disguising its policing powers and intimating the possibility of a freedom it cannot really demonstrate parallel the way money operates in these books. While money is for the most part regarded with moral horror, Micawber has it right: happiness and success depend on money.

are Mrs Morgan's thoughts as the book draws to a close and as the perpetual curate has stopped being perpetual and is awarded the position as Rector that wipes out all money problems (it is obviously no accident that Oliphant arranges the narrative so that the curate, Mr Wentworth, gets the position that Mr Morgan leaves):

> Once more the familiar thought returned to her of what a different woman she would have been had she come to her first experiences of life with the courage and confidence of twenty or even of five-and-twenty, which was the age Mrs Morgan dwelt upon most kindly. And then she thought with a thrill of vivid kindness and a touch of tender envy of Lucy Wodehouse, who would now have no possible occasion to wait those ten years.[3]

So the novel sets up the question and refuses to answer it: it allows the reader the pleasure of the romantic comic resolution made possible by the money that comes with the Rectorship, but does not suggest that romantic marriage despite poverty, would work, or is even a good idea.

In Thackeray and Trollope, rare Victorian birds in this respect, there would be less chance of that kind of evasion. For Thackeray, indeed, marriage is a sure passage to disillusion, with or without money. It is hard to forget the conclusion to *Vanity Fair*, in which Dobbin marries Amelia but the romance is gone, and Amelia fully realizes that he is much fonder of their daughter, Janey, than he is of her. But this does not imply that an early romantic marriage would have ended much better.[4] Penn, unlike David Copperfield, is cynical about his own art—as Thackeray often is, explicitly, in other of his novels. The priority of money over romance is also central to Trollope's work and to his self-description in the *Autobiography* and it is often thematized in his novels. Mrs Greenow in *Can You Forgive Her?*, for example, is both a good person and a very practical one on questions of money, for she frankly admits that she allows herself 'rocks and valleys' only because she has enough 'bread and cheese'. She chooses the dashingly romantic rascal rather than her more prosperous suitor because the death of her first husband, a much older man who was loaded with 'bread and cheese', left her with more than enough money to free her for indulgence in 'rocks and valleys'.

Most often, however, Victorian novels imply that the moral and the romantic can triumph over the exigencies of money. Agnes is forever pointing upwards—and the problems posed by the importance of money, as in *The Perpetual Curate*, are evaded. But money is there in all sorts of guises, doing all sorts of work: it is a question, a source of conflict, a morally erosive force, an aspiration, a temptation. And yet, at critical moments it either drops from attention or suddenly turns up (often through inheritance), and the problems its absence had raised along the way tend to disappear. Just

---

[3] Margaret Oliphant, *The Perpetual Curate*, 2 vols. (Leipzig: Tauchnitz, 1870), 2: 333.

[4] Thackeray's very funny and very cynical story, 'Rebecca and Rowena', makes a mockery of the 'happily ever after' implication of the comic/romance ending.

when they are coming to terms with the question of money's power and ubiquity, the novels shift focus. At the end of *Our Mutual Friend*, Bella wins Harmon by demonstrating that love matters to her more than money, but she gets the money she originally wanted anyway, by marrying Harmon, whose wealth was dependent on his marrying her, and displacing the honourable and loving Boffins. No further word suggests that money ever after enters the minds of the lovers. Romance trumps money (almost) every time.

Our Mutual Friend makes an excellent example of the evasion with which I am concerned here. Money, or the revulsion from it, drives all the rest of the book, most famously, in the ostentatiously symbolic dust heaps. Money is simply garbage—valuable garbage, but nevertheless garbage (which throws a grubby light on the happiness, or at least secular well-being of John and Bella.) Virtually every subplot of the novel works out so as to undercut the importance of money or to emphasize its nastiness: Wegg gets his comeuppance, the repulsive and hypocritical Fascination Fledgeby is appropriately punished, and the fashionably insidious Lammles are defeated. Wrayburn has to die (or almost) to be purged into marrying down to Lizzie. And yet the central romance is resolved with the remarkable coincidence that marrying Bella is not only the condition for Harmon's inheritance of the money, but that Harmon really loves her and *wants* to marry her, while she has become utterly regardless of the money she sought so intensely at the start and gets only because she doesn't want it any more.

Perhaps less obviously, this kind of contortion of plot and self-contradiction of theme is characteristic of the Victorian novel's consistent effort to reconcile romance and moral value with money. Money cannot be avoided although its implications can be evaded; it determines the shape of plots and the fates of protagonists; and it exerts distorting pressure on novelists who refuse to be Trollopean.

Recent criticism, struck by the importance to the nature of Victorian novels themselves of their obsessive preoccupation with money, has studied in great and often illuminating detail both the literature of political economy and the actual financial conditions prevailing in Victorian times. It has been concerned with the entire financial system[5] and with the things that it comprised—like bank crashes, financial bubbles, limited liability, laws of inheritance, stock market, investments and interest rates, insurance, and the nature and meaning of money itself. This criticism rightly attempts to explore the relation between economic and wider cultural history. It is, as one of the studies puts it, work of 'intense interdisciplinarity'.[6]

---

[5] Mary Poovey has been the leading figure in the study of Victorian finance in relation to literature. Her *The Financial System in Nineteenth-Century Britain* (New York: Oxford University Press, 2003) is a virtual guidebook to the way the system worked, from credit and debt to banking and coinage. It includes a wide range of helpful essays by the Victorians themselves.

[6] Nancy Henry and Cannon Schmitt, *New Perspectives on Finance and Culture* (Bloomington: Indiana University Press, 2009), 3. Poovey's magisterial *Genres of the Credit Economy: Mediating Value in Eighteenth- and Nineteenth-Century Britain* (Chicago: University of Chicago Press, 2008) is the most

What I propose to do here is rather less intensely interdisciplinary. In considering the Victorian novel's tensions between money, romance, and moral value, I begin with the obvious: the 19th century was the age, as Marx rightly saw, of the middle-class revolution—of enormous expansion in commerce, capitalism, and wealth, and thus also the age when the very concept of class warfare emerged. Instability and uncertainty of class status helped give rise to that tradition, familiar to readers of Victorian fiction, of the coming-of-age story transmuted into the peculiarly English version of the *Bildungsroman*, invariably a story of upward social mobility, or, very occasionally, its thwarting.[7] As Franco Moretti put it, the *Bildungsroman* emerges when 'status society starts to collapse'.[8] The emerging middle class, with its base in commerce and industry, and with cultural values different from that of a society based in land and aristocracy and long traditions of religion, law, and social organization, so scrambled the balance of power that established hierarchies were constantly under threat. Money displaced land as the basis of power. Markets expanded globally, colonial expansion became the norm, and in the general restructuring the condition of women became a critically important question. Many of the Victorian novel's central subjects—domesticity itself, 'great expectations', romance across classes, *Bildung*—reflect a new apparent fluidity of social movement,[9] new possibilities of social arrangements, the transformation of agrarian into urban populations, and changes in the nature of work itself. Under these conditions, money was the common denominator—an object to be obtained and a condition for success and happy endings. Money can't buy happiness! You couldn't prove that by reading Victorian novels (even the famous story of Scrooge in *A Christmas Carol*), although the moral of their story is often just that.

The details of the financial system, which expanded so rapidly at the end of the century, are of course important for anyone wanting to talk about Victorian economics or about how money can be made to perform its work in the Victorian novel. But I want to consider 'money' as a many-faceted element *inside* of fiction which, though it necessarily reflects the political and social activities of its moment, has very particular work to do inside the novels. I am not so much concerned with the real details of Victorian money-handling as I am with the fact of its pervasive presence and with the *attitudes*

authoritative deployment of the materials relating to finance in a study of the splitting off of economic and literary discourses.

[7] In *Upward Mobility and the Common Good: Toward a Literary History of the Welfare State* (Princeton: Princeton University Press, 2009), Bruce Robbins shows how upward mobility, that narrative of individualist self-reliance and self-help, implies dependence on the social system. The curious paradox parallels the one that I am wanting here to emphasize: that is, the narrative of revulsion from money almost always entails a system in which money is essential to happiness—and therefore to the Victorian form of comic realism.

[8] See Franco Moretti, *The Way of the World: The Bildungsroman in European Culture* (London: Verso Books, 1987), 2; and Julia Prewitt Brown's 'The Moral Scope of the English *Bildungsroman*' in this volume.

[9] The title of one of Samuel Smiles's most successful books tells the story: *Self Help; with Illustrations of Conduct and Perseverance* (1859). Smiles's book, telling the story of famous people who worked their way up from the lower classes begins this way: 'Heaven helps those who help themselves.'

towards it manifested in the novels—with the way characters get it or lose it, act towards it and think about it; with the way the narrators themselves talk about it, and their narratives are shaped in relation to it; and most importantly, with the way the novel's necessary, indeed inevitable, preoccupation with money forces to the surface contradictions and tensions in Victorian ethical and religious beliefs, and in so doing affects the form of the novel. Behind all of this lies my large guess that having to deal with money (or finding various devices to avoid dealing with it) pushed the Victorian novel towards a secularism that it often tried to deny. As I will later show in my reading of *Silas Marner*, the novel attempts to reconcile lucre and morality by turning money itself into evidence of God's grace. But the price of this reconciliation is the very morality that the Victorian novel sought to promote.

II

What I call my 'large guess' is partly supported by Max Weber's discussion of the relation of capitalism to religion in *The Protestant Ethic and the 'Spirit' of Capitalism*. He suggests an ironic consequence of the fact that 'Protestant asceticism works with all its force against the uninhibited *enjoyment* of possessions': that is, one can then acquire wealth as long as one doesn't indulge oneself with it, so that Protestant asceticism 'has the effect of liberating the *acquisition of wealth* from the inhibitions of traditionalist ethics; it breaks the fetters on the striving for gain by not only legalizing it, but…seeing it as directly willed by God'.[10] Much of the tension in Victorian novels when good characters acquire wealth or morally marginal characters seek it can be attributed to this ironic state of things. The fight, as Weber puts it, 'against the lusts of the flesh' follows willy-nilly from the accumulation of wealth, however austerely gotten and used, and, as with the monastic orders of the Middle Ages, the history of Quakers and Puritans in developing capitalist cultures is 'one of constant wrestling with the problem of the secularizing influence of wealth' (118). 'The secularizing influence of wealth' is manifest in the Victorian novel, even as it too might be described as a battleground against it.

Weber's book forms an almost uncanny guide to the place of money in Victorian fiction, whose overt resistance to it and implication in it replay, or rather anticipate, the history of capitalism as Weber, at least, understands it. The irony that Weber pursues in finding religious 'spirit' in the history and the continuing practice of capitalist enterprise plays itself out inside the novels. Thus, the secularizing influence of wealth seeps into pious novels almost without exception. It is not that when the good characters finally do acquire wealth they lapse into secular self-indulgence, but that the very shape and

---

[10] Max Weber, *The Protestant Ethic and the 'Spirit' of Capitalism and Other Writings* (New York and London: Penguin Books, 2002), 115. Subsequent citations appear in the text.

direction of novels, particularly those with comic endings, implicitly accept, as they must, the absolute necessity of wealth and money in modern society. The Calvinist insistence on revulsion from things of this world runs counter to realist descriptions of a society in which money is a condition, if not of happiness, then at least of survival. Stories with happy endings must almost invariably, if usually quietly, send the happy lovers off to a life of material comfort.

If one pauses to consider those novels whose comic endings seem to be largely determined by the renunciation of money and the triumph of romantic love and the moral life, like *Little Dorrit*, or *North and South*, or *Middlemarch*, or even so rigorously pious a book as *The Heir of Redclyffe*, one is likely to find that enough money quietly remains to leave the protagonists comfortable, or that there is some distortion of plot—as we have seen in *Our Mutual Friend*—that makes the (more or less) happy resolution possible and involves the appearance of money (the old pre-capitalist inheritance plot is always handy), or that there is a touch of the tragic, even of the embittered, in the happy ending. The stunningly beautiful and moving ending of *Little Dorrit* contains within it a rather bitter recognition that the lives of Amy and Clennam will be conducted among 'the arrogant and the forward, and the vain'. The Calvinist spirit remains uncontaminated—sacrifice and hard work, not worldly indulgence, mark the 'good' characters. But the narrative itself—although it always punishes the pursuit of money—is only possible because the protagonists can live *in* society with sufficient material means to allow the readers, themselves dwellers in a burgeoning capitalist economy, to believe in their happiness.

But unlike the novelists, Weber frankly confronts the paradox of his argument. How is it possible to think of capitalism, with its unquenchable quest for money, as somehow fuelled by a world-denying Calvinism, a religious pietism, for which the ultimate and virtually only value was personal salvation? How could capitalism 'save' anyone— spiritually, that is? Weber's thesis has been the subject of sustained debate by social scientists and historians for many years. The problem was to account for the fact that 'business leaders and owners of capital, as well as the skilled higher strata of the labor force ... tend to be predominantly *Protestant*' (1). Whatever the truth about history, the thesis works for the Victorian novel.

Weber begins by invoking Carlyle, who describes the early bourgeois defence of Puritan authority ('tyranny') as 'one of the last of our heroisms' (3). Carlyle's moral authority over much of early Victorian culture notoriously plays out Weber's secularized version of Calvinism: 'work while it is day, for the night cometh in which no man can work'. Carlyle several times invokes this version of John: 9.4, and the gospel of work was notoriously a leitmotif of Victorian culture. But Weber seeks to understand this phenomenon in terms of 'the distinct mental characteristics which have been instilled' in workers 'by the influence on them of the religious atmosphere of their locality and home background' (4). Carlyle scholarship focuses on his Calvinist roots; Weber finds those Calvinist roots in capitalism itself.

Given the austerity of the Protestantism of Luther and Calvin, Weber thought that the relation between Protestantism and capitalism has to be found not in the worldly

wealth of capitalism, but in 'purely religious features'(7).[11] Just as Weber sought explanation of capitalism in religion, so it seems to me fruitful to find explanation of the novel's
secularism in *its* religion. Although the primary attention to 'religion' in most Victorian
literary study is to 'the Victorian crisis of faith', historians have long been demonstrating
that the Victorian period was perhaps the most intensely religious in English history.[12]
Boyd Hilton argues that the 'surrounding culture' was in the 19th century saturated with
'traces of religion...Before 1850, especially, religious feeling and biblical terminology
so permeated all aspects of thought (including atheism) that it is hard to dismiss them
as epiphenomenal.'[13] This religiosity is evident in the Victorian novel, well after 1850,
even in implicitly secular novels and often in the work of those writers who are regularly
invoked as indicators of the 'crisis'.

Weber takes Benjamin Franklin's *Autobiography*, which claims that 'The aim of a
man's life is indeed moneymaking', as strong evidence for his thesis. Franklin, he says,
'saw his discovery of the "usefulness" of virtue as a revelation from God'. Hence the
Weberian irony: 'the "summum bonum" of this "ethic" is the *making of money* and yet
more money, coupled with a strict avoidance of all uninhibited enjoyment'(12). Those
who got involved in the developing capitalist system 'had *no wish* to consume, but only
to make profits'(22). Franklin's view is virtually parodied in Dickens' representations
of Bounderby and Gradgrind in *Hard Times*; and yet that novel is itself divided by its
recognition that 'people mutht be amuthed' and its inability to respond to the capitalist
system it shows to be in place. Bounderby and Gradgrind insist on the austerity and difficulty of capitalist work and do not indulge themselves with the money (or at least pretend not to indulge themselves). Dickens offers as an alternative to this austere and nasty
capitalism the amusement of the people. But this response can't adequately address the
kinds of problems the Gradgrinds of the world create, unless one believes that the capitalist programme is fine, but should allow for a little pleasure along the way. Amusement
seems to be Dickens's answer to capitalism, and yet he has no sustained critique of capitalism, except that it disallows self-indulgence. His sentimental and romantic assertion
of amusement and love as opposed to money evades again the fundamental problems.

Another important idea of Weber's reverberates in the Victorian novel: he emphasizes the importance of 'vocation'—a religious concept of 'calling'—to the development
of capitalism. He notes how Franklin's Calvinist father 'constantly drummed into him in
his youth' this biblical text: 'Seest thou a man active *in his calling*, he shall stand before
kings.' 'Moneymaking', Weber goes on, 'is, within the modern economic order, the result

---

[11]   Weber was one of the critical figures in 'the long-standing theoretical debate on the relationship
between religious or cosmological belief and social thought', as Boyd Hilton points out, *The Age of
Atonement: The Influence of Evangelicalism on Social and Economic Thought, 1785–1865* (Oxford:
Clarendon Press, 1988), ix.

[12]   Timothy Larsen calls this emphasis a distortion. 'A distinction needs to be made', he claims,
'between a theme in literature or English studies and a judgment regarding what a historical period
itself was actually like', *Crisis of Doubt: Honest Faith in Nineteenth-Century England* (Oxford: Oxford
University Press, 2006), 3.

[13]   Hilton, *The Age of Atonement*, xi.

and the expression of diligence *in one's calling*' (12). As calling, work becomes its own end, a form of 'piety', and one can feel in the Victorian novel the reverence with which work is imagined.

John Halifax, Gentleman is perhaps the most obvious example. There the impoverished Halifax exudes virtue in every action, refusing money—charity is demeaning—beyond what the work is worth, and giving to work his absolute and total commitment. Victorian novelists celebrate this virtue well beyond the extreme and often implausible conditions of Dinah Mullock Craik's best-selling novel. It virtually initiates George Eliot's writing career; the first chapter of *Adam Bede* finds Adam refusing to stop working just because the closing hour has struck: 'I hate to see a man's arms drop down as if he was shot, before the clock's fairly struck, just as if he'd never a bit o' pride and delight in 's work.'[14] Of course, Adam is no capitalist, but it is just the 'spirit' he shows here that lies, on Weber's account, at the root of developed capitalism. And although Adam is ready to claim that work provides a kind of pleasure, the pleasure is precisely selfless. The actual work is hard (and Mullock Craik spares young John no difficulty, forcing him to work for long hours and years among the awful smelling skins of dead animals). The pleasure is doing it well. It is not by accident that the whole first scene of *Adam Bede* is framed by Adam's singing a hymn as he works:

> Awake my soul, and with the sun
> Thy daily stage of duty run;
> Shake off dull sloth...

But this pious notion of duty, work and 'calling' tends to separate 'money' from the work that produces it. Adam does not work for money but to do the job well: it is the activity not the 'reward' that justifies the work in the first place. 'Shake off dull sloth'.

Ruskin is in effect the great theorizer of this quasi-religious ideal. In his passionate attack on Political Economy and the idea of the economic man,[15] who is 'actuated only by motives of business' and never makes anything except for money, he evokes the likeness of 'vocation'. One must not work just for money, but to serve the consumer as well as possible and fulfil one's own creative possibilities (see the famous passages in *Stones of Venice* that celebrate the unevenness of the work of the labourers on Gothic cathedrals). That requires the best work of which one is capable. As for Caleb Garth in *Middlemarch*, 'business' is a vocation, and Ruskin pushes the idea to its limit by insisting that one must be willing to sacrifice one's life to do one's work right. 'The true function of a merchant

---

[14]   George Eliot, *Adam Bede*, ed. Valentine Cunningham (New York: Oxford University Press, 1996), 10.

[15]   'Political economy', says Walter Bagehot, 'assumes that he always makes that which brings him in most at least cost, and that he will make it in the way that will produce most and spend least; it assumes that every man who buys, buys with his whole heart, and that he who sells, sells with his whole heart, each wanting to gain all possible advantage'. Bagehot anticipates and reacts to Ruskin's kind of objection by explaining that 'Of course we know that this is not so, that men are not like this; but we assume it for simplicity's sakes as an hypothesis. And this deceives many excellent people, for from deficient education they have very indistinct ideas what an abstract science is'. Walter Bagehot, *Economic Studies*, ed. R.H. Hutton (London: Longmans, Green, 1880), 5.

with respect to other people' is certainly not to earn a 'fee', and certainly not to buy low and sell high, or to pass off inferior goods for greater profit—precisely part of Walter Bagehot's definition of the abstract economic man. No, the true functions of a merchant are like the true functions of all the great 'intellectual professions'. The soldier's function is to defend the nation, the pastor's to teach it, the physician's to keep it in health, and so on, and they must be ready, on due occasion, 'to die for it'. While the doctor should be willing to die rather than leave his post in plague, or the lawyer 'rather than countenance Injustice', so the merchant has a vocation for which he should be ready to die: to 'provide' for the nation, and to do that, the merchant must strive 'to understand to their very root the qualities of the thing he deals in, and the means of obtaining or producing it, and he has to apply all his sagacity and energy to the producing or obtaining it in perfect state, and distributing it at the cheapest possible price where it is most needed'.[16]

Weber himself saw the current practice of capitalism utterly beyond this sort of idealism. The system now, says Weber, is

> a monstrous cosmos, into which the individual is born and which in practice is for him, at least as an individual, simply a given, an immutable shell, in which he is obliged to live. It forces on the individual, to the extent that he is caught up in the relationships of the 'market', the norms of its economic activity. The manufacturer who consistently defies these norms will just as surely be forced out of business as the worker who cannot or will not conform will be thrown out of work. (13)

The capitalist system, 'economic selection', is a social Darwinian system—business red in tooth and claw. Capitalism has grown in a process of 'rationalization' (and this rationalization produces the very idea of 'the economic man'), in which the entrepreneur, sensibly enough, tries to set a low price and get a high turnover: 'you either prospered or you went under' (22).

And yet, Weber recognizes that beyond the 'economic man' there is a deep irrational tug still, which is, in a way, the spiritual descendant of religious vocation. Capitalists, he argues, would answer the question of 'why they are never satisfied with what they have acquired (something that must seem inexplicable to those who are entirely oriented to *this* world)' by explaining 'that business, with its ceaseless work, had quite simply become "indispensable to their life." That is, in fact their only true motivation, and it expresses at the same time the *irrational* element of this way of conducting one's life, whereby a man exists for his business, not vice versa' (23, original emphasis).

There is a further irony in this complex of motives and ideology. Ruskin's argument that economics must be understood in terms of human value, of wealth as defined as 'what avails for life', actually might be understood, from a practical and not very cynical perspective, as a way to sustain the ideology of capitalism. If Weber is right that

---

[16] John Ruskin, *Unto this Last: Four Essays on the Principles of Political Economy*, ed. Lloyd J. Hubenka (Lincoln: University of Nebraska Press, 1967), Essay I, 25–26.

capitalism is infused with the 'spirit' of Protestantism, part of that spirit emerges in the irrationally intense sense of vocation that the successful capitalist almost invariably has. In encouraging work as a self-fulfilling activity without reference to money, Ruskin moralizes and justifies the capitalist irrational passion for ever more profits. The money comes not because it is sought directly, but as a sign of grace, or in more secular terms, as a sign of moral worth. Perhaps a nasty and reductive—and yet in some sense correct—way to put it is that Adam Bede is something of a scab, insisting on work without compensation, and benefitting the employer without easing the life of the worker. 'The capitalist economic order', says Weber '*needs* this uncompromising devotion to the "vocation" of money making' (24, original emphasis). It encourages work without worry about pay, carries economic life into the centre of personal life, and produces great rewards of moral satisfaction. This inversion of traditional Christian values in the carrying out of the Christian spirit helps produce just those ethical tensions and paradoxes that the Victorian novel regularly plays out. (Consider the way strikes are often conceived in Victorian novels. At best, they are the product of the ignorance— indeed childishness—of the workers, and at worst, the product of scheming and wicked exploiters. In *John Halifax*, the food strike is led by childish men who don't know what they want—except for a little bread—and need; they are tamed by a little charity; in *Hard Times* the strikers are misled by wicked union leaders; in *North and South*, strikers simply don't know enough about how industry works.) The capitalist system may be devoted to money making, but novels require both sides to think of something other than money. Weber's theory implies a strange divorce between money and the capitalism whose object is to accumulate as much of it as possible. The capitalist who works irrationally to accumulate it, and the moralist who works humanely to turn it to the saving use of others are not interested in money as an instrument of exchange. Money is a *sign* of something else.

In a sensitive and cogent sequence exploring the historical consequences of the Calvinist doctrine of 'election by grace', Weber notes how it left each individual powerless to act for his own salvation, and 'engendered, *for each individual*, a feeling of tremendous inner *loneliness*' (73, original emphasis). This very sense of powerlessness tended, on Weber's account, to develop a strong 'individualism', even if, as he puts it, an individualism '*disillusioned* and *pessimistically* tinted' (74, original emphasis). That sort of darkness settles over Arthur Clennam at the start of *Little Dorrit*. At the same time, the doctrine encouraged a fundamental hostility to all things of this world, 'all sensual and *emotional* elements' (74, original emphasis). The question for the lonely, world-despising, and helpless Calvinist believer was not what he could do to achieve salvation, but what kind of assurances he could find that he was in God's grace. On the one hand, Calvinists were enjoined simply to believe that they were in a state of grace, for not believing was evidence that one was not saved. But one could also *work* simply to find evidence that one was saved: '*tireless labor in a calling* was urged as the best possible means of *attaining* this self-assurance' (77–78, original emphasis). Good works cannot 'serve as a means of attaining salvation' but 'they are indispensable as *signs* of election' (79, original emphasis).

There is no need here to follow this contorted path from Calvinist asceticism to capitalist greed, but only to keep in mind that worldly pleasure and money are never goals along the way. The Calvinist capitalist watches out with minute attention for the signs of grace, and, according to Weber, keeps a very careful accounting of the signs, many of them internal: conscience and accounting run parallel paths.[17] And in the Victorian novel it is interesting to follow how money is thus consistently moralized and almost always an important indicator of something other than itself. It functions symbolically, like the dust heaps in *Our Mutual Friend*, or, as I take up below, like the gold coins in *Silas Marner*, or even like the £20 cheque in *The Last Chronicle of Barset*, and despite its obvious connection with the material world tends to provoke a deep subjectivity—the capitalist's (or the sinner's) reflections on his own condition—or the state of his business.

Regarded as a merely material thing, money is a distraction and an evil because attachment to the world is evidence of the absence of God's grace, evidence that one prefers the world to its creator. On the other hand, *success* in the world, earned by hard work and the refusal of self-indulgence, helps turn the world to praise of God, and is evidence of God's favour. Value (and meaning) is not in the money; it is in the very act of austere striving; it is in the something else for which money always stands, and often *that* is God's favour. And so it is in the Victorian novel.

III

The enormous paradox that is Weber's thesis, which depends upon the strained fusion of religious with worldly value, of ethical practice with economic selection, of spiritual salvation with successful business, emerges in the Victorian novel wherever it has to deal with money, which is virtually everywhere. Whatever else goes on in any Victorian novel, it is likely to be engaged with middle-class life in a social and economic climate that requires attention to money, and that deals with it within a moral framework that inevitably entails—overtly or not—tensions and contradictions. It is to be despised as a sign of worldliness; it is to be sought as a sign of grace.

In attempting to lay out in rough form the nature of Weber's paradox, I have tried to suggest by allusion to a range of novels how widespread in Victorian fiction these

---

[17] Looking back over his argument, Weber summarizes some of the points on which I have been focusing: 'what has been crucial for our consideration was always the view (which recurs in all denominations) of the religious "state of grace" as a status that separates man from the depravity of the creaturely and from the "world". Possession of this status ... could only be guaranteed by *proving oneself* in a specific form of conduct unambiguously distinct from the style of life of the "natural" man [think Bulstrode]. The consequence for the individual was the drive to keep a *methodical check* on his state of grace as shown in how he conducted his life and thus to ensure that his life was imbued with *asceticism*. This ascetic style of life, however, as we have seen, meant a *rational* shaping of one's whole existence in obedience to God's will ... This *rationalization* of the conduct of life in the world with a view to the beyond is the *idea of the calling* characteristic of ascetic Protestantism' (104).

Weberian conditions were. It is time now to look more closely at a single novel for a more detailed consideration of the way narrative, confronting money as a secular fact, but bearing the burden of genre (realist comedy) and driven by the Protestant ethic and (often) piety, runs into contradictions. While no single novel can adequately represent the range of Victorian writers' responses to the centrality of money, there are certain characteristic patterns of response that tend to anticipate Weber's analysis and in so doing expose both formal and ethical difficulties. Such patterns are transparently evident in George Eliot's *Silas Marner*, and it is to that book, despite its pre-capitalist setting, that I want now to turn. Because it is intensely realist—almost anthropological—in its contextual framing and at the same time has a deliberately fabulous structure, *Silas Marner* allows for very clear and bold dramatization of Weber's paradox, and makes strikingly visible the kinds of contradictions and tensions that I am claiming make the overt Victorian revulsion from money inadequate to the novel's keen dramatization of the moral issues exacerbated by the economic transformations of the period.

Despite its apparent simplicity, *Silas Marner* anticipates most of George Eliot's larger, more complex, and more intensely realist novels. Alexander Welsh, for example, talks of how 'the double plot and the theme of discontinuity become her principal means of testing the relation of individuals in society'.[18] The double plot in *Silas Marner* juxtaposes (and occasionally mixes) the realist and the fabulous modes, anticipating the contrasts in the double plot of *Daniel Deronda*, in which, notoriously, the strongly realist plot around Gwendolen Harleth runs parallel to and crosses with the more ideal, even fabulous plot around Daniel himself. On the one hand, there is the 'realist' story of Godfrey Cass, of a type familiar in various forms from the start of George Eliot's career, beginning with Arthur Donnithorne; it works towards a severe recognition of the fall, guilt, fallibility, and irrevocable harm. Near the end, commenting on Godfrey's continuing desire for the baby he had rejected and is now unable to replace in his infertile marriage, the narrator speaks with the voice of that autumnal realism: 'I suppose it is the way with all men and women who reach middle age without the clear perception that life never can be thoroughly joyous.'[19]

On the other hand, there is the over-the-top happy ending of the Silas story, which seems indeed to imply that life can in fact be thoroughly joyous. The two stories threaten to belie even as they echo each other. Silas's banishment parallels Godfrey's secret marriage, the one unjustly accused of crime, the other successfully hiding his secret; on the night of the new year's celebration, Godfrey denies his paternity, while Silas takes the infant for his own; for fifteen years, Silas nurtures Godfrey's daughter; for fifteen years, Godfrey lives in an infertile marriage with Nancy Lammeter. At the crossroads of the two stories, there is the idea—often a motif of Victorian realism—that 'everything comes to light...sooner or later' (150), an idea that works equally well in both narrative modes.

---

[18] Alexander Welsh, *George Eliot and Blackmail* (Cambridge, MA: Harvard University Press, 1985), 164.
[19] George Eliot, *Silas Marner* (New York: Barnes and Noble, 2005), 151. Subsequent citations appear in the text.

By framing the realist narrative in the fabulous one, George Eliot makes almost immediately visible the tensions and contradictions that a strictly realist treatment would likely produce, but more evasively and subtly.

The book's preoccupation with money, inevitably part of a story about a miser, extends into the realist narrative, and with contradictory implications. 'Money' has, in this novel as in much of the more ambitious work of George Eliot, at least a double valence. *Silas Marner* is, after all, no more concerned with money than *Middlemarch*, all the plots and subplots of which spin on money: gambled for, illegitimately won, inherited (or not), overspent, sought through blackmail, given as tacit bribe, withheld out of jealousy, rejected for honour and for love, all as in *Silas Marner* too. In addition, however, Mr Garth seems the perfect example of Weber's 'spirit' of capitalism. For him, 'business' is a holy word, a vocation marked by his indifference to money. Again the happy irony: Caleb's being good at what he does, being honest, refusing to stint at his work, earns him money, after all. Caleb's is the realist version of Silas's fabulous story.

Although *Silas Marner* is set back even further in time than *Middlemarch*, to a pre-capitalist economy, 'in the days when spinning-wheels hummed busily in the farmhouses'(3), or perhaps more precisely, an economy in the background of which one can sense an emerging capitalism, the major motifs of Weber's theory are already anticipated there as money pervades the double plotting and the moral drama. Comic realism, with narratives ending in reconciliation, reward, and, usually, marriage and harmony (as for example, Eppie's or Mary Garth's), common among early Victorian novelists, implies that there is something inherent in the world it describes that, with whatever difficulties, is coherent with the moral values that are rewarded. The world George Eliot imagines in such narratives answered to the one she tried hard to believe in without Christian faith, one that was compatible with Christian ethics. Seeing *Silas Marner* in *Middlemarch* exposes the fabulous nature of that hyper-realist text: it requires fable to make the Weberian narrative work in fact (as Weber suggests, it *doesn't* work, since the capitalist, once smelling money, begins pursuing it greedily). The idea that vocation, financial success, and sustained virtue can come together is the stuff of fable, the crack in the realist representation of money, which the realist mode itself anticipates. Like it or not, money and its distribution in this secular world tend to be the key to justice.[20]

Money is at the centre of both the realist and fabulous narratives in *Silas Marner*, and not only in Silas's hoarded coins. (The point, well taken, that for Silas the gold coins aren't really 'money' since they have no exchange value for him and are merely objects for his displaced relations with humans, does not in the end diminish the fact that the coins are also money, and are treated in that way outside of Silas's consciousness everywhere else

[20] Elsewhere, I will be discussing how changes in the distribution of money in narrative tend to signify a significant generic change. The tendency of mid-century Victorian comic realism to give way, even in George Eliot herself, to tragic or disenchanting realism, like Hardy's, obviously, or James's, or Conrad's, plays out in part on the question of how their narratives allow money to be distributed. Money implying something well beyond its material nature, often becomes a test of the degree to which the world can be understood as consistent with moral ideals, or characters' aspirations.

in the book.) The novel's preoccupation with money begins with the betrayal of Silas by William Dane, who steals the church money in Lantern Yard, a theft that leads to Silas's expulsion from the community; it continues in Raveloe, which, 'speaking from a spiritual point of view, paid highly-desirable tithes' (5) and where Silas begins his lonely accumulation of the gold coins. In the subplot the narrative begins with Dunstan's blackmailing of Godfrey, and the problem created because Godfrey had used the tenants' money to pay off Dunstan; the two plots intersect over Silas's coins, for fortune (good or bad) sets Dunstan down at Silas's home while Silas is in a cataleptic fit; they intersect again when fortune (good or bad) kills Godfrey's wife in the snow within sight of Silas's home, when he is in another cataleptic trance, and Eppie crawls into the light and substitutes for the golden coins with her golden hair. The theft of Silas's money thrusts him into the society of Raveloe, and the appearance of Eppie, as replacement for money, begins his total integration into that society. So the loss of money is the beginning of redemption; the replacement of money by human love *is* the redemption. The two plots converge a final time after the discovery of the stolen money and Godfrey's confession, and the convergence climaxes with Eppie's rejection of Godfrey's paternity, which means the rejection of his money ('you'd like to see her taken care of by those who can leave her well off, and make a lady of her' (159)).

The pattern, though apparently of fable, is a familiar one in mainstream Victorian realism, culminating in the moment in which hero or heroine rejects money, surrenders it, turns from it. The rejection of money is the ultimate moral confirmation that money has no value in comparison with that of love. So the act is often redemptive (when the protagonist needs redemption). There is Pip risking all to save Magwitch; there are Clennam and Little Dorrit rejoicing in their mutual bankruptcy, able to express their love only because neither has money; there is Margaret Hale giving up her money to Thornton, which he takes as a gesture of love; there is the almost egregiously triumphant (to this reader, at least) austerity of Amy Morville, happy to surrender her inheritance from her husband in *The Heir of Redclyffe* and punishing the man, Philip Morville, who tried to undermine her husband, Guy Morville, by making him heir to all of Guy's wealth; and, in Margaret Oliphant's *Hester*, there is Catherine's loss of her wealth in order to save the bank and the town—corresponding to her reconciliation with Hester and leading to her death; and there is, of course, Dorothea marrying Ladislaw in defiance of Casaubon's will and the consequent loss of her inheritance from him. The climactic moment of *Silas Marner* simply participates in the tradition of the triumph of goodness and love over money. Money lost is spirit saved.

The contradiction almost always emerges clearly after the renunciation, for one way or another the protagonists tend to get it back after all, or get enough back to make a happy ending possible. In most cases, money disappears as a subject so that it is easy not to notice that, for example, Dorothea still has more than enough money to live on in her diminished condition with Ladislaw, or that Amy Morville also has more than enough, while she enjoys the luxury of watching Philip squirm with guilt and misery under the burden of all that money, or that even Pip and Little Dorrit will do fine, if without riches. Just as the reward for Caleb Garth's lack of interest in money is the very well-paid responsibility for the best estates all around Middlemarch, so the reward for Silas's no longer wanting it is the return of the stolen money itself: 'I should have thought it was a curse come again', says Silas to Eppie, 'if it had drove you from me'. The choice between money and love is absolute and money becomes a 'curse'. 'It takes no hold of me now', says Silas (157). He gets back all that he lost and more at the moment when he no longer wants it. When Godfrey makes his proposal, the exchange value of Silas's gold coins becomes prominent: 'that money on the table, after all, is but little', says Godfrey, 'It won't go far either way' (158). Silas, defensively, responds, knowing well what they are worth: 'There's few working-folks have got so much laid by as that. I don't know what it is to gentlefolks, but I look upon it as a deal—almost too much. And as for us, it's little we want.'

All the familiar moves and implicit contradictions are here. Wealth, as the wealthy imagine it, is denigrated. At the same time, it is clear that some money is indispensable, and our protagonist has more than he needs, even if the money must not be used for luxury or self-indulgence. And even as Silas prides himself on what he has, he pushes it (morally speaking) away—'almost too much'. He and Eppie want only 'little'. Dramatically, the novel's emphasis on the proper austerity and the importance of love tends to obscure the inescapable fact that money is required for the happy ending. Silas not only has the stolen money restored, but Godfrey decides that he must 'do what I can for her' and Eppie gets 'a larger garden than she had ever expected' and other improvement 'at the expense of Mr. Cass' (172). Although Eppie foregoes the wealth that living with her real father might have brought her, she and Silas do remarkably well.

With money renounced and reappearing in this way, there is the odd effect of making the reader aware that money, as for Weber's Calvinist capitalists, isn't what it's really about, after all (or at least, that was the ideal). Money does its work in this narrative because it so clearly is meant to represent something other than itself. Money really stands for moral significance—Eppie's loyalty, Silas's reward for nurturing, Godfrey's barrenness. In this respect, it anticipates Weber's point that money is never the object of the Calvinist/capitalist's energies, but merely evidence for—or a symbol of—God's grace. Silas Marner provides a clear example of how, in working out the moral emphases of their work, Victorian novelists aspired to what we might call—anachronistically—the Weberian ideal. That is, it is not money that matters in the striving capitalist's pursuit of it, but signs of salvation; it is not money that the idealized Caleb Garth pursues but the best possible (and perhaps hardest) work. It is not money that Silas the miser seeks, but human connection. Although Weber sees that the consequence of the accumulation of wealth is the production of a class of ferociously powerful and money-obsessed capitalists, the Victorian novel stops short of that by means of what in Silas Marner takes the shape of fable. When it finds a Scrooge-like figure, it moralizes him into goodness (that is, the willingness to part with money), or it punishes him fiercely—think of Mr Dombey, or the suicidal financiers Melmotte and Merdle.

In Silas Marner there are no extravagantly powerful capitalists, of course. But its fable manages to punish wealth and reward hard work and austerity and community so that its happy ending is about as happy as any ending in Victorian fiction ('"O father," said

Eppie, "what a pretty home ours is! I think nobody could be happier than we are" (172)). *Silas Marner* and most Victorian comic realist novels do not attack directly the vicious power of wealth, as it is dramatized, for example, in Osborne's hatred of Sedley, the loser of the financial wars in *Vanity Fair*. If such viciousness is represented in these novels, it is usually to punish the greedy capitalist. *Silas Marner* pulls down the curtain before the rough secular work of accumulated wealth does its job: and they lived happily ever after. The comic ending tends to require the core of fable, which Northrop Frye long ago identified as always latent in realist narrative, because it is constrained by the demands of art rather than the demands of reality, whatever that might be. There is a Silas Marner fable at the core of Victorian comic realism, even if it usually does not announce itself as fable.

The trick for George Eliot was to find a way towards Eppie's happy ending while still aspiring 'to give no more than a faithful account of men and things as they have mirrored themselves' in her mind.[21] This entailed a distribution of rewards and punishment that, in effect, runs counter to the directions implied in the early scenes of Silas's betrayal by his best friend, who speaks with a Calvinist assurance of his salvation. While Silas lived with 'hope mingled with fear', his friend William 'possessed unshaken assurance ever since, in the period of his conversion, he had dreamed that he saw the words "calling and election sure" standing by themselves on a white page in the open Bible' (9). And nothing in his worldly condition challenges William's confidence even after he steals the woman to whom Silas was engaged and then the church money. In the casting of lots, favourable chance—that is, favourable to William—points to Silas's guilt. The tough measure of George Eliot's realist narratives is that there is no relation between mind, desire, morality, and the results of gambling. This is a realist narrative set inside Silas's fable. The bad guys gambled, and won.

Godfrey, closer to the fabulous centre of Silas *Marner* gambles (in a way) and loses: 'his conscience, never thoroughly easy about Eppie, now gave his childless home the aspect of a retribution' (151). Dunstan drowns with his stolen money; the church built on superstition that exiled Silas disappears into the developing urban landscape. If there are accidental casualties (why should Nancy Lammeter have to pay in sterility for Godfrey's sins?) they do not diminish the 'justice' of the books' main lines, although they do tend to suggest something of the tensions and contradictions that are built into a vision of the world that—divinely intended or not—produces justice *in* this world.

The need for this pattern and the recognition that gambling does *not* respond to moral merit, makes chance a key theme of the novel, and there too the narrative conflicts about money are exposed. 'Favourable Chance' is a subject that preoccupies George Eliot from *Adam Bede* to *Daniel Deronda*, which opens with Gwendolen Harleth at the gambling tables—waiting, like Godfrey Cass (and for a long time successfully) for favourable chance. Chance, whether thematized or not, is a central element in any narrative, either in being eschewed for probability and cause and effect, or in being employed for aesthetic

---

[21]   George Eliot, *Adam Bede*, 175.

or moral reasons, to work out issues otherwise more difficult to resolve. The prevalence of coincidence, emphasized or not, in Victorian fiction, often points to cracks in narrative consistency, or strains on the values implicitly endorsed. The most famous such 'chancy' moment in George Eliot comes in Raffles's discovery of Bulstrode's presence in Middlemarch by way of a scrap of paper, and George Eliot's elaborate justification of that moment, in her attempt to assimilate to the narrative of realism and probability, is a sign of how much is at stake in any narrative use of chance:

> As the stone which has been kicked by generations of clowns may come by curious little links of effect under the eyes of a scholar, through whose labours it may at last fix the date of invasions and unlock religions, so a bit of ink and paper which has long been an innocent wrapping or stopgap may at last be laid open under the one pair of eyes which have knowledge enough to turn it into the opening of a catastrophe. To Uriel watching the progress of planetary history from the Sun, the one result would be just as much of a coincidence as the other.[22]

George Eliot knew that the dependence on chance in various elements of *Middlemarch* threatened the realist basis of the book. Much was at stake in demonstrating that there are secular ways to understand chance (which favours the directions the novel wants to take) as compatible with realism. Thomas Vargish's description of literary coincidence in fiction is useful here: coincidence 'carries with it an element of surprise or astonishment that derives from the lack of apparent causal connection'. Vargish's argument that coincidence in Victorian fiction tends to imply some larger providential narrative is one way to see the struggle that I am imputing to George Eliot.[23] That is, she is attempting to imagine, while not believing in traditional religion, an empirically verifiable natural world that is, nevertheless, infused with the values of traditional religion—which Nemesis operates, and in which deeds bring forth seed after their kind, and in which 'everything comes to light', and evil is exposed. This requires explanation of providential forms as compatible with secular, scientific understanding, and therein lies the strain of such a passage as this. The leap beyond knowable 'cause' is a leap from narrative realism to fable, just the leap that is built into the two plot structure of *Silas Marner*.

The narrator talks of Godfrey's 'trusting to some throw of fortune's dice', reminding us that Godfrey's behaviour is not 'old-fashioned' but obviously common to human nature itself:

> Favourable Chance is the god of all men who follow their own devices instead of obeying a law they believe in. Let even a polished man of these days get into a

[22] George Eliot, *Middlemarch*, ed. David Carroll (Oxford: Oxford University Press, 1998), 386.
[23] See Thomas Vargish, *The Providential Aesthetic in Victorian Fiction* (Charlottesville: University of Virginia Press, 1985), 7. For an interesting critique of Vargish's view, see Leland Monk, *Standard Deviations: Chance and the Modern Novel* (Stanford: Stanford University Press, 1993).

position he is ashamed to avow, and his mind will be bent on all the possible issues that may deliver him from the calculable results of that position. Let him live outside his income, or shirk the resolute honest work that brings wages, and he will presently find himself dreaming of a possible benefactor, a possible simpleton who may be cajoled into using his interest, a possible state of mind in some possible person not yet forthcoming. [69]

This is the language of George Eliot's realism, and it forms the core of novel after novel, the shattering of self-centred readings of experience, from Arthur Donnithorne, to Tito Melema, to Esther Lyon, to Casaubon and Gwendolen. Protagonists, good or bad, need to learn that the world is not shaped to their desires. When, in the early stages, chance does seem favourable to Godfrey, killing his ill-chosen wife, depositing Eppie in Silas's home, making Dunstan mysteriously disappear, the narrator notes with irony how Godfrey excuses himself: 'when events turn out so much better for a man than he has had reason to dread, is it not a proof that his conduct has been less foolish and blameworthy than it might otherwise have appeared?' (114). Godfrey is allowing himself to think of the world as somehow designed in accordance with his wishes—it is virtually a Providential vision, as opposed to a recognition that chance is just chance, a kind of moral accident.

While the working out of Godfrey's fate in the realist plot demonstrates that nature works without regard to individual desire, and that deeds produce their consequences irrevocably, it also suggests that the understanding of the world as organized in any relation to justice, order, and merit requires an element of 'fable' even in the most rigorous realism. There is a residue of Christianity in George Eliot's secularism and in the way she can tell stories. The moral stance is not to 'follow one's own devices', a curious way of signifying a merely subjective, desire-ridden view of the world; rather, it is to 'obey a law' one believes in. The moral position, then, is to recognize a reality that transcends the limits of self, that is objectively there, that operates according to regular law, and that, in effect, eliminates 'chance' entirely.

This conjunction of the epistemological and the ethical implies, though in a different language, the Protestant ethic. It certainly implies the primary importance of work. As I argued earlier, to do good work, as Caleb Garth and Adam Bede certainly do, is to follow a calling, a vocation. But both Caleb and Adam also understand the effect of the work they do; understanding cause and effect becomes part of Eliot's moral universe. Adam sees Arthur as an immoral man not simply because he ruins Hetty but because he blinded himself to the likely 'effect' of his act. The 'irreversible laws' of nature that George Eliot had invoked in *The Mill on the Floss* are moral laws as well, and thus the nature that, in a religious tradition, would be infused with the spirit of God, is in George Eliot's imagination, infused with an ethical spirit.

One instrument of this ethical spirit turns out to be money. Chance and money combine in the novel to produce its very shape and moral significance, but at the same time the combination lays bare the incoherence of the very idea that an ethic inheres in the nature of things, in cause and effect. When money and chance come together, the contradiction between the realist and the fabular rises to the surface. The distribution of rewards and punishments in the 'realist' part of the story, already suggests that realism requires fable to imply that the world has inherent moral laws. The full appearance of the fable that underlies the realism emerges as just about full-scale fable in Silas's story, where chance makes the story come out 'right' (enough money goes to the right people), regardless of the regularity of laws of cause and effect. Every important moment in Silas's story is determined by chance, his catalepsy whenever money enters or leaves his life, Dunstan's stumbling on Silas's home, Eppie crawling through the door, Godfrey's wife's death, and then the recovery of the money.

And yet, despite the extravagance of these chance moments, the narration has not a word to say about it, certainly not in anything like the way, in *Middlemarch*, the narrator felt obliged to explain coincidence away. The form of fable frees the narrator of the responsibility to explain; the issue is addressed primarily in Godfrey's story. In fact, there is an overt effort to describe a world that is fully consonant with Silas's desire, that links his good behaviour to his social redemption, and equally important for my purposes, to his fiscal redemption. The ancient Mr Macy was 'of opinion that when a man had done what Silas had done by an orphan child, it was a sign that his money would come to light again, or leastwise that the robber would be made to answer for it' (34). While the voice of the narrator regularly gives a sense of looking back and down on the community with anthropological wisdom and a sharp sense of a reality beyond the comprehension of the citizens of Raveloe, she is careful to confirm Mr Macy's sense of the relation between moral merit and financial reward. It is not, in the end, chance that rewards Silas, but merit. The normal George Eliot connections between cause and effect are only partly invoked in the fable narrative of *Silas Marner*; favourable chance, eschewed for Godfrey, is precisely a condition of that narrative. How else could Silas and Eppie end so blissfully happy—and so financially comfortable?

The distanced and knowing narrative voice of *Silas Marner* implies an intellectual superiority to Silas and Dolly, even with a (not quite) condescending affection for them. But it is where George Eliot has to go as she plays out in Silas's story the renunciation of money for love. Money gets displaced or forgotten, as the narrator tells us that Eppie, the replacement for money, 'was not quite a common village maiden, but had a touch of refinement and fervour which came from no other teaching than that of tenderly-nurtured unvitiated feeling' (139). It is the fairy-tale pattern in which the true royal blood manifests itself even when isolated from all the conditions of royalty. Love protects from the consequences of poverty and the vulgarity that is its inevitable condition:

> The tender and peculiar love with which Silas had reared her ... aided by the seclusion of their dwelling, had preserved her from the lowering influences of the village talk and habits and had kept her mind in that freshness which is sometimes falsely supposed to be an invariable attribute of rusticity. Perfect love has a breath of poetry which can exalt the relations of the least-instructed human beings. [139]

The narrator recognizes that in a realist narrative Eppie would talk and act like a country girl. The fable exempts her. It is Oliver Twist speaking like an educated middle-class young man. Value is built-in and has nothing to do with money, with wealth, with what these can buy.

The fable thus skirts the implications of the realist narrative, where chance does not respond either to desire or love, but only to the law of nature. Insisting that the law of nature is itself a moral law, George Eliot imports into her secular world the values she had absorbed from the Christian world she knew she had to reject. It is money, not nature, that would allow Eppie to grow into the perfect young woman she is shown to be, ending in that perfect happiness, and with enough money to live happily ever after.

In those marvellous discussions between Silas and Dolly Winthrop, George Eliot is happy to fall back on an unknowingness that isn't quite licit in the Godfrey sequences: 'that drawing of the lots is dark', says Silas, 'but the child was sent to me: there's dealings with us—there's dealings' (38). Indeed there is!

Suggested Reading

Henry, Nancy and Cannon Schmitt, eds. *Victorian Investments: New Perspectives on Finance and Culture*. Bloomington: Indiana University Press, 2009.

Hilton, Boyd. *The Age of Atonement: The Influence of Evangelicalism on Social and Economic Thought, 1785–1865*. Oxford: Clarendon Press, 1988.

Moretti, Franco. *The Way of the World: The Bildungsroman in European Culture*. London: Verso Books, 1987.

O'Gorman, Francis, ed. *Victorian Literature and Finance*. Oxford: Oxford University Press, 2007.

Poovey, Mary. *Genres of the Credit Economy: Mediating Value in Eighteenth- and Nineteenth-Century Britain*. Chicago: University of Chicago Press, 2009.

——. *The Financial System in Nineteenth-Century Britain*. Oxford: Oxford University Press, 2003.

Weber, Max. *The Protestant Ethic and the 'Spirit' of Capitalism and Other Writings*. New York: Penguin Books, 2002.

19

THE VICTORIAN NOVEL AND THE PROFESSIONS

JENNIFER RUTH

The Victorian novel is crowded with professionals—think of Anthony Trollope's parsons, Charles Dickens's barristers, George Eliot's doctors—but is there an underlying dynamic between the mid-Victorian novel and the ascendance of the professional class? The best, most durable works of literary criticism—Ian Watt's *The Rise of the Novel* (1957) and Georg Lukács's *The Historical Novel* (1937)—proffer theories about the relationship between literary forms and social formations. Watt famously suggested that the emergence of the middle class with its ethos of individualism fostered the realist novels of Defoe, Fielding, and Sterne. Lukács argued that the creation of a historical consciousness as developed in the novels of Sir Walter Scott and others was integral to the construction of the nation state out of feudalism.[1] Because it followed the fortunes of a 'middle of the road hero', the genre captured the new social totality as it shaped itself into collectivities organized by national boundaries as much as by class identities. Might a similar argument be made about the Victorian novel and the rise of the modern professional class? How did the novel imagine a new kind of identity based on credentials and ethical standards? And how did it contribute to the state's evolution into an entity run by this new figure and his cohorts—experts and professionals who administered the nation's internal welfare on the one hand and its imperial territories on the other?

Readers familiar with Lukács know that for him the novel degenerated after 1848 into the brittle objectivism of naturalism and the decadent solipsism of modernism. Neither genres in his view engaged in any meaningful way with the forces of history. This strangely defeatist and undialectical account of the trajectory of the 19th-century novel has been widely criticized but few critics have asked whether this narrative can be rewritten to reveal a 'living' relationship between social and economic transformations

---

[1] Ian Watt, *The Rise of the Novel* (Berkeley: University of California Press, 2001); Georg Lukács, *The Historical Novel* (Lincoln: University of Nebraska Press, 1983).

and the new forms the novel takes after mid-century. There is no doubt more than one way to do so, but one of the most intriguing must be by way of the professional.[2] How did the bourgeoisie's increasing differentiation into two groups as the century wore on—one group working primarily with economic capital, the other using intellectual capital—manifest itself in the novel? If, as Bruce Robbins persuasively argues, professionalism has a 'peculiar ability to produce bonds among detached, institutionally scattered subjects', might it be particularly well suited for the modern imperial nation-state and for a novel imagining new socio-economic relations based not on blood and patronage but on affiliations, credentials, and services?[3]

The last twenty-five years have seen a growing attention to the relation between the novel and the professions, so much so that one can now identify a subgenre in literary critical work. To view this work collectively is to see how more recent work has dismantled particular oppositions (about which more anon) that have come to define criticism of the Victorian novel. My aim here is to analyse the key developments in literary criticism with regard to the novel and the professions and then conclude by reading Charles Dickens's *A Tale of Two Cities* as a kind of implicit answer to the question I've posed above by way of Lukács: how did the novel help bring these new social relations to life?

Although most sociologists and historians agree that the middle of the 19th century is the key moment for the formation of professional ideology, literary critics of the Romantic period have convincingly placed professionalization at an earlier moment of cultural production. Jerome Christenson's *Romanticism at the End of History* (2004), Brian Goldberg's *The Lake Poets and Professional Identity* (2007) and Thomas Pfau's *Wordsworth's Profession: Form, Class, and the Logic of Early Romantic Cultural Production* (1997) bring questions of professional identity to bear on the Romantic poets. In *Romanticism at the End of History*, for instance, Christenson argues that 'the logic of professionalism in which the producer is the product returns us to ... the correlation between an emergent, eighteenth-century middle-class consciousness and significant transformations in the theories of political economy and aesthetic representation'.[4] Bypassing the Victorian period for a moment and jumping to the turn of the century, critics such as Jonathan Freedman in *Professions of Taste: Henry James, British Aestheticism, and Commodity Culture* (1990) find literature's contribution to the emergence of the professional class in the waning years of the 19th century. Nicholas Daly's *Modernism, Romance, and the Fin de Siècle: Popular Fiction and British Culture, 1880–1914* (2007) to take another example, finds in *Dracula* (1897) that the vampire, an obsolete model of greedy individualism, calls into being that which supersedes individualism—the association of experts. 'What if', Daly asks, 'the threat of the vampire has largely been

    [2] For another way, one focusing on imperialism and globalization, see Jed Esty's 'Global Lukács', *Novel: A Forum on Fiction* 42, no. 3 (2009): 366–72.

    [3] Bruce Robbins, 'The Village of the Liberal-Managerial Class', *Cosmopolitan Geographies*, ed. Vinay Dharwadker (New York: Routledge, 2001), 15–32, 23.

    [4] Jerome Christenson, *Romanticism at the End of History* (Baltimore: Johns Hopkins University Press, 2004), 27.

an instrument for the formation of an association between these men?'[5] In *Imperial Archive: Knowledge and the Fantasy of Empire* (1996) Thomas Richards's argument about the centrality of information to imperialism in late 19th-century novels intersects with analyses of the development and expansion of the professions during that period.[6] Thomas Strychacz's work in both *Modernism, Mass Culture, Professionalism* (1993) and *Dangerous Masculinities: Conrad, Hemingway, and Lawrence* (2008) foregrounds and explores the similarities between modernism and elite professional discourses.

Nonetheless, most scholars consider the mid-19th-century period the moment of heightened interest in the professions as a 'loose federation of middle-class professionals was just coming into its own at the middle of the century, increasing in numbers but still struggling for respect and recognition.'[7] Consider another telling historical detail: reformers introduced seventeen different bills in Parliament between 1840 and 1858 as they struggled to organize and control medical practice, succeeding finally with The Medical Act of 1858 which defined practitioners' qualifications and instituted a General Medical Council for regulating licensing.[8] Or the fact that, as Perkin writes, 'between 1841 and 1881 professional occupations trebled in number, compared with a two-thirds increase in general population'.[9]

'These "new" [professional] middle classes', Immanuel Wallerstein explains, 'were very difficult to describe in the 19th-century categories of analysis.'[10] Professional work was and was not *labour* since work was involved but the body often was not. It was and was not invested capital since education was often required but this was an indirect form of investment. Fiction, in which contradictions and paradoxes need not be smoothed into rational solutions but rather generate a semblance of reality, could work around and through this difficulty. Deploying a combination of aesthetic and economic figures, novelists did with fiction what was not possible with non-fiction: they staged and then imaginatively resolved ideological obstacles to the formation of a professional class. The Victorian novel contributed to the emergence of the professional class by developing, analysing, and circulating the paradox that sustains professional identity even as it renders precarious the professional class: professionalism's simultaneous immersion in and dissociation from market society.

Susan E. Colón's recent book *The Professional Ideal in the Victorian Novel: The Works of Disraeli, Trollope, Gaskell, and Eliot* (2007) might be seen to consolidate what is now arguably a subgenre on the novel and the professions in Victorian criticism. This subgenre sketches the emergence and theorization of the modern professional in the

[5] Nicholas Daly, *Modernism, Romance, and the Fin de Siècle: Popular Fiction and British Culture, 1880–1914* (Cambridge: Cambridge University Press, 2007), 37.

[6] Thomas Richards, *Imperial Archive: Knowledge and the Fantasy of Empire* (London: Verso, 1996).

[7] John M. Picker, 'The Soundproof Study: Victorian Professionals, Work Space, and Urban Noise', *Victorian Studies* 42, no. 3 (2000): 427–53, 434.

[8] On the novel and medicine, see Meegan Kennedy's chapter in this volume.

[9] Harold Perkin, *Origins of Modern English Society* (London: Routledge, 1969), 428–9.

[10] Immanuel Wallerstein, 'The Bourgeois(ie) as Concept and Reality', in *Race, Nation, Class*, ed. Etienne Balibar and Wallerstein (London: Routledge, 1991), 135–52, 141.

Victorian imagination, and in addition to the aforementioned texts a brief list of its major works would include Alan Mintz's *George Eliot and the Novel of Vocation* (1978), Bruce Robbins's *Secular Vocations: Intellectuals, Professionalism, Culture* (1993), Cathy Shuman's *Pedagogical Economies: The Examination and the Victorian Literary Man* (2000), Alan Rauch's *Useful Knowledge: The Victorians, Morality, and the March of Intellect* (2001), Amanda Anderson's *The Powers of Distance: Cosmopolitanism and the Cultivation of Detachment* (2001), Lauren M.E. Goodlad's *Victorian Literature and the Victorian State: Character and Governance in Liberal Society* (2003), my own *Novel Professions: Interested Disinterest and the Making of the Professional in the Victorian Novel* (2006). While not all of the above works focus explicitly on the professional, all of them distinguish this figure from his class counterparts in Victorian fiction and work towards explaining the various ideologies which he both embodied and reconfigured. Colón's book crystallizes the discussion begun by these works into the question of the professional ideology's 'complex relationship to idealist and materialist rationalities.'[11]

The professional is presumed to be above the profit motive. Yet, to make a living, he translates his labour into just the market values he claims to reject. Professional services are, in other words, much like works of art: functionally inside but symbolically outside the market, they are such valuable commodities in part because of their apparent exemption from commodity status. In the last twenty years of the last century, Victorian novel criticism interpreted the double quality of professionalism negatively, not as a paradox but as a hypocrisy—following the work of Michel Foucault, particularly *Discipline and Punish* (1975) and *The History of Sexuality* (1978). D.A. Miller's *The Novel and the Police* (1988) and Mary Poovey's *Uneven Developments* (1988) argued that liberal discourses of 'freedom' and/or 'disinterest' misled Victorians into maintaining reassuring but ultimately false oppositions between, say, freedom and incarceration or disinterest and self-interest. Such arguments take for granted that these oppositions, and the related one between exchange and aesthetic value, developed over the course of the 19th century and ask to what extent such oppositions are ideological in nature.

A number of more recent studies—most notably, Daniel Hack's *The Material Interests of the Victorian Novel* (2005) and Clare Pettitt's *Patent Inventions* (2004)—argue, by contrast, that these oppositions were not as aggressively asserted in the first place as the Foucauldian critics presume. Whereas the earlier critics operate on the assumption that the Victorian artist/professional envisioned himself within the Kantian and Romantic tradition, opposing art to commerce and the ideal to the material, Hack and Pettitt explore their many explicit and conscious points of intersection. Contrary to our expectation, the artist and the manufacturer in fact often functioned as analogues for one another in Victorian texts, according to Pettitt. Hack further undermines our presumptions of hard oppositions by showing that 'prominent novels and treatments of authorship often treat the "material" parts and props of writing—including writing designated as "literary"—as neither insignificant and transcendable nor as scandalous and

[11] Susan E. Colón, *The Professional Ideal in the Victorian Novel: The Works of Disraeli, Trollope, Gaskell, and Eliot* (Basingstoke: Palgrave, 2007), 3.

regrettable, but rather as potential sources of meaning, value, and power'.[12] According to these critics, the Victorian artist-professional underscored his position as market agent as often as he obscured it.

Bruce Robbins's work deserves its own paragraph in a chapter on the novel and the professions as he is the Victorian scholar who has kept the 'professions' most consistently and explicitly in mind, from his *Secular Vocations: Intellectuals, Professionalism, Culture* (1993) to *Upward Mobility and the Common Good: Toward a Literary History of the Welfare State* (2007). Throughout his career, Robbins has been acutely aware of the degree to which literary critics have oscillated between asserting the professional-artist's transcendence of exchange value and demonstrating his complicity.[13] Indeed, in many respects, Robbins's *Upward Mobility* answers the question with which this chapter began, the question of how, contrary to Lukács's narrative of alienation, the post-1848 novel engaged the social and political transformations of its time. Whereas the Marxist critic asks why the revolution never happened and diagnoses naturalism and modernism as symptoms of stagnation, Robbins looks at the way cultural texts in Britain and America helped each country imagine and develop its welfare state. A literary history of the welfare state, *Upward Mobility* identifies an archive of British and American novels and movies spanning the 19th and 20th centuries which enabled society to fashion imperfect but, nonetheless, welcome socio-political alternatives to freewheeling market capitalism. 'I will be assuming', Robbins writes at the outset of his book, 'that upward mobility under capitalism is not restricted to the single option of playing and winning at the game of profit-and-loss... Actual capitalist markets have always required immense infrastructural investment and the continuing support of various institutions... All of [these institutions], while supporting capitalism, also interfere with it.'[14] Robbins's *Upward Mobility* allows us to see the ways in which the novel and other cultural texts helped society develop humane checks on the market by, in part, envisioning protagonists with professional values that transcend the market.

With Robbins's argument for inspiration, we might look at *A Tale of Two Cities* as an emblematic moment in the Victorians' development of a professional logic. Before turning to Charles Dickens's novel, though, I want to contrast two invocations of the professional—one from the start of the century and one from the middle—to sketch the shift professional identity undergoes, a shift from a peripheral and indistinct role to a central one in the social imaginary. In her novel *Patronage* (1814), Maria Edgeworth writes:

> A man who has received a liberal education may maintain himself with honor by the exertion of his abilities in respectable professions, and in a variety of employments,

[12] Daniel Hack, *The Material Interests of the Victorian Novel* (Charlottesville: University of Virginia Press, 2005), 2.

[13] See, for example, his 'Presentism, Pastism, Professionalism', *Victorian Literature and Culture* 27, no. 2 (1999): 457–63, in which he analyses the slippery way the term 'professional' comes to stand simplistically for market in many discussions of the state of both Victorian studies and cultural studies more generally.

[14] Bruce Robbins, *Upward Mobility and the Common Good: Toward a Literary History of the Welfare State* (Princeton: Princeton University Press, 2007), 9.

which are allowed to be gentlemanlike. In doing this he continues to be on a footing with his equals in birth; his personal merit and mental qualifications ensure him admission into the first societies.[15]

What concerns Edgeworth is high society, class status, the way one might manage to keep a foothold in the upper castes through one's own meritorious exertions. The default world-view here is one in which individuals struggle to circulate in the right class bracket among the right kind of people. Contrast this with J.S. Mill's context for the professional forty-five years later in *Thoughts on Parliamentary Reform* (1859). After explaining that while he believes in principle in one-man-one vote, until all men are in fact equal (a man who can read is worth more than a man who cannot, a man who can read and write is worth more, and so on), all men's votes are not—or should not be—equal. It is necessary, he says,

> that some means by which the more intrinsically valuable member of society, the one who is more capable, more competent for the general affairs of life, and possesses more of the knowledge applicable to the management of the affairs of the community, should, as far as practicable, be singled out, and allowed a superiority of influence proportioned to his higher qualifications.

Mill then ranks individuals by employment, handing out numbers of votes accordingly. The unskilled labourer receives one vote, the skilled labourer two, etc. When he arrives at the professional, he says:

> A member of any profession requiring a long, accurate, and systematic mental cultivation,—a lawyer, a physician or surgeon, a clergyman of any denomination, a literary man, an artist, a public functionary (or, at all events, a member of every intellectual profession at the threshold of which there is a satisfactory examination test) ought to have five or six...There ought to be an organization of voluntary examinations throughout the country at which any person whatever might present himself, and obtain, from impartial examiners, a certificate of his possessing the acquirements which would entitle him to any number of votes, up to the largest allowed to one individual. The presumption of superior instruction derived from mere pecuniary qualification is, in the system of arrangements we are now considering, inadmissible.[16]

For Edgeworth, the question was how the professions might help one maintain one's class status even were one to lose one's economic standing. Mill's focus is different: it is not social status that matters but political influence: class status ('mere pecuniary quali-fication') is barred from consideration. The people to be entrusted with society's welfare

---

[15] Maria Edgeworth, *Patronage* in *Works of Maria Edgeworth*, 13 vols. (Boston: Samuel Parker, 1825), 7: 16.

[16] John Stuart Mill, *Thoughts on Parliamentary Reform* (London: John W. Parker and Sons, 1859), 25–6.

are those who can demonstrate superior intellectual quality through the attainment of professional qualifications or through other fair and transparent measures such as an examination.

Admittedly, my sketch is somewhat arbitrary. These invocations address the professional indirectly. Mill, for instance, is asking about the conditions in which democracy might be sustainable, but I want to suggest that these two moments are emblematic of something real, a change in the way social relations are understood, a change that grants the professional and the expert new-found authority and importance for the well-being of the nation such that 'what had seemed a subordinate sector of the middle class made up of managers, professionals, experts of various kinds', as Nancy Armstrong and Leonard Tennenhouse write, 'was running England by the 1860s'.[17]

Take doctor Tertius Lydgate in George Eliot's *Middlemarch* (1871–72). Eliot invites us to trust Lydgate and his authority by describing his passion for his vocation and his professional disinterest. He reforms the profession by refusing to sell drugs the way the old-fashioned doctors do, and he distinguishes himself by pursuing his research with all the imaginative energy and drive of an artist or cleric. Giving her audience a reliable member of the reforming professions, Eliot helps rewrite the political fabric. The experts and professionals keep the rapidly industrializing and imperializing society from unravelling. 'George Eliot', Alan Mintz writes, 'examines both how far the conditions of the age made it possible for the impulse toward self-aggrandizing ambition and the impulse toward selfless contribution to society to be united in a single life, and, in addition, how that union is supported by secularized versions of older Protestant ideas about a man's calling in the world.'[18] One might go further by saying that the conditions of Eliot's age *called for* or even required the development of a professional psyche capable of combining ambition and altruism, a psychology one might say of the *qualified hero*, one who is neither an epic hero, a personage by definition rare, nor is he the self-interested *homo economicus* of the free market. Professional status had to be out of reach for the majority of the people but within the reach of enough people to manage and administer the majority.

Better yet, let's turn now to barrister Sydney Carton of Dickens's *Tale of Two Cities*, published the same year as Mill's *Thoughts on Parliamentary Reform*—1859. Imbedded in Dickens's tale of the French Revolution is a narrative about the moment of the novel's production, the late 1850s when a generation of professional men staged their own 'revolution in government'.[19] Critics understand the novel in two related ways: as Dickens's rejection of a proletarian uprising in favour of middle-class rule, and as a typical Dickens text that raises political questions only to abandon them for sentimental representations of domestic life. The first reading often merges with the second so that the novel presents an idealized portrait of the middle-class family that legitimates the middle class over

---

[17] Nancy Armstrong and Leonard Tennenhouse, 'The Vanishing Intellectual', in *The Imaginary Puritan: Literature, Intellectual Labor, and the Origins of Personal Life* (Berkeley: University of California Press, 1992): 114–39, 120.

[18] Alan L. Mintz, *George Eliot and the Novel of Vocation* (Cambridge: Harvard University Press, 1978), 2.

[19] Harold Perkin, *The Rise of Professional Society* (London: Routledge, 1989), 320.

and above other classes. Such a reading interprets the novel as if it had been written during the century in which it is set—the 18th century. That is, it reads into *A Tale of Two Cities* a strategy more clearly deployed in *Pamela* (1740) or *Clarissa* (1748), one in which domesticity appropriates social authority from an aristocratic class in the name of the greater good. But if the realist family tableau is partially responsible for bringing the middle class into being, as Ian Watt, Nancy Armstrong, and others have argued, then by the time Dickens invents Sydney Carton such a tableau offers only diminishing returns—a fact Dickens understood well as evinced in his representations of the family, which were entirely more complicated than is often assumed. This is not to say that domestic ideology does not still contain immense cultural power at mid-century—it does—but the power of that ideology is primarily exercised not through the family's gradual formation by novel's end but by the family's initial dissolution or violation and the need to call in an expert (professional, social worker, civil servant, etc.) to repair it.

Even in sensation fiction—a genre that has come to be so closely associated with the reaffirmation of the family (which seems to follow inevitably from the transgressive acts of its bigamous wives and murderous husbands)—something more than marriage is often validated by the narrative's end. In *Villette* (1853), *Hard Times* (1854), *Lady Audley's Secret* (1862), *Felix Holt* (1866), and a number of other mid-Victorian novels, the conclusion at the rehabilitated hearth signals not the triumph of the middle-class family over its aristocratic or working-class counterparts, but evidence of a new (middle-class) figure's success in establishing a new (middle-class) market in the private sphere. Many of these novels conclude not by rewarding their protagonists with a family but by attributing to them professional status (or by rewarding them with both, as Ann Cvetkovich has argued of *Lady Audley's Secret*).[20] In these novels, a section of the middle class attacks its own institution, domesticity, in order to offer itself in a new professional guise as the solution. The novels, then, underwrite the emergence of a new middle-class identity based not on the entrepreneur's self-interest but the expert's benevolent service.

In the mid-Victorian period, Harold Perkin identifies 'the gradual segregation of the two allied but increasingly rival ideals [of entrepreneurialism and professionalism], and the growing domination in the governors and administrators themselves of the entrepreneurial by the professional ideal.'[21] For the first half of the 19th century, the interests of the entrepreneurial and the professional middle classes were largely identical. Both groups—the one promoting capital and competition, the other touting expertise and selection by merit—joined together to oppose the "'idle" property and "corrupt" patronage of the aristocratic ideal.'[22] Around mid-century, the two groups began to diverge. One result of that division was that the utilitarian principle of the greatest happiness for the greatest number, an idea initially tied to the market, gets detached and re-attached to the professional ideal, enabling the eventual growth of a welfare society. On his way to developing the cultural authority

[20] Ann Cvetkovitch, *Mixed Feelings: Feminism, Mass Culture, and Victorian Sensationalism* (New Brunswick: Rutgers University Press, 1992).
[21] Perkin, *The Rise of Professional Society*, 325.
[22] Perkin, *The Rise of Professional Society*, 261

necessary to underwrite such a transition, the Victorian professional, whether literally employed by the state or not, convinced the public that he worked in the nation's interests rather than in his own. Not only was he required to appear to set aside any personal ambition or self-interest in his concern for others but he had to convince others that he knew their interests better than they did—even when it came to aspects of life that were once considered private. 'The professional as expert', explains Anita Levy of this period, 'gradually came to stand in for mother and wife as the privileged purveyor of every-day knowledge.'[23]

After mid-century, the professional needed to develop a new identity based not only on market principles of rationality and competition but also on service or duty—in other words, that aspect of the professional ethos that calls on practitioners to place others' interests above their own. While some sociologists and historians assume that such a service component was added to the professional identity by a middle-class incorporation of gentlemanly ideals, others, with whom I agree, argue that the mid-century rejection of certain industrial-capitalist values did not constitute a reversion to aristocratic values but rather signalled the development of a new professional ethos, one which must be understood as a separate, differentiated ideology. By mid-century the middle class had done too thorough a job of discrediting the model of the gentleman, exposing noblesse oblige as a hypocritical cover, or feeble apology, for aristocratic licence and excess.[24] The idea of disinterested service must come from somewhere other than the exhausted stereotype of the civic-minded gentleman, such as from the domestic sphere which was being held up as a space that transcends—and, thus, provides a refuge from—commerce. At home, the logic of domesticity ran, the 'angel in the house' set aside personal ambition and self-interest and worked for the familial collective good. Embodying 'that divine spirit of unselfish rectitude', women 'cultivat[e]the religious and moral portion of [men's] nature, which cultivation no government has yet attempted, over which, in fact, governments and public institutions have little or no control', wrote Sarah Lewis in *Woman's Mission* in 1839.[25] Yet it is around this time, the late 1830s, that what John Frow calls 'the protracted development of a public sector' began, a development in which 'a range of ethico-disciplinary functions—those of education, of public health, and a variety of welfare services—are removed from the family or the kinship network and assumed as State responsibilities'.[26] Rather than turn to an aristocratic ideology to

[23] Anita Levy, *Other Women: The Writing of Class, Race, and Gender, 1832–1898* (Princeton: Princeton University Press, 1991), 111.

[24] See Nancy Armstrong's *Desire and Domestic Fiction* (Oxford: Oxford University Press, 1987) for an explanation of how, in the early years of the century, the middle class successfully casts the aristocracy as corrupt and, thus, in need of middle-class values.

[25] Sarah Lewis, *Woman's Mission* [1839] (Boston, 1840), 19.

[26] John Frow, *Cultural Studies and Cultural Value* (Oxford: Oxford University Press, 1995), 117. This is consistent with Hannah Arendt's observation in *The Human Condition* and elsewhere that after mid-century the state was no longer invested in developing or maintaining a political sphere within which to exercise freedom, but rather became an apparatus to administer the realm of necessity, such that the state as a whole became the aggregate of all the private households. See Hannah Arendt, *The Human Condition* (Chicago: University of Chicago Press, 1958).

find the rhetorical resources for such a monumental shift, one faction of the middle class needed to fold within itself a masculine variant of its own class's domestic ideology. Furthermore, while it appropriated the moral authority of home, or rather in order to appropriate that authority, this group needed to rewrite the terms of domesticity so that the family unit—the businessman and his wife—was no longer self-sufficient. The home became a site unable to sustain itself without government.

In order to convince us that the family was unsustainable on its own, the professional appropriated the moral authority of the wife and mother while also signalling that the capitalist father was unable to succeed in the business world and protect his family. The capitalist father was often a success in his family life in inverse proportion to his success in business—one need only think of Trollope's stock-jobbing Alaric in *The Three Clerks*, who increasingly neglects his wife and child as his illicit fortune accrues, or Dickens's Dombey, who is patently unable to maintain a successful firm and a successful family. The professional trumped the entrepreneur by possessing *both* the rationality of the father and the disinterested sympathy of the mother. Thus, he could function as an external, public figure who was nonetheless allowed into—was, in fact, required by—the private sphere. Calling into question the self-sufficiency of the family and turning to the professional rather than the businessman, these novels underwrite a new professional class.

One result of that division was that the utilitarian principle of the greatest happiness for the greatest number, an idea initially tied to the market, was detached and re-attached to the professional ideal, enabling the eventual growth of a welfare society.

In *A Tale of Two Cities* in particular, the family is not an ahistorical refuge from pressing political problems but the appropriate site upon which to enact a political drama: the rise to power not of the manufacturing but the professional middle class. From the very start, we have a home that has been torn apart and must be brought back together in the reunion of Dr Manette and the daughter who thought him dead. But the domestic family is put together only to be undone again by the French Revolution, which is itself figured as domesticity run amok. In the first place, the Revolution is embodied in Madame Defargue who risks her life to exact revenge. The logic of domesticity—the laying down of one's life for the sake of one's family—is presented in her as revolutionary bloodlust. Secondly, as John Lamb points out, the Revolution is more generally gendered female—a 'fierce, passionate, and raging female, La Revolution'[27]—and women are placed within a domestic context and then presented as either abandoning or perverting the logic of domesticity. 'The women were a sight to chill the boldest', writes Dickens; 'From such household occupations as their bare poverty yielded, from their children, from their aged and their sick, crouching on the bare ground famished and naked, they ran out with streaming hair, urging one another, and themselves, to madness with the wildest cries and actions'.[28] From 'household occupations' the women move to 'the wildest cries

---

[27] John Lamb, 'Domesticating History: Revolution and Moral Management in *A Tale of Two Cities*', *Dickens Studies Annual* 25 (1997): 227–45, 227.

[28] Charles Dickens, *A Tale of Two Cities* (New York: Signet, 1960), 225. Subsequent citations appear in the text.

and actions', not through an evil influence which has invaded the home but through each other's 'urging'. These angels work themselves into demons—domesticity spinning furiously into its opposite. Or perhaps knitting itself into its opposite, as the women sit around the guillotine, 'knitting, knitting, counting dropping heads' (189).

But if the Revolution represents domesticity unbridled, Lucie's family is, nonetheless, the site where Dickens emphasizes domesticity's disappointing limitations. If the family can distort itself out of recognition, one would still expect 'good family' to be the bad family's antidote. One would expect that Lucie, a perfect example of the angel on the hearth, could move analogically from her family to the nation's family, weaving a healing thread around them all. Instead, when confronted with the representative of the latter, Madame Defarge, the wall beyond which 'home sympathies' cannot pass is made painfully obvious. With Darnay held in prison, Lucie uses domestic sentiment to appeal to Madame Defarge, 'O sister-woman, think of me. As a wife and mother!' (271). But Madame Defarge is beyond the melting touch of domesticity. Looking 'coldly as ever', she says, 'Is it likely that the trouble of one wife and mother should be so much to us now?' (271–2). As the events of the novel continue to lead seemingly inexorably to the death of her husband, it is clear that Lucie cannot keep her own family together, much less a national one. When the family finds itself in this crisis, 'Little Lucie'—Lucie and Darnay's daughter—is unable to turn to either her 'self-made' father or her ineffectual mother. Instead she turns to Carton, 'Oh, Carton, Carton, dear Carton…I think you will do something to help mamma, something to save papa!' (338).

We first witness domesticity's limitations when Carton pays a visit to Lucie. Carton is a dissolute attorney—a man, the novel tells us, of 'good abilities and good emotions, incapable of their directed exercise' (95). He embodies the bad habits of the 'learned profession' (89) of law at the end of the 18th century, specifically, its 'Bacchanalian propensities' (89). One would think that he might improve himself as he associates with the Manette family, hanging around 'the quiet lodgings' on the 'quiet street-corner' (95), but he does not: 'If Sydney Carton ever shone anywhere, he certainly never shone in the house of Dr. Manette… When he cared to talk, he talked well; but, the cloud of caring for nothing, which overshadowed him with such a fatal darkness, was very rarely pierced by the light within him' (152).

'I am like one who died young', he tells Lucie; 'All my life might have been' (153). Carton's life is a waste—'waste forces within him', the novel tells us, 'a desert all around' (94). Echoing the passage quoted above in which Carton is portrayed as having a light within him that is invisible to others, Lucie describes him as inherently worthy if unable to behave in a way equal to that worth: 'I am sure that you might be much, much worthier of yourself' (153). 'Can I use no influence to serve you?' she asks (155). 'No, Miss Manette' (154). Lucie can have no effect, Carton says, even had she been his wife rather than his friend:

> If it had been possible, Miss Manette, that you could have returned the love of the man you see before you—self-flung away, wasted, drunken, poor creature of misuse as you know him to be—he would have been conscious to this day and hour, in spite of his happiness, that he would bring you to misery. [154]

Lucie, the novel makes clear, 'can use no influence to serve' Carton. Carton, of course, will serve Lucie.

When in prison, Dr Manette pictured himself as having 'altogether perished from the remembrance of the living, and in the next generation my place was a blank' (192). Having saved Dr Manette only to find in him a one-time professional reduced to an inadequate tradesman, *A Tale of Two Cities* focuses on turning Carton's blank life into something legible, something worthy of his own inner resources. Carton ends his interview with Lucie by saying, 'If my career were of that better kind that there was any opportunity or capacity of sacrifice in it, I would embrace any sacrifice for you and for those dear to you' (156). Rather than flinging his self away ('self-flung away'), he will, of course, end up 'lay[ing] down [his] life' so that the lives of Lucie and her family may be 'useful, prosperous, and happy' (377). By substituting himself for Darnay in the French prison, Carton will embody by novel's end the professional ethos of disinterested service. By making it possible for Lucie's family to re-form, Carton reforms himself, becoming legible: 'I see', says Carton prophetically before his death, 'that child who lay upon [Lucie's] bosom and who bore my name, a man winning his way up in that path of life which once was mine. I see him winning it so well, that my name is made illustrious there by the light of his' (377). Sacrificing himself to prevent injustice, Carton enables, in turn, the reform of his profession: 'I see the blots I threw upon [the law], faded away', he continues; 'I see [Lucie's future son], foremost of just judges and honoured men' (377). Carton embodies the domestic logic better than the domestic Angel does, but he does so very much in association with his 'career', fulfilling his wish early in the novel that his 'career were of that better kind'. He exemplifies what Colón calls the professional's 'zeal to combine rational expertise with sympathetic service'.[29]

Adopting the principle of self-renunciation is not enough in itself to warrant the novel's triumphant conclusion in which Carton is both granted professional status and credited with reforming his profession. 'Professionalization', Thomas Pfau writes, 'involves the elaboration of a distinctive ethos, a new symbolism designed less to display wealth, affluence, and material possession than to signal the proficiency of its practitioners—and, in so doing, to facilitate their mutual affirmation as legitimate members in an identifiable community.'[30] Carton must demonstrate that he possesses other professional resources, such as a talent for observation and discernment. In particular, he must possess the ability to accurately read faces, the ability distinguishing the popular from the professional observer. Seemingly the 'most idle and unpromising of men' (90), Carton sits in court during Darnay's trial, 'his eyes on the ceiling as they had been all day' (80). 'Yet', the narrator tells us, 'this Mr. Carton took in more details of the scene than he appeared to take in' (81). Later in the novel, as the plot heats up, Carton's hidden talent for observation enables him to recognize the petty villain Barsad, a man he met earlier in the novel and whose help he requires to take Darnay's place in prison. 'I lighted on you, Mr. Barsad',

---

[29] Colón, *The Professional Ideal*, 1

[30] Thomas Pfau, *Wordsworth's Profession: Form, Class, and the Logic of Early Romantic Cultural Production* (Stanford: Stanford University Press, 1997), 25.

says Carton, 'coming out of the prison of the Conciergerie while I was contemplating the walls' (300). Appearing to do things 'at random', Carton's behaviour always 'shape[s] itself into a purpose' (300), his 'recklessness of manner' hiding 'a braced purpose...and a kind of inspiration' (301). Indeed, while Madame Defargue possesses a 'watchful eye' (38), Carton boasts something better, a 'practiced eye' (301). The figure whose life must be made legible is the one most adept at rendering others legible. Carton's blankness generates the novel's imperative even as it doubles as a kind of professional qualification. It does not indicate vacancy but rather is the sign of his ability to transcend specificity. 'An expert', Pierre Bourdieu writes, 'is someone who is appointed to produce a point of view which is recognized as transcending individual points of view' (137).

Catherine Waters suggests that Carton's 'aloofness' indicates his 'transgressive' nature, his incapacity for domestication.[31] Yet his apparent indifference not only functions as a useful disguise, it also indicates his respect for certain boundaries or, if you will, his professional discretion. Because the new professional must enter homes, he must learn to be as unobtrusive as possible. He is there to observe and offer expert advice, not to participate. Indeed, far from 'a threat to the family', Carton is its well-worn servant. He asks Darnay, for example, if he might 'come and go' in his home 'regarded as an use-less...an unornamental piece of furniture, tolerated for its old service, and taken no notice of' (209–10). The professional provides his 'service' by masking himself in the domestic interior as a piece of furniture, observing everything but calling no attention to himself. The professional is like the novelist who may 'pry, spy, and expose the secret, the personal, but he manages to do these things while maintaining both propriety and privacy', as Catherine Gallagher writes.[32] It is this very ability to appear inconsequential, a fly on the wall, which allows Carton to eavesdrop on Madame Defargue's plan. With this intelligence, Carton saves Lucie from Madame Defargue's clutches, even as he saves Darnay from the guillotine. What appears transgressive is actually a talent, an ability to observe without being observed. In negotiations between Barsad and Carton, the novel tells us, Barsad's 'smooth manner...received such a check from the inscrutability of Carton—who was a mystery to wiser and honester men than he—that it faltered here and failed him' (305). Dickens preserves the novel's desire to render Carton legible ('a mystery to wiser and honester men') while turning Carton's inscrutability to professional ends. Interestingly, these ends are also political. Much like Mill who sees the professional's cultivated intellectual superiority as qualifying him for both his work and for a privileged role in the political sphere, Dickens has Carton's professionalism operate in the political sphere of the French Revolution.

A Tale of Two Cities begins with a famous passage in which the narrator 'enter[s] a great city by night' and contemplates the secrets locked within 'clustered houses' (17). 'In any of the burial-places of this city through which I pass, is there a sleeper more

[31] Catherine Waters, Dickens and the Politics of Family (Cambridge: Cambridge University Press, 1997), 146.
[32] Catherine Gallagher, 'The Duplicity of Doubling in A Tale of Two Cities', Dickens Studies Annual 12 (1983): 125–45, 128.

inscrutable than its busy inhabitants are, in their innermost personality, to me, or than I am to them?' he asks. Using much the same language as in this early passage, Dickens replaces the narrator with Carton in a passage towards the end of the novel:

> With a solemn interest in the lighted windows where the people were going to rest…in the distant burial places, reserved, as they wrote upon the gates, for Eternal Sleep…with a solemn interest in the whole life and death of the city setting down to its short nightly pause in fury; Sydney Carton crossed the Seine again for the lighted streets. [317]

Carton's 'solemn interest' in the lives of others confers upon him, and the novelist, a particular authority, a particular right to look into lighted windows. As Carton moves through the city, the novel tells us that, 'when he had been famous among his earliest competitors as a youth of great promise', he heard a service at his father's grave. 'I am the resurrection and the life', he heard (316). Now, walking along the streets, that sermon rings in his ears, apparently enabling Carton to realize that he must replace 'competition' with service—or, rather, with the lesson of transcendent sacrifice delivered by the service. While competition lent him 'promise', only sacrifice can fulfil that promise. Moments before his death, the narrator tells us that Carton looks into the future and, indeed, into hearts and souls:

> I see that I hold a sanctuary in [the Manette family's] hearts, and in the hearts of their descendants, generations hence. I see [Lucie], an old woman, weeping for me on the anniversary of this day. I see her and her husband, their course done, lying side by side in their last earthly bed, and I know that each was not more honoured and held sacred in the other's soul, than I was in the souls of both. [377]

Sacrificing himself, Carton refuses to profit from the secrets of hearts and souls and, therefore, is given access to them. In the necessarily circular logic of the professional, Carton's skill in reading interiority enables him to transcend himself in order to inhabit another's place, and, yet, if he is to earn the right to access that interiority, he must first prove himself capable of transcendence—of self-sacrifice. In *A Tale of Two Cities*, the mutually constitutive fantasies of professional omniscience and professional sacrifice are writ large so that the new professionals may gain the trust of a mid-to-late century public finding ever more of its private life placed under their jurisdiction.[33]

Just as *A Tale of Two Cities* fashions a professional protagonist and justifies his necessity, so do a number of other mid-century novels like Charlotte Brontë's *The Professor*

[33] See Simon Petch 'The Business of the Barrister in A Tale of Two Cities', *Criticism* 44, no. 1 (2002): 27–42, and my own 'The Self-Sacrificing Professional: Charles Dickens's "Hunted Down" and *A Tale of Two Cities*', *Dickens Studies Annual* 34 (2004): 283–300, for further argument along these lines. Petch's argument, which I discovered only after finishing my own work on the novel, is remarkably similar: 'As an independent professional and representative of the ideology of service, Carton symbolizes the potential for function that characterizes Dickens's critique of English society' (41).

(1846), Charles Dickens's *David Copperfield* (1850), and Anthony Trollope's *The Three Clerks* (1858). One might say that the novel *theorized* the professions. As various disciplines, including fiction-writing, began to professionalize—by defining objective standards of knowledge, developing processes of evaluation and accreditation, and organizing into communities in the form of chapters, associations, societies—the novel develops a professional logic which differentiates the middle-class businessman from the middle-class professional.

I want to finish this chapter on the novel and the professions with a comment the novelist and civil servant Anthony Trollope made in his *Autobiography* (1875) because it indicates the degree to which the professional class had succeeded, by the last years of the century, in disarticulating class from its embeddedness in economics and attaching it instead to 'nature'. Trollope complained, 'If I say that a judge should be a gentleman ... I am met with a scornful allusion to "Nature's Gentlemen".'[34] In place of class struggle, the professional substituted a hierarchy—a meritocracy that was the putative by-product not of power or money but of an unmediated nature. The ability to do this, the expertise it took to restructure society so that class might shake out from merit or ability rather than birth, necessitated the new class it simultaneously helped to identify. In 1857, H. Byerley Thomson published *The Choice of a Profession*, a guide for young men considering their futures. The 'difficulty in the "choice of a profession" is widely acknowledged', Thomson wrote, 'and it is surprising that hitherto no book has been written to assist in so delicate a matter'.[35] Of course a number of books *had been* written and were continuing to be written to assist in this matter—they were called novels.

SUGGESTED READING

Anderson, Amanda. *The Powers of Distance: Cosmopolitanism and the Cultivation of Detachment.* Princeton: Princeton University Press, 2001.

Arendt, Hannah. *The Human Condition.* Chicago: University of Chicago Press, 1958.

Armstrong, Nancy. *Desire and Domestic Fiction.* Oxford: Oxford University Press, 1987.

Armstrong, Nancy and Leonard Tennenhouse. 'The Vanishing Intellectual'. In *The Imaginary Puritan: Literature, Intellectual Labor, and the Origins of Personal Life.* Berkeley: University of California Press, 1992, 114–39.

Colón, Susan E. *The Professional Ideal in the Victorian Novel: The Works of Disraeli, Trollope, Gaskell, and Eliot.* Basingstoke: Palgrave, 2007.

Dickens, Charles. *A Tale of Two Cities.* New York: Signet, 1960.

Freedman, Jonathan. *Professions of Taste: Henry James, British Aestheticism, and Commodity Culture.* Stanford: Stanford University Press, 1990.

Hack, Daniel. *The Material Interests of the Victorian Novel.* Charlottesville: University of Virginia Press, 2005.

Miller, D.A. *The Novel and the Police.* Berkeley: University of California Press, 1988.

---

[34] Anthony Trollope, *Autobiography* (London: Williams & Norgate Ltd, 1946), 53.
[35] H. Byerly Thomson, *The Choice of a Profession* (London, 1857), iv.

Mintz, Alan L. *George Eliot and the Novel of Vocation*. Cambridge: Harvard University Press, 1978.

——. *The Rise of Professional Society*. London: Routledge, 1989.

Petch, Simon. 'The Business of the Barrister in *A Tale of Two Cities*'. *Criticism* 44, no. 1 (2002): 27–42.

Pettitt, Clare. *Patent Inventions: Intellectual Property and the Victorian Novel*. Oxford: Oxford University Press, 2004.

Picker, John M. 'The Soundproof Study: Victorian Professionals, Work Space, and Urban Noise'. *Victorian Studies* 42, no. 3 (2000): 427–53.

Peterson, M. Jeanne. *The Medical Profession in Mid-Victorian England*. Berkeley: University of California Press, 1978.

Poovey, Mary. *Uneven Developments*. Chicago: University of Chicago Press, 1988.

Rauch, Alan. *Useful Knowledge: The Victorians, Morality, and the March of Intellect*. Durham: Duke University Press, 2001.

Robbins, Bruce. 'Presentism, Pastism, Professionalism'. *Victorian Literature and Culture* 27, no. 2 (1999): 457–63.

——. *Secular Vocations: Intellectuals, Professionalism, Culture*. London: Verso, 1993.

——. *Upward Mobility and the Common Good: Toward a Literary History of the Welfare State*. Princeton: Princeton University Press, 2007.

Ruth, Jennifer. *Novel Professions: Interested Disinterest and the Making of the Professional in the Victorian Novel*. Columbus: Ohio State Press, 2006.

——. 'The Self-Sacrificing Professional: Dickens's "Hunted Down" and *A Tale of Two Cities*'. *Dickens Studies Annual* 34 (2004): 283–300.

Shuman, Cathy. *Pedagogical Economies: The Examination and the Victorian Literary Man*. Stanford: Stanford University Press, 2000.

Strychacz, Thomas. *Modernism, Mass Culture, Professionalism*. Cambridge: Cambridge University Press, 1993.

Watt, Ian. *The Rise of the Novel*. Berkeley: University of California Press, 2001.

20

GENTLEMAN'S LATIN, LADY'S GREEK

KENNETH HAYNES

Novelists, in thinking about their genre, have sometimes sought to establish its relation to those of classical literature, as Fielding did in the preface to *Joseph Andrews* (1742) or Richardson in the postscript to *Clarissa* (1748). For writers and critics of the 19th century, Greek tragedy was the classical model most often invoked (though Scott was commonly compared with Homer).[1] George Eliot and Thomas Hardy partly presumed and partly created a close intimacy between the novel and ancient tragedy, and contemporary reviewers of their novels regularly made the comparison.[2] Novelists have replayed scenes and recast characters from ancient epic and especially from Greek drama; Tom Jones, for example, is told that 'you have been a-Bed with your own Mother' (915),[3] and Becky Sharp impersonates Clytemnestra, perhaps twice (*Vanity Fair* (1848), chapters 51, 67).[4] Sometimes the recasting gains in force through being implied only: the damaged harvest crop in Casterbridge and Michael Henchard's subsequent exposure and reversal recall

[1] See *Victorian Criticism of the Novel*, ed. Edwin M. Eigner and George J. Worth (Cambridge: Cambridge University Press, 1985), 28–29, 58, 78; on Scott compared with Homer, see *Walter Scott: The Critical Heritage*, ed. John O. Hayden (New York: Barnes and Noble, 1970), 91, 93, 317, 425, 487, 501, 503 and Richard Jenkyns, *The Victorians and Ancient Greece* (Cambridge, MA: Harvard University Press, 1980), 209–10; on the Victorian novel and Greek tragedy, see Jeannette King, *Tragedy in the Victorian Novel* (Cambridge: Cambridge University Press, 1978), and Jenkyns, 94, 112–32.

[2] *George Eliot: The Critical Heritage*, ed. David Carroll (London: Routledge and Kegan Paul, 1971), 24, 112; *Thomas Hardy: The Critical Heritage*, ed. R.G. Cox (London: Routledge and Kegan Paul, 1970), xxiv, 265. Gaskell's *Mary Barton* and *Sylvia's Lovers* were compared to Greek tragedy by Maria Edgeworth and Henry Liddell respectively (quoted in Arthur Pollard, *Mrs Gaskell: Novelist and Biographer* (Manchester: University Press, 1965, 55 and 195).

[3] For the specific editions to which this and subsequent page numbers refer, see the 'List of Editions' at the end of the chapter.

[4] Fiona Macintosh, '*Agamemnon* in Nineteenth-Century Britain', *Agamemnon in Performance 458 BC to AD 2004*, ed. Fiona Macintosh, Pantelis Michelakis, Edith Hall, and Oliver Taplin (Oxford: Oxford University Press, 2005), 147–50. John Sutherland, 'Does Becky Kill Jos?' in *Is Heathcliffe a Murderer?* (Oxford: Oxford University Press, 1996), 66–72.

Oedipus at Thebes (*The Mayor of Casterbridge* (1886), chapters 27, 31); and when, in the first chapter of *Middlemarch* (1871–72), Dorothea and Celia Brooke are introduced to us in conversation about their mother's memory and jewels, the contrast is with the bold action—burying their brother—which Antigone proposes to her sister at the beginning of Sophocles' play. Narrators of novels allude to, discuss, and parody works from antiquity, quote or translate from them in both text and paratext,[5] and measure their distance from the present. In the 19th century, historical novels set in antiquity were produced in great number, many of them by women; of these a small number have regularly been reprinted, including Bulwer Lytton's *The Last Day of Pompeii* (1834), Kingsley's *Hypatia* (1853), and Pater's *Marius the Epicurean* (1885).[6] Countless novels drew on ancient examples in order to develop mythological themes or translate figures from myth into a modern setting, to learn lessons about national growth and decline, and to discuss the place of classical art and beauty in the industrial age.[7]

Genre, plot, quotation, historical setting, and the use of myth and classical exemplars are some of the means by which the novel engaged with ancient literature. However, this engagement does not only take place along a vertical or historical dimension of past and present, ancient and modern, it also has a horizontal, or sociological, axis because

[5] The chapter motto is a particularly well-studied paratext. Introduced with the Gothic novel of the 1790s, it was established as a convention for the historical novel by Scott, and his example was followed by Ainsworth, Bulwer Lytton, and Cooper. Other 19th-century novelists also adopted them, notably Elizabeth Gaskell and, in her last three novels, George Eliot. However, with the exception of Peacock and Bulwer Lytton, novelists used classics sparingly as a source for them; see Dieter A. Berger, "'Damn the Mottoe'": Scott and the Epigraph', *Anglia* 100 (1982): 373–96 (for classics, see 378); Rudolf Böhm, *Das Motto in der englischen Literatur des 19. Jahrhundert* (Munich: Fink, 1975), 49–54 and 250; David Leon Higdon, 'George Eliot and the Art of the Epigraph', *Nineteenth-Century Fiction* 25, no. 2 (1970): 147–49; and <http://external.oneonta.edu/cooper/writings/epigraphs.html>. On the subject in general, see Gérard Genette, *Paratexts: Thresholds of Interpretation*, trans. Jane E. Lewin (Cambridge: Cambridge University Press, 1997), 144–60 and Rainier Grutman, 'Quoting Europe: Mottomania in the Romantic Age', in *Time Refigured: Myths, Foundation Texts and Imagined Communities*, ed. Martin Procházka and Ondrej Pilný (Prague: Litteraria Pragensia, 2005), 281–95.

[6] Randolph Faries, *Ancient Rome in the English Novel* (PhD thesis: University of Pennsylvania, 1923); Hannu Riikonen, *Die Antike im historischen Roman des 19. Jahrhunderts* (Helsinki: Societas Scientiarum Fennica, 1978); Frank M. Turner, 'Christians and Pagans in Victorian Novels', in *Roman Presences: Receptions of Rome in European Culture, 1789–1945*, ed. Catharine Edwards (Cambridge: Cambridge University Press, 1999), 173–87. Riikonen, 31, remarks on the 'extraordinary' number of women who set novels in antiquity; he lists forty of the more prominent ones, some of whom wrote under their husbands' names. George Eliot finds their work 'the least readable of silly women's novels' ('Silly Novels by Lady Novelists' (1856), in *Victorian Criticism of the Novel*, 177). To judge from the early 20th-century *Mudie's Library Catalogue* (which classified fiction 'historically, topographically, and topically') and from Ernest A. Baker, *A Guide to Historical Fiction* (London: Routledge, 1914), only a small fraction of historical novels written in the 19th and early 20th centuries were set in classical antiquity. On the long-lasting impact of Bulwer Lytton's novel, see William St Clair and Annika Bautz, 'Imperial Decadence: The Making of the Myths in Edward Bulwer-Lytton's *The Last Days of Pompeii*', *Victorian Literature and Culture* 40, no. 2 (2012): 359–96.

[7] Coningsby in Disraeli's novel (1844) contrasts Athens, which 'embodies the pre-eminent quality of the antique world—Art', with London, which commerce created (134). In Gaskell's *North and South* (1855), Thornton insists to Hale that 'we are of a different race from the Greeks, to whom beauty was everything' (334).

classics—taught in schools, supported by the Church, and advanced by scholarship—played a crucial role in the formation of different sorts of identities, especially in matters of class, profession, gender, and religion. Novelists and their audiences, whatever their own education, would keenly register the actions and attitudes which a classical education made or claimed to make possible. When characters in novels use Greek or Latin, make a classical allusion, or study antiquity, they reveal something about their background, their current context, and their aspirations; so, too, are they revealed when they make errors in the languages, or are excluded because they fail to command an allusion, or when they make one at an inappropriate moment or to the wrong audience.

For centuries, knowledge of Latin (and sometimes Greek) was associated with being a gentleman.[8] This held true despite regular complaints that a classical education was wasteful or pointless[9] and despite periodically intense outbursts of anti-classical sentiment.[10]

---

[8] John Locke, in *Some Thoughts Concerning Education* (1693; enlarged 1695), discusses the education of 'a Gentleman, to whom *Latin* and *French*, as the World now goes, is by every one acknowledg'd to be necessary'; he writes that '*Latin*, I look upon as absolutely necessary to a Gentleman' (§§ 195, 164 (pp. 249, 217); Greek is to be omitted by the gentleman though not by the scholar). Mr Wilson in Fielding's *Joseph Andrews* (1742) 'was born a Gentleman': educated at public school he became 'Master of the *Latin*, and... tolerably well-versed in the *Greek* language' (201–2). Lord Chesterfield advises his son that 'Classical knowledge, that is, Greek and Latin, is absolutely necessary for every body, because every body has agreed to think and to call it so' (May 27, 1748 (p. 1155)). Dorcas, in Scott's *Redgauntlet* (1824), takes Peter Peebles to be a 'gentleman' despite his appearance, 'for he speaks as good Latin as the schulemeaster' (175). Lord Monmouth, in Disraeli's *Coningsby* (1844), tells his grandson that 'A classical education... was a very admirable thing, and one which all gentlemen should enjoy' (177)). In Charles Rowcroft's *Confessions of an Etonian* (1852), the father of the protagonist advises him that 'Every gentleman must understand Greek and Latin' (29). Thackeray in *Pendennis* (1849–50, 25) and Eliot in both *Janet's Repentance* (1857, 197) and *The Mill on the Floss* (1860, 143) describe knowledge of Latin as part of 'the education of a gentleman'. In 'On the Present Social Results of Classical Education' (in F.W. Farrar, *Essays on a Liberal Education* (1867), 373), Lord Houghton goes so far as to say that 'as soon as it became the qualification of a Gentleman to read and write at all, it was Latin that he read and wrote'. In 'Gabrielle de Bergerac' (1869), Henry James's story set in pre-revolutionary France, the Latin tutor Pierre Coquelin, the son of a tailor, explains to his charge that 'Every gentleman learns Latin' (436).

[9] Defoe in *The Compleat English Gentleman* (1728–29) objects to the classical education of the English gentry: he does not believe that scholars, much less gentlemen, need the Latin, much less the Greek, by which they are educated (chapter 5). In Fielding's *Joseph Andrews* (1742), Mrs Slipshod complains to Parson Adams that 'It is very proper that you Clargymen must learn it [Latin], because you can't preach without it: but I have heard Gentlemen say in *London*, that it is fit for no body else' (26). Pamela in Richardson's novel (1740–42) has 'long had the Thought, that a great deal of precious Time is wasted to little Purpose in the attaining of *Latin*' (356). The two letters in Richardson's *Sir Charles Grandison* (1754) concerning classical education (vol. 1, letters 12 and 13) raise a number of objections.

[10] In the 19th century, for instance, the value of classical education was prominently denied or qualified on several occasions: in Sydney Smith's review of R.L. Edgeworth, *Essays on Professional Education* (1809) in *The Edinburgh Review* 15 (October 1809): 40–53 (several authors in *The Edinburgh Review* were criticizing Oxford's devotion to classics in 1808–10); in Macaulay's essay on the foundation of the University of London, 'Thoughts on the Advancement of Academical Education in England', *The Edinburgh Review* 43 (February 1826): 315–41; and throughout the 1860s, the period of the Clarendon and the Taunton Commissions (as, for example, in Higgins's letters on Eton in the *Cornhill Magazine*, Farrar's *Essays on a Liberal Education*, and educational writings by Huxley and Spencer). Towards the end of the century, debate was continual, and often focused on the question of whether Greek should be a requirement for those seeking admission to elite universities (see Judith Raphaely, 'Nothing

Classics has had an uncanny ability to survive and be assimilated within new social for-mations.[11] Yet the nature of the association between Latin and Greek and gentlemanly status was always elusive, and it was in flux for much of the 19th century. Gentlemen, especially country gentlemen,[12] did not need to know Latin at all, and in any case know-ing the language often implied little more than that a gentleman had been taught it as a boy and could recognize famous tags as an adult.[13] Moreover, some women and some members of the working classes also learned the language, and they did so increasingly as their educational opportunities expanded in the latter part of the century.[14]

The real problem was the nature of the gentleman,[15] a topic which Victorian novelists investigated with the same fervour with which Elizabethan dramatists studied nobility, in part for the same reason: the terms refer to a fact about social status while also offer-ing a justification for that status, at a time when both the status and the justification

but Gibberish and Shibboleths?: The Compulsory Greek Debates, 1870–1919', in *Classics in 19th and 20th Century Cambridge: Curriculum, Culture and Community*, ed. Christopher Stray (Cambridge: Cambridge Philological Society, 1999), 71–93). In the United States, debate was prompted by C.F. Adams, *A College Fetich* (1883). See further, Edward C. Mack, *Public Schools and British Opinion 1780 to 1860* (London: Methuen, 1938), 56–60, 145–50, 210–12, and 393–98, and, for a bibliography of 'negative references' to classical education, see Lamar T. Beman, ed., *Selected Articles on the Study of Greek and Latin* (New York: H. W. Wilson, 1921), xliv–li.

[11] See especially Christopher Stray, *Classics Transformed: Schools, Universities, and Society in England, 1830–1960* (Oxford: Clarendon Press, 1998) and also Françoise Waquet, *Latin: or, The Empire of a Sign*, trans. John Howe (London: Verso, 2001).

[12] In 1833, W.M. Praed mocks John Russell by having him claim that 'under the Reform Act, all country gentlemen understand Latin' (note to 'Ode on the Passing of the Reform Bill' (p. 245 of *Political and Occasional Poems*)). In *The Irish Sketch Book* (1843), Thackeray writes that 'if occasionally, in the House of Commons, Sir Robert Peel lets off a quotation [from Horace] . . . depend on it it is only to astonish the country gentlemen who don't understand him' (345).

[13] See e.g. John Chandos, *Boys Together: English Public Schools 1800–1864* (New Haven: Yale University Press, 1984), 155–63; Stray, *Classics Transformed*, 59.

[14] Latin was taught at the London Mechanics Institute (later Birkbeck College), founded in 1823; Sheffield People's College, founded in 1842; the Working Men's College in London, founded in 1854; and elsewhere. On the working classes and Latin, see further Waquet, *Latin*, 227–29. In 1849 the Ladies College in Bedford Square (Bedford College) was founded; Royal Holloway College followed in 1879. Women's colleges were established at Cambridge from 1869 and Oxford from 1879. In 1878 the University of London permitted women to take university examinations and gain degrees; Oxford and Cambridge opened their examinations to women in the 1880s. See further Negley Harte, *The Admission of Women to University College, London* (London: University College London, 1979). In the second half of the 19th century, girls' schools increased in number and rigour, and some began to aim at university entrance. Prominent among them were the North London Collegiate School, founded in 1850, and the Cheltenham Ladies College, founded in 1854. See further Josephine Kamm, *Hope Deferred: Girls' Education in English History* (London: Methuen, 1965); Geoffrey Walford, ed., *The Private Schooling of Girls: Past and Present* (London: Woburn Press, 1993) and Waquet, *Latin*, 223–36.

[15] Compare the definitions of 'gentleman' in successive editions of the *Encyclopaedia Britannica* (collated in the article 'gentleman' in the 14th edn of 1929). 5th edn (1815): 'one, who without any title, bears a coat of arms, or whose ancestors have been freemen'. 7th edn (1845): 'All above the rank of yeoman'. 8th edn (1856): 'By courtesy this title is generally accorded to all persons above the rank of common tradesmen when their manners are indicative of a certain amount of refinement and intelligence.'

were vigorously disputed. The social and moral meanings of the gentleman in the 19th century, like those of the nobility in the 17th, were under pressure as new groups sought to redefine them in order to share in their status. The meaning of the gentleman in the 19th century was subject to a fundamental ambiguity as older notions of rank were overlaid with new ones of class; the ambiguity was not resolved for the middle classes until the last quarter of the century, when education at (a Latin-teaching) public school came to be widely accepted as the mark of a gentleman.[16] For most of the century, the question was live and vexing: who was a gentleman? The label implied a contrast with some other kind of person, but which kind: with women, dependents, the needy; with the uneducated, or lesser educated; with professionals, or with dandies; with the commercial middle class, small shopkeepers and clerks, or the working class? Did it divide the gentry from the bourgeois, or both of these from working classes, and did it further divide the ranks themselves? Sometimes the contrast was between the true and the false gentleman, and this raised intricate questions, especially around mid-century when definitions were changing: what was the right conduct of the gentleman; what were the right professions (if any), the necessary income, the source of income, the appropriate schooling; was gentlemanly status inherited (and if so, did it take three generations), or could a man make himself into a gentleman; under what conditions would the status be forfeited? Was he to be gentle, tender, and sensitive; or reserved, independent, and capable of the disinterested view; or manly, honest, respectable?[17] Was the status worth achieving or retaining, or was the ideal fraudulent and the reality hypocritical? Gentlemanliness was meant to resist precise definition and specification, blurring the boundaries between groups at some moments, but capable of sharpening it at others.

How did exposure to classics create gentlemanly qualities? Latin was a ready means for Victorian men to acquire, advertise, or pretend to a gentleman's status, but it is often difficult to interpret specific uses of the language, in novels and outside them. The historical practice of classical allusion and quotation (perhaps the readiest way

---

[16] Robin Gilmour, *The Idea of the Gentleman in the Victorian Novel* (London: George Allen and Unwin, 1981), 182. It was not until the end of the century that the middle classes in general shared in the classical education of the upper classes; see T.W. Bamford, *Rise of the Public Schools* (London: Nelson, 1967), 168–81 and 252–66.

[17] Gilmour, *The Idea of the Gentleman in the Victorian Novel*, 84–104. In addition to his discussions of novels, Gilmour points to the influence of two famous Victorian definitions of the gentleman: Ruskin's chapter 'Of Vulgarity' in *Modern Painters*, vol. 5, part 9, chapter 7 (1860) and Cardinal Newman's discussion in *Discourses on the Scope and Nature of University Education* (1852). Richardson's *Sir Charles Grandison* was an influential precursor in representing members of the middle class as gentlemanly; a century later, Dinah Craik's *John Halifax, Gentleman* (1856) offered a best-selling depiction of the self-made gentleman. Concepts changed later in the century, accompanied by the rise of athleticism and the 'games ethic' at school and university. The bibliography on the topic is large; for diverse treatments, see: Philip Mason, *The English Gentleman: The Rise and Fall of an Ideal* (London: André Deutsch, 1982); Arlene Young, *Culture, Class and Gender in the Victorian Novel: Gentlemen, Gents and Working Women* (Basingstoke: Macmillan, 1998), 14–44; and James Eli Adams, *Dandies and Desert Saints: Styles of Victorian Masculinity* (Ithaca: Cornell University Press, 1995).

to show one's Latin) varied by period, speaker, venue, purpose, and mood, and even in a period as well documented as the 19th century, these contexts are not always possible to recover.[18] In novels, conventions for representing the practice of classical allusion diverged greatly.[19] Characters in Scott, Eliot, and Hardy quote from classics with some frequency, while those in Austen, Dickens, and Collins do so much less. Classical allusion is especially rich in Thackeray's *Pendennis* (1849–50) and *The Newcomes* (1854–55), and it is abundant in Trollope.[20] A number of reasons lie behind these differences among novelists: sometimes a modern author feels a particular affinity for an ancient one (Scott and Virgil, say, or Thackeray and Horace)[21] but the presence of Greek or Latin also depends on the choice of characters (their gender, class, and education), the arena for the action (public or private), and the novelists' literary ambitions. When the world of the novel foregrounds masculine spheres of activity, classical allusions may be made almost continually. In Bulwer Lytton's *Pelham* (1828), almost all the men quote or refer to Latin: the dandy Pelham, the politically ambitious Lord Vincent, the impoverished 'gentleman of the gin-shop' Gordon (201), the gourmand Lord Guloseton, the poor scholar Rev. Clutterbuck, and even the flash man Job Johnson, who compares an old woman to Hecate because 'you see, Sir, I have had a classical education' (402).

The practice of making classical allusions is widely represented in novels; how should it be understood as a practice? A common answer (one given also in the 19th century) is that they serve as passwords, code phrases, shibboleths to assert one's membership in the class of gentlemen.[22] However, this is an incomplete and misleading response: incomplete, because while classics were indeed used to draw distinctions between the

---

[18] In a few cases, we can measure the distance between oral conversation and print. Henry Silver kept a diary of the conversations of the *Punch* 'Brotherhood' during 1858–70. Their conversational humour was often schoolboyish, with sexual and scatological jokes, and frequent allusions to the classics. None of the former and little of the latter made their way into print. See Patrick Leary, *The Punch Brotherhood: Table Talk and Print Culture in Mid-Victorian London* (London: The British Library, 2010), 42.

[19] On classical allusion in the Victorian novel, see Michael Wheeler, *The Art of Allusion in Victorian Fiction* (London: Macmillan, 1979) (see the Index under 'Allusions: classical allusions'); David Skilton, 'Schoolboy Latin and the Mid-Victorian Novelist: A Study in Reader Competence', *Browning Institute Studies* 16 (1988): 39–55; and Hugh Osborne, 'Hooked on Classics: Discourses of Allusion in the Mid-Victorian Novel', in Roger Ellis and Liz Oakley-Brown, eds., *Translation and Nation: Towards a Cultural Politics of Englishness* (Clevedon: Multilingual Matters, 2001), 120–66.

[20] For a list, see George Newlin, ed., *Everyone and Everything in Trollope*, 4 vols., continuously paginated (Armonk: M.E. Sharpe, 2005), 2063–76 and 2375–480.

[21] On Scott and Virgil, see D.S. Carne-Ross, 'Scott and the Matter of Scotland', in Claudio Véliz, ed., *The Worth of Nations* (Boston: University Professors, 1993), 28–29 and Chris Ann Matteo, 'Spolia from Troy: Classical Epic Allusion in Walter Scott's *Waverley*', *Literary Imagination* 9, no. 3 (2007): 250–69; on Thackeray and Horace, see Elizabeth Nitchie, 'Horace and Thackeray', *Classical Journal*, 13, no. 6 (1918): 393–410; Gordon N. Ray, *Thackeray: The Age of Wisdom 1847–1863* (New York: McGraw Hill, 1958), 92–130; and R.D. McMaster, *Thackeray's Cultural Frame of Reference* (Montreal: McGill-Queen's University Press, 1991), 25–43.

[22] Skilton, 'Schoolboy Latin and the Mid-Victorian Novelist'; Waquet, *Latin*, 215; Stray, *Classics Transformed*, 89–90, quoting William Hogdon in 1853 on 'a smattering of Greek and Latin quotation' as 'the conventional pass-sign among persons of a certain rank and breeding'.

capacities of gentlemen and those of ladies or the working classes, they could at times provide an opportunity for inclusion across those groups, whether in reality or aspiration; and misleading, because classical allusions, far from expressing simple solidarity among gentlemen (who did not constitute a unified group) were used to distinguish among competing claimants to gentlemanly status as well as to introduce new ones. Even when exaggerating the role and frequency of classical allusion, novelists closely observed the social distinctions motivating it. The widespread Latin in *Pelham* marks a moment in the redefinition of gentility: the gentleman was to be a new compound, a member of the emerging noble-bourgeois alliance, marked by the 'aristocratisation of the bourgeoisie combined with the eventual *embourgeoisement* of the aristocracy',[23] where all the men spoke Latin.

Classical allusions are widespread in Thackeray's *Pendennis* and *The Newcomes*, two novels attentive to the experiences and allegiances made possible by school or university (*Pendennis* transformed the university novel);[24] the shared Latin quotations express the emotionally charged public-school sentiments that would be shared by later generations of gentlemen until the Edwardians. In *The Newcomes* the references to classics are made both by the narrator, Arthur Pendennis, and by the characters (though it is not always clear, in cases of free indirect discourse, whether it is the narrator or a character making the allusion). The Latin quotations in particular tend to be trite, placing the emphasis on the performance of the Latin, rather than its content. Colonel Newcome's favourite quotation, which Clive 'trembled' to hear repeated (163), is an ungrammatical version of Ovid's 'ingenuas didicisse fideliter artes emollit mores, nec sinit esse feros' ('to have learned faithfully the liberal arts softens manners and prevents them from being harsh'). The Colonel is a gentleman, the product of a public school, and he does not need scholarship in order to sustain his idealism about classics. The English gentleman in any case is more reliably known by the pronunciation of his Latin quotations than by their accuracy, and the novel repeatedly marks out, through phonetic misspellings, the Latin of those who have not been to an English public school: the Cockney 'Hars est celare Hartem' of the painter Gandish (159), the 'duris urgéns in rébūs égestāss' of the ruined Vicomte Florac (260), the joking 'O Vanitas Vanitawtum' of the Scotsman Binnie (63).[25]

An emotional centre of the novel is the relation between Colonel Newcome and his son Clive, which is shaped by public-school classical education. The Colonel plans to educate Clive at school, so that the boy will have 'at least as much classical learning as a gentleman in the world need possess', and then he would like in turn to become his son's

[23] M.L. Bush, *The English Aristocracy: A Comparative Synthesis* (Manchester: Manchester University Press, 1984), 77; applied to *Pelham* by Maria K. Bachman, 'Bulwer-Lytton's *Pelham*: The Disciplinary Dandy and the Art of Government', *Texas Studies in Literature and Language* 47, no 2 (2005): 167–87, 187.
[24] Mortimer Robinson Proctor, *The English University Novel* (Berkeley: University of California Press, 1957), 69–73.
[25] McMaster, *Thackeray's Cultural Frame of Reference*, 25–42. Ars est celare artem: 'art is to conceal art'. *Duris urgens in rebus egestas* (Virgil, *Georgics* 1.146): 'need that presses in hard circumstances'. *O vanitas vanitatum* (Ecclesiastes 1:2): 'O vanity of vanities'.

'pupil for Latin and Greek' and redeem the time which he wasted at school as an 'idle young scamp' (50–1). Later, when he schemes to find out how much Clive has actually learned, Binnie reports that the young man had the usual experience at public school: Clive will be able to quote Horace respectably, which is to say he spent five years learning about three months' worth of classics, or, equivalently, at about the cost of a thousand pounds, he learned about twenty-five guineas' worth of classical literature (78–79). The renewed intimacy of father and son after the Colonel's bankruptcy is tenderly mediated by Clive's quotation of lines from Horace's Ode 3.29, 'the well-known old school words', which he uttered 'with an emotion that was as sacred as a prayer' (297). The physical setting of Grey Friars punctuates the Colonel's life: his boyhood was spent there (chapter 2), 'at the middle of life' he visits Clive at the school (61), and he dies there, in one of the most famous death scenes in Victorian literature (vol. 2, ch. 42, (ch. 80): 'In Which the Colonel Says "Adsum" When His Name Is Called').[26]

Trollope's frequent recourse to classics is commonly seen as 'a means to entertain a male audience who shared a common culture with male authors', but, as a recent critic has insisted, such a view fails to see how often classical quotation is meant to divide, rather than unite, the classically educated men who read him, and in this way represents elite masculine behaviours ambivalently.[27] In particular, Trollope is intent on depicting classical allusions as a means for deception and delusion. Politicians throw quotations at their opponents not with regard to the subject under discussion but for the 'double pleasure of pulling down an opponent, and of raising oneself' (*Phineas Redux* (1873), 276); cf. the Parliamentary debate of Daubeny and Gresham in chapter 8); *nil admirari* is a maxim not for gentlemanly self-possession but unmanly ambitious comportment, the 'self-remembering assumption of manliness, that endeavour of twopence halfpenny to look as high as threepence' (*Phineas Redux*, 252); a line from Horace ('Nullius addictus jurare in verba magistri', *Epistle* 1.1.14), used as a newspaper motto, justifies opportunistic and profitable censure (*The Way We Live Now* (1875), 415); a speaker, addressing a crowd from a balcony, would shout 'ruat cælum, fiat justitia' but know very well that 'he was talking buncombe' and intending to make a deal behind the scenes (*The Last Chronicle of Barset* (1867), 602).

---

[26] See further Skilton, 'Schoolboy Latin and the Mid-Victorian Novelist'; Osborne, 'Hooked on Classics'; and J.R. de Symons Honey, *Tom Brown's Universe: The Development of the Victorian Public School* (London: Millington, 1977), 128–34.

[27] Margaret Markwick, *New Men in Trollope's Fiction: Rewriting the Victorian Male* (Aldershot: Ashgate, 2007), 192–3. On Trollope's classical allusions, see Skilton, 'Schoolboy Latin'; Osborne, 'Hooked on Classics'; Robert Tracy, '*Lana medicata fuco*: Trollope's Classicism', in John Halperin, ed., *Trollope Centenary Essays* (New York: St Martin's Press, 1982), 1–23; Elizabeth R. Epperly, *Patterns of Repetition in Trollope* (Washington, DC: Catholic University of America Press, 1989 (Index under 'Greek' and 'Latin')). The *Oxford Reader's Companion to Trollope*, ed. R.C. Terry (Oxford: Oxford University Press, 1999), 101, asserts that the point of Trollope's classical quotations and translations 'is to reinforce the notion of a community of like-minded readers; in other words, Trollope is writing as a clubbable, middle-class, classically (and public-school-) educated male, and the readership his fiction takes for granted is of a similar background, culture, and sex'. Cf. Gilmour, *The Idea of the Gentleman in Victorian Fiction*, 182: 'A public school education is not a significant determinant of gentlemanliness in Trollope's fiction.'

That last quotation—'though the heavens fall, let justice be done'—is one of Trollope's favourites.[28] It is intimately tied to prideful self-will: destructive, sometimes courageous, often self-deceived. At one end of its spectrum of implication, John Bold silences 'the suggestion within his breast' that his actions will injure the bedesmen by invoking the phrase (*The Warden* (1855), 43–44); at the other, Josiah Crawley decides to resign his living, depriving himself and his family of their income, after meditating on Hogget's 'it's dogged as does it' and on English versions of the Latin tag ('He could do justice though the heaven should fall', 'Let justice be done, though the heaven may fall': *The Last Chronicle of Barset*, chapters 61 and 62 (664, 675)). It intensifies marital disputes, as husbands or wives become intransigent as they silently invoke the tag, as Mary Germain (née Lovelace) does in *Is He Popenjoy?* (1878), 21 and Palliser in *The Prime Minister* (1876), 303–4, and, most sinisterly, as Louis Trevelyan does in *He Knew He Was Right* (1869), 45.

Thackeray and Trollope are both conscious of the wastefulness of classical education, but for both the waste is to be redeemed by the elusive qualities (decency, stubborn independence, moral courage) of the true gentlemen it sometimes helps create.[29] Dickens and Eliot have greater ambivalence. Dickens accepts the fact that Latin is advantageous, perhaps necessary, for gentlemen in Victorian England, but he does so without enthusiasm, doubting the intrinsic value of a classical education, sceptical about its alleged collateral benefits, and conscious of the harm it may do. After eight years at public school (Winchester), Richard Carstone learned, in Esther Summerson's words, to 'make Latin Verses of several sorts, in the most admirable manner' (*Bleak House* (1853), 151), but the school had no interest in discovering or encouraging his own inclinations or aptitudes, and so it confirmed the habit of purposeless drifting. At Dr Blimber's Academy, ten young gentlemen were force-fed Greek and Latin (Dickens three times attaches 'force' to its pedagogy: 'forcing apparatus', 'system of forcing', 'forcing system', *Dombey and Son* (1843), 142–43, cf. 805). The two indictments against educators—that they neglect and that they forcibly denature children—Dickens makes with much greater intensity in the case of the Charity Schools or the sadism of Dotheboys Hall; classics are not in themselves important enough to provoke him to passionate denunciation. When characters feel affection towards their schooling, as Copperfield does at Dr Strong's school (where he grows 'great in Latin verses' (228)), it is for reasons other than the classical content. Only once in a novel does he depict a Latin teacher who is both kindly and helpful: the

[28] Epperly, *Patterns of Repetition in Trollope*, 59, 81, 86, 160, and 207–8. Besides the instances discussed in this and the previous paragraph, the phrase appears in *Castle Richmond* (1860), 216, 237, 276; *Orley Farm* (1862), chapters 12, 45, and 53 (vol. 1, p. 118; vol. 2, p. 46; vol. 2, p. 130); *Rachel Ray* (1863), 175; *Miss Mackenzie* (1865), 100; and *The Vicar of Bullhampton* (1870), 34.

[29] Later, as Latin, or at least Latin grammar, is taught further down the middle-class scale, the wastefulness of the education may be redeemed by the discipline it instils in British gentlemen, as, for example, in Kipling's story 'Regulus', published in 1926, written in 1908, and set in November 1882 (for the date, see Roger Lancelyn Green, 'The Chronology of *Stalky & Co*', *Kipling Journal* 113 (1955): 8). For discussion, see Judith A. Plotz, 'Latin for Empire: Kipling's "Regulus" as a Classics Class for the Ruling Classes', *The Lion and the Unicorn* 17, no. 2 (1993): 152–67; Julia Haig Gaisser, 'The Roman Odes at School: The Rise of the Imperial Horace', *The Classical World* 87, no. 5 (1994): 443–56.

clergyman Frank Milvey, 'expensively educated and wretchedly paid', who 'was under the necessity of teaching and translating from the classics, to eke out his scanty means, yet was generally expected to have more time to spare than the idlest person in the parish, and more money than the richest' (*Our Mutual Friend* (1865), 103).

Dickens is fascinated by characters with ambiguous social status, who tend to be of three sorts: quasi-aristocratic or dandiacal figures, intelligent and cynical, who are conscious of having come down in the world, disinclined towards work but obliged to find means to live (Steerforth, Skimpole, Harthouse, Gowan, Carton, Wrayburn);[30] those characters who are straining to hold on to a former, more genteel status despite strong downward pressure, and do so especially through displays of elevated language (Micawber, William Dorrit); and those rising towards respectable status through a combination of labour, congeniality, and luck (Pip, David Copperfield), or failing to rise despite ceaseless labour in self-advancement, and deforming themselves as a result (Uriah Heep, Bradley Headstone). Latin plays a part in the struggles of all these types. The first would have gone to public school and are at ease in making classical allusions, the second favours Latinate language and emphatic allusion, while the third may need to acquire Latin in the course of an arduous social advancement. *David Copperfield* (1849–50) gives instances of all the types: Steerforth makes an unthinking allusion to Horace (364) in conversation with Copperfield, who had earlier 'dreamed of ancient Rome, Steerforth, and friendship' (247); Micawber quotes Cato to his wife (221);[31] Copperfield's progress with Latin is charted in several environments (at home, chapter 4; at Salem House, chapter 7; at the pawnbroker's, chapter 11; and at Dr Strong's school, chapter 18), and Traddles's hard-won success is measured at the end by the scholarship of his boys (chapter 64). In contrast Latin only exacerbates the resentful envy which Uriah Heep feels towards Copperfield. When Heep confesses his ignorance of Latin legal terminology, Copperfield offers to teach him Latin, but he refuses, 'writhing modestly'; a little later, when Micawber praises Copperfield's capacity for classical learning, Heep 'made a ghastly writhe from the waist upwards, to express his concurrence in this estimation of me' (217–18, 221); and Heep, in his triumph, exults in the power he exercises, and justifies it on the grounds that he exploited the opportunities available to one in his station, not forsaking it, as he would have done by accepting Copperfield's offer to teach him Latin. Heep is the opposite of a gentleman; he has 'a base, unrelenting, and revengeful spirit' (491), but the gulf between Heep and Copperfield follows naturally from the unbridgeable division between their social classes, between the Latin-less charity-school education of the one and fee-paying Latin instruction of the other.

George Eliot scrutinizes the classical education of Victorian gentlemen with exacting harshness. The curate in 'Janet's Repentance' teaches in the upper grammar school, imparting to his pupils 'the education of a gentleman—that is to say, an arduous inacquaintance with Latin' (*Scenes of Clerical Life*, 197). In *Adam Bede*, Arthur Donnithorne

[30] See Ellen Moers, *The Dandy: Brummell to Beerbohm* (New York: Viking Press, 1960), 232–34.
[31] Mrs Micawber had also (mis)heard Latin tags from her father ('experientia does it [docet]', 136).

tells Mr Irwine that country gentlemen have a more pressing need for knowledge of manures than of classics (chapter 16). The uselessness of classics is a theme echoed throughout *Middlemarch*. Lydgate '"did" his classics' at school (140) but derived little benefit from them; the narrator refers ironically to the 'expensive and highly rarified' medical instruction at Oxford and Cambridge, which Lydgate eschewed in favour of more scientific study in London, Edinburgh, and Paris (142–43); and in any case Lydgate vehemently denies that knowledge of any subject makes one competent in another ('No man can judge what is good evidence on any particular subject, unless he knows that subject well... You might as well say that scanning verse will teach you to scan the potato crops' (155)). Fred Vincy, an indifferent student who reads novels rather than going to 'his Latin and things' (100), finds happiness in the end as a 'distinguished agricultural character... with the Greek and Latin sadly weather-worn' (817).

The Mill on the Floss (1860) is Eliot's most searching study of education and wasted human capacity.[32] Maggie Tulliver is poignantly denied access to the classics for which she shows a greater aptitude and responsiveness than Tom; Miss Firniss's boarding school offers no guidance for her inchoate aspirations for a higher life. Nor does limited schooling harm middle-class intellects alone; Bob Jakins blames his disorderly mind on the fact that 'I niver went to school much. That's what I jaw my old mother for. I says, "you should ha' sent me to school a bit more"' (276). Education in those distant days, the narrator writes, 'was almost entirely a matter of luck—usually of ill-luck' (147). Mr Tulliver intends to give Tom 'a good eddication', to make him a gentleman, and 'a bit of a scholard' (8, 9). He finds a clergyman to teach Tom classics in the belief that such an education will 'be a bread to him', 'an investment', 'so much capital to him' (8, 62). Tom can see no reason for it; when he asked why anybody should learn Latin ('It's no good'), Philip Wakem could answer only that 'It's part of the education of a gentleman... All gentlemen learn the same things' (143). Tom's ill-luck comes not from his disinclination for such schooling or Mr Stelling's unsuitedness for teaching—these were commonplace—but from the family circumstances that made him suffer from the incoherence of the notion of the gentleman. Social status was not actually to be secured by elite knowledge of the classics. After his father's downfall, when Tom must earn money and goes to seek assistance from his uncle, Tom explains that at school he learned Latin, 'a good deal of Latin'. For Mr Deane, however, Latin is 'a luxury much run upon by the higher classes', and Tom's expertise in it fills him with 'a sort of repulsion' towards him (199–200). Tom nonetheless succeeds in business; when he repays the family debt, he gives a short speech and is applauded as a gentleman: 'Tom looked so gentlemanly... that Mr. Tulliver remarked... that he had spent a deal of money on his son's education' (311). Gentlemanly behaviour proves itself to be closely connected with Tom's education after all, but in the bitter sense that they both depend on habits of following arbitrary rules without understanding, on

---

[32] On Eliot and education, see Linda K. Robertson, *The Power of Knowledge: George Eliot and Education* (New York: Peter Lang, 1997).

self-maiming discipline, and on an aversion to a wider or more tolerant vision of life (book 7, chapter 3).

Vanity Fair (1848), though set in the Napoleonic period, shows how classical education informs the emotional life of Victorian gentlemen, especially of boys and their fathers. Actual allusion to antiquity plays relatively little part in the story;[33] learning Latin, not speaking it, is a focus of attention for the male characters. The experience of classics at school is treated ironically at times, and at others with sentimental pathos. At Swishtail Academy, before his victory over Cuff (who 'could knock you off forty Latin verses in an hour') and the ensuing recognition of his moral and physical courage, William Dobbin is regularly humiliated: he is one of 'those gentle souls' whom we 'degrade, estrange, torture, for the sake of a little loose arithmetic, and miserable dog-latin'; who in any case suffers from a marked 'incapacity to acquire the rudiments of the above language' (34). (As the son of a grocer he is vulnerable to greater public humiliation than George Osborne, the son of a tallow merchant who keeps his own carriage; neither could be confused with an Etonian like Crawley). When Lord Steyne wishes to disencumber Mrs Crawley of her son, he arranges for the boy to be sent to public school, on the grounds 'that he was of an age now when emulation, the first principles of the Latin language, pugilistic exercises, and the society of his fellow-boys would be of the greatest benefit to the boy'. The objections of the parents 'disappeared before the generous perseverance of the Marquis of Steyne' (464). In Thackeray such cynicism about public school education frictionlessly coexists with sentimentality about it. Crawley, 'though his chief recollections of polite learning were connected with the floggings which he received at Eton in his early youth', still has 'that decent and honest reverence for classical learning which all English gentlemen feel', and he therefore acquiesces in Rawdon's departure for school, 'although his boy was his chief solace and companion, and endeared to him by a thousand small ties' (465). Georgy Osborne's successful education as a gentleman (his father's qualifications were less secure, his grandfather's thinner still) is evident in his unbounded admiration for Dobbin, who has in the meantime gained or been attributed fluency in Latin:

> Georgy never tired of his praises of the Major to his mother... 'Dob reads Latin like English, and French and that; and when we go out together he tells me stories about my Papa, and never about himself; though I heard...that he was one of the bravest officers in the army'. [541]

By the end of the 19th century, the growth and sustained reform of public schools had met the need for a large governing class by producing gentlemen in a wider sense of the term. Latin-based, public-school education provided a basis for mutual identification as members of the governing class. It was less clear earlier in the century. In *Felix Holt* (1866), set at the time of the 1832 Reform Act, Rev. Lingon is contemptuous of the

---

[33] The most prominent quoter of classics is Sir Pitt Crawley, Rawdon's older brother, who at university spoke 'unceasingly at the debating societies' but 'never advanced any sentiment or opinion which was not perfectly trite and stale, and supported by a Latin quotation' (75).

lawyer Matthew Jermyn, calling him 'one of your educated lowbred fellows; a foundling who got his Latin for nothing at Christ's Hospital; one of your middle-class upstarts who want to rank with gentlemen' (30); Jermyn is similarly scorned by Harold Transome, who refuses to acknowledge the lawyer's Latin quotation ('I don't talk in tags of Latin, which might be learned by a schoolmaster's footboy', 167). Latin in *Felix Holt* is authoritative only in the right hands. The vicar advises Transome to make judicious use of it: 'your calling yourself a Radical...looks awkward—it's not what people are used to—it wants a good deal of Latin to make it go down'. Transome's Tory opponent, the young Debarry, 'is a tremendous fellow at the classics', and so Transome should 'rub up a few quotations...just to show Debarry what you could do if you liked' (39); he recommends a passage from Juvenal's fourth satire.

The domains in which Latin, or the fiction of Latin, has authority are those of the gentlemen, above all in governance and administration: parliamentarians,[34] officers of the army and navy,[35] squires and parsons, civil servants in Britain and the Empire.[36] In contrast, the perverseness of this authority is underscored in novels that exploit the frisson that is provoked when the social meaning of gentleman is divided from its moral meaning, as with the Latin-speaking, classically accomplished dandies, scholar-criminals, 'muscular blackguards', and decadents of Bulwer Lytton, G.A. Lawrence, Wilde, and others (though novelists were not obliged to use classics in depicting such types).[37]

[34] Stray, *Classics Transformed*, 65–67, summarizes the history of classical quotation in the context of Parliament: it had become a minority practice by the 1830s and declined from the 1880s on, with the appearance of working-class MPs. See further, Joseph S. Meisel, *Public Speech and the Culture of Public Life in the Age of Gladstone* (New York: Columbia University Press, 2001), 54–70, 79–85, 90–104. In *Adam Bede* (1859), Arthur Donnithorne will do well 'if I can remember a little inapplicable Latin to adorn my maiden speech in Parliament six or seven years hence' (158).

[35] In *Vanity Fair*, Crawley, Dobbins, and Osborne are all army officers and have all learned Latin at school (though, as Mason points out in *The English Gentleman*, 162, the difference between being a member of the Life Guards and belonging to a marching regiment was as large as that between Eton and Swishtail). The hero of Frederick Marryat's *The Naval Officer, or, Scenes and Adventures in the Life of Frank Mildmay* (1829) was sent to a schoolmaster to learn Latin and Greek by means of a large knotted stick (vol. 1, chapter 1); classics in his case supplied discipline but put him at a disadvantage in the colonies, where he was 'far above the common run of society' until he formed a friendship with a young lieutenant with whom he could read classical authors, recite Latin verses, and fence (253).

[36] Chris Hagerman, 'Secret Ciphers, Secret Knowledge: The Classics in British India, ca. 1800–1900', *Victorian Newsletter* 113 (2008): 3–14.

[37] Bulwer Lytton's dandies show effortless mastery over classics, but this is not essential to the type; Disraeli's Vivian Grey is 'more deficient than most of his own age in accurate classical attainments' (16). The hero of Bulwer Lytton's *Eugene Aram* (1832), 'whose whole life seemed to have been one sacrifice to knowledge' (44), is the most influential example of the scholar-criminal for the Victorians; see Nancy Jane Tyson, *Eugene Aram: Literary History and Typology of the Scholar-Criminal* (Hamden: Archon Books, 1983). In *Catherine* (1839–40) and 'George de Barnwell' (1847), Thackeray ridicules the novelistic depiction of learned criminals. Lawrence's Guy Livingstone, the product of public school, Oxford, and the Guards, is repeatedly admired for his command of classics (e.g. 'Charley looked at his friend admiringly, as he always did when Guy was classical in his allusions' (115)); he is the most prominent instance of the 'muscular blackguard' which Rev. Andrew K.H. Boyd denounced in *Fraser's Magazine* 66 (August 1862): 179). Most of the classical allusions in *The Picture of Dorian Gray* (1890)—Antinous, Messalina, the *Satyricon*, and the emperors Tiberius, Caligula, Nero, and Elagabalus—are common

Latin was a means to distinguish gentlemen from those lower down the social scale, but Greek had the ability to distinguish some gentlemen from others. Those who learned both Greek and Latin had a superior education and higher status than those who learned Latin alone. However, such superiority threatened the shared gentlemanly identity of the upper and some middle classes; as a result, knowledge of Greek was not publicized like knowledge of Latin. Unlike the relatively sharp line that excluded the Latin-less lower classes from the status of gentleman, the line between higher-status (Greek and Latin) and lower-status (Latin only) gentlemen was kept blurred. Quoting Greek was much rarer than quoting Latin, and knowledge of Greek was much less relevant for communicating identities. Despite the greater prestige of Greek, with its connotations of higher culture and higher spiritual life, the language is not prominently used in novels for making distinctions among gentlemen or in marking other kinds of identities, but rather for the appeal it had to people who did not usually receive any classical education at all: women[38] such as Dorothea Brooke and lower-class men like Jude Fawley.

One character-type constitutes the major exception: Greek plays a large role in representations of the scholar. Many elements of these representations are of very long standing, especially the negative ones. The scholar is poor, sickly, melancholy, desiccated; or pedantic, boorish, querulous, conceited, 'vir obscurus'; or again, impractical, cloistered, absent-minded, 'doctor umbraticus'; or sometimes he is powerful, haughty, dangerous, Faustian.[39] (Favourable depictions, the scholar-saint, scholar-courtier, gentleman-scholar, and charismatic professor, are more time- and context-bound.) In 19th-century novels, the convention is to depict the poor scholar with sympathy, to show his pride or indifference to the world as costly and perhaps lamentable, but at least honestly hard-won (Dominie Sampson in *Guy Mannering* (1815), Christopher Clutterbuck in *Pelham*, the hero of Dickens's 'George Silverman's Explanation' (1868), Mordecai in Eliot's *Daniel Deronda* (1878), Josiah Crawley in Trollope's novels).[40] Novelists are harsher with scholars who have gained worldly success. One type in particular comes in for condemnation, the 'Greek play' bishop, the cleric who is raised to the episcopal bench

shorthand expressions for decadent sexuality; the name 'Dorian' is a more academic allusion to Spartan pederastic practice (see Linda Dowling, *Hellenism and Homosexuality in Victorian Oxford* (Ithaca: Cornell University Press, 1994), 124–25 and Paul Cartledge, *Spartan Reflections* (Berkeley: University of California Press, 2001), 185–91).

[38] On women's preference for Greek over Latin, see Stray, *Classics Transformed*, 79, 81. Shanyn Fiske, *Heretical Hellenism: Women Writers, Ancient Greece, and the Victorian Popular Imagination* (Athens: Ohio University Press, 2008) discusses the appeal of classical knowledge to Victorian women as one of 'forbidden knowledge' (5).

[39] *Loci classici* include Juvenal, *Satire* 10.114–32; Petronius, *Satyricon* 2–3; Robert Burton, 'Digression of the Misery of Scholars' (*The Anatomy of Melancholy*); Samuel Johnson, *The Vanity of Human Wishes* 135–64. Combe's and Rowlandson's tours of Doctor Syntax (1812, 1820, 1821) re-invigorated the parodic depiction. In three novels Walter Scott features 'Dr Dryasdust'.

[40] These instances are discussed in John R. Reed, *Victorian Conventions* (Athens: Ohio University Press, 1975), 94–104.

because he has edited a Greek play.[41] Both Bulwer Lytton and Disraeli are contemptuous of the supposed practice, the former in *Ernest Maltravers* (1837), 29, and *Alice: or The Mysteries* (1838), 155; and the latter in *Coningsby* (1844), 315, and *Tancred* (1847), 144. A character in Trollope's *Barchester Towers* (1857) nostalgically defends it (182). George Eliot is severe. In *The Mill on the Floss*, Tom's tutor, the Rev. Walter Stelling, is narrowly ambitious: 'he would become celebrated by shaking the consciences of his hearers, and he would by and by edit a Greek play, and invent several new readings' (119). In *Felix Holt*, Rev. Lingon, who has just advised Transome to quote Latin in his public speeches, makes no objection to Transome's attacking the income of bishops: 'Nobody likes our Bishop: he's all Greek and greediness; too proud to dine with his own father' (38). Casaubon in *Middlemarch*, as clergyman, scholar, and author of a timely pamphlet on the Catholic question, is thought to have good prospects of becoming a bishop, or at least a dean (chapters 4, 7, 30). Parson Irwine, the vicar in *Adam Bede*, is not a scholar, but he reads Aeschylus and is one of those 'rectors who appreciate scholars' (159); without ambition for scholarly or churchly advancement, or desire to provide extensive pastoral care, he is a more sympathetic character than her other Greek-reading churchmen.

The scholar who published works on antiquity was not a classicist in the modern sense. He was most often a cleric, perhaps also a private tutor to a young nobleman, or a schoolmaster; more rarely, an amateur, a gentleman of independent means. Academic careers did not exist for most of the century.[42] Until the discipline was professionalized, classical scholarship was supported mainly by the Anglican Church. Among other consequences, this meant that there was no institutional reason to confine the study of antiquity to Greece and Rome alone, and cross-cultural comparisons were common.[43] In these respects, Edward Casaubon's project is typical of a scholarly endeavour in England around 1830, the period when *Middlemarch* is set.

Eliot's portrait of the failed scholar is the greatest depiction of a classicist in Victorian literature,[44] but the nature of his failure has not been well understood. When he is

---

[41] The best study is by Arthur Burns and Christopher Stray, 'Greek play bishops (act. 1810–1840)', *Oxford Dictionary of National Biography* (added May 2009), expanded in 'The Greek-play Bishop: Polemic, Prosopography and Nineteenth-Century Prelates', *The Historical Journal* 54, no. 4 (2011): 1013–38.

[42] Stray, *Classics Transformed*, 120 and 143, describes and accounts for the rise of the academic career in the 1880s (grounds for the transformation had been laid in the previous generation).

[43] Parson Adams not only 'was a perfect Master of the *Greek* and *Latin* Languages' but to them 'he added a great Share of Knowledge in the Oriental Tongues' (*Joseph Andrews*, 22–23). A foundational work of classical scholarship, F.A. Wolf's *Prolegomena to Homer* (1795), discussed Alexandrian and Masoretic scholarship in tandem, but within a generation classical scholarship ceased to make such comparisons; see Anthony Grafton, *Defenders of the Text: The Traditions of Scholarship in an Age of Science, 1450–1800* (Cambridge: Harvard University Press, 1991), 242–43. For the complexities of this development, see Josine H. Blok, 'Proof and Persuasion in *Black Athena I*: The Case of K. O. Müller', *Talanta* 28–9 (1996–7): 173–208.

[44] Perhaps Mary Augusta Ward's depiction of Roger Wendover, the Squire of Murewell Hall, in her best-selling *Robert Elsmere* (1888), was even more widely known. For a comparison of Casaubon and Wendover, see Elizabeth Hale, 'Sickly Scholars and Healthy Novels: The Classical Scholar in Victorian Fiction', *International Journal of the Classical Tradition* 17, no. 2 (2010): 219–43. Wendover is a more modern (as well as far more distinguished) scholar than Casaubon; he took his doctorate from the University of Berlin (chapter 24).

introduced, the narrator explains that 'His very name carried an impressiveness hardly to be measured without a precise chronology of scholarship' (11). The ironic remark—the narrator knows that readers are liable to pretend to know more than they do about the history of classical scholarship—shows a certain strain,[45] but the point is not only that even well-educated readers may not have heard of the great classical scholar Isaac Casaubon, but that a precise grasp of the chronology of scholarship is necessary to reach a judgement about Middlemarch's Casaubon. Eliot describes his scholarship in such a way that it is finely balanced between the inevitably out of date and the culpably negligent. His field of study, the history of religious mysteries and mythologies, had been inaugurated by the first Casaubon, and it soon became part of the polemical attack against Catholicism;[46] the weapons of this attack were then taken up by sceptics and deists of the Enlightenment and applied to all of Christianity; around the middle of the 18th century, William Warburton was influential in re-interpreting pagan mythology as evidence for the priority of Christian truths.[47] After Warburton, numerous attempts were made to establish the Christian truth behind ancient mythology, and in England the Christian study of syncretic mythography was vigorous, from Jacob Bryant's *A New System, or, An Analysis of Antient Mythology* (1774–76) to George Stanley Faber's *The Origin of Pagan Idolatry* (1816); it was moribund by the 1830s.[48] (The debate over mythology in Germany was of far more lasting significance, but Casaubon, unlike his

---

[45] The narrator repeatedly makes strained references to the classics. By insisting on them in contexts where the justification is strained or far-fetched, the narrator plays with readers' demands for the relevance of antiquity: 'if that convenient vehicle [the phaeton] had existed in the days of the Seven Sages, one of them would doubtless have remarked…' (58); 'much the same sort of movement and mixture went on in old England as we find in older Herodotus, who also, in telling what had been, thought it well to take a woman's lot for his starting-point; though Io, as a maiden apparently beguiled by attractive merchandise, was the reverse of Miss Brooke' (94, referring to the opening of Herodotus' *Histories*, where the Phoenicians, selling their merchandise in Argos, seized Io and other Greek women who were 'intent upon their purchases'); 'Hiram Ford, observing himself at a safe challenging distance [from Fred Vincy], turned back and shouted a defiance which he did not know to be Homeric' (544, presumably a reference to Odysseus at a safe distance from the Cyclops).

[46] Isaac Casaubon's discussion of the relation of early Christianity to the pagan mysteries appears in 'De sacrosancta eucharistia' in *De rebus sacris et ecclesiasticis exercitationes XVI* (1614). On Casaubon's influence until the end of the 19th century, see Jonathan Z. Smith, *Drudgery Divine: On the Comparison of Early Christianities and the Religions of Late Antiquity* (Chicago: University of Chicago Press, 1990).

[47] Mark Pattison gives a devastating portrait of Warburton's scholarly and personal failings in a review-essay of 1863, reprinted in *Essays*, ed. Henry Nettleship, 2 vols. (Oxford: Clarendon Press, 1889). For recent treatments, see Jan Assmann, *Moses the Egyptian: The Memory of Egypt in Western Monotheism* (Cambridge: Harvard University Press, 1997), 96–114 and David Sorkin, *The Religious Enlightenment: Protestants, Jews, and Catholics from London to Vienna* (Princeton: Princeton University Press, 2008), 23–64.

[48] See Albert J. Kuhn, 'English Deism and the Development of Romantic Mythological Syncretism', *PMLA* 71 (1956): 1094–116. In France and elsewhere debate was largely centred on the theories of Charles François Dupuis, who in his *Origine de tous les cultes* (1795) interpreted all religions, including Christianity, as forms of solar mythology. A fully sexual version of solar mythology, launched in England by Richard Payne Knight in *A Discourse on the Worship of Priapus* (1786), had almost no sequel until its 'revival' in the 1860s, according to Joscelyn Godwin, *The Theosophical Enlightenment* (Albany: State University of New York, 1994), 22.

creator, refused to learn from it[49]). Edward Casaubon's intellectual labours are confined to this tradition of Anglican scholarship, which, from Eliot's perspective, not only was obsolete by Casaubon's time but (unlike medicine) may never have been a viable science, capable of progressive self-correction.[50]

Eliot rigorously indicts Casaubon's failure. His self-regard, paralyzing sensitivity to criticism, and inadequate commitment to (and competence for) his work are integral parts of the novel's exploration of mediocrity and self-delusion, and to that extent, his selfishness and vanity are not greatly different from the flaws of other characters. He might even have been included in the vision of redeemed, or half-redeemed, waste at the end of the novel. However, more is said against him. He fails in the fundamental duty of a landed gentleman to protect dependents—women, family, tenants, and others. Will Ladislaw, though hardly disinterested, insists to himself that Casaubon was bound to know the wrong he was doing in binding Dorothea to himself ('It is the most horrible of virgin-sacrifices' (351)). Sir James Chettam is outraged by Casaubon's will, saying that 'there never was a meaner, more ungentlemanly action than this—a codicil of this sort to a will which he made at the time of his marriage with the knowledge and reliance of her family—a positive insult to Dorothea!' (475). Dorothea comes to see Casaubon's treatment of Will and his mother not as a noble provision but as scanting their rightful claims to property (chapter 37). How landlords treat their tenants is a key concern of the novel. From private motives, Chettam (in his affection for Dorothea) and Arthur Brooke (in his political ambitions) are nonetheless brought closer to the lives of their tenants and seek to make improvements; Casaubon, in contrast, remains absorbed in himself and aloof from them, contented with their contentment. Indeed, he causes Dorothea to doubt her understanding of the social duties of a Christian: 'how could she be confident that one-roomed cottages were not for the glory of God, when men who knew the classics appeared to conciliate indifference to the cottages with zeal for the glory?' (63).

---

[49] An influential attempt to reconcile Christianity with ancient mythology was made by Friedrich Creuzer (*Symbolik und Mythologie der alten Völker*, 1810–12); his work was attacked by J.H. Voss (1824–26) and discredited by C.A. Lobeck (1829). A new approach to myth was established with K.O. Müller, *Prolegomena zu einer wissenschaftlichen Mythologie* (1825); on Müller's impact in Britain, see Robert Ackerman, 'K.O. Müller in Britain', in William M. Calder and Renate Schlesier, eds., *Zwischen Rationalismus und Romantik: Karl Otfried Müller und die Antike Kultur* (Hildesheim: Weidmann, 1998), 1–17. For the German context, see George S. Williamson, *The Longing for Myth in Germany: Religion and Aesthetic Culture from Romanticism to Nietzsche* (Chicago: University of Chicago Press, 2004).

[50] Casaubon's tractate on Egyptian mysteries is concerned to correct 'certain assertions of Warburton's' (274), and Will Ladislaw insists that it is no use for Casaubon to bother correcting the mistakes of Bryant (217). Casaubon's interests in Xisuthrus, Dagon, the Cabeiri, and Chus further associate him with his immediate predecessors (Faber on Xisuthrus, Bryant on Chus, Dagon, the Cabeiri). On Casaubon's scholarship, see further Daniel P. Deneau, 'Eliot's Casaubon and Mythology', *American Notes and Queries* 6, no. 8 (1968): 125–27; Richard Ellmann, *Golden Codgers: Biographical Speculations* (New York: Oxford University Press, 1973), 17–38; Lisa Baltazar, 'The Critique of Anglican Biblical Scholarship in George Eliot's *Middlemarch*', *Literature and Theology* 15, no. 1 (2001): 40–60; and Felicia Bonaparte, 'Ancient Paradigms, Modern Texts: Classical Keys to George Eliot's Mythologies', *International Journal of the Classical Tradition* 8, no. 4 (2002): 585–603.

Narrow self-absorption must always be more than a personal failing, but Casaubon's faults are magnified by the scale of the waste they bring about. He has benefited not only from Dorothea's idealistic devotion but also from his country's primary instruments of wealth, receiving a University education, the living of Lowick, and (on his brother's death) the manor of Lowick. The plot of *Middlemarch* offers multiple repudiations of classical learning, above all in the example of Casaubon, but also in Dorothea's collusion with him, in the superficiality of Will Ladislaw's learning, and in Lydgate's and Fred Vincy's rejections of classical studies at university. Only once in the novel are the classics unambiguously valued, and then only in passing, in the 'Finale', when Mary Vincy domesticates them: she writes a book of stories taken from Plutarch for her boys and later publishes it (everyone in town believes her husband was the author).[51] Eliot's vision is directed mainly toward the waste and the hollowness of the nation's devotion to classics, despite the attempt at reparation and partial redemption in the last two paragraphs of the novel.[52]

Except under exceptional circumstances, women and workers were presumed not to have any classical knowledge, which had the potential to de-feminize women and *déclasser* members of the working class. The heroes of Kingsley's *Alton Locke* (1850) and Eliot's *Felix Holt* (1866) have received educations which included Latin and which separated them from their class origins and allied them implicitly, if against their stated intentions, with the middle class.[53] A generation later, Gissing in *New Grub Street* (1891) offers a brief and pathetic glimpse of working-class aspirations to professional advancement through Latin in Biffin's tutorials to uneducated men who 'nourish preposterous

---

[51] On George Eliot and the classics, see Vernon Rendall, 'George Eliot and the Classics', in Gordon S. Haight, ed., *A Century of George Eliot Criticism* (London: Methuen, 1966), 215–26; Jenkyns, *The Victorians and Ancient Greece*, 112–32; P.E. Easterling, 'George Eliot and Greek Tragedy', *Arion* 3rd series, 1, no. 2 (1991): 60–74; Laura McClure, 'On Knowing Greek: George Eliot and the Classical Tradition', *Classical and Modern Literature* 13, no. 2 (1993): 139–56. On classics and *Middlemarch* specifically, see Roger Travis, 'From "Shattered Mummies" to "An Epic Life": Casaubon's Key to All Mythologies and Dorothea's Mythic Renewal in George Eliot's *Middlemarch*', *International Journal of the Classical Tradition* 5, no. 3 (1999): 367–82 and Hilary Mackie, 'The Key to Epic Life?: Classical Study in George Eliot's *Middlemarch*', *Classical World* 103, no.1 (2009): 53–67. Several older studies of Eliot and mythology remain useful, including E.S. Shaffer, *'Kubla Khan' and The Fall of Jerusalem: The Mythological School in Biblical Secular Literature, 1770–1880* (Cambridge: Cambridge University Press, 1975) and Joseph Wiesenfarth, *George Eliot's Mythmaking* (Heidelberg: Carl Winter, 1977).

[52] For criticism of the final paragraphs as dishonest, see Geoffrey Hill, *Collected Critical Writings*, ed. Kenneth Haynes (Oxford: Oxford University Press, 2008), 471–73.

[53] After giving up his apprenticeship, Felix Holt studies in Glasgow (chapter 4). Scottish universities, unlike Oxford and Cambridge, 'were open to anyone who could scrape together a little Latin and mathematics' (R.D. Anderson, *Education and Opportunity in Victorian Scotland* (Oxford: Clarendon Press, 1983), 4); on the requirements for a degree in medicine at the University of Glasgow after 1802 (three examinations conducted in Latin and the composition of a Latin commentary on Hippocrates), see James Coutts, *A History of the University of Glasgow* (Glasgow: Maclehose, 1909), 541. Felix never alludes to the classics and does not see them as a means for advancement ('Why should I want to get into the middle class because I have some learning' (57)). Alton Locke teaches himself Latin (chapter 2), but 'the immense disadvantages of self-education' become clear when he visits Cambridge (150). The class status of the heroes and heroines of the industrial novel has been much debated since Raymond Williams, *Culture and Society, 1780–1950* [1958] (New York: Columbia University Press, 1983), 87–109.

ambitions' to pass examinations that would enable them to become doctors, lawyers, and clergymen (144; for Latin instruction, see chapter 16).[54]

The belief that the study of antiquity could be a means towards a higher life leads to the first tragedy of Hardy's *Jude the Obscure* (1895), the failure and waste of Jude's Christminster aspirations; the belief that the past could be set aside leads to the second, domestic tragedy. Both tragedies are introduced with a pregnant description of the Greek letters on the title-page of the Greek New Testament: the letters Η ΚΑΙΝΗ ΔΙΑΘΗΚΗ regard Jude 'with fixed reproach in the grey starlight, like the unclosed eyes of a dead man' (43). The simile prefigures the corpse of Little Father Time (whose 'glazed eyes' stared into the room in which he hanged himself (325)), as well as the self-immolation of Sue Bridehead when Phillotson's 'amative patience' comes to an end and he has her swear on a copy of the New Testament that it is her wish to 'complete' the 'half-marriage' (385). The past is revenant, uncanny, and cannot be repudiated merely because it is dead.

'Lady's Greek'—meaning Greek written without accents—was the pejorative term applied to women's efforts at the language.[55] It was one of many ways women were condescended to when they attempted to enter the masculine province of classical knowledge. Men in Victorian novels pointedly refrain from making classical allusions around women, or they translate for their benefit;[56] they teach their wives and daughters to respond to their use of Latin tags;[57] or they insist that classical knowledge is distinctly unfeminine.[58] But this was by no means the only convention, and it was not rare for

[54] For a working-class response to Gissing's novel, see Jonathan Rose, *The Intellectual Life of the British Working Classes* (New Haven: Yale University Press, 2001), 418.

[55] For the term, see Elizabeth Barrett Browning, *Aurora Leigh* (1856), book 2, ll. 76–77. In *Middlemarch*, Dorothea has an acute pang of self-doubt in 'woman's reason' after Casaubon dismisses her questions about the value of Greek accents (64). See further, Isobel Hurst, *Victorian Women Writers and the Classics: The Feminine of Homer* (Oxford: Oxford University Press, 2006), 7. Yopie Prins's *Ladies' Greek: Translations of Tragedy* is forthcoming from Princeton University Press.

[56] George Eliot found it necessary to remind a novelist that well-bred men (let alone well-bred women) do not 'quote Latin in mixed parties' ('Silly Novels by Lady Novelists', in *Victorian Criticism of the Novel*, 165). In *Felix Holt*, the lawyer Matthew Jermyn, at a birthday party for his daughter, after quoting humorous remarks from his early Latin reading, 'apologised, and translated to the ladies' (100). Casaubon scrupulously translates the Greek or Latin he uses when talking to Dorothea, 'but he probably would have done this in any case' (24). Gissing several times depicts a man using a Latin quotation to assert control in a quarrel with a woman, Alfred Yule with his daughter (*New Grub Street* (1891), chapter 13) and Harvey Rolfe with his wife (*The Whirlpool* (1897), part 2, chapter 1).

[57] In Trollope's novels, women command and sometimes make classical allusions when they have been instructed by men (Grace Crawley, Mary Lawrie, Lady Ongar; see Osborne, 'Hooked on Classics', 150–51).

[58] Dickens's ghoulish Miss Blimber (suggested, remotely, by the example of the 'amiable' Louisa King) was 'dry and sandy with working in the graves of deceased languages' (*Dombey and Son*, 143). (Louisa King's own story, 'Mother and Stepmother', for Dickens' *Household Words* (1855), shows the perverted result of teaching a woman ancient languages: mental exercise makes her cold, and she becomes a murderer. On King see further Kathleen Tillotson, 'Louisa King and Cornelia Blimber', *The Dickensian* 74, no. 385 (1978): 91–95). Men in George Eliot's novels repeatedly argue that women are unsuited for classical study (Tom and Mr Stelling in *The Mill on the Floss* (book 2, chapter 1); Bardo in *Romola* (chapter 5), and Mr Brooke in *Middlemarch* (chapter 7)). On six occasions, characters in Trollope express the view that familiarity with Latin was unfeminine (according to John Williams Clark, *The Language and Style of Anthony Trollope* (London: André Deutsch, 1975), 187–88).

novelists to depict women in possession of classical literacy. One of George Eliot's complaints against two 'silly novels' of 1856 was the heroines' implausible command and display of classical languages.[59] Other novelists did not bother one way or the other. In Jane Austen's novels, for example, neither men nor women are much concerned with classical learning; a recent critic observes that she does not 'present the effects of education on those of her characters who might be expected to show it. Frank Churchill is the only one to use a Latin tag'.[60]

Austen's abstention from classics was not typical of women novelists of the 19th century, who found numerous occasions to delineate characters through classics (even if reviewers at the time expressed not only contempt for their silliness but also doubts about their competence).[61] Mary Shelley, for example, does so in order to establish the intellectual and social credentials of Victor Frankenstein and Henry Clerval (*Frankenstein* (1818), 21, 50). Elizabeth Gaskell uses the classics in order to introduce the family history and educational background of the manufacturer John Thornton (who left school to work when his father died but continues to read Homer); to motivate his conflict with his mother, who resents the useless languages; and to inform his opinion about the incompatibility of the English and Greek races (*North and South*, 84–5, 240, and 334).

Women novelists powerfully presented the drama of women's limited access to education in the classics.[62] The theme regularly occurs in Charlotte Brontë's novels. Jane Eyre twice adverts to her lack of Greek: when she hears an unknown tongue, she confesses her ignorance by saying 'Whether it were Greek or German I could not tell' (425); and when St John advises her not to waste her ardour on 'trite, transient objects', adding for emphasis 'Do you hear, Jane', she replies 'Yes, just as if you were speaking Greek' (499–500). On two occasions, however, her knowledge of some Latin is implied. At Lowood, she is amazed at Helen Burns's ability to read Virgil, but in the next chapter she herself must be the one responsible for the Latin inscription ('Resurgam') on Helen's grave. Moreover, after remarking on her ignorance of Greek and German, she adds that she knows enough to add that the unknown language is 'neither French or Latin' (425). For Caroline Helstone, the Greek and Latin books in her uncle's library are

---

[59] See 'Silly Novels by Lady Novelists', in *Victorian Criticism of the Novel*, 163–64.

[60] Richard Jenkyns, *A Fine Brush on Ivory: An Appreciation of Jane Austen* (Oxford: Oxford University Press, 2004), 182; see *Emma* (1816), 184.

[61] In an 1860 review of George Eliot's first three works of fiction, the critic finds the tone and the atmosphere 'unquestionably feminine' despite the fact that 'there are traces of knowledge which is not usual among women' (namely, acquaintance with classics); see 'Eliot's Novels', *The Quarterly Review* 108, no. 216 (October 1860): 471. When he complains that some of the classical quotations 'might at least have been more correctly printed', he conveys the common prejudice that women who learned Greek were not able to master its correct accentuation; for Eliot's response see Gordon S. Haight, ed., *The George Eliot Letters*, 9 vols. (New Haven: Yale University Press, 1954–1978), 3: 356–57. In the 1870s, reviewers for the *Athenaeum* repeatedly expressed the belief that women novelists were less likely to write Latin accurately than men (Ellen Miller Casey, 'Edging Women Out? Reviews of Women Novelists in the *Athenaeum*, 1860–1899', *Victorian Studies* 39, no. 2 (Winter 1996): 151–71, 156, 163–64).

[62] See R. Fowler, '"On Not Knowing Greek": The Classics and the Woman of Letters', *The Classical Journal* 78, no. 4 (1983): 337–49.

of no use (*Shirley* (1849), 440), but the novel makes clear that they would indeed have been useful, had she been educated to read them. She argues against the Pauline subordination of women to men, saying that she would not be surprised to find, if she could read the original Greek, that 'many of the words have been wrongly translated, perhaps misapprehended altogether' (371). Lucy Snowe was suspected by M. Emanuel of concealing her knowledge of Greek and Latin, and at times she 'would have given my right hand to possess the treasures he ascribed to me' (*Villette* (1853), 512). Males authors, too, responded to this drama: in her isolation (she is 'construed by not a single contiguous being'), Elizabeth-Jane Newson, strongly resented by her stepfather Henchard, 'read and took notes incessantly, mastering facts with painful laboriousness'; she struggles to learn Latin, 'incited by the Roman characteristics of the town she lived in' (*The Mayor of Casterbridge*, 133).

Girls' education in classics is dramatized in two works of 1856, Elizabeth Barrett Browning's *Aurora Leigh* and Charlotte Yonge's *Daisy Chain*; in both a protagonist receives not only a feminine education but also a masculine one in classics (Aurora Leigh from her aunt and her father respectively, and Ethel May from her governess and her older brother); the heroines reach opposite conclusions about the value of such masculine education for young women.[63] Maggie Tulliver's eagerness and aptitude to learn Latin makes no difference at the time the novel is set because, as her brother Tom says, 'Girls never learn such things' as Euclid or Latin (*The Mill on the Floss*, 127). Girls did, sometimes, learn such things (Lady Jane Grey, Queen Elizabeth, and Anne Dacier were the instances most often adduced in answering 'pretended doubt' about women's capacity for education),[64] and they did so increasingly in the course of the 19th century. In *The Heavenly Twins* (1893), Sarah Grand ensures that Maggie Tulliver's fate is not repeated. Angelica Hamilton-Wells objects to being put off with a 'squeaking governess and long division' when like her twin she should have a tutor and 'be doing mathematics and Latin and Greek'. Diavolo concurs that it is unfair for his sister 'only to have a beastly governess to teach her when she knows as much as I do, and is a precious sight sharper' (125). Later in the novel Grand introduces a new objection to the study of classical literature, casting doubt on its intrinsic moral worth, when Diavolo complains about how it depicts women ('Beastly bad tone about women in the Classics' (272)).

Women's ignorance of classical languages, and conversely Greek and Latin as the languages of educated male sociability, are themes that continued to appeal to novelists

---

[63] June Sturrock, *'Heaven and Home': Charlotte M. Yonge's Domestic Fiction and the Victorian Debate over Women* (Victoria: University of Victoria, 1995), 34–38. See further, Clemence Schultze, 'Charlotte Yonge and the Classics', in Julia Courtney and Clemence Schultze, eds., *Characters and Scenes: Studies in Charlotte M. Yonge* (Abingdon: Beechcroft Books, 2007), 159–88.

[64] For their unusual knowledge of classics, these women are mentioned in Samuel Richardson, *Sir Charles Grandison* (vol. 1, letters 12 and 13); Harriet Martineau, 'Middle-Class Education in England: Girls', *The Cornhill Magazine* 10 (November 1864): 549–68; and Matthew Arnold, 'Literature and Science' [1882], reproduced in *Philistinism in England and America* (Ann Arbor: University of Michigan Press, 1974). In *The History of England* (written in 1791), Austen questions whether Lady Jane Grey deserved her reputation for knowledge of Greek (she imputes it to Grey's vanity; see the paragraph on Edward the Sixth (17)).

in the early 20th century. Knowledge of Greek is a leitmotif that runs through Virginia Woolf's *The Voyage Out* (1915). William Pepper, whose 'ideal was a woman who could read Greek' (20), quotes a passage from a choral ode in Sophocles' *Antigone*, prompting Clarissa Dalloway to say that she would give 'ten years of my life to know Greek' and to settle for permitting Ridley Ambrose to teach her the alphabet (39); Ambrose, at work on his Pindar edition 'from morning to night' (25), asks his niece Rachel Vinrace, 'What's the use of reading if you don't read Greek?', extracting from her a promise that she would learn the alphabet (159–60); and Mrs Flushing, who would rather 'break stones in the road' than learn Greek (185), delights in the Sappho which St John Hirst brings to chapel (chapter 17). In Ford Madox Ford's *Parade's End* (1924–28), Valentine Wannop's knowledge of Latin is part of the initial attraction between her and Christopher Tietjens (*Some Do Not …*, chapter 5) and is an aspect of their flirtation. However, by this time it had become rarer for characters to use classical allusions or a knowledge of Latin (including, as in the case of Wannop and Tietjens, its pronunciation) in order to communicate their identities to each other. It continues mainly in fiction set in schools or universities, in comic or whimsical settings,[65] and in new discussions of sexual identity.[66] For a generation or more after the Victorians, classical allusions by narrators and in representations of consciousness remained a central resource for the novel, and classics a source of wide inspiration; but the possibility of characterizing many kinds of people by their use of the classics declined with the advent of 20th-century education.

LIST OF EDITIONS

Austen, Jane. *Emma*. Oxford: Oxford University Press, 1999.
———. *The History of England from the Reign of Henry 4th to the Death of Charles the 1st*. Chapel Hill: Algonquin, 1993.
Beerbohm, Max. *The Illustrated Zuleika Dobson*. New Haven: Yale University Press, 1985.
Brontë, Charlotte. *Jane Eyre*. Edited by Jane Jack and Margaret Smith. Oxford: Clarendon Press, 1969.
———. *Shirley*. Edited by Herbert Rosengarten and Margaret Smith Oxford: Clarendon Press, 1979.
———. *Villette*. Edited by Herbert Rosengarten and Margaret Smith. Oxford: Clarendon Press, 1984.
Bulwer Lytton, Edward George. *Alice: or The Mysteries*. London: Saunders and Otley, 1838.
———. *Ernest Maltravers*. New York: Harper, 1837.

---

[65] In Forster's 'Other Kingdom' (1909), the conversation turns to the value of the classics, and the narrator Mr Inskip demonstrates the value of even meaningless allusion ('it is part of my system to make classical allusions'(53). In his 'sterner moods', the Duke of Dorset, in Beerbohm's *Zuleika Dobson* (1911), 'gravitated to Latin', while finding 'for his highest flights of contemplation a handy vehicle in Sanscrit' and 'hours of mere joy' writing Greek poetry (200).

[66] Talking about Plato is a means for Clive Durham and Maurice Hall to try to communicate, in E.M. Forster's *Maurice* (written 1913–14); see pp. 38, 44, and 73.

———. *Eugene Aram*. New York: Harper, 1832.

———. *Pelham: The Adventures of a Gentleman*. Edited by Jerome J. McGann. Lincoln: University of Nebraska Press, 1972.

Chesterfield, Philip Dormer Stanhope, fourth earl of. *The Letters of Philip Dormer Stanhope, 4th Earl of Chesterfield*. Edited by Bonamy Dobrée. 6 vols., continuously paginated. London: Eyre and Spottiswoode, 1932.

Dickens, Charles. *Bleak House*. Edited by George Ford and Sylvère Monod. New York: Norton, 1977.

———. *David Copperfield*. Edited by Nina Burgis. Oxford: Clarendon Press, 1981.

———. *Dombey and Son*. Edited by Alan Horsman. Oxford: Clarendon Press, 1974.

———. *Our Mutual Friend*. Edited by Michael Cotsell. Oxford: Oxford University Press, 1989.

Disraeli, Benjamin. *Coningsby, or The New Generation*. Edited by Sheila M. Smith. Oxford: Oxford University Press, 1982.

———. *Tancred, or The New Crusade*. 3 vols. London: Colburn, 1847.

———. *Vivian Grey*. London: Colburn, 1826.

Eliot, George . *Adam Bede*. Edited by Carol A. Martin. Oxford: Clarendon, 2001.

———. *Felix Holt, the Radical*. Edited by Fred C. Thomson. Oxford: Clarendon, 1980.

———. *Middlemarch*. Edited by David Carroll. Oxford: Clarendon, 1986.

———. *Romola*. Edited by Andrew Brown. Oxford: Clarendon, 1993.

———. *Scenes of Clerical Life*. Edited by Thomas A. Noble. Oxford: Clarendon, 1985.

———. *The Mill on the Floss*. Edited by Gordon S. Haight. Oxford: Clarendon, 1980.

Fielding, Henry. *Joseph Andrews*. Edited by Martin C. Battestin. Middletown, CT: Wesleyan University Press, 1967.

———. *The History of Tom Jones, A Foundling*. Edited by Fredson Bowers. 2 vols. continuously paginated. Middletown, CT: Wesleyan University Press, 1975.

Ford, Ford Madox. *Parade's End*. New York: Knopf, 1950.

Forster, E.M. *Maurice*. Edited by Philip Gardner. London: André Deutsch, 1999.

———. *The Machine Stops and Other Stories*. Edited by Rod Mengham. London: André Deutsch, 1997.

Gaskell, Elizabeth. *North and South*. Edited by Angus Easson. Oxford: Oxford University Press, 1998.

Gissing, George. *New Grub Street*. Edited by John Goode. Oxford: Oxford University Press, 1993.

Grand, Sarah. *The Heavenly Twins*. Ann Arbor: University of Michigan Press, 1992.

Hardy, Thomas. *Jude the Obscure*. Edited by Patricia Ingham. Oxford: Oxford University Press, 1985.

———. *The Mayor of Casterbridge*. Edited by Dale Kramer. Oxford: Oxford University Press, 1987.

James, Henry. *Complete Stories 1864–1874*. New York: Library of America, 1999.

Kingsley, Charles. *Alton Locke, Tailor and Poet, An Autobiography*. Edited by Elizabeth A. Cripps. Oxford: Oxford University Press, 1983.

Lawrence, George Alfred. *Guy Livingstone, or 'Thorough'*. New York: Harper, 1857.

Locke, John. *Some Thoughts Concerning Education*. Edited by John W. Yolton and Jean S. Yolton. Oxford: Clarendon Press, 1989.

Marryat, Frederick. *The Naval Officer*. London: Colburn, 1829.

Praed, Winthrop Mackworth. *The Political and Occasional Poems*. Edited by George Young. London: Ward, Lock, 1888.

Richardson, Samuel. *Pamela or, Virtue Rewarded*. 4 vols. Oxford: B. Blackwell, 1929–31.

——. *The History of Sir Charles Grandison*. Edited by Jocelyn Harris. London: Oxford University Press, 1972.

Rowcroft, Charles. *Confessions of an Etonian*. London: Colburn, 1852.

Scott, Walter. *Redgauntlet*. Edited by G.A.M. Wood and David Hewitt. Edinburgh: Edinburgh University Press, 1997.

Shelley, Mary. *Frankenstein, or The Modern Prometheus*. Edited by Marilyn Butler. Oxford: Oxford University Press, 1994.

Thackeray, William Makepeace. *The History of Pendennis*. Edited by Peter L. Shillingsburg. 2 vols. with distinct pagination bound together. New York: Garland, 1991.

——. *The Irish Sketch Book 1842*. Belfast: Blackstaff, 1985.

——. *The Newcomes, Memoirs of a Most Respectable Family*. Edited by Peter L. Shillingsburg. Ann Arbor: University of Michigan Press, 1996.

——. *Vanity Fair, A Novel without a Hero*. Edited by Peter L. Shillingsburg. New York: Garland, 1989.

Trollope, Anthony. *Barchester Towers*. Edited by Michael Sadleir and Frederick Page. Oxford: Oxford University Press, 1980.

——. *Castle Richmond*. Edited by Mary Hamer. Oxford: Oxford University Press, 1989.

——. *He Knew He Was Right*. Edited by John Sutherland. Oxford: Oxford University Press, 1985.

——. *Is He Popenjoy?* Edited by John Sutherland. 2 vols., with distinct pagination bound together. Oxford: Oxford University Press, 1986.

——. *Miss Mackenzie*. Edited by A.O.J. Cockshut. Oxford: Oxford University Press, 1988.

——. *Orley Farm*. Edited by David Skilton. 2 vols., with distinct pagination bound together. Oxford: Oxford University Press, 1985.

——. *Phineas Redux*. 2 vols., with distinct pagination bound together. London: Oxford University Press, 1973.

——. *Rachel Ray*. Edited by P.D. Edwards. Oxford: Oxford University Press, 1988.

——. *The Last Chronicle of Barset*. Edited by Stephen Gill. Oxford: Oxford University Press, 1980.

——. *The Prime Minister*. 2 vols., with distinct pagination bound together. London: Oxford University Press, 1973.

——. *The Vicar of Bullhampton*. Edited by David Skilton. Oxford: Oxford University Press, 1988.

——. *The Warden*. Edited by David Skilton. Oxford: Oxford University Press, 1980.

——. *The Way We Live Now*. Edited by John Sutherland. Oxford: Oxford University Press, 1982.

Woolf, Virginia. *The Voyage Out*. Edited by C. Ruth Miller and Lawrence Miller. Oxford: Blackwell, 1995.

Suggested Reading

Burns, Arthur and Christopher Stray. 'The Greek-play Bishop: Polemic, Prosopography and Nineteenth-Century Prelates'. *The Historical Journal* 54, no. 4: 1013–38.

Chandos, John. *Boys Together: English Public Schools 1800–1864*. New Haven: Yale University Press, 1984.

Collins, Philip. *Dickens and Education*. London: Macmillan, 1963.

Fowler, R. '"On Not Knowing Greek": The Classics and the Woman of Letters'. *The Classical Journal* 78, no. 4 (1983): 337–49.

Hagerman, Chris. 'Secret Ciphers, Secret Knowledge: The Classics in British India, ca. 1800–1900'. *Victorian Newsletter* 113 (Spring 2008): 3–14.

Hale, Elizabeth. 'Sickly Scholars and Healthy Novels: The Classical Scholar in Victorian Fiction'. *International Journal of the Classical Tradition* 17, no. 2 (2010): 219–43.

Jenkyns, Richard. *The Victorians and Ancient Greece*. Cambridge: Harvard University Press, 1980.

McClure, Laura. 'On Knowing Greek: George Eliot and the Classical Tradition'. *Classical and Modern Literature* 13, no. 2 (1993): 139–56.

Meisel, Joseph S. *Public Speech and the Culture of Public Life in the Age of Gladstone*. New York: Columbia University Press, 2001.

Moers, Ellen. *The Dandy: Brummell to Beerbohm*. New York: Viking Press, 1960.

Skilton, David. 'Schoolboy Latin and the Mid-Victorian Novelist: A Study in Reader Competence'. *Browning Institute Studies* 16 (1988): 39–55.

Stray, Christopher. *Classics Transformed: Schools, Universities, and Society in England, 1830–1960*. Oxford: Clarendon Press, 1998.

Wheeler, Michael. *The Art of Allusion in Victorian Fiction*. London: Macmillan, 1979.

PART VII

THE NOVEL AND OTHER DISCIPLINES

21

THE VICTORIAN NOVEL
AND SCIENCE

JONATHAN SMITH

Opening his anonymous 1871 review of Charles Darwin's newly published *The Descent of Man, and Selection in Relation to Sex*, the geologist W. Boyd Dawkins declared that in drawing-rooms throughout the land, Darwin's book was 'competing with the last new novel'.[1] Dawkins's claim was no exaggeration—like the novel, natural science in the 19th century became an increasingly important component of cultural life. Darwin's controversial discussion of human evolution may not have sold quite as well as some of 1871's most popular fiction—Edward Bulwer Lytton's Darwinian-inspired fantasy, *The Coming Race*; the latest sensation novel from Mary Braddon, *Fenton's Quest*; Margaret Oliphant's *Squire Arden*—but *The Descent of Man* was eagerly awaited and widely reviewed, and, as historian Bernard Lightman has shown, it became one of the 19th century's best- and steadiest-selling works of science.[2] Indeed, in the world of Victorian periodicals, serialized fiction and reviews of novels frequently appeared alongside articles about the latest scientific discoveries, reviews of scientific books, summaries of public science lectures, and accounts of the annual meetings of the British Association for the Advancement of Science (the latter memorably satirized by Charles Dickens in a series of sketches for *Bentley's Miscellany* in 1837–38 as The Mudfog Association for the Advancement of Everything).[3] Dickens himself, in the two weekly magazines he edited, *Household Words* (1850–59) and *All the Year Round* (1859–70), regularly positioned articles on natural

[1] [W. Boyd Dawkins], 'Darwin on the Descent of Man', *Edinburgh Review* 134 (July, 1871): 195–235, 195.
[2] Bernard Lightman, *Victorian Popularizers of Science: Designing Nature for New Audiences* (Chicago: University of Chicago Press, 2007), 489–93.
[3] Geoffrey Cantor and Sally Shuttleworth, eds., *Science Serialized: Representations of Science in Nineteenth-Century Periodicals* (Cambridge, MA: MIT Press, 2004); Geoffrey Cantor et al., eds., *Science in the Nineteenth-Century Periodical: Reading the Magazine of Nature* (Cambridge: Cambridge University Press, 2004); Louise Henson et al., eds., *Culture and Science in the Nineteenth-Century Media*

THE NOVEL AND OTHER DISCIPLINES

science cheek by jowl with the most recent chapters of a serialized novel, whether his own or someone else's. Readers of the 7 July 1860 issue of *All the Year Round*, for example, moved from the latest instalment of Wilkie Collins's spectacularly popular *The Woman in White* directly to a review of Darwin's *Origin of Species*.

Nor were *Descent of Man* and *Origin of Species* exceptions as attention-getting works of natural science. Edinburgh phrenologist George Combe's *The Constitution of Man* (1828) sold hundreds of thousands of copies over the course of the century, and Robert Chambers's anonymously published *Vestiges of the Natural History of Creation* (1844), with its evolutionary account of the universe and of life, generated a cultural scandal that Darwin, having just completed a private sketch of his own theory, observed with trepidation.[4] Many prominent scientists wrote works influential with, or popularized for, a general audience: Robert Ball in *The Story of the Heavens* (1885); T.H. Huxley in popular successes like *Physiography* (1877), *Introductory Science Primer* (1880), and *Crayfish* (1880); John Lubbock in works like *Prehistoric Times* (1865) and *Ants, Bees, and Wasps* (1882); and John Tyndall in collections of his lecture courses at the Royal Institution such as *Heat Considered as a Mode of Motion* (1863) and *The Forms of Water* (1872). More prosaic, but even more popular, were E.C. Brewer's *A Guide to the Scientific Knowledge of Things Familiar* (1847) and J.G. Wood's *Common Objects of the Country* (1858), their titles indicating a Wordsworthian focus on the stories of the common and familiar elements of the natural world. Writers like Brewer and Wood, though not professional scientists, were among the most prolific and successful of the army of popularizers from whom most Victorians received their science, often packaged with religious or moral messages. Novelist and Anglican divine Charles Kingsley, inspired by the seaside natural history books of his naturalist friend Philip Henry Gosse, wrote a widely read one of his own in *Glaucus; or, The Wonders of the Shore* (1855). Hugh Miller, the Scottish stonemason turned man of letters, harmonized biblical revelation with recent geological discoveries in his enormously popular narratives of earth history in *The Old Red Sandstone* (1841), *Foot-Prints of the Creator* (1849), and *The Testimony of the Rocks* (1857). Margaret Gatty's *Parables from Nature* (1855), Arabella Buckley's *The Fairy-Land of Science* (1879), and Eliza Brightwen's *Wild Nature Won by Kindness* (1890) brought scientific stories to children and their parents, while Mary Somerville's *On the Connexion of the Physical Sciences* (1834) dazzled readers with its mastery of recent work in physics, astronomy, and Continental mathematics. Richard Procter's *Other Worlds Than Ours* (1870) reignited the 'plurality of worlds' debate over the existence of extra-terrestrial life. Grant Allen was both an energetic popularizer of the ideas of Darwin,

(Aldershot: Ashgate, 2004).

    [4] On *The Constitution of Man*, see Roger Cooter, *The Cultural Meaning of Popular Science: Phrenology and the Organization of Consent in Nineteenth-Century Britain* (Cambridge: Cambridge University Press, 1984) and John van Wyhe, *Phrenology and the Origins of Victorian Scientific Naturalism* (Aldershot: Ashgate, 2004). On *Vestiges*, see James A. Secord, *Victorian Sensation: The Extraordinary Publication, Reception, and Secret Authorship of Vestiges of the Natural History of Creation* (Chicago: University of Chicago Press, 2000).

Huxley, and Herbert Spencer and a writer of popular fiction, including the scandalous bestseller, *The Woman Who Did* (1895).[5] Although Allen combined science with fiction only infrequently, H.G. Wells, himself both a novelist and a writer of popular science, credited Allen with laying out the field of philosophical scientific romance that he sought to cultivate in such works as *The Time Machine* (1895), *The Island of Dr. Moreau* (1896), *The Invisible Man* (1897), and *The War of the Worlds* (1898).[6]

All of which is to say that throughout the Victorian period scientists and novelists, as well as their readers, inhabited a vibrant world of print culture in which scientific and fictional narratives were juxtaposed and infused with each other's content and techniques at least as often as they were contrasted or held to be at odds. Novelists read science, and scientists read novels. Among novelists, Kingsley, Allen, and Wells—and George Eliot, who read the *Origin of Species* within two weeks of its publication, and whose companion, George Henry Lewes, not only wrote his own book of seaside natural history but published works on psychology and the philosophy of science—differed only in degree, not kind, from the bulk of their peers. Among scientists, discussions of novels litter the correspondence between Darwin and his good friend Joseph Hooker, Britain's foremost botanist of the period. The voracious Huxley devoured the novels of George Eliot and George Sand. In writing for their peers as well as for the public, scientists frequently cast their work in narrative forms and deployed the same sorts of narrative techniques to be found in the cosmic histories and apocalyptic visions of Genesis, John Milton, and prophets from the Old Testament's Daniel to Thomas Carlyle; in the imaginary voyages of Defoe and Swift; in the macabre and sinister worlds of Gothic romance; in the parables of Christ; in Wordsworthian accounts of the importance of the humble and the obscure; and in the elaborately mapped societies, whether rural or urban, of Jane Austen, Dickens, Eliot, and Anthony Trollope. Behind the famous image of a Megalosaurus waddling through the streets of London in the opening paragraph of Dickens's *Bleak House*, initially published in 1852, lay the article from *Household Words* of the previous year, 'Our Phantom Ship on an Antediluvian Cruise', a journey through England's deep geological past, with successive descriptions of the landscape and its inhabitants.[7] While 'Our Phantom Ship' evokes both the ghost ship of Samuel Taylor Coleridge's 'Rime of the Ancient Mariner' and the ice-bound vessel captained by Robert Walton in Mary Shelley's *Frankenstein*, it is most dependent in both content and form on works of popular geology, which by the early 1850s had made such a journey into the past, and the conjuring up of its flora and fauna, part of its stock in trade. Throughout the Victorian period, science and the novel were not

---

[5] On these scientific popularizers and the literary elements of their works, in addition to Lightman see Barbara Gates, *Kindred Nature: Victorian and Edwardian Women Embrace the Living World* (Chicago: University of Chicago Press, 1998) and Ralph O'Connor, *The Earth on Show: Fossils and the Poetics of Popular Science, 1802–1856* (Chicago: University of Chicago Press, 2007).

[6] Peter Morton, *'The Busiest Man in England': Grant Allen and the Writing Trade, 1875–1900* (New York: Palgrave Macmillan, 2005), 110.

[7] [Henry Morley], 'Our Phantom Ship on an Antediluvian Cruise', *Household Words* 3 (1851): 492–96.

widely separated countries but adjacent realms, their shared boundary a permeable borderland.

Nor were the realms of science and the novel monolithic and unified. As different forms of fiction flourished, so, too, did different branches of the sciences, many of them new. Darwinism—and more broadly, the scientific naturalism of Darwin and his allies, who proclaimed that all phenomena, but especially natural phenomena, should be investigated and explained solely with reference to natural causes—was not simply synonymous with 'science', despite the best efforts of Huxley and Tyndall. Indeed, the diffusion of knowledge and theories generated by scientific elites into the broader culture was never pure and rarely simple: phrenology, for example, flourished in popular culture long after it had been discredited by 'professional' scientists, and popularizers often packaged the work of elites in ways that elicited responses of discomfort or outrage. To examine science and the novel, then, is more aptly to examine sciences and novels, and to consider both the presence of sciences (and scientists) *in* novels, and the relationships *between* sciences and novels, in terms of methodology, cultural status, and form. For over a generation now, literary scholars and historians of science have been conducting such investigations, and in what follows I will sketch an account of this dynamic and complex relationship that draws on this scholarship and suggests some of the new directions that such work is beginning to take.

To speak of sciences and scientists *in* novels, we need first to note that the Victorian era was the period in which both the novelist and the scientist came of age. Rising literacy rates, technological innovations in publishing, cheap paper, increased leisure time, the development of subscription lending libraries and explosive growth in serialization— all contributed to the production of more novels by more novelists for more readers than ever before. Dickens's *Pickwick Papers*, its serial publication in 1836–37 bracketing Victoria's accession to the throne, helped launch the period's love affair with fiction. Almost simultaneously, the term 'science' began to assume its now current meaning, and the term 'scientist' was coined. Over the previous two centuries, the scientist was generally called a 'natural philosopher' or an 'experimental philosopher', 'science' being used to identify any area of learning. By the early 19th century, however, 'the man of science' was someone specifically interested in the natural world. In recognition of the growing specialization of the sciences, in 1833 the polymathic Cambridge philosopher and man of science, William Whewell, proposed the use of 'scientist' to mean one who cultivates science generally, in analogy with the term 'artist'. Thus those participating in the meetings of the newly formed (1831) British Association for the Advancement of Science could call themselves scientists, whatever their particular areas of interest in the natural or physical sciences. The members of the BAAS were as vulnerable to lampoons like Dickens's as their forebears at the Royal Society had been to the satiric pen of Jonathan Swift in *Gulliver's Travels*, but the same social, economic, and technological factors that so benefitted the novel also proved a boon to science, creating a market for the spread of scientific knowledge to all social classes through books, periodicals, lectures, and various forms of public display. Increasingly, science became a vocation rather than an avocation. Within a generation, science was on its way to obtaining the 'cultural authority'—social reliance on it as a major source of knowledge and guidance—that had typically been reserved for religion.[8]

The science that was by far the most prominent presence in the Victorian novel was biology—or rather, at least until the last decades of the century, 'natural history'. While what we call 'biology' emerged in the early 19th century, the term came into widespread use in Britain only in the 1870s, after Parliament's 1870 Education Act mandated the teaching of elementary science in government schools.[9] To train the required science teachers, the government turned to Huxley, who developed what became the standard curriculum in biology. And 'biology' is what Huxley called it, denying in 1876 that the term was merely 'a new-fangled denomination' for natural history.[10] Whereas natural history often included geology and mineralogy, biology, as its name implied, was the science of life and living things, of zoology and botany. To the biologists, natural history was heterogeneous and empirical, its principal activities observation, collection, and description; biology was unified and theoretical, concerned with underlying structures and functions, and rooted in the laboratory. Natural historians had often been amateurs; biologists were trained professionals. Darwin, sixteen years Huxley's senior, always called himself a 'naturalist'. Courses in natural science had been available to Darwin during his undergraduate years at Cambridge, but he could not take a degree in the sciences (that became possible only in 1851); prior to the *Beagle* voyage he aspired to the life of a country parson, though with more of a mind for the collecting of beetles than the saving of souls. Darwin never took holy orders, of course, but neither did he ever hold an institutional post as a scientist. Although his work provided the framework for the emerging 'biology' trumpeted by Huxley, and his controversial theories and their implications found their way into much of the period's fiction, Darwin, by virtue of his family's wealth, was able to live the life he had envisioned, pursuing his researches just outside a quiet village south of London.

A version of the parson-naturalist's life envisioned by Darwin before the *Beagle* voyage, and of the contrast between the natural historian and the biologist, may be found in George Eliot's *Middlemarch* (1871–72), her 'Study of Provincial Life' set primarily in the early 1830s. Camden Farebrother, the local vicar with a passion for natural history, like the young Darwin at Cambridge, had 'made an exhaustive study of the entomology of the district'. Tertius Lydgate, Middlemarch's new and ambitious young doctor, on the other hand, tells Farebrother that he 'never had time to give myself much to natural history', having been 'early bitten with an interest in structure'.[11] The Paris-educated Lydgate is a researcher eager to discover 'the primitive tissue',[12] the common physical basis of the body's organ systems. Although Eliot and Lewes were aligned intellectually with the Lydgates of the 1870s, Eliot characteristically eschews simple contrast for moral complexity. The impoverished vicar has

---

[8] Frank M. Turner, *Contesting Cultural Authority: Essays in Victorian Intellectual Life* (Cambridge: Cambridge University Press, 1993).

[9] David Elliston Allen, *The Naturalist in Britain: A Social History*, 2nd edn (Princeton: Princeton University Press, 1994).

[10] T.H. Huxley, 'On the Study of Biology', *Science and Education*, vol. 3 of *Collected Essays*, 9 vols. (London: Macmillan, 1893–94), 262.

[11] George Eliot, *Middlemarch*, ed. David Carroll (Oxford: University Press, 1998), 161.

[12] Eliot, *Middlemarch*, 139.

his minor vices, but he is the more humane and generous of the two men, supporting his female relations, advising Lydgate, and even aiding the young Fred Vincy, his romantic rival. Farebrother's natural history is neither pedantic nor reactionary, for he pokes fun at colleagues who author treatises with titles like 'a monograph on the Ant, as treated by Solomon, showing the harmony of the Book of Proverbs with the results of modern research'.[13] Lydgate, however, proves himself to be naïve, arrogant, and an extremely poor judge of living human beings, himself included. If Eliot's portrait of Farebrother owes something to both Darwin and Gilbert White, the country parson whose *Natural History and Antiquities of Selbourne* (1789) was already a classic, then her depiction of Lydgate recalls Victor Frankenstein, another fictional scientist whose egotism estranges him from family and friends.

As the example of Victor Frankenstein suggests, the Victorians inherited both a fascination with the science of life and a fear of that fascination's power. At the beginning of the century, William Wordsworth, despite his own interests in natural science and natural history, decried the scientist-physician who would 'peep and botanize/ Upon his mother's grave',[14] and declared that 'Our meddling intellect/Mis-shapes the beauteous forms of things—/We murder to dissect'.[15] Even the well-meaning naturalist could become consumed by his interests to the detriment of his connections with, and responsibilities towards, family, friends, and community. In Kingsley's Darwinian fairy-tale, *The Water-Babies* (1863), in a chapter headed with the Wordsworthian epigraph about murdering to dissect, the kindly Professor Ptthmllnsprts (whose scientific views are quite similar to Huxley's) goes mad after his refusal to accept the existence of water-babies leads to the death of the angelic little girl whom he has befriended. Throughout the Victorian period, however, it was the laboratory biologist in particular who risked becoming, in his quest for knowledge and fame, a despoiler rather than a respecter of life. From the 1870s on, the figure around whom this risk crystallized, in both fiction and real life, was the vivisectionist, the dissector of live animals. Nathan Benjulia of Wilkie Collins's *Heart and Science* (1883) and Wells's Dr Moreau are powerful examples of the way the laboratory scientist's humanity could be lost. In a realistic novel like Eliot's *Middlemarch*, the result for a Lydgate is a thwarting of ambitions and the compromising of principles, but in sensation fiction and the late-century scientific romance, the result is death. Benjulia commits suicide; Moreau is destroyed by the puma he has been vivisecting. In *The Strange Case of Dr Jekyll and Mr Hyde* (1886), Robert Louis Stevenson's Henry Jekyll, though figured as a chemist rather than a biologist, has purchased his home from 'the heirs of a celebrated surgeon' and pursues his researches in the detached, windowless building 'indifferently known as the laboratory or dissecting rooms" ('Incident of the Letter').[16] Jekyll must kill himself to prevent the

---

[13] Eliot, *Middlemarch*, 161–62.

[14] William Wordsworth, 'A Poet's Epitaph', ll. 19–20, in *William Wordsworth*, ed. Stephen Gill (Oxford: Oxford University, 2010), 125.

[15] Wordsworth, 'The Tables Turned', ll. 26–28, p. 48.

[16] Robert Louis Stevenson, *The Strange Case of Dr. Jekyll and Mr. Hyde and Other Tales of Terror*, ed. Robert Mighall (London: Penguin, 2002), 26.

murderous Hyde from completely taking over his personality. In contrast, the figure of a Farebrother—the naturalist, often a clergyman or doctor, abreast of current theories but not consumed by them—frequently appears in the novel as a moral touchstone, recognizably modern but also sensitive to local ways and traditional institutions. Roger Hamley, the Cambridge-educated naturalist of Elizabeth Gaskell's unfinished last novel, *Wives and Daughters* (1865), is another example.

If Farebrother recalls the Darwin who might have been, Hamley, as a Cambridge man who travels to Africa on a lengthy scientific expedition, recalls the Darwin who was. And Darwin's theories of natural and sexual selection were of course the scientific ideas that appeared most frequently in Victorian fiction after 1859. Natural selection captured and troubled public imagination for three main reasons. First, its depiction of a natural world characterized by violent, competitive struggle—what Darwin famously came to call, after Herbert Spencer, 'survival of the fittest'—seemed both to mirror the economic world of laissez-faire capitalism, particularly in the burgeoning industrial towns, and to undermine the image of the bucolic, harmonious countryside as an orderly haven. The 'struggle for life' was constant and ubiquitous—even in apparently tranquil settings. Second, although in the *Origin of Species* Darwin had avoided anything more than an oblique reference to the implications of natural selection for human history, contemporaries had no trouble making the inference: humans were animals, and had once been, or were descended from, apes and monkeys. With the *Descent of Man*, Darwin confirmed that inference: humanity's progenitors were probably hairy, tree-dwelling African quadrupeds with pointed ears, sharp teeth, prehensile feet, and long tails. More shockingly, Darwin argued that our intellects, our moral sense, our aesthetic sense, and (in *The Expression of the Emotions in Man and Animals*, lopped off from the *Descent* and published separately in 1872) our emotions were an evolutionary inheritance from animals. Man's place in nature (to use the title of Huxley's 1863 book on the subject) was neither special nor divinely ordained. And third, because the source of the slight physical variations on which natural selection operated was shrouded in mystery, Darwinism seemed rooted in chance and contingency. Living things were not the product of design, the realization of a blueprint, but the result of random change in both organism and environment. The 'fittest' were best only in terms of adaptation to their surroundings.

Sexual selection was in some ways even more unsettling. The battle among males for the right to select a female provided additional evidence of a natural world full of violence, but the notion that in many cases—with birds, in particular—the female did the choosing was deeply troubling. That the peacock's tail was the result of the aesthetic preferences and sexual desires of untold generations of peahens rather than the work of an artistically sophisticated deity seemed impossible to most of Darwin's contemporaries. To make the future of the species dependent on female taste—notoriously fickle and irrational in the Victorian mind—seemed positively dangerous. Whether they lamented or celebrated these ideas, the public thus saw Darwin's views as examples of materialism—explanations of natural phenomena relying solely on physical causes, to the exclusion of supernatural ones, even in areas traditionally accounted for by recourse to God.

Novelists, charting the development of individuals through an increasingly complex and interconnected society, tracing their own accounts of inheritance and courtship, could hardly ignore the narratives being offered by Darwinism. Darwinism's presence in the Victorian novel was thus multiple and varied, sometimes reshaping existing concerns, sometimes introducing new ones. The crises of faith already induced by historical criticism of the Bible and the revelations by geologists were heightened by the authority and plausibility of Darwin's account of the origin of species. A liberal Anglican like Kingsley, quoted by Darwin in the second edition of the *Origin* to confirm that natural selection need not shock or undermine religious belief, could make that sense of harmony a central premise of *The Water-Babies*. More commonly, however, natural selection was presented, to greater or lesser degree, as faith-shaking, in works like Mary Augusta Ward's bestseller, *Robert Elsmere* (1888), Samuel Butler's *The Way of All Flesh* (1903, but mostly written in the 1870s and 1880s), and *Father and Son* (1907), Edward Gosse's memoir of his naturalist father, Philip Henry Gosse, fervent Evangelical and inspirer of Kingsley's seaside writings. For those novelists mapping the social landscape of Britain's provincial towns, the great urban metropolis that was London, or the rapidly expanding industrial cities where spectacular wealth was juxtaposed with horrific poverty, Darwin provided new ways of thinking about the relationships among individuals and social classes. Are we responsible for the welfare of others, or merely for our own survival? Eliot's *The Mill on the Floss* (1860), with its almost taxonomic account of the 'emmet-like'[17] Dodson and Tulliver families and its extended treatment of human marriage in language typically reserved for animal husbandry, examines these issues in similar ways to, if on a smaller scale than, the even more ambitious *Middlemarch* and *Daniel Deronda* (1876). (*Middlemarch*, Henry James complained in a review, 'is too often an echo of Messrs. Darwin and Huxley'.)[18] Dickens's sprawling, multi-plot novels, in which seemingly unrelated characters turn out to be connected, whether literally through birth or marriage, or socially through such means as communicable diseases or financial collapses, seem in many ways a reflection of the Darwinian 'entangled bank', dynamic and full of life, yet interdependent and, ultimately, knowable. When Pip declares in the opening paragraphs of Dickens's *Great Expectations* (1861) that his five younger brothers, all of whom died in childhood, 'gave up trying to get a living, exceedingly early in that universal struggle', the quiet and comic Darwinian reference to the 'universal struggle' points ironically to what will be one of the novel's central themes: the often corrosive effects of money and wealth on human relationships and human society. If both *Great Expectations* and Dickens's last completed novel, *Our Mutual Friend* (1865), in the end offer a restrained hope that individuals can forge and maintain meaningful bonds in a competitive society, the novels of Thomas Hardy are of course much bleaker. While his characters make choices that shape their destinies, Hardy also frequently draws attention to the ways they are constrained and damaged by forces—natural, social, and economic—beyond their control or understanding. In Hardy's *Tess of the D'Urbervilles* (1891),

---

[17] George Eliot, *The Mill on the Floss*, ed. A.S. Byatt (London: Penguin 2003), 284.
[18] *Galaxy* 15 (March, 1873): 424–28, 428.

the revelation that the Durbeyfields are the last surviving descendants of an old aristocratic family long 'extinct in the male line'[19] only leads to disaster for Tess and her family. Tess's lineage 'did not help [her] in her life's battle';[20] beset by representatives of rapacious new wealth, rigid Evangelicalism, and illiberal agnosticism alike, she is hanged for murdering the supposed kinsman who had raped and impregnated her years earlier, a man from a parvenu family that had merely appropriated the D'Urberville name.

Tess's fellow dairymaids are also oppressed by another element of 'cruel Nature's law': their 'hopeless passion'—the 'torture…almost more than they could endure' that 'burn[s] the inside of their hearts out' and causes them to 'writhe feverishly'[21]—for Angel Clare, the man who has chosen Tess for his wife but will soon abandon her when he learns her sexual history. Although Darwin's theory of sexual selection was widely rejected, it dealt directly (if carefully) with sexual desire, made even clearer the importance of reproduction in the development of species, and raised the question of the extent to which male competition and female choice existed in human mate selection.[22] While no single scholar has attempted the comprehensive analysis of sexual selection's presence in the British novel that Bert Bender has offered for American fiction, critics have analysed the appropriations of and reactions to sexual selection in a range of Victorian novels, moving beyond an initial focus on the mating games in Hardy and Eliot. Darwin's reading of courtship plots in nature was heavily shaped by his reading of courtship plots in novels (including those of Austen, Charlotte Bronte, and Trollope), yet his theory also helped shape the subversive women of sensation fiction and the liberated heroines of 'New Woman' novels.[23] One of the earliest, most extensive, and most explicit deployments of the language of sexual selection in the novel appear in George Meredith's *The Egoist* (1879). The title character, Sir Willoughby Patterne, seeking the hand of the lovely Clara Middleton, underscores his narcissism in the way he understands and applies the theory:

[Sir Willoughby] appreciated Nature's compliment in the fair one's choice of you. We now scientifically know that in this department of the universal struggle, success

[19] Thomas Hardy, *Tess of the D'Urbervilles*, ed. Juliet Grindle and Simon Gatrell (Oxford: Oxford University Press, 2008), 15.
[20] Hardy, *Tess*, 23.
[21] Hardy, *Tess*, 162.
[22] Gowan Dawson, *Darwin, Literature, and Victorian Respectability* (Cambridge: Cambridge University Press, 2007).
[23] Gillian Beer, *Darwin's Plots: Evolutionary Narrative in Darwin, George Eliot, and Nineteenth-Century Fiction*, 3rd edn (Cambridge: Cambridge University Press, 2009), Chapter 7; Bert Bender, *The Descent of Love: Darwin and the Theory of Sexual Selection in American Fiction, 1871–1926* (Philadelphia: University of Pennsylvania Press, 1996) and *Evolution and 'the Sex Problem': American Narratives during the Eclipse of Darwinism* (Kent, OH: Kent State University Press, 2004); Richard A. Kaye, *The Flirt's Tragedy: Desire without End in Victorian and Edwardian Fiction* (Charlottesville: University Press of Virginia, 2002), Chapters 2–3; George Levine, *Darwin Loves You: Natural Selection and the Re-enchantment of the World* (Princeton: Princeton University Press, 2006), Chapter 6; Angelique Richardson, *Love and Eugenics in the Late Nineteenth Century: Rational Reproduction and the New Woman* (Oxford: Oxford University Press, 2003); Ruth Bernard Yeazell, *Fictions of Modesty: Women and Courtship in the English Novel* (Chicago: University of Chicago Press, 1991), Chapters 12–13.

is awarded to the bettermost. You spread a handsomer tail than your fellows, you dress a finer top-knot, you pipe a newer note, have a longer stride; she reviews you in competition, and selects you. The superlative is magnetic to her. She may be looking elsewhere, and you will see—the superlative will simply have to beckon, away she glides. She cannot help herself; it is her nature, and her nature is the guarantee of the noblest races of men to come of her. In complimenting you, she is a promise of superior offspring. Science thus—or it is better to say—an acquaintance with science facilitates the cultivation of aristocracy.[24]

Willoughby's confidence that sexual selection insures the continuation of the aristocracy also points to the potential eugenic applications of Darwin's theories that became so common in the ensuing decades, and that was frequently yoked to socialist or feminist agendas, as in Allen's *The Woman Who Did* or novels by Mona Caird, George Egerton, and Sarah Grand.

Concern for the future of the race and the nation also provided the basis for another major group of novels with clearly Darwinian themes: fantasies, fairy tales, and scientific romances set in distant futures or exotic, isolated civilizations of the present day that afforded visions of how human evolution might unfold. In his pre-Darwinian long poem, *In Memoriam* (1850), Alfred Tennyson, influenced by the progressivist optimism of *Vestiges*, had imagined humans leaving behind their animal heritage, 'working out the beast' and becoming a 'higher race'.[25] After Darwin, however, the fear that the beast within might just as easily regain primacy, that humans might degenerate rather than progress, was a fear reflected insistently in fiction. Kingsley's *Water-Babies*, while tracing the moral and physical development of the illiterate chimney sweeper Tom into a great engineer and man of science, also contains the cautionary tale of the Doasyoulikes, a once-great people who abandoned hard work and reverted into apes. Marie Corelli offered a glimpse of a reassuring future for humanity, and even an 'Electric Principle of Christianity', in *The Romance of Two Worlds* (1886), but seeming Utopias like Butler's Erewhon, Bulwer Lytton's subterranean world of the Vril-ya in *The Coming Race*, and the lost African kingdom of Ayesha in H. Rider Haggard's *She* (1887) presented dystopic satires of what Victorian society was or sought to become. In Wells's *The Time Machine*, humans have evolved into two species: the peaceful, delicate surface-dwellers, the Eloi, and the brutish Morlocks, who live underground. The Eloi, however, are not the masters of the Morlocks, as the Time Traveller initially surmises, but their food. Nine years before Huxley contrasted the struggle between gardener and nature in the Prolegomena to *Evolution and Ethics*, Richard Jefferies in *After London, or Wild England* (1885) imagined the reversion of both city and country to a state of nature following an unspecified catastrophe that decimates the population. The example of Stevenson's Mr Hyde

---

[24] George Meredith, *The Egoist*, ed. Richard C. Stevenson (Peterborogh, ON: Broadview, 2010), 91.

[25] CXVIII, ll. 14, 17; Alfred Tennyson, *In Memoriam*, in *Tennyson: A Selected Edition*, ed. Christopher Ricks (Berkeley, University of California Press, 1989), CXVIII, 465.

chillingly suggests that criminal man is not an easily identifiable atavism but walks among us in respectable garb, while in *The Island of Dr. Moreau* the reversion of the beast people is merely more obvious than that of the novel's human characters.

Although responses to evolutionary ideas constituted the major scientific motifs in the Victorian novel, they were hardly unique. Indeed, in the first half of the 19th century, geology was the popular science *par excellence*. As geologists unearthed the evidence of our planet's long history, of the strange creatures that had once inhabited it, and of humanity's own past, they almost inevitably cast the results of their discoveries in narrative terms. By the time the Victorian period opened, elite geologists like the young Darwin accepted the implications of these discoveries—even those like William Buckland and Adam Sedgwick who sought to retain a Providential understanding of earth history were hardly religious reactionaries attempting to salvage literalist readings of Genesis. The same can be said of the work of the much maligned Richard Owen, the powerful comparative anatomist who became the bête noire of Huxley and the Darwinians, but whose skill at reconstructing the skeletons of fossil 'monsters' so captivated Dickens, providing us not just with the Megalosaurus of *Bleak House* but the metaphor of articulation as story-telling in *Our Mutual Friend*. The re-framing of the geological imagination from one rooted in catastrophic upheavals—global floods, the sudden raising of whole mountain ranges—to one based on the gradualist power of small forces operating over long periods of time cannot be underestimated. We can watch this re-framing happen before our eyes in Darwin's account of the voyage of the *Beagle*, and it was of course essential for Darwin's theorizing on species. Darwinism, coupled with palaeontology's explicit link between the study of the rocks and the fossils entombed within them, often led to the close association of geology with evolutionary conceptions of life in the fiction of Eliot, Trollope, Hardy, and others, as well as in popular accounts of geology and in the public mind. Eliot's *The Mill on the Floss* enacts all of this: a web of geological metaphors standing alongside those of organic development and animal husbandry, a seemingly catastrophic flood, and the carefully charted influences of slowly operating forces.[26] So, too, does the classic scene in Hardy's *A Pair of Blue Eyes* (1873), when Henry Knight, hanging precariously from a coastal cliff, contemplates the fossilized trilobite in the strata before him, his geological knowledge enabling him 'to take in, by a momentary sweep, the varied scenes that had had their day between this creature's epoch and his own'.[27] Although he survives, Henry confronts the palaeontological evidence that had so appalled Tennyson a generation earlier, of a nature careless not only of the species, but of the single life.

The physical sciences were also vivid to the minds of Victorians and Victorian novelists. The development and popularization of the first and second laws of thermodynamics,

---

[26] Sally Shuttleworth, *George Eliot and Nineteenth-Century Science: The Make-Believe of a Beginning* (Cambridge: Cambridge University Press, 1984); Jonathan Smith, *Fact and Feeling: Baconian Science and the Nineteenth-Century Literary Imagination* (Madison: University of Wisconsin Press, 1994), Chapters 3–4.

[27] Thomas Hardy, *A Pair of Blue Eyes*, Intro. Tim Dolin, ed. Alan Manford (Oxford: Oxford University Press, 2005), 200.

particularly as a result of William Thomson's writings for magazines like *Macmillan's* and the Royal Institution lectures that became John Tyndall's *Heat Considered as a Mode of Motion*, reflected the tension between two ways of interpreting Britain's rapid industrialization. The first law showed that energy is never created or destroyed, but merely transformed. The energy of the sun, stored in coal, is released when the coal is burned, the heat used to boil the water that becomes the steam that powers the engines of industrial machinery and locomotives. The second law, however, asserted that in every transformation, some energy is lost in terms of its capacity to do useful work—no engine is completely efficient, 'dissipation' is inevitable. Awareness that Britain's coal supplies were finite, that the sun's heat was not limitless, led to the realization that Britannia's industrial might, and thus its empire, was not guaranteed, and that the world itself would one day end with a whimper rather than an apocalyptic bang. As Wells's Time Traveller explores the distant future, he encounters this dying sun, and an earth slowly growing colder, its life reduced to a primitive slime. Such awareness, however, also added a new dimension to the moral imperative of working, and of working productively, efficiently, and well. If many of the novels of the 1840s and 50s—such as Benjamin Disraeli's *Sybil* (1845), Gaskell's *Mary Barton* (1848), and *North and South* (1855), Kingsley's *Alton Locke* (1850), and Dickens's *Hard Times* (1854)—depicted the dangers of amassing this new industrial wealth to the detriment of workers, much Victorian fiction exhorted the middle-class individual not just to work, but to work in humane and socially responsible ways. Dickens's Pip in *Great Expectations* and Eugene Wrayburn in *Our Mutual Friend* (the latter's name explicitly suggestive of solar combustion) must learn the dangers of wealth and idleness, and embrace work. Indeed, in the Victorian *Bildungsroman*, the importance of the youthful protagonist finding a calling and working well takes on special urgency, and that urgency was shaped not just by social and economic factors, but by the science of thermodynamics.

If thermodynamics raised questions about the Victorians' working lives, the radical changes in optics and acoustics challenged the very nature of reality itself. The eye and ear, as Wordsworth had said in 'Tintern Abbey', really do 'half create' the world around us. Our perception is not direct but mediated through the physical action of waves of light and sound and the electrical impulses carried along the nerves to the brain—an understanding with implications for the burgeoning world of Victorian psychology as well.[28] Reality is truly subjective, relative, and physiological. Whereas the human eye had traditionally served as an example of divine design, a wonderfully precise and complex mechanism that could only have been created by a superior and beneficent intelligence, Darwin was able in the *Origin of Species* to invoke its imperfections, failures, and clumsy construction as part of his case that it, too, had evolved. These physiological accounts of the human senses were, like Darwinism itself, widely disseminated in Victorian culture. Their influence can be found not only in the novels of a writer such as Eliot concerned with issues of epistemology and perception, but in popular forms like detective fiction and ghost stories,

[28] On the novel and psychology, see Suzy Anger's chapter in this volume.

where sight and vision, hearing and sound—and the interpretation of optical and acous-
tical phenomena—was often literally as well as figuratively at stake.[29] From Collins's *The
Moonstone* (1868) and the writings of Sheridan Le Fanu, to Bram Stoker's *Dracula* (1897)
and Conan Doyle's Sherlock Holmes stories, fictional accounts of the interface between
the natural and supernatural—whether ultimately affirming, debunking, or leaving unresolved the status of the latter—reflected a fresh scientific context.

The reliability of visual evidence, the powerful desire to be able to 'read' character, and
the status of the individual will were also in evidence in fields like phrenology, physiognomy, mesmerism, and spiritualism. Phrenology and physiognomy claimed to be able
to interpret personality, character, and mental ability from the shape of the skull or face,
respectively. The mesmerist, much like the hypnotist, purported to exert control over
subjects by manipulating the body's magnetic fluid. Spiritualists believed it was possible
to communicate with the dead and to verify the existence of spirits empirically. These
practices tend to be dismissed today as 'pseudo-sciences', but such a label obscures the
seriousness with which they were taken, the prominent scientists (like the physicist
Oliver Lodge and the evolutionist Alfred Russel Wallace) who supported them, and how
closely they were connected to less contested scientific work. While phrenology, physiognomy, and mesmerism were developed or reinvigorated in the 18th century, they drew
in the 19th century on the latest research in medicine, electricity and magnetism, and
chemistry, much as Victor Frankenstein combined alchemy with modern chemistry,
anatomy, and physiology. Spiritualists similarly buttressed their claims with data from
the physical sciences, mathematical work on higher dimensional spaces, and evidence
derived from new technologies like the camera and the telegraph. The world of popular
science in Victorian Britain was full of such demonstrations and displays, particularly in
the cities, and both novelists and their readers absorbed them. While the 'bumpology'
of the phrenologists and the spirit-rapping and table-turning of the spiritualists' séances
were often targets for lampoon, these 'pseudo-sciences' casually permeate a multitude
of Victorian novels. The works of Dickens, Charlotte Brontë, and Collins are especially
full of them, while at the end of the century George du Maurier's *Trilby* (1894), with its
portrait of the manipulative mesmerist, Svengali, caused a sensation. Although these
'pseudo-sciences' are viewed most productively in relation to medicine and the emerging field of psychology, their development and reception were shaped powerfully by the
physical sciences and the public culture of electrical, magnetic, and chemical display.[30]

[29] Luisa Calè and Patrizia di Bello, eds., *Illustrations, Optics, and Objects in Nineteenth-Century
Literary and Visual Cultures* (New York: Palgrave, 2010); James Krasner, *The Entangled Eye: Visual
Perception and the Representation of Nature in Post-Darwinian Narrative* (New York: Oxford University
Press, 1992); John M. Picker, *Victorian Soundscapes* (Oxford: Oxford University Press, 2003); Srdjan
Smajić, *Ghost Seers, Detectives, and Spiritualists: Theories of Vision in Victorian Literature and Science*
(Cambridge: Cambridge University Press, 2010).

[30] Iwan Rhys Morus, *Frankenstein's Children: Electricity, Exhibition, and Experiment in
Early-Nineteenth-Century London* (Princeton: Princeton University Press, 1998); Sally Shuttleworth,
Charlotte Brontë and Victorian Psychology (Cambridge: Cambridge University Press, 1996); Alison
Winter, *Mesmerized: Powers of Mind in Victorian Britain* (Chicago: University of Chicago Press, 1998).

Turning to the relationship between science and the Victorian novel, as should by now be abundantly clear, the notion of a monolithic 'Science' is as misleading as a notion of 'the' Victorian novel. There were, rather, different types of sciences in Victorian Britain, and different kinds of novels. Benefitting from many of the same social and economic forces, sciences and novels proliferated over the course of the Victorian period, and scientists and novelists professionalized. By the end of the century, both could point to an increased place in the lives of individuals of all social classes, a greater voice in issues of public concern, and a larger claim on the nation's economic resources. Scientists and novelists were alike capable of stirring controversy, or of upholding and reinforcing traditions. If novelists often turned a troubled eye on science and scientists, and on science's anticipated and unanticipated consequences, they also cast them as truth-tellers, problem-solvers, and careful evidence-gatherers, willing to question prejudice. The naturalist-voyager and naturalist-explorer—the young Darwin circumnavigating the globe aboard the *Beagle*, Hooker in his *Himalayan Journals* (1854), the entrepreneurial Henry Walter Bates in *The Naturalist on the River Amazons* (1863), Wallace in the jungles of *The Malay Archipelago* (1869)—as well as fictional counterparts like Roger Hamley, displayed both good sense and heroic virtue, their narratives combining the romantic personal quest with public service to science and to Britain. Their examples continued to resonate even as more ironic accounts of the nexus of science and imperialism, whether in the fictional narratives of Butler and Rider Haggard or a non-fiction work like Mary Kingsley's *Travels in West Africa* (1897), began to mount, culminating in the demonic Kurtz of Joseph Conrad's *Heart of Darkness* (1902). The scientist-detective like Sherlock Holmes, Stoker's Van Helsing, Collins's Cuff, and Dickens's Bucket, whatever their limitations, were presented as forces for order, protectors not just of vulnerable individuals, but of nation and empire as well.[31] Even when Victorian novels displayed suspicion or hostility towards science and scientists, there was little sign of the 'gulf of mutual incomprehension' between scientists and literary intellectuals (including novelists) that C.P. Snow famously lamented in his 1959 lecture on 'The Two Cultures'.[32] More representative of the Victorian state of intellectual affairs were John Tyndall's widely reprinted and widely discussed 1870 British Association address on 'The Scientific Use of the Imagination', which argued that science both depends on and cultivates the imagination, and the critic and poet Edward Dowden's 1877 essay on 'The Scientific Movement and

---

[31] David Amigoni, *Colonists, Cults, and Evolution: Literature, Science and Culture in Nineteenth-Century Writing* (Cambridge: Cambridge University Press, 2007); Jim Endersby, *Imperial Science: Joseph Hooker and the Practices of Victorian Science* (Chicago: University of Chicago Press, 2008); Laura Otis, *Membranes: Metaphors of Invasion in Nineteenth-Century Literature, Science, and Politics* (Baltimore: Johns Hopkins University Press, 2000); Cannon Schmitt, *Darwin and the Memory of the Human: Evolution, Savages, and South America* (Cambridge: Cambridge University Press, 2009).

[32] C.P. Snow, *The Two Cultures* (Cambridge: Cambridge University Press, 1998), 4.

Literature', which declared 'the significance of science for the imagination and emotions of men' to be both 'large and deep'.[33]

That science and the novel were often regarded as complementary endeavours should not surprise us. Both relied on close observation and careful description of the human and non-human worlds. Both employed the imagination—and could be condemned for employing too much or too little of it. Both constructed narratives. In the case of the sciences, this latter point was most obviously true with historical sciences like geology, but nebular astronomy helped turn 'the story of the heavens' into a tale involving more than observation and Newtonian mechanics, the transformations of energy in thermodynamics looked both backwards and forwards in time, and evolutionary theory seemingly converted everything it touched, from the emerging fields of archaeology and anthropology to the classificatory sciences, into narrative.[34] The title of Michael Faraday's 1848 Christmas Lectures at the Royal Institution—'The Chemical History of a Candle'—points to the ubiquity of the narrative impulse in Victorian science. The fact that Dickens wrote to Faraday to obtain his notes for these and other lectures, had them converted into articles for *Households Words*, and then littered *Bleak House* with poorly combusting candles—sources of illumination but also markers in the novel of foul air, impurity, and moral and interpretive ambiguity—is a small but telling example of the traffic between the two enterprises. Their society undergoing rapid change, and with much of that change induced, directly or indirectly, by science, Victorian novelists and scientists sought to make sense of it, and to discern order in it, through narrative.

Was there, then, a relationship between the very form of the novel, and the form of natural science? Here, too, we must be wary of treating 'the novel' and 'science' as monolithic entities. That the latter half of the Victorian period marked both a high point for the realist novel and the ascendency of the scientific naturalism of Darwin, Huxley, Tyndall, Hooker, W.K. Clifford, et al. has seemed hardly coincidental. With its close attention to the details of everyday life, its sensitivity to connections and to cause-and-effect, and its frequent adoption of an objective narrative voice, the realist novel appears virtually to take science as its model. Literary historians often point to George Eliot as the classic case of this conjunction. She lived and worked in an intellectual milieu that included not just the works of the scientific naturalists but the men themselves, and her novels seemed to many contemporaries to attempt a similar account of human life to that given

---

[33] John Tyndall, 'Scientific Use of the Imagination', in *Essays on the Use and Limit of the Imagination in Science* (London: Longmans, Green, 1870), 13–51; Edward Dowden, 'The Scientific Movement and Literature', *Contemporary Review* 30 (June/November, 1877): 558–78, 558. For modern discussions, see Tess Cosslett, *The Scientific Movement and Victorian Literature* (New York: St Martin's, 1982); Peter Allan Dale, *In Pursuit of a Scientific Culture: Science, Art, and Society in the Victorian Age* (Madison: University of Wisconsin Press, 1989); Dawson, *Darwin, Literature, and Victorian Respectability*; Smith, *Fact and Feeling*.

[34] George W. Stocking, *Victorian Anthropology* (New York: Free Press, 1987); Virginia Zimmerman, *Excavating Victorians* (Albany: State University of New York Press, 2008).

by Huxley of cuttlefish or Darwin of pigeons. With literary naturalism, the roots of which of course lie in Émile Zola's 'roman expérimentale', this methodological conjunction between novel and science is explicit: the novelist acts as the laboratory scientist does, subjecting characters to the action of internal and external forces, and mapping their responses, in an effort to discern the laws of human nature and human society, with the generally bleak result that individual will is relatively if not wholly powerless. While naturalism was not nearly as popular in Britain as it was in France and America, both Eliot and Hardy reflect elements of it, and Gissing was perhaps Britain's most successful writer of naturalist novels at the end of the century.

Indeed, since the groundbreaking studies by Gillian Beer (*Darwin's Plots*) and George Levine (*Darwin and the Novelists*) in the 1980s, the connection between realism and Victorian science, and in particular Darwinian science, has become a truism.[35] Although they did not confine themselves to realist writers or to those with demonstrable connections to Darwin's work—Beer used *The Water-Babies* to investigate Darwinian transformations and myths, Levine examined Dickens and Trollope as Darwinian novelists—both came to Victorian science through Darwin, and to Darwin via George Eliot. So persuasive and compelling was the connection to realism, however, that it is difficult to appreciate that prior to Beer and Levine the link was barely noted, let alone lingered over. Leo Henkin's *Darwinism in the English Novel, 1860–1910* (1940), the first comprehensive study of the topic, adopted a thematic approach, tracing Darwinism's impact primarily on crisis-of-faith novels and depictions of Utopian and dystopian societies. Peter Morton's *The Vital Science: Biology and the Literary Imagination* (1984), which appeared just after *Darwin's Plots*, was a richer and more historically precise study than Henkin's, but it followed a similar thematic approach and covered many of the same writers. Alternatively, critics like Jacques Barzun, Stanley Edgar Hyman, and Dwight Culler debated whether Darwinism's characteristic literary form was tragedy (for its concern with struggle and death) or comedy (for its celebrations of life and satiric reversals of orthodoxies).[36]

That the recognition of a deep formal connection between Darwinism and the Victorian realist novel has only become established over the last generation should give us pause on at least two counts. It reminds us, first, that Darwinism, and scientific naturalism generally, were not simply co-extensive with 'science' in the Victorian period. Darwinism didn't deal a death-blow to natural theology, and for all his hammering against 'ecclesiasticism', Huxley couldn't prevent his fellow Victorians from having much of their science served up with a religious sauce, as it had been for centuries.

[35] Beer's book first appeared in 1983, Levine's *Darwin and the Novelists: Patterns of Science in Victorian Fiction* (Cambridge, MA: Harvard University Press) in 1988.

[36] Jacques Barzun, *Darwin, Marx, Wagner: Critique of a Heritage*, 2nd edn (Garden City, NY: Doubleday, 1958); Stanley Edgar Hyman, *The Tangled Bank: Darwin, Marx, Fraser and Freud as Imaginative Writers* (New York: Atheneum, 1962); A. Dwight Culler, 'The Darwinian Revolution and Literary Form', in *The Art of Victorian Prose*, ed. George Levine and William Madden (New York: Oxford University Press, 1968), 224–46.

The intellectual and novelistic propensities of popular writers like Bulwer Lytton and Corelli were aligned neither with scientific naturalism nor with realism, and their scientific analogues might best be found in Proctor's *Other Worlds Than Ours* and Balfour Stewart and Peter Guthrie Tait's *The Unseen Universe* (1875), the latter a work by two leading physicists endeavouring to show that the principles of modern science confirmed Christian belief in the immortality of the soul. Second, it reminds us that neither Darwinism, nor scientific naturalism, nor science as a whole was cast in a single form. One might say, in fact, that Darwinism generated plots rather than a plot because it drew on multiple literary forms. Darwin's botanical writings of the 1860s and 1870s—the fruit of his dominant experimental interests after the *Origin*—with their accounts of macabre violence and complex sexuality, had more in common with the hybrid genre of sensation fiction, flourishing in the same decades and being read to Darwin in the evenings, than with the realism of Eliot or Trollope.[37] More broadly, the scientific romance wasn't invented by novelists—the discourse and techniques of narrative wonder were already in use, in works of science, popularizations, and journalistic accounts. And this was true across the spectrum of the sciences, from geology and biology and to astronomy, chemistry, and the various branches of physics.

A different and more recent approach to the issue of Victorian science's formal relations to Victorian fiction has been taken up by Nicholas Dames in *The Physiology of the Novel*.[38] Dames recovers the 19th-century matrix in which, for a wide range of critics and writers, the forms of novels, the nature of reading practices, and the study of human physiology and psychology converged. Rather than examining science in relation to various fictional genres and subgenres, Dames investigates how Victorian novels and Victorian science shaped the ways Victorians understood what happens to the body and mind when we read. The unfolding of time and the building of comprehension, in this view, were central to the reading act, and more central than aspects of structure to novelistic form. The forms that Dames calls intermittent, elongated, discontinuous, and accelerated thus correspond to issues of reading practice: attention and distraction, duration, fragmentation, and acceleration. The novel thus became, Dames argues, 'a training ground for industrialized consciousness'.[39] In this convergence of science, psychology, medicine, reviewing, reading, and industrialism, we are reminded how inseparable science was from these other practices in Victorian culture. And, returning to Boyd Dawkins's proclamation that Darwin's *Descent of Man* was 'competing' with the latest novel for attention, we can more deeply appreciate the complexities at which Dawkins's Darwinian language—slyly reflective of the very theory of sexual selection Dawkins is about to review and critique—hints: not only the various

---

[37] Jonathan Smith, 'Domestic Hybrids: Ruskin, Victorian Fiction, and Darwin's Botany', *SEL: Studies in English Literature, 1500–1900* 48 (2008): 861–70.

[38] Nicholas Dames, *The Physiology of the Novel: Reading, Neural Science, and the Form of Victorian Fiction* (Oxford: Oxford University Press, 2007). See also Anne Stiles, ed., *Neurology and Literature, 1860–1920* (New York: Palgrave, 2007).

[39] Dames, 7.

ways in which the novel and science might be said to compete, but that their competition for the attention of readers might hinge on the science behind the meaning of attention itself.

Suggested Reading

Amigoni, David. *Colonists, Cults, and Evolution: Literature, Science and Culture in Nineteenth-Century Writing.* Cambridge: Cambridge University Press, 2007.

Beer, Gillian. *Darwin's Plots: Evolutionary Narrative in Darwin, George Eliot, and Nineteenth-Century Fiction.* 3rd edn. Cambridge: Cambridge University Press, 2009.

Chapple, J.A.V. *Science and Literature in the Nineteenth Century.* Houndmills: Macmillan, 1986.

Cosslett, Tess. *The Scientific Movement and Victorian Literature.* New York: St Martin's, 1982.

Dale, Peter Allan. *In Pursuit of a Scientific Culture: Science, Art, and Society in the Victorian Age.* Madison: University of Wisconsin Press, 1989.

Dames, Nicholas. *The Physiology of the Novel: Reading, Neural Science, and the Form of Victorian Fiction.* Oxford: Oxford University Press, 2007.

Krasner, James. *The Entangled Eye: Visual Perception and the Representation of Nature in Post-Darwinian Narrative.* New York: Oxford University Press, 1992.

Levine, George. *Darwin and the Novelists: Patterns of Science in Victorian Fiction.* Cambridge: Harvard University Press, 1988.

Lightman, Bernard. *Victorian Popularizers of Science: Designing Nature for New Audiences.* Chicago: University of Chicago Press, 2007.

O'Connor, Ralph. *The Earth on Show: Fossils and the Poetics of Popular Science, 1802–1856.* Chicago: University of Chicago Press, 2007.

Otis, Laura. *Membranes: Metaphors of Invasion in Nineteenth-Century Literature, Science, and Politics.* Baltimore: Johns Hopkins University Press, 2000.

Richardson, Angelique. *Love and Eugenics in the Late Nineteenth Century: Rational Reproduction and the New Woman.* Oxford: Oxford University Press, 2003.

Secord, James A. *Victorian Sensation: The Extraordinary Publication, Reception, and Secret Authorship of Vestiges of the Natural History of Creation.* Chicago: University of Chicago Press, 2000.

Shuttleworth, Sally. *George Eliot and Nineteenth-Century Science: The Make-Believe of a Beginning.* Cambridge: Cambridge University Press, 1984.

Smajić, Srdjan. *Ghost Seers, Detectives, and Spiritualists: Theories of Vision in Victorian Literature and Science.* Cambridge: Cambridge University Press, 2010.

Smith, Jonathan. *Fact and Feeling: Baconian Science and the Nineteenth-Century Literary Imagination.* Madison: University of Wisconsin Press, 1994.

22

THE VICTORIAN NOVEL AND MEDICINE

MEEGAN KENNEDY

INTRODUCTION: CHANGES AND EXCHANGES

With the emergence of what came to be known as 'scientific medicine', Victorians witnessed remarkable changes in medical theory and practice, chronicled in the pages of newspapers and periodicals, both medical and general-circulation or literary, during the explosion of print media that marks the 19th century. This marks a significant change from earlier models of medical authority and publication. As Roy Porter and others have shown, 18th-century doctors had to negotiate a collaboration between medical and lay experience, sometimes deferring to their patients, who were (after all) their employers.[1] Medical columns in magazines like the *Gentleman's Monthly* allowed educated men to be well informed in the 'heroic medicine' of the time. However, with the new scientific medicine of the 19th century came increased specialization and authority for physicians and new publications designed to bring the new methods to physicians and surgeons. Many scholars have explored the movement towards increased professionalism in medicine, but this narrative of widening distance between lay and professional knowledge is complicated by the mushroom growth of mainstream periodical publishing during the 1840s and 1850s, the most active decades of medical change. It was not only the *Lancet* and *British Medical Journal* that published details of the new medicine; literary and popular periodicals and the news media also published news, editorials, advice columns, stories, and educational articles about the changes in medical theory, training, technology, practice, and professional oversight.

---

[1] Roy Porter, 'Laymen, Doctors and Medical Knowledge in the Eighteenth Century: The Evidence of the "Gentleman's Magazine"', in *Patients and Practitioners: Lay Perceptions of Medicine in Pre-Industrial Society*, ed. Roy Porter (Cambridge: Cambridge University Press, 1985), 283–314.

The combination of the radical changes in medical practice and their expanded visibility in periodical publishing allowed the new medicine to become a significant current of discussion among Victorians. Novelists accordingly made use of these broadly circulating medical facts, narratives of cure or decline, and techniques of observation and representation. In turn, medical authors—who were, after all, readers as well—demonstrate a continued awareness of novelistic tropes and conventions despite an increasing pressure to render their prose scientific.

New in the 19th Century

While the work of a doctor in 1790 was not significantly different from that of his 17th-or even 16th-century forebear, the life of a doctor in the 1890s had been transformed: his education, practical training, tools, techniques, theories, practices, reading, writing, and community all had changed; his methods of prevention and (by the early 20th century) treatment were likewise revolutionized. In 1790, many physicians relied on the so-called 'heroic' medicine of bleeding and purging through harsh and often harmful medicines like mercury, and despite the Evangelical fervour of the new empiricists, many medical books still relied heavily on the 'authorities' of previous eras. Treatment was symptomatic at best, and when (in 1793) George Fordyce published a voluminous chart to record the history of the patient's illness and make medicine more systematic, he didn't even include a place to record 'diagnosis'.[2] Medical observations and advances were published in books or in the general-subject *Philosophical Transactions* if anywhere. Medical education was haphazard and did not require familiarity with what we now consider 'science' (a field and term that also changed radically over the century).[3]

The founding of the reformist periodical *The Lancet* in 1828 by Thomas Wakley helped bring about many changes of the 1830s and 1840s, with the backlash against heroic treatments, the rise of 'first do no harm' or 'watchful waiting', and a surge of hotly debated alternative medicines. The Anatomy Act of 1832 finally provided adequate numbers of donated cadavers so that medical students could learn through dissection; students trained in this method would also be better prepared to carry out autopsies, increasingly common in this period. Joseph Jackson Lister solved the problems of chromatic and spherical (optical) aberration with the compound microscope by 1830, making this instrument now both reliable and affordable. Continental education and experimental medicine advocated the use of the microscope, although it was not until mid-to-late-century that English universities started establishing chairs in anatomy,

---

[2] George Fordyce, 'An Attempt to Improve the Evidence of Medicine', *Transactions of a Society for the Improvement of Medical and Chirurgical Knowledge* (1793): 243–93.

[3] For a reliable and readable traditional history of British medicine, see Roy Porter, *The Greatest Benefit to Mankind: A Medical History of Humanity* (New York: W.W. Norton, 1997) or Christopher Lawrence, *Medicine in the Making of Modern Britain, 1700–1920* (London: Routledge, 1994).

physiology, and other medical sciences; Edinburgh and Dublin adopted Continental methods earlier. A few courageous women pioneered the category of the 'lady doctor', obtaining a medical education and qualifying as a doctor, whether by training in America or France or masquerading as a man.[4] Victorian doctors were also the first generations to undergo the rigours of professionalization, including the institutionalization of the Medical Register in 1858 and (by the end of the century) required examinations in scientific fields like biology and chemistry.[5] Nineteenth-century doctors also discussed plans to regularize how they examined their patients and recorded their cases.[6] It is hard to describe how different everyday practice had become. Even the stethoscope was new to British doctors in this period.

The social reforms of the 1840s and 1850s also opened a vast new field for medical work, prompting public health initiatives for better living conditions, including, crucially, clean air and water. This proved important for national defence, too, after the astounding losses to disease during the Crimean War. The growing use of 'man-midwives' (male obstetricians) became controversial when Ignaz Semmelweis, Oliver Wendell Holmes, and others charged that these doctors—who, unlike female midwives, were trained to perform autopsies on their deceased patients—were actually transmitting the childbed (puerperal) fever on their unwashed hands. Although British physicians were reluctant to acknowledge their role in puerperal fever epidemics, their growing acceptance of statistical analysis (the 'numerical method') forced them to acknowledge the links between dirt and disease, which influenced Florence Nightingale's advocacy for sanitary reform and culminated in Joseph Lister's efforts to secure an antiseptic environment for surgery. Louis Pasteur and Robert Koch, among others, established the failure of the theory of spontaneous generation and the evidence for germ theory. By the turn of the century, X-rays offered a spectacular view inside the body and specific germs and viruses had been identified. British physicians had settled down into a model that is still recognizable: trained and licensed practitioners of various sorts and classes struggle to

---

[4] See, for example, Kristine Swenson, *Medical Women and Victorian Fiction* (Columbia: University of Missouri Press, 2005).

[5] Susan Faye Cannon, *Science in Culture: The Early Victorian Period* (New York: Dawson and Science History Publications, 1978); M. Jeanne Peterson, *The Medical Profession in Mid-Victorian London* (Berkeley: University of California Press, 1978); W.F. Bynum, *Science and the Practice of Medicine in the Nineteenth Century* (Cambridge: Cambridge University Press, 1994); John Harley Warner, 'The Idea of Science in English Medicine: The "Decline of Science" and the Rhetoric of Reform, 1815–45', in *British Medicine in an Age of Reform*, ed. Roger French and Andrew Wear (London: Routledge, 1991), 136–64; Terrie M. Romano, *Making Medicine Scientific: John Burdon Sanderson and the Culture of Victorian Science* (Baltimore: Johns Hopkins University Press, 2002).

[6] For representative 19th-century discussions of case-taking, see, for example, H.M. Bullitt, 'The Art of Observing, or the Proper Method of Examining Patients, with a View to Correct Diagnosis', *Western Lancet* 3, no. 3 (1845): 397–409; John Southey Warter, *Observation in Medicine, or the Art of Case-Taking* (London: Longmans, Green, 1865); James Finlayson, 'Examination and Reporting of Medical Cases', in *Clinical Manual for the Study of Medical Cases*, ed. James Finlayson (London: Smith, Elder, 1878), 33–49; Francis Warner, *The Student's Guide to Medical Case-Taking* (London: J. & A. Churchill, 1881); W.B. Cannon, 'The Case Method of Teaching Systematic Medicine', *Boston Medical and Surgical Journal* 142, no. 2 (1900): 31–36.

combine the art of medical experience with the science reported in the new professional journals or revealed by technologies like the microscope, the ophthalmoscope, or the myograph (machine to record muscle contractions).

The genre of the British novel was likewise transformed over the century. Different as Jane Austen's domestic realism is from Walter Scott's historical romance, both of these early-19th-century novelists take 18th-century narrative conventions—whether of sensibility, the Gothic, the travel narrative, or the experiments in realist reportage, among other possibilities—as a point of departure. Charles Dickens, especially early in his career with novels like *Oliver Twist* or *Nicholas Nickleby*, reinvents such familiar 18th-century narratives as the Newgate calendar, the man of feeling, or the maiden adrift in London, even as the Brontës rework the psychological sublime of the Romantic period. But by mid-century, the Victorian novel is marking out a new territory. What we now term classic or high literary realism emerges from the social reformist blend of realism and sentiment that runs through Benjamin Disraeli, Dickens, and Elizabeth Gaskell; and from the domestic and psychological realism and social satire of novelists like William Makepeace Thackeray, Anthony Trollope, and Margaret Oliphant. However, genre distinctions can be misleading: George Eliot's *Adam Bede* and *Mill on the Floss*—central volumes in the realist canon—were published in the same moment that the sensation fiction of Wilkie Collins and Mary Elizabeth Braddon burst upon the scene. Thomas Hardy flirted with sensation fiction before turning to naturalism; and authors like Braddon wrote for various audiences, publishing realist fiction, middle-brow sensation fiction, and 'penny dreadfuls'. The serious novels produced by and about the New Woman at the end of the century were countered by a surge of male-authored romances—imperial, scientific, fairy—lashing back against the perceived hegemony of realist fiction.

Although it may seem, from this race through history, that literary and medical cultures were entirely distinct, in fact the 19th-century novel and medical writing have much in common. Both follow a similar (although not precisely simultaneous) trajectory, first rejecting the narratives of the 18th century as overly curious or naïve, in favour of a new empiricism linked to realist reporting; then experimenting with ways to nuance or expand the purview of a merely mechanical objectivity; finally turning inward with the psychological narratives of Freud and a late-century fascination with consciousness and its transcription.

Most important, both novelists and doctors read, and wrote, in some of the same textual spaces and in response to some of the same pressures of the new print media. Both medicine and the novel were profoundly changed by the accelerating creation of new periodicals as artificial restraints on print (taxes on paper and on the printing, sale, and distribution of printed matter) were lifted. While this is most evident in the creation of specialist journals in medicine as part of the material production of new professional medical societies, doctors remained men of letters even as they became 'men of science'. Many of them read and contributed to a proliferating list of mainstream literary periodicals, providing essays and reviews that explore medical topics in detail. Their articles go beyond the simple personal health advice one might expect; instead they tackle an array of medical and scientific questions with the air of addressing an intellectual and practical curiosity about the human body and its workings. George Henry Lewes's articles for *Blackwood's Edinburgh Magazine* on human physiology (published in volume form in 1859 as *The Physiology of Common Life*) are typical, but many such articles were provided not by popularizers like Lewes but by physicians and scientists themselves.[7] The physician and public health official Edwin Lankester published hundreds of scientific articles and reviews of medical books in general-circulation periodicals like *The Athenaeum*. Other physician-writers contributing to periodicals like *The Athenaeum*, *The Cornhill Magazine*, *The Fortnightly Review*, *Macmillan's Magazine*, *St. James's Magazine* included Francis Anstie, Walter Butler Cheadle, Daniel Noble, Douglas Spalding, James Sully, and Andrew Wynter. Excerpts from medical texts were also sometimes republished in general-interest periodicals. Even special-interest periodicals, such as the *Chinese Repository* in the 1830s, which largely tracked the efforts of missionary groups in China, included periodical updates, with statistics, of the cases treated at the Ophthalmic Hospital in Canton.[8] And *The Graphic*, which serialized Thomas Hardy's novels, also satisfied readers' curiosity with illustrations of 'Monsieur Pasteur in his laboratory'.[9]

If 19th-century novels often first appeared in periodical form—and if those periodicals also published work by 19th-century physicians—then it is clear how both writers and readers of Victorian novels could be affected by the drastic changes in medicine. The remarkable changes in Victorian medical writing and practice offered a number of productive strategies for novels, whether appearing literally (as actual content affecting plot or character), as a figurative device, as a narrative method inspired by clinical observation and medical-realist case reports, as a theory of human behaviour, or even as a model for the very structure of narrative. Less obviously, physicians—readers of Victorian novels and participants in the literary commons of periodical publishing—also repurposed conventional novelistic structures in their medical writing. Although content and form are of course deeply imbricated, in this chapter I take up each of these strategies separately. Distinguishing these entwined elements of narrative will allow me to trace out the most significant links between Victorian literary and medical culture.

THE USES OF MEDICINE: LITERAL

Medical elements, appearing in fiction as literal doctors, patients, illnesses, and deaths, often motivate plot and delineate character in Victorian novels as they did in earlier periods; certainly Defoe, Richardson, Burney, and Austen have used illness to anchor a plot development or prompt a character's moral or spiritual revelation. However, the changes

---

[7] George Henry Lewes, *The Physiology of Common Life* (Edinburgh: William Blackwood and Sons, 1859).

[8] See, for example, Peter Parker, 'Ophthalmic Hospital at Canton: The Ninth Report, Being for the Quarterly Term Ending December 31st, 1838', *Chinese Repository* 7 (1839): 569–88.

[9] 'Monsieur Pasteur in his Laboratory', *The Graphic* 32 (1885): n.p. (opposite p. 561).

in 19th-century medicine allowed Victorian writers to draw from a more diverse and in many ways more topical range of medical elements. These changes—discussed in not only specialty but also literary and popular periodicals—meant that novels could now consider not just the role but also the training and professional standing of the doctor and nurse; not just the skill but also the new technologies they used; not just the suffering of private illness but also the risks to a wider public health. Victorian medicine offered new ways for novelists to make links to intellectual questions over psychology, religion, materialism, gender, and ethics as well as social debates over regulation, reform, science and technology, education, urban and rural poverty, the class system, the factory system, and the role of the government in ensuring the public welfare. As a result, Victorian novels can be crowded with medical events, providing an almost-too-rich resource for the scholar of 19th-century medical culture.

In a famous example, Dickens's editorial complaint about Elizabeth Gaskell—'I wish to Heaven her people would keep a little firmer on their legs!'—reflects the impressive line-up of sickbeds and deathbeds in her novels.[10] *Mary Barton* provides a good example of how ailments can pile up in a Victorian novel. Here, the staggering toll includes death in childbed (1, plus the baby), and of scarlet fever (1), drink (1), typhus (3), unspecified 'fever' (2), murder (1), paralytic stroke (1), consumption (1), and, apparently, remorse (1), as well as two relatives who died years ago and one major character who simply drops dead. The population of the novel is also afflicted by illness, industrial accident, addiction, and other disabilities such as loss of sight and hearing.

Dickens's critique is a little unfair, however; almost all of these ailments and deaths are productive for the novel. Not only do isolated events, like Mary's mother's death in childbed or Harry Carson's murder, precipitate watershed moments in the plot, but other elements, like Margaret's increasing blindness or Alice's retreat into a childish old age, sustain plot momentum and develop a richer psychology for the characters. More important, one can argue that this saturation of the text with morbidity crucially grounds and amplifies Gaskell's critique of the unhealthy conditions of factory workers in industrial towns like Manchester. Of a number of elements in the novel—tone, description, dialogue, characterization, action—the drumbeat of illness and death more than anything else conveys the brutal realities endured by the Manchester working class in a largely unregulated industrial economy and makes the point that such an economy is, in the long run, unsustainable. Like Benjamin Disraeli's *Sybil*, Charles Dickens's *Hard Times*, and other mid-century reform novels, *Mary Barton* binds illness and noxious politics in a memorable new genre.

Sickness and death were, of course, household occurrences for many Victorians. Unhealthy living conditions, periodic epidemic fevers, fear of hospitals, and high child and perinatal mortality meant that most Victorian readers had at some point housed, perhaps been a caretaker for, someone who was ill or dying. While this had been true for generations, certain kinds of patient are new to Victorian culture. Maria Frawley traces

---

[10] Fred Kaplan, *Dickens: A Biography* (Baltimore: Johns Hopkins University Press, 1988), 268.

the historical development and cultural work of that central figure of Victorian life, 'the invalid'.[11] Victorian authors explored other new roles, too: the victim of occupational accident and disease, in novels like Gaskell's *North and South*; the consumptive, as in Dickens's *Dombey and Son*;[12] the syphilitic, as in Sarah Grand's *Heavenly Twins*; and of course the hysteric. Hospital patients, though increasingly common in Britain, remain relatively under-represented in the novel, perhaps because hospitals were still avoided by those who had the means to do so, or because novels can more readily explore the family dynamic in a domestic setting. Even Lydgate's fever hospital enters *Middlemarch* more as a public work, a high-minded endeavour, a business proposition, and a political minefield than as a physical site for the novel to explore human experience.

At the same time, new medical figures like the professionalized physician, the medical or chemical researcher, the hospital doctor, the medical student, the female doctor, and the professionalized nurse take their place in the pages of Victorian novels, while older roles like the female family member/nurse or the lower-class nurse take on new meanings (female self-sacrifice as an indicator of traditional values, for example) or fade from view. Critics like Miriam Bailin and Athena Vrettos examine the culture of illness more generally in its relation to Victorian novels. While Bailin focuses on the imagined space of the sickroom as a place where novels allow social conflicts to be resolved, Vrettos argues that narratives of illness, actual or fictional, profoundly shaped Victorians' real-life experiences of living and reading.[13]

The high rates of sickness and accident meant that disability was equally common in Victorian life and in novels of the period. Martha Stoddard Holmes demonstrates that literary narratives offer a rich resource from which we can study how medicalized bodies, especially non-normative or disabled bodies, were imagined in the Victorian period.[14] Dickens and his friend Wilkie Collins are well known for playing up the dramatic possibilities in their characters with unconventional bodies, adopting a grotesque as often as a sentimental presentation in characters like Jenny Wren, Quilp, Miserrimus Dexter, or Oscar Dubourg; but as Yonge's *The Clever Woman of the Family* and Dinah Mulock Craik's *A Noble Life* demonstrate, Dickens and Collins were hardly the only authors to feature disabled characters in their fiction. And while sensation fiction, fascinated with the odd and the outré and determined to shock its audience, was best positioned

---

[11] Maria H. Frawley, *Invalidism and Identity in Nineteenth-Century Britain* (Chicago: University of Chicago Press, 2004).

[12] Consumption can seem to be everywhere and nowhere in the Victorian novel: widely implicit, rarely explicit. For discussion of consumption, see Susan Sontag, 'Illness as Metaphor', in *Illness as Metaphor and Aids and Its Metaphors* (New York: Farrar, Straus and Giroux, 1990), 1–87 and Katherine Byrne, *Tuberculosis and the Victorian Literary Imagination* (Cambridge: Cambridge University Press, 2011). Syphilis is similarly mutable in and out of the novel.

[13] Miriam Bailin, *The Sickroom in Victorian Fiction* (New York: Cambridge University Press, 1994); Athena Vrettos, *Somatic Fictions: Imagining Illness in Victorian Culture* (Stanford, CA: Stanford University Press, 1995).

[14] Martha Stoddard Holmes, *Fictions of Affliction: Physical Disability in Victorian Culture* (Ann Arbor: University of Michigan Press, 2004).

to use death, disease, and disability for dramatic effect, novelists from Charlotte Brontë in *Villette* to Thomas Hardy in *Jude the Obscure* and Bram Stoker in *Dracula* made such elements central to the plot of their novels.

The wide range of medical plots and characters, and of the genres of novels adopting them, continued to expand over the course of the century. The historicist bent of much recent literary-critical work has encouraged scholars to dig into these links as a way to understand medical and literary culture as well as Victorian culture more generally; but this work has been limited by disciplinary differences between literary critics and historians of medicine, and by the continuing tendency to read medical writing simply as a historical source rather than a written text published in the same cultural moment as literary texts and rewarding the same kinds of close critical analysis.

THE USES OF MEDICINE: FIGURATIVE

The proliferation of new medical techniques, theories, and roles in the 19th century offered an embarrassment of riches to novelists seeking subject matter. While medical elements are scattered generously throughout many Victorian novels, any individual medical instance often serves multiple functions in the narrative. In particular, as with the 'diseased' conditions of the working class in Gaskell, a medical reference will signify on both a literal and figurative level. For example, Esther, a fallen woman in *Mary Barton*, dies of a consumption that is brought about by her wretched living conditions but also represents her corrupted moral state. The horror of John Boucher's 'determined' suicide in *North and South*, drowning in a few inches of water polluted by the mills, allows his disfigured face to serve in the novel as both a material consequence and a moral indictment of his working conditions.[15]

The ease with which illness takes on multivalent functions in the Victorian novel is especially vivid in a novel like *Hester* (1883), where Oliphant uses headache interchangeably as real pain and as a metaphor for Hester's emotional distress over her romantic entanglement. Oliphant shifts back and forth fluidly between literal and metaphorical suffering in this scene. Hester, overwhelmed with fears about Edward's shameful secret, excuses herself from dancing at a social gathering and sits near her chaperone with 'a headache...her mother's way of getting free of every embarrassment'.[16] To her mother she also prevaricates, saying, 'My head ached...I scarcely danced at all' (373). Oliphant sets up a complex set of relations here between the physical world, Hester's emotional world, and the notion of headache, which mediates between them. Hester claims to have a literal instance of headache. However, this supposed headache is not

---

[15] Elizabeth Gaskell, *North and South* (Oxford: Oxford University Press, 1998), 294.

[16] Margaret Oliphant, *Hester*, ed. Philip Davis and Brian Nellist (Oxford: Oxford University Press, 2003), 372. Subsequent citations appear in the text.

only fraudulent but also a conventional escape, rendering it more a figure of this ill-ness than an actual case. Moreover, the narrator's careful tracing of Hester's supposed headache back to an emotional cause gives the headache a metonymic relation to her emotional pain.

Oliphant complicates matters further when this false headache becomes at once more literal (it becomes real physical pain) and more figurative (it stands in metaphorically for Hester's emotional pain). While Hester's expedient relieves her of the discomfort of feigning interest in the dance, it 'opened only another kind of torture, for poor Mrs. John [Hester's mother], well used to the feminine indulgence of headaches, had a whole surgery of little remedies, and bathed her child's forehead, and drew back her hair, and would have administered sal-volatile, tea, eau-de-cologne—there was no telling how many other cures—if she had been allowed' (373). Hester suffers regardless, 'her brain throbbing, all inaccessible to eau-de-cologne' (374). The 'headache' that began as a fic-tion evolves, with Mrs John's fuss over Hester, into a real physical suffering, even as its work in the novel accumulates not just literal but also figurative significance (as an acute symbol of Hester's confused and anxious state). Medical metaphor works so well here for Oliphant in part because it is so common in the Victorian novel; readers readily under-stand these shifts between physical and mental distress, especially when the ailment is one, like headache, that has been established as readily somatized.

Victorian novels also often figure illness without anchoring it distinctly in material suffering. In *Hester* a discourse representing 'fever' evokes the excitement and poor judgement associated with economic and romantic speculation, as when Edward uses a medical metaphor to express the feeling of physical vitality endowed by his 'fever' for gambling. The promise of speculation for personal gain, as he turns over the possibil-ity in his mind, seems 'like pouring in new blood to stagnant veins...new life coming in, new energy' (249). Unlike Gaskell's *Ruth*, where physical fever has figurative effects, cleansing the protagonist of her sin, Edward does not suffer from any physical ailment (although Hester's headache is a displaced 'symptom' of his 'fever'): gambling fever is a figurative disease with material effects.

While the vague and ill-understood diagnoses of headache or fever are particu-larly useful in representing psychic strain, even well-defined physical ailments read-ily carry symbolic freight, as when Lucy Morris, in Trollope's *The Eustace Diamonds* (1873), considers her hopeless love for Frank Greystock. '[S]he regarded this passion of hers', Trollope explains, 'as a healthy man regards the loss of a leg or an arm. It is a great nuisance, a loss that maims that whole life,—a misfortune to be much regretted. But because a leg is gone, everything is not gone.'[17] Lucy does not lose a limb, of course; but this example shows how easily, and as if naturally, Victorian novelists elide the dis-tinctions between physical and psychic pain, bodily and spiritual disease, failures in the mechanism of the body and the brain.

[17] Anthony Trollope, *The Eustace Diamonds*, ed. W.J. McCormack (Oxford: Oxford University Press, 1998), 26.

THE USES OF MEDICINE: THEORIES
OF SEEING AND STATING

If the medical fact or event often signals some less tangible disorder, the diagnostic gaze often stands in for the work undertaken by the narrator and/or the novel as a whole. The narrative method most often associated with Victorian medical texts—clinical observation recorded by medical realism—establishes ideals that also shape literary realism and can provide authority for a novel's narrative voice. The techniques of clinical observation, which scholars link to the rise of hospital medicine and the autopsy, also grew out of the empirical fervour of the late 18th and early 19th centuries. Advocates of empirical medicine like James Sims and Alfred Stillé prized fact and close observation in a reaction against the theoretical fads of 18th-century doctors, with their over-reliance on paper 'authorities'.[18] In order to assure accurate reports of their painstaking observations, empiricist physicians explored more rigorous and standardized formats for recording their cases. Although the early empiricists' arguments could be clunky and overwrought, the resulting backlash toward the 'art of medicine' did not prove permanent, and debates over the relative importance of art and science in medicine continued in medical journals and textbooks throughout the century. The genre of clinical realism, inspired by those early empiricists, did become the standard for medical observation and writing. However, it was invoked more often than actually achieved, because it attempted to realize impossible ideals: an objective observer producing a formal, distanced, and dispassionate record written in plain speech (a holdover from the 18th century) with exhaustive (especially visual) description and quantifiable details. Objectivity, accuracy, precision, comprehensiveness, and reliability were crucial to both seeing and stating, and these qualities should be not only achieved in practice but also attested to in the written record.

Clinical observation and clinical realism were not stable or static concepts at this time, of course. Lorraine Daston and Peter Galison's work is instructive here as they trace the development of scientific notions of objectivity (and, by association, realism) from the 18th to the 20th centuries.[19] Most useful to scholars of Victorian medicine is Daston and Galison's identification of 'mechanical objectivity', an important phase in the history of clinical observation. Mechanical objectivity, drawing on contemporary research into the vagaries of human perception and reasoning, aspires to prevent even inadvertent interference with absolutely accurate recording. Accordingly, the highest scientific virtues under mechanical objectivity are diligence, laboriousness, and selflessness. Such a combination assures the commitment to record everything that comes under observation, suppressing the observer's agency to prevent any mediation between the world

---

[18] James Sims, *Discourse on the Best Method of Prosecuting Medical Enquiries* (London: J. Johnson, 1774); Alfred Stillé, *Elements of General Pathology* (Philadelphia: Lindsay & Blakiston, 1848).

[19] Lorraine Daston and Peter Galison, *Objectivity* (New York: Zone, 2007).

and its representation. While an unmediated image is of course impossible, scientists attempting the ideal of mechanical objectivity attempt to eschew any kind of interference with the record, whether through focus, framing, or even correction. Mechanical objectivity met its own corrective adjunct in the experimental medicine that was most forcefully argued in the 1860s, with researchers like William Whewell, Claude Bernard, John Tyndall, and George Henry Lewes making the case that scientists needed to direct their factual observation using a new tool: hypothesis, or the scientific imagination.[20] By the time George Eliot wrote *Middlemarch* in 1872, medicine was a long way from the naïve empiricism of the novel's setting in 1830–32.

Lawrence Rothfield demonstrates how 19th-century literary realism developed in relation to the contemporaneous discourse of clinical medicine. That discourse offered, he argues, a powerful cultural authority as well as a useful model of narrative mimesis and 'an ideology of…exactitude', all of which helped novelists eager to professionalize their work and to mark it off as distinct from low-brow popular fiction.[21] George Levine, one of the first and most influential critics on science and the Victorian novel, has recently explored how a self-effacing scientific ideal of distanced observation shaped, among other things, what the mid-to-late-Victorian realist novel tries to achieve through fiction.[22] Among Victorian realist novelists, George Eliot has attracted by far the most critical attention to the connections between her novels and mid-Victorian medical and scientific theory, sparked by Sally Shuttleworth's landmark work on the subject.[23]

Much has also been written about the 'clinical gaze' since Foucault's influential *Birth of the Clinic* was published in 1963.[24] The term refers to Foucault's understanding of specific aspects of clinical observation. Like clinical observation, the clinical gaze prioritizes an assessing perception linked to the physician's observations—both his sensory

[20] William Whewell, *History of the Inductive Sciences, from the Earliest to the Present Times* (London: John W. Parker, 1837); Claude Bernard, *An Introduction to the Study of Experimental Medicine* (New York: Schuman, 1947); John Tyndall, *Essays on the Use and Limit of the Imagination in Science* (London: Longmans, Green, 1870); George Henry Lewes, *Problems of Life and Mind* (London: Trübner, 1874). For discussion, see George Levine, *The Realistic Imagination: English Fiction from Frankenstein to Lady Chatterley* (Chicago: University of Chicago Press, 1981), especially chapter XV; Sally Shuttleworth, *George Eliot and Nineteenth-Century Science: The Make-Believe of a Beginning* (Cambridge: Cambridge University Press, 1984), especially chapter 7; Richard R. Yeo, 'Scientific Method and the Rhetoric of Science in Britain, 1830–1917', in *The Politics and Rhetoric of Scientific Method: Historical Studies*, ed. John A. Schuster and Richard R. Yeo (Boston: D. Reidel, 1986), 259–97; Richard Yeo, *Defining Science: William Whewell, Natural Knowledge, and Public Debates in Early Victorian Britain* (Cambridge: Cambridge University Press, 1993), chapters 3 and 6; Jason H. Lindquist, '"The Mightiest Instrument of the Physical Discoverer": The Visual "Imagination" and the Victorian Observer', *Journal of Victorian Culture* 13, no. 2 (2008): 171–99; Meegan Kennedy, *Revising the Clinic: Vision and Representation in Victorian Medical Narrative and the Novel* (Columbus: Ohio State University Press, 2010), especially chapter 5.

[21] Lawrence Rothfield, *Vital Signs: Medical Realism in Nineteenth-Century Fiction* (Princeton: Princeton University Press, 1992), xiv.

[22] George Levine, *Dying to Know: Scientific Epistemology and Narrative in Victorian England* (Chicago: University of Chicago Press, 2002).

[23] Shuttleworth, *George Eliot and Nineteenth-Century Science.*

[24] Michel Foucault, *The Birth of the Clinic: An Archaeology of Medical Perception*, trans. A.M. Sheridan Smith (New York: Vintage, 1973).

observations and those obtained through questioning the patient. Foucault describes an ideal of exhaustive, rigorous, precise, regular, and distanced reportage. Such an ideal presumes a ready correlation between seeing/sensing and telling, and it promotes and depends upon a physical and philosophical dissection: the opening up of previously invisible surfaces and systems, deep within the body, to human knowledge. The physician's sensory observations (visual, auditory, tactile) make possible a broader analytic perception that controls the disparate symptoms of disease by comprehending them within the physician's authoritative knowledge. The clinical gaze as Foucault describes it is a means of mastering the body and the subject, by mastering this predominantly visual field and its meanings. Visual mastery and specialized knowledge are thus crucial elements of building hegemonic authority within a culture.

The clinical gaze is most clearly identified in Victorian novels with the physician's diagnostic gaze—whether it is put to use by a physician character, another character, or the narrator—and a detached, formal, and rational report of his observations. The clinical gaze (in the Foucauldian sense) and the diagnostic gaze (as it appears in Victorian novels) both emphasize a particularizing and evaluative visuality as a means of apprehending the world. Critiques of the realist novel that see the realist narrator as controlling, even totalizing in his visual mastery of the narrative space would be likely to agree with a reading of this narrator's gaze as a Foucauldian clinical gaze.[25]

However, while Foucault's theory of the gaze productively reminds us of the historical imbrication of power and certain kinds of visuality, Victorian novels also use and depict the gaze in ways that differ significantly from the theory. Most basically, while Foucault's broader interests are of course in tracing larger social and cultural shifts, his discussion of the theory of the gaze emphasizes how it helps discipline the subject (both a body and a body of knowledge) at a particular historical moment. Novels, however, adopt a clinical gaze to examine not just persons and psyches (as doctors do) but also communities and social institutions: consider George Eliot's *Middlemarch* as a dissection of small-town life, uncovering the intricate connections between individual subjects, families, generations, social and political circles, and cultural systems.

More important, while Foucault describes the gaze as substantively unidirectional—describing a power dynamic in which physicians, maintaining a moral distance, wield visual authority over the messy and recalcitrant body—novels are often interested in recording and even celebrating a multidirectional social dynamic. Here 'the body' (symptoms, patients, caregivers, family members) or the narrator looks back at and talks back to the observer. The authority of the gaze can also readily be undercut within the complex signification of a novel, where images and actions function on multiple,

---

[25] See, for a typical poststructuralist critique of realism, Colin MacCabe, 'Realism and the Cinema: Notes on Some Brechtian Theses', in *Tracking the Signifier: Theoretical Essays: Film, Linguistics, Literature* (Minneapolis: University of Minnesota Press, 1985), 33–57. Perspectives on realism that are more sympathetic to the project of the 19th-century realist novel have been articulated in, for example, George Levine, 'George Eliot's Hypothesis of Reality', *Nineteenth-Century Fiction* 35 (1980): 1–28 or Harry E. Shaw, *Narrating Reality: Austen, Scott, Eliot* (Ithaca: Cornell University Press, 1999).

sometimes conflicting, levels. The diagnostic gaze is not, then, necessarily controlling, nor is it uniquely powerful or even authoritative; used within a heterogeneous genre like the novel, it must be read as one of a range of possible ways of seeing and understanding drawn from diverse discursive settings like allegory, lyric poetry, aesthetic theory, and the law. Indeed, when clinical reportage appears in a novel, it often works in juxtaposition with other modes of description, including sensational, sentimental, Gothic, or other romantic approaches. This is evident in, for example, the novels of Wilkie Collins. In *Armadale*, for example, the doctor at Wildbad sets up the scene of Armadale's deathbed by combining clinical medical discourse ('The paralysis is fast spreading upwards, and disease of the lower part of the spine has already taken place') with sentimental details ('I saw the tears on his cheeks when he asked for his child') and sensational drama (when the doctor ventriloquizes the wife's entreaties, 'I implored him for God's sake to let me in').[26] The diagnostic gaze serves here more as a ground from which Collins's outré plot may spin out into its intricate fantasies, than as a tool implementing the speaker's authoritative mastery over the scene. Indeed, it is as much the pathos as the professional authority of the doctor's narrative that finally compels his audience (the reluctant Mr Neal) to assist in the dying man's wishes.

The effect of the gaze in Victorian novels is thus surprisingly various; rather than reliably collecting and channelling hegemonic power, observers' various uses of the diagnostic gaze can augment their individual humanity and indicate their resistance to hegemonic institutions. Indeed, the diagnostic gaze can even undercut the very notion of hegemonic authority. Some of the ways in which the diagnostic gaze both does and doesn't work as a clinical (Foucauldian) gaze are evident in a novel like Oliphant's *Miss Marjoribanks* (1866). It is clear that the physician's visual assessment does carry cultural authority, as when Dr Marjoribanks asks, '"Health all right, I hope?" looking at Mr. Cavendish with that critical medical glance which shows that a verbal response is quite unnecessary.'[27] But other characters—even the narrator—appropriate that 'critical medical glance' with crucial, and varying, results. When Lucilla Marjoribanks's cousin Tom proposes marriage to her, she claims to misdiagnose his love as fever and delirium, responding,

> 'Have you gone out of your senses, Tom...If you have any feeling as if fever was coming on...I think you should go up-stairs and lie down a little till papa comes in. I heard there had been some cases down about the canal....' When Miss Marjoribanks said this, she herself took fast hold of Tom's hands with a motherly grasp to feel if they were hot, and looked into his eyes with a certain serious inspection, which, under the circumstances, poor fellow! was enough to drive him out of the little rationality he had left. [74]

   [26] Wilkie Collins, *Armadale*, ed. John Sutherland (New York: Penguin, 1995), 15–18.
   [27] Margaret Oliphant, *Miss Marjoribanks*, ed. Elisabeth Jay (New York: Penguin, 1998), 386–87. Subsequent citations appear in the text.

Because medicine is not an exact science, Lucilla can pretend misdiagnosis here to shunt the conversation in a safer direction. She sees but refuses to acknowledge his real condition; her diagnostic skills are actually as keen here as any physician's.

Lucilla's (mis)use of diagnosis allows Oliphant to bring it to the forefront of the narrative, to make evident its usefulness as a narrative stance even as she recognizes its vulnerability to error. Indeed, the narrator also 'diagnoses' Lucilla in the aftermath of this episode, in an ambivalent passage that considers this young woman's equanimity and apparent control over herself and her little world:

> She stood in the middle of the room... with a heart which kept beating very steadily in her bosom. On the whole, perhaps, she was not sorry to have had it out with Tom. So far as he was personally concerned, Miss Marjoribanks, being a physician's daughter, had great faith in the *vis medicatrix* [healing powers of nature], and was not afraid for her cousin's health or his morals, as a less experienced woman might have been... 'But, after all, everything is for the best,' Lucilla said to herself, with that beautiful confidence which is common to people who have things their own way. [75]

While this passage is not diagnosing a physical ailment, as Dr Marjoribanks might, nor a mental or spiritual one, as Lucilla also claims to do with Tom, it records not just one but several instances of the diagnostic gaze. Lucilla's determined misdiagnosis of Tom's 'madness' in the previous passage disguises an accurate assessment of his lovesickness; but the novel suggests in this passage that Lucilla's abilities do not extend to herself: the narrator's own diagnostic stance here surfaces to indicate that Lucilla misdiagnoses her own case of love, relying too heavily on her apparently steady character. By the end of the novel, indeed, the fever has spread to the young doctor herself. When—during the course of a proposal by one wooer—she hears the arrival of cousin Tom,

> Miss Marjoribanks... all at once changed colour, and [gave] a great start, and put her hand to her breast, where her heart had taken such a leap that she felt it in her throat... Her heart gave another jump, and, if such a thing were possible to a heart, went off from its mistress altogether, and rushed down-stairs bodily to see who was coming. [467]

Miss Marjoribanks's true state is all too clear to the reader, and it is fitting that Tom announces his triumphant return by clanging on 'Papa's bell' (468), signalling the presence of his (and her) urgent case of 'fever'. But the novel's triumphant fulfilment of its prognostications about Lucilla's Emma-like propensity to overreach ironically echoes Lucilla's own serene confidence. Like her, the novel both plays with the possibility of error and refuses to countenance any suggestion that its own assessments might be faulty.

As *Miss Marjoribanks* suggests, diagnosis is no panacea. In particular, novelists often warn that diagnosis, relying as it does on a particular kind of focused, evaluative, and unwavering gaze, must be disinterested or it will be wrong. Thus, diagnosis would seem to be especially useful in social-realist novels dedicated to reform (as it is), but Charlotte Yonge's *The Clever Woman of the Family* turns this convention on its head by demonstrating how political or social 'interest' in a particular outcome can derail accurate diagnosis. Her strong-minded protagonist Rachel, a fervent reformer of village life and a self-taught homeopathic 'doctress', diagnoses everything from 'curatocult' to abuse of child workers (lace-makers) in her bucolic surroundings.[28] However, Yonge critiques the narrative structure of diagnosis by making Rachel's declarations either comically misguided or tragically wrongheaded. The novel is indeed engaged in a diagnostic enterprise, but it is Rachel's overgrown cleverness that most needs diagnosing—and lancing. The novel does not, however, put any sustained pressure on Yonge's apparently severe diagnosis of Rachel, an assessment that feminist readers might argue is itself one-sided.

The tendency towards diagnosis in Victorian novels draws upon the well-established tradition of the novel as moral compass. Even in realist critiques of the sentimental novel, this orientation often remains. After George Eliot published *The Mill on the Floss*, comparing the bourgeois Dodson family to 'dead-tinted, hollow-eyed, angular skeletons of villages',[29] contemporary critics denounced the Dodsons as 'coarse' and 'sordid', 'degraded' and 'brutish'.[30] Such characterizations index the Dodsons's moral failures along not only class-based but also racial and physiological lines. Although Eliot herself claimed to be 'rather aghast to find [her characters] ticketed with such very ugly adjectives',[31] the critical response demonstrates that readers understood the novel to be identifying bourgeois materialism as a disorder of modern life, a moral illness readily assimilable to a physiological state.

I do not mean to suggest that diagnosis is the only medical stance available to the Victorian novel, although the reformist impulse of much Victorian fiction allows it to appear frequently. Novels also adopt the stance of a patient, most strikingly in the wilfully 'diseased' or degenerate narratives of the *fin-de-siècle*; of a nurse or caretaker, especially in the sentimental novel; a germ of disease itself, as in the fearfully infectious narratives of the sensation novel; an expert witness of forensic medicine, again as in the sensation novel; a medical anthropologist, as in Haggard's exoticizing novels of Africa; or an experimental researcher, as when George Eliot writes in a letter in 1876, 'my writing is simply a set of experiments in life'.[32] Many of these stances derived from new medical developments: debates over the transmission of disease; forensic medicine

[28] Charlotte Mary Yonge, *The Clever Woman of the Family*, ed. Claire A. Simmons (Peterborough, Ontario: Broadview, 2001), 56, 130.

[29] George Eliot, *Middlemarch* (New York: Penguin, 2003), 283.

[30] 'Coarse' (*Westminster Review* 74 [July 1860]: 24–32); 'sordid' (*Spectator* 33 [7 April 1860]: 330–1); 'degraded' and 'brutish' (E.S. Dallas [unsigned], The *Times* [19 May 1860]: 10–11). Available in David Carroll, ed., *George Eliot: The Critical Heritage* (London: Routledge & Kegan Paul, 1971): 'coarse', 140; 'sordid', 112; 'degraded' and 'brutish', 135.

[31] Eliot reacts here to the Dallas review, Letter to William Blackwood, 27 May 1860, in George Eliot, *The George Eliot Letters*, ed. Gordon S. Haight, 9 vols. (New Haven: Yale University Press, 1954–78), 3: 299.

[32] 25 January 1876 in Eliot, *The George Eliot Letters*, 6: 216.

itself (medical jurisprudence), which came into prominent use at mid-century; medical anthropology and the study of tropical environment and disease, a development of the Victorian empire; and the experimentalist techniques adopted from the practices of Claude Bernard and others. The changes in Victorian medicine thus provided novelists with not only new incidents for their plots, new kinds of characters, and new metaphors for the ailments of the human condition, but also radically new ways to position the eye of narration.

THE USES OF MEDICINE: THEORIES OF THE SELF

The emphasis on visual observation in clinical realism reflects not only the dominance of vision among the human senses, but also 19th-century researchers' investigations into perception and the senses, visuality chief among them. Reading work by Johann Wolfgang von Goethe and David Brewster, Johannes Müller and Hermann von Helmholtz, John Tyndall and John Herschel, 19th-century doctors worked in an international context of intensified curiosity and scepticism about the mechanics of perception, especially (with new work on the microscope and telescope) optics and visual perception.[33] This focus on physical function did not mean that work on mental function was neglected. Researchers on the senses, because of their interest in nerve action and its correlation to mental experience, were allied with those examining brain function, including both physiologists and psychologists. Physicians (Forbes Winslow, for example) made reference to both physiological and psychological elements in discussing rare mental disorders.[34] Other work, like the capacious *Problems of Life and Mind* of George Henry Lewes or the early neuropathology of Freud, attempted to understand the links between the nervous system and the mind. Many studies examined how human knowledge was founded on a sensory experience that was shown to be potentially illusory or defective, suggesting larger questions about the nature of subjectivity itself. As a result of this extended interest in human physiology and psychology, Victorian researchers created a decades-long seminar on human subjectivity and the construction of the self.

Novelists were quick to draw upon these new medical theories suggesting how human physiology and psychology help to form the individual subject. Such theories had obvious relevance for a long narrative genre like the novel, which often aspires to comment

---

[33] See Jonathan Crary, *Techniques of the Observer: On Vision and Modernity in the Nineteenth Century* (Cambridge, MA: MIT Press, 1990); Jutta Schickore, *The Microscope and the Eye* (Chicago: University of Chicago Press, 2007); Isobel Armstrong, *Victorian Glassworlds: Glass Culture and the Imagination 1830–1880* (Oxford: Oxford University Press, 2008); Chris Otter, *The Victorian Eye: A Political History of Light and Vision in Britain, 1800–1910* (Chicago: University of Chicago Press, 2008).

[34] Forbes Winslow, *On Obscure Diseases of the Brain, and Disorders of the Mind* (Philadelphia: Blanchard & Lea, 1860; London: John Churchill, 1860).

on human behaviour. Both high- and low-brow novelists incorporated this material into their work in distinct ways, from the literary realism valorized by George Eliot and Thomas Hardy, to the spectacular incidents elaborated by sensation novelists like Wilkie Collins and Charles Reade (occasionally Eliot and Hardy as well), to the earnest discussions of New Woman novelists like Sarah Grand and Mona Caird or the swashbuckling forays of scientific romancers like Robert Louis Stevenson, Bram Stoker, or H.G. Wells.

Recent critics productively examine the links between 19th-century novels and contemporaneous research on how the brain connects to the world. These scholars read 19th-century studies of sensibility, nerves, hysteria, sensation, attention, and the like in order to demonstrate how these early theories of mind are in conversation with 19th-century literary methods. One of the earliest and most influential of this group, Peter Melville Logan, argues for a crucial connection between the medical discourse of 'nerves' and the literary process of authorship, in particular the production of narratives. Logan argues that nervousness or excessive sensibility to one's cultural environment, a constituent ailment of the early 19th century and an important component of middle-class identity, included as a central symptom the compulsion to talk about oneself. While texts told by nervous narrators ostensibly warned the reader of the risk hysteria posed to the subject, in fact these narratives implicitly promote it as a precondition for the narrator's speech. In the Victorian period, he argues, this model shifted as nervousness was attributed to the urban working-class body as well, and researchers developed a theory of the nerves that was less reliant on the single dominant organ of the brain.[35]

Critics writing on the sensation fiction of the 1860s and beyond have demonstrated this genre's particular debt to contemporary medical theories of nerves and sensory function. While novelists from Charlotte Brontë to Thomas Hardy drew upon theories of excess and mental pathology,[36] D.A. Miller influentially argued that the sensation novel in particular is 'one of the first instances of modern literature to address itself primarily to the sympathetic nervous system'.[37] Later critics have shown how new technologies like the railroad and film, and the fears of sensory overload they prompted, underlay the strategies of sensation fiction; or how 19th-century theories of shock helped direct both Victorian researchers and novelists in constructing their models of interiority, even as these researchers drew upon novelistic conventions of the self.[38]

[35] Peter Melville Logan, *Nerves and Narratives: A Cultural History of Hysteria in Nineteenth-Century British Prose* (Berkeley: University of California Press, 1997).

[36] Jane Wood, *Passion and Pathology in Victorian Fiction* (Oxford: Oxford University Press, 2001). Critics working on fiction of the 1890s, especially New Woman fiction and the scientific romances of Stevenson, Stoker, and the like, also frequently note the importance of medical theories and methods—from contagion and eugenics to symptomatology and the case history—in the plot and construction of these novels.

[37] D.A. Miller, '*Cage aux folles*: Sensation and Gender in Wilkie Collins's *The Woman in White*', *Representations* 14 (1986): 107–36, 107.

[38] For 19th-century railways and film, see Nicholas Daly, *Literature, Technology, and Modernity, 1860–2000* (Cambridge: Cambridge University Press, 2004); for Victorian theories of mental trauma and interiority, see Jill Matus, *Shock, Memory and the Unconscious in Victorian Fiction* (Cambridge: Cambridge University Press, 2009).

Medicine also shaped 19th-century theories of reading and attention. Victorian authors used medical theories or metaphors to account for and in some cases restrict how authors and audiences engaged one another. In particular, it was considered dangerous for those considered physically and mentally vulnerable (such as women, children, and members of the working classes) to read certain types of books, whether romances, sensation fiction, or the like.[39] Victorian theories of the interface between the brain, the nerves, and the physical world raised new concerns about how reading novels changed our ability to focus and sustain mental effort.[40] Overall, scholars have found fertile ground examining the relations between Victorian theories of subjectivity and literary methods. The flowering of provocative work in Victorian physiology, neurology, and psychology was more than matched by the creativity of the novelists who picked up, played with, adapted, and revised that work in their novels. Novelists' conventional constructions of the interior self also helped frame 19th-century medical research into the function of the senses, nerves, and brain.

THE USES OF MEDICINE: AS NARRATIVE MODEL

If medicine offers narrative stances and theories of self that prove fruitful for novelists seeking diverse ways to delineate unique worlds, it also provides persuasive models of narrative genre. Most commonly, novels can use the narrative structure of diagnosis—with its attention to detail, its insistent quest for knowledge, its tantalizing divagations into dead-ends, its suspense, and its revelatory teleology—to structure the entire narrative. This often occurs in the sensation novels of Wilkie Collins, where typically the narrator leads the reader through close reading of various clues to a hypothesis regarding a secret crime or social disorder. In Arthur Conan Doyle's *The Hound of the Baskervilles* (1901), the novel makes its governing interest in diagnosis clear at the outset, opening with Sherlock Holmes's spectacularly correct reading of an errant walking stick. The novel as a whole is concerned with diagnosing the cause of the horror hanging over Baskerville Hall and its environs, afflicting the baronet with 'quivering' nerves and a 'black reaction' to the sounds and sights of this 'fatal' place.[41] The suggestion of disease, at first only an undercurrent in Watson's many Gothic descriptions of the gloomy, melancholy moor, acquires momentum with increasing references to the baronet's physical and psychological state. It breaks the surface of the novel at the climactic moment when

---

[39] Kate Flint, *The Woman Reader, 1837–1914* (Oxford: Clarendon, 1993); Pamela K. Gilbert, *Disease, Desire, and the Body in Victorian Women's Popular Novels* (Cambridge: Cambridge University Press, 1997); Patrick Brantlinger, *The Reading Lesson: The Threat of Mass Literacy in Nineteenth-Century British Fiction* (Bloomington, IN: Indiana University Press, 1998).

[40] Nicholas Dames, *The Physiology of the Novel: Reading, Neural Science, and the Form of Victorian Fiction* (Oxford: Oxford University Press, 2007).

[41] Arthur Conan Doyle, *The Hound of the Baskervilles*, ed. Christopher Frayling (New York: Penguin, 2001), 97, 99, 74. Subsequent citations appear in the text.

the hound bursts upon the scene and Watson says, 'Never in the delirious dream of a disordered brain could anything more savage, more appalling, more hellish be conceived than that dark form and savage face which broke upon us out of the wall of fog' (149). The uncanny spirit haunting the moor, and especially the 'miasmatic' Grimpen Mire (153), is thought to be the Hound of the Baskervilles, but proven (by Holmes's superior observation and logical skill) to be a murderous plan to gain a valuable property. The clinical stance governs not just one or two scenes but drives the entire premise of the novel, with varying 'diagnoses', offered by Holmes, Watson, and Dr James Mortimer, vying for supremacy. That clinical observation can now be practised outside a strictly medical context is evident in the diminished authority of the physician here. Watson's nerves are even more susceptible than those of the baronet, and both Watson and Mortimer, unlike Holmes, misread the events. More interesting, while Doyle presents Holmes's diagnostic skill as critical in moving the investigation forward and unmasking the villain, the novel (like Doyle's other Holmes stories) presents Holmes's deductions not in the disinterested manner of a scientific report, but in the most suspenseful, spectacular manner possible, deflecting attention from the possibility that the truth might have been arrived at by other routes.

Nineteenth-century medicine also offers a genre ready-made for the reporting of human experience, especially the human response to suffering. That genre is the case history or case report. Physicians from the 1790s to the 1890s (George Fordyce, John Haygarth, Charles Cowan, Thomas Laycock, John Southey Warter, Samuel Fenwick, Alfred Hills, and Byron Bramwell, to name a few) offered to their colleagues a series of questions, tables, forms, strictures, instructions, and other improvements all designed to wrench the inherently messy business of individual sickness into some kind of regularity, to permit each case to be recalled and studied at will.[42] Most of their advice focused on ways to prompt detailed observations, record them quickly and accurately, and sometimes collate the information to allow the physician to detect general trends in disease.

Critics have found it productive to study this kind of medical writing as a genre that developed in tandem with the 19th-century novel and that still grapples with some of the same challenges of perspective, voice, and audience, among other things. Julia Epstein was the first recent critic to offer a sustained history of the case history in relation to its cultural context.[43] Other critics have focused more specifically on its links to

[42] Fordyce, 'Attempt to Improve the Evidence of Medicine'; John Haygarth, *A Clinical History of Diseases* (London: Cadell and Davies, 1805); Charles Cowan, 'Translator's Introduction', in *Pathological Researches on Phthisis*, by Pierre Charles Louis, trans. Charles Cowan (Washington: Duff Green, 1836), 9–26; Thomas Laycock, *Lectures on the Principles and Methods of Medical Observation and Research* (Philadelphia: Blanchard and Lea, 1857); John Southey Warter, *Observation in Medicine, or the Art of Case-Taking* (London: Longmans, Green, 1865); Samuel Fenwick, *The Student's Guide to Medical Diagnosis* (London: J. & A. Churchill, 1869); Alfred K. Hills, *Instructions to Patients for Communicating with Physicians* (New York: Henry M. Smith [1870]); Byrom Bramwell, 'The Value of Cultivating the Habit of Minute Observation', in *Studies in Clinical Medicine* (Edinburgh and London: Young J. Pentland, 1890), 235–46.

[43] Julia Epstein, *Altered Conditions: Disease, Medicine, and Storytelling* (New York: Routledge, 1995).

literary work. Looking at the bipartite 'history and physical examination' that combines patient and physician narrative, Janis Caldwell argues that literary and medical authors in the first half of the century both worked with literary and scientific ways of knowing.[44] Jason Tougaw focuses on the generic ties between case histories and novels as ways to negotiate troubling pathologies of identity in Victorian culture.[45] Rick Rylance argues that the form of the case history remains 'porous' to other influences, such as that of the theatre. In my own work on Victorian medical narrative and the novel, I argue that the divisions between 'literary/lay' and 'medical' discourse are less important than the interpenetration of strategies of 'seeing and stating', which occurs alike in the case history and the novel. The theories of vision most important to Victorians emerge from the curious observation they inherited from 18th-century authors; from the clinical observation performed for popular audiences in mid-century shilling monthlies; from the surprisingly sentimental medicine of certain medical specialties, as well as Dickens and Gaskell; from the mechanical observation and speculation of mid-19th-century realists like George Eliot; and even from the labyrinthine mapping and speculative insight of Freud and the late-century romance. Close reading of medical case histories alongside novels reveals how the hegemonic 'clinical gaze' works in print; this reading practice reminds us that the gaze operates often under question, and always within a range of other possible modes of vision and narration.[46]

THE USES OF FICTION

Finally, if novelists borrowed elements ranging from facts to entire narrative genres from medicine, physicians also borrowed from the novels that they, like many other Victorians, read in their spare time. For much of the century, after all, physicians were 'men of letters' as much as or more than they were 'men of science'. Despite the increasing pressures on medical authors to produce a regularized, scientific prose, literary norms and conventions—even those drawn from romantic genres like the Gothic or the sentimental novel—persist intermittently in medical texts.

These commonly appear for a sentence or two in moments of strain where a strictly medical knowledge is not adequate to the task of explaining a poor or unexpected outcome, or where the physician may even have erred. In such a case, the conventional narratives, phrases, and roles of romance can offer a familiar structure that makes sense of what is otherwise troubled and troubling. The medical man who carried the germs of

---

[44] Janis McLarren Caldwell, *Literature and Medicine in Nineteenth-Century Britain: From Mary Shelley to George Eliot* (Cambridge: Cambridge University Press, 2004).

[45] Jason Daniel Tougaw, *Strange Cases: The Medical Case History and the British Novel* (New York and London: Routledge, 2006).

[46] Kennedy, *Revising the Clinic*.

puerperal (childbed) fever to a birthing mother becomes a virtuous and sympathetic caregiver as she suffers and dies; Charles Meigs, a vocal opponent of the contagion theory of puerperal fever (American but referenced by British physicians), notes gravely, in an obstetrical textbook:

> It is obvious that the death of a puerperal patient is, in general, more to be deplored than the ordinary fatalities met with in practice. A woman, under these circumstances, appears to have a stronger claim on life; and the disruption of the ties which bind her to society and to her friends is more painful, from the new relations just established with them. If the child survives, it suffers, during the long period of infancy, childhood, and puberty, the bitter fruits of this terrible privation; while the breaking up of the domestic establishment, which usually follows that event, appeals, with irresistible power, to the public sympathy. Each family is a little patriarchate, state, or kingdom; and the domestic catastrophe has, within its proper pale, all the importance of a great political overthrow. It is a great misfortune to lose a patient in childbed.[47]

From Meigs's sombre reflections on the tragedy of a new mother's death to his sentimental prophecies of the 'bitter fruits' for the orphaned child, to the remarkable understatement of his final sentence, revealing that his ultimate concern as a professional may be the public opinion of his work—these elements, many borrowed from the sentimental or romance novel, aim to distract us from the debate he avoids acknowledging here, but which is surely in his reader's minds: the charges of many respected physicians that doctors themselves spread the fatal filth of puerperal fever by failing to clean their hands after performing a post-mortem. '[The doctor] is a gentleman…', Meigs asserts elsewhere, 'and a gentleman's hands are clean'.[48] Clearly literary tropes and conventions could be instrumental in framing the terms of medical controversies.

In this way, inexplicable disorders may be transformed into comprehensible—even predictable—romantic fates, as if in a novel with stock characters (the rural craftsman, the decadent aristocrat, the driven researcher or impetuous sailor). Frederick Harington Brett, attempting to explain 'Amaurosis, or Palsy of the Optic Nerve', writes:

> This disease, involving so often total blindness… is the disease, par excellence, of the poor laborious artizan [sic], or the epicurean; in the former, from over fatigue of the organ, and too often from poverty and care; in the latter, from a deranged state of the system, brought on by luxury and excess; but the former class are much the more frequently attacked… Astronomers and naval officers are not exempt from this affection, from imprudent examination of the more luminous heavenly bodies.[49]

---

[47] Charles D. Meigs, The History, Pathology, and Treatment of Puerperal Fever and Crural Phlebitis (Philadelphia: Ed. Barrington & Geo. D. Haswell, 1842), 13.

[48] Charles D. Meigs, On the Nature, Signs, and Treatments of Childbed Fever (Philadelphia: Blanchard and Lea, 1854), 104.

[49] Frederick Harington Brett, A Lecture on the Eye (London: Hatchard and Son, 1847), 31–32.

As with the distressed gentlewoman in the earlier Meigs passage, the characters here are all too familiar to the reader of romantic fiction. Less obvious is how deftly these conventions divert the responsibility for 'total blindness', from a medicine still struggling to understand the causes of optic palsy, to specific and expected behaviours—overwork (for the artisan), overindulgence (for the aristocrat), overstrain (for the astronomer or naval officer)—with predictable results.

Such conventions also prove useful in suggesting the physician's skill in cases that, against all expectation, end in success. Here a risky surgery becomes the surgeon's and patient's jointly waged heroic battle against that wily opponent, infection, towards that shining goal, knowledge. In a case of 'operation for empyema in an almost moribund patient', the *London Medical Record* describes M. Moutard-Martin's operations on

> a little girl, aged 5, who eight days previously had been attacked with pleuro-pneumonia. He found the patient in a very serious condition. Her face and lips were blue, the cheeks pale, respiration incomplete and jerky, and the pulse was no longer perceptible…It was doubtful whether any action should be taken, or whether it was not too late, and risk would be incurred of seeing the little patient succumb during the operation. M. Moutard-Martin, however, resolved to operate…The child did not die on the spot as was expected [but] on the third day…the spark of life which still remained seemed about to be extinguished, and complete asphyxia seemed imminent. One resource remained—the operation for empyema…The patient felt absolutely nothing, so far advanced was the asphyxia, and a tube was inserted into the pleura. The operation was followed by a veritable resurrection.[50]

The sentimental rhetoric here of the contributor 'H' who transmits this report defends Moutard-Martin's decision to operate although the situation is 'doubtful', the 'risk' clear. H. depicts Moutard-Martin as resolute in this venture; the intrepid surgeon succeeds in securing the little innocent's literal 'resurrection'. To understand the subtext of this case, which is in reality an argument for an aggressive style of surgical practice, we must recognize that many surgeons of the time believed it unethical to operate if chances were high that the surgery would be futile. The procedure would probably not help and would certainly harm the patient (violating Hippocrates' injunction to 'first do no harm'); and it would injure the practice of surgery itself by abandoning rational methods, making patients and families more fearful, wasting valuable time and energy, and (not least) denting the surgeon's reputation. Dr M. Price, an American surgeon, argued, 'many of us are now taking high ground and refusing to operate at the eleventh hour. It is not fair to surgery to operate on dying patients.'[51] In this context, it is clear that H.'s sentimental rhetoric works to shift Moutard-Martin's actions from potentially disastrous to bold and salvific.

[50] 'H', 'Recent Papers [Review of Moutard-Martin, 'On Operation for Empyema,' *Revue Médicale*, Nov. 1879]', *London Medical Record* 7 (15 December 1879): 498.
[51] W.W. Keen, 'Four Operations for Appendicitis: Three Recoveries, One Death from a Very Small Concealed Abscess', *Proceedings of the Philadelphia County Medical Society* 12 (1891): 497. Price's comment appears in the Discussion following the case.

By drawing on novelistic conventions, the medical practitioner, patient, family members, and fellow readers could find comfortable agreement in familiar narratives that made sense of difficult and hopeless cases. These romantic conventions help to reframe error as effort, ignorance as mystery, failure as fate. By sentimentalizing the features of disease, physicians register their sympathy for the patient and their affiliation with her family as common readers of a sad tale. And in the event that the imperilled patient recovers, the physician is figured as the intrepid hero whose intervention snatched her from death. The revision of sentimental tropes in clinical settings sheds new light on how these tropes function even in fiction and forces a re-evaluation of genre as it demonstrates the mobility of many supposedly 'literary' methods.

As digital databases now begin to make 19th-century treatises and (especially) periodical literature more accessible to all kinds of readers, increasing primary source research into this vast archive may radically change our understanding of the imbrication of medicine and the novel in the Victorian period. Literary criticism and historical scholarship to date addresses only a fraction of the type printed on paper in the 19th century. Like their Victorian colleagues, 21st-century critics—even the historicists—tend to circulate some of the same cases. These may be symptomatic or even representative, but that can be best established in the context of a diverse range of examples rather than re-readings of the same useful canon. Critics have, of course, had to restrict the scope of their work given understandable practical limitations, with relatively few having access to an extensive print archive. While the digitization of Victorian medical treatises and obscure novels may, if properly structured and financed, extend the gift of a good library to a much wider range of readers, scholars in periodical studies may find digitization most useful. It is the ephemeral matter of periodical publication—individual medical cases, short fiction, news, essays, editorials, letters, reviews—that we are most likely to miss. This represents an immense untapped resource, useful to critics of all callings. And in this vast river of periodicals, where novelists and physicians could read and publish in the same journals, the unmapped interfiliation of medicine and the novel certainly resides.

Suggested Reading

Bailin, Miriam. *The Sickroom in Victorian Fiction*. New York: Cambridge University Press, 1994.

Caldwell, Janis McLarren. *Literature and Medicine in Nineteenth-Century Britain: From Mary Shelley to George Eliot*. Cambridge: Cambridge University Press, 2004.

Dames, Nicholas. *Physiology of the Novel: Reading, Neural Science, and the Form of Victorian Fiction*. Oxford: Oxford University Press, 2007.

Foucault, Michel. *The Birth of the Clinic: An Archaeology of Medical Perception*. Translated by A.M. Sheridan Smith. New York: Vintage, 1973.

Frawley, Maria H. *Invalidism and Identity in Nineteenth-Century Britain*. Chicago: University of Chicago Press, 2004.

Gilbert, Pamela K. *Disease, Desire, and the Body in Victorian Women's Popular Novels*. Cambridge: Cambridge University Press, 1997.

Logan, Peter Melville. *Nerves and Narratives: A Cultural History of Hysteria in Nineteenth-Century British Prose*. Berkeley: University of California Press, 1997.

Rothfield, Lawrence. *Vital Signs: Medical Realism in Nineteenth-Century Fiction*. Princeton: Princeton University Press, 1992.

Tougaw, Jason Daniel. *Strange Cases: The Medical Case History and the British Novel*. New York and London: Routledge, 2006.

Vrettos, Athena. *Somatic Fictions: Imagining Illness in Victorian Culture*. Stanford: Stanford University Press, 1995.

....

23

NATURALIZING THE MIND IN THE VICTORIAN NOVEL: CONSCIOUSNESS IN WILKIE COLLINS'S *POOR MISS FINCH* AND THOMAS HARDY'S *WOODLANDERS*— TWO CASE STUDIES

....

SUZY ANGER

> How it is that anything so remarkable as a state of consciousness comes
> about as a result of irritating nervous tissue, is just as unaccountable as the
> appearance of the Djin, when Aladdin rubbed his lamp.
>
> (Thomas Huxley)[1]

The production of consciousness out of matter is as baffling to 19th-century science, says Thomas Huxley, as are the fantastic occurrences related in the imaginative stories that consciousness creates. Victorian fiction makes both problems its own. Literary criticism has frequently regarded the novel, with its capacity to register the inner life, as the genre most suited to representing consciousness.[2] Narrative can imaginatively move beyond the limitations of sense experience to reveal the interiority of another mind. Fiction can depict feelings, perceptions, and unspoken thoughts, that is, render in words private mental states. As new scientific knowledge about the mind developed in the 19th century, consciousness—what it is, how it works, how it came into being—exploded as a cultural problem, and was widely discussed in generalist periodicals as well as in specialized

---

[1] *Lessons in Elementary Physiology*, 2nd edn (London: Macmillan and Co., 1968), 210.
[2] See, for instance, Dorrit Cohn, *Transparent Minds* (Princeton: Princeton University Press, 1978).

scholarly works in medicine, psychology, and philosophy. In recent years, commentators on Victorian literature have demonstrated how the literature of the period responded to (and itself influenced) the new scientific psychology that transformed the conception of mind in the 19th century, in critical studies on topics such as mesmerism, hysteria, memory, the unconscious, and the evolutionary development of consciousness.[3] This work has extended our understanding of the Victorian novel, drawing our attention to language that had been overlooked or misinterpreted and deepening our understanding of Victorian views on the nature of the self.

The new physiological psychology inevitably bore upon long-standing questions about human consciousness and the relations between body and mind. As science and medicine moved towards an increasingly materialist understanding of the mind, sometimes even asserting the reducibility of mental processes to brain processes, arguments concerning the workings of consciousness affected the novel in ways that have now been obscured. The larger issues were far from new, but were given a particular shape and urgency as the new physiology and psychology revealed the nature of reflex action and the extent of unconscious thought processes, and studies on conditions such as aphasia and apraxia made undeniable the link between brain injury and changes in perception and character. Theories of automatism suggested a radical diminishment of the role of volition in human action, and in so doing brought fresh challenges to longstanding popular notions about the unity, immortality, and freedom of the self. New experimental studies on the physiology and psychology of sense perception re-energized traditional questions about the role of experience in knowledge but they also introduced radically new methodologies for the investigation of the mind.

Not only did the dramatization of particular psychological phenomenon become important to the content of fiction, but as the mind was increasingly naturalized and the new science further challenged the concept of a soul separate from brain and body, attempts to understand the connection between the mental and the physical shaped the very form of narrative. While Victorian popular fiction tended to present the insights of psychological investigations primarily as content, major writers such as George Eliot and Thomas Hardy incorporated the debates into their novels in more complex ways, not only as subject matter and plot element, but also in their dramatization of character and in their construction of narrative point of view. Many novels manifest the genre's

---

[3] See Sally Shuttleworth, *Charlotte Brontë and Victorian Psychology* (Cambridge: Cambridge University Press, 1996); Jenny Bourne Taylor and Sally Shuttleworth, eds., *Embodied Selves: An Anthology of Psychological Texts 1830–1890* (Oxford: Oxford University Press, 2003); Rick Rylance, *Victorian Psychology and British Culture: 1850–1880* (New York: Oxford University Press, 2000); Alison Winter, *Mesmerized: Powers of Mind in Victorian Britain* (Chicago: University of Chicago Press, 1998); Anne Harrington, *Medicine, Mind, and the Double Brain: A Study in Nineteenth-Century Thought* (Princeton: Princeton University Press, 1987); Robert Young, *Mind, Brain, and Adaptation in the Nineteenth Century: Cerebral Localization and Its Biological Context from Gall to Ferrier* (New York: Oxford University Press, 1990); Mark S. Micale, *Approaching Hysteria: Disease and Its Interpretations* (Princeton: Princeton University Press, 1995); L.S. Jacyna, *Lost Words: Narratives of Language and the Brain, 1825—1926* (Oxford: Princeton University Press, 2000); and Joel Peter Eigen, *Unconscious Crime: Mental Absence and Criminal Responsibility in Victorian London* (Baltimore: Johns Hopkins University Press, 2003), among many other fine studies.

engagement with psychology, and I could spend the following pages moving from one example to another simply to give a sense of the topic's pervasiveness and fictive range. But rather than doing that, I have opted to offer, first, a brief consideration of the scientific and psychological milieu of the culture, and then a more detailed exploration of how two very different novels and novelists represent the mind. I begin with Wilkie Collins's *Poor Miss Finch* where I will be looking at his close attention to the psychology of sense perception. Next, I consider Thomas Hardy's *The Woodlanders*, focusing in particular on Hardy's attempt to represent both the physical and the mental aspects of mind. In both instances I trace the shaping effect of specific problems in the debate on the development of Victorian narrative.

I

As physiology and mental philosophy came together in a scientific psychology that would become a new academic discipline, consciousness, as I have already suggested, was increasingly understood as a function of the brain. Historians of psychology, such as Kurt Danziger, Graham Richards, and Roger Smith, argue that changes in the meaning of psychological concepts, which attended the formation of the discipline, reflect radical shifts in the ways in which human thought and behaviour were constructed.[4] Those concepts gave non-specialists—that is, the general reader—access to these new theories of self and other, and as a result, the lines drawn between the emerging discipline of psychology and the culture at large were initially less distinct than those in more technical fields. Folk psychology—that is, common sense or naïve psychology—and the literary texts that both reflect and help create our ordinary ways of understanding ourselves inevitably influenced scientific psychology, and vice versa.[5]

Consciousness and its relation to the body became a topic of acute interest in the Victorian periodical press by mid century, in articles in widely read journals such as the *Fortnightly Review* and *Nineteenth Century*; in specialized scientific, medical, and psychological journals such as *Nature*, *Brain*, and *The Journal of Mental Science*; and, after 1876, in the newly founded philosophy journal *Mind*. As Huxley points out, that there exists a close relationship between the physical and the mental is clear, but how to explain that relationship remains unclear. Almost every serious Victorian commentator on consciousness makes a version of the 'explanatory gap' argument, admitting that we

---

⁴ In *Naming the Mind: How Psychology Found Its Language* (London: Sage, 1997), Kurt Danziger asserts that concepts such as "'intelligence'", "personality", "behaviour" and "learning" were given such radically changed meanings by modern psychology that there simply are no earlier equivalents' (36). See also Graham Richards, *Mental Machinery: The Origins and Consequences of Psychological Ideas, 1600–1850* (London: Athlone Press, 1992), and *Roger Smith, Inhibition: History and Meaning in the Sciences of Mind and Brain* (London: Free Association Books, 1992).

⁵ See Steven Stich and Shaun Nichols, 'Folk Psychology', in *The Blackwell Guide to Philosophy of Mind*, eds. Steven Stich and Ted A. Warfield (Oxford: Blackwell, 2003), 235–55, for further discussion of the concept of folk psychology.

must recognize that we are unable to bridge the chasm in our understanding between brain and mind. The scientific naturalist John Tyndall, for instance, concedes that while 'accepting fearlessly the facts of materialism…I bow my head in the dust before the mystery of mind'.[6] It is not surprising that this fundamental problem that challenges both our conceptual and linguistic resources would trouble fiction, which has long been understood to be one of our primary modes of exploring the mind.

Fiction indeed did explore the problem with a fervour that equalled that exhibited in contemporary non-fiction. Dickens's novels register his awareness of the controversies. Sally Shuttleworth has demonstrated Charlotte Brontë's knowledge of early-century developments in psychology.[7] Popular writers such as Edward Bulwer Lytton earlier in the century and Grant Allen later on put psychological investigations of mind at the centre of much of their work. George Eliot's interest in the new psychology has long been noted. Given that her partner, her 'husband' as she called him, George Henry Lewes was an active participant in the development of the new physiological psychology, producing works such as *The Physical Basis of Mind* (1877) in his series *Problems of Life and Mind*, and given her friendships with the psychologists Herbert Spencer and James Sully, we might expect George Eliot's novels to register a nuanced understanding of those debates. From her early first-person narrator Latimer in 'The Lifted Veil' who is able—apparently by means of extended perceptual knowledge—to share the consciousnesses of those around him, through close renderings of unconscious mental processes unregistered by the characters themselves in *Middlemarch*, to a narrator that advances the technique of free indirect discourse in *Daniel Deronda*, Eliot's novels examine the workings and problems of consciousness.

George Eliot's contemporaries well recognized the context of her fiction, George Willis Cooke writing as early as 1883:

> In literature, the new method as developed in recent years consists in an application of psychology to all the problems of man's nature. George Eliot's intimate association with the leaders of the scientific movement in England, naturally turned her mind into sympathy with their work, and made her desirous of doing in literature what they were doing in science. In the special department of physiological psychology, no one did more than George Henry Lewes, and her whole heart went out in genuine appreciation of his work. He studied the mind as a function of the brain, as being developed with the body, as the result of inherited conditions, as intimately dependent on its environment. Here was a new conception of man, which regarded him as the last product of nature, considered as an organic whole. This conception George Eliot everywhere applied in her studies of life and character.[8]

---

[6] John Tyndall, 'Apology for the Belfast Address', *Fragments of Science: A Series of Detached Essays, Addresses, and Reviews* (London: Longmans, 1992), 202–23, 222.

[7] See note 3, above.

[8] George Willis Cooke, *George Eliot: A Critical Study of Her Life, Writings, and Philosophy* (Boston: Houghton Mifflin and Co., 1883), 396.

Late century fiction, if often less subtle than George Eliot in its understanding of the 'new conception of man', took up topics related to the mind with a vengeance, in sometimes humorous stories of consciousness transmitted by means of electricity (Rudyard Kipling's 'Wireless'), of one consciousness impressed into the brain of another like a hard drive, of memories extracted and shared (Israel Zangwill's 'Memory Clearing House'), of consciousnesses swapped between bodies (H.G. Wells's 'Story of the Late Mr. Elvesham'), of hereditary determinism (Grant Allen's 'Two Carnegies'), and of consciousness controlled from afar (Arthur Conan Doyle's 'The Parasite' and Richard Marsh's *Beetle*). The psychological ideas that had captured the imagination of the great novelists, and that worked to transform Victorian fiction on its way into modernism, pervade the popular literature of the 1890s.

II

While presently lesser-known authors like Marsh and Allen indulged in fantastic plots that exploited new ideas of the mind, other novelists like Robert Louis Stevenson and Wilkie Collins, whose novels occupy an unstable position between low and high, more earnestly considered problems of consciousness.

Jenny Bourne Taylor has established Collins's concern with 19th-century psychology, demonstrating his attention in his fiction to issues of the unconscious, insanity, inheritance, and memory, among others.[9] Collins's 1872 novel *Poor Miss Finch* shows that he was also concerned with developments in the psychology of sense perception, the area that was foundational to the new psychology from 1860 onwards. Experimental sensory psychology furnished much of the groundwork for basic questions about what the mind is and how we can investigate it.

Of Collins, Algernon Swinburne complained in 1889 that he 'could not, as a rule, get forward at all, without the help of some physical or moral infirmity in some one of the leading agents and patients of the story... If the hero in this story or the heroine in another had not been blind, there could have been no story at all.'[10] For Swinburne, that amounted to a serious limitation in Collins as a novelist. Great writers do not make their books depend upon characters 'abnormally and constitutionally deficient in nerve and brain'. But Swinburne misses the mark here. Collins was not merely in thrall to ingenious plot device and remarkable character. Rather he explored in his fiction an idea that the new psychology was in the process of elucidating, that nerve, brain, and the senses make us what we are.

Theodule-Armand Ribot, known as the founder of French scientific psychology, in his 1870 study *English Psychology* (English translation, 1873) calls for a '*Psychological Teratology*', that is, a study of significant physical divergences from the 'normal' type: 'A

---

[9] Jenny Bourne Taylor, *In the Secret Theatre of the Home: Wilkie Collins, Sensation, Narrative, and Nineteenth-Century Psychology* (London: Routledge, 1988).

[10] 'Wilkie Collins', *Fortnightly Review* 46, no. 275 (1889): 589–99, 590.

deaf man, a blind man, a man originally deprived of any sense, is he not a ready-made subject for observation?'[11] He criticizes the new discipline for overlooking that aspect of psychological inquiry. Excluding Denis Diderot's 1749 *Letter on the Blind* and Dugald Stewart's 1827 remarks on James Mitchell (a deaf and blind child operated on for cataracts), psychology, Ribot says (drawing on a telling visual metaphor), 'has completely shut its eyes ("*ferme les yeux*") to exceptions and anomalies'.[12] Composed in the years in which the interest in the new psychology was burgeoning in Britain, Collins's novel might almost seem to be written to meet Ribot's demand. It is an informed dramatization of the psychology of a blind woman who temporarily recovers sight. In writing *Poor Miss Finch*, Collins draws upon extensive scientific, philosophical, and psychological research on the blind and on cataract surgery. If it is a novel that less successfully plays upon the reader's sensations than many of Collins's works, as early reviewers complained, it is one that, in exchange, offers the beginnings of a phenomenology of sense perception.

First, a little background to the theories of visual perception that Collins considers in his novel.[13] In a 1693 letter to John Locke, the Irishman William Molyneux posed his soon-to-be famous question, asking whether a man blind from birth who suddenly gained vision would be able to distinguish between a cube and a sphere by sight alone. Both Locke and Molyneux answered in the negative, Locke believing that perception is modality specific and developed only by experience. Molyneux's question became central to 18th-century perceptual philosophy. Most importantly, Bishop Berkeley drew upon Molyneux's problem in formulating his *New Theory of Vision* (1709), a work that came to dominate thought on perception into the Victorian period. Berkeley writes that 'a man born blind would not at first reception think the things he saw were of the same nature with the objects of touch, or had anything in common with them',[14] because visual representations exploit different concepts than tactual representations. Tactual experiences must first be correlated with visual experiences in order for the subject to understand what he is seeing. Further, distance, magnitude, and relation are not immediately given in vision, but are the products of association and interpretation.

In 1728, William Chesselden published in the *Philosophical Transactions* an account of a successful cataract operation he carried out on a teenage boy, a medical narrative that has more than once been identified as the most famous case study to precede Freud.[15]

---

[11] Theodule-Armand Ribot, *English Psychology* (London: Henry S. King & Co., 1873), 30.

[12] Ribot, *English Psychology*, 30. See also Dugald Stewart, 'Appendix to Part Third-Chapter Second', Stewart, *Elements of the Philosophy of the Human Mind*, 3 vols. (Philadelphia: Carey, Lea & Carey, 1829), 3: 259–317.

[13] For excellent historical, philosophical, and psychological considerations of Molyneux's problem, see M.J.L. Degenaar, *Molyneux's Problem: Three Centuries of Discussion on the Perception of Forms*, trans. Michael J. Collins (Dordrecht: Kluwer Academic Publishers, 1996); Shaun Gallagher, *How the Body Shapes the Mind* (Oxford: Oxford University Press, 2005); and Michael J. Morgan, *Molyneux's Question: Vision, Touch, and the Philosophy of Perception* (New York: Cambridge University Press, 1977).

[14] *An Essay Towards a New Theory of Vision* (Dublin: Jeremy Pepyat, 1709), Sec. 128.

[15] 'An Account of Some Observations Made by a Young Gentleman, Who Was Born Blind, or Lost His Sight so Early, That He Had no Remembrance of Ever Having Seen, and Was Couch d between 13 and 14 Years of Age', *Philosophical Transactions* 35, no. 402 (1728): 447–50.

Chesselden's report, although it did not involve an experiment with a cube and a sphere, was immediately taken as providing evidence related to answering Molyneux's question, which had originally been conceived of as a thought experiment rather than a question that could be answered empirically. Chesselden described his patient's experiences, observing that the boy could not judge distance, shape, or size. His account was henceforth repeatedly cited in philosophical and later in psychological texts, although by the 19th century, the primary interest had shifted away from issues pertaining to shared concepts to the question of whether visual concepts were innate or acquired. Medical practitioners who performed successful cataract operations later in the 18th and 19th centuries did actual experiments on their patients' vision, the best-known account after Chesselden's being that of J.C.A. Franz, published in the *Philosophical Transactions* in 1841 (and read to the Royal Society by physiologist and psychologist Benjamin Brodie whose book *Psychological Inquiries* (1855) was one of only two psychological texts found in Collins's library after his death). Franz carried out a test with a sphere and a cube on his eighteen-year old patient, concluding that the young man's experience confirmed the negative answer to Molyneux's question; the patient could tell that the two objects he was shown were not the same, but he could not identify them as the objects he knew through touch. Although there were two noted books published in the Victorian period, by Samuel Bailey and Thomas Abbott, which reinterpreted the cataract cases in support of a positive answer to Molyneux's question, with the aim of re-establishing the 'common-sense' notion that our visual perception of space is direct and immediate, Collins, along with John Stuart Mill, Alexander Bain, William Carpenter, and others, dismissed such a view, asserting that one must learn how to see, with experience teaching one how to interpret the percepts provided by vision.

In *Poor Miss Finch*, Collins places Molyneux's problem at the centre of his narrative. Testing Lucilla Finch's vision after the removal of her bandages following a cataract operation, the oculist, Dr Grosse, asks her to distinguish between a sphere and a cube, a task which it turns out she can accomplish only through touch. In addition, Lucilla has no idea of visual perspective and is unable to judge distance. Introducing Molyneux's problem into his fictional exploration of Lucilla Finch's mental processes allows Collins to comment upon some of the fundamental concerns of the new physiological psychology. As scientific psychology emerged as a discipline, spurred on by physiology's intense interest in perception following on the differentiation of sensory and motor nerves early in the century, there was a move away from thinking about sense perception primarily as an epistemological, philosophical problem to thinking about it in psychological terms. Experimental study of sense perception, and particularly visual perception, dominated the new psychology in the second half of the century, with sensation widely taken to be the foundation of consciousness. Even in Britain, notoriously slow in setting up psychological laboratories, vision was studied experimentally in the second half of the century, with the comparative psychologist Douglas Spalding, for instance, announcing the results of his experiments on chicks hooded at birth, as he attempted to prove that visual orientation in space is innate. It was in this context that Collins developed his novel of sense perception, and one need only compare his representation of Lucilla with Dickens's portrayal of his blind protagonist Bertha in *The Cricket on the Hearth* to appreciate the depth of Collins's interest in the new sensory psychology.

Some of Collins's contemporaries recognized his direct borrowings from Chesselden's famous account (as does Catherine Peters in her introduction to the Oxford edition of the novel) in his description of Lucilla's experiences. From Chesselden, Collins takes Miss Finch's preference for scarlet and white, her sensitivity to differences in brightness before her surgery, her inability to distinguish between her dog and her cat following her surgery, and even her aversion to dark colours and to people with dark skin. While Lucilla's 'morbid fancy' about dark-skinned people has been figured as Collins's commentary on the irrationality of racism (and he may well mean to suggest that also), this trait of Lucilla's is borrowed directly from Chesselden's account: '[T]he first Time [the young Gentleman] saw Black, it gave him great Uneasiness, yet after a little Time he was reconcil'd to it; but some Months after, Seeing by Accident a Negroe Woman, he was struck with great Horror at the Sight'.[16]

When Collins claimed in his dedicatory Preface to the novel that he consulted 'competent authorities of all sorts' and that whenever '"Lucilla" acts or speaks ... with reference to her blindness, she is doing or saying what persons afflicted as she is have done or said before her', he stood on far firmer ground than his friend Charles Dickens had when defending the veracity of spontaneous combustion in his own Preface.[17] Collins drew not only on Chesselden's study, but on many of the later reports of successful cataract surgery, as well as on autobiographies written by the blind, and in so doing he transferred the issues from their earlier philosophical context to the new psychological one. Almost every statement made about Lucilla's subjective experience of her perceptual capacities both before and after her surgery finds corroboration in the contemporary literature on the blind. To take a few instances: Oscar's assertion that Lucilla 'has eyes in the tips of her fingers' (156) is found in the French ophthalmologist Pierre-Armand Dufau's 1851 edition of the *Memoirs of a Woman Born Blind*.[18] Collins most likely takes Lucilla's repeated laments about her 'stupidity' in confusing objects from J. Wardrop's 1826 case study and he borrows her mistaking of a horse for a dog directly from E. Home's 1807 report, both recorded in the *Philosophical Transactions of the Royal Society*.[19] Collins's own doctor was the distinguished eye specialist George Critchett, whose best-known account of cataract surgery appeared in his article on the restoration of sight in a female at the age of twenty-two (1855)—that is, a woman exactly the age of Miss Finch. The even more distinguished researcher T. Nunneley's *On*

---

[16]   Chesselden, 'An Account', 448.

[17]   Wilkie Collins, *Poor Miss Finch* [1872] (New York: Oxford University Press, 1995), xxxix. Subsequent citations appear in the text.

[18]   *Souvenirs d'une Aveugle-Née*, edited by Dufau, in which the writer asks: 'Had not nature, in fact, in my case placed my eyes at my finger ends.' The passage is quoted in a review article on works on the blind in 'The Blind', *National Review* 19 (1860): 75–106, 97.

[19]   'He immediately went to the window, and called out, "What is that moving?" I asked him what he thought it was? He said, "A dog drawing a wheelbarrow. There is one, two, three dogs drawing another. How very pretty!" These proved to be carts and horses on the road, which he saw from a two pair of stairs window' (Everard Home, 'An Account of Two Children Born with Cataracts in Their Eyes, to Shew That Their Sight Was Obscured in Very Different Degrees; With Experiments to Determine the Proportional Knowledge of Objects Acquired by Them Immediately after the Cataracts Were Removed', *Philosophical Transactions of the Royal Society of London* 97 (1807): 90). Lucilla: 'I saw my first horse and cart from an upper window, and took it for a dog drawing a wheelbarrow!' (334).

the Organs of Vision (1858) appears to have supplied the precise details of Lucilla's attempts to distinguish between cube and sphere. Collins's friend the novelist Charles Reade, also a careful researcher, sent Collins some articles on the blind, for which Collins belatedly thanks him in a letter: 'I shall certainly use them in "Poor Miss F." The fact I knew—but of the manner in which touch felt the difference in colours I was quite ignorant.'[20] The clippings apparently explain how the blind are able to detect differences in colour (as Lucilla does). The contemporary literature suggested, among other things, that different dyes have different tactile feelings or, more far-fetched, that touch is so far developed in the blind that they are able to distinguish the different rays of light reflected.

In his classic piece, 'What Is It Like to Be a Bat?' Thomas Nagel writes that 'the subjective character of the experience of a person deaf and blind from birth is not accessible to me'.[21] Collins seems to have accepted a similar view, and so went to great lengths in his attempt to represent Lucilla's consciousness by borrowing the point of view of someone who could know the subjective experience of doing without a sense. An anonymous article on 'The Blind' in the *National Review* in 1860, anticipating Ribot's comment, argued that it was Diderot's 'Letter on the Blind' that 'first distinctly suggested and exemplified the manner in which the study of the experience and feelings of the blind might be made to throw light upon some of the most interesting problems of mental science'.[22] Collins was of the same mind: his novel relies heavily on Diderot's remarkable text. He owned Diderot's *Complete Works* in 22 volumes, and as William Baker shows in his reconstruction of Collins's library, those volumes were among the few philosophical texts that Collins did possess at his death.

From the 'Letter', Collins took not only Lucilla's preference for elongating her arms over gaining sight, but also the detail about her absent sense of modesty. Madame Pratolungo, wife of an Italian revolutionary, asserts: 'Modesty is essentially the growth of our own consciousness of the eyes of others judging us' (70), a remark that has been taken to be Collins's own slightly risqué comment on Victorian propriety, but which in fact is derived from one of Diderot's observations on the blind man of Puiseaux, 'who makes little fuss about modesty' and 'sees no reason to cover one part of the body more than another'.[23] Pratolungo's comment registers the way that the objects of our social emotions can be determined by the contingencies of our embodiment, as do Diderot's.

But most significantly, Collins's general perspective on Lucilla's lack of sight owes much to the materialist Diderot who writes: 'I have never doubted that the influence of our organs and our senses has a considerable influence upon our metaphysics and morals, and that even our most purely intellectual ideas, if I may express the matter in that

[20] Collins to Charles Reade, 19 November 1871, in *The Public Face of Wilkie Collins: The Collected Letters*, ed. William Baker, Andrew Gasson, Graham Law, and Paul Lewis, 4 vols. (London: Pickering and Chatto, 2005), 2: 300.

[21] *The Philosophical Review* 83 (1974): 435–50, 440.

[22] 'The Blind', 80. Denis Diderot, 'Letter on the Blind, for the use of those who see' [1749], quoted in *Molyneux's Question: Vision, Touch, and the Philosophy of Perception*, trans. Michael J. Morgan (New York: Cambridge University Press, 1977), 19.

[23] Diderot, 'Letter', 37.

way, are closely dependent on the structure of our bodies.'[24] What Diderot gets at in his letter, and what Victorian psychology was fast determining, was the embodied nature of mind. Nugent, Miss Finch's unsuccessful suitor, who speaks like 'a man profoundly versed in physiology' (170), declares of the surgery that 'the physical result will not be the only result, if her sight can be restored. There will be a new mind put into her as well as a new sense' (188). Consider how far this conception of mind is from Dickens's description in his *American Notes* of Laura Bridgman, the child without sight or hearing, and with greatly diminished senses of smell and taste. '[T]he immortal spirit', Dickens writes, 'which had been implanted within her could not die, nor be maimed nor mutilated; and though most of its avenues of communication with the world were cut off, it began to manifest itself through the others.'[25] Dickens describes a consciousness that is not of the body, but that instead struggles to reveal itself from within a mechanism whose lines of transmission to the external world have been shut down. Spalding writes in his 1873 article on 'Instinct': 'Educated men, even materialists—their own positive statements to the contrary notwithstanding—have not yet quite escaped from the habit of regarding mind as independent of bodily organization.'[26] Collins, however, seems aware that consciousness is inseparable from sense experience. John Morley, editor of the *Fortnightly Review*, argued in the 1870s that the radical Diderot had used his 'Letter' to show 'that all knowledge is relative' and 'that our experience is not the limit to the possibilities of things',[27] and Collins interpreted him in the same way in his borrowings for *Poor Miss Finch*.

It needs to be asked, however, why, after the integration into his story of his extraordinarily careful research, Collins makes his plot depend upon an event that thoroughly undercuts the science that he went to such lengths to establish. That is the scene in which Miss Finch, her bandages just removed, mistakes her fiancé's twin brother Nugent for Oscar himself. It is absurd in realist terms to depict Lucilla as capable of immediately identifying by sight and then throwing herself into the arms of the young man, as Collins knew, and in the pages that follow the narrative straightaway resumes its careful descriptions of her difficulties judging distance and shape. Critchett, in fact, explains that his young woman patient suffers from prosopagnosia: 'Her greatest difficulty was with the human face: although she could see and describe and name each feature, she seemed unable to take it in as a unity, and was unable to recognize a person except by voice or touch; and after two years of education she had not acquired this faculty.'[28] Collins increases the offence by supplying through Madame Pratolungo, Lucilla's companion, the reasons for Lucilla's immediate identification of her lover (or, rather, his identical twin, as it turns out). 'Of the three persons who had offered themselves to view on the right-hand side of the door, one (Mrs. Finch) was a woman; another (Mr. Finch) was

---

[24] Diderot, 'Letter', 37.

[25] Charles Dickens, *Pictures from Italy; American Notes* (London: Chapman and Hall, 1880), 216.

[26] Douglas A. Spalding, 'Instinct', *Macmillan's Magazine* 27 (Feb. 1873): 282–93, 289–90.

[27] 'Diderot', *Fortnightly Review* 17, no. 101 (1875): 680–701, 681.

[28] G. Critchett, 'Operation for Congenital Cataract on an Adult', *Medico-Chirurgical Transactions* 38 (1855): 51–58, 56.

a short, grey-headed, elderly man; the third (Nugent), in his height—which she could see—and in the color of his hair—which she could see—was the only one of the three who could possibly represent Oscar' (284). But as the narrative later shows, the newly sighted Lucilla cannot name colours—so how would she recognize grey versus brown hair?—cannot judge distance or size; cannot tell where in space an object is in relation to herself; cannot transfer perceptions between touch and vision. That she knows male and female, young and old as represented in vision is implausible.

In a review essay, 'The Psychology of the Blind', Edmund Gosse criticizes Andre Gide's *Pastoral Symphony* (which like Collins's novel involves a young blind woman's recovery of sight following an operation) for its abandonment of psychological realism: 'To bring down a surgeon in a machine from the skies is to resign ourselves to melodrama.'[29] As Elisabeth Gitter has shown, the blind lover, vision restored, who immediately recognizes the loved one is a stock scene from 19th-century melodrama.[30] By resorting to a recognizably melodramatic scene that Collins knew would signify for Victorian readers, he was, as he often did, negotiating between narrative realism and melodrama. His ultimate debunking of the convention of immediate recognition (given that Lucilla has in fact mistaken her lover's identical twin for himself) does not work to reinstate narrative realism but instead further disrupts it with an implausible representation of Lucilla's super-sensory powers when sightless, which allows Collins to establish that touch is superior to sight for Lucilla. Her eyes deceive her in a way that touch would have avoided: while blind, she can tactually discriminate between the identical twins Nugent and Oscar. Narrative exigency trumps scientific realism. Collins likewise declines to offer a realist explanation for Lucilla's second loss of sight, interpreted by Lucilla *not* as a loss, but instead as a restoration of blindness. Against a culture that regards vision as the highest of the senses (a point made in nearly every Victorian study on the senses), Lucilla proclaims: 'Thank God I am blind!' (445). The moral of the story is that in gaining sight, Lucilla loses something she regards as more valuable to her: her extreme sensitivity of touch. As Grosse says, she gives up vision in her fingers when she gains it in her eyes, and with that exchange she loses the possibility of feeling the difference between the true loved one and the false. Never mind that by the time she regains sight, Oscar is definitively marked apart visually from his brother Nugent by his blue stained skin, as a result of his treatment for epilepsy following a brain injury (epilepsy was another topic of great interest in the research in psychology); it is not so much sight that fools Lucilla but rather every other character's complicity in hiding from her the substitution of one brother for the other. It also turns out that the visual image of Oscar—even when she mistakes his identical twin, the pristine Nugent, for Oscar—has turned out to be disappointing in comparison with the 'charming ideal picture which she

---

[29] Edmund Gosse, 'The Psychology of the Blind', *Books on the Table* (New York: Scribner and Sons, 1921), 290.

[30] Elizabeth Gitter, 'The Blind Daughter in Charles Dickens's "Cricket on the Hearth"', *Studies in English Literature, 1500–1900* 39, no. 4 (Autumn 1999): 675–89. Gosse further writes in 'The Psychology of the Blind': 'Blind girls who miraculously recover the use of their eyes are common objects at the Lyceum Theatre' (290).

had formed of her lover in the days of her blindness' (431). In allowing Lucilla's mental 'vision' to be more appealing to her than the one provided by sight, Collins seeks to validate different modes of perceptual awareness. Lucilla's 'ideal' is only metaphorically a picture: not a visual representation but a tactile and auditory one. She experiences beauty not through vision (although Oscar—at least before he turns blue–is 'such a handsome young man' (39) according to Pratolungo), but instead through different forms of sense perception. Collins's claim in the Preface that he intends to show that Miss Finch's happiness depends on her bodily condition works to underscore the idea that the beauty that Lucilla perceives as a blind person, in an aesthetic that is in no way connected to visual representation, is as valuable as that which depends on the eyes. Just as Lucilla delights in music, so she derives greater aesthetic pleasure from touch, form, the sound of voice, and language than she does from her restored sight. With that assertion, Collins questions Victorian ocularcentricism, which regarded vision as the highest of the senses and aesthetic experience as above all based in vision.[31] Collins's challenge to the dominant hierarchy of the senses also helps explain why the more competent and visually appealing of the twins, Nugent, becomes the story's villain. It is Nugent who organizes the attempt to restore Lucilla's sight, and he is associated throughout the novel with vision, as a painter who mourns Lucilla's inability to see his work while expounding at length on the 'intellectual perception of beauty' (140). Accepting the pre-eminence of vision and regarding Lucilla's blindness as a deficit that must be corrected, Nugent is marked as contemptible.

In the years following the publication of Collins's novel, a number of psychological 'teratologies' were published in the literature, most frequently studies of Laura Bridgman, the girl who was effectively left with the single sense of touch after an illness in her infancy. G. Stanley Hall, the important American psychologist and founder of the *American Journal of Psychology*, published a long article in the British journal *Mind* in 1879 on Bridgman that might be taken to be one of the studies that Collins borrowed from when writing his novel, if Hall's piece had not appeared a number of years after *Miss Finch*. But despite the striking parallels between Hall's case study of Laura and Collins's representation of the fictional Lucilla there is an important difference between the two authors' stances. *The Journal of American Psychology* could announce that it would publish 'studies in abnormal psychology, including the insane, criminals, idiotic, blind, deaf, or other defectives or degenerates'. Ribot speaks of 'monstrosities'. Collins does not pathologize Lucilla. Instead in *Poor Miss Finch* he takes the melodramatic plot of the blind girl regaining her sight and uses it to offer a realistic representation of the psychology of sense perception—tactile, auditory, and visual—that resists the visual bias of the new psychology and of his culture

---

[31] Most Victorian writing on sense perception takes for granted that vision is the highest of the senses. See Martin Jay's important work *Downcast Eyes: The Denigration of Vision in Twentieth-Century French Thought* (Berkeley: University of California Press, 1993). For discussion of the blind and aesthetic experience, see Constance Classen's chapter 'A Feel for the World: Lessons in Aesthetics from the Blind', in *Worlds of Sense: Exploring the Senses in History and across Cultures* (New York: Routledge, 1993) where Classen writes: 'The Western privileging of sight as *the* aesthetic sense has led philosophers and psychologists to question whether persons who lack sight can have any aesthetic experience' (139). H.G. Wells examines the assumed pre-eminence of the visual sense in his fine short story 'The Country of the Blind', *Strand Magazine* 27 (April 1904): 401–15.

at large. Negotiating between melodrama and realism, he also negotiates between the mental and the physical, dramatizing the complexities of the embodiment of mind.

In 1892 the young French experimental psychologist Alfred Binet published an article in the *Fortnightly Review*, in which he sought to show that thoughts are not always visual images, that thinking does not necessarily involve the pictorial reproduction of objects in one's mind, as, he argued, the philosophers Hobbes and Hume and their successors in 19th-century studies of the mind had often assumed. 'They failed to perceive', Binet writes, 'that thought may take on a number of different forms.'[32] A blind person's thinking will necessarily depend on auditory images. 'The whole present tendency of psychological research', he continues, 'is to show not that the mental operations of all persons are of similar nature, but that immense psychological differences exist between different individuals. In a word, the study of mind has entered of late years upon a new phase.'[33] Collins had come to a similar conclusion in his rendering of consciousness in *Poor Miss Finch* two decades earlier.

III

Thomas Hardy also well recognized the embodiment of mind.[34] Consciousness might be said to be Hardy's central concern in his writing, from *Desperate Remedies* through *The Dynasts*. Hardy's interest in consciousness has not gone unnoticed among critics, who approach the topic from a literary point of view.[35] What has until recently been less remarked upon is the way in which Hardy's representations of consciousness are grounded in a consideration of the psychological, medical, and philosophical

[32] Alfred Binet, 'Mental Imagery', *Fortnightly Review* 52 (1892): 95–104, 97.

[33] Binet, 104.

[34] See Elaine Scarry, 'Work and the Body in Hardy and Other Nineteenth-Century Novelists', *Representations* 3 (Summer 1983), 91: 'Human consciousness is always, for Hardy, embodied human consciousness: hence all states of being—not just overt, physical activity but even what appear to be forms of physical inactivity like reading or perceiving or feeling—inevitably entail reciprocal jostling with the world'. For other fine discussions of Hardy and the body see J.B. Bullen, *The Expressive Eye: Fiction and Perception in the Work of Thomas Hardy* (Oxford: Oxford University Press, 1986), on 19th-century theories of perception and William Cohen, *Embodied: Victorian Literature and the Senses* (Minneapolis: University of Minnesota Press, 2009), on Hardy's 'material account of perception and interiority' (88) in his representations of faces.

[35] Ian Gregor, *The Great Web: The Form of Hardy's Major Fiction* (London: Faber and Faber, 1974), for instance, discusses Hardy's 'rendering of a consciousness which both observes the natural world and is itself an inescapable part of all that it contemplates' and Hardy's 'fresh awareness of the recording consciousness' (143). J. Hillis Miller, in *The Form of Victorian Fiction: Thackeray, Dickens, Trollope, George Eliot, Meredith, and Hardy* (Notre Dame, IN: University of Notre Dame Press, 1968), considers Hardy's narrator as 'general consciousness', arguing that for Hardy, 'to be conscious is to be detached. Consciousness is a passive power of observation which cuts a man off from everything' (61). George Levine, in *Dying to Know: Scientific Epistemology and Narrative in Victorian England* (Chicago: University of Chicago Press, 2002), regards Hardy as Cartesian in his mind/body dualism, and concludes that for Hardy consciousness is almost always mistaken. Levine maintain that Hardy believes that the 'ideal is all there is for human consciousness' (201) and so turns to human creation and art. The latter point is related to my own sense of Hardy's valuation of subjective experience.

discussions of mind that were raging in the years in which he wrote.[36] Hardy's notebook entries manifest his intense interest in those matters. He quotes, often extensively, from nearly every prominent figure in the debates, and we can get a sense of the views that Hardy found most compelling by the weighting of what he includes in his notebooks and the ideas that make their way into his literary texts. I want to insist, however, that Hardy does not promote a coherent view on the mind but instead rethinks narrative and the representation of human character in light of ideas explored in the new psychology.

Hardy regards consciousness as an aspect of the natural world, a development of complex physical organization (a view shared by Herbert Spencer and Henry Maudsley among other prominent Victorian writers on psychology). More than once Hardy characterizes consciousness as a kind of evolutionary mistake:

> A woeful fact—that the human race is too extremely developed for its corporeal conditions, the nerves being evolved to an activity abnormal in such an environment. Even the higher animals are in excess in this respect. It may be questioned if Nature, or what we call Nature, so far back as when she crossed the line from invertebrates to vertebrates, did not exceed her mission. This planet does not supply the material for happiness to higher existences. Other planets may, though one can hardly see how.[37]

Consciousness is an effect of neural processes. What is most important to Hardy here is that consciousness gives rise to feelings and imaginings that are out of accord with the scientific reality of the world we inhabit, and for that reason brings pain and is to be regretted. Elsewhere he writes: 'The mystery of consciousness having appeared in the world when apparently it would have done much better by keeping away is one of the many involved in the whole business [of existence].'[38] The distance between scientific reality and subjective conscious experience leads to his contention that the mental cannot be described in terms of the language of physical science. Much of his work dwells on

---

[36] For criticism attentive to the psychological and philosophical contexts of Hardy's thought on consciousness, see G. Glen Wickens's analysis of *The Dynasts* as Hardy's exploration of the new monism in *Thomas Hardy, Monism, and the Carnival Tradition: The One and the Many in The Dynasts* (Toronto: University of Toronto Press, 2002). In an insightful essay, 'Tree and Machine: *The Woodlanders*', in *Critical Approaches to the Fiction of Thomas Hardy*, ed. Dale Kramer (London: Macmillan Press, 1979): 116–34, Mary Jacobus claims that Hardy is '[c]ommitted to a Spinozistic monism' and writes that 'Hardy shows particular interest at this moment in a subject of topical concern, the attempt to establish mind or consciousness in the context of scientific rationalism' (129). Tim Armstrong, in *Haunted Hardy: Poetry, History, Memory* (New York: Palgrave, 2000), considers Hardy's relation to Henry Maudsley, W.K. Clifford, and others. In 'Science and Art in *Jude the Obscure*', in *The Novels of Thomas Hardy*, ed. Anne Smith (London: Vision Press, 1979), 126–44. Patricia Gallivan argues for Maudsley's influence on *Jude*. See also Shuttleworth's fine work on Hardy and child psychology in *Jude* in *The Mind of the Child: Child Development in Literature, Science, and Medicine, 1830–1900* (Oxford: Oxford University Press, 2010).

[37] Florence Emily Hardy, *The Early Life of Thomas Hardy 1840–91* (London: Macmillan Co., 1928), 285–86.

[38] *The Collected Letters of Thomas Hardy*, ed. Richard Little Purdy and Michael Millgate, 7 vols. (Oxford: Clarendon Press, 1978–98), 5: 153.

that issue, but it is *The Woodlanders*, published in 1887, when the issues were discussed pervasively in the periodicals, that best presents the problem of reconciling objective and subjective perspectives on the mind, in its deliberations on the brain in relation to the world that consciousness constructs.

In the years leading up to and surrounding the writing of *The Woodlanders*, Hardy considers closely a range of positions on the mind emerging from the new physiological psychology, taking up questions concerning the relationship between the body and the mind, the physical understanding of states of consciousness, volition and freewill, and the distinction between humans and automata. In his literary notebooks, he quotes George Henry Lewes from an 1878 article in the *Fortnightly Review* on the relation between the mental and the physical:

> Physiology began to disclose that all the mental processes were (mathematically speaking) *functions* of physical processes, i.e.—varying with the variations of bodily states; & this was declared enough to banish for ever the conception of a Soul, except as a term simply expressing certain functions.[39]

As Lewes has it, the new science demonstrates that there is no separate, non-physical substance—a soul, and that the mental emerges from the physical, a view that Hardy accepts.

In Hardy's notes and diary entries, we see him considering theories on how consciousness emerges from the physical and the relationship that exists between the two. After taking notes from the comparative psychologist George Romanes's 1886 *Contemporary Review* article, 'The World as Eject', in which Romanes opposes W.K. Clifford's non-theistic views on matter and mind, Hardy adds the following: '[QY. How much complication is necessary to produce consciousness]'.[40] Again in 1886 he writes a long notebook entry on Thomas Huxley's *Fortnightly Review* article, 'Science and Morals', in which Huxley famously denies that he is a materialist dispite his scientific naturalism; Hardy quotes Huxley's pronouncement: 'It seems to me pretty plain that [beyond force and matter] there is a third thing in the universe, to wit, consciousness.'[41] Consciousness remains something special on that view, something that appears to be over and above the material regardless of his physicalist stance, again a position that seems largely in accord with Hardy's nonsystematic view.

Theories of unconscious reflex action gave rise to anxieties about the role of volition in human behaviour, as Lorraine Daston and Roger Smith have shown. Hardy alludes more than once to the debates over conscious automatism—the view upon which consciousness is merely a by-product of the physical—which were carried on with fervour in the 1880s following Thomas Huxley's promotion of the theory:

---

[39] *The Literary Notebooks of Thomas Hardy*, ed. Lennert A. Bjork, 2 vols. (New York: New York University Press, 1985), 1: 899.

[40] Hardy, *Literary Notebooks*, 1: 1383.

[41] Hardy, *Literary Notebooks*, 1: 1399.

> *Another hypothesis* … represents mind as never interfering in the course of physical events, but at best representing a mere inner aspect of the outward frame of things—a sort of backwater from the stream of physical forces.[42]

It is a theory that fully denies the efficacy of consciousness and makes volition an illusion. In the *Life and Work of Thomas Hardy* (notoriously composed by Hardy but attributed to his wife Florence), he includes an entry that projects the writing of a work that shows: 'Action mostly automatic, reflex movement, etc. Not the result of what is called *motive*, though always ostensibly so, even to the actors' own consciousness.'[43] The question of the role of will in human action is one that haunts Hardy's writing, leading of course ultimately to *The Dynasts*. Think of the many descriptions of characters who act 'mechanically', 'automatically', and 'unconsciously' in Hardy's fiction. Attentive to mental operations, Hardy's narrator also reminds us that actors are often unaware of the contents of their own minds. That consciousness itself cannot deliver accurate knowledge of the self is an idea that becomes central in later Victorian fiction. The observer who knows the truth about the workings of the mind is no longer, as on the common-sense view, the inward looking I. If in the earlier philosophical tradition, our knowledge of our own minds was never doubted, the scientific psychologist denies that one can get an accurate view of one's own mental life by introspection. Authority shifts from the first-person to the third-person observer, when the science of mind temporarily vanquishes introspection.

A comparable formal shift is reflected in Hardy's novels in the often noted fact of his infrequent use of free indirect discourse and his avoidance of the introspective mode, at a time when novelists were widely adopting those innovations in point of view. Free indirect discourse both registers the first-person perspective while at the same time distancing it by maintaining the effect of a third-person view that renders that perspective questionable. It might, then, be regarded as a narrative mode that begins to undercut the authority of the inward looking self, at a moment at which the reliability of introspection in providing evidence for psychological science was increasingly challenged. Yet Hardy only occasionally grants even a suspect fully subjective viewpoint. He is far from unconcerned with representing the consciousnesses of his characters, but his narrator typically separates himself from that interiority, using narratorial report when describing characters' minds, and notoriously offering a detached, distanced, or disillusioned perspective on the thoughts and sense perceptions he describes.[44] Hardy—like George Eliot elsewhere—can remind us of his character Marty in *The Woodlanders* that 'her

---

[42] Hardy, *Literary Notebooks*, 1: 1282.

[43] *Early Life*, 191.

[44] J. Hillis Miller has influentially discussed Hardy's detached narrator in *Thomas Hardy, Distance and Desire* (Cambridge, MA: Harvard University Press, 1970). Miller argues that both Hardy's narrator and his characters view their minds as one views something external, 'not as something known from the inside with special intimacy…His self-awareness and that of his characters are always inextricably involved in their awareness of the world. Their minds are turned habitually outward' (1).

own existence, and not Mr. Melbury's, was the centre of Marty's consciousness'.[45] But only rarely does the narrative grant direct access to that mind, only rarely does Hardy's prose slip into the point of view of that consciousness. More frequently, consciousness is described and analysed from without, as in this description of Giles Winterborne: 'Had he regarded his inner life spectacularly...he might have felt pride in the discernment of a somewhat rare power in him—that of keeping not only judgment, but emotion, suspended in difficult cases. But he noted it not' (31). Giles, the narrator pointedly states, does not look inward into a theatre of the mind, does not directly examine his consciousness. The narrator is left to analyse that consciousness and to describe it from a third-person viewpoint, and he frequently gestures at a character's interiority through descriptions of actions and behaviour, as though discerning another's mind from external signs, as we are normally constrained to do. Similarly, critics have noted Hardy's use of tactics that work to undercut narrative omniscience, for instance, in his frequent use of a hypothetical embodied viewer or in his use of a narrator who expresses uncertainty about his characters' thoughts.[46]

Perhaps the most striking connection between Hardy and the new psychology is one that has as yet gone unrecognized: the very first page that Hardy inserted into his literary notebooks as he began to compile them in 1876 is a two-sided leaf comprised of notes and drawings that he completed in 1863, with the heading 'Diagrams Shewing Human Passions, Mind, & Character'. Lennard A. Bjork in his edition of *The Literary Notebooks* attributes the ideas Hardy incorporates into the diagrams solely to the French socialist Charles Fourier, based on Hardy's parenthetical note 'See Fourier', written on one corner of the verso page of diagrams. But in fact, all but one of the diagrams represent ideas in Alexander Bain's 1861 text, *On the Study of Character*, and the notes that precede the diagrams contain headings taken directly from that work, and which reflect Bain's analysis of character.[47] Bain's central terms are 'intellect', 'emotion', and 'action' or 'energy', the latter of which Bain sometimes refers to as 'will', the term that Hardy adopts in his tree diagrams. Only the first diagram alone represents Fourier's ideas (and their organization reflects Bain's discussion of Fourier at the start of *On the Study of Character*). While Fourier's thinking inspired the tree diagrams—he presented his own theories in that form, as Bain explains—after drawing one tree representing Fourier's views, Hardy borrows the representational system in order to sketch out Bain's contrasting ideas on character in his 'science of mind'. The notes and the diagrams exhibit a careful reading of Bain's text, and it would be fair to say that Hardy is influenced strongly by that early reading of Bain, in his views on the relations between will, emotion (passion), and intellect in the representation of character, terms which recur in Hardy's work from first to last.

[45] Thomas Hardy, *The Woodlanders* [1887] (New York: Oxford University Press, 2005), 19. Subsequent citations appear in the text.

[46] See David Lodge's important article 'Thomas Hardy and Cinamatographic Form', *Novel; A Forum on Fiction* 7, no. 3 (Spring, 1974): 246–54.

[47] Alexander Bain, *On the Study of Character, Including an Estimate of Phrenology* (London: Parker, Son, and Bourne, 1861).

Hardy's fiction, then, was shaped by the debates on mind, although he more than once asserted that he did not hold a coherent position on the science of the mind and was a literary artist rather than a philosophical writer, as here in a late letter:

> A friend of mine writes objecting to what he calls my 'philosophy' (though I have no philosophy—merely what I have often explained to be only a confused heap of impressions, like those of a bewildered child at a conjuring show)... [Y]ou see that the assumption that intelligent beings arise from the combined action of unintelligent forces is sufficiently probable for imaginative writing, and I have never attempted scientific. It is my misfortune that people will treat all my mood-dictated writing as a single scientific theory.[48]

Unconstrained by the necessity of holding to a unified theory, Hardy says that it is the imaginative, the aesthetic—that subjective view produced by consciousness—that is his mode. Yet he contextualizes his rendering of subjective experience—what philosophers currently call qualia or the 'what it is like to me'—by also representing the 'scientific' view. In his notes from Romanes's 'World as Eject', Hardy copies and alters one of Romanes's sentences as follows: 'The objective explan [scientific] given by Helmholtz of the effects of a sonata on a human brain [e.g. number of vibrations, &c.] was no doubt perfectly sound within its category; but the ejective explan of these same effects which is given by a musician is equally sound within *its* category.'[49] Romanes attempts in the essay to show that his monistic theory of mind allows simultaneously for an objectivist perspective on mind presented in physical terms and an ejective one (here he adopts Clifford's term) involving the projection of subjective mental states, which Romanes calls 'hyper-physical';[50] both modes are interpretations of the same reality and both valid in their own terms. The word 'scientific' (a descriptive term that Romanes uses nowhere in the essay) to gloss 'objective explanation' is Hardy's own addition to the quotation. Hardy carries out an experiment in representing these dual aspects of mind, 'material and mental' (20), from the scientific and the subjective points of view, in *The Woodlanders*, in its depictions of the brain and the conscious experience it produces.

The novel's heroine, Grace Melbury, begins her ill-fated romance with Edred Fitzpiers, when she calls on him to ask him to release her old servant, Grammer, from a bargain she has made to bequeath her brain to him for study after her death. The doctor, 'a gentleman fond of science, and philosophy, and poetry' (28), in his physiological mood is interested in examining her brain, because it is large for a woman's (ostensibly based on her skull

---

[48] Florence Emily Hardy, *The Later Years of Thomas Hardy 1892–1928* (London: Macmillan Co., 1930), 219.

[49] The original, 'The World as an Eject', *Contemporary Review* 50 (July 1886): 44–59, 58, reads: 'The objective explanation which was given (as we supposed) by Helmholtz of the effects produced on the human brain by hearing a sonata, was no doubt perfectly sound within its own category; but the ejective explanation of these same effects which is given by a musician is equally sound within *its* category.' For Hardy's version, see *Literary Notebooks*, 1: 1383

[50] 'The World as an Eject', 58.

size?). Fitzpiers, in agreement with contemporary physiology, mistakenly believes that '[a] woman's is usually four ounces less than a man's' (46); but Grammer's brain is man sized, according to the doctor. Consenting to dissolve his agreement with Grammer, he invites Grace to take a look at a sample of what may be a diseased brain on a microscope slide: 'She applied her eye, and saw the usual circle of light patterned all over with a cellular tissue of some indescribable sort' (119). When Fitzpiers explains that the tissue is from the brain of John South, one of the woodlanders recently deceased, Grace's surprise induces laughter in Fitzpier and then a protest. 'Here am I . . . endeavoring to carry on simultaneously the study of physiology and transcendental philosophy, the material world and the ideal, so as to discover if possible a point of contrast between them; and your finer sense is quite offended!' (119). Although Fitzpiers is not a sympathetic character, his project of simultaneously studying the physical—brain matter—and the ideal can be connected to Hardy's own thought, at least to a degree. Hardy's notebooks and his *Life* include entries related to his own shuttling between materialism and idealism; at one moment his narratives are grounded in a Darwinian world view, while at the next the ideal trumps material reality for Hardy. The *Early Life* includes this diary snippet written at the time at which he was composing *The Woodlanders*: 'I was thinking a night or two ago that people are somnambulists—that the material is not the real—only the visible, the real being invisible optically.'[51] Drawing again on a concern of the new psychology in his allusion to somnambulism, a central topic in the 19th-century investigation of consciousness and volition, Hardy reverts to a Platonic idealism that imagines that the physical world we know is a creation of the mind, behind which stands the real, undetectable by the senses. Unlike Collins who has firmly resisted an idealist conception of the real through his representation of Lucilla by insisting that knowledge is always embodied, Hardy in some of his moods abandons the view that knowledge is sensory, suggesting instead that our knowledge of the real is purely rational. Such a position is not far from that which Hardy attributes to Fitzpiers, who 'was in a distinct degree scientific, being ready and zealous to interrogate all physical manifestations but primarily he was an idealist' (120).

Fitzpiers seems to entertain briefly the idea that an examination of the physical matter might reveal the connection between brain states and diseased consciousness. (Hardy quotes Maudsley's 1886 text *Natural Causes and Supernatural Seemings* in his literary notes: 'In hallucination & illusions a certain tract of the brain has taken on a morbid function.')[52] The narrator tells us in an offhand way, however, that Fitzpiers soon wearies of his investigation of the fragment of South's brain, 'which perhaps was not so interesting under the microscope as might have been expected from the importance of that organ in life' (120). Yet it is the novel's attention to both South's brain, as physical object, and the mentality to which it gives rise, that best conveys the movement between the objective and the subjective views that Hardy undertakes to represent, particularly as it is rendered in the complex image of the tree, the object of South's delusion, which with

[51] *Early Life*, 243.
[52] *Literary Notebooks*, 1: 1505.

its multiple associations concentrates a range of views on the mind. South, who believes that a tree outside his door is threatening his life, is diagnosed by Fitzpiers, in his physician role, as a case of aberrant psychology. Grammer's anxieties about selling her brain ('not my soul—my body' [46] as she explains) are also read by Fitzpiers as morbid delusion: 'Grammer's is a nervous disease too—how singular' (119). When Fitzpiers orders the tree to be cut down, wrongly believing it will relieve South of the worries that are destroying his health, South instead dies. Either he was correct about the essential connection between the tree and himself; or the novel endorses the inseparability of the mental and the physical, showing that South's belief strongly affects his body.

But South's brain and the consciousness it produces work on several levels simultaneously. South's beliefs about the tree confuse the usual distinction between sentient and non-sentient creatures, between mind and matter. Bain begins his seminal work *The Senses and the Intellect* by remarking: 'A tree, which possesses extension, is a part of the object world; a pleasure, a volition, a thought, are facts of the subject world, or of mind proper.'[53] For South, such a clear division is impossible. His tree is not only a part of the object world, but also feels and acts, that is, possesses mentality. As his daughter Marty explains: 'The shape of [the tree] seems to haunt him like an evil spirit. He says that it is exactly his own age, that it has got human sense, and sprouted up when he was born on purpose to rule him and keep him as its slave' (93). South projects consciousness into the tree, accepting both that the tree has volition and that there is a causal connection between the tree's consciousness and his own. His convictions bring to mind James Frazer's emphasis on tree worship in his anthropology, particularly in *The Golden Bough* (1890). Hardy records his reading of it in 1891, and he encountered related folklore in his own experience. Frazer was later to write that Hardy had described to him an incident in which Hardy was told that the reason the trees outside his house 'did not thrive, was that he looked at them before breakfast on an empty stomach. He told me this himself.'[54] Hardy also took notes from his reading of Herbert Spencer on primitive people in 1886, and in his literary notebook copied Spencer's borrowings on animism from Edward Tylor's 1871 *Primitive Culture*.[55] It may appear, then, that Hardy sought to show, along with many Victorian intellectuals, that a central error of primitive consciousness is the confused attribution of its own state to non-sentient things, and that he derived his ideas from work in the new anthropology.[56]

But South's is also the view of the poet, that is, the subjective and imaginative perspective that Hardy says belongs to the literary artist. Havelock Ellis finds in

[53] Alexander Bain, *The Senses and the Intellect*, 3rd edn (New York: D. Appleton and Company, 1874), 1.

[54] Martin Ray, *Thomas Hardy Remembered* (Aldershot: Ashgate, 2007), 64–65. Hardy related the piece of folklore to his friend Edward Clodd in a letter on 30 October 1896, Thomas Hardy, *The Collected Letters*, 2: 136.

[55] *Literary Notebooks*, 1: 1336.

[56] See Andrew D. Radford, *Thomas Hardy and the Survivals of Time* (Aldershot: Ashgate, 2003) and Michael A. Zeitler, *Representations of Culture: Thomas Hardy's Wessex & Victorian Anthropology* (New York: Peter Lang, 2007) for readings of *The Woodlanders* in relation to anthropology.

Hardy's perspective something akin to the primitive outlook, writing in 1883 in the *Westminster Review*: 'It seems scarcely fanciful even to find in it some lingering echoes of the old tree-worship.'[57] Hardy often lends sentience to his trees. Notably in *The Woodlanders*, he speaks of 'the vocalized sorrows of the trees' (15) and tree trunks appear to be locked in 'mesmeric passivity', their [h]elpless immobility…combined with intense consciousness' (150). The personification here is the stuff of poetry, the emotive seemings of the human mind that Hardy values despite the pain consciousness brings. Hardy was later to write that the young Jude 'could scarcely bear to see trees cut down or lopped, from a fancy that it hurt them';[58] like Jude, the overly sensitive Hardy also projected consciousness and the capacity to feel pain onto the insentient.

In his usual manner of shuttling between views, Hardy also incorporates something akin to a scientific perspective in his representation of tree life, with the Darwinian associations of the description of the woods in this well-known passage:

> Here, as everywhere, the Unfulfilled Intention, which makes life what it is, was as obvious as it could be among the depraved crowds of a city slum. The leaf was deformed, the curve was crippled, the taper was interrupted; the lichen ate the vigor of the stalk, and the ivy slowly strangled to death the promising sapling. (48)

Of course, the gloom and the intensity of the human valuations—'depraved', 'deformed', 'crippled'—remove the passage from 'objectivist' discourse, but the description is meant to express the hard reality of the natural world, although it is apparent that for Hardy even the scientific must be refracted through the seemings of human consciousness. The dismal naturalist view recurs in Hardy's poem 'In a Wood: See *The Woodlanders*' (written in 1887, revised and published in *Wessex Poems*, 1898), where nature is again represented as brutal:

> Heart-halt and spirit-lame,
>   City-opprest,
> Unto this wood I came
>   As to a nest;
> Dreaming that sylvan peace
> Offered the harrowed ease—
> Nature a soft release
>   From men's unrest.
>
> But, having entered in,
>   Great growths and small
> Show them to men akin –
>   Combatants all!
> Sycamore shoulders oak,
> Bines the slim sapling yoke,

---

⁵⁷ Havelock Ellis, 'Thomas Hardy's Novels', *The Westminster Review* 119 (April 1, 1883): 334–64, 362.
⁵⁸ *Jude the Obscure* (Oxford: Oxford University Press, 2005), 11.

Ivy-spun halters choke
Elms stout and tall.[59]

Nature carries out the survival of the fittest. There is no community between non-sentient tree and human, and there is no comfort in nature for the speaker of the poem, no 'grace' found in the trees, just as, in more corporeal form, Giles Winterborne learns while lopping off the 'shuddering' branches of South's tree that there will be no Grace for him.

South's tree, then, works to crystallize multiple aspects of Hardy's exploration of mind, physical and mental. As I have said, discussions of animism were to be found in the work of the great anthropologists. But I believe that Hardy's use of the ideas was most strongly influenced once again by a psychologist, this time James Sully, close friend of Leslie Stephen in the years in which Stephen was editor (and Hardy was serializing his novels) at *Cornhill Magazine*. (Hardy describes Leslie Stephen as 'the man whose philosophy was to influence his own for many years, indeed, more than that of any other contemporary.'[60] Hardy began writing *The Woodlanders*, with the intent of serializing it in *Cornhill*, soon after the success of *Far from the Madding Crowd*, but, as is well known, Stephen began to worry about the propriety of Hardy's work, and the publishing association ceased after the serialization of *The Hand of Ethelberta*. The final number of *The Hand* was run alongside Sully's anonymously published article, 'Poetic Imagination and Primitive Conception' in July 1876. There can be little doubt that Hardy was influenced in his early thinking on consciousness, animation, and imaginative writing by that article.[61]

Sully's careful examination of mental processes—dreaming, abstraction, projections of consciousness—is echoed in Hardy's *Woodlanders* depictions of his characters' minds. Sully comments on the mental operations involved in animism, explaining that his use of the term goes beyond Tylor's in *Primitive Culture*: 'In this extended meaning animism would denote the habit of thought, so prevalent in early stages of culture, of conceiving all existence as compounded of the bodily and the spiritual. Thus all inanimate objects are supposed by the primitive man to be inspired with conscious feeling and will.'[62] He goes on to describe what he takes to be the 'anthropomorphic bent of the poetic mind': 'Heine, for example, is continually spiritualizing trees.'[63] Sully ultimately ties this tendency of 'imaginative minds' to transmute 'the operations of conscious mind and lifeless matter'[64] to the human ability to do precisely what the realist novel does, enter into the

[59]   *Wessex Poems* (New York: Harper and Brothers, 1898), ll. 9–24.

[60]   *Early Life*, 100.

[61]   Hardy does not mention Sully's article in his literary notebooks. There are no entries whatsoever for material published between July and October of 1876. We know that Hardy burned many of his notes at Max Gate, and we also know that Hardy did some cribbing when composing his novels and tended to obscure his sources, after some critics of his earliest works suggested plagiarism

[62]   James Sully, 'Poetic Imagination and Primitive Conception', *Cornhill Magazine* 34 (1876): 294–306, 295.

[63]   Sully, 'Poetic Imagination', 298, 295.

[64]   Sully, 'Poetic Imagination', 296.

feelings of those who do possess consciousness, which we are unable to perceive directly. For Sully, that imaginative aspect of human mentality is an evolutionary development: 'Consequently it may be said that the delight of poetic contemplation springs from the satisfaction of a deeply rooted mental impulse, a radical instinct which scientific culture may obscure, but can never wholly eradicate.'[65] That 'instinct' may not accord with the scientific view, but it is an endowment of the mind that is crucial for aesthetics. In late 1890 Hardy writes that he received a response from Edward Clodd, friend and anthropologist, to his question 'why the superstitions of a remote Asiatic and a Dorset labourer are the same'. Clodd explained that the: 'attitude of man … at corresponding levels of culture, before like phenomena, is pretty much the same, your Dorset peasants representing the persistence of the barbaric idea which confuses persons and things'. Hardy adds this note following his quotation of Clodd in the *Life*: '(This "barbaric idea which confuses persons and things" is, by the way, also common to the highest imaginative genius—that of the poet)'.[66] His note repeats Sully's argument and also reminds us of Hardy's own South-like propensities. More than a decade later, Hardy was to write to Clodd that the 'theory of consciousness in plants is an arresting one: but I have always known it intuitively, & hate maiming trees on that account'.[67] The letter expresses Hardy's longing to close the gap between the world that science gives us and the world that consciousness creates.

Hardy's treatment of the issues demonstrates that his interest resides not in the old debate over the material versus the supernatural origin of self, but in a newer view, one that maintains dualist leanings despite its grounding in naturalism, and that was developed in the context of the rise of scientific psychology in the 19th century. It is a compromise position, which seeks to hold on to something special in consciousness. While accepting that consciousness can no longer be regarded as evidence of an immortal soul, it continues to regard it as the bearer of a unique, subjective experience. For Hardy, that experience is largely opposed to scientific truth, but nevertheless prized.

The influence of the new psychology ultimately had two effects on the novel. The first was to move literature away from the direction of supernatural accounts of the mind and self and to bring to it a concern with the mechanism of the mind. The second, a backlash that followed, returned fiction to an interest in the subjective realm of the mind. If, on the one hand, the new scientific psychology threatened to diminish the value of consciousness by leading towards a thoroughly physicalist and behaviourist theory of mind, on the other hand it opened the way to a new emphasis on individual subjective experience, intensifying interiority in stream of consciousness writing that works to create the effect of leaving out the third person altogether. Thus Virginia Woolf was to denigrate the Victorian novelists that she found to be overly 'materialist' in her 1919 essay on 'Modern Novels', calling for an imaginative writing that banishes the objective perspective: 'Let us record the atoms as they fall upon the mind in the order in which they fall, let us trace the pattern, however disconnected and incoherent in appearance,

---

[65] Sully, 'Poetic Imagination', 299.
[66] *Later Years*, 27.
[67] *Letters*, 3: 331.

which each sight or incident scores upon the consciousness.'[68] In so doing, she leaves behind Huxley's scientific worry—the how—to focus on the rendering of the subjective experience of consciousness alone.

SUGGESTED READING

Bain, Alexander. *On the Study of Character, Including an Estimate of Phrenology*. London: Parker, Son, and Bourne, 1861.

Chesselden, Will. 'An Account of Some Observations Made by a Young Gentleman, Who Was Born Blind, or Lost His Sight so Early, That He Had no Remembrance of Ever Having Seen, and Was Couch d between 13 and 14 Years of Age'. *Philosophical Transactions* 35, no. 402 (1728): 447–50.

Collins, Wilkie. *Poor Miss Finch* [1872]. Edited with an Introduction by Catherine Peters. New York: Oxford, 1995.

Danziger, Kurt. *Naming the Mind: How Psychology Found Its Language*. London: Sage, 1997.

Hardy, Thomas. *The Literary Notebooks of Thomas Hardy*. Edited by Lennart A. Bjork. 2 vols. New York: New York University Press, 1985.

——. *The Woodlanders* [1887]. New York: Oxford University Press, 2005.

Morgan, Michael J. *Molyneux's Question: Vision, Touch and the Philosophy of Perception*. New York: Cambridge University Press, 1977.

Nagel, Thomas. 'What Is It Like to Be a Bat?' *The Philosophical Review* 83 (1974): 435–50.

Rylance, Rick. *Victorian Psychology and British Culture: 1850–1880*. New York: Oxford University Press, 2000.

Scarry, Elaine. 'Work and the Body in Hardy and Other Nineteenth-Century Novelists'. *Representations* 3 (Summer 1983): 90–123.

Shuttleworth, Sally. *Charlotte Brontë and Victorian Psychology*. Cambridge: Cambridge University Press, 1996.

——. *Mind of the Child: Child Development in Literature, Science, and Medicine, 1830–1900*. Oxford: Oxford University Press, 2010.

Taylor, Jenny Bourne. *In the Secret Theatre of the Home: Wilkie Collins, Sensation, Narrative, and Nineteenth-Century Psychology*. London: Routledge, 1988.

Taylor, Jenny Bourne and Sally Shuttleworth, eds. *Embodied Selves: An Anthology of Psychological Texts 1830–1890*. Oxford: Oxford University Press, 2003.

Wells, H.G. 'The Country of the Blind'. *Strand Magazine* 27 (April 1904), 401–15.

——. 'The Story of the Late Mr. Elvesham'. *Idler* 9, no. 4 (May 1896), 487–96.

Winter, Alison. *Mesmerized: Powers of Mind in Victorian Britain*. Chicago: University of Chicago Press, 1998.

[68] Virginia Woolf, 'Modern Novels', *Times Literary Supplement* (10 April 1919): 189–90.

24

THE VICTORIAN NOVEL
AND THE LAW

JAN-MELISSA SCHRAMM

The Victorian novel, like the law, was drawn towards regular engagement with criminality. Both discourses sought to probe its aetiology, its prevention, and its punishment, entering thereby into a dynamic relationship which left an indelible impression upon both disciplines at mid-century. With Elizabeth Gaskell's first novel *Mary Barton* (1848) as my point of departure, in this essay I will sketch out, firstly, the appeal of transgression for the literary author, the implications of the novel's transformation of the formal elements of the law (particularly the trial and the reception of evidence), the novel's treatment of the rise of the legal professional, its responses to the growth of democracy, and finally, its representations of the civil law. My investigations of these expansive interdisciplinary areas are of necessity brief, and my analysis is centred upon each discipline's commitment to ethical thought—how and why both the novel and the law invite us to experience vicariously the lives of others.

I. THE TRIAL OF JEM WILSON: A CASE STUDY

Towards the end of *Mary Barton*, the virtuous Jem Wilson is tried for a murder that he did not commit. Lest her readers are misled by Jem's procedurally enforced silence to suspect that his conduct on this occasion may not have been consistent with his good character, Gaskell offers us the following assurance of Jem's worthiness as an object of narrative sympathy, in the form of a letter that Jem passes to his friend Job Legh as the trial opens:

DEAR FRIEND,—I thank you for your goodness in finding me a lawyer, but lawyers can do no good to me, whatever they may do to other people. But I am not the less obliged to you, dear friend. I foresee things will go against me—and no wonder. If

I was a juryman I should say the man was guilty as had as much evidence brought against him as may be brought against me tomorrow. So it's no blame to them if they do. But, Job Legh, I think I need not tell you that I am as guiltless in this matter as the babe unborn, although it is not in my power to prove it. If I did not believe that you thought me innocent, I could not write as I do now to tell you my wishes. You'll not forget that they are the words of a man shortly to die.[1]

Gaskell's management of Jem's defence tells us much about the appeal of the legal 'case' for Victorian authors, and an elucidation of the multivalent functions of this brief passage will introduce the formal features of narrative which are most tellingly illuminated by a study of literature's engagement with the law. Take, for instance, the trope of wrongful accusation. The trope allows for an exaggerated expression of innocence (borrowed perhaps from theatrical melodramas and the earlier novels of Samuel Richardson), and serves in structural terms to stimulate the detective work that must then be undertaken to prove the solidity of Jem's alibi and to probe the affinities between his character and his alleged conduct. That there will be both correlations and disjunctions between what the law and the novel can tell us about a protagonist's character invites us to consider the complex roles of motive and intention in the execution of morally charged actions: like the law, the novel depends upon the arrangement and interpretation of certain types of evidence, and to uncover their shared rhetorical history—their mutual commitment to the language of proof, fact, doubt, judgement—affords particular insight into the discursive competition which characterized the novel's relation with the law in the Victorian period. The representation of legal themes and forms in fiction brings into focus questions of ethics, politics, and justice in both the public and the private spheres, as well as the aesthetic choices which serve most effectively to embody them. In what follows, I will focus particularly on how Jem's imagining himself a juryman allows Gaskell to model novelistically both an improved legal process and a better society. The vicarious experiences that *Mary Barton* produces through the murder trial and its aftermath suggest not only the competitive relations between the novel and the law, but also the way the novel positioned itself to participate in debates about the future of England more generally.

To return, then, to this passage from *Mary Barton*—there is a certain rhetorical bravado here, as well as a nostalgia for the plain speaking of the untutored Protestant mechanic whose artless tales are often privileged in English fiction for their 'sincerity' (an ambiguity which suggests Gaskell's attentiveness to, and perhaps ambivalence about, the rhetorical sophistication of fictional advocacy, too). But perhaps most importantly, the letter also draws attention to, and, indeed, undertakes, a double act of substitution: just as the jury must stand in judgement of Jem, imagining his motives and reconstructing his intentions in his final quarrelsome exchanges with Harry Carson, he has the generosity of mind to substitute himself for the jurors and acquit them of

---

[1] Elizabeth Gaskell, *Mary Barton* [1848] (Oxford: Oxford University Press, 1991), 373–74.

malice in their anticipated conviction of him. As she renders visible the complex means by which judgement is passed, Gaskell gestures towards the mutual accommodations on which social concord should ideally be based: a civilized society depends in large part on a moral education in which, in Adam Smith's analysis, we learn to 'change places in fancy' with another.[2] Although the imaginative suffering of the jurors in their apprehension of Jem's plight can never rival that of Jem's own, some correspondence can nevertheless be achieved which should foster in turn the development of mutual sensibilities and communal understanding. As Jem appeals to the second-person perspective of the neighbourly Job Legh, he thus performs the sympathetic substitution on which wider social relations should be based: he divests himself of an obsessive preoccupation with the particulars of his own case and moves towards a commitment to the general good. As Smith observed in his *Theory of Moral Sentiments* (1759):

> In order to produce this concord, as nature teaches the spectators to assume the circumstances of the person principally concerned, so she teaches this last in some measure to assume those of the spectators. As they are continually placing themselves in his situation, and thence conceiving emotions similar to what he feels; so he is as constantly placing himself in theirs, and thence conceiving some degree of that coolness about his own fortune, with which he is sensible that they will view it. As they are constantly considering what they themselves would feel, if they actually were the sufferers, so he is as constantly led to imagine in what manner he would be affected if he was only one of the spectators of his own situation. As their sympathy makes them look at it, in some measure, with his eyes, so his sympathy makes him look at it, in some measure, with theirs...[3]

In a sense, trial process fails in *Mary Barton* to elicit the truth—the wrong man is accused (albeit not convicted), the real murderer dies before his guilt can be publicly disclosed, counsel commit all the rhetorical excesses which aroused such public ire during the so-called licence of advocacy controversy of the 1840s, and Mary's testimony (of love rather than of 'fact') stages a displacement of empiricism by the domains of affect and sentiment.[4] Given that Gaskell is clearly well informed regarding the controversies surrounding criminal advocacy in the period, the novel could be read as a dramatization of the defeat of legal methodologies at the hand of a literary form that offers us fuller and more sympathetic accounts of individual human behaviour: as Mary says to Jem after his acquittal, the wrongful accusation should never had arisen—'They might have known thee better, Jem.'[5] It is the genre of the novel which offers such full knowledge of character: legal knowledge, based on inference, will always be at best partial. Yet the representation of character in the novel is also dependent on evidence, and

---

[2] Adam Smith, *The Theory of Moral Sentiments* [1759], ed. by Knud Haakonssen (Cambridge: Cambridge University Press, 2002; repr. 2007), 12.

[3] Smith, 27–28.

[4] See Hilary Schor, 'Show-Trials: Character, Conviction, and the Law in Victorian Fiction', *Cardozo Studies in Law and Literature* 11, no. 2 (1999): 179–95.

[5] Gaskell, *Mary Barton*, 425.

there is a sense in which the novel needs the law in order to organize in formal terms its investment in the human costs of transgression, judgement and exculpation: Jem, after all, does not die on the scaffold—legal process does not generate that degree of injustice—and Mary grows in stature from the efforts required to evidence his alibi. But most importantly, perhaps, the model of social concord articulated in Jem's letter to Job prevails, and Jem's gesture—to sympathize with the jurors who may be compelled to condemn him—dramatizes the way forward for England's 'two nations' of the rich and the poor:[6] in Carlylean terms, a mutual commitment to the imaginative apprehension of each other's plight leads inexorably to the possibility of ameliorative action.[7] Away from the impersonal scrutiny of the public sphere, John Barton and Edward Carson move towards a hard-won (and essentially Unitarian) reconciliation based upon a recognition of fellow-feeling and shared humanity in grief, and the final word is left to Job Legh: 'I can see the view you take of things from the place where you stand [Mr. Carson]. I can remember that when the time comes for judging you.'[8]

For many Victorian writers, Christian theology offered a specific language in which to consider the ethical obligations of neighbourliness, but Gaskell's modelling of the means by which reconciliation may be effected is not above critique. Whilst Aristotle had hoped that friendship could underpin the civic life of the polis and thus act as a foundation for the formation of just ideals, philosophers such as Jacques Derrida, Gillian Rose, and Paul Ricoeur have in recent years queried the ways in which rights-based conceptions of justice can arise from the more immediate obligations created by second-person address.[9] But there is no doubt that the emphasis placed upon sympathy in the Victorian novel sought to close this gap between ethics and the law as more abstractly conceived, between friendships and political affiliations, between intimacy and ideology.[10] It is precisely this kind of gap which Esther's manifesto of neighbourly action seeks to address in *Bleak House* (1852–53): 'I thought it best to be as useful as I could, and to render what services I could, to those immediately about me; and to try to let that circle gradually and naturally expand itself.'[11] To focus on charity in the abstract—the 'telescopic philanthropy' of Mrs Jellyby and Mrs Pardiggle—is to overlook the local 'cases' of those like Jo, upon whose suffering the novel compels us to dwell. In the courts, juries and spectators practised this kind of judgement and rehearsed the application of their fellow-feeling, acquiring in the process an equitable flexibility of thought which allowed them to move between the universal and the particular, the abstract and the singular—whilst

⁶ The phrase is from Benjamin Disraeli's *Sybil* [1845] (Oxford: Oxford University Press, 1998), 65–66.

⁷ See Thomas Carlyle, *Chartism* (London: James Fraser, 1840), 5.

⁸ Gaskell, *Mary Barton*, 456.

⁹ See Jacques Derrida, *The Politics of Friendship*, trans. George Collins (London: Verso, 1997; repr. 2005), Paul Ricoeur, *The Just*, trans. David Pellauer (Chicago: University of Chicago Press, 2000), and Gillian Rose, *The Broken Middle: Out of our Ancient Society* (Oxford: Blackwell, 1992).

¹⁰ For two excellent studies on the value of sympathy in literature, see Brigid Lowe, *Victorian Fiction and the Insights of Sympathy: An Alternative to the Hermeneutics of Suspicion* (London: Anthem, 2007) and Sophie Ratcliffe, *On Sympathy* (Oxford: Oxford University Press, 2008).

¹¹ Charles Dickens, *Bleak House* [1852–53] (Harmondsworth: Penguin, 1985), 154.

prioritizing the value of the individual to whom suffering comes. The role of the jury in novels like *Mary Barton* and *Bleak House*, then, suggests the importance of public opinion and lay participation in the administration of justice in an age of mass literacy, increasing democratization, and the expansion of the franchise—an opinion which is shaped in part by the act of reading. Recent critical work has attempted to position the body of modern literature as an equitable supplement to the law's formalism, but, as Dieter Paul Polloczek has observed, the value of the aesthetic text will always exceed its purported corrective function, and it is perhaps more useful to think of both discourses as preoccupied with the drive to reconcile the needs of the individual and the competing claims of a wider community at a time of great social change.[12]

In the double dynamic which accounts for the representation of the law in *Mary Barton*—as the antagonistic foil by comparison with which Gaskell, like Dickens, defines her own philosophy of fiction, and simultaneously as a powerful means for the ordering of 'reality' which the novel empowered itself by imitating—we see the role of the law in Victorian fiction more generally. In Kieran Dolin's analysis, the novel's rise to social prominence in the 19th century can be explained in part by its interrogation of more instrumental public discourses.[13] Between 1830 and the end of the century, public regulation of private affairs had increased significantly: commercial life had been shaped by the enactment of the Limited Liability Act (1855), and the Bankruptcy and Insolvency Act (1861); the criminal law had been altered by the progressive dismantling of the Bloody Code in the 1830s and 40s and the professionalization of the criminal trial; the position of women and the availability of divorce had also been addressed by Parliament, with the enactment of the Matrimonial Causes Act (1857), and the two Married Women's Property Acts (1870 and 1882)—society was changing rapidly, and the novel, like the law, wanted to play a part in debate about the direction of that progress. The representation of legal material is thus of crucial significance to the status and function of the novel throughout the Victorian period as both professions debated the types of knowledge generated by and enacted within their respective narrative economies. The interdisciplinary enquiries of the transatlantic 'Law and Literature' movement are widely understood to have been initiated by the publication, in 1973, of James Boyd White's study, *The Legal Imagination*, but it is perhaps the translation into English of Michel Foucault's *Discipline and Punish* in 1977 which has proven to be more fruitful for literary criticism. For Foucault, both literary and legal discourses are concerned to monitor and discipline their subjects: following the absorption of this insight, in Clare Pettitt's analysis, '[c]ontemporary developments in the law no longer formed merely a

---

[12] Dieter Paul Polloczek, *Literature and Legal Discourse: Equity and Ethics from Sterne to Conrad* (Cambridge: Cambridge University Press, 1999), 244. See also Gary Watt, *Equity Stirring: The Story of Justice Beyond Law* (Oxford: Hart Publishing, 2009); Wai Chee Dimock, *Residues of Justice: Law, Literature and Philosophy* (New Haven: Yale University Press, 1996); and Martha Nussbaum, *Poetic Justice: The Literary Imagination and Public Life* (Boston: Beacon Press, 1995).

[13] Kieran Dolin, *Fiction and the Law: Legal Discourse in Victorian and Modernist Literature* (Cambridge: Cambridge University Press, 1999), 1–3.

kind of "semi-detached" historical context to the Victorian novel, they were the living stuff of which literature was made'.[14]

II. THE NOVEL AND THE LAW (1):
INTERSECTIONS OF CONTENT

That engagement with the law shapes both fictional content and narrative form is an axiom of critical study of the English novel. To begin with the common interest in content: both the novel and the law-courts have long been fascinated by the representation and vicarious consumption of human passions expressed in tragic or transgressive action, and whilst the Victorians took this interest to new heights (empowered by modern technologies of print culture and the public appetite for news in all its forms) it is important to remember that crime has had a long history of imaginative dramatization and fictional elaboration.[15] The formal arraignment and trial of the protagonists were dominant organizational principles of the earliest Greek romances (the Helleno-Roman narratives perfected during the first two centuries AD): Renaissance dramatists later reworked and extended plots of tragic and comic recognition borrowed from the classical tragedians, pioneering in the process a new forensic vocabulary based on theological notions of trial, Aristotle's *Poetics*, and the language of the Inns of Court, where many of these plays were first performed. Given such an inheritance, it is unsurprising that narrative interest in crime was confirmed by the appearance of the first recognizably modern English novels in the early 18th century. Texts like Daniel Defoe's *Moll Flanders* (1722) were closely allied to the non-fictional form of the criminal biography (confessional morality tales sold around the foot of the scaffold on days of public executions), and Defoe and his successors may well have tried to appropriate the biography's established readership by allowing some of the same narrative patterns to shape their own work (albeit with significant departures, most notably in respect of novelistic endings). Fictional fascination with transgression and its punishment (either earthly or divine) generates what Patrick Brantlinger calls the contending impulses of much 18th- and 19th-century fiction: the reader can identify within the text both the celebration of criminal propensity (particularly when articulated in the first-person form) and the conservative policing and expulsion of such elements at the point of narrative closure with the reassertion of economic and Providential order.[16]

---

[14] Clare Pettitt, 'Legal Subjects, Legal Objects: The Law and Victorian Fiction', in *A Concise Companion to the Victorian Novel*, ed. Francis O'Gorman (Oxford: Blackwell, 2005), 71–90, 74.

[15] On Victorian literature and crime, see for example, Keith Hollingsworth, *The Newgate Novel, 1830–47: Bulwer, Ainsworth, Dickens and Thackeray* (Detroit: Wayne State University Press, 1963), and Phillip Collins, *Dickens and Crime*, 3rd edn (Basingstoke: Macmillan, 1962; repr. 1994).

[16] Patrick Brantlinger, *The Reading Lesson: The Threat of Mass Literacy in Nineteenth-Century British Fiction* (Bloomington: Indiana University Press, 1998), 82.

Whilst it is easy to dismiss some Victorian fictional representations of legal process as merely populist or sensationalist—a cheap trick to enhance or sustain the profitability of serial publications in particular—it is also important to remember that the deployment of legal material in a novel performs valuable intertextual work (revealing the ways in which the Victorians read and rewrote the *Oresteia*, or *Hamlet* or *Macbeth*, for example) and it draws attention to the existential commitments of English literature—its abiding interests in what it means to be placed on trial for one's life in a theatre of heroic moral endeavour where judgement of some kind must be passed.

From the first, English novelists were aware of the potential criticisms which could be voiced in response to their interest in the representation of criminality. The power of the novel to render vivid the attractions or repulsions of vicarious experience—particularly, though not only, the vicarious experience of the private lives of others—had significant ethical implications. For Mikhail Bakhtin, the history of the novel itself records 'the formal contradictions' which arose when private life entered the public forum of literature: because the personal lives of individuals were largely sealed off from public enquiry, '[t]he literature of private life is essentially a literature of snooping about, of overhearing "how others live"'.[17] Novelists were quick to realize the ethical and educative value of overhearing 'how others live': as George Eliot observed, 'Art is the nearest thing to life: it is a mode of amplifying and extending our contact with our fellow men beyond the bounds of our personal lot.'[18] And such covert exposure to vicarious experience is of methodological significance: whilst we can choose to imitate or reject the templates of behaviour afforded by their example, we also learn to exercise judgement. For Eliot in particular, such an education should teach the need for self-sacrifice rather than the pursuit of (economic or social) self-interest: in the inhabiting of characters other than their own, readers should be encouraged to cultivate and extend their powers of compassion. The ideological battle concerns what is transmitted to the reader, and what lessons are learnt amongst a socially diverse readership from a contemplation of the pain and sufferings of others.

Reading a novel, then, could ideally teach a reader to feel more fully for their fellow men, to judge actions with a more equitable discrimination. But with the advent of mass literacy and the perceived breakdown of hegemonic interpretative practices shared by an intellectual reading elite, commentators became increasingly preoccupied with the ways in which novels could lead working-class readers and women into acts of social deviancy: if consumption of a text moved a reader to transgressive action, who was to blame? The Victorian period began with the so-called 'Newgate novel' controversy of the late 1830s, in which authors including Edward Bulwer Lytton, William Harrison Ainsworth, Charles Dickens, and William Thackeray were accused of an overly sympathetic representation of criminal conduct in novels as diverse as *Eugene Aram* (1832), *Oliver Twist* (1836–37), *Jack Sheppard* (1838), and *Catherine* (1839). As I will discuss further below,

---

[17] Mikhail Bakhtin, 'Forms of Time and of the Chronotope in the Novel', in *The Dialogic Imagination*, trans. Caryl Emerson and Michael Holquist (Austin: University of Texas Press, 1981), 123.
[18] *The Essays of George Eliot*, ed. Thomas Pinney (London: Routledge, 1963), 271.

the 'Newgate novel' controversy coincided with both the rise of Chartism and the implementation of the Prisoners' Counsel Act of 1836 which extended full legal representation to those accused of felony and which acted to silence the accused when counsel were retained (thereby enforcing a replacement of the first-person speech of the accused with the 'third-person' voice of the professional representative).[19] That criminality itself was contagious—that the 'Newgate novels' were inherently corrupting—seemed more likely when convicted criminals such as François Courvoisier, condemned to death for murder in July 1840, described their reading habits prior to execution: he claimed to have been inspired to kill the uncle of the Prime Minister, Lord William Russell, by a reading of *Jack Sheppard*—an allegation which added spice to a trial already rendered controversial by the fact that his counsel, Charles Phillips, allegedly lied to the court in an attempt to win his acquittal.[20] Although the reliability of both these allegations were later contested, the intense discursive competition of barristers and lawyers in the mid-Victorian period, in which each profession accused the other of a narratological defence of violence, seems particularly self-reflexive as a consequence. On the other hand, as Defoe noted in his famous 'Preface' to *Moll Flanders*, there was scope for gestures of exculpation in the responsibility of the reader for the creation of literary meaning: if a reader acts under the stimulus of the 'wicked' part of the story rather than allowing himself to be disciplined by its penitential conclusion, then 'the difference lyes not in the real worth of the Subject, so much as in the Gust and Palate of the Reader'.[21] The locus of anxiety, then, is not only the subject matter of the controversial narratives themselves, but also the class and gender of the reader, and as Juliet John notes, the unpredictable 'power of popular culture at the dawn of a "modern" age'.[22]

III. The Novel and the Law (2): Epistemology, Evidence, and Narrative Form

But more interesting perhaps than the novel's shared interest in the types of human behaviour subject to legal regulation is the participation of narrative fiction in the very

---

[19] On the history of the amendments to criminal trial procedure in the period, see David Cairns, *The Making of the Adversarial Criminal Trial, 1815–1865* (Oxford: Oxford University Press, 1999), and John Langbein, *The Origins of Adversary Criminal Trial* (Oxford: Oxford University Press, 2003).

[20] On Courvoisier's trial, see Cairns, 67–95; Jan-Melissa Schramm, *Testimony and Advocacy in Victorian Law, Literature, and Theology* (Cambridge: Cambridge University Press, 2000), 101–44; and Allyson May, *The Bar and the Old Bailey, 1750–1850* (Chapel Hill and London: University of North Carolina Press, 2003), 214–15.

[21] Daniel Defoe, 'Preface' to *Moll Flanders* [1722] (Oxford: Oxford University Press, 1981), 3.

[22] Juliet John, *Dickens's Villains: Character, Melodrama, Popular Culture* (Oxford: Oxford University Press, 2001), 123.

epistemological debates which shaped the emergence of the laws of evidence and legal procedure in the first place. The law, admittedly, works rather hard to suppress evidence of reciprocal influence, but an investigation of the ways in which narrative form responds to legal change reveals much about the cultural and contextual pressures which shape choices of emplotment and characterization.

The need to respond to an accusation—to construct a compelling exculpatory tale— drives many a Victorian novel, and critics such as Alexander Welsh and Jonathan Grossman remind us that the history of the English novel can be read as an investigation of the ways in which we seek to pardon and understand protagonists from Henry Fielding's Tom Jones to Thomas Hardy's Tess. The deployment of such formalities as arraignment, judgement, and most often, acquittal (or pardon) enables an assessment of the ways in which characters respond to reversals of fortunes and circumstances. The implications for the novel at this period in its history were primarily theological— Anglican apologists such as Bishop Joseph Butler had long argued that life was a state of probation involving temptation and trial, culminating in the finality of an omniscient verdict.[23] But fiction registered secular pressures as well: that an accusation against a protagonist in a Victorian novel is most likely to be revealed as wrongful at the point of narrative closure tells us much about the indebtedness of narrative fiction to theatrical convention, but also suggests the novel's interest in the affirmation of a character's initial ethos rather than a genuine commitment to discontinuity and growth. E.M. Forster noted in his study *Aspects of the Novel* that an organically mature and whole character, a so-called 'round' individual, is one who 'is capable of surprising in a convincing way', who can convey something of the 'incalculability of life':[24] whilst many Victorian protagonists are often considered the quintessential 'round' characters, the trope of acquittal following a wrongful accusation tends to work against a confirmation of this fullness—it enhances a text's popular appeal, with an endorsement of the types of plot featured in both theatrical melodrama and the daily newspapers, but it also lessens the opportunity for an exploration of the types of change in character wrought by a confrontation with guilt and moral ambiguity.

A comparison with early romance illuminates these anxieties of narrative stasis. Bakhtin describes the dominant form of romance as 'the adventure novel of ordeal', a template designed to test such qualities as the heroes' chastity, fidelity, nobility, and courage, and often dependent upon judicial intervention for its resolution. In Bakhtin's analysis, 'the trials are somewhat external and formal', leaving little imprint upon the psychological makeup of the protagonists: 'The hammer of events shatters nothing and forges nothing—it merely tries the durability of an already finished product. And the product passes the test.'[25] Franco Moretti sees precisely the same dynamic at work in the mid-Victorian *Bildungsroman* which he describes, in *The Way of the World: The*

[23] Bishop Joseph Butler, *The Analogy of Religion, Natural and Revealed to the Constitution and Course of Nature* [1736] (Oxford: Oxford University Press, 1907), 124.

[24] E.M. Forster, *Aspects of the Novel* [1927] (Harmondsworth: Penguin, 1962; repr. 2000), 81.

[25] Bakhtin, 'Forms of Time', 106–107.

Bildungsroman in European Culture, as less a 'novel of initiation' than a 'novel of preservation': 'in the English novel, the most significant experiences are not those that alter but those which *confirm* the choices made by childhood "innocence".[26] According to Moretti, recourse to legal persecution in the Victorian novel is simply the stimulus necessary for the initiation of plot in a comfortable political context. Democracy, he argues, is 'rather anti-heroic',[27] producing an 'essentially conservative' investment in the rhetoric of the law as the force that legitimates the socialization of the novelistic individual.[28] The result, he rather provocatively concludes, 'was the worst novel of the West, and the boldest culture of justice'.[29]

Yet, the quality of the novels aside, Moretti's reading can be challenged on several counts. Firstly, the mid-Victorian period was not necessarily a period of political stability: contemporary commentators seem to have experienced the 1840s and 1850s as vulnerable to continuing social upheaval at home and unrest abroad, in the form of the Crimean War (1854–56) and the Indian Mutiny (1857). Alex Woloch is surely right to note that Victorian realism 'registers the competing pull of inequality and democracy within the nineteenth-century bourgeois imagination', reflecting in its choice of a single protagonist 'acute economic and social stratification' and 'actual structures of inequitable distribution', and simultaneously acknowledging, 'in the claims of minor characters on the reader's attention . . . the democratic impulse that forms a horizon of nineteenth century politics'.[30] And secondly, Moretti is too quick to assume an easy correspondence between law and justice. The inclusion of trial scenes in fiction serves a structural purpose—exposing sometimes private transgressions to the publicity of forensic inquiry—but it also allows for the novelistic interrogation of various epistemologies, and for fine discriminations to be made about which types of knowledge are the most reliable foundations for judgement and action. What the reader may learn from such cross-examinations is not the equivalence of law and justice, but the friction between them and the wastage and inequity generated by attempts to shoehorn material from one category into another. Hence the interest of the Victorian novel in all that the law represses—the voices which cannot be heard in a court of law, the evidence that cannot be recovered, the testimony that is excluded from consideration. To suggest that the providential aesthetic inevitably erases this tension at the point of narrative closure is to ignore very real Victorian anxieties about the persistence and prevalence of injustice, and indeed the implications for fiction of the weakening of the providential guarantees themselves.

---

[26] Franco Moretti, *The Way of the World: The Bildungsroman in European Culture*, trans. Albert J. Sbragia (London: Verso, 1987), 182. For a more detailed treatment of this material, see Schramm, *Atonement and Self-Sacrifice in Nineteenth-Century Narrative* (Cambridge: Cambridge University Press, 2012), 66–72 and 222–36.

[27] Moretti, 192.

[28] Moretti, 207.

[29] Moretti, 214.

[30] Alex Woloch, *The One Versus the Many: Minor Characters and the Space of the Protagonist in the Novel* (Princeton: Princeton University Press, 2003), 31.

John Bender has claimed that 'novelistic knowledge resides in the genre's staging of the act of assessment as ongoing probabilistic judgement'[31]—that our investment in the types of vicarious knowledge acquired through the act of reading is epistemologically equivalent to that performed in any formal experiment—and as a consequence, procedural questions (who can speak in a court of law, what can be said) are integral to the ways in which that assessment is undertaken. In his famous study *The Rise of the Novel*, Ian Watt reminds us of the epistemological assumptions shared by readers and jurors: 'both want to know all the particulars of a given case—the time and place of the occurrence: both must be satisfied as to the identity of the parties concerned...and they also expect the witnesses to tell the story in "his own words".[32] Whilst criticism can be made of Watt's analysis—for his elevation of the genre of 'realistic' writing above other forms less indebted to the discourse of empiricism, and for the exceptions which undermine his thesis that the novel 'arises' as a consequence of the union of Protestantism and capitalism (*Don Quixote*, for example)[33]—his insight into the nature of the reading process possesses explanatory power at both a historical and a theoretical level. Many Victorian authors possessed legal training: Charles Reade and Wilkie Collins were called to the Bar (in 1843 and 1851 respectively), William Thackeray enrolled at the Middle Temple as a young man (though he later abandoned the law to write), and Charles Dickens began his career as a legal clerk and a reporter in the Court of Doctors' Commons. Victorian authors clearly experienced anxieties about the anonymity of their mass readership in an age of industrial progress and addressed their own readers with much of the rhetorical intimacy that can also be identified in courtroom speech by barristers in the period—one well-known example is the appeal to the singular reader (a heartfelt call to action) which closes *Hard Times* (1854). And both the literary and the legal audiences shared a commitment to the language of evidence as the basis of human judgement and knowledge: hence we see George Eliot's narrator in *Adam Bede* (1859) telling the story 'as if I were in the witness-box, narrating my experience on oath',[34] and Collins flattering his readers with the assertion that 'as the Judge on the bench might have heard it once, so the reader will hear it now'[35]—a legally imitative methodology that served him well in *The Woman in White* (1860), *The Moonstone* (1868), and *The Law and the Lady* (1875). Watt's early, pioneering work has since engendered a number of valuable studies which have affirmed the intense inter-relationship of theologico-legal language and the conventions of narrative realism in the period. Alexander Welsh, author of the seminal study, *Strong Representations: Narrative and Circumstantial Evidence in England* (1992) has drawn attention to this pronounced discursive engagement by uncovering what he

---

[31] John Bender, 'Novel Knowledge: Judgment, Experience, Experiment', in *Fictions of Knowledge: Fact, Evidence, Doubt*, ed. Yota Batsaki, Subha Mukherji, and Jan-Melissa Schramm (Basingstoke: Macmillan, 2011), 131–51, 148.

[32] Ian Watt, *The Rise of the Novel* (London: Chatto & Windus, 1957), 31.

[33] Margaret Anne Doody, *The True Story of the Novel* (London: Fontana, 1998), 12.

[34] George Eliot, *Adam Bede* [1859] (Harmondsworth: Penguin, 1994), 174.

[35] Wilkie Collins, *The Woman in White* [1860] (Oxford: Oxford University Press, 1996), 5.

calls 'the evidentiary basis of... realism'.[36] Like the legal treatise and the theological tract, the novel was deeply implicated in the rhetoric of empiricism: as standards of proof were sharpened in response to the application of utilitarian and scientific pressures, authors as well as jurists were concerned to establish what constituted evidence sufficient to justify the performance of action.

The cultural preference for a vocabulary of plain fact which eschewed ornament had traditionally been associated with Puritanism and the work of the Royal Society in the seventeenth century: in Barbara Shapiro's analysis, '[a]ll the discourses of "fact" became suspicious of rhetoric and often voiced this suspicion in connection with announcing their dedication to the norm of impartiality'.[37] This celebration of 'artlessness' or the language of 'plain fact' can be seen in some of the earliest English novels: Samuel Richardson's *Pamela* (1740) and *Clarissa* (1747–8) both suggest that their eponymous heroines 'speak and write the sincere dictates of [their] hearts'.[38] Yet if the epistolary novel can be seen to share certain characteristics with trial methodologies—its interest in the assessment of competing 'witness' statements, for example (even whilst that testimony is cast into differing forms)—the Victorian novel is marked by an engagement with expanding domains of professional knowledge; the representation of witness testimony in the mid-Victorian period was inflected by what Ivan Kreilkamp has identified as a wider suspicion of oratory fostered by the seditious language of Chartism and the struggle for cultural domination enacted in the early Victorian period by an increasingly prolific print culture, and it also reveals a persistent and deeply embedded nostalgia for the power of the voice.[39] Yet this is not to suggest that literature's relation to politico-legal discourse is purely imitative: as Welsh notes, Fielding in *Tom Jones* (1749), for example, almost imagines and anticipates the later 'lawyerization' of the criminal trial, as the narrator sifts the evidence for and against the eponymous protagonist.[40] It is possible to think fruitfully about the ways in which free indirect discourse, for example, may have arisen in tandem with the professionalization of the (criminal) courts, but it is perhaps more accurate to think of both disciplines as responsive to wider currents of epistemological change.

IV. The Law, the Novel, and the Rise of the Professions

The 19th century was characterized by increased specialization of knowledge and greater degrees of professionalization in law, medicine, and science: there is little need

---

[36] Alexander Welsh, *Strong Representations: Narrative and Circumstantial Evidence in England* (Baltimore: Johns Hopkins University Press, 1992), 49.

[37] Barbara Shapiro, *A Culture of Fact: England 1550–1720* (Chicago: University of Chicago Press, 2001), 29.

[38] Samuel Richardson, *Clarissa* [1747–8] (Harmondsworth: Penguin, 1985), 240.

[39] Ivan Kreilkamp, *Voice and the Victorian Story-teller* (Cambridge: Cambridge University Press, 2006).

[40] Welsh, *Strong Representations*, 67–76.

here to repeat the careful taxonomic work undertaken by John Reed and William Holdsworth in their documentation of the classes of professional men represented in various works of fiction[41]—from family solicitors, like Tulkinghorn in *Bleak House* and Jermyn in *Felix Holt* (1866), to the aggressive lawyers contaminated by contact with their criminal clients, like Jaggers in *Great Expectations* (1861), to the bombastic members of the Bar, like Serjeant Buzfuz in *The Posthumous Papers of the Pickwick Club* (1836–37), and the Attorney-General in *A Tale of Two Cities* (1859) and Chaffanbrass in Anthony Trollope's *Orley Farm* (1861–62). Following Foucault, David Miller and John Bender have shown that narrative strategies were also responsive to changing methods of detection and punishment,[42] and Ronald Thomas has suggested that, as a consequence, the very experience of human subjectivity altered in this period. With the professionalization of the police force in 1829, and the emergence of a dedicated detective unit in 1842, the disciplinary forces of the bureaucratic, industrial state ensured that ideas of 'character' were increasingly supplemented by notions of 'identity' based upon documentary material (such as birth and death certificates, medical records) that were capable of verification only by trained medical and legal personnel.[43] At the same time, authors were now seeking to earn a living from their writing (whilst earlier generations had relied more heavily on patronage and private incomes), and, to give but one example, Dickens's treatment of his legal characters habitually suggests that he envied the status and respectability of the other gentlemanly professions.[44]

The sense that, in modern bureaucratic society, identity now required professional validation, is related to broader questions about the ways in which character is presented in narrative—whether, for example, character is best revealed by the voice of the accused individual or the disinterested intervention of the trained professional. According to Bakhtin, the very history of the novel suggests that 'in a human being, there is always something that only he can reveal, in a free act of self-consciousness and discourse, something that does not submit to an externalizing, second-hand definition':[45] in John Kucich's analysis, 'in cultures influenced by Christianity self-cultivation demands an authentic relation to interiority, in which the self must be fully deciphered in order to be either affirmed or renounced'. But as Kucich notes, this Foucauldian model fails to account for the 'inherent undependability' of confession—'the new spaces for lying that

[41] See William Holdsworth, *Charles Dickens as a Legal Historian* (New Haven: Yale University Press, 1929); John R. Reed, 'Laws, the Legal World, and Politics', in *A Companion to the Victorian Novel*, ed. Patrick Brantlinger and William Thesing (Oxford: Blackwell, 2002), 155–71; and Schramm, 'Dickens and the Law', in *The Companion to Charles Dickens*, ed. David Paroissien (Oxford: Blackwell, 2007), 277–94.

[42] D.A. Miller, *The Novel and the Police* (Berkeley: University of California Press, 1988) and John Bender, *Imagining the Penitentiary: Fiction and the Architecture of Mind in Eighteenth-Century England* (Chicago: Chicago University Press, 1987).

[43] See Ronald Thomas, *Detective Fiction and the Rise of Forensic Science* (Cambridge: Cambridge University Press, 1999), 289.

[44] See Jennifer Ruth, 'The Victorian Novel and Professions', in this volume.

[45] Mikhail Bakhtin, *Problems of Dostoevsky's Poetics*, trans. Caryl Emerson (Minneapolis: University of Minnesota Press, 1984), 58.

it opens'.[46] The fundamental antagonism between testimony and so-called circumstantial evidence (and, later, forensic trace) identified in 18th- and 19th-century prose narrative by Welsh and his successors is part of this larger epistemological enquiry about the most effective means by which to account for apprehensions of our own individuality. Authors like Dickens, Gaskell, and Eliot ascribe only to fiction the power to read correctly both physiognomy and interiority, to correlate that troublesome binary of conduct and character. To do so, they often appropriated a professional lexis—most notably that of the law or of medical science—but as Lisa Rodensky points out in *The Crime in Mind: Criminal Responsibility and the Victorian Novel*, 'the Victorian novel's investment in the third person narrator marked its distinction from and at moments superiority to other disciplines... that had to infer knowledge', resulting in a display of narrative power 'that no other discourse could display so fully'.[47]

At stake was not only the assessment of character—the regret Mary expressed to Jem that wrongful arraignment would not have occurred had they but 'known thee better, Jem'—but the boundaries of individual responsibility itself. The mid-Victorian period saw significant developments in the law of insanity (with two prominent trials, *R. v. Oxford* and *R. v. McNaughten*, capturing the public and legal imaginations in 1840 and 1843 respectively), and the three great controversies of the late 1830s–1840s—Chartist unrest, the 'Newgate novel' debates, and the licence of counsel controversy which followed the implementation of the Prisoners' Counsel Act in 1836—all turned on issues of individual accountability.[48] Seditious, inflammatory addresses to torch-lit processions could move a mob to riotous action: unethical barristers could enable guilty clients to evade the gallows and thus offend again: novels could potentially inspire a reader to an act of violence—in each case, rhetoric, improperly employed, could afford potentially transgressive agents new and extended opportunities for criminal conduct. Quantifying professional responsibility for such vicarious violence was difficult: radical orators, barristers, and authors noted with discomfort the similarities of their praxis—the mid-Victorian novel in particular registers anxieties about the perceived amorality of (political and) legal advocacy. In addition to *Mary Barton*, ringing announcements of a defendant's innocence (and concomitant rejections of legal assistance) are to be found in George Eliot's *Felix Holt*, in Charlotte Yonge's *The Trial* (1864) and in Dickens's *Posthumous Papers of the Pickwick Club* (albeit in the context of a civil trial for breach of promise of marriage), in *Bleak House*, and in *Hard Times*, though Stephen Blackpool's innocence is only established posthumously. *Bleak House* dramatizes George Rouncewell's vigorous denial of both guilt and legal assistance when wrongfully charged with the murder of Tulkinghorn. Dickens's own anxieties about the morality of advocacy can be traced through his pseudonymous

[46] John Kucich, *The Power of Lies: Transgression in Victorian Fiction* (Ithaca: Cornell University Press, 1994), 18–19.

[47] Lisa Rodensky, *The Crime in Mind: Criminal Responsibility and the Victorian Novel* (Oxford: Oxford University Press, 2003), 23.

[48] For discussion of the novel's involvement in the formation of the discourse of criminal responsibility in the period, see Rodensky, 3–91.

letters to the *Morning Chronicle* as early as 1840, and George sees the representation of his interests by another as opening up the possibility of a 'sham defence', which could lead in turn to an acquittal based upon a technicality. Instead, George wants his innocence established on substantive grounds: 'I must come off clear and full or not at all.'[49] True, transparent innocence should establish itself despite the manipulation of evidence by the prosecution, and there must be an authentic correspondence between testimony and verdict, conduct and character. Unlike the Victorian courtroom, which, after the enactment of the Prisoners' Counsel Act in 1836, could not hear the accused if he chose to defend himself by proxy, Victorian fiction insists repeatedly on access to the first-person speech of the accused at the point at which a verdict is obtained[50] (though *Adam Bede* is an exception here, as Eliot prioritizes the theological significance of the confession Dinah elicits from Hetty). On the whole, in Victorian fiction a nostalgia persists for an innocence that requires no professional interpretation.

That goodness or innocence should require no casuistical defence suggests the influence of melodrama, a theatrical form which began in France shortly after the Revolution, and which depended upon 'the dramaturgy of virtue misprized and eventually recognized':[51] according to John, this type of dramatic 'ostension', particularly popular with Dickens, eroded distinctions between high and low art 'as a point of ideological principle'.[52] Peter Brooks has categorized melodrama as essentially a secular subgenre, but for the mid-Victorian author conversant with the moral economies of Evangelicalism, the endangerment of virtue, followed by its final triumph, could be seen to affirm the tenacious hold exerted upon the imagination by forensic Protestantism. That the characters acquitted in these novels are, on the whole, working-class men—the very embodiment of potential Chartist menace—is surely no coincidence: the novels defuse any threat they may embody for the middle classes by suggesting that the law has 'tried' their speech and declared it trustworthy.[53]

V.   THE LAW, THE NOVEL, AND DEMOCRACY

Victorian fiction is marked by a unique attentiveness to what J.S. Mill in *On Liberty* (1859) called the competing ethical and political claims of the 'one' and 'the many'.[54] In fiction, the voice of the 'one' is often expressed in compelling first-person terms, and the views of the many in the more statistically based, tabular or objective viewpoints of the sociologist or historian (I mean to suggest considerable but not complete overlap

---

[49]   Dickens, *Bleak House*, 706–7.
[50]   See Schramm, *Testimony and Advocay*, 180–92.
[51]   Peter Brooks, *The Melodramatic Imagination* (New Haven: Yale University Press, 1976; repr. 1995), 27.
[52]   John, *Dickens' Villains*, 3.
[53]   See Schramm, 'Towards a Poetics of (Wrongful) Accusation: Innocence and Working-Class Voice in Mid-Victorian Fiction', in *Fictions of Knowledge*, 193–212.
[54]   J.S. Mill, *On Liberty* [1859] (Cambridge: Cambridge University Press, 2000), 181.

between first- and third-person 'perspectives' and 'voices' here, for clearly free indirect discourse can offer privileged access to individual interiority). The newly professionalized criminal court-room afforded unique opportunities for the staged juxtaposition of first- and third-person perspectives—this relentless interrogation of different ways of knowing which privilege alternately individual and group-based experience (the former in the voice of the various witnesses, the latter in the voice of the expert witnesses, and the legal professionals in so far as they seek to interpret and apply laws in the abstract).[55] Art has long been concerned with a movement or a mediation between the claims of the particular and the general, in Aristotelian terms, but the contrast assumed new force in an age which saw the passage of the First and Second Reform Bills and the advent of mass literacy.[56] In contradistinction to what Jacques Derrida calls the enumeration of 'votes and subjects' and the group-based consensus which characterizes a democracy, lies what Emmanuel Levinas sees as the foundational ethical claim made upon one individual by another, experienced as a relationship between singularities.[57] This is the problem of incommensurability, the often tragic irreconcilability of first- and third-person ways of knowing that is probed in novels like *Bleak House* and *Hard Times*. *Bleak House* can only just contain this epistemological tension in its formal innovations (the parallel construction of Esther's retrospective autobiographical extract and the present tense account of the perhaps professional third-person narrator), but *Hard Times* reveals perhaps even more clearly the standard trajectory of many a Victorian novel, in which a largely sympathetic protagonist gradually acquires first-hand experience of his or her social 'other'. The outcome of this encounter is only partly successful—Louisa, representative of the middle-classes, gains the knowledge which enables her to differentiate the body of industrial 'hands' into individual units, but for Stephen, the working-class exemplar of 'perfect integrity', the betrayal which follows serves to initiate his journey towards a tragic death redeemed only by a shift of genre and an imitation of Christ's passion. In Andrew Miller's terms, Victorian interest in the reconciliation of claims based on love and intimacy and those based on contract and distance places 'overwhelming pressure' on 'second-person relationships such as friendship and marriage': the risks involved in a journey towards mutual recognition and relationship are great, and '[i]n such a light, the period's defining domestic ideology appears as a means of forestalling the scepticisms of abandonment and abstraction'.[58]

---

[55] See Schramm, *Testimony and Advocacy*, 101–44.

[56] On the relationship between political and aesthetic representation of working-class interests at the time of the extension of the franchise, see Catherine Gallagher, *The Industrial Reformation of English Fiction: Social Discourse and Narrative Form 1832–76* (Chicago: Chicago University Press, 1985), 187–218.

[57] See Derrida, *The Politics of Friendship*, x; John Bowen, 'Counting on: *A Tale of Two Cities*', in *Charles Dickens, A Tale of Two Cities and the French Revolution*, ed. Colin Jones, Josephine McDonagh, and Jon Mee (Basingstoke: Macmillan, 2009), 104–25; and for the most compelling philosophical account of the other, see Emmanuel Levinas, *Otherwise than Being, or Beyond Essence*, trans. Alphonso Lingis (Dordrecht: Kluwer Academic Publishers, 1974; repr. 1991).

[58] Andrew H. Miller, *The Burdens of Perfection: On Ethics and Reading in Nineteenth-Century British Literature* (Ithaca: Cornell University Press, 2008), 25.

It is arguably the trial scene in which the Victorian novel places the potential reconciliation of interior and exterior readings of character under the greatest stress—
what the progress towards a verdict often stages, in the fractured relationships of the
litigants themselves, is their potential irreconcilability across the spectrum of public
and private contexts that are distorted by adversarial combat. Prose works from *Caleb
Williams* (1794) to *Tess of the D'Urbervilles* (1891) attempt to understand whether an
embrace between litigants is more valuable than a verdict based on evidence: whether
private reconciliation (or indeed private revenge) is more admirable than recourse to
the courts: whether mercy and Christian forgiveness are of greater efficacy than public prosecution—and which, if any, of these outcomes reveals most about the contested
'authenticity' of a litigant's character.[59] For in a criminal trial, and in the fictional elabora-
tions of such contests, one perspective inevitably compromises the other—forensic dis-
putation resists an easy resolution, and even those novels which dramatize some form of
personal reconciliation between the parties acknowledge the affective cost of recourse
to professional adjudicative measures. Readers of fiction are called to be aware of the
educative value of feeling, but they are also shown the necessity of action, of judgement,
with all of its potentially tragic implications.

VI. Civil Law and the Novel

The predominance of plots involving the criminal law in the Victorian period may perhaps be accounted for by the ways in which evangelical Christianity licensed a continuing preoccupation with the lessons to be learnt from the dramatization of death: the
scaffold scene, in which death could be confronted with some degree of preparation,
allowed for the interrogation of different types of consolation, and different sources of
hope. The civil courts, in contrast, dealt largely with commercial disputes which, at first
glance, seemed to have made less of an impression on the Victorian public imagination.
But Dickens was fascinated by copyright law and questions of inheritance, and Eliot by
inheritance as a metaphor for wider cultural and spiritual concerns—not only the identity of those who shall inherit England, but what values should be transmitted to the
next generation, and more darkly, whether industrialism would bring an end to human
succession and demand instead the sacrifice of Victorian youth. Simon Petch has skil-
fully analysed the constitutional climate of mid-Victorian England (and its relation to
the operation of individual conscience), and Clare Pettitt has addressed insightfully the
impact of copyright debates on conceptions of intellectual property in the period: there

---

[59] On the relationship of morality and the law in the period, see Simon Petch, 'Law, Equity and
Conscience in Victorian England', *Victorian Literature and Culture* 25, no. 1 (1997): 123–39. On tensions
between mercy and judgement in the literature and theology of the period, see Schramm, *Atonement and
Self-Sacrifice*, 25–33 and 216–36.

is little that can be added here to their perceptive assessments.[60] But it remains to mention in conclusion the ways in which plots of inheritance are marked in mid-Victorian fiction particularly by an obsession with many of the same issues of character, conduct and identity which govern emplotment in novels of crime and detection. For inheritance, too, is initiated by a death, and depends upon testamentary 'will' and intention for the transmission of something of value to those left behind.

Preoccupied with the exploitation of his work by rogue publishers, Dickens sought an injunction in January 1844 to prevent the piracy of *A Christmas Carol* (1843): he won the case but lost money when the defendants sought refuge in bankruptcy, and his subsequent writing was characterized by an extraordinary indignation at the activities of the Court of Chancery (historically the home of Equity law). *In Bleak House*, the Chancery suit of *Jarndyce* v. *Jarndyce* performs a number of functions within the text: structurally, it serves to unite the otherwise socially disparate cast of characters—to bring into contact the one and the many—by linking Jo to Lady Dedlock and Tom-all-Alone's to Chesney Wold; theologically, its dependence upon chance and lottery-like risks rather than steady Protestant application contrasts with the providentially driven benevolence of Esther and John Jarndyce, whilst simultaneously drawing attention to the absence of God from the court of conscience and its parody of a Day of Judgement. But perhaps most poignantly in a novel shaped by the tensions between first- and third-person narration, Dickens's satirical treatment of the case enables him to protest against the law's dependence upon statistics, averages and anonymity and to proclaim the supreme value of singularity—of the very individuality which the law (seemingly) works hard to overlook. Although the case of *Jarndyce* v. *Jardyce* 'has been a death to many,...it is a joke in the profession': lawyers in training have 'been in the habit of fleshing their legal wit upon it',[61] but the exhausted litigant Gridley asserts the fundamental incommensurability of this movement from particulars to precedent:

> 'Go into the Court of Chancery yonder, and ask what is one of the standing jokes that brighten up their business sometimes, and they will tell you that the best joke they have is the man from Shropshire. I', he said, beating one hand on the other, passionately, 'am the man from Shropshire'.[62]

As readers of the novel we are asked to care passionately about 'the man from Shropshire': Dickens compels us to attend Gridley's deathbed and calls upon us to ensure that such wastage—such injustice—shall cease to be. On the one hand, *Bleak House* contains little legal detail—as Mr Jarndyce explains, 'the original merits of the case have long disappeared from the face of the earth. It's about a will, and the trusts under a Will—or it

---

[60] See Petch, 'Conscience in Victorian England', and Petch, 'Walks of Life: Legal', in *A Companion to Victorian Literature and Culture*, ed. Herbert Tucker (Oxford: Blackwell, 1992), 275–99: for Pettitt, see n. 14.

[61] Dickens, *Bleak House*, 52.

[62] Dickens, *Bleak House*, 553.

was, once. It's about nothing but costs now'.[63] But on the other hand, Chancery's role in the novel is more than symbolic; Dickens grounds his vigorous critique of self-interest in a well-informed and finely nuanced assessment of the types of financial 'interest' in a cause that a party had to have if he was to be represented in Chancery proceedings. What he champions in place of self-interest or an interest in property is the 'national interest' which all people should be entitled to feel in the future of the British constitution. In this way, Equity is prised away from its institutional home, the Court of Chancery, and reclaimed as a property of the novel and by extension the individual reader.[64] It is Esther who practises most effectively the neighbourly equity which Dickens advocates, and she in turn voices the repugnance in which all men of feeling must hold the law: *Bleak House* reminds us that 'the noun-substantive goodness' is often 'of the feminine gender',[65] and it is women like Esther Hawdon and George Eliot's Esther Lyon who embody the valuable qualities of mercy and charity.

In placing such emphasis upon the 'goodness' of Esther, and in subjecting Lady Dedlock to the persecution of the law, *Bleak House* draws attention to the gendered implications of the rise of the professions at mid-century. Dickens represents Tulkinghorn's misogyny as institutional, a pathological by-product of professional work which invariably exposed the female body (and the language of sensibility, sentiment and passion) to the rational scientific gaze of the male clinician or lawyer. In *Felix Holt*, Eliot was to develop further this trajectory of narrative scrutiny: in his willingness to expose Mrs Transome's disgrace for his own ends, the family solicitor Matthew Jermyn must simultaneously disclose that he is her child's father—to publicly assert what the son registers as 'the hated fatherhood', the 'hardship of an ignominy which was not of his own making'.[66]

English fiction is deeply interested in the economic implications of such paternity: the novel from *Tom Jones* onwards is concerned to establish not simply the legal identity of inheritors or beneficiaries, but the moral character of the claimant as well. The Victorian novel is attentive to both physical evidence of identity (scars on the body, but also portable tokens) and broader questions of moral culpability expressed in consistent, persuasive stories which address, and account for, any suspicious severance from kin, but which also serve to confirm a claimant's inherent 'virtue'. To give but one example from amongst many, Oliver Twist can only inherit under the terms of his father's will because he is located within a precise family genealogy (confirmed by the existence of the standard classical tokens, a locket and a ring), and simultaneously innocent of 'any public act of dishonour, meanness, cowardice or wrong' in his minority.[67] There are numerous variations on this theme of moral and commercial creditworthiness: contrary to expectations

---

[63] Dickens, *Bleak House*, 145.

[64] See Polloczek, *Equity and Ethics*, 242–44; Dolin, *Fiction and the Law*, 71–86; Petch, 'Conscience in Victorian England', 130–39; and Schramm, 'Dickens and the National Interest: On the Representation of Parties in *Bleak House*', *Law and the Humanities* 6, no. 2 (2012): 217–42.

[65] Dickens, *Bleak House*, 721. On the identification of Esther and equity, see Watt, *Equity Stirring*, 169–94.

[66] George Eliot, *Felix Holt* [1866] (Harmondsworth: Penguin, 1972; repr. 1987), 581–82.

[67] Charles Dickens, *Oliver Twist* [1837–39] (Harmondsworth: Penguin, 1966; repr. 1985), 458. See also Rodensky, 3–34.

which suggest that Esther in *Bleak House* should inherit the sins of her unwed parents, she in fact inherits the 'goodness' repeatedly attributed to Captain Hawdon in his treatment of Jo: inheritance follows the contours of moral value in Anthony Trollope's *Is he Popenjoy?* (1873) but not *Ralph the Heir* (1875): Eliot's Esther demonstrates her ethical value in *Felix Holt* by the renunciation of her claims to the Transome estate, and Pip chooses to relinquish his wealth when he discovers the identity of his criminal benefactor in *Great Expectations* (only to learn thereby to love him the more). Eliot's *Daniel Deronda* (1876) offers an extraordinary study of the prophetic directedness of spiritual inheritance, but it is perhaps the curious literary afterlife of *Felix Holt* which best illustrates these shared moral and political concerns. Compelled to speak in his own defence at his trial for manslaughter (as the action of the novel pre-dates the implementation of the Prisoner's Counsel Act), Felix demonstrates the sincerity of a working-class rhetoric free from criminal taint. Eliot's publisher, John Blackwood then called upon her to allow 'Felix' to offer a first-person address to the working men of Britain in *Blackwood's Magazine* with an invocation to use wisely the extension of the franchise: 'when the new Reform Bill comes into operation, the working man will be on his trial, and if he misconducts himself, it will go hard with the country'.[68] Eliot's Felix had proven himself ideally placed to promote self-improvement and self-restraint: inequities of distribution must not be overthrown by force because it is the educated classes who will transmit to the next generation the inheritance of the nation's cultural patrimony—to injure them will be to 'injure your own inheritance and the inheritance of your children'.[69] Eliot's radical speaker embraces here a very Burkean conservatism as he calls for gradual change, moral probity in civic affairs, and political moderation. In this vision of popular involvement in public life as an inheritance to be passed on intact to the next generation, class interests are (seemingly) united.

In *Strong Representations*, Welsh argues that by the 1870s, first-person speech in novels began manifesting itself in its weaker form as 'stories of personal experience'[70] and not as evidence to be assessed and judged (the way, for instance, Eliot invites us to assess and judge Felix's speeches). This development (and others) moves Welsh to conclude that the intensity of fiction's engagement with the law was diminishing at the end of the century, and, further, that recourse to the language of empirical proof in fiction was also in decline (perhaps in part because the rationalist phase of theological enquiry may also be seen to end at mid-century). Post-Darwin, the particulars of the 'case' were also to be understood as a scientific 'study'; by the final decades of the 19th century, aesthetic innovation increasingly arose from the interface of literature and Darwinian science (which offered new perspectives on inheritance and transmission, in *Middlemarch* (1871–72)), for example, and a concomitant loss of belief in models of theological omnipotence

---

[68] John Blackwood to George Eliot, 14 November 1867, in *The George Eliot Letters*, ed. G. S. Haight, 9 vols. (New Haven: Yale University Press, 1954–78), 7: 367.

[69] 'Address to Working Men, by Felix Holt,' *Blackwood's Magazine*, December 1867, reproduced in *Felix Holt*, 607–22 (quotation at 622).

[70] Welsh, *Strong Representations*, 198–201.

(in, say, the mature works of Thomas Hardy) and a displacement of the trial as model. Whilst literature, in its protean generativity, found new materials with which to stake its claims to the fullest and richest account of human experience, there remains much to be done in uncovering the Victorian novel's relationship to other forms of public discourse and instrumental oratory which will require, in turn, a new engagement with the law. Further interdisciplinary interrogation is needed of the ways in which Victorians constructed the semiotics of subjectivity and apprehended the claims of ethics or the demands of justice: new work in the field will continue to illuminate for us the role of religion and philosophy in shaping the common language of the Victorian novel and the law.

SUGGESTED READING

Bender, John. *Imagining the Penitentiary: Fiction and the Architecture of Mind in Eighteenth-Century England*. Chicago: Chicago University Press, 1987.

Dolin, Keiran. *A Critical Introduction to Law and Literature*. Cambridge: Cambridge University Press, 2007.

———. *Fiction and the Law: Legal Discourse in Victorian and Modernist Literature*. Cambridge: Cambridge University Press, 1999.

Frank, Catherine. *Law, Literature, and the Transmission of Culture in England, 1837–1925*. Farnham: Ashgate, 2010.

Foucault, Michel. *Discipline and Punish: The Birth of the Prison*. Translated by Alan Sheridan. London: Allen Lane, 1977.

Grossman, Jonathan. *The Art of Alibi: English Law Courts and the Novel*. Baltimore: Johns Hopkins University Press, 2002.

Kertzer, Jonathan. *Poetic Justice and Legal Fictions*. Cambridge: Cambridge University Press, 2010.

Langbein, John. *Origins of Adversary Criminal Trial*. Oxford: Oxford University Press, 2003.

Miller, Andrew H. *The Burdens of Perfection: On Ethics and Reading in Nineteenth-Century British Literature*. Ithaca and London: Cornell University Press, 2008.

Miller, D.A. *The Novel and the Police*. Berkeley: University of California Press, 1988.

Petch, Simon. 'Law, Equity, and Conscience in Victorian England'. *Victorian Literature and Culture* 25, no. 2 (1997): 123–39.

Pettitt, Clare. *Patent Inventions: Intellectual Property and the Victorian Novel*. Oxford: Oxford University Press, 2004.

Polloczek, Dieter Paul. *Literature and Legal Discourse: Equity and Ethics from Sterne to Conrad*. Cambridge: Cambridge University Press, 1999.

Rodensky, Lisa. *The Crime in Mind: Criminal Responsibility and the Victorian Novel*. Oxford: Oxford University Press, 2003.

Schor, Hilary. 'Show-Trials: Character, Conviction, and the Law in Victorian Fiction'. *Cardozo Studies in Law and Literature* 11, no. 2 (1999): 179–95.

Schramm, Jan-Melissa. *Atonement and Self-Sacrifice in Nineteenth-Century Narrative*. Cambridge: Cambridge University Press, 2012.

———. 'Dickens and the National Interest: On the Representation of Parties in *Bleak House*'. *Law and the Humanities* 6, no. 2 (2012), 217–42.

———. *Testimony and Advocacy in Victorian Law, Literature, and Theology*. Cambridge: Cambridge University Press, 2000.

Thomas, Ronald. *Detective Fiction and the Rise of Forensic Science*. Cambridge: Cambridge University Press, 1999.

Ward, Ian. *Law and Literature: Possibilities and Perspectives*. Cambridge: Cambridge University Press, 1995.

Watt, Gary. *Equity Stirring: The Story of Justice Beyond Law*. Oxford: Hart Publishing, 2009.

Weisberg, Richard. *Poethics: And Other Strategies of Law and Literature*. New York: Columbia University Press, 1992.

———. *The Failure of the Word: The Protagonist as Lawyer in Modern Fiction*. New Haven: Yale University Press, 1984.

Welsh, Alexander. *George Eliot and Blackmail*. Cambridge, MA: Harvard University Press, 1985.

———. *Strong Representations: Narrative and Circumstantial Evidence in England*. Baltimore: Johns Hopkins University Press, 1992.

White, James Boyd. *The Legal Imagination: Studies in the Nature of Legal Thought and Expression*. Boston: Little, Brown & Co., 1973.

25

THE NOVEL AND RELIGION: CATHOLICISM AND VICTORIAN WOMEN'S NOVELS

PATRICK R. O'MALLEY

'When I mention religion', declares Mr Thwackum in Henry Fielding's *Tom Jones*, 'I mean the Christian religion; and not only the Christian religion, but the Protestant religion; and not only the Protestant religion, but the Church of England.'[1] As absurd a character as Thwackum is, he nonetheless speaks to a sense, in the middle decades of the 18th century, of the stability of England's relationship to a national sectarianism. Religion, in some ways, *is* the Established Church, and it is precisely through its establishment that Britishness itself finds its basis. Indeed, in *Britons*, Linda Colley has claimed that Protestantism was the very ground of emergent British identity by the end of the 18th century: 'Protestantism was the foundation that made the invention of Great Britain possible.'[2] That striking assertion goes to the very heart of British identity at the dawn of the 19th century. Colley argues that Protestantism did not—and could not—completely overcome the cross-currents of other affiliations (those of social class, for example, or of the different cultures that constituted Welshness or Englishness or Scottishness), but it was a force that loosened and reformed those ties, binding them by the middle of the 18th century into a broader sense of *Britishness*.

Indeed, as Colley suggests, the undergirdings of English (and British) national identity were, at least from the end of the 17th century, defiantly Protestant. The 1673 Test Act required all persons who held any civil or military position to subscribe to the Oath of Supremacy (which named the monarch the Supreme Governor of the Church

---

[1] Henry Fielding, *Tom Jones*, ed. John Bender and Simon Stern (Oxford: Oxford University Press, 2008), 109.

[2] Linda Colley, *Britons: Forging the Nation 1707–1837* (New Haven: Yale University Press, 1992), 54.

of England and denied papal authority in either temporal or spiritual matters) and to disavow belief in transubstantiation; the 1678 Test Act further required all members of the House of Commons and the House of Peers to reject transubstantiation, the invocation of saints, and the sacrifice of the Mass. The 1689 English Bill of Rights specifically excluded Catholics from the royal succession; the so-called 'Disabling Act' of 1695 barred Catholics from many fields of the law (including the professions of barrister, attorney, and solicitor), and a 1700 Act excluded Catholics from the inheritance or purchase of land, although it does not seem to have been frequently enforced.[3]

Some of that began to change as the 18th century came to its conclusion. The Relief Act of 1778, one of the events that led to the 1780 Gordon Riots, allowed Catholics in Britain and Ireland to inherit and purchase property and repealed the penalty of life imprisonment for priests. A 1791 Relief Act allowed Catholics to practise law and to run schools (although the endowment of such schools was still forbidden, as was the existence of monastic orders); assembly for worship was now permitted, although the buildings which housed those meetings could not have a steeple or bell. In 1793, male Catholics who met the income requirements could vote in Ireland, and after the 1800 Act of Union, Catholics throughout the United Kingdom who otherwise met the qualifications could vote.[4] In general, as Bernard Ward has observed, the admission of Ireland into the newly formed 'United Kingdom' significantly changed the pressure on the various 'Catholic questions' at Westminster: 'from that date until Emancipation was finally won in 1829, hardly a year passed without one or more petitions being presented from English or Irish Catholics, or from both'.[5]

In fact, the changing status of Catholics in Britain was one of the signal trends of the 19th century. Ward estimates that there were fewer than 200,000 Catholics in England in 1805; by 1851, according to Edward Norman, there were probably almost 700,000.[6] Norman notes that 'According to the Catholic Directory there were in 1850, the year of the restored Hierarchy, 587 [Catholic] churches in England and Wales, and 788 clergy...In 1870, the year of the Vatican Council, there were 1151 churches and 1528 clergy...In 1900 there were 1529 churches in England and Wales, with 2812 clergy'.[7] Similarly, 'Between 1850 and 1874 the number of Catholic schools in the country rose from 99 to 1,484.'[8] Norman points out that 'To an age fascinated by the statistics

---

[3] See John Miller, *Popery and Politics in England 1660–1688* (Cambridge: Cambridge University Press, 1973), esp. 55–64; Edward Norman, *Roman Catholicism in England* (Oxford: Oxford University Press, 1985), esp. 37–41; and David Mathew, *Catholicism in England 1535–1935* (London: Longmans, Green, 1936), esp. 118–21.

[4] See Colin Haydon, *Anti-Catholicism in Eighteenth-Century England, c.1714–80* (Manchester, UK: Manchester University Press, 1993), 204–44; Mathew, 156; Bernard Ward, *The Eve of Catholic Emancipation*, 3 vols. (London: Longmans, Green, 1911), 1: 1–19; and John Wolffe, *The Protestant Crusade in Great Britain 1829–1860* (Oxford: Clarendon Press, 1991), 10–28.

[5] Ward, 5.

[6] Ward, 18; Edward R. Norman, *The English Catholic Church in the Nineteenth Century* (Oxford: Clarendon Press, 1984), 206.

[7] Norman, *English Catholic Church*, 205.

[8] Norman, *English Catholic Church*, 206.

of growth these were all indications of an astonishing achievement, proportionately comparable, indeed, to the multiplication of religious institutions within the Protestant Established Church in these decades, but accomplished without the financial resources of the Church of England.'[9]

The Victorian period itself might be thought of as structured around the debates about Catholicism and its relationship to English identity. The Catholic Emancipation Act, due to which Nicholas Wiseman later asserted that the 'year 1829 was to us what the egress from the catacombs was to the early Christians',[10] was enacted just three years before the first Reform Act and eight years before the accession of Victoria to the throne. The Oxford Movement's attention to bringing 'Catholicizing' elements (such as auricular confession, the veneration of saints, and an emphasis on Sacramental theology) into the Church of England reached a kind of climax with the conversion of John Henry Newman to Roman Catholicism in 1845, and seems to have convinced Wiseman that the wide-scale conversion of England was possible.[11] Related to, although not identical with, the Oxford Movement was the rise of Anglican Ritualism, a development that emphasized 'Catholic' aesthetics and aesthetic practices in religious music, architecture and interior design, vestments, and other elements of worship and life, what John Shelton Reed has called 'the ceremonial froth [the Oxford Movement] stirred up'.[12] The year 1850 witnessed the re-establishment of English territorial titles by the Catholic hierarchy (with Wiseman as Cardinal of Westminster), a move condemned as the 'Papal Aggression'; it led not only to the enactment of the 1851 Ecclesiastical Titles Act (which made illegal the assumption of territorial titles by Catholic bishops in the United Kingdom) but also to the consternation of Victoria herself, who is said (perhaps apocryphally) to have exclaimed in frustration, 'Am I Queen of England or am I not?'.[13] In 1871, the Church of Ireland was disestablished,[14] and in that same year the University Test Act opened Oxford and Cambridge to non-Anglicans, although the Catholic Church itself continued for a number of years to ban Catholics from attending those schools.[15] As Walter L. Arnstein has argued:

> In England during the early and mid-Victorian years, the Roman Catholics admittedly remained a small minority... Yet, during these same years, that church was transformed from a tiny, isolated, quietist vestige into a rapidly growing

[9] Norman, *English Catholic Church*, 206.

[10] Quoted in Norman, *English Catholic Church*, 29.

[11] See Norman, *English Catholic Church*, 149–50.

[12] John Shelton Reed, *Glorious Battle: The Cultural Politics of Victorian Anglo-Catholicism* (Nashville: Vanderbilt University Press, 1996), 15.

[13] See Norman, *English Catholic Church*, 103; for more responses to the 'Aggression', see Michael Wheeler, *The Old Enemies: Catholic and Protestant in Nineteenth-Century English Culture* (Cambridge: Cambridge University Press, 2006), 9–46.

[14] For background on the disestablishment of the Church of Ireland, see Wolffe, 295–96 and Walter Arnstein, *Protestant Versus Catholic in Mid-Victorian England* (Columbia, MO: University of Missouri Press, 1982), 84–87.

[15] See Arnstein, 157 and Norman, *English Catholic Church*, 294–301.

organization that demanded a major role in the political, social, and intellectual life of the nation.[16]

That shift in power, both real and symbolic, was certainly reflected in Victorian literature, in which Catholicism could stand either as alien threat or as spiritual possibility. I cannot here offer an overview even of the most significant religious developments and debates of the Victorian period, encompassing as they do such questions as the forms and practices of evangelical Christianity, the status of Jewishness and of Jewish converts within British culture and civic life, the challenge of Darwinism—and science more broadly—to traditional Christian tenets, the interaction of England with its colonies (from Ireland to India and beyond) of differing dominant religious practices, and the notion (expressed by Matthew Arnold in 'Dover Beach') that the 'Sea of Faith' itself was ebbing. Nor can I detail the many representations of Catholicism in various novelistic genres, from the conversion narrative to the 'early Christian' novel to the lurid 'Black Robe' plots, with their Gothic-inflected Jesuitical villains.[17] Instead, I will focus on a specific issue: the complicated place of Roman Catholicism in novels written by women as a trope both for submission and for resistance to patriarchal norms. I hope that this focus will illuminate a central crux at the heart of these texts as well as stand as a sort of case study for the complexities—and even paradoxes—of the literary representations of religion in the Victorian period.

This question is part of an important recent direction in Victorian studies, as critics of cultural history have paid increasing attention to the ways in which the debates over the place of Catholicism in Victorian British culture were significantly intertwined with notions of class, nation, gender, and sexuality. James Eli Adams, for example, has noted that Newman's charismatic Tractarianism (that is, his moves to bring Catholicizing images and practices back to the Church of England in the years before his own conversion to Rome) could, at least in the 1840s, be troped as a Carlylean masculinity, a characterization that may be surprising given Tractarianism's later association with effeminacy and homoerotics.[18] And others have pointed out that the paradoxical claims (masculine/effeminate, foreign/domestic, aristocratic/impoverished, chaste/sexually threatening) that 19th-century Catholicism posed to British identity became central to late Victorian Decadence and, in particular, to such figures as Oscar Wilde.[19]

Conservative in its theology and patriarchal in its institutions, Roman Catholicism would seem to be a natural villain in the works of women challenging the orthodoxies of gender roles—and, in fact, it often was. Other analysis, however, has noted that the

[16] Arnstein, 40.
[17] For many of these genres, see Maureen Moran, *Catholic Sensationalism and Victorian Literature* (Liverpool: Liverpool University Press, 2007).
[18] James Eli Adams, *Dandies and Desert Saints* (Ithaca, NY: Cornell University Press, 1995), 81–83.
[19] See, for example, Ellis Hanson, *Decadence and Catholicism* (Cambridge, MA: Harvard University Press, 1997) and Patrick R. O'Malley, *Catholicism, Sexual Deviance, and Victorian Gothic Culture* (Cambridge: Cambridge University Press, 2006).

paradoxical associations of Catholicism—both reactionary and transgressive, restrictive and liberating—offered particular opportunities (both material and symbolic) to Victorian women, who were already more firmly bound than men by an ideology of domesticity that (in England) was deeply intertwined with a Protestant ethos. In *Suggestions for Thought*, Florence Nightingale observed that

> The Church of England has for men bishoprics, archbishoprics, and a little work (good men make a great deal for themselves). She has for women—what?...Luther gave us 'faith', justification by faith, as he calls it; and the Church of Rome gives us 'works'. But the Church of England gives us neither faith nor works.[20]

Martha Vicinus has pointed out that, in fact, Tractarian Anglican sisterhoods, modelled on those of the Catholics, 'were clearly in the vanguard of women's single-sex organizations, in both their organizational autonomy and their insistence upon women's right to a separate religious life'.[21] In general, as Maureen Moran has observed, 'in the prolonged Victorian debate about the Woman Question, the nature of a nun's experience became a key means of portraying the advantages and disadvantages of an empowered, independent version of the feminine'.[22]

Moran's *Catholic Sensationalism and Victorian Literature*, one of the best of the recent books arguing for a more complex understanding of the status of Victorian Catholicism, insists that while Catholicism in 19th-century writing might represent the oppression of women, it frequently does so precisely because it is *like* Victorian Protestant domesticity, not because it is opposed to it: 'the Roman cloister and the English hearth cast remarkably similar shadows'.[23] Indeed, as Moran points out, ambivalence rather than unalloyed condemnation seems to be the key stance for a number of Victorian woman writers. We can see the tensions even in one of the most famously anti-Catholic scenes in one of the most famously anti-Catholic novels of the Victorian period, Lucy Snowe's description of the confessional in Charlotte Brontë's *Villette* (1853). In *Confessional Subjects*, Susan David Bernstein contextualizes this scene within a series of anti-Catholic novels of the 1840s and 1850s, typically grounded to a large degree in Gothic scenes and narratives:

> Through the enclosed space of the confessional...the father confessor converts an Englishwoman from a life of innocence to one of sin. Or the conversion plot functions through an inversion of this narrative. Instead of inducting a woman of unprotected sexual virtue into service as a prostitute, the tyrant priest coerces a young woman of unprotected material wealth to assume the vocation of virginal sisterhood where she

[20] Florence Nightingale, *Cassandra and Other Selections from Suggestions for Thought*, ed. Mary Poovey (New York: New York University Press, 1993), 88.
[21] Martha Vicinus, *Independent Women: Work and Community for Single Women 1850–1920* (Chicago: University of Chicago Press, 1985), 48.
[22] Moran, 80.
[23] Moran, 126.

is imprisoned in a convent so that the church can claim as its property all her worldly goods.[24]

Bernstein argues that this characterization of the power the priest holds over his (typically female) confessant demonstrates a persistent cultural interest in the play of power as it manifests itself in gender relations:

> [I]t is Lucy's act of ecclesiastical confession that signifies the novel's most salient correlation of anti-Catholic tropes with a critique of untoward repression of the passions that hamper Lucy's narrative career of self-revelation… That Lucy's confession embeds a furtive criticism of conditions about which she is not licensed to speak is implied by her first words in the confessional booth to the father confessor: 'Mon père, je suis Protestante.' Using a foreign tongue, a foreign setting, a foreign culture, Lucy can assume this posture of *protest* precisely as a 'Protestante'—that is, a Protestant woman—in a Catholic country. Here the very act of confession is transgressive as a kind of remonstrance against her own vulnerable domestic circumstances, against the plight of unmarried Englishwomen.[25]

Bernstein's analysis shows how a proto-feminist resistance to Protestant domestic norms can be enacted from within the very structures of patriarchal authority (here, the Catholic confessional) that most vividly trope those norms. But that proto-feminism can also be a characteristic of Catholic structures themselves, as Moran has suggested: 'In *Villette*, the adaptation of the popular convent exposé and the feminized convent space provides a new model of female autonomy that challenges marriage and domesticity as a woman's sole destiny'.[26] Maria LaMonaca, whose 2008 book likewise analyses Lucy Snowe (along with Georgiana Fullerton's Ellen Middleton) in relationship to a confessional that allows female expression of a range of human emotions, similarly claims that

> the practice of secret confession validates for each heroine the existence of a 'secret' self at odds with her public persona… In a culture that divided women into angels or fallen creatures, the confessional was possibly the only realm in Victorian culture that recognized that female sanctity was *not* incompatible with real, constant struggles against natural human drives of aggression and sexuality.[27]

In LaMonaca's account, Lucy's Catholic confession represents not submission to male-dominated forms of surveillance—or even a remonstrance against that surveillance—but rather an appeal to a structure that, paradoxically, actually admits the

[24] Susan David Bernstein, *Confessional Subjects: Revelations of Gender and Power in Victorian Literature and Culture* (Chapel Hill: University of North Carolina Press, 1997), 49–50.
[25] Bernstein, 66–67.
[26] Moran, 79.
[27] Maria LaMonaca, *Masked Atheism: Catholicism and the Secular Victorian Home* (Columbus: Ohio State University Press, 2008), 77.

possibility of female desire, both erotic and other: 'Although the novel does suggest that confession can be employed to manipulate and control women, confession also represents for Lucy Catholicism's most compelling aspect: its acknowledgment and understanding of female desire, in contrast to the austerity of English Protestantism, which recognizes only pure angels or corrupt whores'.[28] While that is, surely, a rather reductive description of Victorian Protestantism, the point is a good one: the strongly dichotomous tropes of Catholicism both as restriction and as unnatural libertinism allowed some authors, both male and female, to deploy it as a kind of stealthy transgression. Investigating these tensions has opened up a new and rich direction in Victorian work on the novel and religion, and what I want to look at here are two novels—George Eliot's *Romola* (1863) and Sarah Grand's *The Heavenly Twins* (1893)—that raise in especially telling ways the question of Catholicism's relationship to women's desire and agency, particularly given its complicated and even con-tradictory cultural status as both the upholder and the transgressor of patriarchal regimes.

Barry Qualls, among others, has observed that despite her personal disavowal of reli-gion, Eliot's novels are structured, from the beginning, by Christian tropes and symbolic narratives, that she, 'from *Scenes of Clerical Life* through *Daniel Deronda*, used the language and tropes of the Bible';[29] as Qualls notes of *Daniel Deronda*, 'The novel is her last rewriting of the story she had told so often: the story of men and especially women seeking texts by which to live, sources in historical and cultural memory that would sustain the private life and allow one to be a part of a moral community'.[30] Eliot's investment in the binding of the individual into history, tradition, and community led her, Qualls points out, perhaps inevi-tably to the iconography of medieval Roman Catholicism: 'George Eliot's art of naturaliza-tion of the sacred committed her to the use of traditional religious iconography, especially the emblem tradition (which originated in medieval Catholic Europe and achieved high popularity in the English Renaissance…)'.[31] After all, it is Roman Catholicism that provides the web of cultural unity that underwrites the possibilities for a woman like St Teresa at the opening of *Middlemarch*: 'these later-born Theresas were helped by no coherent social faith and order which could perform the function of knowledge for the ardently willing soul'.[32]

Among Eliot's novels, it is of course *Romola*—set in 15th-century Catholic Florence during the rise and fall of the Dominican mystic and enforcer of orthodox practices, Girolamo Savonarola—that engages most directly with the representation of Roman Catholicism, as both restriction and possibility. Near the beginning of the novel, Romola herself rejects the prophetic claims of Catholic mysticism, offering instead what looks like a crypto-Enlightenment (and English Protestant) emphasis on reason and nature: 'What is this religion of yours', she bitterly asks her brother, a monk, 'that places visions

---

[28] LaMonaca, 85–86.
[29] Barry Qualls, 'George Eliot and Religion', in *The Cambridge Companion to George Eliot*, ed. George Levine (Cambridge: Cambridge University Press, 2001), 119–37, 124.
[30] Qualls, 121–22.
[31] Qualls, 125.
[32] George Eliot, *Middlemarch*, ed. David Carroll (Oxford: Oxford University Press, 1997), 3.

before natural duties?' (153).[33] Indeed, 'There was an unconquerable repulsion for her in that monkish aspect; it seemed to her the brand of the dastardly undutifulness which had left her father desolate—of the grovelling superstition which could give such undutifulness the name of piety' (152). Dino's passionate mysticism disavows the earthly father for the one on the cross: 'so strangely hard', Romola observes, 'not a word to my father…And yet it was so piteous—the struggling breath, and the eyes that seemed to look towards the crucifix, and yet not to see it' (176). The symbolism here is not subtle: in focusing so intensely on the rituals and iconography of Catholicism, Dino fails to see Christianity itself. Throughout this section of the novel, Eliot's narrator explicitly contrasts the conventual and the familial, even Dino's monastic name (Fra Luca) both reflecting and distorting, as though in a glass darkly, the nomenclature of the natural family:

> The prevision that Fra Luca's words had imparted to Romola had been such as comes from the shadowy region where human souls seek wisdom apart from the human sympathies which are the very life and substance of our wisdom; the revelation that might have come from the simple questions of filial and brotherly affection had been carried into irrevocable silence. (160)

Nonetheless, the pull of Catholic mysticism persists: after her husband, Tito, encloses a crucifix in a triptych bearing mythological figures, symbolically burying Catholicism behind classicism, Romola observes, 'it is still there—it is only hidden' (201). As the novel continues—and as Savonarola's presence seeps across its terrain—Catholic iconography begins to infect the very bodies of the novel's characters; Baldassarre, for example, 'clutched his own palms, driving his long nails into them' (230), transforming himself—in his despair and madness—into the image of Catholic-inflected martyrdom, his very corporeality ('nails') transfigured into the instruments of Christ's crucifixion. The narrator muses on 'that force of outward symbols by which our active life is knit together so as to make an inexorable external identity for us, not to be shaken by our wavering consciousness' (319). While the specific 'symbol' at issue here is Romola's wedding ring, the reflection also hints at the ties that religious custom exerts on its practitioners; it occurs only after Romola puts on the 'grey serge dress of a sister belonging to the third order of St Francis' (318). Indeed, Eliot's account of Romola's internal struggle over casting off her ring echoes and transforms the debate over tradition that structures one of the keynotes of Protestantism's rejection of Catholic doctrine, as well as Romanism's insistence upon the power of sacramental acts of memorialization: 'why should she return to him the sign of their union, and not rather retain it as a memorial? And this act, which came as a palpable demonstration of her own and his identity, had a power unexplained to herself, of shaking Romola' (320).

---

[33] Quotations from *Romola* will be cited parenthetically in the text as they appear in George Eliot, *Romola*, ed. Dorothea Barrett (London: Penguin, 2005).

Romola's removal of the ring suggests a rejection of that sticky web of Catholicism, a gesture of proto-Protestantism that forswears 'wretched superstition', 'the company of the howling fanatics and weeping nuns who had been her contempt from childhood till now' (327). But that protest is short-lived, as Savanorola proves to have a hypnotic power that, for example, the amiable Dr Kenn of *The Mill on the Floss* does not. Whereas the Anglican Kenn is utterly unable to grapple effectively with the interplay of desire and renunciation that seizes Maggie Tulliver, Savanorola's Catholicism, materially figured in the crucifix's image of the suffering Christ, can account for the paradox of Romola's desires precisely because it, too, is paradoxical: its alchemy transfigures desire into renunciation and renunciation into desire. While some critics have seen in Eliot's Savonarola the impulse of purification that drove the Protestant Reformation, Philip Fisher has aptly observed his strong associations with incarnational Catholic practice: 'Like the host in Catholic rituals, Savonarola appears only in the most theatrical settings. One third of his force is personality, one third is theater, and the final third is miracle.'[34] While Romola, 'in a tone of anguish, as if she were being dragged to some torture', makes a Protestant stand against his claims of authority with her assertion that 'Father, you may be wrong' (360)—implicitly echoing Lucy Snowe's declaration 'Mon père, je suis Protestante'—she moves swiftly towards submission: 'Father, I will be guided. Teach me! I will go back' (362).

It is shortly thereafter that Eliot's novel moves explicitly to align Romola with the Catholic Madonna, although continuing also to resist their conflation. In the chapter entitled 'The Unseen Madonna', Eliot's narrator describes the movement of a procession through Florence, figured insistently in terms of Catholic iconography and veneration not only of saints but also of their relics, a medievalism that has seized the imagination of the present, and a theology of mystery that slides into the magical. Following 'a sacred relic—the very head, enclosed in silver, of San Zenobio, immortal bishop of Florence, whose virtues were held to have saved the city perhaps a thousand years before', comes the icon of the Virgin: 'the mysterious hidden Image—hidden first by rich curtains of brocade enclosing an outer painted tabernacle, but within this, by the more ancient tabernacle which had never been opened in the memory of living men, or the fathers of living men. In that inner shrine was the image of the Pitying Mother, found ages ago in the soil of L'Impruneta, uttering a cry as the spade struck it' (380). This unseen Madonna finds its correlate in Romola, who, discovering that an approaching horseman bringing information about the delivery of necessary food and military assistance is in fact Tito, moves to cover her features like those of the Pitying Mother herself: 'Romola, instead of making any effort to be recognised by him, threw her black drapery over her head again, and remained perfectly quiet' (383). And—in the next chapter, entitled 'The Visible Madonna'—as she leaves the procession to serve the poor, removing the veil from her head, the association is clinched: '"Bless you, Madonna! bless you!" said the faint chorus,

---

[34] Philip Fisher, *Making Up Society: The Novels of George Eliot* (Pittsburgh: University of Pittsburgh Press, 1981), 128; Moran notes that Eliot's 'curious mixture of Protestant-Catholic discourse creates a figure [Savonarola] who is as culturally "double" as he is "other" for Victorian readers' (Moran, 163).

in much the same tone as that in which they had a few minutes before praised and thanked the unseen Madonna' (387). Romola here has become a form of the Catholic Virgin herself.[35]

Catholicism in *Romola* is, at times, monstrous: it appears as the burning of books (421) and, metaphorically, in the twisted psyche of the prophetess Camilla, 'whose faculties seemed all wrought up into fantasies, leaving nothing for emotion and thought', whose 'tightening grasp' on Romola's arm is 'like a crab' (442). It easily shrinks to a cramped sectarianism, as when Savonarola—in a kind of mirror image of Thwackum's assertion—insists that 'The cause of my party *is* the cause of God's kingdom', a claim to which Romola, finally, issues a kind of anti-*Credo*: 'I do not believe it!' (492). But there is, in the end, something mystically powerful about it. In any case, it cannot be dismissed. It is Tito who takes the strongly rationalist stand against the religion of 'monks and their legends', scoffing that 'servitude agrees well with a religion like theirs, which lies in the renunciation of all that makes life precious to other men' (66).[36] But Tito is hardly an exemplary character, and what makes life precious to him seems inevitably to lead to the passions, ambitions, and weaknesses that threaten to destroy the men—and especially the women—around him. Indeed, renunciation—fundamental to Eliot's notion of Catholicism and its narratives—is a central issue particularly for women, as it is ever in Eliot, from Maggie Tulliver to Dorothea Brooke. As Eliot's contemporary Richard Simpson noted, 'That which gives the religious charm to George Eliot's novels is the way in which she handles the doctrine of renunciation and self-sacrifice for the benefit of others. In this she speaks as a Christian, even as a Catholic.'[37]

Moran notes that Simpson's assertion 'ignores the extent to which Romola's heroism also demands qualities of assertion and resistance', not only submission.[38] But that does not require a disavowal of Catholicism but rather a reconceptualization of its resonances. Kimberly VanEsveld Adams has noted,

> As a 'Protestant' heroine, a citizen of Florence, Romola anticipates the arguments of the Reformation by claiming moral equality with men. Yet her role as a Madonna-figure is rooted in Catholic thought and experience; she is seen as the living impersonation of the Church's art, doctrines, and legends. These two roles are not wholly separable.[39]

---

[35] Carol Marie Engelhardt has pointed out that, outside of Tractarian circles, Victorian Anglicans tended to view the iconography of the Virgin Mary with suspicion, particularly in terms of its challenge to gendered norms. See Engelhardt, 'The Paradigmatic Angel in the House: The Virgin Mary and Victorian Anglicans', *Women of Faith in Victorian Culture*, ed. Anne Hogan and Andrew Bradstock (Houndmills, Basingstoke: Macmillan, 1998), 159–71, 162.

[36] In context, this comment relates most directly to Greek Orthodox rather than Roman Catholic belief and practice, but neither Eliot nor her characters seem particularly interested in that distinction.

[37] Richard Simpson, 'George Eliot's Novels', in *George Eliot: The Critical Heritage*, ed. David Carroll (New York: Routledge, 1971), 247.

[38] Moran, 166–67.

[39] Kimberly VanEsveld Adams, *Our Lady of Victorian Feminism: The Madonna in the Work of Anna Jameson, Margaret Fuller, and George Eliot* (Athens, OH: Ohio University Press, 2001), 181.

THE NOVEL AND RELIGION 539

It is that inseparability, in fact the very intertwining of proto-feminist protest and Catholic tradition, that gives *Romola* its power as an exploration of religious experience and practice.

In Eliot's work, that rich sense of paradox finds its fullest expression displaced both temporally and spatially from its Victorian English audience. For example, in *Adam Bede*, the extravagant display of Catholic iconography is precisely the very mark of cultural alterity:

> I have often thought so when, in foreign countries, where the fields and woods have looked to me like our English Loamshire...I have come on something by the roadside which has reminded me that I am not in Loamshire: an image of a great agony—the agony of the Cross.[40]

In contrast, although for Sarah Grand, born in Ireland and writing three decades after Eliot, Roman Catholicism still seems rather outré, it can hardly be relegated to the Continent or to past ages. The Oxford Movement and its aftermath is, in Grand, a fait accompli, and she recognizes that by the end of the 19th century, Catholicism has found a home in the heart of Britain itself. The world of *The Heavenly Twins* is contemporary and urbane, caught between a dying reactionary old guard and a forward-looking, scientifically driven progressivism. It is, in Grand's own terms, 'modern', a word that appears nine times in the novel, describing everything from 'modern civilization' (188) to 'modern dress' (611) to 'modern methods of inquiry' (177) to, of particular centrality, 'modern women' (347).[41] When another character asks one of the eponymous 'Heavenly Twins' whether the nickname refers to the 'signs of the Zodiac', she responds, with a kind of portentous prophecy, 'No, signs of the times' (383), an exchange that Grand abstracted from the narrative to make her epigraph for the entire novel.

Much less frequently read and analysed than Eliot's *Romola*, *The Heavenly Twins* narrates the coming into adulthood of three young and wealthy women: Angelica Hamilton-Wells, Evadne Frayling, and Edith Beale. Angelica's grandfather, the Duke of Morningquest (Grand's fictionalized Norwich), is himself—along with his daughter, Lady Fulda—a convert to Romanism, a fact of modern British life that Grand's cosmopolitan Anglicans, even children, can muse over. When Angelica (a 'Heavenly Twin', along with her brother Theodore, called Diavolo) asks the wife of the (Anglican) Bishop of Morningquest about conversion to Catholicism, the result is a bit of humour at the orthodox churchwoman's expense:

> 'I suppose you wouldn't like us to be converted?' Angelica asked.
> 'We call it *perverted*, dear child,' said Mrs. Beale.

---

[40] George Eliot, *Adam Bede*, ed. Margaret Reynolds (London: Penguin, 2008), 394–95.
[41] Quotations from *The Heavenly Twins* will be cited parenthetically in the text as they appear in Sarah Grand, *The Heavenly Twins*, ed. Carol A. Senf (Ann Arbor: University of Michigan Press, 1992).

'Well, they call it *converted* just as positively up at the castle,' Angelica
            rejoined, not argumentatively, merely stating the fact.
'I wonder what the angels call it,' said Diavolo, looking up in their
            direction out of a window opposite, and then glancing at
            the bishop as if he thought he ought to know.
'I don't suppose they care a button what we call it,' Angelica decided off-
            hand, out of her own inner consciousness. [153]

The implication of Grand's situating of this discussion among children is that sectarian-ism makes, after all, not very much difference, and the idle conversation merely domes-ticates what, earlier in the century, might have been the province of controversialist debate and calumny.

Grand doesn't resist the easy stereotypes of Catholicism as a sort of moral perver-sion; for the Duke (as for Wilde's Dorian Gray) it is a kind of exquisite decadence, a sub-stitute for and intensification of erotic desire (complete with a gender-bending simile): 'Their theory was that, having grown too old for worldly dissipation, he had entered the Church in search of new forms of excitement, and to vary the monotony generally, as so many elderly coquettes do when they can no longer attract attention in any other way' (253). The Duke's private confessor is, similarly, a voluptuary, his Catholicism quickly sliding into the failings of his flesh: Father Ricardo is

a man of middle age, middle height, attenuated form, round head with coarse black hair, piercing dark eyes, aquiline nose somewhat thick, and the loose mouth characteristic of devout Roman Catholics, High Church people, and others who are continually being wound up to worship an unseen Deity by means of sensuous enjoyment; the uncertain lines into which the lips fall in repose indicating fairly the habitual extent of their emotional indulgences. [143]

Even as it has entered the discourse of her progress-driven modernity, Catholicism for Grand is a kind of throwback, an anachronism in a world that is striving forward. And that play of modernity and medieval superstition (as Grand presents Catholicism) is one that she highlights at length in her description of the conversion of the Duke of Morningquest to Rome:

For when his youngest daughter, the beautiful Lady Fulda, became a Roman Catholic, she wrought upon him by her earnestness so as to make him fear the flames, and drove him in that way to seek solace and salvation in the Church as well; and when he had done so himself, he rather expected, and quite intended, that everybody else should do likewise. But the people of Morningquest who had adopted his vices did not fear the flames themselves, and would have nothing to do with his piety. They were like the children in 'Punch,' who, when threatened with the policeman at the corner, exclaimed in derision: 'Why, that's father!' And, besides, the times were changing rapidly, and the influence which remained to the aristocracy was already only dominant so long as it went the way of popular feeling and was human; directly it retrograded to past privileges, ideas, superstitions, and tastes, the people laughed at it. They knew that the threatened rule of the priest was a far-fetched anachronism which they need not fear for themselves in the aggregate, and they therefore gave themselves up with interest to the observation of such evidences of its effect on the individual as the duke should betray to them from time to time. [253]

The casual invocation of the expression 'from time to time' is not as insignificant as it might seem. Even in a novel as focused as this one is on the tropes and experience of modernity, this passage stands out for its condensation of temporal markers. There is the contrast between the historical past and the modern present (echoed to some extent in the counterpoint of the standard narrative past and the past perfect), but there is also the *tempo* of historical change, which itself seems to be accelerating. 'The times were changing rapidly', Grand's narrator tells us, and one of the results of that is that the sort of 'retrograde' attachments that Catholicism represents ('past privileges, ideas, superstitions, and tastes') looks humorously anachronistic. That *Punch*, one of the most persistently anti-Catholic of prominent Victorian popular publications, can become a trope for the relationship between a Protestant populace and a Catholic aristocracy is only one of the effects of the topsy-turvy world that this temporal acceleration has left in its wake. And for the Catholic Duke, history itself has collapsed: 'His difficulty was to disconnect the past from the present, the two having a tendency to mix themselves up in his mind' (253).

Catholicism's temporal disruptions in *The Heavenly Twins* suggest that, for Grand, it represents a sort of backward pull, a reactionary force resisting modernity's moves towards the future. Like Eliot, Grand turns to Darwinian evolution as a trope for both narrative and for the development of society; indeed, she takes an epigraph for each of the first two books of *The Heavenly Twins* from Darwin. Unlike Eliot's, Grand's embrace of Darwinism is less ambivalent (and less nuanced): the word *evolution*, typically in Grand synonymous with 'progress', appears in the first chapter of the novel as a kind of retort to Evadne's father's self-satisfied misogyny:

He was quite ignorant of the moral progress of the world at the present time, and ready to resent even the upward tendency of evolution when it presented itself to him in the form of any change, including, of course, changes for the better, and more especially so if such change threatened to bring about an improvement in the position of women, or increase the weight of their influence for good in the world. [6]

Like their author, Grand's enlightened female characters tend to be liberal on gender politics and conservative on sexual politics; the social double standard should be resolved by opening employment and the franchise to women, but the sexual double standard should be resolved by a regime of universal chastity rather than by making men's sexual practices common to all. And that stance, as Angelique Richardson has observed, derives to some extent from Grand's understanding of evolution: 'Positioned among social purists, Social Darwinists, and eugenists, these [New Woman] writers were concerned less with examining the unstable, socially constructed nature of self-hood and the body, than with grounding both the body and sex roles in the flesh and blood of evolutionary narrative'.[42] When the corrupt and erotically dangerous Lord Groome warns Evadne about the contagion of another woman's 'revolutionary ideas', Evadne counters with Darwinian assurance: 'Not "revo"—but evolutionary' (230). Religion also, in Grand, follows an evolutionary path, away from ritual and towards a more general liberal civic faith; it mirrors in reverse the retrograde path of conversion to Catholicism, and it is the path that such positively portrayed characters as Ideala, Lord Dawne, and Lady Claudia take.

To some extent, Grand misreads Darwin, seeing in him an account of what we might distinguish as Lamarckian rather than actual Darwinian evolution. Of Evadne's father, Mr Frayling, Grand's narrator notes darkly that

> He was very particular about the human race when it was likely to suffer by an injurious indulgence on the part of women, but when it was a question of extra port wine for himself, he never considered the tortures of gout he might be entailing upon his own hapless descendants. [103]

The central trope for this Lamarckian inheritance is syphilis, a disease which writes itself upon the flesh and mind of the innocent child of the sexually corrupt (or violated) adult; for Grand, it is the perfect evidence that the sins of the fathers are indeed visited upon the sons, but here it has become a genetic rather than religious inheritance, speaking to the truth of evolutionary biology rather than of the Bible. The brutal descriptions of Edith's suffering and death from syphilis (and the deformity of her child) represent a sustained attack on the regimes of male authority and male sexuality that Grand sees as the enemies of progress. In a haunting scene, Angelica finds herself observing three men gathered around the body of the ailing Edith. They are Sir Mosley Menteith, Edith's husband, the Bishop of Morningquest, her father, and Dr George Galbraith, her physician. That is, they stand allegorically for the military (in which Menteith served), the clergy, and the medical professions, three manifestations of male-dominated spheres whose collusion, in Grand's novel, functions to destroy women's agency and, indeed, their lives. Edith herself, dangerously naïve throughout the early pages of the novel, recognizes this: 'That is why I sent for you all ... you who represent the arrangement of society which has made it possible for me and my child to be sacrificed in this way' (300).

The sacrifice in this case is a secular one, and yet it echoes and amplifies the iconic sacrifices of Christian narrative and hagiography. In particular, it functions as a sort of correlative to Edith's own Catholicizing impulses. Before she is syphilitic, Edith is a ritualist:

---

[42] Angelique Richardson, 'The Eugenization of Love: Sarah Grand and the Morality of Genealogy', *Victorian Studies* 42, no. 2 (2000), 227–55, 228.

[T]he bedroom of the only daughter of the Bishop of Morningquest would have made you think of matters ecclesiastical…The pictures consisted of photographs or engravings of sacred subjects, all of Roman Catholic origin. There was a 'Virgin and Child,' by Botticelli, and another by Perugini; 'Our Lady of the Cat,' by Baroccio; the exquisite 'Vision of St. Helena,' by Paolo Veronese; Correggio's 'Ecce Homo'; and others less well-known; with a ghastly Crucifixion too painful to be endured, especially by a young girl, had not custom dulled all genuine perception of the horror of it. [158]

As in Eliot's *Romola*, Catholicism can be either quaint Continental background (at least to those of vitiated perception) or vividly Gothic foreground. Intellectually and emotionally cloistered as she is, Edith's sexuality explodes into crypto-Catholic adoration of the physical body of Christ:

It was a religious exercise she had taught herself, not knowing that the Roman Catholics practise it as a duty always…She called him by name caressingly: 'Dear Lord!' She confessed her passionate attachment to him. She implored him to look upon her lovingly. She offered him the devotion of her life. And then she sank into a perfect stupor of ecstatic contemplation. This was the way she worshipped, dwelling on the charms of his person and character with the same senses that her delicate maiden mind still shrank from devoting to an earthly lover; calling him what she would have had her husband be: 'Master!' [169]

All religion in *The Heavenly Twins* can serve as a sort of excuse for quietism in the struggle for human advancement, but the eroticism of self-abasement, even of a sort of masochistic relinquishment of any control seems to be the particular province of Edith's strongly Catholic-inflected ritualism. It is defiantly physical in its effects, even as it corrupts the mind. Given the tendencies of her religious life—and given Grand's explicit alignment of religious choice with the sexual object choice of marriage—it is, then, perhaps no wonder that Edith's choice for a husband is the seductive, domineering, powerfully male—and syphilitic—Mosley Menteith.

Like syphilis, Roman Catholicism is for Grand a symptom of male control over women—sexualized, erotic, even attractive, and yet ultimately deadly; Edith's syphilis—troped as a sacrifice to patriarchal power—is her Crucifixion. In this novel, both are also counter-evolutionary, syphilis because of its degenerate symptoms and Catholicism because of its fundamental anachronism. As the rationalist Ideala declares to Father Ricardo when asked where the 'true spirit of God' is:

It is in us *women*. *We* have preserved it, and handed it down from one generation to another of our own sex unsullied; and very soon we shall be called upon to prove the possession of it, for already…already I—that is to say Woman—am a power in the land, while you—that is to say Priest—retain ever less and less even of the semblance of power. [267]

It may happen slowly, but the principle of the survival of the fittest is on the side of political progress—and *explicitly* opposed to the archaic power of the Catholic priest—as
Ideala's genealogically-troped narrative makes clear. It is no accident that the book
that contains the narrative of Edith's suffering, the account of the duke's conversion to
Catholicism (and the description of Catholicism as anachronistic) and Ideala's excla-
mation—in addition to a Gothically-tinged scene of exorcism, a dream of Angelica's in
which she defies both the Pope and the ritualist Archbishop of York, and, ultimately,
Evadne's burning of her books and her retreat into a stiflingly proper womanhood—is
entitled 'Development and Arrest of Development'.

Ideala is one of the most ideological of the anti-Catholics of *The Heavenly Twins*,
declaring 'Just consider the state of degradation, and the dense ignorance of the people
of every country upon which the curse of Catholicism rests!' (266).[43] That comfortably
chauvinistic (and quintessentially English) observation, of course, ignores the compli-
cating effects of social class, and it is there that Grand's novel displays its own ambivalence. It is, to be sure, a text that itself rarely ventures out of the ranks of those with titles
or money or both, but the hints of a broader society at the margins of that prosperous
world suggest that the anti-Catholicism that its characters maintain is not the complete
picture, especially for women. Father Ricardo is petty, superstitious, and selfish, and he
is easily bested in argument by children, but it is not he who leaves a sick and dying
woman (herself Continental and Catholic and suffering from syphilis) on the road; it is
the Anglican bishop's wife and daughter (159–61). In contrast, Lady Fulda, the daughter of the Duke of Morningquest, does in fact demonstrate her Catholic faith through
works, particularly those that help the most miserable of Grand's women, the prostitutes. Angelica, dressed in boy's clothing, watches Fulda take Marie Cruchot, who sold
her sister Louise (the woman whom Edith and Mrs Beale pass by) into a sexual relationship with Mosley Menteith, off the streets and into a Catholic refuge:

> A tall and graceful lady of most dignified bearing, with a countenance of peculiar
> serenity and sweetness, had approached from the opposite direction, and was
> standing beside the girl, speaking to her evidently, but the Boy was too far off to
> hear what was said. He could see, however, that the girl's whole attitude had
> changed. She was no longer dejected, but eager: and she gazed in the lady's face as
> she listened to her words with an expression of admiration and wonder, one had
> almost said of adoration, upon her own, as though it were a heavenly visitant who
> had hailed her. [377]

---

[43] That said, she also avoids the polemically charged term 'pervert' for converts to Catholicism
'because I know that it really cannot matter, so long as they are agreeable' (264). In fact, for Ideala,
the 'religion of the future' transcends Christianity itself, although it especially must evolve beyond
Catholicism's attachment to ceremony and what looks like idolatry (see e.g. 265).

Fulda herself, like Angelica, wants change, although she couches her version of gradual evolution in a religious idiom: 'It will come right, I know... But, Lord, how long?' (441).

Lady Fulda represents a critique of Protestantism in a way that Father Ricardo cannot—and it is precisely because she offers a Catholicism that speaks to women. When Angelica overhears an Anglican clergyman call Fulda 'a pervert as we say' and observe that 'We require such women now, though; but somehow we do not keep them', she comes upon her own answer: 'Too cold... Hollow, shallow, inconsistent—loveless. Catholicism equals a modern refinement of pagan principles with all the old deities on their best behaviour thrown in; while Protestantism is an ecclesiastical system founded on fetish' (489). In Angelica's account, there is a bloodlessness to Protestantism, and while Grand is certainly not the exponent of neo-paganism that some of her aestheticist contemporaries were, she admits the attraction, especially in contrast with the alternative. Fulda is, it must be said, a conservative, although her conservatism aligns in important respects with Grand's own. (For one thing, she convinces Angelica to return to her husband and to focus her energies on her marriage, passionless though it seems to be.) But Angelica does not, it is important to note, recant the attack on Catholic institutional misogyny that she makes in the course of her weird dream during Edith's illness; rather, she admits the ambivalence of nuance: the Anglican Bishop of Morningquest did not save Edith, but Fulda can save Marie.

In *Romola*, Eliot writes that 'Savonorola's nature was one of those in which opposing tendencies coexist in almost equal strength' (523). And much the same can be said for Roman Catholicism itself as it appears in the works of these two authors. Grand's Evadne responds to her aunt's suggestion that she cease her angry refusal to live with her husband despite his sexual failings with a short meditation on capitulation and resistance: 'You mean *submit*... No, that word is of no use to me. Mine is *rebel*' (95). The submission of women to male authority is a concept that the novel has already strongly associated with orthodox Christianity and medieval piety: 'All right minded women have submitted and suffered patiently, and have had their reward', Evadne's mother had written her; '[t]hink of the mother of St. Augustin!' (91). For Qualls, this sort of submission represents a concession to the cultural insistence upon women's purity that Eliot critiques:

> Among George Eliot's women, only Romola is totally successful in turning herself into that emblem of divine love that so much marks Dickens's and his contemporaries' celebration of the angel in the house... [O]nly Romola, floating passively on a river, and wishing for death, brings rescuing life—and becomes a Madonna of the Italian rocks.[44]

But Roman Catholicism also functions in these works—especially for women—as an almost impossible alchemy of submission and rebellion, of a relinquishment of women's

---

[44] Qualls, 128.

agency to a foreign and male-dominated power *and* simultaneously as a rebellion against the domestic restrictions of Protestant domesticity that LaMonaca has described. Certainly in *Romola*, Catholicism represents a sort of submission, as the repeated drumbeat of that term makes clear: of Savonarola, the narrator notes that Romola 'had submitted her mind to his and had entered into communion with the Church, because in this way she had found an immediate satisfaction for moral needs which all the previous culture and experience of her life had left hungering' (388). And when she later leaves the cult of his personality, she tells him much the same in her own words: 'I submitted because I felt the proffered strength—because I saw the light. *Now* I cannot see it' (490). Rebellion, however, in this text both opposes and mirrors submission. On the one hand, it represents Romola's proto-feminist resistance to monkish male authority, particularly when she first meets Savonarola: 'Romola's disposition to rebel against command, doubly active in the presence of monks, whom she had been taught to despise, would have fixed itself on any repulsive detail as a point of support' (156). But on the other, it becomes in itself—as in Angelica's vision in *The Heavenly Twins* of an uprising of new women against the power of the Pope—a kind of sacredness, a ritual of resistance through which Romola (and *Romola*) reworks the very terms of Catholicism by reusing them: 'The law was sacred. Yes, but rebellion might be sacred too. It flashed upon her mind that the problem before her was essentially the same as that which had lain before Savonarola—the problem where the sacredness of obedience ended, and where the sacredness of rebellion began' (468).

This paradox is one that Eliot situates at the very heart of Catholicism's threat and promise, particularly for women:

> The question where the duty of obedience ends, and the duty of resistance begins, could in no case be an easy one; but it was made overwhelmingly difficult by the belief that the Church was—not a compromise of parties to secure a more or less approximate justice in the appropriation of funds, but—a living organism, instinct with divine power to bless and to curse. [457]

As LaMonaca argues, 'Even as Madonna Romola comes across as an essentialist vision of sacred womanhood, it is a vision of womanhood that eclipses male authority'.[45] Certainly for Eliot, the value of Catholicism is not about adherence to doctrine, but neither is it in soulless technocratic distribution of goods; instead, it lies in the possibilities of human relationships that it opens up. The *Oxford English Dictionary* points out that the etymology of the term 'religion' itself is murky, being made up of:

> RE-*prefix* + a second element of uncertain origin; by Cicero connected with *relegere* to read over again ... so that the supposed original sense of 'religion' would have been

---

45 LaMonaca, 176.

'painstaking observance of rites', but by later authors (especially by early Christian writers) with *religāre* ... 'religion' being taken as 'that which ties believers to God'.[46]

The word 'religion' thus subsumes, buried in its own history, both a kind of mindless submission to ritual *and* the notion of binding without which a redemptive sympathy is impossible, an etymology that Nightingale stresses: 'What is the meaning of the word "religion"? Is it not the tie, the *binding*, or connexion between the Perfect and the imperfect, the eternal and the temporal, the infinite and the finite, the universal and the individual?'.[47] As Romola reflects, following her 'new baptism', 'if the glory of the cross is an illusion, the sorrow is only the truer. While the strength is in my arm I will stretch it out to the fainting; while the light visits my eyes they shall seek the forsaken' (560). In that claim is not only a kind of rapprochement to Catholicism but also a new type of realism, both ethical and narrative, that does not see women's submission and rebellion as opposites but as wary allies.

Once the novel has aligned Romola with the Virgin Mary, it is an association that persists. Living among the Jewish survivors of the plague after she has left Florence, Romola becomes, even iconographically, a type of Madonna: 'Only a little while ago, the young acolyte had brought word to the *padre* that he had seen the Holy Mother with the Babe, fetching water for the sick: she was as tall as the cypresses, and had a light about her head, and she looked up at the church' (556). But the redemption that she brings is less doctrinal than material; while the baby that she bears does in fact become 'a tottering tumbling Christian, Benedetto by name, having been baptised in the church on the mountain-side' (558), when the narrator gestures towards the theologically loaded term 'saved', it is insistently a physical salvation: 'but all of these were comforted, most were saved, and the dead were buried' (558). It is survival—and sympathy—and not conversion that represents the beating heart of this kind of Catholicism. As Romola notes, in the last words of the novel, 'There are many good people who did not love Fra Girolamo. Perhaps I should never have learned to love him if he had not helped me when I was in great need' (583).

As Moran has observed, 'In contrast to the alien "Jesuit" style of lurid sensationalism, the conventions of realist practice are held to be synonymous with English native tradition and culture'.[48] Although *Romola* certainly has elements of romance, both Eliot and Grand explore the relationship between Catholicism and women within the narrative expectations of realism, moving away from the Catholic plots and allusions of the Gothic and the sensation novel. To some extent, Catholicism in these novels still counters realism, acting as a sort of Gothic pull into the past that has particular ramifications for

---

[46] *Oxford English Dictionary Online*, s.v. 'religion' (accessed 12 January 2013).
[47] Nightingale, 108.
[48] Moran, 40.

women, but—through them—it also enters the mainstream of realist Protestant fiction, as—through the Oxford Movement and its aftermath—it had British culture. They make possible an understanding of Catholicism not as impossibly alien but as familiar—and thus open it up to the experiences and the ambivalences of women's lives and desires.

SUGGESTED READING

Adams, Kimberly VanEsveld. *Our Lady of Victorian Feminism: The Madonna in the Work of Anna Jameson, Margaret Fuller, and George Eliot.* Athens: Ohio University Press, 2001.

Bernstein, Susan David. *Confessional Subjects: Revelations of Gender and Power in Victorian Literature and Culture.* Chapel Hill: University of North Carolina Press, 1997.

Griffin, Susan M. *Anti-Catholicism and Nineteenth-Century Fiction.* Cambridge: Cambridge University Press, 2004.

Hogan, Anne and Andrew Bradstock. *Women of Faith in Victorian Culture: Reassessing the Angel in the House.* Houndmills, Basingstoke: Macmillan, 1998.

LaMonaca, Maria. *Masked Atheism: Catholicism and the Secular Victorian Home.* Columbus: Ohio State University Press, 2008.

Moran, Maureen. *Catholic Sensationalism and Victorian Literature.* Liverpool: Liverpool University Press, 2007.

Paz, D.G. *Popular Anti-Catholicism in Mid-Victorian England.* Stanford: Stanford University Press, 1992.

Vanita, Ruth. *Sappho and the Virgin Mary: Same-Sex Love and the English Literary Imagination.* New York: Columbia University Press, 1996.

Wheeler, Michael. *The Old Enemies: Catholic and Protestant in Nineteenth-Century English Culture.* Cambridge: Cambridge University Press, 2006.

26

THE VICTORIAN NOVEL AND HORTICULTURE

LYNN VOSKUIL

Two common geraniums growing on Mary Barton's windowsill attest to the significance of horticulture for our understanding of the Victorian novel. Among the very few living, green things in a book filled with the squalor and debris of industrial culture, the geraniums elude the ubiquitous grasp of mechanization and furnish the Bartons' flat with a cheerful, middle-class sensibility. Along with the blue-and-white gingham curtains, they defend the Bartons against 'out-door pryers', cloaking the family in the domestic privacy so crucial to our readings of the Victorian novel. At the same time, as an exotic species imported from South Africa, the geraniums—or *pelargoniums*, as Victorian horticulturists were more likely to call them—reference the British novel's imperial provenance, its emergence as a cultural institution in the clutches of empire. Perhaps most significantly, the geraniums reflect an ethos of improvement that motivated Victorian horticulturists and novelists alike in their shared pursuit of growth and individual development, a narrative arc familiar to us as the *Bildungsroman*. While the Bartons' geranium is 'unpruned'—a potent index to their lack of leisure time for such pursuits—its leafiness signals their moral and ideological ambitions, ambitions Gaskell underscored in order to advance her own sympathetic program.[1] In the Bartons' humble, potted geranium, we are thus provided with a powerful icon of the novel's role in Victorian culture—and a testament to how closely the Victorian novelist's enterprise was linked to that of the horticulturist.

The practice of horticulture in Victorian England was affiliated with a number of related disciplines and pursuits, most notably natural history and botany. These pursuits were less clearly distinct than they are today, in large part because a culture-wide process of professionalization—a process that seeded the forms of many professions as

---

[1] Elizabeth Gaskell, *Mary Barton* [1848], ed. Jennifer Foster (Peterborough, ON: Broadview Press, 2000), 45.

we now know them—was actively reshaping how their related practices were perceived, categorized, and executed. Each of them involved expert knowledge of plants, and their practitioners often engaged in the overlapping activities of collecting plant specimens, conducting experiments in genetic manipulation, studying plant behaviour, and publishing their findings. The career of John Lindley manifests the complexities of separating 'amateur' and 'professional' at this time in history. Appointed Professor of Botany at London University in 1829, Lindley also collaborated with Joseph Paxton—the landscape gardener and architect of the Crystal Palace—on both the *Botanical Dictionary* and *The Gardeners' Chronicle*, a popular gardening magazine. And when sales of his 1840 book *The Theory of Horticulture* were lower than expected, Lindley shrewdly renamed it *The Theory and Practice of Horticulture* and captured the popular audience he sought.[2]

At the same time, however, distinct spheres of theory and practice were beginning to emerge and increasingly to harden as the century progressed. As Jim Endersby has shown so persuasively, figures like Darwin, Huxley, and especially Joseph Hooker—the botanist who succeeded his father William Hooker as the Director of the Royal Botanical Gardens, Kew—were keen to develop botany as a 'science' that moved beyond the descriptive practices and fieldwork of natural history and was allied with the more prestigious sciences of physics and astronomy. This goal gradually constricted the practice of botany to a narrower, more theoretical concern with the classification and distribution of plants, and gradually created the figure of the 'metropolitan expert' who used data gathered by collectors to speculate, to draw larger conclusions, and to write for a similarly expert, scientific reader.[3]

In contrast to the intensifying concerns with professional prestige that shaped the work of botanists in the 19th century, Victorian horticulturists were preoccupied with practical and aesthetic outcomes. Although they were often knowledgeable plantsmen and women who collected their own specimens, conducted experiments with them, and wrote articles on the results, horticulturists dedicated themselves to the cultivation and healthy growth of plants in the landscape, whether the landscape was as small as a cottage garden or as large as an entire estate. And their practices involved germinating, pruning, and cultivating plants as well as studying or collecting them, with the very utilitarian goal of providing sustenance and the aesthetic goal of creating beauty. While landscape gardening was itself beginning to be defined as a circumscribed, quasi-professional field of practice, with men like Joseph Paxton eager to occupy the post of head gardener for wealthy landowners,[4] innumerable amateur Victorian horticulturists exercised great skill and expertise in the creation of the many garden spaces, small and large, that extended over the British Isles and dotted the Empire's colonial outposts. And however utilitarian and mundane the tasks required to cultivate them, these

[2] Tom Carter, *The Victorian Garden* (London: Bell & Hyman, 1984), 105.
[3] Jim Endersby, *Imperial Nature: Joseph Hooker and the Practices of Victorian Science* (Chicago: University of Chicago Press, 2008), 12–17.
[4] Brent Elliott, *Victorian Gardens* (Portland, OR: Timber Press, 1986), 13–16

garden spaces achieved a certain mystique in Victorian culture at large as well as in novels (which Victorians often read in their gardens). Gardening was thought to be a fundamentally moral activity, with the potential to promote sympathy among the classes, make its practitioners better observers and more industrious workers, and improve the prospects of the soul and the psyche as well as the landscape.[5] In theological terms, it evoked Eden and Gethsemane, the greatest gardens of all for biblical Victorians. 'O heaven and O earth!' apostrophized the horticultural writer Shirley Hibberd. 'In the Garden is your meeting-place, for there God talked with Adam, and there the Saviour wept in agony for all.'[6] In the garden, Victorians believed they could find themselves by finding God and each other. It is no wonder, then, that most of Alice's adventures in Wonderland were prompted by her efforts to get into 'the loveliest garden you ever saw', a garden she could barely glimpse through the tiny, mysterious, curtained door she was so frequently thwarted from entering.[7] For someone so preoccupied with proper conduct and the pursuit of her own identity, a garden was the place to be.

HORTICULTURAL AND SOCIAL IMPROVEMENT

Victorian horticulture was involved in many of the same discourses that shaped the Victorian novel, most notably discourses that entailed the development and improvement of self, others, and society. Literary scholars are very familiar with Victorian novelists' aspirations to use fiction as a vehicle of reform and improvement, whether 'improvement' was construed in social, moral, ethical, or imperial terms. Dickens's well-documented urge to address and ameliorate social problems, for example, led him to critique a wide range of Victorian institutions, including philanthropy, education, child welfare, and the 19th-century legal system. Also widely known are George Eliot's explorations of the novel writer's moral and aesthetic goals in both her fiction—the Prelude to *Middlemarch* (1871), for example—and her journalism. 'Art is the nearest thing to life', she wrote famously in her essay 'The Natural History of German Life'; 'it is a mode of amplifying experience and extending our contact with our fellow-men beyond the bounds of our personal lot'.[8] For many Victorian novelists, fiction was a powerful mode of self-knowledge, social critique, and moral improvement.

Victorian horticulturists shared many of these beliefs about the value of their discipline. The belief that 'improvement' could be achieved by means of horticulture

[5] Carter, 7–12.
[6] Shirley Hibberd, *Brambles and Bay Leaves: Essays on Things Homely and Beautiful*, 3rd edn (London: Groombridge and Sons, 1872), 67, <http://books.google.com>.
[7] Lewis Carroll, *Alice's Adventures in Wonderland and Through the Looking-Glass*, ed. Peter Hunt (New York: Oxford University Press, 2009), 13.
[8] George Eliot, 'The Natural History of German Life', *Westminster Review* 56 (July 1856): 28–44, in George Eliot, *Middlemarch*, ed. Gregory Maertz (Peterborough, ON: Broadview Press, 2004), 658.

and landscape gardening, however, did not originate with the Victorians or singularly inspire Victorian novelists. By the time Jane Austen published *Mansfield Park* in 1814, the practice of hiring landscape gardeners to 'improve' one's estate had become faddish among the landed gentry—so much so that Humphry Repton, the real-life, self-styled successor to Capability Brown and the improver *du jour*, could become an object of satire in the novel when he was selected to 'improve' Sotherton, the massive estate of the oafish Rushworth. In Georgian England, the very concept of improvement, a feature of Enlightenment thought, had purchase far beyond the individual novel or estate, permeating English culture with what has recently been described as 'a series of overlapping resonances—financial, pragmatic, moral, educational, aesthetic'.[9] The particular affiliation of improvement with agriculture and horticulture was a strong one, however, and was bolstered by George III's enthusiasm for the concept of improvement and for the practice of agriculture, most notably on the grounds of the Royal Botanical Gardens, Kew.[10] For people like George III and Joseph Banks, the king's collaborator at Kew, improving plants and animals through the linked practices of horticulture, agriculture, and animal husbandry were patriotic activities that contributed to Britain's global ascendency.[11]

If the idea of 'improvement' did not originate with the Victorians—though it did take new forms in the Victorian discourses of 'progress' and 'self-help'—what *was* unique to the Victorian period was an explosive growth of the popular horticultural press. Enabled by new technologies of printing and circulation, the rapid emergence of popular horticultural and gardening journals made horticulture a well-chronicled hobby within the grasp even of working-class cottagers like the Bartons, a condition that gave garden horticulture wide currency in the Victorian novel. When J.C. Loudon started *The Gardener's Magazine* in 1826, it was the first periodical to address the concerns of amateur gardeners and horticulturists and 'the first periodical devoted exclusively to horticultural subjects', to use the words of one of Loudon's many Victorian admirers.[12] When *The Gardener's Magazine* became *The Gardener's Chronicle* in the 1840s, its circulation increased exponentially, and it began to address wider popular interests. Several other very successful horticultural journals also emerged in the decade of the 1840s, including *The Cottage Gardener* (which went through a number of incarnations before becoming *The Journal of Horticulture* in 1861), *The Horticultural Magazine*, and *The Gardener's Gazette*. By the 1870s, when William Robinson launched *The Garden* and *Gardening*

⁹ S. Daniels and S. Seymour, 'Landscape Design and the Idea of Improvement 1730–1990', in *An Historical Geography of England and Wales*, ed. RA. Dodgshon and R.A. Butlin, 2nd edn (London: Academic Press, 1990), 487–520, 488.

¹⁰ Richard Drayton, *Nature's Government: Science, Imperial Britain, and the 'Improvement' of the World* (New Haven: Yale University Press, 2000), 85–90.

¹¹ Stephen Daniels, Susanne Seymour, and Charles Watkins, 'Enlightenment, Improvement, and the Geographies of Horticulture in Later Georgian England', in *Geography and Enlightenment*, ed. David N. Livingstone and Charles W.J. Withers (Chicago: University of Chicago Press, 1999), 345–71, 345–48.

¹² 'Early Writers on English Gardening, No. 30: John Claudius Loudon', *Journal of Horticulture, Cottage Gardener, and Country Gentleman*, n.s., 32 (8 May 1877): 334.

Illustrated, it was in a periodical marketplace saturated with horticultural literature; Victorians had become voracious readers of any number of gardening magazines, some long-lived and successful and others brief start-ups that were quickly composted.

Many of these periodicals took 'improvement' as their stated goal. In 1849, for example, in the first number of *The Cottage Gardener*, editor George Johnson aimed 'to improve the gardening of the many'. The specific audience he targeted, however, suggests that his goals far transcended the improvement of the individual garden. 'Whilst no gardener, we believe, will turn from our pages without receiving some ray of light', he wrote, 'yet we shall especially trim our lamp for the amateur of moderate income, and the cottager'.[13] Loudon shared Johnson's belief that horticulture could improve the material and economic conditions of cottagers and the working poor. He advocated giving labourers the use of good, arable land for cultivating their own food crops and ornamental plants, arguing that such activities 'will stimulate [their] industry, and ultimately ... link each class of society in inseparable bonds for the preservation of national order and tranquillity'.[14] Loudon's arguments on behalf of the working poor expanded into a full-blown mid-century debate about the value of gardens and horticulture for cottagers, a debate that focused in particular on the use of allotment gardens for the improvement of living conditions. In the late 1840s, during the concluding years to a decade of financial privation and unrest for the working classes, this debate gained special force as allotment gardens came to be seen as a panacea for everything from poverty to working-class (im)morality and national welfare on a large scale. 'The grand machinery of vegetation', proclaimed one horticultural journalist in 1848, would be the saviour of the nation—no small thing in a year when Chartism seemed to be the harbinger of a European-style working-class revolution in Britain. 'If we want more trade and commerce, or accumulation of capital', he wrote, linking horticulture directly to the health of the capitalist system in the United Kingdom as a whole, 'they increase with our productions from the soil, in an accumulating ratio, that grows with our growth, and spreads wealth and happiness to every class of society, not in England alone but to the Scotch and Irish also'.[15]

The widespread idea that cottagers could improve themselves and the nation as they improved their land and gardens found its way into a number of Victorian novels. Readers of *Middlemarch* are familiar with Dorothea's plans to improve the cottages of the tenants on Sir James's estate. While Dorothea is more concerned with architecture than horticulture per se, the two were perceived as part of the same whole, with cottage gardens deemed at least as crucial to cottagers' moral well-being as their interior domestic spaces. Once again, *Mary Barton* (1848) is illuminating, with its dramatization of this

---

[13] [George W. Johnson], 'Introductory', *The Cottage Gardener; Or, Amateur and Cottager's Guide to Out-Door Gardening and Spade Cultivation* 1, no. 1 (5 October 1848): n.p.

[14] J.C. Loudon, *The Cottager's Manual of Husbandry, Architecture, Domestic Economy, and Gardening* (London: Baldwin and Cradock, 1840), 56.

[15] 'Allotments: Pauperism', *The Gardener's Chronicle and Agricultural Gazette* (8 January 1848): 27.

linkage at both beginning and end, where cottage gardens are prominently portrayed. In Green Heys Field at the outset, the narrator takes her readers on a tour through the rural regions outside Manchester, stopping next to 'an old black and white farm-house, with…rambling outbuildings…'. More important than the house itself is 'the little garden surrounding it', which is 'covered with a medley of old-fashioned herbs and flowers, planted long ago, when the garden was the only druggist's shop within reach, and allowed to grow in scrambling and wild luxuriance—roses, lavender, sage, balm (for tea), rosemary, pinks and wallflowers, onions and jessamine, in most republican and indiscriminate order'.[16] If this reads like a set-piece, with some of the same manufactured charm that characterizes landscape designer Gertrude Jekyll's writing about cottage gardens at the very end of the 19th century, Gaskell's strategy was a canny one: by portraying her working-class subjects at home in this captivating landscape, she could ground them in an English pastoral history and more easily humanize and distance them from the bestialized, urban squalor in which they were forced to live and work—and which the novel would soon portray in graphic detail.

At the end of the novel, when Mary and Jem have emigrated to Canada, a cottage garden is once again significant. This garden space, though, has not been 'planted long ago', but has been claimed from the wilderness, heralding a new era; and the gardener's hand has clearly been at work. 'The old primeval trees are felled and gone for many a mile around; one alone remains to overshadow the gable-end of the cottage', the narrator writes. 'There is a garden around the dwelling, and far beyond that stretches an orchard.'[17] While we might dispute the ideological meanings of this conclusion, Gaskell's re-invocation of the cottage garden signals its iconic significance for her readers. Almost as certainly as the birth of children (which appear in the succeeding paragraph of *Mary Barton*), Jem and Mary's cultivation of their Canadian cottage garden bespeaks growth and improvement—of the landscape, of the self, of the social order—and underscores the ability of Gaskell's working-class subjects to cultivate productive lives for themselves.

Like *Mary Barton*, Gaskell's first novel, *Wives and Daughters* (1865), her last novel, also makes significant use of horticulture and related disciplines. *Wives and Daughters* is a novel full of garden scenes and many types of gardens. From the 'exquisite cultivation' of the formal gardens at the Towers to the small gardens of surroundings cottages, Gaskell emphasizes the centrality of horticulture to the 'every-day story' she announces in her subtitle.[18] The Hamleys' garden is the most important one, however. When Molly Gibson first visits the Hamleys' estate in her teens and tours the grounds with Squire Hamley, we are given the portrait of a squirearchy from an earlier era. 'They went in and out of old-fashioned greenhouses, over trim lawns, the squire unlocked the great walled

[16]   Gaskell, *Mary Barton*, 33, 34.
[17]   Gaskell, *Mary Barton*, 481.
[18]   Elizabeth Gaskell, *Wives and Daughters* [1866], ed. Angus Easson (New York: Oxford University Press, 2009), 11.

kitchen-garden, and went about giving directions to the gardeners.'[19] The squire's active interest in the care and particularly the drainage of his gardens and grounds bespeaks a man whose knowledge and expertise is put to the practical use of managing an estate; he is, in other words, an accomplished horticulturist in every sense of the word, and the bond between him and Molly grows strong in their rambles over the Hamley property.

In this novel of gardens, however, the practices of Squire Hamley are distinguished sharply from the pursuits of his son, Roger Hamley, who becomes a professional scientist in the course of the novel. Modelled on Darwin, a friend of Gaskell, Roger confirms her life-long interest in the overlapping pursuits of botany, horticulture, and natural history (which also show up in *Mary Barton*, in the figures of Job Legh and Alice Wilson).[20] At the same time, Roger embodies the complexities of the Victorian relationships among these disciplines. Skilled in the care of his father's land, he shows no interest in taking over its management after the death of his older brother Osborne; instead, he is interested in the study of plants and animals for their own sake, pursuing this interest as a vocation that is funded by others and requires him to spend much time abroad on harrowing expeditions. His choice of profession instigates a number of social and familial predicaments involving the ongoing maintenance of the ancient family seat, his ability to support a wife and children on a naturalist's earnings, and his place in Victorian society. When the aristocratic Cumnor family adopts him socially after his initial professional success, the class issue is quickly addressed, and the novel (which Gaskell had almost finished when she died) concludes with the expectation that his next voyage will give him the means to marry Molly and start a family. Nonetheless, many of the obstacles in this marriage plot ensue from the disciplinary tensions between father and son, between practical horticulturist and professional botanist—tensions that are also reflected in the pages of the Victorian horticultural press.

Tellingly, many of these tensions are muted in the novel's garden scenes. Like many horticultural writers, Gaskell underscores the widespread Victorian belief that gardens promoted emotional well-being and moral rectitude; as spaces that are at once organic and manufactured, gardens like the Hamleys' provided opportunities both for social interaction and for private withdrawal from worldly getting and spending, two states of being that carried related and sometimes competing ideological weight in 19th-century England. Squire Hamley thus finds solace pondering the drainage problems on his own grounds, while the young Roger is happiest examining plants and insects in the family garden. And given the soothing prominence of gardens in this novel, it is no surprise that the teenage Molly would seek a secluded nook in the Hamleys' garden where she could release her tears over her father's impending remarriage. It is here, surrounded by

---

[19] Gaskell, *Wives and Daughters*, 71–2.
[20] See Amy King, 'Taxonomical Cures: The Politics of Natural History and Herbalist Medicine in Elizabeth Gaskell's *Mary Barton*', in *Romantic Science: The Literary Forms of Natural History*, ed. Noah Heringman (Albany, NY: SUNY Press, 2003), 255–70, <http://www.netlibrary.com.ezproxy.lib.uh.edu/Reader/>.

the natural overgrowth of a neglected corner, that she meets Roger for the first time and the groundwork is laid for their future union.

Gaskell's use of gardens at crucial plot points in both *Mary Barton* and *Wives and Daughters* suggests the importance of horticulture to the generic conventions of Victorian fiction, especially to the contours of the marriage plot. In Gaskell's novels, the organic abundance of gardens promotes the growth and development of sympathetic bonds between people—like Roger and Molly—who are meant to be together. In some novels, however, the very fecundity of garden spaces engenders a sense of disorientation and confusion that has similarly crucial implications for plot development. Hall Farm in *Adam Bede* (1859) is just such a place. Early in the novel, the earthy sensuality of the farm's dairy provocatively frames Hetty Sorrel's 'false air of innocence', initiating the ill-fated relationship with Arthur Donnithorne that ends tragically for her.[21] The steady, manly Adam is similarly bewitched by Hetty, this time provoked by the prodigal, heavy-laden, late-summer garden at Hall Farm.

Like the cottage garden in Gaskell's Green Hey's Field, this farmhouse garden mixes its plants indiscriminately, 'with hardy perennial flowers, unpruned fruit-trees, and kitchen vegetables growing together in careless, half-neglected abundance'. Eliot's narrator goes on at length in these paragraphs, belabouring the point that the plants, and the garden itself, are 'large and disorderly for want of trimming': hollyhocks are tall and dazzling, scarlet runner beans and late peas are climbing with abandon over garden walls, and the 'very rose-trees...looked as if they grew wild...all huddled together in bushy masses, now flaunting with wide open petals'. In fact, as the narrator notes, visitors to the garden could lose themselves, literally and figuratively, among all this ripeness and sensuality—which is exactly what happens to Adam. After wandering through all manner of produce and flowers, Adam finds Hetty among the currants, and experiences what he believes to be a moment of epiphany. 'Hetty bending over the red bunches', the narrator writes, 'the level rays piercing the screen of apple-tree boughs, the length of busy garden beyond, his own emotion as he looked at her and believed that she was thinking of him, and that there was no need for them to talk— Adam remembered it all to the last moment of his life.' Of course, Adam has mistaken Hetty's shyness and blush as evidence of feelings for him; the superabundant plenitude of the scene produces an uncontrolled growth of emotion, as if the plants and Adam's feelings partake of the same organic essence. There is no suspense here, for the narrator reminds us immediately that we can see what Adam cannot: 'And Hetty? You know quite well that Adam was mistaken about her.' This moment of pointed dramatic irony, however, heightens both the symbolic significance of the over-ripe garden and its crucial role in this plot. This fecund farm garden is no mere setting; is it instead a necessary ingredient in the growth and eventual improvement of Adam's self-knowledge,

---

[21] George Eliot, *Adam Bede* [1859], ed. Mary Waldron (Peterborough, ON: Broadview Press, 2005), 146.

creating an obstacle that he must uproot before the novel can end with 'wedding bells' (the title of the final chapter) for him and Dinah.[22]

THE *BILDUNGSGARTEN*

Many of Gaskell's and Eliot's plots are structured by a process of *Bildung*: the moral, intellectual, and social growth of an individual (to put it very simply). While scholars don't usually classify the novels I've discussed thus far as *Bildungsromane*—as they do Eliot's *Mill on the Floss* (1860), for example—their plots, like those of many Victorian novels, take it as one of their primary goals to highlight a process that entailed not only controlled growth but also training, discipline, and maturation into a recognizable and acceptable social specimen.[23] Tellingly, the verbs we use even today to discuss this process of development—grow, cultivate, root, engender—are derived from the practices of horticulture. In this context, it is worth recalling that 19th-century understandings of the term 'culture', as Raymond Williams has pointed out, had their origins in a more literal process of culture or cultivation, 'the tending of natural growth', as he puts it, as well as 'a process of human training'.[24] While today we might think of both novels and gardens as cultural artefacts, we don't usually think of people and plants as subject to the same sorts of cultivation and pruning, or novelists and horticulturists as carrying out closely related activities: in a world like our own, where 'gardening' often means simply mowing the lawn—or, perhaps more likely, paying someone else to mow the lawn—the parallels between 'natural growth' and 'human training' have receded significantly. In Victorian England, however, where the idea of 'culture' had a somewhat different resonance, *Bildung* could occur in both novels and gardens.

Victorians didn't equate people and plants, of course, but there is evidence, outside of novels, that they understood the development of each as a process of pruning and control. Consider, for example, a piece by landscape gardener Donald Beaton simply entitled 'Geraniums', published in an 1849 issue of *The Cottage Gardener*—one of the many popular horticultural magazines available to the amateur Victorian gardener—in the ongoing column 'Greenhouse and Window Gardening'. The column is addressed to the unnamed niece of 'Aunt Harriet', a young woman nonplussed with her failure to grow geraniums like those of her aunt; and, at an approximate length of 2,500 words, it spares no detail in its advice for the cultivation of model geraniums, acknowledging implicitly that many home gardeners had the same problem with gangliness that the Bartons did with their potted geranium. Even Aunt Harriet, the model gardener in the piece, confessed that

---

[22] George Eliot, *Adam Bede*, 280, 282, 283.

[23] On the *Bildungsroman*, see Julia Prewitt Brown's chapter in this volume.

[24] Raymond Williams, *Culture and Society, 1780–1950* (New York: Columbia University Press, 1983), xvi.

it was many years before she knew how to prune them right; they used to get so long in the branches and so naked below, for want of leaves, that she often resolved, to break off the points of the shoots, to see what effect that would have...At last the geraniums became so tall and unsightly, that she had some thoughts of throwing them away altogether, and to buy a fresh lot of young ones.

But Aunt Harriet persisted, says Beaton, learning by experience how to prune both shoots and roots, to repot at the right time, and to let the plants recover naturally from periods of riotous blooming. Before she learned how to prune properly, Aunt Harriet almost killed the plants outright by exposing them to the winter cold. She noticed, though, that bark at the base of the plants was still fresh, and said to herself, 'as long as there is life there is hope'. Aunt Harriet then removed the frosted bits and soon the geraniums were producing new leaves and growth. 'When she thought upon them after this', Beaton tells us, 'she could breathe freely.'[25]

   In Beaton's column, Aunt Harriet and the geraniums are volitional partners in their growth and welfare. While Beaton's tone is meant to be droll, his purpose is sincere, even serious. Aunt Harriet and her geraniums share both a certain agency and a sympathetic connection, a common bond that unites them in the hard work of cultivation and growth. While Aunt Harriet is clearly the enforcer of this partnership, the tender plants are nurtured with the same commitment one might apply to a child, with concern for its health, its well-being, and its proper development. Clearly far more than a decorative accessory, the geranium is a living, almost breathing thing that must work diligently, be disciplined, endure growing pains, and wait patiently for its maturation. These qualities, however, describe both the geranium and Aunt Harriet's niece, to whom the column is addressed: the teenage grower and the geranium are both given their own little *Bildung* plot, a narrative parallel that highlights the gendered aspects of *Bildung*, whether it occurred in novels or gardens. Just as the geranium would become unacceptably gangly and even die without proper pruning, so Aunt Harriet's niece could not develop her own decorative and reproductive capacities, or grow into a viable social specimen, without enduring a similar process of discipline and training, a process she is clearly meant to infer from the column and her own cultivation of the geranium. Particularly striking about this parallel is the forcible discipline entailed by a maturation process that models human growth on horticultural pruning. Aunt Harriet 'often resolved', Beaton tells us, 'to break off the points of the shoots, to see what effect that would have'—a pruning process that encodes, but doesn't acknowledge, the ideological violence inflicted on Victorian women-in-training. As an exemplar of feminine *Bildung*, Aunt Harriet's initially unruly but eventually compliant geranium models precisely the stages of disciplined growth and aestheticized cultivation required of Victorian girls—a form of discipline that was

[25] D[onald] Beaton, 'Geraniums', *The Cottage Gardener; Or, Amateur and Cottager's Guide to Out-Door Gardening and Spade Cultivation* 1, no. 14 (January 4, 1849): 150–3.

not bestowed on the profligate Hetty Sorrel, who is associated with rambling, luxuriant, unpruned plants.

In this ideological context, it is no surprise that horticulture and *Bildung* often occur together in Victorian novels, especially novels that feature girls as protagonists. The paradigm in this vein is *The Secret Garden* (1910), of course, Francis Hodgson Burnett's story of Mary Lennox's geographical, intellectual, and emotional pilgrimage from an alien India to the heart of the British countryside. (Though technically an Edwardian novel, *The Secret Garden* may be considered as belonging to the long 19th century.) Much like Aunt Harriet's niece from the column in *The Cottage Gardener*, Mary matures by tilling and tending the plants she discovers in her own private garden space.[26] More trenchant in their absurdity and critique, however, are the gardens Alice visits in the search for her own identity in both of Lewis Carroll's *Alice* books. In *Alice's Adventures in Wonderland* (1865), when she finally gains admission to the Red Queen's garden, Alice immediately encounters the card-pack gardeners painting white roses red in a desperate attempt to correct their horticultural mistake before the Queen discovers it. Spilling paint, sniping and carping, mistaking tulip bulbs for onions, the three spades are the three stooges of Wonderland, parodying the parallel I've just drawn between horticulture and *Bildung* and thereby suggesting how widely that parallel applied in Victorian England. If horticulture for Mary Lennox is a slow process that requires patient observation and experiential knowledge, it is here reduced to a slapdash paint job in a scene that takes a little jab at overzealous breeding of both single plant specimens and individual young girls.

In *Through the Looking-Glass* (1871), the story opens once again with Alice seeking access to a garden. This time, though, she must contend with the contradictory, reverse logic of the looking-glass world—a logic that converts a simple walk to the hilltop, where she can enjoy a clear, open view of the garden, into a confusing maze of dead-ends and returns to the house. Like Adam Bede, she gets lost in the garden, and her search for the path is in part a search for self-knowledge. But from the outset, Alice's journey is absurd rather than intellectual or emotional; and, like Alice herself, we are often hard-pressed to know what she will learn and whether maturity, the traditional endpoint of the *Bildungsroman*, will ever be reached. Soon, she finds herself in the Garden of Live Flowers, a scene that literalizes the pursuit of *Bildung* through horticulture. Here, rather than cultivating herself by cultivating plants, Alice is trained by the flowers themselves, who take on human characteristics and scold Alice about her ignorance and appearance. Unlike Alice, who tries desperately to gain self-knowledge in this upside-down world, the flowers know themselves well and manifest traits that are in keeping with their genus and species: the tall, showy Tiger-lily is the bossy spokesperson for the crowd of flowers in the ornamental border, while the Rose is concerned about Alice's colour and the Violet sleeps most of the time with its head beneath the leaves. Their rootedness, moreover, gives them an advantage over Alice, who must wander in search of herself; she is,

---

[26] Francis Hodgson Burnett, *The Secret Garden* [1911], ed. Dennis Butts (New York: Oxford University Press, 2008).

in fact, soon to enter the 'woods...where things have no names', where she risks losing her identity altogether.[27] The flowers also teach Alice some rudiments of horticulture, at least as it is practiced in the looking-glass world. When Alice wonders how they can talk, the Tiger-lily tells her to touch the soil, which is untillably hard. "'In most gardens," the Tiger-lily [says] absurdly, "they make the beds too soft—so that the flowers are always asleep".'[28]

Alice's conversation with the mixed border incisively cuts through a number of Victorian common-places, pertaining not only to horticulture but also to the training of young girls. Flowers were widely associated with women and girls in Victorian England, so much so that the association prompted what was sometimes called 'The Language of Flowers', to invoke the title of a manual illustrated by Kate Greenaway in 1884. What Amy King has called the 'botanical vernacular' shaped the way Victorian novelists wrote about their female characters, especially eroticized young women like Hetty Sorrel.[29] And, as Beverly Seaton has argued, 'Flowers...were seen as the most suitable aspect of nature to represent women, or to interact with them, reflecting as they do certain stereotypical qualities of the female being: smallness of stature, fragility of mind and body, and impermanence of beauty.'[30] In books like the little Greenaway manual, the 'language of flowers' was scripted quite literally. The 'Damask Rose', for example, meant 'Brilliant Complexion'; the four kinds of Violets indicated, respectively, 'Faithfulness', 'Watchfulness', 'Modesty', and 'Rural Happiness'; and the 'Garden Daisy', was associated with the phrase 'I share your sentiments'.[31] By representing looking-glass flowers as scolds, Carroll undercuts the sentimentality that characterized many Victorian versions of 'the language of flowers' and goads Alice into expressing her frustration with floral training. When both she and the Tiger-lily grow impatient with the noisy daisies, Alice leans over and says acerbically, 'If you don't hold your tongues, I'll pick you'[32]—a wonderfully irreverent swipe at Victorian 'flower language' and the paradoxical idea that seven-year-old girls like Alice were in training to become fragile and delicate by means of an enforced process of growth and discipline. Modelling her conduct on the Red Queen's deportment rather than on Kate Greenaway's, Alice threatens to take revenge by beheading her floral trainers.

Focusing on Alice and Mary Lennox might suggest that horticulture was almost exclusively the province of women, and that only girls experienced *Bildung* through horticulture. Flowers and femininity, as we've seen, were certainly thought to be

---

[27] Carroll, 155.

[28] Carroll, 140.

[29] Amy M. King, *Bloom: The Botanical Vernacular in the English Novel* (Oxford: Oxford University Press, 2003).

[30] Beverly Seaton, *The Language of Flowers: A History* (Charlottesville, VA: University of Virginia Press, 1995), 17.

[31] Kate Greenaway, *The Language of Flowers* (London: George Routledge and Sons, 1884), 15, 37, 42, <http://www.illuminated-books.com/books/flowers.htm>.

[32] Carroll, 139.

naturally compatible: Ruskin's dictum from 'Of Queen's Gardens'—that a girl grows 'as a flower does'—was very familiar and widely accepted as a metaphorical and descriptive mode.[33] And more women were beginning to garden quasi-professionally and to author gardening manuals; Jane Loudon, the wife of J.C. Loudon, for example, published widely read manuals with titles like *Instructions in Gardening for Ladies* and *The Lady's Country Companion; Or, How to Enjoy a Country Life Rationally*.[34] Even a cursory look at Victorian gardening manuals and horticultural journals, however, challenges any rigid, culture-wide associations between women and horticulture that we might want to make, even where floriculture was concerned. The rising professional science of botany, as Jim Endersby has pointed out, required the cultivation of qualities like sympathy that we usually associate with 19th-century women, a condition that challenges some of the tenets of separate sphere ideology as we know it.[35] The qualities of what I have nicknamed the *Bildungsgarten*, moreover, applied to both girls and boys, women and men. We might recall that in *The Secret Garden*, it is Dickon who teaches Mary to garden, and Colin who perhaps benefits most from the enclosed garden's therapeutic aura. While the symbolic language of horticulture was frequently and variably gendered, both men and women were avid horticulturists in Victorian England.

EXOTIC PLANTS, IMPERIAL NOVELS?

By 1848, when *Mary Barton* was published, the geranium was a familiar flower in England, widely planted not only in window boxes and flower pots but also in gardens. Given the geranium's common homeliness—its place on the Bartons' window sill beside other domestic objects like tea caddies and gingham curtains—it is easy to forget that it was a foreign import. In fact, it originated in South Africa and was probably first brought to England, via Leiden, as early as the 1630s. By the 19th century, along with lobelias, *agapanthus*, and other familiar tropical species, it had become the backbone of the Victorian practice called 'bedding-out', a practice that dominated domestic garden design at mid-century and involved the use of colourful but tender flowers to define

[33] John Ruskin, 'Of Queen's Gardens', in *The Works of John Ruskin*, ed. E.T. Cook and Alexander Wedderburn, 39 vols. (London: George Allen, 1905), 18: 131, <http:// books.google.com>.

[34] Jane Loudon, *Instructions in Gardening for Ladies* (London: Longman, 1840), <http://books. google.com>; and *The Lady's Country Companion; Or, How to Enjoy a Country Life Rationally* (London: Longman, 1852), <http://books.google.com>. See also Sarah Bilston, 'Queens of the Garden: Victorian Women Gardeners and the Rise of the Gardening Advice Text', *Victorian Literature and Culture* 36, no. 1 (2008): 1–19, doi: 10.1017/S1060150308080017; and Barbara Gates, *Kindred Nature: Victorian and Edwardian Women Embrace the Living World* (Chicago: University of Chicago Press, 1998).

[35] Jim Endersby, 'Sympathetic Science: Charles Darwin, Joseph Hooker, and the Passions of Victorian Naturalists', *Victorian Studies* 51, no. 2 (Winter 2009): 199–320, <http://muse.jhu.edu.ezproxy.lib.uh.edu/journals/victorian_studies/toc/vic.51.2.html>.

separate sections of gardens beds and form intricate designs.[36] Like the Bartons' ging-ham curtains, their geranium would thus have had some of the metonymic qualities that Elaine Freedgood has attributed to what she calls 'Victorian "thing culture"', qualities that would reference the geranium's exotic provenance for Victorian readers and speak as well to the novel's place in imperial culture.[37] As Edward Said has argued controver-sially, the English novel cannot be fully understood apart from its participation in a long history of Western imperialism.[38] It would be fair to say the same for English horticul-ture, especially as it was practised by the Victorians. To understand both Victorian gar-dens and Victorian novels, it is necessary to see them as part of a complex global and imperial cultural system.

As the provenance of the geranium makes clear, Victorians were certainly not the first Britons to import exotic plant species from far-flung regions of the globe. In fact, the practice had been common for centuries by the time the Bartons were able to secure a geranium plant (or at least a cutting) in working-class, mid-century Manchester. What was new in the 19th century, however, was an entrepreneurial spirit that saw profit in the collection and breeding of new botanical species. In 1804, Joseph Banks, William Forsyth, and John Wedgwood were among the founding members of the Horticultural Society, a group whose goal in part was to collect exotic plants and seeds not prima-rily for scientists but for the amateur, practical gardener. Throughout the 19th century, the Society subsidized a large number of plant-hunting expeditions. Later in the cen-tury, the large horticultural establishment of the Veitch family nurtured even greater commercial ambitions. Known as an expert breeder of orchids, James Veitch was also a Fellow of the Horticultural Society, and thus had access to the seeds and plants they acquired; nonetheless, in the 1840s, he conceived a scheme to fund his own expeditions and to control the market for the specimens his collectors found. His plan was spec-tacularly successful. His first two plant-hunters—the brothers William and Thomas Lobb—discovered a number of new species. 'In the first parcel [William] sent home', *The Cottage Gardener* reported, 'was that magnificent orchid *Phaelaenopsis grandiflora*, not before known in England, *Vanda suavis*, and numerous others.'[39] More importantly, as Mary and John Gribbin have discussed, the Lobb brothers identified seemingly bottom-less global sources for what became many of the Veitch's most commercially successful plants. In 1850, for example, Veitch was able to sell a large number of cuttings of *Vanda caerulea* (the blue orchid) for £10 per cutting, which was just one of the many profitable

[36] Joan Morgan and Alison Richards, *A Paradise Out of a Common Field: The Pleasures and Plenty of the Victorian Garden* (New York: Harper and Row, 1990), 16–17.

[37] Elaine Freedgood, *The Ideas in Things: Fugitive Meanings in the Victorian Novel* (Chicago: University of Chicago Press, 2006), 8.

[38] Edward Said, *Culture and Imperialism* (New York: Knopf, 1993).

[39] *The Cottage Gardener; Or, Amateur and Cottager's Guide to Out-Door Gardening and Spade Cultivation*, January, 1855, quoted in James H. Veitch, *Hortus Veitchii: a history of the rise and progress of the nurseries of Messrs. James Veitch and sons, together with an account of the botanical collectors and hybridists employed by them and a list of the most remarkable of their introductions* (Chelsea: James Veitch and Sons, Ltd, 1906), 10, <http://www.archive.org/details/hortusveitchiihiooveitrich>.

exotic species they sold. In 1851, James Veitch & Sons received a Gold Medal at the Great Exhibition, in large part based on the specimens collected by the Lobbs, for a display that was one of the most popular at the Exhibition.[40] Like the horticultural press that emerged and flourished in Victorian England, commercial nurseries and horticulturists had a large, seemingly insatiable market for their exotic wares.

What did this global horticultural marketplace have to do with the Victorian novel? On one level, it provided material for the creation of characters. Early in *Wives and Daughters*, for example, the amateur botanist Lady Agnes Cumnor betrays her own ill breeding by delivering a tedious lecture on the breeding of orchids—complete with Latin nomenclature—to her bored guests in the Towers greenhouse, thus setting the stage for the appearance of the much more sympathetic expert botanist Roger Hamley and signalling the change from an old landed society to an emergent professional one. In a larger cultural sense, popular Victorian genres like travel literature and overseas adventure novels helped create demand for exotic horticultural species, and their authors in turn were instrumental in using new horticultural knowledge to modify various literary conventions. Isabella Bird's travel book *The Hawaiian Archipelago* (1875), for instance, is filled with detailed descriptions of lush tropical vegetation in its native habitat, including a number of species that many Victorians eagerly sought to cultivate.[41] Perhaps most widely read by all ages, however, were novels that portrayed young boys seeking adventure on the high seas, a genre that was popular throughout the Victorian period. While Robert Louis Stevenson's *Treasure Island* (1881–82) is probably the best-known example of this genre, R.M. Ballantyne also found a large and enthusiastic Victorian audience. In his enormous body of work (he published over a hundred adventure stories during his career), *The Coral Island* (1857) is useful for its representations of lush tropical scenes that Victorians would have clamoured to replicate, or at least evoke, in domestic English settings.

The Coral Island may be classified as both a *Bildungsroman* and a Crusoe tale, with the recognizable contours of the familiar adventure plot. Its three young English protagonists—Ralph Rover, Jack Martin, and Peterkin Gay—join the junior ranks of *The Arrow*, a merchant ship bound for the South Pacific. Already in chapter 2, the ship sinks in a horrific storm, but our three heroes survive and reach one of the Coral islands, where the story proper begins. Shipwrecked for years, they build their own dwelling, learn how to find food and keep house, help convert a number of savage natives to Christianity, and survive a number of dangerous but always entertaining adventures; at the end, they are rescued by a missionary and returned to England. Along the way, Ralph, who narrates the story, describes their island home at great length, expatiating on its wealth of natural resources and drawing parallels with his other, native island home. If Victorians

[40] Mary Gribbin and John Gribbin, *Flower Hunters* (Oxford: Oxford University Press, 2008), 131–32, 163–87.

[41] Isabella Bird, *The Hawaiian Archipelago: Six Months Among the Palm Groves, Coral Reefs, and Volcanoes of the Sandwich Islands*, 6th edn (New York: G.P. Putnam's Sons, 1886), <http://books.google.com/>.

in Britain hoped to evoke little Edens in their back gardens, Ralph, Jack, and Peterkin may have stumbled onto the real thing in their Coral Island home. 'My dear boys, we're set up for life', rejoices Peterkin early in the novel, after they've discovered the many useful properties of the cocoa-nut palm. 'It must be the ancient Paradise,—hurrah!'[42]

The scenes Ralph describes at length do indeed evoke the Eden familiar to all Victorians. 'Meanwhile the sun began to descend', he narrates in a typical example,

> so we returned to the shore, and pushed on round the spouting rocks into the next valley... It was by far the largest and most beautiful that we had yet looked upon... Some trees were dark glossy green, others of a rich and warm hue, contrasting well with those of a pale light green, which were everywhere abundant. Among these we recognised the broad dark heads of the bread-fruit, with its golden fruit; the pure, silvery foliage of the candle-nut, and several species which bore a strong resemblance to the pine; while here and there, in groups and in single trees, rose the tall forms of the cocoa-nut palms, spreading abroad, and waving their graceful plumes high above all the rest, as if they were a superior race of stately giants keeping guard over these luxuriant forests. Oh! it was a most enchanting scene, and I thanked God for having created such delightful spots for the use of man.[43]

Striking in this description is the sense that no horticulture is necessary, for God has already completed this Edenic garden before Ralph and his friends arrive. Instead of achieving *Bildung* through gardening, as Mary Lennox and her cousin Colin do, they must make use of their new island home, a mission Ralph notes here in the final line. Accordingly, they teach themselves how to use the various fibres, fruits, and tissues of the plants in their environment to make a civilized home on Coral Island, the achievement of which marks their maturity. Even the local cannibalistic tribes that visit Coral Island from time to time may be said to experience their own *Bildung* plot after converting to Christianity. Like the three boys, they create civilization in the tropics, a condition signalled by cottage gardens planted in their Samoan village, where they fulfil a narrative function similar to the one fulfilled by Mary and Jem's cottage garden in Canada. Jack writes:

> The village was about a mile in length, and perfectly straight, with a wide road down the middle, on either side of which were rows of the tufted-topped ti tree... The cottages of the natives were built beneath these trees, and were kept in the most excellent order, each having a little garden in front, tastefully laid out and planted, while the walks were covered with black and white pebbles.[44]

[42] R. M. Ballantyne, *The Coral Island* (London: T. Nelson, 1858; repr., New York: Garland Publishing, Inc., 1977), 42.
[43] Ballantyne, 111–12.
[44] Ballantyne, 373.

Ralph's sense that they must responsibly use their Garden of Eden distinguishes *Coral Island* from the contemplative garden spaces imagined by some horticultural writers—by Shirley Hibberd, for example, when he describes the garden as 'a Divine institution, a Biblical reminiscence, a present solace, a refuge, a retreat'.[45] In fact, the mission of the three boys is compatible not only with the charge given to Adam in the biblical Garden of Eden but also with the practical and commercial ambitions of horticulturists at home. Although Ballantyne does not voice the same strong support for laissez-faire capitalism that Harriet Martineau does in *Dawn Island* (1845)—a novel in which natives are converted to the virtues of Christianity and free trade alike—it does exude a proprietary sensibility.[46] England is planted abroad in the form of the natives' cottage gardens and the boys' domestic establishment. If the three boys do not collect specimens to cultivate (and sell) in England, Coral Island was seemingly given to them by God, as Ralph sees it, to use in the best way they could, a calling that would resonate with English horticulturists who did indeed greatly advance the knowledge and use of plants in the 19th century. It is not a stretch to imagine a sequel to *The Coral Island*, which would centre on the adventures of plant-hunters collecting and naming new species on the island the boys had found—and bringing the cuttings back to England for (re)propagation there.

Island novels that portrayed virgin territories rich in natural resources and undiscovered botanical species were not the only Victorian genres to feature exotic garden spaces. Victorians were equally fascinated with well-developed, sophisticated urban gardens in remote regions of the world. One such garden plays a significant role in Benjamin Disraeli's novel *Tancred* (1847), a novel whose protagonist, Tancred de Montacute, tours the Middle East, surveying its representative cultures along the way. Like *The Coral Island*, *Tancred* is something of a *Bildungsroman*, with the young Tancred seeking answers on a 'New Crusade', as the subtitle proclaims, to what Tancred calls 'the Holy Land'.[47] Much of the political intrigue of this novel, as well as the eccentricities relating to race and theology, concerns Disraeli's own convictions about the Jewish roots of Western Christianity and his emerging commitment to a conservative state and foreign policy. Certain important scenes, however, occur in a garden in Bethany, a village near Jerusalem and a key site in the ministry and passion of Christ. Tancred stumbles upon this garden, tucked among the hills near the Mount of Olives and 'surrounded by high stone walls', after meditating in the Garden of Gethsemane. Still flushed with 'pious ecstasy' from his visit to Gethsemane, he notices that the gate is open; like countless enclosed gardens in both life and literature—those in the *Alice* books and *The Secret Garden* are only a few of many—this one beckons alluringly with a portal that permits only a glimpse of the wonders within. And, located near Jerusalem, this garden, Tancred suspects, has special qualities: 'an eastern garden, a garden in the Holy Land, such as

45 Hibberd, 68.

46 Harriet Martineau, *Dawn Island. A Tale* (Manchester: J. Gadsby, 1845), <http://books.google.com>.

47 Benjamin Disraeli, *Tancred; Or, The New Crusade* (London: Longmans, Green, and Co., 1877; repr., Westport, CT: Greenwood Press, 1970), 54.

Gethsemane might have been in those days of political justice when Jerusalem belonged to the Jews; the occasion was irresistible...'.[48]

In his description of the garden itself, the narrator underscores its profound effect on the young, impressionable pilgrim.

> Like a prince in a fairy tale, who has broken the mystic boundary of some enchanted pleasaunce, Tancred traversed the alleys which were formed by the lemon and pomegranate tree, and sometimes by the myrtle and the rose. His ear caught the sound of falling water, bubbling with a gentle noise... The walk in which he now found himself ended in an open space covered with roses; beyond them a gentle acclivity, clothed so thickly with a small bright blue flower than it seemed like a bank of turquoise, and on its top was a kiosk of white marble, gilt and painted; by its side, rising from a group of rich shrubs, was the palm whose distant crest had charmed Tancred without the gate.

While this scene is gorgeous and alluring in its lushness, it differs significantly from the naturalistic paradise of *The Coral Island*. This garden is carefully designed, with pathways and parterres, waterfalls and sculpture, and strategically planned sight-lines. Located in a region with a significant past, moreover, it has an air of antiquity, giving the questing Tancred the sense that he has found his original home. Lulled by the sounds of water and his feeling of ease, he sinks, Adam-like, into 'a deep and dreamless repose'— only to awaken, sometime later, with a beautiful woman waiting nearby. Her name, of course, is Eva.[49]

Sculpted, trained, and pruned in a style close to that of European formal gardens, the garden in Bethany is not a source of new species, such as those sought by the plant-hunters of James Veitch & Sons for commercial profit. The specimens on display, in fact—lemon trees, pomegranates, roses—were well known to Victorian gardeners at mid-century and had already been planted in greenhouses and the more temperate climate zones of Britain (though pomegranates didn't usually set fruit). There is, nonetheless, a proprietary aura about Tancred's relation to this garden as well, just as there was in *The Coral Island*. Though it is a private garden that Tancred has entered without invitation—and is, in fact, of recent vintage, with palm trees contributed by Eva's Arab grandfather—Disraeli incorporates it into Tanred's (and his own) story of origin, appropriating it to make sense of his past and his future. Lest readers miss the fact that this is a new Eden, the narrator makes it patently clear with his extensive description of Tancred's Eve, an Eve 'whose face presented the perfection of oriental beauty; such as it existed in Eden, such as it may yet occasionally be found among the favoured races in the favoured climes'.[50] At the end of the novel (perhaps needless to say), Tancred ends his

---

[48] Disraeli, 185.
[49] Disraeli, 183–86.
[50] Disraeli, 187.

quest by proposing to Eva in this very same garden, aiming to reinvigorate the primal story by returning to this Anglicized Eden and figuring himself as Adam.

Exotic gardens in remote regions, like the cottage gardens of the English midlands, thus play a significant role in Victorian novels, perceived as crucial not only to the cultivation and growth of individuals but also to that of the British empire as a whole. If the proprietary and commercial urge—one that drove many Victorian horticulturists and novelists alike—is not always admirable, the history of horticulture and gardening nonetheless benefited greatly from the efforts of Victorian gardeners. Exotic plants, however, were seen not only as a free source of profit. In some cases, they also raised the spectre of runaway growth, the prospect of an invasive species gaining control of the native English landscape. After all, what plant-hunters sometimes experienced abroad was a sense of awe and even disorientation when they saw English greenhouse plants growing naturally and often in massive luxuriance in tropical climates.[51] In H.G. Wells's *The War of the Worlds*, published in 1898, at the very end of Victoria's reign, the frightening 'Red Weed' offers a novelist's perspective on just such a horticultural invasion—and a comment on the problematic possibilities of exotic horticulture. The Red Weed comes to earth with the invading Martians; and its vivid crimson colour, says the narrator, is what gives Mars its tint, blood-red and repellent next to the Earth's living green. In Britain, its adopted habitat, the Red Weed grows 'with astonishing vigour and luxuriance' wherever it encounters water, choking rivers and streams with its 'swiftly growing and Titanic water fronds'.[52] The Red Weed, in other words, is a horticultural disaster, a plant that cannot be eaten or used in any way, but will choke everything in its path.

The Red Weed has been aptly interpreted as an emblem of the ecological calamity engendered by the West in the global regions it colonized.[53] But it might also be read as a horticultural sign of what Stephen Arata has called 'reverse colonization', the perception that a late-century England-in-decline was vulnerable to 'attack from more vigorous, "primitive" peoples'.[54] Acutely and knowledgeably attuned to the possibilities that biology (and other sciences) offered for both good and ill, Wells portrays a horticultural specimen as perhaps the greatest threat not merely to England but to the planet itself. While a terrestrial bacterium finally kills the Red Weed and the Martians alike, the plant creeps over and suffocates everything in its path before it dies, from the landscape to buildings to other plants, invulnerable even to the firepower of the British military. The narrator describes the scene as he surveys the desolate British countryside. 'I stood on a mound of smashed brickwork, clay, and gravel, over which spread a multitude of

[51] See [John Veitch], 'Extracts from the Journal of Mr. John Gould Veitch, During a Trip to the Australian and South Sea Islands', *The Gardeners' Chronicle and Agricultural Gazette* (6 January 1866): 7.
[52] H.G. Wells, *The War of the Worlds* [1898], ed. Martin A. Danahay (Peterborough, ON: Broadview Press, 2003), 147, 161.
[53] Alan Bewell, *Romanticism and Colonial Disease* (Baltimore: Johns Hopkins University Press, 1999), xi–xii.
[54] Stephen Arata, 'The Occidental Tourist: *Dracula* and the Anxiety of Reverse Colonization', *Victorian Studies* 3, no. 4 (Summer 1990): 623, <http://www.jstor.org/stable/3827794>.

red cactus-shaped plants, knee-high, without a solitary terrestrial growth to dispute their footing. The trees near me were dead and brown, but further a network of red thread scaled the still living stems.'[55] It is the landscape from a *fin-de-siècle* nightmare, a perversely ironic re-enactment of the proprietary Eden scenes from island novels, and an ecological comment on the calamitous potential of unrestricted horticultural 'improvement'.

Wells's Red Weed is a sober but fitting counterpart to the Bartons' cheery red geranium, for it shows us where both horticulture and fiction had arrived by the end of the Victorian century, with the world on the verge of decolonization and global war. The Victorian discourses of improvement and self-knowledge that involved both gardens and novels would persist, at least in fragmented forms, into the Edwardian period and well beyond. Never again, however, would novelists and horticulturists so readily take moral and social improvement as their shared goal. As Wells had suggested, even growth and cultivation, if unchecked, could become the vanguard of crisis.

Suggested Reading

Carter, Tom. *The Victorian Garden*. London: Bell & Hyman, 1984.

Daniels, Stephen and Susanne Seymour. 'Landscape Design and the Idea of Improvement, 1730–1990'. In *An Historical Geography of England and Wales*, edited by R.A. Dodgshon and R.A. Butlin, 2nd edn. London: Academic Press, 1990, 487–520.

Elliott, Brent. *Victorian Gardens*. Portland, OR: Timber Press, 1986.

Endersby, Jim. *Imperial Nature: Joseph Hooker and the Practices of Victorian Science*. Chicago: University of Chicago Press, 2008.

Drayton, Richard. *Nature's Government: Science, Imperial Britain, and the 'Improvement' of the World*. New Haven: Yale University Press, 2000.

Gribbin, Mary and John Gribbin. *Flower Hunters*. Oxford: Oxford University Press, 2008.

Grove, Richard H. *Green Imperialism: Colonial Expansion, Tropical Island Edens and the Origins of Environmentalism, 1600–1860*. Cambridge: Cambridge University Press, 1995.

Helmreich, Anne. *The English Garden and National Identity: Competing Styles of Garden Design, 1870–1914*. Cambridge: Cambridge University Press, 2002.

King, Amy M. *Bloom: The Botanical Vernacular in the English Novel*. Oxford: Oxford University Press, 2003.

Musgrave, Toby and Will. *An Empire of Plants: People and Plants that Changed the World*. London: Cassell & Co., 2000.

Seaton, Beverly. *The Language of Flowers: A History*. Charlottesville, VA: University of Virginia Press, 1995.

---

[55] Wells, 159.

PART VIII

DRAMA, POETRY, AND CRITICISM

27

THE VICTORIAN NOVEL AND THEATRE

EMILY ALLEN

The Victorian novel—and theatre? What to the Victorians was an obvious and natural match appeared during much of the 20th century as a pair of strange bedfellows, given the high-profile visibility of the novel and the relative obscurity of Victorian theatre. After all, the Victorian period has long been proclaimed the Age of the Novel, while few outside Victorian theatre scholars—or actual Victorians—have given theatre equal billing. But if we want to understand the novel in its full complexity, which means returning it to its proper historical and cultural context, we must take theatre into account, as novels and novelists of the period most certainly did.

Victorian theatre was the novel's ally, inspiration, and competitor. The two forms, so different in many ways, so similar in others, shared storylines, techniques, audiences, and authors. But, most importantly, they shared a time period to which each form responded in complex ways and with a particular generic signature. How and why the Victorian novel and theatre shared such a productive and friendly rivalry are what this chapter hopes to suggest. How we forgot about theatre in our obsessive focus on the novel, and why we now remember it, is a story the chapter will also tell.

VICTORIAN THEATRE

The Victorian world was rich in theatre. Playgoers could choose from 'high' drama, melodrama of all stripes, pantomime, burlesque, extravaganza, farce, equestrian plays, dancing animals, puppets and even pyrodrama—plays in which large things were set on fire. Or they could opt for some combination of the above during a six-hour evening at the theatre that offered a varied bill of fare to suit all tastes.

While the Victorian theatrical scene was easily as diverse as the novelistic one, when Victoria took the throne in 1837, London had only two sorts of theatres: major and minor ones. The 'major' theatres, Covent Garden and Drury Lane, had since the Licensing Act of 1737 carried the patent to stage spoken or 'legitimate' drama, while the 'minor' or 'illegitimate' theatres could stage only drama with music, otherwise known as melodrama. This distinction was more legal than practical, since the minors were allowed to offer great chunks of spoken drama with only a light dusting of melody and the majors had long since been forced to stage melodrama to attract audiences and their money, thus remaining financially afloat in a world that increasingly favoured the melodramatic and spectacular. When the theatres were deregulated in 1843, then, it was largely business as usual.

Business itself was hit-and-miss during the early Victorian period, when theatres struggled for revenue in a generally depressed economy. Covent Garden, for example, cashed in its dramatic chips in 1847, when it became a premiere opera house and bet its fortunes on a bourgeois audience. The surest bets, however, were on theatres producing extravagant spectacle for lower-class audiences and those paratheatrical enterprises so popular with the Victorians and which we class together as 'spectacle': dioramas, panoramas, magic lantern shows, stereoscopes, balloon ascents, freaks, and curiosities. In a trend that continued throughout the century, the Victorian world had given itself over to the business and pleasure of show, and popular places such as the music hall and the pleasure garden gave revellers a venue to see and be seen, while new technologies such as plate glass allowed the spectacular impulse to spill over into the very streets of the city. New media such as photography and advertising upped the visual ante even farther, until all of London seemed in thrall to the eye.[1]

Some Victorians took to the eyeball more readily than others. While many were eager to sample the visual delights of the city and even to bring those delights home by way of the mass-produced commodities newly available to the public, and while others still were keen to take advantage of the business opportunities created by new spectacular technologies and an overriding culture of spectacle, this embrace of the visual was constantly shadowed by the horror of over-exposure. Critics and reformers worried about the effects of rampant looking, especially on those impressionable young women who were considered both more susceptible to the lure of the eye and more likely to become the object of its gaze. Even Victorian men, so long accustomed to the privilege of looking, seemed to fear the reversal of the gaze inherent in the new culture of spectacle. We can catch a glimpse of this visual anxiety, for example, in the rather astonishing encounter with the human eye maker in Henry Mayhew's *London Labour and London Poor* (1861), an early example of urban anthropology that serves also to exhibit to middle-class readers the human curiosities of the London streets. When the eye maker displays his boxed wares to Mayhew, the author staggers under their collective glare:

> The whole of 380 optics all seemed to be staring directly at the spectator, and occasioned a feeling somewhat similar to the bewilderment one experiences on

---

[1] The classic text on Victorian spectacle is Richard D. Altick's *The Shows of London* (Cambridge, MA: Belknap Press, 1978). On visuality in the Victorian city, see especially Lynda Nead's *Victorian Babylon: People, Streets, and Images in Nineteenth-Century London* (New Haven: Yale University Press, 2005).

suddenly becoming an object of general notice; as if the eyes of a whole lecture-room were crammed into a few square inches and all turned full upon you. The eyes of the whole world, as we say, literally appeared to be fixed upon one, and it was almost impossible to look at them without instinctively averting the head.[2]

In a scene that appears symptomatic of Victorian spectacular culture in general, the uncanny and concentrated effect of eyes upon eyes looking back at the spectator produces an aversion to being seen. It is the author's job to exhibit others, not himself. Or, as Charles Baudelaire had it in his essay on the flâneur, 'the spectator is a prince who everywhere rejoices in his incognito'.[3]

In the theatre proper, this anxiety over exposure, unrestricted viewing, and masculine sovereignty was felt as the friction between 'low' forms of spectacle, including melodrama, and 'high' drama, largely represented by that stalwart guardian of cultural capital and proper Englishness: the great Bard. While legally separated by the Licensing Act of 1737, these levels had become mixed in theatrical practice. To elude spectacle, then, the serious drama of the Romantic period (roughly 1789–1832) went so far as to enter the closet. Unstaged and unstageable dramas that were written for readers rather than spectators, also known as 'closet dramas' or 'mental theatre', were only the most extreme products of the turn away from spectacle that critics call 'Romantic anti-theatricalism', which represented the triumph of certain Romantic 'virtues'—interiority, genius, intellect, masculinity, authorship, individuality, print—over the vices of theatre, associated with the emotions and bodies of women, and with the play-going crowds and working-class patrons who were both feminized and infantilized in anti-theatrical rhetoric of the period.[4]

One obvious target of this rhetoric was melodrama, which had ties both to the French Revolution and to the unrest of the British working classes, and which in its many forms staged the triumph of the downtrodden.[5] Melodramas were criticized for being overly spectacular, emotionally manipulative, badly written, and banal, although this banality was clearly key to the success of these formulaic dramas. The claim that melodrama stimulates the eyes and nerves rather than the intellect runs through criticism throughout the century, from an 1818 essay 'On Melo-drama' arguing that melodramatic taste 'must arise from an inertness in the minds of spectators and a wish to be amused without

[2] Henry Mayhew, *London Labour and London Poor* (London: Penguin Classics, 1985), 345.

[3] Charles Baudelaire, 'The Painter of Modern Life' [1863], in *'The Painter of Modern Life' and Other Essays*, trans. and ed. Jonathan Mayne (London: Phaidon Press, 1964), 9.

[4] On Romantic anti-theatricalism, see especially Julie Carlson's *In the Theatre of Romanticism: Coleridge, Nationalism, Women* (Cambridge: Cambridge University Press, 1994).

[5] On the history and politics of melodrama, see especially Peter Brooks's *The Melodramatic Imagination: Balzac, Henry James, Melodrama, and the Mode of Excess* (New York: Columbia University Press, 1985) and Elaine Hadley's *Melodramatic Tactics: Theatricalized Dissent in the English Marketplace, 1800–1885* (Stanford: Stanford University Press, 1995).

the slightest exertion on their own parts or any exercise whatsoever of their intellectual powers' to Henry Arthur Jones's 1882 lecture, 'The Theatre and the Mob'.[6] Here is Jones:

> In melodrama we find that those plays have been most successful that have contained the most prodigious excitement, the most appalling catastrophes, the more harrowing situations, and this without reference to probability of story or consistency of character. The more a play has resembled a medley of these incidents and accidents which collect a crowd in the streets, the more successful it has been.[7]

In Jones we find not only the common criticism that melodrama substitutes sensation for story and character, but also the crowd phobia that propelled many attacks against popular theatre in general and melodrama in particular. That this fear of massed people and mass taste is a form of class politics is as clear throughout the 19th century as it is in 20th-century critic Allardyce Nicholl's rueful claim, 'melodrama, like the poor, will always be with us'.[8]

Although it continued to be criticized, melodrama's wild success with audiences made it much more the hero than the villain of the Victorian stage, and it quickly became the backbone of the theatrical repertoire. Melodramatic genres proliferated madly. Victorian playgoers could enjoy Gothic, nautical, Oriental, domestic, urban, canine, or disaster melodrama, all of which offered the thrill of seeing virtue imperilled and saved, while hearts and hands were wrung and people sang. Melodramatic plots often turned on a 'sensation scene', in which high-tech effects (storms, floods, fire, explosions, avalanches, etc.) matched the high emotional key of the drama. In Dion Boucicault's wildly popular *The Colleen Bawn* (1860), the heroine is saved from a watery death—she is being drowned, naturally, by a hunchback—in a moonlit sensation scene that left audiences breathless and led to an extended run for the play. Melodramatic audiences witnessed some of the most distressing issues of the day (poverty, unemployment, worker exploitation) restaged in a morally legible universe where moustache-twirling villains met their match in the end. John Walker's *The Factory Lad* (1832) staged the immoral conditions of industrial work, for example, while Douglas Jerrold's *Black Ey'd Susan* (1829) featured a lower-class heroine at the mercy of her more powerful tormentors. The success of melodrama enabled the rise of the extravaganza, lavish theatrical displays that were shorter on plot than melodrama and considerably longer on fairies. Based on the pantomime, an exceedingly popular holiday entertainment that featured a 'transformation scene' in which the characters changed into the figures from *commedia dell'arte*, the extravaganza downplayed the potential subversion of 'panto' in favour of pure spectacle. If melodrama was big, extravaganza was even bigger.

---

[6] 'On Melo-drama', *Theatrical Inquisitor* (March, 1818): 160.

[7] Reprinted in *The Nineteenth Century* 14 (September, 1883): 441–56, 445–46.

[8] Allardyce Nicoll, *A History of English Drama, 1600–1900*, 6 vols. (Cambridge: Cambridge University Press, 1963), 4: 100.

Indeed, much about Victorian era theatre was big: emotions, spectacle, even the theatres themselves, which could be vast. Drury Lane had a seating capacity of 3,600, and Astley's could seat 3,800 in a theatre that included a large circus ring designed for equestrian performance.[9] Cavernous theatre architecture naturally influenced acting style, for to be heard in a house such as this, an actor had to favour vocal projection over nuance. And because it was often impossible to be heard, actors relied on a language of gesture that allowed the body to speak directly to the eye. This gestural performance was strongly associated with the over-the-top emotions of melodrama, which could be communicated, some thought literally, from the body of the actor to the body of the playgoer.

Bodies were very much at issue for Victorian theatre audiences. An evening at the theatre was a highly social event, at which patrons expected to see and hear each other, even if they could not hear the actors. Victorian audiences were boisterous—especially in the pit and the gallery, the areas on the floor and near the ceiling of the theatre, where tickets were at their cheapest—and the theatre experience could be quite tactile. Theatres were thronged with bodies, some of them polite, some less so, but all of them scrutinized. The most suspect bodies were also the most visible: actors and actresses, whose very presence on the stage set them apart from polite society; audience members whose behaviour drew attention to themselves; and those professionals, from fruit sellers to prostitutes, who plied their trade in the shadow of the stage on any given evening.

And what an evening it was. A night at the theatre might last for five or six hours and include an array of entertainments: a tragedy leavened with musical farce, exotic animals, a bit of burlesque, and a spectacular melodrama. In a single night, a Victorian playgoer could take in *King Lear*, a menagerie of lions, and a light opera, all under one roof and while socializing with other members of the audience. At Astley's, the crowd was treated to such spectacles as an historical re-enactment of the battle of Waterloo on horseback, which might be played after an aerial acrobatic performance and before a troupe of dancing monkeys. By contemporary standards, the offerings were overwhelming in number and wildly varied in tone.

The perceived alternative and antidote to dancing monkeys was, of course, Shakespeare, who received continued staging throughout the Victorian period. A taste for the Bard cut across all classes, from the working-class audiences who enjoyed Shakespeare as part of an evening's varied bill to Queen Victoria, who attended Charles Kean's Shakespearean evenings at The Princess in the 1850s, and whose royal patronage did much to renew theatre's tarnished image in the eyes of bourgeois society. What distinguished one Shakespearean staging from another was often the other entertainments on the playbill, the type of spectacle involved, and its perceived relation to the drama itself. For the Victorians, Shakespeare was almost synonymous with spectacle, and in the better theatres his plays received highly pictorial staging, with

---

[9] Michael R. Booth, *Theatre in the Victorian Age* (Cambridge: Cambridge University Press, 1991), 61.

giant panoramas commissioned for backdrops and tremendous attention paid to scenic detail. Indeed, Shakespeare was at the centre of an archaeological movement in Victorian theatre, which called for painstaking historical research and historical accuracy. For *The Merchant of Venice* at the Prince of Wales's in 1875, for example, the Bancrofts took plaster casts of the pillars at the Doge's Palace to recreate the splendour of Venice on the London stage; the resulting set was so large that part of the theatre's wall needed to be cut away to accommodate it.[10] The theatrical manager and actor most associated with historical fidelity was Kean, although he was also no stranger to spectacle for its own sake: his 1854 *A Midsummer Night's Dream* featured seventy fairies dancing around a maypole that rose from the stage floor amidst a profusion of flowers; *Henry VIII* (1855) had flying angels; *King Richard II* (1857) had real horses; and *The Tempest* (1857) opened with a massive on-stage shipwreck.[11] While Kean claimed an instructional purpose for his plays, and while his historical fidelity impressed audiences, critics in general were suspicious of Shakespearean spectacle, which they saw as substituting for drama and acting the more simple pleasures of the eye. Theatre critic Clement Scott exemplified a common refrain when he complained of an 1884 staging of *Romeo and Juliet* at the Lyceum that, 'the whole of the stage seems to be sacrificed to the harvest of the eye'.[12] While audiences appeared to find the sacrifice worthwhile, critics patrolled the Shakespearean perimeter throughout the period, reserving harsh judgement for plays that subordinated—or outright mutilated—the text in favour of gratuitous visual effect. Whether played in a posh theatre or on horseback in the circus ring at Astley's, Shakespeare remained a flashpoint for cultural anxieties over 'low' versus 'high' theatre, and for the class warfare that was coded as anti-spectacular rhetoric. His plays, however, succeeded with audiences at all levels.[13]

Shakespeare's cross-class success was not enjoyed by all who wrote for the Victorian stage, or attempted to do so. Both Romantic and Victorian critics were dismayed that the century's most famous poets and novelists were not also its top dramatists, and these critics called out for serious drama that would engage more than the eye and the nerves. These calls became increasingly audible towards the end of the century, when playwrights like Henry Arthur Jones and theatre critics like William Archer championed an elevated drama distinct from popular, spectacular entertainment. In an 1884 lecture on 'The Modern Drama', Jones insisted that drama should pass two tests: 'Does it truly paint character?' and 'Is it literature?'[14] Archer called for a drama that would be 'not only

---

[10]   Michael R. Booth, *Victorian Spectacular Theater, 1850–1910* (Boston: Routledge, 1981), 40.

[11]   Booth, *Victorian Spectacular Theater*, 39–51.

[12]   'Our omnibus-box', *Theatre* (December, 1884), 310.

[13]   Victorian Shakespeare has, like all Shakespeare, received a great deal of critical attention. Two notable recent titles are Richard Foulkes's *Performing Shakespeare in the Age of Empire* (Cambridge: Cambridge University Press, 2002) and Gail Marshall's *Shakespeare and Victorian Women* (Cambridge: Cambridge University Press, 2009).

[14]   Doris Arthur Jones, *Taking the Curtain Call: The Life and Letters of Henry Arthur Jones* (New York: Macmillan, 1930), 68.

acted, but printed and read'.[15] This new literary drama would have 'at least an undercurrent of seriousness, which would generally arise from the relation of the work to some moral, social, political—may I say religious?—topic of the day'.[16]

Archer's dream would come true, but during the first half of the 19th century, the nerves still had a far stronger record for tickets sales than did the intellect. Theatre owners could not risk the financial hardships of investing exclusively or even primarily in serious drama. Because of the taint of spectacular theatre and its popularity with the lower classes, the upper bourgeoisie of the early Victorian period opted largely to stay away from the theatres and to go elsewhere (the opera, the diorama, the pleasure garden) or simply to stay home.

While not at all unacquainted with display, the commercial market, or class conflict, the Victorian home was seen as a private haven from these public things, and when affluent, early-Victorian audiences withdrew into their parlours and to the strange hybrid form of the home theatrical, theatres sought to woo them back by making them feel more 'at home'. This domestication of theatre, also called the *embourgeoisement* of theatre, took place on several levels during the mid decades of the century: some strains of melodrama became more 'polite' and high-minded, focusing on middle-class characters and toning down extremity in favour of more realistic, less startling situations; some theatre spaces were redesigned to offer a more intimate, homelike setting, with smaller, finely decorated houses like the Prince of Wales's offering up-market alternatives to the barnlike spaces of the early century; and new acting styles, once geared towards huge spaces in which patrons could see but not hear the actors, became more nuanced, favouring realistic expression over extravagant gesture. Where orange girls and prostitutes once roamed, the potted palm now reigned supreme. Theatre spaces were made safe for bourgeois customers, who thrilled to the mid-century melodramas of Boucicault, which coupled sensation with 'real' history and 'real' life, applauded the historical and domestic dramas of Tom Taylor and his sometimes collaborator Charles Reade in the 1850s and 1860s, and who flocked to see representations of themselves in productions such as T.W. Robertson's groundbreaking 'cup and saucer' dramas of the 1860s, so called for their realistic depiction of the habits of the Victorian parlour. This elevating trend towards realism progressed with the century and reached its pinnacle in the late-Victorian plays of Henrik Ibsen, Henry Arthur Jones, Arthur Wing Pinero, and George Bernard Shaw. These later plays were remarkable for their social and psychological (as opposed to scenic or pictorial) realism, which ushered in what many considered a new golden age of drama and acting—once again figured in opposition to the dross of stage spectacle. As Henry James sniffed in 1889, while commenting on

---

[15] William Archer, *English Dramatists of Today* (London: Sampson Low, Marston, Searle and Rivington, 1882), 4.

[16] William Archer, *English Dramatists of Today*, 4.

the 'perversion and corruption' of theatrical machinery, 'It is so much less easy to get good actors than good scenery.'[17]

For those seeking visually stronger stuff, storms were still howling and volcanoes were still exploding on stages elsewhere in London and across England. Massive theatres like Drury Lane in the West End and the Standard in the East continued to stage elaborate pantomimes and spectacular melodramas throughout the century to full audiences.[18] The return of the bourgeoisie—who themselves liked a good Christmas panto—led to a redistribution, rather than an eradication, of theatrical spectacle. Indeed, spectacle put its stamp so firmly on Victorian theatre, as it did on the Victorian period altogether, that it serves along with the melodrama to characterize what is quintessentially 'Victorian' about the period's theatrical scene. The sheer exuberance and diversity of that scene are also among its leading characteristics, as are its dependence on a popular market that was itself diverse, sometimes fickle, and its ability to register, if sometimes only in fantastical inversion, the contradictions of its cultural moment. Those animating contradictions—between 'high' and 'low' culture, mimetic realism and over-the-top spectacle, polite and rude audiences, intellectual sophistication and emotional sensation, interior and exterior space—are not only what kept Victorian theatre so tremendously alive but also what drove the development of the novel and critical discussions about it, as we shall now see.

VICTORIAN NOVELS AND THEATRE

Cue the novel, an undeniable star of the Victorian cultural stage. In preparation for its own Victorian run, the novel had itself undergone an elevation that allowed it to live down its ties to the low, the sensational, and the spectacular. This elevation, the product of nearly a century and of the nascent field of literary criticism, worked to obscure the 18th-century novel's origins in scandal sheets, erotic writing, and the European Continent.[19] Looking back over what later critics would dub 'the rise of the novel', critics like Clara Reeves—whose *The Progress of Romance* (1785)[20] was an early attempt to provide a pedigree for prose fiction as a discrete category—retroactively defined an 18th-century canon in which the domestic fiction of Samuel Richardson loomed large and sensational, popular fiction disappeared. So did female novelists, like Eliza

---

[17] Henry James, 'After the Play', *New Review* I (June 1889): 34–35.

[18] On the Standard, see Allan Stuart Jackson's *The Standard Theatre of Victorian England* (Rutherford, NJ: Fairleigh Dickinson University Press, 1993); on late-century spectacle at Drury Lane, see Booth, *Victorian Spectacular Theatre*.

[19] On the elevation of the novel, see William B. Warner's *Licensing Entertainment: The Elevation of Novel Reading in Britain, 1684–1750* (Berkeley: University of California Press, 1998).

[20] Clara Reeve, *The Progress of Romance, through times, countries, and manners; with remarks on the good and bad effects of it, on them respectively; in a course of evening conversations* (Colchester: W. Keymer, 1785).

Haywood and Delarivier Manley, who were written over by a canon that included Richardson, Henry Fielding, Tobias Smollet, and Thomas Sterne, who if not all equally family-friendly were at least male. Certain women were allowed to join, but only those with proper moral or artistic seriousness, like Frances Burney, whose sparkling novels paved the way for Jane Austen and the comedy of manners. In Austen and Sir Walter Scott, the early 19th century found answers to the problem of the novel's potential way-wardness. Austen's comedies were domesticated, feminine, and private in ways that elevated them over the popular throng, and Scott's historical romances were masculine and vigorous enough to make him the clear successor to the 18th-century male canon.[21] Both Austen's and Scott's novels were considered healthy reading, and in Scott in partic-ular critics were able to formulate a mass literary alternative to that *other* mass culture, cheap popular entertainment. (If Scott's novels were quickly and easily translated to the theatrical stage, as they were, this need only remind us that stage and page were never all that far apart in the 19th century.)

While tremendously different, Austen and Scott were both constructed as elevated novelists, and their elevation helped fuel the Romantic era turn-away from public, spec-tacular culture towards private reading and experience. It is no coincidence, for exam-ple, that Austen's heroines are so often found with their attractive noses in books, or that the scene of private or voiced reading is so critical to her development of character, as it is in *Sense and Sensibility* (1811), when Edward Ferrar's inability to read aloud in a theat-rical manner is sure proof of his interior value. The elevated novel, as it was marketed to the early 19th-century reading public, was a training ground in deep feeling and sympa-thetic identification; it was culturally and morally uplifting, and it was suitable for both sexes and for family reading.

By the beginning of the Victorian period, then, Britons were trained in reading novels both for pleasure and for moral, cultural, and educational profit. The Victorian novel became central to Victorian life, enjoyed as it often was in serial instalments and around the family hearth, and it developed as both a mirror and an agent of proper cultural formation. As any reader of the current volume knows, however, the Victorian novel was not a monolithic category. There were many different types of novels, at many dif-ferent cultural and aesthetic levels. While, for example, domestic realism focused on the cultivation of proper interiority and suitably restrained feeling, other forms like Newgate fiction from the 1830s and 1840s, the sensation novel of the 1860s, and the gothic novels that were written throughout the century were invested in pulling out the sensational and emotional stops. As in the theatre, 'serious' novel forms were pitted against more popular ones, and popularity brought with it critical charges of pandering to the lowly masses with sensational, even spectacular, effects. This separation would have made the novelistic field easy to define and regulate had it not been so difficult to tell the serious from the popular. Charles Dickens, for example, was clearly both, and

---

[21] See Ina Ferris, *The Achievement of Literary Authority: Gender, History, and the Waverley Novels* (Ithaca, NY: Cornell University Press, 1992).

his novels combine domestic realism with social satire, criminal sensation, and Gothic fantasy. And while Dickens was remarkable for the ease with which he traversed the high–low boundary, he was certainly not alone. Serious novelists like Charlotte Brontë and William Makepeace Thackeray were also widely read, if not perhaps with the familial warmth of Dickens.

The uneasy high–low split that governed novelists and novel forms pertained also to their audiences, who were considered polite or rude depending not only on class affiliation, but also on what sorts of novels they read and how they read them. Good readers were characterized as engaged but controlled, and their investments in the novelist world were thought to pay off in proper moral action in the real one, while bad ones glutted themselves on cheap sensation and lost themselves in escapist fictions from which there was no moral or civic gain. Nowhere is this formulation made more bluntly than in the panic of the 1860s, when critics feared that sensation novels would degrade their readers. The critic for the *London Quarterly Review* articulated the prevailing opinion that 'instead of refining, [sensation novels] deprave the taste, that they enfeeble rather than strengthen the intellect, that they stimulate the very feelings which they should have sought to repress, and the recreation which they profess to furnish frequently degenerates into the worst forms of intellectual dissipation'.[22] Indeed, the only perceived gain of low reading was the money lining the pockets of unscrupulous writers and publishers who spewed forth such illegitimate novels.

It is easy to see how simplifying critical narratives about novels and their readers layer over the familiar and often-repeated story about plays and their goers that had such currency with some Victorian and most 20th-century critics. 'Good' readers, who turn out to be bourgeois ones, invest themselves in the moral uplift of reading and eschew the coarser pleasures of the drama. 'Bad' readers, outclassed by their betters in every conceivable way, are as agog before cheap pulp fiction as they are at the cheap theatrical spectacles they savour and which have instructed them in a kind of degraded, sensational reading process that thrills the nerves and blunts true sensibility. Bad novels, in other words, shared with bad theatre a low audience with very strong tastes, while good novels catered solely to the refined palates of the middle and upper classes and dominated their leisure time. Only when theatre had remade itself in the image of the realist novel and the parlour did it regain its place in the bourgeois breast, which in turn led to the elevation and salvation of the art form.

This is a good story, with a strong narrative line, which is why it is so familiar. But, like other cultural and critical fictions that favour the upper classes and work to establish their distinction, it is not entirely, or even mostly, true. Students of the Victorian period will quickly spot its inconsistencies: first, as we have seen, Victorian theatre is not so easily classed into 'serious' and 'spectacular' categories, as pretty much any playbill would make clear, and spectacle in its many forms remained popular with all classes even after the drama's elevation from 1860 onwards; second, Victorian theatre audiences were a mixed bunch, more strongly lower than upper class for the first part of the

---

[22] 'Recent Novels: Their Moral and Religious Teaching', *London Quarterly Review* 27 (October 1866): 102.

century, perhaps, but in no way homogenous in their make-up or their tastes; third, and quite crucially, novels and their writers, publishers and audiences were just as hard to pin down in terms of cultural level and practice. Victorian novel forms were not simply high or low, and they were never generically pure: Charlotte Brontë's *Jane Eyre* (1847) is both domestic realist and Gothic; Dickens's Great Expectations (1861) is a *Bildungsroman* and a sensation novel; both are highly melodramatic. It is, moreover, notoriously difficult to know just how the Victorians read, and there is no reason to assume that they read everything in the same way. A very 'good' reader, for example, might read a realist novel in one way, a Gothic novel in another, and view a pantomime in quite another; a supposedly bad one might similarly distinguish among forms or receive uplift in the 'lowest' places.

The truth makes for a less ripping tale than the story of the novel's abrupt divorce from and eventual heroic rescue of the theatre: we do not know entirely how these two forms developed in terms of and influenced each other, if only because they have such a complex relation to each other, to their producers, and to their overlapping audiences. Some things, of course, we do know. Long after novels were supposed to have written out and over theatre, they were borrowing theatrical language and using theatre as both a thematic and structural device. Examples are everywhere, from Brontë's claim in *Jane Eyre* that 'a new chapter in a novel is something like a new scene in a play' to Olive Schreiner's disavowal of 'the stage method' in her theorization of novelistic realism in *The Story of an African Farm* (1883).[23] Thackeray provides a preamble 'Before the Curtain' in his 1848 novel, *Vanity Fair*, and novels from up and down the Victorian period and the high–low gamut are littered with professional performers, including Geraldine Jewsbury's *The Half Sisters* (1848), Charlotte Brontë's *Villette* (1853), Wilkie Collins's *No Name* (1862), George Eliot's *Daniel Deronda* (1876), George Moore's *A Mummer's Wife* (1885), and Oscar Wilde's *The Picture of Dorian Gray* (1890). Acclaimed novelists were not only assuming theatrical knowledge and interest on the part of their polite readers but were also themselves writing for the stage. A public so deeply schooled in the ways of spectacle did not simply leave behind this training at the stage door, but lived it in their daily lives, of which novels were a big part. The connections between theatre and the novel, in other words, went way beyond adaptations, although these too were highly popular and went in both directions, from page to stage and the reverse. As fascinating a pairing as one could find in either fiction or drama, these two forms of public entertainment remained entwined throughout the century.

The novels of the period publish this relationship in their pages. Some novels, and some novelists, had a more obvious investment in theatre than others. Charles Dickens, for example, not only sent his characters to the play in novels like *Great Expectations* (1861) and *Nicholas Nickleby* (1839), in which Nicholas performs with the Crummles theatrical troupe, but also adopted the authorial pose of the showman in his dramatic reading tours. Dickens's novels were widely adapted for the stage, sometimes by Dickens,

[23] Charlotte Brontë, *Jane Eyre* (London: Penguin Classics, 1996), 108; Olive Schreiner, *The Story of an African Farm*, ed. Patricia O'Neill (Peterborough, Ontario: Broadview Press, 2003), 41.

and the author himself wrote plays. Claiming famously that, 'every writer of fiction, though he may not adopt the dramatic form, writes in effect for the stage', Dickens was the flashiest and most theatrical fictional stylist of the age, and, indeed, no Victorian novelist has been better served by the critics, who have documented this theatricality in detail and with gusto.[24]

William Makepeace Thackeray has also been well served, and his *Vanity Fair*, which features actress-adventuress Becky Sharp, is acknowledged as one of the most theatrical novels of the century. Using puppet-theatre as his conceit for literary authorship, Thackeray frames the novel as a form of role-play. That the creator of the famous 'Becky Puppet', the self-proclaimed 'Manager of the Performance', was himself infamously anti-theatrical should come as no surprise, given the strong push-pull that existed between Victorian novelists and the theatre. Indeed, Thackeray is a perfect example of how often vexed and sometimes contradictory the authorial relationship to theatre could be. As David Kurnick has recently demonstrated, Thackeray was repelled by theatricality but attracted by the actual theatre; his frustrated desire to write for the stage is felt in his novels as a melancholic turn inward from the public sphere.[25]

While Thackeray's arch theatricality was a hit with novel critics, the more heavy-handedly melodramatic style of the sensation novel was considered a threat to the reading public. Shocking, emotional, and flamboyant, these popular novels of the 1860s tingled spines up and down the class ladder but were aligned by outraged critics with low spectacle. Not surprisingly, these novels enjoyed popular success in theatrical adaptation: Mrs Henry Wood's *East Lynne* (1861) and Mary Elizabeth Braddon's *Lady Audley's Secret* (1862) were widely adapted for the stage, and Wilkie Collins wrote his own adaptations of *The Woman in White* (1860), *No Name*, and *The Moonstone* (1868). The melodramatic 'sensation scene' here brought together popular fiction and theatre for the palpitating masses.

The brouhaha over the melodramatic nature of sensation fiction worked to eclipse a more obvious fact: melodrama was not only the backbone of Victorian theatre by mid-century, but also of the novel. Less overtly theatrical novelists than Dickens, Thackeray, or the sensation crew trafficked in melodrama, and both popular romance and domestic realism drew directly from the melodramatic well. Indeed, as such critics as Peter Brooks and Elaine Hadley have shown, the 'mode of excess' that was melodrama was virtually inescapable in Victorian life and certainly in Victorian novels.

The least obviously melodramatic of these novels, penned by the most highly acclaimed authors of the period, nonetheless demonstrate how deep theatre went under

---

[24] Dickens said this in a speech to the Royal General Theatrical Fund on March 29, 1858. Studies of Dickensian theatricality began in the early 20th century and run up to the present, with notable recent additions by Malcolm Andrews, *Charles Dickens and His Performing Selves: Dickens and the Public Readings* (Oxford: Oxford University Press, 2006); John Glavin, *After Dickens: Reading, Adaptation, Performance* (Cambridge: Cambridge University Press, 1999); and Deborah Vlock, *Dickens, Novel Reading, and Victorian Popular Theatre* (Cambridge: Cambridge University Press, 1998).

[25] David Kurnick, 'Empty Houses: Thackeray's Theater of Interiority', *Victorian Studies* 48, no. 2 (Winter 2006): 257–67.

the novel's skin. Charlotte Brontë's novels, from *Jane Eyre* to *Villette*, all demonstrate a strong sense of theatre. Lucy Snowe, the introspective narrator of *Villette*, takes to the boards early in the novel and vows never to act again because she enjoys it too much; later, a theatre catches fire during the blazing performance of an actress and appears to confirm Lucy in linking acting with dangerous passions. But the interiority that the novel proffers as an alternative to spectacle itself operates as a form of internalized theatricality, as Joseph Litvak has shown.[26] No less a champion of interiority and introspection than George Eliot, in whose works the 'serious' Victorian novel reaches its apex, similarly depends upon theatre, both as novelistic foil and stylistic mode. Many have commented on the theatrical subplots of *Daniel Deronda*, Eliot's last published novel, but we need look no further than her first, *Adam Bede* (1859), to see Eliot working out the dynamics of theatrical spectacle in her preaching and courtroom scenes.

Witness, for example, our introduction to Dinah Morris, the Methodist heroine of *Adam Bede*. The scene is packaged in visual terms: a traveller on horseback lifts his eyes from the picturesque beauties of the pastoral landscape to take in an 'unusual scene' unfolding on a village green.[27] A beautiful young woman stands upon a cart and preaches, surrounded by both an 'expectant audience' and a group of naysayers who, shocked and somewhat titillated by the spectacle of a woman preaching, have come not to *hear* but to *see*.[28] The 'pretty preacher woman' in her 'Quakerlike costume' confounds audience expectations: Dinah's 'total absence of self-consciousness' and extraordinary vocal performance move even her strongest critics. The gentleman traveller is 'interested in the course of her sermon as if it had been the development of a drama—for there is this sort of fascination in all sincere unpremeditated eloquence, which opens to one the inward drama of the speaker's emotions'.[29] Framed both in the language of picturesque tourism and theatrical criticism, this scene provides a close description of Dinah's performance in terms familiar to mid-Victorian acting theory. Her vocal tone and rate, her facial mannerisms, the physical discipline seen in her lack of obvious stage gesture: all produce the effect of sincere artlessness and vocal prowess that rivets her audience. While Eliot disavows staginess here and elsewhere in the novel—she, for example, chides the picturesque tourist for thinking that 'nature has theatrical properties and, with the considerate view of facilitating art and psychology, "makes up," her characters, so that there may be no mistake about them'—she here works the theatrical scene for everything it is worth.[30] In a book about the development (and narration) of the interior life, Dinah proves her own through her dramatic resistance to the gaze of her audience, who come for the bodily spectacle of a pretty woman and stay for the 'inward drama of the speaker's emotions'. Dinah's debut performance not only prefigures the emotionally gripping

[26] Joseph Litvak, *Caught in the Act: Theatricality in the Nineteenth-Century English Novel* (Berkeley: University of California Press, 1992).
[27] George Eliot, *Adam Bede*, ed. Stephen Gill (London: Penguin Books, 1980), 63.
[28] George Eliot, *Adam Bede*, 63.
[29] George Eliot, *Adam Bede*, 66, 76.
[30] George Eliot, *Adam Bede*, 67.

scenes in the courtroom, where people once again gather to hear a woman bear witness, but also the truly spectacular climax, in which Dinah and her cousin Hetty Sorrel ride to the gallows in a open cart, surrounded by a 'waiting watching multitude', the eagerly 'gazing crowd'.[31] The surprise return of the picturesque traveller as Hetty's courtroom judge further invites us to conflate the scenes and to consider the politics and morality of visual spectacle, focalized—we see only in retrospect—not only through the theatrical but also the juridical gaze.

Eliot used theatre to develop and refine the 'interior drama' of high novelistic realism. Others would later use theatre to take high realism down. At the end of the Victorian period, novelist and playwright Oscar Wilde favourably contrasts the romantic thrill of theatre with prosaic realism in *The Picture of Dorian Gray*, the title character of which falls in love with an actress, Sybil Vane, because she is a living work of art, something Wilde himself aspired to be. In Wilde, the bloom is off the rose of Victorian realism, and theatrical style becomes a tonic for nerves and novels worn down by too much sincerity. Here, in this most theatrical of fictions, history has already begun its retroactive construction of the dour Victorian period, which would eventually rewrite the century so as to eclipse its theatrical wonders. But if we look closely at the period and its novels, if we look at the whole range of popular Victorian entertainments, as the Victorians did, we see a century brimming with theatre and a novel no less captivated by it.

Novels, Theatre, and Critics

We should return in closing to the various stories circulated about the novel and its relation to theatre. The first is that the novel simply overcame theatre, taking its audience and sending it into the pit. This clearly did not happen, as the robust field of Victorian theatre history proves. Victorian theatre was very much alive long after it was supposedly bumped off by the novel, and it continues its long run in vivid critical afterlife. The second and more sophisticated story is that the novel broke along class lines in the same way that theatre did, with the upper classes choosing serious drama and finally serious novels over their spectacular alternatives and the lower classes gorging themselves on both forms of low spectacle. In this narrative, spectacle both separates and unites, dividing high from low and pulling together the lower levels of society and sensational culture. In a backlash against all that low spectacle, the story goes, serious novels and theatre became more interior and realistic, with Victorian theatre becoming in fact increasingly novelistic as it became culturally elevated.

This story has an obvious appeal in so far as it performs the work of cultural elevation while simultaneously obscuring a number of things it cannot afford to know, such as the novelistic debts owed to theatre, the rough and ready origins of the novel, the

---

[31] George Eliot, *Adam Bede*, 507.

novel's continued ties to theatre and to the working classes, and the magnificent complexity of both the theatrical and novelistic fields. What this story misses altogether is
the continued popularity of spectacle both in and outside the theatre, which amounted
to a thorough theatricalization of public life, the continued theatricality of novel, and
the diversity of taste among Victorian audiences.

Why then has this story been repeated, and what is at stake in its repetition? To answer
the first, we should ask a second question: *Cui bono?* Who benefits? Critics, for one, since
the narrative requires a disciplinary turn away from the popular and towards the 'serious' texts of high culture, which require a critical establishment to review and explain;
and the novel, for another, since it comes off as the conquering hero of the Victorian culture wars. At stake in narrating these wars is, of course, nothing less than culture itself,
and the ability to describe it, to fix its level, to plumb its depths. Culture, like history, is
written by the victors—or, in this case, by those whose act of victory was merely outliv-
ing the Victorians. Like most historical narratives about the Victorians, this one has a
clear modernist bias, one that reads generic development as teleology and posits high
modernist aesthetics as the answer to Victorian low populism. However ironically, the
narrative that performs this triumph is clearly a melodrama—one written by people who
disliked melodrama perhaps, but a melodrama nonetheless, with easily defined levels,
clear conflicts, and a rousing generic rescue performed by a former underdog, the novel.
If nothing else should convince us of the importance of theatrical forms not only to the
novel but also to novel criticism, the persistence of melodrama as critical mode allows
us to see the heroic narratives in which we cast ourselves. The anti-spectacular bias of
this narrative repeats two very common and ultimately complementary ways of looking
back at the Victorians: (1) they were stuffy and prudish; and (2) they were childlike and
naïve. In the first view, the Victorians are the boring parents who never liked spectacle
to begin with; in the second they are the wide-eyed children who need to be weaned off
spectacle for their own good and ours. Either way, the next generation wins.

What have been the effects of this narrative? The critical desire to be serious and
important, not popular, led in the first half of the 20th century to a privileging of
Victorian high culture. The most intellectually ambitious artists and forms fared well,
and serious novels fared very well. In *The Great Tradition* (1948), for example, F.R.
Leavis famously and influentially connected novelistic 'greatness' to high moral purpose
and formal complexity, which put George Eliot and Henry James on top and everyone
else (including Dickens) on the bottom. The Victorian canon as it was then formed in
the criticism of Leavis and others favoured high over low, realism over romance, male
over female, interior over exterior. This bias had effects on the valuation of particular
authors—'dark' Dickens, for example, was acknowledged to be far greater than 'light',
comic Dickens—and entire genres—sensation novels, for example, pulled a disappear-
ing act worthy of their own shock effects. Victorian spectacular theatre dropped out of
sight, and Victorian drama also left the canonical stage, with a few notable, late-century
exceptions (Ibsen, Pinero, Wilde, Shaw) that proved the rule. While tremendously
important theatre research was published in the middle of the 20th century, most notably by Michael Booth and George Rowell, this work did not lead to a reappraisal of

Victorian theatre's importance to the novel until the canon was being rethought altogether in the late 20th century under the pressure of, among other things, feminism, Marxism, new historicism, and popular culture studies. The dominant view for the bulk of the previous century, then, was that the Victorian novel was a deeply anti-theatrical genre, with pockets of theatricality located around Dickens, Thackeray, and Wilde, where it could be contained.

This view of the novel has changed as has our sense of the Victorians and our interest in their spectacular and theatrical pursuits. Richard Altick's encyclopedic *The Shows of London* (1978), and Peter Bailey's *Leisure and Class in Victorian England* (1978) and *Music Hall* (1986)[32] turned the critical gaze on popular pleasures, while Martin Miesel's magisterial *Realisations* (1983) made connections between the novel and the visual arts and David Marshall's *The Figure of Theatre* (1986) traced representations of theatre from the 18th century into the high Victorian novel. Connections between the arts were further explored in the 1990s, when a number of studies appeared on the theatricality of Victorian novels and Victorian life. Nina Auerbach's *Private Theatricals* (1990) examined theatricality as the mode of Victorian public and private life, and Elaine Hadley's *Melodramatic Tactics* (1995) argued for melodrama as a major political force in theatre, novels, and public life. Most influentially, Joseph Litvak's *Caught in the Act* (1992) made the persuasive case for theatricality within the very house of fiction. In Litvak's treatment, the realist novels that most appear to embrace surveillance over spectacle, which is to say those novels most concerned with interiority and propriety, perform their cultural work through theatrical means. Following Litvak, scholars at the turn of the 21st century argued for the crucial position of theatre and theatricality in Victorian fiction. J. Jeffrey Franklin's *Serious Play* (1999) reads Victorian novels in contest with and formed by their relationship to theatre, and my *Theatre Figures* (2003) argues that Victorian novels and novelists actually required theatre to establish categories of distinction within a diverse novelistic field. Lynn Voskuil's *Acting Naturally* (2004) shows performance at the very heart of the Victorian's most sincere enterprises, including the novel, and undoes completely the idea that the century was at its base anti-theatrical.

Where are we now? Victorian theatre studies is and has been on the move, leaving the traditional focus on London and moving into provinces, leaving the stomping grounds of the privileged in London's West End for the diversity of the East, thinking across levels of high and low, and exploring the tremendous diversity of Victorian audiences and theatrical fare. Pioneering work by Jacky Bratton, Jim Davis and Victor Emeljanow, Tracy Davis, Gail Marshall, Katharine Newey, and Kerry Powell, among others, has shown us again the Victorian stage in all of its wonders, which should inspire literary critics and scholars of the theatre/novel connection to continue revising their picture of the

---

[32] Peter Bailey, *Leisure and Class in Victorian England: Rational Recreation and the Contest for Control, 1830–1855* (London: Routledge, 1978) and *Music Hall: The Business of Pleasure* (Philadelphia: Open University Press, 1986). On Altick, see note 1.

Victorian novel.[33] A new generation of scholars now comes to the novel assuming connections to the other arts. David Kurnick, for example, examines Victorian novelists who also wrote plays and argues for the novel form's fundamental longing after the theatrical.[34] Much work is now being done tying the novel to various forms of visual media, in particular photography.[35] What we require for theatre to get into the act on a permanent basis are novel historians with training in theatre history, or at least lively interest in the field, and better and more regular communication between the fields. We have talked the talk of interdisciplinarity for some time now; it is time to walk the walk.

If the Victorian novel were to tell the story of its own relationship to theatre, we would be somewhere in the third volume, at the point where the insurmountable differences that had broken apart the principles in the first and second volumes turn out to be perfectly surmountable, a happy ending in the offing. What happens next? We go back to the beginning, pages flipping towards the novel's theatrical past.

SUGGESTED READING

Allen, Emily. *Theater Figures: The Production of the Nineteenth-Century British Novel*. Columbus: The Ohio State University Press, 2003.

Auerbach, Nina. *Private Theatricals: The Lives of the Victorians*. Cambridge: Harvard University Press, 1990.

Barish, Jonas. *The Antitheatrical Prejudice*. Berkeley: University of California Press, 1981.

Brooks, Peter. *The Melodramatic Imagination: Balzac, Henry James, Melodrama, and the Mode of Excess*. New York: Columbia University Press, 1985.

---

[33] Recent publications in Victorian theatre attest to the vibrancy of the field. See especially, Jacky Bratton's *New Readings in Theatre History* (Cambridge: Cambridge University Press, 2003), Jim Davis and Victor Emeljanow's *Reflecting the Audience: London Theatregoing, 1840–1880* (Iowa City: University of Iowa Press, 2001), Tracy Davis's *The Economics of the British Stage* (Cambridge: Cambridge University Press, 2000), which joins her *Actresses as Working Women* (London: Routledge, 1991), and edited collections, *Women and Playwriting in Nineteenth-Century Britain* (Cambridge: Cambridge University Press, 1999), *Theatricality*, ed. Tracy Davis and Ellen Donkin (Cambridge: Cambridge University Press, 2003), and *The Performing Century: Nineteenth-Century Theatre History*, ed. Tracy Davis and Peter Holland (Houndmills: Palgrave Macmillan, 2008) as must-reads in the field; Gail Marshall's *Actresses on the Victorian Stage* (Cambridge: Cambridge University Press, 2006), Katherine Newey's *Women's Theater Writing in Victorian Britain* (Houndmills: Palgrave Macmillan, 2005), and Kerry Powell's *Women and Victorian Theatre* (Cambridge: Cambridge University Press, 1997).

[34] Kurnick, 'Empty Houses'.

[35] On the novel and new media systems, see Richard Menke's *Telegraphic Realism: Victorian Fiction and Other Information Systems* (Stanford: Stanford University Press, 2008). On Victorian fiction and photography, see Jennifer Green-Lewis, *Framing the Victorians: Photography and the Culture of Realism* (Ithaca: Cornell University Press, 1996); Nancy Armstrong, *Fiction in the Age of Photography: the Legacy of British Realism* (Cambridge, MA: Harvard University Press, 1999); Daniel Novak, *Realism, Photography, and Nineteenth-Century Fiction* (Cambridge: Cambridge University Press, 2008); and Linda M. Shires, *Perspectives: Modes of Viewing and Knowing in Nineteenth-Century England* (Columbus: The Ohio State University Press, 2009).

Franklin, J. Jeffrey. *Serious Play: The Cultural Form of the Nineteenth-Century Realist Novel.* Philadelphia: University of Pennsylvania Press, 1999.

Hadley, Elaine. *Melodramatic Tactics: Theatricalized Dissent in the English Marketplace, 1800–1885.* Stanford: Stanford University Press, 1995.

Kurnick, David. *Empty Houses: Theatrical Failure and the Novel.* Princeton: Princeton University Press, 2012.

Litvak, Joseph. *Caught in the Act: Theatricality in the Nineteenth-Century English Novel.* Berkeley: University of California Press, 1992.

Marshall, David. *The Figure of Theatre: Shaftesbury, Defoe, Adam Smith, and George Eliot.* New York: Columbia University Press, 1986.

Miesel, Martin. *Realisations: Narrative, Pictorial, and Theatrical Arts in Nineteenth-Century England.* Princeton: Princeton University Press, 1983.

Voskuil, Lynn. *Acting Naturally: Victorian Theatricality and Authenticity.* Charlottesville: University of Virginia Press, 2004.

28

VERSE VERSUS THE NOVEL

JAMES NAJARIAN

INTRODUCTION: THE CONTEST

Though we think of Victorian poets and novelists as distinct entities, in their time, writers we know as poets attempted prose fictions, and novelists wrote poetry.[1] With the exception of George Meredith, who was both poet and novelist, those who were successful in both genres did them separately in distinct quadrants of their lives, largely in response to the market. Sir Water Scott and Thomas Hardy, who might serve as the start and end points of the Victorian novel, were successful in writing both genres as entirely opposite responses to changes in the market. The market for poetry started to fall and the novel to rise around 1820; Scott turned from poetry to prose at just this time to relieve himself of debts he contracted when his publisher went under. Thomas Hardy turned away from his vocation as a poet at mid-century and returned to it at the end of the century, after *Tess of the D'Urbervilles* and *Jude the Obscure* were rejected by critics. By that time he no longer needed to depend on the sales of new novels, and could write what ended up being the great poetry of his old age at his leisure.

Though there is the small genre of the verse novel, primarily represented by Elizabeth Barrett Browning's *Aurora Leigh*, this chapter will concentrate on the role of verse within the novel, and within that on a particular repeating theme.[2] Some novelists did include verse: one of Sir Walter Scott's most anthologized lyrics, 'Proud Maisie', is sung by Madge Wildfire on her deathbed in *The Heart of Midlothian*. George Eliot carefully larded *Middlemarch* with poetic epigraphs of her own and others' composition. But I

[1] Of the poets, Christina Rossetti wrote some short fiction and a novella, Swinburne two unpublished novels, and Thomas Hood a single novel. Of those whom we know as novelists today, figures as various as George Eliot, Charles Kingsley, and William Makepeace Thackeray wrote a substantial amount of verse.

[2] On the verse novel, see Dino Felluga, 'Verse Novel', in *A Companion to Victorian Poetry*, ed. Richard Cronin, Alison Chapman, and Antony B. Harrison (Malden: Wiley-Blackwell, 2002), 171–86.

am talking about a more synthetic inclusion of poetry in the novel—the character of the poet and the uses of poetry through that character. Although the novel became the central cultural form in the nineteenth century, poetry still held a certain kind of esteem—of cultural capital, to use John Guillory's phrase.[3] Poets and poetry in the Victorian novel are often dismissed and gently or not-so-gently ridiculed—their ambitions thwarted, their aims not met. When characters quote poetry, it is often garbled or half-understood. Moreover, a consistent effort is made in the Victorian novel to show how poetry is retrograde, non-generative, and sexually borderline.

As several critics have argued, Victorian writers increasingly attempted to stabilize masculine categories because writing is not a particularly manly activity: it is not physical, and authorship was a profession certainly open to both sexes.[4] For Herbert Sussman and James Eli Adams, writers projected ideal masculine or feminine stances.[5] Jeffrey Weeks locates the shift to an aggressive masculinity to the 1860s.[6] So one way of minimizing the cultural power of poetry is to question the poet's gender stance: as a result, the novelist's position, both in relation to an idealized vision of gender and cultural authority, gains more power. This demotic criticism of poetry, particularly in the novel itself, exploits a long line of writing about Romanticism in its time, of 'Cockney' poetry, the 'immoral' Byron, the 'effeminate' Keats, and the 'unmanly' Shelley and Hunt: turns that would be redeployed in criticism of the young Tennyson in the 1830s.[7] Poets, however gifted, are depicted as civically and naturally effeminate, to deprive them of cultural weight and to promote the works of the Victorian novelist: prose fiction.

DICKENS, HUNT, AND SKIMPOLE'S MASCULINITY

The depiction of Harold Skimpole in *Bleak House* (1853), universally recognized as the poet Leigh Hunt, is one of the chestnuts of English literary study—though verse-making is only one of Skimpole's many tiny accomplishments, and it seems to have been diverted

---

[3] See John Guillory, *Cultural Capital: The Problem of Literary Canon Formation* (New York: Columbia University Press, 1995).

[4] See Thais Morgan, 'Victorian Effeminacies', in *Victorian Sexual Dissidence*, ed. Richard Dellamora (Chicago and London: University of Chicago Press, 1999), 109–26, 113 and James Eli Adams, *Dandies and Desert Saints: Styles of Victorian Manhood* (Ithaca and London: Cornell University Press, 1995), 1–5.

[5] Herbert Sussman, *Victorian Masculinities: Manhood and Masculine Poetics in early Victorian Literature* (Cambridge: Cambridge University Press, 1995), 3. For Adams, Victorian writers claim their authorship as a masculine discipline on the lines of the roles of the prophet, dandy, priest, and soldier (Adams, 2).

[6] Jeffrey Weeks, *Sex, Politics, and Sexuality: The Regulation of Sexuality since 1800* (London: Longman, 1981), 40. Connections between the novel's authority and perceptions of its 'manliness' at the beginning of the 19th century have been persuasively set out in Ina Ferris's *The Achievement of Literary Authority: Gender, History, and the Waverley Novels* (Ithaca: Cornell, 1991). Ferris demonstrates that Scott, backed by reviewers, successfully distinguished his masculine writing of the historical novel from the 'common' novels often authored by women.

[7] See Jeffrey Cox, *Poetry and Politics in the Cockney School: Keats, Shelley, Hunt and their Circle* (Cambridge: Cambridge University Press, 1999).

into lyrics for song. He also sketches, makes excellent conversation, and borrows money. Investigations of this old topic have examined it mostly in personal terms.[8] Dickens had a substantial acquaintance with Hunt and eagerly admitted that Skimpole was based on the poet. Dickens wrote in a letter of 25 September 1853, 'I suppose he is the most exact portrait that was ever painted in words!...It is an absolute reproduction of a real man.'[9] He denied it, though, to Hunt's face. Friends of the two tried to get Dickens to soften the caricature, which they recognized instantly—to little avail.

In *Bleak House*, Skimpole's immaturity is economic and social: while the text registers his lack of maturity, it does not call him 'effeminate'. The appellation used repeatedly for him is the 'child', which is a different mode of indicating a lack of male fullness. Skimpole lives largely in the houses of other people, including John Jarndyce, who repeatedly calls him a 'child'. The implication is that Skimpole has not reached real citizenship, defined here in economic and personal terms. Once could even argue that his immaturity accelerates; by chapter 37 Richard is calling Skimpole (whom he admires) an 'old infant'.

The ways that Dickens depicts Skimpole are not only personal (and questions about their accuracy still hover); they are also ideological and selective, and they have a fairly long history of anti-Romanticism behind them. Skimpole's delight in ephemera deploys many of the terms of opposition to the second generation of Romantic poets, chiefly as represented by Hunt, Keats, and their allies. Hunt's earlier career—which began long before Dickens was born—was controversial from the start. He edited liberal papers like the *Examiner* and the *Liberal* and became in some quarters a radical hero. Imprisoned for 'libeling' the Prince Regent, who very much deserved it, Hunt held a central place in Radical politics and poetic thought: a sometime close friend of Byron, Keats, Procter, and Shelley. He was a central figure of the 'Cockney' school. As a result, the conservative literary press of the 1810s and 1820s targeted him as cultural upstart and malign sexual influence. Hunt was also a poet, and a deeply divisive one at that. His verse is self-consciously decorative, and it dwells on ornament, interiors, and cozy suburban rather than empty rural landscapes. His poetry and prose praise leisure, domestic pleasure, and the availability of poetry to the middle classes as an escape from the cares of daily life. Hunt was writing well into the 1840s: his *Autobiography* came out in 1850. In recent years, critics have been reading Hunt's domestic interests as ideological; they counter control of cultural production by the very rich.[10] Hunt's most famous poem was his verse-tale *The Story of Rimini*, which depicts—and explicitly condones—a love affair between a man and his brother's wife. The poem is also full of delicious domestic

---

[8]   An excellent treatment of the subject on a textual and personal level is found in Richard D. Altick, 'Harold Skimpole Revisited', in *The Life and Times of Leigh Hunt*, ed. Robert A. McCown (Iowa City: Friends of the University of Iowa Libraries, 1984), 1–15. A compelling recent account, sympathetic to Hunt, is found in Anthony Holden, *The Wit in the Dungeon: The Remarkable Life of Leigh Hunt* (New York and Boston: Little, Brown 2005), 292–319.

[9]   Dickens to Mrs Richard Watson, 21 September 1853, quoted in Holden, 306.

[10]   See, for example, Ayumi Mizukoshi, *Keats, Hunt and the Aesthetics of Pleasure* (Houndmills and New York: Palgrave Macmillan, 2001) and the essays in Nicholas Roe, ed. *Leigh Hunt: Life, Poetics, Politics* (London and New York: Routledge, 2003).

spaces—spaces in which the couple becomes more and more intimate. Condemnation of the tale and its author reached a fever pitch in the late 1810s. In Romantic-era criticism, Hunt's views were depicted as degenerate and unmanly. As 'Z' (John Gibson Lockhart) writes:

> One feels the same disgust at the idea of opening Rimini, that impresses itself on the mind of a man of fashion, when he is invited to enter, for the second time, the gilded drawing-room of a little mincing boarding-school mistress, who would fain have an At Home in her house. Everything is pretence, affectation, finery, and gaudiness...[11]

The passage implies that Hunt is not only a woman not of the highest class, but one with bad, second-hand taste. She is not supposed to attempt an 'At Home' in her house; she is not of the proper class. The passage links Hunt with the commemoration of domestic interiors and small-scale pleasures. *Rimini*, incidentally, was republished in 1850.

It is in this context that I think we can read Dickens's mean-spirited caricature of Hunt in *Bleak House*. It is not only personal, but ideological in interesting ways, and it removes the real accomplishments of Hunt the radical hero as it re-stations him within the terms of the criticism of an earlier era. For Dickens, Skimpole's refusal to accept normative masculine responsibility is more than a personal failing. Dickens adds, or demonstrates, the social threat of the immature male: the male who will not reach full civic masculinity. J.G.A. Pocock has described the construction of civic masculinity and its lack.[12] Skimpole's laxness is a social threat. In the terms of the novel, it is infectious—both in terms of Skimpole's short, cozy views and in terms of his place in the plot. Skimpole is a poor companion for Richard, as his praise of procrastination and idleness discourages Richard from leading his life. Skimpole repeatedly terms his delight in his lack of knowledge of the world in himself and others as 'poetry': 'Our young friends, losing the youthful poetry which was once so captivating in them, begin to think, "This is a man who wants pounds".'[13] And of course Skimpole's willed blindness, what he classes as 'poetry'—his inability to see outside the terms of his own personal comfort—cause him to take his terrible part in the novel: betraying Jo to Inspector Bucket, and introducing Richard to the sinister Voles for the personal loan of five pounds. Because he professes ignorance about money and even an inability to count, he is not able to see that he will cause far more than five pounds' worth of trouble for Richard.

Though there is no question about Skimpole's sexual object-choice, there are many signs that he is a failure, too, at normative heterosexuality. At first meeting, Esther is

---

[11] 'On the Cockney School of Poetry I', *Blackwoods's Edinburgh Magazine* 2 (October 1817): 38–41, p. 38.

[12] As J.G.A. Pocock has noted, 'effeminacy' has a long history in Western culture's attempts to define civic and moral responsibility as normative masculinity. See Pocock, *The Machiavellian Moment: Florentine Political Thought and the Atlantic Republican Tradition* (Princeton: Princeton University Press, 1975).

[13] Charles Dickens, *Bleak House* [1853] ed. Norman Page (Harmondsworth: Penguin Books, 1985), 883. Subsequent citations appear in the text.

charmed by Skimpole, but her uneasiness begins to show itself not only because he bor-rows money or expounds proudly on his inability to support himself, but because he does not talk about his family, a family Esther knows he has: 'I always wondered on these occasions whether he ever thought of Mrs. Skimpole and the children, and in what point of view they presented themselves to his cosmopolitan mind. So far as I could under-stand, they rarely presented themselves at all' (397–98). That is, Skimpole is not only economically and increasingly morally immature, he is sexually and socially retrograde: his family has not become part of his identity or his responsibility. He lives as a bachelor does, making long solo visits at the expense of other people. He does not take his part in heterosexual society.

When Esther does meet his family, we find out (unsurprisingly) that Skimpole does not support them. His family seems to support him, in his need for interior delight and middle-class delicacies:

> Mr. Jarndyce without further ceremony entered a room there, and we followed. It was dingy enough and not at all clean, but furnished with an odd kind of shabby luxury, with a large footstool, a sofa, and plenty of cushions, an easy-chair, and plenty of pillows, a piano, books, drawing materials, music, newspapers, and a few sketches and pictures. A broken pane of glass in one of the dirty windows was papered and wafered over, but there was a little plate of hothouse nectarines on the table, and there was another of grapes, and another of sponge-cakes, and there was a bottle of light wine. [650]

The 'shabby luxuries' that Esther notices are the interior comforts that Hunt's poetry and prose celebrated: the cushions and pillows there for bodily comfort, the drawing materi-als and piano for the leisure of the middle-class domestic mind. These are just the little delights that Hunt's poetry and prose valorizes and that Romantic-era criticism took him to task as 'unmanly' for celebrating. Someone had to pay for the hothouse nectarines, and their presence with the grapes and wine and tiny comforts—regardless of the real Hunt—perform a kind of leisure that middle-class people, and the indebted Skimpole especially, do not have the money (and Romantic-era criticism would say the right) to have. A pane of the window to the outside world has been shut off with paper and wax. The space is marked as feminine and feminized—Esther notes that the sons have 'run off at various times'—presumably to escape this enclosure. What we have left are Skimpole and his lightly employed daughters, whom he regards as literary themes and genres:

> 'This,' said Mr. Skimpole, 'is my Beauty daughter, Arethusa—plays and sings odds and ends like her father. This is my Sentiment daughter, Laura—plays a little but don't sing. This is my Comedy daughter, Kitty—sings a little but don't play. We all draw a little and compose a little, and none of us have any idea of time or money'. [653]

With that 'we all' Skimpole seems to include himself with his daughters, who at least have these expected ladylike accomplishments. In civic terms, Skimpole emasculates himself.

There is a hint, too, that Skimpole is not only weakening Richard's mind by encouraging him to postpone any efforts in his career—(that is, in investing in normative masculine citizenship)—in hopes of receiving a settlement from Jarndyce and Jarndyce, but that Skimpole is also postponing Richard's expected initiation into heterosexuality and marriage. Esther becomes wary of Skimpole's infectious idleness: '…this captivating looseness and putting-off of everything, this airy dispensing with all principle and purpose' (578). But Skimpole's presence also seems to weaken Richard's affection for Ada, so much that Esther comes to doubt it exists:

> I almost mistrusted myself as growing quite wicked in my suspicions, but I was not so sure that Richard loved her dearly. He admired her very much—any one must have done that—and I dare say would have renewed their youthful engagement with great pride and ardour but that he knew how she would respect her promise to my guardian. Still I had a tormenting idea that the influence upon him extended even here, that he was postponing his best truth and earnestness in this as in all things until Jarndyce and Jarndyce should be off his mind. [578]

That 'influence' is the intertwined effect of the Chancery case and Skimpole's attitude. Skimpole actually seems to work on Richard's affections, weakening his love for Ada and thus his normative heterosexuality and his expectations of marriage. Having less love for Ada, Richard listens to her less, and the combined effect of Skimpole's legal and sexual influence leads to Richard's downfall.

The question we might ask is what this does for Dickens the writer. Donald D. Stone is certainly correct when he sees Dickens's satire on Hunt as a satire of high-Romantic ideals of the artists as above society:

> the Romantic idealization of the artist reaches its ultimate exaggerated expression in Skimpole, to who the Shelleyan doctrine of the poet's innate superiority to others…has been divorced from the Shelleyan view that the poet's imagination will make him feel deeply with humanity and hence enable him to become its benefactor.[14]

(I would add that this view is as much Wordsworthian and Huntian as Shelleyan.) But Dickens also gains as a writer through his castigation of Skimpole as a sexual and moral black hole. 'Poetry' gets defined here as an excuse, a misprision, and a mere domestic accomplishment. And the admirer of poetry is a social threat. *Bleak House* becomes the genuine text of reform; Hunt's real political work is completely superseded.

---

[14] Donald D. Stone, *The Romantic Impulse in Victorian Fiction* (Cambridge, MA: Harvard University Press 1980), 266–67. Stone's fine discussion of *Bleak House* is on 266–71.

CHARLES KINGSLEY AND THE
OPPOSITE OF MASCULINITY

Like Dickens, Charles Kingsley was a central public intellectual in the Victorian era. An Anglican clergyman, he wrote well-regarded novels, sermons, essays, and poetry. The establishment celebrated him: he was eventually appointed tutor to the Prince of Wales. Kingsley's novels, among them *Alton Locke* (1850), *Hypatia* (1853), *Westward Ho!* (1855), and *Hereward the Wake* (1866) (all except the first historical novels) held such a grip on the public imagination that he was awarded the Regius Professorship of History at Cambridge University in appreciation for them. Today they are read mostly by scholars. Kingsley is known for his children's book *The Water Babies* (1863) and for precipitating the writing of John Henry Cardinal Newman's *Apologia Pro Vita Sua* (1864) as a response to his ill-calculated (and anti-Catholic) personal remarks on Newman's integrity.

Alton Locke has a central place in the formulation of Kingsley's position as a moderate reformer and a Christian socialist. The fictional autobiography of a poor tailor, the novel exposes the sweatshop conditions that were taking over the making of men's clothing in the 1840s (Kingsley would also write a pamphlet on the subject, *Cheap Clothes and Nasty*, which serves as a preface to later editions of the novel). Alton, the somewhat attenuated hero of the story, tends towards Chartism, a parliamentary and electoral reform movement that existed from 1837 to 1848, that listed these reforms in 'The People's Charter'. He educates himself as best he can with the help of a Scottish bookseller rather obviously modelled after Thomas Carlyle. Eventually, with the assistance of highly connected people, Alton publishes a successful book of poetry. He forms an idealized attachment to one of these people, an upper-middle-class young woman named Lillian. His work with the Chartists, however, gets him caught up in political hack-writing for the left-wing press and eventually in a riot, which leads to his arrest, and eventually to a conversion to Christian socialism and emigration.

Most writing on *Alton Locke* has focused on its efforts as a social-problem novel. As such it is intensely ambivalent—emotionally and effectively exposing the formation of the sweatshop system and the complicity of affluent people who buy inexpensive, sweatshop-made clothing. Yet its complete repudiation of the rights listed in the Charter, and its embrace of a more abstract compromise between the workers and the established Church, is hard for the contemporary reader to accede to. The long passages of sermonizing at the end of the book are undeniably tiresome. *Alton Locke* is also a highly literary novel—saturated with poetry, both of Alton's and that of actual English poets. Suzanne Keen has called the novel 'multivocal', with its sermons, original poetry, dream-sequence, reportage, and long stretches of Scots dialect; one might also simply say the work is at fascinating cross-purposes with itself.[15] The novel can be best read as a struggle with several problems at once: religious, economic, parliamentary, formal, and literary.

---

[15] See Suzanne Keen, *Victorian Renovations of the Novel: Narrative Annexes and the Boundaries of Representation* (Cambridge: Cambridge University Press, 1994), 114–27.

Kingsley was deeply invested in his Christian ideals of manliness (known as 'muscular Christianity') and undeniably positive about sex: committed heterosexual sex, which in part defined manliness. John Maynard has excavated Kingsley's religio-sexual ideology, complete with Kingsley's own illustrations.[16] Kingsley's manliness was at once fiercely Protestant and Anglican. He was savagely critical of Catholic celibacy. His brand of masculinity was nationalist (manliness gets defined as essentially English, and Jews come in for savage caricature in *Alton Locke*), and seemingly always contested. Manliness, perhaps even as much as sweatshops, is at issue in the novel. As in *Bleak House*, poetry complicates a relationship to manliness. If in Dickens's novel the poet's lack of civic masculinity is infectious, eventually, leading to the downfall of others, here the lack is not only civic, but bodily. As Alton says of himself:

> ... I was weak, as every poet is, more or less. There was in me, as I have somewhere read that there is in all poets, that feminine vein—a receptive as well as a creative faculty—which kept up in me a continual thirst after beauty, rest, enjoyment.[17]

That passivity might be taken from Wordsworth—his 'wise passiveness'—and Kingsley identifies it as a form of masculine lack, feminine and feminizing. And 'every poet' manifests that weakness. Alton dwells on his small size and frame, and he is continually comparing his own bodily masculinity to others his sees: he calls himself (as well as Crosswaithe) 'small, pale, and weakly' (20), and he often pauses to look at groups of athletic men to his own detriment. When a Cambridgeshire farmer offers him a ride, Alton spends his time noting his physique and comparing the farmer's large hands to his 'wasted, white, womanlike fingers'. When Alton first meets Sandy Mackae, the latter subjects him to a phrenological examination, which concludes with a bodily diagnosis: poetry is written into the body in Alton's 'general want o' healthy animalism' (33).

Kingsley's own effort to define masculinity has a curious effect in the novel. While Alton notices and remarks on the praiseworthy specimens of English manhood, giving vent to Kingsley's own need to establish and re-establish what real masculinity is supposed to look like, it comes across as Alton's fascination with the muscular male body. A trip through London becomes a moment of same-sex contemplation, if not desire:

> We were going through the Horse Guards, and I could not help lingering to look with wistful admiration on the huge mustachoed war-machines who sauntered about the courtyard.

[16] See John Maynard, *Victorian Discourses on Sexuality and Religion* (Cambridge: Cambridge University Press, 1994), 85–140.

[17] Charles Kinglsey, *Alton Locke, Taylor and Poet. An Autobiography* [1850], ed. Elizabeth Cripps (Oxford and New York: Oxford University Press, 1983), 228. Subsequent citations appear in the text.

A tall and handsome officer, blazing in scarlet and gold, cantered in on a superb horse, and, dismounting, threw the reins to a dragoon as grand and gaudy as himself. Did I envy him? Well—I was but seventeen. And there is something noble to the mid, as well as to the eye, in the great strong man, who can fight…[44]

Crosswaithe, Alton's companion, is much more critical of the soldier's role as enforcer of the law: Alton's 'admiration'—which really seems to be about musculature—'huge', 'tall and handsome', 'grand'—even the horse is 'superb'—seems to be a little stronger than 'wistful'. It is nearly obsessive. So too his cousin George is first introduced to us through his lively and athletic body: 'capital skater, rower, pugilist…this tall powerful figure showed the fruit of these exercises in a stately and confident, almost martial, carriage and figure' (68). The trip to Cambridge is marked by a disquisition that is pure Kingsley:

And yet, after a few moments, I ceased to wonder either at the Cambridge passion for boat-racing, or at the excitement of the spectators. 'Honi soit qui mal y pense.' It was a noble sport—a sight such as could only be seen in England—some hundred of young men, who might, if they had chosen, been lounging effeminately about the streets, subjecting themselves voluntarily to that intense exertion, for the mere pleasure of toil. The true English stuff came out there; I felt that, in spite of all my prejudices—the stuff which has held Gibraltar and conquered at Waterloo—which has created a Birmingham and a Manchester, and colonized every quarter of the globe—that grim, earnest, stubborn energy, which, since the days of the old Romans, the English possess alone of all the nations of the earth. I was as proud of the gallant young fellows as if they had been my brothers—of their courage and endurance (for one could see that it was no child's-play, from the pale faces, and panting lips), their strength and activity, so fierce and yet so cultivated, smooth, harmonious, as oar kept time with oar, and every back rose and fell in concert—and felt my soul stirred up to a sort of sweet madness, not merely by the shouts and cheers of the mob around me, but by the loud fierce pulse of the rowlocks, the swift whispering rush of the long snake-like eight oars, the swirl and gurgle of the water in their wake, the grim, breathless silence of the straining rowers. My blood boiled over, and fierce tears swelled into my eyes; for I, too, was a man, and an Englishman; and when I caught sight of my cousin, pulling stroke to the second boat in the long line, with set teeth and flashing eyes, the great muscles on his bare arms springing up into knots at every rapid stroke, I ran and shouted among the maddest and the foremost. [132]

The passage propagandizes for English masculinity and the importance of sports, and also separates Alton from this class and its bodies and makes him obsessed by them. By the end of the passage he is the most excited he ever gets in the novel, including during the riot. His sexual object-choice may be called into doubt, especially as there are no such similar passages about women.

Perhaps the strangest and most pointed incident is complicated by Alton's first meeting with Lillian. The two of them meet at the Dulwich College picture gallery, where Alton is admiring—of all paintings there—Guido's Saint Sebastian:

> The breadth and vastness of light and shade upon those manly limbs, so grand and yet so delicate, standing out against the background of lurid night, the helplessness of the bound arms, the arrow quivering in the shrinking side, the upturned brow, the eyes in whose dark depths enthusiastic faith seems conquering agony and shame, the parted lips, which seemed to ask, like those martyrs in the Revelations, half-resigned, 'O Lord, how long?'—Gazing at that picture since, I have understood how the idolatry of painted saints could arise in the minds even of the most educated, who were not disciplined by that stern regard for fact which is—or ought to be—the strength of Englishmen. [70]

Alton has clearly committed the painting—and exactly how Guido's technical skill works with the body—to memory. Richard Kaye, in an extensive essay on images of St Sebastian, argues that Alton identifies with the painting because it enables him to imagine being liberated from the social and religious constraints of his position.[18] To Alton, as to Kingsley, this muscular man represents a physical idea for English masculinity. But Alton's enthusiasm for it seems somewhat unconditioned by its ideological purpose. The bodily precision in this description—from limbs to arms to eyes to lips, becomes more and more erotic as the passage goes on. Yet through this painting he meets Lillian, the ostensible love of his life. The long passage of his description of her (on the page just after the above) seems entirely more aesthetic and less sexual. Lillian is reacting to Alton's fascination with the painting, which puts his paragraph describing her in nice contrast with his words on St Sebastian:

> 'You seem to be deeply interested in that picture?'
>   I looked round, yet not at the speaker. My eyes before they could meet hers, were caught by an apparition the most beautiful I had ever yet beheld. And what— what—have I seen equal to her since? Strange, that I should love to talk of her. Strange, that I fret at myself now because I cannot set down on paper line by line, and hue by hue, that wonderful loveliness of which—. But no matter. Had I but such an imagination as Petrarch, or rather, perhaps, had I his deliberate cold self-consciousness, what volumes of similes and conceits I might pour out, connecting that peerless face and figure with all lovely things which heaven and earth contain. As it is, because I cannot say all, I will say nothing, but repeat to the end again and again, Beautiful, beautiful, beautiful, beyond all statue, picture, or poet's dream.

---

[18] Richard Kaye, '"Determined Raptures": St. Sebastian and the Victorian Discourse of Decadence', *Victorian Literature and Culture* 27, no. 1 (1999): 269–303.

Seventeen—slight but rounded, a masque and features delicate and regular, as if fresh from the chisel of Praxiteles—I must try to describe after all, you see—a skin of alabaster (privet-flowers, Horace and Ariosto would have said, more true to Nature), stained with the faintest flush; auburn hair, with that peculiar crisped wave seen in the old Italian pictures, and the warm, dark hazel eyes which so often accompany it ... [71]

When Alton does try to describe Lillian his literary powers falter: here he simply gives up: 'beautiful, beautiful, beautiful, beyond all measure'. He has to reference other works of art and literature, and his list of her physical attributes is a series of commonplaces. His interest in Lillian seems entirely aesthetic and almost asexual. At another point he says of his inclination to her:

Every time I looked at her, my eyes dazzled, my face burnt, my heart sank, and soft thrills ran through every nerve. And yet, Heaven knows, my emotions were pure as those of an infant. It was a beauty longed for, and found at last, which I adored as a thing not to be possessed, but worshipped. [161]

This conventional idealization of the feminine would be unremarkable were it not for the presence of those passages fascinated by the male body. It is possible that like the praise of the masculine, they may be entirely in line with Kingsley's sexual ideology. Kingsley believes thoroughly in the active value of sexuality within heterosexual marriage. Lillian, after all, will turn out to be the wrong girl for Alton, and perhaps his asexual descriptions of her are supposed to signal that. But the effect is to mark the poet and his art as not only weak and unmasculine, but sexually other.

Alton never marries in the novel. One could see this lack of generation as Darwinian (his weak bloodline dies off) but nobody in the novel actually creates a bloodline but Mackae. Alton's real relationship may be with the fellow Chartist and fellow Christian Socialist convert Crosswaithe. When they meet some kind of attraction, at least on Alton's side, is clear: 'Crosswaithe fascinated me. I often found myself neglecting my work to study his face' (29). It is also clear that this couple (whom death will split) are the spiritual (we well as the legal) heirs to both Eleanor's Christian socialism and to Sandy Mackae: 'still we were together, to live and die; and as we looked into each other's eyes, and clasped each other's heads above the dead man's face, we felt that there was love between us, as of between David and Jonathan, passing the love of woman' (320).

While the social messages of *Alton Locke* are not completely in unison, Kingsley's propagandizing for his version of masculinity at once exploits and diminishes Alton the poet. Alton's intellectual, aesthetic, political, and religious views must be downgraded or changed, and Kingsley's manipulation of them assists him both in his Christian socialist ideals and his eventual solution to England's problems—which is simply to expel them from England. Emigration at once praises the intellectually converted and gets rid of the bodily and emotionally unsuitable.

GASKELL AND THE USES OF
POETIC EFFEMINACY

Ideas about the relationship of the novel to poetry and poets, I want to argue, go further than the few depictions of the poet in the novels discussed above. Dickens emphasizes the poet's lack of civic masculinity, and Kingsley creates an intensely ambivalent portrait of the poet Alton Locke. I now turn to a novel that few have recognized poetry in at all, Elizabeth Gaskell's *Cranford* (1851). Cranford is an unusual Victorian novel in many ways: it is short, and it was not intended to be even as long as that from the start. Its narrative is largely pre-industrial and domestic, and it seems to put itself forward as a 'minor' and distinctly female narrative. Almost all of its characters are women. Many readings of *Cranford* have stressed the novel's role in the theorization of the place of the woman writer.[19] For some, *Cranford's* history as a series of sketches that only later were worked into a novel, plus its fascination with oral narratives—digressions, ghost stories, tall tales, and gossip—provided Gaskell with an opportunity to create a new kind of feminine narration, what Linda K. Hughes and Michael Lund call 'open spaces within contemporary ideology for readers to explore'.[20]

But emphases on the novel's communality and its 'accidental' form can soften the sharpness, even the ferocity, of Gaskell's claims to authorship, and in part these claims depend on marking readers and writers of poetry as both heterosexual and masculine failures.[21] With few exceptions, literary production is made fun of, interrogated, and left behind. And poetry takes a familiar place in this project.

In *Cranford*, Mr Holbrook, a great reader of poetry, almost married Miss Matty years before the action of the novel takes place. Deborah and the Rector, Matty's sister and father, squelched their incipient amour when Matty was a young woman. Holbrook, a mere yeoman farmer, did not have the aristocratic connections they thought suitable. Early in the novel, Matty and her old swain meet again as elderly people. Even though Mary Smith (the story's narrator, a a friend of Miss Matty's who stays with her while visiting Cranford) praises his reading voice and his diverse literary tastes, that praise becomes awfully back-handed as the scene develops. Holbrook's profound love of poetry

---

[19] Hilary Schor, *Scheherezade in the Marketplace: Elizabeth Gaskell and the Victorian Novel* (New York and Oxford: Oxford University Press, 1992), 84. Some readers, including Nina Auerbach and Joseph Alan Boone, see the novel as defending 'communal' values against a marketplace of male writers. See Nina Auerbach, *Communities of Women: An Idea in Fiction* (Cambridge, MA: Harvard University Press, 1978), 77–97 and Joseph Alan Boone, *Tradition Counter-Tradition: Love and the Forms of Fiction* (Chicago: University of Chicago Press, 1987), 295–304.

[20] Andrew Horton Miller, 'The Fragments and Small Opportunities of *Cranford*', Genre 25 (1992): 91–111; and Linda K. Hughes and Michael Lund, *Victorian Publishing and Mrs. Gaskell's Work* (Charlottesville and London: University Press of Virginia, 1999), 6.

[21] For Hilary Schor, *Cranford* 'is most fully read as a woman writer's experiment with narrative' and is finally 'a novel about reading', Schor, 87, 110.

screens him from life, to immure him in his celibate, countrified ways. His relationship to language seems oddly obsessive; it substitutes and even disables him for human companionship—he names his twenty-six cows after the letters of the alphabet. His literacy has only enforced his isolation. Mr Holbrook is certainly a reader, but a peculiar one: 'As we went along, he surprised me occasionally by repeating apt and beautiful quotations from the poets, ranging from Shakespeare and George Herbert to those of our own day.... and their true and beautiful words were the best expression he could find for what he was thinking or feeling.'[22] Even as the text praises Holbrook's knowledge of poetry and the beauty of his quotations, it implies that he has no language of his own. His reading seems to replace the personal creation of authorship, the authorship that 'Mary Smith' the narrator of the novel, aspires to. The lines he repeats are the best expressions that *he* is able to find, but the narrator offers her readers better expressions—not merely repeated but created.

Holbrook's fascination with poetry has dominated and even twisted his life: the reading of poetry has pushed out or substituted for other interests. Though Holbrook is supposed to be a yeoman farmer, his dwelling seems to be less a working farmhouse than a messy library. Books take over the house: 'The room...was filled with books. They lay on the ground, they covered the walls, they strewed the table... They were of all kinds,— poetry, and wild weird tales prevailing' (32). Holbrook's love of poetry and 'weird tales' is at once an attraction and a verdict; Holbrook lives in the language of the poets and does not seem to have a life outside them—the trip out of his library (all the way to France) will result in his death.

Holbrook reads Tennyson's 'Locksley Hall' to the women, an interesting choice since its subject, a marriage suppressed because of a difference in class, might appeal to Matty in particular. Matty's family put a stop to her relationship with Holbrook for just this reason. But she falls asleep within minutes, and Miss Pole, her companion, uses the opportunity to count her crochet stitches. Critics have read this scene in productive ways. For Patsy Stoneman, Matty falls asleep because she is enervated by male language.[23] Yet the inattentive audience does not just expose the women's faulty literary education; it also points out a problem with the literature that they are hearing. The poetry cannot be understood by anyone but a select, and here distinctly odd, male audience. The gap between Holbrook and Matty is not only of class but of mutually unintelligible stances towards the written word: when Matty wakes the only terms she can think of to praise what she has snoozed through are those of her father's and sister's aesthetics—'It is so like that beautiful poem of Dr. Johnson's my sister used to read—I forget the name of it' (35)—a decorum that she can just reference but cannot even remember. (It is clear from earlier in the novel that this is Johnson's *Vanity of Human Wishes*, which of course is not at all like 'Locksley Hall'.) If I am dating this properly, Holbrook was not only a yeoman

[22] Elizabeth Gaskell, *Cranford* [1851], ed. Elizabeth Porges Watson (Oxford and New York: Oxford University Press, 1972), 32. Subsequent citations appear in the text.
[23] Patsy Stoneman, *Elizabeth Gaskell* (Brighton: Harvester Press, 1987), 92.

farmer and thus below Matty's station when he was courting her, but he would have been reading the Romantic poets at that time. His reading would have been quite unfamiliar to Matty even as his background made him socially inferior to her. And perhaps even then he might have been so obsessed that the two may not have been able to connect. Poetry seems to immure their readers from actual heterosexual contact with other people. And Holbrook will never get another chance with Matty; he dies soon after his performance of Tennyson. The poetry has some role in the collapse of the possibility of even a late marriage.

In *Wives and Daughters* (1866), her last, unfinished novel, Gaskell puts poetry in its place largely through her depiction of Osborne Hamley. Osborne is the eldest of Squire Hamley's two sons, and much of the action of the novel revolves around these two men and their relationships with the two daughters (step-sisters) of the family of Dr Gibson. Gibson's second wife is frankly mercenary about her plans for the possible marriages. At first, Gaskell introduces the elder Osborne as the most promising of the two sons. As the novel continues, Osborne seems to lose his credentials: he fails his university examinations and speculates on the estate to pay his debts. Osborne's gender position gets more and more questionable, as Gaskell not only identifies him with the maternal but also calls him out for his effeminate features and dress: 'He was beautiful and languid-looking, almost as frail in appearance as his mother, whom he strongly resembled. This seeming delicacy made him appear older than he was';[24] 'Osborne... was what is commonly called "fine"; delicate almost to effeminacy in dress and manner; careful in small observances' (288). The degeneration of Osborne is often observed by his father the Squire, who at one point in their deteriorated relationship says to him, 'When I was a young man I should have been ashamed to have spent as much time at my looking-glass as if I'd been a girl' (292) and at a later point reflects 'I sometimes think he's half a woman himself' (439). The effeminate man is a political liability, unable to take up the citizen's civil and military duties. Linda Dowling has expanded on the political and social role of the effeminate man: 'The effeminatus in classical republican theory is thus always a composite or protean figure, the empty or negative symbol at once of civic enfeeblement and of the monstrous self-absorption that becomes visible in a society at just the moment at which... private interest has begun to prevail against those things that concern the public welfare.'[25]

It is this civic effeminacy that comes into play in Molly's eyes. As she gets to know Osborne, Molly finds him more and more of a conundrum:

> Molly was altogether puzzled by his manners and ways. He spoke of occasional absences from the Hall, without exactly saying where he had been. But that was not

---

[24] Elizabeth Gaskell, *Wives and Daughters* [1866], ed. Frank Glover Smith (Harmondsworth: Penguin, 1986), 202. Subsequent citations appear in the text.

[25] Linda Dowling, *Hellenism and Homosexuality in Victorian Oxford* (Ithaca and London: Cornell University Press, 1994), 8.

her idea of the conduct of a married man; who, she imagined, ought to have a house
and servants, and pay rent and taxes, and live with his wife. [271]

As in *Bleak House*, Osborne's masculinity is put in question through his civic failures: he
does badly at University, has debts, and contracts a secret marriage. For Molly, Osborne's
behaviour is surprising: it is at once social (his absences, his failure to have a household),
economic (he does not pay rent and taxes), and sexual (he is unmarried). As the novel
explicates, poetry, Osborne's real ambition, seems to have had a part in these failures:
Osborne's efforts are diverted into verse production and unrealistic expectations about
its possible publication. Poetry is deeply involved in his double life. When we see a list of
the titles of his poetry, most are addressed to his secret wife, as if his poetic interests are
involved in the unwise marriage.

We are led to believe, too, that Osborne's poetic fancy is not a masculine trait: it seems
to derive from his mother, who is a great reader of poetry:

> Mrs. Hamley had written many a pretty four-versed poem since she lay on her sofa,
> alternately reading and composing verse. She had a small table by her side on which
> there were the newest works of poetry and fiction; a pencil and a blotting-book, with
> loose sheets of blank paper; a vase of flowers always of her husband's gathering; winter
> and summer, she had a sweet nosegay every day. Her maid brought her a draught of
> medicine every three hours, with a glass of clear water and a biscuit. [76]

Mrs Hamley is also a poet, thought she does not have the ambitions of Osborne: her
poetry is clearly marked as feminine and domestic, a poetry of the indoors, of weakness
and illness. When she praises Osborne's poetry 'so like that of Mrs. Hemans', she ends up
labelling it as feminine and domestic, though perhaps more public than her own.

Mrs Hamley seems both the genetic and the social source for Osborne's condition.
The Squire is brusque and uneducated. Of their two sons, the heir, Osborne, seems to
have inherited his mother's qualities and Roger his father's. These gender characteristics
are the most significant aspect of their respective inheritances. The Squire identifies with
Roger (Roger is named after him) and he can understand his achievements as a natural
historian. The Squire calls this trick of inheritance 'a queer quip of nature' (106). The
physical differences between men and women extend to behaviour—here we have the
macho, outdoorsy Roger and the feminine, literary Osborne. As Osborne's poetic stance
comes from his mother, it seems his illness does too. Both are frail and die off. Osborne's
feminine stance is part and parcel of his disease: Osborne is 'handsome, elegant, languid
in manner and look' (249); the 'languid, careless, dilettante Osborne' (395); he speaks
'languidly' (481). For the Squire, Osborne's fatigue, a physical symptom, is also a symptom of his sexual liminality: 'He [Osborne] would saunter out on the sunny side of the
house in a manner that the Squire considered as both indolent and unmanly' (477).
Osborne's body seems to have become fatally feminized, while his handsomeness evidences and punishes his liminal gender stance. As we are introduced to Osborne the
narrator tells us 'he was the heir, he was delicate, and he was the clever one of the family'

(120) as if all three characteristics—his descent, his literary cleverness, and his physical delicacy—are different facets of the same inherited trait. Osborne's weak poetic gift is inherently feminizing, and it is inherited from his mother. His illness is more of a literary condition than any diagnosable malady—he pines away, becoming more sexually indeterminate as the illness progresses.[26]

In both *Cranford* and *Wives and Daughters*, poetry is presented in ways that question its readers and writers, and that eventually dismiss them as cultural and social forces. Osborne's complex difficulty is at once bodily and literary, and it is diagnosed through his androgynous appearance, weak body, and 'effeminate' habits. Even as the secret marriage stations him as normatively masculine, it also effectively removes him from the marriage market and marriage plot—the plot that seems to begin to work at the start of the novel and that Molly's step-mother is so diligently concerned about. Only Roger and (eventually) Molly know marriage causes Osborne's failure to engage that plot. Gaskell's manipulates Osborne's gender presentation in order to separate her own work from that of the poet.

CONCLUSION

What these discussions hope to show is that poetry and the novel are not comfortable bedfellows in the 19th century, and that the novelist's discomfort with poetry takes some predictable and interesting manifestations. Novelists use poets and poetry to mark themselves as different and superior writers: manliness is one of the issue used in the creation of this performance. With the rise of the literary decadence of the 1890s, one might argue that the dissolute, homoerotic version of the poet figured in these mid-century novels is not merely accepted by, say, Oscar Wilde, Lord Alfred Douglas, and the young John Gray, but positively owned and promoted by them. But the decadent work of such figures was countered by the 'manly' verse of Rudyard Kipling and W.E. Henley. The battle-lines were drawn, sometimes played out in the pages of Punch. The novel too was contending more with competition from within than from without: New Grub Street's talented literary novelist Edwin Reardon cannot hope to prosper in a world that only wants hack novels. For Gissing, the challenge to the novel as a work of art comes not from the poet but from the publisher—the censorial figure who drove Hardy from the novel altogether.

---

[26] For more detailed investigations of sexuality and poetry in *Wives and Daughters*, see James Najarian, "'Mr. Osborne's Secret': Elizabeth Gaskell, *Wives and Daughters*, and the Gender of Romanticism', in *Romantic Echoes in the Victorian Era*, ed. Andrew Radford and Mark Sandy (Aldershot, England and Burlington, VT: Ashgate, 2008), 85–101; and Julia M. Wright, "'Growing Pains': Representing the Romantic in *Wives and Daughters*', in *Victorian Recollections of Romanticism*, ed. Joel Faflak and Julia M. Wright (Albany NY: State University of New York Press, 2004), 163–88.

SUGGESTED READING

Alderson, David. 'An Anatomy of the British Polity: *Alton Locke* and Christian Manliness'. In *Victorian Identities: Social and Cultural Formations in Nineteenth Century Literature*. Edited by Ruth Robbins and Julian Wolfreys. Houndmills, Basingstoke and London: Macmillan, 1996, 43–61.

Beer, John. *Romantic Influences: Contemporary-Victorian-Modern*. New York: St Martin's, 1993.

Clayton, Jay. *Romantic Vision and the Novel*. Cambridge: Cambridge University Press, 1987.

Douglas-Fairhurst, Robert. *Victorian Afterlives: The Shaping of Influence in Nineteenth-Century Literature*. Oxford and New York: Oxford University Press, 2004.

Faflak, Joel and Julia M. Wright, eds. *Victorian Recollections of Romanticism*. Albany NY: State University of New York Press, 2004.

Felluga, Dino Franco. *The Perversity of Poetry: Romantic Ideology and the Male Poet of Genius*. Albany, NY: State University of New York Press, 2005.

Hall, Donald, ed. *Muscular Christianity: Embodying the Victorian Age*. Cambridge: Cambridge University Press, 1994.

Radford, Andrew and Mark Sandy, eds. *Romantic Echoes in the Victorian Era*. Aldershot, England and Burlington, VT: Ashgate, 2008.

Stone, Donald D. *The Romantic Impulse in Victorian Fiction*. Cambridge, MA and London: Harvard University Press, 1980.

Vance, Norman. *The Sinews of the Spirit: The Ideal of Christian Manliness in Victorian Literature and Religious Thought*. Cambridge: Cambridge University Press, 1985.

29

POETIC ALLUSION IN THE VICTORIAN NOVEL[1]

PHILIP HORNE

In the dying world I come from quotation is a national vice.

(Dennis Barlow in Evelyn Waugh, *The Loved One*)[2]

One text leads to another, in the ordinary way of literature.

(Karl Miller, *Authors*)[3]

Allusion—literary, and here specifically poetic allusion—is a highly flexible and unpredictable process, with opportunities for strong individual variations of style and technique (like revision, perhaps). It is by reading with a mind open to its possibilities, this chapter argues, that we are likely to see most in it, and get most from it. There is some dispute over the correct use of the term allusion (as against 'quotation' or 'reference'); I here take it in the way Christopher Ricks does in *Allusion to the Poets*, as 'the calling into play . . . of the words and phrases of earlier writers'—whether the allusion is marked or unmarked by quotation marks, and whether or not the 'play' into which the earlier words and phrases

[1] I would like to thank a number of people for help of various kinds in the writing of this chapter: Robert Douglas-Fairhurst and Stephano Evangelista as convenors of the Oxford Victorian Seminar, and various people who attended that seminar; Rosella Mamoli Zorzi of Ca' Foscari in Venice, as well as Sergio Perosa, Simone Francescati, and Gene M. Moore. I am equally grateful to Judith Hawley, Matt Ingleby, John Mullan, Seamus Perry, Alicia Rix, and Sarah Wintle. In particular, I am grateful to several readers of the piece: Oliver Herford and Rebekah Scott, both sharp-eyed yet kindly close readers; the patient and brilliant Lisa Rodensky, who has made splendid suggestions; the encouraging but properly discriminating Adrian Poole; the immensely knowledgeable and suggestive but also bracingly sceptical Michael Slater; the prompt, incomparable Toru Sasaki; and Christopher Ricks, whose enduring engagement with the subject of allusion has been an inspiration, and who has made me think harder about the subject than, most of the time, it had occurred to me to do.

[2] Evelyn Waugh, *The Loved One* [1948] (Harmondsworth: Penguin, 1985), 108–9.

[3] Karl Miller, *Authors* (Oxford: Oxford University Press, 1990), 6.

are called is evidently intended to be recognized by the reader.[4] The field addressed is potentially vast: there are so many Victorian novels, so full of allusions to English poetry, and such a variety of styles and purposes, that I have only attempted to suggest the complexity of the work some poetic allusions do in a handful of canonical novels.

This essay limits itself to a consideration of allusions to poetry, including poetic drama—partly but not only for reasons of space. There is no absolute difference between the ways Victorian novels can allude to other prose works (including other Victorian novels), to the words of the Bible and the Book of Common Prayer, and to poetry and poetic drama. With due adjustments, the present argument could be adapted for allusion to original texts in prose rather than in verse. But there are reasons to draw certain boundaries. For one thing, it is more often the words of the Bible and of poetry that are learned by heart than those of prose fiction; for another, the Holy Writ of the Bible is a special case, raising particular questions of belief, and especially in the Victorian period. And then the formal properties of poetry, associated with its memorability and its concision, give a special interest to the processes by which it enters the differently ordered world of prose fiction. In the case of Shakespeare and dramatic poetry, the rituals and intensities of theatrical performance strengthen the communal bonds of memory; as Edmund says in Jane Austen's *Mansfield Park* (1814), 'His celebrated passages are quoted by everybody.'[5]

Matthew Arnold in his essay of 1880 on 'The Study of Poetry' gave one reason for knowing bits of the great poets by heart: that it helps us to judge all the poetry we read:

> There can be no more useful help for discovering what poetry belongs to the class of the truly excellent, and can therefore do us most good, than to have always in one's mind lines and expressions of the great masters, and to apply them as a touchstone to other poetry... Short passages, even single lines, will serve our turn quite sufficiently.[6]

This may remind us that rote-learning, or learning by heart, had a special value for many Victorians (not that it is entirely extinct, or began with them); canons were not for them primarily oppressive, and 'touchstones'—in the form of passages and lines and phrases of poetry—had a profound significance for many of them. The 'best that is known and thought in the world',[7] moreover, had a moral as well as aesthetic point. If Arnold's remarks, just quoted, seem a touch priggish and over-didactic (this *was* his Introduction to an improving edition of *The English Poets*), then for a different, more informal and

[4] Christopher Ricks, *Allusion to the Poets* (Oxford: Oxford University Press, 2002), 1.
[5] Quoted in Marianne Novy, *Engaging with Shakespeare: Responses of George Eliot and Other Women Novelists* (Athens and London: University of Georgia Press, 1994), 22.
[6] Published as General Introduction to *The English Poets*, ed. T.H. Ward, repr. in *The Complete Prose Works of Matthew Arnold*, vol. 9: *English Literature and Irish Politics*, ed. R.H. (Ann Arbor: University of Michigan Press, 1973), 161–88, 168.
[7] 'The Function of Criticism at the Present Time' [1864], *Essays in Criticism: First Series* (1865), repr. in *The Complete Prose Works of Matthew Arnold*, vol. 3: *Lectures and Essays in Criticism*, ed. R.H. Super, with the assistance of Sister Thomas Marion Hoctor (1973), 258–85, 268.

intimate sense of what it is 'to have always in one's mind lines and expressions of the great masters', we might recall the moment in *Great Expectations* where Pip, close to delirium, struggles to retain consciousness:

> I counted up to high numbers, to make sure of myself, and repeated passages that I knew in prose and verse.[8]

Pip clings to passages he knows in prose and verse—'to make sure of myself'—as if what one knows by heart *is* one's heart. Identity, it seems, can attach to the passages one knows (and 'high numbers' here itself punningly suggests the elevated diction of poetry).[9]

A notable precursor in treating this subject is Michael Wheeler, who wrote his authoritative *The Art of Allusion in Victorian Fiction* in 1979. His book deals with a small group of selected novels in depth, and charts methodically, and very helpfully, shifts in practices of quotation over the Victorian period. Though indebted to his work, this chapter tries not to overlap too much either in material or in approach. The only one of Wheeler's main texts that occurs here at any length is one of the inevitable landmarks of the Victorian novel, and a vital text for thinking about literary allusion in the period—*Middlemarch*.[10]

One should register how the scene has changed over the decades. It is piquant to look back from the age of the Internet to 1979, when concordances and their memories were all scholars had to help them in tracing allusions. Wheeler imagined then something like the situation that obtains now:

> if the standard works of literature were all on tape, and if limitless computer time were available, he [the reader] could make use of computers to locate numerous examples of particular collocations in the way that the dictionary of quotations supplied me with one earlier example of 'dead bones' in Shakespeare.[11]

Successive annotated editions of Victorian texts have appeared and recorded many allusions previously not identified in print; and the standard works of literature are all now online. However, I think there's a sort of old-fashioned radar still needed for us to sense

---

[8] Charles Dickens, *Great Expectations*, ed. Angus Calder (London: Penguin Classics, 1984), 443. Subsequent citations appear in the text.

[9] Dickens's memory of his reading was legendary; he remarked in 'Lying Awake' (1852), of his childhood reading, that 'I recollect everything I read then.' The passage is quoted in Valerie L. Gager's fine *Shakespeare and Dickens: The Dynamics of Influence* (Cambridge: Cambridge University Press, 1996), 48–49. The whole second chapter of Gager's study is concerned with Victorian reading practices.

[10] There are, however, some fine studies of Shakespearean allusion in Victorian novels, one of the more recent and most agile being Adrian Poole's fine chapter, 'Three Novelists: Dickens, Eliot, Hardy', in his *Shakespeare and the Victorians* (London: Arden Critical Companions, 2003), 116–53. Anyone interested in the subject must consult Valerie L. Gager (see note 9); and also Marianne Novy's finely inflected feminist survey, *Engaging with Shakespeare*.

[11] Michael Wheeler, *The Art of Allusion in Victorian Fiction* (London: Macmillan, 1979), 6.

just where and when to look for the source of something like 'dead bones' that we suspect might be an allusion—we need a sense for style and context which allows dictional
variation and the way a word or phrase is pitched to alert us to a sense that the language
is in some way double—that it points somewhere. Wheeler seems to regret the passing
of the Victorian way of allusion:

> The reader's response to an allusion which he recognises as he reads, and whose
> context in its adopted [i.e. original] text is familiar to him, is obviously more
> spontaneous, and generally stronger and more rewarding, than his response to an
> allusion located with the help of reference books or computers can ever be.[12]

This may be true; but once one has looked up the source of an allusion, it is then possible
to reread with a fuller understanding; and one can recognize and appreciate other allusions to the same source with spontaneity, strength, and rewardingness. The Internet
and electronic databases also make it possible to follow up and investigate possibilities
that would have seemed (would have been) insanely unreachable in 1979. A case from
The Portrait of a Lady: in the early stages of their friendship, Mme Merle asks Isabel
about whether she has had suitors, and Isabel admits there was one (Caspar Goodwood,
though she doesn't name him). Mme Merle says,

> I congratulate you. Only, in that case, why didn't you fly with him to his castle in the
> Apennines?[13]

The particularity of this formulation is striking—and James is a more allusive writer than
he is generally taken to be. If one searches, it turns out that Part III Scene 1 of Byron's
unfinished poetic drama *The Deformed Transformed* (1824) starts with a bridal scene in
'A Castle in the Apennines, surrounded by a wild but smiling country'. At once a chorus
of peasants sings:

> The wars are over,
> The spring is come;
> The bride and her lover
> Have sought their home:
> They are happy, we rejoice;
> Let their hearts have an echo in every voice!
> [Byron, *The Deformed Transformed* (1822)][14]

---

[12] Wheeler, *The Art of Allusion*, 7.

[13] Henry James, *The Portrait of a Lady* (London: Macmillan, 1882), 175. Subsequent citations appear in the text.

[14] George Gordon, Lord Byron, *The Complete Poetical Works*, 7 vols., eds. Jerome J. McGann and Barry Weller (Oxford: Clarendon Press, 1991), 6: 517–77, 571.

It is only a stage direction, but the fact that the scene begins with a bridal song gives some colour to the proposition that James's use of this phrase is more than an accident (and it is not the only gesture towards Byron in the novel).

What is particular about the Victorian uses of poetic allusion? There is too much to say—and this chapter sets out to show that each allusion is a unique case, a concentrated intersection of authors, topics, histories, contexts, and meanings. But we can also see allusion as affected by the larger changes in the course of the period we're familiar with—in matters of faith, because of Darwin and the effect of historical biblical scholarship and other tendencies, throwing into doubt the status of Holy Writ and by extension the words of traditional authorities; and in social attitudes, because problems of inheritance become so fraught, especially amid the ramifications of increasing democracy, that the common literary heritage becomes a battleground at times. Victorian allusion is therefore often attended by anxiety.

Wheeler outlines the history of allusion in the Victorian novel:

> Allusions in Victorian novels can at once have important functions, noticed by those who recognise them, and yet be ignored if they are not recognised, because they themselves are dependent for their effects upon their relationship to the main thematic or plot lines of the novel, which can be followed without paying attention to the allusions. Moreover, many allusions which have an important function in a novel were easily recognisable, drawing on the literary classics with which the majority of readers would have been familiar: the Authorised Version of the Bible, the Book of Common Prayer, the *Pilgrim's Progress*, translations of the *Arabian Nights*, and others. The foundations of most early- and mid-Victorian novels were built on common ground which was familiar to a wide range of mainly middle-class readers.[15]

While undoubtedly true (though the first three of his listed 'literary classics' arguably have a primarily devotional importance), this flattens out some of the more challenging divisions implicit in the practice of novelistic allusion. Though Wheeler shows how a set of allusions to a single text (e.g. to *Paradise Lost* in *Jane Eyre*) makes the novel, and particularly the mid-Victorian novel, more of a coherent whole, which is a major aspect of their importance, serious allusions nearly always convey some tension or ambivalence beyond their easily explicable textual or narrative function.

Wheeler offers a suggestive sketch of changes in the practice of allusion in the course of the period: broadly speaking, from jocular and polite and earnest to ironic and closed and increasingly modernistic. As the century draws on, he argues, there's a kind of dissociation of sensibility as far as allusion is concerned.

> Until the last quarter of the nineteenth century, when Meredith and Hardy narrowed the scope of the reader-narrator contract, using allusion in more obscure ways than

[15] Wheeler, *The Art of Allusion*, 11.

their precursors, these sets of allusions were usually drawn from adopted texts which were part of the 'shared culture' mentioned earlier, thus being familiar to most Victorian readers if not to many of their modern descendants …

In fact, Wheeler's book ends on this note:

> Allusion is increasingly used ironically as the tension between the real and the ideal becomes explicit and problematic in a post-Darwinian world, where faith in God and belief in the value and purpose of human life is increasingly under threat. Unselfconsciousness in the handling of allusion tends to give way to self-consciousness, directness to obliqueness. Changes in the art of allusion in Victorian fiction mirror changes in both the genre and the age.[16]

In other words it's all heading for *The Waste Land* and its shored-up fragments, many of them not 'shared', indeed dauntingly obscure, and for Joyce's opposition to the British 'gentlemanly' Edwardian world of familiar quotations; the world Virginia Woolf shows in *To the Lighthouse*, where Mr Ramsay symptomatically repeats what are represented as the now useless—'cracked', broken or crazy—words of Tennyson

> as if he were trying over, tentatively seeking, some phrase for a new mood, and having only this at hand, used it, cracked though it was. But it sounded ridiculous— 'Someone had blundered'—said like that, almost as a question, without any conviction, melodiously.[17]

Though Woolf's mockery hardly put an end to the practice of poetic allusion. As John Morton shows, the tradition even of Tennysonian allusion has remained alive in Agatha Christie and even Michel Faber, with titles like *The Mirror Crack'd from Side to Side* (1962) and *The Crimson Petal and the White* (2002).[18] However, the confidence that most readers will catch even a reference to *Paradise Lost* or *King Lear* is gone.

The chief interest of allusions for this chapter, and especially of allusions to poetry and poetic drama (as against the Bible and other novels or various kinds of prose texts), is the economy and compression of thought they permit, and the way in which the power and intensity commonly associated with the language of poetry can be brought into prose. When poets allude to poetry, however appreciatively, the act may always be attended by a suspicion of rivalry, Oedipal or generational, and can always be haunted by status anxiety. When prose writers, and for our present purpose novelists, allude to poetry, direct competition seems ruled out. However, in the Victorian period, allusion could be read also as a potentially rivalrous appropriation by the novel of poetry's richness—one which

---

[16] Wheeler, *The Art of Allusion*, 26, 165.
[17] Virginia Woolf, *To the Lighthouse*, ed. Margaret Drabble (Oxford: World's Classics, 1992), 46.
[18] John Morton, *Tennyson Among the Novelists* (London: Continuum, 2010).

crosses over suggestively with Victorian poetry's attempts to win back for itself something of the popular narrative energy (and the large readership) more generally associated with the novel—in particular in the Victorian long narrative poem, for example *Maud* and *Amours de Voyage*. Such rivalries are not the focus here, but, as one might say, the art of the sentence: what poetic allusion brings to the sentences of Victorian novels.

There is often an edge to the process. Sometimes the word 'allusion' or 'allude' occurs in close proximity to acts of poetic allusion—as if acts of poetic allusion demand a marker or trace even if it is not inverted commas, signalling that something is in or at play. (It also suggests that the process of literary allusion—with its shocks of recognition of a direct link to something outside the text (another text)—could be read as an emblem of referentiality more generally understood, and maybe especially of the surprising extent of the play of imagination and interpretation into which novel-readers are being drawn.) Here is Becky Sharp early in *Vanity Fair*, singing at a Sedley family evening, with great pathos, a song about 'an orphan boy', playing up the parallel pathos of her impending departure as she has done earlier in the chapter, and working on the feelings of the impressionable Joseph Sedley. Thackeray quotes two full verses of the song; then:

> It was the sentiment of the before-mentioned words, 'When I'm gone', over again. As she came to the last words, Miss Sharp's 'deep-toned voice faltered'. Everybody felt the allusion to her departure, and to her hapless orphan state.[19]

The phrase marked by inverted commas is from a different song, one by Thomas Haynes Bayly (1797–1839) about an unhappy bride meeting her true love in a crowd: 'I knew how much he felt, for his deep-toned voice faltered'—'deep' here being tweaked to mean not bass or baritone but profoundly in earnest (which she isn't). The allusion is as pointed as one might expect from Becky Sharp herself.

Silas Wegg in *Our Mutual Friend*, with his guest the unhappy Mr Venus, is driven to a positive babble of quotation, or misquotation, proposing that

> '...crushing a flowing wine-cup—which I allude to brewing rum and water—we'll pledge one another. For what says the Poet?
> "And you needn't Mr Venus be your black bottle,
> For surely I'll be mine,
> And we'll take a glass with a slice of lemon in it to which you're partial,
> For auld lang syne."'
> This flow of quotation and hospitality in Wegg indicated his observation of some little querulousness on the part of Venus.[20]

[19] William Makepeace Thackeray, *Vanity Fair*, ed. J.I.M. Stewart (Harmondsworth: Penguin Classics, 1968), 73. The earlier moment recalled here also finds Rebecca hesitating for effect: '"I'll do it when— when I'm gone." And she dropped her voice, and looked so sad and piteous, that everyone felt how cruel her lot was, and how sorry they would be to part with her' (69).

[20] Charles Dickens, *Our Mutual Friend*, ed. Adrian Poole (Harmondsworth: Penguin Classics, 1997), 471–2. Subsequent citations appear in the text. The relevant (5th) stanza in the original 'Auld Lang Syne' of Robert Burns:

> And surely ye'll be your pint-stowp,
> And surely I'll be mine;

The compulsion to quote—and to accommodate his guest (whom he has not known very long) by stretching the metre of Burns's song to fit in his tastes—becomes farcical. 'A flowing wine-cup—which I allude to brewing rum and water' shows the impulse to make connections, to ritual. In both Thackeray and Dickens the elevating effect of verse, and of song, is summoned for enjoyably ironic scrutiny—the act of allusion being placed in a social and interpersonal context, being exposed in its possible manipulativeness, among other kinds of 'allusion'—to the great enrichment of the novel in which it occurs.

Even the more straightforward uses of allusion in novels mostly remain straightforward only as long as they are not probed too deeply; few instances belong solely or comfortably to a single category. We are told in Trollope's *The Vicar of Bullhampton* (1870) that among her other literary predilections, his heroine Mary Lowther's favourite heroine is Rosalind in *As You Like It*.[21] This comes under the heading of characterization through literary taste, which Trollope uses elsewhere—as in *The Eustace Diamonds* (1873), where there's a set-piece discussion by Lizzie Eustace and Frank Greystock of the characters in Tennyson's *Idylls of the King*.[22] Parallels are raised, and moral debates conducted, which can be worked into the symbolic structure of the fiction to a greater or lesser extent. *How* characters allude—or, less playfully, just quote— can also be telling. In *Middlemarch*, for instance, we learn that during the courtship of Casaubon and Dorothea, 'He assented to her expressions of devout feeling, and usually with an appropriate quotation'.[23] Quotation is a marker of knowledge and conformity to the dead hand of the past here—that word 'appropriate' strikes a deathly chill. Where Mr Micawber in *David Copperfield* quotes, in contrast, it is in the key of florid extravagance: in this instance he is reading out a letter he has prepared denouncing Uriah Heep:

> '... This was bad enough; but, as the philosophic Dane observes, with that universal applicability which distinguishes the illustrious ornament of the Elizabethan Era, worse remains behind!'
> Mr Micawber was so very much struck by this happy rounding off with a quotation, that he indulged himself, and us, with a second reading of the sentence, under pretence of having lost his place.[24]

And we'll tak a cup o' kindness yet
For auld lang syne.
[*The Poems of Robert Burns*, ed. J. Logie Robertson (Oxford: Oxford University Press, 1960), 329].

[21] Anthony Trollope, *The Vicar of Bullhampton*, ed. David Skilton (Oxford: The World's Classics, 1988), 53.
[22] The first four *Idylls of the King* were published in 1859, another four in 1869, one in 1871, and another in 1872.
[23] George Eliot, *Middlemarch*, ed. Rosemary Ashton (London: Penguin Classics, 2003), 33. Subsequent citations appear in the text.
[24] Charles Dickens, *David Copperfield*, ed. Jeremy Tambling (London: Penguin Classics, 2004), 756. Subsequent citations appear in the text. *Hamlet* III.4.179 (Hamlet to Gertrude): 'This bad begins

The repetition with variation that is allusion here finds itself repeated at once without variation. Micawber indulges himself first and foremost; his indulgence of David and the others present is submitted to a kindly irony. Dickens, though, is not indulging himself, but creating a character who does, whose transparent theatricality (pretending to lose his place so as to repeat a 'happy' allusion to *Hamlet*) is a humane pleasure to us. And what could be more characterizing than the gulf between Casaubon's 'appropriate quotation' and Micawber's mouthful: 'that universal applicability which distinguishes the illustrious ornament of the Elizabethan Era'?

When a character makes an allusion, it sometimes registers as thematic signposting in the action. A comically overt case: Bucket putting the jealous Mrs Snagsby right in *Bleak House*. 'What does Mr Bucket mean?', she wonders. 'I'll tell you what he means, ma'am. Go and see Othello acted. That's the tragedy for you.'[25] For her, yes—her poor spouse is impeccable—but *Othello* isn't the main tragedy in *Bleak House*. On a rough count, there are twice as many allusions in this novel to *Macbeth* as there are to *Hamlet*, which latter is the play said, doubtless correctly, to be Dickens's favourite.[26] This comparative profusion of reference can be taken as tipping the wink to this novel's reader about *Macbeth*—'That's the tragedy for you.' (An allusion to *Macbeth* in *Bleak House* will be considered later.)

Let us investigate what we might think a dull area, where there's not much sign of the ludic in the allusion—where 'quotation' is more the word. This is the area of 'fine quotations', borrowed embellishments that appear to have a chiefly ornamental or polite function. *Middlemarch* tells us at the start that the heroine Dorothea's plain garments 'by the side of provincial fashion gave her the impressiveness of a fine quotation from the Bible,—or from one of our elder poets,—in a paragraph of to-day's newspaper' (7).

The interest of this subject, then, lies partly in the setting of the high and highly charged words of the Bible (the language at its Sunday best), or of those 'elder poets', presumably including the illustrious ornament of the Elizabethan Era, in and against the quotidian, less conventionally heightened, language of prose—and in the vicissitudes of 'fine quotations' in other contexts, where their 'impressiveness' may often be compromised

and worse remains behind' (3.4.179) in *The Riverside Shakespeare*, ed. G. Blakemore Evans (Boston: Houghton Mifflin, 1974), 1169. Subsequent Shakespeare quotations from are from this edition.

[25] Charles Dickens, *Bleak House*, ed. Norman Page, Intro. J. Hillis Miller (London: Penguin Classics, 1971), 862–3. Subsequent citations appear in the text. 'Othello', incidentally, is not italicized: it is the character of Othello in particular Bucket wants her to see.

[26] Adrian Poole notes that '*Hamlet* and *Macbeth* are the two great Shakespearean plays about the murder of kings, about being haunted, about great expectations. They are the two plays of Shakespeare's that run most vividly in Dickens's memory and imagination' (*Shakespeare and the Victorians*, 123).

or qualified. In Eliot's 'Janet's Repentance', in the early *Scenes of Clerical Life*, we find a marked quotation—'And so the autumn rolled gently by in its "calm decay"'—that sends us back to Wordsworth's 'Memorials of a Tour in Scotland, 1803': '… the memorial majesty of Time/Impersonated in thy calm decay!'[27] A topic like Autumn seems to demand the embellishment, the impressiveness, of poetry. The association of decay with autumn hardly needs the support of Wordsworth. Yet the allusion even in this fairly routine example gives also an intriguing mild oxymoronic twinge to the moment—transferring a phrase for the very slow decay of the stone-built Kilchurn Castle to the more rapid and more all-embracing organic decay of the seasons. Eliot is capable, in this same work, of much subtler—and unmarked—allusions to Wordsworth, as I will show later in this chapter.

Eliot, with her loaded, often elusive epigraphs or 'poetical mottoes' from Chaucer, Shakespeare, Dante, or herself (though they are never attributed to her), likes the elevating effects of allusion, though seeing the dangers of cliché and affectation.[28] The conveniently conventional Dr Minchin in *Middlemarch*, who 'quoted Pope's *Essay on Man*' (181) when theological controversy threatens, is described as 'preferring well-sanctioned quotations, and liking refinement of all kinds' (181). The imputation shadows Eliot herself, who can also appear to be laboriously 'well-sanctioned' in her quotations. Dorothea's sister is engaged, and her blushing calls up a choice extract of Elizabethan verse:

> Celia's colour changed again and again—seemed
>   To come and go with tidings from the heart,
>   As it a running messenger had been.
> It must mean more than Celia's blushing usually did. [277]

The two indented lines are *The Faerie Queene* Book I, Canto IX, st. 51.[29] The comment 'it must mean more' could be admitting rather disarmingly the awkwardness of a narratorial intrusion, and makes the rather heavy gesture of so blatantly, typographically, interrupting the flow and layout of prose and reaching back to the authority and beauty of Spenser into a comic equivalent of Celia's unusual blushes and flushes. *If* a narratorial intrusion is what it is. Because this case raises the issue of point of view—of whose

---

[27] George Eliot, 'Janet's Repentance', in *Scenes of Clerical Life*, ed. Thomas A. Noble (Oxford: Oxford University Press, 2000), 298. William Wordsworth, 'Memorials of a Tour in Scotland, 1803' (X. 'Address to Kilchurn Castle, upon Loch Awe', *The Poetical Works of William Wordsworth*, 2nd edn, ed. E. De Selincourt and Helen Darbishire, 5 vols. (Oxford: Clarendon Press, 1954), 3: 78–79, 76 (ll. 20–21).

[28] George Eliot to Alexander Main in 1877, quoted in Leah Price, *The Anthology and the Rise of the Novel: From Richardson to George Eliot* (Cambridge: Cambridge University Press, 2000), 116.

[29] Spenser's knight is here drawn into despair and on the verge of suicide: 'And troubled blood through his pale face was seene/To come and go …'. *The Faerie Queene*, ed. A.C. Hamilton (London: Longman, 1977), 129.

allusion we're getting; for we're in the middle of a scene where the free indirect style is giving us light occasional indications of Dorothea's perceptions (as in 'It must mean more . . .'); so perhaps Eliot is suggesting that the well-read Dorothea herself is experiencing her sister's heightened emotion through her memory (a not particularly appropriate one) of 'one of our elder poets'. As very often, an allusion is at once a very obvious act and one which brings into play questions of interpretation that make us engage with the intimacies of what we're reading.

Many of George Eliot's allusions are overtly signalled, if not often by actual indentation: she takes care, hospitably, solicitously, that readers who do not recognize the original context should not be disadvantaged by losing much richness of implication. To quote Michael Wheeler, 'A *marked quotation* is one whose nature is indicated by means of punctuation or typography, whereas an *unmarked quotation* is one whose nature is not thus indicated.'[30] Wheeler tells us that in manuscript there were often no inverted commas round her allusions, but that in revising—sometimes between editions—she would often introduce them, with some tag like 'to use Sir Thomas Browne's phrase'.[31] However, that's not to say that they don't have their own kind of subtlety and ambiguity, their own richness. Here's another of her 'marked quotations': Casaubon has the previous moment implied disapprovingly—and unjustly, gratuitously—that she wants Will Ladislaw to pay a visit. Dorothea's anger is understandable:

> Dorothea had thought that she could be patient with John Milton, but she had never imagined him behaving in this way; and for a moment Mr Casaubon seemed to be stupidly undiscerning and odiously unjust. Pity, that 'newborn babe' which was by-and-by to rule many a storm within her, did not 'stride the blast' on this occasion. With her first words, uttered in a tone that shook him, she startled Mr Casaubon into looking at her, and meeting the flash of her eyes. [316]

The Milton comparison is part of an explicit pattern in the book (and something of a sad irony at the idealizing Dorothea's expense, now she has lost faith in Casaubon's work— the biographical Milton, even with the great justification of his poetic project, having been a notoriously difficult man for his daughters to put up with).[32] The salient phrases for us occur in the next sentence, not formally identified as coming from *Macbeth*, but marked with inverted commas to detach them from the texture of the surrounding prose, giving a formality to the gesture. The subject of discussion in the *Macbeth* context is the anticipated murder of Duncan:

---

[30] Wheeler, *The Art of Allusion*, 2–3.

[31] Wheeler, *The Art of* Allusion, 171 n. 2.

[32] Johnson quotes (though he disbelieves it) an account of Milton's demanding behaviour: 'he would sometimes lie awake whole nights, but not a verse could he make; and on a sudden his poetical faculty would rush upon him . . . and his daughter was immediately called to secure what came' ('Milton', *The Lives of the Poets*, in *The Works of Samuel Johnson*, ed. Arthur Murphy, 12 vols. (London: Longman et al., 1796), 5: 132.

His virtues
Will plead like angels, trumpet-tongu'd, against
The deep damnation of his taking-off;
And pity, like a naked new-born babe,
Striding the blast, or heaven's cherubim, hors'd
Upon the sightless couriers of the air,
Shall blow the horrid deed in every eye,
That tears shall drown the wind. [1.7.18–25][33]

This Shakespeare passage is itself wonderfully complex, its piling-up of mixed metaphors and similes conveying the would-be murderer Macbeth's hysterical sense of the hideousness and pathos of his intended act (he doesn't explicitly state, but the tempestuous imagery maybe suggests, that this pity will turn quickly to vengeance). How does the original context infuse the Eliot passage? It is more complicated than at first it seems. The main thrust is clear: in *Macbeth*, pity for the virtuous old man will be universal— guaranteed by various aerial agencies (angels trumpeting, flying babes, cherubim); and that is what *doesn't* happen in *Middlemarch*, and in Dorothea.

The associative link seems to be 'pity', then—the pity for Casaubon that Dorothea does not yet feel—and it is related to Eliot's great value in the novel, sympathy.[34] Dorothea does not yet understand her husband's deep unhappiness and irritable sense of failure, which her admiration only aggravates. Nearly a hundred pages earlier, on the honeymoon in Rome, their first quarrel has revealed to us that 'She was as blind to his inward troubles as he to hers; she had not yet learned those hidden conflicts in her husband which claim our pity' (200). 'Our pity'—'*we*', then, the community of readers following Eliot's penetrating narration, come to 'pity' Casaubon before Dorothea does. And this running theme of pity has been picked up again earlier in this later chapter where the 'newborn babe' allusion occurs: we're told of Casaubon that 'His experience was of that pitiable kind which shrinks from pity, and fears most of all that it should be known: it was that proud narrow sensitiveness which has not mass enough to spare for transformation into sympathy' (279). Casaubon, lacking sympathy, does not wish for pity; we soon find that Dorothea as yet does not pity him; but Eliot's word 'pitiable', one might argue, forces pity upon Casaubon against his will—he's the object of 'our pity' whether he likes it or not. Eliot's narrator declares straight out on the next page that 'For my part I am very sorry for him' (280). This is the lesson that Dorothea has to learn; to feel sorry for Casaubon.

I think Eliot reads 'stride the blast' in the Macbeth passage a little perversely; for the 'naked new-born babe' in Shakespeare doesn't 'rule', in the sense of *restrain*, the storm, but if anything helps drive it onwards, combining with the cherubim to cause gusts of

[33] *Macbeth*, 1317.
[34] Eliot had written as early as the time of *Scenes of Clerical Life* that 'My artistic bent is directed … to the presentation of mixed human beings in such a way as to call forth tolerant judgment, pity, and sympathy' (quoted by Novy in *Engaging with Shakespeare*, 48–9).

618   DRAMA, POETRY, AND CRITICISM

weeping. Pity, in other words, is presented by her as a restraining, controlling force—whereas in Shakespeare's original context it is a passionate, uncontrollable gale. Much in the original context is not being allowed through, then, in this highly filtered and selective adducing of so turbulent a source-passage—but I wonder whether there isn't a subliminal suggestion that Dorothea's blast of anger (could 'the flash of her eyes' be a lightning-flash, part of the storm?) is driven by self-pity on her part at the injustice done her, by *Casaubon's* 'horrid deed' (implied in his 'behaving in this way'). Or, if we think the Shakespeare passage describes pity as having a hurricane-like fury that makes it feel closer to rage than to, say, the quality of mercy, we could read it as implying something about the relation in Eliot's authorial attitude between punitive anger and benign forgiveness. But these are deep waters, of the kind allusions so often lead one into entering.[35]

Dickens takes a different approach to this same passage in *Macbeth*. Compare how, in *Bleak House*, he evokes Lady Dedlock's reaction to the discovery that her child Esther is alive (she was told she was dead):

> Words, sobs, and cries, are but air; and air is so shut in and shut out throughout the house in town, that sounds need be uttered trumpet-tongued indeed by my Lady in her chamber, to carry any faint vibration to Sir Leicester's ears. [466]

(The cry is about Esther—'my child, my child! Not dead...'.) Dickens positively encourages a complex contamination by the original source—but through that single (or double) word, 'trumpet-tongued', with 'air' in the offing—neither of them marked by inverted commas, but conveying a 'faint vibration' of *Macbeth* nonetheless; and 'trumpet-tongued *indeed*' marks the spot where another text makes itself felt. We may here think of Esther as herself 'a naked new-born babe'; of Esther's 'taking-off' and the 'deep damnation' of that act; and of the 'horrid deed' that may be blown 'in every eye'—in *Macbeth* a murder, in *Bleak House* a love-affair and an illegitimate child, a scandal to be avoided... and not unconnected, a murder.

Eliot can be glancing and richly suggestive in her more intimate, inward—unmarked—allusions, as when Dorothea quails before the dying Casaubon's chilling expectations of her: '"Yes," said Dorothea, rather tremulously. She felt sick at heart' (477)—an unobtrusive, perhaps even an unconscious echo of the sentinel Francisco's words ("Tis bitter cold,/And I am sick at heart' (I.i.7–8))[36] at the opening of the Shakespearian work which is probably most full of quotations. The echo subliminally suggests the fatal weight of Casaubon's ghost-like pressure on the living. (Some may want to say here that Shakespeare's phrase has simply 'entered the language'.) And a more recent precursor, Wordsworth, informs 'Janet's Repentance'—more subtly, more unmarkedly, than in her

---

[35] Adrian Poole, whose fine analysis of this passage I read after drafting my own, ingeniously sees a further possibility: 'there is also an undercurrent of thought about what children and childlessness mean to this couple. The effect of invoking Macbeth's "new-born babe" is to flash a sudden light on the murderous intensity of Dorothea's reaction' (*Shakespeare and the Victorians*, 140).

[36] *Hamlet*, 1141.

quotation from 'Memorials of a Tour in Scotland, 1803', discussed earlier. Here is the way Eliot renders Janet's sudden decision to defy her drunken bully of a husband:

> There are moments when by some strange impulse we contradict our past selves— fatal moments, when a fit of passion, like a lava stream, lays low the work of half our lives.[37]

This is not operating in the same way as that *Faerie Queene* allusion parachuted into the text from above. The under-presence of Wordsworth's Lucy poem, 'Strange fits of passion I have known', not necessarily conscious on Eliot's part, implies connections between Janet's impulse—which results in her being cruelly thrown into the street on a cold night at risk to her life—and the night-journey of the speaker of the poem, with his sudden intuition of Lucy's death.[38]

Wordsworth is yet again a presence later in the same story, as Eliot reflects on the 'Blessed influence of one true human soul on another!':

> Ideas are often poor ghosts…But sometimes they are made flesh…Then their presence is a power, then they shake us like a passion, and we are drawn after them with gentle compulsion, as flame is drawn to flame.[39]

The presence that is a power here, the something more deeply interfused that elevates the prose, is 'Lines (Written a few miles above Tintern Abbey)', where 'the sounding cataract/Haunted me *like a passion*' (my emphasis), Wordsworth tells us; and the poem describes

> hearing oftentimes
> The still, sad music of humanity,
> Nor harsh nor grating, though of ample *power*
> To chasten and subdue. And I have felt
> A *presence* that disturbs me with the joy
> Of elevated thoughts; a sense sublime
> Of something far more deeply interfused…[40]

Incorporating the language of poetry—especially Wordsworth's, perhaps—can be a means for the prose of novels to gain access to an additional level of suggestiveness about inner processes of the mind—by offering a depth of reference that is not normally available to the more exclusively functional language of, say, 'a paragraph of to-day's newspaper'. One might speculate that one aspect of this richness of psychological suggestion is

---

[37] Eliot, 'Janet's Repentance', 244.
[38] William Wordsworth, 'Strange fits of passion I have known', *Lyrical Ballads*, 2nd edn, ed. Michael Mason (London: Longman, 2007), 243–44.
[39] Eliot, 'Janet's Repentance', 263.
[40] 'Lines (Written a few miles above Tintern Abbey)', *Lyrical Ballads*, 207–14, 211, 212 (ll. 77–78, 91–97).

the very process—always in some degree inscrutable, always a reminder of the mysteries of memory and imagination—by which a passage or phrase or word from a charged context occurs to the writer in the process of composition, drawing him or her on 'with gentle compulsion'. And there is also a potency in the way in which the words both apply to the immediate subject of the sentence in the novel and feel as if they apply to something else as well: Eliot's description here could be an account of the way Wordsworth's words—an idea made flesh—work on her, and then on us as sensitive readers, drawing us after them. Eliot's allusion has the effect of presenting Wordsworth's words about presence, disturbance and elevation as an account of how an allusion works; so that the reader is overcome by a sense, sublime or not, of something far more deeply interfused.

This sense of the power of words might recall the Preface of Bishop Richard Chenevix Trench's *On the Study of Words*, published in 1851, the year after *The Prelude*, where he quotes himself, saying,

> I am persuaded that I have used no exaggeration in saying, that for many a young man 'his first discovery that words are living powers, has been like the dropping of scales from his eyes, like the acquiring of another sense, or the introduction into a new world'.[41]

Words are living powers, and in allusion they can lead to the 'acquiring of another sense', bringing in another context and a set of underlying meanings that resemble, in a way, the etymological roots revealed by Trench that nourish the words we are reading; they intensify our experience by linking it to the past, in this case to particular usages in the past. From one point of view this could be read as a sacramental process, a ritual, with its symbolic richness, its intrinsic doubleness—as itself and as a re-enactment of a past utterance.

Each allusion defines a community of knowledge in the readership which receives it, a community which can be positively viewed as well as negatively, for not every group is necessarily an élite. A given set of allusions in a work of literature defines the range of reading in its ideal readership. Like other communities, those of allusion can be malign or benign. They can help to enforce a complacent circularity among insiders, or can define communal identity less by generous inclusiveness than by unkindly exclusions. Or, they can be a means towards the achievement of the strength of a reassuring solidarity and a fuller articulacy. Having a common language and a common set of references means you have common values to appeal to, common ground to tread on, helpfully defining though not settling the terms of debate. On 8 May 1781, Samuel Johnson pronounced quotation 'a good thing; there is community of mind in it. Classical quotation is the *parole* [common language] of literary men all over the world.'[42] English and its

---

[41] Richard Chenevix Trench, *On the Study of Words*, 21st edn [1851] (New York: Macmillan, 1891), viii.

[42] Boswell, *The Life of Dr. Johnson* [1791], introduction by John Wain, 2 vols. (London: Dent, 1973), 2: 386.

literature offers in the Victorian period an even broader community of mind, a common language that brings together people through the value they jointly place on the best that has been known and thought.

The community of allusion may be a club, to which it feels good just to belong. The jocular and clubbable literary allusion can work, that is, like a friendly masonic handshake or the glimpse of an old school tie.[43] It need not be invidious. In 'Amos Barton' in George Eliot's *Scenes of Clerical Life* the parasitic Countess Czerlaski, who billets herself on the impoverished Amos Barton,

> kindly consented to dine as early as five, when a hot joint was prepared, which coldly furnished forth the children's table the next day. ['Amos Barton', *Scenes of Clerical Life*, I 98]

Which is *Hamlet* I.ii.179–80:

> Thrift, thrift, Horatio, the funeral bak'd-meats
> Did coldly furnish forth the marriage tables.[44]

George Eliot keeps a satirical edge, though there's nothing funereal about the celebration that the Countess's selfishness demands. The pleasure of the joke is partly our recognition, partly the incongruity of importing anything serious from the original Shakespearean context of murder and incest and revenge into the Shepperton Vicarage. This is the pleasure of mock-epic, of conscious trivialization. So too we appreciate the neatness of the way George Eliot revises Shakespeare and matches 'hot joint' (for 'baked meats') against 'coldly furnished forth'—so those who don't know *Hamlet* so well won't be troubled by the sense of missing something.

Another case of the familiar quotation, flashed like a badge of membership, but not in such a way as to exclude non-initiates: Hamlet's father is murdered while in an unrepentant state, so that his spirit is in purgatory. He was sent to his account, he says,

> With all my imperfections on my head. [I.v.79][45]

We may recall this and see the joke of the twist when in chapter 2 of *Bleak House* we read that

> With all her *perfections* on her head, my Lady Dedlock has come up from her place in Lincolnshire... [58, emphasis added]

---

[43] Wheeler says that while 'habits of worship and Bible study had the greatest influence upon Victorians in their approach to allusion, the use of a knowledge of classical and modern literature to strengthen the sense of group identity shared by the better educated came a strong second' (*The Art of Allusion*, 16).

[44] *Hamlet*, 1145.

[45] *Hamlet*, 1150.

The jocular side of this is that it extends the satirical portrait of Lady Dedlock as just *too* perfect, at least in the view of the 'fashionable intelligence' (58), and perhaps also too conscious of her own perfection. The serious, richer side is that it is her inhuman aspiration to be perfect, her reluctance to acknowledge her humanity and imperfection, that makes Lady Dedlock so unhappy; her 'perfection' *is* her imperfection, in that sense. We should note that we do not absolutely have to recognize that the (quasi-proverbial) allusion is to *Hamlet*. It is often possible to be half-included—to gather that the words used are receiving a special kind of emphasis, are allusive, without quite getting the full joke; and, even if we do not, the words themselves, in this *Bleak House* instance, mean what they want to say on their own.

When a novelist's characters themselves allude, what is at stake alters, for they place themselves by their allusions, identifying themselves in terms of the communities to which they belong. George Eliot is interested in the relation between the psychology of her characters and the matter of their own habits of quotation or allusion. Here is the relatively unlettered Caleb Garth thinking about why old Featherstone hated Bulstrode the banker, and alluding not to poetry but to the Bible, which has a greater social reach as it is familiar not just to readers but to all the church-going classes:

> 'The soul of man,' said Caleb, with the deep tone and grave shake of the head which always came when he used this phrase—'the soul of man, when it gets fairly rotten, will bear you all sorts of poisonous toad-stools, and no eye can see whence came the seed thereof.'
>
> It was one of Caleb's quaintnesses, that in his difficulty of finding speech for his thought, he caught, as it were, snatches of diction which he associated with various points of view or states of mind; and whenever he had a feeling of awe, he was haunted by a sense of Biblical phraseology, though he could hardly have given a strict quotation. [411]

The phrase 'the soul of man' occurs only once in the King James Bible, in Romans 2.9: 'Tribulation and anguish, upon every soul of man that doeth evil, of the Jew first, and also of the Gentile'. To that degree Caleb's utterance is 'a strict quotation'; but 'no eye can see whence came the seed thereof' is just a combination of snatches of biblical diction. George Eliot here nicely evokes the effort of expression, the way language is no one's singular property; and the way the *shapes* of certain phrases, and the associations of particular words ('snatches of diction'), take hold of the mind. Caleb, who has the root of the matter in him, is not wrong about Featherstone. But some readers will feel uncomfortable with Eliot's edge of comic condescension: 'quaintnesses' tells the reader how to view Caleb's incapacity—indulgently, with a knowing smile; while the suspended quotation—'the soul of man . . . the soul of man'—sets him up for the bathos of 'all sorts of poisonous toad-stools'.

One could say that Dickens, a less analytic psychologist, treats this territory—the solecisms and oddities of the uneducated or less educated—with more verve and daring and less condescension. Compare Jenny Wren in *Our Mutual Friend* (1865) saying of her 'child' (actually her alcoholic father Mr Dolls), 'I wish I had never brought him up. He'd be sharper than a serpent's tooth, if he wasn't as dull as ditch water. Look at him' (523). This is a delightfully (and benignly) self-cancelling combination of *King Lear* I.iv.288–9—'How sharper than a serpent's tooth it is/To have a thankless child!'[46]—with the proverbial voice of the people—'as dull as ditch water'. The clash of registers here is made Jenny Wren's own doing, which gives her creative agency and what one might call opacity; whereas Caleb Garth is deadly serious, and *seen through*; we view his comicality from outside and above.[47]

More broadly, Dickens is profoundly aware of allusion's potency as a marker of the exclusivities of literary culture, its uses in the circulation of social power and in the preservation and enforcement of hierarchies. Increasingly, he handles allusion of the genteel, ornamental and jocular kind with a darker, more ironic edge, in a beady-eyed critique of allusion's clubbability. We can see this in *Our Mutual Friend* where one of Dickens's most highly educated characters, the cynical Eugene Wrayburn, manages to allude both to *Twelfth Night* and to *Macbeth* in one short speech to his disapproving friend Mortimer Lightwood about the self-destructively alcoholic Dolls. Wrayburn has been mocking and abusing and giving drink to Dolls, and has just sent him out into the night:

> Don't be like Patience on a mantelpiece frowning at Dolls, but sit down, and I'll tell you something that you really will find amusing. Take a cigar. Look at this of mine. I light it—draw one puff—breathe the smoke out—there it goes—it's Dolls!—it's gone—and being gone you are a man again. [531]

Wrayburn is trying to be funny. First he invokes Viola in *Twelfth Night* II.iv.114–15, in male disguise as Cesario, telling Orsino, whom she secretly loves, how stoically her putative sister 'never told her love'; it is a veiled way to declare her own love:

> She sate like Patience on a monument,
> Smiling at grief. Was not this love indeed?[48]

The allusion says that Lightwood's attitude of gloomy displeasure is a monumental pose, and the switch of 'smiling at grief' to 'frowning at Dolls' says that Dolls is comic. Then Wrayburn turns to a darker source: *Macbeth* III.iv.105–7 and the scene of Banquo's ghost:

> Hence, horrible shadow!
> Unreal mock'ry, hence! Why, so; being gone,

---

[46] *King Lear*, 1264.

[47] As Adrian Poole suggests, 'Perhaps she has heard Lear's famous curse on stage' (*Shakespeare and the Victorians*, 121).

[48] *Twelfth Night*, 420. This particular allusion had been a cliché for at least half a century. Catherine Morland in *Northanger Abbey* (1818), reading 'all such works as heroines must read to supply their memories with those quotations which are so serviceable and so soothing in the vicissitudes of their eventful lives', is said to gather from Shakespeare 'that a young woman in love always looks/—"like Patience on a monument/Smiling at Grief"'(Jane Austen, *Northanger Abbey*, ed. Barbara M. Benedict and Deirdre Le Faye (Cambridge: Cambridge University Press, 2006), 7, 9).

I am a man again.[49]

But this respite for Macbeth is only temporary.

How funny we should find Wrayburn's allusive attempts at jollying his friend Lightwood along, in his would-be insouciant upper-class way, may become clearer when we come about two hundred pages later to the death of Mr Dolls in Jenny Wren's doll shop:

> there, in the midst of the dolls with no speculation in their eyes, lay Mr Dolls with no speculation in his. [712]

Dickens's imagination finds a near-rhyme for this hideous resemblance: 'Midst of the dolls...Mister Dolls'. And the actual repeated phrase takes us back—in what could be read as a double allusion, to Eugene's bad joke as well as to Shakespeare—to Banquo's ghost a dozen lines earlier (III.iv.93–5):

> ... thy blood is cold;
> Thou hast no speculation in those eyes,
> Which thou dost glare with![50]

As so often with Dickens's allusions, there is more of a gleam and a glint if we know the original context: we are left and incited to imagine the awful expression in Mr Dolls's eyes—'which thou dost glare with'. Dickens's narration does not allow Wrayburn to get away with laughing off his brutality through the Macbeth-like self-deception of 'being gone you are a man again'; he brings back the terrible guilt of the corpse's stare in a rebuke to the elusiveness of allusiveness.

Dickens seems to regard parts of allusive culture as an inheritance to be at least questioned, if not repudiated, and one that especially has its roots in the previous century. In *Bleak House* we again find allusions close together, and in relation—in relation to the matter of relatedness:

> Hence the fashionable intelligence proclaims one morning to the listening earth, that Lady Dedlock is expected shortly to return to town for a few weeks... [V]ery red blood of the superior quality, like inferior blood unlawfully shed, *will* cry aloud, and

---

[49] *Macbeth*, 1327. Another of Dickens's dubious upper-class young men, Steerforth in *David Copperfield*, makes the same allusion when talking to David (nicknamed 'Daisy' by him), in Mr Peggotty's boat-cum-house, just after being overcome by 'the horrors' at his own moral and psychological instability:

> 'So much for that!' he said, making as if he tossed something light into the air, with his hand.
> "Why, being gone, I am a man again,"
> like Macbeth. And now for dinner! If I have not (Macbeth-like) broken up the feast with most admired disorder, Daisy' [330]

[50] *Macbeth*, 1327.

will be heard. Sir Leicester's cousins, in the remotest degree, are so many Murders, in the respect that they 'will out'. [445]

This is first animated by hyperbolic mockery, and again by an allusion that when we trace it down goes deep, being imagined with a rich sense of the original context. It is Addison's ode 'The spacious firmament on high'. In Addison,

> The Moon takes up the wondrous tale;
> And nightly, to the listening Earth,
> Repeats the story of her birth.[51]

The idea that the whole earth is listening for news of Lady Dedlock makes sense without knowledge of the Ode—as for most readers it must; but the peculiar rightness, for Dickens himself, seems to come from recalling, partly in the rhyme of 'earth', Addison's phrase (so suggestive in many ways for *Bleak House*) 'Repeats the story of her birth'—insisting on her rank, above all. Then the Dedlock poor relations—in a startling association of aristocratic blood with the blood of murder (suggestions of murder run through *Bleak House* even in places where there doesn't seem to be any)—start repeating the story of *their* birth. '[V]ery red blood of the superior quality, like inferior blood unlawfully shed, *will* cry aloud' recalls the Lord's words to Cain after Abel's murder in Genesis 4.10: 'What hast thou done? the voice of thy brother's blood crieth unto me from the ground'.[52] The purportedly noble blood of the poor relation crying for recognition is ironically equated with the spilt blood of the fratricide's victim demanding justice. And then there's a marked quotation: as Lancelot Gobbo says in *The Merchant of Venice*, 'murder cannot be hid long; a man's son may, but in the end truth will out' (II.ii.79–80).[53]

The Esther plot perhaps shows that not only 'a man's son' but also 'a woman's daughter' *may* 'be hid long' but 'will out' in the end. It is one of these Dedlock cousins whom Dickens, in a ventriloquial *tour de force* recalling Mr Jingle in *The Pickwick Papers*, shows later in the novel referring to Lady Dedlock as resembling the sleepwalking Lady Macbeth of *Macbeth* V.1:

> The debilitated cousin says of her that she's beauty nough—tsetup Shopofwomen—but rather larming kind—reminding-manfact—inconvenient woman—who *will* getoutofbedandbawthestablishment—Shakspeare. [706]

'The establishment' this drawling, affected aristocrat means that Lady Macbeth gets out of bed and bores is the theatre, or perhaps the Macbeth household within the play; but even before the 20th-century usage, the phrase could mean the settled creatures and

[51] Addison, 'The spacious firmament on high' (st. 2), *The Poetical Works of Joseph Addison: Gay's Fables; and Somerville's Chase*, ed. Rev. George Gilfillan (Edinburgh: James Nichol, 1859), 140.

[52] I am grateful to Michael Slater for pointing this out to me.

[53] *The Merchant of Venice*, 261.

office-holders of the state. Dickens's generosity of allusive imagination encompasses the gesture of reductive Shakespearean allusion by which the cousin tries to cope with Lady Dedlock's excessive, 'inconvenient' haughtiness.

In Book I, chapter 12 of *Our Mutual Friend*, Dickens's narration—introducing a chapter about Wrayburn and Lightwood—flirts with the genteel elevating tradition of embellishment by allusion to the Augustan poetic canon, only to deviate mockingly into the everyday reality of Tom, Dick and Harry:

> It was not summer yet, but spring; and it was not gentle spring ethereally mild, as in Thomson's Seasons, but nipping spring with an easterly wind, as in Johnson's, Jackson's, Dickson's, Smith's and Jones's seasons. [147][54]

For a moment, with 'Johnson's', we may wonder if it is Samuel Johnson's works we are being referred to—but the piling up of ever more common names thereafter comically enforces the point that the London spring is commonly experienced as a chilling blast from Siberia—that Wrayburn and Lightwood along with everyone else in London have to undergo the common hardships of life. The youthful Pip in *Great Expectations* starts by being easily impressed by the declamatory, unstoppably quoting tradition associated with the 18th century. The account in chapter 31 of Mr Wopsle's absurdly affected performance as Hamlet tells us:

> I had a latent impression that there was something decidedly fine in Mr Wopsle's elocution—not for old associations' sake, I am afraid, but because it was very slow, very dreary, very up-hill and down-hill, and very unlike any way in which any man in any natural circumstances of life or death ever expressed himself about anything. [276]

The unnaturalness and artificiality of it all is Dickens's point; Pip is born into a small provincial world which rates highly such pretensions, on stage and in poetry. Pip's later perspective, though, which incorporates more of the test of experience, proves Wopsle wanting. The point has been made earlier in the novel. Here Pip recalls the time when he was at Wopsle's great-aunt's school:

> There was a fiction that Mr Wopsle 'examined' the scholars, once a quarter. What he did on those occasions was to turn up his cuffs, stick up his hair, and give us Mark Antony's oration over the body of Caesar. This was always followed by Collins's Ode on the Passions, wherein I particularly venerated Mr Wopsle as Revenge, throwing his blood-stained sword in thunder down, and taking the War-denouncing trumpet with a withering look. It was not with me then, as it was in later life, when I fell into the society of the passions, and compared them with Collins and Wopsle, rather to the disadvantage of both gentlemen. [74]

---

[54] The first line of 'Spring' (1728), the first of James Thomson's *The Seasons*, is: 'Come, gentle Spring, ethereal Mildness, come…' (*The Seasons*, ed. James Sambrook (Oxford: Clarendon Press, 1981), 3).

Dickens quotes a sufficient measure of Collins's original 'The Passions, An Ode for Music'—in his own prose measure—to convey Pip's youthful relish of what he supposes to be Wopsle's grandeur:

> Revenge impatient rose;
> He threw his blood-stain'd sword in thunder down,
> And with a withering look,
> The war-denouncing trumpet took,
> And blew a blast so loud and dread,
> Were ne'er prophetic sounds so full of woe.[55]

We might think back here to the formal, respectful manner in which George Eliot quotes—with careful, correct indentation—the verse of the two lines of *The Faerie Queene* in her narration in *Middlemarch*. In *Great Expectations* Dickens works three lines of Collins, with verve, into the body of his prose: the free indirect style gives free rein to the comic, questioning effect of the swerves and inversions vented on Collins's original, which change the word-order into that of prose. The punchline about later falling into the society of the passions, with its brilliant pairing of Collins and Wopsle, both of whom fail to convince, applies the tests of comedy and of realism to the performance that has been imposed upon Pip, and gives a withering look at both these grand authorities. Such moments contribute to the way in which *Great Expectations* charts, among many other processes, a movement from an induction into a hierarchically ordered world partly characterized by the circulation and exchange of fine quotations, of grandiose declamation, dominated by Mr Wopsle, towards a modest liberation from illusion, partly registered in a difference of perspective, the narrating Pip's distance from his earlier credulities, and recognition of the mixed character of the community of mind to be found in quotation. Comedy is a test here of the pretensions of the gentlemanly, or would-be gentlemanly, quoting world.

Great Expectations can present the ability to quote as an invidious class marker of clubbability, of social inclusion. Pip's ambiguous and blighting friend, the coarse, brutal but decent convict Magwitch, describes how his ex-partner in crime Compeyson, despite his greater guilt, got half the length of sentence Magwitch did at their trial by appearing a gentleman:

> And when it come to character, warn't it Compeyson as had been to the school, and warn't it his schoolfellows as was in this position and that, and warn't it him as had been know'd by witnesses in such clubs and societies, and nowt to his disadvantage.

---

[55] William Collins, 'The Passions, An Ode for Music' [1746], in *The Poems of Thomas Gray, William Collins, Oliver Goldsmith*, ed. Roger Lonsdale (London: Longman, 1969), 477–85, 481–82 (ll. 40–45). Dickens likes the absurdity of 'Collins and Wopsle', and returns to it in chapter 13, where Pip recalls 'That, rather late in the evening Mr Wopsle gave us Collins's ode, and threw his blood-stain'd sword in thunder down, with such effect, that a waiter came in and said, "The Commercials underneath sent up their compliments, and it wasn't the Tumblers' Arms"' (134).

And warn't it me as had been tried afore, and as had been know'd up hill and down
dale in Bridewells and Lock-Ups? And when it come to speech-making, warn't it
Compeyson as could speak to 'em wi' his face dropping every now and then into his
white pocket-handkercher—ah! and wi' verses in his speech, too—and warn't it me
as could only say, 'Gentlemen, this man at my side is a most precious rascal'? [365]

'Ah! and wi' verses in his speech, too': Compeyson's artful adoption of a genteel educated
alluding manner wins him the indulgence of a court that has one law for the gentleman
and another for the seeming ruffian. Dickens knows very well the class configurations of
literacy: think of the illiterate Krook who has the vital papers in *Bleak House*, or later the
pathos and stigma of illiteracy in *Our Mutual Friend*. Or, with a sly cringe from him (and
a cringe of embarrassment from us) of the unctuous Uriah Heep renouncing culture in
David Copperfield:

I should like it of all things, I assure you; but I am far too umble. There are people
enough to tread upon me in my lowly state, without my doing outrage to their
feelings by possessing learning. Learning ain't for me. A person like myself had better
not aspire. [264]

Dickens is as conscious as Heep that the pleasures of allusion, which admit us to the interior of a cosy club, are mostly denied to the classes who, often through no fault of their
own, are doomed to remain on the chilly outside. His whole career—constantly troubled
by the questionable definition of the 'gentleman', and by issues of literacy and education,
and conducted in the face of a vast popular audience but driven by a verbal imagination
of extraordinary intensity—makes him a powerful thinker about, and a crucial test case
for our thinking about, allusion.

Dickens is far from the only Victorian novelist attuned to the potency of allusion as
a badge of class membership and privileged knowledge. Thomas Hardy, another auto-
didact, has a less active, more doom-laden sense of social exclusion than Dickens.
'Characters within Hardy's fiction who consciously cite Shakespeare', as Adrian Poole
observes, 'are rarely if ever to be trusted.'[56] Not that Hardy is always mournful about it.
Alec D'Urberville, fancying Hardy's most famous heroine, first says he has been watching her in her struggles to whistle tunes to the hens, as she is supposed to, while she is 'sitting like *Im*-patience on a monument' (the *Twelfth Night* reference we have already seen
Wrayburn, another dissolute aristocrat, making); and then, showing her how, whistles
a line of 'Take, O take those lips away', the song which the Boy sings for the seduced and
abandoned Mariana in *Measure for Measure* (IV.1.1).[57] 'But the allusion was lost upon
Tess', Hardy observes.[58] If it weren't, maybe Tess herself would not be lost.

---

[56] *Shakespeare and the Victorians*, 145.
[57] *Measure for Measure*, 572.
[58] Thomas Hardy, *Tess of the D'Urbervilles*, ed. Juliet Grindle and Simon Gatrell, with a new
Introduction by Penny Boumelha (Oxford: Oxford World's Classics, 2005), 67.

We have heard from Samuel Johnson that allusion is a 'good thing' because of the 'community of mind' it promotes, and that, in particular, 'classical quotation is the *parole* of literary men all over the world'. While in a sense this is true, it is not the whole story, and some 'literary men' are more included than others. There's an extraordinary moment where the tensions are traceable very near the end of Hardy's *Jude the Obscure* (1895). Poor dead Jude Fawley, after a miserably blighted career in which his working-class background has kept him from getting into Oxford (called Christminster in the book), is mocked in his coffin by the sounds of a university honorary degree ceremony going on outside his window. He is self-taught, and his little classical library is described, with great metaphorical daring, as turning pale at the sounds of the world from which he has been cruelly excluded:

> the old, superseded, Delphin editions of Virgil and Horace and the dog-eared Greek Testament on the neighbouring shelf, and the few other volumes of the sort that he had not parted with, roughened with stone-dust where he had been in the habit of catching them up for a few minutes between his labours, seemed to pale to a sickly cast at the sounds.[59]

Citing this passage, Michael Wheeler comments that 'Hardy incorporated a set of class-cultural allusions'; he goes on: 'The right to the benefits of studying the kind of books to which Hardy refers belongs to the doctors who are conferring degrees and to the gentry who are receiving them, but not to a stonemason. Allusion marks the class barriers of Christminster.'[60] This is quite true, keeping the 'class' in 'classical'. But there's a further effect Wheeler does not comment on, which lies in the insidious way in which Hardy here draws on the words of a more readily available, English-language work, by including an echo of the words of Hamlet in his 'To be, or not to be' speech, at the point where he gives the reason why more people don't commit suicide, that they don't know what will happen to them after death:

> And thus the native hue of resolution
> Is sicklied o'er with the pale cast of thought… [*Hamlet* III.i.83–4][61]

'Sicklied o'er with the pale cast' is given a twist and turned to 'pale to a sickly cast', so that 'roughened with stone-dust' explains the pallor, moderating the pathetic fallacy. The connection of the dead, baffled Jude with the tragic Hamlet is the prime thing to note; both are in some sense 'literary men' whose worldly position frustrates their resolutions,

---

[59] Thomas Hardy, *Jude the Obscure*, ed. Patricia Ingham (Oxford: Oxford World's Classics, 2002), 396.

[60] Wheeler, *The Art of Allusion*, 18, 19.

[61] *Hamlet*, 1160. Shakespeare was accessible in ways the Classics were not, as Dickens argued in a speech of 1853 where he stated his belief that 'there are in Birmingham at this moment many working men infinitely better versed in Shakespeare and in Milton than the average of fine gentlemen in the days of bought-and sold-dedications and dear books' (quoted in Gager, *Shakespeare and Dickens*, 57).

paralyses their will, and leads them to an early death. Allusion, so often a medium of community and inclusion, here conveys despair and exclusion.

Let us close by teasing out just a little more, through close reading, how creatively sustaining or stimulating, as for Pip, the recourse to 'passages that I knew' could be for the Victorian novelist. Look at Pip, in his youth, left waiting alone in the courtyard at Satis House:

> All the uses and scents of the brewery might have evaporated with its last reek of smoke …
>
> Behind the furthest end of the brewery, was a rank garden with an old wall: not so high but that I could struggle up and hold on long enough to look over it, and see that the rank garden was the garden of the house, and that it was overgrown with tangled weeds... [93]

This description seems to have grown out of *Hamlet* I.i.133–7 (I italicize for clarity.):

> How weary, stale, flat, and unprofitable
> Seem to me all the *uses* of this world!
> Fie on't, ah fie! 'tis an *unweeded garden*
> That *grows* to seed, things *rank* and gross in nature
> Possess it merely.[62]

Part of the beauty of Dickens's passage is the way it restores what in Shakespeare is a metaphor to a physical reality, but retains some of the world-weariness of its dramatic context. This use of *Hamlet*, I think, takes us deeper than Juliet John, in her chapter on 'Dickens and Hamlet' in *Victorian Shakespeare*, quite allows when she says that 'Dickens's fascination with Hamlet... was fuelled... by anxieties that the nineteenth-century valorisation of Shakespeare's Hamlet promoted a model of intellectual and aristocratic disengagement from the public sphere unhelpful in an age of burgeoning democracy and mass culture'.[63] This claim may hold good for Wopsle's posturing as the Prince of Denmark, but in the passage quoted there is more inwardness, more doubleness, more private ambivalence, in Pip and the reader than are dreamt of in the philosophy of social policy, with its category of the 'unhelpful'.

Mortality and immortality are always in the frame with allusion to poetry: people die, we remember them, our memories of them die, though maybe not till we die, we are remembered, we too are forgotten. If we put them—or ourselves—in poems, then perhaps we are remembered for longer. The soul may or may not be immortal—may or may not last forever; even the most 'immortal' poem probably won't, as

---

[62] *Hamlet*, 1145.

[63] Juliet John, 'Dickens and Hamlet', *Victorian Shakespeare*, vol. 2: *Literature and Culture*, ed. Gail Marshall and Adrian Poole (Basingstoke and New York: Palgrave Macmillan, 2003), 46–60, 46. More richly and suggestively, Adrian Poole calls *Hamlet* and Hamlet 'the supreme model for what it might mean to be a character or to have a character of your own' (*Shakespeare and the Victorians*, 123).

Tennyson knew; nor can it, except metaphorically, 'immortalize' its subjects. And yet we're drawn to poetry's precious extensions of memory, which correspond to our yearnings. Though words are insubstantial compared with the things they are about, there is a way in which they last better than their subjects and their authors. Much of the most poignant poetry we remember is concerned with remembering, with saving things or people or moments or feelings from an engulfing oblivion (in elegies and epitaphs, lyrics inspired by intense feeling or the fleeting appearances of nature). The words of the great writers are preserved with care from generation to generation; they are something we can have in common with those of earlier times, and we can feel they have accumulated weight by being felt and valued by many before us. These words, often in themselves acts of commemoration, attempts to preserve in verse what will otherwise go unrecorded and become forgotten, can in allusion be kept alive a little more.

So at last, with these Tennysonian reflections, we get to James again, for my last case. Isabel Archer is in Italy for the first time:

> she felt her heart beat in the presence of immortal genius, and knew the sweetness of rising tears in eyes to which faded fresco and darkened marble grew dim.[64]

Isabel's powerful emotion gets its charge here because we are, so to speak, 'in the presence of immortal genius': of two immortal geniuses. 'Immortal', 'fade', and 'dim' all occur in Keats's 'Ode to a Nightingale' ('immortal Bird!', st. VII; 'fade away into the forest dim', st. II);[65] while 'Sweet', 'rise', 'tears', 'grows', 'eyes', and 'dark' coincide in Tennyson's short lyric 'Tears, idle tears', from *The Princess* (1847)—to which James reverts even more notably over 200 pages later, towards the end of the novel, where Isabel's beloved cousin Ralph Touchett, who has opposed her marriage to the ghastly Gilbert Osmond, is finally dying of his long disease in England. She is afraid he will die abroad:

> She had a constant fear that he would die there...Ralph must sink to his last rest in his own dear house, in one of those deep, dim chambers of Gardencourt, where the dark ivy would cluster round the edges of the glimmering window...the tears rose to her eyes.[66]

Isabel's imagining of Ralph's end—like her response to Italy—comes through a set of echoes of 'Tears, idle tears' (drawing on all four stanzas). I italicize the nine repeated words:

---

[64] *The Portrait of a Lady*, 215.

[65] John Keats, 'Ode to a Nightingale', *Keats: The Complete Poems*, ed. Miriam Allott (London: Longman, 1970), 523–32, 529, 526.

[66] *Portrait of a Lady*, 435. Christopher Ricks points out how the name of George Eliot's hateful Grandcourt in *Daniel Deronda* recurs in sweetened form as Gardencourt in this novel inspired by it; while Osmond's first name, Gilbert, also reproduces the original's initial and terminal letters, G—t.

> *Tears*, idle tears, I know not what they mean,
> Tears from the depth of some divine despair
> *Rise* in the heart, and gather to the *eyes* …
> Fresh as the first beam glittering on a sail,
> That brings our friends up from the underworld,
> Sad as the *last* which reddens over one
> That *sinks* with all we love below the verge …
> Ah, sad and strange as in *dark* summer dawns
> The earliest pipe of half-awakened birds
> To dying ears, when unto dying eyes
> The casement slowly grows a *glimmering* square …
> *Dear* as remembered kisses after death,
> And sweet as those by hopeless fancy feign'd
> On lips that are for others; *deep* as love,
> Deep as first love, and wild with all regret … [67]

Tennyson is a frequent presence in James.[68] But this is a remarkable case of a compressed and economical and pretty well submerged set of reminiscences that is likely to work on the reader below the level of conscious recognition. It is hard to say here, with the free indirect style, how much this represents Isabel's conscious or unconscious memory of Tennyson's words and how much it is James's own. Is it an 'allusion' as such? As so often, it's a matter of shadings. The most unusual word here, 'glimmering'—for James, who so often looks back through Tennyson's 'glimmering square'—is perhaps the float bobbing on the surface to mark the movement beneath. And as Matthew Arnold says, short passages, single lines—even single words—will serve our turn quite sufficiently.

SUGGESTED READING

Arnold, Matthew. 'The Function of Criticism at the Present Time' [1864]. In *Essays in Criticism: First Series* (1865). Reprinted in *The Complete Prose Works of Matthew Arnold*. Vol. III: *Lectures and Essays in Criticism*. Edited by R.H. Super, with the assistance of Sister Thomas Marion Hoctor. Ann Arbor: University of Michigan Press, 1973, 258–85.

Davis, Philip. 'Implicit and Explicit Reason: George Eliot and Shakespeare'. In *Victorian Shakespeare*. Volume 2: *Literature and Culture*. Edited by Gail Marshall and Adrian Poole. Basingstoke and New York: Palgrave Macmillan, 2003, 84–99.

Douglas-Fairhurst, Robert. *Victorian Afterlives: The Shaping of Influence in Nineteenth-Century Literature*. Oxford: Oxford University Press, 2002.

Eliot, George. *Middlemarch*. Edited by Rosemary Ashton. London: Penguin Classics, 2003.

Gager, Valerie L. *Shakespeare and Dickens: The Dynamics of Influence*. Cambridge: Cambridge University Press, 1996.

---

[67] 'Tears, idle tears,' ll. 1–3, 6–9, 11–14, 16–19; *The Poems of Tennyson*, ed. Christopher Ricks, 3 vols., 2nd edn (London: Longman, 1987), 2: 232–3.

[68] As I've argued in a piece called 'Henry James Among the Poets', in the *Henry James Review*, 26, no. 1 (Winter 2005): 68–81.

Horne, Philip. 'Henry James Among the Poets'. *Henry James Review* 26, no. 1 (Winter 2005): 68–81.

———. '"Where Did She Get Hold of That?" Shakespeare in Henry James's *The Tragic Muse*'. In *Victorian Shakespeare*. Volume 2: *Literature and Culture*. Edited by Gail Marshall and Adrian Poole. Basingstoke and New York: Palgrave Macmillan, 2003 , 100–113.

John, Juliet. 'Dickens and Hamlet'. In *Victorian Shakespeare*. Volume 2: *Literature and Culture*. Edited by Gail Marshall and Adrian Poole. Basingstoke and New York: Palgrave Macmillan, 2003, 46–60.

Miller, Karl. *Authors*. Oxford: Oxford University Press, 1990.

Morton, John. *Tennyson Among the Novelists*. London: Continuum, 2010.

Novy, Marianne. *Engaging with Shakespeare: Responses of George Eliot and Other Women Novelists*. Athens and London: University of Georgia Press, 1994.

Poole, Adrian. *Shakespeare and the Victorians*. London: Arden Critical Companions, 2003.

Ricks, Christopher. *Allusion to the Poets*. Oxford: Oxford University Press, 2002.

Slater, Michael. 'Dickens's Shakespeare'. Hilda Hume Memorial Lecture, University of London, 7 July 2010.

Welsh, Alexander. *Hamlet in his Modern Guises*. Princeton: Princeton University Press, 2001.

Wheeler, Michael. *The Art of Allusion in Victorian Fiction*. London: Macmillan, 1979.

30

THE NOVELIST AS CRITIC

CHRISTOPHER RICKS

A Petition to the Novel-Writers

(Communicated by a Romantic Old Gentleman.)

I hope nobody will be alarmed if I confess that I am about to disclose the existence of a Disreputable Society, in one of the most respectable counties in England. I dare not be more particular as to the locality, and I can not possibly mention the members by name. But I have no objection to admit that I am perpetual Secretary, that my wife is President, that my daughters are Council, and that my nieces form the Society. Our object is to waste our time, misemploy our intellects, and ruin our morals—or, in other words, to enjoy the prohibited luxury of novel-reading.

(Wilkie Collins, *Household Words*)[1]

I

It was in Ezra Pound's 1922 review of *Ulysses*, the-novel-to end-Victorian-novels, that he issued one of his many remarkable insistences:

The best criticism of any work, to my mind the only criticism of any work of art that is of any permanent or even moderately durable value, comes from the creative writer or artist who does the next job; and *not*, not ever from the young gentlemen who make generalities about the creator.[2]

---

[1] Wilkie Collins, *Household Words*, 6 December 1856, in 2 vols. *My Miscellanies* 2 vols. (London: S. Low, 1863), 1: 72.

[2] Ezra Pound, *The Dial* 72 (June 1922), in *Literary Essays*, ed. T.S. Eliot (London: Faber and Faber, 1954), 406.

Pound, who was fifteen when Queen Victoria died, never meant to be a gentleman, young or old, nor was meant to be. He knew—as a Victorian novel might have set itself to demonstrate—that it takes three generations to make a gentleman. Meanwhile, his ear, pricked, told him that gentlemen make generalities. As was his practice, he particularized at once: 'Laforgue's *Salomé* is the real criticism of *Salammbô*; Joyce and perhaps Henry James are critics of Flaubert.'[3]

The real and durable form that criticism takes, then, is *the next job*, creation at once subsequent and consequent. Creation is itself the highest, widest, and deepest form of criticism. This, whether or not the artistic medium or the literary kind happen to stay the same. The poems of Baudelaire, no less than his *Le Peintre de la Vie Moderne*, are critiques of connoisseurship and of its arts. T.S. Eliot's 'Portrait of a Lady' canvases not only Edwardian portraiture and Winthrop Mackworth Praed's benign light verse, 'Portrait of a Lady', but James's novel too, *The Portrait of a Lady* with its connoisseur of weighty malignity. Gilbert Osmond is soulless and sterile, but the novelist who imagined him into existence was the soul of creativity.

> Our echoes roll from soul to soul,
> And grow for ever and for ever.[4]

When Tennyson wrote *The Princess* (1847), his medley with political education, he knew himself to be the heir to Machiavelli's *The Prince*. Likewise with James's *The Princess Casamassima* (1886) in relation to both of those predecessors. And *The Portrait of a Lady* (1881) would echo and roll and grow, being a coherent apprehension of a riven novel by George Eliot.

Henry James wrote to his brother William James in 1876: 'Daniel Deronda (Dan'l. himself) is indeed a dead, though amiable failure. But the book is a large affair; I shall write an article of some sort about it.'[5] Write an article of some sort about it, James did. Reprint this article as the appendix to a critical study of the Victorian novel, Dr F.R. Leavis did.

The Great Tradition found itself in straitened circumstances: George Eliot, Henry James, and Joseph Conrad had only Jane Austen to look briefly back upon, and D.H. Lawrence (reserved by Leavis for a later occasion) to look forward to. But the process of retrospect and prospect that *The Great Tradition* illuminated was simultaneously creative and critical. James's article of some sort, 'Daniel Deronda: A Conversation', staged the shrewd reflections of Theodora, Pulcheria, and Constantius on the new George Eliot novel that the three of them had been (by and large) enjoying. James had

[3] *Salomé* (1887); Flaubert's *Salammbô* (1862). Italicizing, as Pound did not, the titles.
[4] Alfred Tennyson, *The Princess*, Eversely Edition, 9 vols. (London: Macmillan, 1907–8), 4: 57.
[5] Henry James to William James, 29 July 1876, in *Letters: Volume II, 1875–1883*, ed. Leon Edel (Cambridge: Belknap Press, 1975), 59. The period concluding Dan'l. is supplied from William James, *The Correspondence of William James*, vol. 1: *William and Henry: 1861–1884*, ed. Ignas K. Skrupskelis and Elizabeth M. Berkeley (Charlottesville: University Press of Virginia, 1992), 271.

issued an interim report, a holding operation of a page or so, on the first instalment of *Daniel Deronda*, but it was to be the eighteen-page Conversation in which, a few months later, he invested himself.[6] Yet James's greatest investment in *Daniel Deronda*, with compound interest, was the novel that he floated next year, 1877, and launched in 1881. *The Portrait of a Lady* does not exactly observe George Eliot's conventions, but its acumen is an observation of her aims and accomplishments. It is also, with the right peculiar gratitude, an observation of the misjudgements and infelicities in *Daniel Deronda*.

Much first-rate criticism has derived from Leavis's demonstration (more widely than in just this one case, too) that 'It is not derivativeness that is in question, but the relation between two original geniuses.' Thanks to the imaginary Conversation, 'it can be shown, with a conclusiveness rarely possible in these matters, that James did actually go to school to George Eliot'.[7] *The Portrait of a Lady*, like any novel that *succeeds*, owes its achievement not only to what a predecessor had achieved but also to that which she or he had not achieved. Perhaps the predecessor had left something unattempted, still to be done. Or perhaps some part of the enterprise had been ill-essayed, as with the whole half, so to speak, of *Daniel Deronda* that Leavis lopped: 'It will be best to get the bad half out of the way first.' You know, Dan'l. himself, Judaism, Zionism, and so on and so forth. Which leaves '*Gwendolen Harleth* (as I shall call the good part of *Daniel Deronda*)'.[8]

Leavis argued, and he often argued that a critical conversation naturally took the form of *Yes, but* ... If there were not some kind of agreement, some sort of *Yes*, conversation stalled at once; but if there were no *but*, it was forestalled at once. What, then, might a *Yes, but* ... sound like, in reply to his account of James's engagement with George Eliot? It need not primarily (however disputable the judgement) be Leavis's assurance that James is much the lesser genius. Though the presence of George Eliot's novel, a presence that amounts to inspiration, is convincingly substantiated by Leavis, not so much substantiated as asserted is James's falling short of her achievement in her '*Gwendolen Harleth*', especially his being held to do so in every single respect. For Leavis's word *subtilized* is far from a compliment: 'The moral substance of George Eliot's theme is subtilized into something going with the value James sets on "high civilization"; her study of conscience has disappeared.'[9]

---

[6] Henry James, *Nation*, 24 February 1876, in *Essays on Literature: American Writers: English Writers*, ed. Leon Edel and Mark Wilson (New York: Library of America, 1984), 973–74. '*Daniel Deronda*: A Conversation' first published in *Atlantic Monthly* 38 (December 1876): 684–94; repr. *Partial Portraits* (London: Macmillan, 1888) and in *Essays on Literature: American Writers: English Writers*, 974–92.

[7] F.R. Leavis, *The Great Tradition* (London: Chatto & Windus, 1948), 14, 16.

[8] Leavis, *The Great Tradition*, 80, 85. *Daniel Deronda*: 'As things are, there is, lost under that damning title, an actual great novel to be extricated', 122. But then Leavis has his damnable titles: spavined, *English Literature in Our Time and the University* (1969), and half-cock, *Nor Shall My Sword* (1972), pleading for a sequel, *Sleep in My Hand*.

[9] Leavis, *The Great Tradition*, 15.

I need to say at once that I agree (*have always agreed* ..., as one says on these occasions) with some of Leavis's caveats about this particular novel of James's, especially as to Isabel Archer and James's estimation of her, his esteem for her. Leavis: 'The differences, however, as I see them are fairly suggested by saying that Isabel Archer is Gwendolen Harleth seen by a man.' There is much there that invites a *Yes, but* ... and that would require a reply that is patiently attentive (for Leavis is more patient in these pages than was his wont). 'It isn't that George Eliot shows any animus towards Gwendolen; simply, as a very intelligent woman she is able, unlimited by masculine partiality of vision, and only the more perceptive because a woman, to achieve a much *completer* presentment of her subject than James of his.'[10] Leavis's recourse to *simply* betrays a simple coercion. After all, an intermittent animus towards—*against*—some of her women characters has often been glimpsed or plausibly imagined, and this by critics respectful and responsible. But the more immediate matter, bearing as it does upon *the novelist as critic*, is the way in which this account of James might accommodate Pound's emphasis. On this occasion, *the next job* turned out to be a bit of a botched job. James 'largely mistakes the nature of his inspiration, which is not so much from life as he supposed', with the result that 'he fails to produce the fable that gives inevitability and moral significance. He can remain unaware of this failure because he is so largely occupied (a point that can be illustrated in detail) in transposing George Eliot, whose power is due to the profound psychological truth of her conception, and the consistency with which she develops it.' By contrast, James's *in*consistency 'partly empties the theme of *The Portrait of a Lady* of moral substance.'[11] Not that, when it comes to *the next job*, Pound's position would require Pound to deny such a possibility. The situation would be (though it would not *simply* be) that, should the next job prove botched or bitched, this next creation could not rise to constituting the best criticism of its predecessor.

The limits of James's achievement in *The Portrait of a Lady* may be as Leavis maintains. For present purposes, though, I do need to utter a further *Yes, but* ..., this time to myself. In what respects can James's novel be held to be, not only a novel that went to school to George Eliot, but a critique of her novel?

First and foremost is James's sense (a creative understanding that anticipates Leavis's critical understanding) of how fatal to her venture it had been for her to embark upon the heavily freighted religiously rigged half of *Daniel Deronda*. The germane tribute to James was voiced by the author of 'Portrait of a Lady', T.S. Eliot: 'James's critical genius comes out most tellingly in his mastery over, his baffling escape from, Ideas; a mastery and an escape which are perhaps the last test of a superior intelligence. He had a mind so fine that no idea could violate it.'[12] James had seen that the objection to the ideas in

[10] Leavis, *The Great Tradition*, 86–87.

[11] Leavis, *The Great Tradition*, 111.

[12] T.S. Eliot, 'In Memory', *Little Review* 5, no. 4 (August 1918): 44–47, 46; previously published in 'In Memory of Henry James', *The Egoist* 5, no. 1 (January 1918): 1–2.

Daniel Deronda is that they are Ideas, and that the objection to George Eliot is that she permits her mind to be violated by them. Alerted and even warned by George Eliot's misjudgement, James is fortified in his determination that *The Portrait of a Lady* escape all such servitudes and grandeurs. There is less to the Judaism in the many, many pages of *Daniel Deronda* than there is in a single moment in *Our Mutual Friend*. Not, as it happens, the figure itself of the good Jew, Mr Riah, which has something of George Eliot's well-meaning ill-judgement (and is even by way of being a reparation by the fashioner of Fagin), 'CHARACTERS' being identified by Dickens at the head of the book: 'Mr. Riah, a venerable Jew, of noble and generous nature'.[13] No, the great Dickens is not to be found in Mr Riah, who is not a Character but an Idea; rather, the great Dickens flashes out in a remark cast at Mr Riah, dubbing him with a name that is not his name but the badge of all his tribe, despatching Mr Riah at the moment of despatching the chapter:

> 'Do I go, sir?'
> 'Do you go?' sneered Fledgeby. 'Yes, you do go. Toddle, Judah!'[14]

Those are the authentic accents not only of Fascination Fledgeby but of Fascination Dickens.

The gait (*Toddle!*) is just one of the many gaits observed within the movements of compassion and dispassion.

> And now, among the knot of servants dressed in mourning, and the weeping women, Mr. Dombey passes through the hall to the other carriage that is waiting to receive him. He is not 'brought down,' these observers think, by sorrow and distress of mind. His walk is as erect, his bearing is as stiff as ever it has been. He hides his face behind no handkerchief, and looks before him. But that his face is something sunk and rigid, and is pale, it bears the same expression as of old. He takes his place within the carriage, and three other gentlemen follow. Then the grand funeral moves slowly down the street. The feathers are yet nodding in the distance, when the juggler has the basin spinning on a cane, and has the same crowd to admire it. But the juggler's wife is less alert than usual with the money-box, for a child's burial has set her thinking that perhaps the baby underneath her shabby shawl may not grow up to be a man, and wear a sky-blue fillet round his head, and salmon-coloured worsted drawers, and tumble in the mud.[15]

Such is the genius that inspired the critical insight of Edward FitzGerald when he was alert to this novel:

---

[13] Charles Dickens, *Our Mutual Friend* (London: Chapman & Hall, 1901), 11.

[14] Dickens, *Our Mutual Friend*, 661.

[15] Charles Dickens, *Dombey & Son* (London: Chapman & Hall, 1901), 289–90.

The intended Pathos is, as usual, missed: but just turn to little Dombey's Funeral, where the Acrobat in the Street suspends his performance till the Funeral has passed, and his Wife wonders if the little Acrobat in her Arms will so far outlive the little Boy in the Hearse as to wear a Ribbon through his hair, following his Father's Calling. It is in such Side-touches, you know, that Dickens is inspired to Create like a little God Almighty.[16]

This is masterly criticism in the tradition of Samuel Johnson, without envious malignity or superstitious veneration. Fitz has no pleasure in finding the pathos to be a failure, though he takes a quiet pleasure in the various things that *missed* might hit. How lovingly *suspends* catches both the acrobat and the juggler. How understated is the word *passed* in the procession of a funeral (picking up but not just repeating, and certainly not pastiching, Dickens's own touch, 'Mr. Dombey passes through the hall'). How deftly the little Acrobat proceeds to a little God almighty. How entirely without condescension or sarcasm is the word *calling*, for the baby's relation to the juggler's livelihood: 'following his Father's Calling'. (Fitz is following Dickens's steps: 'He takes his place within the carriage, and three other gentlemen follow'.) And how central in its understanding of Dickens is the touch that gives us not only *Side-touches* but the assurance, the reassurance, the *it-is-so-isn't-it?* in which Leavis would sometimes unexpectedly delight, of *you know*: 'It is in such Side-touches, you know, that Dickens is inspired to Create like a little God Almighty.' We know all right, we really do. The continuity of Fitz's criticism with Dickens's creation is itself creative, and is true criticism. Not only is Dickens's art proved upon our pulses, so is the critic's art. I am thinking of Keats's praise of Wordsworth: 'we find what he says true as far as we have experienced and we can judge no further but by larger experience—for axioms in philosophy are not axioms until they are proved upon our pulses: We read fine—things but never feel them to the full until we have gone the same steps as the Author.'[17] (*His walk is as erect...*) If this is true of philosophy, it cannot be less true of the art of a poet or novelist. Not Ideas about the thing but the thing itself.

W.B. Yeats was to begin his account of the philosophy of Shelley (1900) with a section headed 'His Ruling Ideas', the trouble being that Ruling Shelley is what his Ideas did. As for T.S. Eliot and 'the last test of superior intelligence', it was in his journal, *The Criterion*, that William Empson characterized (not defined) intelligence in a reflection on Aristotle, Copernicus, and the parallax: 'I find this a pleasing historical fact because it shows that both these great men were more intelligent (less at the

[16] FitzGerald to Fanny Kemble, 3 February 1880, in *The Letters of Edward FitzGerald*, ed. A. McK. Terhune and A.B. Terhune, 4 vols. (Princeton: Princeton University Press, 1980), 4: 288; included in *Charles Dickens: A Critical Anthology*, ed. Stephen Wall (Harmondsworth: Penguin, 1970), 211.

[17] Keats to John Hamilton Reynolds, 3 May 1818, in *The Letters of John Keats, 1814–1821*, ed. Hyder Edward Rollins, 2 vols. (Cambridge: Harvard University Press, 1958), 1: 279.

mercy of their own notions) than Mr Burrt wishes to think them.'[18] George Eliot in *Daniel Deronda* was no less at the mercy of her notions because they were not her notions alone. For his part, James skirts notions. To him, the role of notions, ideas, and (in ascending order) Ideas in the Victorian novel was all staged, high-minded to the point of loftiness, mounting aerially to the emptily didactic and the fully dictated. Take John Henry Newman's novel of ideas, *Loss and Gain*, 1848, the year of quite some novels: *Dombey and Son*, for one, *Mary Barton*, *Vanity Fair*, and *The Tenant of Wildfell Hall*, for some others. *Loss and Gain*? As art, a dead loss. 'The Story of a Convert' is not converted into a novel. This story of Charles Reding does not make for charismatic reading. This is not a novel of ideas, it is Newman's Idea of a Novel.

There is a second respect in which *The Portrait of a Lady* may be seen as a critique of *Daniel Deronda*, allied with Leavis's 'limiting judgments' (an imitable nasality of his) about James. For Leavis, it is unremittingly the case, in this comparison with George Eliot, that James's presentment is 'partial in both senses of the word—controlled, that is, by a vision that is both incomplete and indulgent', one that 'entailed much excluding and simplifying': 'The difference between James and George Eliot is largely a matter of what James leaves out.' It is true that Leavis immediately hastens to a concession—'The leaving out, of course, is a very positive art that offers the compensation.'[19] But the concession is empty (*of course* is the mere twaddle of graciousness), since the compensation never gets actually specified or substantiated. So I should like to turn the argument through 180 degrees, along the same axis but in the opposite direction, in the matter of Isabel's hideous mismarriage, as against Gwendolen's, for the latter was brought about by economic necessity or pressure. This pressure is a condition of George Eliot's deep sympathy with Gwendolen's plight, the novelist's unsentimental compassion enabling her to give fully realized life to one of her most firm and most famous beliefs: 'Pity and fairness—two little words which, carried out, would embrace the utmost delicacies of the moral life.'[20]

But what, then, is made artistically available to James once he decides to do otherwise and to grant an ample freedom from financial pressures to his mismarrier, Isabel Archer, when she gives to Gilbert Osmond not only her hand but—unless she is careful, or perhaps even if she is—her soul? (Freedom from financial pressures, thanks to Ralph Touchett's munificence.) The answer is one form that artistic freedom may take in its turn, a freedom from one perilous need or impulse, to *explain*. To Gwendolen, there did belong the tragedy and the pathos that attend upon a decision's being explicable,

[18]   William Empson, review of *The Metaphysical Foundations of Modern Science*, by E.A. Burtt, *Criterion*, October 1930, in William Empson, *Argufying*, ed. John Haffenden (London: Chatto & Windus, 1987), 531–32.

[19]   Leavis, *The Great Tradition*, 86, 91, 110.

[20]   George Eliot to Mrs H.F. Ponsonby, 17 October 1877, in *The George Eliot Letters*, ed. Gordon S. Haight, 9 vols. (New Haven: Yale University Press, 1978), 4: 407.

explainable, humanly on the cards even if the card is the Queen of Spades. But James holds his cards very close to his chest, and sometimes declines, wisely, to play them at all. And so to Isabel, on the losing hand, there belongs the tragedy and pathos that attend upon a decision's remaining obdurately beyond explanation. The gap between what she chooses and any guess as to why she chooses it will remain a constant abyss in the world of a novel in which constancy is itself dark and mysterious.

What is the first thing that the Wife of Bath needs to say?

> Experience, thogh noon auctoritee
> Were in this world, is right inogh for me
> To speke of wo that is in mariage.[21]

The prologue to marriage is a wedding. (Is a wedding assuredly a weal and not a woe, or a weal as against a *weal*?) And the prologue to a wedding is a plighting. (Is this assuredly a plighting, as against a plight?) It is not so much a refusal in James to explain Isabel's acceding to Osmond's proposal, as a refusal by James to be held to be in the explaining business. Osmond can explain, and he expends some glacially laconic energy in doing so; and we can to some extent explain the desirability to him of her. Her money, for a start. For her part, she remains apart from certain kinds of comprehension or certain ambitions that comprehension, in us or in novelists, may nurse; naturally we are allowed and even invited to presume some psychological likelihoods, but on the understanding that we waive any claim to a full understanding, to comprehension's presumption. Far from indulging Isabel Archer in any such respect, *The Portrait of a Lady* is declining to indulge the reader. It conveys that it may be childish to keep asking *Why?*

Leavis gives a summing-up as to Isabel: 'She is merely to make a wrong choice, the wrongness of which is a matter of an error in judgment involving no guilt on her part, though it involves tragic consequences for her.'[22] It is the word *merely* that is the error in judgement by the critic here. The words that Leavis rightly uses in praise of George Eliot, 'inevitability' and 'consistency', are indeed the conditions of her art, but the conditions of James's art include an immitigable scepticism as to inevitability and consistency whether in life or in art—scepticism, not cynicism, because of James's dislike of cynicism's pleasure at the thought of its own omniscience. James does not play what we misleadingly call the omniscient narrator. As to *the omniscient narrator*, all we usually mean is that the narrator is alone in knowing certain things, particularly thoughts. This, God knows, is a far cry from omniscience. I know from Kenneth Graham that it was as long ago as 1894 that Sir Walter Raleigh characterized such a narrator: 'He is invisible and omniscient.'[23]

---

[21] Geoffrey Chaucer, 'Wife of Bath's Tale', *The Canterbury Tales*, in *The Complete Works of Geoffrey Chaucer*, ed. F.N. Robinson, 2nd edn (London: Oxford University Press, 1957), ll. 1–3.

[22] Leavis, *The Great Tradition*, 98.

[23] Kenneth Graham, *English Criticism of the Novel 1865–1900* (Oxford: Clarendon Press, 1965), 121.

It is a complicated matter, the Jamesian claim in the matter of knowing, with the knots of its *nots*. In *What Maisie Knew*, 'I may not even answer for it that Maisie was not aware of how, in this, Mrs. Beale failed to share his all but insurmountable distaste for their allowing their little charge to breathe the air of their gross irregularity'.[24] What is the price paid for James's withholdings as against the profit made from Eliot's demonstrations? Leavis had a way of immediately following one question with another, not staying for an answer, prosecutorially. 'Isn't there, in fact, something evasive about James's inexplicitness; something equivocal about his indirectness and the subtlety of implication with which he pursues his aim of excluding all but the "essential"? What, we ask, thinking by contrast of the fullness with which ...' etc.[25] Insufficiently permitting of response, and using the phrase *in fact* of what is not a fact but a judgement, this does nevertheless identify the charge to which James is often open and of which he is sometimes guilty. For Empson was not out of court when he remarked, of a Milton/James contrast adduced by T.S. Eliot, 'It seems to me that Mr Eliot does not know when Milton is good, and I certainly do not know when Henry James is good; I always feel sure he is jabbering like that only to make the reader as helplessly confused about the rights and wrongs of the case as he is himself'.[26] The rights and wrongs of the case: the wrong charge against James was the one made, as it happens, by T.S. Eliot himself in judging *Roderick Hudson*: James 'too much identifies himself with Rowland, does not see through the solemnity he has created in that character, commits the cardinal sin of failing to "detect" one of his own characters'.[27] What is wrong with this is T.S. Eliot's unmisgiving assumption, as *the* point of principle, that there is a cardinal sin for a novelist and that failing to detect one of his characters is it. James was very good on suspicion and detection, and not because he respected them to the heights.

Conversely, the rights and wrongs of the case when it comes to George Eliot have to do with the limits within which Leavis's values of inevitability and consistency should themselves be valued. George Eliot's determination to understand, and to fashion a plot (a *fable*, Leavis is happy to call it) such as to ensure understanding and explanation, makes visible some truths while it occludes some others. It cannot but prompt on occasion the charge to which she in her turn is often open and of which she is sometimes guilty. And guilt is the nub. (Leavis deprecated James for supposing that his Isabel could be both believable and guiltless.) The prosecution of George Eliot in this matter is led by W.B. Yeats, who calls Balzac to witness against her:

> In *La Peau de chagrin* Balzac spends many pages in describing a coquette, who seems the image of heartlessness, and then invents an improbable incident that her chief victim may discover how beautifully she can sing. Nobody had ever heard her sing, and yet in her singing, and in her chatter with her maid, Balzac tells us, was

[24] Henry James, *What Maisie Knew* (London: W. Heinemann, 1898), 171.
[25] Leavis, *The Great Tradition*, 110.
[26] William Empson, *Milton's God* (London: Chatto & Windus, 1961), 27.
[27] T.S. Eliot, 'The Hawthorne Aspect', *Little Review* 5, no. 4 (August 1918): 47–53.

her true self. He would have us understand that behind the momentary self, which acts and lives in the world, and is subject to the judgment of the world, there is that which cannot be called before any mortal judgment seat, even though a great poet, or novelist, or philosopher be sitting upon it. Great literature has always been written in a like spirit, and is, indeed, the Forgiveness of Sin, and when we find it becoming the Accusation of Sin, as in George Eliot, who plucks her Tito [in *Romola*] in pieces with as much assurance as if he had been clockwork, literature has begun to change into something else. George Eliot had a fierceness hardly to be found but in a woman turned argumentative, but the habit of mind her fierceness gave its life to was characteristic of her century, and is the habit of mind of the Shakespearian critics.[28]

To this, too, one want wants and needs to ask, by way of rebuttal, *Yes, but* ... Those capital letters of Yeats's to heighten Forgiveness, Accusation, and Sin; the injustice to George Eliot's Tito Melema, who is indeed inspected but not as clockwork, rather as a geological specimen, the strata of his indurated habituated selfishness; the injustice to so much else of George Eliot; the exultant misogyny of Yeats, and its confidence of applause: all these raise resistance. But the comparison with Balzac, including the admission of his imperfection as a novelist ('invents an improbable incident'), is on to something, and it has its bearing on whether the determination to *understand* does not preclude some forms or channels that sympathetic imagination may take. Inevitability can harden the heart, and it is the opposite of what T.S. Eliot valued in James: his power to *escape*. And it is what James set his fine face against in George Eliot.

II

A tour of the considerations that attend upon *the novelist as critic* might set out, then, from the belief that the succeeding novelist achieves an imaginative critique of his or her predecessors. But to the critique of a predecessor must immediately be added self-criticism, the novelist as self-critic. For Pound's declaration asks to be understood as complemented by inward self-criticism, such as might be devoted either to one's previous work (predecessor not *of* but *by* oneself), or to the work in progress, the here and now. John Keats, a superb reviser, was eloquent in the belief that creation itself has to be unremittingly critical:

> 'My judgment, (he says,) is as active while I am actually writing as my imagination. In fact all my faculties are strongly excited & in their full play—And shall I afterwards, when my imagination is idle, & the heat in which I wrote, has gone off, sit down

---

[28] W.B. Yeats, 'At Stratford-on-Avon' [1901], in *Selected Criticism*, ed. A. Norman Jeffares (London: Macmillan, 1964), 97–98. Adducing this in an essay for the centenary (1980) of George Eliot's death ('She Was Still Young'), I remarked Yeats's snitching of one of her loved words, *argumentative* (Christopher Ricks, 'Victorian Lives', in *Essays in Appreciation* (Oxford: Oxford University Press, 1996), 229).

coldly to criticise when in Possession of only one faculty, what I have written, when almost inspired.'[29]

Dickens's imagination was never idle and he never sat down, let alone coldly. His revisions are strongly excited criticism. They are therefore themselves open to criticism, not always appreciative. Happily, the evidence that was mounted a while ago (1957) as *Dickens at Work*, a succinct precise study by John Butt and Kathleen Tillotson that has been augmented but not superseded, mostly bears witness to Dickens as a superb novelist–self-critic. This may be a matter of a particular crystallization, as when the entertained title *Nobody's Fault* found itself improved into *Little Dorrit*.

> It seems likely that Little Dorrit was not at first intended to be so important a character; indeed, in manuscript, proofs and letters we can trace the way she grew in importance, and even see her acquiring her name. She was introduced in the third chapter, merely as an unknown girl seen in Mrs Clennam's room and inquired about by Arthur Clennam. In the manuscript her name does not appear; Affery only says 'Oh! *She's* nothing; she's a whim of hers.' Her name is added in proof as 'Dorrit', which is then altered in a different coloured ink to 'Little Dorrit.'[30]

Whereupon Butt and Tillotson identify, with affectionate respect, not only the process by which the name established itself for Dickens as entitled to the novel, but the grounds for believing that the title that duly found itself replaced, *Nobody's Fault*, would have been slighter, belittling.

Other revisions by Dickens have proved enduringly controversial, most famously or most notoriously his changing the end of *Great Expectations*. The account of the matter that I have found both the clearest and the fullest is that of Edgar Rosenberg in his excellent Norton Critical Edition of the novel (1999). Occupying thirty pages, 'Putting an End to *Great Expectations*' sets out the facts crisply before scrupulously adjudicating the understandable disputes that the textual history has occasioned.

Great Expectations, as we now meet it, closes with expectations still opening for Pip:

> 'Glad to part again, Estella? To me parting is a painful thing. To me, the remembrance of our last parting has been ever mournful and painful.'
>   'But you said to me,' returned Estella, very earnestly, '"God bless you, God forgive you!" And if you could say that to me then, you will not hesitate to say that to me now—now, when suffering has been stronger than all other teaching, and has taught me to understand what your heart used to be. I have been bent and broken, but—I

[29] No question-mark to complete 'And shall I...' (there is no question as to the answer); recorded by Richard Woodhouse, July (?) 1820. *The Keats Circle*, ed. by Hyder Edward Rollins, 2 vols. (Cambridge: Harvard University Press, 1965), 1: 128–29. Woodhouse's revisions are not given above.
[30] John Butt and Kathleen Tillotson, *Dickens at Work* (London: Methuen, 1957), 231.

hope—into a better shape. Be as considerate and good to me as you were, and tell me we are friends.'

'We are friends,' said I, rising and bending over her, as she rose from the bench.

'And will continue friends apart,' said Estella.

I took her hand in mine, and we went out of the ruined place; and, as the morning mists had risen long ago when I first left the forge, so the evening mists were rising now, and in all the broad expanse of tranquil light they showed to me, I saw no shadow of another parting from her.[31]

But at the proof stage for the volume publication of 1862, the ending had been significantly other. Pip is in London, with 'little Pip', Joe Gargery's child, and they meet Estella; her first, brutal, husband having died, she has married again:

I was in England again—in London, and walking along Piccadilly with little Pip— when a servant came running after me to ask would I step back to a lady in a carriage who wished to speak to me. It was a little pony carriage, which the lady was driving; and the lady and I looked sadly enough on one another.

'I am greatly changed, I know, but I thought you would like to shake hands with Estella too, Pip. Lift up that pretty child and let me kiss it!' (She supposed the child, I think, to be my child.)

I was very glad afterwards to have had the interview; for, in her face and in her voice, and in her touch, she gave me the assurance, that suffering had been stronger than Miss Havisham's teaching, and had given her a heart to understand what my heart used to be.[32]

This ending first saw the tranquil light of day within the third volume of John Forster's *Life of Charles Dickens* in 1874. It has come to be characterized as the unhappy ending. (Not that this would be an easy or simple judgement.) The so-called happy ending (likewise) had replaced it for publication in 1862. Dickens wrote to Forster on 1 July 1861, crediting or debiting Edward Bulwer Lytton:

You will be surprised to hear that I have changed the end of *Great Expectations* from and after Pip's return to Joe's, and finding his little likeness there. Bulwer, who has been, as I think you know, extraordinarily taken by the book, so strongly urged it upon me, after reading the proofs, and supported his views with such good reasons, that I resolved to make the change. You shall have it when you come back to town. I have put in as pretty a little piece of writing as I could, and I have no doubt the story will be more acceptable through the alteration.[33]

[31] Previously, 'I saw the shadow of no parting from her.' This is the reading in 'all texts earlier than 1862 (the serial versions, first edition [1861], and early American editions based on *All the Year Round*)', Charles Dickens, *Great Expectations*, ed. Edgar Rosenberg (New York: Norton, 1999), 501.

[32] John Forster, *The Life of Charles Dickens*, 3 vols. (London: Chapman and Hall, 1872–4), 3: 336.

[33] Charles Dickens, *The Letters of Charles Dickens*, ed. Graham Storey, 12 vols. (Oxford: Clarendon Press, 2002), 9: 432–33.

Ominous, the blithe invoking there of the 'more acceptable' and of 'as pretty a little piece of writing as I could'. Whose novel is it anyway? Before setting about Dickens's novel, Bulwer Lytton had entitled one of his own *My Novel*.

How self-critical is Dickens's self-criticism here? It is sometimes the mark of genius to be provoked into reconsideration by the urgings of someone who is no genius. But here there is a sense that Dickens, one of the least deferential of men, is deferring to Bulwer Lytton. And deferring to a public, or a guess about the public, in a way that falls short of Dickens's usual ability to respect his readers. Ever since Forster's revelation of the earlier ending, the hearts of readers have had to engage with what Dickens's novel used to be.

> Do I know how I feel? Do I know what I think?
> Let me take ink and paper, let me take pen and ink...[34]

T.S. Eliot thought about 'intelligence, of which an important function is the discernment of exactly what, and how much, we feel in any given situation'.[35] All the more taxing when we find ourselves not in a given situation but in two different situations given by a novelist of genius. (If only the novel were a performing art, permitting of multiple versions, like the art of song...)

Constituting creative self-criticism on the most ample scale is the entire re-fashioning of an enterprise. This, which never comes easily to any creator, is sometimes precipitated by effective criticism from others (as it is on a smaller scale with Dickens, Bulwer, and *Great Expectations*). One of the most effective forms of criticism may of course be censorship, or worse; one recalls Shelley on *Paradise Lost*:

> Milton gives the Devil all imaginable advantage; and the arguments with which he exposes the injustice and impotent weakness of his adversary are such as, had they been printed distinct from the shelter of any dramatic order, would have been answered by the most conclusive of syllogisms—persecution.[36]

A differently effective form of criticism is the rejection slip. Yet this may then turn out to be something that posterity will have cause to welcome. For had not the publishers in 1932 rejected *Dream of Fair to middling Women*, we should never have had Beckett's *More Pricks than Kicks* (1934), which comparison shows to be an incomparably more

[34] T.S. Eliot's ellipsis in *Inventions of the March Hare: Poems 1909–1917*, ed. Christopher Ricks (New York: Harcourt Brace, 1996), 80–81, 274–78. Eliot briefly thought himself entitled to *He do the police in different voices* for *The Waste Land*; he had an uncertain respect for Dickens ('the terribly serious, even savage comic humour, the humour which spent its last breath in the decadent genius of Dickens'); T.S. Eliot, 'Christopher Marlowe' [1919], *Selected Essays* [1932] (London: Faber & Faber, 1951), 123.

[35] T.S. Eliot, 'Reflections on Contemporary Poetry, III', *The Egoist* 4, no. 10 (November 1917), 151.

[36] Percy Bysshe Shelley, 'Essay on the Devil and Devils', *Shelley's Prose*, ed. D.L. Clark (Albuquerque: University of New Mexico Press, 1954), 267.

successful conversion of chaos into cosmos.[37] And had not *The Professor* been repeatedly rejected, we should never have had what is for some of us a novel greater even than *Jane Eyre*, Charlotte Brontë's *Villette* (1853). The editors of the Oxford edition (1987) of *The Professor*, Margaret Smith and Herbert Rosengarten, record that on 15 July 1847, after the manuscript had suffered its sixth rejection, Charlotte Brontë sent it to the London firm of Smith, Elder. They add that, writing as *he* (Currer Bell), she described the publisher's response in the 'Biographical Notice' of 1850:

> Ere long, in a much shorter space than that on which experience had taught him to calculate—there came a letter, which he opened in the dreary expectation of finding two hard hopeless lines, intimating that Messrs. Smith, Elder and Co. 'were not disposed to publish the MS.,' and, instead, he took out of the envelope a letter of two pages. He read it trembling. It declined, indeed, to publish that tale, for business reasons, but it discussed its merits and demerits so courteously, so considerately, in a spirit so rational, with a discrimination so enlightened, that this very refusal cheered the author better than a vulgarly-expressed acceptance would have done.[38]

Jane Eyre being published in October 1847, within two months Charlotte Brontë returned to the novel that had been rejected:

> A few days since I looked over 'the Professor.' I found the beginning very feeble, the whole narrative deficient in incident and in general attractiveness; yet the middle and latter portion of the work, all that relates to Brussels, the Belgian school &c. is as good as I can write; it contains more pith, more substance, more reality, in my judgment, than much of 'Jane Eyre.' It gives, I think, a new view of a grade, an occupation, and a class of characters—all very common-place, very insignificant in themselves, but not more so than the materials composing that portion of 'Jane Eyre' which seems to please most generally—.
>
> My wish is to recast 'the Professor,' add as well as I can, what is deficient, retrench some parts, develop others—and make of it a 3-vol. work; no easy task, I know, yet I trust not an impracticable one.[39]

Far from scrapping *The Professor*, Brontë imagines in strikingly practical terms how to make it into a publishable three-volume novel. She has no doubt as to the value of the Belgian part of the novel (so much 'more' than the successful *Jane Eyre*), so the recasting and retrenching do not present themselves as a re-envisioning. To re-envision would be to begin again, which she in due course does. 'Much of the Brussels material would

---

[37] *Dream of Fair to middling Women*, ed. Eoin O'Brien and Edith Fournier, was published by the Black Cat Press in 1992 and by John Calder in 1993.

[38] Charlotte Brontë, *The Professor*, ed. Margaret Smith and Herbert Rosengarten (Oxford: Clarendon Press, 1987), xvii.

[39] Brontë to W.S. Williams, 14 December 1847, in *Selected Letters of Charlotte Brontë*, ed. Margaret Smith (Oxford: Oxford University Press, 2007), 93.

reappear, though greatly transformed, in *Villette*.' It was in 1855 that Charlotte Brontë's first and deepest biographer,[40] E.C. Gaskell, was told by the widower, Mr A.B. Nicholls, that 'he had the manuscript of *The Professor* in his possession; but he would not let Mrs. Gaskell see it, "saying that whole pages of it had been embodied in *Villette*".'[41] Two years later, *The Professor* was published, with a Preface by Nicholls. *The Professor* is alive with things to be grateful for, but we should be even more grateful to the publishers who rejected it and who thereby made possible *Villette*, a work not only of genius, genius that, prompted by criticism from without, duly profited by criticism from within, the novelist as self-critic.

III

Those of us who engage in literary studies have come to adopt the term *poet-critic* in paying homage to a noble line within English literature, from Ben Jonson, Dryden, Samuel Johnson, Wordsworth, Coleridge, and Keats, through the pre-eminent Victorians Matthew Arnold and Gerard Hopkins, and on to T.S. Eliot, William Empson, W.H. Auden, Robert Graves, Donald Davie, and Geoffrey Hill. If the present essay on *the novelist as critic* turns now for a few pages to the Victorian *poet-critic*, this is not (or not mostly) in order to change the subject to one where the essayer believes himself to be better qualified, but to provide a reminder of how criticism is felt on the pulses, and to provide touchstones of the kind that Arnold proposed, on this occasion not from poetry but from criticism of poetry.

Tennyson is here the poet, Arnold the critic:

> Yet all experience is an arch wherethro'
> Gleams that untravell'd world, whose margin fades
> For ever and for ever when I move.[42]

It is no blame to the thought of those lines, which belongs to another order of ideas than Homer's, but it is true, that Homer would certainly have said of them, 'It is to consider too curiously to consider so'. It is no blame to their rhythm, which belongs to another order of movement than Homer's, but it is true that these three lines by themselves take up nearly as much time as a whole book of the *Iliad*.[43]

---

[40] The artistic achievement that is Gaskell's *Life of Charlotte Brontë* (1857), which has suffered condescension of late, is esteemed by me in *Essays in Appreciation*, 118–45.

[41] Brontë, *The Professor*, xxiv–xxv.

[42] Tennyson, 'Ulysses', Eversley Edition, 2: 27.

[43] Matthew Arnold, 'On Translating Homer, III' [1861], *On the Classical Tradition*, in *The Complete Prose Works of Matthew Arnold*, 11 vols. ed. R.H. Super (Ann Arbor: University of Michigan Press, 1960–77), 1: 147. Yet the commentator on Homer nods, misquoting five words of the three lines (corrected above).

Arnold here achieves something no less remarkable than 'What oft was *Thought*, but ne'er so well *Exprest*', for he expresses, with succinct simplicity, something (something mysterious, moreover) that I for one had not thought, would not have been capable of thinking, but can now never *not* have in mind—while no longer needing *consciously* to have it there—whenever I read these lines from one of Tennyson's greatest poems or the many other lines in Tennyson that evince this haunting quality, this extraordinary disposition towards time. Arnold's characterization of the Tennyson lines is neither blame nor acclaim; it is an appeal, pure and simple, from a sensibility to other sensibilities, that is accompanied by a surge of explanatory power. It is itself a touchstone. It is curiously yet aptly tinged with comedy, in the asseveration that Homer would certainly have said some words that would come to be said in an age between Homer's and Tennyson's, the words not of Homer but of Horatio in *Hamlet*. In no way a digression from Arnold's central question—in what verse-form might it be best to translate Homer?—the critical demonstration is persuasively at one with the account elsewhere in Arnold of a principle creative and critical: 'The superior character of truth and seriousness, in the matter and substance of the best poetry, is inseparable from the superiority of diction and movement marking its style and manner. The two superiorities are closely related, and are in steadfast proportion one to the other.'[44] Exactly valuable, this, in its not permitting *inseparable* to slide into the distortive sentimentality of *indistinguishable*. The two superiorities are distinguishable though not distinct.

Again Tennyson, but this time with Hopkins the critic. Again, a classic achievement of criticism, with a principle that precipitates an instance that then itself flowers into a further principle:

> Great men, poets I mean, have each their own dialect as it were of Parnassian, formed generally as they go on writing, and at last,—this is the point to be marked,—they can see things in this Parnassian way and describe them in this Parnassian tongue, without further effort of inspiration. In a poet's particular kind of Parnassian lies most of his style, of his manner, of his mannerism if you like. But I must not go farther without giving you instances of Parnassian. I shall take one from Tennyson, and from *Enoch Arden*, from a passage much quoted already and which will be no doubt often quoted, the description of Enoch's tropical island.

> > The mountain wooded to the peak, the lawns
> > And winding glades high up like ways to Heaven,
> > The slender coco's drooping crown of plumes,
> > The lightning flash of insect and of bird,
> > The lustre of the long convolvuluses

---

[44] Matthew Arnold, 'The Study of Poetry' [1880], *English Literature and Irish Politics*, in *The Complete Prose Works of Matthew Arnold*, 9: 171.

> That coil'd around the stately stems, and ran
> Ev'n to the limit of the land, the glows
> And glories of the broad belt of the world,
> All these he saw.

> Now it is a mark of Parnassian that one could conceive oneself writing it if one were the poet. Do not say that *if* you were Shakespear you can imagine yourself writing *Hamlet*, because that is just what I think you can*not* conceive.[45]

The contrast of Parnassian with inspiration is itself inspired, markedly in the last leap. For it is a mark of Hopkins's genius that though I could, I suppose, conceive of myself coming up with some distinction between the inspired and the not inspired, I cannot conceive of myself creating the penetrating terms of this principle itself. Do not say that *if* you were Hopkins you can imagine yourself writing these sentences, because that is just what I think you can*not* conceive.[46]

Criticism as humanely penetrating as Arnold on Tennyson, or Hopkins on Tennyson, is of rare value. But among the poet-critics, it is to be found. Before turning to the related question—can criticism of such worth be found among the novelist-critics?—there are clearly concessions that have to be made. For although the tradition of the poet-critic is a remarkable one, there is no point in denying that there have always been poets who are *not* critics, and perhaps that it is the Victorian age where this is most manifestly the case. Take Browning. An uninspired essay on Shelley, or rather on Shelley's letters. Take Tennyson. Although he exercised fine critical judgement in helping F.T. Palgrave to create the best anthology of English verse, *The Golden Treasury* (1861), and although his off-the-cuff remarks were right on target (Shelley seems to go up and burst, Wordsworth is thick-ankled), Tennyson did not write criticism, and neither he nor we should repine at this.[47] Or take Hardy. His love of William Barnes did triumph over his disinclination to set his pen to critical papers, but that was about it. So we should not exaggerate the poet-critic into ubiquity, especially in Victorian England.

The term *critic-poet* (used by Herbert Read in 1938) yielded to *poet-critic*, the provenance being the learned journals: *Essays in Criticism* (1956), 'Poet-critics as dissimilar as Arthur Symons and Mr. Eliot', and *English Studies* (1964), 'Of course a poet-critic may be allowed to speak in images'.[48] We may be allowed to speak in homages, but the homage that is *poet-critic* does not have a parallel that is *novelist-critic*, or

---

[45] Hopkins to A.W.M. Baillie, 10 September 1864, *Further Letters of Gerard Manley Hopkins*, 2nd edn, ed. Claude Colleer Abbott (London: Oxford University Press, 1956), 216–17 (*Enoch Arden* had been published the previous month).

[46] I draw on an essay of mine, 'Literary Principles as against Theory', *Essays in Appreciation*, 329.

[47] For the collaboration, see my edition of *The Golden Treasury* (London: Penguin, 1991).

[48] *OED*.

critic-novelist, come to that, although *critic-dramatist* is recorded in the *Westminster Gazette*, 1906.[49]

IV

The compounded compliment *novelist-critic* would recognize, as *poet-critic* often does, genius doubly manifested. Perhaps we rarely feel the need for the term *novelist-critic* because we rarely encounter the phenomenon. Granted, each of the great Victorian novelists incarnates the particular element of *the novelist as critic* with which this outline began: creation as itself criticism, whether of others' art or of one's own. But what of the further, the discursive, activity, valuable and indispensable in its way?

Criticism is the art of noticing things that the rest of us may well not have noticed for ourselves and might never have noticed. It asks tact, of itself and of its readers, for it must neither state nor neglect the obvious. And whether something is obvious may not be obvious. At its best, criticism participates in the higher reaches of art itself: noticing relations between the things that it notices. But so far as criticism goes, the attending is primarily to art, more than to all the other things which together with art make up the world. Criticism is not a service industry but a service art, one that begins with the asking of crucial questions, a necessary (not a sufficient) condition of seizing crucial answers.

It is not difficult to adduce criticism of the novel, by Victorian novelists of genius, for which one can be grateful. But the gratitude is for the serviceable, the shrewd, the apt, and the historically pertinent, all fine in their way but all falling short of the penetrative surprise that characterizes criticism that is, in both senses, *of genius*, and that can then amount to a touchstone of the critical art.

For instance, George Eliot's essay on 'Silly Novels by Lady Novelists' (*Westminster Review*, October 1856) is never less than markedly intelligent, and it is—as her modern editor says—'of special interest as a record of George Eliot's thoughts about the writing of fiction made just at the time when she began her first story'.[50] It has the value that attends upon any critical enterprise that is essentially hygienic, given that the fashionable

---

[49] Leavis dubs Henry James *poet-novelist* (*The Great Tradition*, 12). A different story, though not a persuasive one as characterized by Leavis: 'It was the profundity of the pondering that I had in mind when I referred to him as a "poet-novelist"' (*The Great Tradition*, 128). Aware of the unthinking disparagement of the novel, Leavis sought to raise the standing of novels by calling them dramatic poems ('The Novel as Dramatic Poem', a series in *Scrutiny*), but there was a price to be paid in the misleading implication that poetry is inherently better than prose and that a truly great novel attains poemhood. I contested such prejudice against prose in my inaugural lecture as Professor of Poetry at Oxford, 'All Praise to Proper Words', in *Times Literary Supplement*, 25 February 2005, 13–15.

[50] Thomas Pinney, *Essays of George Eliot* (New York: Columbia University Press, 1963), 300–301.

novels that George Eliot deplores, of 'the *maid-and-millinery* species', are deplorable. But silly novels by lady novelists cannot, by their nature, elicit the greatest criticism, any more than a bad play can elicit the greatest acting. 'The Natural History of German Life', three months earlier in the *Westminster Review* (July 1856), can briefly breathe a larger air because of the spirit of Dickens: 'We have one great novelist who is gifted with the utmost power of rendering the external traits of our town population; and if he could give us their psychological character—their conceptions of life, and their emotions— with the same truth as their idiom and manners, his books would be the greatest contribution Art has ever made to the awakening of social sympathies.'[51] (Yes, the next word is *But.*) Not self-evidently true, this characterization of Dickens's genius, but self-evidently worth thinking about. Yet it does not acknowledge any critical problems. Dickens tells the truth in idiom and manners, we are assured; are these, then, so assuredly separable from truth of psychological character, of emotions, and of conceptions of life? Do not idioms and manners often prove to be character in action?

The gratitude we may feel for such criticism is of a lesser order than that which George Eliot's novels elicit. The notable critic W.W. Robson used to say in class, when something from Victorian literature was found wanting, 'Well, yes, of course, but better than you or I could do.' Agreed, as to George Eliot on Dickens. But now compare the better to the best. Do not say that *if* you were Eliot you can imagine yourself writing *Middlemarch*, because that is just what I think you can*not* conceive.

For to read the Victorian novelists on the Victorian novel may entail concluding, regretfully and respectfully, that they mostly duck wholehearted critical engagement. Trollope offered advice to George Eliot: 'Do not fire too much over the heads of your readers.'[52] It was in this spirit that he himself penned 'On English Prose Fiction as a Rational Amusement' (1870), which, although it may now have its historical interest, offers as criticism little more than rational amusement.

If we call to mind the many volumes in the *Critical Heritage* series, responsibly representative as they are, and duly eager to muster distinctive criticism, it is remarkable how seldom the novelists themselves achieve criticism that is remarkable, anything that moves beyond summary, the under-described, the unimpinging. *Needless to say*, one finds oneself saying to oneself. Needless to say, the patent and patient exception is Henry James, the novelist-critic *par excellence*.

It is not that Dickens forbore to write criticism, for there stand *Household Words* and *All the Year Round*, journals of his that are not exactly alive with criticism but are on occasion alive to it, and there are the letters and the prefaces to the novels. But, as criticism, he never noticed anything about a novel (as against his having a genius for noticing things within his own novels) that could begin to compare with what he

---

    [51] Pinney, *Essays of George Eliot*, 271.
    [52] Trollope to George Eliot, *The Letters of Anthony Trollope*, ed. N. John Hall, 2 vols. (Stanford: Stanford University Press, 1983), 1: 187.

registered, for instance, about what might seem to be the poor relation of a novel, the art of pantomime:

> How came I, it may be asked, on the day after Christmas Day, of all days in the year, to be hovering outside Saint Luke's [Hospital for the Insane], after dark, when I might have betaken myself to that jocund world of Pantomime, where there is no affliction or calamity that leaves the least impression; where a man may tumble into the broken ice, or dive into the kitchen fire, and only be the droller for the accident; where babies may be knocked about and sat upon, or choked with gravy spoons, in the process of feeding, and yet no Coroner be wanted, nor anybody made uncomfortable; where workmen may fall from the top of a house to the bottom, or even from the bottom of a house to the top, and sustain no injury to the brain, need no hospital, leave no young children; where every one, in short, is so superior to the accidents of life, though encountering them at every turn, that I suspect it to be the secret (though many persons may not present it to themselves) of the general enjoyment which an audience of vulnerable spectators, liable to pain and sorrow, find in this class of entertainment.[53]

It is *or even from the bottom of a house to the top* that does it, a feat not just of acrobatic wording but of critical acumen, soaring into the ways of the imagination within this class not just of entertainment but of art. The leap is from a Hospital for the Insane to what, wrongly considered, might be taken for the insanity of the goings-on in the jocund world of Pantomime, a world that understands the therapeutic as finely as does the world of the circus.

Sometimes it will be anger's freeing power that liberates critical writing from the conventional, the craven, or the pious.[54] So it is that Charlotte Brontë's low estimate of Jane Austen rises to substantial criticism that is worthy of the enterprise of substantiation:

> I have likewise read one of Miss Austen's works 'Emma'—read it with interest and with just the degree of admiration which Miss Austen herself would have thought sensible and suitable—anything like warmth or enthusiasm; anything energetic, poignant, heart-felt, is utterly out of place in commending these works: all such demonstration the authoress would have met with a well-bred sneer, would have calmly scorned as outré and extravagant. She does her business of delineating the surface of the lives of genteel English people curiously well; there is a Chinese fidelity, a miniature delicacy in the painting: she ruffles her reader by nothing vehement, disturbs him by nothing profound: the Passions are perfectly unknown to her; she rejects even a speaking

[53] Charles Dickens, 'A Curious Dance Round a Curious Tree', *Household Words*, 17 January 1852 (with W.H. Wills), in *The Uncollected Writings of Charles Dickens: Household Words 1850–1859*, ed. Harry Stone, 2 vols. (Bloomington: Indiana University Press, 1968), 2: 383–84.

[54] See Stevie Smith's powerful poem about a freed bird, concluding: 'Anger it was that won him hence/ As only Anger taught him sense.//Often my tears fall in a shower/Because of anger's freeing power', Stevie Smith, *Collected Poems* (New York: Oxford University Press, 1976), 321.

acquaintance with that stormy Sisterhood; even to the Feelings she vouchsafes no more than an occasional graceful but distant recognition; too frequent converse with them would ruffle the smooth elegance of her progress. Her business is not half so much with the human heart as with the human eyes, mouth, hands and feet; what sees keenly, speaks aptly, moves flexibly, it suits her to study, but what throbs fast and full, though hidden, what the blood rushes through, what is the unseen seat of Life and the sentient target of Death—this Miss Austen ignores; she no more, with her mind's eye, beholds the heart of her race than each man, with bodily vision sees the heart in his heaving breast. Jane Austen was a complete and most sensible lady, but a very incomplete, and rather insensible (not senseless) woman; if this is heresy—I cannot help it. If I said it to some people (Lewes for instance) they would directly accuse me of advocating exaggerated heroics; but I am not afraid of your falling into any such vulgar error.

    Believe me
    Yours sincerely
    C. Brontë[55]

Believe her, this is said sincerely. We are in the presence of a classic statement of a perennial judgement that must not be waived, particularly by those who would contest it; itself deserving at least the compliment of rational opposition; and at one point, in its imaginative depth, achieving the power of a critical touchstone: 'what throbs fast and full, though hidden, what the blood rushes through, what is the unseen seat of Life and the sentient target of Death'.

    Yet when she confronted a novel that did comprehend 'the unseen seat of Life and the sentient target of Death', she could not but vacillate. Writing the Editor's Preface to the New Edition of her sister's *Wuthering Heights* (1850), she half-acknowledges 'what are termed (and, perhaps, really are) its faults'; she adduces Austen-type readers (men and woman 'naturally very calm, and with feelings moderate in degree'), understandingly enough though not without condescension; and she is concessive to the point of all-but-surrender: 'Whether it is right or advisable to create beings like Heathcliff, I do not know: I scarcely think it is.' (*Advisable*: such a word belongs rather to the world of Jane Austen.) She continues: 'But this I know; the writer who possesses the creative gift owns something of which he is not always master—something that at times strangely wills and works for itself.' And she concludes: 'If the result be attractive the world will

---

[55] Brontë to W.S. Williams, 12 April 1850, in *Selected Letters of Charlotte Brontë*, 161–62. (Retaining this edition's underlining, not converted to italics.) A similar vein had been opened in a letter to G.H. Lewes, 12 January 1848: 'I had not seen "Pride & Prejudice" till I read that sentence of yours, and then I got the book and studied it. And what did I find? An accurate daguerreotyped portrait of a common-place face; a carefully-fenced, highly cultivated garden with neat borders and delicate flowers—but no glance of a bright vivid physiognomy—no open country—no blue hill—no bonny beck. I should hardly like to live with her ladies and gentlemen in their elegant but confined houses. These observations will probably irritate you, but I shall run the risk', *Selected Letters of Charlotte Brontë*, 99.

praise you, who little deserve praise; if it be repulsive, the same world will blame you, who almost as little deserve blame.'[56]

Repulsive: it is in such terms that Matthew Arnold blames *Villette*:

> Miss Brontë has written a hideous undelightful convulsed constricted novel—what does Thackeray say to it. It is one of the most utterly disagreeable books I ever read— and having seen her makes it more so. She is so entirely—what Margaret Fuller was partially—a fire without aliment—one of the most distressing barren sights one can witness. Religion or devotion or whatever it is to be called may be impossible for such people now: but they have at any rate not found a substitute for it and it was better for the world when they comforted themselves with it.[57]

> Why is Villette disagreeable? Because the writer's mind contains nothing but hunger rebellion and rage—and therefore that is all she can in fact put into her book. No fine writing can hide this thoroughly—and it will be fatal to her in the long run.[58]

Such writing is itself convulsed, constricted, and disagreeable—particularly from a critic who justly prided himself on urbanity. But Arnold has manifestly seized upon *something* that a reader needs to reckon with, not as a matter of the authority attaching to Arnold but as inviting attention not only to 'spilt religion'[59] and its acids, but to how a work of art may indeed *contain* (a pregnant word), and not merely vent, the satanic trinity of hunger, rebellion, and rage.

A caveat: that it is a marked feature of such living criticism as Brontë on Austen, or Arnold on Brontë, that it is to be found in letters, which permit of indiscretion. Discretion may be the better part of valour but it is the worst part of criticism.

V

If, then, the Victorian novelists of genius do not show themselves to be novelist-critics of genius, where is the most illuminating and challenging criticism of the Victorian novel to be found? It is to be found then and thereabouts, in the guild of writers who constitute one of the accomplishments of Victorian England: the men of letters. It is in John Ruskin and Edward FitzGerald, in Sir James Fitzjames Stephen and Richard Holt Hutton, in Walter Bagehot and G.H. Lewes, plus those who are not their likes (there is no such

---

[56] Included in *Emily Brontë: A Critical Anthology*, ed. Jean-Pierre Petit (Harmondsworth: Penguin, 1973).

[57] Arnold to Clough, 21 March 1853, *The Letters of Matthew Arnold*, ed. Cecil Y. Lang, 6 vols. (Charlottesville: University of Virginia Press, 2001), 1: 258.

[58] Arnold to his sister Jane ('K'), 14 April 1853, *The Letters of Matthew Arnold*, 1: 262.

[59] T.E. Hulme: 'Romanticism then, and this is the best definition I can give of it, is spilt religion', ('Romanticism and Classicism' [1911–12], *Speculations* (1924), in *The Collected Writings of T.E. Hulme*, ed. Karen Csengeri (Oxford: Clarendon Press, 1994), 62.

thing as a *like* to Ruskin or FitzGerald . . .), that we encounter critics who delight us with the power to notice and to make us think.

Take Bagehot on Thackeray and his thinking:

> He could gauge a man's reality as well as any observer, and far better than most: his attainments were great, his perception of men instinctive, his knowledge of casual matters enormous; but he had a greater difficulty than other men in relying only upon his own judgment. 'What the footman—what Mr. Yellowplush Jeames would think and say,' could not but occur to his mind, and would modify, not his settled judgment, but his transient and casual opinion of the poet or philosopher. By the constitution of his mind he thought much of social distinctions, and yet he was in his writings too severe on those who, in cruder and baser ways, showed that they also were thinking much.[60]

Or the studied thoughtfulness with which the English novel is compared to the French:

> We pay our writers to be moral, and they are moral. But the French have no such custom; on the contrary, a French novelist is rather expected to be immoral. Among the purchasers of such works, probably the majority would feel *hurt* if they contained no scenes which English morals would forbid, and which English women would shrink from. A mere infraction of the marriage vow is too trifling a peccadillo, if indeed it is even a peccadillo, to be the subject of an exciting narrative. Dumas *fils* has indeed contrived to render it proper for modern art. His '*Roman d'une Femme*' entirely turns on such an event; but he escaped the vice of commonplace by making the wife love her husband, and *not* love her lover all the while that she is guilty of adultery with her lover; and thus contrived to make the situation sufficiently *piquant*.[61]

It is delicious that the word is not piquant but *piquant*, and that the word is in audible touch with that repeated 'peccadillo'. Such acknowledgement of titillation plays its sly part within the national distinction that the critic is drawing and drawing upon.

Bagehot has his apt levity, Ruskin his gravity, his deep dismay at the death-dealing world of Dickens, which Ruskin challenges in the conviction that such both is and is not the world, for it is the world sensationalized and indurated:

> The monotony of life in the central streets of any great modern city, but especially in those of London, where every emotion intended be derived by men from the sight of nature, or the sense of art, is forbidden for ever, leaves the craving of the heart for a sincere, yet changeful, interest to be fed from one source only.

---

[60] Walter Bagehot, 'Sterne and Thackeray', *National Review*, April 1864, in *Literary Essays*, ed. Norman St John-Stevas, 2 vols. (London: The Economist, 1965), 2: 309–10.

[61] From a review of *La Griffe Rose* (by Armand Renaud) in *The Spectator*, 13 September 1862; the attribution to Bagehot, proposed by W.D. Paden, is credited by Stevas in *Literary Essays*, 2: 263–64.

Ruskin's convictions and indictments inhabit the tragic city-world of Tennyson's *Maud*, of Baudelaire, and of T.S. Eliot:

> It might have been thought by any other than a sternly tentative philosopher, that the denial of their natural food to human feelings would have provoked a reactionary desire for it; and that the dreariness of the street would have been gilded by dreams of a pastoral felicity. Experience has shown the fact to be otherwise; the thoroughly trained Londoner can enjoy no more excitement than that to which he has been accustomed, but asks for *that* in continually more ardent or more virulent concentration; and the ultimate power of fiction to entertain is by varying to his fancy the modes, and defining for his dullness the horrors, of Death. In the single novel of *Bleak House* there are nine deaths (or left for deaths, in the drop scene) carefully wrought out or led up to, either by way of pleasing surprise, as the baby's at the brickmaker's, or finished in their threatenings and sufferings, with as much enjoyment as can be contrived in the anticipation, and as much pathology as can be concentrated in the description. Under the following varieties of method:

One by assassination	Mr Tulkinghorn
One by starvation, with phthisis	Joe
One by chagrin	Richard
One by spontaneous combustion	Mr Krook
One by sorrow	Lady Dedlock's lover
One by remorse	Lady Dedlock
One by insanity	Miss Flite
One by paralysis	Sir Leicester

> Besides the baby, by fever, and a lively young French woman left to be hanged.[62]

It is the grim comedy of *One by chagrin*, and *Besides the baby*, and *lively*, that brings this home. We should ask of such criticism not only 'Is this true?' but 'What truth is there in it?' For Ruskin has assuredly seized upon something, and in such criticism we experience what Empson admired in pastoral: 'the sense of richness (readiness for argument not pursued)'.[63]

But waiting in the wings throughout these pages there has been the exception, unignorable because of what he gave that is unignorable: Henry James, the Victorian novelist of genius who is the novelist-critic of genius, the first such (*first* in both senses). As the reviewer of Dickens and *Our Mutual Friend* ('it is one of the chief conditions of his genius not to see beneath the surface of things'); of George Eliot and *Middlemarch* ('If we write novels so, how shall we write History?'); of Trollope and *Can You Forgive Her?* ('The question is, Can we forgive Miss Vavasor? Of course we can, and forget her,

---

[62] John Ruskin, 'Fiction, Fair and Foul', *Nineteenth Century*, June 1880, in *Charles Dickens: A Critical Anthology*, ed. Wall, 211–15.

[63] William Empson, 'Marvell's Garden', in *Some Versions of Pastoral* (London: Chatto & Windus, 1935), 145.

too, for that matter'); of Hardy and *Far from the Madding Crowd* ('Everything human in the book strikes us as factitious and insubstantial; the only things we believe in are the sheep and the dogs'): these become touchstones not only because of their memorability but because they are points not scored or made but raised in the service of authentic criticism.[64] The same goes for James's critical commentaries on his own novels, for instance in the Preface (1908) to *What Maisie Knew*, in the New York Edition:

> To live with all intensity and perplexity and felicity in its terribly mixed little world would thus be the part of my interesting small mortal; bringing people together who would be at least more correctly separate; keeping people separate who would be at least more correctly together; flourishing, to a degree, at the cost of many conventions and proprieties, even decencies; really keeping the torch of virtue alive in an air tending infinitely to smother it; really in short making confusion worse confounded by drawing some stray fragrance of an ideal across the scent of selfishness, by sowing on barren strands, through the mere fact of presence, the seed of the moral life.[65]

This is the real thing. See the felicity, and surprise, of the word *felicity* there. Here is a genuinely imaginative attention to the ways of the imagination, James's but not James's alone. And the same is true of his engagement with *the novel*, as against a particular novel by himself or by another. 'The Art of Fiction' demonstrates the art of criticism. When James says, in 1884, that such-and-such is still the case, we need to acknowledge that it still remains the case and moreover needs to do so, since these are the contentions and the contentiousness that the novel insists are at stake and that it must not make the mistake of wishing away:

> It is still expected, though perhaps people are ashamed to say it, that a production which is after all only a 'make-believe' (for what else is a 'story'?) shall be in some degree apologetic—shall renounce the pretension of attempting really to represent life. This, of course, any sensible, wide-awake story declines to do, for it quickly perceives that the tolerance granted to it on such a condition is only an attempt to stifle it disguised in the form of generosity. The old evangelical hostility to the novel, which was as explicit as it was narrow, and which regarded it as little less favourable to our immortal part than a stage-play, was in reality far less insulting.[66]

It is in large part thanks to James that what in due course succeeded the Victorian novelists' protracted inability to illuminate the novel with enduring criticism (as against the admittedly even more valuable thing, their ability to write enduringly illuminating

[64] James, *Essays on Literature: American Writer, English Writers*, 856, 965–66, 1048, 1318.
[65] Henry James, *The Novels and Tales of Henry James*, vol. 11: *What Maisie Knew, In the Cage, The Pupil. Literary Criticism*, vol. 2: *French Writers, Other European Writers, The Prefaces to the New York Edition*, ed. Leon Edel and Mark Wilson (New York: Library of America, 1984), 1158–59.
[66] James, *Essays on Literature: American Writers, English Writers*, 45.

novels) was the extraordinary burst of critical energy in Edwardian and Georgian times: the expansive criticism of the novel and of novels by Henry James himself still, by Virginia Woolf, by D.H. Lawrence, and by E.M. Forster.

Suggested Reading

Arnold, Matthew. 'On Translating Homer, III' [1861]. *On the Classical Tradition*. In *The Complete Prose Works of Matthew Arnold*. Edited by R.H. Super. Ann Arbor: University of Michigan Press, 1960–77.

——. 'The Study of Poetry' [1880]. *English Literature and Irish Politics*. In *The Complete Prose Works of Matthew Arnold*. Edited by R.H. Super. Ann Arbor: University of Michigan Press, 1960–77.

Brontë, Charlotte. *The Professor*. Edited by Margaret Smith and Herbert Rosengarten. Oxford: Clarendon Press, 1987.

——. *Villette*. Edited by Herbert Rosengarten and Margaret Smith. Oxford: Clarendon Press, 1984.

Dickens, Charles. *Great Expectations*. Edited by Edgar Rosenberg. New York: Norton, 1999.

Gross, John. *The Rise and Fall of the Man of Letters*. London: Macmillan, 1969.

James, Henry. *Literary Criticism: Essays on Literature, American Writers & English Writers*. Vol. 1. Edited by Leon Edel. New York: Library of America, 1984.

Leavis, F.R. *The Great Tradition*. London: Chatto & Windus, 1948.

Stang, Richard. *The Theory of the Novel in England, 1850–1870*. New York: Columbia University Press, 1969.

PART IX

··

DISTINGUISHING THE VICTORIAN NOVEL

··

31

THE MORAL SCOPE OF THE ENGLISH *BILDUNGSROMAN*

JULIA PREWITT BROWN

Seeing youth as the most decisive phase of life is a relatively new phenomenon in history. Social historians tell us that it began in the late 18th century, when traditional, agrarian society gave way and the new generation had to contend with a far more uncertain life in the city. Before then, being young simply meant not yet being an adult. You followed a prescribed pattern, and did what your parents did. But with the advent of industrial capitalism, youth became, as Franco Moretti puts it, 'a *problem*'.[1] The coming of age novel or *Bildungsroman* famously appears at this time with the publication of Goethe's *Wilhelm Meister's Apprenticeship* (1795) as a response to the new uncertainties and possibilities of youth.[2] The title of Goethe's novel alone suggests what the experience of maturation now entailed—a particular kind of work undertaken in return for instruction, a test or journey that prepared the hero for life in society.

Yet *Bildungsromane* differ from other novels in more complicated ways than an exclusive attention to historical context would suggest. Whereas one dominant impulse of the nineteenth-century English novel is to reveal the social system as having a life of its own, independent of the human stories with which it may be intertwined, in the Victorian novels that we list under the heading *Bildungsroman*, the development of the individual is integrated with that system. *Bildungsromane* offer something like what Walter Benjamin calls *Rat* or *counsel*.[3] They aim, at least in part, to teach people how to live in the world. Through the archetypal figures of 19th-century *Bildungsromane*—the young man who travels from the provinces to the

---

[1] Franco Moretti, *The Way of the World* (London: Verso, 2000), 4.

[2] The emergence of an idea of youth in Rousseau's *Confessions* and *Émile* influenced Goethe.

[3] Walter Benjamin, 'The Storyteller', in *Illuminations*, trans. Harry Zohn (London: Schocken, 1969), 86–87.

big city and the young woman who has yet to commit herself romantically—the novelist proposed to help readers navigate the new, more democratic and multifaceted social scene. We see this beginning to happen in the *Bildung* plots of Jane Austen and in *Bildungsromane* internationally; the subgenre has a wide reach. It's not so much that in reading, say, Austen's *Northanger Abbey* or Balzac's *Père Goriot* the youthful reader gained advice on how to be a social success; rather, she received counsel as to what she was up against if she wanted to create a meaningful life. When Catherine Morland attends one of her first balls, the narrator alludes to the difficulty of distinguishing sincerity of speech from mere politeness in the increasingly mobile, anonymous social world of Bath. Throughout *Père Goriot*, the narrator periodically interrupts the cynical advance of his narration to point the reader's attention to his hero's compromises of conscience.

Because the *Bildungsroman* imagines the necessity of a narrator-as-moral-guide who often seems like a storyteller in a traditional community of listeners, we can distinguish it from novels that limit this sort of instruction—novels we classify roughly as 'realist'. Consider, for example, the differences between two novels published in the same decade, one a classic *Bildungsroman*, the other a landmark in the history of realism: Dickens's *David Copperfield* and Flaubert's *Madame Bovary*. David's moral growth makes for the central artery of the novel's plot; in telling the story of his life in retrospect, the first person narrator of the *Bildungsroman* illustrates basic truths about falling in love, finding meaningful work, and managing money responsibly that parents in any generation often want their children to know. By the end of the novel, he has created a place for himself in the world, whereas Madame Bovary learns nothing she can profit from and dies by her own hand.

I recognize the baldness of this comparison. As will be shown, David's moral development is by no means simple when placed in the context of fiction as elaborate as that of Dickens. The novel is not a fairy-tale but a realist work with the instructional emphasis of a fairy-tale. The orphaned hero tells the story of his suffering to illustrate his ultimate triumph, but the social landscape against which his moral journey is set is not the landscape of fairy-tale but of class-riven industrial England. The psychological landscape—that of Victorian sexual mores and stereotypes—is equally intractable.

Nevertheless, it is because of this instructional element, this diminished legacy from the archaic tradition of storytelling, that Benjamin suggests that the *Bildungsroman* constitutes a 'modification in the novel form'. The *Bildungsroman* 'does not deviate in any way from the basic structure of the novel', he writes, but by 'integrating the social process with the development of a person, it bestows the most frangible justification on the order determining it. The legitimacy it provides stands in direct opposition to reality. Particularly in the *Bildungsroman*, it is this inadequacy that is actualized.'[4] The *Bildungsroman* then is like a blip in the history of the novel genre: it faces both ways:

---

[4] Walter Benjamin, 'The Storyteller', 88. Benjamin shows the influence of Georg Lukács in these formulations.

backward, towards story, tale, and myth, and forward, towards modern social reality.[5] As a form, it continually undercuts itself in its pursuit of reality, presenting the reader with a tale of the hero's integration into a social process that has all along been represented as inhospitable to human meaning. To take examples from works I shall focus on in this chapter: Austen's caustic evocation of social reality in *Emma* is undermined by the happy marriage ending.[6] Gritty portraits of social subordination in Charlotte Brontë's *Jane Eyre* and *David Copperfield* are subverted by the rags-to-riches story of the protagonists. In *Great Expectations*, the romance of Estella and Pip is given a happy resolution that contradicts all that has preceded it. From their origins in Goethe's novel, the *Bildungsheld* lives under a cloud that never hangs over the hero of a fairy-tale: the storm-cloud of 19th-century social reality. Not that he or she lets this ominous state of affairs get him down for very long, which is where the fairy-tale component of the *Bildung* plot comes into play.

According to Benjamin, fairy-tales communicate 'the earliest arrangements that mankind made to shake off the nightmare which the myth had placed upon its chest'. Take, for example, the familiar tale of Rumpelstiltskin, the dwarf who spins all night turning straw into gold in order to save the miller's daughter from death. Every morning at daybreak she shows the gold to the king, who spares her life. The image suggests sunrise, implying that the older myth embedded in the tale and preceding its invention is a myth explaining why the sun rises and makes things grow. The fairy-tale outwits the myth, shaking off the terrors of the natural world that afflicted our primitive ancestors. 'The wisest thing—so the fairy-tale taught mankind in olden times, and teaches children to this day—is to meet the forces of the mythical world with cunning and with high spirits.'[7]

---

[5] Perhaps for this reason critics of the *Bildungsroman*, such as Jerome Buckley, Gregory Castle, George Levine, and Franco Moretti, tend to either announce its demise or celebrate its longevity. The idea that the *Bildungsroman* tradition either ends or is radically altered with *Jude the Obscure* is common among Victorianists. See George Levine, *How to Read the Victorian Novel* (London: Blackwell, 2007); Jerome Buckley, *Season of Youth: The Bildungsroman from Dickens to Golding* (Cambridge and London: Harvard University Press, 1974), and Gregory Castle, *Reading the Modernist Bildungsroman* (Gainesville: University Press of Florida, 2006).Critics working in a broader European context argue that it ends later, as does Moretti in the new edition of the influential study from which I quoted earlier, *The Way of the World*, when he asserts his belief that the *Bildungsroman* ended in 1914. Yet critics of 20th-century literature locate its reappearance. In *Reading the Modernist Bildungsroman*, Castle establishes that modernist writers effected a 'rehabilitation of the *Bildungsroman* genre' when they adopted the aesthetic educative focus of the original German *Bildungsromane*. (See Moretti, 239 and Castle, 2.) Such 'rehabilitations' persist to the present. Reviews of Benjamin Kunkel's widely praised coming of age novel *Indecision* (2005) characterized it as a postmodern *Bildungsroman*, even while suggesting that this is a contradiction in terms. Considered *en masse* these interpretations contradict one another, yet each is persuasive because of the intrinsically divided nature of the form.

[6] Austen is included here not simply because she is so crucial to the development of the *Bildungsroman* in the 19th century, but also because her work enacts the preoccupation with moral conduct and one particular strain of that preoccupation (discussed in detail later in this chapter) that I see as central to the project of the specifically Victorian *Bildungsroman*.

[7] Benjamin, 'The Storyteller', 102.

What kind of a tale, and by extension, what myth, underlies the *Bildungsroman*? Fairy-tales about growing up—'Snow White', 'Cinderella', 'Hansel and Gretel', and many more—characteristically begin with the loss of a parent. The myth underlying these tales then is one that seeks to explain why parents die, the brutal fact of generational passing. This is the terror that myth imposed on primitive man and that the coming of age fairy-tale so brilliantly beguiles. So close is the *Bildungsroman* to this myth that, like the tales of old, *Bildungsromane* often open by describing the hero's orphaned status. In both tale and novel we are led to believe that if the natural parent had survived, the hero would not have experienced the hardship we witness; the death of the parent is compensated for by the ultimate triumph of the child.

English, French, and German *Bildungsromane* of the 19th century are alike in integrating such fairy-tale elements with the social realities of modern urban life, in spite of the different socio-economic and political contexts informing them. The question then arises: what specifically did the English Victorian *Bildungsroman* bring to this international genre? The answer is deceptively simple: what distinguishes the Victorian or 19th-century *Bildungsroman* from the French and German is its overriding ethical concern, its preoccupation with questions of *conduct* as distinct from questions of personal feeling or romance (what today we call 'relationships')—a distinction, I might add, that is far from obvious to a postmodern generation. (At issue in the proto-Victorian *Emma*, for example, is not Emma's feeling for or friendship with Harriet Smith as much as her conduct in relation to her.) Set beside the German *Bildungsroman*, at any rate, this ethical focus will always seem philosophically naïve. We may recall Nietzsche's scathing dismissal of George Eliot's project to found a 'religion of humanity' or ethical system independent of faith in God.[8] Yet Nietzsche's critique, which I shall return to at the end of this chapter, becomes less daunting when placed beside the English tradition of intense ethical inquiry into secular life, a tradition that I believe begins in the 18th century with writers like Swift and Johnson and continues up through the Victorian novelists and prose writers. Swift, Johnson, Austen, Dickens, and other English writers may themselves have been practising Christians, but their characters (Gulliver, Rasselas, Emma, David Copperfield—to take four examples) do not inhabit a social world in which the Church has living import.

Set beside the French *Bildungsroman* the ethical concerns of the Victorians seem overwrought, the consequence of Puritan repression. To take an example from *Great Expectations*: an early image of Pip's guilt, the bread he steals from Mrs Joe, easily lends itself to psycho-sexual interpretation. Here are Pip's musings about the stolen object he carries in his trousers: 'Conscience is a dreadful thing when it accuses man or boy; but when, in the case of a boy, that secret burden co-operates with another secret burden down the leg of his trousers, it is (as I can testify) a great punishment.'[9] One could read

[8] Friedrich Nietzche, *Twilight of the Idols*, in *The Portable Nietzsche*, ed. Walter Kauffmann (London: Penguin, 1977), 515–16.
[9] Charles Dickens, *Great Expectations* (New York and London: W.W. Norton & Co., 1999), 16.

such assertions of conscience as expressions of sexual guilt were it not for the intricate problems of lying and telling the truth, love and failures of trust—in short, all of the critical human concerns that Pip's obligations to Joe and Magwitch confound him with and that override (without cancelling) the novel's many other strains. My point is that to see the English *Bildungsroman* for what it is and to understand the distinct place it holds in the international house of fiction we need to examine its ethical preoccupations as such.

With this in mind I propose two types of Victorian *Bildungromane*: the *novel of accountability* and the *novel of empowerment*. In the purest examples of the former, *Emma* and *Great Expectations*, the main character's recognition of his or her culpability is the single dramatic event informing all others: the point to which all else either leads up or from which it follows as a consequence. In *novels of empowerment*, like *Jane Eyre* and *David Copperfield*, the main character tries and fails until he or she succeeds in staking his claim to a place in the world. So intrinsically hostile to one another are the twin challenges of coming of age—that of boldly seizing one's place versus that of moral self-scrutiny—that most novels must elevate either one or the other of these tasks. For the two types of *Bildungsroman* derive from the twofold origin of the genre. The drive for empowerment looks back to the fairy-tale; the demands of accountability look forward to modern social experience.

To begin with the novel of accountability: it need hardly be said that the psychological and moral development of the protagonist up to the moment when his humiliation takes place is well-tilled critical ground. What has been overlooked is the novelist's ethical concentration on the aftermath of enlightenment. Eight chapters follow Emma's realization of guilt; nineteen follow Pip's. In the cruder terms of what Oscar Wilde called 'poor, probable, uninteresting human life'—life, unlike art, which is 'terribly deficient in form'—these chapters simply show how people manage to pick themselves up, dust themselves off, and start all over again after they have at last become morally self-sustaining adults.[10] In the language of fiction, however, the post-enlightenment period is not so much a matter of the character's specific conduct or of a resounding plot development, such as a marital engagement, than of the entire ethical situation the author chooses to leave the reader with or that the reader takes away after finishing the story—in short, what Benjamin calls 'counsel'.

In the latter chapters referred to above, both Austen and Dickens are far more invested in exploring the ethical situation of their characters than in the marriage plot. Compare, for example, Austen's famously curt treatment of Emma's response to Mr Knightley's proposal of marriage: 'What did she say?—Just what she ought, of course. A lady always does.' When Emma learns of Harriet's engagement to Robert Martin, however, or when she is at last convinced that in her childish machinations she has not irreparably injured her friend, Austen elaborates on the far more ecstatic Emma: 'She was in dancing, singing, exclaiming spirits; and till she moved about, and talked to herself, and laughed and

---

[10] Oscar Wilde, *The Artist as Critic: Critical Writings of Oscar Wilde*, ed. Richard Ellmann (New York: Vintage Books, 1968), 305, 375.

reflected, she could be fit for nothing rational.'[11] Emma's response shows how fully conscious she now is of the risk she wantonly took with another human being's happiness.
And, given the seriousness of her disastrous undertaking to raise Harriet on the social
scale, it would appear that Austen lets her off the hook when she rewards her with the
classical comic ending of marriage. In so extended an examination of the question of a
young woman's moral obligations within a community as we see in *Emma*, isn't it strange
(critics have often wondered) that Emma isn't punished? The answer is that Austen does
punish her; Emma's failure to improve Harriet's prospects *is* her punishment. As misguided as her ambitions were, they do constitute an effort to act positively within and
for the community. No private happiness can compensate for the loss of independent
action within a community. From a moral point of view, the heroine is now as isolated as
the later Victorians felt they were. In 'Rugby Chapel', Matthew Arnold characteristically
describes this situation as one in which the modern individual can save only himself; his
actions no longer have wider impact. Matthew Arnold's father, Thomas Arnold, whose
confidence in his moral connection to others is commemorated in the poem, might
have delivered Mr Knightley's powerful defence of *noblesse oblige* at Box Hill. Emma, the
restless modern self, hears Mr Knightley's words and weeps, just as Matthew Arnold can
only mourn his father, not follow in his footsteps. The establishment of democratic individualism rendered impotent these social-ethical impulses by isolating the individual
and shattering the traditional communities in which they might be realized.

Emma earns the title of heroine because she accepts her moral isolation. After recognizing her errors, her 'conduct' and 'heart' are at last aligned with one another and
she refuses to intervene further in Harriet's life, even knowing this may result in her
own misery.[12] She silently guards Harriet's secret at the expense of Mr Knightley's feelings when he proposes marriage to her. These moral acts constitute an inner practice
that would seem insignificant in traditional society, but in Highbury, which has already
begun to register the social changes that were to destabilize any moral consensus, they
are precisely what distinguish Emma from characters like Mrs Elton and Jane Fairfax.

If the question driving much criticism of Emma worries over her punishment, then
the question preoccupying critics of *Great Expectations* concerns its problematic ending.
The original ending, as we know, envisioned the chance encounter of Pip and Estella on
a London street, after which they go their separate ways. Dickens supposedly changed it,
on Bulwer Lytton's advice, to the more optimistic and traditional romantic ending. His
readiness to alter the ending of this his most tightly constructed novel suggests that the
question of how to resolve the Estella plot was not nearly as urgent to Dickens as critics
seem to believe. Whether Estella is the reward of Pip's education or part of the education
itself may have been something Dickens could not decide, but the question seems not to
have greatly concerned him once that education had taken place. The later chapters are

---

[11] Jane Austen, *Emma* (Middlesex: Penguin, 1974) 418, 456.
[12] Jane Austen, *Emma*, 398: 'Her own conduct, as well as her own heart, was before her in the same few
minutes.'

instead centred on working out Pip's relations with himself after he has been born out of his moral stupidity, and the great quandary with which the novel leaves us is not that between Estella and Pip, not one of gender relations, but of Pip's moral situation as it is elaborated by means of his two *Doppelgänger*, Orlick and Trabb's boy.

In the climactic scene in the sluice house, when Orlick tries to murder him, Pip symbolically confronts his own self-hatred. From the moment Orlick is introduced in chapter XV, he is conceived as the embodiment of that self-hatred: the sleazy, slouching, criminally violent upstart that Pip knows he is capable of becoming. After Orlick knocks him out and Pip regains consciousness, the face that appears before him is not that of Joe or Herbert, a loving face, but of Trabb's boy, a mocking face, the face that had ridiculed him so mercilessly earlier in the novel. The sluice house scene proposes only two ways for the morally advanced individual to see himself: self-hatred and self-mockery. This is why Pip's successful effort to help Herbert at the end of *Great Expectations* is crucial to the ethical resolution of the novel in a way that his equivocal romance with Estella is not. Given the symbolic realizations presented in the sluice house scene, any moral act on Pip's part is heroic. As in the final chapter of *Emma*, such acts are performed secretly— his decision to keep Magwitch in ignorance of the fate of his wealth and the resolve not to lay claim to it after Magwitch's death—and constitute an inner practice that Dickens alludes to up to the final moment of the original ending, when Pip allows Estella to believe he has a son so as to shield her from the knowledge of his isolation.

Distinguishing the *Bildungsromane* of accountability from those of empowerment means both recognizing their common ethical impulses and confronting the troubling ways that the *Bildungsromane* of empowerment represent violence. As in novels of accountability, in those of empowerment the moral cultivation of the hero is a fully cogitated theme, yet it is often carried forward in the context of savage violence and of social injustices that the hero escapes but that themselves remain fundamentally unchallenged. On the surface, novels of empowerment do not appear to scrutinize the environment in which the hero realizes himself with the same critical intensity that we see at work in novels of accountability, in which the 'world' must be judged clearly if the protagonist's tendency to project his wishes onto it is to be exposed. What are we to make of the contrast between the highly civilized educational subject matter of novels like *Jane Eyre* and *David Copperfield* and the circumstances in which it is realized? If the primary achievement of the English *Bildungsroman* lies in its ethical realization, how is such violence justified? Why aren't social injustices that are fully featured more fully condemned?

In fairy-tales, the protagonist's rise is of course often accompanied by the violent defeat of enemies, and we could say that *Bildungsromane* merely share this archaic feature of storytelling and read it as one of many signs of the hero's gathering empowerment. In *Jane Eyre* we are never surprised that the tyrant who appears in chapter I, John Reed, meets a miserable death later in the novel. In the realistic context of *Jane Eyre*, however, the fairy-tale convention takes on a complicated and contradictory political significance. A contemporary reviewer of the novel complained that the heroine's 'tone of mind' is the same that 'fostered Chartism and rebellion' and critics have long recognized that the words Jane uses in chapter I to combat her oppressor are those of class rebellion.[13] The contradiction becomes apparent, however, when we recall that Jane's conviction of her *entitlement* is also introduced in the early chapters. For Jane's social origins are in fact not beneath those of her cousin John.[14] From a class point of view, she is no less 'entitled' to the comforts of station than he and is being denied them only because of Mrs Reed's deception and jealousy.

When the apothecary, Mr Lloyd, is called in to treat the abused Jane and asks her if she would like to leave Gateshead and reside with poor relations, she flatly refuses. 'I was not heroic enough to purchase liberty at the price of caste', she frankly admits as she recalls with distaste the coarse speech, filth, and lack of education of the village poor.[15] Much later in the story, now mistress of a village school for poor children, she again admits to feeling 'degraded' by these 'heavy-looking gaping rustics', as if she had 'taken a step which sank instead of raising me in the scale of social existence'.[16] Jane's admission that such sentiments are morally wrong does nothing to qualify the condescension in her description of the poor, and she soon abandons her role as their educator to assume the position of Mrs Rochester.

The novel makes perfectly clear then that Jane's Chartist vocabulary does not extend to the very class from which Chartism arose. It applies only to herself. Brontë imbues the archaic theme of empowerment—always so intoxicating to the naïve reader—with suspect claims of social entitlement, fully acknowledging their dubious character by having Jane openly admit that such sentiments are questionable.

Before proceeding further with *Jane Eyre* let us consider the similar and more famous ethical impasse presented in Dickens's most autobiographical novel, *David Copperfield*. When the young David is sent to work in a blacking factory, his sense of injustice does not appear to extend to the other children being exploited there. As a gentleman's son, he alone is degraded in being 'put to work not fit for [him]', as he later complains to his aunt.[17] Long ago noted by George Bernard Shaw and George Orwell, the moral evasion at work in the blacking episode is generally understood among Dickens critics to have been overcome in *Great Expectations*, when, through Pip, Dickens at last fully confronted his own class consciousness.[18]

The critical premise behind this reading would appear to ignore the comprehensive critique of social privilege that is evident in Dickens's writings from *Pickwick Papers*

---

[13] Elizabeth Rigby, '*Vanity Fair*—and *Jane Eyre*', *Quarterly Review* 84, no. 167 (December 1848): 153–85, 174.

[14] Charlotte Brontë, *Jane Eyre* (New York and London: W.W. Norton & Co., 1971), 78; Bessie alludes to the gentility of Jane's relations ('as much gentry as the Reeds are').

[15] Charlotte Brontë, *Jane Eyre*, 20.

[16] Charlotte Brontë, *Jane Eyre*, 306, 312.

[17] Charles Dickens, *David Copperfield* (New York and London: W.W. Norton & Co., 1990), 167.

[18] Bernard Shaw, 'Introduction to *Great Expectations*', in *Great Expectations* by Charles Dickens (New York and London: W.W. Norton & Co., 1999), 632. In a comparison between the two novels, Shaw writes that the 'reappearance of Mr. Dickens in the character of a blacksmith's boy may be regarded as an apology to Mealy Potatoes', one of David's workmates in the blacking factory.

forward. When Pickwick enters the Fleet, for example, which is explicitly conceived of as a microcosm of society, he can live in comfort there while others starve only because he has money. In fully realizing this in a way he never had before, Pickwick can forgive even his enemies, and when he returns to society Dickens wisely allows him to re-enter the domain of comedy—for the same reason, perhaps, that the hero of Preston Sturges's *Sullivan's Travels*, a film director, decides that he cannot compose a tragedy after having seen what he has seen in prison: 'I haven't suffered enough', he admits. Are we to assume that Dickens became desensitized to the reality of privilege as he moved into his middle period? That he underwent a moral devolution between the writing of his first novel and *David Copperfield* and then recovered himself before writing *Bleak House, Little Dorrit*, and *Great Expectations*?

David Copperfield is Dickens's second autobiographical rendering and the first of his novels to be composed in the first person. The self-narrating hero has a more varied set of tasks before him than that of the protagonist of an omniscient narration; for if the protagonist's self-cultivation is to carry the necessary weight of the *Bildungsroman*, he 'must' become the hero, as David puts it in the opening sentence of the novel. How then did Dickens prevent David from becoming an insufferable bore, as anyone telling us of his heroic virtue is likely to become? It is not simply an achievement of style—not that style is simple. As Garrett Stewart has suggested, *David Copperfield* is a 'stylist's autobiography' in which the hero's sincerity is established by means of contrast with other voices.[19] *David Copperfield* registers at the level of content the sacrifices that David's worldly success is costing him. On the day that David is articled, he goes to see a play entitled *The Stranger* and upon returning home does not recognize himself in the mirror; and, in the illustrations, David's face is often averted, particularly in images that allude to injuries done to other characters in which he himself was silently implicated: the firing of Mr Mell and the introduction of Steerforth to the Peggotty household.[20] These images haunt the novel like guilty dreams, as does David's *Doppelgänger* Heep, who has been deformed by the same impulses driving David—personal and professional ambition. And what of the children left behind at the blacking factory? Here is David's description of his encounter with the other boys on his first day of work:

> There were three or four of us, counting me…the oldest of the regular boys was summoned to show me my business. His name was Mick Walker, and he wore a ragged apron and a paper cap. He informed me that his father was a bargeman, and walked, in a black velvet head-dress, in the Lord Mayor's Show. He also informed me that our principal associate would be another boy whom he introduced by the—to me—extraordinary name of Mealy Potatoes. I discovered, however, that this youth had not been christened by that name, but that it had been bestowed upon him in the warehouse, on account of his complexion, which was pale or mealy. Mealy's father

[19] Garrett Stewart, 'Mr. Micawber's Novels', in *David Copperfield* by Charles Dickens (New York and London: W.W. Norton & Co., 1990), 836.
[20] Dickens, *David Copperfield*, 325; 'I hardly knew myself in my own glass when I got home.'

was a waterman, who had the additional distinction of being a fireman, and was engaged as such at one of the large theatres; where some young relation of Mealy's—I think his little sister—did Imps in the Pantomimes.

No words can express the secret agony of my soul as I sunk into this companionship...[21]

Potatoes grow in the earth, and Mealy's father is both a waterman and a fireman. Earth, fire, and water: like the elements, the poor will always be with us. The root of the word *imp* (the Greek: in + *phyton* or growth) suggests *not to grow*. That these references inhabit the quiet domain of David's memory make us all the more conscious of the forgotten world of withered and malnourished children. The passage implies, not that there is nothing wrong with Mealy working in the factory, but that it is so far distant from middle-class experience that no consciousness operating in the realm of a self-generating drama of genteel heroism can possibly relate to it.

Placed in the context of so abject a social reality, there is no more loaded word in all of Dickens than the imperative *must* in the opening sentence of *David Copperfield*. The novel may open on a condition—'Whether I shall be the hero of my own life'—but it follows with an imperative: 'these pages must show'—a more unyielding judgement than the tentative opening clause would seem to propose.

A similar moral imperative is at work in *Jane Eyre*, however securely it is veiled by gothic convention. Jane's *Doppelgänger* is the insane and libidinous wife Bertha Mason. When Jane looks in the mirror on the eve of her wedding she sees Bertha and, when Bertha's presence is finally revealed by Mr Rochester, the image of her locked up and strapped to a chair recalls the hysterical child Jane of the Red Room. It is telling that Bertha's violent death is accompanied by the maiming and blinding, or symbolic castration, of Mr Rochester. In the language of Freud, the violence of these plot developments addresses the guilt of Jane's incestuous desire for the fatherly Rochester, a reading that may well seem overdetermined because Freud, arriving later in the century, read the novel (as he did *David Copperfield*) and may have been influenced by it in the formulation of his theories. A psychoanalytic reading of the subtext, however, needs to be considered in relation to the more explicit meditations on Jane and Rochester that appear in the novel. One such meditation is the prophecy suggested in the image of the ruined chestnut tree, carefully elaborated in chapter XXV. Struck by lightning, the tree is split in half but the base and roots remain unsundered. The boughs are dead—'community of vitality was destroyed—the sap could flow no more'—but the two halves 'hold fast to each other' nonetheless. Brontë's meaning could not be clearer: the price Jane must pay for companionship is loss of erotic pleasure: 'the time of pleasure and love is over with you', Jane thinks, gazing on the tree.[22] In a society that subordinates women, in which every man assumes the symbolic role of father to every woman, these are the conditions

[21] Dickens, *David Copperfield*, 137.
[22] Brontë, *Jane Eyre*, 235–36.

on which relations between men and women can be sustained. Moreover, the next generation will bear the burden of this sacrifice. The marriage of mind and heart with which the novel ends—a chestnut is a nut in the chest—produces a child for whom Jane appears to have no affective response, and young Adèle ('the emblem of my past self', as Jane calls her on the eve of her wedding)[23] is returned to boarding school, the site of female discipline and restraint.

The strange and unsatisfying plot configurations with which *Jane Eyre* concludes are essential to its ethical integrity. Whether Brontë was fully conscious of their implications or not, these configurations speak to her conception of what marriage cost women in patriarchal society. What then do we make of the tearful happiness with which *David Copperfield* draws to a close? This is not the wise comedy with which *Pickwick Papers* ends but a sentimental image of the hero surrounded by family and enjoying the greater community's approval. In Orwell's view, the final chapters of the novel are pervaded by 'the cult of success'.[24] Even characters David has indirectly injured, like Mr Peggotty and Mr Mell, are brought back into the novel as if to say a forgiving hello.

Perhaps these chapters have a deeper moral resonance than Orwell was willing to consider. The loving remembrance of those one has injured: is such remembrance a grotesque luxury or one of the most profound moral acts one can accomplish? It's a psychological necessity to retain some sort of friendship with oneself in adulthood, to create some protective shield against the self-criticism that accompanies mature reflection. In a letter to John Forster, Dickens wrote: 'Why is it, that as with poor David, a sense comes always crushing on me now, when I fall into low spirits, as of one happiness I have missed in life, and one friend and companion I have never made?'[25] As my teacher Lionel Trilling once remarked: we can have little doubt as to who that unattained friend is.[26] No one will fault Dickens for seeking that friend in *David Copperfield*, the novel he called his 'favourite child'; the gentle conclusion of his *Bildungsroman* may be a consequence of that search.[27]

The biological metaphor is telling. In the Preface to the 1869 edition of *David Copperfield*, in which this appellation appeared, Dickens describes himself as a 'fond parent'. Written a year before his death Dickens blesses his imaginary child, who happens to be himself—a character with the same initials as his own name in reverse and one whose life experiences closely parallel his own. According to the logic of metaphor, it is Dickens's own father, the mercurial and disastrously irresponsible John Dickens, who is blessing him here. Is this what Pip is seeking, we may ask, when he stands over his parents' graves in chapter I of *Great Expectations* at the start of his re-evaluation of his

[23] Brontë, *Jane Eyre*, 244.

[24] George Orwell, 'Charles Dickens', in *The Dickens Critics*, eds. George H. Ford and Lauriat Lane, Jr (Ithaca, NY: Cornell University Press, 1961), 169.

[25] Charles Dickens, 'Passages from Dickens' Letters Relating to *David Copperfield*', in *David Copperfield* (New York and London: W.W. Norton & Co., 1990), 773.

[26] Lionel Trilling, *Sincerity and Authenticity* (Cambridge, MA: Harvard University Press, 1971), 4.

[27] Charles Dickens, 'Preface to 1869 Edition', *David Copperfield*, 766.

life, at the precipice of his great reckoning? In any case Dickens advances the fairy-tale convention into more humane territory, for *David Copperfield* and *Great Expectations* do not so much explain why parents die as show why we retain them in our consciousness. The blessing of the dead imaginary parent is always sought and never bestowed.

Friendship compensates, the friendship the author has for the *Bildungsheld*. The authors I have discussed here were highly conscious of possessing this friendship, if we recall Austen's well-known comment that Emma was likely to have only one ally, the author; Dickens's openly expressed fondness for David Copperfield; and Brontë's protectiveness towards Jane Eyre's virtue.[28] When Herbert dresses Pip's wounded hands after he has been injured in the fire, Pip asks him: 'Herbert . . . can you see me best by the light of the window, or the light of the fire?'[29] As if to ask: Is human character seen most clearly when looked at in an impersonal light or through the eyes of friendship? Severe and yet gentle, the morality of the great English *Bildungsromane* encompasses both perspectives. The *Bildungsheld*—Emma, Jane, David, Pip—is held to a strict but not impersonal standard, and for that very reason the 'counsel' with which the *Bildungsroman* leaves the reader cannot be translated into any system. It always awaits a human example. In a sense, the conclusion of Nietzsche's judgement against George Eliot holds true: 'For the English, morality is not yet a problem.'[30] Morality becomes a problem only with each particular case. The 'counsel' readers then take away from *Bildungsromane* lies in the value that the stories themselves, like all stories that are passed on, place on human experience; such value is not by definition moral but the precondition for morality. (When stories are *not* told, as Benjamin states at the opening of 'The Storyteller', 'experience has fallen in value'.)[31]

One cannot know one's 'duty' until the individual case presents itself. As England underwent the great transformations of the late 18th and early 19th centuries, it moved from a concept of duty based on 'the morality of role fulfillment, where we judge a man *as* farmer, *as* king, *as* father, to the point at which evaluation has become detached, both in the vocabulary and in practice, from roles, and we ask not what it is to be good at or for this or that role or skill, but just what it is to be "a good man"; not what it is to do one's duty as a clergyman or landowner, but as "a man"'.[32] The content of duty therefore cannot be filled in or articulated until a particular case declares itself. According to the ethical philosopher Alasdair MacIntyre, from whom I have just quoted, this kind of situation

[28] Austen wrote in 1816: 'I am going to take a heroine whom no one but myself will much like', quoted in J.E. Austen-Leigh, *A Memoir of Jane Austen* (London: Bentley, 1870), 204. For Brontë's protective attitude toward Jane Eyre, see Gaskell's description of the author's distress over the suggestion that her novel was illicit: Elizabeth Gaskell, 'Charlotte Brontë and her Publishers, Reviewers, and First Biographer', in *Jane Eyre*, ed. Richard J. Dunn (New York and London: W.W. Norton & and Co., 1971), 458.

[29] Dickens, *Great Expectations*, 303.

[30] Nietzsche, *Twilight of the Idols*, 516.

[31] Benjamin, 'The Storyteller', 83–84.

[32] Alasdair MacIntyre, *A Short History of Ethics* (New York: Macmillan Publishing Co., 1966), 94.

provides the background to the kind of moral dilemma we see examined in fiction, particularly in the novels of Austen. All the *Bildungsromane* I have discussed here succeed in arriving at the specific content of duty for the hero or heroine. In these narratives the 'moral' is defined as dynamic and context-specific, residing not in a general, normative truth but in the particulars of lived experience.

In ethical philosophy today, narrative appears to be playing an increasingly important role in providing an alternative to the either/or opposition between faith in an ideal good and a sceptical pluralism that insists on 'rival, incommensurate, mutually exclusive goods'. As Jil Larson has shown, however different the work of Alastair MacIntyre, Martha Nussbaum, Margaret Urban Walker, and Richard Rorty, each emphasizes the narrative context of ethical life. In giving us stories of concrete, socially embedded characters, novels do not refer us to 'totalizing theories that attempt to escape contingency and to unify incommensurable values'; rather, they encourage us to reflect on the often contradictory choices and actions that constitute moral life as it is experienced over time.[33] According to Walker's narrative paradigm, for example, these choices inevitably leave 'moral remainders', 'genuine moral demands that, because their fulfillment conflicted with other genuine moral demands, are "left over" in episodes of moral choice, and yet are not just nullified'.[34] In the novels I have discussed here, 'moral remainders' are essential to narrative structure. Surely all moral imperatives, like the imperative with which David Copperfield begins the story of his life, produce moral consequences or unsettling 'remainders'—or 'reminders', as we might call the illustrations in *David Copperfield*.

But does narrative fiction in general really help us to determine concrete answers to the ancient ethical question of how to live? How instrumental to our actual moral choices, made in this time, this place, is the knowledge we derive from reflecting on novels? While any serious work of literature can deepen one's sympathetic imagination and while studying the moral choices and actions that take place in fiction in particular can sharpen our awareness of ethical difficulties, this is not the same as teaching us how to live a moral life. As any parent knows, if morality can be taught, it is taught by example. The only modern literary genre that by definition offers examples of individual development integrated with the social process is the *Bildungsroman*. From its origins in the story of Wilhelm Meister's 'apprenticeship' the *Bildungsroman* begins with the moral imperative to craft or model a meaningful life in society. In exemplifying the discovery of the content of duty in the life of a particular man or woman by means of sacrifices peculiar to a specific time and place, these storytellers neither universalize that content (by laying claim to a fixed set of moral principles) nor present it as one among a plurality

---

[33] Jil Larson, *Ethics and Narrative in the English Novel, 1880–1914* (Cambridge: Cambridge University Press, 2001), 8–10.

[34] Margaret Urban Walker, 'Moral Understanding: Alternative "Epistemology" for a Feminist Ethics', in *Explorations in Feminist Ethics: Theory and Practice*, ed. Eve Browning Cole and Susan Coultrap-McQuin (Bloomington: Indiana University Press, 1992), 170.

of options (giving way to a potentially nihilistic relativism). Instead, they offer a model, irreplaceable and unrepeatable, but one that can be grasped as a standard. To word this another way: the 'standard' that emerges is that of a life in society made meaningful, not by obedience to abstract principle, but by virtue of each individual's discovery of his or her duty. From a moral point of view, the example realizes itself only if it is superseded.

Another word for 'moral remainders' is of course the word I use above—*sacrifices*—and no discussion of the moral vision of the English novel would be complete without recognition of the Christian origins of this morality. Austen, Brontë, and Dickens were practising Christians well versed in Christian literature and theology, yet their representations of institutionalized Christianity are often openly derisive. Even likable clergy in Austen—Henry Tilney, Edward Ferrars, and Edmund Bertram are the three examples—prove to be morally obtuse at a critical moment. As the century unfolds, amoral and spiritually deaf English clergymen become the norm in Victorian novels, as if rejection of the English Church is the precondition of any genuine morality. In this respect, the novelists may be said to express the paradox arising out of the contradiction between obedience to law and internalizing law that is at the centre of Judeo-Christian thought, and the novels they have left us are clearly aligned with an internal religion. In novels of accountability, this alignment is evident in what I have called the inner practice achieved by Emma and Pip, and in novels of empowerment, it is suggested in each author's damning characterization of evangelicals who enforce the laws or conventions of religion most adamantly—Brontë's Mr Brocklehurst and Dickens's Mr and Miss Murdstone. Organized religion actually produces the opposite of the '*practice* of life' that is Christ's real 'legacy to mankind', and genuine religiosity is a 'state of the heart', one that 'resists all formulas' and '*lives*' not as 'a faith but a doing; above all, a *not* doing of many things, another state of *being*'.[35] These words are from Nietzsche, who might have been less dismissive of 'English morality' if he had recognized the extent to which Victorian novelists attempt to guide their characters to this paradoxical 'state of being' and 'practice', one that is so specific to their inner lives and circumstances as to be virtually hidden or 'obscure'—to borrow Hardy's word for the last Victorian *Bildungsheld*, Jude Fawley.

The novel in which these ideas come to full fruition is not *Jude the Obscure*, however, but E.M. Forster's *Howards End*. Because of the inner practice of the half-German, morally independent Margaret Schlegel, a small, 'obscure' community, set apart from the 'world', comes about at the conclusion of the novel that is England's best hope. ('The inner life had paid', writes Forster.)[36] In both Nietzsche and Forster the 'fundamental laws of self-preservation and growth' demand that each person 'invent *his own* virtue, *his own* categorical imperative'. In the novelists I have discussed here, this is not a form of advanced or decadent individualism; it involves a community of individuals; in Forster it becomes a national idea, as indeed it was to Nietzsche. ('A people perishes

[35] Friedrich Nietzsche, 'The Antichrist', in *The Portable Nietzsche*, ed. Walter Kauffmann (London: Penguin, 1977), 605–13.

[36] E.M. Forster, *Howards End* (New York: Vintage Books, 1921), 336, 299.

when it confuses *its* duty with duty in general', writes Nietzsche.)[37] In the fiction, a sense of English identity most often communicates itself in meditations on concrete images of the landscape or home. Against the backdrop of these images, an implicit warning is sounded against conceiving of duty as independent of the local and human context. Like Dorothy in *The Wonderful Wizard of Oz* (itself a modern fairy-tale published in 1900), Emma, Jane, David, and Pip find what they were unknowingly seeking in their own back yard. In *Howards End*, however, published in 1910, the question of what happens when duty becomes abstract and impersonal is posed with a new urgency. History would answer the question four years later.

Thus it is tempting to assert that the *Bildungsroman* comes to an end with this last reimagining of it by Forster. The Schlegel sisters' retreat from the social world seems a recognition of the impossibility of integrating the *Bildungsheld* into the world; moreover, the 'world' as they understood it is about to be swept away. Yet coming of age novels continued to be written during and after the world wars and the coming of age plot was early adapted to film. Most recently, the appearance of Benjamin Kunkel's *Indecision* (2005) is proof that a deeply meditated *Bildung* narrative may realize itself in a contemporary 'world' context that is uncertain at best. The extraordinary resilience of the form owes itself to the simplicity of the definition of it that has come down to us from Goethe. The *Bildungsheld* is any young man or woman with the moral courage to apprentice himself to the world and the 'world' is the horizon of possibilities that both restricts and is created by this morally reckless act. Setting the stage for future *Bildungsromane*, Forster did not lay claim to great expectations. Of the Miss Schlegels he writes:

> In their own fashion they cared deeply about politics, though not as politicians would have us care; they desired that public life should mirror whatever is good in the life within ... Not out of them are the shows of history erected: the world would be a grey, bloodless place were it entirely composed of Miss Schlegels. But the world being what it is, perhaps they shine out in it like stars.[38]

SUGGESTED READING

Austen, Jane. *Emma*. Edited by Ronald Blythe. Middlesex: Penguin Books, 1974.

Benjamin, Walter. 'The Storyteller'. In *Illuminations*. Translated by Harry Zohn. London: Schocken, 1969.

Brontë, *Jane Eyre*. Edited by Richard J. Dunn. New York and London: W.W. Norton & Co., 1971.

Buckley, Jerome. *Season of Youth: The Bildungsroman from Dickens to Golding*. Cambridge and London: Harvard University Press, 1974.

Castle, Gregory. *Reading the Modernist Bildungsroman*. Gainesville: University Press of Florida, 2006.

---

[37] Nietzsche, 'The Antichrist', 577.
[38] Forster, *Howards End*, 28.

Dickens, Charles. *David Copperfield*. Edited by Jerome H. Buckley. New York and London: W.W. Norton & Co., 1990.

———. *Great Expectations*. Edited by Bernard Shaw. New York and London: W.W. Norton & Co., 1999.

Larson, Jil. *Ethics and Narrative in the English Novel, 1880–1914*. Cambridge: Cambridge University Press, 2001.

Levine, George. *How to Read the Victorian Novel*. London: Blackwell, 2007.

Lukács, Georg. *The Theory of the Novel*. Translated by Anna Bostock. Cambridge, MA: MIT Press. 1996.

Moretti, Franco. *The Way of the World*. London: Verso, 2000.

Shaw, Bernard. 'Introduction to *Great Expectations*'. In *Great Expectations* by Charles Dickens. New York and London: W.W. Norton & Co., 1999.

Walker, Margaret Urban. 'Moral Understanding: Alternative "Epistemology" for a Feminist Ethics'. In *Explorations in Feminist Ethics: Theory and Practice*, edited by Eve Browning Cole and Susan Coultrap-McQuin. Bloomington: Indiana University Press, 1992, 165–75.

....

32

THREE MATTERS OF STYLE

....

MARK LAMBERT

On the basis of language alone, a reader could likely identify a great many passages in novels as coming from early or mid-Victorian fiction, and it is good to think about what it is in those passages which says 'Victorian' to us. No one essential thing, probably, no feature unique to and universally present in novels of the age. The prose style of Victorian fiction is better approached—more enjoyably and profitably approached—by appropriating the very useful 'family resemblance' model, with many features variously distributed among members of the family. With members of a human family, of course, shared biological features (a predisposition to a disease, say, or an inherited talent) will sometimes be meaningful in the life of the individual, but more often they simply are: a particular shape of ear lobe, the contours of a thumb. With fictional style, we'll do well to work from the assumption that in one way or another, or in several ways at once, features likely have meaning, and that this is no less so when they are features of period style rather than the style of a particular author, or a particular book, or (as in *Bleak House*) particular sections of a book. 'No less so', in fact, asserts too little: when an author uses a device one has encountered in other works, there is a more muted version of the effects one find in poems—T.S. Eliot's, say—that glancingly allude to other poems. It is an immensely rich field, the study (in itself, and in relation to individual style) of Victorian period style, and the richest work in that rich field is still to be done. In this chapter we will attempt not even the sketchiest treasure map of that territory, but rather give three examples of the sorts of things one may attend to in looking at the style of Victorian fiction, and some of the questions one might ask about those things. We will start with one very small feature, then move on to a very large one—a feature which is actually one particular use of a whole set of features—and then look at one of middling size. These three matters of style are suggestive when taken together, all of them having to do, it seems to me, with the relationship between writer, characters, and the reader. What's more to the point, though, is that all three are interesting in themselves—and in that, certainly, representative of the large field of Victorian fictional style.

I

The first, and smallest, of the three features is a matter of vocabulary. In chapter XL of *Barchester Towers*, the odious Mr Slope is trying to propose to Trollope's heroine, Eleanor Bold. He receives no encouragement, but Mr Slope persists. He has drunk too much champagne, and 'no doubt' decides that at this point 'some outward demonstration of that affection of which he talked so much' is in order. Mr Slope 'contrive[s] to pass his arm round her waist'. And then

> She sprang from him as she would have jumped from an adder, but she did not spring far; not, indeed, beyond arm's length; and then, quick as thought, she raised her little hand and dealt him a box on the ear with such right good will, that it sounded among the trees like a miniature thunder clap.[1]

Trollope will imagine criticism of Eleanor's action by some readers, but he assures us that in boxing Slope's ear, Eleanor had 'a true instinct as to the man; he was capable of rebuke in this way and in no other'.[2] That jumping from an adder also tells us this is a moment of instinct and the natural, and the miniature thunder clap among the trees that it is natural and just, and perhaps sanctioned by nature's God. It is a moment whose sudden, instinctive moral certainty, whose freedom from niggling doubts, will be a special relief and pleasure to readers of Trollope, but it is a passage which even a reader unacquainted with *Barchester Towers*, and attending to language alone, and not content, might identify as Victorian. What in the paragraph about Mr Slope and Mrs Bold would allow the reader to do this? The monosyllabic 'right' might be enough as it occurs in 'and dealt him a box on the ear with such right good will...'. And what is this 'right'? It is not a word that is likely to stop us as we read: here 'right' is an archaic synonym for 'very'. But 'very', itself though not impossible, would be rather flat here, neither noticeably nor significantly Victorian. Consider another Victorian 'right' passage, one similar to Trollope's in situation and phrasing. This is from Dickens's *Barnaby Rudge*, and in it Eleanor Bold's predecessor is Dolly Varden, and Mr Slope's, the wild and dangerous Hugh:

> 'Nay, mistress,' he rejoined, endeavouring to draw her arm through his. 'I'll walk with you.'

> She released herself, and clenching her little hand, struck him with right good will.[3]

---

[1] Anthony Trollope, *Barchester Towers*, ed. Michael Sadleir and Frederick Page (Oxford: Oxford University Press, 1998), 144.

[2] Trollope, *Barchester Towers*, 145.

[3] Charles Dickens, *Barnaby Rudge*, ed. Gordon Spence (London: Penguin, 1973), 219.

It is conceivable that Trollope is alluding to this passage in his description of Eleanor and Mr Slope, but perhaps more likely that both Dickens and Trollope are drawing upon the same stock of phrases expressing attitudes appropriate to a situation. (Here we may actually feel closer to Old English heroic poetry than to T.S. Eliot.) In both Victorian passages that 'little hand' makes the woman's blow at once pitiful and cute. 'Right good will' does a number of things, and one of the things it does is heighten the conspicuousness of 'right'. And as for that adverbial 'right' in the two passages; … well, here we might take the 'very', or 'in a high degree' of the OED[4] and expand it to 'in a high degree; in a manner earnest and hearty, from the good old days, from a vigorous peasantry, from the harmonious society that (from its "right honorables" on down) not only includes but appreciates that vigorous peasantry; in a manner Saxon, muscular, not vitiated by complexities, instinctive'. This expanded Victorian 'right' will cover much of what we have in our two passages, but also contains some features not clearly relevant to what we have in those two passages: particular contexts limit the importance of particular items in this gloss; at the same time, though, one does not want to be too sure about which associations of a word that echoes through the fiction of a period are utterly irrelevant to a particular occurrence of that word. And one would want, ideally, to be able to think about a striking feature of this Victorian 'right'. When it occurs in a narrative passage, or in the speech of a character with whom the writer sympathizes, it is in effect a shibboleth, identifying the novel itself, and its author, with the values the word suggests, and with the values of other books which use the word.

Ideally, we would also think about places in Victorian fiction where this word (or any stylistic feature which we were studying) is avoided, or viewed with suspicion. We may notice, in a consideration of 'right', that there is the occasional use of the word by an unsympathetic character: in *Oliver Twist*, for instance, Mr Gamfield offers to take on Oliver as an apprentice in the 'right pleasant trade' of chimney-sweeping.[5] Some Victorian novels—e.g. *Jane Eyre*, *Vanity Fair*, *Alton Locke*—do not use adverbial 'right' at all.[6] Thackeray, indeed, seems actively to dislike it: in chapter 30 of *Pendennis* he assigns the word—in the extended form 'right good'—to Doolan, an Irish journalist such as one might expect to find in a Thackeray novel, one 'whose speech was unctuous and measured, his courtesy oriental, his tone, when talking to the two Englishmen, quite different to that with which he spoke to his comrade…', and the context is a weave of a hack's banalities:

> 'Your servant, Mr. Warrington—Mr. Pendennis. I am delighted to have the honour of seeing ye again. The night's journey on the top of the Alacrity was one of the most agreeable I ever enjoyed in my life, and it was your liveliness and urbanity that made

---

[4] *OED* (first edition; adv. 9).

[5] Charles Dickens, *Oliver Twist*, ed. Peter Fairclough (New York: Penguin, 1966), 61.

[6] The time needed to find out things like this is very much reduced by consulting the concordances in Mitsuharu Matsuoka's *The Victorian Studies Archive*, <http://victorian.lang.nagoya-u.ac.jp/>, an invaluable resource.

the trip so charming. I have often thought over that happy night, sir, and talked over it to Mrs. Doolan. I have seen your elegant young friend, frequenter of this hostelry, and a right good one it is...'[7]

And this makes sense, really: the vision of an archaic golden age of effort, enthusiasm and social harmony which is to be teased out of the use of adverbial 'right' would surely be, for Thackeray, a vision for quacks and fools.

We learn most from studying period style, then, when we consider which books avoid or dislike a particular device, as well as which books sympathetically employ it. Here, though, we will concentrate on novels in the latter group. Some, like Gaskell's *Mary Barton*, have 'right' only as a feature in the dialectal speech of characters, and not in authorial statements: 'Well, Margaret, you're right welcome...'; 'Yes, I was right weary of waiting...'; 'I'm now right thankful I held my peace...'.[8]

We should notice that these occurrences of adverbial 'right' in *Mary Barton* do not weigh, in the scales of period style, as simple, morally neutral philological observation: dialectal 'right' seems to be used considerably more often by sympathetic characters than by scoundrels. (We may also recall how frequently the glosses on dialectal words in *Mary Barton* go on to connect a seemingly uncouth, non-standard, low prestige form with the deep antiquity of 'Anglo-Saxon', or the high prestige of Chaucer, or Ben Jonson, or the Book of Common Prayer.)

'Right' displays some of its more specific associations—with the land, with physical health and vitality—in this passage from Sheridan Le Fanu's *Uncle Silas*:

'Country air, Miss Ruthyn, is a right good kitchen to country fare. I like to see young women eat heartily. You have had some pounds of beef and mutton since I saw you last,' said Dr. Bryerly.[9]

In *Jorrocks' Jaunts and Jollities*, the hero at one point has finally recovered from the effects of a heavily alcoholic dinner-party:

He was up long before me the next morning, and had a dip in the sea before I came down. 'Upon my word,' said he, as I entered the room, and found him looking as fresh and lively as a four-year-old, 'it's worth while going to the lush-crib occasionally, if it's only for the pleasure of feeling so hearty and fresh as one does on the second day. I feel as if I could jump out of my skin, but I will defer the performance until after breakfast. I have ordered a fork one, do you know, cold 'am and boiled bacon, with no end of eggs, and bread of every possible description. By the way, I've acquaintance

    [7] William Makepeace Thackeray, *The History of Pendennis*, ed. Peter L. Shillingsburg, 2 vols. (New York: Garland, 1991), 306.
    [8] Elizabeth Gaskell, *Mary Barton*, ed. Edgar Wright (Oxford: Oxford University Press, 1987), 49, 75, 117–18.
    [9] Joseph Sheridan Le Fanu, *Uncle Silas: A Tale of Bartram-Haugh*, ed. Victor Sage (London: Penguin, 2000), 238.

with Thorpe, the baker hard by, who's a right good fellow, and says he will give me some wery nice beagles wot he shoots to.....'.[10]

'Right' occurs in both passages, and Surtees's 'hearty' anticipates Le Fanu's 'heartily'. But, even less than with the *Barchester Towers* and *Barnaby Rudge* scenes does one suspect conscious borrowing here: both the shared words express the same sense of life, the same values, however different Dr Bryerly and Mr Jorrocks may be. And we should also notice that if Victorian 'right' is associated with shared values of high and low, 'low' need not mean 'lowest', and need not mean rural low: Jorrocks may be a cit, and absurd, but he is loved rather than sneered at.

One of Jorrocks's winning features is his bluff physical energy: the central part of heartiness. We might compare Kit in *The Old Curiosity Shop*:

> All day long, it blew without cessation. The night was clear and starlight, but the wind had not fallen, and the cold was piercing. Sometimes—towards the end of a long stage—Kit could not help wishing it were a little warmer; but when they stopped to change horses, and he had had a good run, and what with that, and the bustle of paying the old postillion, and rousing the new one, and running to and fro again until the horses were put to, he was so warm that the blood tingled and smarted in his fingers' ends—then he felt as if to have it one degree less cold would be to lose half the delight and glory of the journey: and up he jumped again, right cheerily, singing to the merry music of the wheels as they rolled away, and, leaving the townspeople in their warm beds, pursued their course along the lonely road.[11]

Especially interesting for its cultural and political context is this use of 'right' in Disraeli's *Sybil*. The speaker is Walter Gerard, the heroine's father, who mourns that better, Saxon England lost at the Norman conquest. He is not a man who thinks highly of, for instance, reading:

> '...I can manage a book well enough, if it be well written, and on points I care for; but I would sooner listen than read anytime,' said Gerard. 'Indeed I should be right glad to see the minstrel and the storyteller going their rounds again...'.[12]

In *Bleak House*, we'll remember the great last paragraph of chapter XLVII, and notice that what might seem too obvious a piece of word-play can call up for us not simply an archaic formula of respect, but all the associations of earnestness and simplicity in the adverbial 'right':

> Dead, your Majesty. Dead, my lords and gentlemen. Dead, Right Reverends and Wrong Reverends of every order...[13]

---

[10] Robert Smith Surtees, *Jorrocks' Jaunts and Jollities*, ed. Herbert Van Thal (London: Cassell, 1968), 221.

[11] Charles Dickens, *The Old Curiosity Shop*, ed. Elizabeth M. Brennan (Oxford: Oxford University Press, 1997), 541.

[12] Benjamin Disraeli, *Sybil, or The Two Nations* (London: Peter Davies, 1927), 198.

[13] Charles Dickens, *Bleak House*, ed. Patricia Ingham (Peterborough, ON: Broadview Press, 2011), 575.

Earlier in the novel, in a scene celebrating good, simple characters, Mrs Rouncewell comes upon Mr Bagnet and George, and says she thinks they are military men:

> Mr. Bagnet takes upon himself to reply, 'Yes, ma'am. Formerly.'
> 'I thought so. I was sure of it. My heart warms, gentlemen, at the sight of such. God bless you, gentlemen! You'll excuse an old woman; but I had a son once who went for a soldier. A fine handsome youth he was, and good in his bold way, though some people did disparage him to his poor mother. I ask your pardon for troubling you, sir. God bless you, gentlemen!'
> 'Same to you, ma'am!' returns Mr. Bagnet, with right good will.
> There is something very touching in the earnestness of the old lady's voice, and in the tremble that goes through her quaint old figure.

Later in *Bleak House*, after Sir Leicester's stroke, Mrs Rouncewell will be 'right thankful… that she happened to come to London and is able to attend upon him'.[14] We are considering the uses of adverbial 'right' as a feature of the style of Victorian fiction, but should remember that such a view must be something of a simplification. Other genres count. Tennyson's *Idylls of the King* will be part of the story. It is decidedly a 'right' work (e.g. 'right well I know'; 'All of one mind, and all right-honest friends'; 'Sweet lord, ye do right well to whisper it'; 'Right well I know that fame is half-disfame').[15] To the Victorian word, Tennyson's poems add associations with his Arthur, and the moral dignity of his Arthur. But the 'other genres' author one particularly wants to look at for the combination of the use of adverbial 'right' and visions of greatness, earnestness and vitality in history is Carlyle, especially in *On Heroes and Hero Worship*, a book that seems nearly as taken with the word 'right' as the Victorians were taken with the book's author. We read there, for instance, of Norse mythology:

> Sincerity is the great characteristic of it. Superior sincerity (far superior) consoles us for the total want of old Grecian grace. Sincerity, I think, is better than grace. I feel that these old Northmen were looking into Nature with open eye and soul: most earnest, honest, childlike, and yet manlike; with a great-hearted simplicity and depth and freshness, in a true, loving, admiring, unfearing way. A right valiant, true old race of men.[16]

We are told that Mohammed communed with his own heart, in the silence of the mountains: 'it was a right natural custom'. In the *Divine Comedy*, 'The noblest idea made real hitherto among men is sung, and emblemed forth abidingly: are we not right glad to

[14] Dickens, *Bleak House*, 445, 662.
[15] Alfred Lord Tennyson, *Idylls of the King*, ed. J.M. Gray (New Haven: Yale University Press, 1983), 108, 112, 139, 154.
[16] Thomas Carlyle, *Sartor Resartus; On Heroes and Hero Worship* (London: Dent, 1967), 267.

possess it?' Of a more recent figure, Carlyle says, 'Boswell venerates his Johnson right truly, even in the Eighteenth Century.'[17]

The words we are likely to think of as 'typically' Victorian—'earnest', let us say, or 'trifling'—are denotatively strong. Victorian 'right' is not: it means, as we have said, 'very'; beyond that it is all connotation and social association. If we tried to modernize the language of a Victorian novel, we could deal pretty well with 'earnest' and 'trifling'. But 'right' would give us trouble. It carries a whole sense of a good life led in a good society. It is a pastoral vision in a single word.

II

A pastoral vision in a single word. A maritime vision too. *HMS Pinafore* memorably gets the Victorian 'right' and its sense of vitality, historical continuity, and social harmony: the crew recognizes a right good captain, the captain recognizes a right good crew. In Victorian 'right' novels, an enthusiastic author uses the same term as the speaker of local dialect. The word represents an ideal. Nineteenth-century novels, however, are not typically about utopias. They concern areas of conflicted attitudes and social states. We want to consider now, as representing this other side of things in the language of Victorian prose fiction, not one particular word, but a particular use of a set of features, which set of features we may call the elaborated style, for example:

> The petticoat was short, displaying well a pair of feet and ankles which left much to be desired in the article of symmetry.[18]

> Now the reader may perhaps remember, that in an early part of our veracious chronicle we hinted that Mr Verdant Green's equestrian performances were but of a humble character.[19]

It is easier to recognize this style than to give a complete catalogue of the linguistic devices it can employ, but we might say that among the most notable of these devices are Latinate diction, 'elegant variation' of noun phrases, conspicuously formal syntax, and also complex prepositions and related forms,[20] with their enticing suggestion of

---

[17] Carlyle, *On Heroes and Hero Worship*, 290, 331, 251.

[18] Charlotte Brontë, *Shirley*, ed. Herbert Rosengarten and Margaret Smith (Oxford: Oxford University Press, 2007), 54.

[19] Cuthbert Bede, *The Adventures of Verdant Green* (London: Nathaniel Cooke, 1853), 92.

[20] On these, see Randolph Quirk, Sidney Greenbaum, et al., *A Comprehensive Grammar of the English Language* (London and New York, 1985), sec 9.7–9.13. Just a few of the forms occurring in Victorian fiction are: *as a means of; as permitted by; by dint of; for the convenience of; in a tactile examination of; in acknowledgment of; in the matter of; in the way of; on pain of; through the medium of; to the amount of; with an air of; with some admiring surprise at; under the superintendence of; with a view towards; without expense of; with respect to; with the design of; with the intention of; with the most serious results to.*

saying things in a way just a bit more complicated than it has to be. The tone of passages in this style will be light rather than solemn. Generally the elaborated style does not, like adverbial 'right', work to bring the character, the writer, and the reader together, but to divide them. It can represent prestigious, educated usage, or merely the will to prestigious, educated usage, and in a given example in a given novel, one may not be sure if it is intended as true high style, the language of humane law, literature, politics, and medicine, or as the parodied style of obfuscating authority, and the shabby gentility of merchandising and journalism.[21] The author moving into this elaborated style may be seeking the reader's admiration for his or her fine language, or for his or her strength as a parodist, or, disconcertingly, for both at once. Might the reader's sense of linguistic refinement be greater than the writer's? Might the writer, on the other hand, be assuming an audience able to make linguistic discriminations too subtle for the actual, and now humiliated reader? A very interesting and complex development, the elaborated style of the Victorians. Here, though, we want to concentrate on just one way in which that style is used. This way we will call the arch style: it is what we have when a novelist moves into elaborated language in a narrative passage concerning some character who certainly would not employ such language and might not even understand it. It is the arch style we find, for instance, in this passage from *Dombey and Son*, in which Dickens presents the consciousness of Major Bagstock's servant:

> ... the ill-starred Native had already undergone a world of misery arising out of the muffins, while in connection with the general question of boiled eggs, life was a burden to him.[22]

'Ill-starred', 'a world of misery', 'in connection with the general question of', 'life was a burden to him': we are certainly not struck by the brilliance or originality of these phrases, and the use of this dubiously elegant vocabulary in connection with muffins and boiled eggs does not help matters. The point here might seem to be simply that in the mind of the servant, the preparation of breakfast has become a matter of tragic dignity and importance, what is wrong with the language comically indicating what is wrong with the thought—except that the language is so conspicuously not the language this character would use, and on the other hand, not the language of genuine tragedy either. This is language the author and the reader can understand, can judge, but which the character cannot. It is a very complicated kind of satire we have here: satire both at the expense of those who not only could, but actually and unironically would use such tinny phrases, and at the expense of those who would not be able to use or even understand them. But just what have the two targets to do with one another? And why, in any case, should we at just this point have satire aimed at those who would employ shabby

[21]   See my *Dickens and the Suspended Quotation* (New Haven: Yale University Press, 1981), 94–97, and the works cited in the notes to those pages.

[22]   Charles Dickens, *Dombey and Son*, Intro. Lucy Hughes-Hallett (New York: Knopf, 1974), 271.

genteel phrasing? Similar questions may come to mind when we read, for instance, these sentences from the two last paragraphs of a chapter in Braddon's *The Doctor's Wife*:

> Long ago, when her brothers had been rude to her, and her stepmother had upbraided her on the subject of a constitutional unwillingness to fetch butter, and 'back' teaspoons, she had wished to die young...But in the midst of such thoughts as these she found herself wondering whether the hands of Mr Gilbert the elder were red and knobby like those of his son, whether he employed the same bootmaker, and entertained an equal predilection for spring-onions and Cheshire cheese.[23]

The 'she' is both cases is Isabel, and 'entertained an equal predilection for' is decidedly not the language in which Isabel would do her callow wishing and wondering.

In a passage from *Great Expectations*, the expression 'connubial missile' describes what Mrs Joe had made of the younger Pip:

> My sister, Mrs. Joe, throwing the door wide open, and finding an obstruction behind it, immediately divined the cause, and applied Tickler to its further investigation. She concluded by throwing me—I often served her as a connubial missile—at Joe, who, glad to get hold of me on any terms, passed me on into the chimney and quietly fenced me up there with his great leg.[24]

Clearly 'connubial missile' is not Mrs Joe's style, but is it a phrase that shows the older, narrating Pip's sense of truly elegant language? Is Dickens indicating a linguistic vulgarity in even the oldest Pip? Might Dickens himself think the phrase rather elegant as well as absurd? Might we? Should we? If we smile at the phrase—and I think we do—are we smiling complacently, because we, unlike Mrs Joe, understand? Can we be quite sure about all of this?

Now clearly these questions of good taste that seem so often to come with arch-style passages, and indeed with the elaborated style generally, also have, especially in arch-style passages, a social and moral dimension. The one clear loser in arch-style passages is the character whose association with this high-reaching language is simply implausible. But isn't there something snobbish and smug here? Ought we, really, to be enjoying a kind of linguistic triumph over these characters in which the victory often suggests—as in the Mrs Joe passage—superior education at least as much as superior imagination? Consider, together with the Mrs Joe passage, one about the hero's mother in George Eliot's *Felix Holt*:

> Mrs. Holt was not given to tears: she was much sustained by conscious unimpeachableness, and by an argumentative tendency which usually checks the too

---

[23] Mary Elizabeth Braddon, *The Doctor's Wife*, ed. Lyn Pickett (New York: Oxford University Press, 1998), 198–99.

[24] Charles Dickens, *Great Expectations*, ed. Edgar Rosenberg (New York: Norton, 1999), 13–14.

great activity of the lachrymal gland; nevertheless her eyes had become moist, her fingers played on her knee in an agitated manner, and she finally plucked a bit of her gown.[25]

Here the language, because it would mystify, controls the exasperating and uneducated, but not inhuman Mrs Holt. The author does what Felix does within the novel when he uses high language to keep his mother at bay—he often, Eliot tells us, 'amused himself and kept good-humoured by giving his mother answers that were unintelligible to her' (321)—and what the older Pip does to keep his remembered, powerful sister at a distance.

In such passages as these, we certainly don't have the triumph of evil and confusion, but neither do we have a triumph which is right good. The author/narrator is bullying the character: that character—a Mrs Joe, a Mrs Holt—*may* deserve some sort of literary punishment; but still, we would like the punishment to fit the crime more exactly, and the crime has not been the possession of a limited vocabulary. True, we can say Mrs Holt is too sure of her own knowledge, just as we can say that in *The Doctor's Wife* Isabel is shallow and self-dramatizing; but that doesn't seem enough to make the particular (and various) crimes unproblematically match this one widely favoured punishment.

We friends of Victorian fiction are made uneasy, if also amused, by arch-style passages, and when (or if) we think about the matter, we assume that what makes us uneasy is an unfortunate side effect of a device whose main purpose is to amuse and flatter us. But I believe that on a deep level almost the reverse is true. It is the aesthetic, social and moral strains we have been looking at in the last pages, the air of bad faith and divisions around reader and author and character, that have most to do with the frequent occurrence of arch-style passages in Victorian fiction: the arch style is popular, it is there, not in spite of, but because of these embarrassing features. It is *about* the strains and uncertainties of judgement. We might say that the arch style functions as a sort of union card for Victorian novelists, and that this card bears a strange device. It presents the arrogance of the novelist and shows by how much the writer's linguistic range exceeds the character's. But look at it more closely, and this image of arrogance and power becomes an image of humility.

Of humility; authorial humility. In a great age of literary realism, where writers want to be able to present every kind of consciousness, to show people in their own thoughts and language, the occasional arch-style passage is at once a time-out and a conspicuous example of failure. It is exaggerated, comic failure, or failure comically acknowledged. And the real failure would be the failure not of the character to possess the full language of the author, but of the author to imagine, or to be strong enough to keep trying to imagine what this character's thought and language might really be. Behind the joke

[25] George Eliot, *Felix Holt, the Radical*, ed. Peter Coveney (London: Penguin Classics, 1987), 136. Subsequent citations appear in the text.

there is perhaps a sense that the difference between the author's consciousness and the character's may be too great to overcome.

That understanding of others may not be possible, or possible only in an imperfect and feeble way, is something Dickens knows, or fears, and so too, I think, does Eliot—the novelist we particularly associate with the ideas of the importance of sympathy, and the effort sympathy requires. We might consider here (turning aside from elaborated syntax and diction for a moment) chapter XVI in *Bleak House* and the paragraph in which Dickens tries to imagine Jo's understanding of the world around him:

> It must be a strange state to be like Jo! To shuffle through the streets, unfamiliar with the shapes, and in utter darkness as to the meaning, of those mysterious symbols, so abundant over the shops, and at the corners of streets, and on the doors, and in the windows!…It must be very puzzling to see the good company going to the churches on Sundays, with their books in their hands and to think (for perhaps Jo *does* think, at odd times) what does it all mean…His whole material and immaterial life is wonderfully strange; his death, the strangest thing of all.[26]

And the threadbare 'strange' and 'very puzzling' represent the best we can do: Jo cannot get written language; our written language cannot get (or should we go on to say, we cannot get?) Jo's illiteracy. With George Eliot we might think of what at first seems a more narrowly literary comment the author makes about Hetty Sorrel in *Adam Bede*: 'Hetty had never read a novel; if she had even seen one, I think the words would have been too hard for her; how then could she find a shape for her expectations?'[27] But if a key character in a novel could not have understood the language of a novel, aren't we going to suspect that the language of novels won't quite get the experience of such a character?

That arch style, then, may be an emblem, an acknowledgement, of this kind of failure. We don't get it all right, and it may be the writers who come closest to getting it right, who would feel this most. The best in this kind are but shadows, as Shakespeare's Theseus says, perhaps speaking for his maker.[28] But rather than leave the question just at this point, we might look at something George Eliot does with the arch style, most notably in *Adam Bede*.

Eliot likes to use that arch style in descriptions of animals and small children. She is not unique in so using it. We may remember that Dickens tells us Bill Sykes' dog 'appear[ed] to entertain some unaccountable objection to having his throat cut',[29] and

---

[26] Dickens, *Bleak House*, 239.

[27] George Eliot, *Adam Bede*, ed. Margaret Reynolds (London: Penguin Classics, 2008), 148.

[28] And perhaps for other great writers, earlier as well as later. Shakespeare's line is quoted by E.T. Donaldson as he considers what Chaucer might have meant in assigning the (deliberately) crude *Sir Thopas* to himself in *The Canterbury Tales*. See Donaldson's *Chaucer's Poetry: An Anthology for the Modern Reader*, 2nd edn (New York and Chichester, 1975), 1100.

[29] Dickens, *Oliver Twist*, 153.

there is a stunning passage in one of the great essays of the period, De Quincey's *Suspiria de Profundis*, in which we are knocked from dog as furry person to dog as beast:

> It happened that we had received, as a present from Leicestershire, a fine young Newfoundland dog, who was under a cloud of disgrace for crimes of his youthful blood committed in that county. One day he had taken too great a liberty with a pretty little cousin of mine, Emma H—, about four years old. He had, in fact, bitten off her cheek, which, remaining attached by a thread, was, through the energy of a governess, replaced, and subsequently healed without a scar.[30]

But when Eliot renders animals in the arch style, as she not infrequently does, it is without the sardonic tone, that muted authorial growl, of the *Oliver Twist* passage, and her descriptions don't suddenly turn on the lulled reader in the way De Quincey's does. By contrast, she seems rather sweet-tempered, quite at ease, and eager (perhaps more eager than all of her readers have been) to simply play with the otherness of the other's consciousness. Thus, towards the end of the first chapter in *Adam Bede*, Eliot says of the hero's dog:

> Gyp ran forward and looked up in his master's face with patient expectation.
> If Gyp had had a tail he would doubtless have wagged it, but being destitute of that vehicle for his emotions, he was like many other worthy personages, destined to appear more phlegmatic than nature had made him. [16]

A few lines later we have moved on to chickens:

> On the door-stone stood a clean old woman, in a dark-striped linen gown, a red kerchief, and a linen cap, talking to some speckled fowls which appeared to have been drawn towards her by an illusory expectation of cold potatoes or barley. [16]

In *The Mill on the Floss*, Bob discusses dogs ('they're better friends than any Christian') and in particular his own dog, with Maggie:

> 'I can't give you Mumps 'cause he'd break his heart to go away from me—eh, Mumps, what do you say, you riff-raff?'—(Mumps declined to express himself more diffusely than by a single affirmative movement of his tail.) 'But I'd get you a pup, Miss, an' welcome.'[31]

[30] Thomas De Quincey, *Suspiria de Profundis*, in *Confessions of an Opium-Eater and Other Writings*, ed. Grevel Lindop (Oxford: Oxford University Press, 1996), 122.
[31] George Eliot, *The Mill on the Floss*, ed. A.S. Byatt (London: Penguin Classics, 2003), 295. Subsequent citations appear in the text.

The praise of Mumps continues on the next page:

> The expression of Mump's face, which seemed to be tolerating the superfluous existence of objects in general, was strongly confirmatory of this high praise. [296]

In the same novel, the horse Tancred begins 'to make ... spirited remonstrances against this frequent change of direction' (466) while in *Adam Bede*, when dogs bark, 'the half-weaned calves that have been sheltering themselves in a gorse-built hovel against the left-hand wall, come out and set up a silly answer to that terrible bark, doubtless supposing that it has reference to buckets of milk' (78–9); in *Silas Marner*, we are told that 'a sharp bark inside, as Eppie put the key in the door, modified the donkey's views...'.[32] Turning to babies and small children, we might notice that the first paragraph of *Middlemarch* gives us the young Saint Theresa 'and her still smaller brother' toddling out from rugged Avila 'until domestic reality met them in the shape of uncles'.[33] In *Adam Bede*, Eliot writes of a small boy:

> the sturdy fellow of five in knee-breeches, and red legs, who had a rusty milk-can round his neck by way of drum, and was very carefully avoided by Chad's small terrier. This young olive-branch, notorious under the name of Timothy's Bess's Ben, being of an inquiring disposition, unchecked by any false modesty, had advanced beyond the group of women and children, and was walking round the Methodists, looking up in their faces with his mouth wide open, and beating his stick against the milk-can by way of musical accompaniment. But one of the elderly women bending down to take him by the shoulder, with an air of grave remonstrance, Timothy's Bess's Ben first kicked out vigorously, then took to his heels and sought refuge behind his father's legs. [25]

In *Middlemarch*, Celia's baby is 'that unconscious centre and poise of the world' (461), but does not receive the arch attention lavished on Totty in *Adam Bede* in passages like:

> This errand was devised for Totty as a means of checking certain threatening symptoms about the corners of the mouth; for Tommy, no longer expectant of cake, was lifting up his eye-lids with his fore-fingers, and turning his eyeballs towards Totty in a way that she felt to be disagreeably personal. [524–25]

and

> But here her aunt's attention was diverted from this tender subject by Totty, who, perceiving at length that the arrival of her cousins was not likely to bring anything

---

[32] George Eliot, *Silas Marner* (New York: Harcourt, Brace, 1962), 169.
[33] George Eliot, *Middlemarch*, ed. David Carroll (Oxford: Oxford University Press, 1986), 3. Subsequent citations appear in the text.

satisfactory to her in particular, began to cry, 'Munny, munny,' in an explosive manner. [159]

There is no attempt to 'get' the child's consciouness (as there is, for instance, early in Joyce's *Portrait of the Artist as a Young Man*). And of course there is no attempt actually to get the language and consciousness of animals. The foreign consciousness may finally be out of reach: this, we have suggested, is a possibility the 'union card' arch style acknowledges. But with the things we can unproblematically love—with a Totty, rather than a Hetty—well, that love is enough, and it can be enjoyed effortlessly. And that would seem to be an important, one might say, an importantly comforting fact, to the novelist most conscious of the general need for people to work towards sympathy with other people.

Effortlessly enjoyed. Turning away from animals and small children again, one might think about the Harvest Supper chapter in *Adam Bede* and how much affectionate arch-style passages are part of that chapter's texture. Harvest Supper. It is a festive chapter: for now the hard-working farm-labourers can enjoy themselves, and the author can turn away from the hard work of trying to get other minds right.

III

The arch style plays with the linguistic distance between characters and author. It displays a command of ranges of language, often themselves involving parody of, and thus superiority to, banal literary, or journalistic or commercial uses of language, which puts the user of this arch style above the characters socially, even as it conspicuously fails to get—indeed, seems to mock the idea of getting—the consciousness of those characters realistically, in a way they themselves would recognize. One might say this arch style is a complement to the much-studied free indirect style: with the free indirect style, the language of the character moves markedly into the statements of the author; with the arch style, conspicuously authorial language moves into descriptions of characters. What we want to look at now is another common device of Victorian fiction which also plays with the different voices of character and author and the superior power of the author. This third device is on the arch style rather than the adverbial 'right' side of things. It is what I have called the 'suspended quotation' in novelistic dialogue.[34]

The device has to do with the presentation of characters' speech in direct discourse, and here, in direct discourse, the Victorian novelist has a range of choices. Before looking at these options, though, we should consider a point at which there is little variation. The general rule in the fiction being written in this period is that a new speech, a change of voice, requires a change of paragraph, as it did not in the more varied practice

[34] Lambert, *Dickens and the Suspended Quotation*, 6.

of the 18th century. Compare, with Victorian presentation of speech, this passage from Goldsmith's *The Vicar of Wakefield*:

> —'What signifies minding her,' cried the host, 'if she be slow, she is sure.'—'I don't know that,' replied the wife; 'but I know that I am sure she has been here a fortnight, and we have not yet seen the cross of her money.'—'suppose, my dear,' cried he, 'we shall have it all in a lump'—'In a lump!' cried the other, 'I hope we may get it any way; and that I am resolved we shall this very night, or out she tramps, bag and baggage.'—'Consider, my dear,' cried her husband, 'she is a gentlewoman, and deserves more respect.'[35]

A change of speaker is important in, and a major pleasure of, the Victorian novel, and paragraphing emphasizes the importance of the change.

Now, as to the choices a Victorian novelist does make in presenting direct discourse: if a character, Tom, is to say, 'Yes, I see what you mean', the new paragraph in the novel might begin with, or simply be, 'Yes, I see what you mean.' Or it could be,

> Tom said, 'Yes, I see what you mean'.

or,

> 'Yes, I see what you mean', said Tom.

or,

> 'Yes', said Tom, 'I see what you mean' [Sometimes, here and with the previous possibility, using the newer 'Tom said' word order.]

Or, with an initial focusing on the new speaker,

> Tom continued to stare at his coffee cup. 'Yes, I see what you mean'.

Apart from the uses of that 'said he' word order, these forms are still quite familiar to us. What is not as familiar to us now, and seems archaic, is the expansion of the *inquit*, the medial identification of the speaker. We don't feel swept out of our own time if an authors adds, say, an adverb or so to the *inquit*—we will accept '"Yes", Tom said irritably, "I see what you mean"' as the workaday language of either our own fiction (at least in its more conservative ranges) or the fiction of a not-too-distance past, but something like,

---

[35] Oliver Goldsmith, *The Vicar of Wakefield*, ed. Arthur Friedman (New York: Oxford University Press, 2006), 107.

'Yes', said Tom irritably, looking down once again at the coffee-stain spreading over his gorgeous and far too expensive new shirt, 'I see what you mean'.

is an exotic for us, and even more foreign is a variety like

'Yes', said Tom, irritably, looking down once again at the coffee-stain spreading over his gorgeous and far too expensive new shirt, 'yes, I see what you mean.'

These are suspended quotations: the second of them, with the opening of the character's speech repeated after the authorial interjection, being a variety we may call the catch-word suspended quotation. We will also find varieties in which there is an authorial interjection but no explicit 'he said'. Now the suspended quotation, in its various forms, is much favoured in the Victorian period.

'A sulky state of feeling,' said Squeers, after a terrible pause, during which he had moistened the palm of his right hand again, 'won't do. Cheerfulness and contentment must be kept up. Mobbs, come to me!'[36]

and

'What I want to know, George,' the old gentleman said, after slowly smacking his first bumper,—'what I want to know is, how you and—ah—that little thing upstairs are carrying on?'[37]

and

'What do you think them women does t'other day,' continued Mr. Weller, after a short pause, during which he had significantly struck the side of his nose with his fore-finger some half-dozen times. 'What do you suppose they does, t'other day, Sammy?'[38]

In these three examples we notice one use of the suspended quotation: a dramatic pause before a character speaks will be more dramatic if it is not mentioned in its natural place, before the speech, but during the speech, interrupting the speech and making us (now the reader and the character) wait. In 'The Harvest Supper' chapter of *Adam Bede* discussed earlier, we find George Eliot doing something similar:

'As for this peace,' said Mr Poyser, turning his head on one side in a dubitative manner, and giving a precautionary puff to his pipe between each sentence, 'I don't know. Th'

[36]   Charles Dickens, *Nicholas Nickleby*, ed. Michael Slater (New York: Penguin, 1978), 159.

[37]   William Makepeace Thackeray, *Vanity Fair, A Novel without a Hero*, ed. Peter L. Shillingsburg (New York: Garland, 1989), 111.

[38]   Charles Dickens, *The Pickwick Papers*, ed. James Kinsley (Oxford: Clarendon Press, 1986), 326.

war's a fine thing for the country, an' how'll you keep up prices wi'out it? An' them French are a wicked sort o' folks, by what I can make out; what can you do better nor fight 'em?' [569]

It is often comic, this Victorian suspended quotation, but need not be. Thus this passage from Disraeli's *Sybil*:

'So you see, my father,' said Sybil with animation, and dropping her book, which, however, her hand did not relinquish, 'even then all was not lost. The stout earl retired beyond the Trent, and years and reigns elapsed before this part of the island accepted their laws and customs.'[39]

Indeed it can be used to increase pathos:

'Has my dream come true?' exclaimed the child again, in a voice so fervent that it might have thrilled to the heart of any listener. 'But no, that can never be! How could it be—Oh! how could it!'[40]

But its casualness about the integrity of a given speech also suits the novel of dandyism very well. So in Bulwer-Lytton's *Pelham* we find:

'Let me,' I said, when I found myself alone with my second, 'let me thank you most cordially for your assistance; and allow me to cultivate an acquaintance so singularly begun....'[41]

And in Disraeli's *Sybil* again, where Egremont is a Regency aristocrat becoming a Victorian hero:

'You were speaking of the election, George,' said Egremont, not without reluctance, yet anxious, as the ice had been broken, to bring the matter to a result. Lord Marney, before the election, had written, in reply to his mother consulting him of the step, a letter with which she was delighted, but which Egremont at the time could have wished to have been more explicit. However, in the excitement attendant on a first contest, and influenced by the person whose judgment always swayed, and, in the present case, was peculiarly entitled to sway him, he stifled his scruples, and persuaded himself that he was a candidate not only with the sanction but at the insistence of his brother. 'You were speaking of the election, George,' said Egremont.[42]

[39] Disraeli, *Sybil*, 196.
[40] Dickens, *The Old Curiosity Shop*, 548.
[41] Edward Bulwer Lytton, *Pelham: The Adventures of a Gentleman*, ed. Jerome J. McGann (Lincoln: University of Nebraska Press, 1972), 40.
[42] Disraeli, *Sybil*, 79.

And in Marryat's satire of books like *Pelham*, the hero of a fashionable novel, rebuking his servant, might be presented in this way:

> 'Coridon,' said he, surveying his attendant from head to foot, and ultimately assuming a severity of countenance, 'Coridon, you are becoming gross, if not positively what the people call *fat.*'[43]

But when the suspended quotation form is used to present the speech of an unsympathetic character, and the expanded *inquit* ruins the character's desired effect both by the information it brings us and the way its rhythm ruins the rhythm of that speech, the thing may be at its best, as, for instance, in this passage from Thackeray's *The Virginians*:

> 'Our hostess,' said my lord Chesterfield to his friend in a confidential whisper, of which the utterer did not in the least know the loudness, 'puts me in mind of Covent Garden in my youth...'.[44]

Dickens loves such effects:

> 'And how,' asked Mr. Pecksniff, drawing off his gloves and warming his hands before the fire, as benevolently as if they were someone else's, not his: 'and how is he now?'[45]

> 'I am proud to see,' said Mr. Carker, with a servile stooping of the neck, which the revelations making by his eyes and teeth proclaim to be a lie, 'I am proud to see that my humble offering is graced by Mrs. Dombey's hand...'.[46]

And, turning once again to the treatment of Mrs Joe by the older, narrating Pip:

> 'What did you say?' cried my sister, beginning to scream. 'What did you say? What did that fellow Orlick say to me, Pip? What did he call me, with my husband standing by? O! O! O!' Each of these exclamations was a shriek; and I must remark of my sister, what is equally true of all the violent women I have ever seen, that passion was no excuse for her, because it is undeniable that instead of lapsing into passion, she consciously and deliberately took extraordinary pains to force herself into it, and became blindly furious by regular stages; 'what was the name he gave me before the base man who swore to defend me? O! Hold me! O!'[47]

[43] Frederick Marryat, 'How to Write a Fashionable Novel', in *Nineteenth-Century British Novelists on the Novel*, ed. George L. Barnett (New York: Appleton-Century-Crofts, 1971), 65.

[44] William Makepeace Thackeray, *The Virginians*, 2 vols. (London: Dent, 1965), 2: 228.

[45] Charles Dickens, *Martin Chuzzlewit*, ed. Margaret Cardwell (Oxford: Clarendon Press, 1982), 33–34.

[46] Dickens, *Dombey and Son*, 444.

[47] Dickens, *Great Expectations*, 92.

In such Dickensian passages as these, the interjected comment by the narrator does indeed proclaim the suspended statement of the character to be a lie, destroys, for the reader, the impression the character is trying to create with his or her speech. And what we see quickly in these hostile suspensions of characters' speeches, is, I think, what we eventually come to feel is more subtly present in all of Dickens' suspended quotations, even the most benign, sympathetic and simply helpful. The author who keeps interrupting others in a novel, impresses us in much the way someone does in life who keeps officiously, helpfully, sympathetically, interrupting other speakers: this is someone who loves having our attention even more than she or he seeks our enlightenment. With the Dickensian suspended quotation (and perhaps with all frequent uses of suspended quotations) we seem to have what we seemed to have with the arch style in Victorian fiction: an exploitation of the author's linguistic superiority to characters. With the arch style, though, the literary device used drew much of its oddly disturbing force from the way it was modelled upon a real-life social situation, with a disproportion between the author's breadth of linguistic knowledge and the character's. What suspended quotations in a novel echo is less tensions between social classes than simply bad manners—if anything, the interrupting author might seem less well behaved than the interrupted character! But it is perhaps more useful to say that the essential tension in the Victorian (and especially Dickensian) suspended quotation is a literary one rather than a 'real-life' social one. The important classes here are writers and characters, competing for the reader's attention and affection.

The character has certain advantages in such a competition. In his *Autobiography*, Trollope says that 'the dialogue is generally the most agreeable part of a novel', and I think this is true.[48] In narrative and description we can only read *about* what characters do, or *about* the rooms or town in which they live; dialogue *is* what they actually say. Then again, we have the fun of differentiated voices in exchanges of dialogue. With the new speaker/new paragraph layout we seem to pick up speed as we move from comparatively long narrative paragraphs to clusters of shorter dialogue paragraphs, with more airy white paper around them. We may recall that Lewis Carroll's Alice views matters rather as Trollope does:

> Alice was beginning to get very tired of sitting by her sister on the bank and of having nothing to do: once or twice she had peeped into the book her sister was reading, but it had no pictures or conversations in it, 'and what is the use of a book,' thought Alice, 'without pictures or conversations?'[49]

Alice need not even skim pages of the book to see that there are no conversations in the book: with Victorian paragraphing, it is enough to peep once or twice.

---

[48] Anthony Trollope, *An Autobiography* (London: Oxford University Press, 1953), 205.
[49] Lewis Carroll, *The Annotated Alice*, ed. Martin Gardner (New York: Bramhall House, 1960), 25.

But even if dialogue is generally the most agreeable part of a novel, that dialogue is itself the invention of the author. What is the difficulty? With Dickens, I think—and here, as in the whole matter of the suspended quotation, he seems less a unique than a clarifyingly extreme case—the problem is that the author is someone who wants as little as possible coming between him and the audience's love and admiration. We can think of all that is flamboyant in Dickens's narrative style (including of course elaborated style passages and sentences): we can think of his private theatricals, and especially of his public readings, where admiration by a physically present audience actually became dangerous to his health; we can think of the farce *Mr. Nightingale's Diary*, written by Dickens in collaboration with Mark Lemon, in which Dickens got to play six different characters and, as Edgar Johnson writes, 'The second-night audience screamed with laughter...and were flabbergasted near the end to discover that Dickens in rapid succession had disguised himself to play...a lawyer, a Sam Wellerish waiter, a maniacally enthusiastic walker, a hypochondriac, a gabbling Sairey Gamplike old woman, and a deaf sexton':[50] the author/actor breaks through the characters as in a suspended quotation the author breaks through the rhythms of the character's speech. And perhaps it is worth recalling that Dickens's career began with the actual reporting of speeches: where what was said was often fatuous, but needed to be taken down accurately, where speed was essential, and far from being able to interrupt the speakers, the writer had to master a difficult system of shorthand (including what were called 'arbitrary characters') to get the job done.

With the suspended quotation, then, the writer—and we do need to feel that this is truly the writer, not a ghostly 'narrator'—seems to be competing with his or her characters for the reader's attention and affection. A sense of that authorial will to upstage the character and court and charm and win the reader is part of the readers' experience with fiction from the earlier 19th century, and is most strikingly so when they are reading Dickens. Or perhaps we should say when they are reading the earlier Dickens. There is a general sense that Dickens's later novels are colder, or darker, or less fun, or more mature than the ones from the first half of his career, and one notices that Dickens uses suspended quotations more sparingly in his later than in his earlier novels. One would not say that Dickens seems colder in his later works mostly because he uses the suspended quotation less frequently there, but it does seem clear enough that the heavy use of the suspended quotation, with its suggestions of an eager, jealous courting of the reader, suggests a warmer author than does a more neutral, self-concealing way of presenting dialogue.

[50] Edgar Johnson, *Charles Dickens: His Tragedy and Triumph*, 2 vols. (New York: Simon and Schuster, 1952), 2: 735.

Suggested Reading

Bevis, Matthew. *The Art of Eloquence: Byron, Dickens, Tennyson, Joyce*. New York: Oxford University Press, 2007.

Brook, G.L. *The Language of Dickens*. London: André Deutsch, 1970.

Clark, John W. *The Language and Style of Anthony Trollope*. London: Andre Deutsch, 1975.

Dickens, Charles. *Bleak House*. Edited by Patricia Ingham. Peterborough, ON: Broadview Press, 2011.

———. *Great Expectations*. Edited by Edgar Rosenberg. New York: Norton, 1999.

Eliot, George. *Adam Bede*. Edited by Margaret Reynolds. London: Penguin Classics, 2008.

———. *Felix Holt, the Radical*. Edited by Peter Coveney. London: Penguin Classics, 1987.

Hori, Marahiro. *Investigating Dickens' Style: A Collocational Analysis*. Basingstoke: Palgrave, 2004.

Lambert, Mark. *Dickens and the Suspended Quotation*. New Haven: Yale University Press, 1981.

Mahlberg, Michaela. 'Corpus Linguistics and the Study of Nineteenth Century Fiction'. *Journal of Victorian Culture* 15 (2010): 292–98.

Phillipps, K.C. *Jane Austen's English*. London: André Deutsch, 1970.

———. *Language and Class in Victorian England*. Oxford: Blackwell, 1984.

———. *The Language of Thackeray*. London: André Deutsch, 1978.

PART X

ENDINGS

33

THE NOVEL, ITS CRITICS, AND THE UNIVERSITY: A NEW BEGINNING?

ANNA VANINSKAYA

I

There is no doubt that the Victorian university made its mark on the Victorian novel, and it was but natural that *Tom Brown's Schooldays* (1857) should be followed by *Tom Brown at Oxford* (1861). But was the opposite also true: can one say that the Victorian novel made an equally important mark on the Victorian university? Few critics or historians have asked themselves this question, if only because the early incarnation of English studies is regarded in the history of the discipline as a kind of Dark Ages, when two now extinct species, the pedantic philologists and the dilettante belletrists, fumbled about trying to constitute a subject neither of them knew what to do with. But those who have asked, like Francis O'Gorman in *The Victorian Novel*, have assumed that the answer is no.[1] Was this indeed the case?

It is possible to make a persuasive argument that it was. The debates which accompanied the introduction of English literature into institutionalized higher education, though they at times spilled over into the periodical press and into the national consciousness, had little to do with the familiar questions of 19th-century literary history, so many of which centred on the novel. The Victorian novel was, by definition, 'contemporary' literature, and that it could furnish a serious object of study in the university was for many conceivable only in the context of satire. The following 1895 sketch from *Punch*, entitled 'A Novel Education' (pun intended), is worth quoting in full:[2]

---

[1] Francis O'Gorman, ed., *The Victorian Novel* (Oxford: Blackwell, 2002).
[2] 'A Novel Education', *Punch* (30 November, 1895), 255. The parody mocks W.L. Phelps's groundbreaking Modern Novels course at Yale (thanks to Alexandra Lawrie for the information).

['One of the latest of the new academic studies instituted in the United States is 'a course of modern fiction.'... The modern fiction class in Yale University numbers no fewer than 258 members.'—*Daily Telegraph*.]

The tutor of St. Mary's, Cambridge, was sitting in his rooms after Hall interviewing a succession of undergraduates.

'Sit down, please, Mr. Jones,' he said to the last comer; 'I wish to speak to you very seriously on the subject of your work. The College is not at all satisfied with your progress this term. For instance, Professor Kailyard tells me that your attendance at his lectures has been most irregular.'

'Well, Sir,' said Jones, fumbling with the tassel of his cap, 'I didn't think they were important—'

'Not important? How do you expect to be able to get up difficult authors like Crockett and Maclaren unless you've attended a course of lectures on Scotch dialect? Do you know the meaning of "havers," "gabby," or "yammering"? I thought not. Then your last paper on "Elementary Besantics" was very weak. Have you really been giving your energies to your work, or have you been frittering away your time over other books?'

Jones looked guilty, but said nothing.

'Ah,' resumed the Don, 'I see how it is. You've been wasting your time over light literature—Homer and Virgil, and trash of that sort. But you really must resist temptations of that kind if you wish to do creditably in the Tripos. Good evening.'

Jones departed, to be succeeded by another undergraduate.

'I sent for you, Mr. Smith,' said the Tutor, 'because—though your work on the older writers is pretty good—your acquaintance with modern realism is quite insufficient. You will attend the course of anatomy lectures at the hospital, please. You can't study your "keynotes" intelligently without them.'

A third student made his appearance in the doorway.

'Mr. Robinson, I'm sorry to say that your work is unsatisfactory. On looking at your Mudie list, I find that you've only taken out ten novels in the last month. In order to see whether you can be permitted to take the Tripos this year, I'm going to give you a few questions, the answers to which must be brought me before Saturday. You will find pen and ink on that table. Kindly take down the following questions, as I dictate them.'

The tutor cleared his throat, and began:

'*Question one*. Explain "P.W.D. accounts," "a G.T.," "G.B.T. shin-bones." Trace the bearing of the history of Mowgli on the Darwinian theory.

'*Question two*. "The truth shall make us free." Give context, and comment on this statement. Conjugate, in accordance with the library catalogue, *The Woman who* —, noting which of the tenses are irregular.

'*Question three*. "There were two *Trilbys*" (Trilby, Part VIII.). Explain this statement. What had Mr. Whistler to do with it?

'*Question four*. Give the formulae for the employment of (*a*) the Mad Bull; (*b*) The Runaway Horse; (*c*) the Secret Marriage. What would you suggest as the modern equivalents of these?

'*Question five*. Rewrite the story of *Jack and Jill*,—(*a*) in Wessex dialect; (*b*) as a "Keynote"; (*c*) as a "Dolly Dialogue."

'That will do for the present,' concluded the tutor. And, as his pupil left the room, he seated himself at the writing-table and began Chapter XXIX of his "Prolegomena to *Three Men in a Boat*."

The types of questions were perfectly realistic, the absurdity stemmed from the reversal of the roles of Classics and light literature, and from the devastating up-to-datedness of the references: the 1890s Kailyard school of Scottish sentimental fiction; Thomas Hardy's regional Wessex novels; Grant Allen's New Woman text *The Woman Who Did*, published in the Bodley Head 'Keynote' series in 1895; George Du Maurier's phenomenal best-seller *Trilby* of the previous year (and the best-selling Anthony Hope's *The Dolly Dialogues*, also 1894); Jerome K. Jerome's New Humour; Rudyard Kipling's children's books; Walter Besant's East End romance; and so on. *This* was the contemporary novel, the butt of numerous jokes elsewhere in *Punch*'s pages, and the thought that it was comparable to Homer and Virgil provoked nothing but ridicule. To admit that the novels on Mudie's list were material worthy of examination in the Tripos was, *Punch* seemed to imply, tantamount to cultural suicide.

Some university dons agreed. It was not coincidental that the *Punch* vignette took place in a (fictional) Cambridge college. The ancient university was the last bulwark to yield. G.C. Macaulay, one of the main movers behind the introduction of more modern literature into the Tripos, observed that Cambridge 'came absolutely last in the field' of all other universities in both Britain and the United States in providing a Professor of English Literature.[3] When finally in 1910, none other than Harold Harmsworth, the king of New Journalism, had endowed the King Edward VII Professorship of English Literature in Cambridge, with the mandate 'to deliver courses of lectures on English Literature from the age of Chaucer onwards', voices were raised in protest.[4] It 'would be simply a Professorship of English literature dating from the beginning of the latter half of the nineteenth century', objected Dr James Mayo, 'and the effect of that would be that the Professorship would be a Professorship of English fiction, and that of a light and comic character. For that reason . . . [it was] unworthy of that university.'[5] Dr Mayo—who in any case believed that students of English literature required no training except the ability to read—had earlier opposed the extension of the period covered by the 'Outlines of English Literature' exam paper to 1850, for it 'was perfectly sure to result in the inclusion of Dickens and Thackeray, an extension he most firmly believed to be detrimental to the studies of the University, and entirely below its dignity'.[6] The would-be reformers gave in, and scaled back the scope of the paper to 1832.

---

[3] 'Discussions of Reports. On the Report of the Council of the Senate on the Establishment of the King Edward VII Professorship of English Literature', *Cambridge University Reporter* (13 December, 1910), 407.

[4] 'Report of the Council of the Senate on the Establishment of the King Edward VII Professorship of English Literature', *Cambridge University Reporter* (1 December, 1910), 327.

[5] 'On the Report of the Council of the Senate', 407.

[6] 'Discussions of Reports. On the Report, Dated 13 October 1909, of the Special Board for Medieval and Modern Languages on the Regulations for the Medieval and Modern Languages Tripos', *Cambridge University Reporter* (30 November, 1909), 316. Others objected that 1832 was a 'natural break, with the death of Scott', whereas '1850 brought them to the middle of the productive career of almost every active name in the Victorian era. That was not a good place at which to stop', though instead of going forward it was assumed that the solution was to go back (314).

The problem was not just modern fiction, but modern (i.e. post-medieval) English literature more generally. This was the ultimate late-Victorian 'soft' option, and if 'chatter about Shelley' was disparaged, it was obscene even to contemplate chatter about Mrs Humphry Ward.[7] As the Oxford Regius Professor of Modern History, E.A. Freeman, famously argued (and so had numerous others before him), literature was something people read for pleasure, it was a matter of taste and fashion. If it were to be recognized as a subject fit for systematic and rigorous study, which could be examined like other subjects, it would need to be approached in a philological light, or risk being reduced to the worst species of cram. But we do not want it to be examined, replied his opponents, we do not wish to see literature escape the 'easy' label if that comes at the expense of burdening it with too much language and history in the attempt to make it 'hard' or 'solid'. 'I think it would do no irreparable harm to anyone if English Literature were never examined on from now to the crack of doom', announced Walter Raleigh, the future Oxford Merton Professor of English Literature.[8] 'There is danger in submitting the delicate flowers of English literature to the methods of the lecture room, the schedules and tests of the examination room', wrote Stanley Leathes, a Civil Service commissioner and former Cambridge lecturer responsible for the English papers in the Civil Service examination. 'Examination, like mines and manufacture, is necessary; but to examine in English literature is like opening a coal mine in the Lake District.'[9]

But whether one was against the introduction of English literature or in favour of it, whether one wanted to preserve the pleasure from being ruined by the drudgery of the schoolwork—the novelist Grant Allen contemplated with horror the prospect of Oxford students being examined on 'the nice question why Richard Feveril [*sic*] did not return to Lucy'—or to preserve the schoolwork from being ruined by the frivolity of the pleasure, the Victorian novel per se was rarely the apple of discord.[10] For many, especially earlier in the century, it was outside the equation altogether. As the Earl of Harrowby put it to the Taunton Commission on the reform of middle-class education (1864–68): 'How many of our higher classes there are who pass away from Eton and Harrow without having read any one English classic and who know nothing of English but Dickens and Thackeray? It is a scandal. English reading of the highest order ought to enter into every part of every English education.'[11] Novels obviously did not count as 'reading of the

[7] Victorian and Edwardian critics habitually referred to women writers as 'Miss' or 'Mrs'.

[8] Not to be confused with the Merton Professorship of English Language and Literature which was created in 1885, and to which a philologist was appointed. See Alan Bacon, 'Attempts to Introduce a School of English Literature at Oxford: the National Debate of 1886 and 1887', *History of Education* 9, no. 4 (1980): 303–13.

[9] Walter Raleigh, *The Study of English Literature: Being the Inaugural Lecture Delivered at the University of Glasgow on Thursday, October 18th, 1900* (Glasgow: James MacLehose and Sons, 1900), 16; Stanley Leathes, *The Teaching of English at the Universities, With a Note by Professor W.P. Ker* (Oxford: Horace Hart, 1913), 9, 12.

[10] Repr. in Alan Bacon, ed., *The Nineteenth-Century History of English Studies* (Aldershot: Ashgate, 1998), 273. The reference is to George Meredith's *The Ordeal of Richard Feverel* (1859).

[11] Repr. in Bacon, ed., *The Nineteenth-Century History of English Studies*, 119.

highest order'. The Liberal Cambridge philosopher Henry Sidgwick was wholeheartedly in favour of teaching the English classics, but popular novels were no part of the English literature whose study he advocated, and he lamented the fate of those schoolboys 'who temper small compulsory sips of Virgil, Sophocles, Tacitus, and Thucydides, with large voluntary draughts of [G.P.R.] James, Ainsworth, Lever, and the translated Dumas'. He even quoted the conservative *Quarterly Review* in support of his view that while great English literature was 'still a desideratum in nearly all our great places of education', 'the future gentry of the country are left to pick up their mother tongue from the periodical works of fiction which are the bane of our youth, and the dread of every conscientious schoolmaster'.[12] Ironically, by the 1890s, the baneful authors listed by Sidgwick would figure on a par with the worthiest names in the new literary histories.

Another closely related debate which had been rumbling on since at least the mid-century, and showed no signs of dying on the eve of the Great War, concerned the struggle between 'language' and 'literature', between the philologists and those implacably opposed to the privileging of 'narrow', 'pedantic', and 'specialized' language learning at the expense of the appreciation of literature for its own sake. The dismemberment of the classic literary texts of William Shakespeare, John Milton, or Daniel Defoe into mere gobbets for grammatical and etymological analysis, for 'parsing' of the most mechanical kind, was a feature of examinations at every level of the educational system. Elementary school pupils and teachers-in-training had to put up with it as much as Army commission and Civil Service candidates, or university students sitting matriculation and degree exams. The domination of the philologists at ancient seats of learning like Oxford and Cambridge in particular raised the ire of the literary camp. 'Is the interest of the average student who enters the English school principally philological, or is it literary, historical, humanistic? Is it archaeological or is it modern?' asked Leathes in 1913.[13] He was echoing sentiments expressed many times before by teachers, school inspectors, syllabus reformers, and university professors, and most notoriously by John Churton Collins, the most vociferous campaigner on behalf of the introduction of English literature at Oxbridge in the late 19th century. Collins wrote hundreds of pages objecting to the treatment of literature as 'mere material for the study of words', 'mere pabulum for philology', and to the excessive concentration on the 'barbarous' experiments of the 'infancy of civilization' and the 'niceties of the various Romance and Teutonic dialects'.[14]

But while one would expect this debate to figure centrally in a discussion of the place of novels in the curriculum, this was not in fact the case. The proponents of 'literature' had, on the whole, as little interest in Victorian novels as the philologists. Even Collins failed to find a place for fiction in his scheme of what that literature consisted of, and he

[12] Henry Sidgwick, 'The Theory of Classical Education', in *Essays on a Liberal Education*, ed. Rev. F.W. Farrar (London: Macmillan, 1867), 108, 110. Sidgwick was also an influential promoter of women's higher education.

[13] Leathes, 10.

[14] John Churton Collins, *The Study of English Literature: A Plea for its Recognition and Organization at the Universities* (London: Macmillan and Co., 1891), 22, 8.

was merely following in the footsteps of those predecessors who bewailed the neglect of English in school and university education, but who would have been incredulous at the thought of studying the Victorian novel. Raleigh, who in his inaugural lecture at Glasgow (where he spent four years as Professor of English Literature and Rhetoric before moving to Oxford) railed against 'minute antiquarian researches and historical grammar—[teaching] English, in short, as if it were a dead language', did not think it was the purpose of a 'literary class-room' to teach someone to write novels like a Mr George Meredith either. The end of a university education was to produce good men of letters and readers of books, who preferred the classics to 'the Novel of the Season'.[15] Indeed, when he composed his own study of the English novel, he name-checked every-one from Samuel Richardson and Henry Fielding to Fanny Burney, Jane Austen, and Maria Edgeworth, but stopped short at Walter Scott.[16]

The Scylla to the Charybdis of philology in these debates was 'cram'. Literature could be reduced to language or to superficial lists of facts for memorization, and neither approach required a proper acquaintance with the primary texts. Frequently, the two went hand in hand: the teaching of literature, it was feared, would end in 'the getting up of little annotated text-books, with their scraps of philology and ready-made criticism and antiquarianism, for purposes of examination, very often at the expense of neglect-ing the text'.[17] The 'masterpieces [of literature] have been resolved into exercises in gram-mar, syntax, and etymology', Collins complained, 'Its history has been resolved into a barren catalogue of names, works, and dates. No faculty but the faculty of memory has been called into play in studying it.' The general history of English literature was a sub-ject tailor-made for cramming. If something were not done, the future would be grim:

> An elaborate apparatus of mnemonic aids would be devised. Such works as Mr. Morley's would be summarized into tables for facts, and such works as M. Taine's would be reduced to epitomes for generalizations. Criticism as applied to particular authors would be got by heart from essays and monographs, and criticism on its theoretical side would be got by heart from the analyses of crammers.[18]

The number of times these fears recurred over the course of the second half of the 19th and the first decade of the 20th century is beyond count. 'When I read in a syllabus that one subject is the outlines of English literature from 1350–1832, I do not see how a student can come before the examiners without cramming a text-book', Leathes still complained in 1913.[19] The syllabus he was reading must have been the Cambridge Modern and Medieval Languages (MML) one (under whose aegis English Literature appeared). The

---

[15] Raleigh, *Study of English Literature*, 6–7, 10.
[16] Walter Raleigh, *The English Novel: A Short Sketch of Its History from the Earliest Times to the Appearance of Waverley* (London: John Murray, 1894).
[17] The Headmaster of Clifton College quoted in Collins, *Study of English Literature*, 102.
[18] Collins, *Study of English Literature*, 22, 27.
[19] Leathes, 11.

regulations made it clear that 'connected outlines would be required rather than detailed knowledge': the examiners obviously expected the students to cram.[20] Cambridge was not alone in this. Many university syllabuses featured 'period' and 'outlines' papers—like the University of London 'History of English Literature, 1660–1850' paper—whose coverage corresponded exactly to the subject matter of the literary historical surveys which flooded the market. Handbook provision and exam design enjoyed a perfectly reciprocal relationship. The length of the handbook entry even matched the length of the required response: it is difficult to envision any other way of replying to a question which asked the candidate to write 'brief descriptive notes, in the manner of an entry in a dictionary, on each of the following…' than by memorizing the said dictionary.[21] In fact, the inordinate and therefore superficial coverage necessitated by the cramming of English literary history was a subject of government inquiry, and the kinds of problems revealed by the testimony to the Taunton Commission with regard to the English section of the Civil Service exams were still being invoked in arguments against the introduction of a separate English School at Oxford in the late 19th century.[22]

Cramming was not just something the students and their tutors bore responsibility for. It was the result of a whole culture which militated against first-hand engagement with literary texts, a culture embodied not just in the endless exam-oriented 'manuals, primers, sketches, charts…designed to facilitate [their] study', but in what Walter Raleigh called that 'debased and debasing invention', the 'literary time-saving contrivance in the shape of "Elegant Extracts"'.[23] Although novelists professionally involved in education, such as Charles Kingsley and E.A. Abbott, denounced them in no uncertain terms, in the academic study of English extracts were all the rage. Sir Henry Craik's *English Prose: Selections* came out in five volumes from 1893 to 1896 (volume five was devoted to the 19th century), and it was merely the admired top of an enormous iceberg whose foundations rested in the literary extracts of the elementary school readers which sold in the millions. Edmund Gosse expressed the prevailing view when he insisted that the general reader did not have time to read all of English literature, and therefore needed useful selections. And if this was true of the general reader, how much

[20] 'Report of the Special Board for Medieval and Modern Languages on the Regulations for the Medieval and Modern Languages Tripos', *Cambridge University Reporter* (2 November, 1909), 181.

[21] Question from the 'History of English Literature, 1600–1700' paper in the 1914 Oxford University Final Honour School exam in English Language and Literature. See John Dixon, *A Schooling in 'English': Critical Episodes in the Struggle to Shape Literary and Cultural Studies* (Milton Keynes: Open University Press, 1991), 67, for another example of the correspondence between exam questions and Austin Dobson's *Handbook of English Literature* (rev. edn, 1897).

[22] For the cramming debate see the documents reproduced in Bacon's *History of English Studies* as well as Collins *passim*.

[23] Collins, *Study of English Literature*, 17; Raleigh, *Study of English Literature*, 14. Ironically enough, given his views, Collins served as a general editor of the publisher Edward Arnold's' Shakespeare and British Classics for Schools' series. See Fred Hunter, 'Collins, John Churton (1848–1908)', *Oxford Dictionary of National Biography*, Oxford University Press, 2004, <http://www.oxforddnb.com/view/article/32504> (accessed 9 December 2009).

more so of the student, feverishly preparing for his exams! That student could also turn to another product of a busy publishing industry dedicated to intervening between the 'whole book' and its reader: the educational edition of the 'English Classic with Notes and Introductions', constructed on the model taken from Classical scholarship. The typical edition of a canonical author like Milton, Francis Bacon, or Samuel Johnson, adapted for the use of the pupil, came packaged with prose paraphrase, parsing, specimens of analysis, interpretation and commentary, annotations, and perhaps a book of examination questions. Adverts at the back of handbooks listed not just etymological dictionaries and introductions to English composition, but texts such as *Shakespeare's Plays for Schools. With Introductions, Copious Notes, Examination Papers, and Plan of Preparation* or an *Outline of the History of the English Language and Literature, Showing Sources and Growth, with Roots and Derivatives, List of Principal Authors and Their Works, Figures of Speech, &c.*[24] The philologist W.W. Skeat's recommendations for further reading in his selection of English exam papers set in various Cambridge colleges in the 1860s and early 1870s included literary historical surveys such as the ubiquitous Robert Chambers, George Lillie Craik, Hippolyte Taine, and Henry Morley, as well as selections with notes and illustrative matter, and 'modern' prose-writers and poets 'Edited for Middle-Class Examinations, with Notes on the Analysis and Parsing, and Explanatory Remarks'. Skeat consciously situated himself as part of the mid-Victorian campaign for breaking the monopoly of Classics in favour of the national language and literature—embodied in the oft-repeated rhetorical question: 'Why should we not know our Shakespeare as the Greeks knew their Homer?'—but he saw no contradiction in simultaneously speaking out in favour of cramming.[25]

It was no wonder if the Victorian novel got lost amid all the shouts and bickering about philology, cramming, and examining. And it certainly did not help that there

---

[24] See e.g. Thomas Page, ed., *Moffatt's Pupil Teachers' Course, Fourth Year*, New Edition, Revised and Enlarged (London: Moffatt and Paige, 1883), as well as Collins's intemperate reviews of the Clarendon editions.

[25] Rev. Walter W. Skeat, *Questions For Examination in English Literature, Chiefly Selected from College-Papers Set in Cambridge, With an Introduction on the Study of English* (London: Bell and Daldy, 1873), vii. The authors (usually headmasters) of other cram books had something to say for themselves as well. For extensive treatments of cramming from their point of view see, for example, Rev. Thomas Stantial, *A Test-Book for Students; Comprising Sets of Examination Papers Upon Language and Literature, History and Geography, and Mathematical and Physical Science; Designed for Students Preparing for the Universities or for Appointments in the Army and Civil Service, and Arranged for General Use in Schools, Part II. Language and Literature* (London: Bell and Daldy, 1858), and Rev. Robert Demaus, *English Literature and Composition: A Guide to Candidates in those Departments in the Indian Civil Service. With Examination-Papers and Specimens of Answers* (London: Longmans, Green, and Co., 1866) and *The Prose and Prose Writers of Britain from Chaucer to Ruskin, with Biographical Notices, Explanatory Notes, and Introductory Sketches of the History of English Literature* (Edinburgh: Adam and Charles Black, 1860). Demaus was a fellow of the Educational Institute of Scotland, and the latter work was a literary historical anthology of illustrative extracts from the best authors, aimed at the general public. Bulwer Lytton and Dickens were the two Victorians who made the cut, and the usual mixture of critical and laudatory opinion rounded out the sketches of their life and works. With regard to Dickens in particular, the clichés of the later university critics were already in place.

was a glaring lacuna at the centre of power—the Victorian novel was not canonized in the English literature curricula of Oxford and Cambridge; it had to encroach from the margins and from below. Its introduction at Oxbridge was but the capping stone, the end of the story, rather than the beginning it is so often taken to be.[26] In fact, the Oxbridge-attending male elite would have been exposed to the Victorian novel in absolutely tiny numbers, for even once lectures and examinations which mentioned it had been introduced, the numbers of students attending and sitting them could usually be counted on the fingers of one hand (the same did not hold for the women's colleges, but an influx of male students finally took place only after the Great War). Only two entered for the newly instituted Final Honour School exam in Oxford in 1896, and neither succeeded. No more than ten, and frequently fewer candidates sat the MML Tripos in Cambridge from 1886 to 1891, and there were 'six Examiners...to an average of four examinees'.[27] Things were not much better in 1909, when there were still fewer than ten students sitting the exams. That year an advanced section A2 was introduced to give those who desired to specialize in literature rather than language (covered by section B) an alternative. But though the section included a paper on post-1500 literature, it was not eligible for the Ordinary BA degree, thus making it highly unlikely that anyone would bother with it. The reformers themselves acknowledged this: 'they did not expect [the candidates] to be many'.[28]

But Oxford and Cambridge were not the whole educational system. English literature held 'a foremost place' in the Army, Civil Service, and India Civil Service exams, and the Oxford and Cambridge Local examinations, for which many hundreds of boys and girls answered questions on 'the Victorian novelists'.[29] It had been taught and examined by professors of English at University College, King's College, and Queen's College, London, virtually since the institutions' inception, at Northern 'provincial' universities (the 'newer' universities as the Cambridge syllabus reformers called them), and Scottish universities such as Glasgow, Aberdeen, and Edinburgh, which had always been receptive to the novel.[30] In most of these places, especially towards the end of the century, overworked lecturers had to deal with hundreds of students on a daily basis. 'In the Extension Lectures', aimed since the 1870s at 'ladies' and the lower middle class

---

[26] All such statements, of course, need to be qualified. Colleges set their own papers in literature and offered English prizes for decades before the English Schools were formed, or any professorships of English were established, and Victorian poets like Tennyson were co-opted for this purpose almost instantaneously, though the intercollegiate examinations in Cambridge did not go beyond 1815 as late as 1910 (*Cambridge University Reporter*, 1340). In Oxford, English was one of the subjects that could be taken for the lesser pass examination from 1873, and a special exam for women was instituted in 1881.

[27] Collins, *Study of English Literature*, 25.

[28] 'On the Report, Dated 13 October 1909', 312.

[29] See the 'Fifty-first Annual Report of the Local Examinations and Lectures Syndicate', *Cambridge University Reporter* (15 March, 1909): 668–69.

[30] See Franklin E. Court, *Institutionalizing English Literature: The Culture and Politics of Literary Study, 1750–1900* (Stanford: Stanford University Press, 1992) and Alan Bacon, 'English Literature Becomes a University Subject: King's College, London as Pioneer', *Victorian Studies* 29, no. 4 (Summer 1986): 591–612.

(they were generally too expensive for all but the upper echelons of the working class), literature 'fill[ed] a wider space than either Science or History', and Extension lecturers such as R.G. Moulton and J.A. Hobson specifically focused on the novel.[31] Collins, a professional Extension lecturer himself before he became an English professor at the University of Birmingham, claimed that the reason the leaders of the Extension Movement were always calling upon Oxbridge to teach literature was that demand for courses in their most popular subject was not being met by the teaching supply. English literature was central to women's higher education: many more women candidates than men attended the lectures and sat the English exams at Oxbridge—whether the special examinations for women, the college papers, or the proper degree examinations once they were instituted. It was also central to colonial universities, to Mechanics' Institutes and Working Men's Colleges. Walter Raleigh started his career in India in 1885 as the first professor of English literature at the Mohammedan Anglo-Oriental College in Aligarh, and his trajectory from there to Liverpool, Glasgow, and finally Oxford embodied the slow movement of English itself from the colonies and the provinces to the 'centre'. [32]

The national literature, in particular the 'English classics', had long been considered suitable for those whose path in life did not necessitate a knowledge of Greek and Latin, and although this did not guarantee exposure to the contemporary novel so much as to Shakespeare and William Wordsworth, a middle-class female student's chances of encountering the novel in an educational setting were much higher than those of her upper-class male peers. Advocates of English rarely failed to make the disclaimer that the subject was most suitable for the average majority, rather than the exceptional few, for whom the Classical languages (or philology, if the context was syllabus reform at Oxbridge) were still the way to go. In his inaugural lecture at Queen's College in 1848, Charles Kingsley explicitly advocated the study of 'the recent and living authors', for 'the authors which really interest and influence the minds of the young are just the ones which have formed no part of their education, and therefore those for judging of which they have received no adequate rules'. He called for the establishment of 'a really entire course of English Literature . . . up to the latest of our modern authors', with lectures devoted to the criticism of the most influential in 'the last fifty years of English literature'.[33] Perhaps it helped that Kingsley himself was a modern novelist, but his insistence on guiding judgement is not surprising when one considers that the pupils in question were young women studying to be governesses.

---

[31] Collins, *Study of English Literature*, 16. See Dixon, *A Schooling in 'English'* and Lawrence Goldman, *Dons and Workers: Oxford and Adult Education Since 1850* (Oxford: Clarendon Press, 1995). Thanks to Alexandra Lawrie for the information on Moulton and Hobson.

[32] See D.N. Smith, 'Raleigh, Sir Walter Alexander (1861–1922)', rev. Donald Hawes, *Oxford Dictionary of National Biography* (Oxford: Oxford University Press, 2004), <http://www.oxforddnb.com/view/article/35656> (accessed 9 December 2009).

[33] Charles Kingsley, 'On English Literature', repr. in Bacon, ed., *History of English Studies*, 90–1.

Of course, the middle and upper classes always remained much more likely to encounter the Victorian novel in their leisure reading than in the classroom. It was the working class—by far the largest portion of the population, and the one which had the least say in the processes of canon-formation, as taste-makers, if not as customers—which benefited from the greatest educational exposure to the Victorian novel. Despite the fact that the Revised Code of 1862 only provided for the recitation of poetry, and English did not come into its own as a separate 'specific' subject until the very end of the century, by the 1890s selections from Victorian fiction were already established as an integral part of elementary school reading books, in both the state and voluntary sectors. Full-text and abridged versions of Victorian novels were also issued by educational publishers for school use alongside editions of the English 'classics'.[34] By the 1900s this was no longer just a school phenomenon. A.J. Wyatt's *The Tutorial History of English Literature*—a 'smaller text-book of literature' issued in the 'University Tutorial' series—came in tandem with the publisher's 'English Classics' series, which the student was recommended to read.[35] The series included not just the usual pre-Victorian staples but Charles Dickens's *David Copperfield*, *A Tale of Two Cities*, *The Pickwick Papers*, and *Dombey and Son*; W.M. Thackeray's *Vanity Fair*, *The Newcomes*, and *Esmond*; George Eliot's *The Mill on the Floss*, *Adam Bede*, and *Middlemarch*; and Charlotte Brontë's *Jane Eyre* and *Shirley*. The Victorian novel was finally taking its proper place among the literary historical handbooks and university-oriented classics editions: in other words, it was becoming as worthy of being crammed as Shakespeare. The development was due in no small part to the efforts of those new professors of English who, unlike Dr Mayo, did not think Dickens and Thackeray below the dignity of a university.

II

Few professors at London and the Red Bricks were specialists in the Victorian novel. In fact, the majority could best be described as generalists and comparatists. Oliver Elton,

---

[34] The teaching of English (and the novel) in elementary schools is a huge subject in itself. See Anna Vaninskaya, Christopher Stray, Alice Jenkins, James A. Secord, and Leslie Howsam, 'What the Victorians Learned: Perspectives on Nineteenth-Century Schoolbooks', *Journal of Victorian Culture* 12, no. 2 (Autumn 2007): 262–85; J.M. Goldstrom, *The Social Content of Education 1808–1870: A Study of the Working Class School Reader in England and Ireland* (Shannon: Irish University Press, 1972); Christopher Stray and Gillian Sutherland, 'Mass Markets: Education', in *The Cambridge History of the Book in Britain, 1830–1914*, ed. David McKitterick (Cambridge: Cambridge University Press, 2009), 6: 359–81; David Shayer, *The Teaching of English in Schools 1900–1970* (London: Routledge & Kegan Paul, 1972); Robin Peel, Annette Patterson, and Jeanne Gerlach, *Questions of English: Ethics, Aesthetics, Rhetoric and the Formation of the Subject in England, Australia and the United States* (London: Routledge Falmer, 2000).

[35] A.J. Wyatt, *The Tutorial History of English Literature*, 3rd edn (1900; London: University Tutorial Press Ltd, 1910), v.

Professor of English Literature at the University of Liverpool, for instance, phrased his opposition to medievalist philology in terms of the importance of modern French and Italian literature, and in his consideration of George Meredith in *Modern Studies* contrasted him not just with Dickens, Thackeray, Eliot, Hardy, and Henry James, but with Honoré de Balzac, Émile Zola, Guy de Maupassant, Maxim Gorky, Gabriele D'Annunzio, and Leo Tolstoy.[36] But specialist or not, the greatest champion of the Victorian novel at the turn of the century was George Saintsbury, Professor of Rhetoric and English Literature at the University of Edinburgh. The reason for his enthusiasm was not far to seek. Before he was appointed to his post in 1895, Saintsbury spent twenty years as a reviewer of contemporary literature for big periodicals such as the *Fortnightly*, *Macmillan's*, and the *Saturday Review*.[37] His early critical and review work was dedicated to French novels, and later he broadened his remit to include most contemporary European and American fiction, so Balzac, Gustave Flaubert, Zola, Tolstoy, and James were as much on his radar as the English novelists. Although he conscientiously abandoned reviewing upon his appointment, thus taking his finger off the 'pulse' of modern literature, his interest in it did not wane. He was not unique in this respect: many of his professorial contemporaries were also journalists and men of letters, and the boundary between their activities in the two capacities was often blurred. Elton's collection of *Modern Studies*, dedicated 'to the makers of the University of Liverpool', was composed of articles reprinted from periodicals and newspapers such as the *Quarterly*, the *Fortnightly*, and the *Manchester Guardian*, and so was Collins's *Ephemera Critica, or Plain Truths About Current Literature*.[38] The third volume ('Modern Criticism') of Saintsbury's *History of Criticism and Literary Taste in Europe* contained pronouncements not only on novelists like Dickens, Thackeray, and Walter Pater, but on journalist and professor critics of his own vintage such as William Minto: 'A journalist for one-half of his working life, and a professor—partly—of literature for the other, [he] executed in both capacities a good deal of literary work: but his most noteworthy contribution to our subject consisted in the two remarkable manuals of English literary history which, as quite a young man, he drew up.'[39]

Minto was not the only one: Elton produced two *Surveys of English Literature* of two volumes each (*1780–1830* and *1830–1880*); Raleigh published *The English Novel* in the

[36]   Oliver Elton, *Modern Studies* (London: Edward Arnold, 1907), 129.

[37]   George Saintsbury, *The English Novel* (London: J.M. Dent & Sons Ltd, 1913), 273: 'In regard to a large part of the subject of the present chapter ["The Fiction of Yesterday—Conclusion"] the present writer possesses the knowledge of a reviewer, week by week and almost day by day, of contemporary fiction between 1873 and 1895.' See also his essay 'Twenty Years of Reviewing (1873–1895)' in *The Collected Essays and Papers of George Saintsbury, 1875–1920*, 4 vols. (London: J.M. Dent and Sons Ltd, 1923–24). *The English Novel* was part of a series called 'The Channels of English Literature', whose contributors were mostly professors from Scottish, American, or new English universities.

[38]   Elton, v; John Churton Collins, *Ephemera Critica, or Plain Truths About Current Literature* (Westminster: Archibald, Constable and Co., Ltd, 1901).

[39]   George Saintsbury, *A History of Criticism and Literary Taste in Europe: From the Earliest Texts to the Present Day* (Edinburgh: William Blackwood and Sons, 1904), 3: 553.

'University Extension Manuals' series; and Saintsbury himself was a master of the genre.[40] Unlike the narrowly targeted cramming handbooks, the literary histories penned by the professors were often geared at both a student and a general audience. 'Some have described these volumes as "school-books," and others have been good enough to call them a "popular series"', Saintsbury wrote in the Preface to his survey of *The Later Nineteenth Century*.[41] Collins, in his attack on Saintsbury's *A Short History of English Literature*, confirmed that it was

> evidently designed . . . for the ordinary reader who will naturally look to it for general instruction and guidance in the study of English Literature, and to whom it will serve as a book of reference; for students in schools and colleges, to many of whom it will, in all likelihood, be prescribed as a textbook; for teachers engaged in lecturing and in preparing pupils for examination.[42]

Saintsbury's surveys were indeed assigned in universities: in the 1900s the recommended texts for the 'History of Criticism' exam paper in the School of English Literature at Liverpool included his *History of Literary Criticism* alongside the works of Pater and Matthew Arnold.

What had these histories to say of the novel? 'There are numerous monographs on parts of the subject: but nothing else that I know even attempting the whole', Saintsbury claimed in *The English Novel* of 1913:

> Dunlop's *History of Fiction*, an excellent book, dealt with a much wider matter, and perforce ceased its dealing just at the beginning of the most abundant and brilliant development of the English division . . . The late Mr. Sidney Lanier's *English Novel and the Principle of its Development* is really nothing but a laudatory study of 'George Eliot', with glances at other writers.

One of the reasons for this relative neglect, according to Saintsbury, was the lateness in Western literature of prose fiction, and its 'comparative absence' in Greek and Latin: not until the 19th century did it really come into its own.[43] Although Saintsbury did not say so, the Classical biases and affiliations of so many advocates of English literature as

---

[40] For a discussion of the literary history genre see Lynne Walhout Hinojosa, 'Shakespeare and (Anti-German) Nationalism in the Writing of English Literary History, 1880–1923', *English Literature in Transition* 46, no. 3 (2003): 227–49, as well as Stefan Collini, 'The Whig Interpretation of English Literature, Literary History and National Identity', in *Public Moralists: Political Thought and Intellectual Life in Britain* (Oxford: Clarendon Press, 1991), 342–73 on Brooke, Henry Morley, the 'English Men of Letters' series, and other canon-formation exercises.

[41] George Saintsbury, *The Later Nineteenth Century* (Edinburgh: William Blackwood and Sons, 1907), xiii. The volume appeared in the 'Periods of European Literature' series that Saintsbury edited for Blackwood.

[42] Collins, *Ephemera Critica*, 93.

[43] Saintsbury, *English Novel*, v, 1.

an academic study would not have helped. Fiction barely figures in Collins's polemics: his entire claim for the importance of linking English to Classical studies—the fact that English literature is incomprehensible without the Classical models which influenced it—rests upon this wilful exclusion.[44] For these scholars English literature was constructed solely in terms of pre-Victorian genres: poetry, drama, and non-fiction prose (sermons, political and historical treatises, oratory, and so on). Saintsbury was saddled with no such prejudices, nor did he bemoan the fact that 'there is a very large number of educated people to whom "reading" simply means reading novels ... for whom the novel exhausts even the very meaning of the word "literature"'. On the contrary, he concluded his book with this typical peroration:

> In the last fifty or sixty years of the nineteenth century [the novel] did, as it seems to me, very great things—so great that ... there is no division of the world's literature within a time at all comparable to its own which can much, if at all, excel it. ... In the finest of its already existing examples [the novel] hardly yields in accomplishment even to poetry.[45]

This was an opinion which had remained unaltered since the 1880s, when Saintsbury claimed in an article entitled 'The Present State of the English Novel' that it had 'produced some of nearly the greatest things in literature'.[46]

In fact, Saintsbury's critical judgements in the histories rarely went beyond the standard clichés of periodical literary criticism, though he had as much interest in book historical questions (periodical serialization, circulating libraries, the triple-decker) as in generic ones (the mid-Victorian 'domestic' novel, the return to romance, the fortunes of the historical novel, and numerous other subgenres from the Tractarian or Evangelical novel, to the naval, sporting, and school one). He placed the greatest flowering of the novel in the mid-Victorian period (1845–70), seeing if not quite a falling-off, then a levelling out of the field in the last decades of the century. In terms of particular favourites, he admitted to a life-long love of Dickens and proclaimed Fielding, Scott, Austen, and Thackeray 'the Four Masters of the whole subject'. To get a feel for his style of criticism (and its roots in reviewing) one need only look at the following assessment of Charlotte Brontë:

---

[44] 'Some of our most distinguished Professors of English literature have been trained in a Classical School', wrote Leathes in 1913 (9). Ironically, given Collins's fierce opposition to philology, it was precisely the wish to model the study of English on the Classics that resulted in English books being studied as 'pretexts for philological pedantry' rather than literature: 'the plays of Shakespeare are subjected to the method of instruction habitually applied to the plays of Aeschylus or Euripides, that is to say, they are treated not as literature, but as exercises in grammar and philology' (Lord Lytton quoted in Collins, *Study of English Literature*, 114). Classics were Janus-faced: they could be invoked as a bad example of meaningless philological learning, or the national classics' worthier counterparts.

[45] Saintsbury, *English Novel*, 299, 312–13.

[46] Saintsbury, *Collected Essays*, 3: 149.

> Deprive Thackeray and Dickens of nearly all their humour and geniality, take a portion only of the remaining genius of each in the ratio of about 2 *Th.* to 1 *D.*, add a certain dash of the old terror-novel and the German fantastic tale, moisten with feminine spirit and water, and mix thoroughly: and you have something very like Charlotte Brontë.[47]

This is more outré than the general run of Saintsbury's characterisations (his treatment of Brontë in his other surveys is more balanced), but it is also typical of the kind of statement one could encounter on opening any one of his many volumes.

But whatever his other failings, Saintsbury could not be accused of exclusivity, as even a partial list of the Victorian novelists he discusses shows: Edward Bulwer Lytton, Benjamin Disraeli, W.H. Ainsworth, G.P.R. James, Frederick Marryat, G.W.M. Reynolds, Frances Trollope, George Borrow, Dickens, Thackeray, Wilkie Collins, Charles Lever, the Brontës, the Kingsleys, Charles Reade, Ouida, Charlotte Yonge, Elizabeth Gaskell, George Eliot, Anthony Trollope, R.D. Blackmore, Margaret Oliphant, Dinah Mulock Craik, George MacDonald, J.H. Shorthouse, Richard Jefferies, James Payn, Besant, Meredith, Hardy, R.L. Stevenson, William Morris, and scores of 'minor' names. Some of these receive but a few lines, others are dwelt on at length. Bulwer Lytton, Dickens, Thackeray, Charlotte Brontë, Charles Kingsley, Reade, Eliot, Anthony Trollope, Stevenson, Morris, and a few others appear and reappear from book to book, not just in *The English Novel*, but in *The Later Nineteenth Century*, *A History of Nineteenth Century Literature (1780–1895)* (published in 1896 in Macmillan's 'History of English Literature' series), *A History of English Prose Rhythm*, *A Short History of English Literature*, *Corrected Impressions*, as well as numerous periodical essays collected in other volumes. Some obvious names are missing, but Saintsbury took it as a matter of principle not to write on living authors: a position he defended in virtually every preface, and which accounted for the absence of the likes of Hardy and Meredith from the earlier monographs and surveys.

Although his assessments of the novelists were by no means always positive, this mere repetition, reflecting to a great extent the critical consensus on the figures in question, is probably the clearest instance of canon-formation in the 'literary history' genre that we have. All the stereotypes are there. Dickens is the popular master of humour and fantastic character drawing, of vulgar sentimentalism and theatrical melodrama, who failed at realism and was now falling out of fashion. Thackeray, one of the 'greatest novelists' of the century, is better at character creation than plot construction, and deserves to be remembered for *Esmond*, his brilliant foray into the historical novel. George Eliot ruined her reputation when she exchanged the admirable observation of her earlier rustic novels for the mechanically constructed plots of *Middlemarch* and *Daniel Deronda*, marred by scientific phraseology, elaborate and erudite but dead. Charlotte Brontë's classic status is due to a limited genius which only throve on personal experience; Trollope

---

[47] Saintsbury, *English Novel*, 299, 243.

is notable for his professional but commonplace circulating-library prolixity; Morris's prose romances are under-appreciated …

None of this was particularly original stuff. Edmund Gosse's *Short History of Modern English Literature*, published in the 'Short Histories of the Literatures of the World' series he himself edited, was practically a carbon copy of any Saintsbury volume, though Gosse had more of a theoretical commitment to applying the evolutionary ideas of Charles Darwin and Herbert Spencer to literary criticism, viewing literary history as a growing organism, defined by adaptation, natural selection, and individual variation.[48] Gosse—a man of letters rather than a literature professor—was in close enough proximity to the academic world to be invited as a Clark lecturer to Trinity College, Cambridge, and to be published by university presses, but he prided himself on his awareness of the subjectivity of critical opinions, which was 'patent to every one whose brains have not become ossified by vain and dictatorial processes of "teaching"'. Nevertheless, his chapters on 'The Early Victorian Age (1840–1870)' and 'The Age of Tennyson' (a typical formulation in many post-1892 books) peddled exactly the same versions of the same authors as the ossified teachers. He also endorsed the familiar trajectory of Victorian literary history in which fiction took a 'new and brilliant turn' at mid-century: 'In the hands of three or four persons of great genius, it rose to such a prominent place in the serious life of the nation as it had not taken since the middle career of Scott. Among these new novelists who were also great writers, the first position was taken by William Makepeace Thackeray'. George Eliot—the most prominent novelist in England after the death of Dickens—was 'an agreeable rustic writer, with a charming humour and very fine sympathetic nature, [who] found herself gradually uplifted until, about 1875, she sat enthroned on an educational tripod, an almost ludicrous pythoness'. Since then her reputation had quickly fallen, as readers reacted against the artificial mechanical construction and the abstruse philosophical and scientific pretension of her later work. Mrs Gaskell, on the other hand, was 'technically faultless' but undervalued.[49]

In surveys of this sort, whether the author under consideration received a discursive essay to him- or herself or a mere paragraph summary, the tone was always impressionistic and opinionated, and the aim was to offer an appreciation of particular works as well as a summary of the critical reactions. This kind of 'appreciation' did not call for extensive scholarship or research: it belonged to and it had come from the world of the periodical. Although Saintsbury did not fall prey to the journalistic weakness of self-plagiarism, and each of his treatments of a particular Victorian novelist was a genuinely new piece of work, the overall shape of his critical opinions did not change from the *Fortnightly* essays of the 1880s to the surveys of the 1900s. Except in terms of scope,

---

[48] Edmund Gosse, *A Short History of Modern English Literature* (1897; London: Heinemann, 1903). It was reproduced verbatim, though with additional anthology-style biographies, illustrations, and selections of primary texts for each writer, in Richard Garnett and Edmund Gosse, *English Literature: An Illustrated Record in Four Volumes* (London: Heinemann 1903).

[49] Gosse, *A Short History*, 386, 352, 370, 355.

there was little to differentiate the supposedly more 'academic' works from the reviews which had appeared in the *Pall Mall Gazette*. As he wrote in the Preface to the first volume of his *Collected Essays and Papers*, in reference to his reprinted lectures: they are 'really spoken Essays and not in the least the sort of thing that I used to utter to my class in Edinburgh'.[50] Whatever he may have said in class, in his writings Saintsbury remained the periodical critic. On the rare occasions that he alluded to actual university work in his books and essays, it was not in its relation to the Victorian novel, but to rhetoric, in line with the first part of his professorial title. But even in his publications on prose style he found a place for the novelists: comparing Thackeray's and Dickens's mastery of 'English prose-rhythm' for instance, examining Kingsley's Ruskinian prose and quasi-metrical rhythm, the 'specially feminine *crudity* which accompanied all Charlotte's unquestioned power and passion', Eliot's 'later quasi-scientific jargon [which] was not so *arrhythmic* as it was in other ways inartistic', the 'fantastic' and 'elaborate' prose of Meredith, or Morris's 'Wardour Street' lingo (of which he was an all-out fan).[51]

But if the academic literary history was simply an outgrowth of the periodical essay in the aspect directed at the general reader, when it faced the student it revealed that it was also a near cousin of the handbook. Collins's criticism of Gosse's *A Short History of Modern English Literature* was phrased in precisely these terms:

> Described simply, the work is an ordinary manual of English Literature in which, with Mr. Humphry Ward's *English Poets*, Sir Henry Craik's *English Prose Writers*, Chambers' *Cyclopaedia of English Literature*, the *Dictionary of National Biography*, and the like before him, the writer tells again the not unfamiliar story of the course of our Literature from Chaucer to the present time.

Beyond the few areas that he knows first-hand, 'he is at the mercy of his handbooks'.[52] One of these handbooks, though Collins did not list it, was Stopford Brooke's famous primer of *English Literature*.[53] The original appeared in 1876, and stopped short before the Victorian period. The Victorian chapter dealing with 'Prose Literature from the Death of Scott to the Death of George Eliot, 1832–1881' was only added to the revised edition of 1900, and was written by an American from Columbia University. It gave the standard account, very much in the mode of a Saintsbury or an Andrew Lang periodical essay, of the Victorian battle between romance and realism: the novel of 'stirring incidents' and 'striking types' vs. the novel of 'observation of the facts of life'.[54] All the old

---

[50] Saintsbury, *Collected Essays*, 1: vi.

[51] George Saintsbury, *A History of English Prose Rhythm* (London: Macmillan and Co., Ltd, 1912), 382, 406–407, 408–409, 437.

[52] Collins, *Ephemera Critica*, 111.

[53] Stopford A. Brooke, *English Literature, With Chapters on English Literature (1832–1892) and on American Literature by George R. Carpenter* (1900; London: Macmillan & Co., Ltd, 1906).

[54] Brooke, 257–58. See Anna Vaninskaya, 'The Late-Victorian Romance Revival: A Generic Excursus', *English Literature in Transition* 51, no. 1 (January 2008): 57–79.

truisms are out in force: on the Continent the novel focused on vice and crime, while in England it was more fanciful and idealistic; and the last two decades of the century 'revived the novel of romantic adventure, returning to the field opened by Scott; and the public, perhaps a little weary of novels of society, reform, and ethics, has welcomed the change. Of the new writers of tales of adventure by sea and land the chief was Robert Louis Stevenson.' The resemblance of this passage to something Saintsbury could have written is absolutely uncanny. The chapter then cycles through the familiar list, from Marryat, Lever, Disraeli, Bulwer Lytton, Borrow, Gaskell, Trollope, Reade, and Kingsley, to Charlotte Brontë's *Jane Eyre*—the 'most typical English novel of the Romantic school'. Dickens—'one of the great English story-tellers'—receives a hero-worshipping paragraph with the expected platitudes about odd characters and dramatic qualities. Thackeray is, of course, equally good, while Meredith, who belongs to the class of Dickens and Thackeray, is not as popular because of his strange style. George Eliot is 'a country girl of great power of mind and much learning', though 'less famous than Scott, Dickens, and Thackeray'.[55] Henry James is mentioned briefly together with W.D. Howells as an American realist, and the rest of the chapter is devoted to other traditional kinds of non-fiction prose.

A.J. Wyatt's *The Tutorial History of English Literature* is a handbook of a different type, but its contents are barely distinguishable from Brooke's. Wyatt himself was a Cambridge lecturer of the philological persuasion and examiner in English in the University of London, but as with Brooke's primer, the chapter on Victorian literature ('The Age of Tennyson') was only added to the third edition of 1909 and was written by someone else (a Mr H. Clay, BA Oxon.). Like the supplementary material in Brooke, the chapter surveys the whole Victorian age in retrospect, and reads like nothing so much as a critical essay on the lines and of the quality of an article in one of the reviews. It also puts the novel at the centre as 'the most important section of Victorian literature' and echoes the literary concerns of the previous decades: romance vs. realism, the growth of the uneducated reading public, and the rise of the 'great mass of magazines and other serial publications' to cater for its desire for popular fiction. Saintsbury's voice can be heard throughout:

> The novel is perhaps the most elastic and adaptable medium that the literary artist has discovered...the variety of subject it treats is so great that the works of, for example, Dickens and Thackeray give us a more complete picture of the England of their time than we could have got in any other way...Moreover, the novel appeals to a wider audience than any other form of literature...since about 1860 the big audience has been for the novel and only the novel.[56]

---

[55] Brooke, 266, 260, 262–64.
[56] Wyatt, 226.

The familiar judgements of the familiar authors follow in the familiar terms: Dickens's humour and mastery of the grotesque; his great contemporary Thackeray's cynicism; Charlotte Brontë's limited genius; Eliot's 'over-fondness for scientific and philosophical jargon. Her intellect was apt to get the better of her.' 'A much more powerful thinker and a greater novelist [was] George Meredith', whose difficult fiction inspired imitators in the new genre of the psychological novel.[57]

The grand literary histories and the compact handbooks essentially replicated the same narrative on different scales, but though they may have authored them, few university-affiliated academics were satisfied with this status quo. Collins, Raleigh, and Elton had all called for something to replace the inadequate handbooks then in existence, something which offered a proper overview of English literary history, and many believed that their prayer would be answered by the new *Cambridge History of English Literature*. 'The great syndicate-history of English literature, which we have delayed so long to make, is now promised from Cambridge', Elton wrote, and scholars would no longer have to be 'coerced…by the market rage for manuals'.[58] But was the *Cambridge History* itself anything more than a glorified manual, the crowning achievement of the Victorian literary history handbook genre? The volumes of the *History*, edited by A.W. Ward (Master of Peterhouse and major contributor to the Cambridge English syllabus reform debates) and A.R. Waller, began appearing from the Cambridge University Press in 1907. The two parts of the 'Victorian Age' finally came out in 1916, although the preceding volume on the 'Romantic Revival' also contained relevant sections—the 'Lesser Novelists' included names (G.P.R. James, Ainsworth, and Marryat) which often figured in the literary histories under the Victorian rubric. Saintsbury contributed chapters on Dickens and 'The Prosody of the Nineteenth Century', A. Hamilton Thompson on Thackeray, and Ward himself on 'The Political and Social Novel: Disraeli, Charles Kingsley, Mrs. Gaskell, "George Eliot"'. A.A. Jack, Professor of English Literature in the University of Aberdeen, wrote on the Brontës, and W.T. Young, lecturer in English Language and Literature at Goldsmiths' College, University of London, on the 'Lesser Novelists', including Bulwer Lytton, Trollope, Reade, Mrs Henry [Ellen] Wood, Oliphant, Blackmore, Wilkie Collins, MacDonald, Du Maurier, Ouida, Mark Rutherford, and several others—all staples of the 'Short History' genre. Young also contributed the final chapter of the volume on Meredith, Samuel Butler, and George Gissing. Du Maurier, Butler and Gissing were the only new names on the list; in all other respects this could have been a product of the 1890s, the kind of thing Saintsbury had been churning out single-handedly for over twenty years previously. But the editors thought they were being original. This was not a handbook of 'great' literature limited to poetry, drama, and non-fiction prose, they insisted, it was a genuine 'history'. As they explained to the contributors, their aim was to give 'a connected account…of the successive movements

---

[57] Wyatt, 250–51, 255–58.
[58] Elton, 'The Meaning of Literary History', in *Modern Studies*, 137–38.

of English literature, both main and subsidiary.... Note was to be taken of the influence of foreign literatures upon English and (though in a less degree) of that of English upon foreign literatures.' In neither of these respects were they actually breaking new ground. Although the editors acknowledged the 'cooperation of many scholars', not just British and American, but Continental, 'whose labours in the field of our national literature entitle them to the gratitude of Englishmen', the home-grown literary survey—from Chambers's *Cyclopaedia of English Literature* to the works of Brooke and Morley—was equally prominent among the listed sources.[59] The line of descent from the older handbooks was quite straightforward.

In one respect, however, the editors were not exaggerating. It was indeed the case that among the lower reaches of instructional literature—the pupil-teacher manuals or Civil Service exam cram-books—the novel barely ever figured.[60] Yet even here progress was evident. By 1905, the regulations for the Board of Education's compulsory exam paper on English Language and Literature for pupil-teachers stipulated Scott and Dickens (*David Copperfield*) for general reading. In 1907 the novel component was made even more explicit: 'All candidates should have undertaken as wide a course as possible of general reading, which should include, amongst other books, one or two of Shakespeare's plays, some historical novels, and an anthology of verse.'[61] This was quite an advance over the qualifications required of pupil-teachers in the 1880s, when 'To read with fluency, ease, and just expression, and to recite 100 lines of Shakespeare or Milton, with clearness and force, and knowledge of meanings and allusions' was the official limit.[62] But novels had sometimes appeared in the suggestions for course material even then. *Moffatt's Pupil Teachers' Course* was particularly exemplary in this regard. The section on English Language and Literature, besides going quite deeply into comparative philology, offered a literary history-style survey of the main authors of each period. 'One of the most remarkable features in modern literature, both in England and other civilized countries, is the novel...In England this species of composition has been developed to an extraordinary degree. Many of our best writers have devoted their talents to it.' There were no surprises among the Victorians—this was squarely the territory that

[59] A.W. Ward and A.R. Waller, eds. *The Cambridge History of English Literature* (Cambridge: Cambridge University Press, 1907), 1: v, viii.

[60] See e.g. Rev. Henry Lewis, *The English Language, Its Grammar and History: Together with a Treatise on English Composition, and Sets of Exercises and Examination Papers for the Assistance of Teachers and Students*, 3rd edn (London: Edward Stanford, 1872); W.J. Dickinson, *Hughes's Pupil Teachers' Examination Manuals. A Complete Set of Pupil Teachers' Government Examination Questions in English Grammar, Paraphrasing, Parsing, Analysis, Composition, and Notes of Lessons, To September 1879 (Inclusive)* (London: Joseph Hughes, 1879) (Joseph Hughes's Educational List was 'Specially recommended by Her Majesty's Inspectors of Schools'); James Beveridge, *Guide-book for Pupil-Teachers: Two Years' Papers for Candidates and Pupil-Teachers Embracing All the Questions Set, With Numerous Additions, Solutions, and All the Answers to the Arithmetic* (Edinburgh: W. & R. Chambers, 1885). The authors were usually school headmasters or lecturers in teacher training colleges.

[61] Board of Education, *Regulations for the Instruction and Training of Pupil-Teachers (From 1st August, 1905, to 31st July, 1906)* (London: Wyman and Sons, Limited, 1905), 5–6, 47.

[62] See the 'New Code—Schedule V', in Page's *Moffatt's Pupil Teachers' Course*, 1.

Saintsbury and other professors would tread to smoothness at the turn of the century: Marryat and Bulwer Lytton; Disraeli and Dickens (still a wonder of popularity rather than a battleground for critical factions); Thackeray and the Brontës; George Eliot ('one of the greatest writers of fiction of the present century', though even here her intellectuality was remarked upon); Gaskell, Kingsley; Trollope; Reade; Oliphant; Elizabeth Braddon, 'authoress' of sensational tales; and Charlotte Yonge, 'authoress' of novels of 'quiet, domestic English life'. The only unexpected inclusion was Braddon, a name usually omitted from the more extended surveys. The historical novel received particular attention, and the aspiring pupil-teacher was warned of the 'erroneous impression of historical persons and events' it could produce. 'Low, worthless novels should especially be avoided... There are, however, many excellent works of fiction which the pupil teacher may read with great advantage.' The author of the manual also wished to 'impress on young students [that]... the object of acquiring knowledge is not simply to pass examinations. Such a view of learning is nothing less than a desecration of it.'[63] Nevertheless, when it came to offering sample questions selected from previous examination papers, there was no sense of combating the desecration: questions were mainly of the factual and grammar type based on gobbets, and Shakespeare and Milton readers full of annotated extracts were recommended in place of the general reading alluded to before.

III

The road from cramming manual to exam was a short one, and both were characterized by a certain uniformity. At all levels the types of questions and the types of things tested were the same. The Rev. Thomas Stantial's *Test-Book for Students... Preparing for the Universities or for Appointments in the Army and Civil Service* from the 1850s included several questions on novelists ('Write also a list of writers of fiction, and their works, who have flourished since Sir Walter Scott') which were absolutely typical of the cramming style picked apart by Collins in his articles.[64] To what extent did this style still prevail at the other end of the educational and chronological spectrum: in the Oxford and Cambridge degree examinations over half a century later?

Cambridge offered two relevant examinations in which an unwary candidate could meet with a novel: the Special Examination in Modern Languages for the Ordinary BA Degree and the Examination for the Medieval and Modern Languages Tripos. During the period from 1908 to 1914 (when the 'literary' A2 section was introduced), Victorian novels did indeed make a showing, but not in the English literature papers as one would expect. These were just as limited and philologically focused as Collins's complaints had made out—the novels appeared, instead, in the foreign-language sections of the

---

[63] Page's *Moffatt's Pupil Teachers' Course*, 295, 298, 301, 300.
[64] Stantial, 29.

exam. The French, German, Russian, and Spanish papers were, comparatively speaking, broader, more literary and more focused on modern writing: the student encountered Special Period topics like 'The History of the Romantic Movement in France (1820–1850)', and questions like 'Outline the history of the modern Spanish novel', or 'Why is Tolstoy considered the greatest Russian writer?'[65] But in addition to questions on European 19th-century novelists (Stendhal, Balzac, Victor Hugo, Flaubert, Nikolai Gogol, Mikhail Saltikov-Schedrin, Ivan Turgenev, Fyodor Dostoevsky, Tolstoy, Gorky) there were the Composition papers, which called for the translation of English passages into a given language, and it was here that Victorian novels came to the fore. The sources of selected passages ranged from Bulwer Lytton to Charlotte Brontë's *Villette* and *The Professor*; Thackeray's *Pendennis*, *The Newcomes*, *The Virginians*, and *Esmond*; Dickens's *A Tale of Two Cities*; Borrow's *Lavengro*; Gaskell's *Wives and Daughters*; George Eliot's *Romola*; Hardy's *Tess of the D'Urbervilles*; Henry James's *The American*; W.H. Mallock's *A Human Document: A Novel*; J.M. Barrie's *When a Man's Single: A Tale of Literary Life*; Joseph Conrad's *Under Western Eyes*; as well as Stevenson's essays, G.B. Shaw's plays, and Kipling's children's book *Puck of Pook's Hill*. *Three Men in a Boat*, as the *Punch* satire had it, would not have looked much out of place in this list. The English literature section, by contrast, only stretched to questions of the 'Give some account of the following novels' type, dealing mainly with the standard 18th-century novelists and genres, as well as Austen and Scott. Special Period papers did not go beyond 1830 (nor, of course, did 'The History of English Literature (1500–1832)' paper which was the occasion for so much debate during the syllabus reform attempts of 1909). The Victorian novel only entered once or twice as a topic for essays, with prompts like 'Thackeray', 'The genius of Meredith', and 'What has Criticism to say on the present vogue of the Novel?'

It did not leave much of a footprint in the Cambridge English lecture list either: the General Course of English Literature officially ended at 1832. The sole exception was one lecture course scheduled for Michaelmas Term, 1914 on 'Romance and Realism, with illustrative lectures on Charlotte Brontë and George Eliot', by A.C. Benson (an ally of Arthur Quiller-Couch), who also lectured on Robert Browning, John Ruskin, Thomas Carlyle, and William Morris. In the event, even this was 'postponed until further notice' (perhaps due to the outbreak of the war).[66] The foreign-language lectures, on the other hand, addressed 'Modern Period' literature in greater detail. French lectures featured Hugo, Alexandre Dumas *fils*, the Romantic Movement, and 'Outlines of French Literature 1800–1850', as did German lectures, including even German literature after 1848. When Arthur Quiller-Couch began his course of lectures in 1913 as the newly appointed Edward VII Professor of English Literature, he dealt with topics such

---

[65] All information is quoted from the Cambridge University Special Examinations in Modern Languages for the Ordinary BA Degree and the Examinations for the Medieval and Modern Languages Tripos for the years 1908–14.

[66] 'Lectures proposed by the Special Board for Medieval and Modern Languages, 1914–1915', *Cambridge University Reporter* (21 April, 1915): 778.

as 'The Lineage of English Literature', 'Literature in the Universities', 'The Colonisation of English Literature', 'Patriotism in English Literature', 'On the terms "Classical" and "Romantic"', as well as canonical authors such as Thomas More and Shakespeare. Dr Mayo's fears about the Professor holding forth on Dickens and Thackeray did not come to pass.

The Oxford Final Honour School of English Language and Literature exam was, at least as far as the Victorian novel was concerned, much more advanced. The School itself was only established in 1894, and was intended for candidates (not counting women) who had already taken Classical Honour Moderations or another Honours course. The first exam was offered in 1896 (lectures had begun in 1895 with Ernest de Selincourt's 'English Literature from 1789'), and from that year until 1914, the same authors and questions reappeared again and again, though shunted at times from paper to paper.[67] The questions required the student to comment on gobbets, 'trace the growth, origins or development', 'assess the influence', 'estimate the part played', 'define the position occupied', 'give a short sketch', 'list with dates', and illustrate x by analysing y. Their phrasing often presupposed agreement with accepted critical judgements—an author's greatness, originality, or novelty, or the fact that a book or character occupied 'the highest place in the living world of literature', were taken for granted. But though conventional in this respect (as the crammers' opponents had predicted), the exam was more wide-ranging than its Cambridge equivalent when it came to modern literature, especially in its historical and comparative contexts. Here Victorian novels made a relatively strong showing. Over the years, the Special Subject paper on 'Wordsworth and his Contemporaries (1797–1850)' included the following questions:

'Show from the earlier novels of Dickens his sympathy with social reforms.' (1896)
'Distinguish between the "realism" of Jane Austen and of Dickens.' (1898)
'How far can the working of "realism" be traced in the literature of this period?' (1900)
'Contrast, as students of Human Nature, Charlotte Brontë and Jane Austen.' (1907)

The 'History of English Literature' paper asked the student to

'Compare the dominant ideals of the novel represented by English and French literature respectively.' (1899)
'Discuss the influence of Sterne upon Carlyle and Dickens.' (1901)
'Compare *Tom Jones* and *Vanity Fair*. How far is a general comparison of Fielding and Thackeray possible?' (1903)
'Characterize the art and style of any *one* of the following novelists: Richardson, Goldsmith, Dickens.' (1904)

[67] All information is quoted from the Oxford University Final Honour School examinations in English Language and Literature for the years 1896–1914.

'Discuss the relation of Thackeray with the chief novelists of the eighteenth century.'
(1905)
'Discuss the treatment of life and nature to be found in the poems or novels of George
Meredith.' (1905)

The successor to this paper was the 'Outlines of English Literature' paper introduced
in 1908 (its name changed slightly from year to year), when the syllabus was revised by
Walter Raleigh. But though Raleigh was an implacable enemy of handbooks, the questions requested the examinee to reproduce exactly the kind of thing that was liable to be
crammed from them:

'Trace briefly the growth of the English novel during the first half of the nineteenth
century.' (1908)
'Sketch in outline the history of the novel from *Castle Rackrent* to *Pickwick*' (1912)
'Consider Tennyson as the poet of Victorian England, *or* Thackeray as its critic.'
(1914)

A 'History of English Literature After 1700' paper (known by different names thereafter, such as 'History of English Literature III') was also introduced in 1908; questions
included:

'Describe the main features of the English novel since the time of Thackeray and
Dickens, and indicate what you consider to be its present tendencies.' (1908)
'How far are the works of Dickens or Tennyson representative of the Victorian age?'
(1909)
'Trace the influence of *Don Quixote* on the English literature of the eighteenth and
nineteenth centuries.' (1909)
'In what principal ways was the English literature of the nineteenth century affected
by the progress of scientific discovery?' (1909)
'Mention any works in prose or verse that were in high esteem during the first half of
the nineteenth century, but are now scarcely, or not at all, read, and account for their
loss of popularity.' (1911)
'Indicate the chief models or sources drawn upon by any one of the following:- Defoe,
Sir Walter Scott, R. L. Stevenson.' (1913)

A Special Subject paper on 'Literary Relations of England and France, 1789–1850', first
offered in 1909, asked the student to 'Trace the growth of "realism" in England and in
France, and discuss the connexion between the two movements.'
    It would be possible to undertake a similar survey of the examination papers of
every university that offered a degree in English literature, going back to the University
of London exams of the mid-19th century. One could also study the syllabi of colonial institutions, or look at the lecture courses of the Extension Movement, or the topics of postgraduate theses like the Oxford BLitt. The list of potential sources one could

scour for appearances of the Victorian novel is long, but in all likelihood such sources would yield similar results. By the 1900s, in relation to the entire sweep (chronological and generic) of English literary history covered by the surveys, and tested in the various exams, the Victorian novel still did not occupy more than a tiny section. Although this chapter has not dealt with them, the 18th-century novelists along with Jane Austen were more prominent, while the novelist who received the most attention by far was Walter Scott. But within its own circumscribed realm—a realm which champions like Saintsbury were helping to enlarge—a Victorian canon was quickly established, and perpetuated until at least the Great War. Dickens and Thackeray emerged as the undoubted favourites, followed at some distance by Charlotte Brontë and George Eliot, and occasionally George Meredith, whose cult was at its height at the turn of the century. This was a canon initially constructed outside the walls of the university, for the direction of influence was from the wider literary world (whence so many of the professors came) to the educational institution, rather than the other way around. The late-Victorian and Edwardian university did not initiate literary trends: it co-opted them, often belatedly. If an *Oxford Handbook of the Victorian Novel* had appeared at the beginning of the 20th, rather than the 21st century, it would have looked very different indeed, but it too would have touched on 18th-century influences, serialization, gender, communication networks, scientific disciplines, Classical literature, international cross-currents, style, and new reading publics, as the existing handbooks had actually done. Such issues had been debated for decades in the literary culture at large, and they were duly reflected in the student manuals and surveys of 19th-century literature. A hundred years ago the Victorian novel was just beginning its long journey to the heart of university English study, but it already came equipped with the cultural baggage of the Victorians who created it.

Suggested Reading

Baldick, Chris. *The Social Mission of English Criticism 1848–1932*. Oxford: Clarendon Press, 1983.

Collini, Stefan. 'The Whig Interpretation of English Literature, Literary History and National Identity'. In *Public Moralists: Political Thought and Intellectual Life in Britain*. Oxford: Clarendon Press, 1991, 342–73.

Court, Franklin E. *Institutionalizing English Literature: The Culture and Politics of Literary Study, 1750–1900*. Stanford: Stanford University Press, 1992.

Daunton Martin, ed. *The Organisation of Knowledge in Victorian Britain*. Oxford: Oxford University Press, 2005.

Dixon, John. *A Schooling in 'English': Critical Episodes in the Struggle to Shape Literary and Cultural Studies*. Milton Keynes: Open University Press, 1991.

Doyle, Brian. 'The Invention of English'. In *Englishness: Politics and Culture 1880–1920*. Edited by Robert Colls and Philip Dodd. London: Routledge, 1986, 89–115.

Litz, A. Walton, Louis Menand, and Lawrence Rainey, eds. *The Cambridge History of Literary Criticism*. Vol. 7. Cambridge: Cambridge University Press, 2000.

Mathieson, Margaret. *The Preachers of Culture: A Study of English and Its Teachers.* London: George Allen & Unwin Ltd, 1975.

Palmer, D.J. *The Rise of English Studies: An Account of the Study of English Language and Literature from Its Origins to the Making of the Oxford English School.* London: Oxford University Press, 1965.

Potter, Stephen. *The Muse in Chains.* London: Cape, 1937.

Tillyard, E.M.W. *The Muse Unchained: An Intimate Account of the Revolution in English Studies at Cambridge.* London: Bowes & Bowes, 1958.

34

THE VICTORIAN NOVEL
AND THE NEW WOMAN

TALIA SCHAFFER

The New Woman novel, like 'chick lit' novels a century later, was a wildly popular literary genre about middle-class women's daily lives, and critics have condemned both for their supposedly poor quality and commercial appeal to a female readership. Today, however, scholars recognize that the New Woman novel not only provides unparalleled insight into late-Victorian women's roles, but also marks significant stylistic shifts from the realist novel. The New Woman novel documents a fascinating period of transition away from Victorian separate spheres, recording the stresses, anxieties, and freedoms women experienced as they rebelled against traditional roles. In order to convey these inchoate feelings, New Women novelists invented innovative literary techniques that actually prefigured modernist texts. Moreover, the New Woman novel is a particularly fascinating subject, because it is not just a body of important texts, but also a case study of critical trends. By exploring the history of the New Woman novel's reception, we can see how literary critics' ideas of value, politics, and style have altered in the past century. This chapter, then, will read the New Women novel, but it will also read its readers, offering an account of how and why the movement achieved recognition, and suggesting where the field might be moving.

First, we need to understand how the New Woman novel fits with other women's novels in the 19th century. After all, one might well ask just what was 'new' about 19th-century women's writing. As Virginia Woolf wrote, 'towards the end of the eighteenth century a change came about which, if I were rewriting history, I should describe more fully and think of greater importance than the Crusades or the Wars of the Roses. The middle-class woman began to write.'[1] The 19th century was, of course, famous for its women's novels: *Pride and Prejudice* (1813), *Jane Eyre* (1847), and *Middlemarch* (1871–72). Not only did the 19th century see the work of the Brontë sisters, George

---

[1] Virginia Woolf, *A Room of One's Own; and, Three Guineas* (Oxford: Oxford University Press, 2008), 84.

Eliot, and Jane Austen, but also the highly respected writings of Harriet Martineau, Charlotte Yonge, Margaret Oliphant, and Elizabeth Gaskell, and the wildly popular fiction of Rhoda Broughton, Marie Corelli, Mary Elizabeth Braddon, Ellen Woods, and Catherine Gore. So we may well ask how the late-Victorian New Woman novel relates to earlier women's novels.

The New Woman novel should not be treated as an entirely separate movement, but as the culmination of this history of women's fiction. The New Woman novel can be read for the same reasons we read Mary Wollstonecraft's *Maria, or, The Wrongs of Women* (1798), Florence Nightingale's *Cassandra* (written 1852), or, of course, *Jane Eyre* (1847). Like these predecessors, the New Woman novel passionately exposes the oppression of middle-class women's lives and eloquently pleads for what Brontë called 'a power of vision that might overpass that limit'.[2] Indeed, two of the most popular examples of women's writing among college students, Kate Chopin's *The Awakening* and Charlotte Perkins Gilman's 'The Yellow Wallpaper', are American New Women stories. The New Woman novel fits into a history of passionate outcries about injustice and desperate desires for a wider view. No history of women's writing can be complete without an example of the New Woman genre.

Along with depicting women's situations in their writing, New Women writers often worked for progressive causes. They resembled their mid-century predecessors, female activists like Frances Power Cobbe, Barbara Bodichon, Bessie Rayner Parkes, Jessie Boucherett, and Elizabeth Garrett Anderson, who fought for widespread social reform of major public issues (employment, education, and legal rights). But unlike these mid-century reformers, their New Women successors often agitated for alterations of individual feeling, especially regarding sexual behaviour. As I have noted elsewhere:

> This dangerous 'New Woman' was a middle-class woman agitating for such 'dynamite' ideas as the right to walk without a chaperone, to hold a job, to live alone in a flat, to go to college, and to wear sensible clothing. Moreover, they wanted to remake Victorian marriage. New Women asked men to exercise sexual self-discipline, demanded women have access to honest sex education, and tried to popularize alternatives to marriage (ranging from free unions to easier divorces).[3]

New Women's emphasis on personal independence and marriage reform were key components of their mission. Their writing was linked to their activism in ways that were unusual for other 19th-century literary movements.

Technological and cultural changes in the late 19th century facilitated such changes. New forms of transportation, for instance, allowed women to move freely about a city that was increasingly safe, due to electric lighting and modern police presence. The

[2] Charlotte Brontë, *Jane Eyre* (Oxford: Oxford University Press, 2008), 109.
[3] Talia Schaffer, 'The New Woman: Introduction', *Literature and Culture at the Fin de Siècle*, ed. Talia Schaffer (New York: Longman, 2007), 203–5, 203.

subway and the bicycle allowed women unprecedented freedom. That recent invention, the typewriter, allowed women to work as secretaries or clerks (now that their feminine handwriting would not give them away). Department stores consolidated goods in one place, offering women the chance to serve as shop clerks. Nursing and philanthropy were traditional occupations for women, but they were now becoming professionalized. And the progressive girls' schools required teachers. A young woman who wished to work in one of these modern occupations could rent a flat or a room in a boarding house where meals were provided, or eat at the Aerated Bread Company's cafeterias (designed to offer a safe non-alcoholic alternative to pubs). The literature of the New Woman described the excitements and frustrations of these young women's lives, popularizing the idea of an energetic, self-sufficient, hard-working woman.

It is important to remember that these were middle-class young women who felt stifled by Victorian etiquette. Working-class women already had many of the freedoms their middle-class sisters wanted; nobody felt it necessary to chaperone them, marriage rules were not enforced so strictly, and nobody was questioning their participation in the labour markets open to them, primarily factory work and domestic service. Working-class and impoverished women had a very different set of needs in the late 19th century, having to do with making workplaces safe and creating humane environments.

The idea of the New Woman was one of the great causes of the 1890s. Although the term 'New Woman' had previously been used in a rather affectionately self-deprecating manner in the feminist press, it seems to have entered public discourse as an opprobrious term in articles by Sarah Grand and Ouida (Mary Louise de Ramé) in the *North American Review* of 1894.[4] In this crucial article, Ouida began by grousing, 'the Workingman and the Woman, the New Woman, be it remembered, meet us at every page of literature written in the English tongue, and each is convinced that on its own especial W hangs the future of the world'.[5] Rapidly becoming a cultural stereotype, a media creation, pilloried in *Punch* and condemned in articles, the New Woman was a threateningly unattractive, aggressive figure, through which ambitious women of the period could be lampooned. While New Woman debates were played out most prominently in journalism and fiction, there were also poems, dramas, and art about this figure. And in the fin de siècle, the New Woman shows up in popular and canonical novels alike. From Mina in *Dracula* (1897) to Sue in *Jude the Obscure* (1895), we find the New Woman figure. Just as 1960s fiction is fascinated with the counter-cultural hippie figure, so too 1890s fiction interrogates the New Woman.

If we turn now to the specific genre of fiction designated 'New Women novels', we will be looking at texts centred on this controversial female figure. In 1999, Sally Mitchell pointed out that 'despite some twenty years of scholarship in the field, core questions such as "what is a New Woman?" and "what is New Woman fiction?" still remain vexed

  4 Schaffer, 'Introduction'.
  5 Ouida, 'The New Woman' [1894], *Literature and Culture at the Fin de Si ècle*, ed. Talia Schaffer (New York: Longman, 2007) 210–17, 210.

and all too often need more precise definition'.[6] New Women novels used to be identi-
fied as those works by canonical male authors that interrogated the modern woman:
Thomas Hardy's *Jude the Obscure*, George Gissing's *The Odd Women*, and H.G. Wells's
Ann Veronica. However, today the consensus seems to be that the most important New
Woman novels and stories are those by Sarah Grand (Frances McFall), Olive Schreiner,
George Egerton (Mary Chavelita Dunne Bright), and Mona Caird, while other New
Women fiction worth examining includes work by George Paston (Emily Morse
Symonds), Ella Hepworth Dixon, Elizabeth Robins, and Amy Levy. As Mitchell asked,
however, what makes us identify these authors as 'New Women' and their work as 'New
Woman fiction'?

Because the 1890s press used 'New Women' as an all-purpose accusation, it comes as
no surprise that some women distanced themselves from the moniker, rendering it hard
for us to get a sense of just how many people might have been real-life New Women. In
Mitchell's words:

> Like 'feminist' today, the term could mean just about anything the writer wanted it to
> mean. The New Woman was a seductive temptress and a man-hater, over-educated
> and empty-headed, mannishly athletic or languidly anorexic, poised to take over the
> House of Commons but hysterically unable to decide which necktie to wear.[7]

Such contradictions showed up in fictional depictions of New Women as well. In George
Paston's *A Writer of Books*, Bess lures men to their doom to expose unfair marriage laws.
Yet Bess's friend, the 'writer of books' Cosima Chudleigh, deplores Bess's vigilante activity. The conflicting impulses on display here, especially around female sexual freedom,
appeared in journalism by New Woman activists too. Sarah Grand held the male sex
drive accountable for prostitution, syphilis, and bad marriages, and depicted women
as wise, high-minded guides to help man, who is 'morally, in his infancy'.[8] Meanwhile,
George Egerton infamously described 'the eternal wildness, the untamed primitive
savage temperament that lurks in the mildest, best woman'.[9] While Grand and Egerton
disagreed about which sex was more savage, Mona Caird took the liberal position that
women's sexual desires and vocational needs equalled men's and therefore deserved
comparable outlets. It is, of course, possible—and true—to say that New Women thinking accommodated a wide range of attitudes towards female sexuality. But this wide
range of ideas leaves us wondering whether it is really legitimate to lump them all

[6] Sally Mitchell, 'Review: New Women, Old and New', *Victorian Literature and Culture* 27, no. 2 (1999):
579–88, 579.
[7] Sally Mitchell, 'Review', 583.
[8] Sarah Grand, 'The New Aspect of the Woman Question' [1894], in *Literature and Culture at Fin de
Siècle*, ed. Talia Schaffer (New York: Longman, 2007), 205–10, 207.
[9] George Egerton, 'A Cross Line' [1893], in *Literature and Culture at the Fin de Siècle*, ed. Talia Schaffer
(New York: Longman, 2007), 251–64, 259.

together as New Woman notions. Can Egerton and Grand both be New Women? Can Bess and Cosima?

Similarly, one would assume that New Women would endorse extending the vote and educational and vocational opportunities to women. However, 19th-century gender politics looked very different from our own. Because 19th-century thinkers often believed that women had their own essential sphere, they could support activism that seemed to extend women's 'natural' abilities while fighting against activism that seemed to contradict it. Thus people might support women's right to become doctors (because it was a good feminine skill to nurse the sick), but deny women's right to vote (because involvement in government was seen as profoundly anti-feminine). The novelist Mary Ward, for instance, fought against votes for women—yet Ward demanded access to education and the medical profession for women, and her novel *Marcella* depicts, with powerful sympathy, a strong woman who works as a nurse and a socialist organizer. Similarly, Ouida and Eliza Lynn Linton published famous denunciations of New Women but wrote novels with sympathetic strong female characters and personally lived as independent, self-supporting women. This variety of positions makes it very hard to pin down one set of beliefs as the definitive marker of New Womanhood. While critics should not establish an ideological loyalty test that authors must pass to be admitted into the New Woman club, it seems fair to say that if the term 'New Woman' is to mean anything at all, it must stand for some core values with which we can identify its members.

It should also stand for a particular way of writing. As Lyn Pykett and Ann Ardis pointed out twenty years ago, New Women writers pioneered many of the stylistic experiments we associate with modernism. Working with fragmentation, dream sequences, non-realist narrative, streams of consciousness, shifting and multiple points of view, and narratives without conventional plot or closure, the New Women writers were trying out some very new ideas about literature indeed. Shifting the terms to style rather than personal politics also offers us a different cadre of New Woman writers. This definition allows us to include male writers like Hardy, Gissing, or Wells, who may have been indifferent or even inimical to feminist activism, but who employed these characteristically innovative techniques to depict strong women in their fiction. They form part of a generation of transitional writers between the 1880s and 1910s whose extent we are only now beginning to recognize. Although many modernists liked to portray themselves as brave rebels against hidebound Victorians, with a 'chasm' between the two periods, today the critical consensus is that Victorian style gradually evolved into modernist style, and we can now see that New Women texts formed part of that transition.

One specific innovation is that many New Women incorporated non-fiction manifestos into their novels. Indeed, as Hugh E.M. Stutfield complained, New Women novels 'are for the most part merely pamphlets, sermons, or treatises in disguise'.[10] Because many New Women writers were orators and publishers of pamphlets and journalism,

---

[10] Hugh E.M. Stutfield, 'Tommyrotics' [1895], *A New Woman Reader: Fiction, Articles, and Drama of the 1890s*, ed. Carolyn Christensen Nelson (Peterborough: Broadview Press, 2001), 234–43, 238.

they were accustomed to writing in a hortatory style. It can be disconcerting for readers to hit one of these manifestos in the midst of a fictional world. In Sarah Grand's *The Heavenly Twins*, a group cries, 'Make us a speech! *Do!*' to the American reformer Mr Price, which impels him to strike an attitude and deliver a two-page oration about true womanliness in its relation to reform.[11] Ella Hepworth Dixon's *The Story of a Modern Woman* proclaims, 'all we modern women mean to help each other now' and points out episodes in which characters live up to that slogan.[12] If one assumes the novel ought to be a realistic fictional world in which the reader is immersed, these examples of passionate argument seem to violate the novel's verisimilitude. They violently plunge the reader into a quite different reading experience.

New Woman novels could also use another disconcerting style embedded within the realist novel: the allegory. Schreiner is the most famous practitioner of this technique. In *The Story of an African Farm*, the section called 'Times and Seasons' describes the childhood of a universal 'we' who is and yet is not any of the characters in the novel (an example of its style: 'we cry as though our heart was broken. When one lifts our little body from the window we cannot tell what ails us').[13] Another chapter consists of a tale about a hunter's lifelong quest for Truth, told by a stranger. Schreiner prized this mode of writing, subsequently publishing a collection of allegorical tales called *Dreams*. But Sarah Grand also used it to talk about the music of the bells in Morningquest, in a Proem and a three-page dream sequence in which a character can proclaim 'I am Judith. I am Jael. I am Vashti. I am Godiva. I am all the heroic women of all the ages rolled into one, not for the shedding of blood, but for the saving of suffering.'[14] Her universalism contradicts the novel's usual work of establishing individuation. Lucas Malet (Mary St Leger Kingsley Harrison) studded *The Wages of Sin* with recurrent dreamlike descriptions of a character falling through endless space. As Patricia Murphy explains, 'the verbal art of allegory is particularly suggestive of monumental time in its departure from the realistic settings that tend to characterize nineteenth-century linear novels'.[15] Murphy reads New Women novels as particularly concerned with the desire to establish a cyclical sense of time, and reads allegory as one of the main tools such writers employed.

Allegorical language was particularly jarring because it contrasted with one of the main qualities of New Women prose, its journalistic immediacy. Famous for being contemporaneous, casual, swift, and transparent, New Women prose writers made no claims to high art, which differentiates them from their 1890s contemporaries, the aesthetes. Instead they aimed for readability, controversy, and popularity. Frequently, critics took them to task for poor writing. A.G.P. Sykes marvelled at how 'these apologies

---

[11] Sarah Grand, *The Heavenly Twins* [1893] (Ann Arbor: University of Michigan Press, 1992), 196–98.
[12] Ella Hepworth Dixon, *The Story of a Modern Woman* (New York: Cassell Publishing Co., 1894), 304.
[13] Olive Schreiner, *The Story of an African Farm* [1883], ed. Patricia O'Neill (Peterborough: Broadview, 2003), 138.
[14] Grand, *The Heavenly Twins*, 296.
[15] Patricia Murphy, *Time is of the Essence: Temporality, Gender, and the New Woman* (New York: SUNY Press, 2001), 210.

for literature become "popular novels" despite their illiteracy, tautology, slovenliness, slip-shod vernacular, profanity, and reckless, not to say repulsive, exposure of psychological hypotheses and the errors of humanity.'[16] For Sykes, New Women's appalling casualness about intimate subjects was connected to their carelessness in matters of style.

What you may have noticed in all these criteria—manifestos, allegories, and journalistic style—is that they rebel against high Victorian realism. Wildly different from each other, and often disorientingly clashing in the same text, they nonetheless perform the same function: to signal the reader that this is no longer a detailed fictional universe in which to immerse oneself, but rather, a highly constructed text that aims to argue, convince, and override the reader. In the 1890s, aesthetes were writing in ways that drew attention to their writing as a craft, using epigrammatic and archaic and fantasized language. New Women were not so dissimilar. While their writing did not intend to showcase their artistic skill like aesthetic texts, it did draw attention to itself as writing that had an immediate mission.

In rebelling against high Victorian realism, New Women writers also revolted against the norms of narrative structure. They ignored conventions about introducing characters, they flouted the normal marriage plot, and they violated closure. George Egerton's celebrated short stories provided glimpses of intense emotions, often internal psychological dramas, in the midst of obviously complex lives. Yet she often did not situate these feelings via plot events, settings, or characters' names. Hence 1890s critics complained bitterly about characters who were 'dreadfully introspective. When they are not talking of psychology, they are discussing physiology. They search for new thrills and sensations, and they possess a maddening faculty of dissecting and probing their "primary impulses"—especially the sexual ones.'[17] The New Women were, of course, writing in the era of Henry James (who was a friend of Elizabeth Robins and Lucas Malet, among others). But when women focused on female characters' internal feelings it was seen as morbid, whereas James could do it in the name of art. Critics were especially disturbed by the fact that, in New Woman fiction, writers often represented women's reluctance to marry, have sex, or care for her family. One critic commented, 'There is much that is pathetic in the self-questioning and the cravings of the type of women depicted in neurotic fiction.... But while their dolefulness may command our sympathy, the expression of it in hysterical or squalid stories is not to be encouraged.'[18] While one might pity women for having such repulsive feelings, one did not want to read about it.

What we have in New Women fiction, then, is intensive analysis of a woman's discontent, a psychological state of misery and frustration and thwarted ambition, closely limned. Distressingly, this analysis requires forthright discussion of her sexual

---

[16]   A.G.P. Sykes, 'The Evolution of Sex' [1895], *Literature and Culture at the Fin de Si ècle*, ed. Talia Schaffer (New York: Longman, 2007), 230–33, 231.

[17]   Stutfield, 'Tommyrotics', 236.

[18]   Hugh E.M. Stutfield, 'The Psychology of Feminism' [1897], *A New Woman Reader: Fiction, Articles, and Drama of the 1890s*, ed. Carolyn Christensen Nelson (Peterborough: Broadview Press, 2001), 243–53, 251.

feelings—a subject that there is really no safe way to treat in the 19th century. The sexual frankness of New Women fiction affiliated them with French fiction, Ibsen's controversial dramas, or even pornographic publications. It was shocking enough to have sexually explicit fiction, but it was even worse when Englishwomen wrote such scenes and ascribed such feelings to all Englishwomen.

No wonder, then, that these novels met critical outrage. Satirical poems and cartoons in *Punch* perpetuated the image of the New Woman as a bespectacled, angular, ridiculous spinster, making fun of her supposed mannishness, her propensity for riding bicycles, her bad taste in dress, and her humourlessness. This trend supposedly marked a serious threat to British culture. In 1894, the critic W.F. Barry warned dramatically, 'The New Woman ought to be aware that her condition is morbid, or, at least, hysterical; that the true name of science falsely so-called may be 'brain-poisoning'; that 'ideas' and love affairs, when mixed in unequal proportions, may explode like dynamite'.[19] Not only did the defenders of moral high culture attack these upstart women, but the women also fought publically with each other. Most famously, Sarah Grand and Ouida exchanged a series of tart rebuttals in the *North American Review* in 1894 over the identity and value of the New Woman. *The Nineteenth Century* ran a series of ardent debates between mothers and 'revolting daughters', initiated by an article by B.A. Crackanthorpe. Tempers ran high; strong accusations were made; the New Women's internal wranglings amused readers and sold papers and books, but did not conduce to a sense of the movement's coherence.

Other factors contributed to the New Women novelists' low reputation. The number of their novels and their sales worked against them, as Lyn Pykett explains.[20] By producing best-sellers, they gave the impression that they were catering to mass entertainment and did not care about literary quality. They might have found natural allies in the aesthetes, since aestheticism and decadence also (controversially) challenged accepted gender norms. Linda Dowling even claims that 'to most late Victorians the decadent was new and the New Woman decadent'.[21] But aesthetes saw themselves as artists, whereas the New Women writers positioned themselves as popular entertainers. If aesthetes like Oscar Wilde or John Gray issued limited editions bound in vellum with handmade bindings, New Women like Sarah Grand or Mona Caird published cheap paper-covered editions, rushed into print to meet the latest newspaper controversy and sold by the thousands at railroad bookstalls; and such productions affronted the artistic elite. Moreover, New Women tended to write few novels, because they were active in other fields (especially journalistic writing). That meant that they did not accumulate enough work to build a literary reputation. They were seen as dabblers, not serious writers.

---

[19] W.F. Barry, cited in Talia Schaffer, ed., *Literature and Culture at the Fin de Si ècle* (New York: Longman, 2007), 203.

[20] Lyn Pykett, *The 'Improper' Feminine: The Women's Sensation Novel and the New Woman Writing* (New York: Routledge, 1992), 142–43.

[21] Linda Dowling, 'The Decadent and the New Woman in the 1890's', *Nineteenth Century Fiction* 33 (1979): 434–53, 436.

Finally, New Women writers had no interest in conveying moral lessons, sentimental uplift, or timeless truths. Rather, they used their fiction to agitate for immediate social reform. They cited contemporary legislation, they wrote thinly disguised satires of real people, and they alluded to events that were still in the headlines. In other words, New Women hit a number of cultural hot buttons, writing about matters that readers feared and despised, without generating the signs of literary seriousness that might have excused it.

For decades, New Women fiction could not recover from this critical drubbing. These texts are virtually unmentioned in literary criticism until the 1970s. New Women do not appear in the great critical summation of the Victorian era, Jerome Hamilton Buckley's 1951 *The Victorian Temper: A Study in Literary Culture*. The MLA Index lists only one or two publications before 1970 about New Women novels, and none at all about Sarah Grand (to take the most popular New Woman author). After 1970 there are forty-nine articles about Sarah Grand alone. As Elaine Showalter later recalled, 'feminist criticism did not exist' when she began her dissertation research in 1965.[22] Deterred from researching women writers, it took years of radicalization and political action before Showalter felt ready to publish in this field. She remembers attempting to research New Women: 'When I was writing *A Literature of Their Own*, most of these women were completely unknown. In 1971, I went to Bath in search of Sarah Grand, and, on a rainy winter day, opened the cartons in the Municipal Library which had sat untouched since her death.'[23] Showalter thus literally and figuratively opened up Sarah Grand for study.

As Showalter's reminisences make clear, the rediscovery of New Woman writers was part of the feminist work of the 1970s. And Showalter was not alone; her 1977 *A Literature of Their Own* was matched by Gail Cunningham's 1978 *The New Woman and the Victorian Novel* and Lloyd Fernando's 1977 'New Women' in the Late-Victorian Novel. Other fields within Victorian fiction—the realist novel, Dickens studies, the Brontës— had a long evolution from the 19th century to the present. But New Women studies is different. It began in the 1970s, as feminists tore open cardboard boxes, eager to find lost foremothers.

Ever since, New Women criticism has been indelibly marked by its origin in second-wave feminism. As a result, New Women critics have tended to assume three points. First, it was a matter for celebration that women were able to publish these novels against overwhelming patriarchal indifference/hostility. Second, the novels must be expressing barely-controlled rage, rebelliousness, or reformist zeal in the form of feminist manifestos. Third, the novels unfortunately do not constitute truly great literature, a problem that must be acknowledged sombrely, but excused due to the novels' other qualities.

These assumptions are all true. But they are not all that is true.

[22] Elaine Showalter, *A Literature of Their Own* [1977] (Princeton: Princeton University Press, 1999), xi.
[23] Showalter, *A Literature of Their Own*, xxvii–xxviii.

First, in spite of the obstacles against women's publishing, some New Women were highly successful. Sarah Grand and Mona Caird, for instance, were canny self-publicists, accomplished public speakers, self-promoters, and prolific authors of articles and manifestos. They knew exactly what they were doing in marketing their writing; this was not a case of women awakening at dawn to scribble secretly before the family was awake. This image of a successful public celebrity who deliberately fostered public disputes in order to capitalize on the Woman Question is something feminist criticism still has some trouble digesting, because of our attachment to narratives of private women painfully overcoming obstacles to express themselves.

Second, while many of the novels did express recognizably feminist positions, many did not. Some even make apparently anti-feminist arguments. For instance, how do we read Elizabeth Robins's *George Mandeville's Husband* (1894), in which an overbearing literary wife supporting women's causes must eventually acknowledge the superior merits of her neglected husband? It reads like a vicious satire of a New Woman and a passionate defence of beleaguered males. Yet Elizabeth Robins herself was probably the most famous female representative of Ibsen's plays in England. As an actress, she starred in *Hedda Gabler*, *A Doll's House*, and *The Master Builder*. She was a suffragette and a lifelong advocate of women's rights. It is hard to figure out how to reconcile this activist with the apparent message of *George Mandeville's Husband*. Does one simply discount *George Mandeville's Husband* from Robins's corpus? If so, aren't we using a political litmus test to determine what 'counts'—a technique we do not employ for male writers—and misrepresenting the truth about her career?

Because New Woman criticism is still centrally concerned with demonstrating the feminism of a text there are many historical phenomena with which it simply cannot deal. Not only do we have the apparently antifeminist work of supposed feminists, like Robins, but we also have writings by women that show virtually no interest in feminism. Robins's *The Open Question* (1898) is about the urgent question of whether or not cousins in love ought to kill themselves so as not to have a potentially diseased child. Lucas Malet wrote a strong New Woman novel in 1890, the story of a female art student living on her own, *The Wages of Sin*. However, her next two novels, *The Carissima* (1893) and *The Gateless Barrier* (1900), were ghost stories manifesting more interest in spiritual haunting after death than in feminist agitation. Is Malet only a New Woman writer in 1890, but not before or after 1890?

Third, it is true that New Women novels did not obey the rules of good literature popularized by the New Critics (the rules that that second-wave feminists had to work with), but today scholars understand that New Women writers might have followed alternative criteria. *The Heavenly Twins* is a failure by New Critical standards. It is a loosely constructed narrative stuffed full of irrelevancies, caricatures, anomalous materials (dreams, allegories, a whole section lifted from a separately published short story and stuck into the novel). It is not at all realistic, and its characters have little psychological depth. Yet, as we have seen, *The Heavenly Twins* does all this as part of its radical exploration of literary style. New Women were not necessarily interested in psychological depth, realist stories, and narrative logic, but instead in developing a newly fragmented and non-realist style that would be appropriate to women's needs for self-expression in the modern age.

It was in the 1990s that feminist critics first began to take on the challenge of reading New Women differently from the 1970s pioneers. In 1992, Lyn Pykett published *The 'Improper' Feminine: The Women's Sensation Novel and the New Woman Writing* and in 1991, Ann Ardis published *New Women, New Novels: Feminism and Early Modernism.* (Recently, Ardis reminisced that 'when Rutgers published *New Women, New Novels* seventeen years ago, the scholarship on New Women fiction could quite literally be held in one hand. Moreover, almost all of the primary works and the voluminous fin de siècle periodical press writings about New Women were out of print.')[24] Pykett and Ardis made unprecedented claims for the significance of New Women fiction, and together, they presented a very strong case indeed. Pykett showed that it was possible to read New Women novels for their innovative style, and to appreciate them as proto-modernist work rather than inept Victorian writing. Ardis recovered over 150 heretofore lost novels, and catalogued the major elements of the genre for the first time. Scholars are still mining her bibliography, and the terms she set out have shaped New Women criticism. Thanks to Ardis and Pykett, critics had a way to read New Women novels according to a robust alternative criteria of quality. As a result, modern New Woman scholarship took off in the 1990s. Before 1990, an MLA Index search brings up only one article on the New Woman novel. Between 1990 and 2000, however, there are thirty-five.

In 1999, at the end of this notable decade of New Women criticism, Sally Mitchell summed up the state of the field and suggested new directions. Mitchell identified several problems. First, she noted the lack of accessible texts, which not only inhibited criticism, but also meant that too much space was taken up with plot synopses because the critic could never assume any familiarity with the novel on the reader's part. Second, she pointed out that critics still needed to clarify what feminist or New Women meant, including how they related to the previous generation of Victorian female activists in the 1850s–1880s.[25] Mitchell called for more work on race and empire, same-sex relationships, analysis of popular women writers (who may or may not have been New Women), working-class and socialist narratives, more historical and biographical information, and more attention to publishing history.

I have listed Mitchell's ideas at some length, because they predicted, with an almost uncanny accuracy, what New Women critics would pursue in the following decade, 2000–10. In recent New Women criticism, many of her hopes have been realized.

Today, important theoretical developments have made new kinds of readings of New Women texts possible. Above all, the canon no longer holds the power it once did. Indeed, the very idea of sorting texts into 'canonical' and 'non-canonical' categories seems somewhat quaint today. Rather, critics are reading shifting, flexible bodies of work, based on

---

[24] Ann Ardis, 'Landscape for a New Woman, or Recovering Katharine St. John Conway, "Michael Field," and "the author of *Borgia*", *Nineteenth-Century Gender Studies* 3, no. 2, <http://ncgsjournal.com/issue32/roundtable.htm>.

[25] Mitchell, 'Review', 581–83.

the particular cultural formation they want to pursue. Thus if one is interested in the figure of the shop girl, it makes sense to spend a lot of time on Amy Levy's *The Romance of a Shop*, which depicts the kind of labour involved in opening and operating a shop, regardless of how well known it may be. This new emphasis on reading texts for relevance, not status, has liberated scholars. No longer does the New Woman critic need to defend her subject before even discussing it. No longer does the New Women critic have to commence by insisting on the value of the texts, excoriating the literary establishment for ignoring them, pleading for reconsideration, or compensating for perceived deficiencies. That space can be used for more substantive matters. While these concerns do continue to haunt New Women criticism, they are certainly subsiding.

As recent criticism has opened up to non-canonical texts, it has also opened up to non-British readings. New Womanism seems to have been an international movement, with representatives in Italy, Japan, Germany, and America, amongst other places, and scholars are beginning to perform comparative studies. Moreover, a global awareness seems to have shaped the New Women movement from its inception. As Teresa Mangum provocatively suggests, 'the New Woman materialized from uneven cultural exchanges among the British Isles, India, Africa, and other parts of the world'.[26] It was cultural contact, cultural hybridity, and the work of empire that provided alternative ideas of female identity. Some New Women travelled to colonial spaces, accompanying husbands in the civil service, and used this new point of view to reassess domestic and marital life (Flora Annie Steel, Laurence Hope [Adela Florence Nicolson]). Many New Women texts locate a smouldering female sensuality in an Orientalized East (Egerton's 'A Cross Line', Victoria Cross [Annie Sophie Cory]'s 'Theodora: A Fragment'). Female travellers' narratives insisted on women's resilience, courage, and determination. These include Mary Kingsley's justly celebrated *Travels in West Africa* and Isabella Bird's *A Lady's Life in the Rocky Mountains*. Olive Schreiner's *The Story of an African Farm*, arguably the first New Woman novel, places its female character's thwarted drive to self-realization on a rural South African farm run by the labour of unnamed Africans, creating an ironic tension of which Schreiner may have been only intermittently aware. Mangum reminds us that our own criticism has political effects:

> As studies like Lee Ann Richardson's *New Woman and Colonial Adventure Fiction in Victorian Britain* and Iveta Jusová's *The New Woman and the Empire* have followed the New Woman into the places and politics of empire, the consequences of our interpretations of this icon become even more ethically as well as aesthetically insistent. These studies invite scholars to ask whether we can justify building research careers on a figure embedded in all we find most objectionable about Victorian global domination.[27]

---

[26] Teresa Mangum, 'Review: Iveta Jusová, *The New Woman and the Empire*', *Nineteenth-Century Literature* 61, no. 2 (September 2006): 255–69, 256.

[27] Teresa Mangum, 'New Strategies for New (Academic) Women', <http://ncgsjournal.com/issue32/roundtable.htm>.

Mangum's reminder is especially welcome because New Women criticism's roots in second-wave feminism tend to lend it a celebratory tone. It is hard to work against the grain of jubilation at recovering a lost woman's text, in order to perform a serious (self)-inquiry about the larger effects of placing our academic capital behind certain writers.

Queer theory and gender studies have given critics new methods for reading some of the characters in New Women fiction. In *The Heavenly Twins* and in *The Story of an African Farm,* key chapters involve cross-dressing; characters do not perceive themselves as performing another gender, however, but as uncovering the gender that is really theirs. As Angelica puts on boys' clothes and dances down to the river, or Gregory Rose dons a woman's bonnet in order to nurse the sick, we encounter texts that drastically displace the Victorian assumption that biological bodies link with essential traits. Contemporary critics can use Judith Butler's idea of gender performativity to examine how these characters take on the other sex's qualities through masquerade. We also now have ways of reading these novels' passionate same-sex relationships, as in Edith Johnstone's *A Sunless Heart* (1894) or Eliza Lynn Linton's *The Rebel of the Family* (1880). Sharon Marcus's theory of female friendship, and work on lesbian relationships by writers like Terry Castle and Martha Vicinus, help us understand relations between women in this period.

Moreover, contemporary criticism's interest in material and economic history has led to new ways of reading New Woman fiction. Women's ability to produce fiction, and to have that fiction reach readers, depends far less on abstract notions of 'quality' than on material networks of editors, marketing strategies, publishing contracts, and remuneration. The unforgettable scene of Mary Erle seeking a job on a lady's magazine in *The Story of a Modern Woman* teaches us how many impalpable but important obstacles confronted women who wished to publish. Key criticism here includes Margaret Stetz's lively histories of late-Victorian publishing practices, Mary Ann Gillies's exploration of what the rise of the literary agent meant for women writers, Peter Keating's account of the Society of Authors, and the burgeoning field of Victorian periodical studies.

One publishing development of our own times has also played an enormous role in the burgeoning of the field of New Women criticism. The Internet has made it possible, for the first time, to acess rare and obscure women's writing. Websites like the Indiana University Women Writers' Project, Project Gutenberg, archive.org, and Google Books have massively expanded the number of people who can access New Women texts, and search engines now enable scholars to do highly specific searches over a vast quantity of text. As Patrick Leary discusses in 'Googling the Victorians', electronic publication and searching have transformed the field, enabling new forms of research and transforming scholars' techniques for performing matters like annotations or cross-references. We can now find New Women texts, and we can find material about them, that was previously inaccessible except to those few scholars who lived near a major archive.

No matter how much is available online, however, teachers generally prefer to assign hard copies, and Broadview Press has emerged as the press that has made it possible to teach an entire course on New Women writers. Broadview has published two excellent sources for short prose readings (Carolyn Christensen Nelson's *A New Woman Reader* and Susan Hamilton's *Criminals, Idiots, Women, and Minors*). Broadview also offers excellent editions of novels by Ouida, Sara Jeannette Duncan, Mary Ward, Eliza Lynn Linton, Amy Levy, Ella Hepworth Dixon, Olive Schreiner, and Edith Johnstone. Its policy of reprinting very rare books is especially welcome. Take, for instance, that case of Edith Johnstone's *A Sunless Heart*. Before Constance Harsh republished it with Broadview, there were only two surviving copies of the novel (at least according to Worldcat), one in the National Library of Scotland, one in Flinders University Library in Australia. Ever since Carol Poster pointed out that 'Oxidation is a Feminist Issue', critics have recognized that the greatest threat to recovering neglected Victorian women writers might be the physical disintegration of the few surviving copies. Thanks to far-seeing publishers, scanners, and databases, one can hope that this particular anxiety is beginning to be alleviated.

The result is that today's New Women criticism is wide-ranging indeed. Two larger studies deserve special note. Chris Willis's and Angelique Richardson's *The New Woman in Fiction and in Fact*, a much-cited collection, pulls together work on everything from bicycling to Utopian fiction; and Patricia Murphy's innovative *Time is of the Essence: Temporality, Gender, and the New Woman* explores temporality, arguing that New Women fiction obeys a cyclical sense of time rather than a linear masculine chronology. However, one sure sign that New Women criticism has come of age is that scholars are beginning to publish specific studies of particular types: Angelique Richardson analyses New Women's interest in the eugenic movement, Kristine Swenson discusses female doctors, and Lise Shapiro Sanders addresses shop girls. A one-woman New Women criticism industry is Ann Heilmann, author or editor of at least four books on the topic as well as editor of several multi-volume series and special journal issues on the New Woman, all within the past ten years. Heilmann has perhaps done more than anyone else to publicize the New Woman and shape the field. Finally, writers are beginning to break through the history of celebrating New Women as subversive rebels, by paying attention to women whose politics challenge any easy attempt to identify them as feminist. *Anti-Feminism and the Victorian Novel*, edited by Tamara Silvia Wagner, importantly declares that anti-feminist writers are well worth studying. To sum it all up, let me quote Ann Ardis's evaluation:

> I would even venture to suggest that the Victorian fin de siècle has emerged as one of the most exciting arenas of study within Victorian studies, and that scholarship on the New Woman has played no inconsiderable role in a re-valuation of late-nineteenth-century debates about gender, race, national identity, and the 'progress' of modernity that has transformed the way we think about and teach the entire Victorian period, not just the fin de siècle.[28]

[28] Ardis, 'Landscape'.

Ardis's point is important; when New Women scholarship flourishes, our understanding of the entire period benefits. We expand our sense of the whole century when we learn how to articulate the complications of New Women novels' racial and sexual tensions, political ambivalence, and material publishing conditions.

However, there is one last aspect of New Women writing that poses a great problem for modern readers. Ever since New Women were rediscovered in the 1970s, critics have desperately wanted to find triumphant stories of women triumphing over Victorian patriarchy. But in New Women fiction, that does not happen.

New Women had trouble imagining an ending. They could depict the moving distress of a woman entrapped in a loveless marriage that stymied every attempt at self-expression. They could show how social and familial pressures left women no option but marriage, no matter whether or not they were suited to the marital state. But what they could not do, very often, was imagine an alternative.

Ardis has pointed out that virtually all New Women novels end with failure. The woman's brief attempt at freedom backfires, and she is forced to return to her domestic enslavement. Sometimes, in what Ardis dubs 'boomerang books', the woman's failure reinforces the notion that female independence is doomed, extolling the virtues of traditional domesticity instead. The tragic endings of New Women fiction raise the question: what kind of future was there for the New Woman? In *The Heavenly Twins*, of the three main female characters, one dies (horribly) of syphilis, infected by her husband; one ends the novel as a nearly catatonic, suicidal figure subjected to a controlling psychologist's instructions; and the only one with any sort of happy ending is stuck in a marriage to a man she calls 'Daddy'. The best she can do to fulfil her brilliant potential is to ghost-write his parliamentary speeches—no better than the fate Margaret Oliphant had imagined a generation earlier in *Phoebe Junior* (1876) and *Miss Marjoribanks* (1865–66). In *The Story of a Modern Woman*, Mary Erle ends by looking hopelessly out over a dingy, grim London cityscape, foreseeing (no doubt accurately) a future of exhausting hackwork without love or rest. In *The Daughters of Danaus*, the sensitive, brilliant, talented composer Hadria is forced to come home to take care of her family, giving up her musical career. Male-authored depictions of New Women are no happier. Thomas Hardy's Sue Bridehead ends up in a kind of 'fanatic prostitution', literally bowed under the shadow of the cross; Grant Allen's Herminia dies; and of George Gissing's three 'Odd Women', one dies in a loveless, abusive marriage while the other two become alcoholics and nearly starve to death. Writers of New Women fiction could diagnose what was wrong—but quite often they could not imagine an alternative.

There are a few exceptions, however, in which the writer was able to imagine a professional success offsetting the character's romantic failure. In *A Writer of Books* and *The Beth Book*, the female character seems to be in a desperate state at the end of the novel, judging by the traditional rules of the marriage plot. Cosima and Beth have lost the men they love, their marriages have disintegrated, and they are alone. Yet at the same time, Cosima has just reached a peak of successful authorship, and Beth has found her true calling as an orator. The shining delight they take in their professional achievements render their personal tragedies irrelevant. In writing a vocational plot of triumph, then,

Paston and Grand begin to imagine a different shape for women's lives. As Virginia Woolf would write a generation later, 'Chloe liked Olivia. They shared a laboratory together.'[29] When women can have jobs, and collegial relationships made possible by those jobs, other forms of closure become possible beyond marriage, marriage achieved or marriage denied. Yet with the exception of those very few vocational stories, most New Women novels are tragic.

The truncated, disappointing endings of New Women fiction mirror what happened to the New Woman movement itself. Flourishing for not even two decades—arguably from Olive Schreiner's *Story of an African Farm* (1883) through Mary Cholmondeley's *Red Pottage* (1899)—this brief movement received a vast amount of media attention, provoked outraged criticism, and was incessantly mocked. Yet, like any New Woman heroine, the movement bravely faced all this disapprobation to insist on what it felt was right. New Woman fiction expressed the discontent of middle-class women, their frustration at their curtailed lives, their misery at their inability to escape. For a few years in the 1890s, that voice was heard. But just as the New Woman heroine 'boomeranged' back, so too did New Woman fiction disappear in the earliest years of the 20th century, women's discontent subsiding into silence. For the last couple of decades, New Women criticism has been embattled, fighting to represent late-Victorian gender complexities with the broad tools of 1970s feminism and then fighting to move out of 1970s feminist assumptions into a more accommodating framework. The story of the New Women novel's critical fortunes is far from over, and we do not know how it will end. Like New Women fiction itself, it defies closure. But perhaps we can hope that the ending of Grand's *The Beth Book* speaks for the future of New Woman criticism as well. 'Beth was one of the first swallows of the woman's summer. She was strange to the race when she arrived, and uncharitably commented upon; but now the type is known, and has ceased to surprise.'[30]

Suggested Reading

Ardis, Ann. 'Landscape for a New Woman, or, Recovering Katharine St. John Conway, "Michael Field," and "the author of *Borgia*"'. *Nineteenth-Century Gender Studies* 3, no. 2, <http://ncgsjournal.com/issue32/roundtable.htm>.

——. *New Women, New Novels*. New Brunswick: Rutgers University Press, 1991.

Cunningham, Gail. *The New Woman and the Victorian Novel*. London: Macmillan, 1978.

Dowling, Linda. 'The Decadent and the New Woman in the 1890's'. *Nineteenth Century Fiction* 33 (1979): 434–53.

Fernando, Lloyd. *'New Women' in the Late-Victorian Novel*. University Park: Pennsylvania State Press, 1977.

Mangum, Teresa. 'New Strategies for New (Academic) Women'. <http://ncgsjournal.com/issue32/roundtable.htm>.

---

[29] Woolf, *A Room of One's Own*, 108.

[30] Sarah Grand, *The Beth Book* [1897] (New York: Dial Press, 1981), 527.

———. 'Review: Iveta Jusová, *The New Woman and the Empire*'. *Nineteenth-Century Literature* 61, no. 2 (September 2006): 255–60.

Marcus, Sharon. *Between Women: Friendship, Desire, and Marriage in Victorian England*. Princeton: Princeton University Press, 2007.

Mitchell, Sally. 'Review: New Women, Old and New'. *Victorian Literature and Culture* 27, no. 2 (1999): 579–88.

Murphy, Patricia. *Time is of the Essence: Temporality, Gender, and the New Woman*. New York: SUNY Press, 2001.

Nelson, Carolyn Christensen. *A New Woman Reader: Fiction, Articles, and Drama of the 1890s*. Peterborough, ON: Broadview Press, 2000.

Poster, Carol. 'Oxidation is a Feminist Issue: Acidity, Canonicity, and Popular Victorian Female Authors'. *College English* 58 no.3 (March 1996): 287–306.

Pykett, Lyn. *The 'Improper' Feminine: The Women's Sensation Novel and the New Woman Writing*. New York: Routledge, 1992.

Richardson, Angelique. *Love and Eugenics in the Late Nineteenth Century: Rational Reproduction and the New Woman*. Oxford: Oxford University Press, 2003.

Sanders, Lise Shapiro. *Consuming Fantasies: Labor, Leisure, and the London Shopgirl*. Athens: Ohio State University Press, 2006.

Schaffer, Talia, ed. *Literature and Culture at the Fin de Si ècle*. New York: Longman, 2007.

———. '"Nothing But Foolscap and Ink": Inventing the New Woman'. *The New Woman in Fiction and in Fact: Fin de Si ècle Feminism*. Edited by Chris Willis and Angelique Richardson. New York: Palgrave Macmillan, 2002, 39–52.

———. 'The New Women: Introduction'. *Literature and Culture at the Fin de Si ècle*. Edited by Talia Schaffer, New York: Longman, 2007, 203–205.

Showalter, Elaine. *A Literature of Their Own* [1977]. Princeton: Princeton University Press, 1999.

35

THE LAST VICTORIAN NOVEL

I. *Slapstick Noir:* The Secret Agent *Works the Victorian Novel*

ROSEMARIE BODENHEIMER

'This simple tale of the XIX century'. That was the way Conrad described *The Secret Agent* (1907) when he dedicated it to his friend H.G. Wells. The 'of' is intriguing. Set in or concerning the 19th century, a historical tale? Written (as if) in the 19th century, a literary imitation or commentary on the Victorian novel? Approaching those questions through the rubric of 'the last Victorian novel', I want to play out the possibility that the novel's narrator is himself a secret agent who dresses himself in the garb of Victorian narrative and saturates himself in its atmosphere, both to represent and to question its characteristic activity.

Conrad's foray into the streetscapes of 1880s London is immediately recognizable as Dickensian; its tribute to *Bleak House* in particular has often been remarked. It draws upon a variety of 19th-century subgenres: the detective story, the sensation novel, and the anarchist novel.[1] In brilliantly condensed form, Conrad adapts a number of familiar 19th-century topics, including the perspective of a wise-innocent child, the anatomy of a marriage, and the spectacle of poverty. Like his predecessors, Conrad creates a cross-section of the class order that links characters from the bottom to the top of the social

---

[1] For recent discussions of Conrad in relation to 19th-century subgenres, see Jacques Berthoud ('The Secret Agent', in *The Cambridge Companion to Joseph Conrad*, ed. J.H. Stape (Cambridge: Cambridge University Press, 1996), 100–121) on the anarchist novel and Ellen Burton Harrington ('The Anarchist's Wife: Joseph Conrad's Debt to Sensation Fiction in *The Secret Agent*', *Conradiana* 36, no. 1–2 (2004): 51–63) on the sensation novel. Wendy Lesser offers a detailed study of Dickens, *The Secret Agent*, and sentimentality in her 'From Dickens to Conrad: A Sentimental Journey', *ELH* 52, no. 1 (Spring, 1985): 185–208.

hierarchy: the bloated alcoholic cab driver and the expansive but weak-eyed Secretary of State are equally vital (and equally enormous) players in the intricate plot games of this 'simple tale'.

Of course, Joseph Conrad himself can be considered a Victorian of sorts. Born in 1857, he was just twelve days younger than his fellow-novelist George Gissing. *The Secret Agent* features a bleak urban vision supported by a plot in which every human scheme is undermined and destroyed; it might as readily be aligned with the late-Victorian mood of Gissing as with some form of existential modernism. The actual import of the famously ironic narration has been famously difficult to describe, but—unlike Gissing's—it is wonderfully funny to any reader with an ear for Conrad's fluid variations on familiar Victorian narrative practices.[2] However we may want to interpret the vision conjured up by that ironic voice, it is important to recognize its direct descent from mid-Victorian narrators whose perspective may change from sentence to sentence within a paragraph. Thackeray's *Vanity Fair* and George Eliot's *Middlemarch*, to take two major examples, make constant subtle shifts between the double edge of free indirect discourse and definitive narrative judgement, between close-up intimacy and withdrawn generalization. *The Secret Agent* may differ in providing no admirable characters, but it too moves from one interior character zone to another, swinging the reader dizzily between understanding and revulsion. As Conrad put it in his 1920 Author's Note, 'ironic treatment alone would enable me to say all I felt I would have to say in scorn as well as in pity'.[3]

Conrad's impersonation of the Victorian novelist begins with the thickness of material detail. The first page of *The Secret Agent* has us peering into the window of a Soho shop, cataloguing the sleazy goods displayed there as if we were on a walk with the author of *Sketches by Boz*. The incongruous bottle of marking ink sits amid faded pornography like the clue that it is: with this scandalously overpriced ink Stevie's collar will be marked, providing the evidence for the detective story and precipitating the novel's swerve into domestic sensationalism with Winnie as the murdering heroine. Conrad's sly play with that fragment of writing recalls the inkiness of *Bleak House*, as well as its challenge that every material detail might count as evidence in a world of secrets.

More crucially, however, *The Secret Agent* suggests that the world might be made of nothing but matter. London is repeatedly described either as a pile of bricks—building

---

[2] Hugh Epstein gives a fine analysis of Conrad's English style in 'The Fitness of Things'. He defines 'the saving comedy of this very funny book' as dependent upon 'the reader's hearing how the collision between subject matter and the means of conveying it is infused with social inflections that Conrad recognizes but does not necessarily endorse'. See 'A Pier-Glass in the Cavern: The Construction of London in *The Secret Agent*', in *Conrad's Cities: Essays for Hans van Marle*, ed. Gene M. Moore (Amsterdam-Atlanta, GA: Costerus, 1992), 175–96, 9. Ernidast-Vulcan, looking at a similar disjunction between signifier and signified, sees rather its 'corrosive irony' and 'an authorial refusal of containment within the symbolic order'. See Daphna Ernidast-Vulcan, '"Sudden Holes in Space and Time": Conrad's Anarchist Aesthetics in *The Secret Agent*', in *Conrad's Cities*, 207–21, 220.

[3] Joseph Conrad, *The Secret Agent* [1907], ed. Michael Newton (London: Penguin, 2008), 251. Subsequent citations appear in the text.

matter minus architectural form—or as an equally formless watery swamp. Every itera-
tion of these tropes is differently imagined, according to the psychological situation of
the character present in the scene, but the reduction of form into undifferentiated matter is a constant, finding its ironic apotheosis in the blown-up fragments of Stevie's body,
mixed with bits of gravel and bark (70). Conrad imitates the materialism of the realist novel, but instead of furnishing a world with it, he suggests its threat to any illusion
of social order or cohesion. In the alley where the bomb-making Professor encounters
Chief Inspector Heat, 'An unhappy, homeless couch, accompanied by two unrelated
chairs, stood in the open' (66). The pathetic personification in this heartbreaking detail
is pure Dickens, while the notion that the two antagonists spar across dislocated pieces
of orphaned furniture turns the Victorian parlour inside out.

The detailed and close-up descriptions of characters' bodies highlight the fact of human
materiality. Whether the characters are immovably fat or grotesquely thin, their capacities
for motion or immobility are located in a physiological organism that is determined by a
combination of bodily make-up and environmental pressure; so, for example, Michaelis's
fat is the material result of an undeserved solitary confinement made necessary by the pressure of public opinion. Conrad's emphatic readings of characters' bodies call attention to
themselves as exaggerations, not only of the techniques Dickens usually reserves for comic
lower-middle-class characters, but of the long phrenological/physiognomic tradition
of reading heads as if they were clues to a character's moral and psychological trajectory.
Conrad places his attention to bodies in direct conversation with Ossipon's belief in late-
19th-century theories of criminal and degenerate body types, in order to suggest the miserable paucity of such theories compared with the psycho-physiological complexity of every
human body. In Conrad's hands, reading bodies at all levels of society provides a sometimes
savage amusement, but it also suggests that every body is a potential bomb, its nerve-endings
ready to explode into frantic action when triggered by threats to its corporeal stability.

The slapstick quality in the narrative expresses this perfectly. Ossipon, for his sins, gets
the heaviest slapstick role in chapter 12, as he discovers the corpse of Verloc. Assuming
that Verloc has been blown up that morning, he 'discovered Mr Verloc reposing quietly
on the sofa' of the parlour. His reaction is described in comic physiological terms:

> A yell coming from the innermost depths of his chest died out unheard and
> transformed into a sort of sickly, greasy taste on his lips. At the same time the mental
> personality of Comrade Ossipon executed a frantic leap backwards. But his body, left
> thus without intellectual guidance, held on to the door handle with the unthinking
> force of an instinct. [225]

The passage continues in this vein: Ossipon receives 'a kind of optical shock' from
looking at the whites of the dead man's eyes and observing the knife handle upright on
Verloc's left breast. He panics again, and finds himself struggling in the frantic embrace
of an equally terrified Winnie, 'as if theirs had been the attitude of a deadly struggle,
while, in fact, it was the attitude of deadly fear' (226–27).

The comedic moment takes us quickly into the heart of the matter: the fear that turns human bodies into automata. The narrator extends as much dry comedy to the description of Verloc's bodily sensations while he takes in Mr Vladimir's crazy demand that he blow up the Greenwich Observatory as to the description of the player piano in the underground pub that 'executed suddenly all by itself a *valse* tune with aggressive virtuosity' (22–27, 49). The sudden outburst of activity is followed, at the end of the scene, with pathos: 'The lonely piano, without as much as a music stool to help it, struck a few chords courageously, and beginning a selection of national airs, played [Ossipon] out at last to the tune of "Blue Bells of Scotland"' (63). It's the plot of the novel in miniature: injected with fear, the characters take sudden actions to relieve it, leaving an aftermath of loneliness that attempts to cover itself in an outburst of communication. Thus Mr Verloc, after the accidental explosion of Stevie, pours out the banality of his mental life to an unhearing Winnie. Winnie, after she kills her husband in a state of instinctual rage, becomes 'the most lonely of murderers that ever struck a mortal blow' (214) and tries hopelessly to find relief through a confession to Ossipon. The apparent interchangeability of human and non-living matter draws on Dickensian techniques, but Conrad sharpens and condenses his focus to the physiology of fear. Dickens aims to affect his audience's moral imagination with the inhumanity of thing-ish characters and the projected humanity of things. Conrad does this too, but he brings a wry sympathy precisely to the human condition of being trapped in a body–mind system that is to some extent uncontrollable.

In so far as *The Secret Agent* is a political novel, it critiques the manipulation of public fear for political ends—or, more simply, for the sake of personal advancement or survival.[4] Conrad reserves his most forthright disgust for those who, like Verloc, 'live on the vices, the follies, or the baser fears of mankind' (11). He makes little distinction between the so-called anarchists and government employees: Mr Vladimir, the Professor, Ossipon, Inspector Heat, the Assistant Commissioner, and Sir Ethelred are all tainted by the desire to provoke an emotional public reaction—whether it's panic or the illusion of safety. Behind these positions lie, as the narrator says of the Professor, 'personal impulses disguised into creeds' (65). Heat is obsessed by his reputation; the Assistant Commissioner by his wish to keep his wife happy; the Professor by his 'vengeful bitterness' against those who have failed to recognize his self-proclaimed genius (65). Mr Vladimir, who initiates the novel's long chain of infectious fear, sets up the theme in chapter 2 when he appears as the novel's mad theoretician of pubic opinion. The fear comes around to bite Vladimir when the Assistant Commissioner confronts him as the source of the bomb provocation.

Conrad makes little distinction between the political novel and sensation fiction. The bits of newspaper that litter the novel announce a mysterious bombing outrage and a mysterious suicide; both stories evoke in their readers the conflict between fear and the

---

[4] Conrad's actual political sympathies in this novel have been much debated. Berthoud provides useful perspectives on Conrad's avoidance of both conservative and liberal positions.

instinct to remain in peace and normalcy. The presentation of Winnie Verloc and her unnamed mother also collapses the distinction between virtuous and sensational heroines as it addresses that central Victorian question of female self-sacrifice for the sake of others. Mother and daughter are trapped in a life-long anxiety: how to support and care for a mentally ill family member. The sacrifices they make for Stevie's sake are, as the narrator puts it, both 'heroic and unscrupulous' (128). Winnie gives up her lover and the promise of a happy married life, marrying Verloc under the false pretence that she cares for him. Her mother plots her move to an almshouse in order to render Stevie 'destitute and dependent' upon Verloc's good will (123). This secret decision is a calculated risk, made in ignorance of Verloc's character and profession, and it proves to be the first step in the fatal chain of events that lead directly to Stevie's death, Verloc's murder, and Winnie's suicide.

Winnie's transformation into a murderer—a 'free' being momentarily set loose from the order of social decorum and emotional constraint—comes about when she loses the orienting passion of her life. Conrad treats the feeling with compassion rather than comedy or scorn:

> She saw [Stevie] amiable, attractive, affectionate, and only a little, a very little, peculiar. And she could not see him otherwise, for he was connected with what there was of the salt of passion in her tasteless life—the passion of indignation, of courage, of pity, and even of self-sacrifice. [138]

These remarkably poised sentences create understanding and sympathy without coming close to the brink of sentimentality. How carefully Conrad omits the word 'love', even as he piles up the emotions that define Winnie's interior capacities, their heroism sustained only by a deluded view of her brother. The Victorian largesse in that list of emotions will find its answer in the murder scene: no, this method of anchoring to life cannot hold. It is not that Victorian readers were unacquainted with the potentially destructive aspects of self-sacrifice; we need only think of Dorothea Brooke, or Amy Dorrit. But Victorian heroines who indulge in that passion are given interior lives that explain and justify it; then they are normally rescued and rewarded. Conrad reworks the case to its crazed and desperate end.

Conrad makes similar use of Victorian detective stories, especially those that make a point of escorting the reader into dark corners of London. The pitting of stolid policeman against smart detective is a narrative staple that never seems to lose its charm, because it is a plot that raises questions about the capabilities and limits of human knowledge. 'I'll turn him inside out like an old glove', muses the foreign-looking Assistant Commissioner as he watches the steadfast English citizen Inspector Heat; the sentiment suggests both the arrogance and the gamesmanship of detective intellect (95). His appearance, 'with the white band of the collar under the silvery gleams on the close-cropped hair at the back of the head', suggests the priestly confessor (90), and his ability to cross-examine Inspector Heat to the point of confession dramatizes his talent. Like Sherlock Holmes between stories, he has been chafing at the monotony of life; he leaps delightedly into the case of the unidentified body at Greenwich Park, and solves it within the day.

Conrad blows up that generic figure in a number of entertaining ways. It's not only that he has the usual load of hidden motives: the need to protect Michaelis from arrest in order to appease the lady philanthropist who is kind to his wife, or the desire to make himself valued by his new superior, Sir Ethelred. He has simply read too many detective stories, and he wants to star in one himself. Working his case, Conrad's narrator enters into the 'darkest London' mode that had become so popular in the last decades of the 19th century, especially as popular thinking and writing about London's East End were charged with metaphors of penetration into unknown colonial spaces. The Assistant Commissioner, who has practised his detective chops in a tropical colony, parodies that move when he imagines Inspector Heat as equivalent to an African chief who had taken 'some finding out' in his former position (94). When he decides to 'go native' into the darkness of Brett Street, Soho—a few minutes' walk from his office—Conrad's comic exaggerations suggest just how much fun he is having with the atmospherics of London detective fiction. For example: how to get a cab when you're a detective:

> His exercised eyes had made out in the confused movements of lights and shadows thronging the roadway the crawling approach of a hansom. He gave no sign; but when the low step gliding along the curbstone came to his feet he dodged in skilfully in front of the big turning wheel, and spoke up through the little trap door almost before the man gazing supinely ahead from his perch was aware of having been boarded by a fare. [117]

Or, how to look like one:

> When, after paying for his short meal, he stood up and waited for his change, he saw himself in the sheet of glass, and was struck by his foreign appearance. He contemplated his own image with a melancholy and inquisitive gaze, then by sudden inspiration raised the collar of his jacket. This arrangement appeared to him commendable, and he completed it by giving an upward twist to the ends of his black moustache. [118]

Or, what a crime scene (Brett Street) should look like:

> Only a fruiterer's stall at the corner made a violent blaze of light and colour. Beyond all was black, and the few people passing in that direction vanished at one stride beyond the glowing heap of oranges and lemons. No footsteps echoed. They would never be heard of again ... This barrier of blazing lights [a pub], opposing the shadows gathered about the humble abode of Mr Verloc's domestic happiness, seemed to drive the obscurity of the street back upon itself, making it more sullen, brooding, and sinister. [119–20]

The application of melodramatic chiaroscuro to the most ordinary details of city street life creates the amusing charm of such writing. The last three adjectives in particular suggest that Conrad is impishly quoting from his own jungle book, *Heart of Darkness*. Both the narrator and the Assistant Commissioner relish their indulgence in such fantasies, but the narrator knows he's writing the equivalent of spooky mood music, and holds the ironic edge.

The edge is sharpened when the Assistant Commissioner becomes over-enamoured of his own detective powers. After interviewing Verloc for forty minutes, he arrives back 'at the very centre of the Empire on which the sun never sets', an hour or so after setting forth (169). Verloc's easily obtained confession is all he needs to become very certain of his own character assessment; he did not feel it necessary to arrest Verloc, he tells Sir Ethelred, because 'even if there were no obstacles to his freedom of action he would do nothing' owing to his domestic ties. His little joke, 'From a certain point of view we are here in the presence of a domestic drama' is Conrad's joke on him: as the story turns to domestic murder and suicide, the detective will vanish, never to be heard of again (175). His deluded belief that he knows what Verloc will do destroys his case, and with it the presumption of superior psychological penetration that supports both the Empire and the detective genre.

To say that *The Secret Agent* makes fun of Victorian story forms is not an adequate assessment of Conrad's achievement. In a novel about characters who contrive to manipulate the emotions of unknown others, Conrad conducts a serious investigation of the emotions and beliefs stirred up in the reader by certain kinds of fiction. The thrills of readerly apprehension evoked by sensation or terrorist fictions are rewritten as the unromantic action of fear and anxiety in the human psyche. Entering into the detective genre, the novel exposes the reader's desire to identify with a moody figure of uncanny knowledge with the skill to set things right. But the most salient test of Conrad's relation to Victorian novels may lie in his invention of Stevie, the mentally disabled child-man whose sympathy for the suffering recalls a tradition of abused and maimed Dickensian figures—Smike, Little Nell, Jo—who die as victims of cruelty. Is Stevie a figure of Victorian sentiment embedded in an otherwise ironized world of fictions?

'Bad world for poor people', Stevie's single approach to a coherent idea, seems to carry the whole weight of the 19th-century social novel on its verbless spine (136). His sympathy for the suffering of others puts him in a moral universe unshared by any other character, while his own history as an abused child makes him the object as well as the subject of sympathy. Stevie is Conrad's opportunity to consider the vexed questions raised by sympathetic identification in the Victorian novel. His canny retrospective placement of the great cab drive scene in chapter 8, after Stevie has been blown into bits, could be read as an elegy to the sentiments of horror and pity that Victorian social problem novels appeal to. As the narrator gradually transforms the grotesque trio of cab, driver and horse into a 'slow cortège' and then into 'the Cab of Death', 'the last cab drive of Mrs Verloc's mother's life' might suggest a bizarre funeral rite for all the members of her family and their doomed desires to protect sufferers from harm (123, 134, 136).

Conrad is careful both to elicit and to qualify such a reading. Stevie's mental illness may be pitiable, but it is defined as a dangerous susceptibility to rhetoric, especially when that rhetoric arouses his abiding fear of pain. Almost without language himself,

Stevie is the ultimately undefended credulous reader. For him language is a direct representation of reality that creates immediate physiological reactions. Yundt's bloodthirsty metaphor is 'swallowed ... with an audible gulp, and at once, as though it had been swift poison'; the cabman's sob stories about his wife and kiddies at home leave Stevie 'pushing his hands deeper into his pockets with convulsive sympathy' (41, 133). There is nothing benign about that sympathy; as soon as he articulates 'Bad world for poor people' he feels that 'somebody ... ought to be punished for it—punished with great severity' (136–37).

Stevie, I would suggest, is a caricature of the reader that Victorian social novels propose to create: someone whose sympathy will be aroused to the point of social action on behalf of the poor and oppressed. We are by now familiar with the argument that sympathy for suffering characters leads middle-class readers to feel good about themselves, and serves as a substitute for action against social injustice. Stevie is Conrad's answer to the implicit idealism of that argument, with its yearning for the cleansing potential of social action. When 'his morbid dread of pain' is stimulated, 'Stevie ended by turning vicious', becoming a vessel of 'innocent but pitiless rage' (134). That personal reservoir of rage could be tapped by anyone—it happens to be Verloc—who will prey on fear and anger to create an instrument in the public realm.

When Chief Inspector Heat responds with inward horror to the fragments of Stevie's body, the narrator describes his 'force of sympathy' as 'a form of fear' (70). Stevie's story corroborates that vision. So does Ossipon's new understanding after Winnie's suicide: 'Mankind wants to live—to live' he asserts in the face of the terror-mongering Professor. He now sees in Winnie a 'vigour of vitality, a love of life that could resist the furious anguish which drives to murder and the fear, the blind, mad fear of the gallows. He knew' (241, 244). The sympathy he belatedly achieves with Winnie's struggle is also a form of fear, a fear of himself that keeps him frantically walking through London streets as the novel ends.

In 1920, after the First World War had done its part to undermine Victorian views of human perfectibility and progress, Conrad wrote an Author's Note in which he attempted to justify the vision of *The Secret Agent*: 'Not to insist that I was right but simply to explain that there was no perverse intention, no secret scorn for the natural sensibilities of mankind at the bottom of my impulses.' In his critics' revulsion from the 'moral squalor of the tale', the author recognized the subject of his story: the anxiety that clings to surfaces and evades explanations (247–48). When Conrad gets to the bottom of things, he finds fear where his predecessors imagined sympathy or guilt. *The Secret Agent* is no less humane for that.

Suggested Reading

Berthoud, Jacques. 'The Secret Agent'. In *The Cambridge Companion to Joseph Conrad*. Edited by J.H. Stape. Cambridge: Cambridge University Press, 1996, 100–21.

Conrad, Joseph. *The Secret Agent* [1907]. Edited by Michael Newton. London: Penguin, 2008.

Epstein, Hugh. 'A Pier-Glass in the Cavern: The Construction of London in *The Secret Agent*'. In *Conrad's Cities: Essays for Hans van Marle*. Edited by Gene M. Moore. Amsterdam-Atlanta, GA: Costerus, 1992, 175–96.

——, "'The Fitness of Things": Conrad's English Irony in *Typhoon and The Secret Agent*'. *The Conradian* 33, no. 1 (Spring 2008): 1–30.

Ernidast-Vulcan, Daphna. "'Sudden Holes in Space and Time": Conrad's Anarchist Aesthetics in *The Secret Agent*.' In *Conrad's Cities: Essays for Hans van Marle*. Edited by Gene M. Moore. Amsterdam-Atlanta, GA: Costerus, 1992, 207–21.

Harrington, Ellen Burton. 'The Anarchist's Wife: Joseph Conrad's Debt to Sensation Fiction in *The Secret Agent*'. *Conradiana* 36, no. 1–2 (2004): 51–63.

Lesser, Wendy. 'From Dickens to Conrad: A Sentimental Journey'. *ELH* 52, no. 1 (Spring 1985): 185–208.

THE LAST VICTORIAN NOVEL

II. The Quest of the Silver Fleece, *by W.E.B. Du Bois*

DANIEL HACK

There is more than one way to identify the—or a—last Victorian novel. One might, of course, seek to discover which novel was published in closest proximity to January 22, 1901, the date of Queen Victoria's death. Adopting a less literal-minded understanding of the Victorian novel as a category, one might seek to identify the final novel, chronologically, that seems to fully own or inhabit the characteristic preoccupations, formal conventions, and values of the era's fiction, or some subset of that fiction. Or, alternatively, one might choose a novel that aspires to be the last Victorian novel—that aspires, in other words, to put an end to the genre by showing its defining features to be antiquated, unconvincing, false, incoherent, laughable, boring.

While potentially illuminating, these approaches risk down-playing the self-consciousness of Victorian novels, their frequent willingness to interrogate their own values and procedures. Parody, irony, reflectiveness, demystification, and the flouting of readerly expectations are arguably definitive of the form, and especially characteristic of the novels often taken as its greatest achievements, such as *Vanity Fair*, with its cynical, protean narrator; *Bleak House*, with its mutually defamiliarizing first-person, past-tense and third-person, present-tense narrations; *Villette*, with its teasingly ambiguous conclusion; and *Middlemarch*, with its explicit questioning of its own narrative choices ('But why always Dorothea?'). Conversely, to nominate a 'last' Victorian novel also risks obscuring the genre's resilience—that is, its ability to withstand parody and critique, as shown by the tendency of ostensibly discredited, superseded conventions to persist or return or be resurrected. In other words, the Victorian novel is always already dead and not dead yet; it is, like one of its most famous creations, undead. Taking a different tack, then, I will approach the border between the Victorian and the post-Victorian from the opposite direction, by discussing a novel that is plainly not Victorian, by chronological and geographical standards, but that nonetheless *seems* Victorian in many respects. Recalling and adapting specific Victorian novels and 'the Victorian novel', understood as a collection of generic conventions, this novel puts on display the Victorian novel's elasticity—and puts it to the test.

The Elastic Victorian Novel

The Quest of the Silver Fleece, by W.E.B. Du Bois, was published in Chicago in 1911. One of the most influential African American intellectuals of the 20th century, the prolific Du Bois was trained as a social scientist but wrote in and across a variety of genres; *Quest* was the first of five novels he published at intervals over the course of his long lifetime. Born in Massachusetts in 1868—when Victoria still had slightly more than half of her reign ahead of her—Du Bois grew up reading Victorian literature (he bought himself Macaulay's five-volume *History of England* while still in high school), and the influence of Thomas Carlyle and Matthew Arnold on his views has been frequently noted; indeed, it is a commonplace to describe him as in some sense 'Victorian', with that term used with varying degrees of precision—and derision.

It should not be surprising, then, to discover Victorian traces in *The Quest of the Silver Fleece*; the fact that these have gone unexplored is the equally unsurprising effect of literary scholarship's organization along national lines, along with a critical tendency to highlight Du Bois's contribution to a distinctively African American literary tradition. A rare—if fleeting and slighting—acknowledgement of Victorian influence reflects this stance: leading African Americanist William Andrews declares that 'Despite its excursions (often by means of purple prose) into sentimentality and idealism—betraying Du Bois's fondness for Victorian fiction—*Quest*'s main claim for attention today stems from the portrayal of Zora, a breakthrough in the portrayal of black womanhood in modern African American fiction.'[1] As we will see, however, not only is Victorian fiction a more pervasive and constitutive presence in the novel than this comment suggests, but Du Bois's 'fondness' for Victorian fiction also helped him produce the very character identified here as the most original, forward-looking aspect of the novel.

Set primarily in contemporary rural Alabama and Washington, DC, *The Quest of the Silver Fleece* weaves together several narrative strands to: (1) describe the interlocking economic, political, and legal mechanisms that structure a society founded on racial injustice and economic exploitation; (2) convey a sense of what it feels like for differently situated individuals to inhabit this society; and (3) explore the potential for individual development and social change. Four hundred thirty-four pages long in its first edition,

---

[1] William L. Andrews, 'Introduction', in W.E.B. Du Bois, *The Quest of the Silver Fleece* (New York: Oxford University Press, 2007), xxv–xxvii, xxvi–xxvii.

the novel is divided into thirty-eight named chapters and bracketed by a brief authorial 'Note' and 'Envoi'. The story is recounted by a third-person, omniscient, relatively unobtrusive narrator with access to the interiority of multiple characters. In the novel's first chapter, Blessed (Bles) Alwyn, a fifteen-year old African American boy travelling from his home in Georgia to a Negro School in Toomsville, Alabama, encounters Zora, a wild, dark-skinned, twelve-year-old 'elf-girl',[2] in the swamp outside town. The novel tracks the moral and intellectual progress of these two protagonists and the vicissitudes of their relationship. Both begin their education at the school run by Sarah Smith, a white New Englander, and spend their free time together in the swamp, but their blossoming romance is destroyed when Bles learns of Zora's sexual experience. Both protagonists move, separately, to Washington, DC, where Zora becomes increasingly cultured and sophisticated as the maid to a rich white woman, while Bles becomes involved in politics and engaged to a cynical, light-skinned, African American woman.

Intertwined with the stories of Zora and Bles are those of two white families: the Cresswells, the county's leading landowners who strive to keep 'their' blacks in conditions as close to slavery as possible; and the Taylors, a Northern sister and brother who come into contact with the other characters when Mary Taylor takes a job teaching at the Smith School. Mary enters into an unhappy marriage with dissolute heir Harry Cresswell—the man responsible for Zora's sexual 'impurity'—while John Taylor marries Harry's sister Helen and enlists the family in his successful scheme to gain control of the international cotton trade (cotton being the 'silver fleece' of the novel's title).

In the novel's dénouement, Zora breaks from her employer and Bles from his fiancée, and both return to Toomsville, to work on behalf of their race. Under Zora's leadership, and thanks to a series of unlikely events (to which I will return), the Smith School gains financial security and the wild swamp is transformed into farmland communally owned and tended by the area's black population. The novel ends with the betrothal of Zora and Bles.

Much here will be familiar to the reader of Victorian fiction. The narrative is linear, the narrative voice impersonal, authoritative, and telepathic. The novel tracks a process of maturation for its main characters over several years, mainly in adolescence and young adulthood, with maturation consisting in the acquisition (for lower-class protagonists) of middle-class linguistic competence and cultural knowledge, the chastening of youthful ambitions, and the discovery of a proper vocation and spouse. The novel-ending engagement between characters who plainly belong together confirms the narrative's clear narrative arc and provides a strong sense of closure. An interest in characters' interiority is balanced with an interest in their actions, and an interest in individuals is balanced with an interest in larger institutions and social structures, with the stories of these individuals serving to make the latter legible—and at times threatening to obscure it.

---

[2] W.E.B. Du Bois, *The Quest of the Silver Fleece* (Philadelphia: Pine Street Books, 2004), 20. Subsequent citations appear in the text.

As this account suggests, *Quest* displays a particular kinship with two subgenres pioneered by the Victorians: the *Bildungsroman* and the industrial or condition-of-England novel. But the full measure of Du Bois's adherence to the basic protocols of the traditional, realist Victorian novel—protocols which Victorian novels manipulate and challenge, but rarely ignore—also reveals itself at a more granular level, in the way he constructs scenes and delineates characters and social and physical spaces. Consider, for example, the opening of chapter 13, 'Mrs. Grey Gives a Dinner':

> The Hon. Charles Smith, Miss Sarah's brother, was walking swiftly uptown from Mr. Easterly's Wall Street office and his face was pale. At last the Cotton Combine was to all appearances an assured fact and he was slated for the Senate. The price he had paid was high: he was to represent the interests of the new trust . . .
> As Mr. Smith drew near Mrs. Grey's Murray Hill residence his face had melted to a cynical smile. After all why should he care? He had tried independence and philanthropy and failed. Why should he not be as other men? He had seen many others that very day swallow the golden bait and promise everything. They were gentlemen. Why should he pose as better than his fellows? . . . Mr. Smith snapped his fingers and rang the bell. The door opened softly. The dark woodwork of the old English wainscoting glowed with the crimson flaming of logs in the wide fireplace. There was just the touch of early autumn chill in the air without, that made both the fire and the table with its soft linen, gold and silver plate, and twinkling glasses a warming, satisfying sight. [146–47]

Charles Smith is a minor character appearing here for the first time in the novel (although he has been mentioned previously). The third-person narrator immediately orients the reader by identifying the character in relation to a more prominent one ('Miss Sarah's brother') and situating him geographically and socially ('walking swiftly uptown from Mr. Easterly's Wall Street office'). The narration swiftly moves from this external view to Charles's interiority, as an event with significant implications for the society as a whole—the establishment of the 'Cotton Combine', or cartel—is reported by means of the ethical dilemma it creates for this one particular character. The character's thoughts are reported largely through free indirect discourse, clearly marked as such ('why should he care?'), and the content of those thoughts is a yielding to temptation, a self-serving rationalization the narrator does not hesitate to label 'cynical'. Such a passage would not be out of place in a novel by George Eliot or Anthony Trollope. With the return at the end of the passage from the character's interiority to description of the external world he inhabits, we perhaps edge closer to the late-Victorian fiction of Thomas Hardy, in so far as the balance begins to tip from metonymic realism towards fairly ostentatious symbolism: even as 'the dark woodwork of the old English wainscoting' conjures a specific social milieu, the crimson flames align this mansion in Murray Hill with a much more radically 'warming' place.

Of course, there is one respect in which such a passage *would* be out of place in a novel by Eliot or Trollope or Hardy: it is literally—that is, geographically—out of place. When Victorian novels venture abroad, they almost invariably do so in pursuit of British characters: virtually all non-historical Victorian novels have British protagonists.[3] Like the builders of Mrs. Grey's mansion, we might say, Du Bois transports 'old English' patterns and craftsmanship to the New World, and houses his American characters in a Victorian structure. This combination recalls the pattern that Franco Moretti proposes as typical of the modern novel as it expands from Western Europe to other cultures: 'foreign *plot*; local *characters*'.[4] What is perhaps most striking about *Quest*, however, is its reversal of this pattern: on the one hand, as suggested earlier, the novel's most strikingly original, 'local' character is also the character in the novel most indebted to Victorian fiction, while on the other hand—and despite what was suggested earlier—a closer look at the plot will reveal that it ultimately departs from its Victorian models in significant and revealing ways.

The character of Zora inspired comparison to the heroines of Victorian fiction from the moment *Quest* was published. One of the novel's first reviews, published in the journal Du Bois himself edited, compared Zora to Jane Eyre and Becky Sharp, while an essay by Alice Dunbar-Nelson a few years later placed her 'by the side of Maggie Tulliver'.[5] To be sure, such comparisons were commonplace in the early 20th century; as one American reviewer of a now-obscure novel complained in 1909, 'The dark-haired child with elf-locks and an imagination [is] a type often done before . . . whether we think of her as Jane Eyre or Maggie Tulliver or Rebecca [from *Ivanhoe*].'[6] As critical frames of reference have shifted, however, Zora's conformity to this type has become less visible—and so too, therefore, does her plot's departure from it. Like *Jane Eyre*, *The Mill on the Floss*, and (to a lesser degree) *Vanity Fair*, *The Quest of the Silver Fleece* recounts its female protagonist's passage from childhood to adulthood. Like Jane, Maggie, and Becky, as a girl Zora is a misfit or outsider who chafes against her society's gendered norms and expectations of proper behaviour. Like Jane and Maggie, her early wildness is fitfully tamed, in part through her experience at school. Just as a despondent Maggie gains a sense of

[3] I should note two salient exceptions to this rule: two of the earliest novels by African Americans—novels which, like *Quest*, have African American protagonists and are set in the United States—were written and first published in England in the 1850s, and are arguably addressed to a British readership: *Clotel* (1853), by William Wells Brown, and *The Garies and Their Friends* (1857), by Frank J. Webb. That these novels have nonetheless never been classified or read as Victorian is presumably a function of the nationality of their authors (who did not settle permanently in Britain, unlike, say, Henry James or Joseph Conrad); one wonders, though, if the presence of British protagonists or a British setting would have overridden these factors. These cases point to some rarely articulated assumptions underwriting the category of 'the Victorian novel'.

[4] Moretti adds 'local *narrative voice*' to this structure as well. Franco Moretti, 'Conjectures on World Literature', *New Left Review* 1 (January–February 2000). Although the United States had a well-developed tradition of fiction by the time Du Bois wrote his first novel, the number of African American novels preceding *Quest* is limited—perhaps a couple of dozen.

[5] William Stanley Braithwaite, 'What to Read', *The Crisis* (December 1911): 77–8; Alice Dunbar-Nelson, 'Negro Literature for Negro Pupils', *The Southern Workman* 51, no. 2 (February 1922): 59–63, 62.

[6] 'Sorting the Seeds: A Survey of Recent Fiction' (review of *Thyrza*, by Alice Brown) (1909), *The Atlantic Monthly* 103 (May 1909): 702–12, 710.

self-sacrificing purpose when she happens upon Thomas à Kempis's *Imitation of Christ*, where she reads that 'the love of thyself doth hurt thee more than anything in the world' (236), Zora gains a similar sense of purpose when she wanders into a church and hears a preacher preach that 'Sorrow is born of selfishness and self-seeking—our own good, our own happiness, our own glory' (294). Unlike Maggie, but again like Jane, Zora is granted a happy ending—and one that takes as much authorial heavy lifting as does Jane's (a point I will return to)—in which she decides to marry the man whom she has earlier rejected, and does so in a way that highlights her own agency, with Jane's 'Reader, I married him' matched by Zora's book-ending proposal: 'Will you—marry me, Bles?' (434).

To this list of Zora's Victorian precursors we can add another, ultimately most revealing one: Tess Durbeyfield. The ways in which Du Bois tropes on Hardy's own, self-consciously 'last' Victorian novel (or one of them, along with *Jude the Obscure*) clarify how the Victorian novel does and does not last in *The Quest of the Silver Fleece*. Like Hardy, Du Bois is intent on redefining female 'purity,' and does so by asserting the 'purity' (the term used in both texts) of a woman who has been sexually violated by the scion of a local wealthy family. Both novels are outraged by society's treatment of such an event as nominally scandalous but utterly typical and implicitly sanctioned. Both make ostentatious use of the colours white and red in their treatment of sexual purity and experience, from the red ribbon in Tess's hair at the beginning of her novel—'the only one of the white company who could boast of such a pronounced adornment'[7]—to 'the white beauty of the cotton' the young Zora and Bles cultivate, which 'glow[s] crimson in the failing sun' when Bles hears Zora described as 'notorious' (164, 167, 166). Like Tess, Zora is first abandoned by her beloved—Blessed to Tess's Angel—when she confesses her sexual history, but is later reunited with him when he learns to reject conventional views of female morality. Indeed, just as Hardy, using free indirect discourse, describes Tess resolving to 'pay to the uttermost farthing' by 'tell[ing]',[8] so too does Du Bois, also using free indirect discourse, show Zora employing the same biblical phrase to describe her sense of self-sacrifice: 'She must be true. She must be just. She must pay the uttermost farthing' (433).

This moment of greatest convergence between *Quest* and *Tess* also marks a particularly significant divergence. The passage in *Quest* comes not at the moment of confession, as in *Tess*, but rather at the very end of the novel, when Zora encourages Bles to marry another woman: 'Emma is a good girl. I helped bring her up myself and did all I could for her and she—she is pure; marry her' (433). Here too, though, *Quest* echoes *Tess*, as the doomed Tess says of her sister, 'Liza-Lu, 'She is so good and simple and pure. O, Angel—I wish you would marry her.'[9] This reordering reflects Du Bois's radical alteration of Tess's story, as he replaces Hardy's tragic conclusion with a happy, indeed Utopian ending. At first glance, this ending looks like a return to earlier Victorian novels,

---

7 Thomas Hardy, *Tess of the d'Urbervilles* (Boston: Bedford Books, 1998), 38.
8 Hardy, *Tess*, 228.
9 Hardy, *Tess*, 381.

as opposed to the shocking, anti-Victorian conclusion to Tess; this is partly true, and yet a closer look will suggest that the ending, and the sequence of events that produces it, put the most pressure on the novel's Victorian-ness, and mark its limits.

THE END OF THE VICTORIAN NOVEL

With their providential plotting and commitment to closure, dénouements and endings are arguably the most heavily regulated narrative components of Victorian novels—the components, that is, most constrained in their range of possibilities. The manner in which Du Bois engineers *Quest*'s conclusion is true to form, as a series of unlikely coincidences and reversals of fortune, along with a timely death, lead to the happy ending the reader of Victorian fiction fully expects: the betrothal of the male and female protagonists who met at the beginning of the novel. (A novel such as *Daniel Deronda* is very much the exception that proves the rule, as it ostentatiously flouts this expectation.) As if to signal the Victorian-ness of the dénouement, the turning point comes when Bles, choosing between his pride and political ambition, on the one hand, and his integrity, on the other (like Charles Smith in the scene discussed above), is swayed to do the right thing by four lines of Victorian poetry: 'It matters not how strait the gate,/ How charged with punishment the scroll;/ I am the master of my fate,/ I am the captain of my soul' (318). Bles reads these lines from W.E. Henley's 'Invictus' in an anonymous note from Zora he receives at just the right moment, when he is conducting 'the battle of his life' (317). This providential intervention is followed by a series of uncharacteristic acts of moral probity on the part of powerful and wealthy members of the white ruling class: a gift to the Smith School from Zora's former employer; a favourable court ruling (thanks to the testimony of John Taylor) requiring the Cresswells to honour a contract with Zora for cotton she has grown; and an enormous bequest from the Cresswell patriarch to the Smith School and Zora's protegée Emma. Colonel Cresswell acts out of guilt for his role in sparking events that lead to a lynching and in belated acknowledgement that he is Emma's grandfather, and he dies almost immediately after revising his will. These events make it possible for Zora to realize her plan to buy the swamp and start 'a free community' of blacks working together on 'our own farm' (362).

Two aspects of this dénouement seem particularly Victorian—besides, of course, the adherence to the older comic convention of the concluding marital match. First, there is the generation of a happy ending by means of the inheritance plot—or rather, what we might call the inheritance plot-device: not prolonged suspense and machinations (also common in Victorian novels) but an unexpected, game-changing bequest, as in *Jane Eyre* or another novel about regionalism and the cotton economy (of England), Elizabeth Gaskell's *North and South*. Second, we have the beneficent intervention of wealthy, and often previously villainous or corrupt, characters, as in many a Dickens novel. These devices seem Victorian not only because they are common in the 19th century but also because they have fallen out of favour by the 20th (at least in canonical modernist fiction); indeed, the lateness of late-Victorian fiction by such writers as Hardy and George Gissing consists in no small part in the interrogation and abandonment of these plot devices. These fall out of favour for many reasons (which are themselves overdetermined): as with much Victorian plotting, they come to seem contrived and heavy-handed; the psychology of moral conversion comes to seem false and sentimental (with sentimentality itself acquiring a very bad reputation); writers move away from providential world-views; and questions of inheritance come to seem less relevant to modern, forward-looking lives and societies.

Yet if the means by which Du Bois engineers his conclusion are among the most markedly Victorian aspects of the book, the Victorian-ness of that conclusion itself is more ambiguous. The endings of canonical Victorian (or at least early- and mid-Victorian) novels tend to be happy, but not too happy. the protagonist ends up married to the right person, but that protagonist is typically disabused of whatever heroic ambitions and idealistic beliefs he or she once had. In addition, the focus is usually on the achievement of domestic stability and contentment rather than a larger impact in the wider world; one version of this tendency, as many critics have noted disapprovingly, is that novels identify social, systemic problems but offer only individualized solutions that rescue key characters while leaving the larger problems untouched, or envisioning merely a kinder, gentler version of the status quo. As George Orwell put it in his influential essay on Charles Dickens, these novels depict and demand 'a change of spirit rather than a change of structure'.[10] Think Scrooge. By contrast, in *The Quest of the Silver Fleece* the change of spirit of several powerful white characters make possible a change of structure, as Zora's commune challenges the established order of the American South (which the novel has depicted as being based on the denial of property rights to African Americans and the exploitation of their labour). Du Bois thus goes further than Gaskell does in the reformist vision she articulates at the end of *North and South*: there, mill-owner John Thornton plans to grant his workers greater control over their work environment, but his vision of cooperation or partnership does not extend to an ownership stake in the business for the workers, or even collective bargaining. *Quest*'s Mary Taylor seems to have in mind an outcome like *North and South*'s, where she would have the moderating, humanizing influence on her husband Harry Cresswell that Margaret Hale has on John Thornton. Du Bois's departure from Gaskell, his replacement of ruling-class reconciliation with underclass autonomy and collectivity, is marked by the complete failure of Mary's plan (and marriage), and her marriage's shunting aside by that of Zora and Bles as the novel-ending, forward-looking union.

Du Bois's ending might be seen as another extension of Victorian practices—as more new content that the older form can accommodate, as it has accommodated the national milieu and racial situations *Quest* depicts. The use of the marriage plot to achieve closure—at the expense of a more sustained representation of the community

---

[10]   George Orwell, 'Charles Dickens', *A Collection of Essays* (San Diego: Harcourt Brace Jovanovich, 1995), 64.

Zora establishes—reinforces this sense of incremental expansion rather than a radical formal break. Indeed, the establishment of this community itself arguably has the same effect, since—despite its departure from Victorian norms and its Utopian potential—it does nonetheless constitute a retreat in scale from the national political and economic manoeuvring the novel details. However, the novel's ending is in tension with the Victorian means by which Du Bois engineers it. The plot devices he relies upon not only underwrite his conclusion but also threaten to undermine it, because—in Victorian fashion—they depend upon members and mechanisms of the established order. In doing so, they suggest that that order is not as corrupt and irredeemable as the novel has previously indicated. Worse, they compromise the self-determination and independence Zora's community is intended to model.[11]

Du Bois seems to have sensed this problem, for his next novel, *Dark Princess* (1928), is in some respects a rewriting of *The Quest of the Silver Fleece*, but with key differences: again, a male protagonist abandons his political careerism and the woman who encourages this path to marry and join forces with a woman committed to bettering the fortunes of their people. In the later work, however, it is African Americans themselves, along with members of non-white races from around the world, who seize transformative agency, in the form of a worldwide, secret conspiracy and, ultimately, nothing less than the birth of a saviour (the son of the Bles-like protagonist and the Indian princess of the title). With this messianic conclusion—the last word's of the novel are 'Messenger and Messiah to all the Darker Worlds!'[12] as opposed to *Quest*'s 'Will you—marry me, Bles?' (434)—the novel drives home its abandonment of Victorian norms and conventions.[13] The last Victorian novel? As *Dark Princess* suggests, at least, *The Quest of the Silver Fleece* is the last Victorian novel by W.E.B. Du Bois.

Suggested Reading

Andrews, William L. 'Introduction'. In W.E.B. Du Bois, *The Quest of the Silver Fleece*. Edited by William L. Andrews. New York: Oxford University Press, 2007, xxv–xxvii.

Byerman, Keith. 'Race and Romance: *The Quest of the Silver Fleece* as Utopian Narrative', *American Literary Realism, 1870–1910* 24, no. 3 (Spring 1992): 58–71.

Du Bois, W.E.B. *The Quest of the Silver Fleece*. Philadelphia: Pine Street Books, 2004.

Moretti, Franco. 'Conjectures on World Literature'. *New Left Review* 1, January–February 2000, <http://newleftreview.org/II/1/franco-moretti-conjectures-on-world-literature>.

---

[11] Keith Byerman argues similarly that 'this utopia comes into being only by means of that patriarchal order it has replaced'. See 'Race and Romance: *The Quest of the Silver Fleece* as Utopian Narrative', *American Literary Realism, 1870–1910*, 24, no. 3 (Spring 1992): 58–71, 70.

[12] W.E.B. Du Bois, *Dark Princess* (Jackson, MS: Banner Books, 1995), 311.

[13] On the modernism of *Dark Princess*, see Ross Posnock, *Color and Culture: Black Writers and the Making of the Modern Intellectual* (Cambridge: Harvard University Press, 1998), 161–77.

INDEX

772 INDEX

Chambers Robert (*Cont.*)
'What Literature Gives Us' 49–50
Chambers, William 43 n. 7, 48–50, 52–58, 60,
62, 64, 722
Memoir of Robert Chambers, with
Autobiographic Reminiscences of
William Chambers 48 n. 18
Chandos, John 416 n. 13, 436
Boys Together: English Public Schools
1800–1864 436
Chapman, Raymond 217 n. 41
Chapple, J.A.V. 458
Charpentier, Gervais 190
Chartier, Roger 102 n. 49
Chartism 514, 518, 553, 595, 669–70
Chase, Karen 17 n. 1
Chasles, Philarète 187, 190, 202
Le Roman politique en Angleterre 194
Chaucer, Geoffrey 55, 213 n. 24, 245, 615,
682, 689 n. 28, 705, 719
The Canterbury Tales 641, 689 n. 28
Cheadle, Walter Butler 463
cheap editions 45
Chekhov, Anton 207, 223
Chernyshevsky, Nikolai 213, n. 20
What Is to Be Done? 210
Chesselden, William 488–90
Chesterton, G.K. 188
Chevrier, Thierry 198
La Plus etrange aventure de Mayne-Reid : sa
traduction 198, 204
children's fiction 143, 192, 198–99, 595, 703,
705, 724; *see also* France
Cholmondeley, Mary 180–81, 744
Red Pottage 180
Chopin, Kate 730
Chorley, Henry 138
Christensen, Allan Conrad 354
Christenson, Jerome 398
Christianity; *see* religion; Protestantism;
Catholicism, Roman
Christie, Agatha 611
The Mirror Crack'd from Side to Side 611
Chudleigh, Cosima 732
Chukovsky, Kornei 216 n. 33

Churton, Edward 38
circulating libraries 115, 131
civil service examinations 711, 722–23;
see also education, classical;
university
Clark, Gregory 364 n. 5, 364 n. 6
Clark, John W. 431 n. 58
Clark, Steve 290
class; *see also* allusion, classics; allusion,
poetic; industrialism, mid-Victorian
novel, money, professions
Classen, Constance 494 n. 31
classics 413–37; *see also* allusion, classical;
education, classical; professions;
university; professions
and Anglican Church 427
and civil service 425
and country gentleman 416
and dandy 417, 422, 425
and gentlemanly status 416–26
and Greek, knowledge of 426, 431–34
history of classical scholarship
425 n. 34
and hostility to women 430–31
and 'Lady's Greek' 431
and military officers 425
and mythology 414, 428–29
and paratexts 414
and quotation 414, 419–20, 425
and the scholar 426–30
and surveys of English literature 46–47
and women 417, 430–34
and women novelists 414 n. 6,
431–34
and working classes 417, 430–31
Claybaugh, Amanda 340
Clayton, Jay 288, 605
Cleere, Eileen 276 n. 2
Cleghorn, Thomas 321 n. 13
Clifford, W.K. 455, 496 n. 36, 497, 500
Clodd, Edward 502 n. 54, 505
closure 761–63
Clough, Arthur Hugh 612
Amours de Voyage 612
Cobbe, Frances Power 730